WE VALUE YOUR OPINION

Take your studying further with 100 FREE flash cards from Cirrus Test Prep

Dear Reader,

Thank you for purchasing from Cirrus Test Prep! We appreciate that you have chosen Cirrus to help you achieve your goals. We want to do everything we can to prepare you for your teacher certification tests.

To show our appreciation, we're offering you **100 FREE digital flash cards**. Designed by teachers for teachers, these flash cards will help you to solidify your understanding of fundamental concepts in social studies and prepare you even more for your certification tests and beyond. All we ask is that you email us your feedback and describe your experience with our product. Amazing, awful, or just so-so: we want to hear your thoughts!

To receive access to your **digital flash cards**, please email us at 5star@cirrustestprep.com. Include "Free 5 Star" in the subject line and the following information in your email:

1. The title of the product you purchased.
2. Your rating from 1 – 5 (with 5 being the best).
3. Your feedback about the product, including how our materials helped you meet your goals and ways in which we can improve our products.
4. An email address so we can send you a link to our digital flash cards.

If you have any questions or concerns, please feel free to contact us.

Thank you, and good luck with your studies!

The Cirrus Test Prep Team
info@cirrustestprep.com

Praxis II World and US History

CONTENT KNOWLEDGE (0941/5941) STUDY GUIDE: TEST PREP AND PRACTICE QUESTIONS FOR THE PRAXIS II (0941/5941) EXAM

Copyright © 2016 by Cirrus Test Prep

ALL RIGHTS RESERVED. By purchase of this book, you have been licensed one copy for personal use only. No part of this work may be reproduced, redistributed, or used in any form or by any means without prior written permission of the publisher and copyright owner.

Cirrus Test Prep is not affiliated with or endorsed by any testing organization and does not own or claim ownership of any trademarks, specifically for the Praxis World and US History: Content Knowledge (0941/5941) exam. All test names (and their acronyms) are trademarks of their respective owners. This study guide is for general information only and does not claim endorsement by any third party.

About the Author

Caroline Brennan spent several years on the front lines of multilateral diplomacy at the United Nations, working with the International Committee of the Red Cross (ICRC) in humanitarian affairs from 2007 – 2012. Previously, she studied international development, postcolonial theory, and history in Canada, Europe, and North Africa; she obtained her master's degree from the University of Pennsylvania in 2007, specializing in Middle Eastern history.

Table of Contents

Introduction i

PART I: REVIEW   1

World History 3

- EARLY CIVILIZATIONS AND THE GREAT EMPIRES 3
- WORLD RELIGIONS 17
- FEUDALISM THROUGH THE ERA OF EXPANSION 19
- ARMED CONFLICTS 41
- GLOBAL CONFLICTS 60
- POST-COLD WAR WORLD 81

United States History 87

- NORTH AMERICA BEFORE EUROPEAN CONTACT 87
- COLONIAL NORTH AMERICA 93
- REVOLUTION AND THE EARLY UNITED STATES 102
- CIVIL WAR, EXPANSION, AND INDUSTRY 115
- THE UNITED STATES BECOMES A GLOBAL POWER 127
- POSTWAR AND CONTEMPORARY UNITED STATES 136

PART II: REVIEW 147

Practice Test One 149
Answer Key 183

Practice Test Two 217
Answer Key 253

Introduction

Congratulations on choosing to take the Praxis World and US History: Content Knowledge (0941/5941) exam! By purchasing this book, you've taken the first step toward becoming a history teacher.

This guide will provide you with a detailed overview of the Praxis, so you know exactly what to expect on test day. We'll take you through all the concepts covered on the test and give you the opportunity to test your knowledge with practice questions. Even if it's been a while since you last took a major test, don't worry; we'll make sure you're more than ready!

What Is the Praxis?

Praxis Series tests are a part of teaching licensure in approximately forty states. Each state uses the tests and scores in different ways, so be sure to check the certification requirements in your state by going to www.ets.org/Praxis/states. There, you will find information detailing the role of the Praxis tests in determining teaching certification in your state, what scores are required, and how to transfer Praxis scores from one state to another. The assessment will measure your aptitude in history and prepare you for a career in teaching world and US history courses.

What's on the Praxis?

The content in this guide will prepare you for the Praxis World and US History: Content Knowledge (0941/5941) exam. The test with code 0941 is a pencil-and-paper test, while the test with code 5941 is a computer-administered test. Both are a multiple-choice tests that assess whether you possess the knowledge and skills necessary to become a history teacher. You have a maximum of two hours to complete the 120-question test.

Praxis World and US History: Content Knowledge (0941/5941) Content		
Concepts	Approximate Number of Questions per Subject	Percentage of Test
World History to 1450 C.E.	30	25%
World History: 1450 C.E. to the present	30	25%
United States History to 1877	30	25%
United States History 1877 to the present	30	25%
Total	**120**	**100% (2 hours)**

The Praxis is comprised primarily of questions intended to test your knowledge of historical facts. Other questions on the Praxis also gauge historical thinking skills. Thinking historically entails constructing historical questions, assessing primary and secondary sources, formulating historical arguments, drawing connections, evaluating causation of historical events, and putting events in a global and historical context. Some of these questions may ask you to interpret maps, cartoons, texts, and/or graphs. Historical thinking skills questions are dispersed throughout the test and subject areas and encompass approximately 25 percent of the test.

You will answer approximately sixty multiple-choice questions (50 percent of the test) on United States history. The test will require knowledge of North American geography, pre-colonial civilizations, the purposes of European colonization of the continent, and how pre-colonial peoples interacted with European colonizers. Be prepared for questions about the American Revolution and the foundations of the United States government and Constitution. The test will cover developments in the nineteenth century, including westward expansion, political division, the Civil War, Reconstruction, industrialization, urbanization, and immigration. The Progressive Era and the New Deal are covered as well. Be aware not only of United States involvement in the First and Second World Wars, but also of their impact on both foreign and domestic policy. Prepare for thematic questions that will test your knowledge of the impact of labor and technology on the economy, changing political trends from the New Deal and Great Society to conservatism, the impact of religion on society, and civil rights and changing perceptions of race, ethnicity and gender roles throughout the twentieth century. Questions are also likely to explore the United States' role as a world power during the Cold War and into the twenty-first century.

You will answer approximately sixty multiple-choice questions (50 percent of the test) on world history. In general, you will be expected to understand how world societies and civilizations have been shaped by conflict, technology, and religion; ideologies like nationalism, totalitarianism, and other political philosophies; economic movements like industrialization and the market economy; and major demographic trends. The test will also presume an understanding of transglobal similarities in gender and family expectations, and the impact of trade within and between cultures. Specific questions may ask about the classical civilizations in Europe and Asia and their transformation from 300 – 1400 C.E.; European developments from the Renaissance through the Enlightenment; colonization, trade, and other global interactions from 1200 – 1750 C.E.; the consequences of nationalism and European imperialism from 1750 – 1914 C.E.; the causes and consequences of the First and Second World Wars (like decolonization and the rise of the Soviet Union); and the important developments of the post-Cold War world (such as globalization and fundamentalism).

How Is the Praxis Scored?

Your scores become available two to three weeks after the exam on your online account; you will be notified via email when they are released. When you register, you may choose four recipient institutions for your scores; they will be sent directly for free. After your scores become available, you may send them to other institutions for an additional charge. Some states are automatic score recipients. Check www.ets.org to determine how this applies to your specific situation.

Each multiple-choice question is worth one raw point. The total number of questions you get correct is added up to obtain your raw score, which is then scaled to result in your final score. Keep in mind that some multiple-choice questions are experimental questions for the purpose of the Praxis test-makers and will not count toward your overall score. However, since those questions are not indicated on the test, you must respond to every question. There is no penalty for guessing on Praxis tests, so be sure to eliminate answer choices and answer every question. If you still do not know the answer, guess; you may get it right!

How Is the Praxis Administered?

The Praxis World and US History test with code 0941 is a pencil-and-paper test, while the test with code 5941 is a computer administered test. You are encouraged to take the version of the test that is most comfortable for you. There is no difference between the two versions; both have the same time-limit and cover the same content. The Praxis website allows you to take a practice test to acclimate yourself to the computerized format.

The Praxis Series tests are available at testing centers across the nation. To find a testing center near you, go to http://www.ets.org/Praxis/register. At this site, you can create a Praxis account, check testing dates, register for a test, or find instructions for registering via mail or phone.

On the day of your test, be sure to bring your admission ticket (which is provided when you register) and photo ID. The testing facility will provide pencils and erasers and an area outside of the testing room to store your personal belongings. You are allowed no personal effects in the testing area. Cell phones and other electronic, photographic, recording, or listening devices are not permitted in the testing center at all, and bringing those items may be cause for dismissal, forfeiture of your testing fees, and cancellation of your scores. For details on what is and is not permitted at your testing center, refer to http://www.ets.org/Praxis/test_day/bring.

About Cirrus Test Prep

Cirrus Test Prep study guides are designed by current and former educators and are tailored to meet your needs as an incoming educator. Our guides offer all of the resources necessary to help you pass teacher certification tests across the nation.

Cirrus clouds are graceful, wispy clouds characterized by their high altitude. Just like cirrus clouds, Cirrus Test Prep's goal is to help educators "aim high" when it comes to obtaining their teacher certification and entering the classroom.

How to Use This Guide

This guide will help you master the most important test topics and also develop critical test-taking skills. We have built features into our books to prepare you for your tests and increase your score. Along with a detailed summary of the test's format, content, and scoring, we offer an in-depth overview of the content knowledge required to pass the test. Our sidebars provide interesting information, highlight key concepts, and review content so that you can solidify your understanding of the exam's concepts. Test your knowledge with sample questions and detailed answer explanations in the text that help you think through the problems on the exam and two full-length practice tests that reflect the content and format of the Praxis. We're pleased you've chosen Cirrus to be a part of your professional journey.

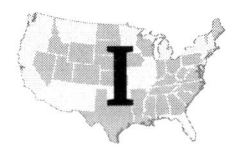

Part I: Review

World History

EARLY CIVILIZATIONS AND THE GREAT EMPIRES

PALEOLITHIC AND NEOLITHIC ERAS

The earliest humans were hunter-gatherers until the development of agriculture in about 11,000 B.C.E. 60,000 – 70,000 years ago, early humans began migrating from Africa, gradually spreading out across the continents in several waves of migration throughout Europe and Asia, eventually into Australia, the Pacific Islands, and the Americas.

Early human history begins with the **Paleolithic Era**, the period before agricultural development and settled communities. During this period, early **hominids** exhibited the use of tools, up to and including our ancestors, *Homo sapiens sapiens*. Other early hominids included *Australopithecus*, from which *Homo habilis*, *Homo neanderthalensis*, *Homo erectus*, and others descended. In fact, evidence suggests that *Homo sapiens sapiens* and *Homo neanderthalensis* coexisted. All are now extinct, save for us, *Homo sapiens*.

During the Paleolithic Era, human technology was rudimentary, based on stone; hence, the term ***Stone Age*** describes this period before metalworking was invented. Between approximately 11,000 – 10,500 B.C.E., humans began changing their behavior; they started settled communities, developed agricultural practices, and began domesticating animals. Notable technological developments occurred: humans began to create tools, weapons, and other objects made of metal. Furthermore, all species of humans except *Homo sapiens sapiens* became extinct. This transition marked the beginning of the **Neolithic** period, characterized by behavioral and technological change like the invention of the wheel. During the **Bronze Age**, humans began working with copper and tin, creating stronger tools and weapons.

Middle East and Egypt

Beginning in the Near East, settled societies organized into larger centralized communities characterized by early social stratification and rule of law; the earliest known examples of these were in the **Fertile Crescent**, the area in North Africa and Southwest Asia stretching from Egypt through the Levant and into Mesopotamia.

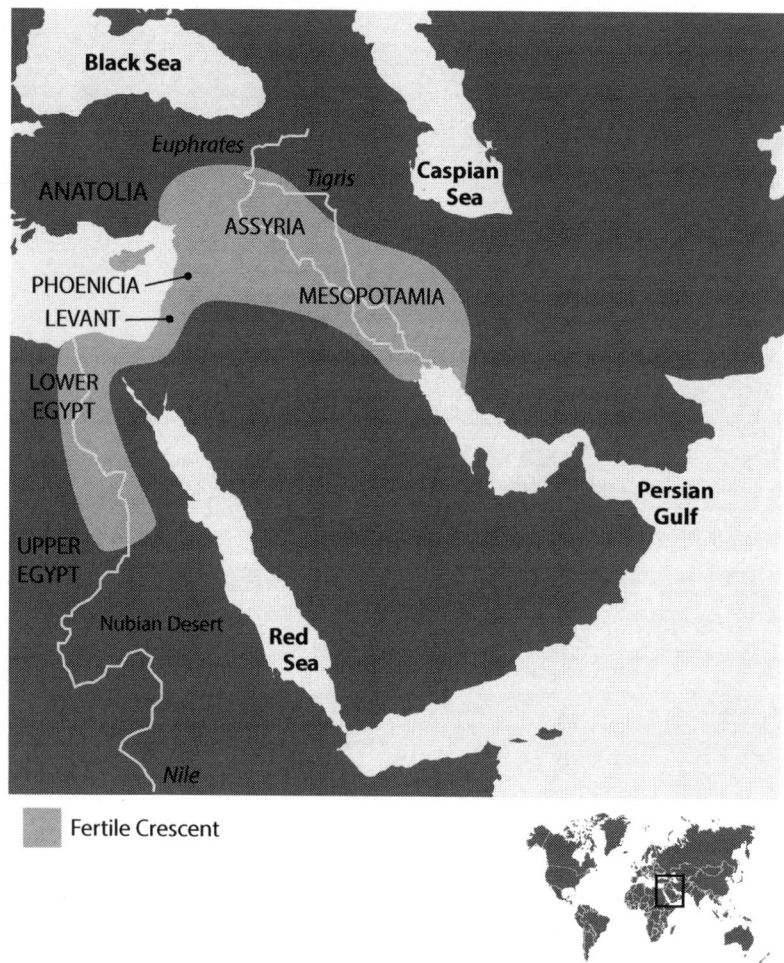

Figure 1.1. Fertile Crescent

Around 2500 B.C.E. (or possibly earlier) the **Sumerians** emerged in the Near East (eventually expanding into parts of Mesopotamia); developing irrigation and advanced agriculture, they were able to support settled areas that developed into city-states and eventually major cities like Uruk.

They also developed **cuneiform**, the earliest known example of writing to use characters to form words; early education, and literary and artistic developments resulted such as the early poetry of *The Epic of Gilgamesh* and architectural achievements like ziggurats. Sumer featured city-states, the potter's wheel, early astronomy

and mathematics, and religious thought. More advanced governance and administration were facilitated by the written language of cuneiform.

Eventually the Sumerians were overcome by Semitic-speaking, nomadic peoples in the Fertile Crescent: the result was the **Akkadian Empire**, which grew to encompass much of the Levant, Mesopotamia, and parts of Persia. One of its major legacies was the Semitic Akkadian language, which adopted cuneiform.

Around the eighteenth century B.C.E., the Akkadians had given way to **Babylonia** in Southern Mesopotamia and **Assyria** in the north. These two civilizations would develop roughly concurrently and remain at odds, with Babylonia eventually coming under Assyrian domination until the final defeat of Assyria by Babylonia in 612 B.C.E. in the battle of **Nineveh**, the Assyrian capital.

> **DID YOU KNOW?**
>
> Settled communities needed the reliable sources of food and fresh water a temperate climate could provide. Surpluses of food allowed for cultural and civilizational development, not just survival.

Before its defeat, Assyria had developed as a powerful city-state in northern Mesopotamia. The Assyrians had based much of their culture on the Sumerian and Akkadian legacies, contributing unique sculpture and jewelry, establishing military dominance, and playing an important role in regional trade. At odds with Babylonia over the centuries, the Assyrian Empire had grown to encompass most of the Fertile Crescent. The Assyrian identity persists to this day among the (widely persecuted) Assyrian people in Iraq, Syria, Turkey, and Iran.

Around 1200 B.C.E. during a time of instability in Mesopotamia, the region became vulnerable to the **Hittites** from Anatolia. The Hittites had developed in the Bronze Age but flourished in the **Iron Age**, developing expertise in metallurgy to create strong weapons; they also mastered horsemanship and invented chariots. These technological developments made the Hittites a strong military power and a threat to both the Assyrians and later the Egyptians (see below); not only did these empires risk losing land but they also lost control of trade routes throughout the Fertile Crescent. Eventually Assyria grew strong enough to overcome the Hittites.

Like Assyria, Babylonia inherited the Akkadian language and used the Sumerian language in religious settings; it also inherited other elements of Sumerian civilization and developed them further. In the eighteenth century B.C.E., King Hammurabi in Babylonia had developed courts and an early codified rule of law—**the Code of Hammurabi**—which meted out justice on an equal basis: "an eye for an eye, a tooth for a tooth."

Babylonia continued settled, urban development supported by organized agriculture, warfare, administration, and justice; **Babylon** became a major ancient city. Babylonia developed more advanced astronomy, medicine, mathematics, philosophy, and art (particularly in working with clay, building bricks, and bas relief).

Furthermore, Babylonian civilization featured literature, developing the Sumerian poetry that was the basis for the *Epic of Gilgamesh* into the extended

work we know today. (In fact, according to the Smithsonian, more lines from the epic have been discovered in stone fragments in Iraq as recently as 2011.) After the fall of Nineveh, Babylonia would control Mesopotamia until the fall of Babylon to the Persian Achaemenid Empire in Persia in 539 B.C.E. (see below).

Meanwhile, development had been under way in the **Nile Valley** in ancient **Egypt.** Known for their pyramids, art, and pictorial writing (**hieroglyphs**), the ancient Egyptians emerged as early as 5000 B.C.E.; evidence of Egyptian unity under one monarch, or **pharaoh**, dates to the First Dynasty, around 3000 B.C.E.

Despite the surrounding Sahara Desert, the fertile land on the banks of the Nile River lent itself to agriculture, and the early Egyptians were able to develop settled communities thanks to agriculture and irrigation. Civilizations developed on the Upper and Lower Nile, unifying under the early dynasties, which established the Egyptian capital at **Memphis**. By the Fourth Dynasty, Egypt's civilizational institutions, written language, art, and architecture were well developed. It was during this period that the famous **pyramids** were erected at Giza; these structures were actually burial tombs for the Pharaohs Khufu, Khafre, and Menkaure circa 2400 – 2500 B.C.E. In addition, the religious framework of ancient Egypt had become established, with a complex mythology of various gods.

Following this period, around 2200 B.C.E. Egypt became increasingly unstable; eventually fighters from the city of Thebes took over, establishing the Eleventh Dynasty. The subsequent Twelfth Dynasty took control of Nubia (now Sudan), an area rich in gold and other materials. Egypt grew in power; it reached its apex during the Eighteenth Dynasty, between 1550 and 1290 B.C.E. Led by the powerful Pharaoh **Thutmose III**, Egypt expanded into the Levant.

Later, **King Akhenaten (Amenhotep IV)** abolished the Egyptian religion, establishing a cult of the sun—Aten—linked to himself. During this period Egypt saw a surge of iconoclastic art and sculpture. However, Akhenaten's successors, particularly Ramesses I and Ramesses II, founded the Nineteenth Dynasty and returned to traditional values. Under **Ramesses II**, Egypt battled the aggressive Hittites in the Levant, reaching a stalemate. Egypt eventually fell into decline, losing control of the Levant and eventually falling to Assyria.

> **QUICK REVIEW**
>
> What were the contributions of the early Middle Eastern civilizations? List several.

INDIA

Meanwhile, early civilizations also developed farther east. The **Indus Valley Civilizations** flourished in the Indian Subcontinent and the Indus and Ganges river basins. The **Harappan** civilization was based in Punjab from around 3000 B.C.E. The major cities of **Harappa** and **Mohenjo-daro** featured grid systems indicative of detailed urban planning; they may be the earliest planned cities in the world. In

addition, Harappan objects found in Mesopotamia reveal trade links between the civilizations.

Centuries later, concurrent with the Roman Empire, the **Gupta Empire** emerged in India. During this period, known as the Golden Age of India, the region was economically strong; there was active trade by sea with China, East Africa, and the Middle East in spices, ivory, silk, cotton, and iron, which was highly profitable as an export.

The Guptas encouraged music, art, architecture, and Sanskrit literature and philosophy. While practitioners of Hinduism, the empire was tolerant of Buddhists and Jains. Organized administration and rule of law made it possible for **Chandragupta II** to govern a large territory throughout the Subcontinent. However, by 550, invasions from the north by the Huns and internal conflicts within the Subcontinent led to imperial decline.

CHINA

In China, the **Shang Dynasty**, the first known dynasty, ruled the **Huang He** or **Yellow River** area around the second millennium B.C.E. and developed the earliest known Chinese writing, which helped unite Chinese-speaking people throughout the region. Like the early civilizations in the Middle East, the Shang Dynasty featured the use of bronze technology, horses, wheeled technology, walled cities, and other advances beyond the Neolithic societies.

Around 1056 B.C.E. the **Zhou** Dynasty emerged. It succeeded the Shang and expanded Chinese civilization to the **Chiang Jiang** (Yangtze River) region. Under the Zhou Dynasty, China developed a social and political infrastructure in which family aristocracies controlled the country, with the capital at **Hao** (near **Xi'an**). Ancestral cults controlled tracts of land throughout the country in a hierarchy similar to later European feudalism, setting the foundation for hierarchical rule and social stratification.

> **DID YOU KNOW?**
>
> Shared customs like the use of silkworms, jade, chopsticks, and the practice of Confucianism also indicate early Chinese unity.

The concept of the **Mandate of Heaven**, in which the emperor had a divine mandate to rule, emerged from the understanding that land was divinely inherited. The unstable period toward the end of the Zhou Dynasty was known as the **Spring and Autumn Period**; during this time **Confucius** lived (c. 551 – 479 B.C.E.). His teachings would be the basis for Confucianism, the foundational Chinese philosophy emphasizing harmony and respect for hierarchy.

Following the chaotic **Warring States Period** (c. 475 – 221 B.C.E.) the short-lived but influential **Qin Dynasty** emerged, unifying disparate Chinese civilizations and regions under the first Emperor, **Qin Shihuangdi**. This dynasty (221 – 206 B.C.E.) was characterized by a centralized administration, expanded infrastructure,

standardization in weights and measures, standardized writing, a standardized currency, and strict imperial control. The administrative **bureaucracy** established by the emperor was the foundation of Chinese administration until the twentieth century. In addition, the Emperor constructed the **Great Wall of China**; Emperor Qin Shihuangdi's tomb is guarded by the famous **terracotta figurines**. During the Qin Dynasty, China expanded as far south as Vietnam.

Figure 1.2. Great Wall of China

Despite the short length of the Qin Dynasty, it had a lasting impact on Chinese organization. The **Han Dynasty** took over in 206 for the next 300 years (206 B.C.E. – 220 C.E.), retaining Qin administrative organization and adding Confucian ideals of hierarchy and harmony. The Han prized education in the Confucian tradition and the idea that educated men should control administrative government began to take root in China. Women were not included in politics or administration.

THE AMERICAS

Prehistoric peoples migrated to the Americas from Asia during the Paleolithic period, and evidence of their presence dates to 13,000 years ago; remnants of the **Clovis** people dating to this time have been found in New Mexico. Recent findings in Canada suggest, however, that prehistoric peoples may have come to North America even earlier, about 13,300 years ago. Migration from Asia was gradual, probably occurring over hundreds or thousands of years; early humans likely crossed by land from Siberia to Alaska, while some may even have had naval capabilities and arrived by boat. Gradually, humans spread throughout the hemisphere.

From around 1200 B.C.E., the **Olmec** civilization developed on the Mexican Gulf Coast. Its massive sculptures reflect complex religious and spiritual beliefs. Later civilizations in Mexico included the **Zapotecs**, **Mixtecs**, **Toltecs**, and **Mayas** in the Yucatán peninsula. Throughout Mesoamerica, civilizations had developed

irrigation to expand and enrich agriculture, similar to developments in the Fertile Crescent.

Meanwhile, in South America, artistic evidence remains of the **Chavin**, **Moche**, and **Nazca** peoples, who preceded the later Inca civilization and empire. The complex Chavin style, which focused on animals, went on to influence Andean art, while the Moche have left behind complicated ceramics comparable to Hellenic artifacts. The construction of the famous Nazca lines, enormous sketches in the ground only visible from the air, remains a mystery.

In North America, the remains of mounds in the Mississippi Valley region may be ancient spiritual structures. For more discussion of precolonial North American peoples, please see Chapter Two, "United States History."

PERSIA AND GREECE

The **Persian** emperor **Cyrus**, founder of the **Achaemenid Empire**, conquered the Babylonians in the sixth century B.C.E. His son **Darius** extended Persian rule from the Indus Valley to Egypt, and north to **Anatolia** by about 400 B.C.E., where the Persians encountered the ancient **Greeks**. Known for its fundamental impact on Western civilization to this day, neighboring Greek or **Hellenic civilization** included political, philosophical, and mathematical thought; art and architecture; and poetry and theater.

> **QUICK REVIEW**
>
> How is Greek philosophy and its focus on reason important in modern culture?

Greece was comprised of **city-states** like **Athens**, the first known **democracy**, and the military state **Sparta**. Historically these city-states had been rivals; however, they temporarily united to come to the aid of Ionian Greeks in Anatolia under Persian rule and drive Persia from Greece. In Anatolia, the Persian king **Xerxes** led two campaigns against Greek forces. The Greeks held the Persians at bay, and much of Greece became unified under Athens following the war. It was during this period, the **Golden Age** of Greek civilization that much of the Hellenic art, architecture, and philosophy known today emerged.

The term *democracy* comes from the Greek word *demokratia*—"people power." It was participatory rather than representative; officials were chosen by groups rather than elected. Athens was the strongest of the many small political bodies (in fact, the word *political* comes from the Greek word *polis* meaning "city-state" or "community"). The Persians had been decisively defeated at the battles of **Marathon** (490 B.C.E.) and **Salamis** (480 B.C.E.) around 460 B.C.E. Athens became a revolutionary democracy controlled by the poor and working classes under the Athenian leaders **Pericles** and **Ephialtes**.

In this period and into the fourth century B.C.E., the **Parthenon** was built, as were other masterpieces of ancient Greek sculpture and architecture. **Socrates**

began teaching philosophy, influencing later philosophers like **Plato** who founded the Academy where figures like **Aristotle** emerged, establishing the basis for modern western philosophical and political thought. Playwrights like **Sophocles, Euripides,** and **Aeschylus** emerged; their work influenced later western literature.

Despite its status as a democracy, Athens was not fully democratic: women did not have a place in politics, and Athenians practiced slavery. Furthermore, those men eligible to participate in political life had to prove that both of their parents were Athenian (the criterion of double descent).

Toward the end of the fifth century B.C.E., Athens and Sparta were at odds once again during the **Peloponnesian War** (431 – 404 B.C.E.), which involved most of the Hellenic world and ultimately crippled the Athenian democracy permanently. Instability permitted the rise of the northern state of Macedon; later in the fourth century B.C.E., Philip II of Macedonia was able to take over most of Greece. His son **Alexander** (later known as Alexander the Great) would go on to conquer Persia, spreading Greek civilization throughout much of Western and Central Asia.

Rome

Meanwhile, in Italy, the ancient Romans had begun consolidating their power. The city of **Rome** was founded as early as the eighth century B.C.E.; it became strong thanks to its importance as a trade route for the Greeks and other Mediterranean peoples. Early Roman culture drew from the **Etruscans**, native inhabitants of the Italian peninsula, and the Greeks, from whom it borrowed elements of architecture, art, language, and even religion.

Originally a kingdom, Rome became a republic under **Lucius Junius Brutus** in 509 B.C.E. As a **republic**, Rome elected lawmakers (senators) to the **Senate**. The Romans developed highly advanced infrastructure, including aqueducts and roads, some still in use today. Economically powerful Rome began conquering areas around the Mediterranean with its increasingly powerful military, expanding westward to North Africa in the **Punic Wars** (264 – 146 B.C.E.) against its rival **Carthage** (in present-day Tunisia). With conquest of territory and expansion of trade came increased slavery, and working class Romans (**Plebeians**) were displaced; at the same time, the wealthy ruling class (**Patricians**) became more powerful and corrupt. Resulting protest movements led by the tribunes **Gaius** and **Tiberius** led to legislative reform and republican stabilization, strengthening the republic by the first century B.C.E.

The increasingly diversified republic, while militarily and economically strong, was still divided between the wealthy ruling class (the **Optimates**, or "the best") and the working, the poor, and the military (now calling themselves **Populare**, "the people," still favoring more democratization). As the Senate weakened due to its own corruption, the **First Triumvirate** of the military leaders **Gaius Julius Caesar** and **Gnaeus Pompeius Magnus (Pompey the Great)**, and the wealthy citizen **Marcus Licinius Crassus** consolidated their rule of the republic. Pompey and Crassus

belonged to the Optimate class, while Julius Caesar, a popular military leader, was firmly of the Populare.

Caesar had proven himself in the widely chronicled conquest of **Gaul** (today, France), and was respected and beloved by the military for his personal devotion to his troops. Meanwhile, Crassus was the wealthiest man in Rome, controlling most of the political class; despite his wealth, he was not popular among the Populare and was not regarded as a military leader on the level of Caesar, though he had played a role in the defeat of the widespread slave rebellion led by the gladiator **Spartacus**. Pompey had led successful missions conquering territory for Rome in Syria and elsewhere in the Levant; he also took credit for defeating Spartacus, though he played less of a role than Crassus, causing a rift between the two.

With resentment between Crassus and Pompey over credit for the defeat of Spartacus, Crassus' insecurity over his perception as a military leader, and Caesar's popularity among the Populare, the Triumvirate was short-lived. Crassus was killed fighting the Parthians in Turkey in 53 B.C.E., at which point Pompey and Caesar declared war upon each other; the two fought in Greece where Pompey was defeated, fled to Egypt, and was assassinated.

Forcing the corrupt Senate to give him control, Caesar began to transition Rome from a republic (if, at that point, in name only) to what would become an empire. Caesar was assassinated by a group of senators led by **Brutus** and **Cassius** in 44 B.C.E.; however, in that short time he had been able to consolidate and centralize imperial control. His cousin, **Marcus Antonius (Mark Antony)**, his friend **Marcus Aemilius Lepidus**, and his nephew **Gaius Octavius Thurinus (Octavian)** defeated Brutus and Cassius two years later at the Battle of Philippi, forming the **Second Triumvirate**.

Lepidus was sent from Rome to Hispania (Spain) and Africa while Mark Antony and Octavian split control of Rome between east and west, respectively. However, the two went to war after Antony became involved with the Egyptian queen **Cleopatra**, upsetting the balance of power; Octavian defeated Antony and Cleopatra, taking control of Rome in 31 B.C.E. He took the name **Augustus Caesar** when the Senate gave him supreme power in 27 B.C.E., becoming the first Roman emperor and effectively starting the Roman Empire.

At this time, Rome reached the height of its power, and the Mediterranean region enjoyed a period of stability known as the ***Pax Romana.*** Rome controlled the entire Mediterranean region and lands stretching as far north as Germany and Britain, territory into the Balkans, far into the Middle East, Egypt, North Africa, and Iberia. In this time of relative peace and prosperity, Latin literature flourished, as did art, architecture, philosophy, mathematics, science, and international trade throughout Rome and beyond into Asia and Africa. A series of emperors would follow and Rome remained a major world power, but it would never again reach the height of prosperity and stability that it did under Augustus.

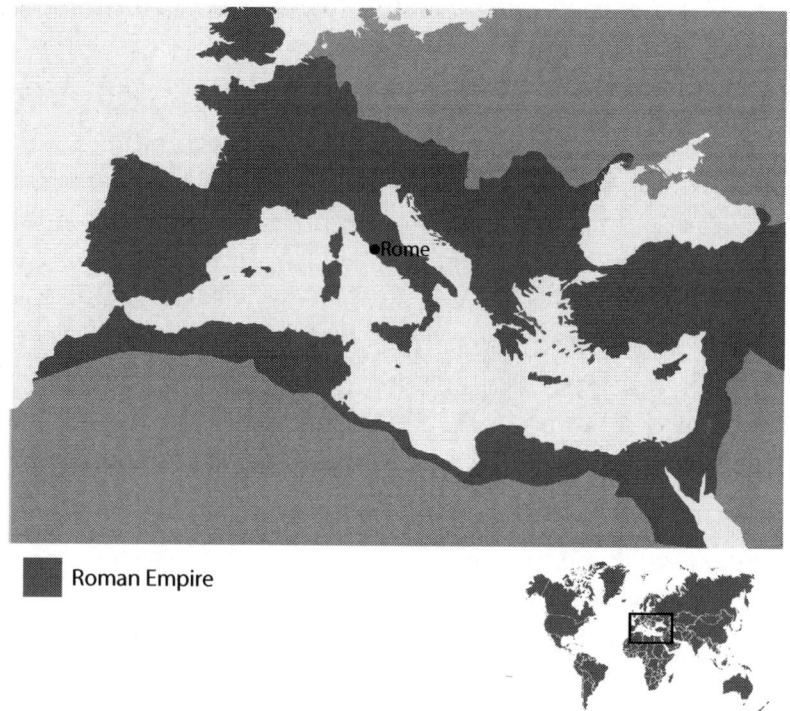

Figure 1.3. Pax Romana

It was during the time of Augustus that a Jewish carpenter named Jesus in Palestine began teaching that he was the son of the Jewish God, and that his death would provide salvation for all of humanity. Jesus was eventually crucified; followers of **Jesus Christ**, called Christians, preached his teachings throughout Rome. Despite the persecution of Christians, the concept of forgiveness of sin became popular and **Christianity** would eventually become the official religion of Rome. Christianity's universal appeal and applicability to people of diverse backgrounds would allow it to spread quickly.

By 300 C.E., Rome was in decline. Following a series of unstable administrations, **Diocletian** (284 – 305 C.E.) took over as Emperor, effectively dividing the empire into two: the Western Roman Empire and the Eastern Roman Empire. Diocletian reestablished some stability and more effective administration, creating a loose power-sharing agreement throughout the empire. The Christian **Constantine** took over the eastern half of the empire, establishing a new capital at **Constantinople**, Christianity as an official religion, and building the **Hagia Sophia**. However, the ambitious Constantine reconquered the Western Roman Empire and reunited the empire in 324 C.E.; the capital remained at Constantinople, and the balance of power and stability shifted to the east.

Figure 1.4. Hagia Sophia

This political shift enabled the western (later, Catholic) Church to gain power in Rome. One of Jesus Christ's followers, Peter, was considered to be the first **Pope**, or leader of Christian ministry. He had been executed in Rome in 67 C.E. after a lifetime of spreading the religion; ever since, the city has been a base of Christianity and home to the **Vatican**, the seat of the Catholic Church. Over time, the Catholic Church would become one of the most powerful political entities in the world; even today, following several schisms in Christianity, there are around one billion Catholics worldwide.

The western part of the Roman Empire gradually fell into disarray: a weakening Rome had created security agreements with different European clans like the **Anglo-Saxons**, the **Franks**, the **Visigoths**, the **Ostrogoths**, and the **Slavs**, among others, to protect its western and northern borders. Eventually, these groups rebelled against the government and what was left of the Roman Empire in the west finally fell. In Western Europe, the last Roman emperor was killed in **476 C.E.**, marking the end of the empire. The west dissolved into territories controlled by these and other tribes.

> **DID YOU KNOW?**
>
> These clans and others from Central Asia were able to defeat the Romans in the north and settle in Europe, thanks to their equestrian skills, superior wheels, and iron technology.

Meanwhile the eastern part of the Roman Empire, with its capital at Constantinople, evolved into the unified **Byzantine Empire**. The Byzantine emperor **Justinian**

(527 – 565 C.E.) re-conquered parts of North Africa, Egypt, and Greece, established rule of law, and reinvigorated trade with China. Ultimately, the Byzantines would control varying amounts of land in Anatolia, the Levant, and North Africa until the conquest of Constantinople by the Ottoman Turks in 1453.

He also continued the establishment of Christianity, rebuilding the Hagia Sophia, and eliminating the last vestiges of the Greco-Roman religion and competing Christian sects. However, over time, differences in doctrine between the church in Rome and Christians in Constantinople would give way to a schism, creating the Roman Catholic Church and the Greek Orthodox Church, as discussed.

During the early Middle Ages in Europe and the Byzantine Empire, the roots of another civilization were developing in the Arabian Peninsula. In the seventh century, the Prophet **Muhammad** began teaching **Islam**. Based on the teachings of Judaism and Christianity, Islam presented as the final version of these two religions, evolving its own set of laws and philosophical teachings. Like Christianity, it held universal appeal.

Conversion was (and is) simple, as is practicing the faith; the religion transcends national and ethnic differences; and it offers the possibility of redemption, forgiveness of sins, and a pleasant afterlife. Furthermore, due to ideological similarities, Muslims were willing to accept Jews and Christians as **People of the Book** rather than forcing their conversion, enabling their later conquest of Southwest Asia and facilitating relationships in the region. Leading a small group of followers out of the desert to conquer the Arabian cities of Mecca and Medina, where they would establish the beginnings of the **Caliphate**, the political embodiment of the society envisioned in Islam, Muhammad's followers would later come to control Southwest Asia and North Africa.

SAMPLE QUESTIONS

1) **What is required for a settled community?**
    A. domesticated animals
    B. a source of fresh water
    C. technology
    D. weapons

Answers:

A. Incorrect. While domesticated animals can be a food source or facilitate production, they are not absolutely necessary for food production or surplus.

B. **Correct.** Fresh water permits a reliable food source, which allows for settlement; people need not travel in search of food.

C. Incorrect. While technology is useful and can improve quality of life, it is not absolutely necessary for a settled society.

D. Incorrect. While weapons are useful for ensuring safety, they are not essential for establishing a settled society.

2) **The earliest known form of writing to use characters to create words was**

A. cuneiform, developed by the Egyptians.

B. cuneiform, developed by the Sumerians.

C. hieroglyphs, developed by the Egyptians.

D. hieroglyphs, developed by the Sumerians.

Answers:

A. Incorrect. The Egyptians did not develop cuneiform.

B. Correct. The Sumerians developed cuneiform.

C. Incorrect. While the Egyptians did develop hieroglyphs, they were pictographs, or images that expressed meaning rather than characters that formed written versions of spoken words.

D. Incorrect. The Sumerians did not develop hieroglyphs.

3) **The Shang and Zhou Dynasties are particularly relevant in Chinese history for their contributions in**

A. developing Chinese administration.

B. centralizing Chinese imperial power as symbolized through the terracotta figurines in the imperial tombs.

C. forming a Chinese identity through the development of written language, the Emperor's Mandate of Heaven, and fostering Confucianism.

D. ensuring China's safety by building the Great Wall of China.

Answers:

A. Incorrect. These developments occurred under the Qin Dynasty.

B. Incorrect. The terracotta figurines are found in the tomb of the Qin Emperor Shihuangdi.

C. Correct. Written Chinese developed under the Shang Dynasty, and the Mandate of Heaven emerged under the Zhou Dynasty; furthermore, traditions like the use of chopsticks also came about during these periods.

D. Incorrect. Again, construction of the Great Wall of China began during the Qin Dynasty.

4) **The Athenian concept of democracy embraced**
   A. participatory democracy, in which local groups made decisions directly by vote, permitting the poor to dominate the process rather than the elites.
   B. an anonymous electoral process similar to that of the United States in which officials were elected.
   C. people of all backgrounds, so that all residents of Athens had a stake in the political process.
   D. an educated electorate in order to ensure the best possible decision-making.

   Answers:
   A. Correct. The Athenian notion of *demokratia*, or people power, was participatory rather than representative.
   B. Incorrect. Voting was not anonymous in Athens.
   C. Incorrect. Only free male Athenians, who could prove Athenian parentage, could take part in the process.
   D. Incorrect. Education was not required to participate.

5) **How did Julius Caesar rise to and retain power?**
   A. He invaded Rome with his armies from Gaul, and used his military resources to control the Empire.
   B. He was elected president of the Senate by the people thanks to political support throughout the Republic.
   C. He took control of the Senate and maintained control of Rome thanks to his charisma and widespread popularity among the people.
   D. As part of the Triumvirate, he was guaranteed a leadership position and the support of Crassus and Pompey.

   Answers:
   A. Incorrect. While Julius Caesar was a powerful military leader, he did not take power purely through military means. Furthermore, when he came to power, Rome was still nominally a republic, not an empire.
   B. Incorrect. There was no president of the Senate and he was not elected as such.
   C. Correct. The Senate's corruption and weakness, and Caesar's popularity with the plebeians, support of the military, and strong leadership, enabled him to take and retain control.
   D. Incorrect. Caesar, Pompey, and Crassus were rivals and their alliance was one of convenience. Furthermore, both Pompey and Crassus were dead by the time Caesar took power.

World Religions

Judaism

Judaism was the first **monotheistic** religion; its adherents believe in only *one* god. It is believed that God came to the Hebrew Abraham and that the Hebrews—the Jew—were to be God's *chosen people*, to serve as an example to the world. Later, **Moses** would lead the Jews out of slavery in Egypt, and God gave him **Ten Commandments** or laws, the basis of what would become Judeo-Christian and Islamic moral codes. Notably, these moral codes applied to all people, including slaves. In addition to confirming the singular nature of God, the Ten Commandments laid out social rules for an organized society under that one god: to refrain from theft and murder and to honor one's parents, among others. Judaism's holy texts are the **Torah** and the **Talmud** (religious and civil law). There are different branches of Judaism with varying teachings, including Orthodox, Conservative, and Reform Judaism, among others.

Christianity

In Roman Palestine, the Jewish carpenter **Jesus** taught that he was the son of the singular, Jewish God. Christians believe that Jesus came to suffer and die for the sins of mankind so that all mankind may be forgiven for sin. He gained many followers for his teaching; ultimately, he was crucified. Christians believe that Jesus rose from the dead three days later (the **Resurrection**) and ascended to heaven. Christians believe that Jesus was miraculously born from a virgin mother (the **Virgin Mary**) and believe in the **Holy Trinity**, that God is made up of the Father, the Son, and the Holy Spirit, all parts of one God. The **Catholic Church** is led by the Pope and descended from the early western Church that followed the **Schism of 1054,** when theological disagreement divided the Church into the western Catholic Church and **Eastern Orthodox** Christianity. Later in Western Europe, the **Protestant Reformation** gave rise to other forms of Protestant, or non-Catholic, Christianity.

Islam

Islam is rooted in the Arabian Peninsula. Muslims believe that the angel Gabriel spoke to the **Prophet Muhammad,** transmitting the literal word of **Allah** (God), which was later written down as the **Qur'an.** Muhammad is considered by Muslims to be the final prophet of the god of the Jews and Christians, and Islam shares similar moral teachings. Islam recognizes leaders like Abraham, Moses, and Jesus, but unlike Christianity, views Jesus as a prophet, not as the son of God. The Prophet Muhammad was a religious, military, and political leader; in conquering the Arabian Peninsula and later other parts of the Middle

> **QUICK REVIEW**
>
> Explain Monotheism. What are the major monotheistic religions and who are their main figures?

East, he protected the **People of the Book,** or Jews and Christians. After his death, discord among his followers resulted in the **Sunni-Shi'a Schism** over his succession and some teachings; to this day, deep divisions remain between many Sunnis and Shi'ites. Like Judaism, Islam also has a book of legal teachings called the **Hadith**.

HINDUISM

Major tenets of Hindu belief include **reincarnation,** or that the universe and its beings undergo endless cycles of rebirth and **karma,** that one creates one's own destiny. The soul is reincarnated until it has resolved all karmas, at which point it attains **moksha,** or liberation from the cycle. Hindus believe in multiple divine beings. Religion is based in the **Vedic scriptures**; other important texts include the **Upanishads,** the **Mahabharata,** and the **Bhagavad Gita.** Hinduism is the primary religion in India and is intertwined with the **caste system,** the hierarchical societal structure.

BUDDHISM

In Buddhism, the Prince **Siddhartha Gautama** is said to have renounced worldly goods and lived as an ascetic in what is today northern India, seeking **enlightenment** around the third century B.C.E. Buddhism teaches that desire—the ego, or self—is the root of suffering, and that giving up or **transcending** material obsessions will lead to freedom, or **nirvana**—enlightenment. While Buddhism originated in India, it is practiced throughout Asia and the world. The main Buddhist schools of theology are the **Mahayana,** which is prevalent in northern and eastern Asia (Korea, parts of China, Mongolia), and **Theravada,** dominant in Southeast Asia and Indian Ocean regions. **Vajrayana** Buddhism is central to Tibetan Buddhism.

> **QUICK REVIEW**
>
> Compare Hinduism and Buddhism.

CONFUCIANISM

Confucianism teaches obedience and adherence to tradition in order to maintain a harmonious society. Ideally, practicing integrity and respecting wisdom would ensure that authority would be used for beneficial purposes. Confucius himself was a Chinese scholar in the sixth century B.C.E.; his philosophy would go on to inform Chinese culture for centuries.

Feudalism through the Era of Expansion

The Middle Ages in Europe

The Byzantine Empire remained a strong civilization and a place of learning. Constantinople was a commercial center, strategically located at the Dardanelles, connecting Asian trade routes with Europe. Later, missionaries traveled north to Slav-controlled Russia, spreading Christianity and literacy. The ninth-century missionaries Saints Cyril and Methodius are credited with developing what would become the **Cyrillic** alphabet used in many Slavic languages. In 988 C.E., the Russian Grand Prince of Kiev, **Vladimir I**, converted to Christianity and ordered his subjects to do so as well. Russian Christianity was influenced by the Byzantine doctrine, what would become Greek Orthodox Christianity.

Despite the chaos in Western Europe, the Church in Rome remained strong, becoming a stabilizing influence. However, differences in doctrine between Rome and Constantinople became too wide to overcome. Beginning in 1054, a series of **schisms** developed in the now-widespread Christian religion between the **Roman Catholic Church** and the **Greek Orthodox Church** over matters of doctrine such as the role of the Pope and papal authority, the use of leavened versus unleavened bread in religious services, and some theological concepts. Eventually the two would become entirely separate churches.

In Europe, the early Middle Ages (or *Dark Ages*) from the fall of Rome to about the tenth century, were a chaotic, unstable, and unsafe time. What protection and stability existed were represented and maintained by the Catholic Church and the feudal system.

Society and economics were characterized by decentralized, local governance, or **feudalism**, a hierarchy where land and protection were offered in exchange for loyalty. Feudalism was the dominant social, economic, and political hierarchy of the European middle ages from the time of Charlemagne (discussed further below).

In exchange for protection, **vassals** would pledge **fealty**, or **pay homage to lords**, landowners who would reward their vassals' loyalty with land, or **fiefs**. Economic and social organization consisted of **manors**, self-sustaining areas possessed by lords but worked by peasants. The peasants were **serfs**, not slaves but not entirely free. Tied to the land, they worked for the lord in exchange for protection; however they were not obligated to fight. Usually they were also granted some land for their own use. While not true slaves, their lives were effectively controlled by the lord.

Warriors who fought for lords, called **knights**, were rewarded with land and could become minor lords in their own right. Lords themselves could be vassals of other lords; that hierarchy extended upward to kings or the Catholic Church. The Catholic Church itself was a major landowner and political power. In a Europe not yet dominated by sovereign states, the **Pope** was not only a religious leader, but also a military and political one.

Small kingdoms and alliances extended throughout Europe, and stable trade was difficult to maintain. The **Celts** controlled Britain and Ireland until the invasion of the **Saxons**; around 600 C.E., the Saxons conquered Britain while the Celts were pushed to Ireland, Scotland, and Brittany in northwest France. While the Church was gaining power, it was insecure in Italy as the **Germanic tribes** vied for control in Germany and France. Monasteries in Ireland and England retained and protected classical documentation in the wake of the fall of Rome and insecurity in Italy. The Germanic tribes themselves were threatened by Asian invaders like the **Huns**, increasing instability in central and eastern parts of Europe, where **Slavs** also fought for supremacy north of Byzantium.

> **DID YOU KNOW?**
>
> There were limits on sovereign power, however. In 1215, long before the revolution, English barons forced King John to sign the Magna Carta, which protected their property and rights from the king and was the basis for today's parliamentary system in that country.

One exception to the chaos was the Scandinavian **Viking** civilization. From the end of the eighth century until around 1100, the Vikings expanded their influence from Scandinavia, ranging from the Baltic Sea to the East to the North Sea through the North Atlantic, thanks to their extraordinary seafaring skills and technology. The Vikings traded with the Byzantine Empire and European powers; Byzantine and Middle Eastern artifacts have been found among Viking excavations in Scandinavia. They traveled to and sometimes raided parts of Britain, Ireland, France, and Russia.

The Icelandic **Erik the Red** established a settlement in Greenland, and his son **Leif Erikson** may have traveled as far as North America. In addition to military prowess and advanced shipbuilding technology, the Vikings had a complex religion with a pantheon of gods and well-developed mythology; they also developed a literary canon of **sagas** in Old Norse, the basis of some Scandinavian languages today. Viking achievements have been documented in literature from other European cultures like the Anglo-Saxons, as well as the Arab historian Ibn Fadlan.

Meanwhile, by the eighth century the North African **Moors**, part of the expanding Islamic civilization, had penetrated Iberia and were a threat to Christian Europe. **Charles Martel**, leader of the **Franks** in what is today France, defeated the Moors at the **Battle of Tours (or Poitiers)** in 732 C.E., effectively stopping any further Islamic incursion into Europe. The Christian Martel had previously consolidated his control of France, leading the Franks in victory over the Bavarians, Frisians, and other tribes and supporting their conversion to Christianity. Instability followed Charles Martel's death, however, and **Charlemagne**, the son of a court official, eventually took over the Merovingian kingdom following disputes over succession, complicated by the Merovingian traditions.

Charlemagne was able to maintain Frankish unity and consolidate his rule, extending Frankish control into Central Europe and defending the **Papal States** in central Italy. In what is considered the reemergence of centralized power in Europe,

parts of Western and Central Europe were organized under Charlemagne, who was crowned emperor of the Roman Empire by Pope Leo III in **800 C.E.** While in retrospect this seems long after the end of Rome, at the time many Europeans still perceived themselves as somehow still part of a Roman Empire. Today Charlemagne's rule is referred to as the **Carolingian Empire**.

Charlemagne brought stability to Western and Central Europe during a period when two powerful, non-Christian, organized civilizations—the Vikings in the north and the Islamic powers in the south—threatened what was left of western Christendom, and when insecurity was growing to the east with the decline of the Byzantines and the emergence of the Umayyad Caliphate based in Damascus. His reign strengthened the Roman Catholic Church and enabled the reemergence of Roman and Christian scholarship that had been hidden in English and Irish monasteries.

It was also under Charlemagne that the feudal system became truly organized, bringing more stability to Western Europe. The Catholic Church would dominate Europe from Ireland towards Eastern Europe—an area of locally controlled duchies, kingdoms, and alliances. In **962 C.E., Otto I** became emperor of the **Holy Roman Empire** in Central Europe, a confederation of small states which remained an important European power until its dissolution in **1806**.

While the Holy Roman Empire remained intact, the Carolingian Empire did not. Spain and Portugal remained under Muslim control, and France dissolved into small fiefdoms and territories. Meanwhile, England and Scotland were controlled by Norsemen (Vikings), especially Danish settlers, and various local Anglo-Saxon rulers, the remnants of the Germanic tribes that had come to rule Europe and led to the fall of Rome.

In 1066, **William the Conqueror** left Normandy in northwest France. The **Normans** established organization in England, including a more consolidated economy and kingdom supported by feudalism. They also consolidated Christianity as the local religion. English possessions included parts of France, nominally a kingdom but consisting of smaller territories with some level of independence. Intermarriage and conquest resulted in English control of Anjou and Bordeaux in France; William had brought control of French Brittany with him when he arrived on the island of Britain. Conflict between Britain and France would continue for several centuries, while rulers in Scandinavia and Northwest Europe consolidated power.

THE ISLAMIC WORLD

Meanwhile, in the wake of the decline of the Byzantine Empire, **Arab-Islamic empires** characterized by brisk commerce, advancements in technology and learning, and urban development arose in the Middle East.

Before the rise of Islam in the seventh century, the Arabian Peninsula was located at the intersection of the Byzantine Empire, a diverse collection of ethnicities, ruled by Greek Orthodox Christians, and the **Sasanians** (Persians), who practiced **Zoroastrianism**. Both of these empires sought to control trade with Central and eastern Asia along the Silk Road; they also sought to establish trade ties with Christian **Axum** (Ethiopia).

In Arabia itself, Judaism, Christianity, and animist religions were practiced by the Arab majority. The Prophet **Muhammad** was born in Mecca around 570; he began receiving messages from God (Allah), preaching them around 613 as the last affirmations of the monotheistic religions, and writing them as the **Qur'an**, the Islamic holy book. Driven from **Mecca** to Medina in 622, Muhammad and his followers were able to recapture the city and other major Arabian towns by the time of his death, establishing Islam and Arab rule in the region.

After Muhammad's death in **632 C.E.**, his followers, led by the first caliph **Abu Bakr**, went on to conquer land beyond Arabia north into the weakening Byzantine Empire. The well-organized Muslim Arabs, based in Arabia, led incursions into Syria, the Levant, and Mesopotamia, taking over these territories. Thanks to military, bureaucratic, and organizational skill as well as their ability to win over dissatisfied minorities, the Arabs eventually isolated the Byzantines to parts of Anatolia and Constantinople and crushed the Persian Sasanians.

> **DID YOU KNOW?**
>
> A caliph was considered both a political and a religious leader.

Muhammad's cousin and son-in-law **Ali**, his wife **Fatima** (Muhammad's eldest daughter), and their followers, had always believed that the leader of the Muslim Arabs should be a blood relative of Muhammad. Since Muhammad had no sons, the logical choice was Ali. However, the Meccan elites had felt differently, and the popular Abu Bakr was chosen as the first caliph.

Abu Bakr was succeeded by the second caliph Umar; upon his death the third caliph Uthman took over. Widely accused of corruption, Uthman was murdered in 656. The Islamic leadership finally settled on Ali to take over as the fourth caliph (the first four caliphs are known as the *Rashidun*, or rightly-guided ones). However, others in power felt differently. **Muawiya**, based in Damascus, led the opposition to Ali; this conflict is at the heart of the **Sunni-Shi'a Schism**.

> **DID YOU KNOW?**
>
> Ali's followers called themselves the *party of Ali* or, in Arabic, the *shiat Ali*, which is the origin of the word *Shia* or *Shi'ite* Muslims.

Ali and Fatima established their base in Kufa, in Mesopotamia. Unable to come to an agreement, the Arabs became embroiled in the First Civil War (656 – 661) over leadership; the conflict ended when Ali was murdered in 661. Unrest continued, and the bloody massacre of

Ali's son Hussein and his family in 680 in Karbala triggered the Second Civil War (680 – 692).

The violence of these years cemented divisions in Islam, and **Shi'ite Islam** emerged in Mesopotamia. The Shi'ites believed that Ali was the rightful heir to Muhammad's early Islamic empire, and maintained a focus on martyrdom, especially that of Ali and Hussein. The followers of the Meccan elites became known as **Sunnis**, "orthodox" Muslims with a focus on community rather than genealogy. Over the centuries, other differences in theology and history would develop.

Muawiya is considered the first caliph of the **Umayyad Caliphate** (empire), named for the leading Meccan tribe that had supported Muhammad from the beginning. The Arabs already controlled Arabia; by 750, they would control parts of Iberia, North Africa, Egypt, Arabia, the Levant, Mesopotamia, Persia, Armenia, and parts of Central Asia into Transoxiana (Uzbekistan) and the Indus River Valley (parts of Pakistan). Spain, or **al-Andalus**, was settled as early as 711.

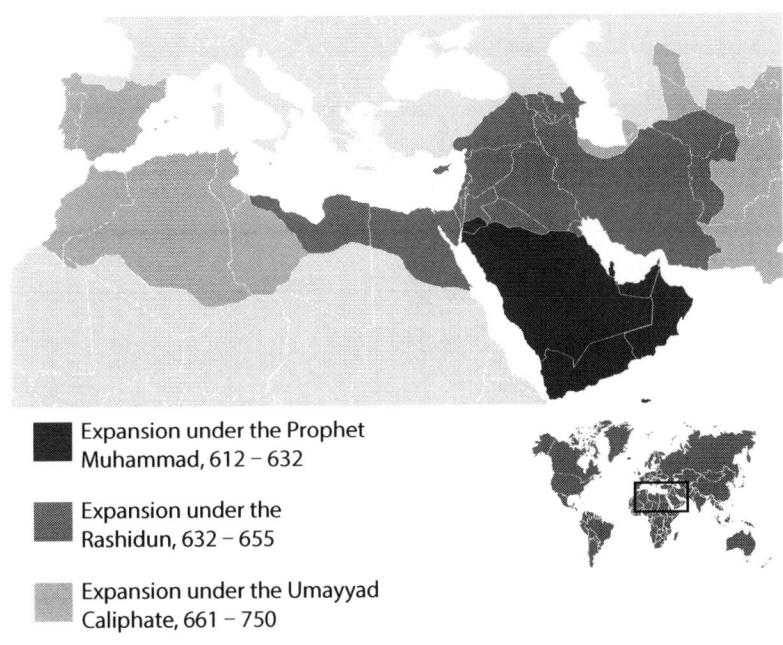

Figure 1.5. Islamic Expansion

Ongoing conflict among Arab elites resulted in the **Abbasid Caliphate** in 750 C.E., based in Baghdad. The Umayyad were overthrown by the Arab-Muslim Abbasid family, which established a new capital in Baghdad. The caliph **al-Mutasim** professionalized the military, creating professional soldiers called **mamluks**, freed slaves usually of Turkish origin. It was thought they would be more loyal with no family or national ties. The mamluks helped al-Mutasim consolidate imperial control and improve tax collection. Abbasid administration was also highly organized, allowing efficient taxation.

The administration and stability provided by the caliphates fostered an Arabic literary culture. Stability permitted open trade routes, economic development, and cultural interaction throughout Asia, the Middle East, North Africa, and parts of Europe. Furthermore, the Abbasid ruler **al-Mamun** fostered cultural and scientific study.

Thanks to the universality of the Arabic language, scientific and medical texts from varying civilizations—Greek, Persian, Indian—could be translated into Arabic and shared throughout the Islamic world. Arab thinkers studied Greek and Persian astronomy and engaged in further research. Arabs studied mathematics from around the world and developed algebra, enabling engineering, technological, and architectural achievements. Finally, Islamic art is well known for its geometric designs.

Around this time, the **Song Dynasty (960 – 1276)** controlled most of China. Under the Song, China experienced tremendous development and economic growth. Characterized by increasing urbanization, the Song featured complex administrative rule, including the difficult competitive written examinations required to obtain prestigious bureaucratic positions in government. Most traditions recognized as Chinese emerged under the Song, including the consumption of tea and rice and common Chinese architecture. The Song engaged not only in overland trade along the Silk Road, exporting silk, tea, ceramics, jade, and other goods, but also sea trade with Korea, Japan, Southeast Asia, India, Arabia and even East Africa.

Conflict and Cultural Exchange

Cultural exchange was not limited to interactions between Christian Europeans, Egyptians, and Levantine Muslims. Indeed, international commerce was vigorous along the **Silk Road,** trading routes which stretched from the Arab-controlled

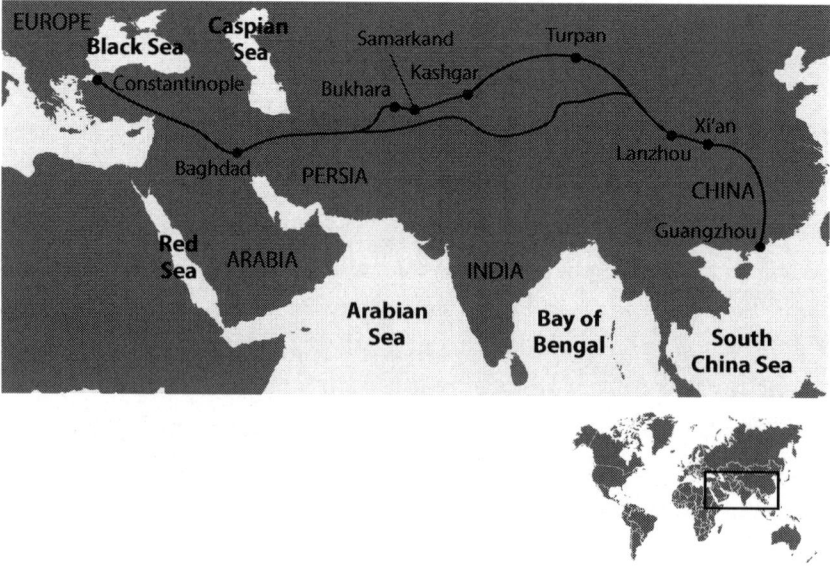

Figure 1.6. The Silk Road

Eastern Mediterranean to Song Dynasty China, where science and learning also blossomed. The Silk Road reflected the transnational nature of Central Asia: the nomadic culture of Central Asia lent itself to trade between the major civilizations of China, Persia, the Near East, and Europe. Buddhism and Islam spread into China. Chinese, Islamic, and European art, pottery, and goods were interchanged between the three civilizations—early globalization. The Islamic tradition of the **hajj**, or the pilgrimage to Mecca, also spurred cultural interaction. Islam had spread from Spain throughout North Africa, the Sahel, the Middle East, Persia, Central Asia, India, and China; peoples from all these regions traveled and met in Arabia as part of their religious pilgrimage.

Islam also spread along trans-Saharan trade routes into West Africa and the Sahel. Brisk trade between the gold-rich **Kingdom of Ghana** and Muslim traders based in Morocco brought Islam to the region around the eleventh century. The Islamic **Mali Empire** (1235 – 1500), based farther south in **Timbuktu**, eventually extended beyond the original Ghanaian boundaries all the way to the West African coast, and controlled the valuable gold and salt trades. It became a center of learning and commerce. At the empire's peak, the ruler **Mansa Musa** made a pilgrimage to Mecca in 1324. However, by 1500, the **Songhai Empire** had overcome Mali and eventually dominated the Niger River area.

> **QUICK REVIEW**
>
> How did the Silk Road and Islam both contribute to global cultural exchange?

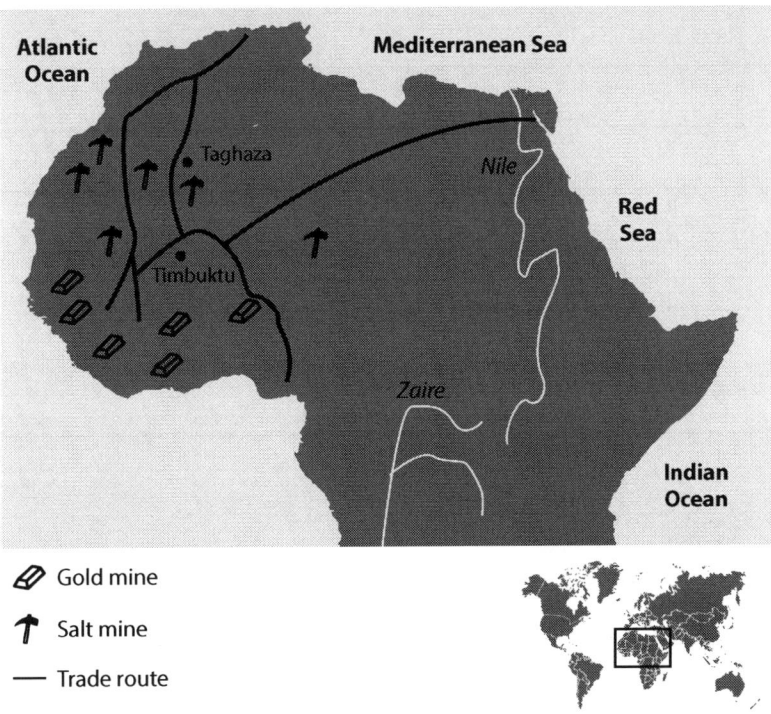

Figure 1.7. Trans-Saharan Trade Routes

Loss of Byzantine territory to the Islamic empires meant loss of Christian lands in the Levant—including Jerusalem and Bethlehem—to Muslims. In **1095 C.E.**, the Byzantine Emperor asked **Pope Urban II** for help to defend Jerusalem and protect Christians. With a history of Muslim incursions into Spain and France, anti-Muslim sentiment was strong in Europe and Christians there were easily inspired to fight them in the Levant, or **Holy Land**; the Pope offered lords and knights the chance to keep lands and bounty they won from conquered Muslims (and Jews) in this **Crusade**. He also offered Crusaders **indulgences**—forgiveness for sins committed in war and guarantees they would enter heaven.

Meanwhile, towards the end of the tenth century, the Abbasid Caliphate was in decline. The Shi'ite **Fatimids** took control of Syria and Egypt, addressing the Shi'ite claim to the caliphate. Other groups took control of provinces in Mesopotamia, Arabia, and Central Asia. In Spain, **Abd al-Rahman III** (891 – 961) had defied the Abbasids and the Fatimids, taking over **al-Andalus** (Spain) himself and fostering a unique Hispano-Arabic culture where intellectual pursuits bloomed. Based in Cordoba, Rahman was responsible for the Great Mosque. In Muslim Spain, the

Figure 1.8. Great Mosque Cordoba

famous Muslim philosopher **Averroes** developed his commentary on Aristotle; likewise, the Jewish **Maimonides** developed religious and philosophical thought. Conflict persisted with the Carolingians and with smaller Christian kingdoms in northern Spain, however.

In Western Europe, instability had been ongoing as control over continental territories passed between England and France. France never regained the strength it had under Charlemagne; while the French monarchy existed, smaller states remained powerful and power was decentralized. In England, despite internal divisions, organization accelerated upon William's 1066 conquest. The two civilizations were at odds.

Despite conflict in Europe, Christians found they had more in common with each other than with Muslims, and were able to unite to follow the Pope's call to arms to fight in the Middle East. The decline of the Abbasids had left the Levant vulnerable, and Christian Crusaders were able to establish settlements and small kingdoms in Syria and on the Eastern Mediterranean coast, conquering major cities and capturing Jerusalem by 1099 in the **First Crusade** as called for by Pope Urban II (see above).

The Crusades continued over several centuries. In 1171, the Kurdish military leader **Salah al-Din** (Saladin) abolished the Fatimid Caliphate; in 1187 he reconquered Jerusalem, driving European Christians out for good. Following Salah al-Din's death and a succession of rulers, elite slave troops took power. The **Mamluks (1250 – 1517)**, whose roots traced back to Abbasid Caliph al-Mutasim's fighting force, controlled Egypt; later they would defeat the Mongols in 1260, protecting Egypt and North Africa from the Mongol invasions.

While the ongoing Crusades never resulted in permanent European control over the Holy Land, they did open up trade routes between Europe and the Middle East, stretching all the way along the Silk Road to China. This increasing interdependence led to the European Renaissance.

Ongoing interactions between Europeans and Muslims exposed Europeans, who could now afford them thanks to international trade, to improved education and goods. However, the **Bubonic (Black) Plague** also spread to Europe as a result of global exchange, killing off a third of its population from 1347-1351. The plague had a worldwide impact: empires fell in its wake.

Back in Europe, conflict reached its height throughout the thirteenth and fourteenth centuries known as the **Hundred Years' War** (1337 – 1453). France was in political chaos during the mid-fourteenth century, decentralized and at times without a king; suffering the effects of the Black Plague; vulnerable to English attack; and periodically under English rule.

> **DID YOU KNOW?**
>
> During the Hundred Years' War, Joan of Arc led the French in the 1429 Battle of Orléans, reinvigorating French resistance to English incursions.

While conflict would continue, England lost its last territory in France, Bordeaux, in 1453 to the French **King Charles VII**.

In **al-Andalus** (Spain), despite some coexistence between Christians and Muslims under Muslim rule, raids and conflict were ongoing during the lengthy period of the **Reconquista**, which did not end until 1492 when Christian powers took Grenada. From the zenith of Muslim rule under **Abd al-Rahman**, Christian raids continued, as did shifting alliances between the small kingdoms of Christian Spain and Portugal. By the second half of the thirteenth century, the only remaining Muslim power in Iberia was Grenada. By the fifteenth century, small Christian Spanish kingdoms were vying for dominance. The marriage of **Ferdinand** of Castilla and **Isabella** of Aragon in 1479 connected those two kingdoms, and the monarchs were able to complete the Reconquista by taking Grenada and uniting Spain.

> **DID YOU KNOW?**
>
> Ferdinand and Isabella launched the Inquisition, an extended persecution of Jews and Jewish converts to Christianity who continued to practice Judaism in secret. Jews were tortured, killed, and exiled; their belongings and property were confiscated. Muslims were also persecuted and forced to convert to Christianity or be exiled.

EMPIRES IN TRANSITION

Beyond Egypt and the Levant, the collapse of the Abbasid Caliphate led to instability and decentralization of power in Mesopotamia, Persia, and Central Asia; smaller sultanates (territories ruled by sultans, regional leaders) emerged, and production and economic development declined. **Tang Dynasty China** closed its borders and trade on the Silk Road declined. In the eleventh century, the nomadic **Seljuks**, Turks from Central Asia, nominally took over the region from Central Asia through parts of the Levant. However, the Seljuks lacked effective administration or central authority.

Despite the lack of political cohesion, Islam remained a unifying force throughout the region, and political instability and decentralization paradoxically allowed local culture to develop, particularly Persian art and literature. Furthermore, Islam was able to thrive during this period: local religious leaders (**ulama**) had taken up community leadership positions following the loss of any powerful central authority, and Islam became a guiding force in law, justice, and social organization throughout the region. Yet political decentralization ultimately left the region vulnerable to the Mongol invasions of the twelfth and thirteenth centuries.

> **DID YOU KNOW?**
>
> During this period, Persian-influenced Sufi (mystical) Islam and poetry developed; Shi'ite theology and jurisprudence also developed as part of a strengthening independent Shi'ite identity.

In the Near East, the **Mongol invasions** destroyed agriculture, city life and planning, economic patterns and trade routes, and social stability. After some time, new patterns of trade emerged, new cities rose to prominence, and stability allowed for prosperity, but the Mongol invasions dealt a blow to the concept that Islam was inherently favored by God.

The **Mongol Empire** was based in Central Asia; led by **Genghis Khan**, the Mongols expanded throughout Asia thanks to their abilities in horsemanship and archery. Despite the rich history of transnational activity across Asia, the continent was vulnerable. Central Asia lacked one dominant culture or imperial power; Southwest Asia was fragmented following the decline of the Abbasids. These weaknesses, along with the disorganization of the Seljuks and the remnants of the Byzantines, allowed the Mongols to take over most of Eurasia—ultimately they controlled Pannonia (Hungary) through the Middle East, Persia, Central Asia, Northern and Western China, and Southeast Asia.

Likewise, in China, the Mongols destroyed local infrastructure, including the foundation of Chinese society and administration—the civil service examinations. However, in order to govern the vast territory effectively, the Mongols in China took a different approach. Genghis Khan's grandson **Kublai Khan** conquered China and founded the Mongol **Yuan Dynasty** in 1271.

Despite abolishing the examinations until 1315, the Yuan Dynasty maintained most of the administrative policy of the preceding Song Dynasty, including the Six Ministries, the Secretariat, and provincial administrative structure. Additionally, in spite of Mongol distrust of Confucianism and Confucian administrator-scholars, Kublai Khan educated his son in the Confucian tradition. The Yuan did, however, upend Chinese social hierarchy, placing Mongols at the top, followed by non-ethnic Han Chinese, and then Han Chinese.

Mongol attempts at imperial expansion in China into Japan and Southeast Asia, coupled with threats from the Black Plague, financial problems, and flooding, led to the decline of the Yuan Dynasty and the rise of the native Chinese **Ming Dynasty** in 1368. **Zhu Yuanzhang** led the Chinese to victory and ruled as the first Ming emperor from Nanjing; the capital later moved to Beijing in 1421. Ming China controlled land throughout Asia, accepting tribute from rulers in Burma, Siam (Thailand), Annam (Vietnam), Mongolia, Korea, and Central Asia.

The Ming reasserted Chinese control and continued traditional methods of administration; however the construction of the **Forbidden City**, the home of the Emperor in Beijing, helped consolidate imperial rule. The Ming also emphasized international trade; demand for ceramics in particular, in addition to silk and tea, was high abroad, and contact with seafaring traders like the Portuguese and Dutch in the sixteenth century was strong. The Ming also encouraged trade and exploration by sea; the Chinese explorer **Zheng He** traveled to India, Sri Lanka, and Asia.

Despite some decline in Mongol hegemony throughout Asia, the military leader **Timur** (also known as **Tamerlane**), a Mongol descendant from Transoxania

(now Uzbekistan) began conquering land in the area around 1364. By 1383, he occupied Moscow and turned toward Persia. Up to the turn of the century he had conquered Persia, Mesopotamia, much of the Caucasus, and Delhi. In the early fifteenth century, Timur took Syria, invaded Anatolia, and extracted tribute from Egypt. He died in 1405 on an expedition to China.

While rarely spending too much time in one place, Timur had contributed to the development of the capital of his empire, **Samarkand**, enriching Central Asia culturally.

Mongol decline was not only isolated to China; in Russia, **Ivan the Great** brought Moscow from Mongol to Slavic Russian control. In the late fifteenth century, Ivan had consolidated Russian power over neighboring Slavic regions. Despite Muscovy's status as a vassal state, Ivan, through both military force and diplomacy, achieved Moscow's independence in 1480. Turning Russian attention toward Europe, he set out to bring other neighboring Slavic and Baltic lands, including Poland-Lithuania and later, parts of Ukraine, under Russian rule. Ivan achieved a centralized, consolidated Russia that was the foundation for an empire and a sovereign nation that sought diplomatic status with Europe.

A century later, **Ivan the Terrible** set out to expand Russia further, to integrate it into Europe, and to strengthen Russian Orthodox Christianity. Named the first **tsar**, or emperor, Ivan reformed government, strengthening centralization and administrative bureaucracy and disempowering the nobility. He led the affirmation of orthodox Christianity, calling councils to organize the church and to canonize Russian saints. Ivan also reorganized the military, including promoting officials based on merit rather than status. However, overextension of resources and his oppressive entourage, the ***oprichnina***, depopulated the state and gave him the reputation as a despotic ruler. However, despite his weaknesses, Ivan's reforms strengthened the apparatus of the Russian state; he also expanded and improved foreign policy and relations, and developed Russian culture and religion.

Farther south in Central Asia, one of Timur's descendants, **Babur**, laid claim to Timur's dominions and would found the **Mughal Empire** of India. Despite his Mongol roots, Babur identified as Turkic due to his tribal origins, and enjoyed support from the powerful Ottoman Empire in Turkey (see below). In 1525, Babur set out for India. By 1529, he had secured land from Kandahar in the west to Bengal in the east; his grandson, **Akbar**, would consolidate the empire, which at the time consisted of small kingdoms. The Mughals would rule India until the eighteenth century and nominally control parts of the country until British takeover in the nineteenth century.

> **DID YOU KNOW?**
>
> The Mughal emperor Shah Jahan built the Taj Mahal in 1631.

During Mughal rule in India, the Ming Dynasty fell in China and the Qing took over. In 1644, the Ming fell to a peasant revolt; the **Manchu**, a non-Han group

from the north, took the opportunity to seize Beijing and take the country. Despite their status as non-Han Chinese, the Manchu were accepted; thus began the **Qing Dynasty**. They would also be China's last imperial rulers, losing power in 1911.

The first Qing emperor, the **Kangxi Emperor**, promoted the arts and education. Under the reign of the **Qianlong Emperor** (1736 – 1796), China grew to its largest size, including Tibet, Mongolia, Xinjiang, and parts of Russia. It became the dominant power in East Asia and a successful multi-ethnic state. Like the Kangxi Emperor, the Qianlong Emperor was a patron of the arts.

Meanwhile, in Persia, the **Safavids** emerged in 1501 in the wake of the Timurid Empire. This dynasty would rule from Azerbaijan in the west through to modern-day Pakistan and Afghanistan. A major rival of the Ottoman Empire, the Safavids were a stabilizing force in Asia. Following Sufism, the Safavids supported art, literature, architecture, and other learning. Their organized administration brought order and stability to Persia throughout their rule, which lasted until 1736, when the **Qajar Dynasty** took over.

Despite the instability inland, Indian Ocean trade routes had continued to function since at least the seventh century. These oceanic routes connected the Horn of Africa, the East African Coast, the Arabian Peninsula, Southern Persia, India, Southeast Asia, and China. The ocean acted as a unifying force throughout the region, and the **monsoon winds** permitted Arab, Persian, Indian, and Chinese merchants to travel to East Africa in search of goods such as ivory and gold—and slaves.

Despite the civilizational achievements of the Islamic empires, Tang and later Ming Dynasty China, and the Central Asian and Indian empires that would emerge from the Mongols, the **East African slave trade** remained vigorous until the nineteenth century. Arabs, Asians and other Africans kidnapped African people and sent them to lives of slavery throughout the Arab world and South Asia. Later, Europeans would take part in the trade, forcing Africans into slavery in colonies throughout South and Southeast Asia, and on plantations in Indian Ocean islands such as Madagascar.

The major East African port was **Zanzibar**, from which slaves, gold, coconut oil, ivory, and other African exports made their way to Asia and the Middle East. However, enslaved persons from Sub-Saharan Africa were also forced north overland to markets in **Cairo**, where they were sold and dispersed throughout the Arab-Islamic, Fatimid, and Ottoman empires.

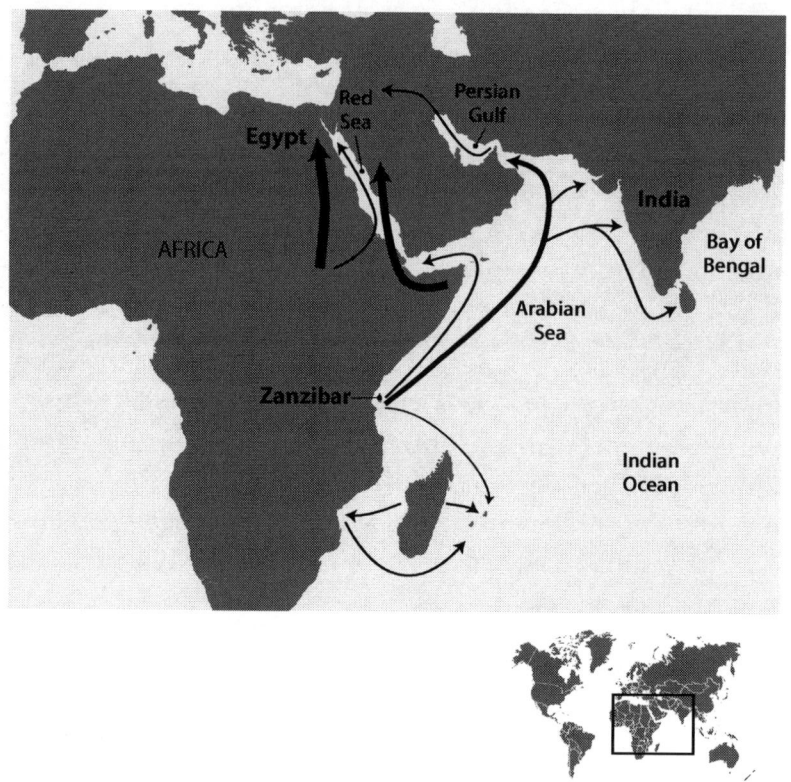

Figure 1.9. Indian Ocean Slave Trade

Islam also spread throughout the African coast and inland; given the cosmopolitan nature of the coastline, the **Swahili** language adopted aspects of Arabic and other Asian languages.

Further north, the Ottoman Turks represented a threat to Central Europe. Controlling most of Anatolia from the late thirteenth century, the Ottomans spread west into the Balkans, consolidating their rule in 1389 at the **Battle of Kosovo**. In 1453 they captured Istanbul, from which the **Ottoman Empire** would come to rule much of the Mediterranean world.

Under the leadership of **Mehmed the Conqueror** in the fifteenth century and his successors, the Ottomans would conquer Pannonia (Hungary), North Africa, the Caucasus, the Levant and Mesopotamian regions, western Arabia, and Egypt. Under **Suleiman the Magnificent** (1520 – 1566), the **Ottoman Empire** consolidated control over the Balkans, the Middle East, and North Africa and would hold that land until the nineteenth century.

The capture of Istanbul (Constantinople) had represented the true end of the Byzantine Empire; the remaining Christian Byzantines, mainly isolated to coastal Anatolia, Constantinople, and parts of Greece, fled to Italy, bringing Greek, Middle Eastern, and Asian learning with them and enriching the emerging European Renaissance.

The European Renaissance

The **Renaissance**, or *rebirth,* included the revival of ancient Greek and Roman learning, art, and architecture. However, the roots of the Renaissance stretched farther back to earlier interactions between Christendom, the Islamic World, and even China, during the Crusades and through Silk Road trade. Not only did the Renaissance inspire new learning and prosperity in Europe, enabling exploration, colonization, profit, and later imperialism, but it also led to scientific and religious questioning and rebellion against the Catholic Church and, later, monarchical governments.

It is important to note that Russia would not experience these cultural changes until the eighteenth century, when **Peter the Great** and **Catherine the Great** copied modern European culture, modernized the military, and updated technology, including building the new capital city of **St. Petersburg,** a cultural center.

Reinvigoration of classical knowledge was triggered in part by Byzantine refugees from the Ottoman conquest of Constantinople, including scholars who brought Greek and Roman texts to Italy and Western Europe. The fall of Constantinople precipitated the development of **humanism** in Europe, a mode of thought emphasizing human nature, creativity, and an overarching concept of truth in all philosophical systems (the concept of **syncretism**). Emerging in Italy, the seat of the Catholic Church, humanism was supported by some popes, including Leo X. However in the long term it represented a threat to religious, especially Catholic, orthodoxy, however, as it allowed for the questioning of religious teaching. Figures associated with humanism included Dante, Petrarch, and Erasmus. Ultimately humanism would be at the root of the **Reformation** of the sixteenth century.

Art, considered not just a form of expression but also a science in itself, flourished in fifteenth century Italy, particularly in **Florence**. Major figures who explored anatomy in sculpture, design and perspective, and innovation in architecture included Leonardo da Vinci, Bramante, Michelangelo, Rafael, and Donatello. Leonardo is particularly known for his scientific pursuits in addition to his artistic achievement. While artists worked throughout Italy and found patrons in the Vatican among other places, the Florentine **Medici family** funded extensive civic projects, construction, décor, and public sculpture throughout Florence, supporting Renaissance art in that city.

Meanwhile, scholars like Galileo, Isaac Newton, and Copernicus made discoveries in what became known as the **Scientific Revolution**, rooted in the scientific knowledge of the Islamic empires, which had been imported through economic and social contact initiated centuries prior in the Crusades. Scientific study and discovery threatened the power of the

> **QUICK REVIEW**
>
> The Scientific Revolution changed European thinking. What was the impact of using reason and scientific methodology rather than religion to understand the world?

Church, whose theological teachings were often at odds with scientific findings and logical reasoning.

Also in the mid-fifteenth century, in Northern Europe, **Johann Gutenberg** invented the **printing press**; the first book to be published would be the Bible. With the advent of printing, texts could be more widely and rapidly distributed, and people had more access to information beyond what their leaders told them. Combined with humanism and increased emphasis on secular thought, the power of the Church and of monarchs who ruled by divine right was under threat. Here lay the roots of the **Enlightenment**, the basis for reinvigorated European culture and political thought that would drive its development for the next several centuries—and inspire revolution.

Transnational cultural exchange had also resulted in the transmission of technology to Europe. During the sixteenth century, European seafaring knowledge, navigation, and technology benefitted from Islamic and Asian expertise; European explorers and traders could now venture beyond the Mediterranean. Portuguese and Dutch sailors eventually reached India and China, where they established ties with the Ming Dynasty. Trade was no longer dependent on the Silk Road. Improved technology also empowered Europeans to explore overseas, eventually landing in the Western Hemisphere, heretofore unknown to the peoples of Eurasia and Africa.

MESOAMERICAN AND ANDEAN CIVILIZATIONS

In the Americas, the **Maya**, who preceded the Aztecs in Mesoamerica, came to dominate the Yucatan peninsula around 300. They developed a complex spiritual belief system accompanied by relief art, and built pyramidal temples that still stand today. In addition, they developed a detailed calendar and a written language using pictographs similar to Egyptian hieroglyphs; they studied astronomy and mathematics. Maya political administration was organized under monarchical city-states from around 300 until around 900, when the civilization began to decline.

Throughout Mayan history there is evidence of interaction with the Mesoamerican city-state of **Teotihuacan**, a major city likely comprised of various Mesoamerican peoples such as Toltecs, Mixtecs, Zapotecs, some Mayans, and other peoples. By around 1400, two major empires dominated Central and South America: the Incas and the Aztecs. These two empires would be the last indigenous civilizations to dominate the Americas before European colonization of the Western Hemisphere.

As smaller Mesoamerican civilizations had weakened and collapsed, the **Aztecs** had come to dominate Mexico and much of Mesoamerica. Their military power and militaristic culture allowed the Aztecs to dominate the region and regional trade in precious objects like quetzal bird feathers. The main city of the Aztec empire, **Tenochtitlan**, was founded in 1325 and, at its height, was a major world city home to several million people.

Aztec civilization was militaristic in nature and divided on a class basis: it included slaves, indentured servants, serfs, an independent priestly class, military, and ruling classes. However, it did allow for upward mobility, especially for those who had proven themselves in battle. The Aztecs shared many beliefs with the Mayans; throughout Mesoamerica the same calendar was used. Central in the Aztec religion was worship of the god **Quetzalcoatl**, a feathered snake.

Figure 1.10. Quetzalcoatl

Meanwhile, in the Andes, the **Incas** had emerged. Based in **Cuzco**, the Incas had consolidated their power and strengthened in the area, likely due to a surplus of their staple crop maize, around 1300. They were able to conquer local lords and, later, peoples further south, thanks in part to domesticated llamas and alpacas which allowed the military to transport supplies through the mountains.

Inca engineers built the citadel of **Machu Picchu** and imperial infrastructure, including roads throughout the Andes. Thanks to highly developed mountain agriculture, they were able to grow crops at high altitudes and maintain waystations on the highways stocked with supplies, keeping track of them through a system called *quipus*, knotted cords. In order to subdue local peoples, they moved conquered groups elsewhere in the empire and repopulated conquered areas with Incas.

COLONIZATION OF THE WESTERN HEMISPHERE

Interest in exploration grew in Europe during the Renaissance period. Technological advancements made complex navigation and long-term sea voyages possible, and economic growth resulting from international trade drove interest in market expansion. Global interdependence got a big push from Spain when King Ferdinand

and Queen Isabella agreed to sponsor **Christopher Columbus'** exploratory voyage in 1492 to find a sea route to Asia, in order to speed up commercial trade there. Instead, he stumbled upon the Western Hemisphere, which was unknown to Europeans, Asians, and Africans to this point.

Columbus landed in the Caribbean; he and later explorers would claim the Caribbean islands and eventually Central and South America for Spain and Portugal. However, those areas were already populated by the major American civilizations (discussed above).

The Aztec ruler **Montezuma II** led the Aztecs during their first encounter with Spain; explorer **Hernan Cortés** met with him in Tenochtitlan after invading other areas of Mexico in 1519. Due to Spanish superiority in military technology, Montezuma attempted to compromise with Cortés; however, Cortés, seeking wealth and prestige in Mexico, had unlawfully left the Spanish stronghold of Cuba, disobeying Spanish colonial authorities. Thus in no position to compromise with the Aztecs, a few days later Cortés arrested Montezuma and took over the city. Spain was especially interested in subduing the Aztec religion, which included ceremonies with human blood and human sacrifice, and in controlling Mexican and Mesoamerican gold. Spain then began the process of colonizing Mexico and Central America, and the Aztec Empire collapsed.

In South America, as in Mexico and Central America, the Spanish were interested in economic exploitation and spreading Christianity, accessing the continent in the early sixteenth century. In 1533, the Spanish conquistador **Francisco Pizzaro** defeated the Inca king **Atahualpa** and installed a puppet ruler, marking the decline of the Inca Empire. While the empire remained nominally intact for several years, the Spanish desecrated important religious artefacts—like mummies important for ancestor worship—installed Christianity, and took economic and political control of the region.

Spain took over the silver- and gold-rich Mesoamerican and Andean territories, and the Caribbean islands where sugar became an important cash crop. Thus developed **mercantilism**, whereby the colonizing or *mother country* took raw materials from the territories they controlled for the colonizers' own benefit. Governments amassed wealth through protectionism and increasing exports at the expense of other rising colonial powers. This eventually involved developing goods and then selling them back to those colonized lands at an inflated price. The *encomienda* system granted European landowners the "right" to hold lands in the Americas and demand labor and tribute from the local inhabitants. Spreading Christianity was another important reason for European expansion. Local civilizations and resources were exploited and destroyed.

> **QUICK REVIEW**
>
> What was destructive about the *encomienda* system?

The **Columbian Exchange** enabled mercantilism to flourish. Conflict and illness brought by the Europeans—especially **smallpox**—decimated the Native Americans, and the Europeans were left without labor to mine the silver and gold or to work the land. **African slavery** was their solution.

Slavery was an ancient institution in many societies worldwide; however, with the Columbian Exchange slavery came to be practiced on a mass scale the likes of which the world had never seen. Throughout Africa and especially on the West African coast, Europeans traded for slaves with some African kingdoms and also raided the land, kidnapping people. European slavers took captured Africans in horrific conditions to the Americas; those who survived were enslaved and forced to work in mining or agriculture for the benefit of expanding European imperial powers.

The Columbian Exchange described the **triangular trade** (Figure 1.3) across the Atlantic: European slavers took kidnapped African people from Africa to the Americas, sold them at auction and exchanged them for sugar and raw materials; these materials were traded in Europe for consumer goods, which were then exchanged in Africa for slaves, and so on.

Enslaved Africans suffered greatly, forced to endure ocean voyages crammed on unsafe, unhygienic ships, sometimes among the dead bodies of other kidnapped people, only to arrive in the Americas to a life of slavery in mines or on plantations. Throughout this period, Africans did resist both on ships and later, in the Americas; **maroon communities** of escaped slaves formed throughout the Western Hemisphere, the **Underground Railroad** in the nineteenth-century United States helped enslaved persons escape the South, and **Toussaint L'Ouverture** led a successful slave rebellion in Haiti, winning independence from the French for that country in 1791.

> **QUICK REVIEW**
>
> Explain the Columbian Exchange.

However, the slave trade continued for centuries. The colonies and later independent countries of the Western Hemisphere continued to practice slavery until the nineteenth century; oppressive legal and social restrictions based on race continue to affect the descendants of slaves to this day throughout the hemisphere.

During the eighteenth century, Spain and Portugal were preeminent powers in global trade thanks to colonization and **imperialism**, the possession and exploitation of land overseas. However, Great Britain became an important presence on the seas; it would later dominate the oceans throughout the nineteenth century.

Though Britain would lose its territories in North America after the American Revolution, it maintained control of the resource-rich West Indies. The kingdom went on to dominate strategic areas in South Africa, New South Wales in Australia, Mauritius in the Indian Ocean, and Madras and Bengal in the Indian Subcontinent, among other places. Later, in the nineteenth century, Britain would expand its empire further. Likewise, France gained territory in North America and in the West

Indies; despite losses to Britain in the eighteenth century, that country would also expand its own global empire in the nineteenth century.

SAMPLE QUESTIONS

6) Which of the following explains why the Eastern Roman Empire remained stable and transitioned to the Byzantine Empire while Rome in Western Europe collapsed?

    A. Feudalism contributed to instability in Western Europe, and so that part of the continent disintegrated into a series of small states.

    B. The schism between the Catholic and Greek Orthodox Churches tore the empire apart.

    C. Muslims entered Constantinople and took it from Christian Roman control.

    D. Imprudent alliances in the West led to Roman collapse, while strong leadership and centralization in the East developed a new empire.

    Answers:

    A. Incorrect. Feudalism actually helped stabilize Western Europe.

    B. Incorrect. The divisions between the Catholic and Greek Orthodox Churches were not integral to the collapse of Rome.

    C. Incorrect. Islam had not yet appeared as a religious movement.

    D. Correct. Security alliances with Germanic and Gothic tribes left Western Rome vulnerable to their attack; meanwhile in the east, centralized power in Constantinople and strong leadership, particularly under Justinian, led to the rise of the powerful Byzantine Empire.

7) Following the death of Muhammad, Muslim leadership became so divided that the religious movement eventually split into Sunnis and Shi'ites. This was due to

    A. disagreement over secession to his place as leader.

    B. disagreement about the importance of conquest.

    C. disagreement over the theological nature of Islam.

    D. disagreement over whether to accept Christians and Jews as *People of the Book*.

    Answers:

    A. Correct. The Meccan elites believed that they should take over leadership of Islam and continue the movement beyond the Arabian Peninsula; however Ali and Fatima, Muhammad's cousin and daughter, believed Ali was Muhammad's rightful successor as his closest living male relative.

    B. Incorrect. All the Muslim leadership believed that they were called to spread Islam beyond the Arabian Peninsula.

C. Incorrect. While the sides had some differences and while major theological differences eventually did develop between Sunni and Shia Islam, the original break was mainly based on the dispute over succession.

D. Incorrect. Accepting the People of the Book was not at issue.

8) **Despite the violence of the Crusades, they were also beneficial for Europe in that they**

   A. resulted in substantial, long-term land gains for European leaders in the Middle East.

   B. introduced European powers to the concept of nation-states, the dominant form of political organization in the Middle East.

   C. exposed Europe to Islamic and Asian science, technology, and medicine.

   D. enhanced tolerance of Islam throughout Europe.

   Answers:

   A. Incorrect. While Europeans retained some territory in the Middle East, this was temporary.

   B. Incorrect. Nation-states did not become a form of governance in Europe for several centuries; furthermore, they were not a form of political organization in the Middle East.

   C. Correct. Europeans who traveled to the Levant to fight returned home with beneficial knowledge and technology.

   D. Incorrect. Christian Europe was not tolerant of Islam.

9) **Which of the following was a result of the rise of the Ottoman Turks?**

   A. Christian Byzantines left Constantinople for Western Europe, bringing classical learning with them.

   B. The Ottomans were able to conquer the Balkans, the Levant, and eventually North Africa and the Middle East, establishing a large Islamic empire.

   C. The Ottomans represented an Islamic threat to European Christendom, given their grip on the Balkan Peninsula.

   D. all of the above.

   Answers:

   A. Incorrect. Byzantine scholars did leave Constantinople and bring classical learning to Europe, especially Rome; this reintroduction of the classics would go on to influence the Renaissance. However, the other answer choices also apply, so this answer is incomplete.

B. **Incorrect.** At its height under Suleiman the Magnificent, the Ottoman Empire stretched from Morocco through Anatolia and the Levant to Persia. However, the other answer choices also apply, so this answer is incomplete.

C. **Incorrect.** The Ottomans represented a serious threat to Europe for centuries, as they controlled the Balkans and much of Pannonia; they even besieged Vienna twice. However, the other answer choices also apply, so this answer is incomplete.

D. **Correct.** All of the answer choices apply.

10) Which of the following best explains the Atlantic Triangular Trade?

   A. American raw materials were transported to Africa, where they were exchanged for enslaved persons; enslaved persons were taken to the Americas, where they turned raw materials to consumer goods for sale in Europe.

   B. European consumer goods were sold in the Americas at a profit; these goods were also sold in Africa in exchange for raw materials and for enslaved persons, who were taken to the Americas.

   C. European raw materials were sent to the Americas to be transformed into consumer goods by people who had been kidnapped from Africa and enslaved. These consumer goods were then traded in Africa for more slaves.

   D. Enslaved African people were traded in the Americas for raw materials; raw materials harvested by slaves went to Europe where they were utilized and turned to consumer goods; European consumer goods were exchanged in Africa for enslaved people.

Answers:

   A. **Incorrect.** American raw materials were transported to Europe where they were turned to consumer goods, not to Africa. Furthermore, American raw materials were converted into consumer goods in Europe.

   B. **Incorrect.** European consumer goods were sold in Africa (and within Europe); the Americas were initially a source of raw materials, though this would later change. Furthermore, Africa was not a major source of raw materials for Europe until the nineteenth century.

   C. **Incorrect.** Raw materials in the Triangular Trade came from the Americas; they were converted to consumer goods in Europe.

   D. **Correct.** American raw materials (like sugar and tobacco) were used in Europe and also turned into consumer goods there. European goods (as well as gold extracted from the Americas) were exchanged in Africa for enslaved persons, who were forced to harvest the raw materials in the Americas.

Armed Conflicts

Reformation and New Europe

While Spain and Portugal consolidated their hold over territories in the Americas, conflict ensued in Europe. With the cultural changes of the Renaissance, the power of the Catholic Church was threatened; new scientific discoveries and secular Renaissance thought were at odds with many teachings of the Church. The Catholic monk **Martin Luther** wrote a letter of protest to the Pope in 1517 known as the **Ninety-Five Theses**, outlining ways he believed the Church should reform; his ideas gained support, especially among rulers who wanted more power from the Church. Triggering the **Reformation**, or movement for reform of the Church, Luther's ideas led to offshoots of new versions of Christianity in Western Europe, separate from the Orthodox Churches in Russia and Greece. Protestant thinkers like Luther and **John Calvin** addressed particular grievances, condemning the **infallibility** of the Pope (its teaching that the Pope was without fault) and the selling of **indulgences**, or guarantees of entry into heaven.

The English **King Henry VIII** developed the Protestant **Church of England**, further consolidating his own power, famously allowing divorce and marrying several times himself. The reign of Henry VIII, of the **House of Tudor**, initiated a chain of events leading to the consolidation of Protestantism in England, and eventually civil war and the empowerment of Parliament.

In Britain, religious and ethnic diversity between Protestant England and Scotland, and Catholic Ireland, made the kingdom unstable. The Catholic **Mary Queen of Scots**, who was the daughter of the Scottish King James V and half French, had been betrothed to Henry VIII's son Edward. However her guardians canceled the arrangement, causing conflict with England. She temporarily married Francis of France, uniting Scotland with that Catholic country; however he quickly died from illness. Mary then married her Protestant cousin the Earl of Darnley, with whom she had a son, **James**. Darnley forced her to abdicate the Scottish throne in 1567 and she fled to England, seeking safety with her Protestant cousin **Elizabeth I**, daughter of Henry VIII and queen of England. Her son, still a baby, became **King James VI** of Scotland.

The Tudor Queen Elizabeth imprisoned the Catholic Mary in England as she—and her son—represented a threat to her power. Not only was James' male sex a liability for Elizabeth's inheritance to the throne, but their religious identities as Catholics threatened Elizabeth's hold over the Catholics of England and Scotland, as well as her tenuous grip on Catholic Ireland. In 1587, Elizabeth had Mary executed following revelations of a Catholic plot to overthrow Elizabeth. Yet on Elizabeth's death in 1603, James succeeded Elizabeth as **King James I** of England and Ireland, ushering in the **House of Stuart**.

James I attempted to balance the diverse ethnic and religious groups in England, Scotland, and Ireland, including the Catholic majority in Ireland and the Calvinist

Scots, who disagreed on many points with the more liberal Church of England (Anglicans). Despite his efforts at maintaining a delicate political balance, instability grew. In fact, despite James' roots in Catholicism, his mother having been the Catholic Mary, oppression of Catholics continued.

Furthermore, James' daughter married into the Bohemian royal family, forcing English involvement in the Thirty Years' War as that family lost power to Catholics in Central Europe—foreign involvement James was loath to initiate. His son **Charles I** continued the anti-Catholic conflict in 1625 upon his succession to the throne; however, upon his withdrawal in 1630, conservative Protestants in England and Scotland (**Puritans**) began to suspect a royal movement to weaken Protestantism and even restore Catholicism in the kingdom. Many began moving to North America as a result.

> **DID YOU KNOW?**
>
> The Gunpowder Plot to blow up the House of Lords and execute King James in the process was planned by Catholic fighters for the fifth of November, 1605. This plot was conceived by a group including the famous Guy Fawkes, who represents rebellion to this day.

Conflict between Protestants and Catholics was fierce on the Continent as well. The **Thirty Years' War** (1618 – 1648) began in Central Europe between Protestant nobles in the Holy Roman Empire who disagreed with the strict Catholic **Ferdinand II**, king of Bohemia and eventually archduke of Austria and king of Hungary (what was not under Ottoman domination). Elected Holy Roman Emperor in 1619, Ferdinand II was a leader of the **Counter-Reformation**, attempts at reinforcing Catholic dominance throughout Europe during and after the Reformation in the wake of the Renaissance and related social change. Ferdinand was also closely allied with the Catholic **Hapsburg** Dynasty, which ruled Austria and Spain.

Later interference in 1625 by Protestant Denmark and Sweden in Poland and Germany stirred further anti-Catholic discontent among local nobles in Germany, who yearned for independence from the imperial Holy Roman Empire. Despite Danish, Dutch, Swedish, and British support, the imperial military leader **Albrecht von Wallenstein** took control of most Protestant German states and Denmark. Ferdinand II issued the **Edict of Restitution**, restoring rebellious Protestant German territory to imperial, Catholic control. 1629 also marked the defeat of Denmark as an important European power at that point in history.

Protestant Sweden engaged in further conflict with Catholic Poland. Polish political ambition drove it to take advantage of instability throughout the region, venturing east into Russia until the 1634 **Peace of Polyanov**; it then battled Sweden for control over Baltic territory.

Meanwhile, farther west, Sweden had quickly reemerged in 1630 to reignite the Protestant cause. Allied with the Netherlands, Sweden reestablished a Protestant revival throughout Germany, driving imperial forces south. Ferdinand sought aid

from the Catholic Spanish Hapsburgs and the Papacy; Sweden was defeated at **Nordlingen** in 1634 and Catholicism was reestablished in the south.

At the same time, despite France's status as a Catholic country, it came into conflict with its neighbors—Hapsburg-ruled Spain and Austria. Spain's victory in Central Europe in 1634 cemented its power in the region; Hapsburg dominance to France's south and east represented a threat to that country, which was now surrounded by a strong military power. As a result, despite their religious commonalities, France declared war on Spain in 1635 and shortly after on the Hapsburg-supported Holy Roman Empire. This political tactic represented a break from the prioritization of religious alliances and a movement toward emphasis on state sovereignty.

The tangled alliances between European powers resulted in war between not only France and Spain, but also Sweden and Austria, with the small states of the weakening Holy Roman Empire caught in the middle. The war had been centered on alliances and concerns about the nature of Christianity within different European countries. However, upon signing the 1648 **Treaty of Westphalia**, the European powers agreed to recognize **state sovereignty** and practice **non-interference** in each other's matters—at the expense of family and religious allegiance. 1648 marked a transition into modern international relations when politics and religion would no longer be inexorably intertwined.

The end of the Thirty Years' War represented the end of the notion of the domination of the Catholic Church over Europe and the concept of religious regional dominance, rather than ethnic state divisions. Over the next several centuries, the Church—and religious empires like the Ottomans—would eventually lose control over ethnic groups and their lands, later giving way to smaller **nation-states**.

As state sovereignty became entrenched in European notions of politics, so too did conflict between states. Upon the death of the Hapsburg Holy Roman Emperor **Charles VI** in 1740, the **War of the Austrian Succession** began, a series of Continental wars over who would take over control of the Hapsburg territories. These conflicts would lead to the Seven Years' War.

Nominally, there was dispute over whether a woman, Charles' daughter **Maria Theresa**, could inherit the Austrian throne; however, it is more likely that **Frederick II** (or **Frederick the Great**) of Prussia took advantage of the instability in 1740 following Charles' death to capture the resource-rich province of Silesia from Hapsburg Austria. Prussia allied with France, Bavaria, and Spain; Maria Theresa sought help from Britain, which would be threatened by French dominance of Europe. Britain and Spain had been in conflict over territory beyond Europe for decades; Britain and France were rivals on the North American continent, in Asia, and in the West Indies. Thus conflict in Europe reflected overseas competition.

Fighting dragged on; forced by dwindling finances to the negotiating table, the European powers signed the Treaty of Aix la Chappelle in 1748, which granted Maria Theresa most Austrian possessions and gave Silesia to Prussia.

However, it was clear that Austria intended to regain Silesia. In an effort to protect its allies in Hannover during Continental instability, Britain formed a pragmatic alliance with Prussia, despite its traditional friendship with Austria. As a result, Austria allied with its former enemy France, in a development known as the *Diplomatic Revolution*.

In 1756, Austria was set to attack Prussia, but Frederick the Great attacked first, launching the **Seven Years' War**. In Europe, this war further cemented concepts of state sovereignty and delineated rivalries between European powers engaged in colonial adventure and overseas imperialism—especially Britain and France. It would kick-start British dominance in Asia and also lead to Britain's loss of its North American colonies, nearly bankrupting the Crown (as discussed below).

On the European front, Frederick the Great invaded Silesia and then Bohemia in 1787; however he was repelled by Austria. Meanwhile, while the English led a Hannoverian army against the French in the west, they too were defeated and the French marched on Prussia. Sweden attacked from the north, and Russia attacked from the east. So Frederick called on Britain for more support. **William Pitt the Elder**, the British political leader (essentially Prime Minister) authorized enormous financial contributions to Prussia; he also began focusing the war overseas against France on imperial possessions in the Western Hemisphere and Asia.

Fortunately for the Anglo-Prussian alliance in Europe, changes in Russian leadership led to Catherine the Great's takeover; she ended hostilities with Prussia and focused on development in Russia instead. Hostilities died down in Europe, but the conflict overseas set the stage for the building of empire (see below).

This time of change in Europe would affect Asia. European concepts of social and political organization became constructed around national sovereignty and nation-states. European economies had become dependent upon colonies and were starting to industrialize, enriching Europe at the expense of its imperial possessions in the Americas, in Africa, and increasingly in Asia.

Industrialization and political organization allowed improved militaries, which put Asian governments at a disadvantage. The major Asian powers—Mughal India, Qing China, the Ottoman Empire, and Safavid (and later, Qajar) Persia—would eventually succumb to European influence or come under direct European control.

THE AGE OF REVOLUTIONS

Monarchies in Europe had been weakened by the conflicts between Catholicism and Protestant faiths; despite European presence and increasing power overseas, as well as its dominance in the Americas, instability on the continent and in the British Isles made the old order vulnerable. Enlightenment ideals like democracy and

republicanism, coupled with political instability, would trigger revolution against **absolute monarchy**. Revolutionary actors drew on the philosophies of enlightenment thinkers like **John Locke**, **Jean-Jacques Rousseau**, and **Montesquieu**, whose beliefs, such as **republicanism**, the **social contract**, the **separation of powers**, and the **rights of man** would drive the Age of Revolutions.

In England, Puritans and Separatists—strict, conservative Protestants—were suspicious of King Charles I, believing he was weakening Protestantism and even possibly supporting Catholic plots. At the same time, more moderate Protestant leaders, including the weak Parliament and aristocratic class, were upset by Charles' dictatorial reign.

The period marked the early days of the **Age of Revolutions**, influenced especially by Enlightenment thinkers like Locke and Rousseau, who believed in the natural rights of man and the social contract between the people and government. Charles I was despotic and sidelined Parliament, causing political and military unrest. Conflict between England and Scotland in the late 1630s and an Irish uprising in 1641 weakened Charles further, as disgruntled English aristocracy, who felt that Charles had become a tyrannical ruler, withdrew support and began consolidating their own power. In 1642, the **English Civil War** broke out between the **Royalists**, who supported the monarchy, and the **Parliamentarians**, who wanted a republic.

Eventually, the Royalists succumbed to the Parliamentarians, and Charles was executed in 1649. Meanwhile, England had lost control over Ireland, and the Parliamentarian military leader **Oliver Cromwell** was sent to reestablish control over the island. Charles II, son of Charles I, had established control as king of Scotland; Cromwell defeated him and England took back control of Scotland in 1651. By 1653, England once again controlled Britain and Ireland; Cromwell was installed as Lord Protector.

Following Cromwell's death, Charles II restored the Stuart monarchy. However, stability was short lived once his Catholic brother James II succeeded him in 1685. By 1688, English Protestants asked the Dutch William of Orange, husband of James II's daughter Mary, to help restore Protestantism in Britain. **William and Mary** defeated James and consolidated Protestant control over England, Scotland, and Ireland under a Protestant constitutional monarchy in the **Glorious Revolution**. The 1689 **English Bill of Rights** established constitutional monarchy, in the spirit of the **Magna Carta**.

The **American Revolution** heavily influenced by Locke, broke out a century later. Please refer to Chapter Two, "United States History," for details.

The French Revolution was the precursor to the end of the feudal order in most of Europe. **King Louis XIV**, the *Sun King* (1643 – 1715), had consolidated the monarchy in France, taking true political and military power from the nobility. Meanwhile, French Enlightenment thinkers like **Jean-Jacques Rousseau**,

Montesquieu, and **Voltaire** criticized absolute monarchy and the repression of freedom of speech and thought; in 1789, the French Revolution broke out.

> **DID YOU KNOW?**
>
> Louis XIV built the palace of Versailles, to centralize the monarchy—and also to contain and monitor the nobility.

The power of the Catholic Church had weakened and the Scientific Revolution and the Enlightenment had fostered social and intellectual change. Colonialism and mercantilism were fueling the growth of an early middle class: people who were not traditionally nobility or landowners under the feudal system were becoming wealthier and more powerful thanks to early capitalism. This class, the **bourgeoisie**, chafed under the rule of the nobility, which had generally inherited land and wealth (while the bourgeoisie earned their wealth in business).

In France, the problem was most acute as France had the largest population in Europe at the time. At the same time, France had one of the most centralized monarchies in Europe and entrenched nobilities. With a growing bourgeoisie and peasant class paying increasingly higher taxes to the nobility, resentment was brewing.

Louis XIV had strengthened the monarchy by weakening the nobility's control over their land and centralizing power under the king. However, his successors had failed to govern effectively or win the loyalty of the people; both the nobility and the monarch were widely resented. Furthermore, the bourgeoisie resented their lack of standing in government and society. Moreover, advances in medicine had permitted unprecedented population growth, further empowering the peasantry and bourgeoisie.

The French government was struggling financially, having supported the American Revolution; in desperation, the controller-general of finances suggested reforms that would tax the nobility. An unwilling council of nobles instead called for the **Estates-General** to be convened in 1787; this toothless body had not come together since 1614.

The Estates-General, a weak representative assembly, reflected French society: the clergy, the nobility, and the **Third Estate**—the middle class and the poor peasants, or *commoners*. The burden of taxation traditionally fell on the Third Estate. In fact, peasants had to **tithe**, paying ten percent of their earnings to the nobles.

After a poor harvest in 1788, unrest spread throughout the country. King Louis XVI permitted elections to the Estates-General and some free speech; momentum against the elites grew. Once the Estates-General convened at Versailles in 1789, disagreement between the nobility and the elite clergy, on the one hand, and the Third Estate and lower-level parish priests, on the other, erupted. The two sides came to terms and formed the **National Constituent Assembly**; still, the king and nobility were suspicious of the other side and Louis XVI planned to dissolve it.

At the same time, panic over dwindling food supplies and suspicion over a conspiracy against the Third Estate triggered the **Great Fear** among the peasants in July 1789. Suspicion turned to action when the king sent troops to Paris, and on July 16 the people stormed the **Bastille** prison in an event still celebrated in France symbolic of the overthrow of tyranny. The peasantry then revolted in the countryside; consequently the National Constituent Assembly officially abolished the feudal system and tithing. Furthermore, the Assembly issued the **Declaration of the Rights of Man and the Citizen**, the precursor to the French constitution assuring liberty and equality, in the model of Enlightenment thought.

Louis XVI refused to accept these developments; as a result, the people marched on Versailles and brought the royals back to Paris, effectively putting the Assembly in charge. Members of the **Jacobins**, revolutionary political clubs, became members of the Assembly; the more extreme of these political figures would play key roles in the immediate future of the country.

> **DID YOU KNOW?**
>
> Charles Dickens' *A Tale of Two Cities* features a fictional account of the storming of the Bastille. Contrary to popular belief, Victor Hugo's *Les Misérables* takes place several decades after the French Revolution.

The Assembly continued reforms, including nationalizing the lands of the Catholic Church to pay off debt, disempowering the Church. It also reorganized the administration of the *ancien régime* (the old government) which allowed the election of judges. When Louis XVI attempted to escape France, he was detained.

The French Revolution inspired revolutionary movements throughout Europe and beyond; indeed, the revolutionary principle of self-determination drove revolutionary France to support its ideals abroad. The country declared war on Austria in 1792, but following severe defeats by joint Austrian-Prussian forces, the people became suspicious of the unpopular queen **Marie Antoinette**. Marie Antoinette was originally from Austria and had, in fact, encouraged an invasion, hoping to suppress the revolution. The people imprisoned the royal family; the Jacobins abolished the monarchy, establishing the republic later that year.

War in Europe dragged on into 1793, with considerable French losses against an alliance between Austria, Prussia, and Great Britain. Within France, the Jacobins—essentially, the government of the Republic—were breaking into two main factions: the more moderate **Girondins**, who favored concentrating power in the hands of the bourgeoisie, and the more extreme **Montagnards**, led by **Robespierre**, who favored radical social policy empowering the poor.

> **DID YOU KNOW?**
>
> An important tenet of the revolutionary ethos in France was the concept of self-determination, or the right of a people to rule themselves, which threatened rulers fearing revolution in their own countries.

Fearful of counterrevolutionaries in France and instability abroad, the republican government created the **Committee of Public Safety** in 1793. Robespierre led the Committee and the **Reign of Terror** began in France, during which time thousands of people were executed by **guillotine**, including Louis XVI and Marie Antoinette. Robespierre himself was executed a year later.

Ongoing war in Europe and tensions in France between republicans and royalists continued to weaken the revolution, but France had military successes in Europe. France had continued its effort to spread the revolution throughout the continent, led by **Napoleon Bonaparte**, who even occupied Egypt in an attempt to threaten British power abroad. In 1799, Napoleon took power in France: the revolution was over.

In 1804 **Napoleon Bonaparte** emerged as emperor of France, and proceeded to conquer much of Europe throughout the **Napoleonic Wars**, changing the face of Europe. French occupation of Spain weakened that country enough that revolutionary movements in its colonies strengthened; eventually Latin American colonies, inspired by the Enlightenment and revolution in Europe, won their freedom.

Napoleon's movement eastward also triggered the collapse of the Holy Roman Empire. However, the powerful state of **Prussia** emerged in its wake, and a strong sense of militarism and Germanic nationalism took root in the face of opposition to seemingly unstoppable France. (Prussia would later go on to unify the small kingdoms of Central Europe that had made up the Holy Roman Empire, forming Germany, as discussed below.)

Napoleon was finally defeated in Russia in 1812 and was forced by the European powers to abdicate in 1813. He escaped from prison on the Mediterranean island of Elba and raised an army again, overthrowing the restored monarch Louis XVIII. Defeated at Waterloo by the British, he was once again exiled, this time to St. Helena in the southern Atlantic Ocean.

By 1815, other European powers had managed to halt his expansion; at the **Congress of Vienna** in 1815, European powers including the unified Prussia, the **Austro-Hungarian Empire, Russia,** and **Britain** agreed on a **balance of power** in Europe. Despite Napoleon's brief reemergence, the Congress of Vienna was the first real international peace conference and set the precedent for European political organization.

Latin American countries joined Haiti and the United States in revolution against colonial European powers. Inspired by the American and French Revolutions, **Simón Bolivar** led or influenced independence movements in **Venezuela, Colombia** (including what is today **Panama**), **Ecuador, Peru,** and **Bolivia** in the early part of the nineteenth century.

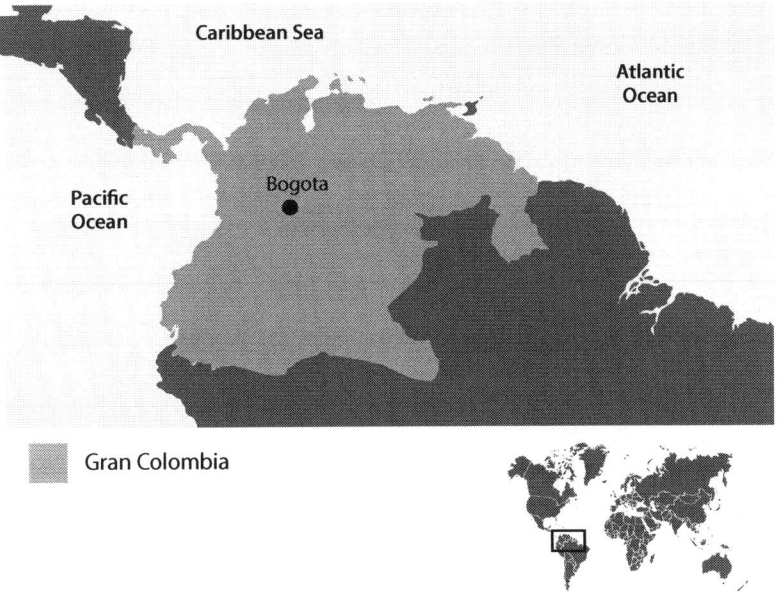

Figure 1.11. Gran Colombia

EUROPEAN DIVISION

The nineteenth century was a period of change and conflict, and the roots of the major twentieth century conflicts—world war and decolonization—are found in it. Modern European social and political structures and norms, including **nationalism** and the **nation-state**, would begin to emerge. Economic theories based in the Industrial Revolution like **socialism** and eventually **communism** gained traction with the stark class divisions brought on by **urbanization** and industry.

Following the Napoleonic Wars, Prussia had come to dominate the German-speaking states that once comprised the Holy Roman Empire. Prussia, a distinct kingdom within the Holy Roman Empire since the thirteenth century, had become a powerful Central European state by the eighteenth century. It had become the main rival of Austria for influence in the Germanic lands of Central Europe. By the nineteenth century and due in part to emphasis on military prowess, Prussia became an important military power and a key ally in the efforts against Napoleon.

Prussia had a particular rivalry with France, having lost several key territories during the Napoleonic Wars. In 1870, the militarily powerful kingdom went to war against France in the **Franco-Prussian War**, during which Prussia took control of **Alsace-Lorraine**, mineral rich and later essential for industrial development.

Following the Franco-Prussian War, **Otto von Bismarck** unified those linguistically and culturally German states of Central Europe. Prussian power had been growing, fueled by **nationalism** and the **nation-state**, or the idea that individuals with shared experience (including ethnicity, language, religion, and cultural practices) should be unified under one government. In 1871, the **German Empire** became a united state. Bismarck encouraged economic cooperation, instituted

army reforms and, perhaps most importantly, created an image of Prussia as a defender of German culture and nationhood, portraying other European states in opposition to that.

Nationalism also led to **Italian Unification**. As a region of small independent states, toward the end of the eighteenth century Italy was occupied by France and then Austria. Later invaded and occupied by Napoleon, the Italian peninsula was divided into three regions. Napoleonic concepts of nationalism, freedom, equality, and justice under the law spread throughout the peninsula, and what was left of feudalism faded.

Despite re-fragmentation throughout the nineteenth century following the fall of Napoleon, a secret movement for reorganization—the *Risorgimento*—began working toward Italian unification. Following the 1859 **Franco-Austrian War**, Austria's loss of territorial control in northern Italy allowed Italian states to unite via elections. **Giuseppe Garibaldi** led the Northern Italian overthrow of Southern Italian monarchies, uniting the Peninsula with the exception of Rome and Venice. The Kingdom of Italy was declared in 1861, under **Victor Emmanuel II**. Thanks to an Italian alliance with Prussia during the **Austro-Prussian War** in 1866, in which Austria lost even more territory, Italy took control of Venice. Finally, the Kingdom of Italy entered Rome and incorporated that city and the Papal States during the Franco-Prussian War.

Conflict in the Balkans

Farther east, as European kingdoms and empires consolidated their power, the Ottoman Empire was in decline. The Ottoman Empire had long been a major force in Europe, controlling the bulk of the Balkans. However, the empire had lost land in Europe to the Austrians and in Africa to British and French imperialists. In the Balkans, rebellion among small nations supported by European puppet masters would put an end to Ottoman power in Europe for good.

Despite previous conflict between some of these powers, deeper rivalries throughout the continent inspired Russia, Germany, and Austria-Hungary to form the **Three Emperors' League** in 1873. If one country went to war, the others would remain neutral, and the powers would consult each other on matters of war. However, the **First Balkan Crisis** in 1874 would put an end to this alliance.

In 1874, Bosnia Herzegovina rebelled against Ottoman rule. Christian peasants in Herzegovina were unwilling to submit to Muslim landlords; neither regional Christians nor Bosnian Muslims were willing any longer to submit to rule by the ethnically-different Turks. Thus began the First Balkan Crisis.

Two years later, the Ottoman autonomous principality of Serbia, joined by Montenegro, rebelled in support of Bosnia. Having come under Russian influence thanks to **pan-Slavism**—the concept that Slavic ethnic groups throughout Eastern and Southeastern Europe should embrace their Slavic heritage and turn toward Russia

for support—Serbian rebellion attracted Russian attention. When the Ottoman **Sultan Hamid II** refused to institute reforms to protect Balkan Christians, Russia declared war.

The **Russo-Turkish War** ended in 1878 with the **Treaty of San Stefano**, which favored Russian territorial gains. However, Austro-Hungarian and British objections to the treaty, which threatened their influence in the region, led to the **1878 Congress of Berlin**, hosted by Otto von Bismarck. Unfortunately for Russia, which was the militarily and financially weaker power, Britain and Austria-Hungary changed the outcome of the war with the **Treaty of Berlin**. While the independence of Serbia and Montenegro was decided, Russia lost influence in Bulgaria as well as territorial gains in Asia. These insults would not be forgotten.

Germany and Austria-Hungary secretly formed the Dual Alliance to respond to fears of pan-Slavism, given developments in the Balkans. In 1882, Italy asked these countries for assistance against France, which had upset Italian imperial ambition in North Africa; thus formed the **Triple Alliance**, a secret political and military alliance. The 1885 **Second Balkan Crisis**, in which Bulgaria declared unification and independence, violating the Treaty of Berlin and Russian interests, further threatened stability in the Balkans and among the great powers. Serbia went to war against Bulgaria, requiring Austro-Hungarian support.

Eventually tension between Russia and Austria-Hungary—which was supported by Germany—led to the breakdown of Russian relationships with those countries, and improvement in Russian relations with Great Britain and France. In 1894, Russia and France became allies. This alliance would culminate in the 1907 **Triple Entente**, setting the stage for the system of alliances at the heart of the First World War.

> **QUICK REVIEW**
>
> List some important European alliances in the nineteenth century.

Continued European involvement in the Balkans accelerated the ongoing loss of Ottoman influence there due to phenomena like nationalism, ethnocentrism (Pan-Slavism), military and political power, and religious influence. The small Balkan nations were empowered to continue rebellion against Ottoman rule, and European powers proceeded into the area.

In 1908, Austria-Hungary annexed Bosnia-Herzegovina, disregarding Russian objections. Russia helped form the **Balkan League**, comprised of Serbia, Montenegro, Greece, and Bulgaria, which went to war with the Ottomans in the 1912 **First Balkan War**. The Ottomans were defeated and lost nearly all their European possessions; however, disagreement over the division of land led to the **Second Balkan War** the following year between Bulgaria and a Serbian-Greek alliance. Serbia wanted to keep Albanian territory, which Austria-Hungary insisted remain independent; Bulgaria wanted control over more land in Macedonia (which had come mainly under Greek and Serbian rule). Eventually, this instability would lead to the First World War which was triggered by the assassination of the Austro-Hun-

garian **Archduke Franz Ferdinand** by the Serbian nationalist **Gavrilo Princip** in Bosnia-Herzegovina in 1914.

Imperialism

As colonialism in the fifteenth and sixteenth centuries had been driven by mercantilism, conquest, and Christian conversion, so was seventeenth, eighteenth and nineteenth century imperialism driven by capitalism, European competition, and conceptions of racial superiority.

Britain and France, historic rivals on the European continent, were also at odds colonizing North America and in overseas trade. During the **Seven Years' War** (1756 – 1763), considered by many historians to be the first truly global conflict, these two powers fought in Europe and in overseas colonies and interests in North America and Asia.

As discussed previously, while the Seven Years' War in Europe was the result of tangled alliances between Britain, Prussia, and Hanover on one side, and France, Austria, Sweden, and Russia on the other, that war's extension into the imperial realm made it a global conflict.

In North America, Britain and France had explored the region and controlled tremendous amounts of territory in what later would become Canada and the United States. Britain controlled the wealthy **Thirteen Colonies** on the Atlantic coast, which were rich in tobacco, rice, vegetables, and other crops. It also controlled major ports like Boston, New York, and Philadelphia.

Meanwhile, the French controlled **Quebec** and northeastern territories rich in natural resources like beaver pelts, valuable in Europe for their water-repellant properties. They also controlled the ports of Montreal and Quebec City, on the St. Lawrence River (leading to the Atlantic Ocean). France also controlled considerable strategic territory in the Midwestern portions of the continent, which allowed products from the interior to reach the oceans. These routes included much of the **Great Lakes** region including the Detroit River (leading to the St. Lawrence and the Atlantic Ocean), and the Mississippi River and the Port of New Orleans (leading to the Gulf of Mexico).

The **French and Indian War**, as the Seven Years' War is called in North America, resulted in net gains for Britain. France formed an important alliance with the powerful Algonquin in the northeast, while Britain was allied with the Iroquois. Thanks to strong military leaders like **George Washington**, Britain eventually took control of French Canada. However, financially exhausted from the costly conflict in Europe, Britain ceded control of the Northwest Territories (Michigan, Ohio, Indiana) to various tribes in the **Treaty of Paris in 1763** (agreements later not honored by the United States). In addition, the financial and military strain suffered by Britain in the Seven Years' War made it particularly vulnerable to later rebellion in the Colonies, helping the Americans win the Revolutionary War there.

According to Pitt the Elder's plan, Britain went to war with France in Asia as well. In India, with the decline of the **Mughal Empire** and the rising power of colonial companies specializing in exporting valuable resources like spices and tea, smaller Indian kingdoms were forming alliances with those increasingly influential corporations.

By the mid-eighteenth century, violence broke out between the **British East India Company** and the **French East India Company** and their allies among the small Indian states in a series of wars known as the **Carnatic Wars** (1746 – 1763). With the end of the Seven Years' War, the Treaty of Paris established British dominance in the Subcontinent as France was allowed some trading posts in the region, but forced to recognize British power there. By 1803, British interests effectively took control of the Subcontinent and the Mughals were pushed to the north.

> **QUICK REVIEW**
>
> The Netherlands was already coming to dominate Indonesia (at the time, the Dutch East Indies) thanks to similar actions by the **Dutch East India Company.**

Despite its loss of the Thirteen Colonies, at the dawn of the nineteenth century Britain retained control of Canada, rich in natural resources like beaver pelts and timber. In addition, it controlled the resource-rich and strategically important Indian Subcontinent. Britain would become the strongest naval power in the world and continue to expand its empire, especially in the search for new markets for its manufactured goods to support its industrial economy.

In 1837, **Queen Victoria** ascended to the throne. During her reign (1837 – 1901) the British Empire would expand to heretofore unseen lengths. In 1788, Britain had begun sending convicts to the penal colony of **Australia**; however in 1851, when gold was discovered there British subjects began to voluntarily settle Australia and the Pacific. In 1857, the **Indian Mutiny** against private British troops controlled by the East India Company caused the British government to intervene, sending in military and eventually resulting in Victoria taking the title of **Empress of India**, cementing the imperial nature of government and the **Raj** (imperial administration).

In 1877, the British annexed **South Africa**; following the Boer Wars, Britain would retain control of diamond- and gold-rich South Africa (see below). The imperialist **Cecil Rhodes** and his company, the British South Africa Company (BSAC), were chartered by Victoria to explore north from South Africa to mine the land. This was despite of conflicting European claims to the land, despite claims by the **Afrikaaners**, (see below) and despite the residence of the **Matabele**, who had lived there for centuries. Rhodes and the BSAC forcefully took over Northern Rhodesia (**Zambia**), Rhodesia (**Zimbabwe**), Nyasaland (**Malawi**) and Bechuanaland (**Botswana**) using treaties, diplomacy, and violence. These territories were under English rule.

In East Africa, the British explorer **David Livingstone** had been working in Kenya; the government had influence over the Sultan of Zanzibar. However, secret

German agreements with coastal leaders and the establishment of the German colony of **Tanganyika** forced the British into more activity in the region. In an agreement with the Germans, the British took control over what would become **Kenya** and **Uganda**, while Germany maintained Tanganyika. Borders were drawn without regard for the **Kikuyu, Masai, Luo,** and other tribes living in the area.

The concept of the **white man's burden,** wherein white Europeans were "obligated" to bring their "superior" culture to other civilizations around the globe, also drove imperialist adventure, popularizing it at home in Britain and elsewhere in Europe.

Despite its small size, **Belgium** controlled the **Congo,** along with its vast resources in Central Africa. Coming into conflict with Rhodes at its southern edges, the Belgian Congo, which reached its heights under **King Leopold II,** was rich in rubber, timber, minerals, and diamonds. Furthermore, this territory was strategically important; controlling the Congo meant controlling the Congo River basin, allowing for the extraction of materials from the interior to the Atlantic Coast.

To gain access to closed **Chinese** markets, Britain forced China to buy Indian opium; the **Opium Wars** ended with the **Treaty of Nanking (1842),** signed between the British and the increasingly impotent Qing government. As a consequence, China lost great power to Britain and later, other European countries, which gained **spheres of influence,** or areas of China they effectively controlled, and **extraterritoriality,** or privileges in which their citizens were not subject to Chinese law.

> **QUICK REVIEW**
>
> List some of the European powers' justifications for imperialism.

Discontent with the Qing Dynasty was growing as Chinese people perceived that their country was coming under control of European imperialists, even though nominally Chinese leadership still governed. Coupled with economic hardship and huge casualties in the Opium Wars and in the **Sino-Japanese War of 1896** (see below), a violent uprising was inevitable. In 1900, the **Boxer Rebellion,** an uprising led by a Chinese society against the Emperor, was only put down with Western (including American) help. The Qing were humiliated further by being forced to pay the West enormous reparations for their assistance; meanwhile, living conditions for Chinese people continued to deteriorate.

> **DID YOU KNOW?**
>
> The *Boxers* were so called because of their belief that physical exercises, like shadow boxing, would make them impervious to bullets. This rebellion was led by a secret society called the *Yihequan,* or *The Society of Righteous and Harmonious Fists.*

The European powers were immersed in what became known as the ***Scramble for Africa***; the industrial economies of Europe would profit from the natural resources abundant in that continent, and the white man's burden continued to fuel colonization. At the **1884 Berlin Conference,** control over Africa was divided among European powers (Africans were not

consulted in this process). Following the **Boer War (1899-1902)** between Afrikaaners of Dutch origin and the English, Britain officially gained control of South Africa, and whites would rule the country until the end of **Apartheid** in the early 1990s. France controlled West Africa and eventually North Africa, especially Algeria, Mali, Niger, Chad, Cameroon, and what has become the Republic of the Congo (not to be confused with Belgian Congo, now the Democratic Republic of the Congo).

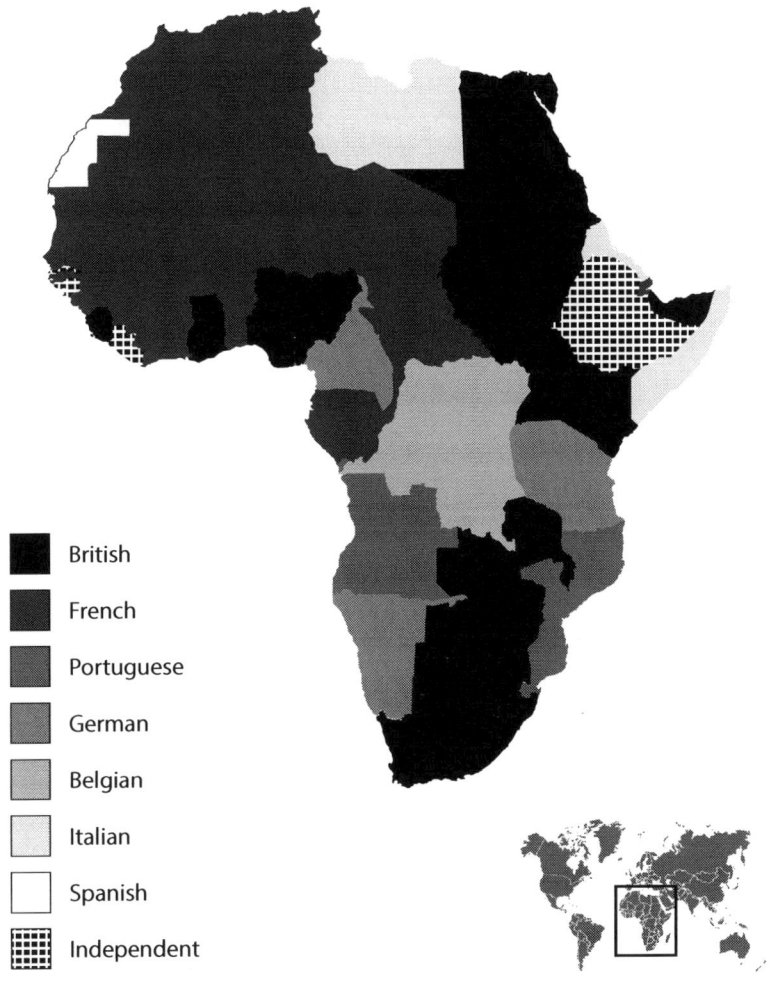

Figure 1.12. Imperial Africa

However, not all non-European countries fell to European imperialism. During the **Meiji Restoration** in Japan in 1868, the Emperor Meiji promoted modernization of technology, especially the military. Japan proved itself a world power when it defeated Russia in the **Russo-Japanese War** in 1905, and would play a central role in twentieth century conflict.

Industrial Revolution

Throughout this entire period, raw goods from the Americas fueled European economic growth and development, leading to the **Industrial Revolution** in the nineteenth century. This economic revolution began with textile production in Britain, fueled by cotton from its overseas territories in North America, and later India and Egypt. The first factories were in Manchester, where **urbanization** began as poor people from rural areas flocked to cities in search of higher-paying unskilled jobs in factories.

Early industrial technology sped up the harvesting and transport of crops and their conversion to textiles. This accelerated manufacturing was based on **capitalism**, the *laissez-faire* (or *free market*) theory developed by **Adam Smith**, who believed that an *invisible hand* should guide the marketplace—that government should stay out of the economy regardless of abuses, as the economy would eventually automatically correct for inequalities, price problems, and any other problematic issues.

Technology like the **spinning jenny** and **flying shuttle** exponentially increased the amount of cotton that workers could process into yarn and thread. The **steam engine** efficiently powered mills and ironworks; factories no longer had to be built near running water to access power. Advances in **iron** technology allowed for stronger machinery and would support the later **Second Industrial Revolution** in the late nineteenth and early twentieth century, which was based on **heavy industry**, railroads, and weapons.

To access the raw materials needed to produce manufactured goods, Britain and other industrializing countries in Western Europe needed resources—hence the drive for imperialism as discussed above. Cotton was harvested in India and Egypt for textile mills, minerals mined in South Africa and the Congo to power metallurgy. Furthermore, as industrialization and urbanization led to the development of early middle classes in Europe and North America, imports of luxury goods like tea, spices, silk, precious metals, and other items from Asia increased to meet consumer demand. Colonial powers also gained by selling manufactured goods back to the colonies from which they had harvested raw materials in the first place, for considerable profit.

Largely unbridled capitalism had led to the conditions of the early Industrial Revolution; workers suffered from abusive treatment, overly long hours, low wages or none at all, and unsafe conditions, including pollution. The German philosophers **Karl Marx** and **Friedrich Engels,** horrified by conditions suffered by industrial workers, developed **socialism**, the philosophy that workers, or the **proletariat,** should own the means of production and reap the profits, rather than the **bourgeoisie**, who had no interest in the rights of the workers at the expense of profit and who did not experience the same conditions.

In his work ***Das Kapital,*** Marx argued for the abolition of the class system, wages, and private property. He argued instead for collective ownership of both the

means of production and products, with equal distribution of income to satisfy the needs of all. Later, Marx and Engels wrote the *Communist Manifesto*, a pamphlet laying out their ideas and calling for revolution. It inspired the formation of socialist groups worldwide.

A different version of socialism would later help Russia become a major world power. The Russian intellectuals **Vladimir Lenin** and **Leon Trotsky** would take Marx and Engels' theories further, developing **Marxism-Leninism**. They embraced socialist ideals and believed in revolution; however they felt that **communism** could not be maintained under a democratic governing structure. Lenin supported dictatorship, more precisely the *dictatorship of the proletariat*, paving the way for the political and economic organization of the Soviet Union.

> **DID YOU KNOW?**
>
> The Communist Manifesto contained the famous words *Workers of the world, unite!*

SAMPLE QUESTIONS

11) **The Treaty of Westphalia**

   A. laid out the final borders of Europe, setting the stage for modern foreign policy.

   B. established the notion of state sovereignty, in which states recognized each other as independent and agreed not to interfere in each other's affairs.

   C. gave the Catholic Church more power in the affairs of Catholic-majority countries.

   D. established the notion of the nation-state, in which culturally and ethnically similar groups would control their own territory as sovereign countries.

   Answers:

   A. Incorrect. Europe's modern borders have only very recently been drawn, and they may continue to change over the course of history.

   B. Correct. The Treaty of Westphalia was based on state sovereignty and non-interference, the core principles of modern international relations.

   C. Incorrect. The political power of the Church had been weakening; the principles of state sovereignty weakened it further.

   D. Incorrect. The notion of the nation-state would more fully develop in the nineteenth century and was not established by a treaty.

12) **An important factor leading to the French Revolution was**
    A. the corruption of Louis XIV.
    B. the strong organization of the Estates-General.
    C. support from the United States of America.
    D. the anti-monarchical philosophies of Enlightenment thinkers like Rousseau and Voltaire.

    Answers:
    A. Incorrect. Louis XIV strengthened the monarchy several decades before the revolution.
    B. Incorrect. The Estates-General was weak and poorly organized, actually facilitating revolution.
    C. Incorrect. While there was support for the revolutionaries, the United States maintained a cautious stance on the revolution given its hesitance to become embroiled in European conflict.
    D. Correct. Enlightenment thinking fueled the Age of Revolutions, and revolutionary French thinkers and writers like Rousseau, Voltaire, and others influenced revolutionary French leaders.

13) **How did Pan-Slavism affect the crises in the Balkans?**
    A. Pan-Slavism led Russia to directly intervene militarily throughout the nineteenth century in the Balkans, leading to violent conflict.
    B. Pan-Slavism generally ensured Russian support for Slavic ethnic groups in the Balkans, which contributed to ongoing tensions there already fueled by competing European and Ottoman interests and diverse nationalities.
    C. Russian interests in Slavic groups in the Balkans strengthened its alliance with Turkey.
    D. Pan-Slavism did not have a major effect on the Balkans, as the major Slavic cultures are located farther north in Europe.

    Answers:
    A. Incorrect. While Russia was very much involved in the Balkans (and continues to be), it was not always necessarily involved in a military capacity.
    B. Correct. Russian support for Slavic ethnic groups in the Balkans—especially Serbia—helped fuel nineteenth century tensions in the region (and continued to do so throughout the twentieth century).
    C. Incorrect. Russia and Ottoman Turkey were not allies; in fact they went to war in the Russo-Turkish War after the First Balkan Crisis.
    D. Incorrect. Pan-Slavism had a tremendous effect on the dynamics of the nineteenth century Balkans, as several Slavic ethnic groups live in Southeast Europe and had alliances with Russia.

14) Which of the following is NOT a way that the white man's burden influenced imperialism?

   A. It inspired Europeans to settle overseas in order to improve what they believed to be "backward" places.
   B. Europeans believed in imperialism as in the best interest of native people, who would benefit from adopting European languages and cultural practices.
   C. Europeans believed it burdensome to be forced to tutor non-Europeans in their languages and customs.
   D. Many Europeans supported the construction of schools for colonial subjects and even the development of scholarships for them to study in Europe.

   Answers:

   A. Incorrect. White Europeans approved of settled colonies; part of the rationale of settlement was the idea that a white European presence was helping "civilize" the area.
   B. Incorrect. According to the idea of the white man's burden, the lives of non-Europeans would improve by adopting European customs and traditions.
   C. **Correct.** The idea of the white man's burden was not meant to suggest a literal burden; it was a paternalistic concept of responsibility used to justify imperial dominance.
   D. Incorrect. Schools were built throughout many colonies (though not all were of high quality, nor were they accessible to all people); furthermore, many colonial subjects moved to England, France, Belgium, and elsewhere in Europe to study.

15) **Marx and Engels believed**

   A. that the proletariat must control the means of production to ensure a wageless, classless society to meet the needs of all equitably.
   B. in the dictatorship of the proletariat, in which the workers would control the means of production in a non-democratic society.
   C. that an organized revolution directed by a small group of leaders was necessary to bring about social change and a socialist society.
   D. that the bourgeoisie would willingly give up control of the means of production to the proletariat.

   Answers:

   A. **Correct.** Marx and Engels believed in abolishing wages and the class structure in exchange for a socialist society where the means of production were commonly held and in which income was equally distributed.
   B. Incorrect. The dictatorship of the proletariat was a Leninist concept.

C. Incorrect. While Marx and Engels believed in revolution, they believed that the workers would be able to bring it about; Lenin would later argue that the proletariat needed direction in revolution.

D. Incorrect. Marx and Engels believed that a socialist society could only be achieved through revolution.

Global Conflicts

Pre-Revolutionary Russia

Russia had gone to war with Japan in 1904 to secure access to the Pacific and secure its interests in Asia. **Tsar Nicholas II**, unpopular at home, also believed that a victory would improve his security as a ruler. Japan, concerned about losing influence in Korea and seeking influence in China, attacked Russia; the **Russo-Japanese War** quickly ended in 1905 due to superior Japanese military technology, including naval technology, training, and leadership.

Russia's loss to Japan in the 1905 Russo-Japanese War was just another example of its difference from other European powers. While technically a European country, Russia had been slow to industrialize, due in part to its size and terrain. A largely agrarian country at the turn of the century, **serfdom**, the practice of "tying" peasants to the land and the last vestiges of feudalism, had only been abolished in 1861. Most Russians were still poor, rural farmers, and industrialization brought wretched conditions to workers in the cities. Russia also continued to have an absolute monarchy, unlike many European powers whose governments had shifted during the Age of Revolution.

Tsar Nicholas faced dissent at home due to the humiliating defeat by the Japanese; discontent was fueled by longer-term economic hardship in the face of a strengthening European industrial economy and limited freedoms in comparison to those enjoyed elsewhere in Europe. Unlawful trade unions appeared; workers began striking; and peasants rose up in protest of oppressive taxation.

Still, many Russians blamed the Tsar's advisors and minor officials for conditions, believing that the Tsar himself would act to improve conditions for Russians. These ideas were shattered in 1905 when a peaceful protest of working conditions in St. Petersburg ended in a bloody massacre of civilians by the Tsar's troops. **Bloody Sunday**, as the event came to be called, resulted in the **Revolution of 1905**, during which the Tsar temporarily lost control of Russia and was discredited.

Following the Revolution of 1905, the Tsar made some reforms in Russia, including the establishment of a **Duma**, or Parliament. However, economic hardship and social discontent continued in Russia.

While not directly involved with the failed Revolution of 1905, the Marxist Social Democrats, made up of the **Bolsheviks**, led by **Lenin**, and the **Mensheviks**, would gain power. They would eventually take over the country in 1917.

World War I

Instability in the Balkans and increasing tensions in Europe culminated with the assassination of the Austro-Hungarian Archduke **Franz Ferdinand** by the Serbian nationalist **Gavrilo Princip** in Sarajevo on June 28, 1914. In protest of continuing Austro-Hungarian control over Serbia, Princip's action kicked off the **system of alliances** that had been in place among European powers.

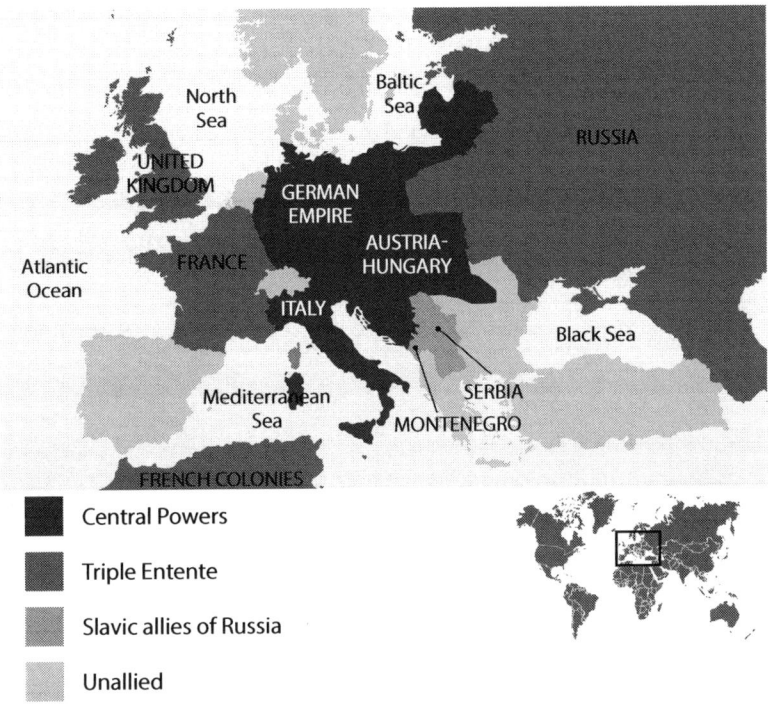

Figure 1.13. WWI Alliances

Austria-Hungary declared war on Serbia, and Russia came to Serbia's aid. As an ally of Austria-Hungary as part of the Triple Alliance, Germany declared war on Russia. Russia's ally France prepared for war; as Germany traversed Belgium to invade France, Belgium pleaded for aid from other European countries and so Britain declared war on Germany.

Germany had been emphasizing military growth since the consolidation and militarization of the empire under Bismarck in the mid-nineteenth century. Now, under **Kaiser Wilhelm II**, who sought expanded territories in Europe and overseas for Germany (including the potential capture of overseas British and French colonies), Germany was a militarized state an important European power in its own right.

Wilhelm, the grandson of Frederick II on his father's side and of Queen Victoria, took over the German Empire in 1888. He had focused on improving naval power and expanding German territory overseas. Despite his connections to Britain, Germany's threat to British overseas power brought the war beyond Europe to Africa and Asia. In **Togo**, Britain and France took over an important German com-

munications point. In **China**, Japan allied with Britain and France, taking control of the German settlement of Tsingtao and of German colonies in the **Pacific Islands**.

Britain's imperial power allowed it to call on troops from all over the globe—Indians, Canadians, Australians, South Africans, and New Zealanders all fought in Europe. France, too, imported colonial fighters from North Africa.

In Europe, the 1914 **Battle of the Marne** between Germany and French and British forces defending France resulted in trench warfare that would continue for years, marking the Western Front. At **Gallipoli** in 1915, Australian and New Zealander troops fought the **Ottoman Empire**, allies of Germany, near Istanbul. Later that year, a German submarine, or **U-boat**, sank the *Lusitania*, a passenger ship in the Atlantic, killing many American civilians. In 1916, the **Battle of Verdun**, the longest battle of the war, ended in the failure of the Germans to defeat the French army. In 1916, the British navy pushed back the German navy in the **Battle of Jutland**; despite heavy losses, Britain was able to ensure that German naval power was diminished for the rest of the war. On July 1, 1916, the **Battle of the Somme** became part of an allied effort to repel Germany using artillery to end the stalemate on the Western Front; after four months, however, the front moved only five miles.

> **DID YOU KNOW?**
>
> The first international war to use industrialized weaponry, WWI was called "the Great War" because battle on such a scale had never before been seen.

Finally, in 1917, the United States caught the **Zimmerman Telegram**, in which Germany secretly proposed an alliance with Mexico to attack the US This finally spurred US intervention in the war; despite Russian withdrawal after the Bolshevik Revolution in October 1917, Germany was forced to surrender in the face of invasion by the US-supported allies.

According to the **Schlieffen Plan**, Germany had planned to fight a war on two fronts against both Russia and France. However, Russia's unexpectedly rapid mobilization stretched the German army too thin on the Eastern Front, while it became bogged down in **trench warfare** on the Western Front against the British, French, and later the Americans. Germany lost the war and was punished with the harsh **Treaty of Versailles,** which held it accountable for the entirety of the war. The Treaty brought economic hardship on the country by forcing it to pay **reparations**. Wilhelm was forced to abdicate and never again regained power in Germany. German military failure and consequent economic collapse due to the Treaty of Versailles and later worldwide economic depression set the stage for the rise of fascism and Adolf Hitler.

The Treaty also created the **League of Nations**, an international organization designed to prevent future outbreaks of international war; however, it was largely toothless, especially because the powerful United States did not join.

CHANGE IN THE MIDDLE EAST

The end of WWI also marked the end of the Ottoman Empire, which was officially dissolved in 1923. From the end of the nineteenth century, the British had been increasing their influence throughout Ottoman territory in Egypt and the Persian Gulf, seeking control over the Suez Canal and petroleum resources in the Gulf. The Ottomans had already lost their North African provinces to France in the mid-nineteenth century.

In 1908, the **Young Turks**, a military government, had effectively taken over the empire in an effort to modernize it. They were especially concerned with nationalism and promoting *Turkishness*, a focus on Turkish ethnicity and culture, throughout the diverse empire. An ally of Germany, the Ottoman Empire had been defeated in the war; tremendous losses led to the collapse of many Ottoman institutions. Poor organization and refugee movements led to starvation and chaos throughout the region.

> **DID YOU KNOW?**
>
> In 1915, the Ottoman Empire launched a genocide against the Christian Armenian people, part of a campaign to control ethnic groups it believed threatened the Turkish nature of the empire. An estimated 1.5 million Armenians were forcibly removed from their homes and killed. To this day, the Turkish government denies the Armenian Genocide.

In 1916, France and Britain concluded the **Sykes-Picot Agreement**, which secretly planned for the Middle East following the defeat of the Ottoman Empire. The Agreement divided up the region now considered the Middle East into spheres of influence to be controlled by each power; Palestine would be governed internationally. In 1917, the secret **Balfour Declaration** promised the Jews an independent state in Palestine, but Western powers did not honor this agreement; in fact it conflicted directly with the Sykes-Picot Agreement. The state of Israel was not established until 1948.

At the end of the war the area was indeed divided into **mandates**, areas nominally independent but effectively controlled by Britain and France. The borders drawn are essentially those national borders that divide the Middle East today. After the First World War, the nationalist **Mustafa Ataturk**, one of the Young Turks who pushed a secular, nationalist agenda, kept European powers out of Anatolia and abolished the Caliphate in 1924, establishing modern Turkey.

After the dissolution of the Ottoman Empire, the future of the Middle East was uncertain. Despite its weaknesses, the Ottoman Empire had been the symbolic center of Islam, controlling Mecca and Medina. The Ottoman sultan held the title of Caliph, or the one entrusted with the leadership of those two holy cities. With the region broken up into European-controlled protectorates and an independent, nationalist, secular Turkey turned toward Europe, the social and political fabric of the region was becoming undone.

There was no more Caliph. Refugees and migrants had traveled throughout the Ottoman Empire over the course of the war, stopping in areas that were now suddenly restricted by international borders from their places of origin. People lacked identification papers. Ethnic and religious groups were divided by what would become the borders of the modern Middle East.

France and Britain backed different political factions in their mandates. While nominally autonomous, Egypt and its ruler, **King Fuad**, were close allies of the British, having essentially been under their control. At the same time, **Husayn ibn Ali (King Hussein)**, the Sherif of Mecca, claimed the title of Caliph, but was eventually driven out of Mecca and granted the title of king of Jordan by the British (his family controls the monarchy to this day). The rest of the Arabian Peninsula, where oil had not yet been discovered, was taken by the **Saudis**, a tribe from the desert which followed an extreme form of Islam, the **Wahhabi Movement**; King Saud would eventually conquer Mecca and Medina but never take the title of Caliph.

The roots of two competing ideologies, **Pan-Arabism** and **Islamism**, developed in this context. According to Pan-Arabism, Arabs and Arabic speakers should be aligned regardless of international borders. Similar to Pan-Slavism, Pan-Arabism eventually became an international movement espousing Arab unity in response to European and US influence and presence later in the twentieth century.

Islamism began as a social and political movement. The **Muslim Brotherhood** was established in Egypt in the 1920s, filling social roles that the state had abandoned or could not fill. Eventually taking a political role, the Muslim Brotherhood's model later inspired groups like Hamas and Hezbollah.

Russian Revolution

By 1917, Russia was suffering from widespread food shortages and economic crisis; morale was low due to conscription and as the military suffered enormous losses and humiliating defeats under the command of Nicholas II. During WWI, this combination of failures at home and on the front only added to widespread dissatisfaction with the rule of the Tsar. An enormous strike in Petrograd in January 1917 commemorating Bloody Sunday ended in revolt; soldiers refused to fire on protesters and the people formed the elected **Petrograd Soviet** (Council) instead in the **February Revolution**. The Tsar was forced to abdicate; the revolutionary movement resulted in the fall of his family, the Romanovs.

A weak provisional government was formed until elections could be held; however, it was widely regarded as working in the interests of the elite, making unpopular decisions like continuing to engage in WWI and putting off land reform. Meanwhile, other Soviets formed beyond Petrograd. The Provisional Government was ineffective in solving economic problems; however, the elected Soviets seemed to better represent the interests of the workers and peasants who suffered the most, and so they became more powerful. At the same time, the Soviets appealed to discontented soldiers fighting in the unpopular war.

The Bolsheviks, unlike the Mensheviks, believed that revolution must be planned and instigated at the right moment, not a phenomenon meant to occur naturally. The Bolsheviks, led by Lenin, consequently were not involved in the February Revolution. Lenin believed that revolution must be planned and that the proletariat needed direction in beginning and pursuing a revolution. However, later in 1917, the Bolsheviks had become a stronger force, and Lenin believed that the time was right to trigger revolution in Russia.

Lenin and the Bolsheviks proposed that power be concentrated in the Soviets, not in the Duma; that Russia would make peace and withdraw from European hostilities; that land would be redistributed among the peasants; and that economic crises in the cities would be solved. Lenin's plan was to take control of the Petrograd Soviet, of which **Leon Trotsky** had become chairman. In the **October Revolution** Lenin, Trotsky, and the Bolsheviks took control of Russia, defeating the Provisional Government in a coup.

In 1918, despite withdrawal from WWI, the **Russian Civil War** was underway; the **White Armies**, former supporters of the Tsar, were in conflict with the Bolshevik **Red Army**. During the war, the communists consolidated their power by nationalizing industry, developing and distributing propaganda portraying themselves as the defenders of Russia against imperialism, and forcefully eliminating dissent. For many, it was more appealing to fight for a new Russia with hope for an improved standard of living than to return to the old times under the Tsar; furthermore, many Russians feared the specter of imperialism or interference by foreign powers. By 1921, the Bolsheviks were victorious and formed the **Soviet Union** or **Union of Soviet Socialist Republics (USSR)**.

Following Lenin's death in 1924, Trotsky and the Secretary of the Communist Party, **Josef Stalin**, struggled for power. Stalin ultimately outmaneuvered Trotsky, who was exiled and assassinated. Under Stalin's totalitarian dictatorship, the USSR became socially and politically repressive; the Communist Party and the military underwent **purges** where any persons who were a potential threat to Stalin's power were imprisoned or executed. This paranoia and oppression extended to the general population: Russians suffered under the **Great Terror** throughout the 1920s. Any hint of dissent was to be reported to the secret police—the **NKVD**—and usually resulted in imprisonment for life.

> **DID YOU KNOW?**
>
> In the 1920s, around twenty *million* Russians were sent to the *gulags*, or prison labor camps, usually in Siberia, thousands of miles from their homes. Millions died.

Stalin also enforced **Russification** policies, persecuting ethnic groups. People throughout the USSR were forced to speak Russian and limit or hide their own cultural practices. Religious practices were restricted or forbidden.

In 1931, Stalin enforced the **collectivization** of land and agriculture in an attempt to consolidate control over the countryside and improve food security. He

had the *kulaks*, or landowning peasants, sent to the *gulags*, enabling the government to confiscate their land. By 1939, most farming and land was controlled by the government, and most peasants lived on collective land. Collectivizing the farms enabled Stalin to encourage more peasants to leave the country and become industrial workers, to produce agricultural surpluses to sell overseas, and to eliminate the *kulaks*. However, systemic disorganization in the 1920s and early 1930s did result in famine and food shortages.

As part of modernizing Russia, Stalin focused on accelerating industrial development. Targeting heavy industry, these **Five Year Plans** increased production in industrial materials and staples like electricity, petroleum, coal, and iron; they also resulted in the construction of major infrastructure throughout the country from 1929 – 1938. These developments provided opportunities for women, but conditions for the workers were dismal. The USSR quickly became an industrial power, but at the expense of millions of Russians, Ukrainians, and other groups who lost their lives in purges, forced labor camps, and famine.

Change in East Asia

Following its victory in the Russo-Japanese War, Japan had become more visible internationally in the early part of the twentieth century. That country had undergone rapid modernization after being closed off from 1600 until the mid-nineteenth century under the **Tokugawa Shogunate**; now, recognized as a military power for defeating Russia, Japan had joined a world focused on industry and imperialism.

Japan, having already embraced industrialization and modern militarization, turned towards imperialism throughout Asia. From 1894 – 1895, Japan had fought the **First Sino-Japanese War** with Qing Dynasty China, establishing trading rights there, gaining influence over China's vassal **Korea**, and controlling **Taiwan** in the **Treaty of Shimonoseki**. This conflict revealed Chinese military and organizational limitations and showed Japanese military superiority.

The Russo-Japanese War had been important not only to solidify Japanese influence in Korea and Manchuria, but also to confirm Japan's status in the eyes of European empires as a world power. In 1910, Japan annexed Korea. After WWI, Japan was granted Germany's **Pacific islands** by the League of Nations.

Following the First World War, despite having provided assistance to the French and British in Asia, Japan began its own imperialist adventure in East and Southeast Asia not only to gain power and access to raw materials, but also to limit and eventually expel European rule in what Japan considered its *sphere of influence*. In 1931, Japan invaded **Manchuria**, creating the puppet state *Manchukuo*.

While Japan was building its global reputation and military and economic strength in Asia, China was undergoing political change. The **Xinhai Revolution** broke out in 1911, resulting in the overthrow of the Qing and the end of dynastic Chinese rule, establishing the short-lived **Republic of China**. Led by **Sun Yat-sen**,

the revolutionaries not only had the support of the disaffected Chinese people; they also had the financial support of millions of Chinese living abroad.

However, despite Republican recognition by major international powers, the power vacuum left by the end of imperial China allowed the rise of warlords throughout the enormous country, and the government was unable to establish total control. The **Kuomintang (KMT)**, or Nationalist Party of the revolutionary government worked to consolidate government power; following Sun Yat-sen's death in 1925, the KMT leader **Chiang Kai-shek** (or **Jiang Jieshi**) went on to take control of much of China back from the warlords.

At the same time, communism was emerging in China. The country felt betrayed by European powers, which had awarded German possessions in China to Japan in the Treaty of Versailles. China refused to sign the treaty, and communism became popular among some Chinese leaders; thus emerged the **Chinese Communist Party**. Temporarily working together, the KMT and CCP were able to bring Chinese territory back under Republican control. However, Chiang turned against the CCP in 1927, driving it south.

The CCP focused its organizing activities in the countryside on the peasants, becoming powerful in southern China. However, KMT attacks on the CCP in the south in 1934 forced the CCP to retreat on the **Long March** north. During this time of hardship, **Mao Zedong** emerged as the leader of the movement.

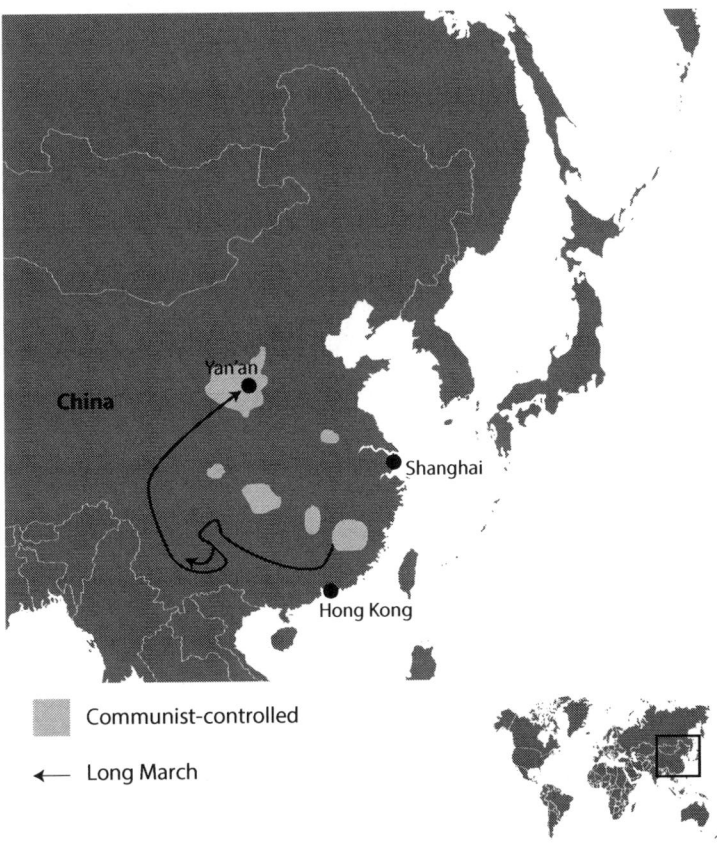

Figure 1.14. The Long March

World War II

Meanwhile, Germany suffered under the provisions of the Treaty of Versailles. In 1919, a democratic government was established at Weimar—the **Weimar Republic**. Germany was in chaos; the Kaiser had fled and the country was torn apart by war. However, the new government could not bring stability.

Blamed for WWI, Germany owed huge **reparations** according to the treaty to pay for the cost of the war, setting off **hyperinflation** and impoverishing the country and its people. The rise of communists and a workers' party that came to be known as the National Socialist Party, or **Nazi Party**, led to further political instability. Following the crash of the stock market in 1929, German unemployment reached six million; furthermore, the United States had called in its foreign loans. Consequently, unemployed workers began supporting communism. On the other hand, the Nazis, led by **Adolf Hitler**, gained support from business interests, which feared communist power in government. Thus, the Nazis became an important force in the Weimar Republic at the beginning of the 1930s.

Hitler maneuvered into the role of chancellor by 1933. His charisma and popular platform—to cancel the Treaty of Versailles—allowed him to rise. Enjoying the support of the wealthy and big business, which feared communism (especially with the development of Soviet Russia), Nazi ideals appealed strongly to both industry and the workers in the face of global economic depression. Finally, the Nazi Minister of Propaganda **Joseph Goebbels** executed an effective propaganda campaign, and would do so throughout Hitler's rule, known as the **Third Reich**.

The following year, Hitler became the *Führer*, or *leader*, of Germany. A series of chaotic events followed: a fire in the Reichstag (German Parliament), which allowed Hitler to arrest communist leaders; the rise of the **Gestapo**, or secret police (which violently enforced Nazi rule among the people); and the banning of political parties and trade unions. As a result, Hitler and the Nazis consolidated total control. They also set into motion their agenda of racism and genocide against "non-Aryan" (non-Germanic) or "racially impure" people.

Jewish people were particularly targeted. Germany had a considerable Jewish population; so did the other Central and Eastern European countries that Germany would come to control. Throughout the 1930s, the Nazis passed a series of laws limiting Jewish rights, including jobs that Jewish people could hold, rights to citizenship, places they could go, public facilities they could use, whom they could marry, even the names they could have. **Kristallnacht** took place in 1938, an organized series of attacks on Jewish businesses, homes, and places of worship, so called because the windows of these places were smashed.

In 1939, Jews were forced from their homes into **ghettoes**, isolated and overcrowded urban neighborhoods; in 1941, they were forced to wear **yellow stars** identifying them as Jewish. Millions of Jewish people were sent to **concentration camps**; the Nazis decided on the **Final Solution** to the "Jewish Question": to murder Jewish

people by systematically gassing them at death camps. At least six million European Jews were murdered by the Nazis in the **Holocaust**.

Roma, Slavic people, homosexuals, disabled people, people of color, prisoners of war, communists, and others not considered "Aryan" were also forced into slave labor in concentration camps and murdered there. Later, this concept of torturing and killing people based on their ethnicity in order to exterminate them would become defined as **genocide**.

Hitler was a **fascist**, believing in a mostly free market accompanied by a dictatorial government with a strong military. He sought to restore Germany's power and expand its reach by annexing **Austria** (the *Anschluss*, or *union*) and the **Sudetenland**, German-majority areas in part of what is today the Czech Republic.

With the collapse of the Weimar Republic and the League of Nations at its weakest state, France and Britain granted the Sudetenland to Hitler in 1938 in a policy called **appeasement** in an effort to maintain stability in Europe and avoid another war. In fact, given the threat posed by the new Soviet Union, Britain and France actually believed that a stronger Germany would be in their interests.

However, appeasement failed when Hitler invaded the rest of **Czechoslovakia** and formed an alliance with **Italy** the next year.

The Soviet Union made a pact with Germany in 1939: Germany would not invade the USSR, and the two countries would divide Poland. Germany then invaded **Poland**; its 1939 invasion is commonly considered the beginning of the **Second World War** (though some historians actually consider the Japanese invasion of Manchuria in 1931 to be the beginning of the war).

War exploded in Europe in 1939 as Hitler gained control of more land than any European power since Napoleon. In 1940, Germany had taken Paris. The **Battle of Britain** began in July of that year; however Germany suffered its first defeat and was unable to take Britain. Despite staying out of combat, in 1941 the **United States** enforced the **Lend-Lease Act** which provided support and military aid to Britain. The two also released the **Atlantic Charter**, outlining common goals.

When Japan joined the **Axis** powers of Germany and Italy, the **Second Sino-Japanese War of 1937** would also be subsumed under the Second World War, ending in 1945. The **Chinese Civil War** between communists led by Mao Zedong and nationalists led by Chiang Kai-shek was interrupted by the Second Sino-Japanese War, when Japan tried to extend its imperial reach deeper into China, resulting in atrocities like the **Rape of Nanking** (1937 – 1938).

> **DID YOU KNOW?**
>
> The Atlantic Charter described values shared by the US and Britain, including restoring self-governance in occupied Europe and liberalizing international trade

At this time, Chiang was forced to form an alliance with Mao and the two forces worked together against Japan. By the end of the war, the CCP was stronger

than ever, with widespread support from many sectors of Chinese society, while the KMT was demoralized and had little popular support.

In June of 1941, Japan, now part of the **Axis** along with Germany and Italy, attacked the United States at Pearl Harbor. Consequently, the US joined the war in Europe and in the Pacific, deploying thousands of troops in both theaters.

Meanwhile, in Asia, Japan continued its imperialist policies. In the early 1940s, it took advantage of chaos in Europe and the weakened European colonial powers to invade and occupy **French Indochina**, **Indonesia**, and **Burma**; it also occupied the **Philippines**. Controlling these strategic areas meant the Axis was a direct threat to British India, Australia, and the eastern Soviet Union, not to mention European imperial and economic interests.

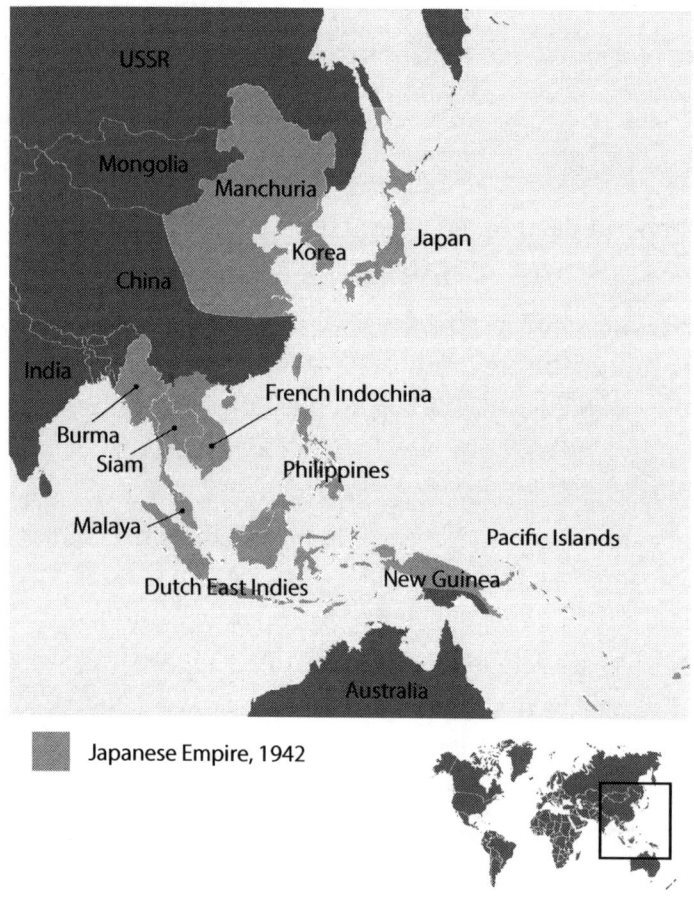

Figure 1.15. Japanese Expansion in Asia

Back in Europe, having broken his promise to the Soviet Union, Hitler invaded Russia. But in 1942, the USSR defeated Germany at the **Battle of Stalingrad**, a turning point in the war during which the Nazis were forced to turn from the Eastern Front. In 1943, Churchill, Roosevelt, and Stalin all met in Teheran to discuss the invasion of Italy; the Allies took Rome later that year.

In 1944, the Allies invaded France on **D-Day**. While they liberated Paris in August, the costly **Battle of the Bulge** extended into 1945. Despite thousands of American casualties, Hitler's forces were pushed back. In the spring of 1945, the US crossed the Rhine while the USSR invaded Berlin; Hitler killed himself and the Allies accepted German surrender.

The war in the Pacific would continue, however. Strategic battles were fought in **Saipan** and **Iwo Jima** to secure landing strips for American bombers. At **Leyte**, the US destroyed most of the Japanese Navy. Despite casualties of up to 400,000, Japan continued to fight the US for territory in the **Philippines**. Finally, even after the war in Europe had ended, the US and Japan fought over **Okinawa**, which the US planned to use as a staging point for an invasion of Japan in order to force Japanese surrender.

An American invasion of Japan would have likely resulted in hundreds of thousands of casualties. **President Truman**, who had succeeded Roosevelt, elected to use the nuclear bomb on Japan instead to force surrender. In 1945, the US bombed the Japanese cities of **Hiroshima** and **Nagasaki**. The tremendous civilian casualties did force the Emperor to surrender; at that point, the Second World War came to an end.

That year in China, the Chinese Civil War recommenced; by 1949 the communists had emerged victorious. The KMT withdrew to Taiwan, while Mao and the CCP took over China, which became a communist country.

WWII and the period immediately preceding it saw horrific violations of human rights in Europe and Asia, including the atrocities committed during the Japanese invasions of China, Korea, and Southeast Asia, and the European Holocaust of Jews and other groups like Roma and homosexuals. The war finally ended with the US atomic bombings of Hiroshima and Nagasaki in 1945, ending years of firebombing civilians in Germany and Japan; devastating ground and naval warfare throughout Europe, Asia, the South Pacific, and Africa; and the deaths of millions of soldiers and civilians all around the world.

The extreme horrors of WWII helped develop the concept of **genocide**, or the effort to extinguish an entire group of people because of their ethnicity, and the idea of **human rights**. The **United Nations** was formed, based on the League of Nations, as a body to champion human rights and uphold international security. Its **Security Council** is made up of permanent member states which can intervene militarily in the interests of international stability.

Allied forces took the lead in rebuilding efforts: the US occupied areas in East Asia and Germany, while the Soviet Union remained in Eastern Europe. The Allies had planned to rebuild Europe according to the **Marshall Plan**; however, Stalin broke his promise made at the 1945 **Yalta Conference** to adhere to that plan and allow Eastern European countries to hold free elections. Instead, the USSR occupied these countries and they came under communist control. The **Cold War** had begun.

The Cold War

At the Yalta Conference in February 1945, Stalin, Churchill, and Roosevelt had agreed upon the division of Germany, the free nature of government in Poland, and free elections in Eastern Europe. However, at the **Potsdam Conference** in July 1945, things had changed. Harry Truman had replaced Franklin D. Roosevelt, who had died in office, and Clement Atlee had replaced Winston Churchill. Stalin felt betrayed by the US use of the nuclear bomb; likewise, the US and the British felt that Stalin had violated the agreement at Yalta regarding democracy in Eastern Europe.

Stalin ensured that communists came to power in Eastern Europe, setting up satellite states at the Soviet perimeter in violation of the Yalta agreement. The Soviet rationale was to establish a buffer zone following its extraordinarily heavy casualties in WWII—around twenty million. With Stalin's betrayal of the Allies' agreement, in the words of the British Prime Minister **Winston Churchill,** an *iron curtain* had come down across Europe, dividing east from west.

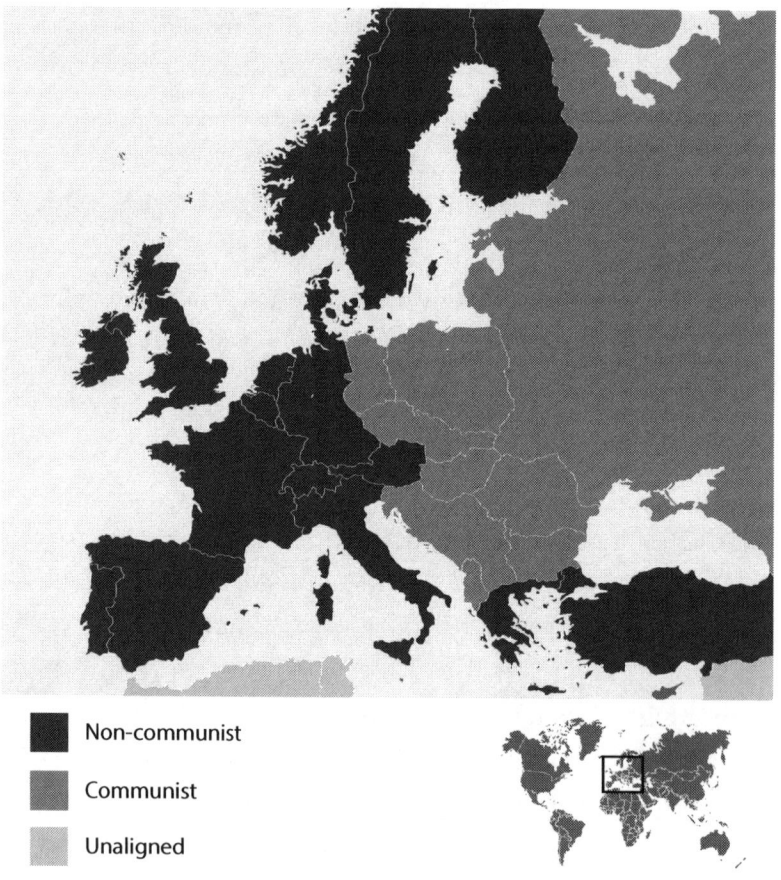

Figure 1.16. Cold War Europe

Consequently, western states organized the North Atlantic Treaty Organization or **NATO**, an agreement wherein an attack on one was an attack on all; this treaty provided for **collective security** in the face of the Soviet expansionist threat. The

United States adopted a policy of **containment**, the idea that communism should be *contained*, as part of the **Truman Doctrine** of foreign policy. The United States also sponsored the **Marshall Plan**, which provided aid to European countries in an effort to restart the European economy and rebuild the continent. Stalin did not permit Soviet-controlled countries to take Marshall aid.

In response, the Soviet Union created the **Warsaw Pact**, a similar organization consisting of Eastern European communist countries. **Nuclear weapons**, especially the development of the extremely powerful **hydrogen bomb,** raised the stakes of the conflict. The concept of **mutually-assured destruction**, or the understanding that a nuclear strike by one country would result in a response by the other, ultimately destroying the entire world, may have prevented the outbreak of active violence.

Germany itself had been divided into four zones, controlled by Britain, France, the US, and the USSR. Berlin had been divided the same way. Once Britain, France, and the US united their zones into West Germany in 1948 and introduced a new currency, the USSR cut off West Berlin in the **Berlin Blockade**. Viewing this as an aggressive attempt to capture the entire city, for nearly a year western powers provided supplies to West Berlin by air in the **Berlin Airlift**.

> **QUICK REVIEW**
>
> How did the Cold War erupt between the Allies and the Soviet Union?

Berlin continued to be a problem for the USSR. Until 1961, refugees from the Eastern Bloc came to West Berlin, seeking better living conditions in the West. Furthermore, West Berlin was a center for Western espionage. In 1961, the USSR, now led by **Nikita Khrushchev**, closed the border and constructed the **Berlin Wall**.

Following the Second World War, Korea had also been divided. In the northern part of the country, the communist **Kim il Sung** controlled territory. South of the **thirty-eighth parallel**, the non-communist Syngman Rhee controlled the rest of the country. In 1950, Kim il Sung invaded the south with Russian and Chinese support, intending to create a communist Korea.

According to the Truman Doctrine, communism needed to be contained. Furthermore, according to **domino theory**, if one country became communist, then more would, too, like a row of dominoes falling. Therefore, the United States, by way of the United Nations, became involved in the **Korean War** (1950 – 1953).

UN troops dominated and led by the US came to the aid of the nearly defeated South Koreans, pushing back Kim il Sung's troops. China supported Kim il Sung, and war on the peninsula continued until 1953, when US President Eisenhower threatened to use the nuclear bomb, ending the war in a stalemate.

Later, in **Cuba**, the revolutionary **Fidel Castro** took over in 1959. Allied with the Soviet Union, he allowed missile bases to be constructed in Cuba, which threatened the United States. During the **Cuban Missile Crisis** in 1962, the world came closer

than ever to nuclear war when the USSR sent missiles to Cuba. Cuba ships faced an American blockade and tension grew as the US considered invading Cuba. President Kennedy and Premier Khrushchev were able to come to an agreement in which the USSR promised to dismantle its Cuban bases as long as the US ended the blockade and secretly dismantled its own missile bases in Turkey. Nuclear war was averted.

Despite this success, the United States engaged in a lengthy violent conflict in Southeast Asia. Supporting anti-communist fighters in Vietnam in keeping with containment and Domino Theory, the United States pursued the **Vietnam War** for almost a decade. The **Gulf of Tonkin Resolution** authorized the US president to manage the ongoing conflict without consulting Congress, so for a period of years troops continued to be deployed to the region, fueling the conflict.

The US had become involved in the war after coming to the aid of Vietnam's old colonial master, France. **Ho Chi Minh**, the revolutionary Vietnamese leader, had actually originally approached the Americans for assistance in asserting Vietnamese independence. He led the North Vietnamese forces (**Viet Cong**) in a guerrilla war for independence throughout the 1960s.

Despite being outnumbered, Viet Cong familiarity with the difficult terrain, support from Russia and China, and determination eventually resulted in victory. Bloody guerrilla warfare demoralized the American military, but the 1968 **Tet Offensive** was a turning point. Despite enormous losses, the North Vietnamese won a strategic victory in this coordinated, surprise offensive. Extreme objection to the war within the United States, high casualties, and demoralization eventually resulted in US withdrawal in 1975.

Toward the end of the 1960s and into the 1970s, the Cold War reached a period of **détente**, or a warming of relations. The US and USSR signed the **Nuclear Non-Proliferation Treaty**, in which they and other nuclear power signatories agreed not to further spread nuclear weapons technology. Later, the USSR and the US signed the **SALT I Treaty** (Strategic Arms Limitation Treaty), limiting strategic weaponry. Some cultural exchanges and partnerships in outer space took place.

At the same time, the United States began making diplomatic overtures toward communist China. This was however, part of a different Cold War strategy. Despite its status as a communist country, China and the USSR had difficult relations due to their differing views on the nature of communism. While Khrushchev was taking a more moderate approach to world communism, Mao believed in more aggressive policies. Following the **Sino-Soviet Split** of the 1960s, China had lost much Soviet support for its modernization programs and despite advances in agriculture and some industrialization, Mao's programs like the **Great Leap Forward** had taken a toll on the people.

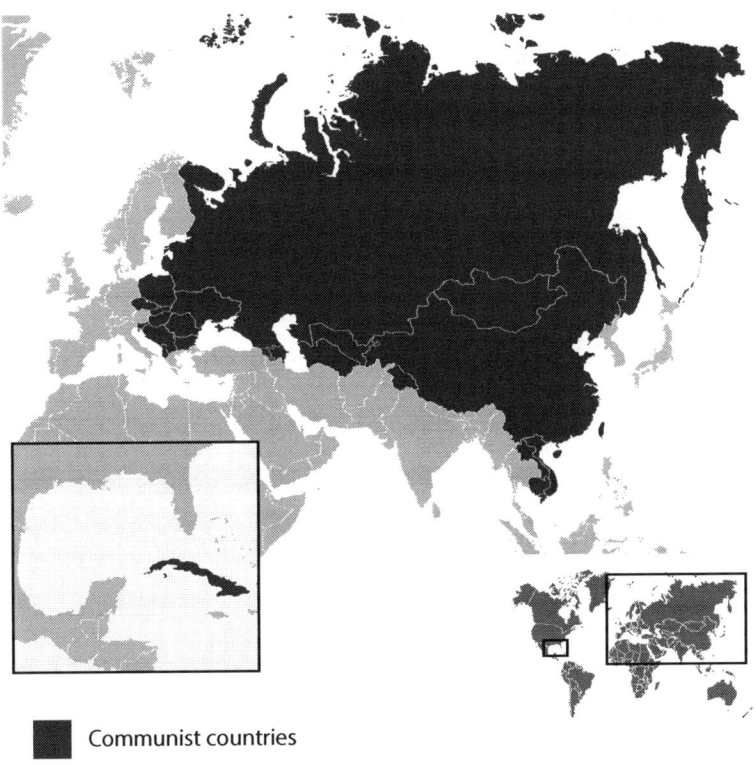

Figure 1.17. The Communist World

In 1972, President Nixon visited China, establishing relations between the communist government and the United States. Communist China was permitted to join the UN (previously, China had been represented by the KMT, which was isolated to Taiwan).

The climate would change again, however, in the 1970s and 1980s. The US and USSR found themselves on opposite sides in proxy wars throughout the world (see below). In addition, and the **arms race** was underway. **President Ronald Reagan** pursued a militaristic policy, prioritizing weapons development with the goal of outspending the USSR on weapons technology.

> **DID YOU KNOW?**
>
> Perhaps the most famous proposal in weapons technology during this time was the Strategic Defense Initiative; popularly known as *Star Wars*, this outer-space based system would have intercepted Soviet intercontinental ballistic missiles.

DECOLONIZATION

Meanwhile, the former colonies of the fallen European colonial powers had won or were in the process of gaining their independence. One role of the United Nations was to help manage the **decolonization** process. Already, the leader **Mohandas Gandhi** had led a peaceful independence movement in **India** against the British,

winning Indian independence in 1949. His assassination by Hindu radicals led to conflict between **Hindus** and **Muslims** in the **Subcontinent**, resulting in **Partition,** the bloody division of India: Hindus fled into what is today India, while Muslims fled to **East Pakistan** (now **Bangladesh** and **West Pakistan**). Instability is ongoing on the Subcontinent.

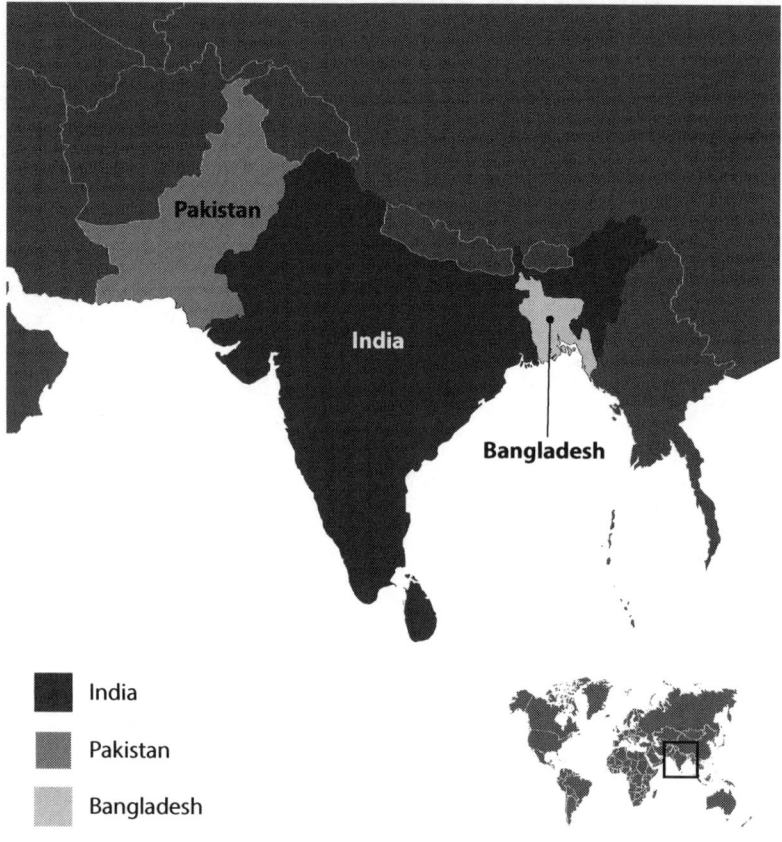

Figure 1.18. Partition

Bloody conflict in Africa like the **Algerian War** against France (1954 – 1962), the **Mau Mau Rebellion** against the British in Kenya in the 1950s, and violent movements against Belgium in the **Congo** ultimately resulted in African independence for many countries in the 1950s, 1960s, and 1970s; likewise, so did strong leadership by African nationalist leaders and thinkers like **Jomo Kenyatta, Julius Nyerere**, and **Kwame Nkrumah.** The apartheid regime in South Africa, where segregation between races was legal and people of color lived in oppressive conditions, was not lifted until the 1990s; **Nelson Mandela** led the country in a peaceful transition process.

In the Middle East, following the fall of the Ottoman Empire after WWI, European powers had taken over much of the area; these *protectorates* became independent states with arbitrary borders drawn and rulers installed by the Europeans. The creation of the state of **Israel** was especially contentious: in the 1917 **Balfour Declaration**, the British had promised the **Zionist** movement of European Jews that they would be given a homeland in the British-controlled protectorate of

Palestine; however, the US assured the Arabs in 1945 that a Jewish state would not be founded there. Israel emerged from diplomatic confusion, chaos, and tragedy after the murder of millions of Jews in Europe, and violence on the ground in Palestine carried out by both Jews and Arabs. This legacy of conflict lasts to this day in the Middle East.

While the Middle East had been divided into protectorates or into nominally independent states like Egypt that were still under strong European influence, these areas had become independent after the Second World War. Liberal activists against monarchical and dictatorial regimes and popular movements like Pan-Arabism and Islamism put pressure on Middle Eastern monarchies. Countries created by artificial borders based on the Sykes-Picot Agreement and comprised of divided and diverse ethnic and religious groups were already vulnerable to political instability; with added unrest, Middle Eastern governments fell. Furthermore, the Middle East became a Cold War battleground, with regimes courting the support of the Cold War powers.

In Egypt, **Gamal Abdul Nasser** led the Pan-Arabist movement in the region, which included creating an Arab alliance against Israel. In 1967, Arab allies launched a war against Israel; they were badly beaten, however, in the **Six Day War**, an embarrassing defeat for the Arab states and one from which Nasser never truly recovered. Furthermore, Israel took control of the Sinai Peninsula, the Golan Heights, and the West Bank of the Jordan River.

During the 1973 **Yom Kippur War**, while the US supported **Israel**, the USSR supported **Syria** and **Egypt**. Syria and Egypt had launched a surprise attack on Israel on the holiest day of the Jewish year in an attempt to gain back territory lost years prior. However, Israel was able to maintain its defenses.

In 1978, the American president Jimmy Carter was able to broker a peace agreement between the Egyptian leader **Anwar Sadat** and the Israeli leader **Menachem Begin** known as the **Camp David Accords**. However, other Arab countries, aside from Jordan, did not make peace with Israel. By the 1970s, Pan-Arabism was no longer the popular, unifying movement it had once been.

The **Non-Aligned Movement** arose in response to the Cold War. Instead of the bipolar world of the Cold War (one democratic, led by the US, the other communist, led by the USSR), the Non-Aligned Movement sought an alternative: the **Third World**. Non-Aligned or Third World countries wanted to avoid succumbing to the influence of either of the superpowers, and many found a forum in the United Nations in which to strengthen their international profiles.

However, throughout the Cold War, **proxy wars** between the US and the USSR were fought around the world. In the 1980s, the United States began supporting the anti-communist **Contras** in **Nicaragua**, who were fighting the communist **Sandinista** government. In 1979, the USSR invaded **Afghanistan**, an event which would contribute to the Soviet collapse; in response, the US began supporting anti-Soviet *mujahideen* forces (some of whose patrons would later attack the US as part of

international terrorist groups). Other examples include the **Angolan Civil War**, the **Mozambican Civil War**, and the **Nicaraguan Revolution**.

In the **Horn of Africa**, Somalia was formed when the Italian-administered UN trust territory of Somalia united with the British protectorate of Somaliland in 1960. Initially supported by the USSR for its socialist leanings, Somalia and its leader, Mohamed Siad Barre, initated a war against Ethiopia in 1977. Ultimately the USSR supported Ethiopia, and the United States supported Somalia.

While never officially colonized, **Iran** had been under the oppressive regime of the western-supported **Shah Reza Pahlavi** for decades. During its imperial era, Britain had begun exploring petroleum interests in what was then Persia, and western oil companies had remained powerful in that country. The **Pahlavi Dynasty** had taken over Persia in 1920 from the Qajars, who had ruled since 1785, and who themselves had been important in administration under the Safavids since the sixteenth century.

> **QUICK REVIEW**
>
> What is a proxy war? Why were proxy wars important in the context of the Cold War?

By the 1970s, the Shah's corrupt, oppressive regime was extremely unpopular in Iran, but it was propped up by the West. Several underground movements worked against the Shah, including communists and Islamic revolutionaries inspired by the Islamism of the early twentieth century. In the 1979 **Iranian Revolution**, these forces overthrew the Shah; shortly afterward, Islamist revolutionaries took over the country. The new theocracy was led by a group of clerics led by the Supreme Leader **Ayatollah Khomeini**. The Ayatollah became Supreme Leader and instituted political and social reforms, including stricter interpretations of Islamic laws and traditions and enforcing those throughout the country as national and local law. Later that year, radical students who supported the revolution stormed the US Embassy and held a number of staff hostage for over a year; the **Iran Hostage Crisis** would humiliate the United States.

> **DID YOU KNOW?**
>
> The revolutionary Iranian government would go on to support Shi'a militants (the *Hezbollah*, or the *Party of God*) in the **Lebanese Civil War** throughout the 1980s; this group is also inspired by Islamism.

Following the Iranian Revolution, the Iraqi leader **Saddam Hussein**, an ally of the United States, declared war against Iran. While governed by Sunnis, Iraq was actually a Shi'ite-majority country, and Saddam feared Iran would trigger a similar revolution there. Iraq also sought control over the strategic Shatt al-Arab waterway and some oil-rich territories inland. The war raged from 1980 – 1990.

SAMPLE QUESTIONS

16) **Which of the following was a weakness of the Schlieffen Plan?**
    A. It overstretched the German army.
    B. It failed to anticipate a stronger resistance in France.
    C. It underestimated Russia's ability to mobilize its troops.
    D. all of the above

    Answers:
    A. Incorrect. While the German army was stretched too thin, the answer is incomplete as the other answer choices are also true.
    B. Incorrect. While the Schlieffen Plan did indeed underestimate resistance on the Western Front, this answer choice is also incomplete as the other answer choices are also true.
    C. Incorrect. While the Schlieffen Plan did fail to anticipate rapid Russian mobilization, this answer choice is incomplete given the other options.
    D. Correct. All of the answer choices are true.

17) **According to the Sykes-Picot Agreement,**
    A. Israel would become an independent state.
    B. Husayn ibn Ali would become Caliph.
    C. Ataturk would lead an independent Turkey.
    D. Palestine would be under international supervision.

    Answers:
    A. Incorrect. Sykes-Picot made no promises of an independent Jewish state.
    B. Incorrect. Husayn ibn Ali, while taken into account in the Agreement in determining positions of power, was never offered the title of Caliph.
    C. Incorrect. Ataturk himself took control of Turkey, having been part of its leadership for some time and having held off European interference.
    D. Correct. Sykes-Picot put Palestine under the supervision of various international powers.

18) **Which of the following led to the rise of the Nazis in early 1930s Germany?**
    A. the impact of reparations and the support of German industrialists
    B. the impact of the Great Depression and the support of the workers
    C. support from the international communist movement and the impact of reparations on the German economy
    D. support from German industrialists and strong backing from other political factions in the Reichstag

Answers:

A. Correct. The Nazis planned to cease paying reparations, so their nationalist approach appealed to many Germans suffering from the hyperinflation that reparations had triggered. Furthermore, the Nazis had the support of German industrialists, who feared the rise of communism among the working classes.

B. Incorrect. While the economic suffering brought on by the Great Depression made the Nazis' promises appealing to many, they did not have the support of the majority of German workers, who mostly supported communists at the time.

C. Incorrect. The Nazis were against communism.

D. Incorrect. While they had support from German industrialists, the Nazis did not have widespread support in government: they were elected by popular vote.

19) **The Cold War was rooted in**

   A. Stalin's unwillingness to cede control of East Berlin to the allies following the fall of the Nazis.

   B. the erection of the Berlin Wall.

   C. Stalin's failure to honor the agreement at Yalta, installing communist regimes in Eastern Europe rather than permitting free, democratic elections

   D. the Cuban Missile Crisis

Answers:

   A. Incorrect. There had never been a plan for the Soviet Union to immediately cede control of East Berlin following the fall of the Nazis; dividing Berlin among the four allied powers had been foreseen.

   B. Incorrect. The Berlin Wall was built in 1961, several years after the Cold War had begun.

   C. Correct. The Cold War was rooted in Stalin's creation of communist satellite states in Eastern and Central Europe.

   D. Incorrect. The Cuban Missile Crisis occurred in 1962, well into the Cold War.

20) **Which of the following precipitated the end of the Cold War?**

   A. the Iran Hostage Crisis

   B. the Soviet War in Afghanistan

   C. the Iran-Iraq War

   D. the Yom Kippur War

Answers:

A. Incorrect. While the Iran Hostage Crisis was an embarrassment for the United States, it did not significantly alter its role in the Cold War nor did it contribute to the collapse of the USSR.

B. **Correct.** The Soviet invasion of Afghanistan and the subsequent ten-year war sapped Soviet financial and military resources—and morale. This draining war, plus the high price of the arms race with the United States, contributed significantly to the fall of the Soviet Union.

C. Incorrect. While the Cold War powers had strong interests and some involvement in this war—particularly the United States, an enemy of the revolutionary Iranian government—it did not significantly affect the balance of power between the US and the USSR. Furthermore, both superpowers supported Iraq.

D. Incorrect. Arguably, the Yom Kippur War was indeed a proxy war: the Soviet Union supported Syria and Egypt, so the United States came to Israel's aid. However this war did not significantly change the balance of power between the superpowers, although it did significantly affect the Middle East.

Post-Cold War World

In 1991, the Soviet Union fell when Soviet Premier **Mikhail Gorbachev**, who had implemented reforms like ***glasnost*** and ***perestroika*** (or *openness* and *transparency*), was nearly overthrown in a coup; a movement led by **Boris Yeltsin**, who had been elected president of Russia, stopped the coup. The USSR was dissolved later that year and Yeltsin became president of the Russian Federation. The war in Afghanistan and military overspending in an effort to keep up with American military spending had weakened the USSR to the point of collapse, and the Cold War ended.

Cold War Consequences

That same year, Saddam Hussein, the leader of Iraq, invaded Kuwait and took over its oil reserves and production facilities. In response, the United States and other countries went to war—with a UN mandate—to expel Iraq from Kuwait and to defend Saudi Arabia in order to regain control of the world's petroleum reserves in the **Gulf War**. This event cemented the US status as the sole world superpower; the global balance of power had changed.

Despite stability throughout most of Europe, the changes following the fall of the Iron Curtain led to instability in the Balkans. In 1992, Bosnia declared its independence from the collapsing state of Yugoslavia, following Croatia and Slovenia. Violence broke out in Bosnia between Bosnian Serbs on one side, and Bosnian Muslims (Bosniaks) and Croatians on the other. The **Bosnian War** raged from 1992

to 1995, resulting in the deaths of thousands of civilians and another European genocide—this time, of Bosnian Muslims.

Also following the Cold War, proxy wars throughout the world and instability in former colonies continued. In 1994, conflict in Central Africa resulted in the **Rwandan Genocide**. Hutus massacred Tutsis, and violence continued on both sides. In **Zaire**, the country descended into instability following the fall of **Mobutu Sese Seko**, the US-supported dictator, in 1997. Renamed the **Democratic Republic of the Congo**, parts of this country and others in Central Africa would remain wracked by poverty and torn by violence for decades.

In the 1980s, drought in the Horn of Africa led to widespread famine; humanitarian affairs and issues came into the public eye and the general public, especially in wealthier families, became more concerned about providing foreign aid to the suffering.

The Somali leader Mohamed Siad Barre was overthrown in 1991 and **Somalia** was broken up under the control of various warlords and clans. The people suffered from starvation with the breakdown of social order. The United States intervened as part of a UN peacekeeping mission in an attempt to provide humanitarian aid; however, strong military resistance from the warlord Muhammad Aideed impacted US public opinion and the effort failed. To this day there is no central government in Somalia, and much of the country is still dependent on aid; however, autonomous areas function independently.

Cooperation and Conflict

Following the end of the Cold War and post-decolonization, the balance of economic and political power began to change. The **G-20**, the world's twenty most important economic and political powers, includes many former colonies and non-European countries. The **BRICS**—Brazil, Russia, India, China, and South Africa—are recognized as world economic and political leaders. With the exception of Russia, all these countries were only recently classified as developing countries. While still wrestling with considerable social, economic, and political challenges, the BRICS are world powers in their own right as independent nations—unthinkable developments a century ago.

Steps toward European unification had begun as early as the 1950s; the **European Union**, as it is known today, was formed after the **Maastricht Treaty** was signed in 1992. As the former Soviet satellite states moved from communism to more democratic societies and capitalistic economies, more countries partnered with the EU and eventually joined it; as of 2015, twenty-eight countries are members, with more on the path to membership.

European Union countries remain independent, but they cooperate in international affairs, justice, security and foreign policy, environmental matters, and

economic policy. Many also share a common currency, the **euro**. According to the **Schengen Agreement**, some EU countries even have open borders.

Continental integration exists beyond Europe. In Africa, the **African Union**, originally the Organization of African Unity, has become a stronger political force in its own right, organizing peacekeeping missions throughout the continent. An organization similar to the EU, the AU is a forum for African countries to organize and align political, military, economic, and other policies.

In this era of **globalization**, international markets became increasingly open through free-trade agreements like **NAFTA** (the North American Free Trade Agreement), **Mercosur** (the South American free-trade zone), and the **Trans-Pacific Partnership**, a proposed free-trade zone between nine countries on the Pacific Ocean. The **World Trade Organization** oversees international trade. Technological advances like improvements in transportation infrastructure and the **internet** made international communication faster, easier and cheaper.

> **DID YOU KNOW?**
>
> While benefits of international trade include lower prices and more consumer choice, unemployment often increases in more developed countries and labor and environmental violations are more likely in developing countries.

However, more open borders, reliable international transportation, and faster, easier worldwide communication brought risks, too. In the early twenty-first century, the United States was attacked by terrorists on **September 11, 2001**, resulting in thousands of civilian casualties. Consequently, the US launched a major land war in Afghanistan and another later in Iraq.

Following the attacks on 9/11, the United States attacked Afghanistan as part of the **War on Terror**. Afghanistan's radical Islamist **Taliban** government was providing shelter to the group that took responsibility for the attacks, **al Qaeda**. Led by **Osama bin Laden**, al Qaeda was inspired by Islamism and also by the radical Wahhabism of the remote Arabian desert followed by the Saudis. Bin Laden had fought the Soviets with the US-supported Afghan *mujahideen* during the 1980s; despite that alliance, bin Laden and his followers were angered by US involvement in the Middle East throughout the 1990s and its support of Israel. While bin Laden was killed by the United States in 2011, and while control of Afghan security was turned over from the US to the US-backed government in 2014, the US still maintains a strong military presence in the country.

The Iraq War began in 2003 when the US invaded that country under the faulty premises that Saddam Hussein's regime was involved with al Qaeda, supported international terrorism, and possessed weapons of mass destruction that it intended to use in pursuit of terrorism. Iraq descended into chaos, with thousands of civilian and military casualties, Iraqi and American alike. While the country technically and legally remains intact under a US-supported government, the ethnically and

religiously diverse country is de facto divided as a result of the disintegration of central power.

Elsewhere in the Middle East, reform movements began via the 2011 **Arab Spring** in Tunisia, Egypt, Bahrain, and Syria. Some dictatorial regimes have been replaced with democratic governments; other countries still enjoy limited freedoms or even civil unrest. In Syria, unrest erupted into civil war between **Bashar al Assad**, who inherited leadership from his father, and opposition fighters. One consequence has been enormous movements of refugees into Europe.

Today, a new group known as the Islamic State of Iraq and al Sham (**ISIS**) referring to Iraq and Syria (or Islamic State of Iraq and the Levant—ISIL) has filled the vacuum in parts of northern and western Iraq and eastern Syria. ISIS has established a de facto state in Iraq and Syria with extremist Islamist policies and presents a global terror threat.

Uprisings in Israeli-occupied West Bank and Gaza have continued sporadically. Israel passed control of **Gaza** to the Palestinian Authority in 2005; however following political divisions within Palestinian factions, Gaza is controlled by Hamas while the Palestinian Authority represents Palestinian interests abroad and in the **West Bank**. In 1999, US President Clinton attempted to broker a final peace deal between the Israelis and Palestinians delineating borders as part of a two-state solution, but these efforts failed and conflict continues.

SAMPLE QUESTIONS

21) While immediately after the fall of the Soviet Union the US emerged as the sole superpower, in the twenty-first century, which phenomenon has so far characterized global governance?

    A. international terrorism
    B. international economic and political organizations
    C. international conflict
    D. the European Union

Answers:

A. Incorrect. While international terrorism has been a major feature of the past fifteen years, it is not a form of governance or political order.

B. Correct. While the United States remains a leading world power, the emergence of international organizations like the BRICS, the EU, the G-20, and the AU has empowered other countries; furthermore, international trade agreements are helping mold the international balance of power.

C. Incorrect. While international conflict has unfortunately been a major feature of the past fifteen years, there has been sufficient political global order to confidently state that the world has not fully descended into chaos.

D. Incorrect. The European Union is an important world power as an international organization, but is not the dominant global superpower.

22) **What was one reason for the Bosnian War?**
   A. attacks by Bosniak Islamic extremists
   B. the dissolution of Yugoslavia
   C. the separation of Yugoslavia from the USSR
   D. attacks by Middle Eastern Islamic extremists

   Answers:
   A. Incorrect. Bosniak Muslims were primarily the victims of genocide during the Bosnian War. Furthermore, while some mujahideen from the Soviet war in Afghanistan did go to the Balkans to fight, Islamic extremism is not traditionally a feature of Balkan Islam.
   B. **Correct.** One reason for the Bosnian War was the Yugoslav government's attempt to force the country to stay together; following the end of the Cold War and the collapse of communism, the formerly communist Yugoslavia had started to break up.
   C. Incorrect. Yugoslavia was never part of the USSR.
   D. Incorrect. No actors from the Middle East triggered the Bosnian War.

23) **What is one major role that the African Union plays?**
   A. The AU is a free trade area.
   B. The AU manages a single currency.
   C. The AU manages several peacekeeping forces.
   D. The AU represents individual African countries in international diplomacy.

   Answers:
   A. Incorrect. The AU is not a free trade zone; it is an organization of fifty-four African countries to convene and act in their common interests. While they may align trade policies, the entire continent is not a free trade zone.
   B. Incorrect. There is no single African currency.
   C. **Correct.** The AU organizes and manages peacekeeping forces in Africa; it also cooperates with the United Nations in peacekeeping.
   D. Incorrect. Individual African countries are sovereign and manage their own international relations.

Go on

24) Which of the following is NOT a reason that the Soviet Union collapsed?

- A. glasnost
- B. perestroika
- C. the war in Afghanistan
- D. the rise of the Taliban

Answers:

- A. Incorrect. Glasnost, or openness, was one of Gorbachev's policies of reform, allowing for more free speech in the USSR; this arguably helped weaken the regime.
- B. Incorrect. Perestroika, or transparency, was one of Gorbachev's policies of reform, providing a more transparent and democratic government under communism; this arguably helped weaken the regime.
- C. Incorrect. The Soviet war in Afghanistan was financially ruinous for the USSR and cost the country much in morale.
- D. **Correct.** The Taliban did not emerge in Afghanistan until well after Soviet withdrawal from the country.

25) Despite his alliance with the US-supported *mujahideen* in the war in Afghanistan against the Soviets, Osama bin Laden sponsored attacks against the United States because

- A. he opposed a US military presence in Saudi Arabia.
- B. he opposed US support of Israel.
- C. he wanted to establish a global Islamist regime in accordance with the extremist, unorthodox beliefs rooted in Wahhabism.
- D. all of the above

Answers:

- A. Incorrect. While this is true, it is incomplete as it is not the only correct answer choice.
- B. Incorrect. While bin Laden opposed the US-Israeli alliance, this answer is incomplete as it is not the only correct answer choice.
- C. Incorrect. While bin Laden did indeed want to establish such a regime, this answer is incomplete as it is not the only correct answer choice.
- D. **Correct.** Bin Laden cited all of these reasons for his violent acts.

United States History

NORTH AMERICA BEFORE EUROPEAN CONTACT

NORTHEASTERN SOCIETIES

Prior to European colonization, diverse Native American societies controlled the continent; they would later come into economic and diplomatic contact, and military conflict, with European colonizers and United States forces and settlers.

Major civilizations that would play an important and ongoing role in North American history included the **Iroquois** and **Algonquin** in the Northeast; the Iroquois in particular were known for innovative agricultural and architectural techniques, including the construction of longhouses and the farming of maize. The Iroquois farmed according to the *three sisters* tradition, farming maize, beans, and squash; these plants complement each other, providing natural protection from pests and the elements, and increasing availability of nitrogen necessary for growth. Both of those tribes would also be important allies of the English and French, respectively, in future conflicts, in that part of the continent.

The Iroquois actually consisted of five tribes. According to tradition, before European contact, five tribes—the **Mohawk**, **Seneca**, **Cayuga**, **Oneida**, and **Onondaga**—made peace thanks to the leadership of the peacemaker **Hiawatha**. Also known as the **Five Nations**, they organized into the regionally powerful **Iroquois Confederacy**, bringing stability to the eastern Great Lakes region including Upstate New York, Southern Ontario, and parts of Quebec and the Midwest. Later, the Tuscarora tribe would join, and the union became known as the **Six Nations**.

While many Native American, or First Nations, people speak variants of the Algonquin language, the **Algonquin** people themselves have historically been a majority in what is today Quebec and the Great Lakes region. Active in the fur trade, the Algonquin developed important relationships with French colonizers and a rivalry with the Iroquois. Many Algonquin in French-controlled North America converted to Christianity.

The Midwest

Later, the young United States would come into conflict with the Shawnee, Lenape, Kickapoo, Miami, and other tribes in the Midwestern region of Ohio, Illinois, Indiana, and Michigan in early western expansion. These tribes formed the Northwest Confederacy to fight the United States, developments discussed in more detail in later sections.

The **Shawnee** were an Algonquin-speaking people based in the Ohio Valley; however their presence extended as far east and south as the present-day Carolinas and Georgia. While socially organized under a matrilineal system, the Shawnee had male kings and only men could inherit property. The Lenape, also a matrilineal society, originally lived in what is today southern New Jersey and the Delaware Valley (but were later driven west by colonization). Also Algonquin-speaking, the **Lenape** were considered by the Shawnee to be their "grandfathers" and thus accorded respect. Another Algonquin-speaking tribe, the **Kickapoo** were originally from the Great Lakes region but would move throughout present-day Indiana and Wisconsin. The **Miami**, also Algonquin-speaking, moved from Wisconsin to the Ohio Valley region forming settled societies and farming maize. They also took part in the fur trade as it developed during European colonial times.

The Southeast

In the South, major tribes included the **Chickasaw** and **Choctaw**, the descendants of the **Mississippi Mound Builders** or Mississippian cultures, societies that built mounds from around 2,100 to 1,800 years ago as burial tombs or the bases for

Figure 2.1. Mississippi Mounds

temples. Both tribes were organized in clans along matrilineal lines, and both spoke languages of the Muskogean family. The Chickasaw were a settled tribe originally based in what is today northern Mississippi and Alabama and western Kentucky and Tennessee, and like the Iroquois, they farmed in the sustainable three sisters tradition. The Choctaw, whose origins trace to Mississippi, Louisiana, Alabama, and Florida, spoke a similar language to the Chickasaw. These two tribes would later form alliances with the British and French, fighting proxy wars on their behalf.

The **Creek**, or **Muscogee**, also descended from the Mississippian peoples, originated in modern Alabama, Georgia, South Carolina, and Florida. Speaking a language similar to those of the Chickasaw and Choctaw, the Creek would later participate in an alliance with these and other tribes—the Muscogee Confederacy—to engage the United States, which threatened tribal sovereignty.

Unlike the Chickasaw, Choctaw, and Creek, the **Cherokee** spoke (and speak) a language of the Iroquoian family. It is thought that they migrated south to their homeland in present-day Georgia sometime long before European contact, where they remained until they were forcibly removed in 1832. Organized into seven clans, the Cherokee were also hunters and farmers like other tribes in the region, and would later come into contact—and conflict—with European colonizers and the United States of America.

GREAT PLAINS, SOUTHWEST, PACIFIC NORTHWEST

Farther west, tribes of the Great Plains like the **Sioux**, **Cheyenne**, **Apache**, **Comanche**, and **Arapaho** would later come into conflict with American settlers as westward expansion continued. Traditionally nomadic or semi-nomadic, these tribes depended on the **buffalo** for food and materials to create clothing, tools, and domestic items; therefore they followed the herds. While widely known for their equestrian skill, horses were introduced by Europeans and so Native American tribes living on the Great Plains did not access them until after European contact. Horseback riding facilitated the hunt; previously, hunters surrounded buffalo or frightened them off of cliffs.

In the Southwest, the **Navajo** controlled territory in present-day Arizona, New Mexico, and Utah. The Navajo were descendants of the **Ancestral Pueblo** or **Anasazi**, who had settled in the Four Corners area, engaging in three sisters agriculture and stone construction, including cliff dwellings. The Navajo also practiced pastoralism, and lived in semi-permanent wooden homes called *hogans*, the doors of which face eastward to the rising sun. The Navajo had a less hierarchical structure than other Native American societies, and engaged in fewer raids than the Apache to the north.

Figure 2.2. Ancestral Pueblo Cliff Palace at Mesa Verde

In the Pacific Northwest, fishing was a major source of sustenance, and Native American peoples created and used canoes to engage in the practice. Totem poles depicted histories. The **Coast Salish**, whose language was widely spoken throughout the region, dominated the Puget Sound and Olympic Peninsula area. Farther south, the **Chinook** controlled the coast at the Columbia River.

Ultimately, through both violent conflict and political means, Native American civilizations lost control of most of their territories and were forced onto reservations by the United States. Negotiations continue today over rights to land and opportunities and reparations for past injustices.

SAMPLE QUESTIONS

1) Which of the following best describes the political landscape of the Northeast before European contact?

   A. Many small, autonomous tribes scattered throughout the region fought over land and resources.

   B. Several organized tribes controlled the region, including a major confederation.

   C. A disorganized political landscape would facilitate European colonial domination.

   D. The land was largely uninhabited, allowing easy exploitation of resources.

Answers:

A. Incorrect. While there were numerous tribes in the region besides the Iroquois and the Algonquin, and while the Iroquois themselves were made up of smaller tribes, regional political organization and alliances were strong before European contact.

B. Correct. Powerful tribes controlled trade and territory; among these were the powerful Iroquois Confederacy.

C. Incorrect. The political landscape was highly organized; European settlers would later have to form alliances and sign treaties with local regional powers.

D. Incorrect. Many people inhabited the land and had done so for centuries.

2) How do the movements of the tribes of the Northwest (throughout present-day Indiana, Illinois, Ohio, Michigan, and Wisconsin) illustrate tribal interactions before European contact and during colonial times?

   A. Having been pushed westward by the Iroquois, the Lenape are just one example of forced migration in early North American history.

   B. The migration of the Miami from Ontario to the Ohio Valley illustrates the diffusion of the Algonquin language throughout the continent.

   C. Despite the wide geographic range of the Shawnee, Kickapoo, Miami and Lenape, all these peoples spoke variants of the Algonquin language; this shows the importance of this language for many Native American tribes whether or not they were Algonquin people.

   D. Ongoing conflict between the Northwest Algonquin Confederacy, based in Ontario and the Upper Midwest, and the Iroquois Confederacy, based in the eastern Great Lakes region and present day Upstate New York, resulted in instability that forced tribes to move throughout the region.

Answers:

A. Incorrect. The Lenape were forced west by European colonization, not by conflict with the Iroquois.

B. Incorrect. While their experience was indeed illustrative of the wide range of the Algonquin language, the Miami moved from present-day Wisconsin, not Ontario.

C. Correct. While the Algonquin people were primarily located in what is today Quebec and southern Ontario, the Algonquin language was spoken widely throughout North America among both settled and semi-settled non-Algonquin peoples.

D. Incorrect. While many tribes did move throughout the region as a result of intertribal conflict, the Northwest Confederacy emerged later in response to the United States; furthermore, it was not rooted in a shared Algonquin experience.

3) **At the time of European contact, the Southeastern United States was mainly populated by**
    A. the Mississippi Mound Builders.
    B. settled tribes who spoke Muskogean and Iroquoian languages.
    C. nomadic tribes who spoke Muskogean and Iroquoian languages.
    D. the Ancestral Pueblo cliff dwellers.

    Answers:
    A. Incorrect. The Mississippi Mound Builders and their civilization had disappeared by European contact; the Chickasaw, Choctaw, Creek, and other tribes were their descendants.
    B. **Correct.** The Choctaw, Creek, Chickasaw, and others were Muskogean-speaking peoples; the Cherokee spoke an Iroquoian language. Both tribes were settled.
    C. Incorrect. While the tribes in the Southeast did speak languages from these families, they were not nomadic.
    D. Incorrect. The Ancestral Pueblo, or Anasazi, lived in the Southwest.

4) **Tribes living in the Great Plains region were dependent on which of the following for survival?**
    A. buffalo for nutrition and materials for daily necessities
    B. domesticated horses for hunting and warfare
    C. access to rivers to engage in the fur trade
    D. three sisters agriculture

    Answers:
    A. **Correct.** The Great Plains tribes depended on buffalo, which were plentiful before European contact and settlement, for food; they also used buffalo parts for clothing and to make necessary items.
    B. Incorrect. Horses were not introduced to North America until European contact.
    C. Incorrect. Great Plains tribes did not depend on the fur trade for survival before European contact or afterwards.
    D. Incorrect. While three sisters agriculture was widely practiced throughout North America, most major tribes living on the Great Plains were hunter-gatherers and depended primarily on buffalo for food.

5) How were the Navajo influenced by the Ancestral Pueblo, or Anasazi?

   A. The Navajo continued the practice of pastoralism, herding horses throughout the Southwest.
   B. The Navajo expanded control over land originally settled by the Ancestral Pueblo.
   C. The Navajo began building cliff dwellings, improving on the Anasazi practice of living in rounded homes built from wood.
   D. The Navajo developed a strictly hierarchical society, abandoning the looser organization of the Ancestral Pueblo.

Answers:

   A. Incorrect. Horses were introduced to North America by Europeans; neither the Navajo nor the Ancestral Pueblo had access to them before contact.
   B. **Correct.** The Ancestral Pueblo had settled in what is today the Four Corners region; the Navajo came to control land extending through present-day Arizona, New Mexico, and Utah.
   C. Incorrect. The Anasazi or Ancestral Pueblo themselves had built cliff dwellings.
   D. Incorrect. The Navajo did not have a strictly hierarchical society.

COLONIAL NORTH AMERICA

The Americas were quickly colonized by Europeans after Christopher Columbus first laid claim to them for the Spanish, and the British, French, and Spanish all held territories in North America throughout the sixteenth, seventeenth, eighteenth, and nineteenth centuries.

SPAIN IN THE WEST AND SOUTHWEST

Spanish **conquistadors** explored what is today the Southwestern United States, claiming land for Spain despite the presence of Southwestern tribes. Prominent *conquistadors* included **Hernando de Soto** and **Francisco Vasquez de Coronado**; Spanish colonization not only included the control and settlement of land but also the mission to spread Christianity. Indeed, **missions** were established in the West and Southwest for this purpose, throughout Mexico and parts of what is today Texas, New Mexico, Arizona, and California. The Spanish Crown granted **encomiendas**, land grants to individuals to establish settlements, allowing the holder to ranch or mine the land. *Encomiendas* allowed colonists to demand tribute and forced labor from local Native peoples, essentially enslaving them, to profit from the land. Spain's holdings ultimately extended through Mexico into Texas, the Southwest, and California, reaching as far north into what are today parts of Montana and Wyoming. Spain also controlled the Gulf Coast, including New Orleans and Florida.

Throughout this region, Spanish colonizers encountered resistance from Native Americans. In 1680, the **Pueblo Revolt**, led by the leader **Popé**, resulted in a two-year loss of land for Spain. Sometimes referred to as part of the ongoing **Navajo Wars**, this revolt included several Native American tribes. (In the literature and in some primary sources, *pueblo* is often used interchangeably with "Indian" to refer to Native Americans; here, the term refers to Navajo, Apache, and other tribes that came together to resist Spanish hegemony in the region.) Spain eventually reconquered the territory, subjugating the peoples living in the region to colonial rule.

The conflict led to friction among Spanish thinkers over the means, and even the notion, of colonization. The priest **Bartolomé de las Casas**, appalled at the oppression of colonization, argued for the rights and humanity of Native Americans. De las Casas lived in the Americas and had first-hand experience with the brutal consequences of colonization. On the other hand, **Juan de Sepulveda**, who never left Spain, argued that the Native Americans needed the rule and "civilization" brought by Spain, justifying their treatment at the hands of colonizers.

Despite ongoing conflict between Native Americans and Spanish colonizers, there was social mixing among the people. Intermarriage and fraternization resulted in a stratified society based on race, not only in North America but throughout Spanish and Portuguese holdings in the Americas. According to the *casta* system, an individual's place in societal hierarchy was determined by his or her race, with white people most privileged. The term *mestizo* referred to people of mixed white European and Native American, who were more privileged than the Native American peoples.

The Spanish also introduced African people to the Americas, and North America was no exception. Forced labor and diseases like **smallpox** had decimated Native American populations in Mexico and the Southwest. Consequently, in order to exploit these resource-rich lands, Spanish colonizers took part in the European-driven **trans-Atlantic slave trade**, kidnapping African people or purchasing them on the West African coast, bringing them to the Americas and forcing them into slavery in mines and plantations in the Western Hemisphere.

French Hegemony in the Midwest and Northeast

Unlike Spain, which sought not only profit but also to settle the land and convert Native Americans to Christianity, France was mainly focused on trade. French explorers like **Samuel de Champlain** reached what is today Quebec, Vermont, upstate New York, and the eastern Great Lakes region as early as the seventeenth century. While the explorer **Jacques Cartier** had claimed New France (present-day Quebec) for France in the sixteenth century, Champlain founded Quebec City and consolidated control of France's colonies in North America in 1608.

France prioritized trade; the **fur** and beaver pelts from game plentiful in the Northeast were in great demand in Europe. French colonists were also more likely to establish agreements and intermarry with local Native Americans than

other European powers; they did not establish settlements based on forced labor or arrive with families. The term *métis* described mixed-race persons; eventually France would control much of the Great Lakes and the Mississippi region through Louisiana and New Orleans, valuable trade routes.

ENGLAND AND THE THIRTEEN COLONIES

While the Spanish and French arrived generally as single men for trade, who would intermarry with local inhabitants, the English brought their families and settled in North America, with the goal of establishing agricultural settlements. In the sixteenth century, Sir Walter Raleigh established the Roanoke colony in present-day Virginia; while this settlement disappeared by 1590, interest in colonization reemerged as **joint-stock companies** sought royal charters to privately develop colonies on the North American Atlantic coast. The first established colony, **Jamestown**, was also located in Virginia, which became so profitable that the Crown took it over as a colony in 1624.

The colonial leader **John Rolfe** introduced **tobacco** to Virginia farmers, which became the primary cash crop. Requiring plantation farming, Virginia required **indentured servants**, who were freed from servitude after a period of work. Some of these indentured servants were from Africa. However in 1660, the **House of Burgesses**, which governed Virginia, declared that all blacks would be lifelong slaves. The South became increasingly socially stratified, with enslaved persons, indentured servants, landowners, and other classes. The Carolinas and Georgia would also become important sources of tobacco and rice; South Carolina institutionalized slavery in North America for the next two centuries by adopting the slave codes from Barbados.

While Jamestown and Virginia were populated by diverse populations of settlers, businessmen, indentured servants, and slaves, the demographics were different farther north. In New England, **Separatists**, members of the Church of England who believed it had strayed too far from its theological roots, had come to North America seeking more religious freedom. The first group of Separatists, the Pilgrims, arrived on the *Mayflower* in 1620 and had drawn up the **Mayflower Compact**, guaranteeing government by the consent of the governed. They were later joined by the **Puritans**, who had been persecuted in England by King Charles I, whom many suspected of weakening the Church of England and even of plotting to restore Catholicism. The colonial Puritan leader **John Winthrop** envisioned the Massachusetts Bay Colony in the model of the

> **DID YOU KNOW?**
>
> Slavery was not as widespread in the northern colonies as it was in the south, as the land and climate in the north did not support plantation agriculture; this led to far less demand for slaves than in the south, where unskilled labor was needed to harvest tobacco and later, cotton.

Biblical *City upon a Hill*, rooted in unity, peace, and what would be a free, democratic spirit; its capital was Boston. These philosophies would later inform the American Revolution.

Despite differences from the South, social stratification existed in New England as well: according to Puritan belief, wealth and success showed that one was a member of the **elect**, or privileged by God. Poorer farmers were generally tenant farmers; they did not own land and rarely made a profit.

The concepts of religious tolerance were not isolated to New England. The mid-Atlantic region was well-suited for agricultural crops and trade, with fertile lands and natural harbors. The settlement of New Amsterdam, an ideal port and trading post, came under English control in 1664 and was renamed New York; in 1682, the Quaker **William Penn** founded the city of Philadelphia, based on tolerance. Penn had been given the land later called Pennsylvania by the Crown to settle a debt; Pennsylvania, New Jersey, and Delaware were founded in the Quaker spirit as part of Penn's **Holy Experiment** to develop settlements based on tolerance.

> **DID YOU KNOW?**
>
> Quakerism promotes equality, community, non-violence, conflict resolution, and tolerance. These tenets are at the root of the name of Philadelphia, the "City of Brotherly Love."

Earlier in the region, in 1649 the **Maryland Toleration Act** had ensured the political rights of all Christians there, the first law of its kind in the colonies. This was due, in part, to the influence of **Lord Baltimore**, who had been charged by Charles I to found a part of Virginia (to be called Maryland) as a Catholic haven—helping him maintain power in an England divided between Catholics and Protestants.

The North American colonial economy was part of the **Atlantic World**, taking part in the **triangular trade** (pictured on the following page) between the Americas, Africa and Europe, where slaves were exchanged in the Americas for raw materials shipped to Europe to be processed into goods for the benefit of the colonial powers, and sometimes exchanged for slaves in Africa. In this way, North America was part of the **Columbian Exchange**, the intersection of goods and people throughout the Atlantic World.

Exploitation of colonial resources and the dynamics of the Columbian Exchange supported **mercantilism**, the prevailing economic system: European powers controlled their economies in order to increase global power. Ensuring a beneficial **balance of trade** is essential; the country must export more than it imports. An unlimited supply of desirable goods obtainable at a low cost made this possible, and the colonies offered just that. In this way, European powers would be able to maintain their reserves of gold and silver rather than spending them on imports. Furthermore, those countries that obtained access to more gold and silver—notably, Spain, which gained control of mines in Central America and Mexico—

exponentially increased their wealth, dramatically changing the balance of economic power in Europe. Long-term consequences included the decline of feudalism and the rise of capitalism.

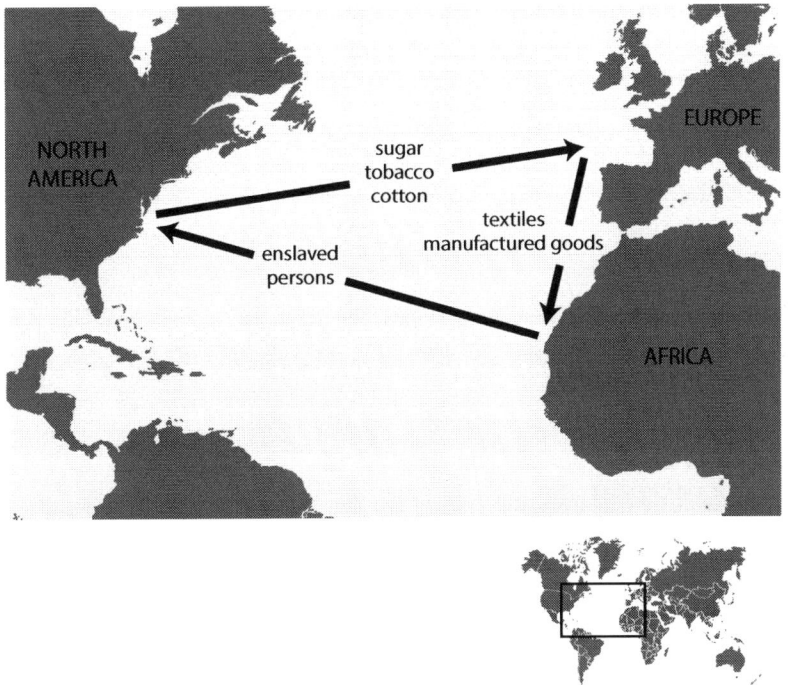

Figure 2.3. Triangular Trade

Colonial Conflict

Throughout the chaos in England during the **English Civil War**, policy toward the Colonies had been one of **salutary neglect**, allowing them great autonomy. However, stability in England and an emerging culture of independence in the Thirteen Colonies caught the attention of the British Crown; to ensure that the British mercantilist system was not threatened, it passed the **Navigation Acts** in 1651 to prevent colonial trade with any other countries. An early sign of colonial discontent, **Bacon's Rebellion** in 1676 against Governor Berkeley of Virginia embodied the growing resentment of landowners, who wanted to increase their own profit rather than redirect revenue to Britain. Following the 1688 Glorious Revolution in England, many colonists thought they might gain more autonomy; however, the new leadership under William and Mary continued to limit self-rule.

American colonists were also increasingly influenced by Enlightenment thought. John Locke's *Second Treatise* was published in 1689; critical of absolute monarchy, it became popular in the Colonies. Locke's concepts of government by consent of the governed and the natural rights of persons became the bedrock of the United States government. Locke argued for **republicanism:** that the people must come together to create a government for the protection of themselves and their property, thereby giving up some of their natural rights. However, should

the government overstep its bounds, the people have the right to overthrow it and replace it.

In the mid-eighteenth century, a sense of religious fervor called the **Great Awakening** spread throughout the Colonies; people became devoted to God beyond the confines of traditional Christianity, attracted to traveling preachers and convinced that they must confess sins publicly to avoid going to hell. Many universities, including some Ivy League schools, were founded during this time to train ministers; the Great Awakening helped develop a more singularly North American religious culture. It also created a divide between traditional European Christianity and emerging North American faiths.

Meanwhile, North America served also as a battleground for France and England, already in conflict in Europe and elsewhere. In the mid-seventeenth century, the Algonquin and Iroquois, allied with the French and Dutch, and English, respectively, fought the **Beaver Wars** for control over the fur trade in the northeastern part of the continent. The Iroquois would ultimately push the Shawnee and other tribes associated with the Algonquin from the Northeast and Great Lakes area farther west to present-day Wisconsin. Given the British alliance with the Iroquois, England would also refer to the Beaver Wars and Iroquois control over the Northeast (today, the Ohio Valley and Great Lakes region) to assert their own claim over this area, which was called the **Northwest Territories**.

France had come to control the vast **Louisiana Territory**, from the Ohio Valley area through the Mississippi Valley, the area down the Mississippi River to its capital of New Orleans, and as far as the reaches of the Missouri River and the Arkansas/Red River stretching west. Not only did France clash with Britain in the northern part of the continent, but the two colonial powers came into conflict in the South as well. In 1736, French forces, allied with the Choctaw, attacked the English-allied Chickasaw as part of France's attempts to strengthen its hold on the southeastern part of North America in the **Chickasaw Wars**.

Following another period of salutary neglect in the Colonies, in 1754, French and English conflict exploded once again in North America as fighting broke out in the Ohio Valley. The British government organized with North American colonial leaders to meet at Albany; **Benjamin Franklin** helped organize the defensive Albany Plan of Union and argued for this plan in his newspaper, the *Pennsylvania Gazette*, using the famous illustration *Join, or Die*. However, the Crown worried that this plan allowed for too much colonial independence, adding to tensions between the Thirteen Colonies and England.

The Seven Years' War broke out in Europe in 1756; this conflict between the British and French in North America was known as the **French and Indian War**. War efforts in North America accelerated under the British leader (essentially, Prime Minister) **William Pitt the Elder**, who invested heavily in defeating the French beyond Europe (see Chapter One, "World History," for details). Ultimately, Britain

Figure 2.4. *Join, or Die.*

emerged as the dominant power on the continent. France had allied with the Algonquin, traditional rivals of the British-allied Iroquois. However, following defeats by strong colonial military leaders like **George Washington** and despite its strong alliances and long-term presence on the continent, France eventually surrendered. Britain gained control of French territories in North America—as well as Spanish Florida—in the 1763 **Treaty of Paris** which ended the Seven Years' War.

SAMPLE QUESTIONS

6) **How did Spanish and French colonization in North America differ?**

   A. Both intermarried with Native Americans; however the Spanish took a more aggressive approach in spreading Christianity.

   B. Spain sought accord and agreement with Native Americans, while France forced marriages as part of settling the land, resulting in the mixed-race *métis* class.

   C. France colonized the Southwest; Spain colonized the Northeast and Midwest.

   D. France imported enslaved Africans as part of the Triangular Trade in order to support New France, while Spain mainly exploited local Native American tribes, forcing them to perform labor and essentially enslaving them.

Go on

Answers:

A. **Correct.** Spain established missions to spread Christianity, in addition to settling and exploiting the land; France worked to establish networks of trade and did not concentrate on religious conversion (although the Church was present and at work in its colonies). Both intermarried locally.

B. Incorrect. Spanish encounters with tribes in the West and Southwest were frequently violent; *métis* were not the result of a campaign of forced marriages.

C. Incorrect. France came to control Northeastern Canada (New France, what is today Quebec and other regions) and parts of the Midwest south through Louisiana. Spain did control some territory through the Gulf Coast, but primarily settled the Southwest.

D. Incorrect. Spain brought African slaves to the Americas and, in North America, forced them to work in mines. Given the nature of the fur trade, which supported New France in the northern part of the continent, there was no real role for slaves; however, slavery was practiced in colonies in the southern parts of North America where plantation farming was profitable. France also practiced slavery widely in other colonies such as Haiti and throughout the Caribbean.

7) On the Atlantic coast of North America, which of the following contributed to demographic differences between North and South?

   A. a climate that supported plantation agriculture in the southern colonies, which resulted in high demand for African slaves

   B. geography favorable to ports in the Northeast, resulting in diverse and tolerant centers of commerce and trade in Boston, New York, and Philadelphia

   C. a climate that supported small-scale agriculture and family farms in the northern colonies, which resulted in a very low demand for African slaves

   D. all of the above

Answers:

A. Incorrect. While it is true that the climate in the former colonies of Georgia, the Carolinas, and Virginia supported plantation agriculture, requiring large numbers of unskilled laborers to grow and harvest crops like tobacco and rice, this choice does not sufficiently answer the question.

B. Incorrect. Indeed, geography in the Northeast lent itself to the establishment of ports and commercial centers in these areas, but this answer choice does not sufficiently respond to the question.

C. Incorrect. It is true that the climate in the Northeast supported crops grown on small family farms rather than those grown on plantations; thus, there was very little demand for African slaves in that area and a preponderance of tenant farmers instead. However, this choice does not completely answer the question.

D. **Correct.** All of the above answer choices are true.

8) **Upon what premise were Mid-Atlantic colonies like Pennsylvania, Delaware, and New Jersey founded?**

   A. A beacon of unity and humanity, reminiscent of John Winthrop's *City Upon a Hill*.

   B. Tolerance, as part of William Penn's *Great Experiment*.

   C. Profit, in accordance with their roots in joint-stock companies seeking profit from the land through royal charters.

   D. Conquest and conversion, in order to take land from Native American tribes and convert those original inhabitants to Christianity.

   Answers:

   A. Incorrect. Winthrop was a leader in Massachusetts and his philosophies applied to development in that region.

   B. **Correct.** William Penn founded these colonies in the spirit of his tolerant Quaker faith.

   C. Incorrect. Joint-stock companies sought profit in Virginia; profit was not Penn's primary motive in founding Pennsylvania, Delaware, and New Jersey.

   D. Incorrect. While conquest was certainly an element of colonization, this was not Penn's primary motive, nor was Christian conversion. Furthermore, spreading Christianity was not a priority of the English as it was for the Spanish.

9) **How did the British and French rivalry spill over into North America?**

   A. While Britain and France were often on opposite sides in European conflict, they found common ground against Native Americans in North America.

   B. European conflicts between Catholics and Protestants affected Catholic French and Protestant English settlers; related violence from the Hundred Years' War broke out between them as a result.

   C. These European powers engaged in proxy wars, supporting the Iroquois and Algonquin, respectively, as well as the Chickasaw and Choctaw, in jockeying for control of land in the Great Lakes and southeastern regions of North America.

   D. France and Britain formed an alliance to prevent Spain from moving eastward on the continent.

Answers:

A. Incorrect. These colonial powers formed alliances with different North American tribes as part of ongoing rivalries on and off the continent in maneuvering for power and control of land.

B. Incorrect. The British colonies were not a religious battleground; furthermore, the Hundred Years' War had ended in Europe before the explorations of Columbus and the beginnings of settlement in the Western Hemisphere.

C. **Correct.** The Beaver Wars, the Chickasaw Wars, and later the French and Indian War, which was part of the Seven Years' War, are all examples of British-French conflict playing out in North America.

D. Incorrect. France and Britain never had a long-term alliance on North America.

10) Which of the following were factors in stirring up colonial discontent?

A. Locke's *Second Treatise*
B. trade restrictions like the Navigation Acts
C. the Great Awakening
D. all of the above

Answers:

A. Incorrect. While Locke's *Second Treatise* criticized absolute monarchy and so became very popular in the Thirteen Colonies, where colonists sought more autonomy, it was only one of many factors; given the other answer choices, this choice is incomplete.

B. Incorrect. Restrictive measures like the Navigation Acts did limit colonial trade to Britain only, to the chagrin of colonial merchants who desired to broaden their commercial enterprises. Still, this choice does not completely answer this question.

C. Incorrect. The Great Awakening was a religious revival that contributed to ongoing cultural differences between the Colonies and Europe in that it deepened divisions between Christian practices in Europe and newer religious thought in North America. However, this choice does not sufficiently answer the question, given the other options.

D. **Correct.** All of the above are true.

Revolution and the Early United States

The American Revolution

Despite British victory in the French and Indian War, Britain had gone greatly into debt. Furthermore, there were concerns that the Colonies required a stronger military presence following **Pontiac's Rebellion** in 1763. The leader of the **Ottawa**

people, Pontiac, led a revolt that extended from the Great Lakes region through the Ohio Valley to Virginia. As this land had been ceded to England from France (lacking any consultation with the native inhabitants) the Ottawa people and other Native Americans resisted further British settlement and fought back against colonial oppression. **King George III** signed the **Proclamation of 1763**, an agreement not to settle land west of the Appalachians, in an effort to make peace; however much settlement continued in practice.

As a result of the war and subsequent unrest, Britain once again discarded its colonial policy of salutary neglect; furthermore, in desperate need of cash, the Crown sought ways to increase its revenue from the Colonies.

King George III enforced heavy taxes and restrictive acts in the colonies to generate income for the Crown and punish disobedience. England expanded the **Molasses Act** of 1733, passing the **Sugar Act** in 1764 to raise revenue by taxing sugar and molasses. Sugar was produced in the British West Indies and widely consumed in the Thirteen Colonies. In 1765, Britain enforced the **Quartering Act**, requiring colonists to provide shelter to British troops stationed in the region.

The 1765 **Stamp Act**, the first direct tax on the colonists, triggered more tensions. Any document required a costly stamp, the revenue reverting to the British government. **Patrick Henry** protested the Stamp Act in the Virginia House of Burgesses; the tax was seen as a violation of colonists' rights, given that they did not have direct representation in British Parliament. In Britain, it was argued that the colonists had **virtual representation** and so the Act—and others to follow—were justified.

As a result, colonists began boycotting British goods and engaging in violent protest. **Samuel Adams** led the **Sons and Daughters of Liberty** in violent acts against tax collectors. In response, the Chancellor of the Exchequer Charles Townshend enforced the punitive **Townshend Acts** which imposed more taxes and restrictions on the colonies; customs officers were empowered to search colonists' homes for forbidden goods with **writs of assistance**. **John Dickinson's** *Letters from a Farmer in Pennsylvania* and Samuel Adams' **Massachusetts Circular Letter** argued for the repeal of the Townshend Acts (which were, indeed, repealed in 1770) and demanded *no taxation without representation*. Samuel Adams continued to stir up rebellion with his **Committees of Correspondence**, which distributed anti-British propaganda.

Protests against the Quartering Act in Boston led to the **Boston Massacre** in 1770, when British troops fired on a crowd of protesters. By 1773, in a climate of continued unrest driven by the Committees of Correspondence, colonists protested the latest taxes on tea levied by the **Tea Act** in the famous **Boston Tea Party** by dressing as Native Americans and tossing tea off a ship in Boston Harbor. In response, the government passed the **Intolerable Acts**, closing Boston Harbor and bringing Massachusetts back under direct royal control.

In response to the Intolerable Acts, colonial leaders met in Philadelphia at the **First Continental Congress** in 1774 and issued the *Declaration of Rights and Grievances*, presenting colonial concerns to the King, who ignored it. However, violent conflict began in 1775 at **Lexington and Concord**, when American militiamen (**minutemen**) had gathered to resist British efforts to seize weapons and arrest rebels in Concord. On June 17, 1775, the Americans fought the British at the **Battle of Bunker Hill**; despite American losses, the number of casualties the rebels inflicted caused the king to declare that the colonies were in rebellion. Troops were deployed to the colonies; the Siege of Boston began.

> **DID YOU KNOW?**
>
> King George III also hired Hessian mercenaries from Germany to supplement British troops; adding foreign fighters only increased resentment in the colonies and created a stronger sense of independence from Britain.

In May 1775, the **Second Continental Congress** met at Philadelphia to debate the way forward. Debate between the wisdom of continued efforts at compromise and negotiations and declaring independence continued. The king ignored the Congress' *Declaration of the Causes and Necessities of Taking Up Arms*, which asked him to consider again the colonies' objections; he also ignored the **Olive Branch Petition** which sought compromise and an end to hostilities. **Thomas Paine** published his pamphlet *Common Sense*; taking Locke's concepts of natural rights and the obligation of a people to rebel against an oppressive government, it popularized the notion of rebellion against Britain.

By summer of 1776, the Continental Congress agreed on the need to break from Britain; on July 4, 1776, it declared the independence of the United States of America and issued the **Declaration of Independence**, drafted mainly by **Thomas Jefferson** and heavily influenced by Locke.

Americans were still divided over independence; **Patriots** favored independence while those still loyal to Britain were known as **Tories**. **George Washington** had been appointed head of the Continental Army and led a largely unpaid and unprofessional army; despite early losses, Washington gained ground due to strong leadership, superior knowledge of the land, and support from France (and to a lesser extent, Spain and the Netherlands). The tide turned in 1777 at **Valley Forge**, when Washington and his army lived through the bitterly cold winter and managed to overcome British military forces. The British people did not favor the war and voted the Tories out of Parliament; the incoming Whig party sought to end the war. In the 1783 **Treaty of Paris**, the United States was recognized as a country, agreeing to repay debts to British merchants and provide safety to those British loyalists who wished to remain in North America. The American Revolution would go on to inspire revolution around the world.

FEDERALISTS AND DEMOCRATIC-REPUBLICANS

Joy in the victory over Great Britain was short-lived. Fearful of tyranny, the Second Continental Congress had provided for only a weak central government, adopting the **Articles of Confederation** to organize the Thirteen Colonies—now states—as a loosely united country. A unicameral central government had the power to wage war, negotiate treaties, and borrow money. It could not tax citizens, but could tax states. It also set parameters for westward expansion and establishing new states: the **Northwest Ordinances** of 1787 forbade slavery north of the Ohio River. Areas with 60,000 people could apply for statehood. However, it soon became clear that the Articles of Confederation were not strong enough to keep the nation united.

> **DID YOU KNOW?**
>
> The Northwest Ordinances also effectively nullified King George III's Proclamation of 1763, which promised Native Americans that white settlement would not continue in the Ohio Valley region. The United States did not recognize the Proclamation, and tensions would build.

The new country was heavily in debt. Currency was weak, and taxes were high: Daniel Shays led **Shays' Rebellion**, a revolt of indebted farmers who rose up to prevent courts from seizing property in Massachusetts and to protest debtor's prisons. Furthermore, debt and disorganization made the country appear weak and vulnerable to Great Britain and Spain. If the United States was to remain one country, it needed a stronger federal government.

Alexander Hamilton and **James Madison** called for a **Constitutional Convention** to write a Constitution as the foundation of a stronger federal government. Madison and other **Federalists** like **John Adams** believed in **separation of powers**, republicanism, and a strong federal government.

To determine the exact structure of the government, delegates at the convention settled on what became known as the **Great Compromise**, a **bicameral legislature**. Two plans had been presented: the **New Jersey Plan**, which proposed a legislature composed of an equal number of representatives from each state (which would benefit smaller states), and the **Virginia Plan**, which proposed a legislature composed of representatives proportional to the population of each state. States with large African American slave populations accounted for those persons with the **Three-Fifths Compromise**, which counted a slave as three-fifths of a person; while represented in a state's population to determine that state's number of representatives in Congress, enslaved persons had no place in the political process. The states adopted both plans, creating the **House of Representatives** and the **Senate**, to most fairly represent the large and small states at the federal level.

Despite the separation of powers provided for in the Constitution, **Anti-Federalists** like **Thomas Jefferson** called for even more limitations on the power of the federal government. The first ten amendments to the Constitution, or the **Bill of Rights**, a list of guarantees of American freedoms, was a concession to the

anti-Federalists, who would later become the **Democratic-Republican Party** (eventually, the Democratic Party).

> **DID YOU KNOW?**
>
> Federalists were generally from the North and were usually merchants or businessmen; Anti-Federalists were usually from the South or the rural west, and farmed the land.

In order to convince the states to ratify the Constitution, Hamilton, Madison, and John Jay wrote the *Federalist Papers*, articulating the benefits of federalism. Likewise, the Bill of Rights helped convince the hesitant. In 1791, the Constitution was ratified. **George Washington** was elected president, with John Adams serving as vice president; Washington appointed Hamilton as Secretary of the Treasury and Jefferson as Secretary of State.

Hamilton prioritized currency stabilization and repayment of debts; he also believed in establishing a national bank—the **Bank of the United States (BUS)**, which Washington signed into law in 1791. He also favored tariffs and excise (sales) taxes, which Anti-Federalists—who became known as **Democratic-Republicans**—vehemently opposed. in 1795, rebellion against the excise tax on whiskey broke out; the **Whiskey Rebellion** indicated unrest in the young country and was put down by militia.

Meanwhile, the French Revolution had begun in Europe. However, President Washington issued the **Neutrality Proclamation** in 1793. Despite this action, British and French ships accosted American ships in the Atlantic and forced American sailors into naval service (**impressments**). John Jay attempted to reinstate neutrality; **Jay's Treaty** was unsuccessful and unpopular, only negotiating the removal of British forts in the western frontier. Furthermore, it concerned Spain, which feared changes in the balance of power on the continent. President Washington had Thomas Pickney negotiate a new treaty with Spain; providing for US rights on the Mississippi River and in the Port of New Orleans, **Pickney's Treaty** was a diplomatic success, ratified by all thirteen states. The ongoing **Northwest Indian Wars** continued conflict with the Shawnee, Lenape, Kickapoo, Miami, and other tribes in the Ohio region; the Americans gained more territory in Ohio and Indiana following the defeat of allied tribes at the **Battle of Fallen Timbers** in 1794.

In President Washington's **Farewell Address**, he recommended the United States follow a policy of neutrality in international affairs, setting a precedent for early American history. Vice President John Adams, a Federalist, became the second president. France continued to seize American ships, so Adams sent representatives to negotiate; however, in what became known as the **XYZ Affair**, the Americans were asked for bribes in order to even meet with French officials. The insulted Americans began an undeclared conflict in the Caribbean until the **Convention of 1800** negotiated a cessation of hostilities.

During the Adams administration, the Federalists passed the harsh **Alien and Sedition Acts**. The Alien Act allowed the president to deport "enemy aliens"; it also increased the residency requirements for citizenship. The Sedition Act forbade criticism of the president or of Congress. Divisions between the Federalists and the Democratic-Republicans were deeper than ever and the presidential elections of 1800 were tense and controversial; nevertheless, Thomas Jefferson was elected to the presidency in 1801 in a non-violent transfer of power.

Jefferson shrank the federal government. The Alien and Sedition Acts were repealed. Economic policies favored small farmers and landowners, in contrast to Federalist policies, which supported big business and cities. However, Jefferson also oversaw the **Louisiana Purchase**, which nearly doubled the size of the United States. This troubled some Democratic-Republicans, who saw this as federal overreach, but the Louisiana Purchase would be a major step forward in westward expansion. **Meriwether Lewis** and **William Clark** were dispatched to explore the western frontier of the territory: Jefferson hoped to find an all-water route to the Pacific Ocean (via the Missouri River). While this route did not exist, Lewis and Clark returned with a deeper knowledge of the territory the US had come to control.

Figure 2.5. Louisiana Purchase

Jefferson was also forced to manage chaotic international affairs. Britain and France, at war with each other in the **Napoleonic Wars**, were attempting to blockade each other's international trade, threatening US ships, as the United States did business with both countries. In an attempt to avoid the conflict, Congress passed the **Embargo Act** under the Jefferson administration in 1807, which limited US international trade; however the Embargo Act only damaged the US economy further. In addition, the United States was fighting North African pirates in the Mediterranean, who were seizing US ships. At the end of Jefferson's presidency,

Congress passed the **Non-Intercourse Act**, which allowed trade with foreign countries besides Britain and France; under President **James Madison**, tensions would remain high.

MONROE DOCTRINE AND MANIFEST DESTINY

British provocation at sea and in the northwest led to the **War of 1812**. Growing nationalism in the United States pressured Madison into pushing for war after the **Battle of Tippecanoe** in Indiana, when **General William Henry Harrison** fought the **Northwest Confederacy**, a group of tribes led by the Shawnee leader **Tecumseh**. The Shawnee, Lenape, Miami, Kickapoo, and others had come together not only out of common interest—to maintain independent territory at the northwest of the United States (present-day Indiana and region) but also because they followed Tecumseh's brother **Tenskwatawa**, who was considered a prophet. Despite the Confederacy's alliance with Britain, the United States prevailed. Congress declared war under Madison with the intent to defend the United States, end chaotic trade practices and treatment of Americans on the high seas, and penetrate British Canada.

The war resulted in no real gains or losses for either the Americans or the British; however **Andrew Jackson** became a popular war hero following the Battle of New Orleans (fought two weeks after the **Treaty of Ghent** was signed, ending the war in 1814). Yet at the war's end, the United States had successfully defended itself as a country and reaffirmed its independence. Patriotism ran high.

The **Era of Good Feelings** began with the presidency of **James Monroe** as a strong sense of public identity and nationalism pervaded in the country. During this period, religious revival became popular and people turned from Puritanism and predestination to Baptist and Methodist faiths, among others, following revolutionary preachers and movements. This period was called the **Second Great Awakening**. In art and culture, romanticism and reform movements elevated the "common man," a trend that would continue into the presidency of Andrew Jackson.

However, not all was well. Federalists had strongly opposed the war. They had also opposed economic policies taken under Jefferson and Madison. At the **Hartford Convention**, Federalists developed an anti-Republican platform; however by the time they completed their discussions and were ready to head to Washington, the War of 1812 had already ended. The Federalists essentially collapsed afterwards.

From a financial perspective, the country would again struggle. Disagreement over the **Tariff of 1816** divided industrialists, who believed in nurturing American industry, from Southern landowners, who depended on exporting cotton and tobacco for profit. Later, following the establishment of the **Second Bank of the United States**, the **Panic of 1819** erupted when the government cut credit following overspeculation on western lands; the BUS wanted payment from state banks in hard currency, or **specie**. Western banks foreclosed on western farmers, and farmers lost their land.

With the Louisiana Purchase, the country had almost doubled in size. In the nineteenth century, the idea of **manifest destiny**, or the sense that it was the fate of the United States to expand westward and settle the continent, pervailed. Also in 1819, the United States purchased Florida from Spain in the **Adams-Onis Treaty**. The **Monroe Doctrine**, James Monroe's policy that the Western Hemisphere was "closed" to any further European colonization or exploration, asserted US hegemony in the region.

Westward expansion triggered questions about the expansion of slavery, a divisive issue. Slavery was profitable for the southern states which depended on the plantation economy, but increasingly condemned in the North. Furthermore, the Second Great Awakening had fueled the **abolitionist** movement. In debating the nature of westward expansion, the Kentucky senator **Henry Clay** worked out a compromise. The **Missouri Compromise**, also known as the **Compromise of 1820**, allowed Missouri to join the union as a slave state, but provided that any other states north of the **thirty-sixth parallel (36°30')** would be free. Maine would also join the nation as a free state. However, more tension and compromises over the nature of slavery in the West were to come.

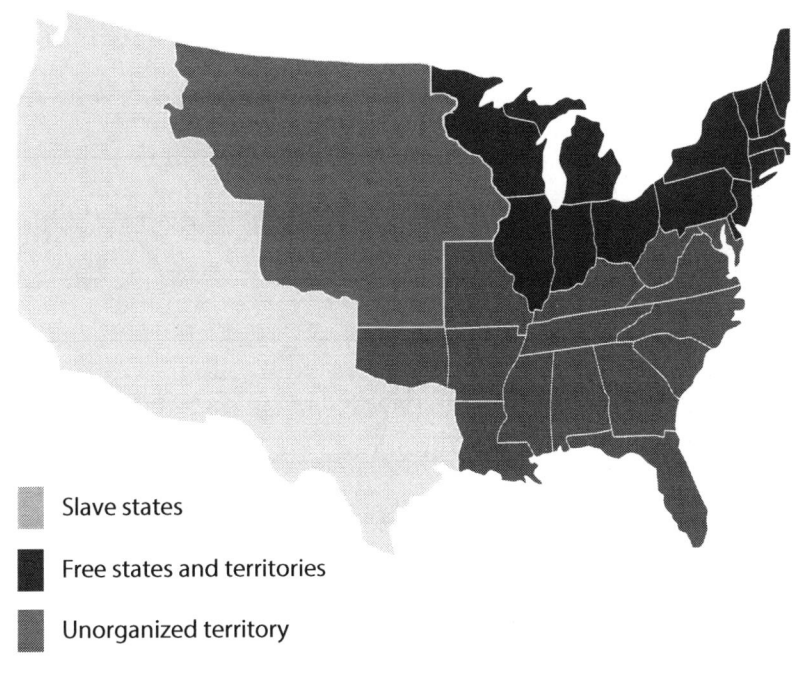

Figure 2.6. Missouri Compromise

Jacksonian Democracy

Demographics were changing throughout the early nineteenth century. Technological advances such as the **cotton gin** had allowed exponential increases in cotton; therefore, more persons were enslaved than ever before, bringing more urgency to the issue of slavery. In addition, **immigration** from Europe to the United States was increasing—mainly Irish Catholics and Germans. Reactionary **nativist** movements like the **Know-Nothing Party** feared the influx of non-Anglo Europeans, particularly Catholics, and discrimination was widespread, especially against the Irish. Other technological advances like the **railroads** and **steamships** were speeding up westward expansion and improving trade throughout the continent; a large-scale **market economy** was emerging. With early industrialization and changing concepts following the Second Great Awakening, women were playing a larger role in society, even though they could not vote.

Most states had extended voting rights to white men who did not own land or substantial property: **universal manhood suffrage**. Elected officials would increasingly come to better reflect the electorate, and the brash war hero Jackson was popular among the "common man."

During the election of 1824, Andrew Jackson ran against **John Quincy Adams**, Henry Clay, and William Crawford, all Republicans (from the Democratic-Republican party); John Quincy Adams won. By 1828, divisions within the party had Jackson and his supporters known as Democrats, in favor of small farmers and inhabitants of rural areas, and states' rights. Clay and his supporters became known as **National Republicans** and, later, **Whigs**, a splinter group of the Democratic-Republicans which supported business and urbanization; they also had federalist leanings. Thus the **two-party system** emerged.

Jackson's popularity with the "common man," white, male farmers and workers who felt he identified with them, and the fact that owning property was no longer a requirement to vote, gave him the advantage and a two-term presidency. Jackson rewarded his supporters, appointing them to important positions as part of the **spoils system**.

Opposed to the Bank of the United States, he issued the **Specie Circular**, devaluing paper money and instigating the financial **Panic of 1837**. Despite his opposition to such deep federal economic control, Jackson was forced to contend with controversial tariffs. The **Tariff of 1828**, or **Tariff of Abominations**, benefitted Northern industry, but heavily affected Southern exports; Senator **John C. Calhoun** of South Carolina spoke out in favor of **nullification**, wherein he argued that a state had the right to declare a law null and void if it was harmful to that state.

Tensions increased with the **Tariff of 1832**; Calhoun and South Carolina threatened to secede if their economic interests were not protected. Jackson managed the **Nullification Crisis** without resorting to violence; paradoxically, he protected the federal government at the expense of states' rights, working out a compromise in 1833 that was more favorable to the South.

Socially and politically, white men of varying levels of economic success and education were able to have stronger political voices and more opportunities in civil society. However, women, African Americans, and Native Americans were oppressed. With continental expansion came conflict with Native Americans. Despite efforts by the Cherokee, who unsuccessfully argued for the right to their land in the Supreme Court in **Cherokee Nation v. Georgia** (1831), President Andrew Jackson enforced the 1830 **Indian Removal Act**, forcing Cherokee, Creek, Chickasaw, Choctaw, and others from their lands in the Southeast. Thousands of people were forced to travel mainly on foot, with all of their belongings, to Indian Territory (today, Oklahoma) on the infamous **Trail of Tears**, to make way for white settlers. Violent conflicts would continue on the Frontier farther west between the US and the Apache, Comanche, Sioux, Arapaho, Cheyenne, and other tribes throughout the nineteenth century.

SAMPLE QUESTIONS

11) How did the Quartering Act impact the colonists?

   A. Colonists were forced to take British soldiers into their homes; protests against the Act led to the Boston Tea Party.

   B. Colonists were forced to build quarters for British soldiers who were stationed locally.

   C. Colonists had to provide one-quarter of their earnings to support British soldiers stationed locally.

   D. Colonists were forced to take British soldiers into their homes; protests against the Act led to the Boston Massacre.

Answers:

   A. Incorrect. While the Quartering Act did require colonists to provide housing for British soldiers, whose numbers were increasing in the Colonies with rising tensions, protests against it did not include the Boston Tea Party; this event protested the Tea Act.

   B. Incorrect. The Quartering Act required colonists to take British soldiers into their own homes to provide them with a place to stay, not to build them housing.

   C. Incorrect. The Quartering Act was not a tax.

   D. **Correct.** Anger at being forced to provide shelter for British soldiers led to protests; in 1770, British soldiers fired on protests against the Quartering Act in what came to be called the Boston Massacre.

Go on

12) What was the impact of Shays' Rebellion?

- A. It showed resistance to imposing excise taxes on whiskey and other consumer goods.
- B. It showed the tenuous nature of governmental control in the young United States and illustrated the need for a stronger federal government.
- C. Inspired by *Letters from a Farmer in Pennsylvania*, Daniel Shays and other farmers rose up to protest taxes and the fiscal policies engineered by Alexander Hamilton during the Washington administration.
- D. Shays, who was concerned about strengthened federal powers under the new Constitution, organized radical Democratic-Republicans to protest the fiscal measures espoused by Hamilton, particularly the Bank of the United States.

Answers:

- A. Incorrect. The Whiskey Rebellion erupted in response to the imposition of excise taxes (in addition to tariffs) under the Federalist Treasury Secretary Alexander Hamilton's fiscal policies, which reflected a stronger federal government.
- **B. Correct.** Shays' Rebellion, in which Daniel Shays led a rebellion of indebted farmers shortly after the end of the Revolution, showed the need for a stronger federal government to ensure national stability and was a major factor in planning the Constitutional Convention.
- C. Incorrect. Shays and his allies—indebted farmers—revolted against seizures of land and debtors' prisons, consequences of post-revolution disorganization and the indebtedness of the new United States. Furthermore, Dickinson's *Letters from a Farmer in Pennsylvania* had stirred up pre-revolutionary protest against the Townshend Acts and the concept of being taxed without proper representation in Parliament; this document was not a factor in Shays' Rebellion.
- D. Incorrect. Shays and his group were driven by personal interest, not politics; furthermore, Shays' Rebellion took place before the Constitution was written and before these fiscal policies were put into place.

13) Despite King George III's agreement with Native American tribes in the Northwest (Great Lakes and Ohio Valley region) in issuing the Proclamation of 1763, the United States did not recognize this deal. What was the impact of that diplomatic reversal?

   A. A series of conflicts between the Americans and the Northwest tribes—the Shawnee, Lenape (who had been pushed west from the Atlantic coast by colonization), Kickapoo, Miami, and others—culminated in the Battle of Fallen Timbers; later, organized into the Northwest Confederacy under the Shawnee leader Tecumseh, inspired by his brother Tenskwatawa, and backed by the British, the tribes once again came into conflict with the Americans, defending their land at the Battle of Tippecanoe and in the War of 1812. Ultimately, the US would control the land.

   B. The French and British were able to form the Northwest Confederacy, allying against the United States in an effort to control more land in North America.

   C. A series of conflicts between the Americans and the Northwest tribes—the Algonquin, Oneida, Mohawk, Onondaga, Cayuga, Seneca, and others—culminated in the Battle of Fallen Timbers; later, organized into the Northwest Confederacy under the Mohawk leader Tecumseh, inspired by his brother Tenskwatawa, and backed by the British, the tribes once again came into conflict with the Americans, defending their land at the Battle of Tippecanoe and in the War of 1812. Ultimately, the US would control the land.

   D. The Northwest Confederacy of British and American soldiers united to drive Native American tribes from what is today the Midwest region of the United States, in order to allow whites to establish settlements in the region.

Answers:

   A. Correct. Despite efforts by the tribes to retain control over their land, they would eventually lose a series of conflicts and the United States would establish states in the Midwest and Ohio Valley region.

   B. Incorrect. While Britain allied with the Shawnee-led Northwest Confederacy, Britain and France did not form an alliance during this time. By the turn of the century, France no longer had a presence at all in North America.

   C. Incorrect. While most of these tribes were Algonquin-speaking, the ethnic Algonquin were not major participants; furthermore, Tecumseh was Shawnee, not Mohawk. In addition, the Mohawk, Seneca, Oneida, Onondaga, and Cayuga composed the Iroquois Confederacy, which did not take part in this conflict.

   D. Incorrect. The British and Americans did not form an alliance in North America; they came into conflict in the region.

14) How did demographics play a part in democratic change during the early and mid-nineteenth century, particularly in the context of Jacksonian Democracy?

   A. The rising strength of industry in the Northeast, coupled with the beginnings of railroads, strengthened support for pro-business politicians and the business class.

   B. Wealthy European immigrants shifted the balance of power away from the "common man" to business owners and the elites, leading to the rise of the powerful Whig party.

   C. Universal manhood suffrage shifted the balance of political power away from the elites; immigration accelerated westward expansion and began to power early industry and urban development.

   D. Jackson's focus on strengthening the federal government dissatisfied the South, leading to the Nullification Crisis.

Answers:

   A. Incorrect. While early industry and railroads were a feature of this era, universal manhood suffrage and the popular notion of the "common man" actually meant that more power went to working people and small rural farmers. Also, rising numbers of poor European immigrants tipped the balance of power away from the rich.

   B. Incorrect. European immigrants were not wealthy; furthermore, their rapid influx led to nativist movements such as the Know-Nothing party. The Whigs emerged later as an offshoot of the Democratic-Republicans.

   C. **Correct.** Universal manhood suffrage allowed all white males, whether or not they owned property, to vote; the "common man" had a voice in government, and Jackson enjoyed their support. Likewise, an influx of poor European immigrants changed the country's demographics, providing more workers for early industry, more settlers interested in populating the west, and a stronger voice in government against the wealthy.

   D. Incorrect. Jackson did not favor a strong federal government. However, the series of tariffs passed during the early nineteenth century, which benefitted the North at the expense of the Southern economy, led to the Nullification Crisis in which John C. Calhoun of South Carolina argued that states could declare federal laws they judged harmful to their own interests null. Jackson managed to negotiate compromises to end the crisis.

15) How did the Missouri Compromise reflect divisions over slavery?
   A. It showed disagreement over the nature of westward expansion.
   B. It showed the impact of the abolitionist movement on politics.
   C. It showed how the Second Great Awakening had influenced society.
   D. all of the above

Answers:

A. Incorrect. While the Missouri Compromise was indeed a compromise over how far west slavery would be permitted to extend, this choice does not fully answer the question, given the other answer choices available.

B. Incorrect. The abolitionist movement did indeed impact politics to the extent that permitting slavery was at the forefront of Congress' agenda. However, given these answer choices, this choice does not fully respond to the question.

C. Incorrect. The Second Great Awakening did indeed influence society by liberalizing thought, including popularizing humanism and the abolition of slavery. However, this answer choice is incomplete given the other options available.

D. **Correct.** All of the answer choices are true.

Civil War, Expansion, and Industry

The Road to Conflict

The Civil War was rooted in ongoing conflict over slavery, states' rights, and the reach of the federal government. Reform movements of the mid-nineteenth century fueled the abolitionist movement. The Missouri Compromise and the Nullification Crisis foreshadowed worsening division to come.

In 1836, Texas, where there were a great number of white settlers, declared independence from Mexico; one reason was because Mexico abolished slavery, an institution white Texans wished to retain. In 1845, Texas joined the Union; this event, in addition to ongoing US hunger for land, triggered the **Mexican-American War**. As a result of the **Treaty of Guadalupe Hidalgo**, which ended the war following the surrender of the Mexican General Santa Ana, the United States obtained territory in the Southwest: the Utah and New Mexico Territories, and gold-rich California. The population of California would grow rapidly with the **gold rush** as prospectors in search of gold headed west to try their fortunes. However, Latinos and Latinas who had lived in the region under Mexico lost their land and were denied many of the rights that whites enjoyed—even though they had been promised US citizenship and equal rights under the Treaty. They also suffered from racial and ethnic discrimination.

Meanwhile, social change in the Northeast and growing Midwest continued. As the market economy and early industry developed, so did an early **middle class**. Social views on the role of **women** changed; extra income allowed them to stay at home. The **Cult of Domesticity**, a popular cultural movement, encouraged women to become homemakers and focus on domestic skills. However, women were also freed up to engage in social activism, and they were active in reform movements. Activists like **Susan B. Anthony** and **Elizabeth Cady Stanton** worked for women's rights, including women's suffrage, culminating in the 1848 **Seneca Falls Convention** led by the **American Woman Suffrage Association.** Women were also active in the temperance movement. Organizations like the Woman's Christian Temperance Union advocated for the prohibition of alcohol, which was finally achieved with the Eighteenth Amendment, although it was later repealed with the Twenty-First.

Reform movements continued to include abolitionism, which ranged from moderate to radical. The American Colonization Society wanted to end slavery and send former slaves to Africa. The former slave **Frederick Douglass** advocated for abolition. An activist leader and writer, Douglass publicized the movement along with the American Anti-Slavery Society and publications like Harriet Beecher Stowe's *Uncle Tom's Cabin*. The radical abolitionist **John Brown** led violent protests against slavery. Abolitionism became a key social and political issue in the mid-nineteenth century.

The industrial change in the North did not extend to the South, which continued to rely on plantations and cotton exports. Nor were the majority of demographic changes occurring in the South. Differences among the regions grew, and disputes over extending slavery into new southwestern territories obtained from Mexico continued. Another compromise was needed.

Anti-slavery factions in Congress had attempted to halt the extension of slavery to the new territories obtained from Mexico in the 1846 **Wilmot Proviso**, but these efforts were unsuccessful. The later **Compromise of 1850** admitted the populous California as a free state and Utah and New Mexico to the Union with slavery to be decided by **popular sovereignty**, or by the residents. It also reaffirmed the **Fugitive Slave Act**, which allowed slave owners to pursue escaped slaves to free states and recapture them. It would now be a federal crime to assist escaped slaves, an unacceptable provision to many abolitionists.

Shortly thereafter, Congress passed the **Kansas-Nebraska Act of 1854** which allowed those two territories to decide slavery by popular sovereignty as well, effectively repealing the Missouri Compromise. A new party, the **Republican Party**, was formed by angered Democrats, Whigs, and others as a result; later, one of its members, Abraham Lincoln, would be elected to the presidency. Violence broke out in Kansas between pro- and anti-slavery factions in what became known as **Bleeding Kansas**.

In 1856, an escaped slave, **Dred Scott**, took his case to the Supreme Court to sue for freedom. Scott had escaped to the free state of Illinois and sought to stay

there; his former "owner" had argued that he could him back regardless of the state he was in. The Court heard the case, *Scott v. Sandford*, and ruled in favor of Sandford, upholding the Fugitive Slave Act, the Kansas-Nebraska Act, and nullifying the Missouri Compromise. The Court essentially decreed that African Americans were not entitled to rights under US citizenship.

In 1858, a series of debates between the presidential candidates, Republican **Abraham Lincoln** and Democrat **Stephen Douglas**, showed the deep divides in the nation over slavery and states' rights. During the **Lincoln-Douglas Debates**, Lincoln spoke out against slavery, while Douglas supported the right of states to decide its legality on their own. In 1860, Lincoln was elected to the presidency. Given his outspoken stance against slavery, South Carolina seceded immediately thereafter, followed by Mississippi, Alabama, Florida, Louisiana, Georgia, and Texas. They formed the Confederate States of America, or the **Confederacy**, on February 1, 1861, under the leadership of **Jefferson Davis**, a senator from Mississippi.

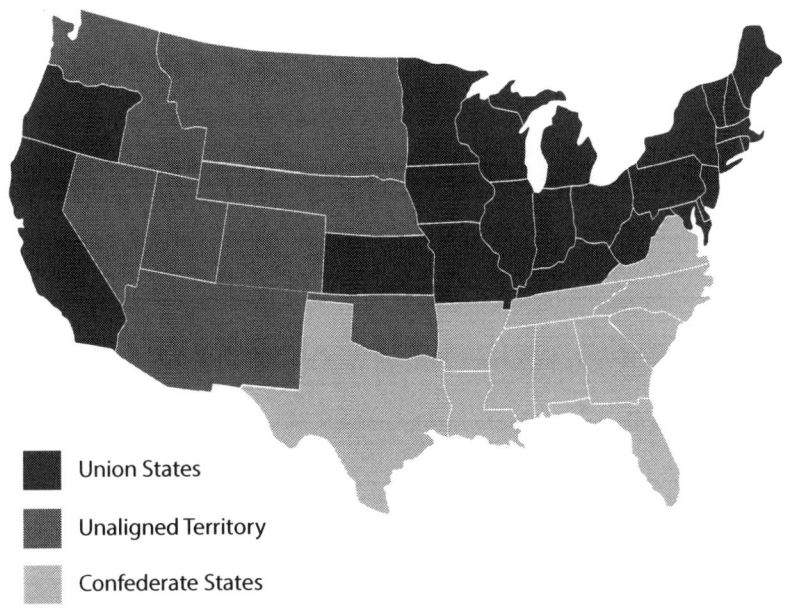

Figure 2.7. Union and Confederacy

Shortly after the South's secession, Confederate forces attacked Union troops in Charleston Harbor, South Carolina; the **Battle of Fort Sumter** sparked the Civil War. As a result, Virginia, Tennessee, North Carolina, and Arkansas seceded and joined the Confederacy. West Virginia was formed when the western part of Virginia refused to join the Confederacy.

Both sides believed the conflict would be short-lived; however, after the First Battle of Bull Run when the Union failed to route the Confederacy, it became clear that the war would not end quickly. Realizing how difficult it would be to defeat the Confederacy, the Union developed the **Anaconda Plan**, a plan to "squeeze" the

Confederacy, including a naval blockade and taking control of the Mississippi River. Since the South depended on international trade in cotton for much of its income, a naval blockade would have serious economic ramifications for the Confederacy.

However, the **Second Battle of Bull Run** was a tactical Confederate victory, led by **General Robert E. Lee** and **Stonewall Jackson**. The Union army remained intact, but the loss was a heavy blow to Union morale. The **Battle of Antietam** was the first battle to be fought on Union soil. Union General **George B. McClellan** halted General Lee's invasion of Maryland, but failed to defeat Confederate forces. Undaunted, on January 1, 1863, President Lincoln decreed the end of slavery in the rebel states with the **Emancipation Proclamation**. The **Battle of Gettysburg** was a major Union victory, led by General George Meade. It was the bloodiest battle in American history up to this point; the Confederate army would not recover.

> **DID YOU KNOW?**
>
> President Lincoln later delivered the Gettysburg Address onsite, in which he framed the Civil War as a battle for human rights and equality.

Meanwhile, following the **Siege of Vicksburg**, Mississippi, Union forces led by **General Ulysses S. Grant** gained control over the Mississippi River, completing the Anaconda Plan. The **Battle of Atlanta**, was the final major battle of the Civil War; following the Union victory led by **General William T. Sherman**, the Union proceeded into the South, and the Confederacy fell. One of the final conflicts of the war, the Battle of Appommatox Court House, resulted in Confederate surrender at Appommatox, Virginia, on April 9, 1865, where General Lee surrendered to General Grant and the war ended.

AFTERMATH AND RECONSTRUCTION

Despite the strong leadership and vast territory of the Confederacy, a larger population (strengthened by immigration), stronger industrial capacity (including weapons-making capacity), the naval blockade of Southern trade, and superior leadership resulted in Union victory. Yet bitterness over Northern victory persisted, and President Lincoln was assassinated on April 15, 1865. Post-war **Reconstruction** would continue without his leadership.

> **DID YOU KNOW?**
>
> Despite ratifying the amendments, Southern states instituted the Black Codes to continue oppression of freedmen, or freed African Americans, who faced ongoing violence.

Before his death, Lincoln had crafted the **Ten Percent Plan**: if ten percent of a Southern state's population swore allegiance to the Union, that state would be readmitted into the Union. However Lincoln's vice president, Andrew Johnson, enforced Reconstruction weakly and the white supremacist **Ku Klux Klan** emerged to intimidate and kill black people in the South; likewise, states developed the oppressive **Black Codes** to limit the rights of African Americans.

As a result, the punitive Congress passed the **Civil Rights Act** in 1866, granting citizenship to African Americans and guaranteeing African American men the same rights as white men (later reaffirmed by the **Fourteenth Amendment**). Eventually former Confederate states also had to ratify the 1865 **Thirteenth Amendment**, which abolished slavery; the **Fourteenth Amendment**, which upheld the provisions of the Civil Rights Act; and the **Fifteenth Amendment**, which in 1870 granted African American men the right to vote. (No women, regardless of race, would receive the right to vote in federal elections until the ratification of the Nineteenth Amendment in 1920.)

Conflict over how harshly to treat the South persisted in Congress between Republicans and Democrats and in 1867, a Republican-led Congress passed the **Reconstruction Acts**, placing former Confederate states under the control of the US Army, effectively declaring martial law. While tensions and bitterness existed between Northern authorities and Southern leaders, Reconstruction did provide for modernization of Southern education systems, tax collection, and infrastructure. The **Freedmen's Bureau** was tasked with assisting freed slaves (and poor whites) in the South.

While technically enslaved African Americans had been freed, many slaves were not aware of this; others still remained voluntarily or involuntarily on plantations. All slaves were eventually freed; however, few had education or skills. Furthermore, oppressive social structures remained: the **Jim Crow laws** enforced **segregation** in the South. Despite the Fourteenth Amendment, the rights of African Americans were regularly violated. In 1896, the Supreme Court upheld segregation in *Plessy v. Ferguson* when a mixed-race man, Homer Plessy, was forced off a whites-only train car. When Plessy challenged the law, the Court held that segregation was, indeed, constitutional; according to the Court, *separate but equal* did still ensure equality under the law. This would remain the law until *Brown v. Board of Education* in 1954.

Black leaders like **Booker T. Washington** and **W.E.B. DuBois** sought solutions. Washington believed in gradual desegregation and vocational education for African Americans, providing it at his **Tuskegee Institute**. DuBois, on the other hand, favored immediate desegregation and believed African Americans should aim for higher education and leadership positions in society. His stance was supported by the advocacy group, the **National Association for the Advancement of Colored People (NAACP)**. These differing views reflected diverse positions within and beyond the African American community over its future. Furthermore, many blacks fled the South for greater opportunities in the North, in cities, and farther West, as part of a greater demographic movement known as the **Great Migration**.

Resentment over the Reconstruction Acts never truly subsided, and military control of the South finally ended with the **Compromise of 1877**, which resolved the disputed presidential election of 1876, granting Rutherford B. Hayes the presidency, and removed troops from the South.

While the Civil War raged and during the chaotic post-war Reconstruction period, settlement of the West continued. California had already grown in population due to the gold rush. In the mid-nineteenth century, **Chinese immigrants** came in large numbers to California, in search of gold but arriving to racial discrimination instead. At the same time, however, the US was opening up trade with East Asia, thanks to **clipper ships** that made journeys across the Pacific Ocean faster and easier. Earlier in 1853, **Commodore Matthew Perry** had used "gunboat diplomacy" to force trade agreements with Japan; even earlier, the United States had signed the **Treaty of Wangxia**, a trade agreement, with Qing Dynasty China.

Despite the racism faced by Chinese immigrants, Americans of European descent were encouraged to settle the Frontier. The **Homestead Act of 1862** granted 160 acres of land in the West to any settler who promised to settle and work it for a number of years; frontier life was difficult, however, as the land of the Great Plains was difficult to farm. Meanwhile, ranching and herding cattle became popular and profitable. White settlers also hunted the buffalo; mass buffalo killings threatened Native American survival.

Meanwhile, the Great Plains and Rockies were already populated with the Sioux, Cheyenne, Apache, Comanche, Arapaho, Pawnee, and others. Conflict between Native American tribes and white settlers was ongoing; the 1864 **Sand Creek Massacre** in Colorado, when US troops ambushed Cheyenne and Arapaho people, triggered even more violence. The United States came to an agreement with the Sioux in South Dakota, offering them land as part of the burgeoning **reservation** system. However, by the late nineteenth century, gold was discovered in the Black Hills of South Dakota on the **Great Sioux Reservation**. The US reneged on its promise, encouraging exploration and seeking control over that gold. The resulting **Sioux Wars** culminated in the 1876 **Battle of Little Big Horn** and General George Custer's famous "last stand." While the US was defeated in that battle, reinforcements would later defeat the Sioux and the reservation system continued. Conflict continued as well: the **Ghost Dance Movement** united Plains tribes in a spiritual movement and in the belief that whites would eventually be driven from the land. In 1890, the military forced the Sioux to cease this ritual; the outcome was a massacre at **Wounded Knee** and the death of the Sioux chief, **Sitting Bull**.

In 1887, the **Dawes Act** ended federal recognition of tribes, withdrew tribal land rights, and forced the sale of reservations—tribal land. It also dissolved Native American families; children were sent to boarding schools, where they were forced to abandon their cultures and assimilate to the dominant American culture.

THE GILDED AGE AND THE SECOND INDUSTRIAL REVOLUTION

Back in the Northeast, the market economy and industry were flourishing. Following the war, the **Industrial Revolution**, accelerated in the United States. The Industrial Revolution had begun on the global level with textile production in Great Britain, had been fueled in great part by supplies of Southern cotton, and was evolving in

the United States with the development of heavy industry—what would come to be called the **Second Industrial Revolution**.

The **Gilded Age** saw an era of rapidly growing income inequality, justified by theories like **Social Darwinism** and the **Gospel of Wealth**, which argued that the wealthy had been made rich by God and were socially more deserving of it. Much of this wealth was generated by heavy industry in what became known as the **Second Industrial Revolution** (the first being textile-driven and originating in Europe). Westward expansion required railroads; railroads required steel, and industrial production required oil: all these commodities spurred the rise of powerful companies like John D. Rockefeller's Standard Oil and Andrew Carnegie's US Steel.

The creation of **monopolies** and **trusts** helped industrial leaders consolidate their control over the entire economy; a small elite grew to hold a huge percentage of income. Monopolies let the same business leaders control the market for their own products. Business leaders in varying industries (monopolies) organized into trusts, ensuring their control over each other's industries, buying and selling from each other, and resulting in the control of the economy by a select few. These processes were made possible thanks to **vertical** and **horizontal integration** of industries. One company would dominate each step in manufacturing a good, from obtaining raw materials to shipping finished product, through vertical integration. Horizontal integration describes the process of companies acquiring their competition, monopolizing their markets. With limited governmental controls or interference in the economy, American **capitalism**—the free market system—was becoming dominated by the elite.

However, the elite were also powering industrial growth. Government corruption led only to weak restrictive legislation like the **Interstate Commerce Act** of 1887, which was to regulate the railroad industry, and the **Sherman Antitrust Act** (1890), which was intended to break up monopolies and trusts, in order to allow for a fairer marketplace; however, these measures would remain largely toothless until President Theodore Roosevelt's "trust-busting" administration in 1901.

Not only were products from the US market economy available in the United States; in order to continue to fuel economic growth, the United States needed more markets abroad. **New Imperialism** described the US approach to nineteenth and early twentieth century imperialism as practiced by the European powers. Rather than controlling territory, the US sought economic connections with countries around the world.

While the free markets and trade of the **capitalist** economy spurred national economic and industrial growth, the **working class**, comprised largely of poor European and Chinese immigrants working in factories and building infrastructure, suffered from dangerous working conditions and other abuses. As the railroads expanded westward, white farmers suffered: they lost their land to corporate interests. In addition, Mexican Americans and Native Americans were harmed and lost land as westward expansion continued with little to no regulations on

land use. African Americans in the South, though freed from slavery, were also struggling under **sharecropping**, in which many worked the same land for the same landowners, leasing land and equipment at unreasonable rates, essentially trapped in the same conditions they had lived in before.

These harmful consequences led to the development of reform movements, social ideals, and change.

POPULISM AND THE PROGRESSIVE ERA

The **People's (Populist) Party** formed in response to corruption and industrialization injurious to farmers (later, it would also support reform in favor of the working class and oppressed groups like women and children). Farmers were suffering from crushing debt in the face of westward expansion, which destroyed their lands; they were also competing (and losing) against industrialized and mechanized farming. Groups like the **National Grange** advocated for farmers. More extreme groups like **Las Gorras Blancas** disrupted the construction of railroads altogether in efforts to protect land from corporate interests.

Farmers were also concerned about fiscal policy. In order to reduce their debt, they believed that introducing a **silver standard** would inflate crop prices by putting more money into national circulation. The **Greenback-Labor Party** was formed in an effort to introduce a silver standard. Debate would continue until the passage of the **Sherman Silver Purchase Act** in 1890, which allowed Treasury notes to be backed in both gold and silver. However, political conflict and continuing economic troubles led to the **Panic of 1893**, the result of the silver standard and of the failure of a major railroad company. **Grover Cleveland**, who had never been in favor of the silver standard, asked Congress to repeal the Act.

Meanwhile, the **Colored Farmers' Alliance** formed to support sharecroppers and other African American farmers in the South. The Jim Crow laws remained in place in much of the South, reaffirmed by the Supreme Court case *Plessy v. Ferguson*. The NAACP was formed to advocate for African Americans nationwide and still functions today.

At the same time, the **labor movement** emerged to support mistreated industrial workers in urban areas. **Samuel Gompers** led the **American Federation of Labor (AFL)**, using **strikes** and **collective bargaining** to gain protections for the unskilled workers who had come to cities seeking industrial jobs. The **Knights of Labor** further empowered workers by integrating unskilled workers into actions. **Mother Jones** revolutionized labor by including women, children, and African Americans into labor actions.

Poor conditions led to philosophies of reform. Many workers were inspired by **socialism**, the philosophy developed in Europe that the workers should own the means of production and that wealth should be distributed equally, taking into account strong economic planning. Other radical movements included **utopianism**,

whose adherents conceptualized establishing utopian settlements with egalitarian societies. More modern philosophies included the **Social Gospel**, the notion that it was society's obligation to ensure better treatment for workers and immigrants. With the continual rise of the **middle class**, women took a more active role in advocating for the poor and for themselves. Women activists also aligned with labor and the emerging **Progressive Movement**.

With the Progressive **Theodore Roosevelt's** ascension to the presidency in 1901 following President William McKinley's assassination, the Progressive Era reached its apex. The *trust-buster* Roosevelt enforced the Sherman Antitrust Act and prosecuted the **Northern Securities** railroad monopoly under the Interstate Commerce Act, breaking up trusts and creating a fairer market. He led government involvement in negotiations between unions and industrial powers, developing the *square deal* for fairer treatment of workers. The Progressive Era also saw a series of acts to protect workers, health, farmers, and children under Presidents Roosevelt and Taft.

Roosevelt continued overseas expansion following McKinley's **Spanish-American War** (1898-1901), in which the US gained control over Spanish territory in the Caribbean, Asia, and the South Pacific.

The Spanish-American War had been the first time the United States had engaged in overseas military occupation and conquest beyond North America, entirely contrary to George Washington's recommendations in his Farewell Address.

During this period, the US annexed Hawaii, Guam, Puerto Rico, and took over the Panama Canal; Cuba became a US protectorate; and the US annexed the Philippines, which would fight an ongoing guerrilla war for independence.

Spanish abuses in Cuba had concerned Americans; however, many events were sensationalized and exaggerated in the media—this **yellow journalism** aroused popular concern and interest in intervention in Cuba. The discovery of a letter from the Spanish minister de Lome, which insulted President McKinley, along with the mysterious explosion of the United States battleship USS. *Maine* in Havana spurred the US into action.

Many Americans did not support intervention, however. According to the **Teller Amendment**, Cuba would revert to independence following the war. The US signed a peace treaty with Spain in 1898. As a result, it controlled Puerto Rico and Guam. Despite having promised independence to the Philippines, McKinley elected to keep it; furthermore, under the **Platt Amendment**, the United States effectively took over Cuba despite previous promises of independence.

The **Roosevelt Corollary** to the Monroe Doctrine, which promised US intervention in Latin America in case of European intervention there, essentially gave the US total dominance over Latin America. Under the **Hay Pauncefote Treaty**, Great Britain granted its claims to the area that would become the Panama Canal (at the time, in Colombia) to the US As Colombia refused to recognize the treaty, President Roosevelt engineered a revolution, creating the new country of Panama,

and beginning construction of the canal. This **new imperialism** expanded US markets and increased US presence and prestige on the global stage.

SAMPLE QUESTIONS

16) Which of the following is true about the roots of the Civil War?

    A. John C. Calhoun used slavery as the reason behind his doctrine of nullification; indeed, disagreements over the institution of slavery precipitated the Nullification Crisis, an early example of Southern discontent with the federal government.

    B. The high numbers of immigrants moving to the North in the early nineteenth century represented a threat to the South, which had a smaller population in comparison, so it wanted to maintain control over the slaves.

    C. Lincoln and Douglas provoked anti-slavery sentiment in their debates around the country.

    D. The Missouri Compromise, the Compromise of 1850, and the Kansas-Nebraska Act all reflected dissent within the Union over the nature of the future of the country—whether slavery should be extended as the United States grew.

Answers:

    A. Incorrect. High tariffs were the impetus behind nullification.

    B. Incorrect. Slavery was an essential part of the plantation economy of the South; its benefit lay in its role in supporting the cotton trade, not in balancing population relative to the North.

    C. Incorrect. The Lincoln-Douglas debates reflected white Americans' conflicted views on slavery; furthermore, Douglas was not against outlawing the institution, believing instead it was an issue best left up to states.

    D. Correct. These pieces of legislation represent ongoing efforts to bridge the gap between differences in views over slavery in determining the future of the country.

17) How did the Dawes Act impact Native Americans in the West?

    A. It forced them to move from their ancestral lands to what is today Oklahoma.

    B. It revoked tribal rights to land and federal recognition of tribes, forcing assimilation.

    C. It granted them land on reservations: for example, the Sioux received deeds to the Great Sioux Reservation in the Black Hills of South Dakota.

    D. It provided 160 acres of land to any settler willing to farm land on the Great Plains for at least five years, threatening Native American rights to land.

Answers:

A. Incorrect. The Indian Removal Act was responsible for this.

B. Correct. The punitive Dawes Act forced assimilation by revoking federal recognition of tribes, taking lands allotted to tribes and dissolving reservations, and forcing children into assimilationist schools (thereby dividing families).

C. Incorrect. The Dawes Act actually dismantled the reservation system.

D. Incorrect. The Homestead Act was responsible for this.

18) **How was a small elite of wealthy businesspersons able to dominate the economy during the Gilded Age?**

A. The Sherman Antitrust Act put a few expert business leaders in charge of economic policy.

B. Monopolies and trusts, developed through horizontal and vertical integration, ensured that the same business leaders controlled the same markets.

C. Industrialization was encouraging the United States to shift to a planned economy in keeping with philosophical changes in Europe.

D. The silver standard allowed specific businesspeople holding large silver reserves to dominate the market.

Answers:

A. Incorrect. The Sherman Antitrust Act, though largely toothless until the Roosevelt administration, was intended to break up monopolies and avoid the concentration of economic power in the hands of a few.

B. Correct. Horizontal and vertical integration of industries allowed the same companies—and people—to control industries, or create monopolies. Those elites who monopolized specific markets organized trusts so that one group controlled entire sectors of the economy.

C. Incorrect. The United States was a capitalist economy (though imperfect, due to strong monopolies). A planned economy would be a socialist economy.

D. Incorrect. The silver standard affected government fiscal policy and backed currency; it did not directly affect class organization.

19) **How did the Progressive Movement change the United States during the Second Industrial Revolution?**

   A. Trade unions fought for workers' rights and safety; the Social Gospel, an early philosophy of charity and philanthropy, developed to support the poor and urban disadvantaged.

   B. The Seneca Falls Convention drew attention to the question of women's suffrage.

   C. Progressives argued to extend rights and protections to Native Americans, particularly those displaced by settlement on the Great Plains.

   D. The Supreme Court ruled segregation unconstitutional in *Plessy v. Ferguson*.

   Answers:

   A. **Correct.** Unions improved conditions for industrial workers; the Social Gospel imparted a sense of social responsibility that eventually manifested in laws and regulations protecting the rights and safety of workers, farmers, the poor, and others.

   B. Incorrect. While women's suffrage continued to be an important issue during the Progressive Era and while women continued to advocate for their rights, the Seneca Falls Convention took place several decades before.

   C. Incorrect. Protection of Native Americans was not a central part of the Progressive platform.

   D. Incorrect. The Supreme Court maintained that segregation was constitutional in *Plessy v. Ferguson*.

20) **How did the Spanish-American War change perceptions of the United States?**

   A. It was clear to Europe and Latin America that the United States had military and territorial, in addition to economic, aspirations as an imperial power.

   B. The United States had begun to prove itself as a military power on the global stage, with strong naval capabilities.

   C. It was clear that nationalism was strong among the American people.

   D. all of the above

   Answers:

   A. Incorrect. Given the failure of the United States to follow through on its promises of independence for Cuba and the Philippines, it was clear that the country had interests in gaining territory. However, this choice does not completely answer the question.

B. Incorrect. The United States had indeed demonstrated formidable naval powers, fighting a war in both the Pacific Ocean and Caribbean Sea. However, this choice does not completely answer the question.

C. Incorrect. While a strong sense of nationalism drove public opinion to favor the war, this choice does not completely answer the question.

D. **Correct.** All of the above answer choices satisfy the question.

The United States Becomes a Global Power

Socioeconomic Change and World War I

Social change led by the Progressives in the early twentieth century resulted in better conditions for workers, increased attention toward child labor, and calls for more livable cities.

The Roosevelt administration focused its attention on economic change at the corporate level. The **Sherman Antitrust Act**, despite its intended purpose—to prosecute and dissolve large trusts and create a fairer market place—had actually been used against unions and farmers' alliances. Under Roosevelt, the Act was used to prosecute enormous trusts like the **Northern Securities Company**, which controlled much of the railroad industry, and **Standard Oil**. Actions like this earned Roosevelt his reputation as a trust-buster.

> **DID YOU KNOW?**
>
> Jacob Riis' groundbreaking book and photo essay *How the Other Half Lives* revealed the squalor and poverty the poor urban classes—often impoverished immigrants—endured, leading to more public calls for reform.

Continuing economic instability also triggered top-down reform. Banks restricting credit and overspeculating on the value of land and interests, coupled with a conservative gold standard, led to the **Panic of 1907**. To stabilize the economy and rein in the banks, Congress passed the **Federal Reserve Act** in 1913 to protect the banking system. Federal Reserve banks were established to cover twelve regions of the country; commercial banks had to take part in the system, allowing "the Fed" to control interest rates and avoid a similar crisis.

During the Progressive Era, while the United States became increasingly prosperous and stable, Europe was becoming increasingly unstable. Americans were divided over how to respond. Following the Spanish-American War, debate had arisen within the US between **interventionism** and **isolationism**—whether the US should intervene in international matters or not. Interventionists believed in spreading US-style democracy, while isolationists believed in focusing on development at home. This debate became more pronounced with the outbreak of World War I in Europe.

Inflammatory events like German **submarine warfare** (U-boats) in the Atlantic Ocean, the sinking of the *Lusitania*, which resulted in many American civilian deaths, the embarrassing **Zimmerman Telegram** (in which Germany promised to help Mexico in an attack on the US), and growing American **nationalism**, or pride in and identification with one's country, triggered US intervention in the war. On December 7, 1917, the US declared war. With victory in 1918, the US had proven itself a superior military and industrial power. Interventionist **President Woodrow Wilson** played an important role in negotiating the peace; his **Fourteen Points** laid out an idealistic international vision, including an international security organization. However, European powers negotiated and won the harsh **Treaty of Versailles**, which placed the blame for the war entirely on Germany and demanded crippling **reparations** from it, one contributing factor to **World War II** later in the twentieth century. The **League of Nations**, a collective security organization, was formed, but a divided US Congress refused to ratify the Treaty, so the US did not join it. Consequently, the League was weak and largely ineffective.

Divisions between interventionists and isolationists continued. Following the Japanese invasion of Manchuria in 1932, the **Stimson Doctrine** determined US neutrality in Asia. Congress also passed the **Neutrality Acts** of 1930s in face of conflict in Asia and ongoing tensions in Europe.

For more information on the First World War, please see Chapter One, "World History."

On the home front, fear of homegrown radicals—particularly of communists and anarchists—and xenophobia against immigrants led to the **Red Scare** in 1919 and a series of anti-immigration laws. Attorney-General Palmer authorized **J. Edgar Hoover** (who would later head the FBI) to lead a series of raids (the **Palmer Raids**) on suspected radicals, precipitating the hysteria of the Red Scare; Palmer was later discredited. In response to widespread xenophobia and a sentiment of isolationism following the First World War, Congress limited immigration specifically from Asia, Eastern Europe, and Southern Europe with the racist **Emergency Quota Act** of 1921 and **National Origins Act** of 1924.

The ongoing Great Migration of African Americans to the North led to differing views on black empowerment. Leaders like **Marcus Garvey** believed in self-sufficiency for blacks, who were settling in urban areas and facing racial discrimination and isolation. Garvey's **United Negro Improvement Association** would go on to inspire movements like the Black Panthers and the Nation of Islam; however, those radical philosophies of separation were at odds with the NAACP, which believed in integration. Tensions increased with 1919 race riots. In the South, the Ku Klux Klan was growing in power, and blacks faced intimidation, violence, and death; **lynchings**, in which African Americans were kidnapped and killed, sometimes publicly, occurred frequently.

Despite race riots and discrimination in northern cities, African American culture did flourish and become an integral part of growing American popular

culture. The **Harlem Renaissance**, the development and popularity of African American-dominated music (especially **jazz**), literature, and art, was extremely popular nationwide and contributed to the development of American pop culture. So did the evolution of early technology like radio, motion pictures, and automobiles—products which were available to the middle class through credit. Furthermore, the women's rights movement was empowered by the heightened visibility of women in the public sphere; the **Nineteenth Amendment**, giving all women the right to vote, was ratified in 1920. However, the **Roaring Twenties**, a seemingly trouble-free period of isolation from chaotic world events, would come to an end.

Great Depression

Following WWI, the United States had experienced an era of consumerism and corruption. The government sponsored **laissez-faire** policies and supported **manufacturing**, flooding markets with cheap consumer goods. Union membership suffered; so did farmers, due to falling crop prices. While mass-production helped the emerging middle class afford more consumer goods and improve their living standards, many families resorted to **credit** to fuel consumer spending. These risky consumer loans, **overspeculation** on crops and the value of farmland, and weak banking protections helped bring about the **Great Depression**, commonly dated from October 29, 1929, or *Black Tuesday*, when the stock market collapsed. During the same time period, a major drought occurred in the Great Plains, affecting farmers throughout the region. Millions of Americans faced unemployment and poverty.

Figure 2.8. Soup Kitchen During the Great Depression

Speculation, or margin-buying, meant that speculators borrowed money to buy stock, selling it as soon as its price rose. However, since the price of stocks fluctuated, when buyers lost confidence in the market and began selling their shares, the value of stocks fell. Borrowers could not repay their loans; as a result, banks failed.

Following weak responses by the Hoover administration, **Franklin Delano Roosevelt** was elected to the presidency in 1932. FDR offered Americans a *New Deal*: a plan to bring the country out of the Depression. During the *First Hundred Days* of FDR's administration, a series of emergency acts (known as an *alphabet soup* of acts due to their many acronyms) was passed for the immediate repair of the banking system. Perhaps most notable was the **Glass-Steagal Act**, which established the **Federal Deposit Insurance Corporation (FDIC)** to insure customer deposits in the wake of bank failures. (Later, to monitor stock trading, the **Securities and Exchange Commission (SEC)** was established; it also has the power to punish violators of the law.) To address the effects of overspeculation on land, the **Agricultural Adjustment Act (AAA)** reduced farm prices by subsidizing farmers to reduce production of commodities. The **Home Owners Loan Corporation (HOLC)** refinanced mortgages to protect homeowners from losing their homes, and the **Federal Housing Administration (FHA)** was created for the long term to insure low-cost mortgages.

The **Tennessee Valley Authority (TVA)**, was the first large-scale attempt at regional public planning; despite being part of the First Hundred Days, it was a long-term project. While intended to create jobs and bring electricity to the impoverished, rural inhabitants of the Tennessee Valley area, one of its true objectives was to accurately measure the cost of electric power, which had been supplied by private companies. The TVA was the first public power company and still operates today.

FDR did not only address economic issues; a number of acts provided relief to the poor and unemployed. The federal government allotted aid to states to be distributed directly to the poor through the **Federal Emergency Relief Act**. The New Deal especially generated jobs. The federal government distributed funding to states through the **Public Works Administration (PWA)** for the purpose of developing infrastructure and to provide construction jobs for the unemployed. Likewise, the **Civilian Conservation Corps (CCC)** offered employment in environmental conservation and management projects. Later, during the **Second New Deal**, the **Works Progress Administration (WPA)** was established. The WPA was a long-term project that generated construction jobs and built infrastructure throughout the country. It also employed writers and artists: the **Federal Writers' Project** and the **Federal Art Project** created jobs for writers and artists, who wrote histories, created guidebooks, developed public art for public buildings, and made other contributions.

The New Deal addressed labor issues as well. The **Wagner Act** ensured the right to unionize and established the **National Labor Relations Board (NLRB)**. Strengthening unions guaranteed collective bargaining rights and protected workers.

FDR was a Democrat in the Progressive tradition; the Progressive legacy of social improvement was apparent throughout the New Deal and his administration. The New Deal and its positive impact on the poor, the working class, unions, and immigrants led these groups to support the Democratic Party, a trend that continues to this day.

INTERNATIONAL AFFAIRS AND WORLD WAR II

The entire world suffered from the Great Depression, and Europe became increasingly unstable. With the rise of the radical Nazi Party in Germany, the Nazi leader Adolf Hitler led German takeovers of several European countries and became a threat to US allies, bombing Britain. However, the United States, weakened by the Great Depression and reluctant to engage in international affairs due to continuing public and political support for isolationism, reinforced by the Neutrality Acts, remained militarily uncommitted in the war. However, the Neutrality Act of 1939 allowed cash-and-carry arms sales to combat participants; in this way, the United States could militarily support its allies (namely, Great Britain).

FDR was increasingly concerned about the rise of fascism in Europe, seeing it as a global threat. To ally with and support Great Britain without technically declaring war on Germany, FDR convinced Congress to enact the **Lend-Lease Act**, directly supplying Britain with military aid, in place of cash-and-carry. FDR and the British Prime Minister **Winston Churchill** met in response to the non-aggression pact between Hitler and Stalin to sign the **Atlantic Charter**, which laid out the anti-fascist agenda of free trade and self-determination. To garner support for his position, FDR spoke publicly about the **Four Freedoms**: freedom of speech, freedom of religion, freedom from want, and freedom from fear.

However, after the Japanese attack on **Pearl Harbor** on December 7, 1941, the US entered the war. While directly attacked by Japan, allied with the fascist Axis powers of Italy and Germany, the United States focused first on the European theater, having agreed with the other Allied powers (Great Britain and the Soviet Union) that Hitler was the primary global threat. The United States focused on eliminating the Nazi threat in the air and at sea, destroying Nazi U-boats (submarines) that threatened the Allies throughout the Atlantic. The US also engaged Germany in North Africa, defeating its troops to approach the fascist Italy from the Mediterranean. On June 6, 1944, or **D-Day**, the US led the invasion of Normandy, invading German-controlled Europe. After months of fighting, following the deadly and drawn-out **Battle of the Bulge** when the Allies faced fierce German resistance, the Allies were able to enter Germany and end the war in Europe.

The United States was then able to focus more effectively on the war in the Pacific. The United States had been able to break the Japanese code; at the same time, Japan had been unable to crack US code thanks to the **Navajo Code Talkers**, who used the Navajo language, which Japan was unable to decipher. The US strategy of **island hopping** allowed it to take control of Japanese-held Pacific islands, pro-

ceeding closer to Japan itself despite **kamikaze** attacks on US ships, in which Japanese fighter pilots intentionally crashed their planes into US ships. President **Harry Truman** had taken power following FDR's death in 1945. Rather than force a US invasion of Japan, which would have resulted in huge numbers of casualties, he authorized the bombing of **Hiroshima** and **Nagasaki** in Japan, the only times that **nuclear weapons** have been used in conflict. The war ended with Japanese surrender on September 2, 1945.

The **United Nations** was formed in the wake of the Second World War, modeled after the failed League of Nations. Unlike the League, however, it included a **Security Council** comprised of major world powers, with the power to militarily intervene for peacekeeping purposes in unstable global situations. With most of Europe destroyed, the victorious US and the Soviet Union emerged as the two global **superpowers**.

> **DID YOU KNOW?**
>
> Japanese-Americans faced oppression and discrimination at home simply due to their race. Forced into internment camps, Japanese-Americans challenged this violation of their rights in *Korematsu v. US*; however, the Supreme Court ruled that this forced displacement was constitutional.

In 1945, Stalin, Churchill, and Roosevelt had met at the **Yalta Conference** to determine the future of Europe. The Allies had agreed on free elections for European countries following the fall of the fascist regimes. However, following the war, the USSR occupied Eastern Europe, preventing free elections. The United States saw this as a betrayal of the agreement at Yalta. Furthermore, while the US-led **Marshall Plan** began a program to rebuild Europe, the USSR consolidated its presence and power in eastern European countries, forcing them to reject aid from the Marshall Plan. This division would destroy the alliance between the Soviets and the West, leading to the **Cold War** between the two superpowers and the emergence of a **bipolar world**.

COLD WAR AT HOME AND ABROAD

With the collapse of the relationship between the USSR and the US, distrust and fear of **communism** grew. Accusations of communist sympathies against public figures ran rampant during the **McCarthy Era** in the 1950s, reflecting domestic anxieties.

President Harry S. Truman's **Truman Doctrine** stated that the US would support any country threatened by authoritarianism (communism), leading to the **Korean War** (1950 – 1953), a conflict between the US and Soviet-backed North Korean forces, which ended in a stalemate. The policy of **containment**, to contain Soviet (communist) expansion, defined US foreign policy; according to **domino theory**, once one country fell to communism, others would quickly follow. Other incidents included the **Bay of Pigs** invasion in Cuba (1961), a failed effort to topple the communist government of Fidel Castro, and the **Cuban Missile Crisis** (1962),

when Soviet missiles were discovered in Cuba and military crisis was narrowly averted, both under the administration of the popular President **John F. Kennedy**.

Meanwhile, in Southeast Asia, communist forces in North Vietnam were gaining power. Congress never formally declared war in Vietnam but gave the president authority to intervene militarily there through the **Gulf of Tonkin Resolution** (1964). However, this protracted conflict—the **Vietnam War**—also led to widespread domestic social unrest, which only increased with US deaths there, especially after the Vietnamese-led **Tet Offensive** (1968). The US ultimately withdrew from Vietnam and the North Vietnamese forces, or **Viet Cong**, led by **Ho Chi Minh**, took over the country.

For more detailed information, please see Chapter One, "World History."

SAMPLE QUESTIONS

21) Which of the following precipitated US entry into the First World War?
    A. the sinking of the *Lusitania*
    B. nationalism stirred up by the Zimmerman telegram
    C. the threat of German U-boats in the Atlantic
    D. all of the above

    Answers:
    A. Incorrect. The sinking of the *Lusitania* had a strong impact on public opinion in the United States, as many American civilians died on board. However, this event alone did not cause the US to enter into the war.
    B. Incorrect. Nationalism was growing in the United States, fueled in part by the legacy of the Spanish-American War and anti-immigrant xenophobia. However, despite its embarrassing nature, the Zimmerman telegram was not the only factor that pushed the US to join the war.
    C. Incorrect. German U-boats threatened American activity and shipping in the North Atlantic Ocean, but this threat was not the only reason the United States was compelled to join hostilities against Germany.
    D. Correct. All of the above events together precipitated US entry into the First World War.

22) How did the United States change in the 1920s?
    A. The Great Migration ceased.
    B. African American culture became increasingly influential.
    C. The Great Depression caused high unemployment.
    D. Thanks to the New Deal, millions of Americans found jobs.

Answers:

A. Incorrect. The Great Migration was an ongoing phenomenon; furthermore, discrimination and violence against African Americans in the South continued to drive black people to northern cities.

B. **Correct.** The Harlem Renaissance is one example of the emergence of African American culture in the public imagination; as US popular culture developed, African American contributions had a strong influence.

C. Incorrect. The Great Depression began in 1929, and mass unemployment followed; it was not a major feature of the 1920s.

D. Incorrect. The New Deal was a consequence of the Great Depression and a feature of the 1930s.

23) **How did the New Deal repair the damage of the Great Depression and help the United States rebuild?**

A. Immediate economic reforms stabilized the economy during the First Hundred Days; later, longer-term public works programs provided jobs to relieve unemployment and develop infrastructure.

B. Social programs put into effect during the First Hundred Days provided jobs for Americans; measures to protect homeowners, landholders, and bank deposits followed to guarantee financial security.

C. Programs like the Tennessee Valley Authority helped the government determine proper pricing and institute price controls for important public goods.

D. FDR proposed supporting banks and big business with federal money in order to reinvigorate the market by limiting government intervention.

Answers:

A. **Correct.** FDR focused on immediate economic stabilization upon taking office, then attacked poverty and unemployment on a sustainable basis.

B. Incorrect. While some social programs were initiated during the First Hundred Days, emergency financial measures like the Glass-Steagal Act, the HOLC, and the AAA were the hallmark of the First Hundred Days, when FDR prioritized immediate economic stabilization.

C. Incorrect. While one purpose of the TVA was indeed to determine the true cost of providing electricity, the government did not enforce price controls on public goods in the long term or on a widespread basis. Furthermore, the TVA was mainly an exercise in regional planning and poverty relief.

D. Incorrect. FDR's focus was on limiting the power of large banks and dramatically increasing government intervention in the market.

UNITED STATES HISTORY 135

24) Why did the former allies, the United States and the Soviet Union, turn against each other following the end of the Second World War?

- A. Stalin felt that the Marshall Plan should have been extended to the Soviet Union.
- B. Because of the fear of communism in the United States, the US had considered invading the USSR following the occupation of Nazi Germany.
- C. Despite assurances to the contrary, the USSR occupied Eastern European countries, preventing free elections in those countries.
- D. The Soviet Union was concerned that the United States would use the nuclear bomb again.

Answers:

- A. Incorrect. The Marshall Plan was not intended for the USSR; it was part of an effort to create a post-war Europe in the model of the Atlantic Charter, espousing free trade and democracy.
- B. Incorrect. During WWII, the US and Soviet Union were allies (despite mutual suspicion), and the US did not plan to invade the USSR.
- **C. Correct.** Stalin's refusal to permit free elections or democracy in the countries of Eastern Europe were seen as a betrayal of the agreement reached by the Allies at Yalta, and a major reason for the collapse of the US-Soviet relationship.
- D. Incorrect. While this was a major concern of the Soviet Union, it was not the precipitating reason for the collapse of the relationship.

25) What was the purpose of the United Nations Security Council?

- A. to provide a means for international military intervention in case of conflict that could threaten global safety, in order to avoid another world war
- B. to provide a forum for the superpowers to maintain a dialogue
- C. to provide a means for countries to counter the power of the US and USSR in an effort to limit the reach of the superpowers
- D. to develop a plan to rebuild Europe and Japan

Answers:

- **A. Correct.** While the UN was modeled in part after the League of Nations, the Security Council was (and is) able to militarily intervene in cases of armed conflict that could pose a global threat, an ability the League of Nations did not have.
- B. Incorrect. While both the US and the USSR had permanent seats on the Security Council, the purpose of the Council was not to facilitate their relationship, nor did it.

C. Incorrect. The Security Council was formed before the Cold War and did not necessarily envision the development of a bipolar world; furthermore, it was not intended as a forum for global dialogue (that is the role of the UN General Assembly).

D. Incorrect. The Security Council was not involved in post-war development; its purpose was (and is) to safeguard international security.

Postwar and Contemporary United States

Civil Rights and Social Change

During the 1960s, the US experienced social and political change, starting with the election of the young and charismatic John F. Kennedy in 1960. Following JFK's assassination in 1963, President **Lyndon B. Johnson**'s administration saw the passage of liberal legislation in support of the poor and of civil rights. The **Civil Rights Movement**, led by activists like the **Rev. Dr. Martin Luther King, Jr.** and **Malcolm X**, fought for African American rights in the South, including the abolition of segregation, and also for better living standards for Blacks in northern cities.

Civil rights came to the forefront with the 1954 Supreme Court case ***Brown v. Board of Education***, when the Warren Court (so-called after Chief Justice Earl Warren) found segregation unconstitutional, overturning its decision in *Plessy v. Ferguson*. *Brown* took place shortly after the desegregation of the armed forces, and public support for civil rights and racial equality was growing.

The **Southern Christian Leadership Conference (SCLC)** and Dr. King, a religious leader from Georgia, believed in civil disobedience, non-violent protest. In Montgomery, Alabama, **Rosa Parks**, an African American woman, was arrested for refusing to give up her seat to a white man on a bus. Buses were segregated at the time, and leaders including Dr. King organized the **Montgomery Bus Boycott** to challenge segregation; the effort was ultimately successful. Building on their success, civil rights activists, now including many students and the **Student Nonviolent Coordinating Committee (SNCC)**, led peaceful protests and boycotts to protest segregation at lunch counters, in stores, at public pools, and other public places.

The movement grew to include voter registration campaigns organized by CORE, the Congress of Racial Equality, supported by students and other activists (both black and white) from around the country—the **Freedom Riders**, so-called because they rode buses from around the country to join the movement in the Deep South. SNCC and activists organized to protest segregation at government and public facilities and on university campuses. The movement continued to gain visibility as non-violent protesters were met with violence by the police and state authorities, including attacks by water cannons and police dogs in Alabama. Undaunted, activists continue to fight against segregation and unfair voting restrictions on African Americans.

The Civil Rights Movement had national public attention, and had become a major domestic political issue. Civil rights workers organized the **March on Washington** in 1963, when Dr. King delivered his famous *I Have a Dream* speech. Widespread public support for civil rights legislation was impossible for the government to ignore. In 1964, Congress passed the **Civil Rights Act**, which outlawed segregation.

Figure 2.9. March on Washington

However, African Americans' voting rights were still not sufficiently protected. According to the Fifteenth and the Nineteenth Amendments, all African Americans—men and women—had the right to vote, but many Southern states had voting restrictions in place such as literacy tests and poll taxes, which disproportionately affected African Americans. Dr. King and civil rights workers organized a march from Selma to Montgomery, Alabama, to draw attention to this issue; however it ended in violence as

> **DID YOU KNOW?**
>
> Today, some states have instituted voter identification laws similar to literacy tests and poll taxes, which disproportionately affect minorities.

marchers were attacked by police. In 1965, led by President Lyndon B. Johnson, Congress passed the **Voting Rights Act**, which forbade restrictions impeding the ability of African Americans to vote, including literacy tests. Separately, the **Twenty-Fourth Amendment** made poll taxes unconstitutional.

Meanwhile, **Malcolm X** was an outspoken proponent of **black empowerment**, particularly for African Americans in urban areas. Unlike Martin Luther King Jr., who believed in integration, Malcolm X and other activists, including groups like the **Black Panthers**, believed that African Americans should stay separate from whites to develop stronger communities.

The Civil Rights Movement extended beyond the Deep South. **Cesar Chavez** founded the **United Farm Workers (UFW)**, which organized Hispanic and migrant farm workers in California and the Southwest to advocate for unionizing and collective bargaining. Farm workers were underpaid and faced racial discrimination. The UFW used boycotts and non-violent tactics similar to those used by civil rights activists in the South; Cesar Chavez also used hunger strikes to raise awareness of the problems faced by farm workers.

The Civil Rights Movement also included **feminist** activists who fought for fairer treatment of women in the workplace and for women's reproductive rights. The **National Organization for Women** and feminist leaders like **Gloria Steinem** led the movement for equal pay for women in the workplace. The landmark case of *Roe v. Wade* struck down federal restrictions on abortion.

The **American Indian Movement (AIM)** brought attention to injustices and discrimination suffered by Native Americans nationwide. Ultimately it was able to achieve more tribal autonomy and address problems facing Native American communities throughout the United States.

In New York City in 1969, the **Stonewall riots** occurred in response to police repression of the gay community. These riots and subsequent organized activism are seen as the beginning of the LGBT rights movement.

President Kennedy had envisioned a liberal United States in the tradition of the Progressives. His youth and charisma were inspiring to many Americans, and his assassination in 1963 was a shock. Kennedy's vice president Lyndon B. Johnson continued the liberal vision with the **Great Society**. LBJ embraced **liberalism**, believing that government should fight poverty at home, and play an interventionist role abroad (in this era, by fighting communism).

Johnson launched a **War on Poverty**, passing reform legislation to support the poor. The **Medicare Act** provided medical care to elderly Americans; the creation of the **Department of Housing and Urban Development** increased the federal role in housing and urban issues. Johnson's **Head Start** program provided early intervention for disadvantaged children before elementary school (and still does today); the **Elementary and Secondary Education Act** increased funding for primary and secondary education. Additionally, the **Immigration Act of 1965** overturned the

provisions of the Emergency Quota Act, ending the racist limitations on immigrants to the US.

At the same time, LBJ's overseas agenda was increasingly unpopular. Adhering to containment and domino theory—US policy toward communism in an effort to stop its spread—Johnson drew the United States deeper into conflict in Southeast Asia. The **Vietnam War** was extremely unpopular in the US due to high casualties, the unpopular draft (which forced young American males to fight overseas) and what seemed to many to be the purposelessness of the war. Student activists, organizing in the mold of the Civil Rights Movement, engaged in non-violent (and, at times, violent) protest against the Vietnam War. The rise of a **counterculture** among the youth—the development and popularity of **rock and roll music**, the culture of **hippies**, and changing concepts of drug use and sexuality—added to a sense of rebellion among Americans, usurping government authority and challenging traditional values.

For more information on the Vietnam War, please see Chapter One, "World History."

THE RISE OF CONSERVATISM

Radical social change in the 1960s, coupled with the toll of the Vietnam War on the American public, many of whom had lost loved ones in the war, or served themselves in combat, led to backlash against liberalism. **Conservatism** strengthened in response to the heavy role of government in public life throughout the 1960s, high rates of government spending, and social challenges to traditional values. Due in great part to the escalation of the Vietnam War, LBJ announced his intention not to run for another term, and the conservative **Richard Nixon** became president in 1970.

During the administration of the conservative President Richard Nixon, the conflict in Vietnam ended and a diplomatic relationship with China began. Nixon also oversaw economic reforms—he lifted the gold standard in an effort to stop **stagflation**, a phenomenon when both unemployment and inflation are high at the same time. Ending the gold standard reduced the value of the dollar in relation to other global currencies, and foreign investment in the United States increased. However, the Nixon administration was found to have engaged in corrupt practices. A burglary at the Democratic National Headquarters, based at the Watergate Hotel, was found to have been connected to the Oval Office. The **Watergate scandal** eventually forced Nixon to resign, and Vice President **Gerald Ford** took office for one term. Nixon's resignation further destroyed many Americans' faith in their government.

During the 1970s, the economy suffered due to US involvement in the Middle East. US support for Israel in the Six Day War and 1973 Yom Kippur War caused **OPEC** (the Organization of Petroleum Exporting Countries), led by Saudi Arabia and other allies of Arab foes of Israel, to boycott the US As a result, oil prices sky-

rocketed. In the 1979 Iranian Revolution and the resulting **hostage crisis**, when the US Embassy in Teheran was taken over by anti-American activists, the economy suffered from another oil shock. (For more information on these events, please see Chapter One, "World History.") While President Jimmy Carter had been able to negotiate peace between Israel and Egypt in the **Camp David Accords**, he was widely perceived as ineffective. Carter lost the presidency in 1980 to the conservative Republican **Ronald Reagan**.

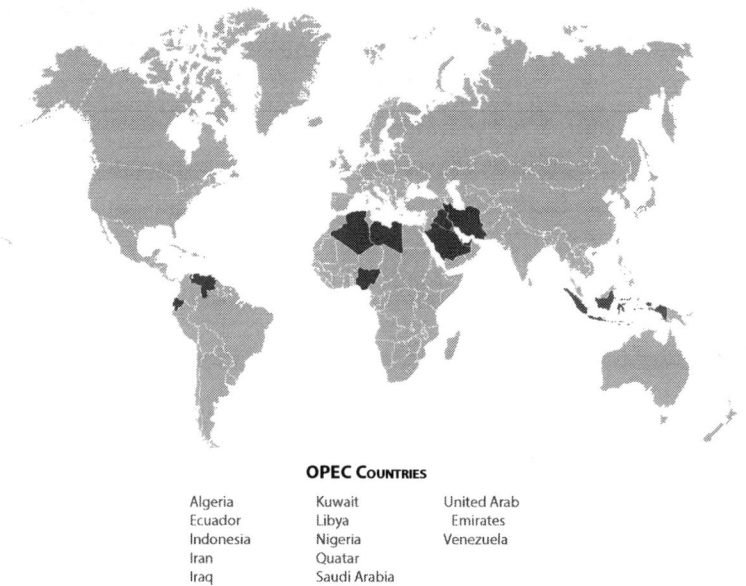

Figure 2.10. OPEC

Reagan championed domestic tax cuts and an aggressive foreign policy against the Soviet Union. The Reagan Revolution revamped the economic system, cutting taxes and government spending. According to supply-side economics (popularly known as *Reaganomics*), cutting taxes on the wealthy and providing investment incentives, wealth would "trickle down" to the middle and working classes and the poor. However, tax cuts forced Congress to cut or eliminate social programs that benefitted millions of those same Americans. Later, the **Tax Reform Act** of 1986 ended progressive income taxation.

Despite promises to lower government spending, the Reagan administration invested huge sums of money in the military. This investment in military technology—the **arms race** with the Soviet Union—helped bring about the end of the Cold War with the 1991 fall of the USSR and later, a new era of globalization. In addition to funding a general arms buildup and supporting measures to strengthen the military, the Reagan administration funded and developed advanced military technology to intimidate the Soviets, despite having signed the **Strategic Arms Limitation Treaties (SALT I and II)** limiting nuclear weapons and other strategic armaments in the 1970s. Ultimately, the US would outspend the USSR militarily,

a precipitating factor to the fall of the Soviet Union. (For more information on the fall of the USSR, please see Chapter One, "World History.")

The Reagan Revolution also ushered in an era of conservative values in the public sphere. After the Civil Rights Era, whose victories had occurred under the auspices of the Democratic Johnson administration, many Southern Democrats switched loyalties to the Republican Party. At the same time, the Democrats gained the support of African Americans and other minority groups who benefitted from civil rights and liberal legislation. During the Reagan Era, conservative Republicans espoused a return to "traditional" values. **Christian fundamentalism** became popular, particularly among white conservatives. Groups like **Focus on the Family** lobbied against civil rights reform for women and advocated for traditional, two-parent, heterosexual families.

THE END OF THE COLD WAR AND GLOBALIZATION

The administration of **George H. W. Bush** signed the Strategic Arms Reduction, or **START, Treaty** with the Soviet Union in 1991, shortly before the dissolution of the USSR.; later, it would enter into force in 1994 between the US and the Russian Federation as an agreement to limit the large arsenals of strategic weapons possessed by both countries.

With the collapse of the Soviet Union, the balance of international power changed. The bipolar world became a unipolar world, and the United States was the sole superpower. The first major crisis occurred in the Middle East when Iraq, led by **Saddam Hussein**, invaded oil-rich Kuwait. The US intervened—with the blessing of the United Nations, and the support of other countries. The resulting **Gulf War**, or **Operation Desert Storm** (1991)—cemented its status as the world's sole superpower; Saddam's forces were driven from Kuwait, and Iraq was restrained by sanctions and no-fly zones.

With the election of President **Bill Clinton** in 1992, the US took an active role in international diplomacy, helping broker peace deals in the former Yugoslavia, Northern Ireland, and the Middle East. Clinton's election also indicated a more liberal era in American society: while conservative elements remained a strong force in politics and sectors of society, changing attitudes toward minorities in the public sphere and increased global communication (especially with the advent of the Internet) were a hallmark of the 1990s.

As part of **globalization**, the facilitation of global commerce and communication, the Clinton administration prioritized free trade. Encouraging open borders, the United States signed the **North American Free Trade Agreement (NAFTA)** with Mexico and Canada, creating a free trade zone throughout North America, removing trade restrictions. The Clinton administration also eased financial restrictions in the United States, rolling back some of the limitations provided for under Glass-Steagal. These changes were controversial: many American jobs went overseas, especially manufacturing jobs, where labor was cheaper. Furthermore, globalization

began facilitating the movement of people, particularly undocumented immigrants from Latin America seeking a better life in the United States. **Immigration reform** would be a major issue into the twenty-first century.

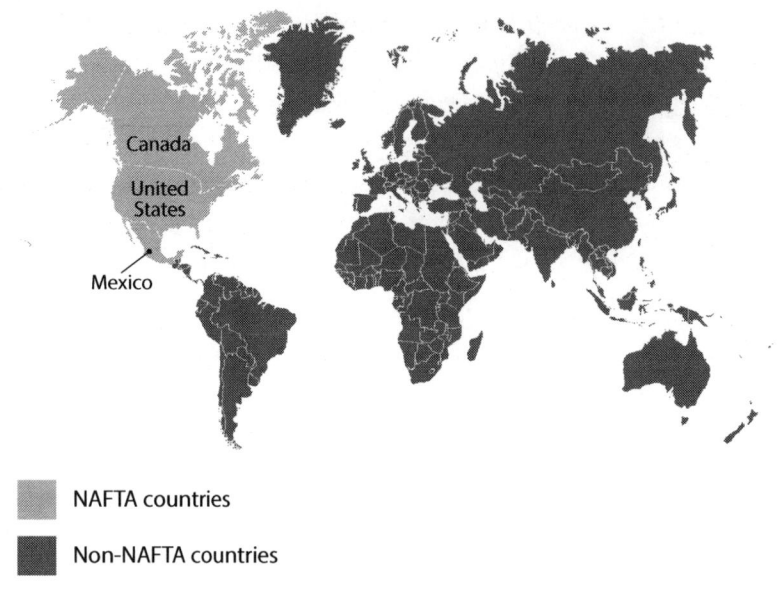

Figure 2.11. NAFTA countries

Clinton faced dissent in the mid-1990s with a conservative resurgence. A movement of young conservatives elected to Congress in 1994 promised a **Contract with America**, a conservative platform promising a return to lower taxes and traditional values. Clinton also came under fire for personal scandals: allegations of corrupt real estate investments in the Whitewater scandal and inappropriate personal behavior in the White House. These scandals fueled social conservatives and Christian fundamentalists who favored a return to the conservative era of the 1980s. Despite these controversies and political division, society became increasingly liberal. Technology like the **Internet** facilitated national and global communication, media, and business; minority groups like the LGBT community engaged in more advocacy; and environmental issues became more visible.

The Twenty-First Century

By the end of the twentieth century, the United States had established itself as the dominant global economic, military, and political power. Due to its role in global conflict from the Spanish-American War onwards, the US had established military bases and a military presence worldwide, in Europe, Asia, the Pacific, and the Middle East. The US dominated global trade: American corporations established themselves globally, taking advantage of free trade to exploit cheap labor pools and less restrictive manufacturing environments (at the expense of American workers). American culture was widely popular: since the early twentieth century, American pop culture

like music, movies, television shows, and fashion was enjoyed by millions of people around the world.

However, globalization also facilitated global conflict. While terrorism had been a feature of the twentieth century, the United States had been relatively untouched by large-scale terrorist attacks. That changed on **September 11, 2001**, when the terrorist group **al Qaeda** hijacked airplanes, attacking New York and Washington, D.C. in the largest attack on US soil since the Japanese bombing of Pearl Harbor. The 9/11 attacks triggered an aggressive military and foreign policy under the administration of President **George W. Bush**, who declared a *War on Terror*, an open-ended global conflict against terror organizations and their supporters.

Following the attacks, the US struck suspected al Qaeda bases in Afghanistan, beginning the **Afghanistan War**, during which time the US occupied the country. Suspected terrorist fighters captured there and elsewhere during the War on Terror were held in a prison in **Guantanamo Bay**, Cuba, which was controversial because it did not initially offer any protections afforded to prisoners of war under the Geneva Conventions.

President Bush believed in the doctrine of **preemption**, that if the US was aware of a threat, it should preemptively attack the source of that threat. Preemption would drive the invasion of Iraq in 2003. In 2003, the US attacked Iraq, believing that Iraq held **weapons of mass destruction** that could threaten the safety of the United States. This assumption was later revealed to be false; however, the United States promulgated the **Iraq War**, deposing Saddam Hussein and supporting a series of governments until it withdrew its troops in 2011, leaving the country in a state of chaos.

At home, Congress passed the **USA Patriot Act** to respond to fears of more terrorist attacks on US soil; this legislation gave the federal government unprecedented—and, some argued, unconstitutional—powers of surveillance over the American public.

Despite the tense climate, social liberalization continued in the US Following the Bush administration, during which tax cuts and heavy reliance on credit (especially in the housing market—the **Subprime Mortgage Crisis**) helped push the country into the **Great Recession**, the first African American president, **Barack Obama**, was elected in 2008. Under his presidency, the US emerged from the recession, ended its occupations of Iraq and Afghanistan, passed the Affordable Care Act, which reformed the healthcare system, and legalized same-sex marriage. The Obama administration also oversaw the passage of consumer protection acts, increased support for students, and safety nets for homeowners.

SAMPLE QUESTIONS

26) Why did the Civil Rights Movement continue to push for legislative change even after the passage of the 1964 Civil Rights Act?

   A. While the Civil Rights Act provided legal protections to African Americans and other groups, many believed it did not go far enough as it did not outlaw segregation.

   B. Leaders like Malcolm X believed further legislative reform would ensure better living conditions for blacks in cities.

   C. Civil rights leaders wanted legislation to punish white authorities in the South that had oppressed African Americans.

   D. Legal restrictions like literacy tests, poll taxes, and voter registration issues inhibited African Americans from exercising their right to vote, especially in the South.

Answers:

   A. Incorrect. The Civil Rights Act of 1965 was the *de jure* end to segregation, even though discrimination was still widespread.

   B. Incorrect. Black empowerment focused on strengthening black communities from within and at the grassroots level, not working for legislative reform from the outside.

   C. Incorrect. Prosecution and punishment was not the goal of the mainstream Civil Rights Movement.

   D. Correct. Despite the end to legal segregation, discrimination was deeply entrenched, and laws still existed to prevent African Americans from voting. Civil rights activists worked to ensure the passage of the Voting Rights Act in 1965.

27) Which of the following best describes liberalism under LBJ?

   A. Liberalism was the philosophy that the government should be deeply involved in improving society at home, and work on fighting communism abroad.

   B. According to liberalism, the US should devote its resources to improving life at home for the disadvantaged, but refrain from direct intervention in international conflict.

   C. Liberals believed in moderate social programs, but that spending should be limited.

   D. Liberalism frowns upon conflict intervention, as shown by the mass demonstrations against the Vietnam War in the 1960s.

Answers:

   A. Correct. LBJ believed in forming a Great Society and launched a War on Poverty, initiating federal government-sponsored social programs to support the disadvantaged; he also actively waged a war against the spread of communism in Southeast Asia, ultimately unsuccessfully.

B. Incorrect. Liberals believe that the federal government should devote resources both to social programs domestically and to fighting communism (or, today, to humanitarian intervention) internationally.

C. Incorrect. Liberals favored government spending.

D. Incorrect. LBJ's liberalism favored overseas intervention; furthermore, demonstrations against the Vietnam War were organized by diverse groups of students and other activists who did not necessarily share all of LBJ's liberal philosophies.

28) **How did Reagan's economic policies affect working class and poor Americans?**

   A. They had little effect on these classes because the United States has a free market economy.

   B. They increased taxes by eliminating the progressive income tax and cut social programs needed by many disadvantaged people.

   C. They benefitted the working and middle classes by cutting taxes and increasing investment opportunities.

   D. Despite Reagan's tax cuts, the government was able to fund all social programs, so lower income Americans who used them were unaffected by changes in revenue.

Answers:

   A. Incorrect. While the US espouses capitalism, it is in practice a mixed economy; the federal government does intervene in the economy to an extent (although in a more limited way than in other economies around the world).

   B. Correct. Supply-side economics theorized that low taxes on the wealthy would encourage investment in the economy; as a result, wealth would "trickle down" to the middle and working classes and the poor. However, in practice, lower taxes meant less government revenue and many social programs that were needed by poor Americans were cut.

   C. Incorrect. These policies benefitted the wealthy more than the working and middle classes.

   D. Incorrect. Tax cuts forced the federal government to cut many social programs, harming low-income Americans.

29) **Which of the following best describes globalization?**

   A. the free movement of goods and services across borders

   B. easier communication worldwide thanks to technology like the Internet

   C. facilitated movement of persons from one country to another

   D. all of the above

Answers:

A. Incorrect. While commercial activity without restrictions or tariffs is a core element of economic globalization, globalization is more than just an economic phenomenon.

B. Incorrect. The Internet, improved telephone and television technology, and other improved communications technology are indeed a part of globalization; however, better global communication is not its only feature.

C. Incorrect. While globalization can include both open borders and socioeconomic structures that facilitate the movement of persons (for example, improved communication can strengthen family ties across borders, and free trade agreements may help migrant workers establish roots in a foreign country, even if temporarily), globalization is more than just international migration.

D. **Correct.** Globalization is a multifaceted phenomenon that takes into account all the factors listed above.

30) **How did the Bush doctrine of preemption affect US foreign policy in the early twenty-first century?**

A. The US believed that in order to contain terrorism, it had to occupy countries that might harbor terrorists.

B. Fearing that the entire Middle East would succumb to terrorists, the Bush administration established a presence in the centrally located country of Iraq to avoid a "domino effect" of regime collapse.

C. The Bush administration justified international intervention and foreign invasion without previous provocation in order to preempt possible terrorist attacks.

D. The US held prisoners captured during the War on Terror at Guantanamo Bay, where they were not given the protections and privileges entitled to prisoners of war under the Geneva Conventions.

Answers:

A. Incorrect. This describes the concept of containment theory, a Cold War philosophy.

B. Incorrect. This describes domino theory, part of US policy during the Cold War.

C. **Correct.** Preemption was used to justify the 2003 invasion of Iraq, on the assumption that Iraq had weapons of mass destruction it intended to use or to provide for terrorist attacks against the United States.

D. Incorrect. While this did occur, it was not part of the Bush doctrine of preemption.

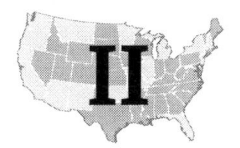

Part II: Practice

Practice Test One

WORLD HISTORY PRE-1450 (30)

1

The Hittites were able to expand from Anatolia due to

A. superior seafaring technology, allowing expansion into the Mediterranean.
B. superior military technology, including chariots and weaponry.
C. advanced technology imported from Greece.
D. their development of bronze metallurgy.

2

During the Peloponnesian War,

A. the dominant Hellenic powers, Crete and Sparta, went to war with each other.
B. the dominant Hellenic powers, Athens and Sparta, went to war with the Ionian Greeks in Anatolia.
C. Greece was able to unite as the dominant powers, Athens and Sparta, fought against Persia and the Ionian Greeks.
D. the dominant Hellenic powers, Athens and Sparta, went to war with each other.

3

How did the Neolithic Era mark a major development in human evolution?

A. the development of agriculture and beginning of settled societies
B. the early use of the wheel
C. the use of bronze to develop basic tools
D. early medical treatment

4

During the Paleolithic Era,

A. *Homo sapiens* was the only species of human in existence.

B. multiple species of human existed.

C. *Homo sapiens* likely eliminated all competition for resources.

D. hominids had not yet evolved.

5

During the Neolithic Era,

A. *Homo sapiens* was the only species of human in existence.

B. multiple species of human existed.

C. *Homo sapiens* likely eliminated all competition for resources.

D. humans had not yet evolved.

6

There is evidence that the Bronze Age

A. was a purely European phenomenon.

B. only occurred in the Fertile Crescent.

C. can be attributed to widespread sources of early bronze metallurgy.

D. was a Chinese development.

7

Which of the following best describes the caste system in India?

A. It is a defined, unchangeable social and religious hierarchy, determined by birth.

B. It is a changeable social hierarchy.

C. It is a hierarchy determined by skills and education wherein one's position can be changed.

D. It is a defined, unchangeable social hierarchy, determined by birth.

8

What concept(s) did early Chinese imperial civilization and early Fertile Crescent civilizations share?

A. centralized government structure

B. written language

C. monotheism

D. A and B only

9

Which of the following statements best explains the relevance of bronze metallurgy in early human civilizations?

- A. Bronze technology allowed early societies in the Fertile Crescent to develop improved irrigation.
- B. The Bronze Age gave rise to the Neolithic Era.
- C. The development of bronze allowed humans to create copper.
- D. Early civilizations like the Sumerians were able to use bronze for tools and weapons; geographic expansion and technological innovation (including in weaponry) resulted.

10

The Qin dynasty was able to consolidate its power in China due to which of the following?

- A. The Qin enforced Confucianism throughout China as a means to consolidate its power.
- B. The Qin developed a common written language, allowing them to unite the disparate Chinese-speaking groups of people throughout China.
- C. Emerging dominant following the Warring States period, the Qin developed standardized weights and measures and a unified bureaucracy.
- D. All of the above are correct.

11

What development under the Shang dynasty contributed to Chinese unity?

- A. early writing, which helped united disparate Chinese-speaking peoples across a wide landscape
- B. the concept of the Mandate of Heaven, which taught that the emperor was chosen by a divine source to rule, helping consolidate his power
- C. the construction of the Forbidden City, which strengthened the power of the emperor and further centralized it
- D. all of the above

12

The Babylonians are known for having developed an early form of

- A. irrigation, increasing agricultural production in the fertile areas near the Tigris and Euphrates Rivers.
- B. cuneiform, the first known example of writing in which characters were connected to form words.
- C. rule of law: the Code of Hammurabi.
- D. iron weaponry and chariots, enabling them to control large areas of land.

13

How would society develop in the civilizations of the Indus Valley region?

A. A society based on respect for wisdom and harmony became entrenched in the region.

B. A hierarchical caste system intertwined with religion came to delineate social roles and status.

C. The teachings of Siddhartha Gautama would become popular and persist in the region until the present day.

D. A strict social system of exams would be established, creating a hierarchy of educated government officials.

14

Buddhism is practiced

A. in parts of the Himalayas, East and Southeast Asia.

B. widely throughout India and the Himalayas.

C. only in Tibet.

D. only in Southeast Asia.

15

Despite the period of relative stability enjoyed by Europe during the High Middle Ages, the Black Death resulted in which of the following outcomes?

A. European powers were made vulnerable to attacks by the Magyars, who toppled the disorganized Holy Roman Empire.

B. Instability in Europe led to military conflict, division within the Catholic Church, and weakening of the Holy Roman Empire.

C. The Mongols were able to expand their empire into Eastern Europe.

D. Islamic powers were able to completely conquer the Iberian Peninsula as a result of instability there.

16

Following the collapse of the Western Roman Empire and the subsequent, disorganized "Dark Ages" in Europe,

A. The Catholic Church based in Rome lost power in Western Europe to the rising Greek Orthodox Church based in Constantinople.

B. The Byzantine Empire was able to conquer unorganized European land in what is today Germany.

C. Charlemagne united parts of Western and Central Europe—what would become the Holy Roman Empire—leading to a period of stability.

D. Charlemagne united parts of Western and Central Europe (including what would become France) under his rule, leading to a period of stability.

17

Many scholars argue that modern banking began in Venice in the fifteenth century. Which of the following strengthens this argument?

- A. Venice was the first major colonial power, developing mercantilism.
- B. Venice was a center of intellectual and cultural development.
- C. Venice was a commercial center, ideally situated to profit from goods imported on the Silk Road and from Africa.
- D. Venice was not badly affected by the plague.

18

Judaism developed in which of the following areas?

- A. Egypt
- B. the Levant
- C. Mesopotamia
- D. the Fertile Crescent

19

In feudal Europe, serfs were

- A. enslaved by the lords and knights.
- B. bonded to the land but under the protection of the lords.
- C. forced to fight for the lords.
- D. able to eventually purchase their freedom from the knights in exchange for support fighting.

20

Which of the following is the main reason for the development of the Sunni-Shi'a schism in early Islam?

- A. Sunnis believed that early Muslims should conquer lands west of the Arabian Peninsula, while Shi'ites thought it would make more sense strategically to invade the Mesopotamian regions and Persia.
- B. Sunnis prioritized military conquest over Muhammad's religious and philosophical teachings, a development with which Shi'ites vehemently disagreed.
- C. Sunnis were more willing to accept Jews and Christians as "People of the Book," but Shi'ites felt that they should be converted to Islam, or forced out of communities controlled by Muslims.
- D. Sunnis and Shi'ites disagreed over the appropriate line of succession following the death of the Prophet Muhammad.

21

While the Crusades enriched Europe in many ways, they did not

A. provide new learning to the West.

B. result in lasting land gains.

C. provide religious indulgences.

D. offer the opportunity to gain personal wealth.

22

How was Russia affected by the schism between Byzantine (Greek Orthodox) Christianity and the Roman Catholic Church?

A. Russia was unaffected.

B. Strong papal influences within Europe extended into Kiev and Russia, and Vladimir I converted to Catholicism, encouraging his subjects to do the same.

C. Byzantine missionaries moved north into Kiev and Russian territories; as a result, Vladimir I converted to Greek Orthodox Christianity and had his subjects do the same.

D. Disagreeing with the Catholic Church, Russia developed Eastern Orthodox Christianity and a separate Russian church.

23

The collapse of the Mongol Empire was due in part to which of the following developments?

I. the rise of Islam and the growing power of the Abbasid Caliphate

II. Ivan the Great's consolidation of power and conquest of Moscow

III. the overthrow of the Yuan dynasty by the Ming dynasty in China

A. I, II, and III

B. I and II only

C. II and III only

D. I and III only

24

One reason Charlemagne was able to retain legitimacy and hold power in an unstable Europe was because

A. He was crowned by the pope and had the support of the Catholic Church.

B. He had the support of the serfs, having pledged to end the feudal system.

C. He encouraged knights to travel to the Middle East to fight the Crusades.

D. He was seen as a counter to the tremendous power of the Catholic Church.

25

As head of the Catholic Church, the pope was particularly influential because

- A. Catholicism had more followers than Greek Orthodox Christianity.
- B. the pope held not only spiritual power, but also political power.
- C. the church had special influence in Europe because it was based in Rome, a city of historical significance.
- D. the pope had direct political control over most lords throughout feudal Europe.

26

Europeans were encouraged to fight in the Crusades for which of the following reasons?

- A. They were promised indulgences by the pope—forgiveness for any sins committed in the Crusades.
- B. They were encouraged to keep wealth they might gain in the Middle East.
- C. They were encouraged to fight against perceived threats to Christianity in the Middle East.
- D. all of the above

27

Following the defeat of the Mongol-backed Yuan dynasty, the powerful Ming dynasty demonstrated its imperial strength in which of the following ways?

- A. expanding military occupation through Central Asia into Mongol-held territories in Russia
- B. consolidating and projecting imperial power by building the Great Wall
- C. accepting tribute from Muslim powers along the Silk Road to strengthen Chinese influence in Central Asia
- D. developing a strong navy to expand its global exploratory capabilities as a counter to Portuguese naval exploration

28

The Kingdom of Mali developed due to

- A. its control over the trans-Saharan trade routes, enabling it to tax traders transporting goods between Morocco and the Atlantic coast.
- B. its ability to repel Islamic influences from the north.
- C. its control over gold and salt resources, generating tremendous wealth for the kingdom.
- D. its control over the trans-Saharan slave trade.

29

Despite never making significant land gains in the Levant, Europe benefitted from the Crusades through which of the following ways?

- A. Many knights returned from the Middle East with Middle Eastern, Muslim wives, bringing religious and ethnic diversity to Europe.
- B. Crusaders returned to Europe with new language skills, helping reinvigorate trade on the Silk Road through Asia and Muslim-held lands into China.
- C. Crusaders returned to Europe with knowledge of Arab-Islamic technology, navigation, and science, contributing to European learning and seafaring capability; this knowledge would eventually contribute to the colonial era and the Scientific Revolution.
- D. Crusaders returned to Europe with more knowledge of Eastern Orthodox Christianity, contributing to the rites and teachings of the Catholic Church after centuries of stagnation following the fall of the Roman Empire.

30

Despite disorganization in the west, the Eastern Roman Empire was able to reorganize into the Byzantine Empire for which of the following reasons?

- A. Emperor Justinian's ability to establish rule of law
- B. a centralized seat of government in the Eastern Mediterranean, thanks to Constantine's having moved the imperial capital to Constantinople
- C. Justinian's consolidation of military power and ability to re-conquer parts of the Middle East and Northern Africa
- D. all of the above

World History Post-1450 (30)

1

Which of the following best describes the motivation for Protestant reformers?

A. Protestants, including Martin Luther, originally sought to develop a new form of Christianity separate from the Catholic Church.

B. Protestants like Martin Luther were unhappy with the teachings of the church, including papal indulgences and corruption in the church, and originally sought reform.

C. Protestants were initially influenced by European political leaders, who used them to limit the power of the church.

D. Protestants, including Martin Luther, originally sought to topple the Catholic Church, believing it to have become too corrupt.

2

The Hundred Years' War

A. is an example of European unity against an outside, non-European invading force.

B. showed the technological dominance of the powers aligned with the Catholic Church, whose resources were massive.

C. indicated a shift in European politics from allegiance to one's ethnicity or nation to allegiance to the empire.

D. described ongoing ethnic conflict in Europe.

3

Major influences on the European Renaissance included

A. cultural discoveries in North America.

B. African music and culture.

C. Greek Orthodox Christianity and learning brought by Byzantine missionaries.

D. scientific knowledge from the Islamic empires and Greco-Roman philosophy and art.

4

Which of the following led to the French Revolution?

A. food shortages, heavy taxation of the peasants and bourgeoisie, and Enlightenment thought

B. the rise of Napoleon and militarization of French culture

C. the Congress of Vienna and shifting diplomatic alliances in Europe

D. the reign of Louis XIV

5

The Treaty of Westphalia

A. marked the end of the Thirty Years' War.

B. was indicative of a shift in European politics, towards international relations based on non-interference and emerging concepts of independent states, rather than empires dominated by the Catholic Church and other forces.

C. is often viewed as the foundation of modern European relations.

D. all of the above

6

Which of the following best describes the Counter-Reformation?

A. The Counter-Reformation was a response to corruption in the church that divided the Catholic Church.

B. The Counter-Reformation was a response to the Protestant Reformation.

C. The Counter-Reformation occurred in response to the discovery of the Americas.

D. The Counter-Reformation occurred in response to the Enlightenment.

7

How was Europe affected by the American Revolution?

A. Fearing a revolution at home, France supported the British.

B. Spain began decolonization in Latin America as a response to revolution in North America.

C. The ideals of the American Revolution inspired later revolutionary movements in Europe.

D. European powers ceased trade with the rebellious colonies.

8

How was Europe affected by the Civil War in the United States?

A. European powers were inspired to make slavery illegal following the American Civil War.

B. Industrializing European powers relied on Southern cotton, but were encouraged not to trade with the Confederacy so as not to support slavery, which had already been abolished in Europe and most European empires.

C. Industrializing European powers relied on Southern cotton, and traded with the Confederacy, supplying them with needed income during the Civil War.

D. None of the above are correct.

9

How did the United Kingdom reflect division in Europe and within Christianity in the seventeenth century?

A. Conflict between Protestants and Catholics over national leadership resulted in ongoing conflict and a series of unstable governments; however, following the Civil War, a Protestant monarchy was finally established in Great Britain and Ireland.

B. The purpose of the Glorious Revolution—to take back Protestant control of a Protestant country—was an example of the idea of the ethnic nation-state that was to take hold in Europe in later history.

C. Conflict between Protestants and Catholics over national leadership resulted in ongoing conflict and a series of unstable governments; however, following the Glorious Revolution, a Protestant monarchy was finally established.

D. While numerous Britons were Protestant, belonging to the church of England, Puritans feared an overwhelming Catholic influence and left for the North American colonies to create a new church.

10

Which of the following best describes the consequences of the Opium Wars?

A. British occupation of China
B. Chinese victory over Britain
C. unequal trade treaties favoring China
D. unequal trade treaties favoring Britain

11

European imperialism in the nineteenth century was a function of which of the following?

I. an effort to gain natural resources to power industrialization in the Americas
II. a way of shouldering the "white man's burden," or helping to improve "backward" societies
III. a competition between European countries to control territory, leading to phenomena like the "scramble for Africa"

A. I and II
B. II and III
C. I, II, and III
D. I and III

12

In the nineteenth century, Britain occupied parts of Somalia, Kenya, and Egypt, and negotiated boundaries and treaties with other colonial powers and local governments. Which of the following best explains why the British prioritized organizing this area?

A. Britain wished to safeguard shipping routes through the Red Sea and into the Indian Ocean.

B. Britain wished to control the valuable and popular routes in the Red Sea to Mecca and Medina.

C. Britain was concerned about instability in Somalia.

D. Britain was unable to consolidate control further inland into Africa.

13

During the 1884 Berlin Conference, European imperial powers

A. established extraterritoriality within important Chinese cities to support their nationals, who were participating in trade in opium, silk, and other Chinese goods.

B. agreed upon spheres of influence whereby each European country would dominate different parts of China.

C. determined which parts of Africa would be controlled by which European powers, a process also called the "scramble for Africa."

D. established the Triple Alliance and the Triple Entente, setting the stage for the system of alliances that would eventually spark the First World War.

14

As part of nineteenth-century European diplomacy in the tradition of the Congress of Vienna, how was the Three Emperors' League meant to maintain a balance of power?

A. Russia, Germany, and Austria-Hungary agreed that if one empire went to war, the other two would remain neutral; furthermore, the powers would consult with each other on matters of war.

B. Russia, Germany, and Austria-Hungary agreed that if one empire went to war, the other two would support it militarily; furthermore, the powers would consult with each other on matters of war.

C. Russia, Germany, and Austria-Hungary agreed that if one empire went to war, the other two would support it financially and with weaponry; furthermore, the powers would consult with each other on matters of war.

D. Russia, Germany, and Austria-Hungary agreed that an attack on one was an attack on all; furthermore, the three empires agreed not to levy taxes on one another to facilitate trade.

15

Choose the best description for the Russian strategy of empire-building.

A. Russia focused on colonizing overseas, strengthening its navy to build a trans-oceanic empire.

B. Russia focused on overland expansion, moving eastward into northern Asia across Siberia and westward into Eastern Europe.

C. Russia remained isolated, avoiding expansion and focusing on industrialization instead.

D. Russia lacked the resources to build an empire and struggled to maintain its agrarian-based society.

16

How were European empires affected by nationalism in the eighteenth and nineteenth centuries?

A. European empires like the Austro-Hungarian Empire benefitted from nationalism, as Austrians and Hungarians were more loyal to the imperial government.

B. The Austro-Hungarian Empire lost its Balkan territories to the Ottoman Empire, which was perceived to be more tolerant of Muslim minorities.

C. Given the nature of empires—consolidated rule over an extended region home to diverse peoples—nationalism threatened empires as ethnic groups began to advocate for representation in imperial government.

D. Given the nature of empires—consolidated rule over an extended region home to diverse peoples—nationalism threatened empires as ethnic groups began to advocate for their own independent states.

17

Following the collapse of the Ottoman Empire after the First World War, European countries took control of the Middle East, establishing protectorates according to arbitrary boundaries and installing rulers in accordance with European strategic interests. What effect has this had on the Middle East in the twentieth and twenty-first centuries?

A. The Middle East has not been greatly affected.

B. Illegitimate national borders and rulers have led to instability in the region.

C. Improved governance, thanks to the protectorates, improved stability following the decline of the Ottoman Empire in the region.

D. European investment in strategic resources supported long-term political stability in the Middle East.

18

The Meiji Restoration was

A. a Japanese attempt to restore traditional Japan and reinvigorate Japanese culture as it had been before Western incursions into the country.

B. a period of modernization and westernization in Japan.

C. the early stage of Japanese imperialism in Asia, when it invaded Korea.

D. a cultural movement in Japan to restore Shintoism and traditional poetry.

19

Choose the answer that presents events in the correct chronology:

A. the French Revolution, the American Revolution, the Industrial Revolution, World War I

B. the American Revolution, the French Revolution, Napoleon's conquests, World War I

C. the French Revolution, the Industrial Revolution, the American Revolution, World War I

D. the Rape of Nanjing, World War I, the Great Depression, World War II

20

Which of the following was not a consequence of nationalism in nineteenth-century Europe?

A. Italian unification

B. the Congress of Vienna

C. German unification

D. the Franco-Prussian War

21

Which of the following statements describes both the French Revolution and the Russian Revolution?

A. Both originated among the wealthiest elites.

B. Both valued agricultural workers over the middle class.

C. Both sought a totally egalitarian society, with publicly owned means of production.

D. Both were based upon ideals articulated by intellectuals who were not members of the working or agricultural classes.

22

Which of the following best explains the economic impact on Germany following the First World War?

A. Overspeculation on German farmland caused the market to crash.

B. Wartime reparations mandated by the Treaty of Versailles and the worldwide Great Depression caused inflation to skyrocket, plunging the German economy into crisis.

C. Germans were forced to pay extra taxes to cover reparations, and due to high prices, many could not afford to do so.

D. The Reichsmark was removed from circulation and replaced with the dollar as a means of punishment, forcing many Germans into poverty.

23

The Sino-Soviet Split was due in part to

A. the Chinese alliance with the United States.

B. the Soviet alliance with the United States.

C. the absence of the People's Republic of China from the United Nations.

D. division between the communist philosophies of Maoist China and the Marxist-Leninist USSR.

24

While the beginning of the Second World War is usually understood to be Hitler's invasion of Poland, some scholars date it even earlier. Which of the following events do some scholars identify as the beginning of World War II?

A. the Rape of Nanjing

B. the Japanese takeover of Korea

C. the Japanese invasion of Manchuria

D. the Chinese Civil War

25

Decolonization

A. was the process of granting independence to the European colonies in Africa, Asia, and the Pacific.

B. was overseen in great part by the United Nations.

C. was violent at times.

D. all of the above

26

Following the Soviet invasion of Afghanistan and subsequent withdrawal, Afghanistan

A. came under Indian influence, making it vulnerable to extremist movements like the Taliban.

B. descended into a period of instability and civil war, making it vulnerable to extremist movements like the Taliban.

C. temporarily joined Pakistan in an effort to regain stability.

D. temporarily came under NATO administration in an effort to regain stability and prevent the development of extremist groups.

27

Which of the following best describes the Warsaw Pact?

A. a defense agreement between the Soviet Union and Eastern Bloc

B. a Soviet alliance with Poland

C. Soviet control over Eastern Europe

D. the division of Eastern Europe after WWII

Read the excerpt and answer the questions that follow.

> Somalia achieved its independence in 1960 with the union of Somalia, which had been under Italian administration as a United Nations trust territory, and Somaliland, which had been a British protectorate. The United States immediately established diplomatic relations with the new country. In 1969, the Somali army launched a coup which brought Mohamed Siad Barre to power. Barre adopted socialism and became allied with the Soviet Union. The United States was thus wary of Somalia in the period immediately after the coup.
>
> Barre's government became increasingly radical in foreign affairs, and in 1977 launched a war against Ethiopia in hopes of claiming their territory. Ethiopia received help from the Soviet Union during the war, and so Somalia began to accept assistance from the United States, giving a new level of stability to the US-Somalia relationship.
>
> Barre's dictatorship favored members of his own clan. In the 1980s, Somalis in less favored clans began to chafe under the government's rule. Barre's ruthlessness could not suppress the opposition, which in 1990 began to unify against him. After joining forces, the combined group of rebels drove Barre from Mogadishu in January 1991.
>
> "Milestones 1993 – 2000: Somalia, 1992 – 1993,"
> Office of the Historian, United States Department of State,
> (last modified October 31, 2013).

28

In what way does Somalia show the impact of colonization on newly independent African countries?

A. Somalia had limited political infrastructure and civil society, making it vulnerable to a military coup by Mohamed Siad Barre.

B. Somalia had limited political infrastructure and civil society, and so it turned to the USSR for support in developing a sense of national unity and identity through socialism.

C. A sense of national Somali identity made it possible for Somaliland and the UN trust territory of Somalia to become a strong, unified nation-state.

D. Due to limited economic development (since most resources had gone to support the colonial powers), Somalia's infrastructure was weak; consequently, it strengthened its ties with the Cold War powers to support its economy by improving its position in international markets.

29

How is Somalia illustrative of a challenge faced by many former colonies in Africa?

A. Somalia's weak internal security has allowed piracy to flourish off of the coast of the Horn of Africa, posing a threat to shipping.

B. Somalia lacks a strong sense of national identity; people are more loyal to their own ethnic groups or clans than to a nation artificially created by colonial powers.

C. Newly independent Somalia, like many other African countries during decolonization, was forced to fight off the Cold War powers that were trying to gain influence in Africa.

D. Like many African countries, Somalia was unable to develop a strong presence at the United Nations.

30

Which of the following best describes the 1977 war between Somalia and Ethiopia in terms of the Cold War?

A. a proxy war in which the Soviet Union supported Ethiopia while the United States supported Somalia—only once did US and USSR military forces come into contact in Africa

B. an example of diplomacy where the USSR and US worked together to try to stop a war

C. a proxy war in which the Soviet Union supported Ethiopia while the United States supported Somalia—US and USSR military forces were not directly involved in the fighting

D. The 1977 war was not relevant to the Cold War.

US History to 1877 (30)

1

Why was the Mayflower Compact an important contribution to the foundation of American government?

A. It provided for equal treatment of all Christians under the law.

B. It was the first treaty between European settlers (the Pilgrims) and Native Americans.

C. It laid out terms for government with the consent of the governed.

D. It allowed people of all faiths to practice their religions freely under the law.

2

How did the colonies in New England differ from southern ones like Virginia, the Carolinas, and Georgia?

A. Farms tended to be larger in the southern colonies and produce cash crops like tobacco using slave labor; in the north, smaller family farms predominated, and early urbanization was more widespread.

B. Farms tended to be larger in the northern colonies and produce cash crops like tobacco, using slave labor; in the south, smaller family farms predominated, and early urbanization was more widespread.

C. The southern colonies were wealthier than the northern colonies, with a more educated population.

D. There were no major differences between the northern and southern colonies before independence.

3

What advantage did the colonists have in the American Revolution?

A. vast financial wealth

B. superior weaponry

C. strong leadership and knowledge of the terrain

D. a professional military and access to mercenaries

4

What resources attracted the French and the British to North America?

A. tobacco

B. rice

C. beaver pelts

D. all of the above

5

The British and French leveraged alliances with which of the following tribes in conflicts in colonial North America?

- A. the Sioux and the Cheyenne
- B. the Algonquin and the Iroquois
- C. the Cherokee and the Seminole
- D. the Apache and the Miami

6

How did the views of the Federalists and the Anti-Federalists differ during the Constitutional Convention?

- A. The views of the Federalists and Anti-Federalists did not significantly differ at the Constitutional Convention.
- B. The Anti-Federalists did not believe in a Constitution at all, while the Federalists insisted on including the Bill of Rights.
- C. The Anti-Federalists favored a stronger Constitution and federal government, while Federalists were concerned that states would risk losing their autonomy.
- D. The Federalists favored a stronger Constitution and federal government, while Anti-Federalists were concerned that states would risk losing their autonomy.

7

The early Democratic Party (the Democratic-Republicans) was mainly concerned with which of the following?

- A. agrarian issues, small landowners, and maintaining a weaker federal government
- B. fiscal policy in support of urban areas and big businesses
- C. limitations on federal oversight of business and banks
- D. maintaining a strong federal government

8

What was one reason for the election of Andrew Jackson?

- A. Jackson was able to find a solution to the first Nullification Crisis.
- B. Allowing those white males who did not own property to vote was a boon to Jackson, who was popular with the "common man."
- C. Jackson's popularity with landowners in Northern states guaranteed him the funds he needed to win the presidency.
- D. Jackson and his vice president, John C. Calhoun, were a strong and popular team when running for election.

9

Which of the following best describes the conditions faced by Latinos and Latinas who had remained in western territories won by the US in the Mexican-American War?

A. They were treated with derision; many lost land and wealth they had held under Mexico, and did not enjoy the same rights under the law as citizens, even though they had been promised American citizenship in the Treaty of Guadalupe Hidalgo.

B. While many had lost land and wealth they had held under Mexico, they were entitled to and received restitution from the government of the United States.

C. They were treated equally in social and political situations under the United States.

D. Most Latinos and Latinas left the western territories for Mexico following the Mexican-American War, due to discriminatory conditions they faced under the United States government.

10

Which of the following is a safeguard against federal overreach built into the US Constitution?

A. a system of checks and balances, in which a president can only be elected to two consecutive terms

B. a system of checks and balances, in which the House, Senate, and president are able to limit each other

C. a system of checks and balances, in which the president—a civilian leader—controls the military

D. a system of checks and balances, in which the three branches of government—executive, legislative, and judicial—are able to limit each other

11

John Adams would have been likely to agree with which of the following statements?

A. A strong federal government is necessary to keep the United States together as one country.

B. States' rights are paramount.

C. The Bill of Rights was always intended to be part of the US Constitution.

D. The Articles of Confederation sufficed to assert the sovereignty of the United States of America.

12

In the first half of the nineteenth century, social change in the US was driven by religious and social organizations that helped to foster political interest in women's rights, abolitionism, and utopianism. This movement was called:

A. the Industrial Revolution
B. the Second Great Awakening
C. the Enlightenment
D. the Glorious Revolution

13

With the Monroe Doctrine, President Monroe attempted to

A. keep the United States involved in European conflicts.
B. isolate the United States from European intervention in its affairs.
C. assert US hegemony in the Western Hemisphere by isolating it from Europe, to prevent European powers from expanding there.
D. increase US involvement in international affairs.

14

The Louisiana Purchase was controversial most especially because of

A. the difficult relationship between the United States and France.
B. concerns about federal overreach, given the scope of the purchase.
C. concerns about maintaining stable relationships with the Native Americans living in the territories west of the Mississippi River.
D. the amount of land it encompassed and the ability of the US to bring it under control.

15

Which of the following best explains the Three-Fifths Compromise?

A. Three-fifths of the states would be permitted to own slaves.
B. Three-fifths of the states needed to ratify amendments before they could go into effect.
C. To account for a state's population size, a slave would count for three-fifths of a person.
D. Three-fifths of the states had to ratify the Constitution before it could go into effect.

16

An important benefit of the Louisiana Purchase was

A. possession of Texas.

B. access to the Pacific Ocean.

C. total control over the Oregon Trail.

D. control over the Port of New Orleans and the Mississippi River.

17

Which group insisted on including the Bill of Rights in the Constitution in order to ratify it?

A. Constitutionalists

B. Revolutionaries

C. Federalists

D. Anti-Federalists

18

The strategic alliance between the British and Tecumseh's Confederacy

A. helped the British win the War of 1812.

B. was part of Tecumseh's plan, along with the allied tribes, to form a sovereign nation northwest of the United States.

C. was intended to mislead the British, when in reality Tecumseh had secretly formed an alliance with the US

D. caused the breakdown of the British army.

19

How did the Fugitive Slave Act empower slave states under federal law?

A. Slave states had the right to take escaped slaves to court under the Fugitive Slave Act; even though the former slaves were safe in free states, they were still subject to prosecution and in danger of being legally returned to their former "masters" if they were unable to prove residency in a free state.

B. Despite the reluctance of states' rights advocates—many of whom were based in slave states—to adhere to federal law, many of these same advocates approved of the federal Fugitive Slave Act because it allowed them to pursue escaped slaves from slave states to free states and to capture them.

C. Slave states were able to send police and military authorities into free states to capture escaped slaves.

D. Slave states were able to prosecute free states in federal court for offering safe haven to escaped slaves.

20

What assets did the Confederacy have during the Civil War?

A. The Confederacy had superior weaponry and production resources.

B. The Confederacy maintained brisk trade with Europe, enabling it to fund the war.

C. The Confederacy benefitted from strong military leadership and high morale among the population.

D. The Confederacy's strong infrastructure allowed it to transport supplies and people efficiently throughout the South.

21

How did the Dred Scott decision affect the Fugitive Slave Act?

A. It weakened the act.

B. It strengthened the act.

C. It had no effect on the act.

D. It abolished the act.

22

The Compromises of 1820 and 1850, and the Kansas-Nebraska Act all revolved around which of the following issues?

A. states' rights to legalize slavery

B. accommodating politicians who protected slavery and the rights of their states to keep its practice legal

C. deep division within the United States over the role of the federal government, as illustrated by the question of states' rights to legalize slavery

D. all of the above

23

Why was the principle of popular sovereignty controversial?

A. Slave owners were concerned that free black Americans would vote against slavery in new states.

B. White settlers were concerned that they would be outnumbered by Native Americans in new states and therefore have less political control.

C. Mormon settlers in the Utah Territory were concerned that non-Mormon settlers moving westward due to the act would have too much influence in local politics.

D. Popular sovereignty allowed the legality of slavery in new states to be decided by those able to vote, when it was originally to have been outlawed in new states.

24

Which of the following effectively repealed the Missouri Compromise?

A. the Dred Scott decision
B. the Compromise of 1850
C. the Kansas-Nebraska Act
D. the Fugitive Slave Act

25

Which of the following best explains the strategy behind the Anaconda Plan?

A. The North would "squeeze" the South by taking control of the Mississippi River and establishing a naval blockade on the Atlantic coast; given the South's reliance on cotton export for revenue, this would be a devastating economic blow.
B. The North would "squeeze" the South by taking control of the Mississippi River and establishing a naval blockade on the Atlantic coast; given the South's reliance on raw materials from overseas to power its industrial growth, this would be a devastating economic blow.
C. The North would crush Southern resistance by fighting primarily in Virginia; by "squeezing" the seat of Confederate government in Richmond, it hoped to cause the entire Confederacy to collapse.
D. The North would surround the South with troops in Kentucky, West Virginia, Missouri, and elsewhere, hoping to outnumber their forces.

26

A major consequence of the Civil War was

A. the rise of the Federalist Party.
B. the destruction of the South's economy and the growth of the North's economy.
C. the emergence of the Republican Party.
D. the growth of the South's economy and the destruction of the North's economy.

27

The Reconstruction Acts

A. immediately improved conditions for African Americans in the South.
B. immediately benefitted the Southern economy.
C. were widely considered fair in Congress and by Southerners.
D. imposed Northern military control over the South.

28

Following the Civil War, the United States ratified the Thirteenth, Fourteenth and Fifteenth Amendments to the Constitution. What did these amendments guarantee?

- A. an end to slavery, equal rights for all Americans, and voting rights for all Americans, respectively
- B. an end to slavery, equal rights for all Americans, and voting rights for all African Americans, respectively
- C. an end to slavery, equal rights for all American men, and voting rights for all African American men, respectively
- D. an end to slavery, equal rights for Americans, and voting rights for African American men, respectively

29

Even after the end of slavery, African Americans in the rural South still suffered due to

- A. sharecropping, which kept them in heavy debt, often to their former "masters."
- B. the Colored Farmers' Alliance, which was organized to limit their efforts to become independent farmers.
- C. the Reconstruction Acts, which specifically punished Southern blacks who did not join the Union army.
- D. labor unions, which advocated for white workers' rights in factories in urban areas and ignored rural issues.

30

How did the Bureau of Indian Affairs break down tribal bonds and weaken Native American societies?

- A. through policies of assimilation
- B. by forcing Native American children to go to white schools and reject their cultures
- C. by forcing Native Americans to move onto reservations
- D. all of the above

US History 1877–present (30)

1

The United States remained relatively neutral in international conflicts for much of its early history; its first major assertion of international power and foreign intervention overseas is considered to be which of the following?

A. the Spanish-American War

B. the First World War

C. the Texan Revolution

D. the War of 1812

2

Within the two years following the WWI, the US would

A. join the League of Nations.

B. join NATO.

C. ratify the Treaty of Versailles.

D. none of the above

3

Antitrust legislation in the US was designed to

A. reduce wealth.

B. redistribute wealth.

C. prevent businesses from monopolizing and thus disrupt the market.

D. prevent price controls.

4

Which of the following best explains why the Temperance movement became popular?

A. Because women were discouraged from public consumption of alcohol, women activists in the Progressive movement felt that prohibition of consumption of alcoholic beverages would encourage social equality.

B. High prices for alcohol were an increasing problem for working class families, for whom this product was one of few affordable luxuries.

C. Alcohol consumption by working men, generally the breadwinners in impoverished urban households, affected their wives and female partners, who were forced to cope with the resulting strain on household budgets and domestic violence.

D. Since most alcohol was imported from overseas, a movement to decrease trade with European powers was popular with nationalists.

5

Women did not receive full suffrage in the United States until which of the following?

- A. The Seneca Falls Convention was held.
- B. The Nineteenth Amendment was ratified.
- C. The Equal Rights Amendment was ratified.
- D. The Voting Rights Act of 1965 was passed.

6

Nineteenth-century workers organized labor unions for all of the following reasons except for which of the following?

- A. they were not paid fairly for their work
- B. their shifts were frequently 12 – 14 hours a day
- C. to overthrow capitalists like Carnegie and Rockefeller
- D. dangerous work conditions

7

Which of the following best describes Social Darwinism?

- A. the belief in evolution
- B. the belief that survival of the fittest applies to communities of people, particularly as regards race or wealth
- C. a rejection of the theory of evolution
- D. the belief that evolution applies only to creatures and not social groups

8

The Cuban Missile Crisis ultimately resulted in

- A. the installation of the Castro regime.
- B. the fall of the Castro regime.
- C. a new opening of dialogue between the United States and the Soviet Union.
- D. the end of a period of détente between the United States and the Soviet Union.

9

SALT and SALT II were indicative of what in the US – USSR relationship?

- A. a stalemate
- B. a period of conflict
- C. glasnost
- D. a period of diplomatic détente

10

President Theodore Roosevelt, a Progressive, was known for which major action?

- A. prosecuting the Northern Securities Company under the Interstate Commerce Act, breaking up this large monopoly and earning his reputation as a "trust-buster"
- B. developing the Works Progress Administration to assist working people in finding jobs and to support mistreated factory workers
- C. ensuring the ratification of the Sixteenth Amendment
- D. limiting the use of the Sherman Antitrust Act only to a few situations, earning his reputation as a "trust-buster"

11

During periods of high tension between the United States and the Soviet Union in the 1950s, how was the US affected?

- A. Fear of communism was pervasive, and during the McCarthy era, accusations were made against public figures.
- B. Fearing Soviet communism, the United States supported Maoism in China as a counterweight to Leninism.
- C. During the McCarthy hearings, several members of Congress were found to be communist and so were removed from office.
- D. During the McCarthy hearings, several members of Congress were found to be Soviet spies and so were removed from office.

12

The Iranian hostage crisis

- A. resulted in the establishment of an anti-American theocracy in Iran.
- B. contributed to the election of Ronald Reagan to the presidency, which led to the escalation of weapons production and the arms race.
- C. resulted in regional instability, forcing the Soviet invasion of Afghanistan.
- D. contributed to the election of Jimmy Carter to the presidency, which led to a period of détente with the Soviet Union.

13

How did internment affect Japanese-Americans?

- A. The US government immediately compensated them after the war.
- B. They did not fight internment in court.
- C. Many lost their property and were treated as potential traitors.
- D. They were forcibly relocated to the East Coast.

14

A consequence of US support for Israel in the Six-Day and Yom Kippur Wars was

- A. OPEC's oil embargo, which was economically harmful for the Middle East.
- B. OPEC's oil embargo, which was economically harmful for many working Americans.
- C. increased Arab support for the United States in international forums like the United Nations.
- D. improved relations between the United States, Saudi Arabia, and Iran.

15

Which of the following were part of the War on Poverty?

I.	Head Start
II.	Department of Housing and Urban Development
III.	Social Security

- A. I and II
- B. I and III
- C. II and III
- D. I, II, and III

16

Cesar Chavez and the United Farm Workers

- A. supported Mexicans who wanted to join the Bracero Program and become guest workers in the United States.
- B. supported Mexican-American agricultural workers in California and the Southwest, and also provided a foundation for later advocacy groups supporting the rights of Hispanic Americans.
- C. worked on behalf of Texas farmers to coordinate agreements with agricultural workers from Mexico.
- D. none of the above

17

Which of the following is generally considered to mark the beginning of the movement for LGBT civil rights in the US?

- A. the first Gay Pride marches in New York, Chicago, and San Francisco
- B. the election of Harvey Milk to the San Francisco Board of Supervisors
- C. activism and dialogue surrounding the AIDS crisis
- D. the Stonewall Riots

18

Which of the following best explains the difference between the philosophies of the Rev. Dr. Martin Luther King Jr. and Malcolm X?

- A. Dr. King believed that African Americans should focus on empowering black communities, while Malcolm X believed that African Americans should focus on racial integration.
- B. Dr. King believed that African Americans should focus on racial integration, while Malcolm X believed that African Americans should focus on empowering black communities.
- C. Dr. King believed that African Americans should focus on political change, while Malcolm X believed that African Americans should focus on social change.
- D. Dr. King and Malcolm X did not differ in their philosophies on civil rights.

19

Which of the following best explains the impact of the Watergate scandal on the United States?

- A. President Nixon was impeached.
- B. President Nixon declined to seek a second term of office.
- C. Americans lost faith in the federal government.
- D. Americans began supporting third-party candidates more.

20

Which of the following is a hallmark of conservative ideology?

- A. open borders to facilitate international trade
- B. low taxes
- C. labor rights
- D. a small, efficient military

21

The United States invaded Afghanistan following the terrorist attacks of September 11, 2001

- A. in order to defeat the Taliban, who had attacked the United States.
- B. in order to capture Osama bin Laden and al Qaeda, who had attacked the United States and who were harbored by the Taliban, the government of Afghanistan.
- C. in order to defeat al Qaeda, the government of Afghanistan.
- D. in order to defeat al Qaeda, which held weapons of mass destruction in Afghanistan.

22

The Patriot Act was controversial because it

A. permitted the US to search for weapons of mass destruction in Iraq, following the terrorist attacks on September 11, 2001; however, many believed that Iraq had not been involved in planning these attacks.

B. expanded the NSA's ability to spy on foreign heads of state, a violation of international law.

C. established Guantanamo Bay as a detention center for suspected terrorists captured in the War on Terror but without allowing them visits from the International Committee of the Red Cross, a violation of the Geneva Convention.

D. broadened the government's powers of surveillance over the activities of American citizens, interpreted as a violation of Americans' rights under the Fourth Amendment and other rights to privacy.

23

Why was the prison opened at the US naval base at Guantanamo Bay, Cuba, following the terrorist attacks of September 11, 2001, so controversial?

A. Surveillance programs secretly run from the prison at Guantanamo were found to have violated privacy laws in the United States.

B. Both Democrats and Republicans argued that prisoners at Guantanamo Bay should be moved to prisons within the United States to save money, as the facility at Guantanamo was enormously expensive.

C. Prisoners at Guantanamo Bay were denied the rights normally granted to prisoners of war under the Geneva Convention, to which the United States is a party.

D. Many US citizens were found to have been mistakenly imprisoned in Guantanamo for crimes they did not commit.

24

The United States invaded and occupied Iraq during Operation Iraqi Freedom in 2003

A. under the faulty premise that Saddam Hussein held weapons of mass destruction and was linked to al Qaeda, which had recently attacked the US.

B. in order to capture Osama bin Laden, who was under the protection of Saddam Hussein.

C. after it was proven that Iraq provided al Qaeda with weapons it used to attack the United States on 9/11.

D. because Iraq attacked the United States on September 11, 2001.

25

Which of the following best describes the approach taken by the Reagan administration to counter the Soviet Union?

A. bilateral diplomacy
B. direct military confrontation
C. engagement in multilateral fora such as the United Nations
D. escalation of arms production and proxy warfare

Read the excerpt and answer the questions that follow.

> To ensure the peaceful development of nations, free from coercion, the United States has taken a leading part in establishing the United Nations. The United Nations is designed to make possible lasting freedom and independence for all its members. We shall not realize our objectives, however, unless we are willing to help free peoples to maintain their free institutions and their national integrity against aggressive movements that seek to impose upon them totalitarian regimes. This is no more than a frank recognition that totalitarian regimes imposed on free peoples, by direct or indirect aggression, undermine the foundations of international peace and hence the security of the United States.
>
> The peoples of a number of countries of the world have recently had totalitarian regimes forced upon them against their will. The Government of the United States has made frequent protests against coercion and intimidation, in violation of the Yalta agreement, in Poland, Rumania, and Bulgaria. I must also state that in a number of other countries there have been similar developments.
>
> At the present moment in world history nearly every nation must choose between alternative ways of life. The choice is too often not a free one.
>
> One way of life is based upon the will of the majority, and is distinguished by free institutions, representative government, free elections, guarantees of individual liberty, freedom of speech and religion, and freedom from political oppression.
>
> The second way of life is based upon the will of a minority forcibly imposed upon the majority. It relies upon terror and oppression, a controlled press and radio; fixed elections, and the suppression of personal freedoms.
>
> I believe that it must be the policy of the United States to support free peoples who are resisting attempted subjugation by armed minorities or by outside pressures.
>
> 80th Cong. 171 (1947) (Statement of Harry Truman, President of the United States) March 12, 1947 (Truman Doctrine)

26

How does Truman differentiate between the two ways of life he discusses in his speech?

A. He describes one as better than the other.

B. He describes one as based on free institutions, speech, elections, religion, but politically oppressive, while the other is based on oppression, suppressed radio, press, and personal freedoms, but with some political freedoms.

C. He describes one free from political oppression, and the other with only limited political freedoms.

D. He describes one as based on free institutions, speech, elections, religion, and freedom from political oppression, while the other is based on oppression, rigged elections, and suppressed radio, press, and personal freedoms.

27

Read this sentence from the text.

> This is no more than a frank recognition that totalitarian regimes imposed on free peoples, by direct or indirect aggression, undermine the foundations of international peace and hence the security of the United States.

In the context of the excerpt, how is this idea comparable to the Bush doctrine of preemption?

A. It argues that communism is a threat to US security.

B. It states that the US must protect its national sovereignty.

C. It argues that the US must intervene in countries before they are taken over by totalitarian forces; otherwise, national security is at risk.

D. It argues that the US must intervene in countries after they are taken over by totalitarian forces; otherwise, national security is at risk.

28

When discussing the "two ways of life," what is Truman describing?

A. the differences between communism and democratic capitalism—that is, between the US and the USSR

B. the differences between communism and democratic totalitarianism—that is, between the USSR and the European Union

C. the differences between communism and fascism—that is, between the USSR and Nazi Germany

D. the differences between democratic capitalism and fascism—that is, between the US and the USSR

29

Read this excerpt from the text.

> The peoples of a number of countries of the world have recently had totalitarian regimes forced upon them against their will. The Government of the United States has made frequent protests against coercion and intimidation, in violation of the Yalta agreement, in Poland, Rumania, and Bulgaria. I must also state that in a number of other countries there have been similar developments.

To which historical developments is Truman referring?

A. the occupation of the Sudetenland and Poland, among other European countries, by Hitler

B. the occupation of several Eastern European countries by Stalin

C. the construction of the Berlin Wall and the occupation of Poland, Romania, and Bulgaria by the USSR

D. the construction of the Iron Curtain

30

A historian of the Cold War would most likely use this excerpt from Truman's speech in order to help answer which of the following questions?

A. How did the United States determine its foreign policy following the Second World War?

B. What were the two ways of life available to the world following the Second World War?

C. What is the purpose of the United Nations?

D. What were twentieth-century American values?

Answer Key

World History Pre-1450

1)

- A. Incorrect. The Hittites expanded overland.
- **B. Correct.** The Hittites were skilled charioteers and were early pioneers of iron weaponry.
- C. Incorrect. The Hittites created their own weapons; furthermore, they preceded ancient Greek development.
- D. Incorrect. The Hittites worked with iron.

2)

- A. Incorrect. The Peloponnesian War was between Sparta and Athens, not Sparta and Crete.
- B. Incorrect. The Peloponnesian War was fought between Greeks in Peloponnesus and Central Greece, not in Anatolia.
- C. Incorrect. The Peloponnesian War did not involve Persia.
- **D. Correct.** The Peloponnesian War was between the major Greek powers.

3)

- **A. Correct.** Developing agricultural practices in the Neolithic Era allowed humans to establish settled societies sustained by reliable food sources.
- B. Incorrect. While the wheel was an important development in the Neolithic Era, it was just one part of the major change in human behavior exhibited in that era: the development of settled societies.

C. Incorrect. The use of bronze was a defining characteristic of the eponymous Bronze Age, which followed the Neolithic Era.

D. Incorrect. While it is likely that early medical treatment developed in the Neolithic Era, again, this was not a defining characteristic of this period; furthermore it was made possible by the development of settled societies.

4)

A. Incorrect. In the Neolithic Era, only *Homo sapiens* would exist, but during the Paleolithic Era, other hominids existed.

B. Correct. During the Paleolithic Era, hominids like *Australopithecus* and later, *Homo habilis, Homo erectus, Homo neanderthalensis* lived.

C. Incorrect. Humans began changing their behavior; eventually *Homo sapiens* would begin to practice agriculture and settle communities while other hominids would die out. It is still not clear why other hominids died out or, indeed, whether they coexisted with our ancestors at all (although it seems possible that *Homo sapiens* and *Homo neanderthalensis* did coexist).

D. Incorrect. A number of early humans coexisted and were evolving.

5)

A. Correct. By the Neolithic Era, other hominids had died out.

B. Incorrect. Other hominids did not survive beyond the Paleolithic Era.

C. Incorrect. It is unclear why other hominids died out.

D. Incorrect. *Homo sapiens* existed.

6)

A. Incorrect. Development of bronze metallurgy was widespread.

B. Incorrect. Evidence of bronze metallurgy has been found throughout Eurasia.

C. Correct. Humans began using bronze globally and concurrently.

D. Incorrect. Several different civilizations used bronze.

7)

A. Correct. The caste system is a social hierarchy rooted in religious tradition. It is not possible to change the caste into which one is born.

B. Incorrect. While the caste system is a social hierarchy, and while there is more social and economic flexibility within it than before, it is not possible to move from one caste to another.

C. Incorrect. One's position in the hierarchy is determined by birth; a person is born into his or her caste, and that position is permanent.

D. Incorrect. While this definition is true, it leaves out the traditionally religious nature of the caste system.

8)

- A. Incorrect. While early Chinese and Fertile Crescent civilizations were both organized under an emperor or king, this answer choice is incomplete.
- B. Incorrect. Again, while these civilizations did both have written languages, this answer choice is also incomplete, given the other possible responses.
- C. Incorrect. Monotheism did not exist in either of these regions, aside from Judaism practiced by the Hebrews, a small tribe in the Levant who were not politically powerful.
- D. **Correct.** China and the Fertile Crescent civilizations like the Sumerians, Assyrians, Babylonians, Egyptians, and Akkadians had imperial or monarchical governments; they also developed written languages.

9)

- A. Incorrect. Early societies in the Fertile Crescent developed irrigation before developing bronze.
- B. Incorrect. The Neolithic Era preceded the Bronze Age.
- C. Incorrect. Copper is a naturally occurring element, from which humans create bronze.
- D. **Correct.** Bronze improved weapons and tools; improved weaponry meant expanded control over territory and more secure societies that could continue to develop.

10)

- A. Incorrect. Confucianism emerged in China during the Spring and Autumn Period, before the Qin dynasty.
- B. Incorrect. Written Chinese is believed to have developed as early as the Shang dynasty period, several centuries earlier.
- C. **Correct.** Under the Qin dynasty, the emperor centralized Chinese bureaucracy and standardized weights and measures in order to centralize and consolidate imperial power.
- D. Incorrect. A and B are incorrect.

11)

- A. **Correct.** Early Chinese writing evolved under the Shang dynasty.
- B. Incorrect. The Mandate of Heaven developed under the Zhou dynasty.
- C. Incorrect. The Forbidden City was constructed under the Ming dynasty.
- D. Incorrect. Only choice A is correct.

12)

    A.   Incorrect. Several early civilizations in the Fertile Crescent developed irrigation.

    B.   Incorrect. The Sumerians developed cuneiform.

    C.   **Correct.** King Hammurabi's code metedized out justice on an equal basis ("an eye for an eye, a tooth for a tooth").

    D.   Incorrect. The Hittites mastered iron weaponry and charioteering.

13)

    A.   Incorrect. This answer describes East Asia.

    B.   **Correct.** This describes the traditional Caste system of the subcontinent.

    C.   Incorrect. While Buddhism emerged in India, it is more widely practiced in East and Southeast Asia.

    D.   Incorrect. China had an exam-based administrative hierarchy.

14)

    A.   **Correct.** Buddhism, though it emerged in India, is mainly practiced throughout the Himalayas, East Asia, and Southeast Asia.

    B.   Incorrect. While Buddhism developed in India, it is not widely practiced there.

    C.   Incorrect. Buddhism is practiced throughout Tibet, East Asia, and Southeast Asia.

    D.   Incorrect. Buddhism is widespread not only in Southeast Asia, but also in East Asia and Tibet.

15)

    A.   Incorrect. The Magyars did not topple the Holy Roman Empire; furthermore, their incursions into Europe had been several hundred years prior.

    B.   **Correct.** The continental—indeed, global—impact of the Black Death destabilized much of Europe.

    C.   Incorrect. The Black Death actually destabilized the Mongol Empire.

    D.   Incorrect. The Umayyads reached Iberia long before the Black Death.

16)

    A.   Incorrect. The Catholic Church gained power and became an important stabilizing force in Western Europe.

    B.   Incorrect. The Byzantine Empire expanded in the Balkans, the Middle East, and North Africa.

C. Incorrect. The Holy Roman Empire was consolidated later under Otto I in 962.

D. **Correct.** Charlemagne was Frankish and stabilized parts of Western and Central Europe; most of the Carolingian Empire eventually became France.

17)

A. Incorrect. Venice was not a major global colonial power, nor did it develop mercantilism.

B. Incorrect. While Venice was a center of intellectual and cultural development, this was not a major reason for development of modern banking there.

C. Correct. As a commercial center and well-situated to handle goods arriving in Europe from the Silk Road and from Africa, Venice developed banking institutions that influenced modern banking.

D. Incorrect. As a center of international trade, Venice was strongly affected by the plague.

18)

A. Incorrect. While the time the Jewish people spent in Egypt is an important part of Jewish history, Judaism developed in Southwest Asia, not North Africa.

B. Correct. Judaism emerged in the area that is today home to Israelis and Palestinians.

C. Incorrect. The Jewish presence in Mesopotamia was a key time in Jewish history; however, Judaism did not emerge there.

D. Incorrect. The Levant can be considered part of the Fertile Crescent; however, B is the better answer because it is more specific. In the case of a question where more than one answer could be chosen, however, both of these answers would be correct.

19)

A. Incorrect. Serfs, while limited in their freedom, were not truly slaves; they could not be bought or sold.

B. Correct. Serfs were bonded to the land—they had to work it for the lord—however, the lord was obligated to protect them.

C. Incorrect. Serfs did not fight.

D. Incorrect. Serfs could not purchase individual freedom by fighting for their lords.

20)

- A. Incorrect. Both Sunnis and Shi'ites believed in extending Islam everywhere beyond the Arabian Peninsula.
- B. Incorrect. Both Sunnis and Shi'ites agreed that military conquest was vital in order to spread Islam.
- C. Incorrect. Both Sunnis and Shi'ites agreed with the teachings of Muhammad, including the philosophy of the "People of the Book."
- **D. Correct.** Sunnis believed that the Meccan elites should take over leadership of Muslims, while Shi'ite believed that Muhammad's cousin Ali was Muhammad's rightful successor.

21)

- A. Incorrect. Crusaders returned to Europe having been exposed to learning and technology in the Middle East that was, at the time, unknown in Europe.
- **B. Correct.** European powers controlled some areas in the Levant, but only temporarily.
- C. Incorrect. Crusaders were entitled to indulgences—forgiveness for any sins committed in conflict.
- D. Incorrect. One incentive for Europeans to fight in the Crusades was the possibility of amassing personal wealth through plunder.

22)

- A. Incorrect. Russia eventually embraced Orthodox Christianity, which was originally introduced to Russia as Greek Orthodox Christianity as practiced by the Byzantines.
- B. Incorrect. Vladimir I did not convert to Catholicism.
- **C. Correct.** Byzantine missionaries spread Orthodox Christianity north; Vladimir I converted and a tradition of Orthodox Christianity took root in Russia and Ukraine.
- D. Incorrect. Russia's Orthodox tradition came from Byzantium.

23)

- A. Incorrect. Mongol power had actually been a factor in the decline of the Abbasids.
- B. Incorrect. The Yuan dynasty was a Mongol dynasty.
- **C. Correct.** Ivan the Great had weakened Mongol power in Northwest Asia, while the Ming had taken control of China from the Mongols.
- D. Incorrect. The Abbasid Caliphate was a non-factor in Mongol decline, while Ivan the Great played an important role in it.

24)

- **A. Correct.** Papal endorsement of Charlemagne gave his rule legitimacy.
- B. Incorrect. Charlemagne did not promise to end the feudal system, which actually brought stability to Europe.
- C. Incorrect. The Crusades did not begin until 1096. Charlemagne was crowned in 800.
- D. Incorrect. Charlemagne was supported by the church.

25)

- A. Incorrect. Both churches were powerful in their respective regions.
- **B. Correct.** At the time, the pope controlled the Papal States in Italy, which were political territories; furthermore, he was extremely influential among European leaders.
- C. Incorrect. While Rome was a significant city, this was not the reason for the church's power; the importance of Christianity among Europeans was.
- D. Incorrect. The pope was extremely influential; however his political control was generally indirect.

26)

- A. Incorrect. While fighters were promised indulgences, this was not the only encouragement they received to fight in the Crusades.
- B. Incorrect. Amassing wealth was an incentive to join the Crusades, but it was not the only one.
- C. Incorrect. Many fighters were driven by their faith to counter perceived threats to Christianity, but this answer choice is incomplete given the other options available.
- **D. Correct.** All of the answer choices are true.

27)

- A. Incorrect. The Ming dynasty consolidated power in China; Ivan the Great controlled Russia as the Mongols went into decline.
- B. Incorrect. The Qin constructed the Great Wall.
- **C. Correct.** Ming power extended into Southeast Asia, Central Asia, and Korea; the Ming developed trade and exacted tribute from local leaders.
- D. Incorrect. While the Ming encouraged oceanic exploration, they did not develop a major navy.

28)

- A. Incorrect. Mali did not control the trans-Saharan trade routes.
- B. Incorrect. The Kingdom of Mali embraced Islam.

C. **Correct.** Mali became wealthy due to gold and salt, valuable natural resources.

D. Incorrect. Mali did not control the trans-Saharan trade routes.

29)

A. Incorrect. Fighters did not return with Middle Eastern wives and diversity in Europe did not increase.

B. Incorrect. While some returning Europeans had learned a new language, this alone was not enough of a widespread phenomenon to impact international trade.

C. **Correct.** Crusaders had gained knowledge of navigation, technology, medicine, and science—incidentally, all knowledge and skills necessary in warfare—and transferred this knowledge to Europe, helping spark the Scientific Revolution and the Renaissance.

D. Incorrect. In fact, at times the Orthodox Church and the Catholic Church worked together against Muslims.

30)

A. Incorrect. Justinian's strong leadership and rule of law undoubtedly contributed to the stability of the Byzantine Empire, but the empire enjoyed other advantages, too.

B. Incorrect. Constantinople was situated very strategically; however, the city's location was not the only reason for Byzantine success.

C. Incorrect. Justinian was able to expand Byzantine territory, but the empire would not have been sustainable without other advantages.

D. **Correct.** All of the answer choices present essential factors in Byzantine organization and stability in the face of decline in the West.

World History Post-1450

1)

- A. Incorrect. Martin Luther was a Catholic monk; he originally sought reform within the Catholic Church.
- **B. Correct.** Martin Luther and his followers opposed corruption in the church and wanted changes.
- C. Incorrect. The Reformation was not originally a political movement.
- D. Incorrect. Again, Martin Luther wanted reform, not to overthrow the papacy or the church.

2)

- A. Incorrect. The Hundred Years' War was an intra-European war.
- B. Incorrect. The Hundred Years' War occurred before the Reformation and was a conflict mainly between England and France; the church was not a major figure.
- C. Incorrect. This was not a factor of the Hundred Years' War.
- **D. Correct.** The Hundred Years' War was really an ongoing conflict between different European ethnic groups (mainly, the French and the English).

3)

- A. Incorrect. While the Americas were of interest to many Renaissance figures, the historical movement did not rely on developments in the Western Hemisphere.
- B. Incorrect. African music and culture had no bearing on the Renaissance.
- C. Incorrect. While Christians came from Constantinople following its conquest by the Ottomans, their influence on the Renaissance came from the classical texts and learning they brought, not from their Christian faith.
- **D. Correct.** Science and technology imported from the Middle East during the Crusades, coupled with a resurgence of classical philosophy, art, and scholarship imported by Byzantine refugees, inspired the Renaissance.

4)

- **A. Correct.** The peasants and bourgeoisie were dissatisfied with bearing the brunt of the heavy tax burden; meanwhile, poor harvests led to food shortages and panic in rural areas. These factors, along with Enlightenment thought and recent revolutions elsewhere, spurred the French Revolution.
- B. Incorrect. Napoleon came to power after the French Revolution, providing stability in a chaotic period.

C. Incorrect. The Congress of Vienna was a conference held after the initial defeat of Napoleon to determine the future of Europe. It occurred after the French Revolution.

D. Incorrect. The reign of Louis XIV weakened the nobility and centralized power under the king. In the long term, weakening the nobility and isolating them at Versailles contributed to the circumstances that enabled the French Revolution. However, his reign alone did not cause it, and he was long dead by the time the Revolution began.

5)

A. Incorrect. While the Treaty of Westphalia did end the Thirty Years' War, this answer choice is incomplete given the other possibilities offered.

B. Incorrect. Again, while this is true, it is incorrect due to the other options presented.

C. Incorrect. The Treaty of Westphalia is considered the foundation of modern international relations as it is based on the idea of state sovereignty; however, due to the other answer choices, this one is incorrect.

D. Correct. All of these answer choices are correct.

6)

A. Incorrect. The Catholic Church was not divided over the Counter-Reformation.

B. Correct. The Counter-Reformation re-converted Protestants back to Catholicism, spread Catholic education, and fought heresy.

C. Incorrect. While the Counter-Reformation embraced spreading Catholicism globally, it did not emerge in response to exploration in the Western Hemisphere.

D. Incorrect. Enlightenment thought did not truly emerge for another century.

8)

A. Incorrect. Some European powers had already made slavery illegal (legally, if not in practice).

B. Correct. Abolitionist European powers were unwilling to support the South economically, due to the Confederacy's stance on slavery.

C. Incorrect. While rapidly industrializing Europe needed cotton, many European countries ceased trade with the states that seceded from the Union and developed sources of cotton elsewhere (in Egypt and India, for example).

D. Incorrect. B is the correct answer choice.

7)

A. Incorrect. France supported the United States in order to weaken the British.

B. Incorrect. Spain retained control over its territories in the Americas, which included substantial land in North America.

C. Correct. The Enlightenment ideals that inspired the American Revolution and the revolution's success helped inspire the French Revolution and other movements.

D. Incorrect. International trade continued with the resource-rich United States.

9)

A. Incorrect. Oliver Cromwell controlled the country following the Civil War, subduing revolt in Ireland and defeating Charles in Scotland.

B. Incorrect. The Glorious Revolution was mainly a religious, not ethnic, movement; in fact, William of Orange was Dutch.

C. Correct. The Glorious Revolution, in which the Protestants William and Mary deposed the Catholic James II, secured a future of Protestant monarchies in Britain.

D. Incorrect. Separatists, not Puritans, wanted to separate from the Church of England; less radical, Puritans sought reform.

10)

A. Incorrect. Britain did not occupy China, although it did control Hong Kong, which remained a colony until 1997.

B. Incorrect. China was not successful in the Opium Wars.

C. Incorrect. Trade treaties at the time did not favor China.

D. Correct. Britain gained economic and commercial privileges in China it had previously not had, including gaining Hong Kong, freedom of movement in China, and access to ports.

11)

A. Incorrect. European control over the Americas was limited by the nineteenth century; furthermore, natural resources gleaned through imperialism went to power industrialization in Europe, not elsewhere.

B. Correct. The philosophy of taking on the "white man's burden" and the competition for global control of territory between European powers (among other factors) drove imperialism.

C. Incorrect. European imperial powers did not fuel industrialization in the Americas.

D. Incorrect. European imperialists sought resources to power industry in Europe.

12)

- **A. Correct.** The valuable routes into and through the Red Sea were essential for the British economy and Britain's connections to its colonies in India, East Africa, South Africa, and Australia. The security of those routes was of paramount importance.
- B. Incorrect. Mecca and Medina are both inland cities and not major centers of global trade.
- C. Incorrect. Inland Somalia, with limited natural resources, was not a major concern.
- D. Incorrect. Britain controlled substantial territory throughout sub-Saharan Africa.

13)

- A. Incorrect. The 1884 Berlin Conference focused on Africa, not China.
- B. Incorrect. Spheres of influence were negotiated over time with China and in the context of instability and conflict there, not between European powers alone; furthermore, the Berlin Conference concentrated on imperialism in Africa, not Asia.
- **C. Correct.** The 1884 Berlin Conference determined the division of Africa into colonies between the European imperial powers. This was done without regard for or consultation with Africans.
- D. Incorrect. The Triple Alliance was rooted in the collapse of the Three Emperors' League (an alliance between Russia, Germany, and Austria-Hungary); after Germany and Austria-Hungary established the secret Dual Alliance and assisted Italy against France, the Triple Alliance was born. Russia later allied with Britain and France, forming the Triple Entente. These relationships were the basis for the system of alliances leading to the First World War; however, they were not developed at the Berlin Conference.

14)

- **A. Correct.** The Three Emperors' League reflected the principles of state sovereignty and non-interference.
- B. Incorrect. The Three Emperors' League was not an active military alliance.
- C. Incorrect. There was no explicit agreement of financial support in the Three Emperors' League.
- D. Incorrect. The Three Emperors' League was not a free-trade agreement, nor was it an active military alliance.

15)

- **A.** Incorrect. Russia's strategy was land-based expansion; it did not have a strong navy until the twentieth century.
- **B.** **Correct.** Russia expanded to the east, taking control of Siberia. Russia also extended westward to an extent, controlling part of Eastern Europe.
- **C.** Incorrect. Russia expanded and employed developmental strategies under a number of czars, including Catherine the Great and Peter the Great. In terms of industrialization, some efforts were made under the Romanovs; however, industrialization accelerated under the Soviets.
- **D.** Incorrect. Russia engaged in empire building throughout Eurasia well into the twentieth century; some argue that it has continued to do so in Crimea and Ukraine today.

16)

- **A.** Incorrect. Nationalism did not benefit the Austro-Hungarian Empire: smaller ethnic groups living in territory controlled by the empire wanted their independence due to nationalism.
- **B.** Incorrect. The Austro-Hungarian Empire began losing control over its Balkan territories due to nationalism and due to interference from Russia, which supported Slavic minorities in the Balkans.
- **C.** Incorrect. Nationalism drove ethnic groups to seek self-rule and independence, not representation in government.
- **D.** **Correct.** Nationalism triggered independence movements and advocacy.

17)

- **A.** Incorrect. Many of the boundaries are the modern borders of Middle Eastern countries today, so the region has been greatly affected.
- **B.** **Correct.** Borders did not take into account history or ethnic groups; installed rulers did not necessarily have legitimacy in the eyes of the people, leading to political instability and violence.
- **C.** Incorrect. The protectorates did not improve governance or stabilize the region following the decline of the Ottoman Empire.
- **D.** Incorrect. Outside investment in strategic resources (like oil) has contributed to instability in the region by providing support to illegitimate rulers and contributing to income inequality and conflict.

18)

- **A.** Incorrect. During the Meiji Restoration, Japan abolished traditional institutions like feudalism and began pursuing western-style development.
- **B.** **Correct.** The Meiji Restoration was a period of industrialization and westernization in Japan.

19)

- C. Incorrect. The Meiji Restoration occurred before Japanese imperialism began throughout Asia.
- D. Incorrect. The Meiji Restoration was a socioeconomic movement, not a return to traditional cultural practices.

19)

- A. Incorrect. The American Revolution preceded the French Revolution. Early industrialization had begun in the late eighteenth and early nineteenth centuries, around the same time as the revolutions; however, the First World War would not break out until 1914.
- **B. Correct.** The American Revolution preceded the French Revolution; resulting instability in France eventually led to the rise of Napoleon. Shifting European alliances triggered the First World War in the early twentieth century.
- C. Incorrect. Like answer choice A, the American Revolution preceded the French Revolution and the Industrial Revolution began at roughly the same time. WWI did not occur until the twentieth century.
- D. Incorrect. The Rape of Nanjing occurred in 1937; otherwise the events are in order.

20)

- A. Incorrect. Italian nationalism inspired unification of the small political entities of the Italian Peninsula.
- **B. Correct.** The Congress of Vienna followed the Napoleonic Wars; it was a meeting of European powers to determine how to manage Europe.
- C. Incorrect. German unification was largely a result of nationalism, as the small territories of Central Europe united under Prussia thanks to shared language, cultural practices, and other commonalities.
- D. Incorrect. During the Franco-Prussian War, Prussia attacked France to regain control over Alsace-Lorraine, which it had lost to Napoleon. Prussian nationalism, in part, inspired this war, as France was a long-time rival.

21)

- A. Incorrect. These revolutions both opposed the wealthiest elites.
- B. Incorrect. Both revolutions took advantage of the discontented and numerous agricultural workers, but the French bourgeoisie was mainly concerned with limiting its overwhelming tax burden and controlling more land; likewise, the Russian revolutionaries focused on organizing urban industrial workers more than the Russian agricultural workers.

C. Incorrect. This was a socialist ideal, not a goal of the French Revolution.

D. **Correct.** While the peasantry revolted in the countryside and the people stormed the Bastille in 1789, the French Revolution was based on the Enlightenment ideals embodied in the *Declaration of the Rights of Man and Citizen* issued by the National Constituent Assembly dominated by the Bourgeoisie of the Third Estate. Likewise, the Russian Revolution was instigated by Lenin and Trotsky, urban intellectuals inspired by the socialism of Karl Marx. Lenin and Trotsky helped organize the proletariat in a communist revolution overthrowing the tsar.

22)

A. Incorrect. This explanation is insufficient.

B. **Correct.** The main factors in post-WWI German economic collapse are all addressed here.

C. Incorrect. This explanation does not account for global economic depression.

D. Incorrect. This is untrue.

23)

A. Incorrect. China was not a US ally.

B. Incorrect. The Soviet Union was certainly not a US ally.

C. Incorrect. While the People's Republic of China was not represented at the UN, this was not the reason for the Sino-Soviet Split; the USSR recognized the PRC.

D. **Correct.** The Soviet establishment became increasingly alarmed at Maoist interpretations of communism, which differed from Marxism-Leninism.

24)

A. Incorrect. Some scholars date the beginning of WWII to Japan's invasion of Manchuria, which occurred before the 1937 Rape of Nanjing.

B. Incorrect. Japan annexed Korea in 1910 following the growth of its influence in East Asia after the Russo-Japanese War and other developments. This was before the First World War.

C. **Correct.** Given Japan's role as an Axis power and the conflict in East Asia, some historians believe that WWII began with Japan's invasion of Manchuria in 1931, earlier than Hitler's invasion of Poland in 1939.

D. Incorrect. The Chinese Civil War took place throughout the 1930s and after WWII; it was not a cause of the Second World War.

25)

A. Incorrect. While decolonization resulted in independence for former colonies (usually following a period of international or United Nations supervision), this answer choice is incorrect given the other options presented.

B. Incorrect. The United Nations took a leading role in decolonization; however, this answer choice is incomplete.

C. Incorrect. Some countries experienced lengthy and brutal conflict in fighting for their independence and periods of violent instability after independence; again, though, this is not a complete answer given the other choices.

D. Correct. All of the answer choices provided are true.

26)

A. Incorrect. Afghanistan did not come under Indian influence, although it did become vulnerable to extremist influences.

B. Correct. Afghanistan became unstable and entered into a period of civil war that ended only with the rise of the extremist Taliban, who brought stability to much of the country—along with an ideology embracing tribalism and extremely traditional Islamic values.

C. Incorrect. While greatly influenced by Pakistan, Afghanistan did not join that country.

D. Incorrect. Technically, neither NATO nor any other international organization governed Afghanistan, though a US-led international presence strongly influenced Afghan politics during the United States' war in Afghanistan in the early twenty-first century.

27)

A. Correct. The Warsaw Pact was a mutual defense agreement between Eastern European countries and the USSR in response to NATO.

B. Incorrect. The Warsaw Pact included more than two countries.

C. Incorrect. While it could be argued that the Warsaw Pact reflected Soviet control over Eastern Europe, this answer choice is not specific enough.

D. Incorrect. The Warsaw Pact was defense agreement, not simply a political division.

28)

A. Correct. Only nine years after independence, Somalia endured a coup and came under a dictatorship. A strong civil society would have strengthened a democratic government, making it less susceptible to a coup.

B. Incorrect. Somalia's alliance with the USSR was clearly strategic as it attacked a Soviet ally and willingly accepted aid from the United States.

C. Incorrect. Somalia was clearly divided among clans, leading to Barre's downfall.

D. Incorrect. Improving ties with the communist Soviet Union would not improve a country's position in the global capitalist market; furthermore, under Barre, conflict and shifting allegiances, not international trade, were priorities.

29)

A. Incorrect. While this is true, it is not typical of most former colonies in Africa.

B. Correct. The boundaries of many African countries were created at the 1885 Berlin Conference when Africa was divided among European powers; as a result, ethnic groups have been separated by international borders and many countries have a limited or no sense of national identity.

C. Incorrect. Somalia experimented with alliances with both Cold War powers.

D. Incorrect. The United Nations provided a forum where many small countries—former African colonies among them—could develop diplomatic blocs (such as the Non-Aligned Movement) and effectively increase their influence in international affairs.

30)

A. Incorrect. As the conflict was a proxy war between the Cold War powers, the United States and Soviet Union never came into military conflict.

B. Incorrect. The US and USSR did not seek a diplomatic solution to resolve the conflict.

C. Correct. The Cold War powers did not take direct military action in the war between Somalia and Ethiopia.

D. Incorrect. As a proxy war between the US and USSR, the conflict was a Cold War phenomenon.

US History to 1877

1)

A. Incorrect. The Mayflower Compact was written by one Christian group—Separatists.

B. Incorrect. The Mayflower Compact articulated terms of governance among European settlers; it was not a treaty with other parties.

C. Correct. As a governing document, the Mayflower Compact was notable in that it provided for governance with the consent of the governed, a departure from British rule.

D. Incorrect. The Mayflower Compact was written by Separatists.

2)

A. Correct. Southern geography and climate lent itself to labor-intensive plantation agriculture, for which the colonists exploited slave labor. Natural harbors in the north fostered urban development, while the land was more appropriate for smaller farms.

B. Incorrect. The reverse was true.

C. Incorrect. All the colonies had wealthy, elite classes, in addition to working classes, indentured servants, and slaves.

D. Incorrect. Economic and cultural differences developed among the colonies.

3)

A. Incorrect. While some colonists were quite wealthy, colonial wealth paled in the face of British wealth.

B. Incorrect. The colonists did not have superior weaponry.

C. Correct. The colonial military did have strong leaders, and an intimate knowledge of the terrain, many having been born there.

D. Incorrect. Britain had an experienced military with substantial experience fighting in Europe and elsewhere. In addition, King George III hired Hessian mercenaries from Germany to supplement British troops.

4)

A. Incorrect. While tobacco was a major source of income for the British, this answer choice does not sufficiently respond to the question.

B. Incorrect. Rice was an important crop in the mid-Atlantic colonies; however, this response is incomplete given the other answer choices.

- C. Incorrect. While beaver pelts were essential to North American trade, particularly throughout Canada, this answer choice is incomplete.
- D. **Correct.** Tobacco, rice, and beaver pelts were all enormously popular in Europe and very profitable North American resources.

5)

- A. Incorrect. The British and French colonial presence did not extend as far west as the Sioux and Cheyenne lands.
- B. **Correct.** During the French and Indian War, the British were allied with the Iroquois and the French with the Algonquin throughout the northeast (today, Ontario, Upstate New York, and the Great Lakes region).
- C. Incorrect. The Cherokee and Seminole were not involved in British-French conflict.
- D. Incorrect. Colonial power did not reach as far west as Apache territory.

6)

- A. Incorrect. The views of the Federalists and Anti-Federalists differed a great deal.
- B. Incorrect. The Bill of Rights was a compromise measure; it was not originally a Federalist contribution.
- C. Incorrect. The reverse was true.
- D. **Correct.** The Federalists were the driving force behind a stronger Constitution that would empower the United States federal government; the Anti-Federalists worked to protect state sovereignty and ensured the passage of the Bill of Rights to protect certain rights not explicitly guaranteed in the Constitution itself.

7)

- A. **Correct.** The Democratic-Republicans, descended from the Anti-Federalists, opposed a strong federal government and urban business interests, focusing on agrarian issues.
- B. Incorrect. The Democratic-Republicans focused on rural constituents.
- C. Incorrect. While the Democratic-Republicans surely did not favor a strong federal government, their priority was not supporting big business or banking.
- D. Incorrect. The Democratic-Republicans were against federalism.

8)

    A.   Incorrect. This did not occur until after Jackson had been elected president.

    B.   **Correct.** Jackson was extremely popular among the lower classes and rural farmers of the South; changing voting laws to allow dispossessed white males to vote expanded the electorate, giving him a huge advantage.

    C.   Incorrect. Jackson was unpopular with the elite landowners of the North.

    D.   Incorrect. Jackson and Calhoun were fierce rivals with a poor personal and professional relationship.

9)

    A.   **Correct.** Hispanic residents of the land the United States gained in the Treaty of Guadalupe Hidalgo did not obtain all they were promised; in fact, many lost their property and were not treated equally under the law or in society.

    B.   Incorrect. Those Hispanic residents of Mexico who were living on territory ceded to the United States did not receive restitution for losses suffered in violation of the Treaty of Guadalupe Hidalgo.

    C.   Incorrect. Latinos and Latinas living in United States territory often experienced unequal treatment under the law and in social situations.

    D.   Incorrect. Many people of Mexican descent stayed in what became the United States following the Mexican-American War.

10)

    A.   Incorrect. An individual president was not limited to two terms of service until the twentieth century.

    B.   Incorrect. The system of checks and balances, as built into the Constitution, includes the judicial branch.

    C.   Incorrect. While civilian oversight of the military is an important part of the American government, this answer choice does not properly describe the system of checks and balances reinforced by the three branches of government.

    D.   **Correct.** The Constitutional system of checks and balances is comprised of the three branches of government, which limit each other, thereby limiting federal power.

11)

    A.   **Correct.** Adams was a staunch Federalist who arguably veered into federal overreach with the Alien and Sedition Acts during his presidency.

    B.   Incorrect. As a Federalist, Adams believed the opposite.

    C.   Incorrect. The Bill of Rights was a concession to Anti-Federalists, who feared the Constitution did not adequately protect states' and individual rights.

    D.   Incorrect. The Constitutional Convention was called upon recognition that the Articles of Confederation were too weak.

12)

- A. Incorrect. The Industrial Revolution began in Britain when new technology allowed the faster and more organized production of goods.
- **B. Correct.** The Second Great Awakening was characterized by religious movements like utopianism; interest in romanticism in the arts and humanism led to abolitionism and early progressive ideals.
- C. Incorrect. The Enlightenment was a seventeenth- and eighteenth-century phenomenon in Europe.
- D. Incorrect. The Glorious Revolution had taken place in England over a century before.

13)

- A. Incorrect. The Monroe Doctrine did not attempt to assert US power beyond the Western Hemisphere.
- B. Incorrect. The Monroe Doctrine encompassed Latin America, not just the United States.
- **C. Correct.** The Monroe Doctrine was a US policy designed to insulate Latin America from European influence, increasing US dominance in the region.
- D. Incorrect. While the Monroe Doctrine did result in increased US international involvement, this choice does not specifically answer the question.

14)

- A. Incorrect. France and the early United States had a complex relationship, but this was not the central reason for US anxiety over the Louisiana Purchase.
- **B. Correct.** Despite Jefferson's position as an Anti-Federalist Democrat, he had used executive powers as president to negotiate the purchase without congressional consultation, considered by many as federal overreach.
- C. Incorrect. The needs of Native Americans were not a pressing issue for most Americans, as they considered strategic control of land and, eventually, westward expansion, to be necessary.
- D. Incorrect. This was not the most pressing concern for most Americans, who were still preoccupied with preventing a dictatorship.

15)

- A. Incorrect. At the time, slavery was legal throughout the United States.
- B. Incorrect. Three-quarters of the states must ratify amendments in order for them to take effect.
- **C. Correct.** The Three-Fifths Compromise accounted for slaves as part of a state's population (although they could not vote or enjoy the same rights as white citizens).
- D. Incorrect. Nine states needed to ratify the Constitution for it to go into effect.

16)

    A.   Incorrect. The Louisiana Purchase did not include Texas.

    B.   Incorrect. The territory did not extend to the Pacific Ocean.

    C.   Incorrect. While Lewis and Clark explored this area, the Louisiana Purchase did not include territory through Oregon—control over this land was disputed by the British.

    D.   **Correct.** The United States gained the valuable Port of New Orleans and Mississippi River.

17)

    A.   Incorrect. Today, Constitutionalists refers to politicians and members of the judiciary who believe in following the Constitution today exactly as it was written; it was not a term used in the late eighteenth century.

    B.   Incorrect. The Revolution was over by the time of the Constitutional Convention.

    C.   Incorrect. Federalists were content with the Constitution as it was written.

    D.   **Correct.** Anti-Federalists would not accept the Constitution without the Bill of Rights, believing it did not go far enough to protect individual and states' rights.

18)

    A.   Incorrect. The War of 1812 is widely considered to have ended in a stalemate.

    B.   **Correct.** Tecumseh and the Confederacy wanted to halt US expansion and maintain control over their land.

    C.   Incorrect. Tecumseh never allied with the US.

    D.   Incorrect. The British army did not collapse.

19)

    A.   Incorrect. The Fugitive Slave Act allowed slave owners, not states, to pursue escaped slaves.

    B.   **Correct.** The Fugitive Slave Act—a federal law—actually benefitted those states' rights advocates who also favored slavery.

    C.   Incorrect. The Fugitive Slave Act did not allow states to carry out police actions.

    D.   Incorrect. The Fugitive Slave Act applied to individuals, not states.

20)

- A. Incorrect. The South's technological resources were inferior to those of the North.
- B. Incorrect. European countries ceased trade with the South, finding alternative sources of cotton in protest of slavery.
- **C. Correct.** The Confederacy had excellent military leaders; many Confederate leaders and much of the population strongly believed in the right of states to make decisions without federal interference, not only about slavery but also about trade and other issues.
- D. Incorrect. The Confederacy had limited infrastructure.

21)

- A. Incorrect. The Supreme Court ruled against Dred Scott, who was an escaped slave.
- **B. Correct.** The ruling reinforced the Fugitive Slave Act by forcing Scott to return to a life of slavery.
- C. Incorrect. The ruling strengthened not only the Fugitive Slave Act, but also the Kansas-Nebraska Act; thus, it effectively abolished the Missouri Compromise.
- D. Incorrect. The court did not abolish the Fugitive Slave Act.

22)

- A. Incorrect. While slavery and states' rights to allow it were essential elements of these pieces of legislation, this answer is incomplete in the context of the other choices.
- B. Incorrect. Indeed, the compromises were reached in order to resolve disagreements among politicians; however, this answer is not sufficient, given the other answer choices.
- C. Incorrect. The United States was deeply divided over the role of the federal government, and this division manifested through slavery; still, this answer choice is incorrect given the other choices available.
- **D. Correct.** All of the answer choices are true.

23)

- A. Incorrect. African Americans could not vote until the Fifteenth Amendment was ratified.
- B. Incorrect. Native Americans did not have a political voice in the US.
- C. Incorrect. Popular sovereignty would still benefit settlers in the territories in the long term by increasing their political power.
- **D. Correct.** Popular sovereignty made the expansion of slavery possible.

24)

A. Incorrect. The Dred Scott decision upheld the Fugitive Slave Act.

B. Incorrect. The Compromise of 1850 only permitted the possibility of slavery in a small section of land north of the thirty-sixth parallel in the far West (parts of Utah).

C. Correct. The Kansas-Nebraska Act allowed slavery north of the thirty-sixth parallel throughout the Plains and the Western territories which the Missouri Compromise had previously forbidden.

D. Incorrect. The Fugitive Slave Act did not determine where slavery was legal.

25)

A. Correct. By blocking the South's access to strategic waterways, the Union was able to prevent cotton exports and other vital trade, "strangling" the Confederacy economically.

B. Incorrect. The South was primarily a rural economy.

C. Incorrect. The Anaconda Plan envisioned surrounding the entire South, not just Richmond.

D. Incorrect. The Anaconda Plan strategically interrupted trade; it did not take a tactical military approach.

26)

A. Incorrect. The Federalist Party had declined in the early nineteenth century and never returned to the political scene.

B. Correct. The Civil War devastated the South's economy due to infrastructural damage and international isolation.

C. Incorrect. The Republican Party appeared before the Civil War.

D. Incorrect. The Southern economy suffered from the Civil War.

27)

A. Incorrect. Conditions for most freed slaves did not immediately improve; they continued to face widespread violence and discrimination.

B. Incorrect. With damage to agricultural land and existing infrastructure, the Southern economy and many Southerners suffered; Reconstruction programs did not immediately take effect.

C. Incorrect. Radical Republicans felt that the Reconstruction Acts did not go far enough in punishing the South; others in Congress felt they were too harsh. Likewise, many in the South felt they were unfair.

D. Correct. The Reconstruction Acts effectively placed the South under martial law.

28)

A. Incorrect. The Fifteenth Amendment only enabled African American men to vote. No American women could vote in national elections until the ratification of the Nineteenth Amendment in 1920.

B. Incorrect. African American women were still unable to vote, even though the Fifteenth Amendment allowed African American men to exercise that right. African American women would not be able to vote until 1920.

C. Incorrect. The Fourteenth Amendment ensures equal protection under the law to all Americans, regardless of race, gender, or other categories.

D. **Correct.** The Thirteenth Amendment abolished slavery; the Fourteenth Amendment promised equal protection under the law to all US citizens; the Fifteenth Amendment ensured that (male) African Americans and former slaves could vote.

29)

A. **Correct.** Sharecropping perpetuated racial inequality in the South.

B. Incorrect. The Colored Farmers' Alliance assisted African American farmers.

C. Incorrect. The Reconstruction Acts did not include this provision.

D. Incorrect. While labor unions championed urban workers, most of whom were white, this was not in direct opposition to efforts to advance African Americans in the South; indeed, the Progressive movement brought together activists for these and many diverse causes.

30)

A. Incorrect. Assimilation destroyed many people's connection with their cultures and traditions, but this answer choice is incomplete in the context of the other options.

B. Incorrect. Again, forcing children to leave their families for white schools destroyed their connection with their languages, cultures, and traditions. Moreover, these actions injured their personal bonds with their families and communities—further weakening tribal societies. However, this answer choice is insufficient, given the other answer choices available.

C. Incorrect. Forcing people to leave their homelands for assigned living spaces on reservations fostered social breakdown by interrupting traditional connections with land and dispossessing people of their homes. Again, however, this answer choice is incomplete.

D. **Correct.** All of the above are true.

US History 1877 – Present

1)

- **A. Correct.** The United States was the aggressor in the Spanish-American War—it was never definitively proven that the *Maine* was actually attacked by Spain. Furthermore, the war was fought in several different theaters worldwide.
- B. Incorrect. The First World War took place after all of these conflicts.
- C. Incorrect. The Texan Revolution occurred before Texas joined the United States.
- D. Incorrect. The War of 1812 was partially due to British provocations and took place entirely on US and British Canadian soil.

2)

- A. Incorrect. The Senate never ratified the Treaty of Versailles, so the United States never joined the League of Nations.
- B. Incorrect. NATO formed after WWII.
- C. Incorrect. The United States did not ratify the Treaty of Versailles.
- **D. Correct.** None of the above are true.

3)

- A. Incorrect. While many businessmen had become extremely wealthy due to trusts, antitrust legislation was not explicitly designed to reduce wealth altogether.
- B. Incorrect. Antitrust legislation was intended to create a fairer marketplace, not redistribute existing wealth.
- **C. Correct.** Trusts had monopolized the marketplace; thus the market required intervention.
- D. Incorrect. While trusts, having monopolized the markets, could effectively control prices, this was not the explicit reason for antitrust legislation.

4)

- A. Incorrect. Temperance activists believed alcohol was harmful to society.
- B. Incorrect. Temperance activists were unconcerned with alcohol prices, believing that it destroyed families and thus should not be consumed at all.
- **C. Correct.** Temperance activists feared the negative impact of alcohol on poor and working class families.
- D. Incorrect. The United States was a major producer of alcohol.

5)

A. Incorrect. The Seneca Falls Convention called for women's suffrage; however, women would not be able to vote for another seventy-two years.

B. Correct. The Nineteenth Amendment allowed women to vote; it was ratified in 1920.

C. Incorrect. The Equal Rights Amendment was never ratified.

D. Incorrect. The Voting Rights Act of 1965 protected the voting rights of African Americans.

6)

A. Incorrect. Labor unions formed to address unfair wages (or non-payment of them altogether).

B. Incorrect. Overwork was an important issue addressed by labor unions.

C. Correct. Labor unions sought improved working conditions, not the overthrow of capitalism.

D. Incorrect. Workers used labor unions to protest dangerous working conditions.

7)

A. Incorrect. Social Darwinism is not related to the theory of evolution.

B. Correct. Social Darwinism was the idea that the wealthiest and more privileged (generally, white people) deserved their power because they were inherently stronger than and more fit for survival and success than poorer people and those of other races.

C. Incorrect. Again, Social Darwinism was unrelated to evolution.

D. Incorrect. Social Darwinism was applied to humans and social groups, not the animal kingdom.

8)

A. Incorrect. Castro was already in power at the time of the Cuban Missile Crisis.

B. Incorrect. Fidel Castro has remained in power, at least in name, through 2015; his brother Raul controls Cuba, and despite many reforms, the same government is in place.

C. Correct. Following the extreme tensions between the two countries, the United States and the Soviet Union improved dialogue in the early 1960s, leading to a period of détente.

D. Incorrect. The Cuban Missile Crisis led to a period of détente; it did not end one.

9)

A. Incorrect. SALT and SALT II were arms agreements, so the two countries were engaged in diplomatic discourse.

B. Incorrect. Given that these agreements led to limitations of strategic arms for both countries, they were not indicative of active conflict.

C. Incorrect. Glasnost was a policy of openness in the Soviet Union under Gorbachev.

D. Correct. SALT and SALT II were reached during periods of diplomatic détente when productive dialogue between the Cold War powers was possible.

10)

A. Correct. Roosevelt actually used the Interstate Commerce Act to carry out its original purpose: to break up trusts. By prosecuting the powerful Northern Securities railroad company, he became known as a "trust buster."

B. Incorrect. FDR developed the Works Progress Administration as part of the New Deal.

C. Incorrect. The Sixteenth Amendment was ratified after Theodore Roosevelt's presidency.

D. Incorrect. Roosevelt implemented antitrust acts widely.

11)

A. Correct. Public paranoia over communism was widespread, and many public figures were accused of being communist.

B. Incorrect. The United States never supported Maoism.

C. Incorrect. No members of Congress were removed from office due to the McCarthy hearings.

D. Incorrect. No members of Congress were revealed to be Soviet spies during the McCarthy hearings.

12)

A. Incorrect. The Iranian Revolution established a theocratic government that would become radically anti-American; the hostage crisis was led by activist students.

B. Correct. President Carter's inability to resolve the crisis helped propel Ronald Reagan to victory in the 1980 presidential election; Reagan took an aggressive stance against the Soviet Union and escalated the arms race, intensifying the Cold War throughout the 1980s.

13)

- C. Incorrect. The Soviet Union's invasion of Afghanistan was unrelated to the Iranian hostage crisis, even though it did occur in the same year.
- D. Incorrect. President Carter lost the election, in part due to ineffective negotiations with Iran; furthermore, the 1980s were a tense period between the United States and the Soviet Union.

13)

- A. Incorrect. The US government did not even acknowledge wrongdoing for another forty years.
- B. Incorrect. In *Korematsu v. US*, the legality of internment came before the Supreme Court; however, it was upheld.
- **C. Correct.** Japanese-Americans were dispossessed and unfairly treated as potential traitors, even though they had lived in the United States for generations.
- D. Incorrect. Most camps were located on the West Coast.

14)

- A. Incorrect. OPEC did place an embargo on the US for supporting Israel. However, even though OPEC is comprised of many Middle Eastern countries, the Middle East did not suffer economically as much as the United States did because it supplies oil to countries worldwide.
- **B. Correct.** In retaliation for its support for Israel, OPEC placed an oil embargo on the United States. OPEC's embargo strongly harmed the US economy, which was very dependent on Middle Eastern oil at the time.
- C. Incorrect. Arab support for the United States decreased due to its support for Israel.
- D. Incorrect. The United States' relationships with Saudi Arabia and Iran were strained by its support for Israel.

15)

- **A. Correct.** Head Start was introduced to provide early childhood support for low-income families; the Department of Housing and Urban Development became a cabinet-level agency in 1965.
- B. Incorrect. Social Security was created as part of the New Deal.
- C. Incorrect. Social Security already existed when Johnson became president.
- D. Incorrect. While Head Start and the Department of Housing and Urban Development were initiatives connected to the War on Poverty, Social Security was not.

16)

A. Incorrect. Cesar Chavez and the UFW organized Mexican and Mexican-American workers already present in the United States. They focused on the rights of workers in the US

B. Correct. Cesar Chavez and the UFW advocated for the rights of Mexican and Mexican-American farmworkers in the US, who were often disadvantaged; moreover, the activism of the UFW set a precedent for later advocacy in support of Hispanic Americans.

C. Incorrect. Cesar Chavez and the UFW were mainly active in California and the Southwest, not Texas.

D. Incorrect. B is the correct answer.

17)

A. Incorrect. Gay Pride rallies and marches were not major features of the public landscape until after the Stonewall Riots.

B. Incorrect. Milk's election was an important development in LGBT rights as openly gay public figures were rare, but his election occurred after the Stonewall Riots.

C. Incorrect. Again, the public discourse and activism that resulted from the AIDS crisis helped bring LGBT issues into the mainstream public sphere, but these events happened in the 1980s and 1990s.

D. Correct. Generally viewed as the beginning of the LGBT rights movement, the Stonewall Riots occurred in response to ongoing police harassment of the gay community in New York City and resulted in a more organized push for civil rights.

18)

A. Incorrect. Each believed the opposite.

B. Correct. Dr. King focused on integration, while Malcolm X focused on black empowerment.

C. Incorrect. Both believed in social change.

D. Incorrect. On some issues, they took very different positions.

19)

A. Incorrect. President Nixon resigned.

B. Incorrect. Watergate unfolded during Nixon's second term.

C. Correct. Watergate destroyed many Americans' trust in the government, which had already been weakened after the turbulent 1960s and the Vietnam War.

D. Incorrect. Watergate did not change the two-party system.

20)

- A. Incorrect. Conservatives believe in free trade, but not in open borders and unrestricted movement of people.
- **B. Correct.** Conservatives believe in low taxes to boost business.
- C. Incorrect. Conservatives believe in minimal interference with businesses and the marketplace.
- D. Incorrect. Conservatives would likely support efficiency in the military, but believe in a large and strong one.

21)

- A. Incorrect. While the Taliban harbored Osama bin Laden, they themselves had not directly attacked the United States and were not the primary reason for the US invasion.
- **B. Correct.** Neutralizing Osama bin Laden and his network—al Qaeda—was the stated objective for the invasion of Afghanistan.
- C. Incorrect. Al Qaeda was not the government of Afghanistan.
- D. Incorrect. Al Qaeda was not believed to have weapons of mass destruction in Afghanistan.

22)

- A. Incorrect. The Patriot Act was created before the invasion of Iraq.
- B. Incorrect. The Patriot Act affected the US domestically.
- C. Incorrect. The Patriot Act did not establish the detention centers at Guantanamo Bay.
- **D. Correct.** The Patriot Act gave the federal government unprecedented surveillance powers over Americans within the United States.

23)

- A. Incorrect. Concerns over privacy were related to the Patriot Act; no known surveillance programs were based in Guantanamo.
- B. Incorrect. Many lawmakers argued vehemently against transferring prisoners to facilities on US soil.
- **C. Correct.** Lack of clarity over the status of prisoners at Guantanamo Bay and their treatment was—and remains—controversial.
- D. Incorrect. This is not known to be the case.

Go on

24)

- **A. Correct.** The invasion and occupation of Iraq was part of the War on Terror and in accordance with President Bush's doctrine of preemption—that the US should preempt terrorist attacks by attacking threats first. Erroneous beliefs that Saddam Hussein had weapons of mass destruction and was linked to al Qaeda were reasons for the invasion.
- **B.** Incorrect. Osama bin Laden was not believed to be in Iraq; some argued that he was linked with Saddam Hussein, but there was very little evidence of such an alliance as the two had divergent ideologies.
- **C.** Incorrect. No partnership between Iraq and al Qaeda was ever uncovered; furthermore, al Qaeda did not use any weapons on 9/11 to attack the United States (aside from box cutters to threaten the airline pilots)—it hijacked airplanes and crashed them into buildings.
- **D.** Incorrect. Iraq had nothing to do with the terrorist attacks on the United States on September 11, 2001.

25)

- **A.** Incorrect. The Reagan administration focused on the arms race, not diplomatic engagement.
- **B.** Incorrect. Under Reagan, the US fought proxy wars in Central America, Afghanistan, and elsewhere, but did not directly confront the USSR militarily.
- **C.** Incorrect. Multilateral diplomacy was not a US priority at this time.
- **D. Correct.** The Reagan administration focused on arms buildup, weapons spending, and supporting anti-Soviet movements around the world.

26)

- **A.** Incorrect. While Truman certainly suggests that one way of life is better than the other, his description is more complicated.
- **B.** Incorrect. He describes one way of life as free from political oppression with personal freedoms; he describes the other as politically and socially limited.
- **C.** Incorrect. Truman paints a picture of starkly different societies, one with political freedoms and the other without.
- **D. Correct.** Truman described two ways of life: one politically and socially repressive, the other politically and socially free.

27)

- A. Incorrect. While this is the general idea, Truman expresses more specific policy objectives.
- B. Incorrect. Truman is alluding to international security, not sovereignty.
- **C. Correct.** Truman suggests that totalitarianism threatens US security; hence, it must be prevented.
- D. Incorrect. Truman offers a more aggressive stance here.

28)

- **A. Correct.** Truman is contrasting the democratic, capitalist United States and the communist Soviet Union.
- B. Incorrect. The European Union did not yet exist.
- C. Incorrect. Nazi Germany no longer existed.
- D. Incorrect. The Soviet Union was a communist, not a fascist, country.

29)

- A. Incorrect. Hitler's occupation of these territories took place years before Truman's speech.
- **B. Correct.** Truman presents the Soviet threat here, not the Nazi threat, which was already eliminated in the Second World War.
- C. Incorrect. The Berlin Wall was not built until 1961.
- D. Incorrect. The Iron Curtain was a figurative description, not a literal construction.

30)

- **A. Correct.** Truman laid out the Truman Doctrine—containment of communism—in this speech.
- B. Incorrect. Truman discusses two ways of life, but goes farther and places judgement upon them.
- C. Incorrect. This is not the main point of the speech.
- D. Incorrect. Again, this is not the main point of the speech.

Practice Test Two

World History Pre-1450 (30)

1

An important civilizational contribution made by the Sumerians was

A. cuneiform, the first known example of writing in which characters were connected to form words.

B. cuneiform, the first known example of writing to use pictographs to indicate words.

C. the Code of Hammurabi, an early form of rule of law.

D. Hieroglyphs, the first known example of writing in which characters were connected to form words.

2

The "Golden Age" of Hellenic civilization was one consequence of

A. Roman influence in Greece as Rome became an important Mediterranean power.

B. the influence of Greek sculpture and philosophy on the developing Etruscan civilization in the Italian peninsula.

C. the end of the Peloponnesian War between Athens and Sparta, and their move toward unity to defend the Ionian Greeks from Persia.

D. the emergence of Alexander the Great to protect Greece from Persian incursions from Anatolia.

3

Civilizations in the Fertile Crescent like the Babylonians and the Sumerians had which of the following in common?

- A. They were primarily agricultural societies, with a few small towns.
- B. They promoted urban growth.
- C. They promoted a decentralized form of government.
- D. They focused on military, rather than administrative, government.

4

Despite its democratic roots as a republic, Rome evolved into an empire because

- A. it was able to conquer so much land that it would have been impossible to maintain the Republic in its original form.
- B. the patricians of Rome amassed so much wealth that they were able to take over the Senate and establish an empire.
- C. Hannibal was able to overthrow the Senate, and establish an empire in its place.
- D. the wealthy patricians of the Senate became corrupt, disregarding the interests of the plebeians, who then supported Julius Caesar's coup.

5

How was the Mandate of Heaven an important concept in early Chinese history?

- A. It taught that the people in the area that became China were divinely fated to unite as one civilization.
- B. It taught that the emperor was given a divine mandate to rule the people in what would become China.
- C. It taught that China was a divinely important world power.
- D. It taught that the emperor was a divine servant of the people of what would become China.

6

In Catholicism, the Virgin Mary is believed to be

- A. a semi-divine being and part of the Holy Trinity.
- B. a symbol of fertility.
- C. a human being who miraculously conceived Jesus as a virgin.
- D. a goddess and the mother of Jesus Christ.

7

Rome was able to maintain imperial control over a vast amount of territory thanks in part to

- A. the idea that the Roman emperor had a divine mandate to rule: the Mandate of Heaven.
- B. advanced engineering and strong infrastructure (like roads) throughout the empire.
- C. the concept of one god, and shared religion throughout the empire.
- D. how easy it was to obtain Roman citizenship and all the benefits that came with it.

8

Ancient Persia, as a military power,

- A. controlled territory from the Levant through Anatolia and into Asia.
- B. would likely have remained strong, had Greece never successfully united under strong leadership.
- C. benefitted from strong hereditary and imperial leadership.
- D. all of the above

9

Under the Roman Republic, which of the following technically held political power?

- A. the Senate
- B. the Triumvirate
- C. a combination of elected officials and military leadership
- D. assemblies representative of all local residents

10

According to Confucianism, an ideal society

- A. is based on respect for authority and wisdom, making harmonious interaction a priority.
- B. allows respectful debate and discussion to encourage learning and the development of wisdom.
- C. encompasses a diverse group of people, to gather wisdom from different cultures.
- D. values hierarchy and enforces a caste system.

11

During the Pax Romana, the Mediterranean region

A. experienced a period of relative peace and stability under Roman rule.

B. was a center of commercial activity.

C. was ruled by Augustus Caesar.

D. all of the above

12

Islam developed in which of the following areas?

A. the Middle East

B. the Arabian Peninsula

C. Egypt

D. Iran

13

How did the spread of Islam affect West Africa?

A. Muslim traders raided the West African coast for slaves in order to profit from the Atlantic triangular trade.

B. Islam spread along trans-Saharan trade routes, eventually influencing West African kingdoms like the Mali and Songhai empires.

C. Islam never had a major presence in West Africa.

D. Despite the influence of Muslim traders on trans-Saharan trade routes, the gold- and salt-rich kingdom of Ghana was able to repel Islamic influence from the region.

14

One reason the Muslim Arabs were able to take over Byzantine- and Persian-controlled areas was

A. Muslims were ambivalent towards Christian minorities who may have opposed the Greek Orthodox Byzantines or the Zoroastrian Persians; these groups therefore preferred Arab-Muslim rule to more oppressive power structures.

B. Arabic-speaking people in the region were more responsive toward Arabic-speaking rulers.

C. Muslims already living in the Byzantine and Persian empires welcomed Islamic rule.

D. A and B only

15

Buddhism places value on

- A. monotheism: the belief in one god—the Buddha.
- B. harmony with nature and the development of wisdom.
- C. transcendence of the ego and desire for material things to relieve suffering and achieve nirvana.
- D. filial piety in order to achieve a harmonious society.

16

Which of the following was a consequence of Persian attacks on Greece?

- A. Athens and Sparta were weakened, eventually coming into conflict in the Peloponnesian War.
- B. The former enemies Athens and Sparta united to form a strong unified state, providing the foundation for the eventual emergence of Alexander the Great.
- C. Athens and Sparta united with the Ionian Greeks to conquer Persia.
- D. Greece and Persia united to form the empire under Alexander the Great that stretched from Greece into Central Asia.

17

Ancient Egypt was able to develop into a civilizational power due to which of the following?

- A. the Indus River valley
- B. the agricultural yield of Mesopotamia
- C. the Yellow River valley
- D. the Nile Valley

18

Choose the best explanation for the origin of the Byzantine Empire.

- A. After the fall of Rome, the Eastern Roman Empire became progressively more powerful, evolving into the Byzantine Empire.
- B. With Rome threatened by northern European forces, the entire Roman government moved eastward and eventually developed into the Byzantine Empire.
- C. After the introduction of Christianity, Byzantium was founded as a Christian empire.
- D. Following the death of Muhammad, his followers conquered lands throughout the Levant and eventually established the Byzantine Empire.

19

What was a consequence of the decline of the Abbasid Caliphate?

> I. the dissolution of Islamic territories into lands dominated by the Seljuks, the Mamluks and Fatimids, and the Ottoman Turks
>
> II. a loss of connection with the Tang dynasty, a center of learning and technology
>
> III. decentralization and disorganization in Central Asia, allowing for the rise of the Mongols and their subsequent empire

A. I, II, and III
B. I only
C. I and II only
D. I and III only

20

Mongol conquest of the Middle East contributed to division between the western (Levantine and Syrian areas) from eastern (Persian) areas. What was one long-lasting result of the Mongol invasions of Southwest Asia?

A. ongoing imperial division of Southwest Asia: the Mamluks and later the Ottoman Empire would eventually control land as far west as Iraq, a contested border area with the Safavid Empire (later, the Persian Empire) to the west.

B. ongoing imperial division of Southwest Asia: the Mamluks and later the Ottoman Empire would eventually control land as far east as Iraq, a contested border area with the Safavid Empire (later, the Persian Empire) to the east.

C. Arab and Persian powers came together in an alliance to drive the Mongols out of Southwest Asia.

D. The Mongol invasions had no major effect on the Middle East.

21

What was a consequence of the fall of the Mongols in the fourteenth century?

A. the rise of the Ming dynasty in China, which led to cultural developments in art and architecture like the construction of the Forbidden City

B. the rise of Ivan the Great in Russia, who gained control of Moscow

C. the expansion of the Ottoman Empire into the Middle East

D. all of the above

22

Following the collapse of the Western Roman Empire, what was the status of serfs in Europe?

- A. Serfs, while bound to the land on the manors where they lived and forced to farm for the lords, were not enslaved, nor were they forced to fight for lords; rather, they were to be protected.
- B. Serfs were agricultural slaves expected to farm the land on manors in order to support lords.
- C. Serfs were peasants on manors, expected to farm the land for lords but also able to farm their own land; they were free to leave manors if they wished but rarely did due to unsafe conditions.
- D. Serfs were agricultural slaves who were also expected to fight for lords when called upon for defense.

23

In approximately the same time period as Charlemagne's foundation of the Carolingian Empire, how did Central Europe become organized?

- A. The Catholic Church took power over a series of small states in Central Europe, organizing them as the Papal States.
- B. Charlemagne expanded his empire into Central Europe, organizing small states there as far east as modern-day Poland.
- C. Otto I became emperor of the Holy Roman Empire, a confederation of small states in Central Europe.
- D. Byzantine missionaries extended organized rule through the Balkans north into Central Europe, organizing the small states under the influence of the Greek Orthodox Church.

24

How did political stability or instability impact trade along the Silk Road?

- A. Stable imperial rule allowed for easier trade and travel, as roads were safe.
- B. Political instability made trading more profitable, since demand for scarce goods would rise.
- C. Political stability led traders to use sea routes, even when navigation technology was limited.
- D. Since trade was so profitable, political conditions did not impact the trade routes.

25

Which of the following fostered learning and the development of scientific knowledge?

- A. China during the Warring States period
- B. China during the Cultural Revolution
- C. Europe under Charlemagne
- D. the Islamic caliphates

26

Of the following, which best describes the impact that the Byzantine Empire had on Russia?

- A. The Russians adopted the Orthodox Church, due to the influence of Byzantine missionaries who traveled north.
- B. The Byzantine Empire protected Russia from the Ottomans, which is why Russia is not a Muslim-majority country.
- C. The Byzantine Empire conquered Russia; as a result of this conquest, its influence in architecture, religion, and language persist to this day.
- D. The Byzantine Empire posed a military threat to Russia, which stimulated Russia to develop a stronger military to protect its borders.

27

What was a consequence of the trans-Saharan trade networks on African empires in West Africa?

- A. The slave trade between the Mediterranean and the Atlantic coast of Africa accelerated.
- B. Islam spread from traders in North Africa to kingdoms in West Africa like the Mali Empire.
- C. Gold and salt in West Africa were overexploited and led to the fall of the West African empires to Muslim invaders.
- D. As trade routes opened up access to landlocked West African empires, these empires became vulnerable to Europeans seeking labor for colonies in the Western Hemisphere.

28

Which of the following is one reason that the Roman Empire collapsed?

- A. the decline of Latin as a common language
- B. lack of interest in traditional Roman religion and the adoption of Christianity by Emperor Constantine
- C. the introduction of gunpowder to the Mediterranean region
- D. incursions by northern European tribes like the Franks, Goths, and the Vandals, who had been originally contracted for military work by the Romans

29

One reason for the Mongols' ability to hold power throughout Asia was

- A. the Mongols' strong, centralized political system of control.
- B. a shared language throughout the region.
- C. the Mongols' decentralized method of governance.
- D. the Mongols' use of Islam as a unifying factor throughout Central Asia.

30

Islamic powers expanding from the Arabian Peninsula were able to

- A. establish the Umayyad Caliphate, based in Damascus, due to the weakening power of the Byzantine Empire.
- B. establish the Abbasid Caliphate, based in Damascus, due to the weakening power of the Byzantine Empire.
- C. establish the Umayyad Caliphate, based in Baghdad, due to the weakening power of the Mongols.
- D. all of the above

World History Post-1450 (30)

1

Slaves were originally brought to the Americas as part of the triangular trade in order to do what?

A. work on cotton plantations

B. work on sugar plantations

C. work in colonists' homes

D. all of the above

2

In addition to being challenged by criticism of papal indulgences and accusations of corruption, what other criticisms did the Catholic Church face during the Reformation?

A. The church was widely criticized for not doing enough to protect the indigenous peoples of the Americas.

B. Due to the discoveries of the Scientific Revolution, church power was compromised because its theological teachings were disproven by science.

C. The church had lost its political power throughout Italy and Spain.

D. The church was damaged by the Crusades.

3

The system of mercantilism

A) enriched Spain by providing it with valuable raw materials, especially gold and silver.

B) placed particular value on merchants, allowing them to trade without taxes or duties.

C) was established in order to take advantage of the African slave trade.

D) was a market strategy to cut off trade between the Aztecs and other regional populations in the Western Hemisphere and Spain's European competitors like the Netherlands and Britain.

4

Encomiendas

A) allowed Spanish colonists to possess land and to demand tribute and labor from its inhabitants.

B) were a traditional Inca labor system in which land was collectively owned.

C) were a form of feudalism in which African slaves belonged to the land.

D) were a political system employed in Spain.

5

In South America, how was the Inca Empire able to consolidate its rule?

A. The Inca used strong military technology and tactics to subdue conquered peoples and expand their empire.

B. Driven by the belief in conversion, the Inca were able to convert Andean peoples to their own religion, gaining followers and therefore loyal subjects.

C. The Inca civilization had grown thanks to a surplus of maize and mastery of high altitude agriculture; due to their domestication of llamas and alpacas, the Inca were able to sustain their military with supplies to travel through the mountains.

D. Due to the mountainous terrain of the Andes, the Inca were unable to expand their empire far.

6

How did the slave trade change after 1500 and the development of the Columbian Exchange?

A. It decreased substantially.

B. It increased substantially.

C. Slaves now came predominately from Africa, rather than from Southeast Asia.

D. Slave traders were increasingly local.

7

Which of the following is the best definition for the Columbian Exchange?

A. The Columbian Exchange describes trading relations between Europe and the Americas.

B. The Columbian Exchange describes the slave trade to the Americas.

C. The Columbian Exchange describes the exchange of foods, people, diseases, and goods between Europe and the Americas.

D. The Columbian Exchange describes the trade in colonial properties.

8

During the colonization of the Americas, the triangular trade across the Atlantic developed, and Africans suffered greatly; however, Africans still developed forms of resistance. Which of the following events or phenomena is an example of African resistance to slavery during this period?

A. Maroon communities

B. the Seminole Wars

C. the Underground Railroad

D. the Ghost Dance movement

9

Despite the strength of the Aztec Empire, it declined rapidly upon the arrival of the Spanish colonizers. This can be attributed to which of the following reasons?

A. Spain's superior weapons technology allowed it to conquer and destroy the Aztec Empire.

B. Europeans brought smallpox to the Americas; having never been exposed to the disease, Native American populations were decimated by it.

C. Spain purposefully broke down Aztec infrastructure in order to gain access to gold, a resource the Aztecs had in abundance.

D. all of the above

10

How did Belgium benefit from colonization?

A. Despite its small size, it controlled the Congo, a vast and remarkably resource-rich territory in Central Africa.

B. Despite its small size, it controlled Indonesia, a vast and remarkably resource-rich archipelago in Southeast Asia.

C. Belgium was not yet an independent country.

D. Belgium was not a major imperial power.

11

Inspired by revolutionary ideals and the revolutions in France, the United States, and Haiti, Simon Bolivar

A. led a movement to implement reforms in the Spanish territories in the Americas.

B. advocated for the rights of indigenous peoples in the Americas.

C. led revolutionary movements in Venezuela, Colombia, Bolivia, and Ecuador; these countries would gain independence as a result.

D. led revolutionary movements in Venezuela, Colombia, Bolivia, and Ecuador that were crushed by the Spanish.

12

Apartheid was

A. strict racial segregation associated with South Africa.

B. a type of slavery.

C. a form of colonial government.

D. rebellion against colonial government.

13

Which of the following best explains Spain's development into an empire?

- A. After consolidating their control over Spain, Ferdinand and Isabella sponsored Columbus' voyage, enabling them to lay claim to most of the Western Hemisphere and profit from mercantilism.
- B. Thanks to mercantilism, Ferdinand and Isabella were able to amass enough money to successfully conquer the Iberian Peninsula.
- C. Spain's military superiority enabled it to take Latin America from Portugal, except for Brazil.
- D. After consolidating their control over Spain, Ferdinand and Isabella sponsored Columbus' voyage, enabling them to lay claim to most of the Western Hemisphere and profit from an allegiance with the Catholic Church.

14

India was often called the "crown jewel" of the British Empire. Why was it such an important colonial possession?

- A. India was rich in important resources like rice, opium (which Britain used to extend its influence in China), tea, silk, and other raw materials.
- B. India's geographic location was strategically ideal for British influence over travel and shipping routes in the Indian Ocean to Australia and overland in Asia.
- C. India was a export destination for British manufactured goods, bringing income to the "mother country."
- D. all of the above

15

The Franco-Prussian War indicated what about Prussia and military power in Europe?

- A. Militarization in society was not successful.
- B. France's smaller and more professional army was suitable for modern conflict at the time.
- C. The balance of power in Europe was not changing.
- D. A militarized society with conscription and a large army could be successful over a small, professional, imperial army.

Go on

16

Which of the following was the result of the Balkan Crises of the nineteenth and early twentieth centuries?

A. The Ottoman Empire gained control over the Balkans, and European powers withdrew from the complex alliances between peoples of the region.

B. The Ottoman Empire lost control of the Balkans, and European powers developed alliances based on ethnic and geographic interests in the region.

C. Russia gained control over the Balkans and formed the Triple Entente with France and Britain in order to expel Hapsburg influence.

D. Austria-Hungary gained control over the Balkans and formed the Three Emperor's League as a result, in order to protect its holdings from Russia.

17

Which of the following best explains how the Russian Empire was able to capitalize on ethnic pride in order to expand its influence in Europe?

A. Russia improved its economic ties with Prussia, Austria-Hungary, and in the Ottoman Empire, thanks to connections with Slavic merchants in these regions who were influenced by pan-Slavism.

B. Russia benefitted from pan-Slavism: Slavic minorities in Prussia and Austria-Hungary rebelling against those imperial rulers were supported militarily by Russia, which was then able to expand its land holdings into those empires.

C. Russia benefitted from pan-Slavism, the concept of unity among Slavic peoples; it was able to gain and maintain influence among Slavic minorities under the control of other empires, notably the Serbs.

D. Russia gained the support of imperial powers like the Ottomans and Austria-Hungary, which wanted to please their sizeable Slavic minority groups.

18

How did the Congress of Vienna affect the balance of power in Europe?

A. Prussia, the Austro-Hungarian Empire, France, Britain, and Russia agreed they would maintain that balance of power in Europe following the Napoleonic Wars and setting a precedent for future European organization.

B. The Congress of Vienna marked the end of the imperial model in Europe; with the decline of the Holy Roman Empire, the last European empire had finally fallen.

C. Prussia, the Austro-Hungarian Empire, Britain, and Russia agreed on a series of sanctions against France following the Napoleonic Wars and French empire-building in Europe.

D. Prussia, Britain, and Russia emerged victorious, while France and the Austro-Hungarian Empire entered periods of decline.

Read the passage and answer the questions that follow.

> **Art. I.**
>
> The Suez Maritime Canal shall always be free and open, in time of war as in time of peace, to every vessel of commerce or of war, without distinction of flag.
>
> Consequently, the High Contracting Parties agree not in any way to interfere with the free use of the Canal, in time of war as in time of peace.
>
> The Canal shall never be subjected to the exercise of the right of blockade.
>
> Convention on Free Navigation of the Suez Canal
Between the European Powers and the Ottoman Empire,
October 29, 1888, Great Britain, Parliamentary Papers,
Commercial no. 2, C. 5623.

19

At the time of this convention, Britain controlled Egypt. What does the passage show about Britain's strategic interests in the late nineteenth century?

- A. The convention shows Britain's interest in taking over Ottoman territories from its foothold in Egypt.
- B. The convention shows Britain's interest in forging a strong trading partnership with the Ottoman Empire.
- C. The convention shows Britain's interest in maintaining open and safe maritime routes between Europe, Africa, and Asia for consistent shipping and international trade.
- D. The convention shows Britain's interest in forging strong trading partnerships with other European powers.

20

Which of the following was true about the Suez Canal in 1888?

- A. The Suez Canal was strategically important to all signatories to the Convention.
- B. The Ottoman Empire did not fully control the Suez Canal.
- C. Britain wished to use the Suez Canal for trade.
- D. all of the above

21

Which of the following was true about the Mediterranean and Red Sea region in the late nineteenth century?

A. European power was limited.

B. Europe dominated North Africa in the late nineteenth century.

C. Europeans expanded overseas thanks to partnership and unity of purpose.

D. The power of the Ottoman Empire in the eastern Mediterranean was unmatched.

22

During Indian Partition, which states were created?

A. India and Pakistan

B. India, Pakistan, and Bangladesh

C. India, Pakistan, and Afghanistan

D. India, Pakistan, Afghanistan, and Bangladesh

23

The Boer War is an example of which of the following?

A. British imperialism in Africa

B. Dutch imperialism in the East Indies

C. South African repression of minority groups under apartheid

D. Dutch imperialism in Africa

24

During the late twentieth century, several Latin American countries, notably Argentina, experienced harsh dictatorships. How were dissidents treated in this specific context?

A. Dissidents were placed under the protection of the Catholic Church.

B. Dissidents were exiled to the Falkland Islands, starting a war with the United Kingdom.

C. Dissidents were given public trials.

D. Dissidents were "disappeared," arrested, and frequently executed in secret.

25

Which of the following best describes the differences between the Russian and Chinese Revolutions?

A. The Russian Revolution focused on industrialization, while the Chinese Revolution focused on agriculture.

B. The Soviet Union used starvation as a means of control, but the Chinese revolutionary government did not.

C. The Soviets used prison camps; the Chinese revolutionary forces focused on protecting human rights instead.

D. The Chinese government tolerated cultural differences; however, the Soviets imprisoned those who refused to accept their ideology.

26

Prior to the First World War, how was the European system of alliances organized?

A. The Three Emperors' League was allied with the Triple Entente against the Triple Alliance.

B. Germany, Italy, and Russia, the Triple Alliance, were allies against the Triple Entente, Great Britain, France, and Austria-Hungary.

C. Great Britain, Russia, and France, allies who had formed the Triple Entente earlier in the twentieth century, were at odds with the Central Powers (formerly the Triple Alliance), composed of Germany, Italy, and Austria-Hungary.

D. Russia was allied with the Ottoman Empire against the Triple Alliance of Austria-Hungary, Germany, and Italy, in order to support Slavic interests in the Balkans.

27

The Warsaw Pact was a supranational organization created in response to:

A. NATO

B. the United Nations

C. the European Union

D. the League of Nations

Read the excerpt and answer the questions that follow.

> Inside South Africa, riots, boycotts, and protests by black South Africans against white rule had occurred since the inception of independent white rule in 1910. Opposition intensified when the Nationalist Party, assuming power in 1948, effectively blocked all legal and non-violent means of political protest by non-whites. The African National Congress (ANC. and its offshoot, the Pan Africanist Congress (PAC., both of which envisioned a vastly different form of government based on majority rule, were outlawed in 1960 and many of its leaders imprisoned. The most famous prisoner was a leader of the ANC, Nelson Mandela, who had become a symbol of the anti-Apartheid struggle. While Mandela and many political prisoners remained incarcerated in South Africa, other anti-Apartheid leaders fled South Africa and set up headquarters in a succession of supportive, independent African countries, including Guinea, Tanzania, Zambia, and neighboring Mozambique where they continued the fight to end Apartheid. It was not until the 1980s, however, that this turmoil effectively cost the South African state significant losses in revenue, security, and international reputation.
>
> "Milestones: 1989 – 1992: The End of Apartheid," Office of the Historian, United States Department of State, http://history.state.gov/milestones/1989-1992/apartheid (accessed August 26, 2015).

28

Why was it most likely that the independent African countries like Guinea, Tanzania, Zambia, and Mozambique, which did not suffer from apartheid regimes like South Africa, unable to provide enough support to the ANC to eliminate apartheid altogether?

A. Independent African countries feared losing their power in the United Nations if they upset South Africa, an ally of the United States.

B. Independent African countries did not want to lose foreign aid from the Soviet Union, which was an ally of South Africa.

C. Nearly all the newly independent African countries felt threatened by the Soviet Union and sought support from the United States, so they were reluctant to lend too much support to anti-apartheid forces, as South Africa was a US ally.

D. Having recently gained their own independence, many African countries were still struggling with the legacy of colonialism, building or rebuilding their own governments, infrastructure, and economies.

29

Why did South Africa come under international criticism in the 1980s for apartheid?

A. It was discovered that the apartheid regime was secretly providing communist insurgents in Central America with financial and military support.

B. The United States began sponsoring anti-apartheid movements throughout Africa.

C. Grassroots movements in the United States and elsewhere in the west against apartheid gained momentum.

D. All of the above are correct.

30

Why was there a large, established population of whites in South Africa, unlike other African countries following decolonization?

A. More whites went to South Africa than to any other part of the continent because it was easy to access geographically, given its wide coastline.

B. Dutch colonizers—known as Afrikaners—had arrived in South Africa and settled there as early as the eighteenth century, even before major European colonization of the rest of Africa in the nineteenth century.

C. English colonizers—known as Afrikaners—had arrived in South Africa and settled there as early as the eighteenth century, even before major European colonization of the rest of Africa in the nineteenth century.

D. Whites from throughout Europe had colonized South Africa since the eighteenth century due to the fertile farmland there.

US History to 1877 (30)

1

All of these were factors in the rise of slavery in British colonies except

A. ample land for agricultural activity.

B. the growing popularity of Quakerism.

C. difficulty enslaving Native Americans.

D. growing demand for colonial goods such as tobacco.

2

The Declaration of Independence

A. is rooted in Enlightenment thought.

B. specified that women and people of color are equal to white men.

C. did not address the specific reasons the United States chose to declare independence from Great Britain.

D. all of the above

3

The Intolerable Acts included all of the following except

A. the Boston Port Act.

B. the Quartering Act.

C. the Alien and Sedition Acts.

D. the Massachusetts Government Act.

4

Which of the following was a major difference between British and French colonization of the Americas?

A. French colonists tended to be single men who intermarried with local residents, while British colonists brought their entire families to settle permanently, forming insular communities.

B. British colonists tended to be single men who intermarried with local residents, while French colonists brought their entire families to settle permanently, forming insular communities.

C. French colonists were more likely to form alliances with Native American tribes, while the British shunned them.

D. British colonists had more economic interests in the Americas than the French did.

5

All of the following contributed to the destruction of Native American populations in North America except

- A. intentional transfer of smallpox from Europeans to Native Americans.
- B. unintentional transfer of smallpox from Europeans to Native Americans.
- C. violent conflict over land and resources between Europeans and Native Americans.
- D. geographical displacement by colonists.

6

Initially, colonists were frustrated with the British government and insisted on

- A. independence.
- B. immediate self-government.
- C. the overthrow of King George III.
- D. repeal of unfair taxes and restrictions.

7

The Whiskey Rebellion

- A. reflected fears that the new government of the young United States would not be strong enough to hold the country together, leading to the Constitutional Convention.
- B. occurred in response to federal taxes and required military action to be halted.
- C. occurred in response to federal taxes but ceased after military action became a possibility.
- D. led to George Washington's decision not to seek a second term of office.

8

An important consequence of the War of 1812 was

- A. the territory gained by the US from Britain in the Northeast, including the state of Maine.
- B. the military technology the US was able to capture from British troops fleeing the unsuccessful siege of Washington, D.C.
- C. the purchase of the Port of New Orleans from the French.
- D. a sense of a strong national identity in the wake of the United States' successful expulsion of the British and defense of its borders.

9

An important consequence of the Alien and Sedition Acts was

A.   the election of John Adams as president.

B.   the election of Thomas Jefferson as president.

C.   the impeachment of John Adams.

D.   the dissolution of the Federalist Party.

10

The Mexican-American War resulted in which of the following gains for the United States?

A.   territory south of the Rio Grande

B.   the Southwest

C.   Oregon and Washington State

D.   western land including Idaho

11

What was one reason for the Mexican-American War?

A.   the possibility of extending slavery to Arizona and New Mexico

B.   disputes over the extension of railroads through agricultural areas in the Southwest

C.   the annexation of Texas by the United States

D.   disputes over the treatment of Mexican-American farm workers

12

Although women did not gain the right to vote until the ratification of the Nineteenth Amendment in 1920, activists like Elizabeth Cady Stanton and Susan B. Anthony began advocating for women's rights as early as the Seneca Falls Convention of 1848. Why did the women's movement gain traction in the mid-nineteenth century?

A.   European literary thought supporting women's rights became popular in the northern states.

B.   As the abolitionist movement grew, abolitionists also came to oppose the oppression of women, recognizing their limited rights under the law and in society.

C.   The development of a middle class gave some women the time and the means to engage in progressive activism.

D.   Women settling the Frontier became increasingly vocal about equality at a national level, since men and women were nominally equal in many remote western settlements due to their small size and isolation.

13

Immigration to the United States, particularly from famine-hit Ireland, increased in the nineteenth century. What was one widespread response?

- A. the nativist movement, which promoted the rights of Native Americans
- B. the Know-Nothing movement, a nativist, anti-immigrant, anti-Catholic society
- C. the Know-Nothing movement, a nativist, anti-immigrant, anti-Protestant society
- D. the privileging of Chinese immigrants over white Irish immigrants

14

Early industrialization in the northern and western states in the first half of the nineteenth century led to which of the following developments at this time in US history?

- A. the beginnings of a middle class in the US
- B. the Progressive movement
- C. the abolition of slavery
- D. the extension of voting rights to women, who were increasingly visible in society

15

In the Emancipation Proclamation, President Lincoln declared an end to slavery

- A. in Kentucky and Missouri.
- B. in the Union only.
- C. in slave states that had not seceded from the Union.
- D. in the rebel states.

16

Ongoing Native American resistance to United States westward expansion effectively ended

- A. with the Northwest Indian Wars at the Battle of Fallen Timbers.
- B. as the Lakota Sioux and others were subdued towards the late nineteenth century with the end of the Sioux Wars and the Massacre at Wounded Knee.
- C. with the Trail of Tears and the forced migration of the Cherokee and other tribes to what is today Oklahoma.
- D. when the Supreme Court heard *Cherokee Nation v. Georgia*.

17

What was the impact of the Battle of Gettysburg?

A. The Confederate Army was victorious but would never fully recover from its losses.

B. The Union was victorious, and the Confederate Army would never fully recover.

C. The Union was victorious, but the Confederate Army was still strong enough to represent a significant threat and did so at the Battle of Bull Run.

D. The Confederacy was victorious, but it would soon lose the war anyway.

18

How did the secession of the Confederacy affect the black population living in the South?

A) Most remained slaves under the Confederacy.

B) While the Confederate States of America was established in the name of states' rights to govern themselves without excessive federal interference, most African Americans remained slaves, without any rights at all, or had very few as freedmen.

C) Slaves were not entitled to any new freedoms under the Confederacy.

D) all of the above

19

What did the Compromise of 1850 accomplish?

A. It admitted California and Maine as free states and strengthened the Fugitive Slave Act.

B. It admitted California as a free state, Utah and New Mexico with slavery to be decided by popular sovereignty, and strengthened the Fugitive Slave Act.

C. It admitted California, Utah, and New Mexico as free states, and strengthened the Fugitive Slave Act.

D. It admitted California, Utah, and New Mexico as states with slavery to be decided by popular sovereignty, and strengthened the Fugitive Slave Act.

20

What was a consequence of the Kansas-Nebraska Act?

A. the Fugitive Slave Act

B. the Compromise of 1850

C. violence between pro- and anti-slavery advocates in Kansas over the legalization of slavery ("Bleeding Kansas")

D. the Missouri Compromise

21

Tecumseh was able to unite which of the following tribes in his Confederacy?

- A. Shawnee, Lenape, Miami, Kickapoo, and others
- B. Shawnee, Algonquin, Iroquois, Miami, and others
- C. Shawnee, Cherokee, Miami, Apache, and others
- D. Shawnee, Lenape, Chickasaw, Choctaw, and others

22

What did the Missouri Compromise accomplish?

- A. It admitted Missouri as a free state.
- B. It admitted California as a free state.
- C. It allowed slavery in New Mexico and Utah to be decided by popular sovereignty.
- D. It banned slavery north of the thirty-sixth parallel, so that new states formed in northern territories would be free.

23

How did the Lincoln-Douglas Debates impact the nation before the 1860 presidential election?

- A. They reflected the national mood: that the country was deeply divided over the question of slavery and whether states had the right to determine its legality.
- B. They reflected the national mood: that the country was deeply divided over the question of slavery—Lincoln called for abolition, while Douglas favored the practice.
- C. They reinvigorated the debate over slavery, which had been overshadowed by debate over states' rights.
- D. They reinvigorated the debate over states' rights, which had been overshadowed by debate over slavery.

24

The Underground Railroad

- A. was a small, elite organization of wealthy Northerners that helped slaves escape to the North.
- B. was an expansive, decentralized network of ordinary people that helped slaves escape to the South.
- C. was an expansive, decentralized network of ordinary people that helped slaves escape to the North.
- D. was an expansive, decentralized network of organized criminals that smuggled alcohol across state borders during Prohibition.

25

Following Lincoln's assassination, the Radical Republicans

A. favored softer measures on the South than Lincoln had planned to take following the war.

B. pushed for harsher measures on the South than Lincoln had wanted following the war.

C. sought compromise in order to more quickly rebuild the country after the war.

D. allied with the Democrats.

26

The Sioux War

A. was instigated by the United States, which wanted to take back land it had granted to the Sioux.

B. resulted in a very bloody battle in which the United States was defeated; however, the US eventually took the land from the Sioux.

C. was an example of unity among western tribes.

D. all of the above

27

Crafted by President Lincoln, the Ten Percent Plan

A. called for the rebel states to pay ten percent of the costs of the war in restitution to the North as a condition of readmission to the Union.

B. ensured that African Americans would be represented by at least ten percent of Congress following the Civil War.

C. re-admitted any rebel state to the Union once at least ten percent of its citizens swore allegiance to the Union.

D. required ten percent of the population of a rebel state to move to the North before it would be re-admitted to the Union.

28

According to the Homestead Act,

A. the Lakota Sioux would be granted a homeland in the Black Hills of South Dakota.

B. white immigrants would be allotted free land in the Plains states.

C. the US government would provide land in the West for free to white settlers willing to farm it for at least two years.

D. the Cheyenne and Arapaho would agree to remain on reservations so that settlers could establish homesteads in Colorado, Nebraska, and Wyoming.

Read the passage and answer the following questions.

> First, it is the duty of black men to judge the South discriminatingly. The present generation of Southerners are not responsible for the past, and they should not be blindly hated or blamed for it. Furthermore, to no class is the indiscriminate endorsement of the recent course of the South toward Negroes more nauseating than to the best thought of the South. The South is not "solid"; it is a land in the ferment of social change, wherein forces of all kinds are fighting for supremacy; and to praise the ill the South is today perpetrating is just as wrong as to condemn the good. Discriminating and broad-minded criticism is what the South needs—needs it for the sake of her own white sons and daughters, and for the insurance of robust, healthy mental and moral development.
>
> W.E.B. DuBois, *The Souls of Black Folk*, 1903.

29

What does DuBois encourage black people to do?

A. to cooperate with all segments of Southern society in the interests of peaceful co-existence between black and white people in the South

B. to consider white, Southern perspectives and then support, challenge, or condemn them as appropriate in order to promote positive change in the South

C. to fear white Southerners who wish to disenfranchise, deport, lynch, and harm African Americans, and to avoid the South

D. to praise the ill of the South and to condemn the good

30

Which of the following best explains how DuBois felt about black men's role in reimagining the United States, according to the passage above?

A. Since African Americans were victims of the brutality of slavery, they should not be expected to interact with Southern whites.

B. African Americans should not be expected to keep an open mind to Southern perspectives because they have often faced oppressive and dangerous conditions in the postwar South.

C. Black men have a duty to remain open-minded to, but critical of, Southern perspectives, for the sake of positive change.

D. Black men should consider being open-minded to Southern perspectives for the sake of positive change.

US History 1877–present (30)

1

During FDR's terms in office, which of the following was created?

A. Medicare

B. Social Security

C. the Federal Reserve

D. all of the above

2

The New Deal was intended to

A. provide immediate economic relief to those suffering from the Great Depression.

B. stimulate longer-term economic and social recovery for US society through various targeted programs.

C. implement permanent reforms in banking and finance to prevent a reoccurrence of the failures that led to the Great Depression.

D. all of the above

3

The Spanish-American War

A. brought the United States territories in Asia, the Pacific Ocean, and the Caribbean.

B. was triggered in part by public support generated by sensationalist yellow journalism.

C. could be viewed as a precursor to Theodore Roosevelt's Roosevelt Corollary to the Monroe Doctrine.

D. all of the above

4

The Interstate Commerce Act and the Sherman Antitrust Act

A. immediately went into effect to regulate the railroad industry and break up monopolies.

B. remained largely toothless until the First World War.

C. remained largely toothless until the administration of Theodore Roosevelt.

D. immediately went into effect to promote congressional efforts to regulate interstate commerce.

5

The US entered WWI largely because of which of the following?

A. the Zimmerman Telegram

B. the rise of Nazi Germany

C. the assassination of Franz Ferdinand

D. the attack on the *Lusitania*

6

Which of the following reduced the ability of railroads to create monopolies and set prices without market interference?

A. Sherman Antitrust Act

B. Interstate Commerce Act

C. International Commerce Act

D. the Sixteenth Amendment

7

According to the Monroe Doctrine, the United States would view European interference in Latin America as a sign of aggression, consolidating US influence in that region. What is different about the Roosevelt Corollary to the Monroe Doctrine?

A. It stationed US troops throughout Latin America.

B. It strengthened commercial ties between the United States and Latin American countries.

C. It limited diplomatic relations between Europe and Latin America.

D. It provided for US military intervention in Latin America.

8

After WWII, the Secretary of State proposed to rebuild Europe with

A. the Organization for Economic Security and Development (OECD), which promoted democracy and free-market capitalism.

B. the North Atlantic Treaty Organization (NATO), which would provide collective security and economic partnership for countries bordering or close to the northern Atlantic Ocean.

C. the Marshall Plan, in order to help Europe recover economically and partner with the Soviet Union in developing a secure sphere of influence over the continent.

D. the Marshall Plan, in order to help Europe recover economically and help secure it from Soviet influence.

9

Which event caused the United States to enter the Second World War?

A. Britain's need for assistance as it came under attack from Germany

B. Nazi atrocities and genocide in Europe

C. the Japanese attack on Pearl Harbor

D. Japanese expansion and atrocities in Asia

10

Which of the following Cold War events is an example of the US foreign policy of containment, in the spirit of the Truman Doctrine, put into effect?

A. the Cuban Missile Crisis

B. the Korean War

C. glasnost and perestroika

D. the Non-Aligned Movement

11

Despite the reluctance of the United States to intervene in the Second World War, it used the Lend-Lease Act

A. as a legal justification to continue trade with Japan, even though it was an ally of Germany.

B. to support American shipbuilders and weapons manufacturers, which had suffered under the Great Depression.

C. to entice Stalin to join the allies in exchange for cash, despite his agreements with Hitler.

D. to provide support to Britain, which was threatened by Nazi Germany.

12

How did the United Nations Security Council differ from the League of Nations?

A. The Security Council is made up of several different countries, but the League of Nations was not.

B. The Security Council is empowered to take military action on behalf of the international community to maintain international security; the League of Nations was not.

C. The Security Council's mission is to maintain international peace and security, but the mission of the League of Nations was to enforce the Treaty of Versailles.

D. The Security Council is only made up of European countries, but the League of Nations included the United States.

13

According to the Gulf of Tonkin Resolution,

A. the United States declared war on Vietnam.

B. the president was empowered to take military action in Vietnam when he deemed it necessary.

C. Vietnam was declared a belligerent state.

D. the United States Army was authorized to begin ground operations in Vietnam.

14

By signing the Atlantic Charter, the United States and Great Britain

A. agreed to divide the world into democratic capitalist and communist regions.

B. decided to jointly occupy Europe indefinitely.

C. established the Atlantic Ocean as a neutral area.

D. agreed on a postwar world characterized by free trade and self-determination.

15

What was the US combat strategy during WWII?

A. Since Japan had attacked the United States, FDR believed it necessary to contain Japan using the tactic of island-hopping before addressing Europe.

B. The United States invaded Europe to defeat Nazi Germany (even though the US had been directly attacked by Japan); following major combat in Western Europe and the defeat of the Nazis, it addressed Japan.

C. Due to the threat of kamikaze attacks from German U-boats, the United States was forced to lead a ground war in Europe, which it had tried to avoid.

D. The failure of island hopping forced a US invasion of Japan; the United States was then better prepared for ground combat in Europe.

16

Johnson's vision of a Great Society

A. included programs to stabilize the economy and promote civil rights, like Social Security.

B. included programs as part of the War on Poverty to support the disadvantaged, like Medicare, Head Start, and the Department of Housing and Urban Development.

C. included programs to strengthen society in the face of communism, like the CIA and the Department of Homeland Security.

D. included a plan to end the war in Vietnam.

17

How did feminist advocacy groups effect empowering change for women in the United States?

A. They obtained ratification of an Equal Rights Amendment to the Constitution guaranteeing equal rights for men and women in public places and affairs in the United States.

B. They advocated for the passage of the Equal Pay Act, which ensured that men and women would be paid equally for equal work done in the same workplace.

C. They supported Supreme Court cases that ensured women would receive certain health benefits throughout the United States.

D. B and C only

18

What was the relevance of the Gulf of Tonkin Resolution?

A. It gave Congress the power to declare war against the North Vietnamese forces.

B. It authorized the president to take military action against North Vietnamese forces.

C. It authorized the military to take action against North Vietnamese forces.

D. It authorized the president to take military action against South Vietnamese forces.

19

The Civil Rights Act of 1964

A. struck down restrictions on voting rights for African Americans.

B. guaranteed equal rights for all Americans, regardless of their race, gender, religion, or sexual orientation.

C. ended segregation.

D. all of the above

20

Segregation was found unconstitutional by which of the following Supreme Court decisions?

A. *Brown v. Board of Education*

B. *Plessy v. Ferguson*

C. *Scott v. Sanford*

D. *Korematsu v. US*

21

In which of the following international conflicts of the 1990s did the United States play a major role in peacemaking?

I. the war in Bosnia
II. the Rwandan Civil War
III. the conflict in Northern Ireland

A. I only
B. I and II
C. I and III
D. I, II, and III

22

The Voting Rights Act of 1965

A. gave African Americans the right to vote in the segregated states.
B. gave Americans under the age of twenty-one the right to vote.
C. ended segregation in voting.
D. ended restrictions that prevented African Americans from voting in many states with histories of institutionalized racism.

23

The Civil Rights Movement made use of which of the following to effect social change?

A. non-violent civil disobedience
B. large-scale demonstrations and marches
C. local community development and empowerment programs in disadvantaged urban areas
D. all of the above

24

In the 1980s, President Reagan and the conservatives theorized that lower taxes would affect the economy in which of the following ways?

A. The economy would grow because there would be less unemployment.
B. The economy would grow because people would have more income to spend and invest.
C. The economy would grow because government social programs would interfere less with consumer behavior.
D. The economy would shrink because military budgets would have to be cut.

25

How has globalization helped the United States remain a world power, even after the Cold War?

- A. the popularity of US pop culture like music, movies, video games, and fashion
- B. the widespread use of US inventions like the Internet
- C. the global presence of active US military bases
- D. all of the above

26

In 2008, a period of economic stagnation in the United States known as the Great Recession began. What was one important cause of this crisis?

- A. the extension of high-risk car loans to borrowers, who were unable to pay back their car loans, resulting in abandoned cars throughout the US, delinquency, and broader financial consequences
- B. the extension of high-interest loans and mortgages to high-risk borrowers who were unable to pay off their mortgages, resulting in defaults, and foreclosure with broader financial consequences
- C. the extension of student loans to borrowers who were unable to find jobs and therefore unable to repay the loans, resulting in forbearance, delinquency, and defaults with broader financial consequences
- D. the extension of high-interest credit cards to high-risk borrowers who were then unable to keep up with payments, resulting in delinquency and defaults with broader financial consequences

27

NAFTA accomplished which of the following?

- A. opened borders between the US, Canada, and Mexico, allowing for free movement of goods and people between these three countries
- B. initiated free trade between the US, Mexico, and Canada, facilitating and strengthening trade between these three countries
- C. created a union similar to the European Union in North America, in which Canada, Mexico, and the US shared similar policy goals and consulted each other on matters of shared concern
- D. established common immigration procedures between Mexico, the US, and Canada

28

A consequence of Operation Desert Storm, or the Gulf War of 1991, was

A. the occupation of Iraq by the United States.

B. the occupation of Kuwait by Iraq.

C. the de facto establishment of the United States as the world's sole superpower in the wake of the fall of the Soviet Union.

D. improved cooperation in the United Nations between the United States and the former Soviet Union, now represented by the Russian Federation.

29

Even though the United States had supported Iraq during the Iran-Iraq War in the 1980s, it went to war with Iraq in 1991 following that country's invasion of Kuwait. Which of the following best explains why?

A. The US wanted to secure access to oil in Kuwait and elsewhere in the Persian Gulf, especially Saudi Arabia.

B. The US wanted to secure the region to prevent a resurgence of war with Iran.

C. The US wanted to stabilize the region to prevent terrorism.

D. The US wanted to effect regime change in Iraq.

30

Despite the resurgence of political conservatism in the twenty-first century under the administration of George W. Bush, United States society became increasingly liberal during his presidency and that of Barack Obama. Which of the following is an example of social liberalism?

A. the ratification of an Equal Rights Amendment to the Constitution guaranteeing equal rights to women and transgender people

B. increased social acceptance of homosexuality and eventual legalization of same-sex marriage throughout the United States

C. reduction in rates of imprisonment and emphasis on rehabilitation over punishment, particularly for non-violent offenders

D. a more equitable, progressive income tax

Answer Key

WORLD HISTORY PRE-1450

1)
- **A.** **Correct.** Cuneiform was a Sumerian innovation.
- B. Incorrect. While cuneiform was Sumerian, it did not use pictographs.
- C. Incorrect. The Code of Hammurabi was Babylonian.
- D. Incorrect. Hieroglyphs were Egyptian; furthermore, they were pictographs.

2)
- A. Incorrect. Rome became a power long after the Greek Golden Age.
- B. Incorrect. Greek influence elsewhere was a consequence of the Greek Golden Age, not a result of it.
- **C.** **Correct.** Stability in Greece permitted art, architecture, literature, philosophy, and science to develop.
- D. Incorrect. Alexander emerged after the Golden Age.

3)
- A. Incorrect. Several large cities flourished in the Fertile Crescent, including Babylon.
- **B.** **Correct.** Cities like Nineveh and Babylon grew in strength and power.
- C. Incorrect. These civilizations were centralized with kings and bureaucracies.
- D. Incorrect. There is evidence of administrative bureaucracies throughout the Fertile Crescent.

4)

- A. Incorrect. The Senate did not chose to dissolve itself and form an empire in order to better control land.
- B. Incorrect. The patricians already controlled the Senate and most Roman wealth when the Republic fell.
- C. Incorrect. Hannibal never overthrew the Senate.
- **D. Correct.** Caesar, with the support of dissatisfied Romans, took over the weak and corrupt Senate.

5)

- A. Incorrect. The Mandate of Heaven did not proscribe Chinese unity.
- **B. Correct.** The Mandate of Heaven legitimized governance.
- C. Incorrect. The Mandate of Heaven did not alter China's world view.
- D. Incorrect. While the Mandate of Heaven imbued the emperor with divinity, he was not perceived as a servant of the people.

6)

- A. Incorrect. Catholics believe that the Holy Trinity is a tripartite God: God the Father, God the son, and the Holy Spirit. Mary is not included.
- B. Incorrect. Mary is not regarded as such in the Catholic mainstream.
- **C. Correct.** Mary, while believed by Catholics to be the mother of Jesus, is still considered human, not divine.
- D. Incorrect. Mary is not considered a goddess.

7)

- A. Incorrect. The Mandate of Heaven was a Chinese concept.
- **B. Correct.** Strong infrastructure facilitated trade, communication, and military movement throughout the empire, ensuring unity and security.
- C. Incorrect. Traditional Roman religion had many gods, and many religious faiths were practiced throughout the empire.
- D. Incorrect. It was not easy to obtain Roman citizenship.

8)

- A. Incorrect. While Darius expanded the Persian Empire from Anatolia to Egypt and as far east as the Indus Valley, this answer choice is insufficient given the other options available.
- B. Incorrect. Xerxes' able leadership would likely have extended Persian rule farther, were it not for Greek resistance; however, bearing in mind the other answer choices, this option is incorrect.

C. Incorrect. Persia did enjoy strong leadership, but this answer choice is incorrect in this context.

D. **Correct.** All of the possibilities presented are correct.

9)

A. **Correct.** The Senate was the governing body of the Republic.

B. Incorrect. Two triumvirates eventually effectively controlled the Senate, but was not the actual governing body of the Republic.

C. Incorrect. The Senate did not include unelected military leaders.

D. Incorrect. Elected leadership only represented Roman citizens.

10)

A. **Correct.** Confucius taught others to respect authority—filial piety—and encouraged group harmony.

B. Incorrect. Confucianism does not encourage the questioning of authority, for that would risk harmonious interaction with others by raising the possibility of conflict.

C. Incorrect. Confucianism does not focus on cultural diversity.

D. Incorrect. While Confucianism values hierarchy, it does not feature a caste system.

11)

A. Incorrect. While the Roman Empire controlled the Mediterranean and much of the land bordering it, given the other answer choices, this response is incomplete.

B. Incorrect. While Rome was enormously commercially powerful during the Pax Romana, this answer choice is incomplete.

C. Incorrect. Rome was ruled by Augustus Caesar during this time period; however, taking into account the other possible responses, this answer choice is also incomplete.

D. **Correct.** All of the answers are true.

12)

A. Incorrect. Islam developed in the Arabian Peninsula; while this area is located in the Middle East, there is a better answer choice available.

B. **Correct.** Muhammad was from Mecca, which is located in the Arabian Peninsula; Islam developed in Mecca, Medina, and that area (the Hijaz).

C. Incorrect. While Islam spread to Egypt, it did not develop there.

D. Incorrect. While Islam spread to Iran, it did not develop there.

13)

A. Incorrect. Triangular trade was driven by Christian Europeans.

B. Correct. Trans-Saharan trade routes brought Islam to West Africa, where it spread throughout the region.

C. Incorrect. Islam was widespread in West Africa.

D. Incorrect. West African empires became Islamic empires.

14)

A. Incorrect. While this is true, it is not the complete answer given the other options presented.

B. Incorrect. Again, while this is true, it is not the complete answer.

C. Incorrect. Islam had not yet spread to these areas.

D. Correct. Even though the peoples living under Byzantine and Persian rule were not Muslim or Arab, the Islamic tradition of tolerance toward the "People of the Book" and, to an extent, Zoroastrians, made them more acceptable rulers than the oppressive and disorganized collapsing regimes; furthermore, many people in the region spoke Arabic, which made it easier to accept Arab rule.

15)

A. Incorrect. Buddha is not considered a god or worshiped the way God/Allah is in the three major monotheistic religions.

B. Incorrect. While many Buddhists likely believe in living harmoniously with nature and value wisdom, the religion is not based on these philosophies. Shintoism values harmony with nature; Confucianism prioritizes developing wisdom.

C. Correct. A core belief of Buddhism is that desire is the root of all suffering. Buddhists believe that nirvana, or a state of peace and joy, is achieved by transcending the ego.

D. Incorrect. Confucianism values filial piety and a harmonious society.

16)

A. Incorrect. The Peloponnesian War occurred before the major Persian attacks.

B. Correct. Athens and Sparta came together to help the Ionian Greeks; as a result, Alexander later built an empire that conquered Persia.

C. Incorrect. Greece did not defeat Persia until the time of Alexander.

D. Incorrect. Alexander defeated Persia.

17)

- A. Incorrect. The Indus River is located in South Asia.
- B. Incorrect. Mesopotamia is located in Southwest Asia.
- C. Incorrect. The Yellow River is located in China.
- **D. Correct.** The Nile River is located in North Africa.

18)

- **A. Correct.** The better-organized Eastern Roman Empire was able to consolidate its power in the Eastern Mediterranean, becoming the Byzantine Empire, while the Western Roman Empire fell to invasions by northern European tribes.
- B. Incorrect. The Roman government (and entire empire) divided into two—the Eastern Roman Empire and the Western Roman Empire.
- C. Incorrect. Christianity did not become widespread until several hundred years following its emergence.
- D. Incorrect. Islam did not emerge until the Byzantine Empire was well established.

19)

- **A. Correct.** Various powers controlled Egypt and Southwest Asia, until the Ottoman Empire took control of the region. Connection with China dissipated as the Silk Road fell out of use and the Mongol invasions destabilized Central Asia.
- B. Incorrect. Ties with China also declined, and the weaknesses of the Seljuks in Southwest Asia left the region vulnerable to the Mongols.
- C. Incorrect. Again, the Mongols were able to take advantage of the decentralized Seljuk-controlled territory and access Southwest Asia.
- D. Incorrect. Vulnerable to disorganization in Central Asia, Tang dynasty China closed its borders.

20)

- A. Incorrect. Iraq is located east of Egypt, which the Mamluks controlled.
- **B. Correct.** Arabs, and later the Ottomans, were able to take control of the Levant; Mesopotamia became a contested border area with Persia.
- C. Incorrect. Persia and the Arabs did not form an anti-Mongol alliance.
- D. Incorrect. The Mongols controlled much of the Middle East for some time.

21)

- A. Incorrect. While the Ming emerged following the fall of the Mongol Yuan dynasty, this answer is incomplete given the other choices.
- B. Incorrect. While Ivan the Great was able to take Moscow, this answer choice is not sufficient in the context of the other options.
- C. Incorrect. The Ottoman Empire was able to expand to the east thanks to Mongol decline; however, this answer is incorrect given the other options available.
- **D. Correct.** All of the above answer choices are true.

22)

- **A. Correct.** Serfs were not slaves, but they were not entirely free as they were bound to the lord's land and had to farm it. However, the lord was obligated to protect them and they were not expected to fight.
- B. Incorrect. Serfs were not slaves and could not be individually bought or sold (although since they were tied to the land, they worked for whomever owned the land).
- C. Incorrect. Serfs could not leave the manor.
- D. Incorrect. Serfs were not slaves nor were they expected to fight.

23)

- A. Incorrect. The Catholic Church directly controlled territory in Italy, but not Central Europe.
- B. Incorrect. Charlemagne did not control territory east beyond parts of Central Europe.
- **C. Correct.** Central Europe became organized into the Holy Roman Empire for several hundred years, beginning under Otto I.
- D. Incorrect. Byzantine missionaries traveled into Russia and Ukraine, not Central Europe.

24)

- **A. Correct.** Stability allowed safer travel and a stronger international economy, with demand for international products.
- B. Incorrect. Instability halted trade as it was unsafe to travel long distances in Asia.
- C. Incorrect. Oceanic routes were not widely used until the fifteenth century as navigation was improved during the European Renaissance and Scientific Revolution.
- D. Incorrect. Despite profit, international commerce was impossible without security.

25)

- A. Incorrect. China's instability during the Warring States period made learning and scientific development difficult, despite the emergence of Confucius.
- B. Incorrect. Reactionary, anti-intellectual forces dominated the Cultural Revolution.
- C. Incorrect. Charlemagne brought stability to Europe, but scientific and academic discovery would come later with the Renaissance.
- **D. Correct.** Under the caliphates, science, technology, medicine, and philosophy flourished in the Middle East and North Africa.

26)

- **A. Correct.** Russia embraced Orthodox Christianity due to Byzantine influence.
- B. Incorrect. The Byzantine Empire eventually fell to the Ottoman Turks.
- C. Incorrect. The Byzantine Empire controlled the Balkans, but not Russia.
- D. Incorrect. Byzantine control did not extend as far north as Russian-majority lands.

27)

- A. Incorrect. This was not a major slave route.
- **B. Correct.** Islam, which had spread across the Sahara from Arabia, arrived in West and West-Central Africa via the trans-Saharan trade routes.
- C. Incorrect. The West African empires benefitted from their control over gold and salt.
- D. Incorrect. Europeans did not encounter the landlocked empires of West Africa as part of the trans-Atlantic slave trade.

28)

- A. Incorrect. Latin remained a common language in academics and liturgy in Europe and in parts of the Mediterranean long after the fall of the Roman Empire; furthermore, it spawned related languages used today in Europe.
- B. Incorrect. While Constantine did adopt Christianity and encouraged its growth, lack of interest in the classical faith did not cause imperial decline.
- C. Incorrect. Gunpowder was not introduced to the region for many centuries.
- **D. Correct.** The empire eventually collapsed due to division and incursions by northern European tribes.

29)

- A. Incorrect. The Mongol Empire was decentralized.
- B. Incorrect. The diverse Mongol Empire included many languages and peoples.
- **C. Correct.** Decentralized governance allowed the Mongols to retain dominance by exacting tribute while leaving functional local organization intact.
- D. Incorrect. The Mongols were not Muslims.

30)

- **A. Correct.** The Muslim Arabs expanded west from the Arabian Peninsula toward the Levant, taking advantage of the weakening Byzantine Empire and eventually establishing the Umayyad Caliphate.
- B. Incorrect. The Abbasid Caliphate emerged after the Umayyad Caliphate.
- C. Incorrect. The Umayyad Caliphate was based in Damascus, not Baghdad.
- D. Incorrect. Only answer choice A is correct.

World History Post-1450

1)

- A. Incorrect. Many thousands of enslaved Africans were kidnapped and taken to the Americas to harvest cotton; however, this was not the only task they were forced to do.
- B. Incorrect. While thousands of slaves from Africa and of African origin were forced to work on sugar plantations, slaves were also forced into labor in other sectors.
- C. Incorrect. Some slaves were forced to do housework. However, given the other answer choices, this answer is incomplete, too.
- **D. Correct.** Slaves were forced to do all of the above work—and more.

2)

- A. Incorrect. While some thinkers, like Bartolomé de las Casas, spoke out against atrocities committed against the indigenous peoples of the Americas, this was not a central issue for most Europeans.
- **B. Correct.** The Scientific Revolution, humanism, and logic brought into question church teachings long regarded as fact, undermining church power.
- C. Incorrect. The church remained politically influential in Italy and Spain.
- D. Incorrect. The church had encouraged the Crusades, but was not directly responsible for them; in addition, while papal indulgences increased during the Crusades, they were not the only context in which they were granted.

3)

- **A. Correct.** Mercantilism enriched colonial powers at the expense of colonies, increasing their power relative to other European countries.
- B. Incorrect. Mercantilism was advanced by the government; it was not market based.
- C. Incorrect. The slave trade was an important element of mercantilism, enabling the cheap exploitation of labor and raw materials.
- D. Incorrect. In a mercantilist economy, the government promoted protectionism and increasing exports.

4)

- **A. Correct.** An *encomienda* was a land grant from the Spanish Crown permitting a colonists to possess land in the Americas and force Native Americans there into labor.
- B. Incorrect. The *encomienda* system was a European, not an Inca, innovation.

C. Incorrect. The *encomienda* system was not initially connected to African slavery.

D. Incorrect. The *encomienda* system was employed in the Americas.

5)

A. Incorrect. Military technology was not the primary reason the Inca Empire became so large.

B. Incorrect. The Inca did not focus on mass conversion as a reason for empire-building.

C. Correct. Agricultural surplus and advanced transportation in high altitude terrain enabled the Inca military to range widely throughout the Andes.

D. Incorrect. The Inca expanded despite the mountainous terrain.

6)

A. Incorrect. Agricultural production in the Americas called for cheap labor; consequently, European colonial powers developed the Atlantic slave trade exponentially.

B. Correct. In order to fulfill the demand for inexpensive labor in the fields and mines of the Americas, the Atlantic slave trade developed to become an enormous phenomenon.

C. Incorrect. The vast majority of slaves in the Americas had always come from Africa.

D. Incorrect. The slave trade was dominated by European colonial powers.

7)

A. Incorrect. The Columbian Exchange does encompass trade, but it also includes cultural and social exchange.

B. Incorrect. The Atlantic slave trade was certainly part of the Columbian Exchange, but this definition fails to address commercial trade, social, and cultural exchange.

C. Correct. The Columbian Exchange was the social, economic, and cultural exchange throughout the Atlantic World.

D. Incorrect. This definition does not accurately or completely describe the magnitude of the Columbian Exchange.

8)

A. Correct. Maroon communities were communities of escaped slaves throughout the Americas.

B. Incorrect. The Seminole Wars were fought between the Seminole tribe and United States forces in Florida in the nineteenth century.

C. Incorrect. The Underground Railroad took place in the nineteenth century, long after colonization and the trans-Atlantic slave trade.

D. Incorrect. The Ghost Dance movement is an example of Native American resistance to westward expansion of the United States.

9)

A. Incorrect. While Spanish *conquistadores* were able to easily subdue the Aztecs and other Mesoamerican peoples, this answer choice is insufficient, given the other options available.

B. Incorrect. Smallpox from Europeans indeed decimated local populations in the Americas, who had never been exposed to the disease. However, this answer is incomplete in the context of the entire question.

C. Incorrect. Spain sought gold at all costs; however, this answer choice does not sufficiently respond to the question.

D. Correct. All of the answer choices are true.

10)

A. Correct. As a colonial power, Belgium took advantage of the resources of the Congo.

B. Incorrect. Belgium did not control Indonesia; the Netherlands did.

C. Incorrect. Belgium was an independent monarchy and colonial power in its own right.

D. Incorrect. While not the strongest European power, Belgium's dominance of the Congo made it an important imperial power.

11)

A. Incorrect. Bolivar led revolutions for independence; he did not seek simply reform.

B. Incorrect. Bolivar's main focus was achieving South American independence from Spain.

C. Correct. Bolivar's revolutionary leadership resulted in the creation of several independent South American countries.

D. Incorrect. Spain did not defeat the revolutions in Latin America.

12)

A. Correct. Apartheid was a policy of racial segregation and unequal treatment in South Africa.

B. Incorrect. While apartheid was a system of oppression against blacks and other people of color, it was not legalized slavery.

C. Incorrect. Apartheid was a policy under independent South Africa.

D. Incorrect. Apartheid was a social policy, not a revolutionary philosophy.

13)

A. **Correct.** Spanish control over Iberia brought it enough stability to support exploration; control over the Americas and profit from mercantilism transformed it into an imperial power.

B. Incorrect. Ferdinand and Isabella had conquered the Iberian Peninsula before they sponsored colonial exploration.

C. Incorrect. Spain and Portugal diplomatically divided control over Latin America.

D. Incorrect. The Catholic Church did not bring economic profit to Spain.

14)

A. Incorrect. India was a rich source of valuable products; however, this answer choice does not sufficiently respond to the question.

B. Incorrect. While India's location was strategically advantageous for the British Empire, given the other answer choices, this one is insufficient.

C. Incorrect. Exporting to India was an important factor in Britain's success during the Industrial Revolution, but this answer choice is not sufficient, given the other options.

D. **Correct.** All of the above are true.

15)

A. Incorrect. Prussia's victory in the Franco-Prussian War proved the benefits of militarization.

B. Incorrect. Prussia's army was victorious.

C. Incorrect. The Franco-Prussian War was an early indication of the changing balance of power in Europe, as Prussia (later, Germany) was becoming an important European power.

D. **Correct.** Militarization and conscription created a fighting force strong enough to guarantee Prussia victory over the French army.

16)

A. Incorrect. The Ottoman Empire lost control over the Balkans, and European powers became increasingly involved in the region.

B. **Correct.** As Ottoman power diminished, European powers became entrenched in geostrategic alliances in the Balkans.

C. Incorrect. Russia did not control the Balkans, although it had a strong alliance with Serbia; furthermore, the Triple Entente was initially a diplomatic alliance, not the start of a military campaign.

D. Incorrect. The Three Emperors' League was a diplomatic agreement; furthermore, Austria-Hungary never controlled the entire Balkan region.

17)

A. Incorrect. Russia's relationships with these countries were tenuous at best, mainly because it supported Slavic independence movements that threatened stability in the Balkans.

B. Incorrect. Russia generally did not support these movements militarily (at least overtly); moreover, Russia did not gain territory following conflict in Eastern and Southeastern Europe in the nineteenth and twentieth century (although it did gain influence among Slavic groups like the Serbs).

C. Correct. Russian influence among Slavic minority groups under imperial control was strong.

D. Incorrect. The Ottoman and Austro-Hungarian Empires were deeply suspicious of Russia.

18)

A. Correct. European countries agreed to affirm their territories and respect sovereignty to stabilize Europe.

B. Incorrect. There were still European empires.

C. Incorrect. The powers agreed to stabilize Europe rather than punish France further, after imprisoning Napoleon.

D. Incorrect. The Austro-Hungarian Empire was still strong.

19)

A. Incorrect. The convention simply states that the Suez Canal should remain open regardless of the circumstances.

B. Incorrect. The convention does not suggest that Britain develop a privileged commercial relationship with the Ottoman Empire.

C. Correct. The convention reflects Britain's interest in protecting the strategic shipping route through the Suez Canal.

D. Incorrect. The convention does not call for stronger intra-European commercial relationships.

20)

- A. Incorrect. While the Suez Canal was immensely strategically important, this answer choice is incomplete given the other options available.
- B. Incorrect. Britain dominated the canal, given its power in Egypt. However, in the context of the other answer choices, this answer is insufficient.
- C. Incorrect. Britain clearly used the canal for trade, but this answer choice does not fully respond to the question.
- **D. Correct.** All of the above answer choices are true.

21)

- A. Incorrect. Imperial Europe was powerful worldwide during the nineteenth century.
- **B. Correct.** In the late nineteenth century, Europe largely controlled North Africa.
- C. Incorrect. European imperial powers expanded overseas, but were in competition, not united.
- D. Incorrect. The Ottoman Empire's influence in the Eastern Mediterranean was weakening.

22)

- **A. Correct.** Immediately following Partition, India and Pakistan were created. Pakistan was divided into two portions: East and West Pakistan.
- B. Incorrect. Bangladesh became independent later; originally, it was known as East Pakistan and was part of Pakistan.
- C. Incorrect. Afghanistan was never part of British India and so was not directly involved in Partition.
- D. Incorrect. Afghanistan was not part of British India, so it was not directly affected politically by Partition; furthermore, Bangladesh was originally part of Pakistan and did not become independent until 1971.

23)

- **A. Correct.** The British fought the Boer War to maintain control of South Africa from the Boers, or Afrikaners, the descendants of Dutch settlers in the region (who themselves had taken control of territory from Africans already living there).
- B. Incorrect. The Boer War took place in South Africa.
- C. Incorrect. South Africa was not yet an independent country.
- D. Incorrect. While the Afrikaners were descendants of the Dutch, the Boer War itself was not the result of Dutch imperialism.

24)

- A. Incorrect. Some members and organs of the church came to the aid of suffering dissidents, but the governments had nothing to do with that.
- B. Incorrect. There was no Argentine prison on the Falkland Islands, which was and remains a British territory.
- C. Incorrect. Dissidents were denied public trials.
- **D. Correct.** Dissidents were "disappeared," subject to extrajudicial treatment and frequently executed in secret.

25)

- **A. Correct.** In Russia, revolutionaries organized the workers; in China, revolutionaries organized the peasants.
- B. Incorrect. People suffered from starvation at times in both countries due to a series of missteps, human rights violations, natural disasters, and policy failures.
- C. Incorrect. Prison camps were widespread in both countries for periods of time.
- D. Incorrect. Ideological differences were not tolerated in China.

26)

- A. Incorrect. The Three Emperors' League had broken down by the time the Triple Alliance and Triple Entente came into effect.
- B. Incorrect. The Triple Alliance included Italy, Germany, and Austria-Hungary; the Triple Entente was comprised of Great Britain, Russia, and France.
- **C. Correct.** The Triple Entente (Russia, France, and Britain) were at odds with the Central Powers (the former Triple Alliance—Italy, Germany, and Austria-Hungary).
- D. Incorrect. Russia did not have an alliance with the Ottoman Empire.

27)

- **A. Correct.** Following the creation of NATO, a military alliance formed to counter the Soviet Union, the USSR, and the countries of the Eastern Bloc came to an agreement on collective defense—the Warsaw Pact.
- B. Incorrect. All Warsaw Pact countries were members of the United Nations.
- C. Incorrect. At the time, the European Union did not exist.
- D. Incorrect. The League of Nations no longer existed.

28)

- A. Incorrect. Independent African countries had a strong voice in the United Nations as a bloc; furthermore, not all African countries were aligned with the United States.
- B. Incorrect. The Soviet Union was not an ally of South Africa.
- C. Incorrect. Many African countries sought alliances with the USSR or bargained with both superpowers.
- **D. Correct.** Internal, post-colonial problems made African support for the ANC difficult.

29)

- A. Incorrect. South Africa was not supporting Central American communists.
- B. Incorrect. The United States did not sponsor anti-apartheid movements, although many Americans participated in anti-apartheid activism.
- **C. Correct.** Popular movements against apartheid became too powerful for governments to ignore.
- D. Incorrect. Only C is the correct answer choice.

30)

- A. Incorrect. Many African countries had lengthy coastlines.
- **B. Correct.** Parts of South Africa had been colonized by a substantial number of Europeans who settled there permanently, rather than taking up temporary residence to establish political and economic control.
- C. Incorrect. Afrikaners were of Dutch origin.
- D. Incorrect. Dutch Europeans had colonized South Africa.

US History to 1877

1)

A. Incorrect. Large-scale agriculture called for mass labor.

B. Correct. Quakers opposed slavery; furthermore, Quakerism did not develop until the Second Great Awakening.

C. Incorrect. Efforts to enslave Native Americans throughout the Western Hemisphere were unsuccessful.

D. Incorrect. In order to meet European demand for plantation-based colonial goods like tobacco, colonial producers needed increasing amounts of cheap agricultural labor.

2)

A. Correct. The Declaration of Independence was inspired by the Enlightenment, especially by John Locke and his theory of natural rights.

B. Incorrect. The Declaration of Independence did not address this issue.

C. Incorrect. The Declaration of Independence laid out specific grievances against the British.

D. Incorrect. A is the correct answer.

3)

A. Incorrect. Closing the Port of Boston was a major blow to the Colonies and one of the Intolerable Acts.

B. Incorrect. Forcing colonists to take British soldiers into their homes outraged colonial subjects.

C. Correct. The Alien and Sedition Acts were implemented during John Adams' administration.

D. Incorrect. The Massachusetts Government Act punished the colonists by revoking local control of Massachusetts.

4)

A. Correct. French colonists were generally single men seeking profit; if they stayed, they were more likely than the British to intermarry.

B. Incorrect. The British were more likely to establish settler colonies; entire families settled and formed communities in the colonies.

C. Incorrect. Both the British and the French formed strategic alliances with tribes as was expedient.

D. Incorrect. Both the British and the French had major economic interests in the Americas.

5)

A. **Correct.** In early exploration of North America, European colonists were interested in spreading Christianity, extracting tribute and labor from Native Americans, and establishing trade agreements, not intentionally spreading disease.

B. Incorrect. Smallpox decimated Native American populations, which had never been exposed to the disease.

C. Incorrect. Ongoing violent conflict between European colonizers and Native Americans over hundreds of years caused thousands of deaths and led to social breakdown among some Native American societies.

D. Incorrect. Colonization and related conflict forced tribes to move from their traditional lands; for example, the Lenape were forced to move from Delaware west to the Great Lakes region. Later, many tribes were forced from their land during the Trail of Tears to Indian Territory (later, Oklahoma).

6)

A. Incorrect. Most colonists did not initially seek independence.

B. Incorrect. Most colonists had more pressing concerns than immediate self-government.

C. Incorrect. Overthrowing the king was not on the colonial agenda.

D. **Correct.** Colonists were upset by what they perceived to be unfair taxes and restrictions on trade.

7)

A. Incorrect. The Whiskey Rebellion occurred in 1795, after the Constitutional Convention.

B. **Correct.** A militia was required to put down the Whiskey Rebellion.

C. Incorrect. The Whiskey Rebellion could not be stopped without a militia.

D. Incorrect. George Washington served two terms as president.

8)

A. Incorrect. The United States did not win any territory in the War of 1812.

B. Incorrect. The United States made no major gains in military technology.

C. Incorrect. The United States already controlled New Orleans.

D. **Correct.** A spirit of patriotism pervaded among many Americans, given that the country had successfully held off the British.

9)

- A. Incorrect. Adams was president while the Alien and Sedition Acts were in effect.
- **B. Correct.** Concerns over federal overreach led to the Democrat Jefferson's election to the presidency.
- C. Incorrect. Adams was not impeached.
- D. Incorrect. The Federalist Party fell apart later in the nineteenth century.

10)

- A. Incorrect. The United States never controlled the land south of the Rio Grande, which remains Mexico to this day.
- **B. Correct.** Following the war, the United States took control of the Southwest (today, Arizona, New Mexico, and adjacent areas), as well as California.
- C. Incorrect. These areas came under US control in the 1846 Oregon Treaty with the British.
- D. Incorrect. Idaho emerged from portions of the Washington and Dakota Territories.

11)

- A. Incorrect. Manifest Destiny and the Monroe Doctrine drove US expansion, not the concept of expanding slavery.
- B. Incorrect. Railroads did not become a major feature of the North American landscape for several decades.
- **C. Correct.** Annexing Texas posed a threat to Mexico's security in the context of Manifest Destiny.
- D. Incorrect. The treatment of agricultural workers became an important social issue in the twentieth century.

12)

- A. Incorrect. There was no major literary movement explicitly supporting women's rights (although significant women writers like Jane Austen and the Bronte sisters wrote novels with strong female characters).
- B. Incorrect. While some abolitionists also believed in improving women's rights, women's suffrage was not part of the abolitionist platform.
- **C. Correct.** Middle- and upper-middle-class women had more time to work in activism and charity, as they did not have to work.
- D. Incorrect. Women's status on the Frontier may have varied, but Frontier women were not a major part of the nineteenth century women's rights movement.

13)

- A. Incorrect. Nativists promoted the rights of white Americans who had been born in North America and whose families had been born there for generations, not Native Americans.
- **B. Correct.** The Know-Nothings were an underground nativist and anti-immigrant group.
- C. Incorrect. The Know-Nothings were particularly anti-Catholic, not anti-Protestant; immigrants from Ireland and Southern Europe were mainly Catholic, while white Americans were mainly Protestant.
- D. Incorrect. Chinese and other Asian immigrants were rarely, if ever, privileged over white immigrants.

14)

- **A. Correct.** Industrialization led to the formation of a new managerial middle class and small business owners.
- B. Incorrect. The Progressive movement emerged in the late nineteenth century.
- C. Incorrect. Slavery was not abolished until the ratification of the Thirteenth Amendment after the Civil War.
- D. Incorrect. Women did not gain voting rights until the ratification of the Nineteenth Amendment in 1920.

15)

- A. Incorrect. The Emancipation Proclamation applied to rebel states; Missouri and Kentucky did not secede.
- B. Incorrect. Lincoln freed the slaves in the Confederacy with the Emancipation Proclamation, not in the Union.
- C. Incorrect. The Emancipation Proclamation applied to the rebel states.
- **D. Correct.** The Emancipation Proclamation freed the slaves in the Confederacy.

16)

- A. Incorrect. Serious and ongoing resistance to US expansion continued long after the Battle of Fallen Timbers.
- **B. Correct.** The end of the Sioux Wars represented the last of the major battles between US and tribal forces in the West; administrative, economic, and military tactics—in addition to the loss of the buffalo—eventually subdued the Plains tribes.
- C. Incorrect. The Trail of Tears occurred after the 1830 Indian Removal Act, sixty years before the Massacre at Wounded Knee.
- D. Incorrect. The Court heard *Cherokee Nation v. Georgia* before the forced migration of Cherokee and other tribes to Indian Territory (Oklahoma).

17)

- A. Incorrect. The Union was victorious.
- **B. Correct.** The battle was devastating for both sides, but the Confederate Army suffered too many losses; the battle was a turning point for the Union.
- C. Incorrect. The Confederate Army was no longer the force it had been; furthermore, both the First and Second Battles of Bull Run had already taken place.
- D. Incorrect. The Union was victorious.

18)

- A. Incorrect. While most African Americans did remain slaves under the Confederacy, with the exception of some freedmen, this answer is insufficient, given the other choices.
- B. Incorrect. Under the Confederacy, most blacks were slaves without rights; those freedmen that did live in the area had very few. However, in the context of the other answer choices, this answer is incomplete.
- C. Incorrect. The Confederacy did not grant any privileges to slaves. Again, however, this answer choice is incomplete, given the other options.
- **D. Correct.** All of the above are true.

19)

- A. Incorrect. Maine was admitted as a free state in the Missouri Compromise.
- **B. Correct.** The Compromise of 1850 admitted California as a free state; however, it strengthened the Fugitive Slave Act. The legalization of slavery in Utah and New Mexico would be decided by the voters.
- C. Incorrect. Slavery in New Mexico and Utah would be decided by popular sovereignty.
- D. Incorrect. Slavery would never be permitted in California.

20)

- A. Incorrect. The Fugitive Slave Act was already in existence.
- B. Incorrect. The Compromise of 1850 had already taken place.
- **C. Correct.** Violence broke out over the question of legalizing slavery in Kansas, where it had previously been prohibited.
- D. Incorrect. The Missouri Compromise had taken place decades before and was essentially undone by the Kansas-Nebraska Act.

21)

- **A. Correct.** Tecumseh, a Shawnee leader, united these tribes in the Northwest Confederacy.
- B. Incorrect. The Iroquois and Algonquin lived farther east in land already part of the United States and British Canada.
- C. Incorrect. The Cherokee did not live in the Northwest, but in the South; neither did the Apache, who lived farther west.
- D. Incorrect. The Chickasaw and Choctaw lived farther south than the tribes of the Northwest Confederacy and were not involved in the Northwest Indian Wars.

22)

- A. Incorrect. The Missouri Compromise allowed slavery in Missouri.
- B. Incorrect. California was not admitted as a state until 1850.
- C. Incorrect. This was a feature of the Compromise of 1850.
- **D. Correct.** The Missouri Compromise prohibited slavery north of the thirty-sixth parallel in new US territories, permitting slavery in Missouri.

23)

- **A. Correct.** The Lincoln-Douglas Debates showed how divided the country was over slavery.
- B. Incorrect. Douglas was not so much in favor of slavery as he was a proponent of states' rights.
- C. Incorrect. Slavery and states' rights were intertwined.
- D. Incorrect. The question of slavery was at the root of the debate over states' rights.

24)

- A. Incorrect. The Underground Railroad was primarily decentralized and made up of working people, churches, and communities, not wealthy people in the North.
- B. Incorrect. The Underground Railroad helped slaves escape from the South.
- **C. Correct.** The Underground Railroad was a decentralized network of African American and other families, individuals, and churches who helped slaves escape to free states.
- D. Incorrect. The Underground Railroad was unrelated to Prohibition.

25)

- A. Incorrect. Radicals in the Republican Party favored harsher treatment for the South.
- **B. Correct.** Radical Republicans wanted to punish the South more harshly than Lincoln had planned.
- C. Incorrect. Radical Republicans sought the opposite.
- D. Incorrect. Radical Republicans were at odds with Democrats.

26)

- A. Incorrect. Following the discovery of gold on the Great Sioux Reservation, which the United States had granted to the Sioux, the US wanted control over the valuable land. However, this answer choice is incomplete in the context of the question.
- B. Incorrect. The Battle of Little Big Horn was a defeat for the US; however, this answer choice is incomplete, given the other options.
- C. Incorrect. Ongoing conflict between Plains tribes and white settlers had helped develop alliances among the western tribes; however, this answer choice is incorrect.
- **D. Correct.** All of the above choices are true.

27)

- A. Incorrect. The Ten Percent Plan was not a financial plan.
- B. Incorrect. No promises of congressional representation were ever made to freed slaves.
- **C. Correct.** The Ten Percent Plan reunited the country by allowing states to rejoin the Union with only ten percent of their populations swearing allegiance to it.
- D. Incorrect. The Ten Percent Plan did not require demographic migration.

28)

- A. Incorrect. The Homestead Act did not apportion land for Native American reservations.
- B. Incorrect. While the Homestead Act provided (mainly white, immigrant) settlers the opportunity to own property in the West, settlers had to meet certain conditions.
- **C. Correct.** White settlers who were willing to farm land for at least two years in the West would be given that property for free by the US government.
- D. Incorrect. There were no agreements made with any Native American tribes who had been living on the land the US government promised to white settlers as part of the Homestead Act.

29)

- A. Incorrect. While DuBois does not necessarily discourage any cooperation, here he encourages constructive criticism.
- **B. Correct.** DuBois believes African Americans can change the South for the better through critical interracial discourse.
- C. Incorrect. DuBois encourages dialogue between races.
- D. Incorrect. DuBois encourages the opposite.

30)

- A. Incorrect. DuBois addresses the need for interaction between races.
- B. Incorrect. DuBois emphasizes the necessity of open-mindedness.
- **C. Correct.** DuBois believes positive change can be attained in the South as long as blacks listen and remain open minded to white perspectives—while maintaining a critical perspective and judging ideas carefully.
- D. Incorrect. DuBois believes that open-mindedness is a duty, not a consideration.

US History 1877 – present

1)

- A. Incorrect. The Medicare Act was passed under the Johnson administration.
- **B. Correct.** The Social Security Act was part of the New Deal.
- C. Incorrect. The Federal Reserve Act was passed in 1913 following the Panic of 1907.
- D. Incorrect. Only answer choice B is correct.

2)

- A. Incorrect. While many New Deal programs targeted impoverished Americans, the New Deal had a wider scope than short-term poverty alleviation.
- B. Incorrect. Several New Deal programs and projects sustained economic and social development in the United States, but this does not describe the breadth of the New Deal.
- C. Incorrect. New Deal legislation did indeed address needed banking reform; however, the New Deal had other components as well.
- **D. Correct.** The New Deal encompassed programs providing immediate relief for impoverished Americans, long-term development projects, and financial reforms to prevent a repeat of the Great Depression.

3)

- A. Incorrect. While the United States gained control over former Spanish colonies in these regions, this answer choice does not completely answer the question.
- B. Incorrect. One of the major driving forces behind the war was public pressure, which had indeed been boosted by yellow journalism; however, this answer choice is incomplete given the other options.
- C. Incorrect. The Spanish-American War asserted United States military dominance in the Western Hemisphere, but this answer choice is inadequate in this context.
- **D. Correct.** All of the answer choices are true.

4)

- A. Incorrect. The Interstate Commerce Act and the Sherman Antitrust Act were ineffective until the Roosevelt administration; they were even used to break up labor unions and farmer's organizations rather than for their intended purpose.
- B. Incorrect. During Theodore Roosevelt's presidency, the Interstate Commerce Act and the Sherman Antitrust Act were finally used to break up monopolies and to ensure a fairer marketplace.

5)

- **C. Correct.** It was not until Theodore Roosevelt came into office that these acts were effectively used for their intended purpose: to create a fair market in the United States by eliminating trusts and monopolies.
- D. Incorrect. They were not immediately implemented.

5)

- **A. Correct.** The Zimmerman Telegram, a German offer to assist Mexico in attacking the US, forced the United States to enter WWI, following a series of other German provocations.
- B. Incorrect. Nazi Germany did not exist until the 1930s.
- C. Incorrect. While the assassination of Franz Ferdinand triggered the First World War in Europe, the United States did not enter the conflict until later.
- D. Incorrect. The attack on the Lusitania angered many Americans but did not alone trigger US entry into the conflict.

6)

- A. Incorrect. The Sherman Antitrust Act was a wide-ranging law intended to break up monopolies.
- **B. Correct.** The Interstate Commerce Act specifically targeted railroads.
- C. Incorrect. The International Commerce Act is not an act of Congress.
- D. Incorrect. The Sixteenth Amendment established a federal income tax.

7)

- A. Incorrect. The Roosevelt Corollary suggested a more aggressive US presence throughout the region, but it did not call for a military presence without some sort of threat.
- B. Incorrect. The Roosevelt Corollary was of a military, not economic, nature.
- C. Incorrect. Roosevelt sought to discourage strong relationships between Europe and Latin America, but the Roosevelt Corollary did not prevent diplomatic ties between the two regions.
- **D. Correct.** According to the Roosevelt Corollary to the Monroe Doctrine, the United States would intervene militarily in Latin America if it felt that its interests were threatened.

8)

- A. Incorrect. The OECD was not a United States program; it is an international organization.
- B. Incorrect. NATO was a security organization, not a rebuilding program.

C. Incorrect. While the Marshall Plan was a program to rebuild Europe, it was not a partnership with the Soviet Union.

D. **Correct.** The United States intended the Marshall Plan to rebuild Europe and protect it from Soviet communism.

9)

A. Incorrect. The United States supported Britain through the Lend-Lease Act, but did not enter the war purely to help defend that country.

B. Incorrect. The breadth of the atrocities committed by the Nazis in the Holocaust was not largely known until the end of the war; still, the United States and other countries had turned away European Jewish refugees, despite knowing they were threatened in Nazi Germany following Kristallnacht and the oppressive measures taken by the Nazi government in the 1930s.

C. **Correct.** The direct attack against the United States at Pearl Harbor in 1941 compelled the United States to enter WWII as a combatant.

D. Incorrect. The Neutrality Acts prevented US interference overseas; while the United States had a special agreement with Great Britain, it did not have any similar treaties in place with China or other East Asian and Pacific countries and maintained a policy of neutrality regarding Japanese expansion.

10)

A. Incorrect. During the Cuban Missile Crisis, the United States and the Soviet Union used diplomacy to defuse a potentially deadly situation.

B. **Correct.** The United States fought Soviet- and Chinese-supported communists in Korea, isolating them in to North Korea and preventing them from establishing an entirely communist Korea.

C. Incorrect. Glasnost and perestroika were liberalizing policies in the Soviet Union during the 1980s under Gorbachev.

D. Incorrect. The Non-Aligned Movement was an international alliance of mainly newly independent former colonies unaligned with either of the Cold War superpowers.

11)

A. Incorrect. The Lend-Lease Act did not apply to Japan.

B. Incorrect. The Lend-Lease Act applied internationally, not domestically.

C. Incorrect. The Lend-Lease Act did not apply to the Soviet Union.

D. **Correct.** The Lend-Lease Act enabled the United States to support Britain without joining the war as a combatant.

12)

- A. Incorrect. Both institutions were and are comprised of many countries.
- **B. Correct.** The Security Council has military powers that the League of Nations did not have.
- C. Incorrect. The League of Nations was intended to provide a diplomatic forum that would prevent another large-scale war.
- D. Incorrect. The Security Council is made up of countries from around the world; furthermore, the United States was not a member of the League of Nations.

13)

- A. Incorrect. The Gulf of Tonkin Resolution allowed the president substantial latitude in committing forces.
- **B. Correct.** The Gulf of Tonkin Resolution gave the president power to commit military troops in Vietnam without congressional authorization.
- C. Incorrect. The head of the military is the president, and Congress empowers the president to take lengthy military action.
- D. Incorrect. The United States was allied with South Vietnamese forces.

14)

- A. Incorrect. Cold War divisions emerged after the war and were unplanned.
- B. Incorrect. The Atlantic Charter did not pursue military occupation.
- C. Incorrect. The Atlantic Charter envisioned a global future; it did not determine current the military or economic status of a region.
- **D. Correct.** The Atlantic Charter embodied the shared vision of the United States and Great Britain for the postwar world.

15)

- A. Incorrect. The United States focused militarily on Europe before the Pacific.
- **B. Correct.** The United States helped ensure the defeat of Nazi Germany before defeating Japan.
- C. Incorrect. Kamikaze attacks were a Japanese tactic, not a German one.
- D. Incorrect. The United States never invaded Japan.

16)

- A. Incorrect. Social Security was a New Deal program.
- **B. Correct.** The Great Society was rooted in Johnson's War on Poverty and in liberalism: the belief that government programs should support those in need (and that the US should be active in fighting communism overseas).

C. Incorrect. The CIA was founded before the Johnson administration and the Department of Homeland Security was created under President George W. Bush.

D. Incorrect. There was no specific plan to end the war in Vietnam in the 1960s.

17)

A. Incorrect. The Equal Rights Amendment was never ratified.

B. Incorrect. Women's rights activists worked for the passage of the Equal Pay Act, but this answer choice is incomplete given the context.

C. Incorrect. Women's rights activists supported Supreme Court cases regarding birth control and abortion, but again, this answer choice is incomplete in the context of this question.

D. Correct. B and C are correct.

18)

A. Incorrect. The Gulf of Tonkin Resolution allowed the president substantial latitude in committing forces.

B. Correct. The Gulf of Tonkin Resolution gave the president power to commit military troops in Vietnam without Congressional authorization.

C. Incorrect. The head of the military is the president, and Congress empowers the president to take lengthy military action.

D. Incorrect. The United States was allied with South Vietnamese forces.

19)

A. Incorrect. The Voting Rights Act of 1965 eliminated restrictions on voting rights of African Americans.

B. Incorrect. The Civil Rights Act of 1964 did not take sexual orientation into account.

C. Correct. The Civil Rights Act of 1964 made segregation illegal.

D. Incorrect. Only answer choice C is true.

20)

A. Correct. *Brown v. Board of Education* found that keeping races separate (in this case, in segregated schools) could not ensure that all people would receive equal treatment, and that segregation was therefore unconstitutional.

B. Incorrect. *Plessy v. Ferguson* upheld segregation.

C. Incorrect. *Scott v. Sandford* upheld and strengthened the Fugitive Slave Act, thereby upholding the Kansas-Nebraska Act and effectively abolishing the Missouri Compromise.

D. Incorrect. *Korematsu v. US* ruled the constitutionality of the Japanese internment camps during WWII.

21)

A. Incorrect. While the United States was deeply involved in making peace in the former Yugoslavia, this answer is incomplete.

B. Incorrect. The United States did not play a major role in making peace in Rwanda.

C. Correct. The United States led peace talks to resolve conflict in Bosnia and the former Yugoslavia as well as in Northern Ireland.

D. Incorrect. Again, the United States did not lead peace talks in Rwanda.

22)

A. Incorrect. Black men won the right to vote with the Fifteenth Amendment; black women could vote after the ratification of the Nineteenth Amendment (although in practice, African American men and women were often denied this right).

B. Incorrect. Americans eighteen years of age and older were able to vote after the ratification of the Twenty-Sixth Amendment.

C. Incorrect. Segregation in public places ended with the Civil Rights Act.

D. Correct. The Voting Rights Act abolished discriminatory restrictions that prevented African Americans from exercising their right to vote.

23)

A. Incorrect. Non-violent civil disobedience was widely used during the Civil Rights Movement. However, this answer choice is incomplete in the context of this question.

B. Incorrect. Large-scale demonstrations and marches were famous for promoting social and political change; however, given the other answer choices, this answer choice is insufficient.

C. Incorrect. Elements of the Civil Rights Movement, especially Black Power, focused on black empowerment in urban areas. Again, however, this answer choice is insufficient given the context of this question.

D. Correct. All of the above answer choices are true.

24)

- A. Incorrect. Lower taxes were thought to drive spending, not necessarily lead to job creation.
- **B. Correct.** Conservative theory postulated that lower taxes would permit people and businesses to spend more, growing the economy.
- C. Incorrect. Conservatives believe in fewer social programs, and the Reagan administration cut many social programs.
- D. Incorrect. Conservatives believe in military spending; lower taxes would not affect military budgets.

25)

- A. Incorrect. People in many countries, many cultures, and of many faiths enjoy US pop culture worldwide. However, in the context of this question, this answer is incomplete.
- B. Incorrect. US innovations are widely used globally; again, though, this answer is insufficient given the other answer choices.
- C. Incorrect. The United States maintains active military bases worldwide. However, this answer does not sufficiently respond to the question, given the other choices available.
- **D. Correct.** All of the above choices are true.

26)

- A. Incorrect. While an important factor in the economic problems of the early twenty-first century, auto loans were not the main reason for the 2008 Great Recession.
- **B. Correct.** The Subprime Mortgage Crisis was a central cause of the Great Recession.
- C. Incorrect. Problems with student loans have been and continue to be an economic concern, but did not drive the Great Recession.
- D. Incorrect. Credit card debt devastated the finances of many Americans and remains an economic issue; however, it was not the main force behind the Great Recession.

27)

- A. Incorrect. NAFTA permitted free trade among the three countries, but national borders remain, and movement of people is restricted.
- **B. Correct.** NAFTA is a free trade agreement among the three countries.
- C. Incorrect. NAFTA is not a political agreement.
- D. Incorrect. NAFTA is not an immigration agreement; it deals only with international trade.

28)

A. Incorrect. The United States did not occupy Iraq until the 2003 Iraq War.

B. Incorrect. Iraq was driven from Kuwait in 1991.

C. Correct. Having led the coalition that defeated Iraq in the 1991 Gulf War, the United States proved its position as the sole superpower following the end of the Cold War with the collapse of the Soviet Union.

D. Incorrect. The relationship between the United States and the Soviet Union, while not destabilized, did not necessarily improve in the context of multilateral diplomacy.

29)

A. Correct. Iraq posed a threat to the biggest oil producers in the Persian Gulf; the United States needed to secure its energy interests there.

B. Incorrect. While stability in the region was in the best interest of the United States, such a situation was unlikely at the time given Iraq's focus on weaker Persian Gulf oil producers over Iran's hardened military.

C. Incorrect. Terrorism did not become a major feature of US policy toward Iraq until the twenty-first century (although US foreign policy did consider terrorism a threat from Iran and other Middle Eastern countries and groups).

D. Incorrect. Regime change in Iraq was not a US policy goal until the twenty-first century.

30)

A. Incorrect. The Equal Rights Amendment was never ratified.

B. Incorrect. The United States does not have a progressive income tax.

C. Incorrect. The United States has one of the highest rates of incarceration in the world.

D. Correct. Same-sex marriage became legal in the United States in 2015 and the LGBT community is more accepted than ever before in many parts of the country.

Made in the USA
Middletown, DE
11 October 2016

MATHEMATICS APPRECIATION

James Magliano
Union County College

Susan E. McLoughlin
Union County College

Middlesex County College
Library
2600 Woodbridge Avenue
Edison, NJ 08818

KENDALL/HUNT PUBLISHING COMPANY
4050 Westmark Drive   Dubuque, Iowa 52002

Copyright © 1996 by James Magliano and Susan E. McLoughlin

ISBN 0-7872-2490-1

All rights reserved. No part of this publication may be reproduced, stored in a retrieval system, or transmitted, in any form or by any means, electronic, mechanical, photocopying, recording, or otherwise, without the prior written permission of the copyright owner.

Printed in the United States of America
10 9 8 7 6 5 4 3 2

CONTENTS

Detailed Contents **iv**
Foreword **xi**
Preface **xiii**

Chapter 1   **Logic**   1

Chapter 2   **Sets**   33

Chapter 3   **Algebra and Matrices**   71

Chapter 4   **Operations Research and Game Theory**   121

Chapter 5   **Number Theory**   153

Chapter 6   **Systems of Numeration**   207

Chapter 7   **Groups**   229

Chapter 8   **The Computer Age**   251

Chapter 9   **Geometry**   277

Chapter 10   **Probability and Counting**   305

Chapter 11   **Statistics**   351

Solutions, Answers, and Hints to Selected Exercises   389

Index   407

DETAILED CONTENTS

Foreword **xi**
Preface **xiii**

Chapter 1   **Logic**   **1**

1.0   **Introduction**   **3**
1.1   **Historical Perspective**   **3**
     Valid Reasoning   **4**
     Fallacies   **4**
     Modern Refinements   **4**
1.2   **Preliminaries; Logical Connectives; Conjunction**   **5**
     Examples and Non–Examples of Statements   **5**
     Symbolic Representation of Statements   **6**
     Conjunction   **6**
     Examples of Conjunctions   **6**
     The Truth Table for Conjunction   **7**
1.3   **More Connectives; Comparing Statements**   **9**
     Disjunction   **9**
     Negation   **10**
     Comparing Statements   **10**
1.4   **Material Implication**   **14**
1.5   **More on Material Implication**   **17**
     Converse of an Implication   **17**
     Inverses and Contrapositives   **17**
1.6   **Rewording Implications**   **18**
1.7   **Logical Proofs**   **20**
     Direct Reasoning   **22**
     An Invalid Argument   **23**
1.8   **The Incompleteness Theorem**   **24**
     Self–reference   **25**
     Self–reference and Literature   **27**
     Self–reference and Art   **27**
1.9   **Chapter Review**   **30**

Chapter 2   **Sets**   33

     2.0   **Introduction**   35
     2.1   **Historical Perspective**   35
     2.2   **Preliminary Concepts; Sets, Elements, and Notation**   36
                  Examples and Non–examples of Sets   36
                  Basic Notation   36
                  The Empty Set   37
                  Universal Sets   38
                  Cardinality of a Set   38
     2.3   **Membership; Subsets**   39
     2.4   **Set Operations**   41
                  Set Union   41
                  Set Intersection   41
                  Properties of Basic Set Operations   42
                  Other Set Operations; Difference and Complements   43
     2.5   **Euler Circles and Venn Diagrams**   45
           2.5.1   **Venn Diagrams and Sets**   45
           2.5.2   **Survey Diagrams**   52
           2.5.3   **Euler Circles and Logical Arguments**   62
                  A Fallacious Argument   65
     2.6   **Infinite Sets**   67
     2.7   **Chapter Review**   69

Chapter 3   **Algebra and Matrices**   71

     3.0   **Introduction**   73
     3.1   **Historical Perspective**   73
     3.2   **Solving Linear Equations**   74
     3.3   **Solving Linear Inequalities**   80
     3.4   **Solving Systems of Linear Equations**   83
     3.5   **Introduction to Matrices**   92
     3.6   **Matrix Arithmetic**   94
                  Addition and Subtraction   94
                  Scalar Multiplication   95
                  Multiplication of Matrices   96
     3.7   **Solving Systems of Linear Equations Using Matrices**   105
     3.8   **Inverses and Some Applications**   112
                  Solving Systems of Equations Using Inverses   114
                  Cryptography   114
     3.9   **Chapter Review**   118

Chapter 4 Operations Research and Game Theory 121

- 4.0 **Introduction** 123
- 4.1 **Historical Perspective** 124
  - *Operations Research* 124
  - *Games* 125
- 4.2 **The Design of Operations Research** 125
- 4.3 **Linear Programming** 127
  - *A Maximization Problem – Baseball Bats* 127
  - *A Minimization Problem – Stocks* 136
  - *The Simplex Method* 138
- 4.4 **Other Operations Research Techniques** 139
  - *Queuing Theory* 139
  - *Sinking Funds* 140
  - *Forecasting* 140
  - *Conclusion* 141
- 4.5 **The Theory of Games** 141
  - *The Toothpaste Example* 142
- 4.6 **Some Examples of Games** 143
  - *Reverse Tic-Tac-Toe* 143
  - *Analysis of the Game* 144
  - *The Game of Sim* 145
  - *A Variation of Sim* 147
  - *The Game of Domineering* 147
  - *Games as Numbers* 148
- 4.7 **Chapter Review** 150

Chapter 5 Number Theory 153

- 5.0 **Introduction** 155
- 5.1 **Historical Perspective** 155
- 5.2 **Some Familiar Classifications of Numbers** 156
- 5.3 **Prime Numbers** 157
  - *Prime and Composite Numbers* 158
  - *Sieve of Eratosthenes* 159
  - *Twin Primes* 160
  - *Mersenne Primes* 161
  - *Goldbach's Conjecture* 161
- 5.4 **Divisibility Tests** 163
  - *Factor Trees* 165
  - *Division* 165
  - *The Least Common Multiple* 166
  - *The Greatest Common Factor* 167
- 5.5 **Other Topics Concerning Primes and Factoring** 170
  - *Perfect Numbers* 170

Deficient and Abundant Numbers **171**
Amicable Numbers **172**
Magic **172**

5.6 Number Sequences 173
5.7 Arithmetic and Geometric Sequences 176
5.8 The Fibonacci Sequence 189
5.9 Patterns and Magic Squares 194
Pascal's Triangle **195**
Magic Squares **196**
5.10 Chapter Review 204

Chapter 6 Systems of Numeration 207

6.0 Introduction 209
6.1 Historical Perspective 209
6.2 Types of Systems of Numeration 210
Repetitive Systems **210**
Multiplicative Systems **211**
Ciphered Systems **212**
Positional Systems **212**
6.3 The Egyptian System 214
6.4 Roman Numerals 216
6.5 The Babylonian Numeration System 219
6.6 The Mayan Numeration System 223
6.7 The Hindu–Arabic System of Numeration 226
6.8 Chapter Review 227

Chapter 7 Groups 229

7.0 Introduction 231
7.1 Historical Perspective 231
Polynomial Equations **232**
The Contribution of Evariste Galois **233**
7.2 The Group Concept 233
7.3 The Definition of a Group 235
Abelian Groups **237**
7.4 Examples and Non–Examples of Groups 239
7.5 Isomorphic Groups 247
7.6 Chapter Review 250

Chapter 8 The Computer Age 251

8.0 Introduction 253
8.1 Historical Perspective 253
Digital versus Analog Computers **254**
The Abacus **254**

The Slide Rule **255**
Early Mechanical Calculators **256**
Control of the Machine – Punched Cards and Data Storage **257**
Other Advances **258**
Modern Electronic Computers **258**
First Generation Machines **259**
Second Generation Machines **259**
Third Generation Machines **259**
Fourth Generation Machines **260**

8.2 Computer Functions 260
Input **261**
Storage **262**
Internal Storage **262**
External Storage **262**
Processing **263**
Output **263**

8.3 The Role of the Computer 264
Numerical Applications **264**
Clerical Applications and Data Processing **264**
The Airline Industry **265**
Other Examples of Data Processing **265**
Pattern Recognition **266**
The Turing Test **267**
Simulation **268**

8.4 Modern Trends in Computing 269
Home Computing **270**
Office Computing **270**
Scientific Computing **271**
Neural Networks, Expert Systems, and Artificial Intelligence **272**
The Arts **272**

8.5 Chapter Review 274

Chapter 9   Geometry 277

9.0 Introduction 279
9.1 Historical Perspective 279
9.2 The Geometry of Euclid 280
The Special Status of Geometry **280**
Definitions **281**
Postulates and Axioms **281**
Theorems **282**

9.3 Plane Analytical Geometry and Other Developments 283
The Coordinate System **283**
Locating Points **284**
The Utility of Analytical Geometry **284**

Projective Geometry **287**

9.4 Non–Euclidean Geometry 289
Girolamo Saccheri's Attempt; Reducio ad Absurdum **290**
The Birth of Non–Euclidean Geometry **290**
Riemannian Geometry **292**
A Model for Elliptic Geometry **292**
A Model for Hyperbolic Geometry **293**
Use of the Models **293**
Differences in Theorems **294**

9.5 Modern Geometry; Fractals 295
Symmetry **295**
Mandelbrot's Contribution **295**
The Nature of Self–Similarity **299**
The Self–Similarity of Nature **300**
Fractal Growth **302**
Fractal Models of Other Processes **302**

9.6 Chapter Review 303

Chapter 10 Probability and Counting 305

10.0 Introduction 307
10.1 Historical Perspective 307
10.2 The Fundamental Counting Principle 308
10.3 Permutations 310
10.4 Combinations 314
More Complex Combinations **317**
Pascal's Triangle **318**
10.5 Counting Trees 320
10.6 Counting Problems 325
Duplicate Items **328**
10.7 Types of Probabilities 331
Preliminaries **331**
Basic Notation **332**
Classical Probability **333**
Relative Frequency Probability **335**
Subjective Probability **337**
10.8 Probability Problems and Basic Facts 339
Facts about Probability **339**
Complements **340**
Probability Involving "or" **341**
Probability of Independent Events **342**
10.9 Odds 345
Converting Odds to Probabilities **347**
Converting Probabilities to Odds **347**
10.10 Chapter Review 349

Chapter 11   Statistics   351

- 11.0   **Introduction**   353
- 11.1   **Historical Perspective**   353
- 11.2   **Some Basic Terminology**   354
- 11.3   **Sampling**   355
  - *Quota Samples*   355
  - *Random Samples*   356
  - *Systematic Samples*   356
  - *Stratified Samples*   356
  - *Unrepresentative Samples*   357
- 11.4   **Graphs**   358
  - *Pie Charts*   358
  - *Bar Charts*   360
  - *Histograms*   362
  - *Frequency Polygons*   365
  - *Scatter Plots*   367
- 11.5   **Measures of Central Tendency**   373
  - *The Mean*   373
  - *The Median*   375
  - *The Mode*   376
- 11.6   **Measures of Dispersion**   378
  - *The Range*   379
  - *The Standard Deviation*   380
- 11.7   **The Truthfulness of Statistics and Graphs**   383
- 11.8   **Modern Methods**   385
- 11.9   **Chapter Review**   386

Solutions, Answers, and Hints to Selected Exercises   389

Index   407

FOREWORD

It is not so easy to carry on a conversation using 103 words of Italian, 49 of which are flavors of ice cream. Nevertheless, I was riding some years ago in a second class coach between Florence and Pisa, trying hard to talk with the only other occupant of the compartment. I think maybe he spoke 103 words of English. "What do you do?" he asked. "I teach mathematics." "Ah," he said, perhaps a little proudly, "mathematics was my worst subject."

Every math teacher I know tells the same story, more or less, but maybe not set on the Ferrovia del Stato. Educated, intelligent, and cultured folks are supposed to know Shakespeare and Aquinas and Mozart, or at least to be able to say something relevant while moving the conversation to more familiar ground. Not so often do we hear, "Oh, I never could understand Polonius."

Why is fear of mathematics acceptable, while fear of Hamlet confers a certain stigma? Why does almost everyone know Beethoven's "Moonlight Sonata," while almost no one has even heard of Carl Friedrich Gauss's *Disquisitiones Arithmeticae*? (Both were published in 1801, but while the "Moonlight" is just another sonata, the *Disquisitiones* is the second greatest mathematics text ever written.)

Probably we know the answers, both as teachers and as students. Most of us can enjoy Hamlet or Beethoven without feeling that we will be examined on our own writing, or our own skill as a composer or performer. Mathematics, on the other hand, frequently appears as an unforgiving taskmaster, a hurdle preceding progress in science and technology, a competency required for graduation or employment. We can choose to participate in literature, music, philosophy, or art, and our rewards increase with the depth of our activity. Many of us, and surely most of our students, do not choose mathematics freely. Typical courses of study in mathematics also do not allow a choice of observation or participation. "Mathematics is learned by doing mathematics." A student who has been unsuccessful at doing mathematics cannot usually be expected to appreciate mathematics.

What can we do as teachers for our students who cannot do mathematics well and who believe they will never be able to do mathematics well? Is there any hope of persuading them that mathematics is not only useful and necessary, but also beautiful? Must competence precede appreciation? On the other hand, will appreciation improve the prospects of competence, especially for those whom competence has eluded for some years?

In *Death at an Early Age*, his book about teaching children surrounded by hopelessness, Jonathan Kozol wrote about his violin lessons. He wanted to achieve some competence in playing the violin, but mostly he wrote experiencing the tension of trying to learn something new and extremely difficult. He tried hard to emulate the feelings his students confronted when faced with a mathematics lesson. We mathematics teachers have to work at sympathy, since math was always easy for us, and sometimes we cannot remember not understanding, in an internalized and almost automatic way, issues which are serious roadblocks for our students. We are not always completely persuaded that we know everything, but most of us, most of the time, believe that given enough time and effort we can figure out what we need to know. If we put in enough hours, we are pretty sure we can get it straight. So, when our

students fail to perform, we wonder if they put in the time, or if they just failed to behave in a conscientious manner.

I admit that not all of my students are conscientious, but I suspect that a lot of them would do better mathematics and enjoy it more if I were better at communicating with them. How can we teach these students? I don't really know very well, but I have some strong convictions. We have to assume that they are willing to work on mathematics, or at least that they would be willing to work if they were not afraid. We have to assume that they are literate. We have to assume that they know a lot, and that they will be more successful in learning mathematics if we can relate mathematics to the world they already know. We have to believe that mathematics is useful and beautiful. We have to believe that given enough time and effort we can figure out how to show our students this utility and this beauty. We have to believe that if we put in enough hours, we can get it straight.

Mathematics Appreciation assumes the right things about our students and helps us believe in our own teaching. I recommend it for teachers, students, and readers. When you finish working through it, you could start on the *Disquisitiones*.

Bostwick F. Wyman
The Ohio State University

PREFACE

In 1959 the British physicist and novelist C.P. Snow introduced the phrase "the two cultures." He regretted that these two cultures, the literary realm of the arts and humanities on the one hand, and the mathematical and scientific community on the other, contained people of similar intelligence, yet had so little in common that communication between them was almost non–existent. The meeting of these two cultures — which would do so much to benefit both — never seemed to take place. Neither culture seemed to be aware of the ways that the other could enrich and even elevate it.

Mathematics Appreciation was written for students whose main interests lie in the areas of the arts, humanities, or education. Its purpose is to show how the understanding and enjoyment of these fields can be enhanced by the insights which the study of mathematics has to offer. This is accomplished both through the development of useful skills, such as those learned in the chapters on statistics and probability, and through exposure to the unexpected and subtle connections between mathematics and other disciplines. The authors' explicit goal in writing this text was to make students more aware of these connections between mathematics and other areas of study, and to help them in the construction of bridges between the "two cultures." The strategic placement of "Questions to Discuss" and "Small Group Exercises" throughout the text is intended to facilitate the construction of these bridges by students. The questions to discuss are designed to inspire students to look more intensely at mathematics and its many relationships to other fields, and to express their resulting thoughts in words rather than mathematical symbols. The small group exercises require students to delve more deeply, to discuss, and to discover mathematics. We hope that through these exercises the students will develop a better awareness of the true nature of mathematics, a better understanding of their own discipline, and a better understanding of the position of mathematics when compared to mankind's other accomplishments.

Accomplishment of our goal would bring with it many attractive benefits. One of the most desirable of these would be a better understanding by the public at–large of the nature and importance of mathematics. The common notion that mathematics is simply a "toolbox" containing formulas and techniques which only a lucky few can utilize is not simply inaccurate, but a gross underestimation of the impact of the subject on the development of human thought. An improved understanding of the role of mathematics is essential if we are to reverse the current trend, which has minimized mathematics so much that our children are not exposed to the benefits and the wonders of the subject.

On a more practical note, the prerequisites needed for understanding this text are minimal. A knowledge of elementary algebra should be more than enough, and even that is not explicitly needed in most sections. Many of the exercises in the text are essay questions, although as indicated above, some chapters do contain more traditional skills problems. Students are given an opportunity to take an active part in the development of the subject.

To The Student

In recent years a mini-revolution has taken place. A number of mathematicians, such as Rudy Rucker (*Infinity and the Mind; Mind Tools*), Ivars Peterson (*The Mathematical Tourist*), Martin Gardner (*Knotted Doughnuts and Other Mathematical Entertainments; Time Travel and Other Mathematical Bewilderments*), Robert Osserman (*Poetry of the Universe—A Mathematical Exploration of the Cosmos*), and John McLeish (*The Story of Numbers—How Mathematics Has Shaped Civilization*) have written books which attempt to bring the wonder and excitement of mathematics to the general public. These books have made some of the natural connections between mathematics and other subjects more explicit. Now it's time to bring some of this excitement into the classroom.

In order to clarify the connections between mathematics and other disciplines, this book will give you the opportunity to build bridges to other fields through "Questions to Discuss" and "Small Group Exercises." Some of these are designed to probe a specific connection with another field, while others are not as focused, aiming for a general understanding of some common principle. These small group exercises may incorporate short essays to focus and guide students in attaining this understanding. We have found that these offer a wonderful chance for students to solidify their understanding of the connection between mathematics and some other area, while at the same time we as teachers never fail to pick up some new and unexpected insight that the students have brought from their field of study. In this way, many of the short essays that result from these exercises will benefit both teacher and student. In addition, each chapter contains a review which includes a list of important terms, a list of important names, and a small set of review exercises. These were designed to help you reinforce your understanding of the chapter, and to place it into the wider context of your knowledge.

Some warnings before you move into the text: First of all, from the preceding two paragraphs it should be clear that this is not a remedial text. Furthermore, although most of the material in the book is not the "mechanical manipulation of symbols" that you may have experienced in earlier mathematics classes, it is demanding. You will be expected to master concepts, to have opinions, and to involve yourself in your study of the subject. You will be asked to write essays because this is the only way that you can make your opinions known, and to clarify for yourself the important relationships that exist between mathematics and other intellectual endeavors. You will work hard, but the results will be well worth the effort. Our experience has been that students are often surprised by what is expected of them, surprised by what is not expected of them, and surprised by the fact that they can understand, and even do, a considerable amount of mathematics.

Acknowledgments

There were many people whose encouragement and assistance were invaluable in the completion of this project. Special thanks go to Steve Kato of the Union County College Media Center and Elizabeth Leppig of the Union County College Faculty Resource Center who worked so hard to assist us in capturing the graphics images in the text; and to Mark Bala and Susan Connelly, computer gurus extraordinaire, whose advice and tips kept the project on track despite impossible odds. Diagrams and graphs were prepared with the assistance of Serif DrawPlus 2.0.

> Thanks to my fiancée Gloria, whose patience, understanding, technical expertise, and encouragement all played key roles in the completion of the manuscript.
>
> — James Magliano

> Thanks to my husband, Peter, and my three daughters, Mary Emily, Kathleen and Patricia, whose encouragement kept me going when unexpected frustrations surfaced and whose patience and understanding showed how much they believed in me and in this project.
>
> — Susan McLoughlin

Chapter One

Logic

"In formal logic, a contradiction is the signal of defeat. But in the evolution of real knowledge it marks the first step in progress toward a victory."

Alfred North Whitehead

Chapter One: LOGIC

Chapter Outline

1.0 Introduction

1.1 Historical Perspective
    Valid Reasoning
    Fallacies
    Modern Refinements

1.2 Preliminaries; Logical Connectives; Conjunction
    Examples and Non–Examples of Statements
    Symbolic Representation of Statements
    Conjunction
    Examples of Conjunctions
    The Truth Table for Conjunction

1.3 More Connectives; Comparing Statements
    Disjunction
    Negation
    Comparing Statements

1.4 Material Implication

1.5 More on Material Implication
    Converse of an Implication
    Inverses and Contrapositives

1.6 Rewording Implications

1.7 Logical Proofs
    Direct Reasoning
    An Invalid Argument

1.8 The Incompleteness Theorem
    Self–reference
    Self–reference and Literature
    Self–reference and Art

1.9 Chapter Review

1.0 Introduction

Mathematical Logic (also called Symbolic Logic, Formal Logic and Analytical Philosophy) is the basis for all mathematical reasoning. In its most abstract form logic deals with the manipulation of symbols with respect to certain rules. The subject was originally developed as a tool to be used in the study of other subjects, and is still used extensively in fields such as computer science. However, careful examination of this tool has recently led to some of the most interesting and surprising results in the history of human thought.

Our study of logic will enable us to understand some of the important questions which are now being discussed in other areas of mathematics and allied fields, such as geometry and computer science. It should also allow us to get a sense of how man's understanding of what mathematics is, and what it can and cannot accomplish, has changed in recent years.

Upon completion of this chapter you should better understand the logical foundation of the sciences and mathematics. You should also be able to distinguish between a good argument and a bad one, and have some idea of the limitations on logical reasoning that have been discovered in recent years. This chapter will conclude with an indication of how the study of mathematical logic can improve your understanding and appreciation of the arts and humanities.

1.1 Historical Perspective

The person generally credited with the development of logic into the instrument which has proved to be indispensable in so many disciplines was the Greek philosopher Aristotle (4th century BC). Motivated by his desire to study the sciences, Aristotle was interested in tracing causes and drawing conclusions from observed events. This led him to the classification of the valid forms of logical deduction. He also pointed out common mistakes in logical arguments, which are called *fallacies*. His idea was that all good arguments would always fit into "approved patterns" in which conclusions were the inescapable result of the form of the argument rather than the content of the statements. Verifying that an argument was valid would simply mean checking to see if it fit into one of the approved patterns.

Valid Reasoning

The design of Aristotle's program was simple. All good arguments, called *valid arguments*, or *syllogisms*, would always lead to true conclusions from true assumptions. The forms of all valid arguments were then listed, and you could decide if the argument you were considering were valid by simply comparing its form with those in Aristotle's list.

The usual first example of a valid argument goes something like this:

Every Greek is a man.
Every man is mortal.
Every Greek is mortal.

In this argument the first two sentences (above the horizontal line) are called the *hypotheses*, or *premises*, of the argument. The third sentence is called the *conclusion*. Because this argument agrees in form with one of the approved patterns in Aristotle's list, it is valid. Assuming that everything was working according to Aristotle's plan, this would still not be enough to guarantee the truth of the conclusion, but *it would guarantee that the conclusion is true whenever the hypotheses are true*. In this way the truth of the conclusion was reduced to the truth of the premises, which presumably were either proved previously or were accepted basic principles.

Fallacies

Fallacies, or arguments that did not agree with the models in Aristotle's approved list, would not always lead to true conclusions, even if all of the hypotheses were true. An example of a fallacious argument follows:

If I win the lottery, then I'll pay you the money I owe you.
I paid you the money that I owed you.
I won the lottery.

This argument is not valid because it is possible for the conclusion to be false even if both premises are true. In other words, I might have paid you the money that I owed you even though I didn't win the lottery. Because the truth of the conclusion does not follow inescapably from the truth of the premises, this type of argument would not appear on Aristotle's "approved list."

Modern Refinements

Aristotle's plan worked quite well. In fact, over the next two thousand years, very few improvements of his methods were found. Some refinements were made in the 17th century by the German *Gottfried Wilhelm Leibniz* (who is more well known as being one of the inventors of calculus), and in the 19th century by the Englishmen *George Boole* and *Augustus De Morgan*. Through these advances, which introduced the modern symbolism used in representing arguments, decisions could be made following rules that were similar to the those learned in elementary algebra to solve equations.

In the late 19th and early 20th centuries the concept of the *truth table* was developed by a number of logicians, including Americans Charles Saunders Peirce and Emil Post, the Pole Jan Lukasiewicz, and the Austrian–English logician Ludwig Wittgenstein. We will be studying truth tables because they give an efficient way of analyzing arguments and testing their validity. This will give us a way to complete Aristotle's program without having to write down his complete list of "approved patterns."

1.2 Preliminaries; Logical Connectives; Conjunction

Very early in the study of logic the importance of clarity and precision were recognized. Without proper care a large number of apparent *paradoxes*, or self–contradictory statements, arose. These cast some doubt on the ability of logic to deal with all possible situations. At one time it was hoped that if enough care was exercised, all paradoxes would be eliminated. It has now been shown that no matter how careful you are some paradoxes will persist, but the need for clear, precise definitions is still seen as important.

One of the paradoxes which came up early was called the *Liar Paradox* (also known as the *Cretan Paradox* and the *Epimenides' Paradox*). Various versions of this paradox are still popular today (at least in mathematics classes). One of the simplest versions of this paradox is the sentence "This sentence is false."

If the words "true" and "false" are used the way we normally use them in everyday speech, then it is impossible to assign either of these two truth values to this sentence. First of all, if we try to assign the sentence the value "true," then we must believe what the sentence says. But it says it is false, so it must also be false.

The only other possibility is that the sentence might be false. This means that we may not believe what it says. It says it is false, so if we are not to believe that, then it must be true.

The result of all this is that the only way for this sentence to be true is if it is also false, and the only way for it to be false is if it is also true. We seem to be in trouble no matter which way we go!

There have been many attempts at trying to circumvent this paradox. One of the simplest is to very carefully limit the scope of what logic deals with by finding a way to exclude this and other troublesome sentences. This is done by carefully defining the types of sentences that logic will be applied to.

Definition: Logic deals with *statements* (or *propositions*). A statement is a sentence which is either true or false, but not both.

This restrictive definition insures that the Liar Paradox will not be a problem, because it simply refuses to let logic have anything to do with this sentence! One problem with this is that certain very reasonable looking sentences which cause problems are simply ignored for no other reason than the fact that they are causing trouble. For now we will content ourselves with this definition, however eventually we hope to get some insight into the real reason why sentences similar to this one cause such difficulties.

Examples and Non–examples of Statements

The following are statements:

1. It is raining. (It is assumed here that the sentence refers to a specific place and time. It also is assumed that there is some empirical way of testing the sentence. That is, that there is some practical way of deciding whether or not it is raining.)
2. $9 + 5 = 45$. (Hopefully we all know whether or not this is true.)
3. The capital of Michigan is Detroit. (Hopefully anyone who is not sure will know a way of finding out if this is true or false.)

The following are not statements:

1. This sentence is false.
2. Go to school.

3. Gloria is pretty. (This is an opinion. There is no test that can be applied to Gloria to decide if the sentence is true or false. Although not a statement, there are times when the rules of logic might be applied to sentences such as this to aid in drawing conclusions. In fact, some of the analysis that we do in chapter 2 will be applied to sentences like this even though they are not really statements.)

Symbolic Representations of Statements

When we analyze statements to decide whether or not they are true we want to make sure that the judgments we make are based solely on logic, and not on our emotions or any other attributes of the statements. One way of making sure that we do not get emotionally involved in the argument we are analyzing is to use letters to represent simple statements. That there are also other reasons for wanting to do this will soon become evident. *It is customary to use the lower case letters p, q, r,... to represent the simple statements that make up the complex statements which we will be studying. It is also standard practice to use the capital letters T and F to represent the truth values "true" and "false."*

To indicate that the variable p will represent the sentence "I like peppermint." we will write

p: I like peppermint.

This may be read as *"p represents 'I like peppermint.'"* *Note how colons are used in a way that is similar to the way equals signs are used in algebra.*

In addition, simple sentences can be combined using *logical connectives* to build more complicated statements. We will also find it useful to have special symbols to represent the logical connectives.

Conjunction

The first of the logical connectives which we will study is called *conjunction*. This type of statement can often be identified by the use of the words *and* or *but*, however other ways of expressing this logical operation are possible. The symbol "$\wedge$" is used to indicate conjunction, the compound statement $p \wedge q$ often being translated as *"p and q."*

Examples of Conjunctions

(1) Let us assign the letters p and q to two simple statements as follows:

p: I like pretzels.
q: I like beer.

Then $p \wedge q$ would represent the compound statement "I like pretzels and I like beer." (or more simply, "I like pretzels and beer.").

(2)   Now let's assign the letters r and s so that

   r: I do not like popcorn.
   s: I like to go to the movies.

Then the statement "I like to go to the movies, but I do not like popcorn." would be represented symbolically by $s \wedge r$.

The Truth Table for Conjunction

We wish to construct a *truth table* for conjunction, that is, a table which reflects the logical properties of this operation. Before doing this we must make absolutely sure that we understand exactly how the word "and" is used in everyday speech, and that we have accounted for every possible alternative in our analysis. To help focus our ideas, we will assume that p and q have the same meaning that they had in example one above, that is, we will assign p and q the meanings

   p: I like pretzels.
   q: I like beer.

Is the sentence "I like pretzels and beer" true, or false? Clearly, this will depend on whether or not the components that make up the sentence (these two components are p and q) are true or false. The analysis must cover a number of different possibilities.

Possibility #1: p is true and q is true.

In this case we are assuming that p is true, so the sentence "I like pretzels." is true. We are also assuming that q is true, so the sentence "I like beer." is also true. Surely if the word "and" is being used the way we usually use it in every day language, we would expect that the sentence "I like pretzels and beer." would be assigned the value "true" in this case. To reflect this, we put a "T" in the first row of the $p \wedge q$ column of the truth table for conjunction (See Table 1.1 below. The $p \wedge q$ column is indicated in **bold** lettering.).

Possibility #2 p is true and q is false.

In this case we are again assuming that p is true, so the sentence "I like pretzels." is true. However, we are now assuming that q is false, so the sentence "I like beer." is false. This time we should *not* want to assign the compound sentence "I like pretzels and beer." the value true, because if we did, we would not only be saying that I like pretzels, but we would also be saying that I like beer (which I don't, since we are assuming that q is false). To reflect the fact that we want to assign the sentence $p \wedge q$ the truth value "false" in this case, we enter an "F" in the second row of the column for the truth table for conjunction. (Again, see Table 1.1 below.)

Possibility #3 p is false and q is true.

In this case p is assumed to be false, and this assumption means that I do not like pretzels. As in Possibility #2 (above), since I don't like pretzels, I certainly can't like both pretzels and beer. Again, the sentence "I like pretzels and beer." is false, so an "F" is entered in the third row of the $p \wedge q$ column of the truth table.

Possibility #4 p is false and q is false.

The same reasoning that works for possibility #3 will again work here. The reader should convince himself or herself that we want to enter an "F" in the fourth row of the $p \wedge q$ column of the truth table.

Table 1.1 given below is nothing more than a summary of the analysis just given, listing the truth value for $p \wedge q$ in each of the four possible cases. Note that each row in the table corresponds to one of the four listed possibilities, and that these four options are the only ones possible.

p	q	$p \wedge q$
T	T	T
T	F	F
F	T	F
F	F	F

←Row #1
←Row #2
←Row #3
←Row #4

Table 1.1 The truth table for conjunction

Before going any further it should be pointed out that what we are doing here is very similar to what we learned how to do in our arithmetic and elementary algebra classes. The algebraic expression $a + b$ has various values depending on the numerical values of a and b. These values, when "acted on" by the arithmetic operator "+" yield a numerical value for $a + b$. In logic, the logical value of $p \wedge q$ (either true or false) depends on the logical value of p, the logical value of q, and the rule governing the logical operator "$\wedge$." The truth table we have just constructed is similar to the addition table or multiplication tables memorized in elementary school.

Rather than memorize the truth table for conjunction given above, it will be more useful to have a working rule that can be used to easily reproduce it whenever necessary. This rule can be stated as follows.

The Rule of Conjunction: The statement $p \wedge q$ is true only when both p and q are true. If either p or q (or both) are false, then $p \wedge q$ is false.

Eventually we will be using truth tables to compare statements and analyze arguments. In order to insure that we are really comparing similar objects in both cases, *we must be sure that our truth tables are always built exactly the same way*. To make sure that we are doing this, *if a truth table contains two basic variables (usually p and q) we will always form the first two columns exactly as we did in table 1.1. That is, the p column will always consist of two T's followed by two F's, and the q column will always contain alternate T's and F's.*

Small Group Exercise

Operating on two simple sentences with the logical operator *and* yields the new sentence "p and q" (or $p \wedge q$) in much the same way that operating on the two numbers 3 and 5 with the arithmetic operator "+" yields the new number 8. Just as there are other arithmetic operators besides "+," there are also other logical connectives besides "and." In fact you are familiar with many of these logical connectives since you use them in your everyday speech.

> Make a list of as many words or phrases as you can think of that can be used as logical operators. That is, make a list of words which can be used to "connect" simple statements in order to construct more complex statements. Group together words that work similarly, such as *and* and *but*.
>
> If you need help in getting started take out any book (except this one) and try to identify those words that the author has used to construct more complicated statements from simpler ones.

1.3 More Connectives; Comparing Statements

Besides conjunction, there are other basic logical connectives that can be used to construct new statements from simpler ones. The most common of these other connectives are called *negation*, *disjunction*, and *material implication*. Hopefully you will soon realize that you discovered many ways of expressing these connectives in the group exercise at the end of the previous section. We will consider disjunction and negation in this section and put off material implication until a later section.

Disjunction

If p and q are statements, then "p or q," denoted by $p \vee q$, is called *the disjunction of p and q*. For example, if p and q again represent the statements

p: I like pretzels.
q: I like beer.

then the disjunction of these two statements would be

$p \vee q$: I like pretzels or I like beer (or both).

A complete analysis of disjunction would look very similar to the analysis of conjunction given in section 1.2. The difference would be that instead of analyzing the statement "I like pretzels *and* beer." we would be analyzing "I like pretzels *or* beer." This sentence would be assigned the value "true" if either p is true or if q is true (or if both p and q are true). The reader should go through each of the four possibilities (as we did for conjunction) and convince himself or herself that $p \vee q$ should be assigned the value "true" *in all cases except for possibility #4*. This is the only case where neither p nor q is true.

Therefore, the truth table for disjunction should look like this:

p	q	$p \vee q$
T	T	T
T	F	T
F	T	T
F	F	F

Table 1.2 The truth table for disjunction.

The Rule of Disjunction: The statement $p \vee q$ is true if at least one of the two statements p and q are true.

Negation

If p is a statement, then "*not p*," denoted by $\sim p$, is called the negation of p. Thus, if

p: I like pretzels.

then

$\sim p$: I do not like pretzels.

The truth table for the negation of p does not contain four columns because only one statement (just p, not both p and q), is used to build up this compound statement. Since there are only two possible truth values for p, the truth table will have only two rows rather than four. In order to construct this truth table it is only necessary to know that $\sim p$ always has the opposite truth value of p. Thus the truth table for negation looks like this:

p	$\sim p$
T	F
F	T

Table 1.3 The truth table for negation.

Rule of Negation: If p is a statement, then $\sim p$ has the opposite of the truth value of p.

One more example, which will be useful shortly, is now given. Let's assign p the meaning "I am at least eighteen years old." Since this means that I am eighteen years of age or older, its negation, $\sim p$, could be translated as "I am less than eighteen years old."

Again, note that if r is any statement, then r and $\sim r$ must have opposite truth values. If r is true, then $\sim r$ must be false; if r is false, then $\sim r$ must be true.

Comparing Statements

Now we can get some idea of how truth tables can be used to analyze statements. Consider the following representations of two statements, each of which is constructed from the same two basic variables p and q:

Statement #1: $\quad \sim (p \wedge q)$
Statement #2: $\quad \sim p \wedge q$ (Note that $\sim p \wedge q$ means the same thing as $(\sim p) \wedge q$, just as in arithmetic $-5 + 3$ means the same thing as $(-5) + 3$.)

For example, if

p: I am at least eighteen years of age.
q: I may vote.

then the two statements above are the symbolic representations of:

It is not the case that I am at least eighteen years of age and that I may vote. (Statement #1)
I am less than eighteen years of age, but I may vote. (Statement #2)

Notice that, as mentioned above, we have chosen to simplify the language here and to translate $\sim p$ as "I am less than eighteen years of age" rather than "I am not at least eighteen years of age."

We wish to decide if the two statements $\sim (p \wedge q)$ and $\sim p \wedge q$ (given above) logically say the same thing. In order to make our decision, we will build truth tables for each of these statements and compare them.

Now that we have working rules for constructing truth tables, the tables that we need can be built in a fairly mechanical fashion. The procedure that we will employ will start with the construction of the first two columns (and they will always look the same if we are building a statement that has the two components p and q). After that, successive columns will be added to the table until the statement that we are trying to analyze is finally built.

In this instance, to construct the table for $\sim (p \wedge q)$ we will first construct a column for $p \wedge q$ using the law of conjunction. (It may help to follow along by checking Table 1.4, below, as you read this analysis.) The "T" is only put in the first row of the $p \wedge q$ column because that is the only row where both p and q are true. Once the $p \wedge q$ column is constructed we can now build the $\sim (p \wedge q)$ column by reversing the truth values in the $p \wedge q$ column. It is important to understand how the final statement is built up in stages — we need to build the $p \wedge q$ column before we can construct the $\sim (p \wedge q)$ column.

p	q	$p \wedge q$	$\sim (p \wedge q)$
T	T	T	F
T	F	F	T
F	T	F	T
F	F	F	T

Table 1.4 The truth table for the statement $\sim (p \wedge q)$ (statement #1).

Similarly, in constructing the truth table for the statement $\sim p \wedge q$ we must first build a column for $\sim p$, since this is a component of the statement we are analyzing. We can then construct the last column by applying the rule of conjunction to the $\sim p$ and q columns. Thus, the only T in the last column appears in row #3, since this is the only row where both components (that is, both $\sim p$ and q) are true.

p	q	$\sim p$	$\sim p \wedge q$
T	T	F	F
T	F	F	F
F	T	T	T
F	F	T	F

Table 1.5 The truth table for the statement $\sim p \wedge q$ (statement #2).

With these two truth tables in front of us, we can now decide whether or not these sentences logically say the same thing. This is easily done by comparing the last columns of each of these tables. Since the last column of Table 1.4 is not the same as the last column of Table 1.5, the statements corresponding to these tables are not logically equivalent. Thus the statement $\sim (p \wedge q)$ is not equivalent to $\sim p \wedge q$.

12   Chapter One: **LOGIC**

> **The Principle of Logical Equivalence**: *Two statements logically say the same thing if the last columns of their truth tables are the same.* When this happens we say that the two statements are *logically equivalent*.

This is a reasonable definition because it means that for two statements to be equivalent they must both be true at exactly the same times. (They will also be false at the same times.) This means that if you replace a statement by its logical equivalent, you will never change the truth value (that is, the logical meaning) of that statement.

Now that we know how to construct truth tables, let's build a truth table for another statement, $\sim p \wedge \sim q$, so that we can compare this to the two statements that we have just examined. Note that if p and q are again assigned the meanings

   p: I am at least eighteen years of age.
   q: I may vote.

then $\sim p \wedge \sim q$ can be translated as "I am less than eighteen years old and I may not vote."

The truth table for this statement can only be constructed after columns for its two components, $\sim p$ and $\sim q$, are first constructed.

p	q	$\sim p$	$\sim q$	$\sim p \wedge \sim q$
T	T	F	F	F
T	F	F	T	F
F	T	T	F	F
F	F	T	T	T

First two columns are always the same   Negations of the first two columns   Conjunction of the 3rd and 4th columns

Table 1.6 The truth table for $\sim p \wedge \sim q$.

Because the last column of the truth table for the statement $\sim p \wedge \sim q$ is not the same as the last column of either of the truth tables constructed earlier (Tables 1.4 and 1.5), we see that this statement is not logically equivalent to either $\sim (p \wedge q)$ or $\sim p \wedge q$.

Before moving on to the next section, let's look at two additional statements and construct their truth tables. The two statements we will look at are $\sim (\sim p)$ and $(\sim p) \vee (\sim q)$.

If p and q represent the same statements that they did earlier in this section, then $\sim (\sim p)$ will represent the statement "It is not true that I am less than eighteen years of age," while $(\sim p) \vee (\sim q)$ would represent "Either I am less than eighteen years of age, or I may not vote."

In constructing the truth table for $\sim (\sim p)$ we will have to build the $\sim p$ column first. The $\sim (\sim p)$ column can then be filled in by reversing the truth values in the $\sim p$ column.

p	$\sim p$	$\sim (\sim p)$
T	F	T
F	T	F

Table 1.7 The truth table for $\sim (\sim p)$.

Notice that the column under p is the same as the column under $\sim(\sim p)$. This means that these two statements are equivalent. This makes sense, because if "It is not true that I am less than eighteen years of age," that must be because "I am at least eighteen years of age." That is, the normal English meanings of these two statements are the same. Since their meanings are the same we should expect the sentences to be logically equivalent, so it is not surprising that their truth tables are the same.

Finally, here's the truth table for $\sim p \vee \sim q$. Again, notice that before we can construct the last column, each of its component parts must be constructed. The two components of this statement are $\sim p$ and $\sim q$.

p	q	$\sim p$	$\sim q$	$\sim p \vee \sim q$
T	T	F	F	F
T	F	F	T	T
F	T	T	F	T
F	F	T	T	T

Table 1.8 The truth table for $\sim p \vee \sim q$.

A comparison of the last column of this truth table with the last column of Table 1.4 reveals that these two columns are the same! This means that we've just proved that the two statements $\sim(p \wedge q)$ and $\sim p \vee \sim q$ *are* logically equivalent.

Questions to Discuss

1. We have found that none of the symbolic statements $\sim(p \wedge q)$, $\sim p \wedge q$, and $\sim p \wedge \sim q$ are equivalent. Make some observations concerning the importance (or lack of importance) of parentheses in symbolic expressions.

2. We have discovered two rules for logical operators. They are:

- p is equivalent to $\sim(\sim p)$
- $\sim(p \wedge q)$ is equivalent to $\sim p \vee \sim q$

Compare and contrast these rules with rules that you know from arithmetic or algebra.

3. (a) Group together those statements in the following list which you think might be equivalent to each other. (Your answer to question #2 above may help you in making your decision. Make as many groups as you think are necessary, and assign as many statements as necessary to each group.)

$\sim(\sim p)$
$\sim(p \wedge q)$
$\sim p \wedge \sim q$
$\sim p \vee \sim q$
p
$p \vee q$
$\sim p \wedge q$

(b) Explain your answer to part (a).
(c) If you wanted to prove your answer to part (a), what could you do?

Exercises

1. Justify the entries in each of the cells in Tables 1.4, 1.5, 1.6, and 1.8.

2. Go through each of the four possibilities (as was done in the previous section for conjunction), explaining the entries in the last column of the truth table for disjunction (Table 1.2).

1.4 Material Implication

The conditional statement, or *implication*, is a type of statement that comes up often in logical arguments (and other places). Part of the difficulty with implications is that there are many different ways of expressing them in English. Another problem is that the logical interpretation of this type of statement may be slightly different from the everyday use of the words involved.

Consider the following statements:

"If you eat too much, then you'll get a stomachache."
"You got a stomachache because you ate too much."
"Since you ate too much, you got a stomachache."
"You ate too much, hence you got a stomachache."

All of these statements are expressing the same idea. One act is "following from" another. ("Follows from" is in quotes because in logic we are not interested in why the second act follows from the first, only that it does.)

As you can see from the above examples, an implication is made up of two parts. These two parts are called the *hypothesis* and the *conclusion* of the implication (or the *antecedent* and the *consequent*). Informally you can think of these as "the cause" and "the effect," however there need not really be any causal connection between the hypothesis and the conclusion. (For example "If I take a walk then you'll read a book." is an implication.) In the first of the statements given above, "If you eat too much then you'll get a stomachache," the hypothesis is "You eat too much." and the conclusion is "You get a stomach ache." If we let

p: You eat too much.
q: You get a stomachache.

then the implication in question is expressed symbolically by

$$p \Rightarrow q.$$

A question now comes up. What does the truth table for material implication look like? In order to give some insight as to why the truth table for material implication looks as it does, it will be advantageous to think of an implication as a commitment, or promise.

The Rule of Material Implication: The implication $p \Rightarrow q$ can be thought of as "p promises q." The implication will be considered true if the promise is kept, false if the promise is broken.

Before constructing the truth table for material implication, let us again assign meanings to the variables p and q in order to clarify our understanding of the symbols. For example, we can assign p and q to the following statements:

p: The batter gets a hit.
q: The Mets win.

Then the implication $p \Rightarrow q$ would represent the statement "If the batter gets a hit, then the Mets will win." As usual, there are four possibilities to consider:

Possibility #1 p is true and q is true

In this case we are assuming that p is true, so the sentence "The batter gets a hit." is true. We are also assuming that q is true, so "The Mets win." is also true. Since we promised that the Mets would win if the batter got a hit, and since they did win as promised, the promise was not broken. Thus $p \Rightarrow q$ is assigned the value "true" in the first row. (As before, it may be helpful to follow along by checking the truth table as you consider these possibilities. Table 1.9 below summarizes the information from these possibilities.)

Possibility #2 p is true and q is false

In this case we are again assuming that p is true, so the sentence "The batter gets a hit." is true. However, we are now assuming that q is false, so the sentence "The Mets win." is false. Since we promised that the Mets would win if the batter got a hit, but they did not win (even though he did get a hit), the promise is broken. For this reason, $p \Rightarrow q$ is assigned the value "false" in row #2.

Possibilities #3 & 4 p is false and q is true
p is false and q is false

The promise cannot possibly be broken in either of these cases, since you are only obligated to follow through on your promise if the condition that was originally agreed to is satisfied. That is, I promised that the Mets would win *if the batter gets a hit*. If the batter does not get a hit, then I am released from any obligation that I might have had. That is exactly what is happening in these cases, since "p is false" means that the batter did not get a hit. It doesn't matter whether or not the Mets win, so the entry in the q column in either of these rows need not even be checked. Since the promise cannot be broken in this case, T's must be assigned to rows 3 and 4 in the truth table.

p	q	$p \Rightarrow q$
T	T	T
T	F	F
F	T	T
F	F	T

Table 1.9 The truth table for material implication.

In order to help facilitate the construction of truth tables, an alternative to The Rule of Implication given above is presented:

Alternate Rule of Material Implication: The implication $p \Rightarrow q$ is always true except when p is true and q is false (the only situation when the promise is broken).

A possibly surprising and unexpected result is that $p \Rightarrow q$ is equivalent to the statement $\sim p \vee q$. This is easily proved by constructing the truth table for $\sim p \vee q$ and comparing its last column to the last column of the truth table for $p \Rightarrow q$.

16   Chapter One: **LOGIC**

p	q	$\sim p$	$\sim p \vee q$
T	T	F	T
T	F	F	F
F	T	T	T
F	F	T	T

Table 1.10 The truth table for $\sim p \vee q$.

Questions to Discuss

1.   Discuss the merits of the statement "Because $p \Rightarrow q$ is true whenever p is false, anything follows from a false statement."

2.   Explain in everyday English why $\sim p \vee q$ is equivalent to $p \Rightarrow q$. The interpretation of an implication as a promise may be helpful.

3.   (a) Explain each entry in the following truth table:

p	q	$p \Rightarrow q$	$q \Rightarrow (p \Rightarrow q)$
T	T	T	T
T	F	F	T
F	T	T	T
F	F	T	T

Table 1.11 A tautology.

Note that the statement $q \Rightarrow (p \Rightarrow q)$ is *always true*, regardless of the truth values of its component statements p and q. Such a statement is called a *tautology*.

(b)   A statement which is always false is called a *contradiction*. That is, a contradiction is a statement which can *never be true* no matter what truth values are assigned to its components.
     Give an example of a logical statement in symbolic form that is a contradiction.

(c)   Look up the definitions of "tautology" and "contradiction" in a dictionary and compare the dictionary definitions to the definitions given above.

4.   Since $p \Rightarrow q$ and $\sim p \vee q$ are equivalent statements, the implication arrow is not essential to logic and could be eliminated. Explain why you may not want to eliminate this symbol, even though it is possible to do so.

Exercise

1.   Justify each entry in Table 1.10.

1.5 More on Material Implication

Consider the following two statements:

If you may vote then you are at least eighteen years of age.
If you are at least eighteen years of age then you may vote.

These two statements cannot possibly be logically equivalent, since the first statement is true, but the second is false (being at least eighteen years of age is only one of the conditions that need to be satisfied in order to be eligible to vote).

We can prove this logically by looking at truth tables. Let

p: You may vote.
q: You are at least eighteen years of age.

Then $p \Rightarrow q$ would represent the statement "If you may vote then you are at least eighteen years of age," and $q \Rightarrow p$ would represent "If you are at least eighteen years of age then you may vote." The two truth tables in question can be condensed into one:

p	q	$p \Rightarrow q$	$q \Rightarrow p$
T	T	T	T
T	F	F	T
F	T	T	F
F	F	T	T

Table 1.12 A comparison of $p \Rightarrow q$ and $q \Rightarrow p$.

Since the last two columns of this truth table are not the same, we have shown that interchanging the hypothesis and the conclusion of an implication changes the meaning of that statement. This is very reasonable indeed, since you wouldn't expect "q follows from p" to mean the same thing as "p follows from q."

Converse of an Implication

The *converse* of the statement $p \Rightarrow q$ is the statement $q \Rightarrow p$. The discussion given above demonstrates that a statement is not logically equivalent to its converse. For this reason, when dealing with implications it is necessary to be careful in identifying the hypothesis and the conclusion of the statement, since mixing them up will change the meaning of the implication. This is usually not a problem if the statement is given in the usual "if ... then ..." form, however implications may be expressed in many different ways, and even accomplished logicians sometimes fall into traps when trying to identify the hypothesis and conclusion of some implications. If you are in doubt, it is often helpful to reword the sentence into the usual "if ... then ..." form.

Inverses and Contrapositives

Every implication $p \Rightarrow q$ has a converse associated with it. The implication also has two other statements associated with it, called the *inverse* of the statement and the *contrapositive* of the statement.

The inverse of the implication $p \Rightarrow q$ is the statement whose form is $\sim p \Rightarrow \sim q$, while the contrapositive of the statement $p \Rightarrow q$ has the form $\sim q \Rightarrow \sim p$.

Let's assign p and q the same meanings that they had earlier in this section, that is,

p: You may vote.
q: You are at least eighteen years of age.

Then the basic implication, $p \Rightarrow q$ would represent the statement "If you may vote then you are at least eighteen years of age." The converse of this statement, $q \Rightarrow p$, would represent "If you are at least eighteen years of age then you may vote." The inverse of the statement, $\sim p \Rightarrow \sim q$, would represent "If you may not vote, then you are less than eighteen years of age." Finally, the contrapositive, or $\sim q \Rightarrow \sim p$, would be the representation of "If you are less than eighteen years of age then you may not vote."

It may not be clear to everyone at this point which of these statements (if any) are equivalent to any of the others. This is exactly why truth tables were developed, as they make answering this type of question easier.

Small Group Exercises

1. (a) Construct truth tables for $\sim p \Rightarrow \sim q$ and for $\sim q \Rightarrow \sim p$.
   (b) Is a statement equivalent to either its inverse or to its contrapositive? Explain your answers.

2. Is the converse of an implication equivalent to the inverse of the same implication? Explain your answer.

1.6 Rewording Implications

As mentioned earlier, it is often advisable to reword implications into a standard usual "if ... then ..." form in order to properly identify the hypothesis and conclusion (and eventually to translate the statement into symbols). This cannot generally be done in any mechanical way, but requires some insight into the intent of the statement.

For example, the statement "Every Greek is a man." may not seem to be an implication, but it is. In fact, it surely has the same meaning as the far less literary sentence "If a person is a Greek, then that person is a man." When reworded in this way, we can see that this is an implication. Thus, to translate "Every Greek is a man." into symbols we could let

p: A person is Greek.
q: A person is a man.

Then $p \Rightarrow q$: would represent our statement "Every Greek is a man."

Please note that whenever you use a letter (such as p or q above) to represent a statement, you must clearly indicate what statement that letter represents. Failure to do this will inevitably lead to confusion.

As a second example, consider the statement "I say what I mean." Is this an implication? If I do say what I mean, then I said what I did <u>because</u> that was what I meant. (That is, the "meaning" was the

cause of the "saying.") Therefore a reasonable way to translate this statement into symbols would be to start with the assignments

p: I mean it.
q: I say it.

Then $p \Rightarrow q$ would represent "If I mean it then I say it," or "I say what I mean." Note how p and q are combined to form the original sentence, and how important it is to identify the cause in order to translate the sentence into symbols.

As a third example let's analyze the statement "I'll go free unless Alice testifies." Here the intent of the statement is that if Alice does testify, then I do not go free; however, if Alice doesn't testify, then I will go free. To translate this into symbols, make the assignments

p: Alice testifies.
q: I go free.

The statement in question then translates as $(p \Rightarrow \sim q) \wedge (\sim q \Rightarrow p)$. Here the first half of the sentence says that "If Alice testifies, then I do not go free." while the second half says that "If Alice doesn't testify then I do go free." Since the original statement required that both of these "halves" be satisfied, these two halves are joined with the conjunction symbol, $\wedge$.

Since this statement turned out to be much more complicated than the original sentence appeared to be, a look at its truth table would be interesting. Remember: before constructing a column for any statement you must first have a column for any "piece" of that statement.

p	q	$\sim p$	$\sim q$	$p \Rightarrow \sim q$	$\sim q \Rightarrow p$	$(p \Rightarrow \sim q) \wedge (\sim q \Rightarrow p)$
T	T	F	F	F	T	F
T	F	F	T	T	T	T
F	T	T	F	T	T	T
F	F	T	T	T	F	F

Table 1.13 The truth table for "p unless q."

The purpose of this section is not to show off complicated problems and let you see how difficult logic can be. It's to help you to realize that even relatively innocent looking statements may be difficult to translate into symbolic form. Many students get the idea that they understand the subject simply because they can construct truth tables in some mechanical way. However, sometimes the most difficult part of the problem is to translate the statements into symbolic form.

Small Group Exercises

Read the following passage, then answer the questions that follow.

"Then you should say what you mean," the Mad Hatter went on.
"I do," Alice hastily replied; "At least —at least I mean what I say — that's the same thing you know."
"Not the same thing a bit!" said the Hatter. "Why you might as well say that 'I see what I eat.' is the same thing as 'I eat what I see.'!"

20   Chapter One: **LOGIC**

---

1.   In order to decide whether Alice or the Mad Hatter is correct, we wish to logically decide whether or not the two statements "I say what I mean." and "I mean what I say." logically say the same thing. To do this, translate the two statements into symbols, carefully identifying the meaning of any letters you use.

Hints: (1) Each statement is an implication.
         (2) It may help to reword the statements.

2.   (a) Make truth tables for each of the two statements that you translated into symbols in problem #1.
      (b) *Using the truth tables* decide who was right, Alice or the Mad Hatter. *Explain* your answer using *complete sentences*.

Questions to Discuss

1.   Instead of using truth tables to prove that the two statements in the above group exercise are not equivalent, the Mad Hatter uses another method. He makes up two new statements which are of the *same form* as the first two statements, but which are obviously not equivalent. What do you think of the Mad Hatter's method? (See below.)

In order to answer this question, consider the following questions:

- Is the Mad Hatter's method easy to understand?
- Could you use it in other problems?
- Why do you think the Hatter uses this method instead of truth tables?
- Which method do you prefer, the Mad Hatter's method or the truth table method? Why?

2.   Make up a rule (similar to the rule of conjunction or the rule of implication) for the statement "p unless q."

3.   (a) Construct a truth table for the statement $(p \Rightarrow q) \wedge (q \Rightarrow p)$. [Note: Sometimes a special symbol is used to translate this statement into symbols, the double arrow. The sentence would then be represented by $p \Leftrightarrow q$, which could be read as "p if and only if q" or "p is equivalent to q."]
      (b) Compare the statement $(p \Rightarrow q) \wedge (q \Rightarrow p)$ [from part (a)] with the $(p \Rightarrow \sim q) \wedge (\sim q \Rightarrow p)$ [analyzed in the section].
         Hint: It may help to consider the negation of $(p \Rightarrow q) \wedge (q \Rightarrow p)$.

1.7 Logical Proofs

We will now use what we know about truth tables to test arguments for validity. Remember, for an argument to be valid it is necessary that true hypotheses will always yield true conclusions.

Consider the syllogism given earlier (see section 1.1):

Every Greek is a man.
<u>Every man is mortal.</u>
Every Greek is mortal.

To test this for validity we will assign each basic statement in the argument a variable, translate the argument into symbols, and then construct a truth table. Investigation of the truth table will then give us our answer as to whether or not the argument is valid.

Earlier we learned that the statement "Every Greek is a man." is an implication which could be reworded as "If a person is a Greek then that person is a man." Repeating the assignment that we made in the last section, we again let

p: A person is a Greek.
q: A person is a man.

As before, $p \Rightarrow q$ then represents the statement "If a person is a Greek then that person is a man." or "Every Greek is a man."

Similarly, "Every man is mortal." can be reworded as "If a person is a man, then that person is mortal." We recognize "A person is a man." as q from the translation of the first statement, but we have not yet assigned a variable to the basic statement "A person is mortal." We will do that now by assigning

r: A person is mortal.

The statement "Every man is mortal." can now be represented as $q \Rightarrow r$.

Finally, the conclusion is "Every Greek is mortal." which may be reworded as "If a person is a Greek then that person is mortal." Checking back on our assignments we see that this translates into the symbolic statement $p \Rightarrow r$.

We are now able to write the entire argument in symbolic form:

$$p \Rightarrow q$$
$$\underline{q \Rightarrow r}$$
$$p \Rightarrow r$$

Our job is to determine whether or not this argument is valid.

To test this we will be making a truth table which contains all of the statements (both the hypotheses and the conclusion) in the argument. This is a bit more complicated than what we did earlier, the main difficulty being that there are three variables in the argument, not just the two that we had in our previous statements. The idea is still the same, however. We still wish to start by listing all possible combinations of "true" and "false" for the basic variables. It turns that this can be done in eight ways, as shown in the list given in Table 1.14 (see below).

Please look this table over carefully and see if you can figure out the pattern that was used to construct it. In particular, you should focus on the first column and the top and bottom halves of the last two columns. The shading in the last two columns is there to help spot the patterns used in their construction. Whenever analyzing statements containing three variables this method should be used to fill in the first three columns of your truth table.

p	q	r
T	T	T
T	T	F
T	F	T
T	F	F
F	T	T
F	T	F
F	F	T
F	F	F

Table 1.14 All possible assignments of T and F to three statements.

We shall now complete the table by building a column for each of the statements in the argument. Each of the added columns are constructed with the help of the "Alternate Rule of Material Implication" from section 1.4.

p	q	r	hypothesis #1: $p \Rightarrow q$	hypothesis #2: $q \Rightarrow r$	conclusion: $p \Rightarrow r$
T	T	T	T	T	T
T	T	F	T	F	F
T	F	T	F	T	T
T	F	F	F	T	F
F	T	T	T	T	T
F	T	F	T	F	T
F	F	T	T	T	T
F	F	F	T	T	T

Table 1.15 A truth table for testing an argument.

It is not essential that the conclusion (the last column) always be true, only that it be true whenever all of the hypotheses are true. There are some rows in the truth table where one or more of the hypotheses are not true, so we should eliminate these rows. Rows 3 and 4 should be eliminated because hypothesis #1 is not true in those rows. Similarly, rows 2 and 6 should be eliminated because hypothesis #2 is not true in those rows. (The rows to be eliminated have been shaded in the above table.) After eliminating these rows all that will remain is those rows where all of the hypotheses of the argument are always true.

p	q	r	hypothesis #1: $p \Rightarrow q$	hypothesis #2: $q \Rightarrow r$	conclusion: $p \Rightarrow r$
T	T	T	T	T	T
F	T	T	T	T	T
F	F	T	T	T	T
F	F	F	T	T	T

Table 1.16 A copy of Table 1.15 with the shaded rows removed.

Notice that in all of the rows that remain the conclusion of the argument is always "true." This means that the argument is valid (that is, the conclusion of the argument will always be true whenever the hypotheses are true).

Truth Table Test for Validity of an Argument: Construct a truth table containing all of the statements (the hypotheses and the conclusion) used in the argument. Eliminate all rows in which any of the hypotheses of the argument are false. For the argument to be valid, the conclusion of the argument must be true in all of the remaining rows.

Direct Reasoning

Now consider the following argument, which we also wish to test for validity:

If Lynda studies hard she will get an A.
<u>Lynda studies hard.</u>
Lynda will get an A.

In order to analyze this argument make the following assignments:

p: Lynda studies hard.

q: Lynda will get an A.

Then the argument becomes

$p \Rightarrow q$
<u>p</u>
q

    This is much easier to test than the last argument. Because there are only two basic variables in this argument, the truth table will only have four rows.

hypothesis #2: p	conclusion: q	hypothesis #1: $p \Rightarrow q$
T	T	T
T	F	F
F	T	T
F	F	T

Table 1.17 The truth table for direct reasoning.

    The following rows are now removed: Row 2 is removed because hypothesis #1 is false in this row; rows 3 and 4 are removed because hypothesis #2 is false in these two rows. (In Table 1.17, all shaded rows should be removed.)

    In the only remaining row (row #1) the conclusion, q, is seen to be true. Therefore this argument, which is called "direct reasoning," is valid.

An Invalid Argument

    Finally, let's test the following argument for validity.

$p \Rightarrow q$
<u>$\sim p$</u>
$\sim q$

Again we build a truth table containing all of the statements contained in the argument:

p	q	hypothesis #2: $\sim p$	conclusion: $\sim q$	hypothesis #1: $p \Rightarrow q$
T	T	F	F	T
T	F	F	T	F
F	T	T	F	T
F	F	T	T	T

Table 1.18 A truth table for an invalid argument.

In row #1 hypothesis #2 is false, so this row should be removed. In row #2 both hypotheses are false, so this row should also be removed. No other rows should be removed, because the hypotheses are all true in each of the other rows. However, after doing this, there will still be an entry in the "conclusion" column which is "false." That means that this argument is not valid, since it is possible for the conclusion of this argument to be false even though all of the hypotheses are true.

Questions to Discuss

1. In your own words, describe the procedure used to fill in the three columns in Table 1.14.

2. We have seen that statements which contain two basic variables (p and q) have truth tables with four rows. We have also seen that statements containing three variables require eight rows. How many rows do you think would be needed in order to analyze statements containing four basic variables? How about five variables? How do you think this might effect the utility of truth tables in analyzing statements containing large numbers of variables?

Exercises

In problems #1–3, test the given arguments for validity:

1. $p \Rightarrow q$
    $\underline{q}$
    p

2. $p \Rightarrow q$ (This is called *indirect reasoning*.)
    $\underline{\sim q}$
    $\sim p$

3. $p \Rightarrow q$
    $q \Rightarrow r$
    $\underline{p}$
    r

1.8 The Incompleteness Theorem

There are many reasons for studying logic. For one thing, it would be nice to be able to judge whether the arguments given by politicians, used car dealers, environmentalists, and others really are valid. To be honest, however, when confronted by such an argument almost no one would consider taking out a pencil and a piece of paper and constructing a truth table to test it. An informal "feel" for the validity of an argument would be enough to decide most questions such as these.

An even more interesting question deals with the validity of logic itself. Incredibly, this question leads to an amazing link between mathematics and many other academic studies, especially with the humanities and fine arts.

Can we be sure that logic (and therefore everything based on it, including mathematics) will never lead us astray? If we were to try to attack a question such as this, what approach would we use? We certainly shouldn't be allowed to use logic to prove the consistency of logic, but what else is left to rely on?

This type of question received little attention until the twentieth century. Before that there was some interest in this problem, mostly revolving about the paradoxes which were mentioned earlier, but just about everyone simply assumed that these paradoxes were minor irritations which could be explained away as soon as mathematicians understood these difficulties better. Then, in the first quarter of the twentieth century, there was a new interest in this area and some very eminent thinkers such as Bertrand Russell, Alfred North Whitehead, and Ludwig Wittgenstein spent a considerable amount of time investigating this type of problem in great depth.

It seems that no one was ready for the surprising answer which was discovered by the Austrian mathematician Kurt Gödel. He showed that mathematics, and its foundation, logic, would never achieve the "perfection" that some had hoped for. He accomplished this by showing how to construct something similar to the Liar Paradox within any mathematical system. Gödel's accomplishment actually shows a connection between mathematics and the arts which may give some insight into the reasons why certain themes in literature, art, music, and many other fields are found to be interesting.

Gödel's construction can be thought of as showing how to construct the sentence

G: This statement has no proof.

within mathematical systems. The problem with the sentence G is very similar to the problem that we ran into when we considered the Liar Paradox in section 1.2.

There are two possibilities, either G can be proved, or it can't be proved. But if it can be proved, then it is false. Since we have just mathematically proved a false statement, we have invalidated all of mathematics. This is so offensive that most mathematicians won't even consider it as a possibility.

The other possibility is that G cannot be proved. In this case G is a true statement which cannot be proved. Although this is certainly not as serious as the first option, it is still very serious. It means that logic, which had been used as the final judge of "truth" for well over two thousand years, is not adequate to decide on the truth of all statements.

So here's the choice that we are faced with. Either *logic*, and therefore all of mathematics, *is inconsistent*, or it is *incomplete*. That is, either it is totally invalid, or we have to accept the fact that there are true statements which we have no hope of proving. It's not surprising that mathematicians have chosen to call this *"Gödel's Incompleteness Theorem."* The alternative of inconsistency is simply too outlandish to even consider.

A number of reasonable questions can now be asked. Among these are:

- Why does this imperfection in logic occur?
- Why is it important that it occurs?
- What impact does this imperfection have on other disciplines?

Self-reference

Apparently the ultimate cause of this interesting problem is the *self-referential nature of logic*. A look back at the definitions and explanations given earlier in this chapter may give some idea of this problem. Notice that as the notions of conjunction, implication, and so on, were being developed, they were already being used in constructing their definitions. (If you need to, go back and look at the

definitions of conjunction, disjunction, implication, etc. in sections 1.2, 1.3, and 1.4. Notice how often the words "and," "or," "not," and "therefore" are used even though these are the words we are trying to define and analyze!) It was assumed that the reader was already familiar with these ideas in an informal way. What seems to be the problem is that the two ways of using language (the formal and the informal) are somehow getting confused. Apparently it is not possible to keep these two levels of usage separated, no matter how careful we try to be. A mathematician (or a linguist) would say that there is a confusion between the *object language* (the language being studied, in this case logic) and the *metalanguage* (the language in which the study is taking place, in this case English). To take this one step further, *logic is being used to analyze logic*. This apparently doesn't happen in other studies, but it is even more important to point out that logic was never intended to be used in this way by the pioneers of the subject. Logic was intended to be used to study arguments in other areas, but it wasn't intended to be "referred to" itself. By doing this we "tangle" things up so much that we end up with inescapable confusion instead of the hoped for certainty. In fact in the book *Gödel, Escher, Bach: an Eternal Golden Braid*, Douglas Hofstadter calls the situation that we've just described a *tangled hierarchy* or a *crazy loop*. In this extraordinary book Hofstadter demonstrates how this self–referential character is really not just a property of logic, but is an essential ingredient in human thought. He identifies the same self–referential characteristic in many other human endeavors, including the music of Johann Sebastian Bach and the art of M. C. Escher. Far from being a defect in logic, the self–referential nature of human thought is seen to be the factor that makes human thinking the special faculty that it is.

The paradoxes that we considered earlier, especially the Liar Paradox, are nothing more than the most blatant of self–referential statements. They make no pretext at all and openly refer to themselves. *This sentence* is false. "*This sentence*" is expected to refer to something even before you have completed writing (or reading) the sentence! In this most flagrant form we have already seen the problems that self–referentiality can cause, but the problems that lie beneath the surface are even more interesting and unexpected. To get some idea of how complicated things can get, let us again consider the sentence

S: This sentence is false.

We have already decided that this, the Liar Paradox, is undecidable. That is, S can be neither true nor false.

Now let us modify this sentence in the most innocent of ways. We will take its subject, "This sentence," and replace it by S. This surely should not change the meaning of the sentence, since S is nothing more than the symbol that we are using to represent "This sentence." The sentence now becomes:

S is false.

But it seems that this does not mean the same thing as S after all! S was neither true nor false, but this "new" sentence surely is false (since it says that S is false, and we know that this is not so). The simple operation of *replacing the subject* of the sentence S *by a new expression that is equivalent to the original subject* has somehow changed the meaning of the original sentence!

Although this seems strange, the explanation is not so complicated — once you know it! All that is happening is that the sentence is being looked at on different levels. *As you move from one level to another the meaning of the sentence does change.* As the meaning changes, so may its truth value. Later on in this section we will see that the same type of thing really does happen in other subjects which you have studied.

It is not currently known whether or not self–reference is essential to this level confusion. As of now, the only known cases of level confusion occur because of self–referentiality, but some mathematicians believe that level confusion without self–reference is possible. If this is so, then other types of sentences besides self–referential ones could be undecidable.

Finally, an important reminder. Although the self–referentiality of the Liar Paradox is very obvious (once you've learned to look for it), other self–referentiality may not be. A sentence which refers to *another* sentence, for example, could be self–referential. (To see why this is, think of what would

happen if the second sentence referred back to the first sentence.) As we've seen, applying logic to try to prove (or even develop) logic is self-referential. The thing that raises human thought above other types of thought, that is, the ability to *think about thinking*, is self-referential. And finally, as we will soon see, it seems that a very subtle self-referentiality is the basis for so much of what people find interesting in many areas in the arts and humanities.

Self-reference and Literature

Although interest in self-referentiality is recent, it is the belief of many that writers have taken advantage of this property (maybe unconsciously) for many years. For example, writing a book about words (or better yet, about language) would be an example of self-referentiality. Even literature, such as novels, plays, and movies are not immune to self-referentiality. Two blatant examples, one a play and the other a movie, may make this situation a bit easier to understand.

Shakespeare's play *Hamlet, Prince of Denmark* contains a "play within the play." In fact, these two levels even get confused, resulting in a situation which would have different meanings at any of the three levels where you might be viewing the action (level 1 is the inner play, level 2 is *Hamlet*, and level 3 is as an observer of *Hamlet*). The situation here is really very similar to what we saw earlier when we viewed the Liar Paradox at different levels and changed its truth value from undecidable to false (see p. 25). As was the case there, the same activity in the innermost play has different meanings when viewed at any of the three different levels. Also notice that each level deeper into the play takes us one step further from "reality." We know Hamlet is not real. Hamlet himself knows that the characters in the inner play ("The Mouse-trap") are not real to him. Yet we willingly "become" a part of the play and have feelings for Hamlet and the other characters, and Hamlet is willing to change his actions based on what he sees in "The Mouse-trap."

A very similar thing happens in the Woody Allen movie *The Purple Rose of Cairo* where "people" in the movie watch a movie, and one even changes places with a "person" in an "inner movie." The inner levels are again confused, this time very flagrantly, and although the observers (of the outer movie) must realize that what they are seeing is impossible, they still must see enough that is realistic about what is going on. The observers of *The Purple Rose* are viewing something that is totally beyond belief, yet they seem to have no problem with the fact that they probably have often identified with other characters and have made just such switches with characters in other movies and novels themselves (at least in their minds). Again notice the similarity to what was happening in the Liar Paradox; a blurring and a confusion between levels (in this case we might say levels of reality) allow for an interesting situation which has different meanings to "people" on each of the levels.

The levels in both of these examples (*Hamlet* and *The Purple Rose*) are very obvious, but the same thing also happens in many, many movies and books in a much more subtle way. Indeed, if writers of novels don't get their readers to feel as though they are part of the action, then they've failed as writers. It is for this reason that one mathematician, Jacob Bronowski, believed that self-referentiality is the source of all good literature. If this is so, then it is not only true that movies and novels are not immune from self-reference. It is more likely that *self-reference is an essential characteristic of all good literature*.

Self-reference and Art

Just as the successful writer attempts to confuse levels (for example by trying to fool the reader into thinking that he or she is a part of the action of a novel), the artist also often tries to make the observer feel as though he or she is a part of the work. In some works this may be done in a subtle way, but again there are examples where this "level confusion" has been taken to the extreme and the effect is easier to see.

One place where this can be most easily seen is in the art of M. C. Escher. Again, the book *Gödel, Escher, Bach: An Eternal Golden Braid* by Douglas Hofstadter is an excellent reference if you wish to get more information on this very interesting subject.

One example of Escher's work, the lithograph *Ascending and Descending*, is shown below. As with many of his works, things are going on on more than one level here. If you follow the monks walking around the perimeter of the building and look at the picture as a whole, you see the impossibility of this situation. The lines of monks are continuously rising (or falling), yet they never seem to get anywhere! On *one level* (for example, viewing each side of the building separately, but never putting them together to get the whole picture) everything is fine. On the *global level* there's a problem (which many people miss until it is pointed out to them) which makes the whole situation impossible. Escher's works are packed with similar interesting mysteries.

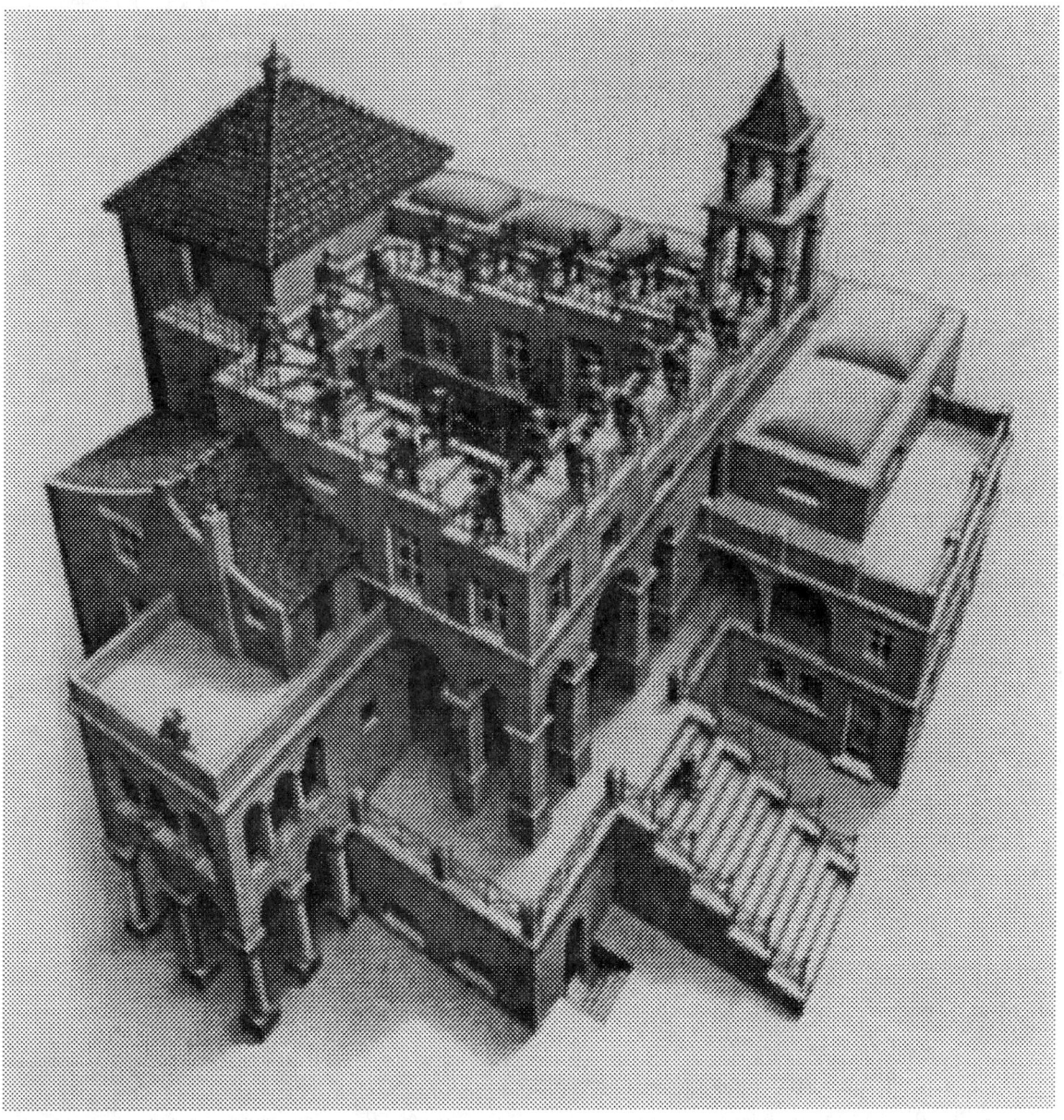

Figure 1.1 M. C. Escher's *Ascending and Descending.*
©1995 M.C. Escher/Cordon Art–Baarn–Holland. All rights reserved.

We might also point out another similarity between this and the Liar Paradox that we first studied in section 1.2. Both look quite innocent at first glance. It is only after careful consideration that one finds a hidden problem that causes concern.

> ### *Small Group Exercise*
>
> Escher's work *Drawing Hands* appears below. This may be viewed from two different levels, either the *level of the observer* or the level of the hands (called the *visible level*). Compare and contrast what is going on in each of the two levels.
>
> *Hints*: For the *visible level* (on the page) consider the following:
>
> 1. What is being done by the hand on the top? What is being done to it?
> 2. What is being done by the hand on the bottom? What is being done to it?
> 3. In light of the first two hints, is there a paradox here?
>
> Douglas Hofstadter has quite a bit to say about this example in his book.

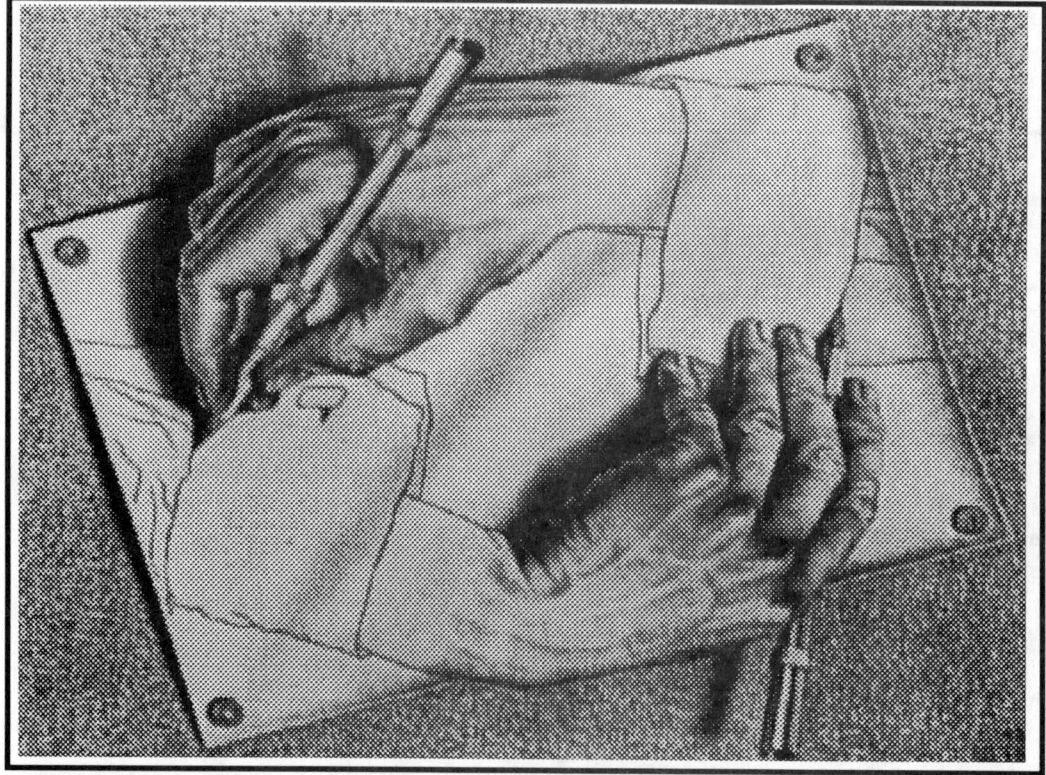

Figure 1.2 M. C. Escher's *Drawing Hands*.
©1995 M.C. Escher/Cordon Art–Baarn–Holland. All rights reserved.

30 Chapter One: **LOGIC**

> *Questions to Discuss*
>
> 1. Explain why the following apparent paradox is not really a paradox. The two sentences
>
> S_1: This sentence contains exactly six words.
> S_2: This sentence does not contain exactly six words.
>
> both appear to be true, yet they also both *appear to be* negations of each other. Negations are supposed to have opposite truth values to one another, yet these do not. Explain how this can be.
> **Hint**: Are these sentences really negations of each other? What is the subject of S_1? What is the subject of S_2?
>
> 2. Explain how the use of flashbacks in movies can cause level confusion that is similar to that found in the two examples given in the text. Can you give an example where such confusion was essential to the plot of a movie?
>
> 3. In *Chapter Two,* Neil Simon's autobiography, the play ends with the author writing his autobiography. Why is this interesting, and what would you expect to happen at the end of the autobiography written by the character in the play? (There is another interesting bit of level confusion here as Simon's ex–wife, Marcia Mason, plays the love interest in the movie adaptation of the play.)
>
> 4. Hofstadter's law states: "Everything always takes longer than you think it will, even when you take Hofstadter's law into account." Explain why Hofstadter's law is interesting.

1.9   Chapter Review

Important Terms to Know

antecedent	Epimenides' Paradox	negation
conclusion	fallacy	paradox
conditional statement	Hofstadter's Law	premise
conjunction	hypothesis	proposition
consequent	Incompleteness Theorem	self-reference
contradiction	indirect reasoning	statement
contrapositive	inverse	syllogism
converse	Liar Paradox	tangled hierarchy
crazy loop	logical connective	tautology
Cretan Paradox	logical equivalence	truth table
direct reasoning	material implication	valid argument
disjunction	mathematical logic	

Important Names to Know

Aristotle
Boole, George
De Morgan, Augustus

Gödel, Kurt
Hofstadter, Douglas
Leibniz, Gottfried Wilhelm von

Russell, Bertrand
Whitehead, Alfred North
Wittgenstein, Ludwig

Review Questions

1. Discuss Aristotle's reasons for developing the subject of logic. How did his interest in other subjects influence his work?

2. Explain the difference between a fallacy and a paradox. Give examples to clarify the distinction.

3. Explain how to construct a truth table analyzing a statement consisting of the two components p and q. Pay careful attention to how you assign values in the first two columns, and how you would use the "working rules" to fill in the rest of the table.

4. Discuss how the truth table for material implication can thought of in terms of promises.

5. Describe how truth tables can be used to decide whether or not an argument is valid.

Chapter Two

Sets

"'Which reminds me—' the White Queen said, looking down and nervously clasping and unclasping her hands, 'we had *such* a thunder–storm last Tuesday—I mean one of the last set of Tuesdays, you know.'
"Alice was puzzled. 'In our country,' she remarked, 'there's only one day at a time.'"

Lewis Carroll

Chapter Two: **SETS**

Chapter Outline

- **2.0 Introduction**
- **2.1 Historical Perspective**
- **2.2 Preliminary Concepts; Sets, Elements, and Notation**
  - *Examples and Non–examples of Sets*
  - *Basic Notation*
  - *The Empty Set*
  - *Universal Sets*
  - *Cardinality of a Set*
- **2.3 Membership; Subsets**
- **2.4 Set Operations**
  - *Set Union*
  - *Set Intersection*
  - *Properties of Basic Set Operations*
  - *Other Set Operations; Difference and Complements*
- **2.5 Euler Circles and Venn Diagrams**
  - **2.5.1 Venn Diagrams and Sets**
  - **2.5.2 Survey Diagrams**
  - **2.5.3 Euler Circles and Logical Arguments**
    - *A Fallacious Argument*
- **2.6 Infinite Sets**
- **2.7 Chapter Review**

2.0 Introduction

As a branch of mathematics, set theory had a troubled beginning. It was first developed in an attempt to deal with problems mathematicians encountered in dealing with the concept of infinity. It has since evolved into a powerful tool which is indispensable in almost every branch of mathematics.

We will not be digging deeply into those difficult problems which led to the origin of set theory, and in this sense our study of the subject will only scratch the surface. We will, however, learn the basic principles of the subject. In so doing we will see how it may be used to answer questions and give insights both within and outside of mathematics.

Upon completion of this chapter you should have a working knowledge of the language of set theory, and an understanding of the relationship between this branch of mathematics and other disciplines. You should also understand how to use Venn diagrams. Although Venn diagrams are often used to help illustrate some of the abstract ideas encountered in set theory, we will also be using them to help resolve logical arguments and to analyze information collected in surveys.

2.1 Historical Perspective

Compared to many of the other branches of mathematics that we will be looking at, set theory is a relative newcomer on the scene. For example, while logic and geometry have been around for thousands of years, set theory was not considered to be a branch of mathematics until the end of the nineteenth century. Even then, as we shall see, it was not accepted by all.

The man credited with creating set theory almost single–handedly, Georg Cantor, was born in St. Petersburg, Russia, in 1845. His father's plans for Georg included training as an engineer, and although Georg hated the idea, he refused to oppose his father's desires because of the family's deep religious beliefs. Fortunately, Georg's father eventually agreed to allow him to study his treasured mathematics at universities in Zurich and Berlin.

Cantor's studies in the branch of mathematics known as Real Analysis (that branch of mathematics that includes and generalizes Calculus) dictated that certain questions about the infinite be clarified. To this end, Cantor developed his theory of sets between the years of 1874 and 1897. Because his theory allowed for the formation and study of infinite sets, which many mathematicians considered to be fictitious, Cantor's ideas came under severe criticism. The infinite was within the domain of religion and philosophy, not mathematics!

36   Chapter Two: **SETS**

By the end of the nineteenth century set theory was finally accepted by most mathematicians. This acceptance was costly to Cantor, who had suffered a series of nervous breakdowns and never got his hoped–for professorship at a major university. Furthermore, even after set theory had gained the approval of the general mathematical community, some very respected mathematicians refused to grant its importance. For example, as late as the 1930's, Ludwig Wittgenstein, possibly one of the most influential philosophers and mathematicians of the twentieth century proclaimed "the theory of classes (sets) is completely superfluous in mathematics" and worked vigorously to tear down the framework that Cantor had built up.

Almost all mathematicians would now agree with Cantor rather than Wittgenstein. Far from being superfluous, the theory of sets has proven to be indispensable in almost all other branches of mathematics.

2.2 Preliminary Concepts; Sets, Elements, and Notation

Cantor described a *set* as a "collection of definite, distinguishable objects of perception or thought conceived as a whole." This is not actually a definition; it leaves the idea of "set" as an intuitive, undefined concept. This is necessary, since the idea of "set" is considered to be so fundamental that it is not definable in terms of simpler concepts.

Although the concept of set will remain undefined, it is still necessary that the objects known as sets satisfy certain conditions. For one thing, it is necessary that a set be a *well–defined* collection of objects. This means that we must have a standard for deciding whether or not any possible object is a member of the set. The objects which are the members of a set are called its *elements*.

Examples and Non–examples of Sets

For example, the collection of "all good mathematics teachers" would not be considered a set, since there is no standard for deciding whether or not someone belongs to this collection. On the other hand, the collection of all universities in the United States is a set, since there is a clear–cut procedure for deciding whether or not a prospective element is a member of this collection. We know that Princeton University, Arizona State University, and the University of Michigan are members of this set, while the Los Angeles Dodgers, the country of Denmark, and Dartmouth College are not. Similarly, the collection of all even integers does form a set, while the collection of all large numbers does not form a set (since there is no clear distinction between numbers which are large and those which aren't).

Basic Notation

If we are going to discuss sets at any length, it's going to be necessary to have a convenient notation which we all agree on. Traditionally, *sets are represented by capital letters*, while the *elements which may be in them are represented by small letters*. Although we will try to stick to this convention as much as we possibly can, the rule cannot be uniformly adhered to because sets can also be considered to be objects, and as such, they may be elements of other sets. Just keep in mind that when a set is considered to be an element of another set the possibility for confusion is present, and extra care may be necessary.

When describing particular sets we will make extensive use of braces in two ways:

1. If there are a small number of elements, or if the elements obey some reasonably simple pattern, a set can be described by simply listing its elements between the braces. Individual elements of the set are separated by commas. This is called the *roster method* of describing sets. For example,

(a) $A = \{2,3,5,7\}$

describes a set that contains exactly four elements (which happen to positive, whole numbers);

(b) $N = \{1,2,3,4,\ldots\}$

defines the set of *natural numbers* (sometimes called the *counting numbers*); and

(c) $P_3 = \{\text{George Washington, John Adams, Thomas Jefferson}\}$

defines the set containing the first three presidents of the United States.

In the example (b) above, the three dots indicate that the pattern of numbers listed will continue indefinitely. N (a bold face capital "n") is the standard way of representing the set of natural numbers.

Please note that when listing or describing a set the order that the elements occur is immaterial to the definition. You also do not have to worry about the number of times that an element is listed in the description of the set, that is, elements may be listed more than once without changing the contents of the set. For example, $\{a,b,c\}$, $\{c,b,a\}$, and $\{a,b,c,b,b,c\}$ all represent the same set. This is because all three of these sets contain exactly the same three elements.

2. If it's inconvenient to use the roster method to describe a set, another method, called *set–builder notation*, may be used. When using set–builder notation we use one variable, say n, or x, to represent a typical element of a set. The set is then described by giving a condition that the variable must satisfy in order for it to be considered an element of the set. For example, the three sets given above may be represented as follows:

(a) $A = \{n | n \text{ is one of the first four prime numbers}\}$

(b) $N = \{x | x \text{ is a positive whole number}\}$

(c) $P_3 = \{n | n \text{ is one of the first three presidents of the United States}\}$

The Empty Set

One set that turns out to be important in many discussions is the *empty set*, or the *null set*. As its name implies, the empty set contains no elements. Some may wonder why it might be necessary to even mention sets that contain no elements, but it turns out to be a simplifying concept in many problems. Furthermore, we have seen how set–builder notation may be used to describe sets; if the condition given is one that cannot be satisfied, such as in $\{n | n \text{ is a teenage president of the United States}\}$, then it would be natural to call this an "empty set." The empty set is represented symbolically by either $\emptyset$ or by $\{\ \}$. Note that any set which contains elements cannot be the empty set. For example, neither $\{\emptyset\}$ nor $\{0\}$ are empty. The first of these sets does contain an element, that element being the empty set! What element does the second of these sets contain?

Universal Sets

In some studies it may be useful to restrict the elements which we wish to deal with. For example, in dealing with mathematical questions it may be that we wish to restrict things so that the only elements we consider are natural numbers. In this case we would say "the universal set for this particular problem is the set of natural numbers", or "the set of natural numbers is the universe." U is usually used to represent the universe, so in this case we could write $U = \{x | x \text{ is a natural number}\}$. If instead of a mathematical problem we were dealing with a problem in marketing for an advertising agency that was studying the sale of a certain type of perfume, we would probably use a different universal set. It might be $\{x | x \text{ is a woman living in the United States}\}$ (or possibly $\{x | x \text{ is a man living in the United States}\}$).

Cardinality of a Set

In some problems the particular elements of a set may not be as important as the number of elements in the set. We will denote the number of elements in a set A, called the *cardinality* of A, by $n(A)$. Cardinality turns out to be an extremely important and useful concept in mathematics, and, in fact, was the reason why Cantor's theory of sets was so controversial. Cantor extended the idea of cardinality to infinite sets, and as we will see later, came up with some very surprising results. For example, he was able to show that in some cases, even though one infinite set might appear to be much larger than another, the two sets could, in some sense, be considered to be the same size (have the same cardinality). He also showed that some infinite sets are larger than other infinite sets, another idea that some found to be surprising.

Some examples of cardinality follow:

1. Let $S = \{n | n \text{ is a state in the United States}\}$. Then $n(S) = 50$.
2. Let $B = \{x | x \text{ is a book in the Old Testament}\}$. Then $n(B) = 39$. (Note: This value depends on which Bible you are using.)
3. Let $C = \{m | m \text{ is a chessman on the board at the beginning of a chess game}\}$. Then $n(C) = 32$.
4. Let $N = \{n | n \text{ is a positive, whole number}\}$. Then $n(N)$ is not finite. Cantor denoted the cardinality of this set by $\aleph_0$ (read aleph–null). $\aleph$ (aleph) is the first letter of the Hebrew alphabet. Cantor used the subscript of 0 on aleph because he had proven that N had the smallest cardinality of any infinite set.

Question to Discuss

Explain the differences between describing sets using the roster method and the set–builder method. Give some examples of sets where the roster method is more appropriate in describing them. Give some examples where set–builder is more appropriate.

Exercises

1. Which of the following collections are sets?

   (a) The collection of all good basketball teams.
   (b) The collection of all professional jockeys over 7 feet tall.
   (c) The collection of all positive whole numbers.
   (d) The collection of positive whole numbers which are less than 0.
   (e) The collection of all diet sodas that taste good.
   (f) The collection of all states in the United States which do not share a boarder with another state.

2. Compare and contrast the sets listed below. Give the cardinality of each set.

   (a) $A = \{\ \}$
   (b) $B = \{\varnothing\}$
   (c) $C = \varnothing$
   (d) $D = \{0\}$
   (e) $E = \{0, \varnothing\}$
   (f) $F = \{\varnothing, 0\}$

3. Discuss the difference between $\{3\}$ and 3.

4. Describe the following sets using the roster method.

   (a) The set of all letters used as vowels in English.
   (b) The set of all prime numbers between 10 and 20.
   (c) The set of all numbers which satisfy the equation $x^2 = 25$.
   (d) The set of all even numbers which satisfy the equation $x + 7 = 10$.

5. Describe the following sets using set–builder notation.

   (a) $\{2,4,6,8,\ldots\}$
   (b) $\{1,2,3,4,\ldots,100\}$
   (c) $\{1,4,9,16,25,\ldots\}$

2.3 Membership; Subsets

The primary relationship between objects and sets is *membership*, denoted by the symbol $\in$. The mathematical sentence "$a \in A$" is shorthand for "a is an element of A." "$a \notin A$" is read as "a is not an element of A." For example,

1. $7 \in \{n | n \text{ is a prime number}\}$.
2. $\dfrac{1}{3} \notin N$.
3. George Washington $\in \{x | x \text{ is a president of the United States}\}$.
4. Benjamin Franklin $\notin \{x | x \text{ is a president of the United States}\}$.

In addition to the relationships between sets and their elements, there are also relationships between sets which may come into play. If A and B are two sets, and every element of A is also an element of B, then A is called a *subset* of B, denoted symbolically by $A \subseteq B$. For example, if $P = \{n | n$ is a president of the United States$\}$ and $A = \{n | n$ is a citizen of the United States$\}$, then $P \subseteq A$. If $Q = \{n | n$ is a prime number$\}$, then $Q \subseteq N$. Finally, using the same sets just defined above, A is not a subset of Q, and Q is not a subset of A. These statements would be written mathematically as $A \not\subseteq Q$ and $Q \not\subseteq A$.

If A is a subset of B which is not equal to B, then A is called a proper subset of B. This is expressed symbolically by $A \subset B$.

If every member of A is a member of B and if, in addition, every member of B is also a member of A, then the sets A and B must contain exactly the same elements. In this case the sets A and B are said to be *equal*, and we write $A = B$.

Keep in mind that the set relation symbols ($\subseteq, \not\subseteq, =$) are always put between two sets, whereas the membership relation symbols ($\in, \notin$) are always put between an object and a set. Thus it is *correct* to say that $3 \in N$, but *incorrect* to say that $\{3\} \in N$. It would, however, be correct to say that $\{3\} \subseteq N$. This is because every element of the set $\{3\}$ (there is only one element in this set) is an element of the set N.

For every set A it is true that $A \subseteq A$ (this simply says that every member of the set A is a member of the set A). It is also true that for every set A, $\emptyset \subseteq A$. The reason that it is true that $\emptyset$ is a subset of any set A is that it is true that every element of $\emptyset$ is an element of A. If this were not true, it would be because some element of $\emptyset$ were not in A. However, we know that this is impossible, because $\emptyset$ has no elements to choose from.

Questions to Discuss

1.
(a) List all of the subsets of the set $\{a\}$. (Remember, every set except $\emptyset$ must have *at least* two distinct subsets, namely $\emptyset$ and the set itself.)
(b) List all of the subsets of the set $\{a, b\}$. (Organize your work as follows: first list all subsets with no elements – there's only one, $\emptyset$; then list all subsets with one element; then list all subsets with two elements; keep going until you have listed all subsets.)
(c) List all of the subsets of the set $\{a, b, c\}$. (Follow the pattern as was given in (b).
(d) Let A be a set containing four elements. Make a guess at the number of distinct subsets that A will have.

2. Explain why it's all right to write both $\{3\} \subseteq \{3, \{3\}\}$ and $\{3\} \in \{3, \{3\}\}$.

3. Explain the difference between the statement $A = B$ and the statement $n(A) = n(B)$.

2.4 Set Operations

Just as numbers can be combined using mathematical operations (addition, subtraction, etc.) to give new numbers, sets may also be combined using set operations to form new sets. The basic set operations are called *union* and *intersection*.

Set Union

If A and B are sets, then *the union of A and B*, denoted by $A \cup B$, is the set of all elements which are either in A or in B (or both). In symbols the definition looks like this: $A \cup B = \{x | x \in A \text{ or } x \in B\}$.

Some examples:

1. If $\mathcal{E} = \{x | x \text{ is a positive, even whole number}\}$ and $\mathcal{O} = \{x | x \text{ is a positive, odd whole number}\}$ then $\mathcal{E} \cup \mathcal{O} = N$.
2. If $R = \{x | x \text{ likes rap music}\}$, and $C = \{x | x \text{ likes classical music}\}$, then $R \cup C = \{x | x \text{ likes either rap music or classical music (or both)}\}$.

You can think of the union of two sets A and B as "throwing together" the elements of A with those of B to form a new set. If A and B are relatively small sets then one way of forming $A \cup B$ is illustrated in the following example:

Example: Let $A = \{1,3,5,7,9,11,13\}$ and $B = \{2,3,5,7,11,13,17\}$. Form $A \cup B$.

We'll start by listing the elements of A: 1,3,5,7,9,11,13

Now we'll go through the elements of B, one by one, to determine if they need to be added to the list. The first element of B is "2." When we check, we see that it is not yet in the list, so we add it in; the list would then look like this: 1,3,5,7,9,11,13,17,2. When we check the next five elements, 3,5,7,11, and 13, we see that they are already in the list, so they need not be added again. However, when we check the last element, we see that 17 is not yet listed. We add it to the list, and since there are no further elements to check, we are done. We add the braces to both sides of the list to indicate that the operation is complete: $A \cup B = \{1,3,5,7,9,11,13,2,17\}$.

Note that in this case, $n(A) = 7, n(B) = 7$, and $n(A \cup B) = 9$.

This example enables us to write down a working rule for forming the union of two sets which have been described using the roster method.

Rule for Forming Unions: If sets A and B have been described using the roster method, then the set $A \cup B$ can be constructed by listing all members of A, and then adding to the list all elements of B which are not yet in the list.

Set Intersection

If A and B are sets, then the *intersection of A and B*, denoted by $A \cap B$, is the set of all elements which are both in A and in B. Symbolically, $A \cap B = \{x | x \in A \text{ and } x \in B\}$.

For example:

1. If $\mathcal{E} = \{x|x$ is a positive, even whole number$\}$ and $\mathcal{T} = \{x|x$ is a positive whole number divisible by $3\} = \{3,6,9,12,15,\ldots\}$, then $\mathcal{E} \cap \mathcal{T} = \{6,12,18,24,\ldots\} = \{x|x$ is a positive whole number which is divisible by $6\}$. Essentially what this says is that the whole numbers which are divisible by both two and by three are simply those numbers which are divisible by 6 (that is, those numbers which are both in $\mathcal{E}$ and in $\mathcal{T}$ are simply those which are divisible by 6).
2. If $C = \{x|x$ likes classical music$\}$ and $R = \{x|x$ likes rap music$\}$, then $C \cap R = \{x|x$ likes both classical music and rap music$\}$.
3. If $\mathcal{E} = \{x|x$ is a positive, even whole number$\}$ and $\mathcal{O} = \{x|x$ is a positive, odd whole number$\}$, then $\mathcal{E} \cap \mathcal{O} = \emptyset$. Two sets such as these, whose intersection is empty, are often called "*disjoint sets.*"

You should compare these last two examples with the ones on the previous page concerned with set union. In particular, note the relationship between the set operations of union and intersection and the English words "and" and "or."

Again, there is a procedure which can be used to form the intersection of two sets which are relatively small. The following example illustrates this.

Example: Let $A = \{1,3,5,7,9,11,13\}$ and $B = \{2,3,5,7,11,13,17\}$. Form $A \cap B$.

We start by checking the first element of the set A, the number "1." Since this member of A does not appear in the set B, we do not include it in the intersection. The next three elements of A, the numbers 3, 5, and 7, are also in B, so they are to be included in the intersection. The element 9 is in A but not in B, so it is not in the intersection. However, the last two elements of A, 11 and 13, are also in B. These two numbers must also be included in the intersection. Thus, $A \cap B = \{3,5,7,11,13\}$.

Note that in this case $n(A) = 7$, $n(B) = 7$, and $n(A \cap B) = 5$.

Again, an examination of this example will enable us to write down a rule that can often be used to form the intersection of sets.

Rule for Forming Intersections: If A and B are sets which have been described using the roster method, then the intersection of A and B can be constructed by checking each element of A in turn to see if it is also in B. If the element being checked is also in B, then that element should be included in $A \cap B$. If the element being checked is not in B, then that element should not be included in $A \cap B$.

Properties of the Basic Set Operations

Just as the familiar arithmetic operations of addition, multiplication, and so on, satisfy certain properties, the set operations of union and intersection also obey certain rules. In many cases these rules are similar to their arithmetic counterparts. For example, *set intersection is a commutative operation* because for all sets A and B, $A \cap B$ and $B \cap A$ are equal. The reason for this is that $A \cap B = \{x|x \in A$ and $x \in B\}$, while $B \cap A = \{x|x \in B$ and $x \in A\}$. Since these two set descriptions are clearly equivalent, $A \cap B$ and $B \cap A$ must represent the same set. The word "commutative" is used here because the rule looks so much like the commutative laws of arithmetic: For all real numbers a and b, $a + b = b + a$ and $a \cdot b = b \cdot a$.

You should also be able to convince yourself that the set operation of union is also commutative, that is, for any two sets A and B, $A \cup B = B \cup A$. Again, this is a direct result of the definition of set union.

Other Set Operations; Differences and Complements

Two other set operations deserve brief mention. We will come back and look at these two operations a little more deeply in later sections in this chapter.

The *difference of two sets* A and B, denoted by $A - B$, is the set of all elements which are in A but not in B. That is, $A - B = \{x | x \in A \text{ and } x \notin B\}$.

For example:

1. If $\mathcal{E} = \{x | x \text{ is a positive, even whole number}\}$ and $\mathcal{O} = \{x | x \text{ is a positive, odd whole number}\}$ then $\mathcal{E} - \mathcal{O} = \mathcal{E}$. (We want to remove from $\mathcal{E}$ those elements which are also in $\mathcal{O}$. There are no elements which are both in $\mathcal{E}$ and in $\mathcal{O}$, so nothing needs to be removed.)
2. $N - \mathcal{E} = \mathcal{O}$. (If we remove the even numbers from the set of positive whole numbers we will be left with the odd numbers.)
3. If $A = \{1,3,5,7,9,11,13\}$ and $B = \{2,3,5,7,11,13,17\}$, then $A - B = \{1,9\}$.

Note that in this last example, $n(A) = 7, n(B) = 7$, and $n(A - B) = 2$.

The rule for forming the difference of two sets would look something like this:

Rule for Forming Differences: Let A and B be two sets which are described using the roster method. To form the difference of the sets A and B, start with all of the elements of A and throw out all elements which are also in B.

The last set operation to be mentioned is complementation. If A is any set, then the *complement* of A, denoted by A', represents all elements of U (the universe) which are not in A. Thus, the complement of A can be defined in terms of subtraction: $A' = U - A$. In order for the complement of a set to make sense in a particular problem the universe must be either clearly stated or implied.

Some examples:

1. The complement of the set of even integers could be the set of odd integers if we were working on problems where the implied (or stated) universe is the set of integers.
2. The complement of the set of all people who like rap music would be $\{x | x \text{ is a person who does not like rap music}\}$. Here the assumed universe would be $U = \{x | x \text{ is a person}\}$.

Small Group Exercises

1. The set operation of union has been called "set addition," while intersection has been called "set multiplication." The reason for this is that many of the properties of these operations are similar to the arithmetical properties that we are more familiar with. For each of the arithmetical laws listed below, try to come up with a *corresponding property* about the set operations which you think might also be true. The first one has been done for you.

ARITHMETICAL PROPERTY

(a) For all real numbers, $a + b = b + a$.
(b) For all real numbers, $a \cdot b = b \cdot a$.
(c) For every real number a, $a + 0 = a$.
(d) For every real number a, $a \cdot 1 = a$.
(e) For every real number a, $a \cdot 0 = 0$.
(f) For all real numbers, $a \cdot (b + c) = a \cdot b + a \cdot c$.

PROPERTY OF SETS

For all sets, $A \cup B = B \cup A$.

Hint: Which set do you think corresponds to 0?

Hint: Try U, the universal set, as the replacement for the number "1."

2. Now that you've made conjectures about some properties of sets in problem #1 above, you'll want to test them to see if they really are true. In each of the prospective properties of sets that you've listed above, make an assignment to the sets named in the property; for example, you might let $A = \{1,2,3,4,5,6,7,8,9,10\}$, $B = \{1,3,5,7,9,11,13,15,17,19\}$, and $C = \{2,3,5,7,11,13,17,19,23,29\}$. After making these replacements, test your properties to see if they are true. (Note that you could not prove that a property is universally true using this method, but at least you could gather evidence for the truth of a property.)

Exercises

1. Let $A = \{2,3,5,7,11,13,17,19\}$, $B = \{1,3,5,7,9,11,13,15,17,19\}$. Form the following sets:

   (a) $A \cup B$
   (b) $A - B$
   (c) $B - A$
   (d) $A \cap B$.

2. Let A be the set of all multiples of 5 (that is, $A = \{5,10,15,20,25,30,\cdots\}$), and let B be the set of all multiples of 10. Describe the sets $A - B$ and $B - A$ in English.

3. Let A be the set of all books with at least 500 pages and B the set of all hard–cover books. Assume that the universe U is the set of all books. Give English descriptions of the following:

   (a) A'
   (b) B'
   (c) $A \cap B$
   (d) $A \cup B$
   (e) $A \cap B'$

(f) $(A \cap B')'$
(g) $(A \cap B)'$
(h) $A' \cup B'$

4. (a) Identify those sets in problem 3 that are the same (if any).
   (b) Identify those sets in problem 3 which contain this book as a member.

2.5 Euler Circles and Venn Diagrams

Because the relationships between sets are abstract, attempts have been made to clarify these relationships through the use of diagrams. An early attempt at using diagrams was made by Leonhard Euler (pronounced "oiler"), a brilliant eighteenth century mathematician. Euler's insights enabled him to make advances in all branches of mathematics known at that time, and his work led to the development of many new branches of mathematics. Euler's diagrams have been used to help analyze logical problems, and we will also be exploring them in this context in a later section. Other types of diagrams, called *Carroll diagrams*, were developed by the mathematician Charles Dodgson, also known as Lewis Carroll (the author of *Alice in Wonderland*).

Euler's circles can be used as a primitive way of visualizing the relationships between sets. In his scheme sets are represented by circles (or ovals), and the relationships between the sets are built into the picture. For example, if A is a subset of B, the circle representing A would be drawn totally within the circle representing B (see Figure 2.1a below). On the other hand, if A and B are disjoint sets (that is, they do not meet, or $A \cap B = \emptyset$) then the circles would be drawn so that they do not intersect (Figure 2.1b).

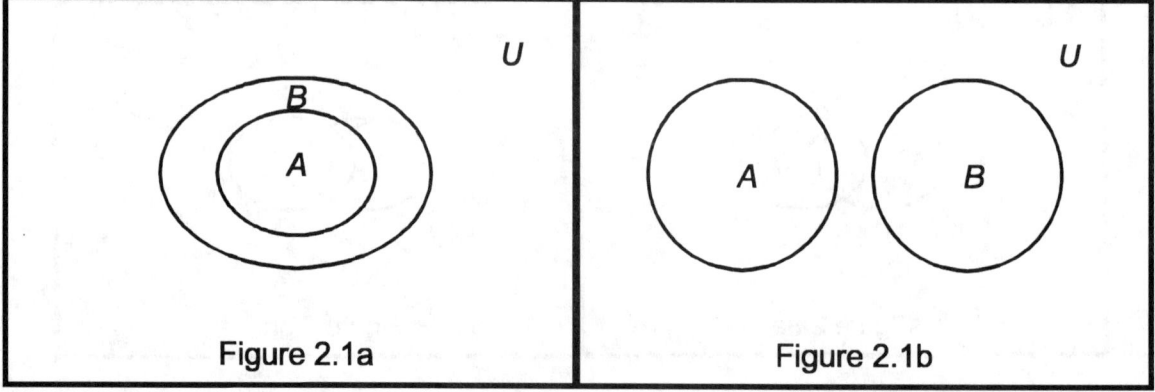

Figure 2.1 Euler's representations for the two statements "A is a subset of B." (Figure 2.1a) and "A and B are disjoint." (Figure 2.1b).

2.5.1 Venn Diagrams and Sets

Although Euler Circles were very helpful in analyzing the relationships between sets, they did present some problems. For example, what diagram would you draw if you weren't sure whether or not there is an element in $A \cap B$? To help solve this problem an English mathematician named John Venn developed an improved version of Euler circles which he introduced in his book *Symbolic Logic* published in 1881. These diagrams, now called *Venn Diagrams*, are in common use today in analyzing problems in

set theory and logic. Venn's improvement on Euler's circles was to draw his circles so that they always intersected. Thus the situations described above would be diagrammed as follows:

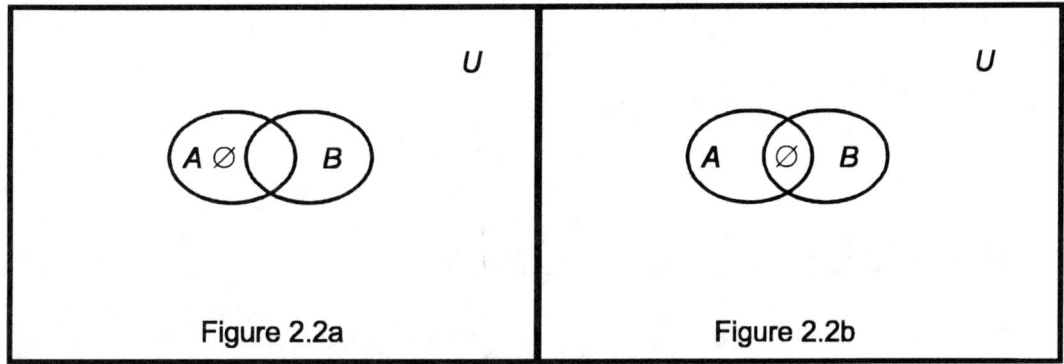

Figure 2.2 Venn diagrams for the two statements $A \subseteq B$ (**Figure 2.2a**) and "A and B are disjoint." (**Figure 2.2b**).

Note that the Venn diagram containing two sets A and B will always divide U into four non–intersecting regions: $A \cap B$; that part of A which is not part of B; that part of B which is not part of A; the rest of U (that part which has elements which are in neither A nor B). If a region is known to be empty, the empty set symbol, $\varnothing$, is entered in that region. If a region is known to be occupied, some symbol representing a typical element of that set (such as x) could be entered. If a particular region is of some special importance in some problem, that region can be shaded. Examples of how this can be put into practice follow:

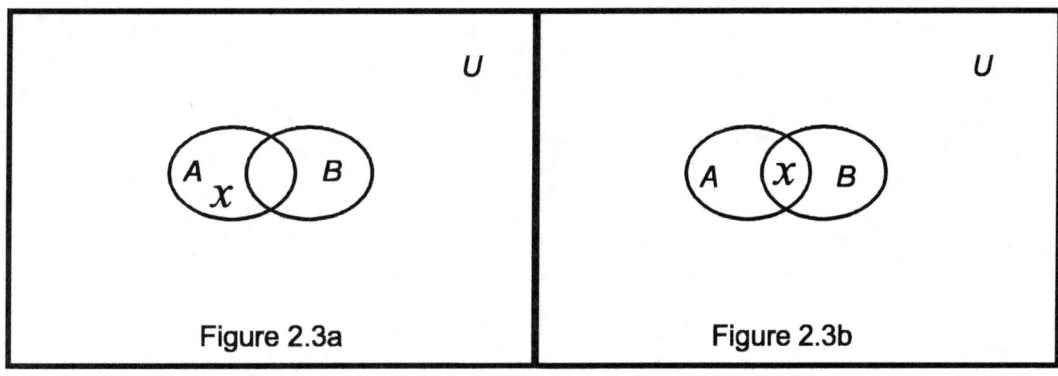

Figure 2.3 Venn diagrams for the two statements $A \not\subset B$ (**Figure 2.3a**) (because that part of A that is outside of B is not empty; it contains some element x) and $A \cap B \neq \varnothing$ (**Figure 2.3b**) (because the region common to A and B contains at least one element x).

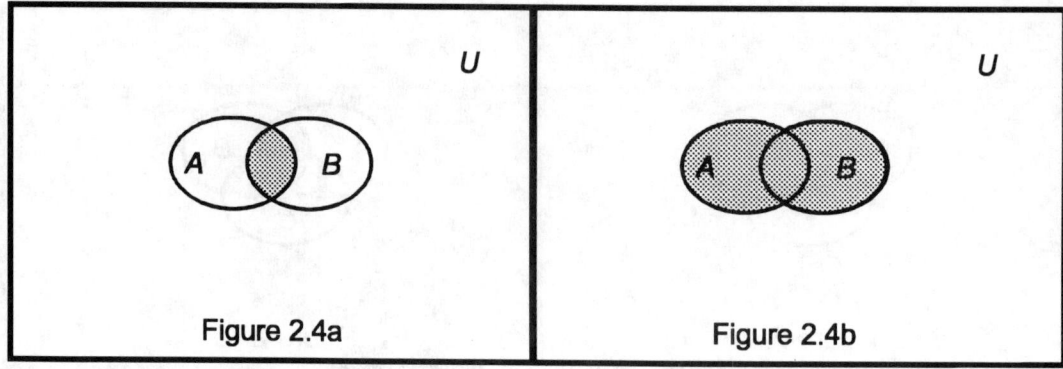

Figure 2.4 Venn diagrams representing the sets $A \cap B$ (Figure 2.4a) and $A \cup B$ (Figure 2.4b).

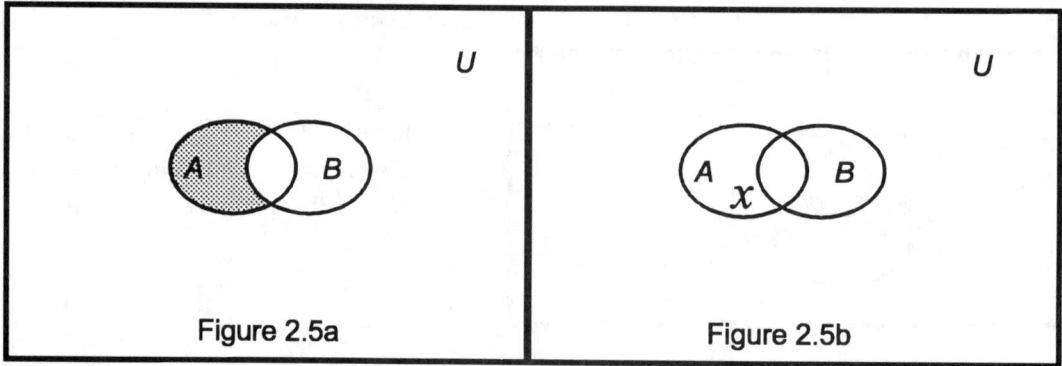

Figure 2.5 Figure 2.5a represents the set $A - B$; Figure 2.5b represents the statement "$A - B$ is nonempty." (Compare this with Figure 2.3a.)

Venn diagrams become most useful when dealing with problems concerning three sets; more than that and the diagrams often become too complicated and hard to read. Here are some examples of situations where three sets are involved:

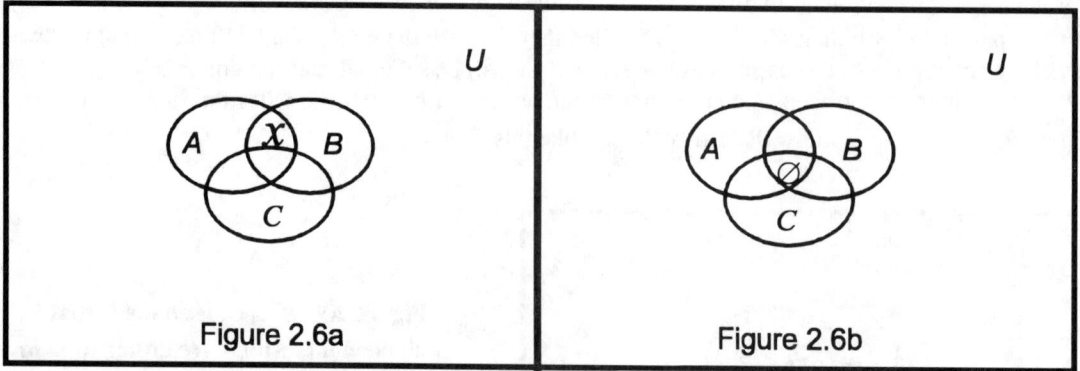

Figure 2.6 Fred (represented by x) is a member of the sets A and B (Figure 2.6a). There is no common element to all three sets A, B, and C (Figure 2.6b); symbolically, $A \cap B \cap C = \emptyset$.

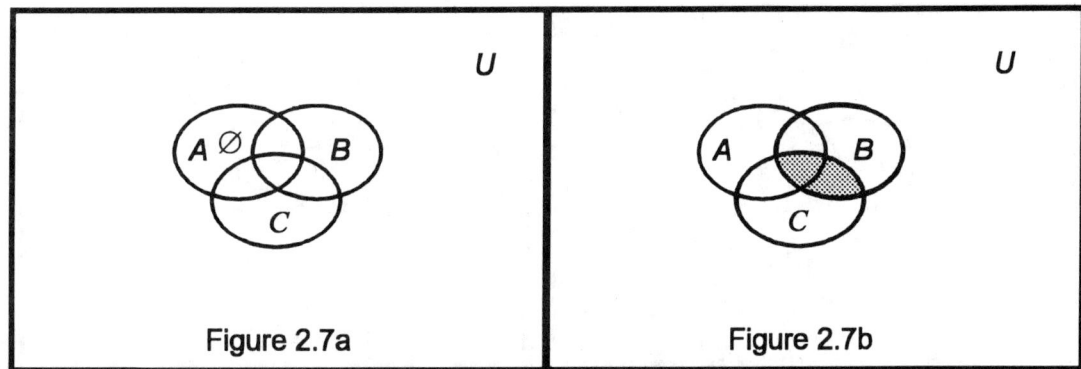

Figure 2.7 In Figure 2.7a, all elements of A are also elements of either B or of C (that is, they are in $B \cup C$). Another way of saying this is $A \subseteq B \cup C$. In Figure 2.7b, $B \cap C$ is shaded.

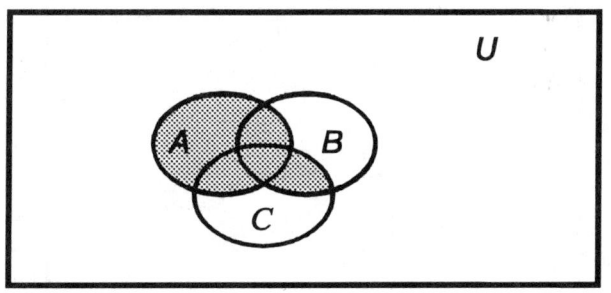

Figure 2.8 $A \cup (B \cap C)$ is shaded. This represents all elements either in $B \cap C$ (from Figure 2.7b) or in A.

Note that every Venn diagram depicting three sets will always divide up the universe into eight non-overlapping sets.

As an example of how Venn diagrams can be used to provide evidence and insight concerning conjectures about set relationships, consider the following demonstration which shows that $A \cap (B \cup C) = (A \cap B) \cup (A \cap C)$ for all sets A, B, and C. (Note that this is a property which you may have guessed during the small group exercises at the end of section 2.4.) The strategy will be to construct a Venn diagram that represents the left-hand side of the equation, $A \cap (B \cup C)$. We will then construct a second Venn diagram to represent the right-hand side of the equation, $(A \cap B) \cup (A \cap C)$. After comparing the two diagrams, we will see that they are both the same. That will mean that the two sides of the equation both represent the same set, and we will be sure that the equation is true.

In order to construct a Venn diagram for the set $A \cap (B \cup C)$, we will first need to construct a diagram for $B \cup C$. We know that this will look like this:

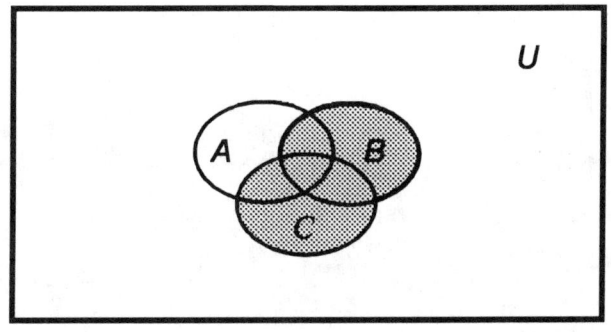

Figure 2.9 $B \cup C$ is shaded (that is, all elements which are either in B or in C or in both).

We wish to take the intersection of this set (shaded above) with A to form $A \cap (B \cup C)$. That is, we wish to diagram the region which is common to both the circles representing A and to the shaded region representing $B \cup C$. A little bit of reflection indicates that what we are looking for is that part of the shaded region which is within the circle representing A. So what we want is this:

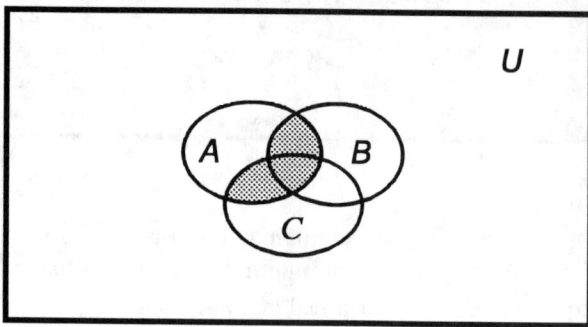

Figure 2.10 $A \cap (B \cup C)$ (Representing all objects that are both in set A and in the shaded area diagrammed in Figure 2.9.)

We shall now draw a diagram representing the set $(A \cap B) \cup (A \cap C)$. In order to do this we will first separately form two diagrams for the sets $A \cap B$ and $A \cap C$. They would look like this:

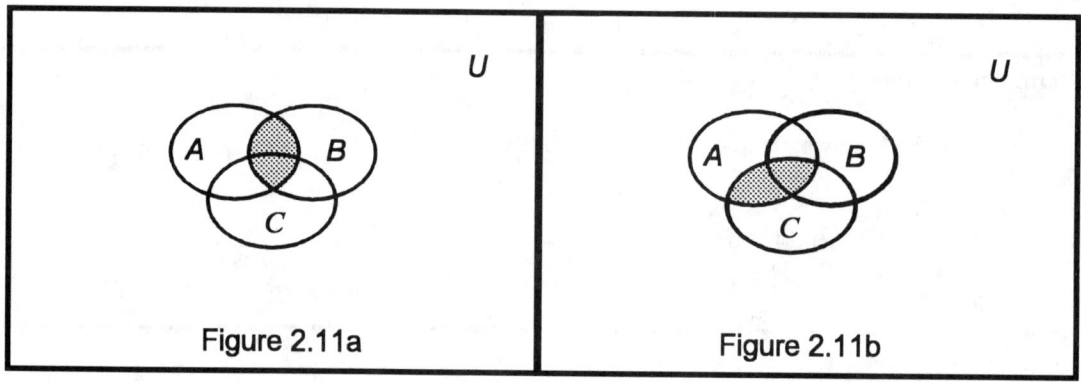

Figure 2.11 Two Venn diagrams, one representing the set $A \cap B$ (Figure 2.11a), and the other representing the set $A \cap C$.

To complete the Venn diagram of $(A \cap B) \cup (A \cap C)$ we need to take the union of the two sets diagrammed in Figures 2.11a and 2.11b. Since we are interested in the elements which are in either the first of these diagrammed regions or in the second of the regions, what we want is the portion of the diagram which is in either of the two shaded regions. This means that what we want is the following:

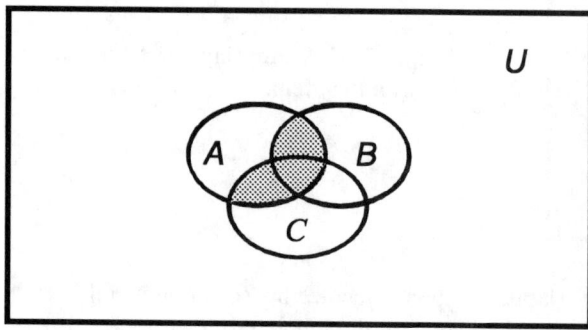

Figure 2.12 The shaded region represents $(A \cap B) \cup (A \cap C)$ because it is the region representing the elements which are either in $A \cap B$ (Figure 2.11a) or in $A \cap C$ (Figure 2.11b).

50 Chapter Two: **SETS**

If we now compare the two diagrams we have constructed, the one for $A \cap (B \cup C)$ (Figure 2.10) and the other for $(A \cap B) \cup (A \cap C)$ (Figure 2.12) we can see that they are the same. This indicates that these two sets which they represent are the same, and that $A \cap (B \cup C) = (A \cap B) \cup (A \cap C)$. By the way, you may have already guessed that this is called a "*distributive law*," because that is the name given to the more familiar and very similar property of arithmetic: $a \cdot (b + c) = a \cdot b + a \cdot c$. The law concerning sets which we just verified is summarized by saying "The operation of intersection is distributive over union."

Small Group Exercise

From arithmetic we know that multiplication is distributive over addition, that is, that $a \cdot (b + c) = a \cdot b + a \cdot c$. We also know that addition is *not* distributive over multiplication, that is that generally $a + (b \cdot c)$ and $(a + b) \cdot (a + c)$ are not equal. We have now learned that intersection is distributive over union, and we verified this fact through the use of Venn diagrams. However, when dealing with sets *it is also true* that union is distributive over intersection. Verify this fact through the use of Venn diagrams.

Question to Discuss

Explain the following mathematical statements in English:

(a) If $A \subseteq B$ then $A \cup B = B$.
(b) If $A \cup B = B$ then $A \subseteq B$.
(c) If $A \subseteq B$ then $A \cap B = A$.
(d) If $A \cap B = A$ then $A \subseteq B$.

Exercises

1. Let $C = \{x | x \text{ likes classical music}\}$ and $R = \{x | x \text{ likes rock music}\}$. Consider the following Venn diagram:

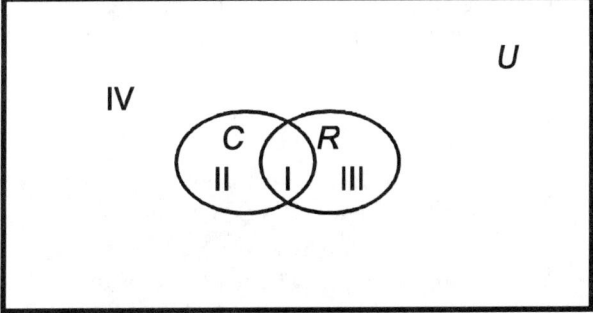

Figure 2.13 Venn diagram for the "Music Problem."

The diagram breaks up the universe into four non–overlapping regions (denoted by Roman numerals). Using the Roman numerals, identify the region *or regions* that represent the following:

(a) The people who enjoy classical music but not rock.
(b) The people who enjoy rock music but not classical.
(c) The people who enjoy one or the other of the two types of music, but not both.
(d) The people who enjoy both types of music.
(e) The people who enjoy neither type of music.
(f) The people who enjoy at least one of the two types of music.
(g) The people who enjoy at most one of the two types of music.

2. In addition to the two sets described in problem #1, let's add an additional set: $W = \{x | x \text{ likes rap music}\}$. Consider the following Venn diagram:

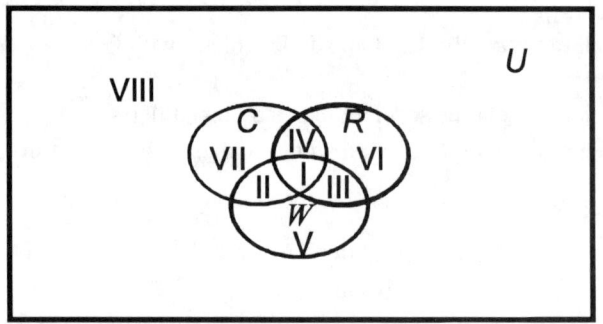

Figure 2.14 Diagram for Problem #2.

The diagram breaks up the universe into eight non–overlapping regions (denoted by Roman numerals). Describe in English the regions which are labeled as indicated:

(a) The people represented by the region labeled I.
(b) The people represented by the region labeled II.
(c) The people represented by the region labeled VII.
(d) The people represented by the region labeled VIII.
(e) The people represented by the regions labeled I and II. (Hint: What kinds of music do the people in this region like?)
(f) The people represented by the regions labeled I, III, IV, and VI.
(g) The people represented by the regions labeled III and VI. (Hint: Describe the likes and dislikes of the people in these regions.)
(h) The people represented by the regions labeled III, V, and VI.
(i) The people represented by the regions labeled II, III, and IV.
(j) The people represented by the regions labeled V, VI, and VII.
(k) The people represented by the regions labeled V, VI, VII, and VIII.
(l) The people represented by the regions labeled I, II, III, and IV.

3. Consider a universe consisting of all people. Let A be the set of all people who are 18 years of age or older and B the set of all people who are college freshmen.
Draw a Venn diagram similar to Figure 2.13, label it similarly, and do the following:

(a) Identify the regions in your diagram which represent the set of all people under the age of 18.
(b) Identify the regions in your diagram which represent the set of all freshmen who are under the age of 18.
(c) Identify the regions in your diagram which represent the set of all freshmen who are age 18 or older.
(d) Where would you place an x in your diagram to represent the following:
- a 22 year–old sophomore

52   Chapter Two: **SETS**

- a 17 year–old who has never been to college
- a 45 year–old housewife?

4.   Consider a universe consisting of all college students. Let A be the set of all college students who play athletics, B the set of college students with a 3.0 GPA or higher, C the set of college students who are married.
Draw a Venn diagram similar to Figure 2.14, label it similarly, and do the following.

(a) Identify the regions in your diagram which represent the set of all single athletes with GPA less than 3.0.
(b) Identify the regions in your diagram which represent the set of all married non–athletes with GPA 3.0 or higher.
(c) Identify the regions in your diagram which represent the set of all single athletes with GPA greater than 3.0.
(d) Identify the regions in your diagram which represent the set of all married non–athletes.
(e) Identify the regions in your diagram which represent the set of all single students who are 18 or older.
(f) Where would you place the following symbols?
- an L for Laurie, an unmarried woman who scores 12.1 points per game for her college's basketball team
- an S for Sam, the shortstop for his college's baseball team. He has a 2.7 GPA and his wife's name is Julie
- an A for Amanda, who is getting married next month and has a GPA of 1.5

2.5.2 Survey Diagrams

We have learned how the use of Venn Diagrams can help us visualize relationships between sets. In other applications it is possible to use a variation of Venn Diagrams to analyze data and count up the number of elements that satisfy certain conditions. When used in this way the diagrams are often called *Survey Diagrams*.

As an example, consider the following problem:

Example #1:   One hundred fifty people were surveyed in order to determine if they liked to watch baseball or football. When the data was analyzed it was found that 62 of the people liked to watch both sports, while a total of 98 enjoyed watching baseball and 87 liked watching football. Determine the following:

(a) The number of people who like watching baseball but not football.
(b) The number of people who like watching football but not baseball.
(c) The number of people who like neither of the sports.
(d) The number of people who like watching only one of these sports.
(e) The number of people who like watching at least one of these sports.

Solution: We will build a Venn Diagram with two intersecting circles to portray the data in the problem. One circle will represent the people who like to watch baseball, while the other will represent those who like to watch football. The universe, U, represents the 150 people who were surveyed.

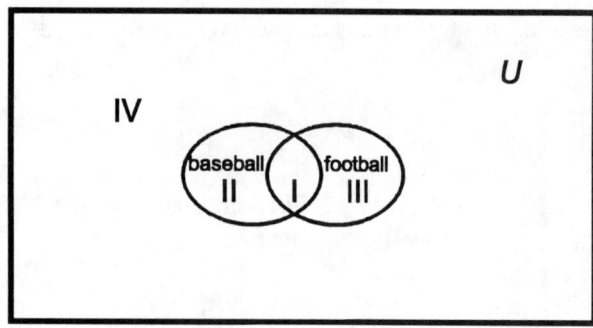

Figure 2.15 Survey Diagram for example #1.

As mentioned earlier, the diagram breaks up U into four non-overlapping regions, which have been labeled with Roman numerals in the above diagram. We will now determine the number of elements from the survey represented by each of the four regions.

Here region I represents those surveyed who enjoy both sports (since it is within both the "baseball" circle and the "football" circle), region II represents those who like only baseball (since this region is within the "baseball" circle, but not within the "football" circle), region III represents those who like only football, and region IV represents those who like neither sport.

An examination of the given information indicates that 62 of those who responded said that they enjoyed both sports. Since this is represented by region I, we will redraw the diagram, placing the number 62 in region I.

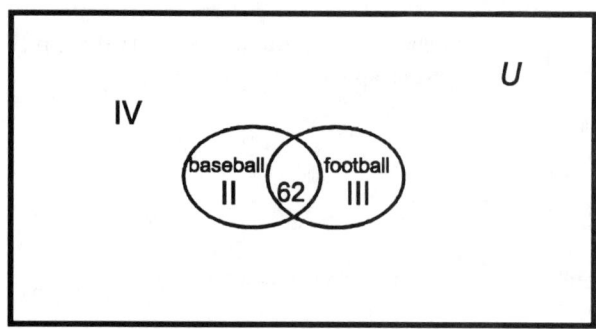

Figure 2.16 Partial analysis of data for example #1.

What number should we enter in region II? There are a total of 98 who enjoy baseball, but 62 have already been accounted for in region I. Thus, there are a total 98-62, or 36, who still need to be assigned somewhere in the baseball circle. These people must be represented by region II. To check, note that after entering "36" in region II, there are total of 98 people accounted for within the "baseball" circle:

62 (people who enjoy both sports, including baseball)
+36 (people who enjoy only baseball)
98 (total assigned to the "baseball" region)

Another way of determining this would be to represent the number of people in region II by the variable x. Then the total number of people who enjoy baseball is the number of people in region I plus the number of people in region II, which is $x + 62$. But we know that this has to equal 98. This gives the equation $x + 62 = 98$, which, when solved, results in $x = 36$.

Using a similar argument, you should be able to convince yourself that region III represents 25 people, the number of people who like football, but not baseball.

We will now redraw the diagram again, including all of the results that we have determined so far:

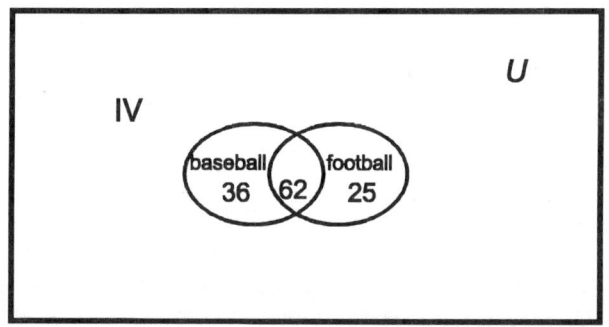

Figure 2.17 Further analysis of the data in example #1.

We've now filled in three of the regions, and accounted for 36+62+25=123 of the 150 people surveyed. 27 people remain to be classified, so they must go into the only region remaining — region IV, those who like neither sport. The final diagram, classifying all of the data in the problem, would look like this:

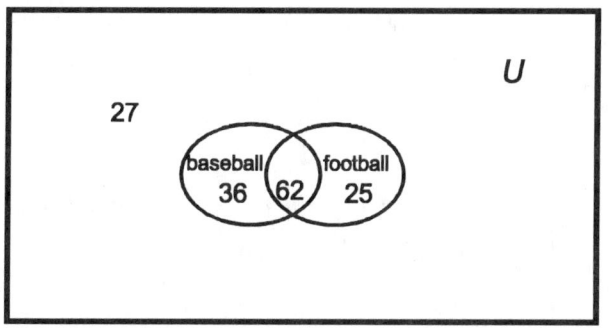

Figure 2.18 Final analysis for the data of example #1.

We can now easily answer the questions which we were asked in the problem by referring to the final diagram.

(a) 36 people liked only baseball (represented by region II).
(b) 25 people liked only football (represented by region III).
(c) 27 people liked neither sport (represented by region IV).
(d) 36+25=61 people liked either baseball or football, but not both (represented by regions II and III).
(e) 36+25+62=123 people liked at least one of the sports (regions I, II, and III).

After completing this example we can see a common mistake that many make. When trying to determine $n(A \cup B)$ (remember: this represents the number of elements in the set $A \cup B$), we may not simply add together $n(A)$ and $n(B)$. (See Figure 2.19). If we add together $n(A)$ and $n(B)$ we will count the elements of region I twice! Hence $n(A)+n(B)$ equals not $n(A \cup B)$, but $n(A \cup B)+n(A \cap B)$. (The last term must be added in to compensate for the fact that we counted the elements of region I, which represents $A \cap B$, twice.) Thus, $n(A)+n(B) = n(A \cup B)+n(A \cap B)$, or $n(A)+n(B)-n(A \cap B) = n(A \cup B)$.

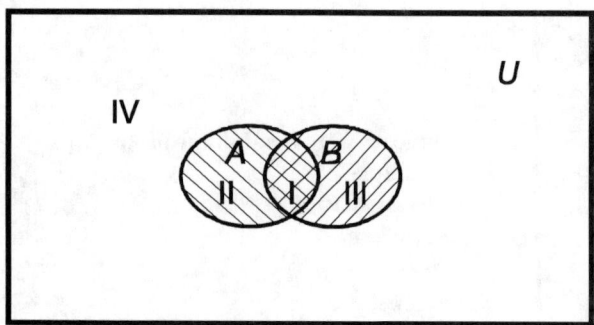

Figure 2.19 Illustration of the difference between $n(A \cup B)$ and $n(A) + n(B)$. $n(A \cup B)$ equals $n(A) + n(B) - n(I)$, because the elements in region I are counted twice if we add together $n(A)$ and $n(B)$.

Counting Principle: If A and B are finite sets, $n(A \cup B) = n(A) + n(B) - n(A \cap B)$.

You should now go back to Example #1 to verify that this equation is satisfied by the data in that problem. There, $n(A) = 98$, because we were told that 98 people enjoyed baseball, and $n(B) = 87$, because 87 people enjoy football. We also were told that 62 people enjoyed both sports, which means that $n(A \cap B) = 62$. Using the formula, $n(A \cup B) = n(A) + n(B) - n(A \cap B) = 98 + 87 - 62 = 123$. But this simply verifies something that we already knew, the result that we got before in answering question (e) of Example #1.

Example #2: If $n(A \cap B) = 7$, $n(A) = 13$, and $n(B) = 11$, find the following:

(a) $n(A \cup B)$
(b) $n(A - B)$
(c) $n(B - A)$

Solution: Drawing a Venn Diagram will help make the data easier to inspect.

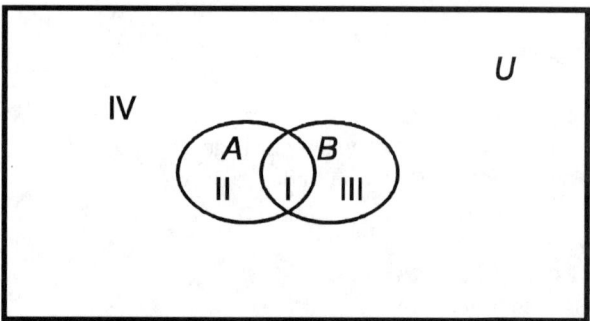

Figure 2.20 Venn diagram for example 2.

We are told that region I has 7 elements, so we can fill that in on the diagram. Since $n(A) = 13$, regions I and II must add up to 13. Because region I has 7 elements, region II must have 6. In a similar manner, region III has 4 elements. The final diagram will look like this:

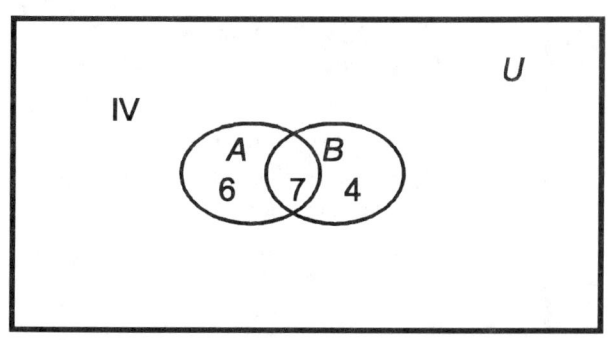

Figure 2.21 Final diagram for example 2.

(a) To get $n(A \cup B)$, either add up all of the elements in regions I, II, and III (to get $6 + 7 + 4 = 17$), or use the formula $n(A \cup B) = n(A) + n(B) - n(A \cap B) = 13 + 11 - 7 = 17$.
(b) $n(A - B) = 6$ (region II).
(c) $n(B - A) = 4$ (region IV).

Example 3: A marketing company has been asked to do research for a soft drink manufacturer in order to help them make decisions on which flavors of soda they should introduce in the coming year. One hundred twenty people who drink soda are surveyed. They are each asked to check off which of the following flavors of soda they would buy:

(1) Peach
(2) Strawberry
(3) Watermelon

When the data was analyzed it was found that 37 people said that they would try all three, 59 people would try Peach and Strawberry, 48 would try Strawberry and Watermelon, 51 would try Peach and Watermelon, 83 would try Peach, 78 would try Strawberry, and 66 would try Watermelon.
    Determine the following:

(a) The number of people who would not try any flavor.
(b) The number of people who would try only watermelon.
(c) The number of people who would try either Watermelon or Peach.
(d) The number of people who would try Watermelon and Strawberry, but not Peach.
(e) The number of people who would try Watermelon or Strawberry, but not Peach.
(f) The number of people who would try at least two of the types.
(g) The number of people who would try two types.
(h) The number of people who would try exactly one of the types.
(i) The number of people who would try at least one of the types.
(j) The number of people who would try only Watermelon.

Solution: In solving this problem it will be advantageous to form a survey diagram containing three mutually intersecting circles. We'll use P to represent the set of people who would try the Peach soda, S for the set of people who would try the Strawberry, and W for the set of people who would try the Watermelon. The Universe, U, represents the 120 people surveyed.

Mathematics Appreciation   57

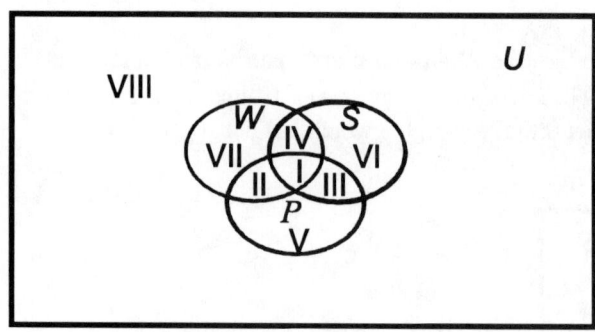

Figure 2.22 Survey diagram for example 3.

As usual, we'll label the regions with Roman numerals for reference.

In putting the numerical values into the regions of these diagrams it is often easiest to start on the innermost region (that is, region I) and work your way out. (If you recheck Examples 1 and 2 you'll see that we did this in those problems too.) It's easy to see that region I should contain the number 37, since this region represents the elements that are common to all three sets (that is, the people who would try all three types of soda). How many people are represented by region II? Since we know that 48 would be willing to try both the Watermelon and the Strawberry, these people would have to be distributed through regions I and II. Since 37 of the 48 are already accounted for in region I, the remaining 11 people must be represented by region II. In a similar way, we determine that region III should contain the number 14 and the that region IV should contain the number 22. (Check these for yourself.) At this point the diagram would look like this:

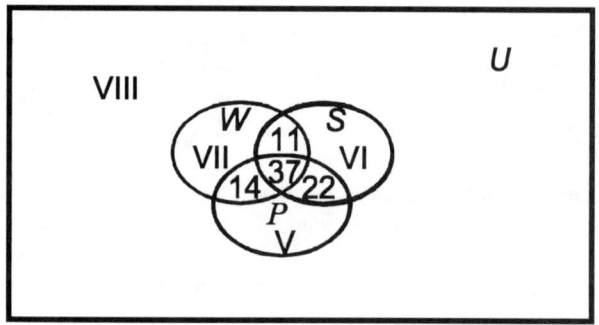

Figure 2.23 Updated survey diagram for example 3.

We will now determine what numbers to place in regions V, VI, and VII. For region V, notice that there are 78 people who are willing to try Strawberry (regions I, II, IV, and V), and of these 78, 70 have already been allocated (37 in region I, 11 in region II, and 22 in region IV). The remaining 8 people must be represented by region V, so we enter an "8" there. In a similar way, we determine that region VI represents 4 people (The 4 of the 66 "Watermelon people" who have still not yet been assigned to regions I, II, and IV must be represented in region VI) and that region VII represents 10 people. An update of the diagram would now look like this:

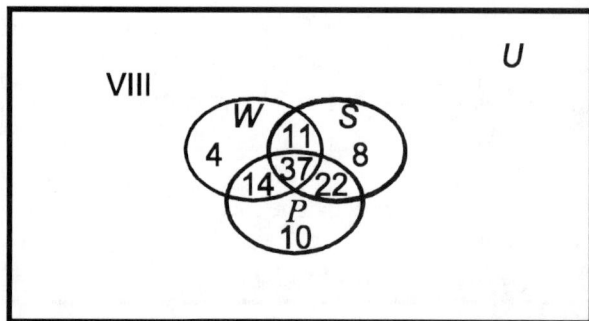

Figure 2.24 Further update of example 3.

By counting up the people accounted for in the seven regions decided upon so far, we see that 106 of the 120 people in the universe have already been assigned. This leaves 14 unassigned people, so that number must be placed in region VIII (since this is the only region which has not yet been determined). The final diagram for the problem would look like this:

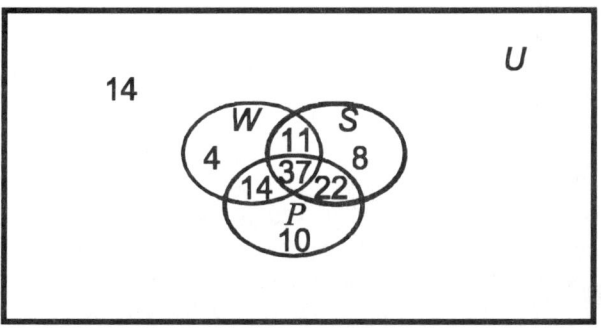

Figure 2.25 The final diagram for example 3.

By referring to this diagram we can now figure out the answer to the questions which we were asked earlier.

(a) Fourteen people would not try any of the three flavors. (Region VIII.)
(b) Four people would be willing to try only Watermelon. (Region VI.)
(c) Ninety-eight people would try Watermelon or Peach. (The sum of the numbers in regions I, II, III, IV, VI, and VII.)
(d) Eleven people would try Watermelon and Strawberry but not Peach. (Region II.)
(e) Twenty-three people would try Watermelon or Strawberry but not Peach. (The sum of the numbers in regions II, V, and VI.)
(f) Eighty-four people would try at least two types (that is, two or more types). (The sum of the numbers in regions I, II, III, and IV.)
(g) Forty-seven people would try two types. (The sum of the numbers in regions II, III, and IV.)
(h) Twenty-two people would try exactly one type. (The sum of the numbers in regions V, VI, and VII).
(i) One hundred six people would try at least one type. (The sum of the numbers in regions I through VII.)
(j) Fifty-one people would try Watermelon and Peach (Region VI.)

Questions to Discuss

1. Explain the following two statements in English. Assume that A and B represent finite sets.

(a) $n(A \cup B) \geq n(A)$
(b) $n(A \cap B) \leq n(A)$

2. Is it possible for $n(A \cup B)$ and $n(A)$ to be equal? How about $n(A \cap B)$ and $n(A)$? Can $n(A \cup B)$ ever equal $n(A \cap B)$?

3. Give an example to show that $n(A \cup B)$ and $n(A) + n(B)$ need not be equal.

4. In your own words, explain why $n(A \cup B) = n(A) + n(B) - n(A \cap B)$.

Exercises

1. *Puzzles Magazine* polls a sample of its readers to determine what kinds of puzzles they enjoy. They ask the sample of 100 readers to indicate their preferences on the following form:

> **Indicate the types of puzzles you enjoy solving. Check as many as apply.**
>
> ☐ Logic Puzzles
> ☐ Word Puzzles

Figure 2.26 Survey for the *Puzzles Magazine* problem.

The results of their survey can be summarized as follows:
- 49 readers liked both types of puzzles
- 69 readers liked logic puzzles
- 75 readers liked word puzzles

Draw a survey diagram illustrating the data in this problem and use it to answer the following questions:

(a) How many readers in the sample liked neither type of puzzle?
(b) How many readers in the sample liked logic puzzles but not word puzzles?
(c) How many readers in the sample liked word puzzles but not logic puzzles?
(d) How many readers in the sample liked only one type of puzzle?
(e) How many readers in the sample liked at least one type of puzzle?

2. A book publishing company surveys 85 people in a mall and asks if they read romance novels or mysteries. They find that 12 of those surveyed read both, 29 read romances, and 33 read mysteries.

Draw a survey diagram illustrating the data in this problem and use it to answer the following questions:

(a) How many of those surveyed read neither?
(b) How many of those surveyed read only romance novels?
(c) How many of those surveyed read only mysteries?
(d) How many of those surveyed read one type, but not both?
(e) How many of those surveyed read at least one of the two types of books?
(f) How many of those surveyed read at most one of the two types of book?

3. The Democratic Party wishes to choose their candidate for the up–coming Presidential Election. The Republicans have selected their candidate, and the Democrats are choosing between two front–runners, candidates A and B. Before they make their selection, the Democratic delegates commission a poll of the voting public to determine which of their candidates stands the best chance of success.

The results of the survey can be summarized as follows:
- 46% would vote Democratic if A is the candidate
- 53% would vote Democratic if B is the candidate
- 41% would vote Democratic if either candidate is the nominee

(a) What percent of the sample would not vote Democratic if A is the candidate?
(b) What percent of the sample would not vote Democratic if B is the candidate?

(c) What percent of the sample would not vote Democratic whether the candidate is A or B?

4. The local YMCA is running a summer program for children. In order to decide which activities to offer, they asked 100 children to complete the following form:

> Indicate the types of activities you would be willing to participate in. Check all that apply.
>
> ☐ Swimming
> ☐ Finger painting
> ☐ Basketball

Figure 2.27
Survey for the YMCA problem.

The results were tabulated, and the following summary was compiled:
- 23 children would participate in all three activities
- 40 children would participate in swimming and finger painting
- 35 children would participate in finger painting and basketball
- 44 children would participate in swimming and basketball
- 54 children would participate in finger painting
- 64 children would participate in swimming
- 61 children would participate in basketball.

Draw a survey diagram illustrating the data in this problem and use it to answer the following questions:

(a) How many of the children surveyed would not participate in any of these activities?
(b) How many of the children surveyed would participate in finger painting and swimming, but not basketball?
(c) How many of the children surveyed would participate in finger painting or swimming?
(d) How many of the children surveyed would participate in finger painting and basketball but not in swimming?
(e) How many of the children surveyed would participate in finger painting or basketball?
(f) How many of the children surveyed would participate in swimming and basketball but not in finger painting?
(g) How many of the children surveyed would participate in swimming or basketball?
(h) How many of the children surveyed would not participate in finger painting or swimming?
(i) How many of the children surveyed would not participate in finger painting or basketball?
(j) How many of the children surveyed would not participate in swimming or basketball?
(k) How many of the children surveyed would participate in swimming only?
(l) How many of the children surveyed would participate in finger painting only?
(m) How many of the children surveyed would participate in basketball only?
(n) How many of the children surveyed would participate in only one of the three activities?
(o) How many of the children surveyed would participate in at least two of the three activities?
(p) How many of the children surveyed would participate in at most two of the three activities?

5. A frozen pizza company surveys perspective customers by sending out a questionnaire asking about the customers' tastes in pizza toppings. They are considering offering sausage, pepperoni, and peppers as possible toppings. 217 people returned their surveys, and the following results were tabulated:
- 61 respondents would eat all three toppings
- 102 respondents would eat pepperoni and sausage

- 81 respondents would eat sausage and peppers
- 93 respondents would eat pepperoni and peppers
- 141 respondents would eat sausage
- 151 respondents would eat pepperoni
- 117 respondents would eat peppers

Draw a survey diagram illustrating the data in this problem and use it to answer the following questions:

(a) What number of respondents would eat none of these toppings?
(b) What number of respondents would eat only sausage?
(c) What number of respondents would eat only pepperoni?
(d) What number of respondents would eat only peppers?
(e) What number of respondents would eat only one type of topping?
(f) What number of respondents would eat sausage and pepperoni, but not peppers?
(g) What number of respondents would eat sausage and peppers but not pepperoni?
(h) What number of respondents would eat peppers and pepperoni, but not sausage?
(i) What number of respondents would eat exactly two types of toppings?
(j) What number of respondents would eat at least two types of toppings?
(k) What number of respondents would eat at most two types of toppings?
(l) What number of respondents would eat at least one type of topping?
(m) What number of respondents would eat at most one type of topping?

6. Caroline's Used Car Company needs to keep its inventory up to date in order to make decisions on how much to pay customers who are selling their cars. They classify their cars in the following categories:
automatic or manual transmission
two door or four door
power or standard steering.

They currently have 68 cars on the lot. A check of the company's database shows that the 68 cars satisfy the following:
- 23 cars have four doors, power steering, and automatic transmission
- 0 cars have four doors, standard steering, and automatic transmission
- 0 cars have four doors, power steering, and manual transmission
- 16 cars have two doors, power steering and automatic transmission
- 31 cars have four doors
- 46 cars have automatic transmission
- 41 cars have power steering

Draw a survey diagram illustrating the data in this problem, labeling the circles "four doors," "automatic transmission," and "power steering." Use the diagram to answer the following questions:

(a) How many cars on the lot have two doors, standard steering, and manual transmission?
(b) How many cars on the lot have four doors, but do not have power steering?
(c) How many cars on the lot have four doors, but do not have automatic transmission?
(d) How many cars on the lot have four doors and neither power steering nor automatic transmission?
(e) How many cars on the lot have two doors, but do not have power steering?
(f) How many cars on the lot have two doors, but do not have automatic transmission?
(g) How many cars on the lot have two doors and neither power steering nor automatic transmission?
(h) How many cars on the lot have four doors and automatic transmission?
(i) How many cars on the lot have automatic transmission and standard steering?
(j) How many cars on the lot have power steering and manual transmission?

2.5.3 Euler Circles and Logical Arguments

Although it is possible to use the Venn Diagrams which we have studied to analyze logical arguments, it is probably a bit simpler to use the Euler Circles first mentioned in section 2.5. To get an idea of how they could be used to do this, let's go back to Aristotle's famous syllogism which we looked at in chapter 1:

Every Greek is a man.
<u>Every man is mortal.</u>
Every Greek is mortal.

In chapter 1 we learned how to translate arguments such as this into symbols, make truth tables for the arguments, and test these truth tables to see if the argument were valid. Euler Circles give a method for analyzing arguments such as this without going through much of this trouble.

The method will work like this: Diagram the hypotheses of the argument. (In this case we would diagram the statements "Every Greek is a man." and "Every man is mortal.") *We will then check the diagram to see if, in the process of diagramming the hypotheses, the conclusion was also diagrammed.* If, in the process of diagramming the hypotheses, we have also diagrammed the conclusion, then the argument is valid. If the process of diagramming the hypotheses has not diagrammed the conclusion, then the argument is not valid. (You may want to go back to chapter 1 to remind yourself what some of these words mean.) If this seems to be complicated now, a few examples will show just how simple it is.

In this case, the first hypothesis, "Every Greek is a man." is diagrammed like this:

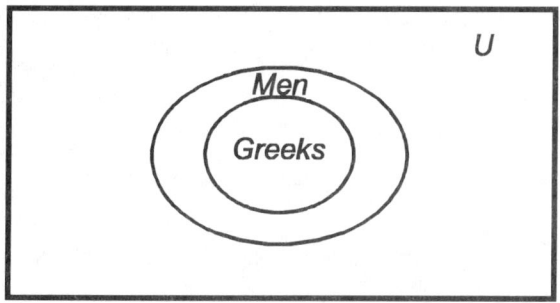

Figure 2.28 Diagram of the statement "Every Greek is a man."

Note that the circle representing "Greeks" is totally contained within the circle representing "men." This is because the statement "All Greeks are men" says that the set of all Greeks is a subset of the set of all men.

The second hypothesis, "Every man is mortal," indicates that the set of all men is a subset of the set of all mortals. As far as the diagram is concerned, this means that the circle representing "all men" should be totally contained within the circle representing "all mortals." Adding this fact to the diagram would update it to look like this:

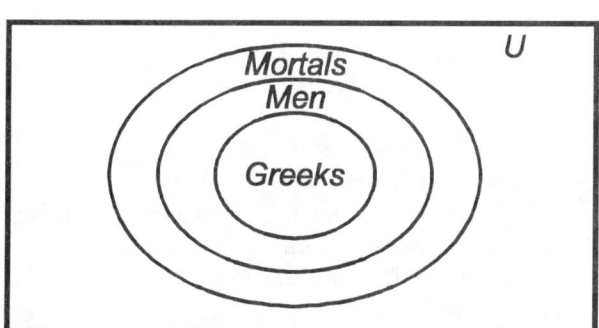

Figure 2.29 Diagram of both hypotheses of the argument.

Has diagramming the two hypotheses also diagrammed the conclusion? If it has, then the statement "Every Greek is mortal" should already be diagrammed in Figure 2.29, above. But this is the case, because all the statement "Every Greek is mortal" says is that the set of all Greeks is a subset of the set of all mortals. This statement is clearly portrayed in the diagram, because the circle representing the set of all Greeks is totally contained within the circle representing "mortals."

Before going over any more arguments, let's see how to diagram a number of different logical statements using Euler Circles. When doing this remember that when translating a statement into logical form, the intent of the statement is much more important than its appearance.

| **Diagram** | **Set Interpretation** | **Statement** |

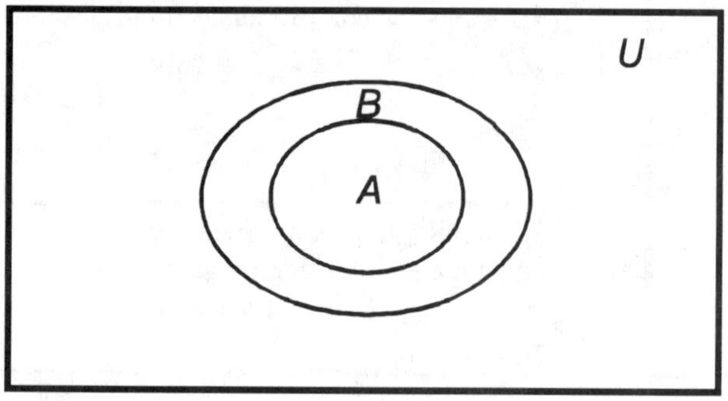

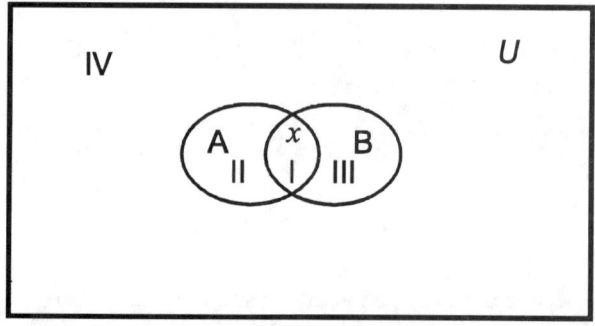

The set of A's is a subset of the set of B's.   All A's are B's.

Figure 2.30 All A's are B's.

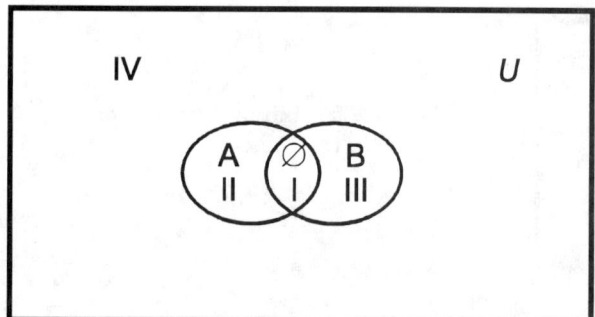

The sets A and B meet. (or "Some B is an A.")   Some A is a B. (or: $A \cap B \neq \emptyset$)

NOTE: This does not mean that any A's are necessarily non–B's. That is, region II may or may not be empty (we don't have enough information to say). Also, region III may be empty or not, we just don't know.

Figure 2.31 The sets A and B meet. They contain the common element x.

The sets A and B do not meet. (or "No B is an A.")   No A's are B's. (or: $A \cap B = \emptyset$)

Note: There may not be any elements in region II either! A may be empty, and it may not. All that we really know for sure is that region I is empty.

Figure 2.32 No A's are B's.

64   Chapter Two: **SETS**

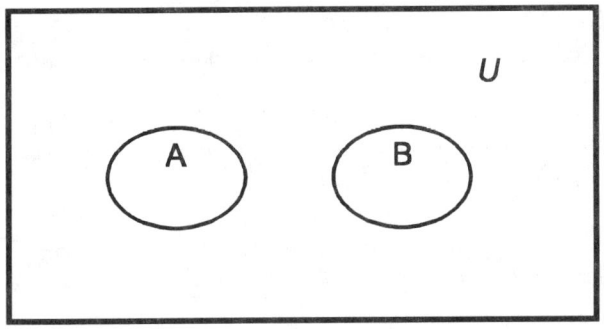

Figure 2.33 Alternate version of "No A's are B's."

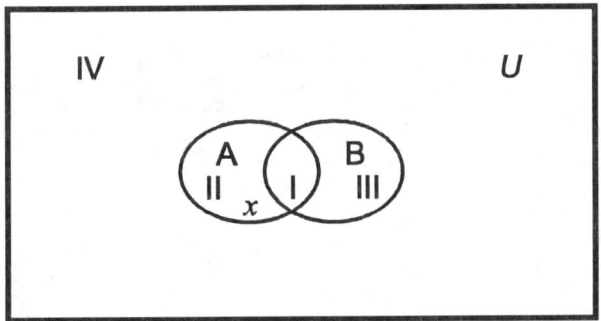

A meets the compliment of B.   Some A is not a B (or: $A \cap B' \neq \emptyset$)

Note: Region I may be empty, and it may not be. All that we really know for sure is that there's at least one element in region II.

Figure 2.34 Some A is not a B.

Example #1

Now let's go over another of the arguments that we looked at in chapter 1 and see how Euler Circles can be used to clarify it. In section 1.7 we looked at the following argument:

If Lynda studies hard she will get an A.
<u>Lynda studies hard.</u>
Lynda will get an A.

In analyzing this argument we see that we need to be concerned with two sets here, the set of people who study hard, and the set of people who get A's. It may not be clear at this point whether or not one of these sets is a subset of the other. Because of this, we'll draw the diagram representing these two sets in the most general way possible.

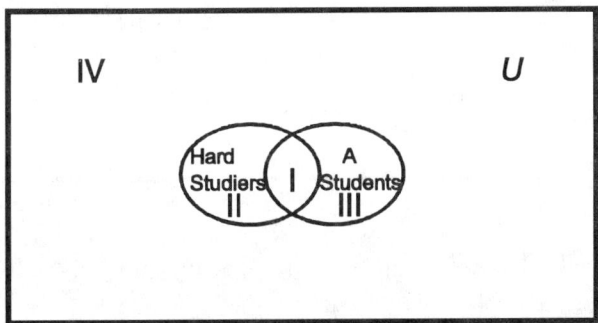

Figure 2.35 Initial diagram for example 1.

We will now introduce a symbol for Lynda, say L, to this diagram. In which region of the diagram should we put the L? Since Lynda does study hard (by hypothesis #2) we know that L has to go

in the "hard studiers" circle. That means that the L needs to go either in region I or region II. But putting the L in region II would contradict the first hypothesis, since then Lynda would be in the set of people who study hard, but not in the set of people who get an A (which is impossible because hypothesis #1 says that if Lynda studies hard then she must get an A). Thus, the only possible region where the hypotheses allow us to place the L is in region I. The diagram would then look like this:

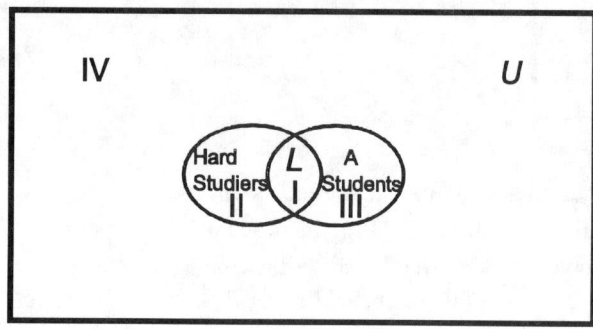

Figure 2.36 Final diagram for example 1.

Has diagramming the hypotheses also diagrammed the conclusion? It has, because in diagramming the hypotheses we were forced to place the symbol representing Lynda inside the circle representing the set of people who got A's. Hence "Lynda gets an A" is diagrammed, and we again conclude (as we did in section 1.7) that this argument is valid.

A Fallacious Argument

Example #2

Consider the following argument, which we will show is not valid:

If Lynda studies hard she will get an A.
<u>Lynda got an A.</u>
Lynda studied hard.

We will start the analysis of this problem with the same diagram as we used in the last example:

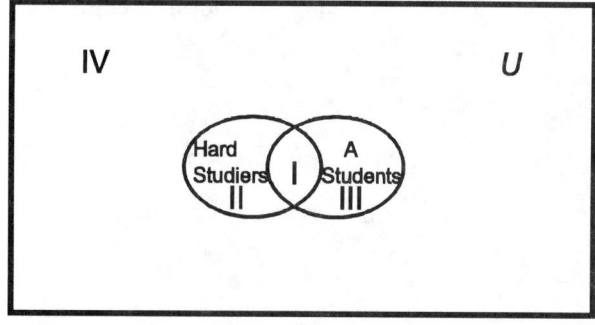

Figure 2.37 Initial diagram for example 2.

The second hypothesis, "Lynda got an A" now needs to be diagrammed. By hypothesis #2, the L representing Lynda can be placed either in region I or in region III. Checking both of these placements against the other hypothesis of the argument, we see that we may place the L in either of these regions and the hypotheses will still be satisfied. To show that the L may be placed in either of these regions we now complete the diagram by placing it right on the boundary between regions I and III:

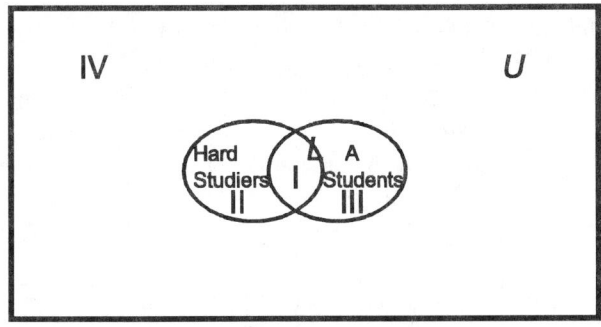

Figure 2.38 *L* may be placed in either region I or in region III.

Has the conclusion, "Lynda studied hard," been diagrammed? Not necessarily, because we are not sure whether the L should be placed in region I or in region III. If the L is in region III, and it may be, then L is <u>not</u> diagrammed to be in the set of people who study hard, and so, the conclusion has not been diagrammed. Since diagramming the hypotheses has not diagrammed the conclusion, the argument is fallacious (not valid).

Exercises

(1)   Using Euler Circles, diagram the following statements:

(a) All Peruvians are South Americans.
(b) Everyone who studied hard got an A.
(c) Jean studied hard, but did not get an A.
(d) All hockey players are tough.
(e) All Brazilians are good soccer players.
(f) No loan sharks are nice people.
(g) Some loan sharks are not nice.
(h) Not all hockey players are Canadian. (You may reword this as "At least one hockey player is not Canadian.")
(i) No Brazilians are Canadians.
(j) Some Americans are Texans.
(k) Alaska is a part of the United States. (You might reword this as "Alaska is a member of the United States.")

(2)   Using Euler Circles, test the following arguments for validity.

(a) All baseball players are rich.
<u>Babe is a baseball player.</u>
Babe is rich.

(b) All baseball players are rich.
<u>Babe is rich.</u>
Babe is a baseball player.

(c) All politicians are unscrupulous.
<u>Amy is not unscrupulous.</u>
Amy is not a politician.

(d) All freshman are 18 years old.
   All wise people are over 18 years old.
   No freshman is wise.

(e) No baseball players are poor.
   No basketball players are poor.
   All baseball players are basketball players.

(f) All Martians are under five feet tall.
   Evelyn is less than five feet tall.
   Evelyn is a Martian.

(g) All rock stars are happy.
   Frank is not a rock star.
   Frank is not happy.

(h) All lions are cats.
   All cats are animals.
   Leo is a lion.
   Leo is an animal.

(i) All negative numbers are less than zero.
   Three is not less than zero.
   Three is not a negative number.

(j) All students who did their homework understand this assignment.
   Maria doesn't understand this assignment.
   Maria didn't do her homework.

(k) All parrots are birds.
   No birds are reptiles.
   No parrot is a reptile.

(l) All winners of the Oscar were great actors.
   Michael did not win an Oscar.
   Michael was not a great actor.

2.6 Infinite Sets

In the beginning of this chapter it was pointed out that one of the reasons that Georg Cantor did not gain general acceptance for this theory of sets was because it led to some unusual results concerning the infinite. Many conclusions which were reached were counter–intuitive, and it took careful definitions and controversial judgments to make sense out of the resulting situations. Without proper care it seemed that paradoxes were inevitable.

To show the kind of problems that Cantor faced, consider the following paradox, which was first discovered by the Italian mathematician Galileo in 1638. Start with the set N of all integers, $\{1,2,3,4,\ldots\}$, and its subset, $\mathcal{E} = \{2,4,6,8,\ldots\}$ of all positive, *even* whole numbers. We know that $\mathcal{E} \subseteq N$. It is also clear that $\mathcal{E}$ does not exhaust all of N; that is, there are additional elements of N which are not in $\mathcal{E}$ (namely, all of the odd integers). Galileo's paradox stated that although $\mathcal{E}$ appears to be considerably smaller than N, in fact, $\mathcal{E}$ and N are, in some sense, the same size! The reason one can say

this is that if we list all of the integers, and then list the even integers directly beneath them, we will see that a natural correspondence will be set up between the elements of N and the elements of $\mathcal{E}$:

```
1  2  3  4  5  6  ...
↕  ↕  ↕  ↕  ↕  ↕  ...
2  4  6  8  10 12 ...
```

Figure 2.39 There are the same number of even integers as there are integers!

Thus we can see that every element n of N corresponds to one and only one element of $\mathcal{E}$ (that element being the double of n), and every element m of $\mathcal{E}$ corresponds to one and only one element of N (that element of N being "half of m," which must be a whole number because m is in $\mathcal{E}$, making it even). In modern terminology, Galileo had exhibited a *one–to–one correspondence* between the elements of N and the elements of $\mathcal{E}$, and it's easy to see why one would want to say that these two sets are the same size. After all, when such a correspondence can be set up between two *finite* sets, then those two sets would have to contain the same number of elements. In this respect, finite sets and infinite sets seemed to act very differently. Because his experience with finite sets did not prepare Galileo for this, he believed that he had discovered a paradox — a statement which seemed to contradict the currently held beliefs about the world.

Cantor realized that there really was no paradox here. It was simply that infinite sets did not always act in ways that we expected of finite sets. In fact, Cantor showed that if $\aleph_0$ (the Hebrew letter aleph with the subscript 0) is used to represent the number of elements of N, then $\aleph_0 + 1 = \aleph_0$, $\aleph_0 + 2 = \aleph_0$, ..., and, in fact, $\aleph_0 + \aleph_0 = \aleph_0$. Actually, Cantor had hit upon a distinctive property of infinite sets: Every infinite set is the "same size" as a proper subset of itself. That is, *if A is an infinite set*, then it would *always* be possible to find *a subset B of A* that had the following property: *even though there are elements of A which are not in B, A and B are still the "same size."* This kind of thing could never happen with finite sets.

As strange as this seemed, things got even stranger. Even though N and $\mathcal{E}$ were the same size, and some other sets which seemed to be considerably larger than N also turned out to be the same size as N, there also were sets which were "larger" than N. For example, the set of all rational numbers (that is, all fractions of the form $\frac{p}{q}$ where p and q are whole numbers and $q \neq 0$), although apparently much larger than N, is actually the same size as N. However, the set of all real numbers (that is, all numbers on the number line) is actually larger than N. This is because Cantor showed that it is impossible to find a one–to–one correspondence between the set of all whole numbers and the set of real numbers. With results as hard to understand and as counter–intuitive as this, it isn't difficult to see why Cantor had trouble getting other mathematicians to accept his theory of sets.

Questions to Discuss
1.
(a)   Explain why in some sense it would be reasonable to say that the set N has more elements than the set $\mathcal{E}$.
(b)   Explain why in some sense it would be reasonable to say that the sets N and $\mathcal{E}$ have the same number of elements.
(c)   What explanation did Cantor offer to the apparent conflict between (a) and (b)?

> 2. The difficulty we face in this section seems to hinge on the question of what the "size" of a set is. See if you can give a satisfactory explanation of what it means for two sets to be of the "same size."

2.7 Chapter Review

Important Terms to Know

aleph–null
cardinality
Carroll diagram
complement
disjoint sets
element
empty set
equal sets
Euler circle
finite set
Galileo's paradox
infinite set
intersection
membership
null set
one–to–one correspondence
roster method
set
set–builder notation
set difference
subset
survey diagram
union
universal sets
Venn diagram
well–defined

Important Names to Know

Cantor, Georg
Carroll, Lewis
Dodgson, Charles
Euler, Leonhard
Galileo
Venn, John
Wittgenstein, Ludwig

Review Questions

1. What were the reservations that mathematicians had that impeded the acceptance of set theory as a branch of mathematics?

2. What contributions of John Venn, Leonhard Euler, and Lewis Carroll simplified the analysis of problems dealing with sets?

3. Compare and contrast the way Euler circles and Venn diagrams represent sets.

4. What is the main difference between a survey diagram and a Venn diagram? Give examples of some situations where survey diagrams might be useful.

5. Briefly explain how Euler circles can be used to analyze logical arguments.

6. Explain the mathematical distinction between finite and infinite sets.

Chapter Three

Algebra and Matrices

"Algebra is generous; she often gives more than what is asked of her."

J. Le Rond D'Alembert

Chapter Outline

- **3.0** **Introduction**
- **3.1** **Historical Perspective**
- **3.2** **Solving Linear Equations**
- **3.3** **Solving Linear Inequalities**
- **3.4** **Solving Systems of Linear Equations**
- **3.5** **Introduction to Matrices**
- **3.6** **Matrix Arithmetic**
  - *Addition and Subtraction*
  - *Scalar Multiplication*
  - *Multiplication of Matrices*
- **3.7** **Solving Systems of Linear Equations Using Matrices**
- **3.8** **Inverses and Some Applications**
  - *Solving Systems of Equations Using Inverses*
  - *Cryptography*
- **3.9** **Chapter Review**

3.0 Introduction

You have seen some algebra in a previous course. Algebra is used in solving everyday problems, such as calculating interest on a savings account. You use it to calculate the quantity needed for each ingredient when you change the number of servings for a recipe. You even apply algebra when reading a road map. It is used in many other fields as well, such as engineering, chemistry, physics, biology and geology.

Algebra is a symbolic language. It enables one to consider many separate cases that share a common property. With algebra, one can generalize and investigate.

Another useful field of mathematics that is closely tied to algebra is the theory of matrices. We will look at some algebra and then explore matrices.

3.1 Historical Perspective

As long ago as 1650 BC, in the time of the Ahmes Papyrus, the Ancient Egyptians were solving linear equations. This papyrus included problems that required solutions of equations of the form $x + ax = b$ or $x + ax + bx = c$ where a, b, c are known and x is unknown. These equations were not solved in the manner we use today, but they were solved.

In the time of the Babylonians, some 4,000 years ago, flexible algebraic operations were developed. The Babylonians did not use letters to represent unknown quantities because their alphabet had yet to be invented. Instead, they used words such as "length" to represent an unknown.

It is remarkable how much algebra the Babylonians knew. They were familiar with many simple forms of factoring and could solve two simultaneous linear equations in two unknown quantities. They could even find a solution of a quadratic or cubic equation if it was a positive solution. They would, however, only find one solution and stop. They did not bother to find additional solutions, if there were any. They were concerned with approximate solutions of equations only. They did not concentrate on finding exact solutions.

Around AD 250 a mathematician named Diophantus wrote *Arithmetica*. This work made use of a different approach. Here he was concerned with determining the exact solution of equations. This work required a high degree of mathematical skill.

Mohammed ibn–Musa al–Khwarizmi, who died before 850 AD, wrote two books on arithmetic and algebra. It is from the title of his book, *Al–jabr wa'l muqabalah,* that the word "algebra" came. In this work, he did not deal with difficult problems. He was concerned with straight–forward expositions of solutions of equations.

There are three basic stages in the historical development of algebra. The first stage was rhetorical. During this stage everything was written out in words. This was the time of the early Greeks.

The second stage was the syncopated stage. At this time there were some abbreviations but no special symbols had been developed yet for operations, relations, or exponential notation. This was the time of Diophantus.

The third and final stage is known as the symbolic stage. Europe did not enter this stage until the late fifteenth century. Rene Descartes, a French mathematician who lived from 1596 to 1650, is known as the "father of modern philosophy." He was born of a good family and was well educated. Symbolic algebra is said to have reached its maturity in Descartes' work *La geometrie*. This is the earliest mathematics text in which the notation would not cause difficulty to an algebra student of today.

Today there is an increasingly abstract view of algebra. The study of matrix algebra has been one of the chief factors in this development. Arthur Cayley, who lived in the nineteenth century, was one of the first men to study matrices. We will look at these in sections 3.5 – 3.8

3.2 Solving Linear Equations

We will begin by reviewing *linear equations* and their solutions. In this section we will look at linear equations in one variable, that is, equations in which the only variable has an exponent of one. Here are examples of several linear equations:

$$3x + 4 = 20; \quad \frac{2}{5}(x - 0.5) = 3x + \sqrt{3}; \quad \sqrt{0.4a} = 12.$$

These are all equations because they each involve two expressions which are set equal to each other. The equations are all linear because in each case the variable (there is only one in each) has an exponent of one. The *solution* of a linear equation is the value or values that make the equation true. We will only consider real numbers for our solutions in this chapter. For example, the value $x = 1$ is a solution of the equation $2x + 3 = 5$ because the statement $2(1) + 3 = 2 + 3 = 5$ is true.

In what follows it is assumed that you will be reviewing principles that were studied in a previous course in elementary algebra. Concepts will not be explained in detail; examples will be used to illustrate ideas that you have previously studied.

There are a series of steps that are often helpful when solving this type of equation.

STEPS TO FOLLOW IN SOLVING A LINEAR EQUATION:

1. Simplify each side of the equation separately.
2. Use addition or subtraction to bring all of the terms involving the variable to one side of the equation.
3. Use addition or subtraction to bring all of the constant terms to the other side of the equation.
4. Divide both sides of the equation by the coefficient of the variable.
5. Check your solution into the given equation. (Optional.)

Example. Solve each of the following equations. Check your solution. State the solution.

(a) $3x = 14$ (b) $x + 7 = 22$ (c) $2x + 4 = 21$
(d) $5x + 7 = 3x - 3$ (e) $3(x - 2) + 7x = 5(x - 3) + 4$

Solution:

(a) Neither side of this equation can be simplified further, all terms involving the variable, x, are already on one side, the left side, and all constant terms are already on the other side, the right side. Thus, we start by performing step 4 — dividing both sides of the equation by the coefficient of x, that is dividing by 3. This gives

$$\frac{3x}{3} = \frac{14}{3}$$
$$x = \frac{14}{3}$$

Now, we will check our solution into the given equation (step 5).

$$3\left(\frac{14}{3}\right) = 14$$

This verifies that the solution is $x = \frac{14}{3}$ or $x = 4\frac{2}{3}$.

(b) In this equation neither side can be simplified, and all terms involving the variable x are on one side of the equation, the left side. Next, we need to bring all constant terms to the right side. Since 7 is added to the left side, we will subtract 7 from each side of the equation in order to isolate the x term. Subtraction undoes addition.

$$\begin{array}{r} x + 7 = 22 \\ -7 -7 \\ \hline x = 15 \end{array}$$

Now, we will check our solution into the given equation (step 5).

$$15 + 7 = 22.$$

The solution is $x = 15$.

(c) In the third equation, it is again impossible to simplify either side of the equation, and the variable appears only on the left side of the equation. However, the constant terms are not grouped on the other side of the equation. Therefore, we begin with step 3 (as we did in the last problem).

$$\begin{array}{r} 2x + 4 = 21 \\ -4 -4 \\ \hline 2x = 17 \end{array}$$
$$\frac{2x}{2} = \frac{17}{2}$$
$$x = \frac{17}{2}$$

Now, we will check this solution. $2\left(\dfrac{17}{2}\right) + 4 = 17 + 4 = 21$.

Thus, the solution is $x = \dfrac{17}{2}$.

(d) With this equation we will need to begin with step 2. Do you see why step 1 is not needed for this equation?

$$
\begin{aligned}
5x + 7 &= 3x - 3 \\
-3x & -3x \\
\hline
2x + 7 &= -3 \\
-7 & -7 \\
\hline
2x &= -10 \\
\dfrac{2x}{2} &= \dfrac{-10}{2} \\
x &= -5
\end{aligned}
$$

Now we will check this solution.

$$
\begin{aligned}
5(-5) + 7 &\;?\; 3(-5) - 3 \\
-25 + 7 &\;?\; -15 - 3 \\
-18 &= -18
\end{aligned}
$$

Thus, $x = -5$ is the solution.

(e) With this equation we must begin with step 1.

$3(x - 2) + 7x = 5(x - 3) + 4$ (expand each side)
$3x - 6 + 7x = 5x - 15 + 4$ (combine like terms)

$$
\begin{aligned}
10x - 6 &= 5x - 11 \quad \text{(step 1 is complete) (bring } 5x \text{ to the left side)}\\
-5x & -5x \\
\hline
5x - 6 &= -11 \\
+6 & +6 \\
\hline
5x &= -5 \\
\dfrac{5x}{5} &= \dfrac{-5}{5} \\
x &= -1
\end{aligned}
$$

Now, we will check if this truly is the solution.

$3(-1 - 2) + 7(-1) \;?\; 5(-1 - 3) + 4$

$$
\begin{array}{ll}
3(-3) - 7 & \quad ?\ 5(-4) + 4 \\
-9 - 7 & \quad ?\ -20 + 4 \\
-16 & \quad =\ -16
\end{array}
$$

Thus, $x = -1$ is the solution.

Each of the equations considered above is known as a *conditional equation* because there are some real numbers that are solutions and some that are not. For example, consider the second equation, $x + 7 = 22$. We found the solution to be $x = 15$. Therefore there is at least one real number that is a solution of the equation, 15. There are also real numbers that are not solutions, such as 2.

Example: Solve $2(x - 4) + 3x = 5(x + 9)$.
Solution: Again, we need to begin with the first step. Why?

$$
\begin{array}{ll}
2(x - 4) + 3x = 5(x + 9) & \\
2x - 8 + 3x = 5x + 45 & \\
5x - 8 = 5x + 45 & \\
\underline{-5x \qquad\qquad -5x} & \\
-8 = 45 &
\end{array}
$$

Now that obviously is not true. -8 does not equal 45. When you get an obviously *false* statement, there is no value of x that will satisfy the equation. This is known as a *contradiction*. A contradiction is an equation that has no solutions.

Example. Solve the linear equation $6(x - 1) - 3(x - 4) = 3(x + 2)$.
Solution: We begin by expanding and combining like terms.

$$
\begin{array}{ll}
6(x - 1) - 3(x - 4) = 3(x + 2) & \\
6x - 6 - 3x + 12 = 3x + 6 & \\
3x + 6 = 3x + 6 & \\
\underline{-3x \qquad\qquad -3x} & \\
6 = 6 &
\end{array}
$$

Now, is this statement like the previous one? No. This statement is always *true*. 6 is always equal to 6 regardless of the value of the variable. Thus, every value of x will satisfy this equation. Therefore, all numbers satisfy the equation.

An equation that has all real numbers as its solution is known as an *identity*. In an identity every number satisfies the equation.

Example. Solve the equation $x(x + 2) + 3x - 4 = 2x(x + 1) - x(x + 3) - 16$
Solution: We begin by expanding.

$$
\begin{array}{l}
x(x + 2) + 3x - 4 = 2x(x + 1) - x(x + 3) - 16 \\
x^2 + 2x + 3x - 4 = 2x^2 + 2x - x^2 - 3x - 16 \\
x^2 + 5x - 4 = x^2 - x - 16
\end{array}
$$

Chapter 3: ALGEBRA AND MATRICES

This does not look like a linear equation. However, notice what happens if we now group the terms involving x^2 on the left side of the equation.

$$\begin{array}{r} x^2 + 5x - 4 = x^2 - x - 16 \\ -x^2 \qquad\quad -x^2 \qquad\qquad \\ \hline 5x - 4 = \quad -x - 16 \end{array}$$

Notice that the terms that were causing all the trouble dropped out. This is now a linear equation. So, we may now proceed with the steps for solving a linear equation.

$$\begin{array}{rl} 5x - 4 =& -x - 16 \\ +x & +x \\ \hline 6x - 4 =& -16 \\ +4 & +4 \\ \hline 6x \;=& -12 \\ x \;=& -2 \end{array} \qquad \text{(How did we get } -2\text{?)}$$

Now, we will check.

$-2(-2 + 2) + 3(-2) - 4 \;?\; 2(-2)(-2 + 1) + 2(-2 + 3) - 16$
$-2(0) - 6 - 4 \;?\; -4(-1) + 2(1) - 16$
$0 - 10 \;?\; 4 + 2 - 16$
$-10 = -10$

Thus, $x = -2$ is the solution.

It is important to remember to always check your work. If the check does not yield a true statement, (for example, if it yields something like $2 = 5$), you know you made a mistake either in the check or in your process of solving the equation. When you do this, it is important to check your solution in the original, untouched equation. This way if you made an error in the first step, you will pick up the problem.

We will consider one last example.

Example. Solve $\dfrac{3 + x}{4} - \dfrac{2x}{12} = \dfrac{1 + x}{15}$.

Solution: We begin by multiplying both sides of the equation by the least common multiple of all of the denominators. This will eliminate the fractions for now. The least common multiple (the smallest number that 4, 12, and 15 divide) is 60.

$$60\left(\frac{3+x}{4}\right) - 60\left(\frac{2x}{12}\right) = 60\left(\frac{1+x}{15}\right)$$

$$15(3+x) - 5(2x) = 4(1+x)$$

$$45 + 15x - 10x = 4 + 4x$$

$$45 + 5x = 4 + 4x$$

$$45 + x = 4$$

$$x = -41.$$

The check is left for you.

This last example shows that the steps for solving linear equations which were given earlier are only a guide and need not be rigorously applied in all problems. Sometimes there is some other strategy, such as multiplying both sides of the equation by 60 in this last problem, that is more efficient than blindly applying the steps.

Exercises

1. Identify each equation as a conditional equation, a contradiction, or an identity. Find and check the solutions for all conditional equations.

   (a) $3(x + 2) - 4 = x - 5$
   (b) $6(x + 5) - 3(2 - x) + 4 = -5(x - 1) - x - 3$
   (c) $4x + 11 = 3x + 2$
   (d) $4(x - 1) + 3(x + 2) = -2(2x - 1) - (5 - 11x)$
   (e) $7x - 3 = 2(x - 1) - 1$
   (f) $-3(x - 2) - (x - 7) = 2(3 - 2x) + 7$
   (g) $4(x - 1) - (x - 1) + 2 = 2(x - 3) - 2(x + 2)$
   (h) $7x - 5(1 - x) = 2(2x - 3) - 4(7 - 2x)$
   (i) $3 - 2[x - 4(3 - 2x)] = 2x + 5$
   (j) $\dfrac{x + 3}{3} = \dfrac{x + 7}{5}$
   (k) $\dfrac{x}{3} + 4 = \dfrac{2x}{5} - 6$
   (l) $x(x - 2) + 3(x - 1) = 2x(x + 1) - x(x + 4)$
   (m) $3x - x(x - 5) = x(x + 1) - x$

2. Kelly would like to earn at least a B in her history class. To do this she needs at least an 80% average in the course. There are five tests. The average of these tests is her average in the course. She has received a 72, 68, 89, and 73 on the first four tests.

   (a) What is the lowest grade she can earn on the fifth test and still earn a B in the course?
   (b) Can she earn an A? (90% average or better)
   (c) What is the lowest grade she can earn on the fifth test and still pass if passing is a 70% or higher?

3. You would like to rent a car for your next trip. The trip will last five days. The rental place charges $27 per day plus $0.19 per mile.

    (a) If you budget $300 for car rental, how many miles can you drive?

    (b) If the trip is 800 miles long, how much should you budget for car rental?

4. Sarah earned a 68, 82, 93, 72, and 80 on the five exams in her Philosophy class. She received a C+ for the course. She believes she should have received a B. She argues that her average exam grade is a 79 and therefore she missed a B (requiring at least an 80 average) by only one point. What is wrong with her argument?

5. Two equations are equivalent if they each have the exact same solution set. Are the following pairs of equations equivalent? Explain.

    a) $3x - 5 = -11$ and $6 - 5x = 16$
    b) $6x - 5 = 10(x + 1) - 17$ and $8x + 2(4x - 1) = 12x + 1$
    c) $2(x - 3) + 4 = 3x - 10$ and $2(10 - x) = x + 3 - (x - 1)$.

6. List three equations that are equivalent.

7. Which of the following are not linear equations? If an equation is not linear, explain why.

    a) $x + 3 = \dfrac{2}{3}x$

    b) $\dfrac{5}{7x} + 3 = 11$

    c) $\sqrt{4x} + 5 = x - 2$

    d) $x(x - 3) + 4x = 2x(x + 7) - 11$

    e) $x^3 + 3x = 12$

    f) $\sqrt{11}x + 3 = 4(x - 0.2)$

3.3 Solving Linear Inequalities

In this section we will consider *linear inequalities*. Linear inequalities are two expressions connected by an inequality sign. We solve linear inequalities in much the same manner as we just solved linear equations. The only difference occurs when we multiply or divide by a negative number. Follow the same steps as we used in solving linear equations. However, we will revise step 4 as follows:

REVISION OF THE STEPS WHEN SOLVING LINEAR INEQUALITIES:

STEP 4: Divide both sides of the equation by the coefficient of x. If this number is positive, the direction of the inequality sign is left unchanged. If this number is negative, change the direction of the inequality sign. (For example, $>$ becomes $<$).

In addition, step 5 usually cannot be performed when solving inequalities. Since the solution to an inequality is generally a range of numbers rather than just one or two, it would be impossible to check all of your solutions in an inequality.

Example. Solve each of the following:

a) $2x + 7 < 13$

b) $5(x - 2) - 8(x + 1) > 3(x + 2)$

c) $\dfrac{2}{3}x - 4 \geq -10$

d) $2(x - 5) - x > x - 3$

Solution:

(a) We begin by bringing the constant term to the side which does not contain x — the right side.

$$\begin{array}{r} 2x + 7 < 13 \\ -7 \quad -7 \\ \hline 2x \quad\ < 6 \end{array}$$

Now, we divide by the coefficient of x, which is 2. Since 2 is a positive number, the inequality sign remains as a less than sign.

$$\dfrac{2x}{2} < \dfrac{6}{2}$$

$$x < 3$$

Thus, the solution is all real numbers that are less than 3.

(b) We must begin by expanding both sides and combining like terms.

$$5(x - 2) - 8(x + 1) > 3(x + 2)$$
$$5x - 10 - 8x - 8 \quad > 3x + 6$$

$$\begin{array}{rl} -3x - 18 & > 3x + 6 \\ -3x & \quad -3x \\ \hline -6x - 18 & > \quad 6 \\ +18 & \quad +18 \\ \hline -6x & > \quad 24 \end{array}$$

(Now, subtract $3x$ from both sides.)

(Now add 18 to both sides.)

Now we need to divide both sides of the inequality by -6, the coefficient of x. Remember, -6 is a negative number, thus our greater than sign will need to change to a less than sign.

$$\dfrac{-6x}{-6} < \dfrac{24}{-6}$$

$$x < -4$$

Therefore, the solution is all real numbers less than -4.

(c) We begin with step 3, bringing all constant terms to one side, in this case the right side.

$$\frac{2}{3}x - 4 \geq -10$$
$$\underline{+4 +4}$$
$$\frac{2}{3}x \geq -6$$

Next we need to divide by the coefficient of x. Recall that dividing by a fraction is the same as multiplying by its reciprocal. For example,

$$\frac{\frac{1}{4}}{\frac{2}{3}} = \frac{1}{4} \div \frac{2}{3} = \frac{1}{4} \cdot \frac{3}{2} = \frac{3}{8}.$$

Thus, we will multiply both sides of the equation by the reciprocal of $\frac{2}{3}$ which is $\frac{3}{2}$.

$$\frac{3}{2}\left(\frac{2}{3}x\right) \geq -6\left(\frac{3}{2}\right)$$
$$x \geq -9$$

Our solution is all real numbers that are greater than or equal to -9.

(d) We begin by expanding and combining like terms.

$$2(x-5) - x > x - 3$$
$$2x - 10 - x > x - 3$$

$$x - 10 > x - 3$$
$$\underline{-x -x}$$
$$-10 > -3$$

  Is this a true statement or a false statement? Recall from the previous section, when we get a statement that is always true, the solution is all real numbers. When the statement is always false, there is no solution. The statement we have reads: -10 is greater than -3. That would mean that -10 is to the right of -3 on the number line. But, -10 is to the left of -3 on the number line. Therefore, -10 is less than -3, not greater than it. Thus, this is a false statement. Therefore, there is no solution.

  An inequality of the form $a < x < b$ is called a *double inequality* or *compound inequality*. An inequality such as $-3 < x \leq 2$ is read -3 is less than x and x is less than or equal to 2.

Example. Solve $-5 < 2(x-1) < 7$
Solution:
$$-5 < 2(x-1) < 7$$
$$-5 < 2x - 2 < 7$$
$$\underline{+2 \quad\quad +2 \quad +2}$$
$$-3 < 2x < 9$$

(Note how we need to add 2 to all three members of the inequality.)

$$\frac{-3}{2} < x < \frac{9}{2}.$$

Therefore, the solution is all real numbers between $\frac{-3}{2}$ and $\frac{9}{2}$.

Exercises

1. Solve each of the following linear inequalities.

   (a) $2(x-3) + 7 < 11$
   (b) $4(x-1) - 5(2x+3) \geq 12$
   (c) $x - 3(x-2) \leq 4(x-1) + 6$
   (d) $2x - (x-3) > 4x - 2(x-1) - (x+3)$
   (e) $-4 < x + 3 \leq 10$
   (f) $-1 \leq 2(x-3) + 5 < 10$
   (g) $4 - x > -5$
   (h) $3(x-2) + 3 \leq -10$
   (i) $3 < x - 5(2-x) \leq 20$
   (j) $11 - 2(x-3) < 3(4-x) + x + 2$

2. Bob goes to the restaurant for dinner with $25. If he needs to pay 6% tax and leave a 15% tip, what is the range of dinner prices he can order? (Assume dinner includes a beverage.)

3. We also have three classifications of linear inequalities. They are conditional, contradiction, and identity. Which type of inequality is each inequality in problem 1 above?

4. Sally works through a word problem algebraically and has 5 < length < 12. She writes the length is greater than 5 or less than 12. Is this correct? If not, why is it incorrect?

3.4 Solving Systems of Linear Equations

Now we will consider a system of linear equations. We want to know what values for the variables will satisfy all of the equations of the system. The solution of a system of linear equations in two unknowns consists of all values of x and y that satisfy both equations of the system. For example, we could consider the system consisting of the following two equations:

$$2x - y = -3$$
$$5x - y = 4$$

Each of these is the equation of a straight line. We will graph these two equations on the same pair of axes. To do this we will find the *x*–intercept and *y*–intercept for each of these equations. Connecting the intercepts will give the equation's graph.

$$2x - y = -3$$

***x*–intercept**: Let $y = 0$. Solving the equation gives $x = \dfrac{-3}{2} = -1.5$. The point $(-1.5, 0)$ is on the graph.

***y*–intercept**: Let $x = 0$. Solving the equation gives $y = 3$. The point $(0, 3)$ is on the graph.

$$5x - y = 4$$

***x*–intercept**: Let $y = 0$. Solving the equation gives $x = \dfrac{4}{5} = .8$. The point $(.8, 0)$ is on the graph.

***y*–intercept**: Let $x = 0$. Solving the equation gives $y = -4$. The point $(0, -4)$ is on the graph.

Now we plot the intercepts for each line and connect them. We purposely graph these two lines on the same set of axes so that we can see where they intersect. The graph of these two lines is shown in Figure 3.1 below.

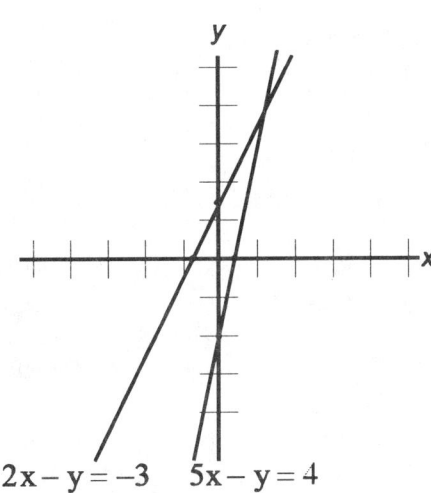

**Figure 3.1 The graph of a consistent system.
(Each mark represents two units.)**

We can see from the graph that these two lines intersect in exactly one point. However, we cannot accurately tell from the graph what the coordinates of that point are (this is a weakness of using graphs to try to solve systems of equations). Since these two lines have exactly one point in common, this is known as a *consistent system* and that one point of intersection represents the solution of the system.

Definition: A system of equations whose graphs intersect in exactly one point is called a *consistent system*. The point of intersection represents the solution.

We have determined that this is a consistent system, but we have not yet found its solution. Fortunately, we have two algebraic methods we can use to find the coordinates of the solution. The first method we will investigate is the *substitution method*. Here are the steps to follow.

> **SUBSTITUTION METHOD**:
> 1. Solve one equation for one of the variables.
> 2. Substitute the quantity found in step 1 for the value of that variable in the other equation.
> 3. Solve this equation for the remaining variable.
> 4. Substitute the value found in step 3 into the equation formed in step 1 to find the value of the other variable.

Example. We will find the point of intersection for the two graphs plotted in Figure 3.1. Recall that the equations of these graphs are

$$2x - y = -3$$
$$5x - y = 4$$

Solution: We will use the substitution method outlined above. We need to solve either of these equations for one of the variables. Let's tackle the first equation and solve it for y.

$$2x - y = -3$$
$$\underline{-2x \qquad\quad -2x}$$
$$-y = -2x - 3$$
$$\frac{-y}{-1} = \frac{-2x}{-1} - \frac{3}{-1}$$
$$y = 2x + 3$$

This completes step 1.

Now, for step 2 we will replace y with $2x + 3$ in the second equation, $5x - y = 4$. The result of this is

$$5x - (2x + 3) = 4.$$

In step 3 we solve this equation for x.

$$5x - (2x + 3) = 4$$
$$5x - 2x - 3 = 4$$
$$3x - 3 = 4 \qquad \text{(add 3 to each side)}$$
$$3x = 7 \qquad \text{(divide both sides by 3)}$$
$$x = \frac{7}{3}.$$

In step 4 we substitute the value we just found for x into the equation found in step 1, $y = 2x + 3$, and compute to find y.

$$y = 2\left(\frac{7}{3}\right) + 3$$

$$y = \frac{14}{3} + \frac{9}{3}$$

$$y = \frac{23}{3} = 7\frac{2}{3}.$$

Thus, the solution of this system is $x = \frac{7}{3}$ and $y = \frac{23}{3}$. This agrees well with our graph above; we now see that the lines in that graph intersected at the point $\left(\frac{7}{3}, \frac{23}{3}\right)$.

The second algebraic method we have is known as the *addition method*. Here are the steps to follow.

ADDITION METHOD
1. Transform both equations into the form $ax + by = c$.
2. Multiply one or both equations by a number or numbers such that when the two equations are added together, one of the variables will drop out.
3. Add together the two equations.
4. Solve for the remaining variable.
5. Substitute the value just found into either of the original equations and solve for the other variable.

Example. We will now solve the same system of equations using the addition method.

$$2x - y = -3$$
$$5x - y = 4$$

Solution: Right now, if we add the two equations together we will not eliminate either variable, but it is still easy to eliminate the y's. If one of the equations contained $+y$ instead of $-y$, then, after adding, the y-terms would drop out. We can change the $-y$ to a $+y$ by multiplying either of the equations by -1. We will multiply the first equation by -1 and add the two resulting equations.

$$-2x + y = 3$$
$$\underline{5x - y = 4}$$ (adding the two equations together yields:)
$$3x \quad\quad = 7$$ (divide both sides by 3)
$$\frac{3x}{3} = \frac{7}{3}$$
$$x = \frac{7}{3}$$

Now, we substitute this value for x into either of the original equations to solve for y. Neither equation looks pleasant; we decide to substitute into the first equation.

$$2\left(\frac{7}{3}\right) - y = -3$$

$$\frac{14}{3} - y = -3$$

$$-y = \frac{-9}{3} - \frac{14}{3} = \frac{-23}{3}$$

$$\frac{-y}{-1} = \frac{-23}{3} \div (-1) = \frac{-23}{3} \cdot \frac{1}{-1}$$

$$y = \frac{23}{3}$$

We have again arrived at the same result. The solution is $x = \frac{7}{3}, y = \frac{23}{3}$.

We can check this solution by substituting these two values for x and y in both equations and seeing that they make both equations true. We will check now.

$$2\left(\frac{7}{3}\right) - \frac{23}{3} ? = -3 \qquad 5\left(\frac{7}{3}\right) - \frac{23}{3} ? = 4$$

$$\frac{14}{3} - \frac{23}{3} ? = -3 \qquad \frac{35}{3} - \frac{23}{3} ? = 4$$

$$\frac{-9}{3} = -3 \qquad \frac{12}{3} = 4$$

Our check shows that we have indeed found the one and only solution for this system.

One algebraic method is not better than the other. There are times when one method may be easier to apply. If, for instance, at least one of the equations is already solved for one of the variables, such as in the system

$$2x + y = 12$$
$$x = 3y - 1$$

it may be faster to apply the substitution method. On the other hand, if you notice that you can add the two equations in the given form and one variable will be eliminated, then the addition method would be faster. For example, the system

$$5x - 6y = 12$$
$$4x + 6y = -30$$

would be solved quickly using the addition method. If you add these two equations, which variable will be eliminated?

Are all systems consistent systems? Let's consider all of the possibilities we could encounter if we graphed two lines. So far, we saw that the two lines could intersect in exactly one point. Now consider the following system.

Chapter 3: ALGEBRA AND MATRICES

$y = 3x + 5$
$3x - y = 2$

To graph these two lines, we again find the intercepts for each of the equations

$y = 3x + 5$

x–intercept: Let $y = 0$. Solving the equation gives $x = \dfrac{-5}{3} = -1\dfrac{2}{3}$. The point $(-1\dfrac{2}{3}, 0)$ is on the graph.

y–intercept: Let $x = 0$. Solving the equation gives $y = 5$. The point $(0, 5)$ is on the graph.

$3x - y = 2$

x–intercept: Let $y = 0$. Solving the equation gives $x = \dfrac{2}{3}$. The point $\left(\dfrac{2}{3}, 0\right)$ is on the graph.

y–intercept: Let $x = 0$. Solving the equation gives $y = -2$. The point $(0, -2)$ is on the graph.

Now we plot the intercepts for each line and connect them. The graphs of these two lines are shown in Figure 3.2 below.

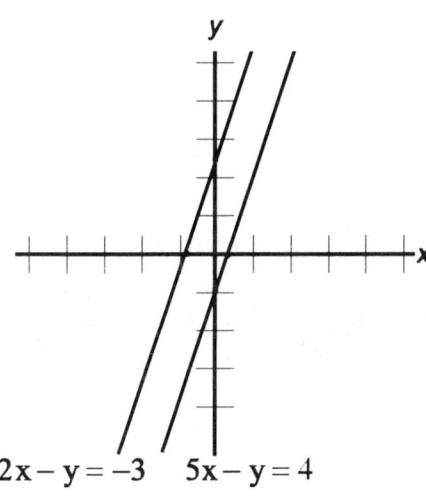

Figure 3.2 The graph of an inconsistent system.

We notice that these two lines do not intersect at all. They are called parallel lines. If the solution set of the system corresponds to the point of intersection, then this system must have no solution. This is known as an *inconsistent system*.

Definition: When the graphs of the equations of the system do not intersect, the system is called an *inconsistent system*. Such a system has no solution.

This system that we have just investigated has no solution. We will now take a look at what happens when we try to apply one of our algebraic methods to this system. Which method should we apply? Is one faster than the other for this system? We will use the substitution method. Why did we choose this method?

Recall that the system is:

$y = 3x + 5$
$3x - y = 2$

We can substitute $3x + 5$ for y into the second equation and solve it for x.

$3x - (3x + 5) = 2$
$3x - 3x - 5 = 2$
$-5 = 2$

This is an obviously false statement. Recall that when we had an obviously false statement when studying linear equations, that meant that there were no solutions. The same conclusion holds when trying to solve systems of equations. This is the same result that we came to when looking at the graph of the system.

We have found two possibilities so far. Two lines may intersect in exactly one point or may be parallel and never intersect. Are these the only two possibilities? Try drawing two lines on a graph and see if you can find any other possibilities.

We will investigate one more system. Consider the system:

$2x - y = -3$
$4x - 2y + 6 = 0$

First, we will attempt to graph these two lines. Again, we will determine the intercepts of these graphs.

$2x - y = -3$

x–intercept: Let $y = 0$. Solving the equation gives $x = \frac{-3}{2} = -1.5$. The point $(-1.5, 0)$ is on the graph.

y–intercept: Let $x = 0$. Solving the equation gives $y = 3$. The point $(0, 3)$ is on the graph.

$4x - 2y + 6 = 0$

x–intercept: Let $y = 0$. Solving the equation gives $x = \frac{-3}{2} = -1.5$. The point $(-1.5, 0)$ is on the graph.

y–intercept: Let $x = 0$. Solving the equation gives $y = 3$. The point $(0, 3)$ is on the graph.

Notice that both of these equations have the same intercepts. This could only happen if both of their graphs were the same. Every point on either line is, in actuality, on both lines. This means that every point on the line $2x - y = -3$ corresponds to a solution to the system. Since there are infinitely many such points, there must be infinitely many solutions to this system. Such a system is called a dependent system.

Definition: When the two equations in the system represent the same line, the system is called a *dependent system*. Such a system has infinitely many solutions, one corresponding to each point on the line.

Now we will consider what happens when we try to solve this system algebraically. Do you have a guess? Think back to the types of solutions we have for linear equations in one variable.

Chapter 3: **ALGEBRA AND MATRICES**

We will apply the addition method this time. Neither method appears to be faster. Recall our original equations.

$2x - y = -3$
$4x - 2y + 6 = 0$

We need both equations to be in the form $ax + by = c$. The first equation already is in this form. The second equation will be once we subtract 6 from both sides of the equation. The second equation then becomes

$4x - 2y = -6$

Now, which variable should we eliminate? If we want to eliminate y, we would want the first equation to contain $+2y$ so it will drop out when added with the $-2y$ in the second equation. To accomplish this, we will multiply both sides of the first equation by -2. We get

$-2(2x - y) = -2(-3)$

which simplifies to

$-4x + 2y = 6$

(If you decided to eliminate the variable x, what would you need to multiply the equation by?) Next, we add the two equations together.

$-4x + 2y = 6$
$4x - 2y = -6$
_____
$0 = 0$

Wow! That's different. But is it really? 0 does equal 0. This is a true statement. Think back to when we solved linear equations in one variable. The solution of an identity was all numbers. It isn't quite that for a system of equations. Not every pair of numbers satisfies this system of equations. But, all points on the line $2x - y = -3$ do. That is our solution.

Are there other possible types of solutions for a system of two linear equations? The answer is no. When you graph two straight lines in the plane, either they intersect in one point, no points, or at every point on a line. Those are the only possibilities.

Why would we be interested in knowing where two equations intersect? They do not have to be equations of straight lines. Many things are not represented by linear equations, but we may still be interested in them and where they intersect. Let me give one example at this time, a business application. Although the equations would not be straight lines, they could still be graphed in the xy–plane.

There is a cost associated with operating a certain shop, say an ice cream parlor. In determining how much it costs to operate the shop, many things need to be considered — wages of employees, rent, utility bills, insurance, etc. This cost could be represented in the xy–plane, where the x–axis would represent amount of ice cream sold and the y–axis would represent cost in dollars. Think about this for a moment. If you only sold one ice cream cone, it would cost a lot of money to run the shop. If you sold two cones, it would cost only a very little bit more. (Why is this?) If you had a really large crowd of customers coming to your shop for ice cream, you would eventually need more employees and the cost

might rise quickly again. Therefore, the cost of producing the ice cream cones isn't a straight line, but a curve.

Now, we need a second equation. Consider revenue this time. What is revenue? Revenue is how much money you collect from your customers. (This is not the same as profit. This is just the money you collect and put into your cash register, before you pay all those bills. So all or some of this money has to go to pay the bills; what is left after you pay the bills is known as profit.) When graphing the equation for revenue, the x–axis would again be labeled amount of ice cream sold and the y–axis would represent revenue in dollars.

If you only sell one ice cream cone, your revenue is very small – the amount you charged for that one ice cream cone. Obviously, your revenue would be much smaller than your cost to produce that one cone. If you sold two cones, your revenue would be more, but still very small. Eventually, for some number of cones sold, your revenue (the amount in your cash register), would hopefully equal your cost (the total of all those bills). This is known as the *break–even point*. How does one find this break–even point? You find the place (or places; since these are not straight lines it's possible that the curves may intersect more than once) where the graphs of the two equations intersect. This point is important to business. This tells a businessperson how much he or she needs to earn to just break–even — to lose no money and make no money.

Hopefully you see that being able to find points of intersection are important in many fields. Mathematics makes it possible to find those points.

Exercises

For exercises #1 – 9, solve each system of equations.

1. $2x - y = 7$
   $3x + 4y = -6$

2. $-2y = 3x + 11$
   $2x - 6y = 22$

3. $x = 5y + 11$
   $-3x + 15y = -25$

4. $2x - 3y = 7$
   $6y = 4x - 14$

5. $-7y - 2x = -17$
   $x + 3y = 2$

6. $3x - 10y = -7$
   $6x + 5y = 6$

7. $2x + 3y = 7$
   $4x - y = -7$

8. $8y = -1 - 9x$
   $-12x - 10y = 1$

9. $10x - 4y = 8$
   $-6y + 15x = 12$

10. Mr. Smith is offered a job and an option for his salary. Under the first option, he would earn $300 per week plus 4% commission on all sales. Under the second option, he would earn $240 per week and 6% commission.

    (a) What is the break–even point?
    (b) Define what this break–even point means for this problem in complete sentences.
    (c) If he sells $2,500 each week, which option will pay more?

11. The police pull over a gray van matching the description of a vehicle seen leaving a robbery scene. Upon a search they find CD players and 75 televisions. The driver shows the police a receipt that states that there were 90 items purchased for a total of $20,000, that each CD player cost $200, and that each television cost $240. Should the police continue to question this driver or should they let him go?

12. Classify each of the systems of equations in problems 1 through 9 above.

3.5 Introduction to Matrices

Arthur Cayley was born in 1821 in England. He was a great mathematician. One of his discoveries was matrices and their algebra. He first wrote about matrices in 1858 in a memoir. He also invented the rules for matrix arithmetic, including the unusual rule for the multiplication of two matrices which we will study in section 3.6. At the time, matrices had no practical uses. However, sixty seven years later Heisenberg utilized the algebra of matrices as tools for his great work in quantum mechanics. Matrices are used to organize and manipulate large amounts of data. With the arrival of the age of computers, the usefulness of matrices has greatly increased. This is because computers can perform calculations on large amounts of data efficiently. Today they are used in many areas, including the social sciences and economics.

A *matrix* is simply a rectangular array of numbers. Because it is rectangular, every row must have the same number of entries and every column must have the same number of entries. Each of the following is a matrix:

$$\begin{bmatrix} 2 & -4 & 0.3 \\ 5 & 27 & -6 \\ 0 & 0 & 44 \end{bmatrix} \quad \begin{bmatrix} 3 & 2 \\ -5 & 1 \end{bmatrix} \quad \begin{bmatrix} 1 \\ 6 \end{bmatrix} \quad \begin{bmatrix} 1 & 8 \\ 9 & -2 \end{bmatrix} \quad \begin{bmatrix} 3 & 6 & 2 \end{bmatrix}$$

In the first matrix, each row contains three entries and each column contains three entries. For example, the first row contains the entries 2, –4, and 0.3. In the third matrix, each row contains 1 entry and each column (there is only one column) contains two entries.

> **Definition:** A *matrix* is a rectangular array of elements. Each entry in the matrix is called an *element*. When you have more than one matrix, they are called matrices.

It is customary to label matrices with capital letters so we can refer to them again in the future. For example, we could let the first matrix above be A, the second matrix be B, the third C, the fourth D, and the last matrix E. For the remainder of this section, whenever we refer to matrix B we will be referring to the matrix

$$\begin{bmatrix} 3 & 2 \\ -5 & 1 \end{bmatrix}$$

When the number of columns is the same as the number of rows, the matrix is called a *square matrix*. In the example above, matrices A, B, and D are square matrices. In matrix A there are 3 rows and 3 columns. In matrices B and D, there are 2 rows and 2 columns. Why isn't matrix C a square matrix?

> **Definition:** A *square matrix* has the same number of rows as columns.

If the matrix is a square matrix, we can refer to something known as the *main diagonal*. This diagonal starts with the top left entry and ends with the bottom right entry. For example, in our first matrix, which is square, the main diagonal consists of the entries 2, 27, and 44. In matrix B, which is also square, the main diagonal consists of the entries 3 and 1. What are the entries on the main diagonal of matrices C and D?

If the square matrix has all ones on the main diagonal and zeros everywhere else, it is known as the *identity matrix*. Here are some identity matrices:

$$[1], \quad \begin{bmatrix} 1 & 0 \\ 0 & 1 \end{bmatrix}, \quad \begin{bmatrix} 1 & 0 & 0 \\ 0 & 1 & 0 \\ 0 & 0 & 1 \end{bmatrix}, \quad \begin{bmatrix} 1 & 0 & 0 & 0 \\ 0 & 1 & 0 & 0 \\ 0 & 0 & 1 & 0 \\ 0 & 0 & 0 & 1 \end{bmatrix}$$

Definition: An *identity matrix* is a square matrix where all of the entries on the main diagonal are 1 and all other entries are 0.

Later on we will see why these matrices are called identity matrices.

The matrix C only has one column and matrix E has only one row. These two matrices are also known as *vectors*. Thus, vectors are simply matrices which have only one row or only one column.

Definition: A matrix that consists of only one row or one column is known as a *vector*. If the matrix has only one row, it is called a *row vector*. If the matrix has only one column, it is known as a *column vector*.

We will often refer to the *dimension* or *order* of a matrix. This is the "number of rows by the number of columns." It is written "*number of rows* × *number of columns*." The "×" is read as "by". For example, matrix A had three rows and three columns. Therefore, its dimension is 3×3, which is read "three by three." The third matrix, matrix C, has two rows and one column. This is a column vector and its order is 2×1, which is read "two by one."

Definition: The *dimension* or *order* of a matrix is the size of the matrix. It is written as the number of rows by the number of columns.

As with numbers and sets, there is also a concept of equality for matrices.

Definition: Two matrices A and B are equal if they have the same dimension (that is, they both have the same number of rows and they both have the same number of columns) and their corresponding entries are equal.

Exercises

1. Refer to the following matrices to answer the questions that follow:

$$A = \begin{bmatrix} 3 & 7 & -2 \\ \frac{1}{2} & 4 & 0.3 \\ 8 & -2.3 & \frac{1}{3} \end{bmatrix}, \quad B = \begin{bmatrix} 1 & 0 & 0 \\ 0 & 1 & 0 \end{bmatrix}, \quad C = \begin{bmatrix} 2 \\ 8 \\ -5 \end{bmatrix}, \quad D = \begin{bmatrix} 6 & 4 & 1 & 11 \\ 8 & 2 & -3 & 12 \\ 1 & 0 & 1 & -15 \end{bmatrix}$$

(a) Which of the above matrices are square matrices? What are the entries on the main diagonal of each of these square matrices.?

(b) What is the dimension of each of these matrices?

(c) Are any of these identity matrices? If so, which?
(d) Are any of these matrices vectors? If so, which are vectors, and which type of vector are they?
(e) What is the value of the entry in the second row, third column of matrix D?

2. Write the identity matrix that is 7×7.

3. Answer "true" or "false" to each of the following.

    (a) An identity matrix must be a square matrix.
    (b) An identity matrix must have zeros everywhere except on the main diagonal.
    (c) A 5×7 matrix has 5 columns and 7 rows.

4. For each part, create a matrix that has the given property or properties.

    (a) A is square and has 6 rows.
    (b) B has dimension 5×8.
    (c) C is a column vector.
    (d) D has every entry on the main diagonal equal to –2.
    (e) I is an identity matrix of order 8×8.
    (f) E is not square and has all negative entries.

3.6 Matrix Arithmetic

Addition and Subtraction

Just as with numbers it is possible to define the operations of addition, subtraction, and multiplication of matrices. We begin with addition and subtraction. In order to add or subtract matrices, the matrices must have the same dimensions. Then you add or subtract the corresponding elements. Let's consider the following four matrices.

$$A = \begin{bmatrix} -1 & 5 \\ 2 & 0.4 \\ \frac{1}{3} & -8 \end{bmatrix}, \quad B = \begin{bmatrix} -5 & 0 & 0 & 1 \\ -1 & 16 & -2 & 8 \end{bmatrix}, \quad C = \begin{bmatrix} 3 & 6 & 8 & -9 \\ 2 & 0 & 0 & 4 \end{bmatrix}, \quad D = \begin{bmatrix} 1 & 6 \\ 2 & 2 \\ \frac{2}{5} & -1 \end{bmatrix}$$

Matrices A and D have the same dimension; they are both 3×2 matrices. Thus, we can add or subtract matrices A and D. Matrices B and C also have the same dimension; they are both 2×4 matrices. Thus, they may be added or subtracted. We cannot, however, add or subtract matrices such as A and B, because they do not have the same dimension.

When adding two matrices (such as A and D above) the sum will have the same dimension as the terms you are adding. Thus, because A and D are 3×2 matrices, we expect that the sum $A + D$ will also be a 3×2 matrix. In computing this sum you simply have to add together the corresponding terms of the two matrices A and D to get the corresponding entry in the matrix $A + D$. For example, to get the entry in the first row and first column of the matrix $A + D$ you would add together the entry in

the first row and first column of A and the entry in the first row and first column of D. Continuing in this way with each of the other entries yields the following result as $A + D$:

$$A + D = \begin{bmatrix} -1+1 & 5+6 \\ 2+2 & 0.4+2 \\ \frac{1}{3}+\frac{2}{5} & -8-1 \end{bmatrix} = \begin{bmatrix} 0 & 11 \\ 4 & 2.4 \\ \frac{11}{15} & -9 \end{bmatrix}.$$

We can also subtract two matrices of the same dimension in a very similar way. For example, we will find $C - B$ now.

$$C - B = \begin{bmatrix} 3-(-5) & 6-0 & 8-0 & -9-1 \\ 2-(-1) & 0-16 & 0-(-2) & 4-8 \end{bmatrix} = \begin{bmatrix} 8 & 6 & 8 & -10 \\ 3 & -16 & 2 & -4 \end{bmatrix}.$$

Note that the entry in row 2, column 3 of the matrix $B - C$ is gotten by subtracting the entry in row 2, column 3 of matrix C from the entry in row 2, column 3 of B.

Small Group Exercises

Using the matrices defined above, do the following:

1. Find $C + B$ and $B + C$. Does $C + B = B + C$?

2. Find $C - B$ and $B - C$. Does $C - B = B - C$?

3. Define two of your own matrices that have the same dimension. What is the dimension? Call one matrix Y and the other matrix W.

4. Find $Y + W$ and $W + Y$. Does $Y + W = W + Y$?

5. Find $Y - W$ and $W - Y$. Does $Y - W = W - Y$?

6. Is matrix addition commutative? Is matrix subtraction commutative?

Scalar Multiplication

In addition to the operations of addition and subtraction defined above there are two types of multiplication that we will study, called scalar multiplication and matrix multiplication. When discussing matrices we will conform with standard practice and call numbers *scalars*. Multiplying the matrix B by the scalar 3 will simply mean multiplying every entry of the matrix B by the number 3. For example, if B is the matrix that we defined at the start of this section, then the matrix $3B$ would be computed as follows.

$$3B = 3\begin{bmatrix} -5 & 0 & 0 & 1 \\ -1 & 16 & -2 & 8 \end{bmatrix} = \begin{bmatrix} 3(-5) & 3(0) & 3(0) & 3(1) \\ 3(-1) & 3(16) & 3(-2) & 3(8) \end{bmatrix} = \begin{bmatrix} -15 & 0 & 0 & 3 \\ -3 & 48 & -6 & 24 \end{bmatrix}.$$

Now find $-2A$ on your own.

Multiplication of Matrices

Before we can consider multiplying a matrix by another matrix, we need to use a general form to denote the elements of a matrix. We will use double subscripts to denote the elements. For example, a_{ij} is the element in row i, column j of matrix A. Thus, we can denote matrix A the following general way.

$$A = \begin{bmatrix} a_{11} & a_{12} & a_{13} & \cdots & a_{1n} \\ a_{21} & a_{22} & a_{23} & \cdots & a_{2n} \\ a_{31} & a_{32} & a_{33} & \cdots & a_{3n} \\ \vdots & \vdots & \vdots & \vdots & \vdots \\ a_{m1} & a_{m2} & a_{m3} & \cdots & a_{mn} \end{bmatrix}$$

As we see here, matrix A has dimension $m \times n$ — it has m rows and n columns.

To illustrate this notation, consider a new matrix C defined as follows.

$$C = \begin{bmatrix} -1 & 5 & 0 & -2 \\ 3 & 11 & -10 & 6 \end{bmatrix}.$$

Then we see the following.

$c_{11} = -1, c_{12} = 5, c_{13} = 0, c_{14} = -2, c_{21} = 3, c_{22} = 11, c_{23} = -10, c_{24} = 6$.

The reason for this notation is to make it easier to find the position of an entry in a matrix. Remember, when referring to the entry c_{ij} the first subscript will always tell you what row the entry is in, and the second subscript will tell you the column it is in. Thus, the entry c_{ij} will always be found in row i and column j.

In order to multiply two matrices, the number of columns in the first matrix must equal the number of rows in the second matrix. For example, if matrix A had dimension 2×3 and matrix B had dimensions 3×6, then we could compute AB because matrix A, the first matrix, has 3 columns and matrix B, the second matrix, has 3 rows. However, we could not find BA. Why? Matrix B has 6 columns and matrix A has 2 rows. (Remember, we listed B as the first factor in this case, so we need to consider the number of columns in B and the number of rows in A.)

The product matrix will have the same number of rows as the first matrix and the same number of columns as the second matrix. Consider for example a matrix A being 2×3 and a matrix B being 3×6. We already determined that we could find AB. What is the dimension of AB? It will have the same number of rows as matrix A, or 2 rows, and the same number of columns as matrix B, or 6 columns. Thus, AB will have dimension 2×6.

Example. Consider the following 5 matrices and decide which products are possible to compute. If a product is possible, give the dimension of the product matrix.

$$A = \begin{bmatrix} 1 \\ -2 \\ 4 \end{bmatrix}, \quad B = \begin{bmatrix} -1 & 0 & 6 \\ 4 & -2 & 9 \end{bmatrix}, \quad C = \begin{bmatrix} -1 & 1 & 2 & 5 \\ 6 & -7 & 10 & -2 \\ 0 & 1 & -3 & 4 \end{bmatrix}, \quad D = \begin{bmatrix} 12 & 23 \end{bmatrix}, \quad E = \begin{bmatrix} 3 & 4 \\ -5 & 6 \end{bmatrix}$$

Solution:
1. Consider AB. Matrix A is 3×1 and matrix B is 2×3. The number of columns of A, 1, is not equal to the number of rows of B, 2. Thus, AB cannot be computed.
2. Consider AC. Matrix A is 3×1 and matrix C is 3×4. The number of columns of A is 1 and the number of rows of C is 3. Again, AC cannot be computed.
3. Consider AD. Matrix A is 3×1 and matrix D is 1×2. The number of columns of A, 1, is equal to the number of rows of D, 1. Thus AD can be computed. The dimension of the product matrix will be the number of rows of A by the number of columns of D, or 3×2.
4. Consider AE. Matrix A is 3×1 and matrix E is 2×2. The number of columns of A, 1, is not equal to the number of rows of E, 2. AE cannot be computed.
5. Consider BA. Matrix B is 2×3 and matrix A is 3×1. The number of columns of B, 3, is equal to the number of rows of A, 3. Thus, BA can be computed. The dimension of the product matrix will be the number of rows of B by the number of columns of A, or 2×1.
6. Consider BC. Matrix B is 2×3 and matrix C is 3×4. The number of columns of B, 3, is equal to the number of rows of C, 3. Thus, BC can be computed. The dimension of the product matrix will be the number of rows of B by the number of columns of C, or 2×4.
7. Consider BD. Matrix B is 2×3 and matrix D is 1×2. Thus, BD cannot be computed.
8. Consider BE. Matrix B is 2×3 and matrix E is 2×2. Thus, BE cannot be computed.
9. Consider CA. Matrix C is 3×4 and matrix A is 3×1. Thus, CA cannot be computed.
10. Consider CB. Matrix C is 3×4 and matrix B is 2×3. Thus, CB cannot be computed.
11. Consider CD. Matrix C is 3×4 and matrix D is 1×2. Thus, CD cannot be computed.
12. Consider CE. Matrix C is 3×4 and matrix E is 2×2. Thus, CE cannot be computed.
13. Consider DA. Matrix D is 1×2 and matrix A is 3×1. Thus, DA cannot be computed.
14. Consider DB. Matrix D is 1×2 and matrix B is 2×3. Thus, DB can be computed. The product matrix will have dimension 1×3.
15. Consider DC. Matrix D is 1×2 and matrix C is 3×4. Thus, DC cannot be computed.
16. Consider DE. Matrix D is 1×2 and matrix E is 2×2. Thus, DE can be computed. The product matrix will have dimension 1×2.
17. Consider EA. Matrix E is 2×2 and matrix A is 3×1. Thus, EA cannot be computed.
18. Consider EB. Matrix E is 2×2 and matrix B is 2×3. Thus, EB can be computed. The product matrix will have dimension 2×3.
19. Consider EC. Matrix E is 2×2 and matrix C is 3×4. Thus, EC cannot be computed.
20. Consider ED. Matrix E is 2×2 and matrix D is 1×2. Thus, ED cannot be computed.

Therefore, we conclude that we can find the following products: AD, BA, BC, DB, DE, and EB. Also, note that although the matrices A^2 (or AA), B^2, C^2, and D^2 are not defined, the matrix E^2, or EE, is defined.

> *Question for Discussion*:
>
> Is matrix multiplication commutative?

Before we consider multiplying two matrices in general, we will investigate the special case of vector multiplication. Suppose matrix A is a row vector of dimension $1 \times n$ and matrix B is column vector of dimension $n \times 1$. Then their product $P = AB$ is a number.

Fact: Let A be a $1 \times n$ row vector and B be a $n \times 1$ column vector. Then their product AB is the number defined by:

$$AB = \begin{bmatrix} a_1 & a_2 & a_3 & \ldots & a_n \end{bmatrix} \begin{bmatrix} b_1 \\ b_2 \\ b_3 \\ \ldots \\ b_n \end{bmatrix} = a_1 b_1 + a_2 b_2 + a_3 b_3 + \ldots + a_n b_n$$

Note: Strictly speaking, the result of multiplying the $1 \times n$ matrix A with the $n \times 1$ matrix B should be a 1×1 matrix. It is common practice to leave off the brackets and refer to this 1×1 matrix as a number.

Example. Let $A = \begin{bmatrix} 3 & -4 & 0 & 2 \end{bmatrix}$, $B = \begin{bmatrix} -2 \\ -5 \\ 10 \\ 6 \end{bmatrix}$. Then the product AB is equal to

$$3(-2)+(-4)(-5)+0(10)+2(6) = -6 + 20 + 0 + 12 = 26.$$

Now, we are ready for the rule for multiplying two matrices. We begin by assuming the product AB is possible to compute. Let the dimension of matrix A be $r \times n$ and the dimension of matrix B be $n \times m$. This way the number of columns of matrix A, n, is equal to the number of rows of matrix B, n. The product matrix, $AB = P$, will have order $r \times m$. Recall our general notation for the elements of a matrix.

$$A = \begin{bmatrix} a_{11} & a_{12} & a_{13} & \cdots & a_{1n} \\ a_{21} & a_{22} & a_{23} & \cdots & a_{2n} \\ a_{31} & a_{32} & a_{33} & \cdots & a_{3n} \\ \vdots & \vdots & \vdots & \vdots & \vdots \\ a_{r1} & a_{r2} & a_{r3} & \cdots & a_{rn} \end{bmatrix}, B = \begin{bmatrix} b_{11} & b_{12} & b_{13} & \cdots & b_{1m} \\ b_{21} & b_{22} & b_{23} & \cdots & b_{2m} \\ b_{31} & b_{32} & b_{33} & \cdots & b_{3m} \\ \vdots & \vdots & \vdots & \vdots & \vdots \\ b_{n1} & b_{n2} & b_{n3} & \cdots & b_{nm} \end{bmatrix},$$

$$P = \begin{bmatrix} p_{11} & p_{12} & p_{13} & \cdots & p_{1m} \\ p_{21} & p_{22} & p_{23} & \cdots & p_{2m} \\ p_{31} & p_{32} & p_{33} & \cdots & p_{3m} \\ \vdots & \vdots & \vdots & \vdots & \vdots \\ p_{r1} & p_{r2} & p_{r3} & \cdots & p_{rm} \end{bmatrix}$$

We can consider each row of matrix A to be a $1 \times n$ row vector and each column of B to be a $n \times 1$ column vector. Since A has r rows, there are r of these $1 \times n$ row vectors in A. Likewise, since B has m columns, there are m of these $n \times 1$ column vectors in B. Thus we can view A and B in the following way:

$$A = \begin{bmatrix} R_1 \\ R_2 \\ R_3 \\ \vdots \\ R_r \end{bmatrix}, \text{ where } R_1 = \begin{bmatrix} a_{11} & a_{12} & a_{13} & \cdots & a_{1n} \end{bmatrix}, R_2 = \begin{bmatrix} a_{21} & a_{22} & a_{23} & \cdots & a_{2n} \end{bmatrix}, \ldots, \text{ and }$$

$$R_r = \begin{bmatrix} a_{r1} & a_{r2} & a_{r3} & \cdots & a_{rn} \end{bmatrix};$$

$$B = \begin{bmatrix} C_1 & C_2 & C_3 & \cdots & C_m \end{bmatrix}, \text{ where } C_1 = \begin{bmatrix} b_{11} \\ b_{21} \\ b_{31} \\ \vdots \\ b_{n1} \end{bmatrix}, C_2 = \begin{bmatrix} b_{12} \\ b_{22} \\ b_{32} \\ \vdots \\ b_{n2} \end{bmatrix}, \ldots, \text{ and } C_m = \begin{bmatrix} b_{1m} \\ b_{2m} \\ b_{3m} \\ \vdots \\ b_{nm} \end{bmatrix}.$$

We can now give the rule for finding the elements of the product matrix $AB = P$.

Fact: The product $P = AB$, where A is a $r \times n$ matrix and B is a $n \times m$ matrix, is a $r \times m$ matrix where the entry in row i and column j is the product of the ith row of A and the jth column of B. That is,

$$P_{ij} = R_i C_j$$

Thus, we can now view matrix $P = AB$ in the following way:

$$P = AB = \begin{bmatrix} R_1 C_1 & R_1 C_2 & R_1 C_3 & \cdots & R_1 C_m \\ R_2 C_1 & R_2 C_2 & R_2 C_3 & \cdots & R_2 C_m \\ R_3 C_1 & R_3 C_2 & R_3 C_3 & \cdots & R_3 C_m \\ \cdots & \cdots & \cdots & \cdots & \cdots \\ R_r C_1 & R_r C_2 & R_r C_3 & \cdots & R_r C_m \end{bmatrix}.$$

That is, the product of A and B is computed by multiplying together the rows of A and the columns of B.

Example: Find the product AB for each pair of matrices.

Chapter 3: ALGEBRA AND MATRICES

1. $A = \begin{bmatrix} 1 & 3 & -11 & 2 \\ 0 & 4 & -2 & 5 \end{bmatrix}$, $B = \begin{bmatrix} 3 & 6 & 1 \\ 8 & -2 & -1 \\ 0 & 0 & 2 \\ 0 & 5 & -7 \end{bmatrix}$

2. $A = \begin{bmatrix} 1 & 8 \\ 6 & -1 \\ 4 & 0 \end{bmatrix}$, $B = \begin{bmatrix} 6 & 8 & 1 \\ -4 & 2 & -1 \end{bmatrix}$

Solution:

1. Since A is 2×4 and B is 4×3, the product AB can be found, and $P = AB$ will have order 2×3.

$$P = AB = \begin{bmatrix} \begin{bmatrix} 1 & 3 & -11 & 2 \end{bmatrix}\begin{bmatrix} 3 \\ 8 \\ 0 \\ 0 \end{bmatrix} & \begin{bmatrix} 1 & 3 & -11 & 2 \end{bmatrix}\begin{bmatrix} 6 \\ -2 \\ 0 \\ 5 \end{bmatrix} & \begin{bmatrix} 1 & 3 & -11 & 2 \end{bmatrix}\begin{bmatrix} 1 \\ -1 \\ 2 \\ -7 \end{bmatrix} \\ \begin{bmatrix} 0 & 4 & -2 & 5 \end{bmatrix}\begin{bmatrix} 3 \\ 8 \\ 0 \\ 0 \end{bmatrix} & \begin{bmatrix} 0 & 4 & -2 & 5 \end{bmatrix}\begin{bmatrix} 6 \\ -2 \\ 0 \\ 5 \end{bmatrix} & \begin{bmatrix} 0 & 4 & -2 & 5 \end{bmatrix}\begin{bmatrix} 1 \\ -1 \\ 2 \\ -7 \end{bmatrix} \end{bmatrix}$$

$$= \begin{bmatrix} 1(3)+3(8)-11(0)+2(0) & 1(6)+3(-2)-11(0)+2(5) & 1(1)+3(-1)-11(2)+2(-7) \\ 0(3)+4(8)-2(0)+5(0) & 0(6)+4(-2)-2(0)+5(5) & 0(1)+4(-1)-2(2)+5(-7) \end{bmatrix}$$

$$= \begin{bmatrix} 3+24+0+0 & 6-6+0+10 & 1-3-22-14 \\ 0+32+0+0 & 0-8+0+25 & 0-4-4-35 \end{bmatrix} = \begin{bmatrix} 27 & 10 & -38 \\ 32 & 17 & -43 \end{bmatrix}.$$

2. Since A is 3×2 and B is 2×3, the product AB can be computed. $P = AB$ will have order 3×3.

$$P = AB = \begin{bmatrix} \begin{bmatrix} 1 & 8 \end{bmatrix}\begin{bmatrix} 6 \\ -4 \end{bmatrix} & \begin{bmatrix} 1 & 8 \end{bmatrix}\begin{bmatrix} 8 \\ 2 \end{bmatrix} & \begin{bmatrix} 1 & 8 \end{bmatrix}\begin{bmatrix} 1 \\ -1 \end{bmatrix} \\ \begin{bmatrix} 6 & -1 \end{bmatrix}\begin{bmatrix} 6 \\ -4 \end{bmatrix} & \begin{bmatrix} 6 & -1 \end{bmatrix}\begin{bmatrix} 8 \\ 2 \end{bmatrix} & \begin{bmatrix} 6 & -1 \end{bmatrix}\begin{bmatrix} 1 \\ -1 \end{bmatrix} \\ \begin{bmatrix} 4 & 0 \end{bmatrix}\begin{bmatrix} 6 \\ -4 \end{bmatrix} & \begin{bmatrix} 4 & 0 \end{bmatrix}\begin{bmatrix} 8 \\ 2 \end{bmatrix} & \begin{bmatrix} 4 & 0 \end{bmatrix}\begin{bmatrix} 1 \\ -1 \end{bmatrix} \end{bmatrix}$$

$$= \begin{bmatrix} 1(6)+8(-4) & 1(8)+8(2) & 1(1)+8(-1) \\ 6(6)-1(-4) & 6(8)-1(2) & 6(1)-1(-1) \\ 4(6)+0(-4) & 4(8)+0(2) & 4(1)+0(-1) \end{bmatrix} = \begin{bmatrix} 6-32 & 8+16 & 1-8 \\ 36+4 & 48-2 & 6+1 \\ 24+0 & 32+0 & 4+0 \end{bmatrix} = \begin{bmatrix} -26 & 24 & -7 \\ 40 & 46 & 7 \\ 24 & 32 & 4 \end{bmatrix}.$$

Small Group Exercise

Create two non–square matrices A and B so that they have the following properties:

- each is non–square
- the dimension of each is different
- each has more than 2 rows
- each has more than 2 columns
- the product AB cannot be computed
- the product BA can be computed

Now, find the product BA.

Suppose we consider a troop of girl scouts. As a fund–raiser, this troop decides to sell four different types of cookies, Minty, Coconut, Creamy, and Comet. We have the following information about the sales given in Tables 3.1 and 3.2 below.

	Minty	Coconut	Creamy	Comet
Kelly	12	10	2	7
Susan	30	25	8	23
Mary	42	38	7	32
Megan	7	8	0	8
Saray	2	3	0	3
Caitlin	27	18	1	8

Table 3.1 The number of boxes of each type of cookie sold by each girl.

	Price per box
Minty	$ 3.00
Coconut	$ 3.25
Creamy	$ 2.50
Comet	$ 3.00

Table 3.2 The price per box for each type of cookie.

We can create two matrices for the information contained in these two tables. The first matrix, let's agree to call it matrix G, will relate each girl to the number of boxes of each type of cookie she sold. The second matrix, which we'll call matrix P, will relate type of cookie to its price per box.

Chapter 3: ALGEBRA AND MATRICES

$$A = \begin{bmatrix} 12 & 10 & 2 & 7 \\ 30 & 25 & 8 & 23 \\ 42 & 38 & 7 & 32 \\ 7 & 8 & 0 & 8 \\ 2 & 3 & 0 & 3 \\ 27 & 18 & 1 & 8 \end{bmatrix} \qquad P = \begin{bmatrix} 3 \\ 3.25 \\ 2.5 \\ 3 \end{bmatrix}.$$

Suppose we wanted to find the following two things:

(a) The amount of money each girl collected.
(b) The girl who collected the most money.

We can find the product AP. Why? To begin, we note that the dimension of matrix A is 6×4 and the dimension of matrix P is 4×1, so the number of columns of A is equal to the number of rows of P. Would this product be reasonable? Yes, because the columns of matrix A and the rows of matrix B both refer to the same thing, the type of cookie. The resulting product will relate the girls in the troop (the rows of matrix A) to the amount of money (the column of matrix P). We will find that product now. From this product matrix, we will be able to find the two facts we are looking for.

$$AP = \begin{bmatrix} 12(3) + 10(3.25) + 2(2.5) + 7(3) \\ 30(3) + 25(3.25) + 8(2.5) + 23(3) \\ 42(3) + 38(3.25) + 7(2.5) + 32(3) \\ 7(3) + 8(3.25) + 0(2.5) + 8(3) \\ 2(3) + 3(3.25) + 0(2.5) + 3(3) \\ 27(3) + 18(3.25) + 1(2.5) + 8(3) \end{bmatrix} = \begin{bmatrix} 94.5 \\ 260.25 \\ 363 \\ 71 \\ 24.75 \\ 166 \end{bmatrix}$$

We can now get the answer to (a). Our product matrix is a column vector where each row represents a different girl scout and the column represents the total amount of money each girl should collect. Since the first row of matrix A referred to Kelly's sales, the first row of matrix AP yields the amount of money Kelly should collect. Therefore, Kelly should collect $94.50, Susan should collect $260.25, Mary should collect $363.00, Megan should collect $71.00, Saray should collect $24.75, and Caitlin should collect $166.00.

To answer part b we notice that the largest number in our product matrix appears in row 3 which is the amount of money Mary should collect. Thus, Mary collected the most money.

In general, when multiplying two matrices that represent tables, the column headings of the first factor must match the row headings of the second factor. After computing the product, the resulting table inherits its row headings from the first factor and its column headings from the second factor.

Small Group Exercises

1.
   (a) Create a 2×2 matrix. Call this matrix A.
   (b) Write the 2×2 identity matrix I. Compute AI and IA.

(c) Create a 3 × 3 matrix called matrix B.
(d) Write the 3 × 3 identity matrix I. Compute BI and IB.
(e) Create a 4 × 4 matrix C.
(f) Write the 4 × 4 identity matrix I. Compute CI and IC.
(g) What can you say in general about the product of a square matrix and its identity?
(h) Why is the identity matrix called the "identity" matrix?

2. The Toy Bid company manufactures four different models, Red Rider, RB, T–Time, and Roger. Each model will be distributed from six different centers. The number of each model (in thousands) to be distributed from each center is given in Table 3.3 below. The cost to store each toy at a distribution center is given in Table 3.4 below.

	MA	NJ	GA	CA	IA	MN
Red Rider	9	20	18	40	11	17
RB	10	18	21	35	8	16
T–Time	8	15	11	30	13	20
Roger	6	30	15	50	9	10

Table 3.3 The number of each model stored at each distribution center.

	Red Rider	RB	T–Time	Roger
Cost	$4	$3	$2	$5

Table 3.4 The cost to store each toy at a distribution center.

(a) How much will it cost to store the toys in the MA distribution center?
(b) At which distribution center will the most money be spent in storage?
(c) Which toy plane costs the most to store per item?

Exercises

For exercises # 1 – 22, use the following matrices.

$$A = \begin{bmatrix} 3 & -2 & -1 \\ 0 & 2 & 4 \\ -6 & 8 & -9 \end{bmatrix} \quad B = \begin{bmatrix} 3 & 2 \\ -2 & 1 \\ -1 & -3 \end{bmatrix} \quad C = \begin{bmatrix} 1 & 6 & 7 & -8 \end{bmatrix}$$

$$D = \begin{bmatrix} -1 \\ 2 \\ 3 \\ 4 \end{bmatrix} \quad E = \begin{bmatrix} 1 & 1 & 6 \\ -2 & -2 & 1 \\ 3 & -1 & 0 \\ 4 & 0 & 2 \end{bmatrix} \quad F = \begin{bmatrix} 3 & 1 & 0 & 2 \\ 1 & 1 & 0 & -2 \end{bmatrix}$$

$$G = \begin{bmatrix} 1 & 0 & 0 \\ 0 & 1 & 0 \\ 0 & 0 & 1 \end{bmatrix} \quad H = \begin{bmatrix} 2 & 4 \\ -1 & 3 \\ 5 & -8 \end{bmatrix} \quad J = \begin{bmatrix} 2 & 1 & 0 \\ 11 & 9 & -8 \\ -7 & 6 & 5 \end{bmatrix}$$

1. Which matrices are square matrices?

2. Determine which matrices are vectors and state what type of vector each is.

3. If possible, compute $A + B$.

4. If possible, compute $A + J$.

5. If possible, compute $3B$.

6. If possible, compute $2A + J$.

7. If possible, compute $2(B + H)$.

8. If possible, compute $2E$.

9. If possible, compute $\frac{1}{2}B$.

10. If possible, compute $A - (G + J)$.

11. If possible, compute $(A - G) - J$.

12. If possible, compute AB.

13. If possible, compute BA.

14. If possible, compute AE.

15. If possible, compute EA.

16. If possible, compute CE.

17. If possible, compute FD.

18. If possible, compute DF.

19. If possible, compute AG.

20. If possible, compute GA.

21. If possible, compute GH.

22. If possible, compute GJ.

23. Write the matrix $\begin{bmatrix} \frac{1}{3} & 1 \\ -2 & \frac{2}{3} \end{bmatrix}$ as the product of a scalar and a matrix whose elements are integers.

24. A new book will be coming out in the spring in two forms, paperback and hard–cover. The cost of each form is given in Table 3.5 below. Copies of this book in both forms are scheduled to be delivered to four different book outlets and sold there. The number of copies of the book in each form to be sold at the four different book outlets is given in Table 3.6 below.

	Cost per copy
Paperback	$ 5.95
Hard–cover	$ 14.95

Table 3.5 The cost per copy of both forms.

	Paperback	Hard–cover
Sell–write	7,000	9,000
Buy–it	23,000	18,000
Got–a–Deal	18,000	7,000
Good–reading	20,000	35,000

Table 3.6 The number of copies in each form sold at each outlet.

(a) How much money will be taken in at each of the distribution centers on the sale of this book?
(b) Which book outlet will receive the most copies of this book?
(c) Are there more paperbacks or hard–covers being sold at the outlets?
(d) How much money will be collected in the sale of the paperback form of this book?

3.7 Solving Systems of Linear Equations Using Matrices

In this section we will revisit an old problem —solving systems of linear equations. We explored two algebraic methods in section 3.4. Now, we will learn how to use matrices to solve such problems. To begin, we need to define some additional terms.

Let us reconsider a system of equations we solved in section 3.4. Recall the system:

$2x - y = -3$
$5x - y = 4.$

We found the solution of this system to be the values $x = \frac{7}{3}$ and $y = \frac{23}{3}$.

We begin by placing our equations in the form $ax + by = c$ and then defining a matrix. Each row of the matrix will represent one of the equations: The first row consists of the coefficients and the constant of the first equation and the second row consists of the coefficients and constant of the second equation. The elements of this matrix will be the coefficients of each variable and the constant term from each equation. We must be careful to list the coefficients of the same variable in the same column for

each equation. In other words, if we begin by putting the coefficient of x in the first equation in the first row, we must also begin the second row with the coefficient of x from the second equation. Remember, if the variable does not appear in an equation, its coefficient is zero. Our last column will consist of the constants from each equation. In our example, the coefficient of x is 2, the coefficient of y is -1, and the constant is -3 in the first equation. In the second equation, the coefficient of x is 5, the coefficient of y is -1, and the constant is 4. Thus, we construct the 2×3 matrix:

$$\begin{bmatrix} 2 & -1 & -3 \\ 5 & -1 & 4 \end{bmatrix}.$$

Our goal is to transform this matrix into the form: $\begin{bmatrix} 1 & 0 & a_1 \\ 0 & 1 & a_2 \end{bmatrix}$. After doing this, we can read the coefficients of x and y and the constant for each equation. From the first row we will get the equation

$$1 \cdot x + 0 \cdot y = a_1, \text{ or } x = a_1$$

while the second row will yield

$$0 \cdot x + 1 \cdot y = a_2, \text{ or } y = a_2.$$

From this we would arrive at the solution to the system: $x = a_1$ and $y = a_2$.

How do we transform the matrix into this desirable form? There are three row operations we can perform on such a matrix that do not affect the solution of the system.

THREE ROW OPERATIONS:

1. Swap two rows. (For example, row 1 moves to row 2 and row 2 moves to row 1.)
2. Multiply a row by any real number other than zero.
3. Add a multiple of a row to another row.

Before we proceed any further, let's take a brief look at these three row operations. We will use the matrix above for our example. Suppose we were to use row operation 1, swap two rows. We only have two rows, so row 2 moves up to become row 1 and row 1 moves down to take the place of row 2. Then we would have the matrix:

$$\begin{bmatrix} 5 & -1 & 4 \\ 2 & -1 & -3 \end{bmatrix}.$$

If we begin with our original matrix and multiply row 1 by -2, (row operation 2), we would have instead:

$$\begin{bmatrix} -2(2) & -2(-1) & -2(-3) \\ 5 & -1 & 4 \end{bmatrix} = \begin{bmatrix} -4 & 2 & 6 \\ 5 & -1 & 4 \end{bmatrix}.$$

Now let's see what happens when we apply row operation 3 to the original matrix. Suppose we take three times row 1 and add this to row 2, or $3R_1 + R_2 \to R_2$ (read as "3 times R_1 plus R_2 replaces R_2"). The result of applying this row operation would be the matrix

$$\begin{bmatrix} 2 & -1 & -3 \\ 3(2)+5 & 3(-1)-1 & 3(-3)+4 \end{bmatrix} = \begin{bmatrix} 2 & -1 & -3 \\ 11 & -4 & -5 \end{bmatrix}.$$

Most times we use operation 1 or operation 2 to get a "1" at a specific place in the matrix, and use operation 3 to convert an entry to "0." It would make sense to want to do these things, since the form that we desire for the matrix has all ones and zeros in it (except for the last column).

Here is the procedure that we will use to convert the matrix of a system of equations into the desired form using row operations.

STEPS FOR TRANSFORMING A MATRIX INTO FINAL FORM:

1.   Change the first row first column entry to a 1 by using row operation 1 or 2. (Swap rows if row two has a 1 in the first column. Otherwise, multiply row 1 by the reciprocal of the first entry in row 1.) If the first entry in row 1 is a zero you will need to interchange rows 1 and 2 before performing this step.

2.   Change the second row first column entry to a 0 by using row operation 3. (Multiply row 1 by the opposite of the second row's first column entry, and add this result to row 2.)

3.   Change the second row second column entry to a 1 by using row operation 2. (Multiply row 2 by the reciprocal of the second column entry in row 2.) If this entry turns out to be a zero, it will be impossible to achieve this step. Look at the examples later in the section to see what happens in this case.

4.   Change the first row second column entry to a 0 by using row operation 3. (Multiply row 2 by the opposite of the first row second column entry and add this result to row 1.)

After performing these steps you will easily be able to read off the solution and check (If desired).

We will now perform this procedure to our original problem (given at the beginning of the section). Recall the matrix we are trying to transform:

$$\begin{bmatrix} 2 & -1 & -3 \\ 5 & -1 & 4 \end{bmatrix}.$$

We would like the entry in row 1 and column 1 to be a 1 rather than a 2. Swapping the rows will not help us. (The 2 would become a 5, not a 1.) Instead, we will multiply row 1 by the reciprocal of 2 which is $\frac{1}{2}$. After applying this row operation, the transformed matrix will look like this:

$$\begin{bmatrix} 2\left(\frac{1}{2}\right) & -1\left(\frac{1}{2}\right) & -3\left(\frac{1}{2}\right) \\ 5 & -1 & 4 \end{bmatrix} = \begin{bmatrix} 1 & \frac{-1}{2} & \frac{-3}{2} \\ 5 & -1 & 4 \end{bmatrix}.$$

Notice how we are moving towards the desired form: The first entry in row 1 is now correct; it is a 1.

We will now work with this resulting matrix and not the original. We must transform the second row first column entry from a 5 to a 0. The opposite of 5 is -5. Therefore, we will multiply row 1 by -5 and add the result to row 2, $(-5R_1 + R_2 \to R_2)$. The result will be:

$$\begin{bmatrix} 1 & \dfrac{-1}{2} & \dfrac{-3}{2} \\ -5(1)+5 & -5\left(\dfrac{-1}{2}\right)-1 & -5\left(\dfrac{-3}{2}\right)+4 \end{bmatrix} = \begin{bmatrix} 1 & \dfrac{-1}{2} & \dfrac{-3}{2} \\ 0 & \dfrac{3}{2} & \dfrac{23}{2} \end{bmatrix}$$

We will now work with this matrix. Next we will concentrate on changing the second column entry in row two from $\dfrac{3}{2}$ to 1. We will do this by multiplying row 2 by the reciprocal of $\dfrac{3}{2}$, which is $\dfrac{2}{3}$. The result would be

$$\begin{bmatrix} 1 & \dfrac{-1}{2} & \dfrac{-3}{2} \\ \dfrac{2}{3}(0) & \dfrac{2}{3}\left(\dfrac{3}{2}\right) & \dfrac{2}{3}\left(\dfrac{23}{2}\right) \end{bmatrix} = \begin{bmatrix} 1 & \dfrac{-1}{2} & \dfrac{-3}{2} \\ 0 & 1 & \dfrac{23}{3} \end{bmatrix}.$$

Notice how close we are getting to the desired form. All we need to do now is to transform one more entry into a 0, and we'll be there.

Now, working with this last matrix, we must change the first row second column entry from $\dfrac{-1}{2}$ to 0. We accomplish this by multiplying row 2 by the opposite of $\dfrac{-1}{2}$ which is $\dfrac{1}{2}$, then adding the result to row 1, $\left(\dfrac{1}{2}R_2 + R_1 \rightarrow R_1\right)$. The result:

$$\begin{bmatrix} \dfrac{1}{2}(0)+1 & \dfrac{1}{2}(1)-\dfrac{1}{2} & \dfrac{1}{2}\left(\dfrac{23}{3}\right)-\dfrac{3}{2} \\ 0 & 1 & \dfrac{23}{3} \end{bmatrix} = \begin{bmatrix} 1 & 0 & \dfrac{7}{3} \\ 0 & 1 & \dfrac{23}{3} \end{bmatrix}.$$

Interpreting the first row gives the equation $1 \cdot x + 0 \cdot y = \dfrac{7}{3}$ or $x = \dfrac{7}{3}$. The second row yields the equation $0 \cdot x + 1 \cdot y = \dfrac{23}{3}$ or $y = \dfrac{23}{3}$. Therefore, the solution to our original system of equations is: $x = \dfrac{7}{3}$ and $y = \dfrac{23}{3}$. This is the same as the solution we derived in section 3.4. We should now check this in both equations to verify that this is indeed the solution. The check is left for the reader.

Analyzing this example turns up a plan. Concentrate on transforming the matrix into the desired form one column at a time. When working on column 1, first get the entry in row 1, column 1 to be a 1, then convert the remaining entry to 0. Next move to column 2. Again, work to get the 1 in the desired position first, then convert the remaining entry to a 0.

Example. Solve the following system of linear equations using matrices. Check the solution.

$2x - 4y = 18$
$- 3y = - x + 13$

Solution: The second equation is not in the form $ax + by = c$. Therefore, we begin by changing its form. We will add x to each side of the equation. Now our system looks as follows:

$2x - 4y = 18$
$x - 3y = 13$

We form our first matrix: $\begin{bmatrix} 2 & -4 & 18 \\ 1 & -3 & 13 \end{bmatrix}$. We need the first row first column entry to be a 1. Notice that the first entry in the second row is a 1. Therefore, we will swap rows 1 and 2. Our new matrix is $\begin{bmatrix} 1 & -3 & 13 \\ 2 & -4 & 18 \end{bmatrix}$. Next we now need to change the first entry of row two from a 2 to a zero. The opposite of 2 is -2, so we will now multiply row 1 by -2 and add the result to row 2 $(-2R_1 + R_2 \rightarrow R_2)$. The result is

$\begin{bmatrix} 1 & -3 & 13 \\ -2(1)+2 & -2(-3)-4 & -2(13)+18 \end{bmatrix} = \begin{bmatrix} 1 & -3 & 13 \\ 0 & 2 & -8 \end{bmatrix}$.

Next, we need to change the second element of the second row from a 2 to a 1. To accomplish this we multiply row 2 by the reciprocal of 2, which is $\frac{1}{2}$.

$\begin{bmatrix} 1 & -3 & 13 \\ \frac{1}{2}(0) & \frac{1}{2}(2) & \frac{1}{2}(-8) \end{bmatrix} = \begin{bmatrix} 1 & -3 & 13 \\ 0 & 1 & -4 \end{bmatrix}$.

Finally, we need to change the second element of row one from -3 to 0. We will do this by multiplying row 2 by 3 (the opposite of -3) and adding the result to row 1 $(-3R_2 + R_1 \rightarrow R_1)$.

$\begin{bmatrix} 3(0)+1 & 3(1)-3 & 3(-4)+13 \\ 0 & 1 & -4 \end{bmatrix} = \begin{bmatrix} 1 & 0 & 1 \\ 0 & 1 & -4 \end{bmatrix}$.

Now we can read the solution. From this matrix, we have the equations: $1 \cdot x + 0 \cdot y = 1$ and $0 \cdot x + 1 \cdot y = -4$. Thus, $x = 1$ and $y = -4$.

Let's check this solution into the original equations. Recall that the original equations were:

$2x - 4y = 18$
$-3y = -x + 13$.

Substituting 1 for x and -4 for y, we obtain

$2(1)-4(-4)=2+16=18$ and
$-3(-4)= -1+13$.

110   Chapter 3: **ALGEBRA AND MATRICES**

Since both of these statements are true, the solution is verified to be $x = 1$ and $y = -4$.

Example. Solve the following system of linear equations using matrices.

$2x - 8y = 10$
$3x - 12y = 15$

Solution: Each of our equations is already in the form $ax + by = c$. Thus, the matrix form of the system is: $\begin{bmatrix} 2 & -8 & 10 \\ 3 & -12 & 15 \end{bmatrix}$. We will now change the first entry of the first row to a 1 by multiplying the first row by the reciprocal of 2, which is $\frac{1}{2}$. This yields:

$$\begin{bmatrix} \frac{1}{2}(2) & \frac{1}{2}(-8) & \frac{1}{2}(10) \\ 3 & -12 & 15 \end{bmatrix} = \begin{bmatrix} 1 & -4 & 5 \\ 3 & -12 & 15 \end{bmatrix}.$$

Now we work with this resulting matrix. We need to change the first entry of the second row from 3 to 1. We will do this by first finding the opposite of 3 which is -3. Now we multiply row 1 by -3 and add the result to row 2, (that is, $-3R_1 + R_2 \to R_2$). This yields:

$$\begin{bmatrix} 1 & -4 & 5 \\ -3(1)+3 & -3(-4)-12 & -3(5)+15 \end{bmatrix} = \begin{bmatrix} 1 & -4 & 5 \\ 0 & 0 & 0 \end{bmatrix}.$$

Now, we would like to multiply row 2 by some number to change the 0 in the second column to a 1. However, 0 multiplied by any number is 0. Thus, this is impossible. This is as far as we can go. This matrix yields one equation : $x - 4y = 5$. (The second row is supposed to give us a second equation, but interpreting that row simply gives the equation $0 + 0 = 0$. As we know, this equation is always true, so it puts no restrictions on our solution.) In other words, there are infinitely many points that are solutions for this system — all points that satisfy the equation $x - 4y = 5$. (Recall that this is called a dependent system.)

Example. Solve the following system of equations using matrices.

$4x + 12y = 20$
$-5x - 15y = 30$.

Solution: The matrix of the system is: $\begin{bmatrix} 4 & 12 & 20 \\ -5 & -15 & 30 \end{bmatrix}$. To begin, we must change the first row first column entry from 4 to 1 by multiplying row 1 by the reciprocal of 4. This yields:

$$\begin{bmatrix} \frac{1}{4}(4) & \frac{1}{4}(12) & \frac{1}{4}(20) \\ -5 & -15 & 30 \end{bmatrix} = \begin{bmatrix} 1 & 3 & 5 \\ -5 & -15 & 30 \end{bmatrix}.$$

Next, we change the first element of the second row from −5 to 0 by replacing R_2 by $5R_1 + R_2$. This yields:

$$\begin{bmatrix} 1 & 3 & 5 \\ 5(1)-5 & 5(3)-15 & 5(5)+30 \end{bmatrix} = \begin{bmatrix} 1 & 3 & 5 \\ 0 & 0 & 55 \end{bmatrix}.$$

Again, we have a problem. We cannot transform the second element in row two from 0 to 1 through multiplication. But this does not look exactly the same as the previous problem either. In the previous problem, the last row consisted entirely of zeros. This is not the case here. Interpreting the rows of this matrix as equations yields

$x + 3y = 5$
$0x + 0y = 55$

or

$x + 3y = 5$
$0 = 55$.

The last equation can never be made true. Zero cannot equal fifty five. Thus, this is an inconsistent system — it has no solutions.

Although it may seem as though the techniques learned in this section are of limited value because these systems are more easily solved by the methods reviewed earlier in this chapter, this is not the case. When large systems are studied, systems with many unknowns and many equations, the methods studied earlier in the chapter become almost useless, and the only way to solve such problems efficiently is through the application of matrix methods

---

Small Group Exercise:

Explain how you could modify the procedure illustrated in the text to solve a system of three equations with three unknowns. In doing this you should be aiming toward a final matrix of the form

$$\begin{bmatrix} 1 & 0 & 0 & a_1 \\ 0 & 1 & 0 & a_2 \\ 0 & 0 & 1 & a_3 \end{bmatrix}.$$

Explain how you would set up your original matrix, how you would transform it into the form given above, and how you would read the solution of the system off of the final matrix. What possible problems might you expect?

Exercises

For exercises # 1 – 8, solve each system of equations using matrices.

1. $2x - 3y = 18$
   $x - 2y = 11$

2. $2y = 10 - 4x$
   $3x - 5y = 1$

3. $x = 10 - 3y$
   $2x + 6y = 7$

4. $8x - y = 12$
   $4x + 3y = -22$

5. $6x - 24y = 48$
   $12y = 3x - 24$

6. $6x + 10y = -3$
   $-21x + 20y = -17$

7. $2x - y = -9$
   $x + 3y = 13$

8. $3x - 10y = 7$
   $12y - 4x = -10$

9. $9x + 6y = -1$
   $6x - 3y = 4$

10. $2x + y = -1$
    $\frac{1}{2}x - y = -14$

11. $x + 5y = 3$
    $2x + 11y = 4$

12. $x - y = 4$
    $\frac{1}{3}x - y = -6$

13. $5x - 3y = 11$
    $10x - 6y = 9$

14. $x - 2y + z = 1$
    $2x + y - z = 0$
    $3y - z = 2$

15. $3x - y - z = -11$
    $x + 2y + z = 1$
    $x + y + 3z = -1$

16. $x + y - z = 1$
    $2x - 2y + z = 3$
    $y - 2z = -7$

3.8 Inverses and Some Applications

Consider the following two matrices:

$$A = \begin{bmatrix} 2 & 4 \\ 1 & 3 \end{bmatrix} \quad \text{and} \quad B = \begin{bmatrix} \frac{3}{2} & -2 \\ \frac{-1}{2} & 1 \end{bmatrix}.$$

Notice that $AB = \begin{bmatrix} 2\left(\frac{3}{2}\right) + 4\left(\frac{-1}{2}\right) & 2(-2) + 4(1) \\ 1\left(\frac{3}{2}\right) + 3\left(\frac{-1}{2}\right) & 1(-2) + 3(1) \end{bmatrix} = \begin{bmatrix} 1 & 0 \\ 0 & 1 \end{bmatrix}$ and

$$BA = \begin{bmatrix} \frac{3}{2}(2) - 2(1) & \frac{3}{2}(4) - 2(3) \\ \frac{-1}{2}(2) + 1(1) & \frac{-1}{2}(4) + 1(3) \end{bmatrix} = \begin{bmatrix} 1 & 0 \\ 0 & 1 \end{bmatrix}.$$ Both products are equal to the identity matrix.

When this happens we say that A and B are *inverses*. The inverse of matrix A is denoted by A^{-1}.

Definition: Let A be a square matrix. If there is a matrix A^{-1} such that $A \cdot A^{-1} = A^{-1}A = I$, then A^{-1} is called the *inverse* of A.

Take note that in order for A to have an inverse it must be square. However, not all square matrices have inverses. If a square matrix A has an inverse, then we say A is *invertible* or *nonsingular*. If it does not have an inverse, we say A is *singular*. Although matrix inverses are extremely useful in applications, it is not at all unusual to have to deal with singular matrices.

We will not concern ourselves with how matrix inverses are computed in this text, however, we will illustrate their usefulness with some examples. If you find this to be interesting, there are many books on linear algebra that you can consult in order to learn how inverses are computed.

Example. Verify that the matrices $A = \begin{bmatrix} 3 & 9 \\ 1 & 2 \end{bmatrix}$ and $B = \begin{bmatrix} \frac{-2}{3} & 3 \\ \frac{1}{3} & -1 \end{bmatrix}$ are inverses of each other.

Solution:

We will compute the products AB and BA to verify that both products are equal to the identity.

$$AB = \begin{bmatrix} \begin{bmatrix} 3 & 9 \end{bmatrix}\begin{bmatrix} -\frac{2}{3} \\ \frac{1}{3} \end{bmatrix} & \begin{bmatrix} 3 & 9 \end{bmatrix}\begin{bmatrix} 3 \\ -1 \end{bmatrix} \\ \begin{bmatrix} 1 & 2 \end{bmatrix}\begin{bmatrix} -\frac{2}{3} \\ \frac{1}{3} \end{bmatrix} & \begin{bmatrix} 1 & 2 \end{bmatrix}\begin{bmatrix} 3 \\ -1 \end{bmatrix} \end{bmatrix} = \begin{bmatrix} 3\left(\frac{-2}{3}\right) + 9\left(\frac{1}{3}\right) & 3(3) + 9(-1) \\ 1\left(\frac{-2}{3}\right) + 2\left(\frac{1}{3}\right) & 1(3) + 2(-1) \end{bmatrix} = \begin{bmatrix} 1 & 0 \\ 0 & 1 \end{bmatrix}$$ and

$$BA = \begin{bmatrix} \begin{bmatrix} \frac{-2}{3} & 3 \end{bmatrix}\begin{bmatrix} 3 \\ 1 \end{bmatrix} & \begin{bmatrix} \frac{-2}{3} & 3 \end{bmatrix}\begin{bmatrix} 9 \\ 2 \end{bmatrix} \\ \begin{bmatrix} \frac{1}{3} & -1 \end{bmatrix}\begin{bmatrix} 3 \\ 1 \end{bmatrix} & \begin{bmatrix} \frac{1}{3} & -1 \end{bmatrix}\begin{bmatrix} 9 \\ 2 \end{bmatrix} \end{bmatrix} = \begin{bmatrix} \frac{-2}{3}(3) + 3(1) & \frac{-2}{3}(9) + 3(2) \\ \frac{1}{3}(3) - 1(1) & \frac{1}{3}(9) - 1(2) \end{bmatrix} = \begin{bmatrix} 1 & 0 \\ 0 & 1 \end{bmatrix}.$$

Since both of these products equal the identity, A and B are inverses of each other, and we could write $B = A^{-1}$.

Remember, for a matrix to have an inverse it must be a square matrix, but the fact that a matrix is square is not enough to guarantee that it will have an inverse.

Solving Systems of Equations Using Inverses

There is another method we can use to solve systems of equations. We begin by placing each equation into the form $ax + by = c$. Then we form two matrices — one consisting of the coefficients of the variables, call it matrix A, and the other a column vector of constants, call it matrix B. Then we find A^{-1} and finally $A^{-1}B$. The values of x and y can be read from the two entries of $A^{-1}B$. In what follows we will assume that it is known that the inverse of the matrix $A = \begin{bmatrix} 2 & -1 \\ 5 & -1 \end{bmatrix}$ is the matrix

$$A^{-1} = \begin{bmatrix} \frac{-1}{3} & \frac{1}{3} \\ \frac{-5}{3} & \frac{2}{3} \end{bmatrix},$$ which you should verify.

For example, again consider the system:

$$2x - y = -3$$
$$5x - y = 4$$

Earlier we found the solution of this system to be $x = \frac{7}{3}$ and $y = \frac{23}{3}$. Now we will use matrix inverses to solve this same system of equations. Each equation in the system is in the form $ax + by = c$, thus we can form the matrices A and B mentioned above. The first row of matrix A will consist of the coefficients of x and y respectively from the first equation and the second row will consist of those from the second equation. The first row element of matrix B will be the constant from the first equation and the second row element will be the constant from the second equation. Thus, we have

$$A = \begin{bmatrix} 2 & -1 \\ 5 & -1 \end{bmatrix} \text{ and } B = \begin{bmatrix} -3 \\ 4 \end{bmatrix}.$$

Next, we compute the matrix product $A^{-1}B$:

$$A^{-1}B = \begin{bmatrix} \frac{-1}{3}(-3) + \frac{1}{3}(4) \\ \frac{-5}{3}(-3) + \frac{2}{3}(4) \end{bmatrix} = \begin{bmatrix} \frac{7}{3} \\ \frac{23}{3} \end{bmatrix}.$$

This final matrix contains the value of x as its top element and the value of y as the bottom element. We find the same solution as before: $x = \frac{7}{3}$ and $y = \frac{23}{3}$.

Cryptography

Cryptography, the art of deciphering coded messages, also can utilize matrices. Secret codes have been used for thousands of years to secure communication. It is hoped that only those who know the secret code can decipher such messages, but a good cryptographer may be able to break a code that was

not intended for him or her. Today these codes are very important. They are used by the government, industry, and financial institutions. Matrices and their inverses can be used to encode and decode secret messages.

Let us consider a simple example. Suppose we use the correspondence set up in Table 3.5 to represent the English alphabet and some other characters.

A	B	C	D	E	F	G	H	I	J	K	L	M	N	O	P
−1	1	−2	2	−3	3	−4	4	−5	5	−6	6	−7	7	−8	8
Q	R	S	T	U	V	W	X	Y	Z	space	.	!	?	,	$
−9	9	−10	10	−11	11	−12	12	−13	13	−14	14	−15	15	−16	16

Table 3.5 Symbols for the English alphabet and some other characters.

We will also need a square invertible matrix A. We will choose a 3×3 matrix, although in practice we would choose a larger square matrix to make it more difficult to break the code. We will use

$$A = \begin{bmatrix} 1 & 1 & 2 \\ 0 & 1 & 3 \\ 1 & 2 & 1 \end{bmatrix}, \text{ which has inverse } A^{-1} = \begin{bmatrix} \frac{5}{4} & \frac{-3}{4} & \frac{-1}{4} \\ \frac{-3}{4} & \frac{1}{4} & \frac{3}{4} \\ \frac{1}{4} & \frac{1}{4} & \frac{-1}{4} \end{bmatrix}.$$

Suppose we wish to encode the message "READER ALERT." We begin by representing each letter and symbol with the corresponding number from Table 3.5 above.

R	E	A	D	E	R	space	A	L	E	R	T
9	−3	−1	2	−3	9	−14	−1	6	−3	9	10

Now we form 3×1 column vectors from this series of numbers (we use 3×1 vectors because our matrix A has dimension 3×3, and we would like to multiply A by each of the vectors). The entries of our first column vector will represent R,E,A; the entries of our second column vector will represent D,E,R; and so forth. If we need additional numbers at the end, we will use −14 to represent a space. Thus, we now have:

$$V_1 = \begin{bmatrix} 9 \\ -3 \\ -1 \end{bmatrix} \quad V_2 = \begin{bmatrix} 2 \\ -3 \\ 9 \end{bmatrix} \quad V_3 = \begin{bmatrix} -14 \\ -1 \\ 6 \end{bmatrix} \quad V_4 = \begin{bmatrix} -3 \\ 9 \\ 10 \end{bmatrix}.$$

Next we multiply A by each vector.

$$C_1 = AV_1 = \begin{bmatrix} 4 \\ -6 \\ 2 \end{bmatrix} \quad C_2 = AV_2 = \begin{bmatrix} 17 \\ 24 \\ 5 \end{bmatrix} \quad C_3 = AV_3 = \begin{bmatrix} -3 \\ 17 \\ -10 \end{bmatrix} \quad C_4 = AV_4 = \begin{bmatrix} 26 \\ 39 \\ 25 \end{bmatrix}.$$

We now copy down the entries in each of these vectors in turn, first writing the entries of C_1, then those of C_2, and so on. The message would be encoded as:

4, −6, 2, 17, 24, 5, −3, 17, −10, 26, 39, 25.

If we received of this message, how would we decode it? We would begin by forming 3×1 column vectors. This simply requires us to copy the numbers in the coded message back into vector form:

$$C_1 = \begin{bmatrix} 4 \\ -6 \\ 2 \end{bmatrix}, \quad C_2 = \begin{bmatrix} 17 \\ 24 \\ 5 \end{bmatrix}, \quad C_3 = \begin{bmatrix} -3 \\ 17 \\ -10 \end{bmatrix}, \quad \text{and} \quad C_4 = \begin{bmatrix} 26 \\ 39 \\ 25 \end{bmatrix}.$$

Next we would multiply each of these matrices by A^{-1}. In this example, we would get:

$$A^{-1}C_1 = \begin{bmatrix} 9 \\ -3 \\ -1 \end{bmatrix} \quad A^{-1}C_2 = \begin{bmatrix} 2 \\ -3 \\ 9 \end{bmatrix} \quad A^{-1}C_3 = \begin{bmatrix} -14 \\ -1 \\ 6 \end{bmatrix} \quad A^{-1}C_4 = \begin{bmatrix} -3 \\ 9 \\ 10 \end{bmatrix}.$$

We can now recreate the original message by writing these numbers in a horizontal line, and using Table 3.5 to translate the numbers back into letters.

9, −3, −1, 2, −3, 9, −14, −1, 6, −3, 9, 10
R E A D E R space A L E R T.

In essence, what is happening here is that multiplying the column vectors by A "scrambles" the message, mixing it up so that it is unrecognizable. Applying the matrix A^{-1} to the coded message unscrambles it again, making the message readable.

Exercises

1. Verify that the matrices $\begin{bmatrix} 2 & -1 \\ 5 & -1 \end{bmatrix}$ and $\begin{bmatrix} \frac{-1}{3} & \frac{1}{3} \\ \frac{-5}{3} & \frac{2}{3} \end{bmatrix}$ are inverses of each other. (This fact was needed to solve the system $\begin{matrix} 2x - y = -3 \\ 5x - y = 4 \end{matrix}$ in the text.)

2. Verify that the matrices $\begin{bmatrix} 1 & 1 & 2 \\ 0 & 1 & 3 \\ 1 & 2 & 1 \end{bmatrix}$ and $\begin{bmatrix} \frac{5}{4} & \frac{-3}{4} & \frac{-1}{4} \\ \frac{-3}{4} & \frac{1}{4} & \frac{3}{4} \\ \frac{1}{4} & \frac{1}{4} & \frac{-1}{4} \end{bmatrix}$ are inverses. (This fact is needed to complete the analysis of the work in the text on cryptography.)

3. Complete all of the matrix multiplications required to verify the section on cryptography.

4. Verify that the matrices $\begin{bmatrix} 2 & 1 \\ -3 & 2 \end{bmatrix}$ and $\begin{bmatrix} \frac{2}{7} & \frac{-1}{7} \\ \frac{3}{7} & \frac{2}{7} \end{bmatrix}$ are inverses. Use this fact to solve the system

$$2x + y = -1$$
$$-3x + 2y = -9$$

5. Verify that the matrices $\begin{bmatrix} 1 & 3 \\ 2 & -4 \end{bmatrix}$ and $\begin{bmatrix} \frac{2}{5} & \frac{3}{10} \\ \frac{1}{5} & \frac{-1}{10} \end{bmatrix}$ are inverses. Use this fact to solve the system

$$x + 3y = -10$$
$$2x - 4y = 0$$

6. Verify that the matrices $\begin{bmatrix} 2 & -3 \\ 5 & 1 \end{bmatrix}$ and $\begin{bmatrix} \frac{1}{17} & \frac{3}{17} \\ \frac{-5}{17} & \frac{2}{17} \end{bmatrix}$ are inverses. Use this fact to solve the

system $\begin{aligned} 2x - 3y &= -3 \\ 5x + y &= 18 \end{aligned}$

7. Verify that the matrices $\begin{bmatrix} 4 & -1 \\ 10 & -2 \end{bmatrix}$ and $\begin{bmatrix} -1 & \frac{1}{2} \\ -5 & 2 \end{bmatrix}$ are inverses. Use this fact to solve the

system $\begin{aligned} 4x - y &= -6 \\ 10x - 2y &= -11 \end{aligned}$

8. Verify that the matrices $\begin{bmatrix} 0 & 1 & 2 \\ 1 & 2 & 3 \\ 1 & 3 & 4 \end{bmatrix}$ and $\begin{bmatrix} -1 & 2 & -1 \\ -1 & -2 & 2 \\ 1 & 1 & -1 \end{bmatrix}$ are inverses of each other.

For exercises # 9–12 use the matrix $A = \begin{bmatrix} 0 & 1 & 2 \\ 1 & 2 & 3 \\ 1 & 3 & 4 \end{bmatrix}$ (from problem #8) and Table 3.5.

9. Encode the message "come now!"

10. Encode the message "help needed"

11. Decode the message:

19, 21, 30, –24, –39, –58, –8, –29, –40, –23, –42, –50

12. Decode the message:

–22, –39, –54, –32, –58, –81, –9, –27, –34, –20, –33, –40

Chapter 3: **ALGEBRA AND MATRICES**

13. Research how matrices are used by financial institutions for cryptography.

3.9 Chapter Review

Important Terms to Know

addition method	double inequality	matrices
break–even point	element	matrix
column vector	equation	nonsingular
commutative	identity	order
compound inequality	identity matrix	row vector
conditional equation	inconsistent system	scalar
consistent system	inequality	singular
contradiction	inverse	solution
cryptography	invertible	square matrix
dependent system	linear equation	substitution method
dimension	main diagonal	vector

Important Names to Know

Cayley, Arthur	Diophantus	Mohammed ibn–Musa al–Khwarizmi
Descartes, Rene		

Review Questions

1. What are the three classifications for linear equations? Give an example of each type and state the solution of each equation.

2. In grading two students' exams, the instructor found the following double inequality solved two different ways. Is either one correct? If so, which? If not, solve them correctly. What mistakes were made by each student, if any?

$$5 < 5 - 2x \leq 11 \qquad\qquad 5 < 5 - 2x \leq 11$$
$$0 < -2x \leq 11 \qquad\qquad\phantom{5 < 5}-2x \leq 6$$
$$0 < x \leq \frac{-11}{2} \qquad\qquad\phantom{5 < 5-2}x \geq -3$$

3. Find a matrix that has all of the following properties:
   (a) Is not square.

(b) All entries on the main diagonal are 1.
(c) Is not the Identity matrix.
(d) Has more than three rows.

4. Is it possible to find two matrices A and B such that all of the following hold:

AB is possible,
$A + B$ is possible,
BA is not possible?

If it is possible, find two such matrices A and B and show that all three of these conditions hold. If it is not possible, explain why two matrices cannot be created that meet all three conditions using complete sentences.

5. You have learned three methods for solving a system of equations. Consider the system:

$$2x = \frac{1}{2}y - 4$$
$$3x + y = 1.$$

Solve this system using all three methods. Which method do you prefer and why? (You will need to know the fact that $A^{-1} = \begin{bmatrix} \frac{2}{7} & \frac{1}{7} \\ \frac{-6}{7} & \frac{4}{7} \end{bmatrix}$, which you should verify.)

Chapter 4

Operations Research and Game Theory

"For when the One Great Scorer comes
to write against your name,
He marks — not that you won or lost —
but how you played the game."

Grantland Rice

Chapter Four: OPERATIONS RESEARCH AND GAME THEORY

Chapter Outline

4.0 Introduction

4.1 Historical Perspective
   Operations Research
   Games

4.2 The Design of Operations Research

4.3 Linear Programming
   A Maximization Problem – Baseball Bats
   A Minimization Problem – Stocks
   The Simplex Method

4.4 Other Operations Research Techniques
   Queuing Theory
   Sinking Funds
   Forecasting
   Conclusion

4.5 The Theory of Games
   The Toothpaste Example

4.6 Some Examples of Games
   Reverse Tic–Tac–Toe
   Analysis of the Game
   The Game of Sim
   A Variation of Sim
   The Game of Domineering
   Games as Numbers

4.7 Chapter Review

4.0 Introduction

The two branches of mathematics that we look at in this chapter, operations research and game theory, have developed side-by-side during the twentieth century. Both fields had their origin in the years following World War I, but it wasn't until the 1940's that they matured into the important and useful tools that are now important in so many areas of study. There were two important events which stimulated the growth of these fields at that time, the second world war and the development of the electronic computer.

Operations research is not actually a branch of mathematics, but rather an interdisciplinary subject whose application usually requires teams of individuals from many different fields. Because of its heavy dependence on mathematics techniques, however, students interested in operations research often find themselves studying in the mathematics department.

Operations research, the application of scientific and quantitative methods to management and administration, uses different techniques than those used traditionally in the solution of problems in other disciplines. Whereas mathematics had been used by scientists, technologists, and engineers to improve their products, the point of view taken by the operations research team was very different. Instead of concentrating on improving the product itself, the goal of the operations research team is to *insure that existing products and resources are utilized as well as they can be*. One of the earliest formal applications of operations research exhibits this point well. In the late 1930's and early 1940's the British were under severe pressure to improve their defense system in order to protect themselves from air attack. Rather than attempting improvements on the radar itself, a team was commissioned to guarantee that the existing system would be employed as effectively as possible. The team was headed by P.M.S. Blackett, a physicist, but it also included physiologists, army officers, mathematicians, and astrophysicists. It was so successful in solving the problem that within three years all three branches of the British military had operations research units, and units were also in the process of being set up in many of the allied armed forces, including that of the United States.

In solving these problems the operations research team has many mathematical tools at its disposal. We will look at linear programming, perhaps the most well-developed and useful of these tools, in more detail than the others. Although linear programming, like other branches of operations research, can get very complex, it has the advantage of being easily understood in theory. We'll be able to look at some simple problems in this area and follow them from their formulation to their final resolution. In this way we will be able to get a better idea of how operations research works in general. Other methods currently in use in operations research include calculus, queuing theory, search patterns, sinking funds, and forecasting. We will look at these branches of operations research only briefly.

The purpose of game theory is very similar to that of operations research — to allow managers access to quantitative techniques in order to enable them to make better decisions. Early in the twentieth century mathematicians and economists made an interesting discovery: when the strategic features of competitive situations were extracted and analyzed quantitatively, a clear resemblance was found with the

strategies used in many actual games such as bridge, poker, and chess. These similarities have been exploited successfully in many fields, including economics, politics, psychology, military planning, and biology. As modern life and its problems got more complex, so did game theory. Game theory is now a highly sophisticated and complex subject requiring the use of high-speed computers to analyze problems involving elaborate conditions and strategies.

4.1 Historical Perspective

Operations Research

Although operations research became a force in the analysis of complex problems in the early years of World War II, the field's history goes back quite a few years before that to the years of the first world war. At that time American and British researchers were interested in improving their ability to locate the German submarines which were terrorizing their shipping. Although the work that was done at that time would now be considered primitive, this problem of analyzing *search patterns* is now one of the principle issues dealt with in operations research. This "search pattern problem" would not now be used to identify the position of a submarine, but rather to locate things like natural resources, missing data on computer disks, escaped convicts, or misshelved books in a library. In fact, just about every operations research problem has some kind of search as part of its solution.

In the 1930's a new branch of operations research started to develop, *linear programming*. The early work in this area, which attracted little attention, dealt with scheduling. The *scheduling problem*, still very important today, deals with assigning manpower to tasks in the most efficient way. Office managers, supervisors of construction teams, and military officers would be some of the people who would be interested in the solution of this type of problem, which is now understood to be more complicated than people once thought. A similar problem, called the *transportation problem*, was studied during the second world war. This problem is concerned with the most effective way of moving goods from one point to another, say from warehouses to retail stores or from ammunition depots to companies of soldiers. The early clarification of these two problems, although important, really only consisted of specialized techniques. More general types of linear programming problems were not addressed until 1947, when George Dantzig introduced the *simplex method*. This powerful method enabled mathematicians to solve a very large class of *optimization problems* which had not been approachable before. Unfortunately, real-world problems often contained hundreds of variables, equations, and inequalities. For these problems even the simplex method was often not enough. The development of the computer helped in solving many of these problems, but for some even this was not sufficient. Recent years have seen new attacks and refinements in this area, and the problems which now can be solved were unthinkable only a few years ago.

Since 1947 operations research has grown in importance, mainly because of the success of linear programming. Courses and programs were developed in mathematics departments and management departments following the introduction of this technique, and after the successful applications of operations research in the military it gained increasing acceptance in industrial and commercial settings. Now there is almost no large organization where this method is not applied.

Some of the other specialties which qualify under the title of "operations research" are *queuing theory* and *forecasting*. Although we won't have the time to get too deeply into these areas, they do represent the future of operations research. Operations researchers should expect the number of tools available to them to grow. The increased number of available techniques will allow for more effective utilization of the world's resources in the future.

Games

The first person to formally consider games of *strategy* from an analytical point of view was the French mathematician Émile Borel in 1921. His work was preliminary since he was not able to prove his results. This, however, was done in 1928 by the brilliant American mathematician John von Neumann, who later would be one of the primary influences in the development of the electronic computer and the atomic bomb. In 1944 von Neumann and the American Economist Oskar Morgenstern published *The Theory of Games and Economic Behavior*, and the modern theory of games was established. Since 1944 the theory of games has advanced significantly both from theoretical and practical standpoints. From the theoretical point of view it has been found that the idea of "game," in some technical sense, could even be considered a more fundamental concept than the idea of "number." This has led to the development of new number systems, and an increased understanding of our familiar number system. On the practical side, games have been used to analyze many competitive situations, and, with the help of computers, have been used to aid in making decisions in large numbers of complicated situations.

4.2 The Design of Operations Research

As mentioned in the introduction to this chapter, operations research is the application of scientific or quantitative techniques to decision making within organized systems. Among others, these systems could be military, political, or commercial. The distinction between the Operations research approach and the traditional engineering/technology approach is that the engineer and technologist are usually concerned with *improvement of the system*, while the Operations research team is usually concerned with *performance of the system*. When the system is performing at its best it is said to be *optimized*. Thus, the optimal utilization of resources is the goal of the operations research team.

Typically a manager faced with a difficult problem would consult with his operations research team in order to assist him or her in finding a "good" solution to a problem. The team's job would consist of a number of different phases. First the problem would have to be *systematized*. In forming this system, the operations research team is standardizing the problem so that scientific and mathematical principles can later be applied. In this phase it is important that the operations research team keep in mind the fact that the system that they are working in must accurately reflect the real–life situation which they are studying. This is one of the places where the interdisciplinary nature of the team is important, since it gives them the opportunity to view the system from many different perspectives.

Once the system that the team will be working in has been established it is possible for the team to move on to the construction of a *model* of the problem. The term "model" here is a technical one, referring to a mathematical description of the important aspects of the problem. Often the model which is constructed contains inequalities which represent limitations of time or other resources imposed on the problem by the organization's environment. The model could consist of equations, inequalities, graphs, and/or computer descriptions of the problem. The construction of theses models often requires the break–down of large amounts of empirical data and the application of advanced statistical and probabilistic methods. The operations research team often has to rely on past experience and analogies with related models in the construction of their model. In addition to being important in the solution of many of these problems, the use of computers is often indispensable in the construction of the model.

The construction of the model still leaves us a long way from our goal. It would be easy to say that all we have to do at this point is to "solve" the model, much the way you have solved equations in your algebra class. However there is quite a bit more to it than this, because the models we are talking about may contain hundreds or even thousands of variables, equations, and inequalities. Even if you were absolutely sure that your model were accurate, high–speed computers would not even be up to the task

presented here. Furthermore, the accuracy of the model is rarely a sure thing, so even if you can solve the mathematical model you have formulated, there's no guarantee that the computed solution is really useful to you. The following list indicates some of the problems that operations research teams need to deal with – although certainly other problems may need to be considered too.

1. When setting up the model, which variables need to be accounted for? If the inclusion of all of the variables will make the model too complex, even for computer analysis, is it possible to omit some of the variables and still have an accurate and usable model?
2. If the model suggests that a certain solution be implemented, is there some way of testing the accuracy of the solution before putting it into action? If tests (often *computer simulations*) indicate a problem with your solution, can you pinpoint which features of your model are causing the problem?
3. If there is a problem, can you refine your model to make it more effective?
4. If a prospective solution is changed a little bit, will it lead you to a better solution? That is, do we have a procedure for improving an approximate solution? Learning how to do this effectively is key in the solution of many operations research problems, including the solution of linear programming problems. This is also the idea behind many popular computer software programs, such as Lotus 1–2–3 and Excel, which allow users to change key numbers in a spreadsheet and see how these changes effect their model. Taken to its extreme, operations research teams can try different policies in computer simulations and observe which policies lead to the best results within the model.

As you can see, there seems to be quite a bit of uncertainty involved in the operations research approach to solving problems. Difficulties can be a result of faulty assumptions in the system, a decision to ignore what turn out to be important variables in the model, or an inability to mathematically solve the model. This means that after the operations research team comes up with a prospective solution to a problem, the biggest decision of all still has to be made: the *manager* who the team is working for needs to decide whether or not to implement the solution, either in whole or in part. If the decision to implement is made, the manager needs to check periodically to make sure that conditions haven't changed so much that modifications are needed. Note that it is the manager, not the operations research team, who decides whether or not to implement the proposed solution.

The key word in making this whole plan work is *cooperation*. Cooperation among the members of the interdisciplinary operations research team is needed if they are to come up with a plan that could be effective, and cooperation between the team and the manager is essential if the plan is to be put into effect.

Questions to Discuss

1. What two events stimulated the growth of operations research and game theory?

2. Define operations research. How does its application differ from the traditional ways that mathematics was used to solve problems?

3. Give some examples showing how operations research can be used to help solve commercial, political, and military problems.

4. What are the typical steps that an operations research team needs to follow in order to analyze a problem?

5. What problems does an operations research team face in the construction and solution of a model?

> 6. How might an operations research team test a proposed model?
>
> 7. In what ways could inaccuracies be introduced into models? What can an operations research team do to safeguard against this?
>
> 8. Who decides whether or not to implement the operation research team's recommendations?

4.3 Linear Programming

In order to better understand what has become the most powerful of the operations researcher's tools, linear programming, we will look at a *simplified version* of a problem that a typical business might give to its operations research team. In the process of analyzing this problem we will review some concepts from algebra, particularly the graphing of linear equations, which we will find useful. As we go through the problem, keep in mind that the problems faced by most managers are considerably more complicated than this one.

A Maximization Problem — Baseball Bats

A sports equipment company produces only two products, *baseball bats* and *softball bats*. Given the company's limited resources in machine time, material, and manpower, the operations research team is asked to determine how many of each type of bat to produce.

The operations research team would take this problem and attempt to build a model reflecting the profit and restrictions that they find to be in effect in the organization. In this particular case the operations research team's research uncovered the following facts which had an impact on their problem:

1. The company reaps a profit of $4 on each baseball bat sold and $3 on each softball bat sold.
2. The sales staff tells the operations research team that they can sell no more than 1100 bats per week. It is assumed that if 1100 bats or fewer are produced per week then the company will be able to sell all of the bats produced.
3. Each baseball bat requires 6 ft^3 of wood while each softball bat requires 4 ft^3 of wood. A total of 4800 ft^3 of wood is available.
4. Each baseball requires 45 minutes of machine time, while each softball bat requires 18 minutes of machine time. A total of 480 hours of machine time is available on the company's machines.

With their research complete, it's now time to attempt to build the model. Although you may never have dealt with so many conditions in one mathematics problem before, you have worked with conditions such as these in your elementary algebra course.

In constructing the model, the team's first step is to set up a formula representing the company's profit. Since the profit depends on the number of baseball bats and softball bats made, and we are not sure of how many of each type that we want to produce yet, we'll use variables to represent these values. Let x be the number of baseball bats produced and y the number of softball bats produced.

Since one baseball bat produces $4 in profits, x baseball bats would generate $4x$ dollars in profits. Similarly, y softball bats, each yielding $3 profit, would produce $3y$ dollars in profits. Therefore the total profit generated, which we will represent by P, will be $4x + 4y$ dollars, the profit from the baseball bats plus the profit from the softball bats. The formula for the profit, $P = 4x + 3y$, is called the

objective function. The operations research team's desire is to *maximize the objective function*. In some problems the team may be asked to minimize a function.

The restrictions uncovered by the operations research team's explorations will now be investigated to see what kind of limitations they put on P. Checking the facts given above we see that three limitations have been introduced, one by the *Sales Department*, one by the *amount of wood available*, and one by the *amount of machine time available*. We will look at each of these restrictions in turn.

1. **Sales Restriction**: Since we know that the number of baseball bats produced is represented by x and the number of softball bats produced is represented by y, the total number of bats produced would be represented by $x + y$. Since research indicated that the total number of bats produced must be less than or equal to 1100 bats, we get the *Sales Inequality*: $x + y \leq 1100$.

2. **Wood Availability Restriction**: Each baseball bat requires 6 ft^3 of wood. Since x bats are produced, this requires $6x$ cubic feet of wood. Similarly, a softball bat would require 4 ft^3 of wood, so y bats would require $4y$ cubic feet of wood. Thus the production requires a total of $6x + 4y$ cubic feet of wood. According to the limitation discovered by the team, this total may be at most 4800 ft^3. This gives the *Wood Availability Inequality*: $6x + 4y \leq 4800$.

3. **Machine Time Restriction**: There are x baseball bats, each requiring 45 minutes of machine time. This gives a total of $45x$ minutes of machine required for processing the baseball bats. In addition, there are y softball bats, each of which requires 18 minutes of machine processing time. This amounts to $18y$ minutes of processing time required by the softball bats. The total amount of processing time needed for both types of bats is therefore $45x + 18y$ minutes. Since we know that this total must be less than 480 hours, or $(480)(60) = 28800$ minutes, the *Machine Availability Inequality* would be $45x + 18y \leq 28800$.

In addition to the inequalities derived above, we make the observation that both x and y must be non–negative — after all, you can't make a negative number of bats! This means that two additional inequalities, $x \geq 0$ and $y \geq 0$, should be added to the ones which we have already developed. The mathematical model we have developed is generally presented something like this:

Maximize $P = 4x + 3y$ (objective function)
Subject to $x \geq 0, y \geq 0$
$x + y \leq 1100$ (sales inequality)
$6x + 4y \leq 4800$ (wood availability inequality)
$45x + 18y \leq 28800$ (machine availability inequality)

As mentioned earlier, the first equation here is called the *objective function*. This will always represent *a quantity which is to be either maximized or minimized*. The inequalities are called *constraints*. These represent the restrictions on the objective function which we've uncovered during our research. *It is the analysis of these constraint inequalities that is key to the solution of the problem*.

Now that the model has been built, a solution can be attempted. Because of the simple nature of this particular problem, it turns out that *a graphical solution is possible*. In more complicated problems this is not the case, but we will not be dealing with any such problems in this book.

We will now graph each of the constraint inequalities in order to see what they can add to our understanding of the problem. The first of the inequalities, $x \geq 0$ and $y \geq 0$, tell us that we should focus our attention on those points in the Cartesian coordinate system which are above the x–axis and to the right of the y–axis. See Figure 4.1 for a graph of this region.

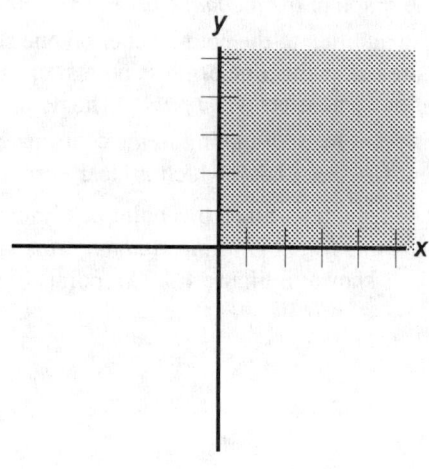

Figure 4.1 The graph of the inequalities $x \geq 0$ and $y \geq 0$. Intervals each represent 400 units.

The *inequality* $x + y \leq 1100$ will be graphed next. How is this done? The procedure consists of two steps: First graph the *equation* $x + y = 1100$. This will form the *boundary* of the inequality. Second, a decision has to be made to decide which side of the boundary the solution is on (see chapter 3 if you need to refresh your memory on this procedure).

To implement the first part of this procedure, recognize the fact that the equation $x + y = 1100$ is a linear equation, so its graph is a *straight line*. In fact, it is because the objective function and the constraints are all linear that this is classified as a *linear programming* problem. As is common with these types of problems, we will graph this equation by plotting its *intercepts*.

x–intercept: Let $y = 0$. Solving the equation gives $x = 1100$. The point $(1100,0)$ is on the graph.

y–intercept: Let $x = 0$. Solving the equation gives $y = 1100$. The point $(0,1100)$ is on the graph.

Plotting these two points and connecting them gives the graph of the *equation* $x + y = 1100$. This graph is shown below in Figure 4.2.

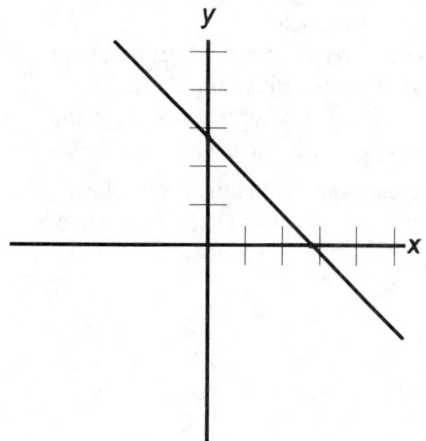

Figure 4.2 The graph of the equation $x + y = 1100$.

As mentioned earlier, this graph is the *boundary* of the graph of the *inequality* $x + y \leq 1100$. The inequality's graph consists of all points on this boundary, in addition to the points either on one side of this boundary or on the other side (that is, those points that are below this line or those points that are above it). In order to determine which side of the line we want, we will select a *test point*. The point $(0,0)$ is often a convenient test point, and we will be using this point here. Plugging in the coordinates of this point into the inequality $x + y \leq 1100$ yields the statement $0 + 0 \leq 1100$, which is clearly true.

This means that the point that we tested, $(0,0)$, does satisfy the inequality. Since this point lies *below* the boundary line that we graphed earlier, it must be that *all of the points lying below the boundary line must also satisfy the inequality*. Thus the graph of $x + y \leq 1100$ is as shown in Figure 4.3. All points in the shaded region satisfy the inequality.

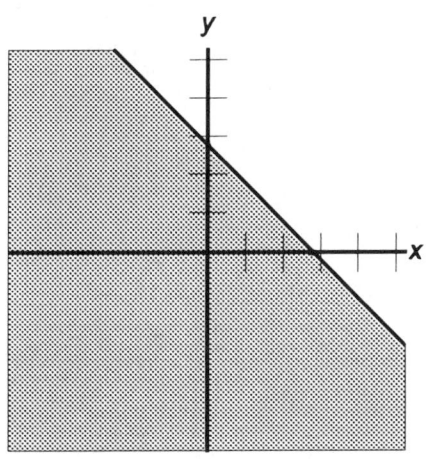

Figure 4.3 The graph of the inequality $x + y \leq 1100$.

Note that if we had tried *any* test point *above the boundary*, for example if we had tried the point $(1200,0)$, we would have gotten a result which is *not true* upon substitution in the inequality. (Replacing x by 1200 and y by 0 in the inequality $x + y \leq 1100$ gives the false statement $1200 + 0 \leq 1100$.)

This would have led us to the same conclusion: Since the point $(1200,0)$ *does not satisfy the inequality*, neither does any other point above the boundary. This means that we do not want to shade in the region above the line, so we must want to shade in the region on the other side, that is, below it.

Remembering that we still have two constraints which we have not yet concerned ourselves with yet, where do we stand now? We graphed the region which represented all points satisfying the inequalities $x \geq 0$ and $y \geq 0$ (see Figure 1), and we also graphed the region which represented all points satisfying the inequality $x + y \leq 1100$ (see Figure 4.3). In order for the point (x,y) to be in consideration in this problem, it is necessary that it satisfy all of these conditions — that is, it must be a point which is shaded in both diagrams. Thus, at this point we have restricted ourselves to consideration of the points which are shaded in Figure 4.4.

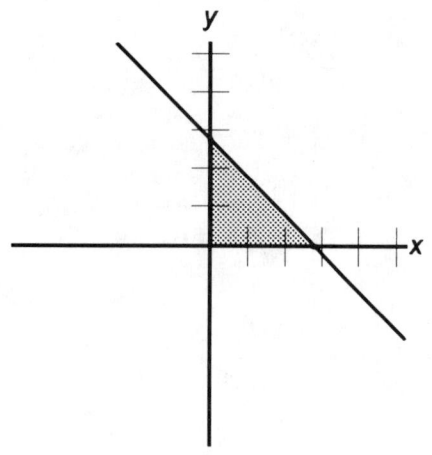

Figure 4.4 The graph of all points satisfying $x \geq 0$, $y \geq 0$, and $x + y \leq 1100$. That is, all points shaded in both Figures 4.1 and 4.3.

The other two constraints will further cut down the size of this region.

The next constraint, $6x + 4y \leq 4800$, is graphed in a manner similar to the way we handled $x + y \leq 1100$. That is, we first graph the boundary by plotting its intercepts, then we decide which side of the boundary that we want to shade in.

The boundary is plotted by graphing the equation $6x + 4y = 4800$. Again, in order to get the intercepts we let both x and y be zero:

x-intercept: Let $y = 0$. Solving the resulting equation gives $x = 800$. The point $(800, 0)$ is on the graph.

y-intercept: Let $x = 0$. Solving the resulting equation gives $y = 1200$. The point $(0, 1200)$ is on the graph.

The boundary of the inequality $6x + 4y \leq 4800$ is shown in Figure 4.5.

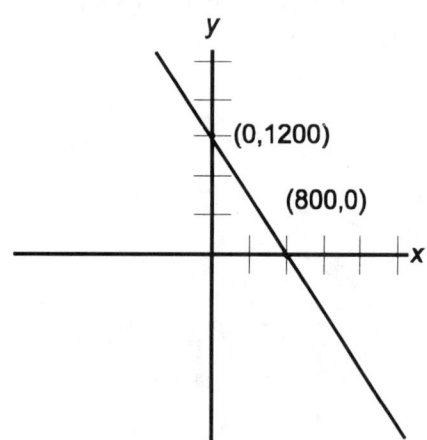

Figure 4.5 The graph of $6x + 4y = 4800$; this is the boundary of $6x + 4y \leq 4800$.

Again, the question of whether to shade above or below this boundary comes up. We answer this question as before, using the point $(0,0)$ as the test point. We again find that it is appropriate to shade in those points below the boundary. This is illustrated in Figure 4.6.

132 Chapter Four: **OPERATIONS RESEARCH AND GAME THEORY**

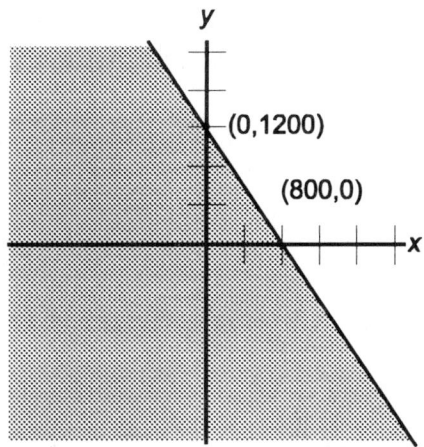

Figure 4.6 The graph of $6x + 4y \leq 4800$.

How does this affect the region that we are interested in? In order for a point to be under consideration it must satisfy all of the conditions that we've looked at so far. That is, it must satisfy $x \geq 0$, $y \geq 0$, $x + y \leq 1100$, and $6x + 4y \leq 4800$. In order for all of these conditions to be satisfied the point must be shaded in both Figure 4.4 (so that we are sure that $x \geq 0$, $y \geq 0$, and $x + y \leq 1100$), and in Figure 4.6 (so that we can be sure that $6x + 4y \leq 4800$). Taking all of this into consideration gives Figure 4.7, shown below.

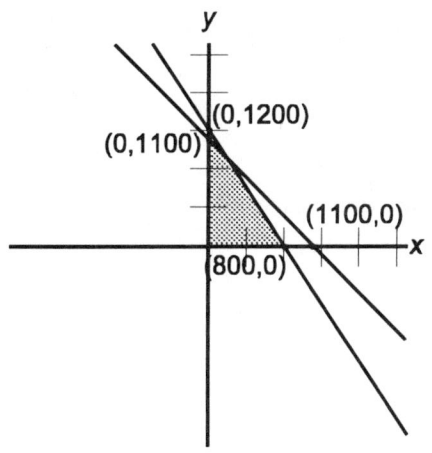

Figure 4.7 The graph of all points shaded in both Figure 4.4 and Figure 4.6.

We're almost there! We still need to consider the last constraint, $45x + 18y \leq 28800$. Treating this as we have the other two inequalities, the boundary is formed by the graph of $45x + 18y = 28800$. This is again graphed by plotting its intercepts.

x–intercept: Let $y = 0$. Solving the resulting equation gives $x = 640$. The point $(640, 0)$ is on the graph.

y–intercept: Let $x = 0$. Solving the resulting equation gives $y = 1600$. The point $(0, 1600)$ is on the graph.

The graph of the boundary is shown in Figure 4.8.

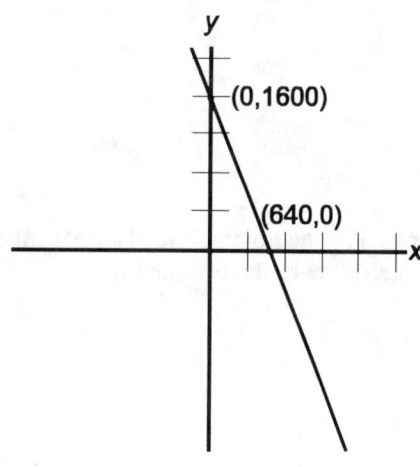

Figure 4.8 The graph of $45x + 18y = 28800$; this is the boundary of $45x + 18y \leq 28800$.

Once again, we use $(0,0)$ as the test point and we determine that the points below this boundary need to be shaded in. This the graph of $45x + 18y \leq 28800$ is as indicated in Figure 4.9.

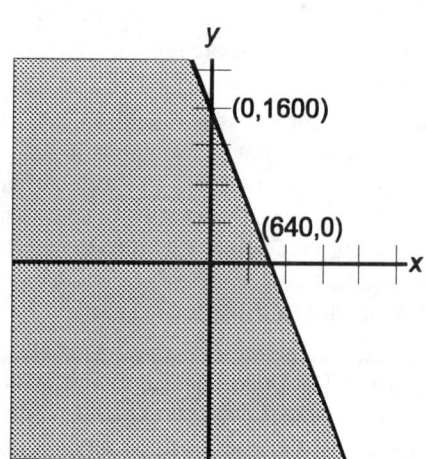

Figure 4.9 The graph of $45x + 18y \leq 28800$.

Putting this together with the information that we had before, we find that all of the constraints will be satisfied only if a point is shaded both in Figure 4.7 and in Figure 4.9. The points which satisfy all of the required conditions are graphed below, in Figure 4.10.

134   Chapter Four: **OPERATIONS RESEARCH AND GAME THEORY**

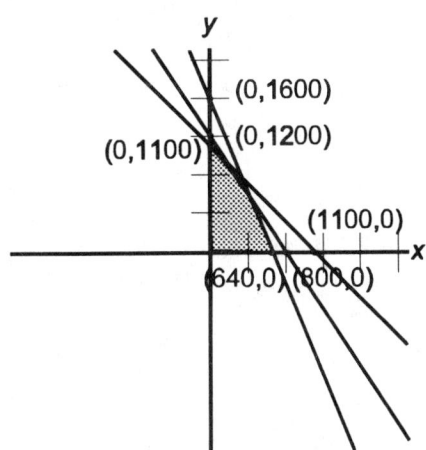

Figure 4.10 The points shaded satisfy all of the constraints in the problem.

The region shaded in Figure 4.10 is called the *feasible region* for the problem. These shaded points represent all values of x and y which satisfy all of the constraints of the problem. We now, at least, can start to get some idea of what a solution to the problem would mean. *Each point (x,y) in the feasible region has a corresponding profit associated with it.* This profit is computed by simply taking the x and y values of the point and substituting them into the formula for P (that is, the formula for profit). The problem can now be formulated as follows: Of all of the points (x,y) in the feasible region, which point will yield the highest value for P?

Although we've done quite a bit in analysis of the problem, it still seems as though we are quite a long way from determining it's solution. After all, there are still an infinite number of points in the feasible region which could yield the maximal profit. If we had to check each one of these to see which gives the best possible solution, we would be no better off than when we started. Actually, once we know one more fact we will see that we won't have to check an infinite number of points after all. In fact, it turns out that we are now quite close to finding the solution that we seek.

The breakthrough in this particular type of problem is contained in the following fact:

THE CORNER POINT RULE: If a linear programming problem has an optimal solution (that is, a maximum or minimum for the objective solution satisfying all of the given constraints), then that optimal solution must occur at a "corner point" of the feasible region. (Note that the same optimal solution may be attained at other points in the feasible region.)

Redrawing the feasible region we see that there are exactly five corner points (labeled P_1 through P_5) for this region (see Figure 4.11). These are the only five points that we will need to check in order to find the maximal value of P. (The minimal value of P in the region will also occur at one of these five points.)

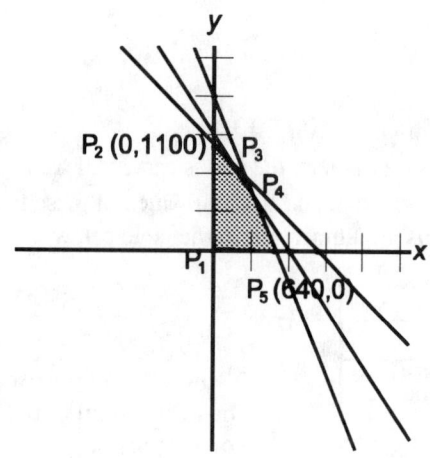

Figure 4.11 The feasible region with all corner points identified.

In this case the five points that we need to check are:

$P_1 = (0,0)$
$P_2 = (0,1100)$
P_3: The point of intersection of the line defined by $x + y = 1100$ and the line defined by $6x + 4y = 4800$.
P_4: The point of intersection of the line defined by $6x + 4y = 4800$ and the line defined by $45x + 18y = 28800$.
$P_5 = (640,0)$

Note that in some problems you may have to deal with more than five corner points, while in other problems you may need to check fewer than five. The important thing to understand here is that the reason that this procedure works is that there will only be a finite number of points that need to be checked. *The "corner point rule" has reduced the number of points that could satisfy the problem from an infinite number to a finite number.*

In order to determine which of these five corner points represents the maximal profit we will need to know the coordinates for all five of these points. In this case that will mean that we need to find the coordinates of points P_3 and P_4, because we already know the coordinates of the other three points.

To find the coordinates of P_3 we need to find the solution of the following system of two equations with two unknowns:

$$\begin{cases} x + y = 1100 \\ 6x + 4y = 4800 \end{cases}$$

(If you need to refresh your memory, check chapter 3 to review how this is done.) Multiplying both sides of the first equation by -4 and adding the two equations will cause the y terms to drop out and we will be able to solve the resulting equation for x. As a result, we find that the x-coordinate of the point of intersection is 200. Substituting this value into either of the original equations and solving for y will give the y-coordinate of the point of intersection. When you do this you will find that $y = 900$. Thus we have determined that P_3 is the point $(200,900)$.

The coordinates of P_4 are found in a similar manner. For that point we need to solve the system

$$\begin{cases} 6x + 4y = 4800 \\ 45x + 18y = 28800 \end{cases}$$

When this is done you will find that P_4 is the point with coordinates $(400, 600)$.

Now that we know the coordinates of all five of the corner points, the rest is easy. All we have to do is substitute the x and y values of each point into the profit function and find out which of these five points gives the maximal value for the profit. The result of this is summarized in the table below.

	Point	Profit
P_1	$(0,0)$	$P = 4x + 3y = 4 \cdot 0 + 3 \cdot 0 = 0$
P_2	$(0,1100)$	$P = 4x + 3y = 4 \cdot 0 + 3 \cdot 1100 = 3300$
P_3	$(200,900)$	$P = 4x + 3y = 4 \cdot 200 + 3 \cdot 900 = 3500$
P_4	$(400,600)$	$P = 4x + 3y = 4 \cdot 400 + 3 \cdot 600 = 3400$
P_5	$(640,0)$	$P = 4x + 3y = 4 \cdot 640 + 3 \cdot 0 = 2560$

Table 4.1 Comparison of the profit at all of the corner points.

Comparing the values of the profit at each of the five corner points we find that the largest value of P, $3500, occurs at point P_3, that is, at the point where $x = 200$ and $y = 900$.

Our problem is finally solved. The operations research team would report to the manager that the company should be producing 200 baseball bats (remember, x represented the number of baseball bats produced) and 900 softball bats per week. The resulting profit to the company, the maximal possible profit that the company can expect, is $3500 per week.

A Minimization Problem — Stocks

A financial consultant is preparing recommendations for a client. The consultant is considering two stocks for purchase, and they have been analyzed in a number of different categories. The result of this analysis has been summarized in the following table.

	Stock #1	Stock #2
Minimum expected growth in stock's value in the next year.	10%	5%
Minimum expected growth in stock's value in the next ten years.	100%	300%
Minimum expected dividend rate.	6%	9%

Table 4.2 Rates of return for the "stocks" problem.

The consultant asks the operations research team to determine the smallest total investment that can be made which will guarantee the following minimum returns:

1. At least $500 growth (that is, increased stock value) in the next year.
2. At least $12000 growth in the next ten years.
3. At least $540 in dividend income per year.

In order to solve this problem, let x be the amount of money invested in stock #1 and y be the amount of money invested in stock #2. The total amount of money invested can then by represented by

the formula $T = x + y$, and our job is to minimize this investment. As in the problem just completed, there are a number of constraints that x and y must satisfy. Getting the inequalities which correspond to these constraints is our first task.

The first restriction on x and y is that they need to generate $500 of increased growth in the value of the stock in the first year. This increased growth comes from the 10% increase in the value of stock #1 (that is, 10% of x, or $.10x$) and the 5% increase in the value of stock #2 (that is, 5% of y, or $.05y$). The total increase, that is, $.10x+.05y$, must add up to at least $500. This gives our first constraint, $.10x+.05y \geq 500$. Since it will be inconvenient to work with decimals in the following analysis, we will eliminate them by multiplying both sides of this inequality by 100. Doing this results in the inequality $10x+5y \geq 50000$.

In a similar manner we get two other constraints, one from the "expected growth over the next ten years" and the other from the annual income generated by the investment (that is, the dividends). These constraints translate into the inequalities $x+3y \geq 12000$ and $.06x+.09y \geq 540$ (which when multiplied through by 100 yields the equivalent inequality $6x+9y \geq 54000$). Remembering that both x and y must be non-negative, this means that the "stocks" problem can be expressed mathematically as follows.

Minimize $T = x + y$
Subject to $x \geq 0, y \geq 0$
            $10x + 5y \geq 50000$
            $x + 3y \geq 12000$
            $6x + 9y \geq 54000$

To solve this problem we proceed just as we did in the "baseball bats" problem. We graph each of the constraints, find the feasible region, and locate its corner points. We then test each of the corner points in the objective function (the formula for T given above) and determine which gives the optimal value (Note that this time we will be attempting to minimize T, but the procedure is the same as before. We will simply keep the corner point that gives the smallest value for T rather than the largest.). The reader should convince herself or himself that the graph given below accurately depicts the feasible regions and the corner points for the problem given above.

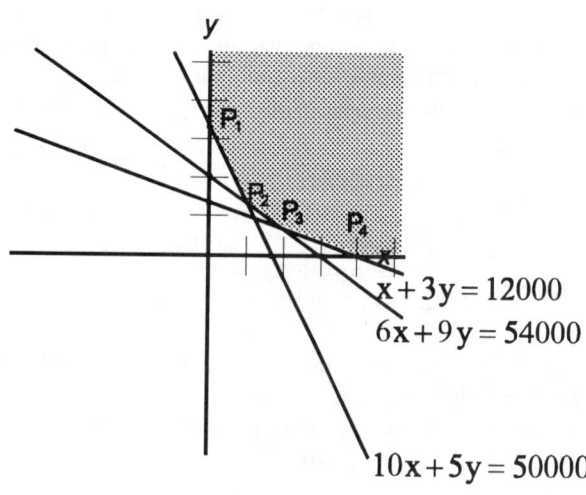

Figure 4.12 The feasible region for the "stocks" problem. Each interval represents 3000 units.

This feasible region contains four corner points. The following table summarizes the value of T at each of these corner points.

	Point	Value of T
P_1	(0,1000)	$T = x + y = 0 + 10000 = 10000$
P_2	(3000,4000)	$T = x + y = 3000 + 4000 = 7000$
P_3	(6000,2000)	$T = x + y = 6000 + 2000 = 8000$
P_4	(12000,0)	$T = x + y = 12000 + 0 = 12000$

Table 4.3 Value of the investment at each of the corner points.

An inspection of this table shows that a minimum investment of $7000 would satisfy all of the conditions of the problem if we invest $3000 in stock #1 and $4000 in stock #2.

The Simplex Method

In concluding this section we would like to point out that the procedure which has been demonstrated here may give considerable insight into how Linear Programming problems are set up and the type of situations that these techniques are useful in, but this procedure cannot be carried out in the problems faced by managers in real life situations. For instance, in the first example of this section we investigated what is called a *product mix* problem for a company that made two products. In a real–world problem we probably would not be dealing with a situation where only two products were competing for the company's resources, but the company would probably have many products drawing on their assets. This changes the problem significantly, because we would no longer be able to rely on graphs in the solution of the problem. Remember, each of the axes represented one of the items in the product mix. What would you do if you had three or more items in your product mix?

Because of this, the real–world problems which are studied and solved by large companies require more advanced techniques. One of the earliest of these methods, the *Simplex Method*, was introduced by George Dantzig in 1947. This powerful method allows operations research teams with access to large computers to solve problems that are similar to the ones we solved, but which deal with a large number of variables and constraints. Recent research has focused on finding new methods which allow for the solution of larger problems (that is, problems containing more variables), solving problems faster, and solving those relatively few problems which caused trouble for the simplex method.

The product mix problem solved earlier in this section is only one of many types of problems that can be solved with linear programming techniques. Other types of problems which can be attacked with linear programming include:

1. Transportation problems (see section 4.1)
2. Scheduling problems (also called assignment problems) (see section 4.1)
3. Advertising problems (What mix of advertising resources should be used to maximize your product's impact on the market?)
4. Diversity of investment portfolio (What mix of financial instruments — stocks, bonds, notes, etc. — should be purchased to maximize your return and/or minimize your risk?)
5. Blending of chemicals (This problem is common in the petroleum industry, the making of perfume, the production of detergents, and in many other industries.)

> *Small Group Exercise*
>
> Algebraically find each of the four corner points in the "stocks problem." Graph each of the constraints in the problem, and verify that the Figure 4.12 accurately depicts the feasible region.

> *Questions to Discuss*
>
> 1. Summarize in your own words the procedure for graphing a linear inequality.
>
> 2. Summarize in your own words the procedure for graphing a model's feasible region.
>
> 3. What is the corner point rule, and what important role does it play in the graphical solution of linear programming problems?
>
> 4. Algebraically solve the system of equations which determine the point P_4 in the baseball bats problem.
>
> 5. Write a brief explanation of the second and third constraints in the "Stocks" Problem.
>
> 6. Graph each or the individual inequalities in the "Stocks" problem. Give a brief explanation of why the feasible region looks as it does.
>
> 7. The point $(3600, 2800)$ is at the intersection of the boundaries of two of the constraints in the "Stocks" problem (namely $10x + 5y \geq 50000$ and $x + 3y \geq 12000$). Explain why this point is not considered in finding the minimum value of T.
>
> 8. Algebraically find the coordinates of each of the points P_1, P_2, P_3, P_4 in the "Stocks" problem.
>
> 9. Select other points at random in the feasible region for the "Stocks" problem. Calculate the value of T for each of the points you selected. Based on this evidence, convince yourself that we really did find the minimum value of T by looking only at corner points.

4.4 Other Operations Research Techniques

Although it's not possible to spend as much time on other operations research techniques as we have on linear programming, we can at least take a quick glance at some of the other procedures used to analyze utilization problems.

Queuing Theory

Queuing theory deals with the analysis of the amount of time people need to wait before being served. Queues are encountered just about everywhere: at the supermarket, the gas station, the post

office, the restaurant, and the video rental store just to name a few. When you call your local cable television company and are put on hold until a customer service representative can talk with you, you are put on a queue. Similarly, when you are lined up (the British would say "queued up") outside of a movie theater waiting to purchase your ticket you are also on a queue.

The analysis of queues has become extremely important in modern business. For example, a bank with too few cashiers on duty during lunch hour runs the risk of losing customers who aren't willing or able to waste time on long lines at that time. One the other hand, if too many cashiers are on duty at that time, the bank is paying employees who are not involved in profitable work for them. Similarly, a company which deals in taking phone orders may have to hire more operators if its callers have to be put on hold for long periods of time. The customer "on hold" is on line in the same sense as the banking customer waiting on line for service.

In a sense, the supermarket manager is employing a primitive form of queuing theory when he or she makes up the schedule for coverage by cashiers for the week. Although the store manager may employ more common sense and experience than mathematics in making up their schedule, the connection is clear. If he schedules too many cashiers for a given hour they will have nothing to do — but they will still have to be paid. If he schedules too few cashiers, the long lines that result may cause his store to lose business, either now or in the future, when prospective customers decide to go elsewhere.

The analysis of queues has become highly technical. The examination of random events (people walk into stores for service in a somewhat random manner) leads to elaborate formulas for things like "the average waiting time on line," "the number of customers served per hour" and the like. This data is then used to assist managers in making their manpower decisions.

Sinking Funds

Organizations, like families, need to plan for the future. If a company owns a factory whose machines will wear out or be outdated at a certain point in time, they need to be ready to replace these machines in a timely manner. This is where the sinking fund comes into play. Managers make decisions concerning the amount of money that needs to be saved each period (week, month, quarter, whatever) in order to *replace* and *maintain* their equipment. These decisions depend on the time available before the equipment will become obsolete, the rate of return they can get on their investments, and the projected cost of the replacement equipment. If we are concerned with repairing machinery, another variable needs to be considered — some kind of average time period between breakdowns. If the breakdown of a machine is due to the failure of a part, this problem can be thought of as the replacement of that part, so in some sense this "maintenance problem" can be thought of as a special case of the "replacement problem."

Forecasting

Forecasting is the name given to the highly specialized field which concerns itself with predictions in the world of finance. Rather than getting too technical, an example may make the job of the forecaster clearer.

In planning its investments for the coming month, a commercial bank needs to know how much money its investors are going to be depositing this month (in certificates of deposit, savings accounts, and so on). The amount of money its depositors will be investing depends on factors like the interest rate and other services the bank is offering its customers. This, in turn, depends on things like the interest rate that the Federal Reserve System is offering and the rate at neighboring institutions. Actually, these problems get very complex, with many variables requiring consideration.

The forecaster, in helping the manager to make his or her decision, has many mathematical tools at his disposal, such as spread sheets and computer simulation (see chapter 8). However, it also must be understood that there are times when forecasters venture into the unknown, because changes in the

economic situation may lead to conditions that no longer satisfy the assumptions built into their models. This means that they need to be continually testing their predictions against current conditions to see how well their predictions are holding up.

Conclusion

There's no doubt that managers now have more tools at their disposal than ever before to help them make their decisions. The few mentioned in this section are only the beginning, as mathematicians, scientists, and managers continue to work together to develop new techniques for use in the future.

Questions to Discuss

1. List some situations where an understanding of queuing theory could be helpful.

2. Discuss how the concept of a sinking fund could be important to a newly married couple.

3. Why are forecasters constantly checking how well their predictions compare with actual market conditions?

4.5 The Theory of Games

As mentioned in section 4.1, modern game theory was essentially founded by John von Neumann, a mathematician, and Oskar Morgenstern, an economist, in 1944 with their publication of *The Theory of Games and Economic Behavior*. Their insight was to identify that economic situations and certain games had three important common features. These three features were:

1. Conflicting interest
2. Incomplete information
3. The interplay of logic and chance

By studying and exploiting these similarities they realized that they could gain an insight into economic situations by analyzing the strategic features of games. Since then game theorists have taken this one step further, and they have incorporated the important strategic features of real-life situations into games which they have developed for the express purpose of analyzing the real-life problems. This type of activity is now commonly employed not only in economics, but also in military science, psychology, sociology, politics, and other areas of decision making. Figure 4.13 illustrates this process. The real-life conflict is studied to determine the important features under consideration. These important features, and the way they interact with each other, are then reproduced in the game, or model, which is being constructed in order to analyze the conflict. After the game has been put together, different strategies can be tested to see which of these strategies leads to the most favorable outcomes in the model. Hopefully this will enable the game theorist to recommend a course of action in the real-life situation by interpreting the play of the game. If the model is complex, the play of the game could be simulated by a computer in order to identify the possible (or probable) outcomes of the different strategies. Replaying a game with the same strategy many times will enable the game theorist to estimate how often that strategy will be successful in real life and the worst possible outcome if things should go wrong.

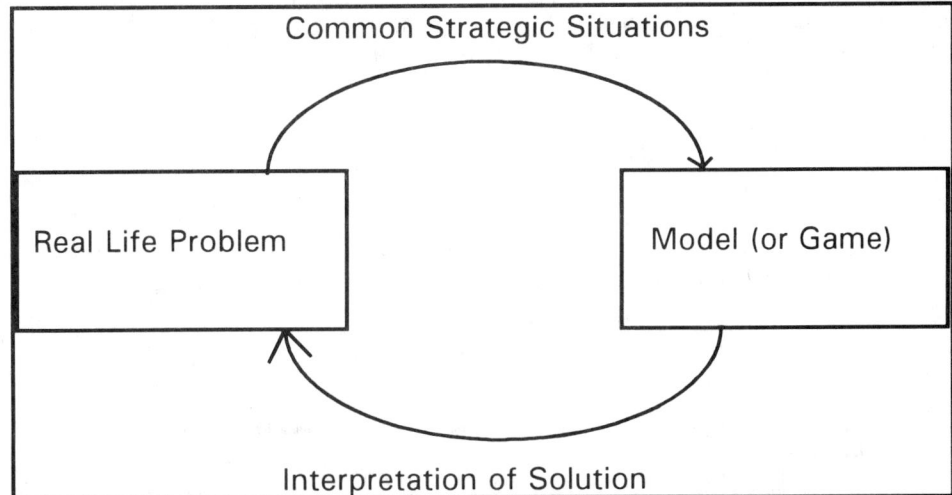

Figure 4.13 Strategis situations are extracted from "real–life" and built into games; solutions are extracted from games and employed in "real–life."

One important pitfall that must be understood is that the game's assumptions play an important role in determining whether the results be useful to the manager. If important assumptions are ignored or downplayed by the model, the game may not be faithful to the way things will actually play out in the real world, and the usefulness of the model would then be questionable.

The Toothpaste Example

As an example, assume that a toothpaste company is interested in increasing its share of the market. They wish to test the strategy that they are considering before putting it into operation. For example, they may be contemplating a price cut of 10% in the hopes that they will make up the difference with increased sales. By considering the way customers and competitors will respond to their action, a game can be designed and the strategy can be replayed many times in a computer simulation. They may find that in 60% of the simulations their company increases profits significantly, in 15% of the simulations their profits stay approximately constant, and in 25% of the cases they lose profits. In 10% of the cases the losses are so bad that their company is put out of business. They now need to decide if the gain that they are hoping for is worth the risk they are taking.

The "Toothpaste Example" points out the difficulties that we are dealing with in the application of game theory. One of the most important of these difficulties is the *incomplete information* that we have at our disposal in planning our strategy. How will customers react to our price decrease? Will they stay loyal to their current brand, or will they switch? Possibly even more important is the question of how competitors will respond to the challenge. If our competitors all follow our lead and also drop their prices by 10%, we've lost any advantage that we may have hoped to gain. It is because of this incomplete information that this problem would be classified as "game theory."

Situations such as the one described above are replayed on a daily basis by military leaders in planning campaigns, by politicians as they plan their international policies, and even by baseball managers as they plan their next play. In all cases the decision makers need to take into consideration a number of different strategic responses by their "opponent," and decide what they think their best course of action will be.

Another example from a familiar game may clarify how von Neumann and Morgenstern discovered the three important common features of games and economic situations. In a card game like

poker there are certainly conflicting interests as each player strives to win as much as possible. There certainly is incomplete information in poker, since players generally don't know for sure the strength of their opponents' hands. Finally, the interplay of logic and chance is also very apparent here. Players have no control over how good their hands will be (unless they cheat), since the cards are dealt randomly. However, players do have strategy at their disposal. They can "fold" if their hand is bad, or "bluff" (make a high bet even when they have a weak hand in hopes of convincing their opponents that their cards are really better than they are so that the opponents will drop out). They could also "sandbag" (make a low bet on a powerful hand to try to convince the other players that their hand is weaker than it really is). This *strategy* is what makes poker a game in the technical sense. Players have at least some control over the outcome of the game, but chance and their opponents play a large part too.

Chess, baseball, Tic–Tac–Toe, and blackjack are all games in the technical sense because all require *strategy*, all feature *incomplete information* (For example, what strategy will your opponent be using?), and all contain *conflicting interests*.

In the next section we will be looking at some special games, most of which were invented by mathematicians — often in an attempt to solve a particular problem. Unfortunately, most games seem to fit into two categories: games that are very difficult (or impossible) to analyze, such as chess and poker; and games that are very easy to analyze, such as Tic–Tac–Toe. Hopefully, the games considered in the next section will not be so hard or easy as to be boring, and yet will still illustrate what strategy and luck are and how they interrelate with each other.

Questions to Discuss

1. What are the three common features connecting games and economic situations?

2. Give some military or political situations where a knowledge of game theory would be helpful.

3. Explain why games such as poker and craps are games in the mathematical sense.

4.6 Some Examples of Games

The complete analysis of games is something that many mathematicians have concerned themselves with since von Neumann and Morgenstern introduced the subject. Many books, such as the classics *The Compleat Strategist* by J.D. Williams (reprinted by Dover Publications in 1986) and *On Numbers and Games* by John Horton Conway (Academic Press, 1976) can be consulted if you are interested in the type of analysis done by mathematicians in order to evaluate games. We will take a different approach, looking at a few games selected because they satisfy some subjective criteria. These few games seem to be reasonably interesting, exhibit some enlightened strategy, or were invented to tackle some interesting but apparently unrelated problem. No attempt has been made to select games that represent any kind of "typical sample."

Reverse Tic–Tac–Toe

Although the game of Tic–Tac–Toe is such a simple game that two rational players (that is, players who always make the best possible move) would always play to a draw, a variation of this game is a bit more interesting. In the game of Reverse Tic–Tac–Toe two players alternate in putting their symbol,

either X or O, into a regular Tic–Tac–Toe board. As Conway does in the book *On Numbers and Games*, we will refer to the two players as "L" and "R" (for "left" and "right").

The difference between Reverse Tic–Tac–Toe and regular Tic–Tac–Toe is that in Reverse Tic–Tac–Toe the first player to put three symbols in a row *loses*.

Although once the players know the best strategy for this game it no longer retains its interest, this strategy is probably not at all obvious unless the players have some familiarity with the theory of games. Before reading the analysis below you might want to try the game with a friend. It's surprising how often one player is forced into the undesirable position of *having* to complete three in a row on their move. Even if you manage to win or draw a game, unless you know the best strategy, the amount of thought that needs to be put in before making a move is also surprising. By the way, this is called an *avoidance game* — the players are trying to avoid a certain losing condition — in this case the completion of three–in–a–row.

Analysis of the Game

In many games one player or the other will have an advantage. For example, one might say that in the game of regular Tic–Tac–Toe the first player to move has an advantage. In this case the first player does not have a decided advantage, because no matter where the first player puts his or her X, the second player always has a strategy at his or her disposal that guarantees at least a draw. But the first player still has some kind of advantage, because even if he or she plays a poor first move, the second player will still not be able to force a win. The second player has no such cushion — any slip by the player number two will always lead to defeat if the first player follows it up with the best moves. Of course the advantage here really amounts to nothing, because if two players master the simple strategy of the game there will never be a winner. Similarly, in chess it is generally accepted that White (who by the rules is always the first to move) has an advantage. Here the strategy is much more complicated than in Tic–Tac–Toe, but there is still no forced win for White and many games end in draws or in wins for Black.

One of the appeals of Reverse Tic–Tac–Toe is that one could argue that the first player is at a disadvantage. In fact, it turns out that the first player must play very carefully just to achieve a draw. A bit of reflection clarifies this; if the game is carried out to its conclusion, L (the first player) will have placed *five* X's on the board, while R would have placed four O's. If there is a line of three symbols anywhere on the board, it would more likely be X's rather than O's simply because there would be more X's than O's on the board.

This means that L (the first player) must play much more carefully than R does. Fortunately, however, there is a simple strategy that allows L to force a draw. Once the players know this strategy, the game ceases to be interesting except for the fact that variations on this strategy are useful in other games.

The first move in L's drawing strategy is to place his or her X in the center square, which we will call square #5 (see Figure 4.14 for a labeling of the squares). This may seem surprising since many consider this to be a good move in regular Tic–Tac–Toe, but it turns out to be the *only move that L can play* which will guarantee that he or she will be able to force a draw! That is, if L makes any other first move, then R will always be able to force a win (that is, to force L to place three X's in a row). If you are interested, the article by Daniel I. A. Cohen entitled "The Solution of a Simple Game" in the September 1972 issue of *Mathematics Magazine* proves this fact.

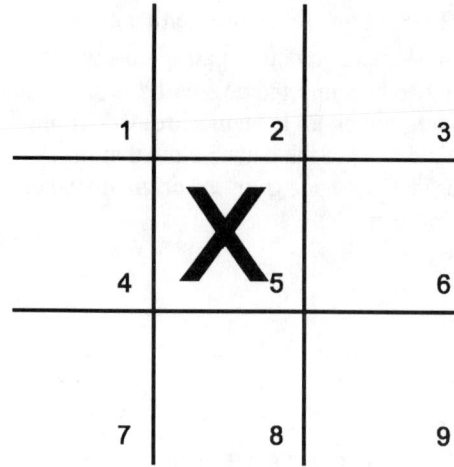

Figure 4.14 The numbering of the squares for Tic–Tac–Toe.

Once L has played in the center, the drawing strategy is easy to understand. After each of R's moves, L replies by placing his or her X in the box that is the mirror image of the one where R placed his or her O. (Squares 1 and 9 are mirror images of each other, as are 2 and 8, 3 and 7, and 4 and 6). By following this strategy it will be impossible for L to place three X's in a row, unless R has placed three O's in a row first.

This "symmetrical strategy" turns out to be useful in many other games. When playing new games that are unfamiliar, it is often wise for the first player to consider a similar strategy. That is, first play to the middle (If the game you are playing has one!), then copy your opponents moves through symmetry.

The Game of Sim

In his book *Knotted Doughnuts and other Mathematical Entertainments*, the respected author Martin Gardner states that the game of Sim is named after a mathematician names Gustavus J. Simmons, the first person to completely analyze the game with the help of a computer. All that is needed to play the game is a piece of paper and two different colored pens or pencils.

Six dots are drawn on the piece of paper forming a regular hexagon. (Although the actual position of the dots on the paper is not important, if you put them in the form of a regular hexagon it may be easier to follow what follows). See Figure 4.15.

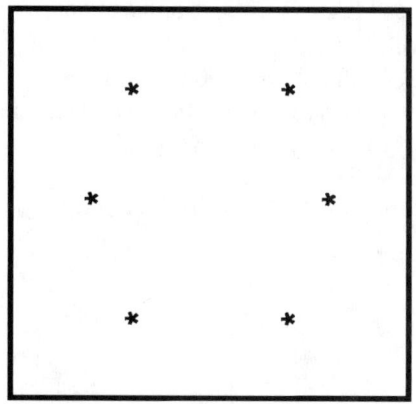

Figure 4.15 The game board for Sim.

The play of the game proceeds as follows: For his or her first turn, L chooses either colored pencil and connects any two of the dots with that color. R then connects any other pair of dots with the other color. Play continues in this way, each player connecting two unconnected dots with his or her color when his or her turn comes up. Play ends when one of the players completes a "monochromatic triangle," that is, a triangle all of one color. The person who does this is the loser of the game. Note that in completing a monochromatic triangle, only triangles whose vertices are made from the original six points on the game board are considered. See Figures 4.16 and 4.17 for examples.

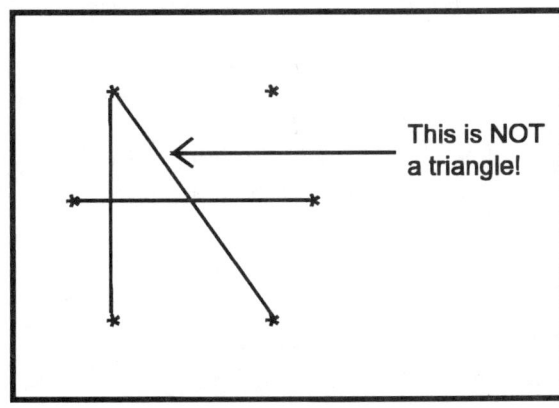

Figure 4.16 An example of a non-triangle. Its vertices are not all from the original six points.

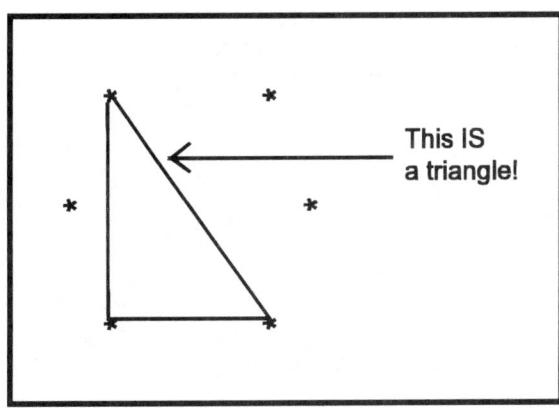

Figure 4.17 An example of a triangle. Its vertices are all from the original six points.

Simmons' analysis of this game established the fact that that this game could not end in a draw — that is, one of the two competing players would eventually be forced to form a triangle of his or her color, thus losing the game. Simmons' analysis did not determine which of the two players, L or R, had the advantage, although it has since been proved that the second player will always be able to win the game if both players always make the best moves when it is their turn. The strategy that the second player should follow in order to insure a win is not as easy to describe as it is in the game of Reverse Tic-Tac-Toe.

Note that Sim is also an example of an avoidance game. In this case both players are trying to avoid the completion of a triangle of one color.

A Variation of Sim

Various variations of Sim have been played. In one variation, L joins any two points with either color, then when R moves he or she does the same – possibly selecting the same color as L. That is, *every* turn in the game consists of two parts: First *selecting a color*, then *connecting* any *two* unconnected *points* with that color. At any turn the color you select is not dependent on any previous color choices either by you or by your opponent. Again, the first person to complete a monochromatic triangle loses, and again *the game cannot end in a draw*. This alternate version of the game is the one referred to in problem #2 at the end of the section.

For other variations of Sim (including one variation that starts with 17 points) see Martin Gardner's article in *The Scientific American* of November 1977. In fact Gardner's series "Mathematical Games", which ran in *The Scientific American* from January 1957 to December 1981, is a source for may interesting mathematical games.

The Game of Domineering

Domineering is another of the games described by John Horton Conway in his book *On Numbers and Games*, where he refers to it simply as "a game with dominoes." The game was invented by Göran Anderson.

A rectangular board is ruled into squares (so in effect we have a checkerboard, but the number of rows and columns are not specified). L and R alternate moves. When it is L's turn to move he or she picks up a domino (which is sized so that it covers exactly two squares of the game board) and covers two squares on the board. *L must place his or her domino vertically.* When it's R's move he or she also picks up a domino and covers two squares of the game board, but *R's domino must be placed horizontally.* Dominoes may not overlap. A player who has no available legal moves at his or her turn is the loser.

Without attempting to fully analyze this game, it's clear that as the game progresses various regions of the board separate themselves out as "subgames." A player can gain an advantage in the game as a whole by analysis of these subregions. For example, the region illustrated in Figure 4.18 affords R an advantage of two moves over L, since R can make two legal moves in this region while L cannot make any.

Figure 4.18 Possible "sub–game" from Domineering.

Of course if R decides to cover the two center squares of this region with a domino he or she has made a serious mistake. R will no longer have the second move at his or her disposal, and will lose a bit of the advantage that he or she held.

The region shown in Figure 4.19 shows another possible region from a Domineering game. If it's L's move, this region allows him or her two possible legal moves, and again one is better than the other.

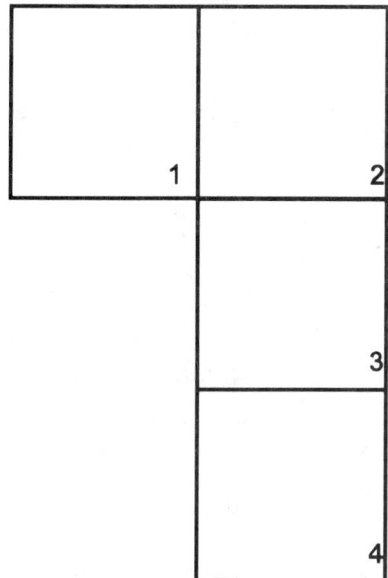

Figure 4.19 Possible "subgame" from Domineering.

If L elects to cover squares 3 and 4 he or she leaves a possible move open to R. On the other hand, if L elects to cover squares 2 and 3 he or she leaves no possible moves open to R in this region, and R is one move closer to defeat.

Games as Numbers

As mentioned in section 4.1, there is a technical sense in which games can be considered to be numbers (This is where the mathematician gets interested!). Although it is impossible to get into the details of what this means here, we can at least give some idea of what it means to "add" games. Suppose we consider two games, such as Sim and Domineering (For the purposes of this discussion, assume that we are playing the second variation of Sim, the one where players may re-select their color each time they make a move.). What would their sum be? The sum of these two games is defined to be the new game with the following rules:

1. L and R alternate turns.
2. A turn consists of a player selecting a game and making a move in that game.

In the case of the sum of Sim and Domineering, L would start the game by selecting either the game of Sim or the game of Domineering. If he chose Domineering, he would pick up a domino and place it vertically over two squares of the Domineering game board, while if he chose Sim he would then select a colored pencil and connect two points on the Sim game board. Then it's R's turn. R selects a game – it need not be the same game that L chose — and makes a legal move in the selected game. It's L's turn next, and the whole process starts all over again.

How would you expect this game — the sum of Sim and Domineering — to terminate? Let's say that the players have been making moves in both games, and we have finally reached the point where any move in Sim causes the player who made that move to form a monochromatic triangle. Since making a move in that game will cause either player to lose, they should now choose to play only in the Domineering game, placing dominoes on its game board. At some point, one of the players will no longer have any moves left in the Domineering game either, so when it is that player's turn to move he or she

will be forced to go back to the game of Sim. This player will have to be the loser, because the only move available to him will force him to complete a monochromatic triangle.

> ### *Small Group Exercise*
>
> Consider the variation of the game that uses the same rules as the second variation of Sim given in the text, but starts with only five points rather than six. Show that this game could end in a draw if both players always select the best moves.

Questions to Discuss

1. (The birth of Sim) Sim was invented to solve a problem from the branch of mathematics known as combinatorics (counting techniques). This was problem #E1321 in *The American Mathematical Monthly* of June–July 1958:

    "Prove that at a gathering of *any six people*, some three of them are either *mutual* acquaintances or *mutual* strangers to one another."

    If the six people in question are represented by dots which are connected by (say) a red line if the dots represent acquainted people and by a blue line if the dots represent strangers, explain how what you know about Sim solves this problem.

2. Using your own words, write out a description of how games are added.

3. The game of "Frogs and Toads" is played on a board that looks like the one pictured in Figure 4.20.

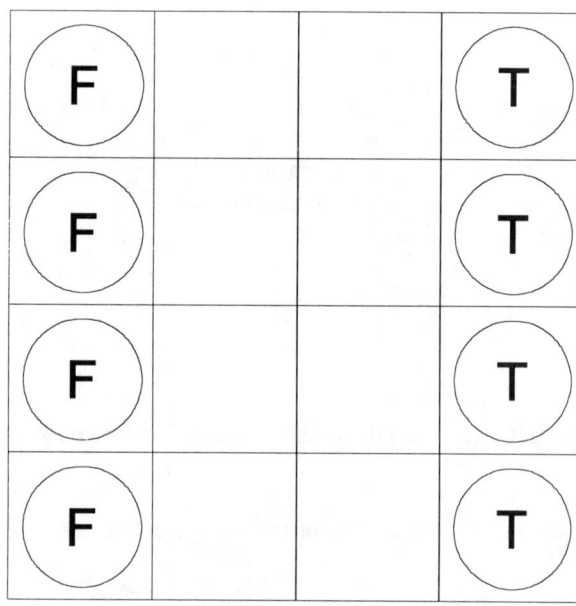

Figure 4.20 The game board for "Frogs and Toads."

The circles containing the F's and T's depict movable markers that represent frogs and toads, respectively. The F markers are controlled by L and move to the right only, while the T markers are controlled by R and only move left. A move consists of moving one of your reptiles in the indicated direction, or, if the square you wish to move to is already occupied, jumping over your opponent's reptile on that square to the next square. Your opponent's piece is not removed if you jump over it. *The first player who can't move loses.*

Describe the sum of the game "Frogs and Toads" and Sim. How would you expect this game to end?

4. How would you attempt to define the sum of three games? Give an example to illustrate your definition.

4.7 Chapter Review

Important Terms to Know

avoidance game	game theory	queuing theory
computer simulation	incomplete information	reverse tic-tac-toe
conflicting interests	interplay of logic and chance	scheduling problem
constraint	linear programming	search patterns
corner point rule	model	Sim
Domineering	objective function	simplex method
feasible region	operations research	sinking funds
forecasting	optimization problem	strategy
Frogs and Toads	product mix	transportation problem

Important Names to Know

Anderson, Goran	Dantzig, George	von Neumann, John
Blackett, P.M.S.	Gardner, Martin	Simmons, Gustavus J.
Borel, Emile	Morgenstern, Oskar	

Review Questions

1. Why do you think it is that managers, rather than operations research teams, have the final say as to whether or not a proposed strategy is implemented?

2. What are the three common features of games and economic situations that led von Neumann and Morgenstern to develop the theory of games?

3. Explain how the corner point rule reduces the work in solving a linear programming problem from checking an infinite number of points to checking a finite number.

4. Contrast operations research with the methods that mathematicians and engineers had previously employed in the solution of real-world problems.

5. Explain why the solution of a problem in a model might not always give a practical solution to the real-world problem under consideration.

Chapter Five

Number Theory

"Mathematics is the queen of the sciences and number theory the queen of mathematics."

Carl Freidrich Gauss

Chapter 5: NUMBER THEORY

Chapter Outline

- **5.0** **Introduction**
- **5.1** **Historical Perspective**
- **5.2** **Some Familiar Classifications of Numbers**
- **5.3** **Prime Numbers**
  - *Prime and Composite Numbers*
  - *Sieve of Eratosthenes*
  - *Twin Primes*
  - *Mersenne Primes*
  - *Goldbach's Conjecture*
- **5.4** **Divisibility Tests**
  - *Factor Trees*
  - *Division*
  - *The Least Common Multiple*
  - *The Greatest Common Factor*
- **5.5** **Other Topics Concerning Primes and Factoring**
  - *Perfect Numbers*
  - *Deficient and Abundant Numbers*
  - *Amicable Numbers*
  - *Magic*
- **5.6** **Number Sequences**
- **5.7** **Arithmetic and Geometric Sequences**
- **5.8** **The Fibonacci Sequence**
- **5.9** **Patterns and Magic Squares**
  - *Pascal's Triangle*
  - *Magic Squares*
- **5.10** **Chapter Review**

5.0 Introduction

We are all familiar with the set of natural numbers, or counting numbers, $\{1,2,3,\cdots\}$. We learned how to count before we entered kindergarten. In grammar school we learned how to add, subtract, multiply, and divide and learned about other sets of numbers, such as the whole numbers and the integers. There is much more to the theory of numbers. There are other types of numbers, properties, and beautiful and useful patterns.

For thousands of years, man has found playing with numbers curious and delightful. As Plato wrote in the *Republic*, "Arithmetic has a very great and elevating effect, compelling the mind to reason about abstract number." Often, someone has posed a number problem or puzzle for amusement. In the process of solving these puzzles, new and very useful properties have been discovered. This is true of Pascal's triangle and the Fibonacci sequence, to name just two. Number theory is the area of mathematics that deals with the properties of numbers, looking for relationships between various numbers. It is a complex and extremely useful area of mathematics, used in such fields as cryptography and computer science.

As Carl Friedrich Gauss (1777–1855) wrote, "Mathematics is the queen of the sciences and number theory the queen of mathematics." Interestingly enough, Gauss has been called the prince of mathematicians.

5.1 Historical Perspective

The Greeks were the first to make a systematic study of the properties of the integers. Among them was a mathematician named Euclid who taught mathematics in Alexandria. He lead a very obscure life, so obscure in fact, that there is no birthplace associated with his name.

He wrote an introductory textbook entitled the *Elements* covering all elementary mathematics of the time (about 300 BC). This work is composed of thirteen books, the fourth of which opens with a list of 22 definitions of various types of numbers, including prime, composite, odd, even, and perfect. The *Elements* is the earliest major Greek mathematics work we have. It is also the most influential textbook of all time.

Much of the language and notation we use today were developed by a great mathematician born in Basel in 1707, Leonhard Euler. He was a broadly trained man, having been trained in theology, medicine, astronomy, physics, and oriental languages besides mathematics. He published more than 500 books and papers in his lifetime, continuing to do research and publish many years after he became blind. He is known as the most successful notation builder of all times.

156 Chapter 5: **NUMBER THEORY**

Since the time of Euclid, the study of patterns and properties of different types of numbers have been of great interest and usefulness to mathematicians. Pierre Fermat, a great French mathematician of the seventeenth century, is credited with setting the modern foundation of number theory.

5.2 Some Familiar Classifications of Numbers

There are some sets of numbers with which we are already familiar. The set of *natural mumbers* is the set $N = \{1,2,3,\cdots\}$. The set of *whole numbers* is the set $W = \{0,1,2,3,\cdots\}$. As you can see, every natural number is a whole number, but not every whole number is a natural number. Thus the set of natural numbers is a proper subset of the set of whole numbers. What element or elements of the whole numbers are not elements of the natural numbers?

Another set of numbers with which we are familiar from algebra is the set of *integers*, $Z = \{\cdots -3,-2,-1,0,1,2,3,\cdots\}$. Are the whole numbers or the natural numbers subsets of the set of integers? Is the set of integers a subset of the whole numbers or the natural numbers?

You also learned about the *real numbers*, which are the numbers on the number line, and the *rational* and *irrational numbers*. Every real number is either a rational number or an irrational number. The Rational numbers can be written in the form $\frac{p}{q}$, where p and q are both integers. The numbers $\frac{11}{7}, -\frac{2}{3}, 0, 6, 0.\overline{3}$ are all rational numbers. The number 6 can be written as $\frac{6}{1}$, so it is rational. The number $0.\overline{3}$ is equivalent to the fraction $\frac{1}{3}$, and thus it is also a rational number.

Sometimes it is not that obvious what the fractional form of a decimal is, such as with $0.\overline{63}$. This is equivalent to the fraction $\frac{7}{11}$ and is therefore a rational number. We would like to have a test which we could use to decide which decimal numbers are rational numbers. The test turns out to be a simple one: Every terminating or repeating decimal can be written as a fraction where the numerator and denominator are integers, and thus is a rational number. For example, the numbers $2.1\overline{34}$ and 7.38956 are both rational numbers.

Those decimal numbers that are nonterminating and nonrepeating are irrational numbers. One such number that you are familiar with is π, which is approximately equal to 3.141592654. It turns out that π is nonterminating (never ending) and nonrepeating (the digits have no pattern). Thus, it is an irrational number. Another example of an irrational number is $\sqrt{7}$, which is approximately equal to 2.645751311. It also is nonrepeating and nonterminating. However the number $\sqrt{169}$ is a rational number because it is equal to 13 which can be expressed as $\frac{13}{1}$.

Exercises

1. Classify each of the following numbers as a natural number, whole number, integer, real number, rational number, or irrational number. (More than one classification may apply.)

(a) 7   (b) −3   (c) 0   (d) $\dfrac{1}{2}$ (e) 3.8

(f) $\sqrt{9}$ (g) $\sqrt{11}$ (h) $2.6\overline{4}$ (i) π

2. Answer "TRUE" or "FALSE" for each of the following.

(a) $N \subset W$ (b) $N \subseteq W$ (c) $W \subset N$ (d) $W \subseteq N$ (e) $N \subset Z$

(f) $N \subseteq Z$ (g) $W \subset Z$ (h) $W \subseteq Z$ (i) $Z \subset N$ (j) $Z \subseteq N$

(k) $Z \subset W$ (l) $Z \subseteq W$

(m) The set of rational numbers is a subset of the set of real numbers.
(n) The set of rational numbers is a proper subset of the set of real numbers.
(o) The set of irrational numbers is a subset of the set of real numbers.
(p) The set of irrational numbers is a proper subset of the set of real numbers.
(q) The set of real numbers is a subset of the set of rational numbers.
(r) The set of real numbers is a proper subset of the set of rational numbers.
(s) The set of real numbers is a subset of the set of irrational numbers.
(t) The set of real numbers is a proper subset of the set of irrational numbers.

3. Explain why every integer is a rational number.

5.3 Prime Numbers

In this section we will restrict ourselves to the set of whole numbers.

We say that the number a is *divisible* by b if b divides into a evenly (that is, with no remainder). In this case we say that "b divides a," and we write $b|a$. For example, 12 is divisible by 4 because 4 divides evenly into 12; that is 12 divided by 4 is 3 with no remainder. This is written as $4|12$. Since 12 is divisible by 4, 4 is said to be a *factor* or *divisor* of 12. The factors of 12 are all those natural numbers that divide into 12 evenly. Thus, the set of factors of 12 is $\{1,2,3,4,6,12\}$ because $1 \times 12 = 12$, $2 \times 6 = 12$, and $3 \times 4 = 12$. What is the set of factors of 30? It is the set $\{1,2,3,4,5,6,10,15,30\}$. The set of factors of a number m contains all natural numbers that divide into m evenly.

The notation $b|a$ means that a is divisible by b. For example we write $3|15$ because $15 \div 3 = 5$. On the other hand, the notation a/b represents "a divided by b." For example $15/3 = 5$.

Now, let's consider what we mean by the *multiples* of 4. Since 4 is a factor of 12, we say that 12 is a multiple of 4. 20 is also a multiple of 4 because 4 divides into 20 evenly, that is, 4 is a factor of 20. This means that the set of multiples of 4 is $\{4,8,12,16,\cdots\}$. We see that every element of this set has 4 as a factor.

Similarly, b is a multiple of a if a is a factor of b, or in other words, if a divides b.

What is the set of multiples of 20? It is the set $\{20,40,60,\cdots\}$.

A natural number is said to be *even* if it is divisible by 2 and *odd* if it is not. The numbers 2, 10, and 120 are all divisible by 2 and are therefore even numbers. The numbers 3, 5, and 17 are not divisible by 2 and are therefore odd numbers.

Prime and Composite Numbers

Now that we understand these terms, we can begin the topic of this section — prime numbers. We will restrict ourselves to the set of natural numbers when dealing with this topic. Recall that the set of natural numbers is the set $N = \{1, 2, 3, \cdots\}$.

> **Definition**: A *prime number* is a natural number that has exactly two distinct factors.

By saying that a prime number has two distinct factors, we mean that the two factors are different numbers. For example, 2 has exactly two distinct factors, 1 and 2, so 2 is prime. The number 7 has exactly two distinct factors, 1 and 7, so 7 is also a prime number. However, the number 4 has three distinct factors, 1, 2, and 4. Thus the number 4 is not prime. This means that the set of prime numbers is the set

> $P = \{2, 3, 5, 7, 11, 13, 17, 19, 23, 29, 31, \cdots\}$

Why did we not include the number 1 as a prime number? We did not include the number 1 because it does not have exactly two distinct factors; it has only one factor, itself. What is the largest prime number? Euclid proved over 2000 years ago that there is no largest prime number by proving the following theorem.

> **Theorem**: There are infinitely many primes.

What do we call numbers such at 4, 6 and 100? They are composite numbers.

> **Definition**: A *composite number* is a number that has at least three distinct factors.

A natural number must have three or more factors to be a composite number. Therefore, none of the prime numbers are composite numbers because they only have two distinct factors each. The number 4 is a composite number because the factors of 4 are 1, 2, and 4. The number 10 is also a composite number because 1, 2, 5, and 10 are its factors. Thus, the set of composite numbers is the set

> $C = \{4, 6, 8, 9, 10, 12, 14, 15, 16, 18, 20, 21, 22, 24, 25, 26, 27, 28, 30, \cdots\}$

As you can see, the number 1 is not a composite number either because it has only one factor, itself. The number 1 is the only natural number that is neither prime nor composite. If we take the union of the set of prime numbers with the set of composite numbers we get the set of natural numbers with the number 1 removed, that is

$$P \cup C = N - \{1\}$$

> ### Question for Discussion
>
> Explain why every even number except the number 2 is a composite number.

Sieve of Eratosthenes

Identifying prime numbers can become a very tedious, time–consuming task. For instance, is the number 817 a prime number or a composite number? One way to approach this problem is to try to divide 817 by each natural number starting with the number 2 until one of the numbers divides 817 or we reach 817. The number 2 does not divide 817, nor does $3,4,5,6,7,8,9,10,11,12,13,14,15,16,$ or 17. If we try 18, it also does not divide 817. But when we try dividing 817 by 19, we find that $817 = 19 \times 43$. Therefore, we know that 817 has at least four factors, that is, $1, 19, 43,$ and 817. Therefore 817 is a composite number.

There is a faster way to determine all of the prime numbers less than a given number. This method was found by a Greek geographer and astronomer named Eratosthenes who lived from about 276 to 192 B.C. It is called the *Sieve of Eratosthenes*.

Suppose you wanted to find all of the prime numbers less than n. You would begin by listing all of the natural numbers from 2 through $n-1$, inclusive. Circle the first prime number on your list, the number 2, and then cross out all of the multiples of 2 (that is, cross out $4,6,8,10,12$, and so on). Now go to the first number on your list that is not crossed out or circled, in this case the number 3. Circle this number and cross out all of its multiples (that is, cross out $6,9,12,15,18$, and so on). Continue in this fashion until the next number not circled or crossed out is greater than the square root of n. For example, if we were finding all of the prime numbers less than $14,400$, we would only need to test for the prime numbers less than 120 because $120 \geq \sqrt{14,400}$. Finally, circle all of the remaining numbers in the sieve that are neither circled nor crossed out. The numbers that are circled are the prime numbers less than n.

Let's consider an example. Suppose we wish to find all of the prime numbers less than 50. We would list the numbers from 2 through 49, inclusive, as shown below in Table 5.1. We begin by circling the number two and crossing out the multiples of two that are not circled, that is, $4, 6, 8,$ and so on.

② 3 ~~4~~ 5 ~~6~~ 7 ~~8~~ 9 ~~10~~
11 ~~12~~ 13 ~~14~~ 15 ~~16~~ 17 ~~18~~ 19 ~~20~~
21 ~~22~~ 23 ~~24~~ 25 ~~26~~ 27 ~~28~~ 29 ~~30~~
31 ~~32~~ 33 ~~34~~ 35 ~~36~~ 37 ~~38~~ 39 ~~40~~
41 ~~42~~ 43 ~~44~~ 45 ~~46~~ 47 ~~48~~ 49

Table 5.1 Step one: The number two is circled, then all multiples of two are crossed out.

Next, we take the first uncircled number, three, and we circle it. All other multiples of this number are then crossed out, so we would cross out $6, 9, 12, 15,$ and so on. (See Table 5.2, below.) Note that some of these multiples of three were already crossed out when we crossed out the multiples of two.

160   Chapter 5: NUMBER THEORY

```
②③ 4̸  5  6̸  7  8̸  9̸ 1̸0̸
11 1̸2̸ 13 1̸4̸ 1̸5̸ 1̸6̸ 17 1̸8̸ 19 2̸0̸
2̸1̸ 2̸2̸ 23 2̸4̸ 25 2̸6̸ 2̸7̸ 2̸8̸ 29 3̸0̸
31 3̸2̸ 3̸3̸ 3̸4̸ 35 3̸6̸ 37 3̸8̸ 3̸9̸ 4̸0̸
41 4̸2̸ 43 4̸4̸ 4̸5̸ 4̸6̸ 47 4̸8̸ 49
```

Table 5.2 Step two: The number three is circled, then all multiples of three are crossed out.

We now repeat this process by circling the number five and crossing out its multiples (that is, we cross out 10, 15, 20, 25, and so on, unless they already have been crossed out). Finally, we perform the procedure once more, circling the number seven and crossing out all of its multiples. We can stop at this point, since the next number to be checked is eleven, which is bigger than $\sqrt{50}$. We now circle all of the numbers that are not circled or crossed out. Table 5.3 below shows the result of this process. The circled numbers in this Table are the prime numbers less than 50.

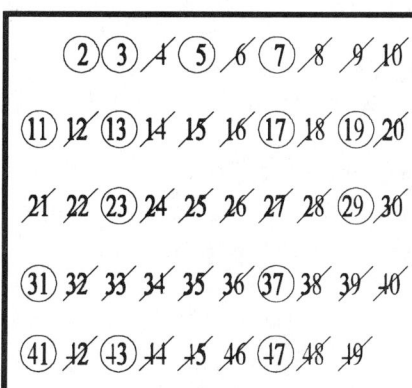

Table 5.3 The circled numbers are the primes less than fifty.

Note that every number in the final sieve is either circled or crossed out, and all of the primes are circled.

Although you may consider this method to be time consuming and tedious, it is much more efficient than the first method that we studied. Today computers are used to find very, very large prime numbers.

Twin Primes

Twin primes are two prime numbers that are exactly two units apart. Thus, if n and $n+2$ are both prime numbers, they are twin primes. The numbers 3 and 5 are both prime and are two units apart, that is, $3+2=5$. Thus, 3 and 5 are twin primes. Another pair of twin primes is 5 and 7. As you consider greater and greater numbers, the occurrence of twin primes becomes fewer and farther apart.

Mersenne Primes

Father Marin Mersenne was an amateur mathematician who lived from 1588 to 1648. He studied numbers of the form $2^p - 1$ where p is prime, and found that it was often the case that $2^p - 1$ was prime when p was. There are, however, cases when p is prime but $2^p - 1$ is not. For example, the number 67 is prime, yet $2^{67} - 1$ is not a prime number. This was shown by the mathematician Frank Cole in 1903.

Because of his interest in questions such as these, when both p and $2^p - 1$ are prime the number $2^p - 1$ is called a *Mersenne prime* in his honor.

The number 3 is a Mersenne prime because $3 = 2^2 - 1$ and 2 is a prime number. The number 7 is also a Mersenne prime because $7 = 2^3 - 1$ and 3 is a prime number. Properties of Mersenne primes are still being studied in Number Theory today.

Goldbach's Conjecture

A *conjecture* is a statement that appears to be true but has not been proven or disproved. Once a statement is proven true, it is called a *Theorem*. Goldbach's Conjecture has never been proven or disproved. There are two parts to this conjecture. The first part concerns even numbers. Goldbach conjectured that *every* even number greater than two can be written as the sum of two prime numbers. (These two prime numbers do not have to be distinct; they can be the same number.) For example:

$4 = 2 + 2$	and 2 is a prime number
$6 = 3 + 3$	and 3 is a prime number
$8 = 3 + 5$	and both 3 and 5 are prime numbers
$10 = 3 + 7$ or $5 + 5$	and 3, 5, and 7 are all prime numbers.

The second part to his conjecture is that *every* odd number greater than 6 can be written as the sum of three prime numbers. (These three prime numbers do not have to be distinct; they can be the same number.) For example:

$7 = 2 + 2 + 3$	and 2 and 3 are both prime numbers
$9 = 2 + 2 + 5$ or $3 + 3 + 3$	and 2, 3, and 5 are all prime numbers
$11 = 2 + 2 + 7$ or $3 + 3 + 5$	and 2, 3, 5, and 7 are all prime numbers.

As you can see, sometimes there is more than one expression for the sum.

This is a conjecture and has never been proven. The interesting fact is that this conjecture was made by Christian Goldbach in 1742, and no one to this date has been able to prove or disprove this conjecture.

One of the appeals of number theory is that there are still conjectures, such as Goldbach's conjecture, which are simple enough to be understood by elementary school children and yet have baffled mathematicians for hundreds of years. A similar situation, which was solved only recently, had to do with a conjecture known as Fermat's Last Theorem. The statement of this conjecture was made by Pierre de Fermat in the seventeenth century, but the proof, by mathematician Andrew Wiles of Princeton University, was not completed until 1995.

162   Chapter 5: **NUMBER THEORY**

Small Group Exercises

1.   What is the smallest natural number that has 2, 4, 5, and 10 among its divisors? How many divisors does this number have?

2.   What is the smallest natural number that has 2, 3, 7, and 8 among its divisors? How many divisors does this number have?

3.   Find the smallest natural number that has exactly eight divisors.

4.   Find the smallest natural number that has exactly ten divisors. What are its divisors?

Exercises

1.   Answer "TRUE" or "FALSE".

   (a) The number 1 is a prime number.
   (b) The number 33 is a composite number.
   (c) The number 0 is a composite number.
   (d) The number 0 is a prime number.
   (e) The number 1 is a composite number.
   (f) $7 \mid 63$
   (g) Eight is a divisor of 72.
   (h) Thirty is a multiple of three.
   (i) Every odd number is prime.
   (j) Every even number is composite.

2.   Find the divisors of 32.

3.   Find the divisors of 24.

4.   Use the Sieve of Eratosthenes to find all of the prime numbers less than 100.

5.   Find five consecutive composite numbers less than 65.

6.   We said that 3 and 5 are twin primes. The next twin primes are 5 and 7. What are the next two pairs of twin primes?

7.   The numbers 2 and 3 are both prime numbers and are also consecutive numbers. Is there another pair of consecutive natural numbers that are prime? Explain.

8.   Are 5, 11, 13, 15, and 31 Mersenne primes? Why or why not?

9.   Find the first five Mersenne primes.

10.   Show that Goldbach's conjecture is true for each of the following numbers.

   (a) 12   (b) 22

(c) 28   (d) 13
(e) 21   (f) 37

11. Does the formula $3^n - 1$ yield prime numbers for $n = 1, 2, 3, 4$?

12. If a natural number has exactly two distinct divisors, must it be prime?

13. If a natural number has exactly three divisors, is it prime?

5.4 Divisibility Tests

Before we begin this section's topics, we need to understand what *digits* are. A number is composed of digits. For example, the number 863 consists of three digits, that is, 8, 6, and 3. The last digit of this number is 3. The number formed by the last two digits is the number 63.

Sometimes we need to determine if a given number a is divisible by another number b. If b is small enough, there are often *divisibility tests* that may be used to quickly answer this question. For example, suppose I wanted to know if 51 is divisible by 3. I could divide 51 by 3. But now, suppose I wanted to determine if the number 178,342,986 is divisible by 3 and my calculator's batteries are dead. Long division would be lengthy and tedious. Besides all I want to know is if 3 is a factor of 178,342,986; I do not need to know the quotient. The divisibility tests listed below often give a quick way of answering this questions such as this.

Value of n	Test The number is divisible by n if
2	the last digit is even, that is, if the last digit is 2, 4, 6, 8, or 0.
3	the sum of its digits is divisible by 3.
4	the number formed by the last two digits is divisible by 4.
5	the last digit is 0 or 5.
6	it is divisible by 2 and 3.
7	it satisfies the following condition. Continue finding the difference of the number with the unit's digit removed and twice the unit's digit to determine if the result is divisible by 7.
8	the number formed by the last three digits is divisible by 8.
9	the sum of the digits is divisible by 9.
10	the last digit is 0.
11	it satisfies the following condition. Find the sum of every other digit: the ones digit, the hundreds digit, the ten thousands digit, and so on. Next find the sum of the other digits: the tens digit, the thousands digit, the hundred thousands digit, and so on. Finally find the difference of these two quantities. If the result is divisible by 11, then the original number is also divisible by 11.
12	it is divisible by 3 and 4.

Table 5.4 Common divisibility tests.

Example 1. Let's determine if the number 711,480 is divisible by
(a) 2   (b) 3   (c) 4   (d) 5   (e) 6   (f) 7   (g) 8   (h) 9   (i) 10   (j) 11   (k) 12

using the above tests for divisibility.
Solution:

(a) The last digit is an even number (it is 0) so the number is divisible by 2.

(b) The sum of the digits is $7+1+1+4+8+0 = 21$, and 21 is divisible by 3. Thus the original number is also divisible by 3.

c) The number formed by the last two digits is 80 and 80 is divisible by 4. Thus the original number is also divisible by 4.

d) The last digit is 0, thus the number is divisible by 5.

e) We found the number to be divisible by both 2 and 3, thus it is must be divisible by 6.

f) Organize your work as shown in Table 5.5.

NUMBER	UNIT'S DIGIT	TWICE THE UNIT'S DIGIT	NUMBER WITH THE UNIT'S DIGIT REMOVED	DIFFERENCE SOUGHT
711,480	0	$0 \times 2 = 0$	71,148	$71148 - 0 = 71148$
71,148	8	$8 \times 2 = 16$	7,114	$7114 - 16 = 7098$
7,098	8	$8 \times 2 = 16$	709	$709 - 16 = 693$
693	3	$3 \times 2 = 6$	69	$69 - 6 = 63$

Table 5.5 The number 711,480 is divisible by 7.

We stop now because we see that 63 is divisible by 7; thus the number 711,480 is also divisible by 7.

(g) The number formed by the last three digits is 480, which is divisible by 8. Thus the original number is also divisible by 8.

(h) In doing part (b) we found that the sum of the digits is 21, which is not divisible by 9. Thus the original number is also not divisible by 9.

(i) The last digit is 0, so the number is divisible by 10.

(j) To test for divisibility by 11:
   Find the sum of the digits in the odd positions: $7+1+8 = 16$.
   Find the sum of the digits in the even positions: $1+4+0 = 5$.
   Check the difference of these two numbers: $16 - 5 = 11$.

Since this result is divisible by 11, so is the original number.

(k) The number is divisible by both 3 and 4, thus it is also divisible by 12.

Every composite number can be written as a product of prime numbers. This is known as the *prime factorization* of a number. For example, $22 = 2 \times 11$. There is no other way to decompose the number 22 into a product of prime factors.

The Fundamental Theorem of Arithmetic: Every composite number has a unique prime factorization.

There are several methods of finding the prime factorization of a number. We will examine two of these methods here.

Factor Trees

This is the first method we will look at. Write the number to be factored with two branches stemming from it. At the end of the branches write two numbers whose product is that number. For example, suppose that we want to factor the number 120 into a product of primes. We can view 120 as 12×10. Now, if any of the numbers just written are prime numbers, circle them. If any are not prime numbers, draw two branches stemming from it, and we again write two numbers at the ends whose product is that number. In our example, 12 and 10 are not prime, so we draw two branches stemming from each of these. At the end of the two branches leading from 12 we will write 3 and 4 because $3 \times 4 = 12$. At the end of the branches leading from 10 we will write 2 and 5 because $2 \times 5 = 10$. Three of the numbers at the base of the tree, 3, 2, and 5 are prime, so we now circle them. The number 4 is not prime, so we will again draw two branches out from the 4 and write two 2's at the ends because $2 \times 2 = 4$. Since number 2 is prime we will circle the numbers at the base, and we are finished. The prime factorization of the original number is the product of all of the prime numbers that we circled. The process is illustrated in Figure 5.2, below.

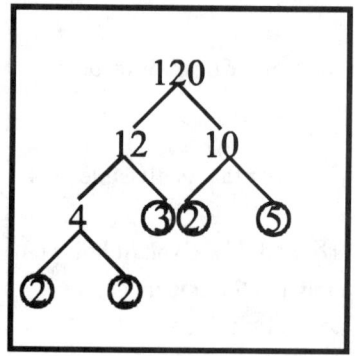

Figure 5.2 A factor tree showing that $120 = 2^3 \cdot 3 \cdot 5$.

Division

With this method we begin by writing down the number we wish to factor into a product of primes, and then we draw a straight line along the left side of the number and another line underneath it. Next we divide the number by its smallest prime factor, writing the prime factor to the left of our number and the quotient of the number and the factor under the line beneath it. We now continue the process, working on this quotient. That is, if this quotient is not a prime number, we draw a line to its left and beneath it. We then identify its smallest prime factor, write it to the left, and again put the quotient beneath it. Note that the prime factor used in this second step could be the same as the one that we used in the first step of the process. We continue in this way until the quotient is finally a prime number.

To illustrate the process, let's again consider the number 120. Start by writing down the number 120 and drawing the two straight lines to the left and beneath it. We know that its smallest prime factor is 2. We write this to the left of the 120 and the quotient, 60, underneath 120. The quotient (60) is not a prime number, so we draw a straight line to the left of 60 and underneath it. We again see that 2 is a factor of this number, so we write a 2 to the left of 60 and write the quotient of 60 divided by 2, which is 30, underneath it. Thirty is not a prime number, so again draw two lines as before and identify its smallest factor. Two is a factor 30, so we write a 2 to the left of 30 and the quotient, 15, underneath it. Again, 15 is not a prime number, so we draw the two lines and identify its smallest prime factor of 15, which is 3. We write a 3 to the left of 15 and write the quotient, 5, underneath it. Since the quotient, 5,

is a prime number, we are finally finished. We find, once again, that $120 = 2^3 \cdot 3 \cdot 5$. Look at Figure 5.3, below, to see what your computation would look like.

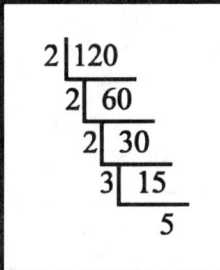

Figure 5.3 The division method for factoring the number 120.

Small Group Exercises

1. Do the following:
   (a) Take another look at the divisibility tests for 6 and 12. What are the similarities? Why do these tests for divisibility hold true?
   (b) What are the prime factorizations of 4, 6, 8, and 12?
   (c) Why is the divisibility test for 4 different from that for 8? Is every number that is divisible by 4 divisible by 8? Explain your answer.
   (d) Based on what you have discovered, state divisibility tests for 15, 18, and 21. Explain how you can devise a divisibility test for a number greater than 12. Does this apply to all numbers greater than 12 or only certain ones? If it only applies to certain ones, what are the limitations?

2. Construct a factor tree for the number 120 by starting with the factors 30 and 4 (instead of 12 and 10 as was done in the text). Then construct a factor tree by starting with the factors 15 and 8. Show that ultimately all of these trees will lead to the same factorization of the number 120 that was found in the text.

Being able to determine the prime factorization of a number is very useful in finding two important quantities, the least common multiple and the greatest common divisor. We will now investigate these two concepts.

The Least Common Multiple

Definition: The l*east common multiple* of a and b is the smallest natural number that is a multiple of both a and b.

Recall that a multiple of a is any number c such that a divides into c evenly. For example, the set of multiples of 10 is $\{10, 20, 30, 40, \cdots\}$, and the set of multiples of 4 is $\{4, 8, 12, 16, 20, \cdots\}$. The least common multiple, or LCM, of 10 and 4, is 20, the smallest number that is a multiple of both 10 and 4. (This is the smallest number that appears in both of the sets of multiples given above.)

Now, suppose we need to find the LCM of 3,960 and 8,316. Listing the multiples of both of these numbers would not be a very appealing idea. These numbers are large, and our lists would be very long before they share a common multiple. Fortunately, there is another method.

Steps for finding the least common multiple of two numbers a and b:

1. Find the prime factorizations of both a and b.
2. List each prime factor with the greater of the exponents that appears in either of the prime factorizations.
3. Find the product of the factors listed in step 2.

Note that if a prime factor appears in only one of the two factorizations that it must still appear in the list.

Example 2. We will now return to the problem just mentioned. We wish to find the LCM of 3,960 and 8,316.

SOLUTION: We start by finding the prime factorizations of both of these numbers. They are:

$$3,960 = 2^3 \cdot 3^2 \cdot 5 \cdot 11$$
$$8,316 = 2^2 \cdot 3^3 \cdot 7 \cdot 11$$

Since the prime number 2 appears with an exponent of 3 in the factorization of 3960 and with an exponent of 2 in the factorization of 8316, we must start our list with 2^3 (2 with the larger of the two exponents). Similarly, we need to include 3^3 in the the list. We also need to include 5, 7, and 11 because these are factors of at least one of the numbers. Accounting for all of these factors we have

$$\text{LCM} = 2^3 \cdot 3^3 \cdot 5 \cdot 7 \cdot 11 = 83,160.$$

The number 83,160 is the smallest number that is divisible by both 3,960 and 8,316.

The Greatest Common Factor

Definition: The *greatest common factor* of a and b is the largest natural number that divides both a and b.

Recall that a factor of a is any number that divides into a evenly. The set of factors of 12 is {1,2,3,4,6,12}. The set of factors of 32 is {1,2,4,8,16,32}. Therefore, the greatest common factor, or GCF, of 12 and 32 is 4. Four is the largest number that appears in both lists of factors.

Now, suppose we wanted to find the greatest common factor of 3,960 and 8,316. Listing all of the factors of these two numbers is no easy task. As early as 300 BC there was an algorithm for finding the greatest common factor, given by Euclid in his work the *Elements*. Fortunately, there is another method.

168   Chapter 5: **NUMBER THEORY**

Steps for finding the greatest common factor of two numbers a and b:
1. Find the prime factorizations of both numbers.
2. List each prime factor that appears on BOTH prime factorizations with its SMALLER exponent.
3. Find the product of the factors listed in step 2.
   Note that a factor will not be included in the list unless it appears in both factorizations.

Example 3. We will now find the GCF of 3,960 and 8,316 (the same two numbers that we looked at earlier in example 2).
SOLUTION: We begin by finding the prime factorization of each. Recall that they are:

$$3,960 = 2^3 \cdot 3^2 \cdot 5 \cdot 11$$
$$8,316 = 2^2 \cdot 3^3 \cdot 7 \cdot 11$$

Since 2 is a factor of both and has exponents 3 and 2, we will need to include 2^2 in our list (Two is the smaller of the two exponents that appear on the factor of 2.). Since 3 is a factor of both, we will need to include 3^2 to the list (2 is the smaller of two exponents which appear). Five and 7 are only factors of one of the numbers and therefore are not part of the GCF. Eleven is a factor of both factors, so we will also need to include 11 in the list, (with an exponent of 1). Therefore, the GCF is:

$$2^2 \cdot 3^2 \cdot 11 = 396.$$

The number 396 is the largest number that divides into both 3,960 and 8,316 evenly.

Small Group Exercises

1.   Multiply together the numbers 3,960 and 8,316, the two numbers analyzed in examples 2 and 3 in the section. Now multiply together the GCF and LCM of these two numbers (as found in the text). Did you find that your answers were the same?
        Now, supposed that you suspected that this was always true. How could you test this conjecture?

2.   Extend the ideas of LCM and GCF to sets of three numbers by doing the following:

   (a) Define what you mean by the LCM of three numbers and the GCD of three numbers.
   (b) Modify the procedure given in the text to get working rules for computing the LCM and GCF of three numbers.
   (c) Show (by giving an example) that the conjecture that you made in problem #1 of this group exercise does *not* hold true for three numbers. That is, if a, b, and c are 3 numbers, then the product of the GCD of these three numbers with the LCM of these three numbers will *not* equal the product of these three numbers.

Question to Discuss

        Assume that the earth circles the sun exactly once every 365 days (the actual value is closer to 365.24 days) and that Mars circles the sun exactly once every 687 earth days. Suppose that the two planets are directly aligned with the sun as shown in Figure 5.4.

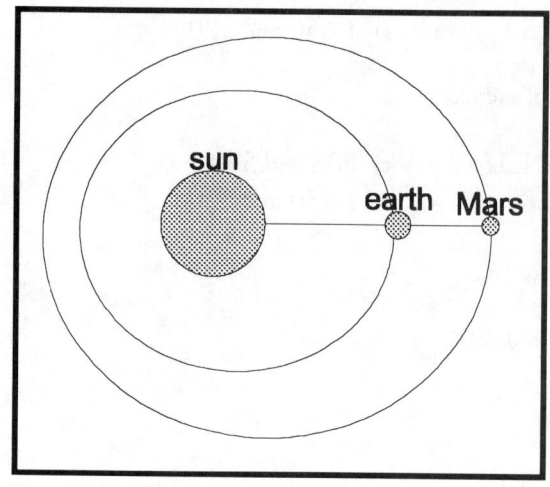

Figure 5.4 **Alignment of the planets (not to scale!).**

How many earth days will pass before these celestial bodies next repeat this exact alignment? (Hint: Explain why the answer to this question must be divisible by both 365 and 687.)

How would this problem change if Mars took only 657 days to circle the sun?

How would this problem change if we added the planet Venus, which circles the sun once every 225 days?

Exercises

1. In the text it was found that the LCM of 3,960 and 8,316 is 83,160. Show that both 3,960 and 8,316 divide into 83,160 evenly.

2. In the text it was shown that the GCD of 3,960 and 8,316 is 396. Show that 396 does divide evenly into both 3,960 and 8,316.

3. Answer "TRUE" or "FALSE".

   a) If a number is divisible by 10, then it must be divisible by 5.
   b) If a number is divisible by 9, then it must be divisible by 3.
   c) If a number is divisible by 3, then it must be divisible by 6.

4. Determine if each of the numbers below is divisible by 2,3,4,5,6,7,8,9,10,11 or 12 by using the tests for divisibility.

   a) 1,728   b) 19,602   c) 39,200   d) 4,620   e) 1,890

5. Find the prime factorization of each number below using both methods — factor trees and division.

   a) 180   b) 440   c) 1,008   d) 1,440   e) 2,250

6. Find the least common multiple of each group of numbers.

   a) 180 and 1,008   b) 175 and 1,375   c) 504 and 540

170   Chapter 5: **NUMBER THEORY**

      d) 4,200 and 2,520 and 924   e) 84 and 280   f) 1,650 and 220

7. Find the greatest common factor of each group of numbers.

    a) 180 and 1,008   b) 175 and 1,375   c) 504 and 540
    d) 4,200 and 2,520 and 924   e) 84 and 280   f) 1,650 and 220

8. Find a natural number that is divisible by 2, 5, and 7.

9. Find a natural number that is divisible by 3, 5, and 20.

10. Find a natural number that is divisible by 4, 5, and 11.

5.5 Other Topics Concerning Primes and Factoring

There are some other classifications of numbers that have fascinated mathematicians. We will look at four of these categories now.

Perfect Numbers

Recall that the *divisors* of a number a are those numbers that divide a, or are factors of a. For instance, the set of divisors of 10 is $\{1,2,5,10\}$ and the set of divisors of 28 is $\{1,2,4,7,14,28\}$.

> **Definition:** The *proper divisors* of a natural number are all of the divisors of the number except the number itself.

Since the set of divisors of 10 is $\{1,2,5,10\}$, the set of proper divisors of 10 is $\{1,2,5\}$. Similarly, the set of proper divisors of 28 is $\{1,2,4,7,14\}$.

> **Definition:** A *perfect number* is a natural number which is equal to the sum of its proper divisors.

For example, 10 is not a perfect number because the sum of its proper divisors is $1+2+5=8$, which does not equal 10. However, 28 is a perfect number. The sum of its proper divisors is $1+2+4+7+14$, which does equal 28.

Example 1. Is 496 a perfect number?
Solution: The set of proper divisors of 496 is $\{1,2,4,8,16,31,62,124,248\}$. The sum of these divisors is $1+2+4+8+16+31+62+124+248$, which equals 496. Therefore, 496 is a perfect number.

Are there many perfect numbers? Comparatively speaking, no. The next perfect number after 28 is 496. The next perfect number after that is 8,128. We also do not know what the largest perfect number is, if indeed there is one. At this time, we do not know if there are infinitely many perfect numbers. Every perfect number that is known today is an even number. We do not know of any odd

perfect numbers. This is not a theorem because it has never been proven. There may be an odd perfect number that has not been found yet, or there may not be. It is also known that all even perfect numbers end in 6 or 8.

Small Group Exercise:

What is the smallest perfect number? Show that it is a perfect number.

Euler proved the following theorem in 1757.

Theorem: An even number is perfect if and only if it is of the form $2^{p-1}(2^p - 1)$, where $2^p - 1$ is prime.

Does this look familiar? Recall that if p is prime, a prime number of the form $2^p - 1$ is a Mersenne prime. Thus, to find all even perfect numbers, one needs to find all Mersenne primes.

The first four perfect numbers are 6, 28, 496, and 8,128. Notice that these are all even numbers and further that

$$6 = 2(3) = 2(4-1) = 2^{2-1}(2^2 - 1). \quad \text{(Here } p = 2.\text{)}$$
$$28 = 4(7) = 2^2(6-1) = 2^{3-1}(2^3 - 1). \quad \text{(Here } p = 3.\text{)}$$
$$496 = 16(31) = 2^4(32-1) = 2^{5-1}(2^5 - 1). \quad \text{(Here } p = 5.\text{)}$$
$$8,128 = 64(127) = 2^6(128-1) = 2^{7-1}(2^7 - 1). \quad \text{(Here } p = 7.\text{)}$$

Deficient and Abundant Numbers

Most natural numbers are not perfect numbers. There are two classifications for these numbers.

Definition: A natural number that is greater than the sum of its proper divisors is called *deficient* and a natural number that is less than the sum of its proper divisors is called *abundant*.

Example 4. Determine whether each of the following is deficient or abundant.
    (a) 10   (b) 12   (c) 15

SOLUTION:
(a) The set of proper divisors of 10 is $\{1,2,5\}$. The sum of these divisors is $1+2+5 = 8$, which is less than 10. Therefore 10 is deficient.
(b) The set of proper divisors of 12 is $\{1,2,3,4,6\}$. The sum of these divisors is $1+2+3+4+6 = 16$, which is larger than 12. Thus 12 is abundant.
(c) The set of proper divisors of 15 is $\{1,3,5\}$. The sum of these divisors is $1+3+5 = 9$, which is less than 15. Thus 15 is deficient.

172   Chapter 5: **NUMBER THEORY**

> *Small Group Exercise*
>
> How many abundant numbers are there between 1 and 100? Find them. (Hint: None are odd numbers.)

Amicable Numbers

> **Definition**: Two natural numbers a and b are *amicable,* or *friendly,* if the sum of the proper divisors of a is b and the sum of the proper divisors of b is a.

In other words, you begin by finding all of the proper divisors of a and then of b. If the sum of the proper divisors of a equals b *and* the sum of the proper divisors of b equals a, then a and b are amicable. Notice that both conditions must be met if the numbers are to be considered friendly.

Example 5. Determine if each pair of numbers is amicable.
 a) 8 and 10   b) 220 and 284

Solution:

   a) The set of proper divisors of 10 is $\{1,2,5\}$ and 1+2+5=8, but the set of proper divisors of 8 is $\{1,2,4\}$ and $1+2+4=7$. Since the sum of the divisors of 8 does not equal 10, these numbers are not amicable.

   b) The set of proper divisors of 220 is $\{1,2,4,5,10,11,20,22,44,55,110\}$, and the sum of these numbers is 284. The set of proper divisors of 284 is $\{1,2,4,71,142\}$ and the sum of the numbers in this set is 220. Thus the numbers 220 and 284 are amicable.

The numbers 220 and 284 are the smallest pair of amicable numbers. This fact was known in the time of Pythagoras, a Greek teacher of mathematics who may have lived around 500 B.C. It took over a thousand years before another pair of amicable numbers was found. That pair is 18,416 and 17,296.

Magic

A natural number is said to be *magic* if when we add the digits and then add the digits of the resulting sum and continue in this manner, the end result is one. For example, 28 is magic. To check this, first we add its digits, $2+8=10$. Now, add the digits of the resulting sum of 10, $1+0=1$.

Exercises

1.   For each number given below, find the set of divisors and the set of proper divisors.

   (a) 18   (b) 20   (c) 22   (d) 24
   (e) 30   (f) 50   (g) 32   (h) 40

2. Explain why 32 is not a perfect number.

3. Explain why 16 is not a perfect number.

4. Verify that 496 is a perfect number by adding its proper divisors.

5. Classify each number as deficient, abundant, or perfect.

   (a) 18   (b) 20   (c) 22   (d) 24
   (e) 30   (f) 50   (g) 32   (h) 40

6) State why the following pairs of numbers are not amicable.

   (a) 18 and 21   (b) 30 and 42

7) Show that the numbers 1,184 and 1,210 are amicable. This pair had been overlooked until 1866 when a sixteen year old Italian boy named Nicolo Paginini discovered them.

8) Verify that the number 496,298 is not magic. Show that the number 8,128 is magic.

9) Find two numbers which are magic but which are not perfect numbers.

5.6 Number Sequences

Another topic of interest in number theory is that of sequences. A *sequence* is any ordered list of numbers

$$a_1, a_2, a_3, a_4, \cdots.$$

The numbers in the list are called the *terms* of the sequence. The small numbers below each a are called subscripts. The subscripts indicate the position of the term within the sequence.

Definition: A *number sequence* is an ordered list of numbers. Each number in the sequence is called a *term*. The nth term of a sequence is denoted by a_n.

The following are examples of sequences.

$1, 2, 3, 4, 5, \cdots$
$3, 7, 11, 15, \cdots$
$7, -14, 28, -56, \cdots$
$2, 5, 4, 7, 6, 9, 8, \cdots$

In each of these examples the terms in the list are related to each other by a rule. In the first sequence each term is arrived at by adding one to the previous term: The first term is 1, and adding 1 to this gives $1+1=2$, the second term; adding 1 to this gives $2+1=3$, the third term; adding 1 to this gives $3+1=4$, the fourth term; adding 1 to this gives $4+1=5$, the fifth term. If we assume that the

rest of this sequence can be generated by using this same rule, the sequence can be extended out as far as we wish.

In the second sequence, the rule for generating the terms is to add 4 to any term to get the next term. In the third sequence, the rule is to multiply a term by -2 to get the next term: $7 \times (-2) = -14$, the second term; $(-14)(-2) = 28$, the third term; and $28 \times (-2) = -56$, the fourth term.

In the last sequence the rule is a bit more complex, but there is a rule. Starting with the first term, the next terms are generated two at a time by first adding 3, and then adding -1. This gives a second term of $2 + 3 = 5$ and a third term of $5 + (-1) = 4$. We now use the third term to generate the next two terms in exactly the same way first adding 3, then adding -1. This gives a fourth term of $4 + 3 = 7$ and a fifth term of $7 + (-1) = 6$. Again, if we make the assumption that this pattern continues we would be able to use this procedure to extend this sequence to any length that we desire.

Now we will take a closer look at the second sequence above,

$3, 7, 11, 15, \cdots$

The first term, 3, is denoted by a_1. The second term, 7, is denoted by a_2. The third term, 11, is denoted by a_3, and the fourth term, 15, is denoted a_4.

If you know a rule for a sequence, you can find any term you want. Keeping with the above sequence, we noted earlier that it could be generated with the rule which says to add 4 to get the next term. What is a_5, the fifth term? It is $a_4 + 4 = 15 + 4 = 19$. What is a_{10}? We could find this by computing the next few terms one at a time until we reach a_{10}:

$a_6 = a_5 + 4 = 19 + 4 = 23$ and
$a_7 = a_6 + 4 = 23 + 4 = 27$ and
$a_8 = a_7 + 4 = 27 + 4 = 31$ and
$a_9 = a_8 + 4 = 31 + 4 = 35$ and finally
$a_{10} = a_9 + 4 = 35 + 4 = 39$.

What if we wanted to find the 53rd term? Would we need to find all 52 terms before it? Right now we would. However, for some sequences we will develop formulas that will help us with this task. For other sequences, we will not be able to do this. The only method for those sequences would be to keep reapplying the rule over and over again.

Example 1. Find a rule which generates each of the following sequences.

(a) $-2, -5, -8, -11, \cdots$
(b) $99, 33, 11, \dfrac{11}{3}, \cdots$
(c) $-12, -8, -4, 0, 4, \cdots$
(d) $5, -20, 80, -320, \cdots$
(e) $1, 1, 2, 3, 5, 8, 13, 21, \cdots$
(f) $1, 3, 11, 13, 21, 23, 31, \cdots$

Solution:

(a) A rule that works is to add -3 to any term to get the next term: $-2 + (-3) = -5$, the second term; $-5 + (-3) = -8$, the third term; $-8 + (-3) = -11$, the fourth term; and so on.

(b) A rule that works here is to multiply a term by $\frac{1}{3}$ to get to the next term. Check for yourself to see that if any term in this list is multiplied by $\frac{1}{3}$ you will get the next term listed.

(c) A rule that works in this case is to add 4 to any term to get to the next term: $-12 + 4 = -8$, the second term; $-8 + 4 = -4$, the third term; $-4 + 4 = 0$, the fourth term; $0 + 4 = 4$, the fifth term.

(d) In this sequence a rule which will work is to multiply any term by -4 to get the next term.

(e) Look at this sequence carefully because it is different from the other sequences in this list. After the first two terms, each succeeding term is computed by adding together the two previous terms in the list. Thus the third term is computed by adding together the first two terms in the sequence, the fourth term is computed by adding together the second and third terms, the fifth term is computed by adding together the third and fourth terms, and so on. This sequence has a special name, the *Fibonacci Sequence*. We will take a closer look at the sequence in Section 5.8.

(f) A rule that works for this sequence is to compute the terms two at a time by first adding 2 and then adding 8:

The first term is 1; add 2 to get 3, then add 8 to get 11. The second and third terms are 3 and 11. The third term is 11; add 2 to get 13, then add 8 to get 21. The fourth and fifth terms are 13 and 21.

The fifth term is 21; add 2 to get 23, then add 8 to get 31. The sixth and seventh terms are 23 and 31.

Sometimes an explicit formula for a sequence may be given. For example, the formula $a_n = 3n + 5$ generates a sequence by replacing n successively by the values 1, 2, 3, 4, and so on. In this case we would get the following:

$n = 1$: $\quad a_1 = 3(1) + 5 = 3 + 5 = 8$.
$n = 2$: $\quad a_2 = 3(2) + 5 = 6 + 5 = 11$.
$n = 3$: $\quad a_3 = 3(3) + 5 = 9 + 5 = 14$.
$n = 4$: $\quad a_4 = 3(4) + 5 = 12 + 5 = 17$.

You can see the advantage of this type of situation: Not only are you relieved of the need to be inspired to come up with a rule for the sequence, but you can easily compute any term you want, such as the 23rd term or the 95th term, without having to figure out all of the terms that come before it.

Small Group Exercise

Create three different sequences. Give the first five terms and a rule for each. At least one rule should involve negative numbers. Use both the operations of addition and multiplication

---

In the next two sections we will investigate three special types of sequences.

Exercises

1. State a rule which can be used to generate each of the following sequences.

(a) $3, 8, 13, 18, \cdots$
(b) $-4, 12, -36, 108, -324, \cdots$
(c) $48, 24, 12, 6, \cdots$
(d) $15, 9, 3, -3, -9, \cdots$
(e) $-6, -3, 2, 5, 10, 13, 18, \cdots$
(f) $1, 5, 6, 10, 11, 15, \cdots$
(g) $90, -30, 10, -\dfrac{10}{3}, \cdots$

2.   Find the tenth term of the sequence $5, -15, 45, -135, \cdots$.

3.   For each of the sequences given, what is a_2? a_5?

(a) $2, 8, 14, 20, 26, 32, \cdots$
(b) $10, 6, 2, -2, \cdots$
(c) $-5, 15, -45$

4.   Create sequences with each of the following rules. Use any first term that you wish, then compute the first five terms of your sequence.

(a) add four to get the next term
(b) multiply by -7 to get the next term
(c) compute terms two at a time by first adding 4 and then subtracting 1
(d) subtract 3 from 5 times the previous term to get the next term
(e) add -6 to get to the next term

5.   Find the first five terms of the sequence defined by each of the formulas given.

(a) $a_n = n + 3$ (b) $a_n = 2n - 7$
(c) $a_n = \dfrac{n}{3}$ (d) $a_n = 3 \cdot 2^n$

(e) $a_n = -3n$ (f) $a_n = 5n - 2$

5.7 Arithmetic and Geometric Sequences

Two special types of sequences are known as arithmetic and geometric sequences. These types of sequences are easier to deal with than most, because there are useful formulas for finding the general term and other information about these sequences.

We will start by taking a look at *arithmetic sequences*. In an arithmetic sequence, you find the next term by adding a set amount to the previous term. For example:

$4, 7, 10, 13, 16, \cdots$

is an arithmetic sequence. The first term is 4. The second term is 7, or $4+3$. The third term is 10, or $7+3$. The fourth term is 13, or $10+3$, and the fifth term is 16, or $13+3$. This is an arithmetic sequence because if you add 3 to the previous term you always arrive at the next term. In this example 3 is the set amount that you need to add. This amount, 3, is called the *common difference*.

> **Definition**: An *arithmetic sequence* is a sequence of numbers where each term is computed by adding a set amount, known as the *common difference*, to the previous term. The common difference is generally denoted by d, so that $a_n = a_{n-1} + d$.

Example 1. Determine if each of the following is an arithmetic sequence. If it is, state the common difference, d.

(a) $5, 16, 27, 38, \cdots$
(b) $3, 4, 5, 7, 8, \cdots$
(c) $-2, 3, 8, 13, \cdots$
(d) $6, 1, -4, -9, \cdots$

Solution:
(a) Apparently this is an arithmetic sequence.

$a_2 = 16 = 5 + 11 = a_1 + 11$.
$a_3 = 27 = 16 + 11 = a_2 + 11$.
$a_4 = 38 = 27 + 11 = a_3 + 11$.

In every one of the cases listed here we see that the term being computed is *always* gotten by adding the common difference of 11 to the previous term.

(b) Look carefully at this one. In this sequence the second term is gotten by adding 1 to the first term, and the third term is computed by adding 1 to the second term. At first glance it may appear as though we may be dealing with an arithmetic sequence with a common difference of 1. However, adding 1 to the third term will not give the correct fourth term, because $a_3 + 1 = 5 + 1 = 6$, which is not a_4. Therefore, this is NOT an arithmetic sequence and there is no common difference. Remember, in an arithmetic sequence it is necessary that *every* term (except the first) is computed by adding the common difference to the previous term.

(c) This is an arithmetic sequence. The common difference is 5.

(d) This is also an arithmetic sequence. Be careful though, the common difference is not 5, but -5. The common difference is the amount that must be ADDED to the previous term to get the next term. Note that $6 + (-5) = 1$ (the correct second term); $1 + (-5) = -4$ (the correct third term); and $-4 + (-5) = -9$ (the correct fourth term).

Example 2. Find the fifth term of the sequence $2, -1, -4, -7, \cdots$.
Solution: This appears to be an arithmetic sequence with $d = -3$. Thus
$a_5 = a_4 + d = -7 + (-3) = -10$.

Now suppose that you wanted to find the fifteenth term for the sequence in example 2 above. Rather than computing each of the first fourteen terms to get to the fifteenth, a little bit of thought will show why it's possible to use the following formula to compute the fifteenth term directly.

178   Chapter 5: **NUMBER THEORY**

Fact: In an arithmetic sequence with first term a_1 and common difference d, the nth term may be computed by using the formula

$$a_n = a_1 + d(n-1).$$

The reason why this simple formula works is easily understood. To get from the first term of an arithmetic sequence to the nth term we would need to add the common difference of d a total of $n-1$ times. But if we add d a total of $n-1$ times, that's the same as adding $d(n-1)$ to a_1. This is exactly what the formula says to do.

Now let's take another look at the sequence in example 2, that is,

$$2, -1, -4, -7, \cdots$$

Using the formula to find the fifteenth term makes computing the fifteenth term much easier than it would have been before.

$$a_{15} = a_1 + d(n-1)$$
$$a_{15} = 2 + (-3)(15-1) \qquad \text{[Replace } n \text{ by 15 and } d \text{ by } -3 \text{ in the formula.]}$$
$$a_{15} = 2 + (-3)(14) = 2 + (-42) = -40.$$

Example 3. Find the tenth term in each of the following sequences.

(a) $6, 9, 12, 15, \cdots$
(b) $7, -4, -15, -26, \cdots$
(c) $1, 2, 4, 8, \cdots$

Solution:
(a)   This is an arithmetic sequence and the common difference is 3, $d = 3$. Thus,

$$a_{10} = a_1 + d(n-1)$$
$$= 6 + 3(10-1)$$
$$= 6 + 3(9)$$
$$= 6 + 27$$
$$= 33.$$

(b) This is also an arithmetic sequence with $d = -11$.

$$a_{10} = a_1 + d(n-1)$$
$$= 7 + (-11)(10-1)$$
$$= 7 + (-11)(9)$$
$$= 7 + (-99)$$
$$= -92.$$

(c) This is NOT an arithmetic sequence, so we must use the iterative method for now. The rule is to multiply the previous term by 2. So,

$a_5 = 2 \cdot a_4 = 2 \cdot 8 = 16.$
$a_6 = 2 \cdot a_5 = 2 \cdot 16 = 32.$
$a_7 = 2 \cdot 32 = 64.$
$a_8 = 2 \cdot 64 = 128.$
$a_9 = 2 \cdot 128 = 256.$
$a_{10} = 2 \cdot 256 = 512.$

Next suppose we wanted to find the sum of the first eight terms of an arithmetic sequence. We could find all of the first eight terms and then simply add them all up. As an example, consider the arithmetic sequence

6,9,12,15,···

To complete the job we would need to know the next four terms, and then add all of the eight terms together.

$a_5 = a_4 + d = 15 + 3 = 18.$
$a_6 = 18 + 3 = 21.$
$a_7 = 21 + 3 = 24.$
$a_8 = 24 + 3 = 27.$

Adding these up gives the sum we seek: 6+9+12+15+18+21+24+27=132. It's customary to denote this, the sum of the first eight terms, by S_8.

This wasn't so bad, but suppose you wanted to find the sum of the first 100 terms and the common difference was $\frac{2}{7}$. Now that wouldn't be at all pleasant! As you may have guessed, there is another way of doing problems such as this.

Fact: In an arithmetic sequence, the sum of the first n terms is given by the formula

$$S_n = \frac{n(a_1 + a_n)}{2}.$$

Now, we can return to the above problem in which we found the sum of the first eight terms of the sequence 6,9,12,15,···. We found this sum to be 132. We will now use the above formula instead of adding together the eight terms. Recall that $d = 3$ and $n = 8$ (n is the number of terms; since we want the sum of the first eight terms, we need to use $n = 8$). We also found $a_8 = 27$ (see above, but it is important to note that we could have computed this directly without computing a_5, a_6, and a_7 by using the formula for a_n).

$$S_n = \frac{n(a_1 + a_n)}{2}$$
$$= \frac{8(6+27)}{2}$$
$$= \frac{8(33)}{2}$$
$$= 4(33)$$
$$= 132.$$

Again, note that in order to use this formula we need to already know the value of a_n. This is not a problem, though, because we also have a formula for finding this value.

Example 4. Find the sum of the first 10 terms for each of the following sequences:

(a) $2, 7, 12, 17, \cdots$
(b) an arithmetic sequence where $a_1 = -10$ and $d = -3$.
(c) $2, 4, 8, 16, \cdots$

Solution:
(a) This is an arithmetic sequence and $d = 5$. If we want to find S_{10}, then we need to know the value of a_{10}, or the tenth term of the sequence. Recall that

$$a_n = a_1 + d(n-1).$$

Therefore,

$$a_{10} = 2 + 5(10-1)$$
$$= 2 + 5(9)$$
$$= 2 + 45$$
$$= 47$$

Now, we can apply the fact that

$$S_n = \frac{n(a_1 + a_n)}{2}$$
$$S_{10} = \frac{10(2+47)}{2}$$
$$= \frac{10(49)}{2}$$
$$= 5(49)$$
$$= 245.$$

(b) In this arithmetic sequence we are only told that the first term is -10 and that $d = -3$. Once again, we will need to find the value of the tenth term before we can find the sum of the first ten terms.

$$a_n = a_1 + d(n-1)$$
$$a_{10} = -10 + -3(10-1)$$
$$= -10 + -3(9) = -10 - 27 = -37.$$

Now we have enough information to use the formula for the sum of an arithmetic sequence.

$$S_n = \frac{n(a_1 + a_n)}{2}$$
$$S_{10} = \frac{10(-10 + -37)}{2}$$
$$= 5(-47) = -235.$$

(c) Notice that this sequence is not an arithmetic sequence. The rule is to multiply the previous term by 2. We will again have to use the iterative method for now. That means that we will need to find the values of a_1 through a_{10} and then add them up.

$$a_5 = 2 \cdot a_4 = 2 \cdot 16 = 32.$$
$$a_6 = 2 \cdot a_5 = 2 \cdot 32 = 64.$$
$$a_7 = 2 \cdot 64 = 128.$$
$$a_8 = 2 \cdot 128 = 256.$$
$$a_9 = 2 \cdot 256 = 512.$$
$$a_{10} = 2 \cdot 512 = 1{,}024.$$

Therefore, the sum of the first 10 terms of this sequence is

$$2 + 4 + 8 + 16 + 32 + 64 + 128 + 256 + 512 + 1{,}024 = 2{,}046.$$

The last sequence of the above example was not an arithmetic sequence because the rule was to MULTIPLY the previous term by a set amount, in this case 2, and not to add. That means that the formulas that we learned earlier in this section could not be used, since they only apply to arithmetic sequences.

When you compute the terms of a sequence by MULTIPLYING the previous term by a set amount to determine the next term, the sequence is called a *geometric sequence*.

Definition: A sequence in which the rule is to *multiply* the previous term by a set amount to determine the next term is known as a *geometric sequence*. The set amount which you multiply by is known as the *common ratio* and is generally denoted by r.

Example 5. Determine if each of the following is an arithmetic sequence, a geometric, or neither. If the sequence is arithmetic, state the common difference d. If the sequence is a geometric sequence, state the common ratio r.

(a) $4, 12, 36, 108, \cdots$

(b) $99, 33, 11, \dfrac{11}{3}, \cdots$

(c) $6, 10, 14, 18, \cdots$
(d) $3, 6, 8, 16, 18, \cdots$
(e) $-3, 6, -12, 24, \cdots$

Solution:

(a) Notice that

$$a_2 = 12 = 3 \cdot 4 = 3 \cdot a_1$$
$$a_3 = 36 = 3 \cdot 12 = 3 \cdot a_2$$
$$a_4 = 108 = 3 \cdot 26 = 3 \cdot a_3$$

Therefore, this is a geometric sequence and the common ratio is $r = 3$.

(b) We observe that

$$a_2 = 33 = \frac{1}{3} \cdot 99 = \frac{1}{3} \cdot a_1$$
$$a_3 = 11 = \frac{1}{3} \cdot 33 = \frac{1}{3} \cdot a_2$$
$$a_4 = \frac{11}{3} = \frac{1}{3} \cdot 11 = \frac{1}{3} \cdot a_3$$

(Notice that 33 is 99 divided by 3 which is the same as 99 times $\frac{1}{3}$.)

Therefore, this is a geometric sequence and the common ratio is $\frac{1}{3}$.

(c) Notice that

$$a_2 = 10 = 6 + 4 = a_1 + 4$$
$$a_3 = 14 = 10 + 4 = a_2 + 4$$
$$a_4 = 18 = 14 + 4 = a_3 + 4$$

This is an arithmetic sequence with the common difference $d = 4$.

(d) We observe that

$$a_2 = 6 = 2 \cdot 3 = 2 \cdot a_1$$
$$a_3 = 8 = 2 + 6 = 2 + a_2$$
$$a_4 = 16 = 2 \cdot 8 = 2 \cdot a_3$$
$$a_5 = 18 = 2 + 16 = 2 + a_4$$

It appears as though the rule for this sequence is to alternately multiply by 2, then add 2, in order to compute the next two terms in the sequence. Thus this can be neither an arithmetic nor a geometric sequence.

(e) In this sequence we notice that

$$a_2 = 6 = -2 \cdot (-3) = -2 \cdot a_1$$
$$a_3 = -12 = -2 \cdot 6 = -2 \cdot a_2$$
$$a_4 = 24 = -2 \cdot (-12) = 2 \cdot a_3$$

Therefore, this is a geometric sequence and the common ratio is $r = -2$.

We will now take a look at finding a particular term of a geometric sequence. Consider example (e) above, the sequence

$$-3, 6, -12, 24, \cdots$$

If we needed to, we could find the eighth term of this sequence, but we will have to use the iterative method. Recall that $r = -2$. Thus

$$a_5 = -2 \cdot a_4 = -2 \cdot 24 = -48,$$
$$a_6 = -2 \cdot a_5 = -2 \cdot (-48) = 96,$$
$$a_7 = -2 \cdot 96 = -192,$$
$$a_8 = -2 \cdot (-192) = 384.$$

This was not too bad, but if we consider example (b) above, the geometric sequence $99, 33, 11, \frac{11}{3}, \cdots$, we would probably all agree that we have better things to do than figure out the next four terms of this sequence! Is there a formula similar to that for the arithmetic sequence that will help with geometric sequences? Yes!

Fact: In a geometric sequence, the nth term, or a_n, can be found using the formula

$$a_n = a_1 r^{(n-1)},$$

where r is the common ratio.

Again, the reason for this rule is simple. To get from the first term to the nth term we need to multiply it by r a total of $n-1$ times. But multiplying a_1 by r a total of $n-1$ times is the same thing as multiplying a_1 by r^{n-1}, which is exactly what the formula says to do!

Now let us again consider the sequence $-3, 6, -12, 24, \cdots$ which we analyzed above. We found the eighth term of this sequence to be 384 using the iterative approach. Now, we will use the above formula instead. Recall that the first term is $a_1 = -3$, that $r = -2$, and that $n = 8$ (because we want to compute the 8th term).

184   Chapter 5: **NUMBER THEORY**

$$a_n = a_1 r^{(n-1)}$$
$$a_8 = (-3) \cdot (-2)^{(8-1)}$$
$$= (-3) \cdot (-2)^7$$
$$= (-3) \cdot (-128)$$
$$= 384.$$

Example 6. Find the tenth term of each of the following sequences.

(a) $1, 2, 4, 8, \cdots$
(b) $88, 44, 22, 11, \cdots$
(c) $3, 5, 7, 9, \cdots$

Solution:
(a) This is a geometric sequence and the common ratio is $r = 2$. Therefore
$$a_n = a_1 r^{(n-1)}$$
$$a_{10} = 1 \cdot 2^{(10-1)}$$
$$= 1 \cdot 2^9$$
$$= 1 \cdot 512 = 512.$$

(b) This is also a geometric sequence and the common ratio is $r = \dfrac{1}{2}$. (Remember, dividing by 2 is the same thing as multiplying by $\dfrac{1}{2}$.) Therefore,
$$a_n = a_1 r^{(n-1)}$$
$$a_{10} = 88 \cdot \left(\dfrac{1}{2}\right)^{(10-1)}$$
$$= 88 \cdot \left(\dfrac{1}{2}\right)^9$$
$$= 88 \cdot \left(\dfrac{1}{512}\right)$$
$$= \dfrac{11}{64}.$$

(c) This is an arithmetic sequence and the common difference is $d = 2$. This time we need to use the earlier formula for the nth term of an arithmetic series.

$$a_n = a_1 + d(n-1)$$
$$a_{10} = 3 + 2(10-1)$$
$$= 3 + 2(9)$$
$$= 3 + 18 = 21.$$

Now we will return to the problem of finding the sum of the first n terms of a given sequence, but this time we will concentrate on geometric sequences. Suppose we have the geometric sequence

$$2, 4, 8, 16, \cdots$$

and we want to find the sum of the first 8 terms. We will use the iterative method again. This means that we will need to first find the fifth through eighth terms so that we can add them up. Recall that the common ratio of this sequence is 2. Thus,

$$a_5 = 2 \cdot a_4 = 2 \cdot 16 = 32$$
$$a_6 = 2 \cdot a_5 = 2 \cdot 32 = 64,$$
$$a_7 = 2 \cdot 64 = 128,$$
$$a_8 = 2 \cdot 128 = 256.$$

Therefore, the sum of the first eight terms is

$$2 + 4 + 8 + 16 + 32 + 64 + 128 + 256 = 510.$$

However, if we were considering the sequence

$$99, 33, 11, \frac{11}{3}, \cdots$$

this approach would not be inviting. Fortunately we do have the following formula to help us.

Fact: The sum of the *first* n terms of the sequence in a geometric sequence, S_n, can be found using the formula

$$S_n = \frac{a_1(1-r^n)}{1-r},$$

provided r, the common ratio, does not equal 1..

Now, let's find the sum of the first eight terms of the sequence

$$2, 4, 8, 16, \cdots$$

once again, this time using the above formula. Recall that $r = 2$ and $n = 8$ (since we want the sum of the first eight terms).

186   Chapter 5: **NUMBER THEORY**

$$S_n = \frac{a_1(1-r^n)}{1-r}$$

$$S_8 = \frac{2(1-2^8)}{1-2}$$

$$= \frac{2(1-256)}{-1}$$

$$= \frac{2(-255)}{-1}$$

$$= \frac{-510}{-1} = 510.$$

This is the same value we found using the iterative approach earlier, but it is much less work.

Example 7. Find the sum of the first 9 terms of each of the following sequences.

  (a) $1, -3, 9, -27, \cdots$
  (b) $40, 20, 10, 5, \cdots$
  (c) $11, 14, 17, 20, \cdots$

Solution:
(a) This is a geometric sequence and the common ratio is $r = -3$. We want to find the sum of the first nine terms, so we apply the above formula with $n = 9$. Thus,

$$S_n = \frac{a_1(1-r^n)}{1-r}$$

$$S_9 = \frac{1(1-(-3)^9)}{1-(-3)}$$

$$= \frac{1(1-(-19{,}683))}{4}$$

$$= \frac{1(19{,}684)}{4} = 4{,}921.$$

(b) The common ratio, r, of this geometric sequence is $\frac{1}{2}$. Thus,

$$S_n = \frac{a_1(1-r^n)}{1-r}$$

$$S_9 = \frac{40\left(1-\left(\frac{1}{2}\right)^9\right)}{1-\frac{1}{2}}$$

$$= \frac{40\left(1-\frac{1}{512}\right)}{\frac{1}{2}}$$

$$= \frac{40\left(\frac{511}{512}\right)}{\frac{1}{2}}$$

$$= \left(\frac{2{,}555}{64}\right) \div \left(\frac{1}{2}\right)$$

$$= \left(\frac{2{,}555}{64}\right) \cdot \left(\frac{2}{1}\right)$$

$$= \frac{2{,}555}{32}.$$

(c) This is not a geometric sequence. It is an arithmetic sequence with the common difference is $d = 3$. Recall that we need to find the ninth term before we can find the sum of the first nine terms for an arithmetic sequence.

$$\begin{aligned} a_9 &= a_1 + d(n-1) \\ &= 11 + 3(9-1) \\ &= 11 + 3(8) \\ &= 11 + 24 = 35. \end{aligned}$$

Therefore,

$$\begin{aligned} S_n &= \frac{n(a_1 + a_n)}{2} \\ S_9 &= \frac{9(11+35)}{2} \\ &= \frac{9(46)}{2} \\ &= 9(23) = 207. \end{aligned}$$

188   Chapter 5: **NUMBER THEORY**

> *Small Group Exercises*
>
> 1.   Find the sum of the second through the twentieth term of each sequence without finding the value of each of the first twenty terms of the sequence.
>
>   (a) $3, 6, 12, 24, \cdots$
>   (b) $-1, 1, 3, 5, \cdots$
>
> 2.   Peter and Ginny each start a job at the same salary of $20,000 per year on the same day. At the end of each year Peter's salary is increased by $1,000 and Ginny's salary is increased by 5%. This pattern is continued for ten years.
>
>   (a) Write a sequence representing Peter's salary at the end of the first year, second year, third year, and so on. What kind of sequence is this? Then do the same for Ginny's salary. (Hint for Ginny's salary: If Ginny earned x dollars in one year, her salary the next year would be 1.05 times x. Determine the type of sequence this is, and, if necessary, use a calculator to compute the terms of the sequence.)
>   (b) What will Peter's new salary (for the eleventh year) be after he has completed his tenth year on the job? How about Ginny's? Who is doing better?
>   (c) Find the total amount earned by each person after having completed ten years on the job (that is, after nine increases).

In the next section, we will consider another sequence, one that occurs in our natural world in many forms.

Exercises

1.   Determine whether or not each of the following sequences is arithmetic, geometric, or neither. If it is arithmetic, state the common difference. If it is geometric, state the common ratio.

   (a) $3, 12, 48, \cdots$
   (b) $2, -1, -4, \cdots$
   (c) $6, \dfrac{13}{2}, 7, \cdots$
   (d) $2, 5, 7, 10, 12, \cdots$
   (e) $-48, 24, -12, \cdots$
   (f) $1, -1, -3, \cdots$
   (g) $4, -12, 36, \cdots$
   (h) $13, 26, 52, \cdots$
   (i) $-6, -9, -12, -15, \cdots$
   (j) $-4, 12, -36, \cdots$
   (k) $23, 19, 15, \cdots$

2.   For each sequence in problem 1 which is either arithmetic or geometric, find the value of the tenth term without finding any of the other unknown terms.

3.   For each sequence in problem 1 which is either arithmetic or geometric, find the value of the sum of the first ten terms without finding all of the first ten terms of the sequence.

4.   For the sequence

   $1.4, 1.6, 1.8, \cdots$

   find the sum of the first twenty terms. (Do not use the iterative method.)

5.   When mathematician Carl Freidrich Gauss was ten years old, his arithmetic teacher put a sequence similar to the following on the board and asked the class to find the sum of the terms.

$$81297, 81495, 81693, \cdots, 100899$$

This problem was given to keep the boys busy. Gauss saw a pattern and found the sum as the teacher finished putting the problem on the board. This shocked the teacher.

   (a) What type of sequence is this?
   (b) If 81297 is the first term of the sequence, which term is 100899?
   (c) Find the sum of the terms of this sequence without finding any of the missing terms.

6. Find the sum of the first hundred counting numbers without adding all of the numbers. Explain how you did this.

7. A man starts a job with an annual salary of $17,500. He receives a raise of $700 each year. Find his salary for his tenth year on the job. What was the total amount that he earned in his ten years on the job?

8. A man starts a job with an annual salary of $18,200. He receives an $850 raise each year. What is his salary in the eleventh year? How much did he earn in his eleven years on the job?

9. A woman rents an apartment for $600 per month. Each year her rent is raised by $25 per month. What is the monthly rent she is paying in her ninth year of renting the apartment? What was the total rent that she has paid out to live in the apartment for the nine years?

5.8 The Fibonacci Sequence

The following problem was posed to an unusually capable mathematician in the medieval times by the name of Leonardo of Pisa (1180–1250), also called Fibonacci, in the thirteenth century.

A certain man put a pair of rabbits in a place enclosed on all sides by a wall. How many pairs of rabbits will be born there in the course of one year if it is assumed that every month a pair of rabbits produces another pair, and that all new rabbits begin to bear young two months after their own birth? (p.185, *1977 Yearbook of Science and the Future, Encyclopedia Britannica*)

Fibonacci published his solution in his famous book *Liber abaci* in 1202. Here is the solution to the problem.

190   Chapter 5: **NUMBER THEORY**

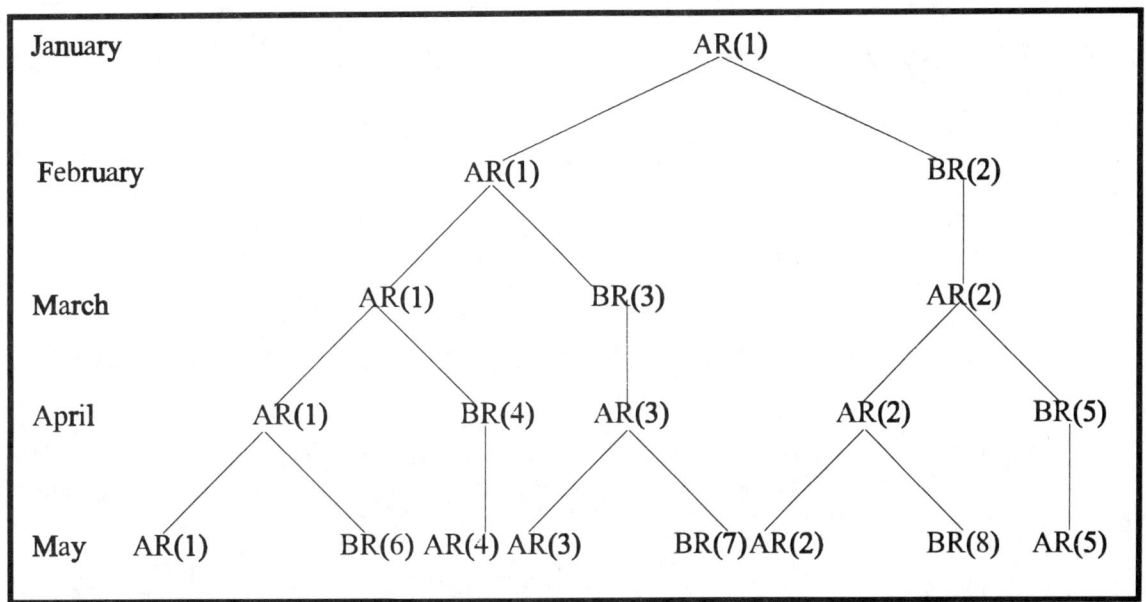

Figure 5.5 The descendants of one pair of rabbits. AR represents a pair of Adult rabbits; BR represents a pair of Baby rabbits.

Each pair is numbered to keep track of it in the diagram (see Figure 5.5). Note that in month two there are two pairs of rabbits, the original adult pair (symbolized by AR(1)) and an immature pair of baby rabbits (denoted by BR(2)). In month three we will have the original adult pair (still denoted by AR(1)); the baby rabbits from February which mature, so their designation is changed (from BR(2) to AR(2)); and a new pair of baby rabbits (denoted by BR(3)). Note that the number designating a pair will never change, but their prefix changes from BR to AR when the pair matures. It is also assumed that rabbits are immortal, that is, no pair ever dies.

The pattern continues in this manner. Each pair of adult rabbits is alive the next month and also bears a pair of baby rabbits. Each pair of baby rabbits becomes a mature pair of adult rabbits the next month. The results are summarized in the following table.

MONTH	PAIRS OF ADULT RABBITS	PAIRS OF BABY RABBITS	TOTAL PAIRS OF RABBITS
January	1	0	1
February	1	1	2
March	2	1	3
April	3	2	5
May	5	3	8
June	8	5	13
July	13	8	21
August	21	13	34
September	34	21	55
October	55	34	89
November	89	55	144
December	144	89	233
January	233	144	377

Table 5.6 Summary of the analysis of the "rabbits problem."

Thus, there were 377 pairs of rabbits twelve months later, one of which was the original pair of rabbits. Therefore, 376 pairs of rabbits were born.

The interesting fact is the relationship among the numbers in any of the three columns above, (excluding the 0 in the second column). Notice the numbers in the column labeled **Pairs of Adult Rabbits**, that is the sequence:

$$1, 1, 2, 3, 5, 8, 13, 21, 34, 55, 89, 144, 233, \cdots$$

If you look closely, you will discover the rule that can be used to generate this sequence. Beginning with the third term, each term is the sum of the two previous terms; that is, the third term is $1 + 1 = 2$; the fourth term is $1 + 2 = 3$; the fifth term is $3 + 5 = 8$; and so on in this manner. This sequence is known as the *Fibonacci sequence*.

Definition: 1, 1, 2, 3, 5, 8, 13, ... is called the *Fibonacci sequence*. Its terms are called the *Fibonacci numbers*. The symbol F_n denotes the nth term of the Fibonacci sequence.

Thus, we notice that

$$F_1 + F_2 = F_3$$
$$F_2 + F_3 = F_4$$
$$F_3 + F_4 = F_5$$

In general we see that $F_{n-1} + F_n = F_{n+1}$.

Example 1. If the 27th and 28th Fibonacci numbers are $196{,}418$ and $317{,}811$ respectively, find the 29th Fibonacci number.
Solution:

$$F_{n-1} + F_n = F_{n+1}$$
$$F_{27} + F_{28} = F_{29}$$
$$196{,}418 + 317811 = 514{,}229.$$

The Fibonacci numbers repeatedly manifest themselves in nature. For example, we will discover this sequence in the genealogy of the male honeybee. With honeybees, all fertilized eggs become females and all unfertilized eggs become male bees. The females either join the worker caste or become queens with special diets. Therefore, the male bee has only a mother and no father, but the female bee has both a mother and a father. Now, let us consider the genealogy of a male bee.

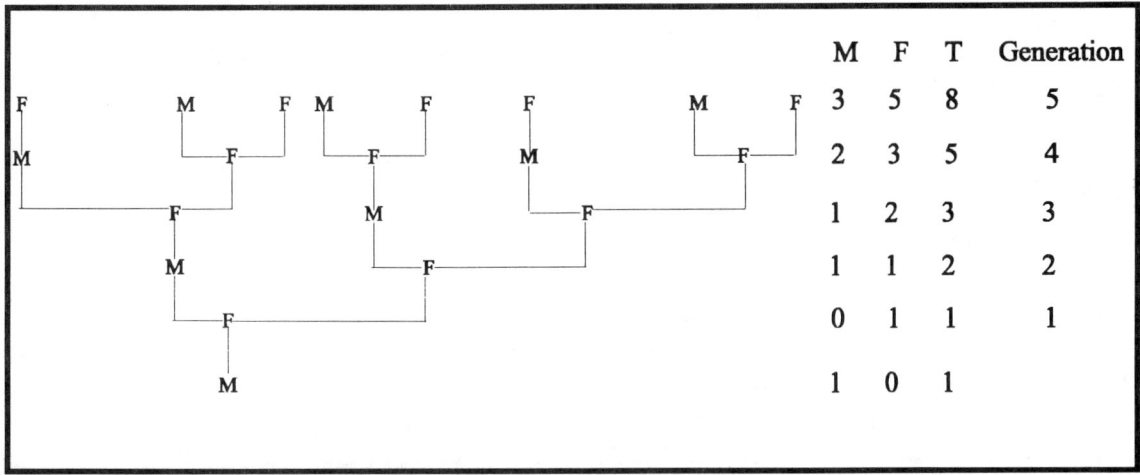

Figure 5.6 The genealogy of a male honeybee.

In Figure 5.6 M stands for a male bee and F represents a female bee. The chart to the right of the diagram gives the total number of male, female, and total number of honeybees for each generation. Notice, that for each generation, the number of male, female, and total number of honeybees is a Fibonacci number.

The Fibonacci numbers also appear in the seed arrangement of many plants, the scale like structures of pine cones, the leaves of a head of lettuce, and in the layers of an onion. Also, they appear in the petal count of flowers. If you were to pluck petal by petal off a daisy, saying "He loves me. He loves me not." more than likely you would pluck 21, 34, 55, or 89 petals off the daisy before you plucked every petal. These are all Fibonacci numbers. If you pick a leaf growing out of the side of a stalk of a plant near the bottom of the stalk and then count the number of leaves up the stalk until you come to the one directly over the original leaf, this is also usually a Fibonacci number.

Now, we will consider the ratio of a term of the Fibonacci sequence with the term immediately preceding it. Remember, the sequence is:

$1,1,2,3,5,8,13,21,34,55,89,144,233,\cdots$.

If we compute the ratio of each term to the term immediately before it, we will get the following values:

$$\frac{F_2}{F_1} = \frac{1}{1} = 1$$

$$\frac{F_3}{F_2} = \frac{2}{1} = 2$$

$$\frac{F_4}{F_3} = \frac{3}{2} = 1.5$$

$$\frac{F_5}{F_4} = \frac{5}{3} \approx 1.67$$

$$\frac{F_6}{F_5} = \frac{8}{5} = 1.60$$

$$\frac{F_7}{F_6} = \frac{13}{8} = 1.625$$

$$\frac{F_8}{F_7} = \frac{21}{13} \approx 1.615384615$$

$$\frac{F_9}{F_8} = \frac{34}{21} \approx 1.619047619$$

$$\frac{F_{10}}{F_9} = \frac{55}{34} \approx 1.617647059$$

$$\frac{F_{11}}{F_{10}} = \frac{89}{55} \approx 1.6181818$$

If you look closely at these ratios, they appear to be nearing $1.618\cdots$ Actually, this sequence of ratios converges toward the number

$$\frac{\sqrt{5}+1}{2} \approx 1.61803\ldots$$

This number is known as the *golden number*. The classical Greeks incorporated the golden number into their architecture and art. Items in this proportion were and still are considered pleasing to the eye. Take for instance a standard index card, which is 3" by 5". The ratio $\frac{5}{3} = 1.\overline{6}$.

Thus, the Fibonacci Sequence plays an important and appealing role in nature and art. The many properties of this sequence is incredibly large and continues to grow.

Exercises

1. Find each of the following.

   (a) F_8 (b) F_{10} (c) F_{12}

   (d) F_{13} (e) F_{14} (f) F_{15}

2. Find the sum of the first ten Fibonacci numbers.

3. Given that $F_{25} = 75{,}025$ and $F_{26} = 121{,}393$, find:

   (a) F_{27} (b) F_{24}

4. Given that $F_{33} = 3{,}524{,}578$ and $F_{35} = 9{,}227{,}465$, find:

   (a) F_{34} (b) F_{36} (c) F_{32}

5. Given that $F_{37} = 24{,}157{,}817$ and $F_{38} = 39{,}088{,}169$ find F_{36} and F_{39}.

6. The eleventh Fibonacci number is 89. Find the first six terms in the decimal expression of $\frac{1}{89}$. What do you find?

194   Chapter 5: **NUMBER THEORY**

7.   Find the ratio of the length to the width of a standard size index card.

8.   The greatest common factor of any two consecutive Fibonacci numbers is one. Show that this is true for the first ten Fibonacci numbers.

9.   Determine whether each is a Fibonacci type sequence (A Fibonacci type sequence is any sequence in which each term after the third is the sum of the previous two terms). If it is, find the next four terms.

(a) $3, 7, 10, 17, \cdots$

(b) $1, 3, 4, 7, 11, \cdots$

(c) $10, 15, 25, 50, \cdots$

(d) $\frac{1}{2}, \frac{1}{2}, 1, \frac{3}{2}, \frac{5}{2}, 4, \cdots$

5.9   Patterns and Magic Squares

When we studied sequences in the previous three sections, we needed to look for patterns to determine the type of sequence with which we were dealing. Looking for patterns and discovering patterns can be enjoyable and also, at times, very useful. You can approach it as a puzzle.

Nicomachus of Gerasa, a mathematician who lived about the year 100, noticed a pattern he wrote about in the *Introductio arithmeticae*. He began by grouping the odd integers as the first one, then the next two, then the next three, and so on in this pattern.

$1; 3 + 5; 7 + 9 + 11; 13 + 15 + 17 + 19; \cdots$

He then noticed that:
$$1 = 1^3$$
$$3 + 5 = 8 = 2^3$$
$$7 + 9 + 11 = 27 = 3^3$$
$$13 + 15 + 17 + 19 = 64 = 4^3$$

The successive sums are the cubes of the integers.

Consider the following arrangement:

$$1 \times 8 + 1 = 9$$
$$12 \times 8 + 2 = 98$$
$$123 \times 8 + 3 = 987$$
$$1234 \times 8 + 4 = 9876$$

Can you find the next five lines? (From November 1992 *Recreational & Educational Computing*, Volume 17, number 7. Reprinted with the permission of Dr. Michael W. Ecker, 909 Violet Terrace, Clarks Summit, PA 18414)

Example 1. Do you see a pattern? Make a conjecture about the next line.

$1 + 1 = 2$

$1 + 2 = 3$

$2 + 3 = 5$

$3 + 5 = 8$

Solution: $1,1,2,3,5,8,\cdots$ is the Fibonacci sequence. We are simply adding consecutive pairs of Fibonacci numbers. The next Fibonacci number is 13 (because 5+8=13). Thus, the next line is:

$5 + 8 = 13.$

Example 2. Do you see a pattern? Make a conjecture about the next line.

$1 = 1^2$

$1 + 3 = 2^2$

$1 + 3 + 5 = 3^2$

$1 + 3 + 5 + 7 = 4^2$

Solution: The terms we are adding are consecutive odd integers. The next odd integer is 9. If we add: $1 + 3 + 5 + 7 + 9$ we have a sum of 25, which fits the pattern on the right of the equal sign perfectly. Thus, the next line is:

$1 + 3 + 5 + 7 + 9 = 5^2$

Pascal's Triangle

Blaise Pascal in the seventeenth century noticed a pattern that became very useful in future mathematics, known as *Pascal's Triangle*. (We mention this triangle again in section 10.4)

The following array of numbers is known as Pascal's Triangle:

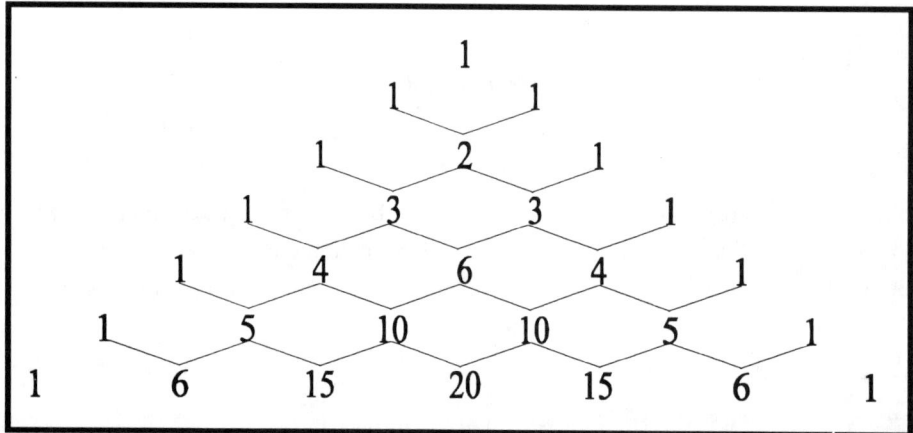

Figure 5.7 Pascal's triangle.

This triangle continues in this manner. The first two rows consist of 1's. Every other row begins and ends with 1. Each other entry in a row is computed by adding together the two entries diagonally adjacent in the row above it (connected to it by lines in Figure 5.7). In the third row from the top, the first entry is 1, then the next entry is 2 (the sum of the two numbers diagonally adjacent in the row above it),

and the next entry is 1. In the fourth row from the top, the first entry is 1, the next entry is 3 (which is the sum of the 1 and 2 immediately to the left and right of this number in the row above it), the next entry is 3 (which is the sum of the 2 and 1 immediately to the left and right of this number in the row above it), and the last entry on the right is 1.

This triangle appeared earlier in the *Precious Mirror* by Chu Shih–chieh, a Chinese mathematician who lived from 1280–1303, long before the time of Pascal.

Magic Squares

Magic Squares come in many shapes, sizes, and more than one dimension. A *magic square* is a square array of numbers such that every row, every column, and every diagonal have the same sum. This sum is known as the *magic number*. (Magic squares do not necessarily have to be square, as we will see later.)

The first recorded magic square, Figure 5.8, is of order 3, meaning it has three rows and three columns. This square originated in China over 4,800 years ago. It "was supposedly brought to man by a turtle from the River Lo in the days of the legendary Emperor Yii, reputed to be a hydraulic engineer." (p.197, 1968 *A History of Mathematics* by Boyer and revised by Merzbach). The magic number is 15.

4	9	2
3	5	7
8	1	6

Figure 5.8 The first magic square.

Suppose we wanted to create a magic square that is three rows by three columns using the counting numbers from 1 through 9 inclusive. We will use each number only once. How could we create this square?

We begin by placing the middle number, 5, in the middle square. We will place the two numbers furthest apart, 1 and 9, in the same row. Place them in the middle row (see Figure 5.9 below). Thus, the magic number will be 15 (because $1 + 5 + 9 = 15$ is one of the row sums).

1	5	9

Figure 5.9 The first row completed.

The next two numbers furthest apart are 8 and 2. Notice that $2 + 5 + 8 = 15$; put these so that 8 and 2 are in the same diagonal as 5. We do not want the 8 in the same row or column as 9 because $8 + 9 > 15$, giving a row or column sum that is too big. Thus, we place the 8 in the same column as the 1 and the 9 with the 2 as in Figure 5.10. So far our square looks like this:

8		
1	5	9
		2

Figure 5.10   One diagonal is completed.

The first column must sum to 15, so we need to place a 6 in the last row of the first column ($8 + 1 + 6 = 15$). Likewise, we place a 4 in the first row last column (because $4 + 9 + 2 = 15$) (see Figure 5.11 below)

8		4
1	5	9
6		2

Figure 5.11 Two columns are completed.

Note that so far we have placed each of the first nine numbers into the diagram exactly once except for the numbers 3 and 7. Since the first row must also sum 15 and $15 - 8 - 4 = 3$, we will place the 3 in the first row and the 7 in the last row. So, our square looks like Figure 5.12.

8	3	4
1	5	9
6	7	2

Figure 5.12 The magic square is complete.

Now, we check that each row ($8 + 3 + 4 = 15$, $1 + 5 + 9 = 15$, $6 + 7 + 2 = 15$), each column ($8 + 1 + 6 = 15$, $3 + 5 + 7 = 15$, $4 + 9 + 2 = 15$), and each diagonal ($8 + 5 + 2 = 15$, $4 + 5 + 6 = 15$) sums to 15. Thus, this is a magic square and the magic number is 15.

If a magic square consists of m rows and m columns, then the magic number, S, is usually

$$S = \frac{m(1+m^2)}{2}.$$

Notice in the square above, $m = 3$ and

$$S = \frac{3(1+3^2)}{2} = \frac{3(10)}{2} = 15.$$

An interesting magic square consists of 25 different *palindromic numbers*. A palindromic number is a number that reads the same both forwards and backwards, such as 939 or 12,321. This magic square, given in Figure 5.13, has magic number 1,991 which is also a palindromic number. (p.4, December 1990 *Recreational and Educational Computing* Volume 5, Number 8 by Dr. Michael W. Ecker, 909 Violet Terrace, Clarks Summit, PA 18411. Magic Square by Allan Wm. Johnson Jr. Reprinted with permission.)

44	323	787	454	383
393	101	898	4	595
484	989	292	171	55
303	545	3	868	272
767	33	11	494	686

Figure 5.13 A palindromic magic square.

Not all magic squares are shaped in this manner. Consider the following magic square.

Example 3. The following "magic square", Figure 5.14, is to use each of the counting numbers from 1 through 25 inclusive exactly once. The magic number is 65. Each line of five circled numbers in the star must sum to the magic number.
(p. 27, 1992 *The Ultimate Book of Number Puzzles* by Kelsey and King).

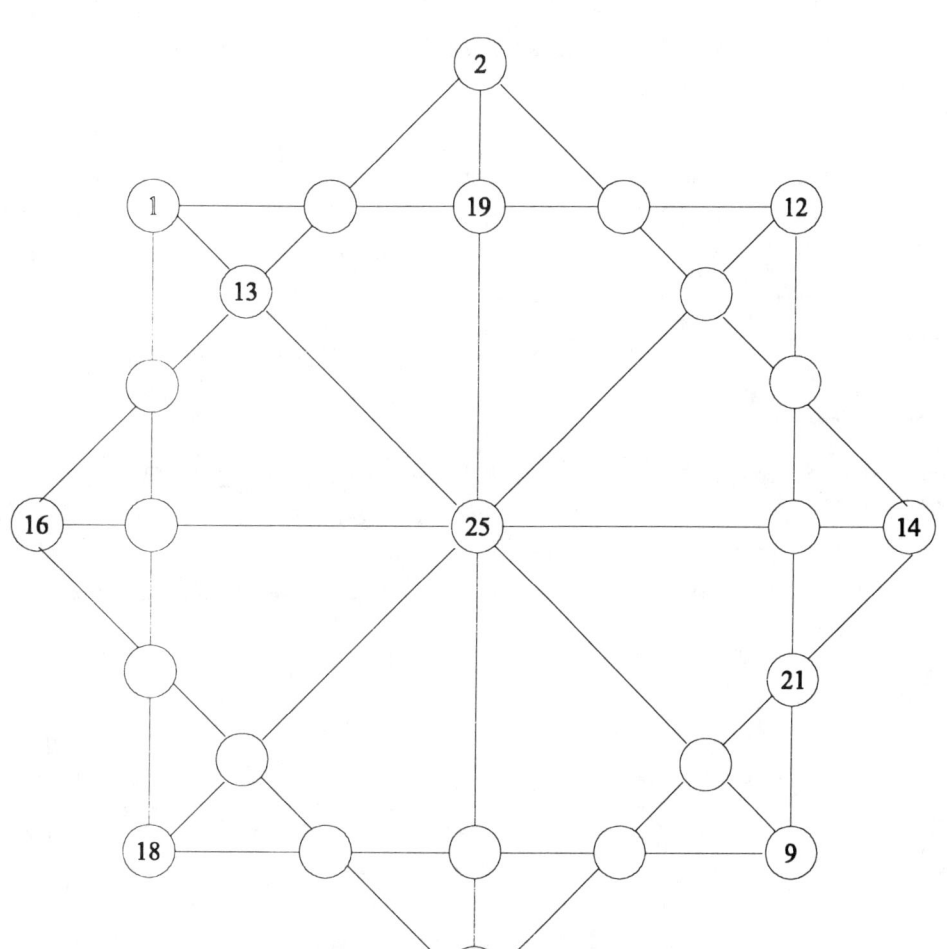

Figure 5.14 Can you complete this magic square? Every line of five circled numbers must sum to the magic number of 65.

For the solution, see figure 5.15 (below) and the explanation following.
Solution:

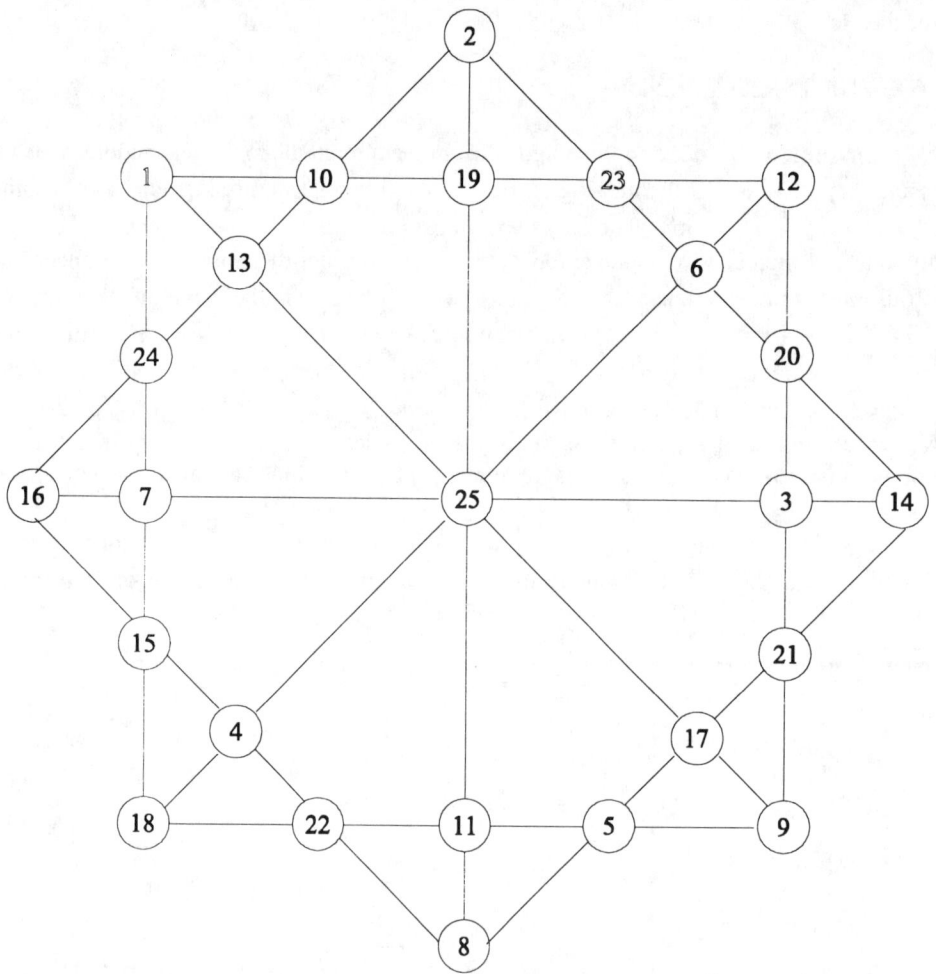

Figure 5.15 The completed magic square for example 3.

We begin by noting the counting numbers that still need to be placed. They are the numbers

3, 4, 5, 6, 7, 10, 11, 15, 17, 20, 22, 23, 24 .

We also notice that the middle column has four of the five circles completed. Thus, in that column we have accounted for all but $65 - 2 - 19 - 25 - 8 = 11$. We fill in the 11 in the empty circle and remove it from our list of available numbers. The diagonal from the top left to the lower right now has four of the five circles completed. This time, we have accounted for all but $65 - 1 - 13 - 25 - 9 = 17$. Thus, we complete the empty circle with 17 and remove it from the list of available numbers.

Our new list of available numbers is

3, 4, 5, 6, 7, 10, 15, 20, 22, 23, 24.

The diagonal from the middle right to the bottom now consists of four completed circles (because we filled in the 17). The remaining circle needs to contain $65 - 14 - 21 - 17 - 8 = 5$. We fill in the 5, and remove it. The bottom row now has four completed circles, so we need to enter $65 - 18 - 11 - 5 - 9 =$

200   Chapter 5: **NUMBER THEORY**

22 into the remaining circle. We fill in the 22, and remove it from the list. Our list of available numbers has been reduced to

   3, 4, 6, 7, 10, 15, 20, 23, 24.

The top row is missing two entries and the diagonal from the top middle to the left middle is also missing two entries and they share one of the missing entries. The top row's two missing entries must sum to 33 (because $65 - 1 - 19 - 12 = 33$). The only two numbers that sum 33 from our list are 10 and 23. The question now is which goes in which empty circle. Now consider the diagonal mentioned. Its two missing entries must sum 34 because $65 - 2 - 13 - 16 = 34$. One of the two numbers must be 10 or 23. Since $34 - 23 = 11$ and 11 is not available, it must be 10. Thus, we place the 10 in the circle shared by the top row and this diagonal. We place the 23 in the other circle of the top row. We place the 24 in the empty circle of the diagonal in consideration (because $65 - 2 - 10 - 13 - 16 = 24$).

We proceed in this manner and eventually get the circles filled as in Figure 5.15 above.

Another interesting example of a magic square is of a three dimensional character.

Example 4. The following "magic square", Figure 5.16, has magic number 170. It consists of 16 planes and four vertical edges, each of which sums to 170 using the multiples of 5 from 5 through 80 inclusive. (p. 13, 1992 *The Ultimate Book of Number Puzzles* by Kelsey and King).

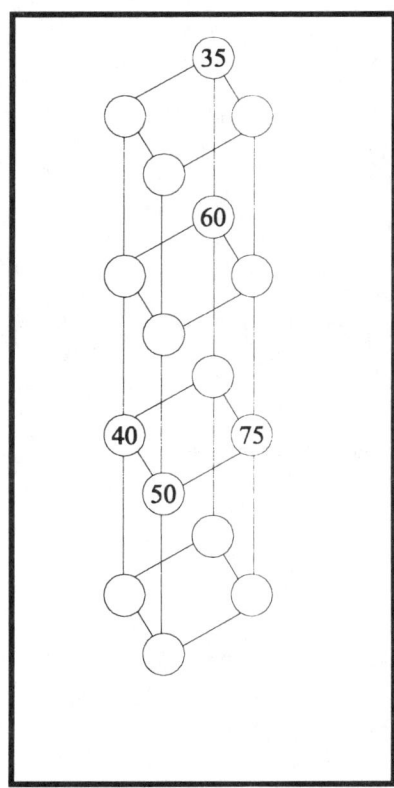

Figure 5.16 A three dimensional magic square puzzle. Fill the circles with the multiples of 5 from 5 to 80 so that each of the four vertical edges and the sixteen planes sum to 170.

Solution: We first note the available counting numbers for placement. They are

   5, 10, 15, 20, 25, 30, 45, 55, 65, 70, 80.

The third shelf from the top has three of the four vertices completed. Thus in this plane, the empty circle is completed by filling in the number $170 - 40 - 50 - 75 = 5$. Now, the back most vertical edge has

four circles completed. The fourth circle must be $170 - 35 - 60 - 5 = 70$. The back left bottom plane now has three of the four vertices completed. Thus the fourth vertex must be $170 - 40 - 5 - 70 = 55$. We continue in this fashion and complete the "magic square" as Figure 5.17 below.

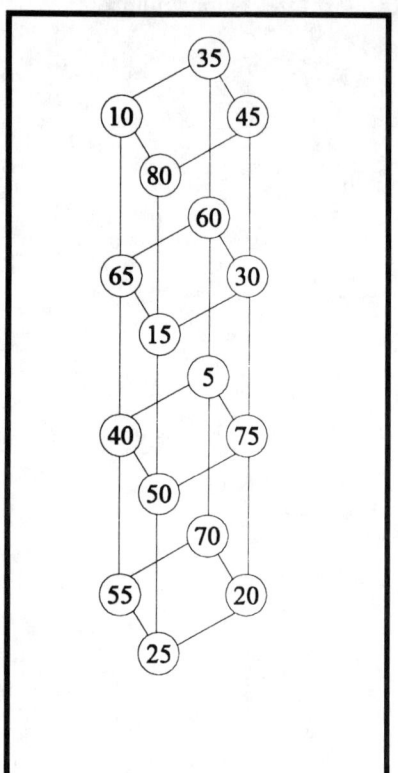

Figure 5.17 The completed three dimensional magic square of example 4.

Question to Discuss

Make a conjecture about the next line of each, then describe each of the patterns in words.

(a)
$$1 + 1 = 2$$
$$1 + 4 = 5$$
$$4 + 9 = 13$$
$$9 + 16 = 25$$

(b)
$$1 + 2 = 3$$
$$1 + 3 = 4$$
$$2 + 4 = 7$$
$$3 + 8 = 11$$

(c)
$$2 = 4 - 2$$
$$2 + 4 = 8 - 2$$
$$2 + 4 + 8 = 16 - 2$$
$$2 + 4 + 8 + 16 = 32 - 2$$

(d)
$$1 + 8 = 9$$
$$1 + 8 + 27 = 36$$
$$1 + 8 + 27 + 64 = 100$$

202   Chapter 5: **NUMBER THEORY**

Exercises

1. An oblong number can be written in the form $n(n+1)$, where n is a counting number. The first four oblong numbers are 2, 6, 12, and 20, as displayed below. Find the next three oblong numbers.

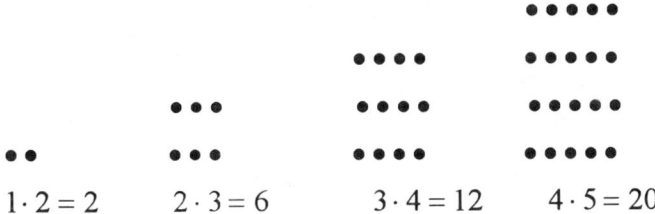

2. Make a conjecture about the next line.

$$1 = \frac{1 \cdot 2}{2}$$

$$1 + 2 = \frac{2 \cdot 3}{2}$$

$$1 + 2 + 3 = \frac{3 \cdot 4}{2}$$

$$1 + 2 + 3 + 4 = \frac{4 \cdot 5}{2}$$

3. Make a conjecture about the next line.

$$1^3 + 2^3 = \frac{2^2 \cdot 3^2}{4}$$

$$1^3 + 2^3 + 3^3 = \frac{3^2 \cdot 4^2}{4}$$

$$1^3 + 2^3 + 3^3 + 4^3 = \frac{4^2 \cdot 5^2}{4}$$

4. Make a conjecture about the next number.

5. Find the next three rows of Pascal's Triangle after those show in Figure 5.7.

6. Create a three row by three column magic square using the counting numbers from 10 through 18 inclusive (each exactly once) with magic number 42.

7. Create a three row by three column magic square using the counting numbers from 3 through 11 inclusive (each exactly once). What is the magic number?

8. Create a four row by four column magic square using the counting numbers from 1 through 16 inclusive (each exactly once) with magic number 34.

9. Complete the following "magic square" using the counting numbers from 1 through 16 inclusive (each exactly once) with magic number 34. (p.14, 1992 *The Ultimate Book of Number Puzzles* by Kelsey and King).

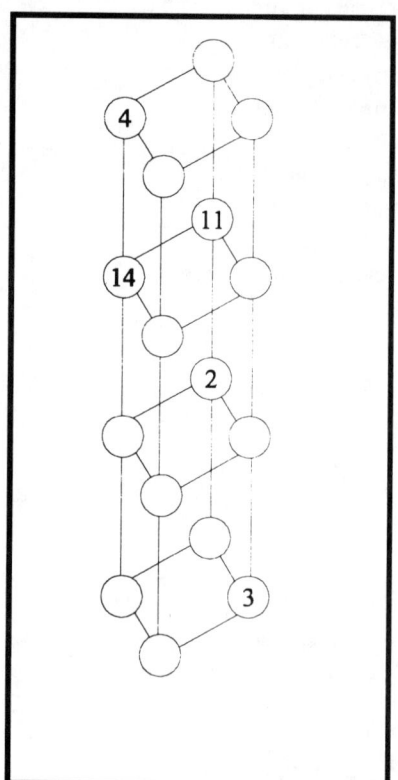

Figure 5.18 Diagram for problem 9.

10. Complete the magic square in Figure 5.19 which is to contain the natural numbers from 1 through 25 inclusive (each exactly once) with magic number 65. (p. 14, 1992 *The Ultimate Book of Number Puzzles* by Kelsey and King).

2	15			8
10				
14			4	
		9		

Figure 5.19 The diagram for problem 10.

5.10 Chapter Review

Important Terms to Know

abundant	geometric sequence	odd number
amicable	golden number	palindromic number
arithmetic sequence	greatest common factor	Pascal's triangle
common difference	integers	perfect number
common ratio	irrational numbers	prime factorization
composite	least common multiple	prime number
conjecture	magic	proper divisor
deficient	magic number	rational numbers
digit	magic square	real numbers
divisible	Mersenne prime	sequence
divisor	multiple	sieve of Eratosthenes
even	natural numbers	term
factor	nonrepeating	theorem
Fibonacci number	nonterminating	twin primes
Fibonacci sequence	number theory	whole numbers
friendly		

Important Names to Know

Cole, Frank	Euler, Leonhard	Mersenne, Father Marin
Chu Shih-chieh	Fermat, Pierre de	Nicomachus of Gerasa
Eratosthenes	Gauss, Carl Freidrich	Pascal, Blaise
Euclid	Goldbach, Christian	Plato
Euler	Leonardo of Pisa	Wiles, Andrew

Review Questions

1. Describe five different classifications of numbers and give an example of each.

2. What is a prime number? State two facts about different types of prime numbers and give examples of each.

3. What is a conjecture? State Goldbach's conjecture in your own words.

4. We studied two methods to find the prime factorization of a number. What are these two methods? Which do you prefer and why?

5. Create your own arithmetic sequence. State the first five terms and the common difference. Find the sum of the first twenty terms of your sequence without finding all of the first twenty terms.

6. Create your own geometric sequence. State the first five terms and the common ratio. Find the sum of the first ten terms of your sequence without finding all of the first ten terms.

7. Fibonacci numbers appear often in nature. Research this topic and write a paper about their occurrence in nature.

8. The diagram below (Figure 5.20) is not a magic square. Explain in complete detail, using the proper terminology, why this is not a magic square.

9	15	2	6
7	1	16	8
3	5	10	14
13	11	12	4

Figure 5.20

Chapter Six

Systems of Numeration

"All the fun's in how you say a thing."

Robert Frost

Chapter Outline

- **6.0**   **Introduction**
- **6.1**   **Historical Perspective**
- **6.2**   **Types of Systems of Numeration**
  - *Repetitive Systems*
  - *Multiplicative Systems*
  - *Ciphered Systems*
  - *Positional Systems*
- **6.3**   **The Egyptian System**
- **6.4**   **Roman Numerals**
- **6.5**   **The Babylonian Numeration System**
- **6.6**   **The Mayan Numeration System**
- **6.7**   **The Hindu–Arabic System of Numeration**
- **6.8**   **Chapter Review**

6.0 Introduction

In the beginning, people only had words for one and two. Any quantity above that was called "many." People eventually began to maintain tallies of things, such as the number of sheep that they owned. These tallies could be used to count and measure *different things*, such as fish, berries, and stones. Numeration systems are the result of this insight. With a numeration system one could use the same symbol to count his sheep, his bags of grain, his berries, or his children.

People have used many numeration systems to answer the question "how many." For example, the question "How many children do you have?" could be indicated using many symbols, such as "7," "seven," "VII," "sieben," or "|||||||." All of these symbols denote the same number. Just as your name is a symbol which represents you, these *numerals* can also be thought of as names for the number that they represent.

Most of the time this distinction between "number" and "numeral" can be blurred without serious consequences. After all, we say things like "Jane left the room." Making no distinction between the name "Jane" and the person that this name represents. No one says "The person represented by the name Jane left the room." Similarly, people talk about "The number 3," sometimes confusing "number" with "numeral," and generally no serious consequences are encountered because of this. This chapter, however, is an exception. Here we will need to be more careful. In the study of numeration systems we must realize that every single system that we study in this chapter was symbolizing the same numbers as every other system. The Babylonians and Romans were not studying different numbers than we do today simply because they represented them differently! On the other hand, as we shall see, an efficient numeration system can be helpful in giving us insights into the properties of numbers. We know more about numbers now than the Babylonians and Romans did in part because of the more efficient way that we have of representing numbers. There's no doubt that proper organization and convenient notational conventions can go a long way toward understanding difficult concepts! That is, a good numeration system will be helpful in discovering facts about numbers.

6.1 Historical Perspective

When people began to develop systems of numeration, they did not immediately invent a neat, compact system. The symbols developed at first related to the life around them – hieroglyphics. They might draw a fish or a flower to represent a number. Or, if they were writing with rough instruments into stone, maybe just a line or a dot.

At first, there weren't many rules like we have today. These developed as their numbers grew larger and they discovered new more compact ways to display their numeration system.

We will begin by investigating some of the different types of numeration systems that have been used by different cultures.

6.2 Types of Systems of Numeration

Before we define the different types of numeration systems, we need to understand the term *base*. The base of a system is the size of a basic group. The base we use in our system today is ten, because our groupings are in powers of ten. Recall that as we move from the decimal point to the left we have the units place $(10^0 = 1)$, then the tens place $(10^1 = 10)$, then the hundreds place $(10^2 = 100)$, the thousands place $(10^3 = 1,000)$, and so forth. We say that we have a base of ten because each position in our representation of a number represents a power of ten. This is the size of a basic group in the system. Any natural number greater than one, $(2,3,\cdots)$, may be used as a base.

To examine the different types of systems, we will use base 4 in our examples in this section. Thus, we will be grouping things by 4 and by powers of 4.

Repetitive Systems

In a *repetitive system*, symbols are written over and over again, as many times as necessary to represent the number. For example, suppose we let > represent 1 and $ represent 4. Then to represent the following values one could write:

VALUE	SYMBOL
1	>
2	>>
3	>>>
4	$
5	$>
6	$>>
7	$>>>
8	$$
9	$$>

Table 6.1 Representations of some values in a repetitive system with a base of four.

Do you see the pattern?

One way of thinking of the symbols in this system is that they are breaking up a value into groups (in this case, into groups of four). For example, if we wished to represent the value 59 in this system we could ask ourselves a question such as this: "How many groups of 4 are contained in 59?" Since 4 goes into 59 a total of fourteen times, we would write down fourteen of our symbols that represent groups of four, that is, we would write down fourteen $'s (We wouldn't want to use fifteen $'s since that would represent $15 \times 4 = 60$, which is too many.). This would account for 56 of the 59 that we are attempting

to represent (because $14 \times 4 = 56$). There is still $59 - 56 = 3$ that needs to be accounted for, so we write down three of the symbols that represent units in our system, that is we write down three >'s. We are thinking of the value 59 in the following way:

$$59 = 14 \times 4 + 3 \times 1$$
$$= (14 \text{ groups of } 4) + (3 \text{ groups of } 1)$$
$$= \$\$\$\$\$\$\$\$\$\$\$\$\$\$>>>$$

    This is a pretty lengthy way of representing the value 59, but it is no doubt better than the way such a value would have originally been represented in early tally systems. In these systems there would have been no groups, and a value such as 59 might have been represented simply by 59 lines. Because a repetitive system allows one symbol to represent a group of objects (in our case a group of four objects), these systems are sometimes referred to as *grouping systems* or as *additive systems*. The Egyptian numeration system, which we will look at shortly, is an example of a repetitive or grouping system.

    In an effort to save space, repetitive systems could be further refined so that larger numbers could be represented more economically. In our system, since we are grouping by fours, the next logical step would be to invent a new symbol for "four groups of four," or sixteen. Suppose that we let the value sixteen be represented by ^. Now how would we represent the value 59? Since 59 contains "three groups of sixteen," we will need to use three of the ^'s in the representation of this number. (Note that $3 \times 16 = 48$, a value which is smaller than 59, but $4 \times 16 = 64$, a value which is larger than 59. Thus, 59 does not contain four groups of sixteen, so we would not need four ^'s.) Of the original value of 59 we have now accounted for 3×16, or 48. That still leaves $59 - 48 = 11$ of the original group that we wanted to represent. Since a group of eleven contains two groups of four (three groups of four are too many), we need to use two symbols for four (that is, we need two of the \$'s), which accounts for eight more elements of the group. That still leaves $11 - 8 = 3$ units for which we have not accounted. We throw in three of the unit symbols (three >'s) to complete the value of the number. In this we get a shorter representation for 59 than we had before:

$$59 = 3 \times 16 + 2 \times 4 + 3 \times 1$$
$$= (3 \text{ groups of } 16) + (2 \text{ groups of } 4) + (3 \text{ groups of } 1)$$
$$= \text{^^^}\$\$>>>$$

Multiplicative Systems

    In a *multiplicative system*, a *multiplier* is used. This multiplier is written next to the symbol and represents how many of the symbol are being represented. This saves space. The results are then added together.

    Let's keep with the base four symbols we used in the previous section on repetitive systems, that is, $> = 1$, $\$ = 4$, and $\text{^} = 16$. Instead of writing a symbol over and over again, we will also use a multiplier. We will let a series of dots be our multiplier. One dot will represent just one of that symbol, two dots will represent two of that symbol, and so on. Consider the number 59 again. Recall that we need three ^'s, two \$'s, and three >'s. Thus, we would write our number 59 as follows:

    ... ^
    .. \$
    ... >

212   Chapter 6: **Systems of Numeration**

We wrote it vertically so you see that a system does not have to be a horizontal system. This is more compact than the previous system, but it would still be inefficient for larger numbers.

There have been some multiplicative systems of numeration, such as the ancient Chinese system of numeration. We will not study that system here.

Ciphered Systems

A *ciphered system* of numeration is more compact than the previous two types, but it requires a lot of memorization because it uses many symbols. These are added together as with the repetitive type systems. The distinguishing feature of this type of system is that there are many symbols. We will create a ciphered system. Consider the system created by assigning symbols the numerical values listed in Table 6.2.

NUMBER	SYMBOL	NUMBER	SYMBOL
1	!	20	#
2	@	25	^
3	$	30	%
4	&	35	*
5	(	40	+
6	>	45	)
7	>	50	=
8	,	55	?
9	/	60	.
10	|	65	}
11	{	70	[
12	]	75	"
13	;	80	'
14	–	85	:
15	~		

Table 6.2 An example of a Ciphered System

This system we just created uses 29 symbols. That is a lot of symbols to memorize, making this is a ciphered system. How would we represent the numbers 16, 28, and 100? Consider 16 first. This is $15+1$. Thus, we would write the symbols for 15 and 1. Therefore, 16 is represented as ~!. The number 28 is the same as $25+3$. Thus, 28 is represented as ^$. Finally, 100 is the same as $85+15$ and would therefore be represented as :~. As you see this is a compact system. There is no base.

The Ionic Greek system from about 3000 BC was a ciphered system of numeration. We will not investigate this system here.

Positional Systems

In a *positional system*, the position of a symbol determines its value. We will again use base 4 and the multiplication symbol of dots that we used in our multiplicative system above. Recall that we represented the number 59 in the multiplicative system as:

```
...   ∧
 ..   $
...   >
```

If this were a positional system, we would only need to keep the multiplicative symbol of dots. The value that a dot is multiplied by would be determined not by the symbol that it precedes, but by its position in the numeral. Our representation would simply be:

```
...
 ..
...
```

Here we would be using the bottom row as the units place; since there are three dots in this bottom row, this would represent $3(1) = 3$. The middle position would represent the four's place; since there are two dots in this position, this would represent $2(4) = 8$. The top place would be the sixteen's place and there are three dots here, so this represents $3(16) = 48$. If we sum these values, $3 + 8 + 48$, we do indeed get 59.

How would we represent 45? This time, we will write it horizontally with the units place on the far right, as we are accustomed to today. 16 divides into 45 two times, so we need two sixteens. Since $2(16) = 32$ and $45 - 32 = 13$, we still have thirteen to account for. Now for the four's place. 4 divides into 13 three times, so we need three fours. Because $4(3) = 12$ and $13-12=1$, we also need one unit. Therefore, our representation would be:

```
 ..     ...    .
```

What about the number 12? Because 4 divides into 12 three times with a remainder of zero, we need three fours and no units. But if we write

```
...
```

it would not be clear that this was intended to mean 3 fours rather than 3 units. This was the main problem that had to be overcome in developing a usable positional system. A symbol was needed to indicate an empty position. For this reason, the concept of the *placeholder* was developed. This is a symbol that represents "none" of a given place value. In this case we have no units. We will use the symbol { as a placeholder in our system. Then we could write 12 as:

```
...     {
```

This tells us there are 3 fours and no units. The placeholder is essential in a successful positional system of numeration.

Small Group Exercises

1. Create your own base 8 repetitive system of numeration.

2. Represent the number 348 using your repetitive system.

3. Create your own base 8 multiplicative system of numeration.

4. Represent the number 348 using your multiplicative system.

5. Create your own base 8 positional system of numeration.

6. Represent the number 348 using your positional system.

7. Create your own ciphered system of numeration.

8. Represent the number 348 using your ciphered system.

9. Which system do you prefer and why?

Questions to Discuss

1. Which types of systems must have a base?

2. Which types of systems must have a placeholder?

3. What is the placeholder we use in our current system of numeration?

4. What is the distinguishing feature of a ciphered system of numeration?

5. What are the advantages and disadvantages of a repetitive system of numeration?

6. What are the advantages and disadvantages of a ciphered system of numeration?

7. What are the advantages of a multiplicative system of numeration as compared to a repetitive system of numeration?

8. What particular problem was encountered before positional numeration systems could be successful? How was this problem solved?

9. The system we use is known as the Hindu–Arabic system of numeration. What type of system is it and why?

6.3 The Egyptian System

The Egyptians were using a repetitive system of numeration at least 5,000 years ago. The discovery of the Rosetta Stone in 1799 enabled people to decipher these symbols, since it contained a message written in three different scripts: Greek, Demotic, and Hieroglyphics. Since Greek was already known and could be translated, the researchers were able to decipher the Hieroglyphics. With this came the ability to read the inscriptions on Egyptian tombs and monuments and the Egyptian system of

numeration. These Egyptian numbers are at least as old as the pyramids. They used a base of ten and had seven symbols. Their symbols are given in Table 6.3.

VALUE	SYMBOL	SYMBOL NAME
1	|	vertical stroke
10	∩	heel bone
100	ϑ	scroll or snare
1,000	⚘	lotus flower
10,000	↑	bent finger
100,000	⌐	burbot fish (or tadpole)
1,000,000	⚘	kneeling or astonished person

Table 6.3 Egyptian symbols for numbers

At first this was a purely repetitive or additive system with a base of 10. They just simply wrote however many of a symbol or symbols they needed to represent the number. For example, to write the number 14, they would write:

∩ ||||

This is because 14=10+4. They would write 356 as

ϑϑϑ ∩∩∩∩∩ ||||||

because 356 = 3(100)+5(10)+6(1).

Example. What is the value that is represented by ⚘⚘⚘⚘ ∩∩∩∩∩∩∩∩ |||?
Solution: Each lotus flower is worth 1,000 and there are four of them, so that is 4,000. Each heel bone is worth 10 and there are eight of them, so that is 80. There are three vertical strokes each worth one, so that is 3. Thus the value is 4000+80+3 = 4083.

Example. Represent the value 732 in Egyptian Hieroglyphics.
Solution: We have seven hundreds (seven scrolls), followed by three tens (three heel bones) and two ones (two vertical strokes). Thus, we should write

ϑϑϑϑϑϑϑ ∩∩∩ ||.

This also may have been written as

∩∩∩ || ϑϑϑϑϑϑϑ.

The Egyptians did not always write the highest valued symbols to the left and the smallest valued symbols to the right. The position of a symbol did not influence its value.

The Ahmes Papyrus or Rhind Papyrus was written about 1650 BC and was about one foot high and eighteen feet long. This Egyptian scroll was not written in hieroglyphic form but in a more cursive script known as *hieratic*. This lent itself better to the use of pen and ink. From this papyrus, we know that the Egyptians eventually introduced ciphers or special signs into their system of numeration to represent multiples of powers of ten. This principle of cipheration was a great contribution of the Egyptians to the formulation of later systems of numeration.

Questions to Discuss

1. What are the advantages and disadvantages of the Egyptian system of numeration?

2. Explain why the Egyptian numeration system described in the text did not need a placeholder.

Exercises

1. What type of system of numeration did the ancient Egyptians use? Did it have a base? If so, what was the base? Did it use a placeholder? If so, what was the symbol?

2. Translate these numerals into the system currently used.

   (a) 𓏲𓏲𓏲 𓆼
   (b) 𓆼 𓆼𓆼𓆼𓆼𓆼 ∩ |||||
   (c) 𓆈 𓆈 𓏥

3. Translate each numeral into Egyptian symbols.

   (a) 38
   (b) 251
   (c) 602

6.4 Roman Numerals

Another repetitive system of numeration is the Roman Numeral System which is still used today for decorative purposes. You will find that roman numerals are used on the faces of some clocks, as chapter headings in some books, and to represent the year films were produced. The Roman system was still commonly used in most of Europe until the eighteenth century, although Fibonacci had tried to introduce the more modern Hindu–Arabic system as early as 1202. See the chapter on number theory for more information on Fibonacci.

The Roman system also uses a base of ten. Its numerals are selected letters of the Roman alphabet. Table 6.4 below gives the Roman numerals and their respective values.

SYMBOL	VALUE
I	1
V	5
X	10
L	50
C	100
D	500
M	1,000

Table 6.4 Basic Roman numerals

As you can see, they saved space by introducing symbols for 5, 50, and 500. They also introduced a *subtraction principle*. If a symbol with a smaller value appears to the right of a larger symbol, the values would be added together as you would expect. However, in some cases a symbol with a smaller value could appear to the left of a larger symbol, and the values of the two symbols would then be subtracted. There were certain rules as to when this would or would not be allowed, but we won't get into them in this text. Because of this innovation, the Roman system is sometimes called a *modified positional system*.

For example, to write the number 4, instead of using four Is, they could use IV. This is more compact. Since I is worth 1, V is worth 5, and the smaller valued symbol is to the left of the larger valued symbol, we subtract and get a value of $5-1=4$. However, VI is 6 because the smaller valued symbol is to the right of the larger valued symbol and so we add: $5+1=6$. The representations of some numbers are given below in Table 6.5.

VALUE	SYMBOL	VALUE	SYMBOL
2	II	16	XVI
3	III	17	XVII
4	IV	18	XVIII
6	VI	19	XIX
7	VII	20	XX
8	VIII	21	XXI
9	IX	22	XXII
11	XI	23	XXIII
12	XII	24	XXIV
13	XIII	25	XXV
14	XIV	26	XXVI

Table 6.5 Representations for some numbers in the Roman system.

As an example, consider fourteen. Here, we view 14 as $10+4$, where 10 is represented as X and 4 is represented as $5-1$, or IV. Thus, 14 is represented as XIV.

Multiples of 1,000 were sometimes represented by placing a bar over the entire numeral. For example, $\overline{\text{LIV}}$ would represent $(1,000)(54) = 54,000,000$. (Recall that L = 50 and IV = $5-1 = 4$.) Also, a double bar over a numeral was used to represent multiples of 1,000,000.

Example. What number do each of the following represent?

1. DLXIV
2. CDXX
3. MMDCVII

Solution:

1. D stands for 500, L stands for 50, X for 10, I for 1, and V for 5. We add the values except for the IV. Since I is smaller in value than V, $IV = 5 - 1 = 4$. Thus, we have a value of $500 + 50 + 10 + 4 = 564$.
2. C represents 100, D is the symbol for 500, and X has the value 10. Since C has a smaller value than D and C is to the left of D, we subtract their two values and then add the result to the rest of the values. So we have $500 - 100 + 10 + 10 = 420$.
3. M represents 1,000, D 500, C 100, V 5, and I 1. We add all of their values in this case, getting $1000 + 1000 + 500 + 100 + 5 + 1 + 1 = 2607$.

Example. Write each of the following numbers using the Roman system of numeration.

1. 74
2. 891
3. 436
4. 80,000,000

Solution:

1. $74 = 70 + 4$, where $70 = 50 + 10 + 10$ and $4 = 5 - 1$. Thus $74 = 70 + 4 = $ LXXIV.
2. $891 = 800 + 90 + 1$. Since 800 is DCCC and 90 is XC, we see that 891 is DCCC "+" XC "+" I, or DCCCXCI.
3. $436 = 400 + 30 + 6$, where $400 = 500 - 100 = $ CD, $30 = 10 + 10 + 10 = $ XXX, and $6 = 5 + 1$. Therefore 436 would be represented by CDXXXVI.
4. $80,000,000 = 80(1,000,000)$. Since $80 = 50 + 10 + 10 + 10$, it is represented by LXXX. Placing a double bar over this numeral indicates that its value is to be multiplied by 1,000,000, so $80(1,000,000)$ is represented by $\overline{\overline{\text{LXXX}}}$.

Question for Discussion

Compare and contrast the Egyptian and Roman systems of numeration.

Question for Discussion

What are the advantages of the Roman system of numeration as compared to the Egyptian system of numeration?

Exercises

1. Represent the following numerals using the Roman system of numeration.

   (a) 954
   (b) 762
   (c) 2,098
   (d) 19,000
   (e) 9,000,000
   (f) 1997

2. Write the following as numerals in the system in common usage.

   (a) MII
   (b) DCCXLI
   (c) XCVII
   (d) $\overline{\text{CM}}$
   (e) CCCXLIV
   (f) DLXXXI

3. What type of system of numeration is the Roman system? Does it have a base? If so, what is the base? Does it have a placeholder? If so, what is the placeholder?

4. Watch a movie. Record the date the movie was released in Roman numerals as it appears on the screen. Convert this to system in common usage.

5. Why do you believe we still use Roman numerals for some purposes?

6.5 The Babylonian Numeration System

The oldest known numeration system that resembled a positional system is that of the Babylonians. It was a *relative positional system*, not an absolute one. We will see why it was called this towards the end of this section. Their system used a base of sixty and originally consisted of only two symbols as given in Table 6.6 below.

SYMBOL	VALUE
▽	1
<	10

Table 6.6 The symbols of the Babylonian numeration system.

The Babylonians used a combination of these two symbols and spacing to represent their numbers. In a Babylonian numeral the group of symbols furthest to the right represented the units portion of the number. Since this was a base sixty system, the group of symbols next to them to the left were in the 60's place.

The next group to the left of that were in the 60^2, or 3600's position. Each time you moved another place to the left, you would multiply the value of the position by another factor of sixty. Unlike more modern systems, however, there could be more than one symbol in a position. Within each position or group, the symbols were additive, that is, the value in that place was the sum of the values of the symbols.

220   Chapter 6: **Systems of Numeration**

Example. What are the values of each of the following?

1. ∇ ∇ ∇ ∇ ∇
2. ∇   < ∇ ∇
3. ∇   ∇   <<<<
4. ∇   ∇ ∇   < ∇ ∇ ∇

Solution:
1.   There is apparently just one grouping of symbols here, and there are 5 of the symbols that represent one unit each. Thus, this represents the value $5(1) = 5$.

2.   There are two groupings of symbols. The grouping furthest to the right is the units position. The other grouping is the 60's place. In the units place, there is one symbol for 10 and two symbols for 1, thus, there is $10 + 1 + 1 = 12$ in the units place. In the 60's place, there is one symbol for 1. This represents "one group of sixty", $1(60)$, or 60. Thus, the value represented is $1(60)+12(1) = 60 + 12 = 72$.

```
∇              < ∇ ∇
1              10+1+1
1              12
1(60)    +     12(1)
```

3.   There are three groupings of symbols. The grouping furthest to the right is the units place. The middle grouping is the 60's place. The grouping furthest to the left is the 3600's place. We set up our work as follows:

```
∇          ∇              <<<<
1          1              10 +10 + 10 + 10
1          1              40
1(3600) +  1(60)    +     40(1)
```

The value of this numeral is $3600 + 60 + 40 = 3,700$.

    An interesting interpretation of a problem such as this is to think in terms of time. We use a system that has sixty minutes in an hour and sixty seconds in a minute. Thus 1 hour = 60 minutes, and 1 minute = 60 seconds. This is similar to the Babylonian numeration system where the value of any symbol is multiplied by sixty when it is moved one position further left. In other words, this problem is very similar to the following: How many seconds are there in 1 hour, 1 minute, and 40 seconds? You could even organize your work similarly:

1 hour	+	1 minute	+	40 seconds
1(60) minutes	+	1(60) seconds	+	40 seconds
1(60)(60) seconds	+	1(60) seconds	+	40 seconds

This totals to $3600 + 60 + 40 = 3700$ seconds.

4.   Again there are three sets of groupings of symbols. We work this in a manner similar to the previous example.

▽		▽ ▽		< ▽ ▽ ▽
1		1+1		10+1+1+1
1		2		13
1(3600)	+	2(60)	+	13(1)

Thus, we have a value of 3600+120+13=3,733.

Example. Write the following numbers using the Babylonian system of numeration.
1.   662   2.   1,801
3.   36,131   4.   7,880

Solution:

1.   We don't need three positions for this number since it is smaller than 3600. How many groups of 60 will we need? Since 662 divided by 60 gives a quotient of 11 with a remainder of 2, we can think of 662 as "eleven groups of sixty plus two units." Now it's easy to construct the corresponding Babylonian numeral: Put the symbol for 11 in the sixties position and the symbol for 2 in the units position.

11(60)	+	2(1)
(10+1)(60)	+	(1+1)(1)
< ▽		▽ ▽

2.   Again, this number is smaller than 3600, so we will only need to plan for two positions, the units position and the sixties position. How many sixties will we need? Since 1801 divided by 60 gives a quotient of 30 with a remainder of one, we will break up 1801 into "thirty groups of sixty plus one unit." Put the symbol representing 30 in the sixties position and the symbol for 1 in the units position.

30(60)	+	1(1)
(10+10+10)(60)	+	1(1)
<<<		▽

3.   36,131 is larger than 3600, in fact it contains ten groups of 3600. This means that the numeral that we are constructing will need three positions — the units position, the sixties position, and the $60^2 = 3600$'s position. Since 36,131 divided by 3600 is 10 with a remainder of 131, we will need to put the symbol for ten in the 3600's place, then allocate the remaining 131 to the other two positions. This is done in exactly the same manner that it was done in the previous two problems.

10(3600)	+	131		
10(3600)	+	2(60)	+	11(1)
10(3600)	+	(1+1)(60)	+	(10+1)(1)
<		▽ ▽		< ▽

Again, note how similar this is to the following familiar problem: Convert 36,131 seconds into hours, minutes, and seconds. Since 36,131 seconds divided by 3600 (the number of seconds in an hour) is 10 with a remainder of 131, we see that 36,131 seconds is 10 hours plus 131 seconds, that is, 10 hours plus 2 minutes and 11 seconds.

4.   When 7,880 is divided by 3600, the result is 2 with a remainder of 680. Thus, we have two groups of 3600's. Next, we take the remainder, 680, and divide it by 60 (the next place value). 680

divided by 60 is 11 with a remainder of 20. Thus, there are eleven 60's and twenty units. We organize our work as follows:

```
2(3600)     +     11(60)      +     20(1)
(1+1)(3600) +     (10+1)(60)  +     (10+10)(1)
∇ ∇               < ∇                <<
```

Example. Write the numerals for 10 and 600 in the Babylonian system.
Solution: Ten is simply 10(1). Thus, we represent 10 as:

<

When we divide 600 by 60 The result is 10 with a remainder of zero. Thus, there are ten 60's and no units. So, it seems that we also represent 600 by

<

As you can see, this could be quite confusing! How do we determine whether < represents 10(1)=10, 10(60)=600, or for that matter 10(3600)=36,000? This is the problem with the early Babylonian system. They had no placeholder. If you saw a single symbol in the Babylonian system there would be no way of knowing in which position it was supposed to be.

By the time of the conquest of Alexander the Great a placeholder had been invented by the Babylonians. They used two small wedges placed obliquely like this ⊥⊥. However, they only used this placeholder for intermediate positions, not the unit's place. Thus, this placeholder did not aide in depicting the value 60. It was still written as <. However, it did help in depicting a number such as 3,601. Early Babylonians represented 3,601 as

∇   ∇

leaving a larger space between the 3600's place and the unit's place to show that there were no 60's. Later, they used the placeholder to show the empty position and represented it as

∇   ⊥⊥   ∇

It helped a great deal, but not enough.

Because the Babylonian system used positional values, but essentially used grouping within a position, it is referred to as a relative positional system of numeration.

Questions to Discuss

1. What are the advantages and disadvantages of the Babylonian system as compared to the Egyptian? the Roman?

2. Are there any vestiges of the Babylonian base sixty numeration system that you can find in modern culture? If so, can you think of any reasons why this base would have survived in these places, but not in other places?

Exercises

1. Write these numbers in the modern system.

    (a) << ▽   (b) ▽ <<   (c) < <▽ ▽▽▽

2. Represent these values using the Babylonian numeration system.

    (a) 203   (b) 7,451   (c) 3,782

3. Why is the Babylonian system of numeration known as a relative positional system? What is the base? Did it have a placeholder? If so, what was the symbol?

6.6 The Mayan Numeration System

The *Mayan*s of the Yucatan were an American Indian people who lived in southern Mexico. They were the first people in the New World to keep historical records. They had a highly evolved lifestyle for their time, with intensive agricultural and sophisticated water management that they developed between 900 and 300 BC. They also had a calendar that consisted of 360 days for one year. Their number system was important to them because they used it to represent time intervals between dates in their calendar.

Their system of numeration is a positional system with a basic base of twenty and an auxiliary base of five. They wrote their numbers vertically, with the smallest valued position on the bottom and the largest on the top. We say it had a basic base of twenty, because it was not a pure base twenty system. The place values of their system are listed in Figure 6.1.

$$\vdots$$
$$18 \cdot 20^4 = 2,880,000$$
$$18 \cdot 20^3 = 144,000$$
$$18 \cdot 20^2 = 7,200$$
$$18 \cdot 20^1 = 360$$
$$20^1 = 20$$
$$20^0 = 1$$

Figure 6.1 The values of the positions in the Mayan numeration system. Read the figure from bottom to top.

Notice that they did not quite follow what one might think is the usual pattern, but replaced $(20)(20)$ with $(18)(20)$. This was done for the purposes of their calendar which consisted of 360 days because $(18)(20)=360$.

The Mayan system worked in a way that was similar to the Babylonian system in the sense that they used two basic symbols to represent values within a position. Their two symbols are given in Table 6.7 below.

224   Chapter 6: **Systems of Numeration**

SYMBOL	VALUE
•	1
———	5

Table 6.7 Mayan symbols

They represented the numbers from 1 to 19 inclusive, which would have required only position, as shown in Figure 6.2. Notice how within the units position they used a bar to represent 5 and a • to represent one.

Figure 6.2 The numerals one through nineteen in the Mayan Numeration System.

They also had a placeholder which looked like the following symbol:

Numbers larger than twenty would have had a representation requiring more than one position. The twenties position would have been placed directly above the units position, and it could contain symbols representing any value up to seventeen — remember, the next position up would be the "(18)(20)" position, the only exception to the rule of grouping by twenties. In any other position you could place a numeral with any value up to nineteen, or a placeholder, if necessary.

Example. Write each of the following Mayan numerals in the modern system.

Solution:

1.   We begin with the bottom place, the units place. The three horizontal lines represent 15, thus we have $15 \times 1 = 15$. The next place above that, the twenty's place, consists of three dots or 3. That represents $3 \times 20 = 60$. The place above that, the 360's place, has two dots, or 2. Thus, we have $2 \times 360 = 720$. Finally, the top place gives us $7 \times 7{,}200 = 50{,}400$. We add these values together to get the value of this numeral:

$$(15 \times 1) + (3 \times 20) + (2 \times 360) + (7 \times 7200) = 15 + 60 + 720 + 50{,}400 = 51{,}195$$

2.   In this numeral we have 5 in the unit's place, 3 in the twenty's place, 9 in the 360's place, 0 in the $18 \times 20 \times 20 \times 20$'s place, and 8 in the $18 \times 20 \times 20 \times 20 \times 20 = 144{,}000$'s place. Therefore this numeral has the value

$$(5 \times 1) + (3 \times 20) + (9 \times 360) + (0 \times 7{,}200) + (8 \times 144{,}000) = 5 + 60 + 3{,}240 + 0 + 1{,}152{,}000$$
$$= 1{,}155{,}305$$

Example. Translate each of the following into Mayan numerals.
1.   363   2.   9,395

Solution:
1.   We begin by finding the largest place value contained in 363, which is 360. Since 363 divided by 360 is 1 with a remainder of 3, we need to place the symbol for 1 in the 360's place. Now we divide the remainder, 3, by the next place value, 20. The result is 0 with remainder 3. We have zero (a placeholder) in the 20's place. Finally, we divide the remainder by 1. We find that the remaining 3 go into the unit's place. Thus, our Mayan numeral is:

2.   The largest place value we can divide 9,395 by is 7,200. The result of this division is 1 with a remainder of 2,195. We put the symbol for 1 in the 7,220's place. Now, we find that 2,195 (the remainder) divided by 360 is 6 with a new remainder of 35. We place the Mayan numeral for 6 in the 360's place. Now, 35 (the new remainder) divided by 20 (the next place value) is 1 with a remainder of 15. Thus, we also place a 1 in the 20's place and the symbol for 15 (the final remainder) in the unit's place. Our Mayan numeral is:

This is an example of a true positional system of numeration, just as the Hindu–Arabic system is.

Question to Discuss

The examples concerning the Mayan numeration system contained generally larger numbers than the examples studied in the other systems. Why do you think that the numbers in this section could be larger than those in the other sections?

Exercises

1. Write each of the following Mayan numerals as numerals in the system currently in common use.

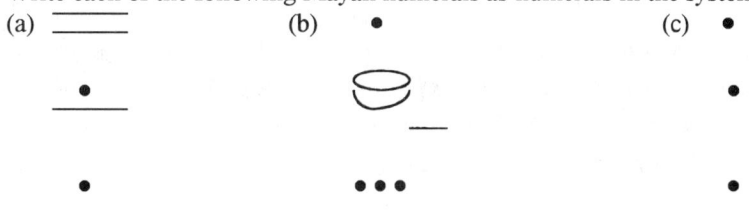

2. Write each of the following values as Mayan numerals.

   (a) 962   (b) 580   (c) 24,448

3. What type of system is the Mayan system of numeration? Does it have a base? If so, what is the base? Does it have a placeholder? If so, what is the placeholder?

4. What are the advantages of the Mayan system as compared to the Babylonian system?

6.7 The Hindu–Arabic System of Numeration

There are many different systems of numeration in use in our world today. The system we use, the Hindu–Arabic system, originated around the sixth century in India and eventually progressed into Europe and the rest of the world. It is the system that is used in all science and international trade today.

Although this is the system we use today, we still have the remains of other systems in our society. Many decorative clocks use the Roman numerals. When we measure an angle or time, we use a base of 60 (a sexagesimal system), a remnant of the Babylonian system. As you can see, other systems still have an influence in our society today.

Small Group Exercise

Complete the following table:

	TYPE	BASE	NUMBER OF SYMBOLS	PLACEHOLDER	VERTICAL VS HORIZONTAL
Egyptian					
Babylonian					
Roman					
Mayan					
Hindu–Arabic					

Table 6.8 Comparison of numeration systems.

Question to Discuss

Compare and contrast the Egyptian, Roman, Babylonian, Mayan, and Hindu–Arabic systems of numeration. Completing Table 6.8 should help you focus your ideas. In particular, focus on the similarities and differences between the Babylonian, Mayan, and Hindu–Arabic systems.

Exercise

What are the disadvantages of the Mayan system as compared to the Hindu–Arabic system we use today?

6.8 Chapter Review

Important Terms to Remember

additive system of numeration
Ahmes Papyrus
base
ciphered system
grouping system
hieratic
modified positonal system

multiplicative system
multiplier
number
numeral
numeration system
placeholder

positional system
relative positional system
repetitive system
Rhind Papyrus
Rosetta Stone
subtraction principle

Review Questions

1. Describe the four different types of systems of numeration discussed in the text.

2. What are the advantages and disadvantages of these four different types of numeration systems?

3. Both The Egyptian and Roman systems are repetitive systems. Compare and contrast the two.

4. The Babylonian, Mayan, and Hindu–Arabic systems are all positional systems of numeration. Compare and contrast the three. State some advantages and disadvantages of each.

5. Create your own hieroglyphic system of numeration. Does it have a base? If so, what is it? What type of system is it? Express 68 in your system.

Chapter Seven

Groups

"We're gonna rock around the clock tonight, rock, rock, rock 'til broad daylight. We're gonna rock, gonna rock around the clock tonight."

Bill Haley and the Comets

Chapter Seven: **GROUPS**

Chapter Outline

- 7.0 **Introduction**
- 7.1 **Historical Perspective**
   Polynomial Equations
   The Contribution of Evariste Galois
- 7.2 **The Group Concept**
- 7.3 **The Definition of a Group**
   Abelian Groups
- 7.4 **Examples and Non–Examples of Groups**
- 7.5 **Isomorphic Groups**
- 7.6 **Chapter Review**

7.0 Introduction

This chapter is different from most of the other chapters in this book. Some other chapters, such as those on statistics, probability, and sets, were designed to teach skills which could be useful in the study of other subjects, or in later life. Other chapters, such as those on logic, geometry, and computers, were intended to give you some idea of how an understanding of mathematics could increase your enjoyment and understanding of other disciplines. This chapter, however, is much more abstract than most of the others. Its purpose is to give students some idea of the types of questions encountered in contemporary mathematics, and the surprising and unexpected places where they sometimes lead.

One of the problems that new students often confront when starting the study of groups is one of focus. The objects studied in group theory (which may be numbers, geometric objects, or even abstract symbols) are generally not the central point of the study. More important than these objects themselves are the relationships between these objects and the rules which they satisfy. In this sense group theory could be considered an abstract model for many modern disciplines, such as sociology. For example, in sociology the focus is on the *interaction* of the objects (in this case people) as they form societies, organizations, and cultures which are governed by formal and informal rules. Similarly, the numbers, geometric objects, and abstract symbols encountered in group theory are generally subordinate to the relationships between them.

Group theory is a major division of the branch of mathematics known as *abstract algebra*. Although its early development was stimulated by purely mathematical considerations (the solution of polynomial equations), the study of groups has proved to be valuable in physics, chemistry, cryptography, and in the exposition of the idea of symmetry. But beyond the effect that the theory of groups has had outside of mathematics, it would not be an exaggeration to say that this subject has been one of the prevalent themes within mathematics over the last two hundred years. It has given mathematicians the ability to recognize and classify important structures, and to identify significant features of systems which might otherwise remain hidden. Eric Temple Bell, in his classic book *Mathematics, Queen and Servant of Science*, said that "Wherever groups disclosed themselves, or could be introduced, simplicity crystallized out of comparative chaos."

7.1 Historical Perspective

Work which modern mathematicians would recognize as group theory can be traced back as far as the late eighteenth and early nineteenth centuries. As usual, the events which led to the emergence of this field go back many years before this.

Polynomial Equations

In some sense, polynomial equations are the simplest equations which are studied in algebra. When put into standard form, they can be made to look like this:

$$a_n x^n + a_{n-1} x^{n-1} + a_{n-2} x^{n-2} + \cdots + a_1 x + a_0 = 0.$$

In this formula the a's (called the coefficients) are real numbers whose values we will assume to be known. Some of the a's may be zero, but a_n, called the *leading coefficient*, is assumed to be nonzero. The terms are arranged so that the exponents are in decreasing order, with x^n being the highest power of x, followed by the next highest power, and so on. The *variable*, or *unknown*, is x. Solving such an equation means finding the values of x which make the equation true. The highest exponent, n, is called the *degree of the equation*.

Example 1. $\quad 3x - 1 = 0$

This equation is a *first degree* equation, because the highest exponent of x that appears in the equation is one. (Remember, x means the same thing as x^1.) First degree equations are also called *linear equations*. In elementary algebra we learn how to solve such equations, and in this particular case we find that the only solution to this equation is $x = \dfrac{1}{3}$.

Example 2. $\quad 2x^2 + 6x - 3 = 0$

This equation is a *second degree* equation in x because the highest exponent for x is two. Second degree equations are also called *quadratic equations*. Such equations are also studied in elementary algebra, and can be solved using the *quadratic formula*. In this case it is possible to show that $x = \dfrac{-3 + \sqrt{15}}{2}$ and $x = \dfrac{-3 - \sqrt{15}}{2}$ are the only two solutions of this equation. The solution of this equation is called a *solution by radicals* because square roots, or radicals, are required to write the general solution of quadratic equations. Methods for solving quadratic equations have been known since antiquity.

Example 3. $\quad 3x^3 - 2x^2 + x - 2 = 0$

This equation is a *third degree* equation in x because the highest exponent for x is three. Third degree equations are also called *cubic equations*. Such equations are not usually studied in elementary algebra, however, using more advanced techniques it can be shown that $x = 1$ is the only real solution to this equation. There are also two other solutions, called *complex solutions*, of this equation. We won't be dealing with complex solutions here, except to note that the complex number system is a generalization of the real number system studied in elementary algebra.

Although the particular equation given above in example 3 is easily solved by people who have studied the appropriate algebraic techniques, a more difficult question went unanswered for many years: Is there a "cubic formula," a formula similar to the quadratic formula, that could be used to solve *all* cubic equations? Such a procedure was finally discovered in the sixteenth century. In fact, two Italian mathematicians, Niccolo Tartaglia and Ludovico Ferrari, discovered techniques which could be used to solve any third or fourth degree equation. (Fourth degree equations are called *quartic equations* or *biquadratic equations*.) These techniques were published by Gerolamo Cardano in 1545 in his famous book, *Ars Magna* (The Great Art). Cardano was probably the greatest mathematician of his time, and he also was an accomplished physician. In medicine he is known for having been the first person to give a

clinical description for typhus fever. In mathematics he is famous for his early investigations into the laws of probability (a hundred years before Fermat and Pascal), and his publication of the general solution of the cubic equation, which he got from Tartaglia only after promising him that he would keep the solution secret.

At this point things start to get quite a bit more complicated. Many years of unsuccessful attempts at trying to solve fifth degree equations (called *quintic equations*) gave some the idea that a procedure for solving such equations might not exist – at least not a procedure involving the basic operations of addition, subtraction, multiplication, division, and the taking of radicals (roots). This was eventually proved by Neils Henrik Abel, a Norwegian mathematician, in 1824. (Although formulas for the solution of fifth degree equations do exist, they require more than the basic operations of addition, subtraction, multiplication, division, and the taking of radicals mentioned above). Not long after this another mathematician, Evariste Galois, was to make an even more impressive contribution to algebra which would lay the foundation for modern group theory.

The Contribution of Evariste Galois

Evariste Galois' life was brief and troubled. He was born near Paris in 1811. His mother educated him at home until 1823, when he entered Collège Royal de Louis–le–Grand. Although his proficiency in mathematics was obvious, his mediocre, rigid teachers could not stimulate him to excel in other areas of study. He applied twice to École Polytechnique, a highly regarded school of mathematics, but failed both entrance examinations. Although he wrote a couple of technical papers, his submissions to the French Academy of Sciences were either lost or rejected.

Now resigned to the reality that he would not be a mathematician, Galois entered a school for training as a teacher and became a political activist. His articles on the revolution earned him a quick expulsion from school and two arrests for "republican activities."

Galois' short life came to an end after a duel which took place on May 30, 1832. Although the date of the duel is known, not much else is. The romantic version of the story is that the duel was to be fought over the honor of a former girlfriend. A second version of the story, proposed by Alexandre Dumas, is that the duel was held for political reasons, his opponent being an advocate of the monarchy. Whatever the reason, Galois knew before the duel that he had very little chance of surviving, so he spent the night before it writing one last mathematical paper. The paper began the development of what is now called *Galois Theory* – a procedure by which polynomial equations could be classified as either "solvable by radicals" or "non–solvable by radicals" depending on the properties of a certain "Galois group" associated with the equation. Galois did, in fact, die of his wounds, on the day after the duel.

Galois' manuscripts were finally published in 1846, but it wasn't until 1870 that the mathematician Camile Jordan published a treatise finally establishing Galois theory as a powerful tool in the solution of equations.

7.2 The Group Concept

Before giving the definition of a group in the next section, an example may help in understanding just what a group is. Consider the following "multiplication table."

Chapter Seven: GROUPS

×	I	A	B	C	D	E
I	I	A	B	C	D	E
A	A	B	I	D	E	C
B	B	I	A	E	C	D
C	C	E	D	I	B	A
D	D	C	E	A	I	B
E	E	D	C	B	A	I

Table 7.1 A multiplication table.

This table is used in the same way as a grade–school multiplication table. Take any letter, say D, from the left hand column, and any letter, say B, from the top row. The *product* of D and B, denoted by $D \times B$, is found by taking the entry where the row headed by D intersects the column headed by B (see Table 7.2). In this case we see that the product of D and B is E.

×	I	A	B	C	D	E
I	I	A	B	C	D	E
A	A	B	I	D	E	C
B	B	I	A	E	C	D
C	C	E	D	I	B	A
D	D	C	E	A	I	B
E	E	D	C	B	A	I

Table 7.2 $D \times B = E$.

A number of interesting comments can be made concerning this table.

1. This multiplication table is defined for elements in the set $\{I, A, B, C, D, E\}$, however, it would be *inaccurate* to say that this set is "the group." The multiplication table is imposing a *structure* on the set, and it is this structure that a mathematician is interested in when he or she studies the group. In fact, one mathematician, Arthur Cayley, said that *any finite group is completely determined by its multiplication table.*
2. Although it is true that every finite group is completely defined by its multiplication table, it is not true that every multiplication table defines a group. As was stated above, the multiplication table imposes a structure on the set of elements. It is only when this structure satisfies certain restrictions that this construction can be called a group. These restrictions, which are stated in the next section, can be verified for the multiplication table given as Table 7.1. When we make these verifications in the next section we will have verified that the system under consideration is a group.
3. In this particular case we found that $D \times B = E$. However, if we use the table to compute $B \times D$ we find that this does not equal E, but instead it equals C. Thus, this particular group does not satisfy the *commutative law* which you are familiar with for the basic operations of addition and multiplication from arithmetic. For this reason the system under consideration here is called a noncommutative group. In fact, this particular example, which can be found in many elementary books on group theory, was selected precisely because it is the simplest example of a noncommutative group.
4. The only entries that appear in the body of the table are the ones that appear on the top row (or equivalently, in the left–hand column).
5. The element I has two interesting properties. First of all, multiplying any element by I leaves that element unchanged. ($x \times I = x$ and $I \times x = x$ for every x in the set. What rows and columns of the table illustrate this?) Furthermore, a more careful look at the table shows that for each element, there is *exactly* one other element in the set that it can be multiplied with in order

to give the answer I. (For example, A needs to be multiplied with B to get the answer I; C needs to be multiplied with itself.) Both of these properties turn out to be essential to the group concept.

7.3 The Definition of a Group

We shall now define a group. In so doing we will often be referring back to the multiplication table, Table 7.1, from the previous section, in order to make these abstract ideas a bit easier to understand.

A group is a collection of objects, S, along with an operation, which we will write as $\circ$. The system satisfies the following conditions, called the *group postulates*:

The Group Postulates:

P1 (The closure postulate): If a and b are any two elements of S, then $a \circ b$ is also in S.

P2 (The associative law): If a, b, and c are any three elements of S, then $(a \circ b) \circ c = a \circ (b \circ c)$.

P3 (Existence of an identity): There is a unique element i of S such that $a \circ i = i \circ a = a$ for every element a in S. i is called the *identity* for the group.

P4 (Existence of unique inverses): If a is any element of S, then there is exactly one element of S, say a', such that $a \circ a' = a' \circ a = i$. a' is called *the inverse of a*.

To review:

Definition: A group is a set of objects together with an operation $\circ$ which satisfies the four group postulates listed above.

Groups may be finite or infinite – that is, the set S that the group is built upon may be either a finite set or an infinite set. As implied in the last section, if S is finite the group postulates may be confirmed by investigation of its multiplication table. Of course if a mathematical system is not a group, that can also be confirmed by investigating its table. Let's look back at the example from the last section and see how a table can be used to check a mathematical system to see if it's a group.

Postulate **P1** is easily checked by simply verifying that each entry in the body of the table is one of the elements of S, that is, that the only entries which appear in the table are elements which appear in the top row (and the left–hand column) of the table. As mentioned earlier, this is certainly true in our example – the only entries in the table are I, A, B, C, D, and E, and these are all elements of S.

Before going to the other postulates, let's introduce some terminology. When we refer to *row–A* we will mean the row in the table with A as its left–most entry. Table 7.3, below, is simply a copy of Table 7.1 with row–A shaded.

×	I	A	B	C	D	E
I	I	A	B	C	D	E
A	A	B	I	D	E	C
B	B	I	A	E	C	D
C	C	E	D	I	B	A
D	D	C	E	A	I	B
E	E	D	C	B	A	I

Table 7.3 Row–A is shaded.

Similarly, a reference to *Column–D* will mean that we are talking about the column of the table that has the element D at the top.

Now, let's discuss how we can check postulate **P3**. If an identity element, i, exists, then *multiplying any element* of S *by i will yield the same element* of S. That is, $i \circ x = x$ for every x in S. What does this mean in terms of the table? The first factor in the product, i, is taken from the left-hand column; the second factor of the product, x, is taken from the top row; the answer, also x, is taken from *the intersection of row–i and column–x*. Thus, the entry in row–i and column–x must be the same as the entry directly above it in the top row (they are both x.) *But this must be true for every entry in row–i!* Thus, *every element in row–i must be the same as the entry directly above it in the top row*. This means that row–i must exactly match the top row of the table. See Table 7.4 to see what this means in terms of our example.

×	I	A	B	C	D	E
I	I	A	B	C	D	E
A	A	B	I	D	E	C
B	B	I	A	E	C	D
C	C	E	D	I	B	A
D	D	C	E	A	I	B
E	E	D	C	B	A	I

Table 7.4 I **is the identity for this system, because row–I (shaded) exactly matches the top row of the table.**

Note that the same would be true of column–I. If I is the identity, then it would have to match the far left-hand column of the table.

Working Rule for Testing Postulate P3: If there is a row of the multiplication table which exactly matches the top row of the table, the element of S corresponding to this row will act as the identity referred to in the postulate. You must then check to make sure that column–S exactly matches the far left column of the table.

In order to test postulate **P4**, it is necessary to verify that every element of S has a unique inverse. That is, we wish to show that if a is any element of S, we can find some unique element of S which we can multiply a by to get the answer i (the identity). But if $a \circ$ (something) is to equal i, then we must be able to *find an i somewhere in row–a*. If the "something" mentioned in the last sentence is to be unique, then we must be able to find *only one occurrence of i* in row–a. Don't forget, this must be possible for every element of S.

Working Rule for Testing Postulate P4: Postulate **P4** is satisfied if the identity element for the operation appears exactly once in each row and each column of the multiplication table for the operation.

Note that **P4** cannot be verified unless we can identify whether or not the identity appears once in each row and each column. To do this, we must know which element is the identity. Thus **P3** must be verified before **P4**.

This leaves one postulate, **P2**, which still needs to be verified. We've left this one for last because it is often the toughest of the postulates to verify. In order to fully confirm this postulate we would have to verify that $(a \circ b) \circ c$ and $a \circ (b \circ c)$ are *always the same* whenever a, b, and c are *any* elements of S. In our example, there are six different elements of S which are possible replacements for a, six elements of S which are possible replacements for b, and six elements of S which are possible replacements for c. That's a total of $6 \cdot 6 \cdot 6 = 216$ different combinations which need to checked in order to verify the postulate. (See Chapter 10 in order find out how the number of possibilities is computed in situations such as this.)

This may seem bad enough, but if we had started with even a slightly larger system you can see that you could spend the greater part of your life verifying this property alone. Obviously this means that a direct verification of this postulate will usually be out of the question. Usually this postulate is verified in an indirect manner, although a computer could also be helpful.

In our example we will content ourselves with verifying **P2** for only a few special cases.

$(a \circ b) \circ c$	$a \circ (b \circ c)$	comment
$(A \circ B) \circ C = I \circ C = C$	$A \circ (B \circ C) = A \circ E = C$	the same
$(C \circ E) \circ A = A \circ A = B$	$C \circ (E \circ A) = C \circ D = B$	the same
$(C \circ B) \circ A = D \circ A = C$	$C \circ (B \circ A) = C \circ I = C$	the same
$(E \circ C) \circ A = B \circ A = I$	$E \circ (C \circ A) = E \circ E = I$	the same

Table 7.5 Verification of some instances of the associative law. In each row, a, b, and c are replaced by different elements of S.

Please note, however, that we have only checked four of the possible 216 different combinations, less than 2%! Although we did verify that the associative law does hold in these four situations, *we have not proved* that it holds in all cases (which it must if this system really is a group). The reality of the situation is that this is probably the best that we can hope for in many problems.

One ray of hope can be injected here. Nonassociative operations (other than the common operations of subtraction and division, neither of which is associative) are unusual in elementary mathematics. When such operations do occur they are generally difficult to deal with and are of limited utility. In most cases we will be restricting ourselves to operations which are associative.

Abelian Groups

Although it is true that groups need not satisfy the commutative law, some groups do. These groups, called *commutative groups*, or *Abelian groups*, satisfy the additional condition given below. Abelian groups are named for the Norwegian mathematician Neils Henrik Abel mentioned earlier in this chapter in relation to fifth degree equations.

> **Definition**: If the two products $a \circ b$ and $b \circ a$ are always equal whenever a and b are in a group, then this group is called an Abelian group.

Again, not all groups are Abelian. However, Abelian groups are important enough and common enough to have considerable attention devoted to them over the years. In the next section, where we look at some examples of groups, we will find that many of these examples are Abelian groups.

Just as with **P1**, **P3**, and **P4**, checking its table in order to determine if a finite group is Abelian is also an easy task. For a group to be Abelian we must always have $x \circ y = y \circ x$ whenever x and y are in S. A little reflection will suggest what this means concerning the group's multiplication table: The entry in row–x and column–y must always equal the entry in row–y and column–x. Let's look at an example of an Abelian group in order to clarify this idea.

∘	0	1	2	3	4
0	0	1	2	3	4
1	1	2	3	4	0
2	2	3	4	0	1
3	3	4	0	1	2
4	4	0	1	2	3

Table 7.6 The operation "addition modulo 5."

Consider the "multiplication table" given in Table 7.6, which is known as the operation "addition modulo 5." It is easy to verify the following facts:

1. (Closure) **P1** is satisfied because the only entries appearing in the table are the entries in the top row of the table, namely 0, 1, 2, 3, and 4.
2. (Existence of identity) **P3** is satisfied by the element 0. (Combining 0 with any element leaves that element unchanged.)
3. (Existence of inverses) **P4** is satisfied because the identity, 0, appears once in each row and each column.

It is also possible to verify that **P2** is satisfied. Although this is easy, it is time consuming since it requires checking $5 \cdot 5 \cdot 5 = 125$ equations. In the next section we will see an indirect way of verifying **P2** which is much less trouble.

To verify that this group is Abelian we need to check to see that $x \circ y$ and $y \circ x$ are always equal for this operation. Although this can be done with little effort here, a little bit of thought will make the task even simpler. Compare the positions in the table of $1 \circ 3$ and $3 \circ 1$. (See Table 7.7 below where these two entries are shaded.)

∘	0	1	2	3	4
0	0	1	2	3	4
1	1	2	3	4	0
2	2	3	4	0	1
3	3	4	0	1	2
4	4	0	1	2	3

Table 7.7 Comparison of the positions of $1 \circ 3$ and $3 \circ 1$ in Table 7.6.

You should also compare the positions of $2 \circ 4$ and $4 \circ 2$ in the table. Note that in each of these cases the two entries are "symmetric" to each other across the *main diagonal* of the table. (The main diagonal of the table goes from the upper left–hand corner to the lower right–hand corner.) Hopefully, this example has clarified the following:

> **Working Rule for Testing a Group for the Commutative Property**: A group is commutative, or Abelian, if its multiplication table is symmetric about its main diagonal. This means that each entry in the table is equal to its *mirror image* through the main diagonal.

The reason why this works is that the product $x \circ y$ is always the mirror image of the product $y \circ x$ in the table (the entry in row-x and column-y will always be the mirror image of the entry in row-y and column-x). If these two mirror images are equal, then $x \circ y$ and $y \circ x$ must be equal.

Exercises

1. For the group defined by Table 7.1, give the inverse of the element A. That is, $A \circ ? = I$. What is the inverse of element B?

2. Describe a procedure that will enable you to find the inverse of any element in a group by investigating its row (or column) in the multiplication table.

3. For the group defined by Table 7.1, are any elements their own inverse? That is, are there any elements which satisfy the equation $x \circ x = i$?

4. For the group defined by Table 7.6, give the inverse of the element 4 and the inverse of the element 3.

5. Are any elements their own inverse in the group defined by Table 7.6?

6. Explain in your own words why the working rules for verifying postulates **P3** and **P4** work. Explain why the working rule for verifying the commutative property works.

7.4 Examples and Non-Examples of Groups

Although the examples used to illustrate the group concept in the last two sections were both finite, not only are infinite groups common, but you are also quite familiar with them. A disadvantage of working with an infinite group is that you can't rely on its multiplication table, because the table would require an infinite number of rows and columns.

Example 1: (An infinite group.) Consider the system of all integers, $\{\cdots,-2,-1,0,1,2,\cdots\}$ along with the operation of addition. This system is an infinite Abelian group.

- **P1** is satisfied because we know that the sum of any two integers must be an integer.
- **P2** is satisfied because we know from our study of arithmetic that the ordinary operation of addition satisfies the associative law.
- **P3** is satisfied by the number "0." 0 is the identity here because adding it to any other integer will leave that number unchanged.
- **P4** is satisfied because every element has an inverse, generally called *the opposite of the element*. Adding any number to its opposite yields 0, the identity. Thus, the inverse of 4 is -4 because $4+(-4)=0$ (the identity); the inverse of -7 is 7; and the inverse of 0 is 0.
- This group is Abelian because we know from our study of arithmetic that addition is a commutative operation — that is, when adding together any two numbers, the order that you write the numbers down will not change the value of the sum. $7+13=13+7$; $x+y=y+x$ no matter what integers x and y represent.

240   Chapter Seven: **GROUPS**

Of course the whole concept of group is nothing more than a generalization of this example, which might be considered the simplest group. All other groups are similar to this one, at least in some respects. Mathematicians are interested how other groups are similar to and differ from this basic one.

Example 2:   (An example of a <u>non–group</u>.) The set of all integers with the operation of multiplication does <u>not</u> form a group. Although **P1**, **P2**, and **P3** are all easily verified from our knowledge of basic arithmetic (the number 1 plays the role of the identity here), **P4** does not hold true. This is because for the operation of multiplication the inverse of an integer is generally not an integer. For example, for the number 3 to have an inverse in this system we would need to find an integer x such that $3 \cdot x = 1$ (the identity). But no such *integer* x can be found. The only solution to this equation is the number $\frac{1}{3}$, which we know is not an integer.

It should be pointed out that even if only one element in the system fails to have an inverse, then that system is not a group.

These first two examples show why statements such as "The integers form a group." are inaccurate. The integers do form a group when the operation under consideration is addition, but they do not form a group when the associated operation is multiplication.

Example 3:   (Addition modulo five.) The system defined by the multiplication table in Table 7.6 was shown to be a group in the last section (although we did not verify the associative property, **P2**). There is another way of looking at this operation which dispenses with the need for the multiplication table and has the advantage of making postulate **P2** obvious.

First of all, the set for this group is $\{0,1,2,3,4\}$. We will use $+_5$ to represent the operation that we were calling ○ in the last section. (This conforms with standard practice.) The operation can be defined by the table that we gave earlier, but we can also define the operation in terms of the following two–step procedure:

The value of $x +_5 y$ is computed by performing the following steps:

1. Add x and y together.
2. Divide this result by 5, but *keep only the remainder*.

Thus to compute $4 +_5 3$, you add together 4 and 3 giving 7. Next, you divide this by 5. The result is a quotient of 1, with a remainder of 2. Keep only the remainder of 2. Thus $4 +_5 3 = 2$. You should check that this is the same answer that you would get for $4 \circ 3$ if you use Table 7.6 to make the computation. You should also check that all other entries in Table 7.6 could be computed in this way.

Note that understanding addition modulo five in this way allows us to give a trivial proof of the associative property, something which we did not complete earlier. It is obvious that $(a +_5 b) +_5 c$ and $a +_5 (b +_5 c)$ must be equal, because $(a+b)+c$ and $a+(b+c)$ are equal in normal arithmetic. Since these two numbers are equal, they must both yield the same remainder when divided by five.

Example 4:   (Multiplication modulo five; a non–group.) Consider the system consisting of the set $\{0,1,2,3,4\}$ (the same set as in example 3) with the operation "multiplication modulo five" defined below. This operation, denoted by $\times_5$, is defined in a manner that is similar to the one used above to describe addition modulo five.

The value of $x \times_5 y$ is computed by performing the following steps:

1. Multiply x and y together.
2. Divide this result by five, but only keep the remainder.

Thus, to compute $3 \times_5 4$, multiply 3 and 4 together to get 12. Now divide this by 5, keeping only the remainder, 2. You should be able to verify the accuracy of the entries in the following multiplication table for "multiplication modulo five."

$\times_5$	0	1	2	3	4
0	0	0	0	0	0
1	0	1	2	3	4
2	0	2	4	1	3
3	0	3	1	4	2
4	0	4	3	2	1

Table 7.8 Multiplication table for "multiplication modulo five."

This system does not form a group, because the number 0 does not have an inverse in this system. (The identity is the number 1, but a look at the table clearly shows that the equation $0 \times_5 x = 1$ cannot be satisfied for any value of x.) Note that all other elements in this system do have inverses.

Exercises

1. What row (and column) of Table 7.8 would you use to convince someone that the number 1 is the identity element for the operation of multiplication modulo five examined in example 4?

2. Explain how you could use Table 7.8 to quickly verify that the number 0 does not have an inverse in the system of example 4.

3. Other than 0, all of the other elements of the system in example 4 do have inverses. Using the table, find the inverses of each of these elements.

4. (Clock arithmetic.) Start with the set $\{0, 1, 2, \cdots, 11\}$.
(a) Explain how you would define the operation of addition modulo 12 on this set.
(b) Verify that this system forms a group.
(c) Discuss why you think this system is often called *"clock arithmetic."*

5. Consider the two element set $\{O, E\}$ and the operation $\oplus$ defined by the following multiplication table:

$\oplus$	O	E
O	E	O
E	O	E

Table 7.9 "Multiplication table" for problem 5.

Determine whether or not this system forms a group. If it is, determine if it is Abelian.
Note: If O abbreviates "odd integer" and E abbreviates "even integer," then the given table summarizes the following facts:
- The sum of two odd integers is even.
- The sum of two even integers is even.
- The sum of an odd integer and an even integer is odd.

242   Chapter Seven: **GROUPS**

6.   Repeat exercise 5 for the multiplication table given below.

$\otimes$	O	E
O	O	E
E	E	E

Table 7.10 "Multiplication table" for exercise 6.

What facts do you think this table summarizes?

7.   Let $\mathcal{E}$ represent the set of all positive and negative even integers with the normal operation of addition. Explain why this system forms an Abelian group.

8.   Let $\mathcal{O}$ represent the set of all positive and negative odd integers with the normal operation of addition. Does this system form a group? Why, or why not?

Small Group Exercises — The Symmetries of the Square

One powerful application of groups that mathematicians have discovered has to do with the way groups can be used to investigate the geometric notion of symmetry.

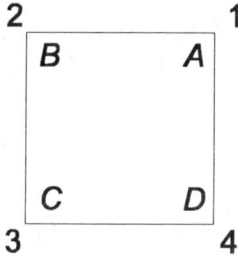

Figure 7.1 Basic diagram for the "symmetries of the square."

Start with the square pictured in Figure 7.1. The letters A, B, C, and D represent the vertices of the square, while the numbers 1, 2, 3, and 4 represent the positions of the vertices. We are going to be moving the square in various ways. These motions will move the vertices (A, B, C, and D), but not the positions (1, 2, 3, and 4) — these positions will stay where they are.

For example, one possible motion would be to pick up the square and rotate it 90° counterclockwise. This will move vertex A from position 1 to position 2, vertex B from position 2 to position 3, and so on. The result of this operation is to move the square from its original layout, pictured in Figure 7.1, to a final arrangement as shown in Figure 7.2.

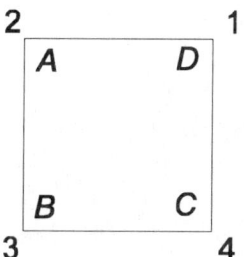

Figure 7.2 The original square after a counterclockwise rotation of 90°.

Note that the final picture here looks exactly like the original one, *except* that the vertices have been moved. If you were to erase the letters representing the vertices, you would not be able to determine any differences at all between the pictures in Figure 7.1 and Figure 7.2. An operation that satisfies this restriction is called a "*symmetry of the square.*" A more formal definition follows:

> Definition: A *symmetry of the square* is any motion which moves the square in such a way that, in its final position, the square takes up *exactly the same space* as it originally did.

To reiterate what is going on when performing a symmetry of the square, we are moving it in such a way that its final position takes up exactly the same space as the square originally did – although the vertices of the square may have been moved.

The motion described above – counterclockwise rotation by $90°$ – satisfies this definition, so it is a symmetry of the square. We will denote this motion by R_1 (for "rotation").

Note that rotating the square $270°$ clockwise moves the square into the exact same configuration that R_1 does. Since rotating the square $270°$ clockwise has the exact same effect as R_1, we will *not* consider this to be a different symmetry of the square.

We now wish to *list all possible symmetries of the square*. There are three other possible *rotations* which are symmetries. We will name them $R_2, R_3,$ and R_0. R_2 will represent a rotation of the square $180°$ in the counterclockwise direction. This rotates the original square (Figure 7.1), to the configuration shown below in Figure 7.3. Vertex A has moved from position 1 to position 3, vertex B has moved from position 2 to position 4, and so on.

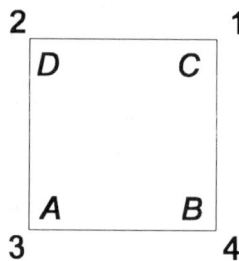

Figure 7.3 The effect of applying R_2 to Figure 7.1.

> 1. R_3 will represent a rotation of $270°$ counterclockwise. Draw a diagram indicating the final configuration of the vertices for this symmetry of the square.

R_0 will represent a rotation of $360°$ counterclockwise. Note that this brings the original square of Figure 7.1 back to its original configuration – all of the vertices are back in their original positions. This is the equivalent of not moving the square at all. (We could just as well have called this a rotation of $0°$.)

We now know four possible symmetries of the square. There are four more, but they are not rotations. These four additional symmetries of the square require us to "flip" the square about an axis.

244   Chapter Seven: **GROUPS**

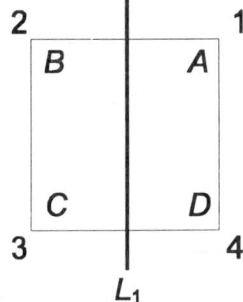

Figure 7.4 The original square with an axis of symmetry indicated.

Figure 7.4 shows our original square with an *axis of symmetry*, L_1, indicated. This axis of symmetry is the vertical line that goes through the center of the square. We will spin the square (in three dimensions), revolving it about L_1, so that it moves to the final position shown in Figure 7.5. This operation is clearly a symmetry of the square since the final square takes up exactly the same space as the original one did. We will call this operation F_1 (for flip). This symmetry of the square interchanges the two vertices at the top of the square, and also interchanges the two vertices at the bottom.

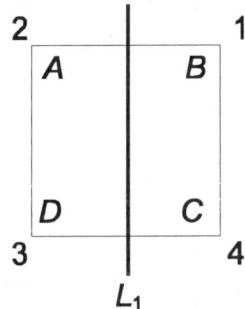

Figure 7.5 Figure 7.4 after being "flipped" about L_1.

There are three other flips which also act as symmetries of the square. F_2 will be a flip about the *horizontal* line through the center of the square (see Figure 7.6).

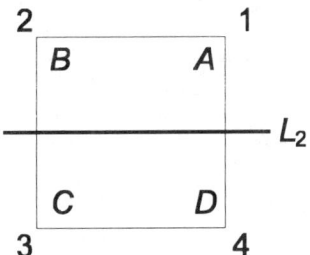

Figure 7.6 Figure 7.1 with a horizontal line of symmetry indicated.

---

2.   Draw a diagram indicating the final configuration of the vertices that results after flipping this diagram about the line L_2. Then describe this operation using complete sentences, and explain why it is a symmetry of the square.

F_3 will represent a flip of the original square (Figure 7.1) about the *diagonal* line L_3 which goes through positions 2 and 4 (see Figure 7.7). Flipping about this axis will interchange the vertices in positions 1 and 3, but leave the vertices in positions 2 and 4 unmoved.

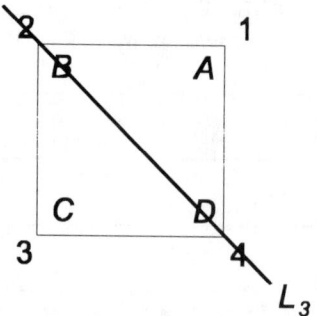

Figure 7.7 Figure 7.1 with the diagonal line of symmetry L_3 indicated.

If we start with the configuration in Figure 7.1, the final position after performing this symmetry of the square is shown in Figure 7.8.

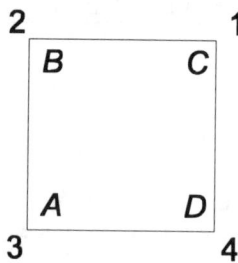

Figure 7.8 The final configuration after applying operation F_3 to the square in Figure 7.1.

F_4 would represent a flip about the other diagonal of the square, the line going through positions 1 and 3.

---

3. Draw a diagram indicating the final configuration of the vertices after applying the operation F_4 to the square in Figure 7.1. Describe the results of this operation in complete sentences.

---

4. The eight operations described above are the only symmetries of the square. Complete the following table, summarizing the eight operations.

OPERATION	DESCRIPTION	RESULT
R_0	Rotate counterclockwise 360°.	No vertices are moved.
R_1		
R_2		
R_3		
F_1	Flip about the vertical line through the center.	Positions 1 and 2 are interchanged. Positions 3 and 4 are interchanged.
F_2		
F_3	Flip about the diagonal line through positions 2 and 4.	Positions 1 and 3 are interchanged. Positions 3 and 4 are left unmoved.
F_4		

Figure 7.9 Summary of the symmetries of the square.

We now propose to form a group whose elements are the eight symmetries of the square listed above. If X and Y are any two of these symmetries, we will define $X \circ Y$ to mean "first do X, then do Y." Thus, $F_3 \circ R_1$ would mean: First flip about line L_3 then rotate 90° counterclockwise. Let's see what the result of this is (see Figure 7.10).

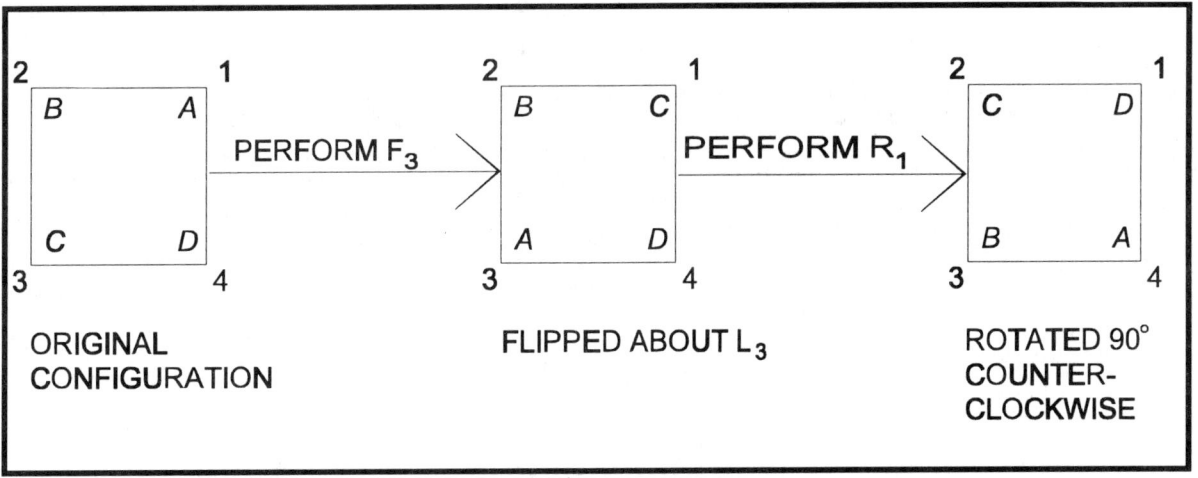

Figure 7.10 The result of performing the operation F_3 followed by the operation R_1 on the original square of Figure 7.1.

Note that the final configuration of the square is the same as if we had simply performed the operation F_2 on the original diagram. Thus, performing F_3 followed by R_1 is the same thing as simply performing F_2; that is, $F_3 \circ R_1 = F_2$.

On the other hand, if we perform $R_1 \circ F_3$ the analysis would look like this (Figure 7.11):

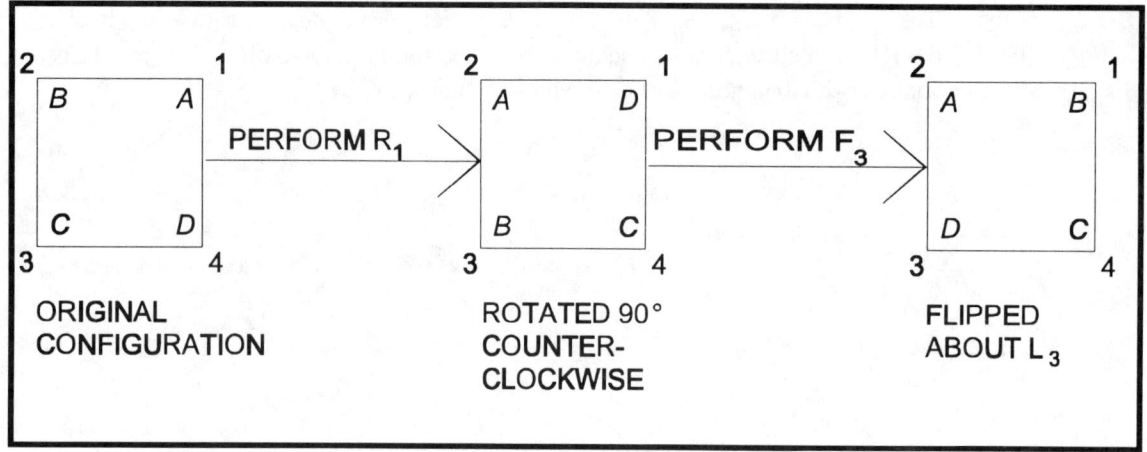

Figure 7.11 The result of performing the operation R_1 followed by the operation F_3 on the original square of Figure 7.1.

Thus $R_1 \circ F_3 = F_1$.

> 5. Complete the entire multiplication table (below) for this system.

∘	R_0	R_1	R_2	R_3	F_1	F_2	F_3	F_4
R_0	R_0	R_1	R_2	R_3	F_1	F_2	F_3	F_4
R_1	R_1						F_1	
R_2	R_2							
R_3	R_3							
F_1	F_1							
F_2	F_2							
F_3	F_3	F_2						
F_4	F_4							

Table 7.11 Multiplication table for the symmetries of the square.

> 6. Verify the group postulates for this multiplication table. In so doing, answer the following questions (don't bother verifying postulate **P2**):
>
>   (a) What is the identity for this multiplication table?
>   (b) Give the inverse for each element of this system.
>   (c) Is this system Abelian? Give a reason for your answer.

7.5 Isomorphic Groups

In order to introduce the concept of *isomorphism*, we will start with an example. If you have competed the small group exercise on the symmetries of the square at the end of the last section, you should find this example easy to follow.

Example: (The symmetries of the equilateral triangle.) We are going to start with an equilateral triangle, that is, a triangle with all three sides equal (and all three angles equal to $60°$). Figure 7.12 is a diagram of such a triangle with a number of axes of symmetry indicated.

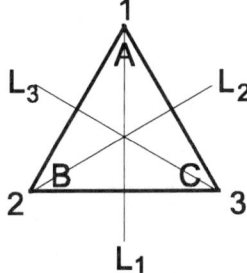

Figure 7.12 An equilateral triangle with its axes of symmetry.

As in the "symmetries of the square" example, there are certain ways of rotating or flipping this figure so that the resulting figure occupies the same space it did before the movement. This time there are three rotations and three "flips" that are possible. We will denote them as follows:

R_1: Rotate the figure $120°$ counterclockwise.

R_2: Rotate the figure $240°$ counterclockwise.

R_3: Rotate the figure $360°$ counterclockwise. (Equivalent to not changing any vertices in the original diagram.)

F_1: Flip the figure through line L_1 (This interchanges the contents of positions 2 and 3 while leaving the contents of position 1 unchanged.)

F_2: Flip the figure through line L_2.

F_3: Flip the figure through line L_3.

The mathematical system we are defining contains these six elements, the symmetries of the equilateral triangle. These are combined in the same way as the symmetries of the square in the small group exercise of the previous section. That is, $X \circ Y$ will mean "first do X, then do Y." With this definition you should be able to verify that the following multiplication table (table 7.12) describes our mathematical system.

$\circ$	R_0	R_1	R_2	F_1	F_2	F_3
R_0	R_0	R_1	R_2	F_1	F_2	F_3
R_1	R_1	R_2	R_0	F_2	F_3	F_1
R_2	R_2	R_0	R_1	F_3	F_1	F_2
F_1	F_1	F_3	F_2	R_0	R_2	R_1
F_2	F_2	F_1	F_3	R_1	R_0	R_2
F_3	F_3	F_2	F_1	R_2	R_1	R_0

Table 7.12 Multiplication table for the symmetries of the equilateral triangle.

It is easy to verify that this multiplication table defines a group (except that, as usual, associativity is difficult to prove). Furthermore, this group is not Abelian because, for example, $R_1 \circ F_1 \neq F_1 \circ R_1$ (see the shaded entries in Table 7.12).

Possibly the most interesting thing about this group is that, believe it or not, we have seen it before. Compare Tables 7.12 and 7.1. Although these tables may not look the same, in some sense they are. If we take each occurrence of R_0 in Table 7.12 and replace it by I, each occurrence of R_1 and replace it by A, each occurrence of R_2 and replace it by B, each occurrence of F_1 and replace it by C, and each

occurrence of F_2 and replace it by D, and each occurrence of F_3 and replace it by E, the result will be the exactly the same as table 7.1 (from section 7.2). This means that, even though we may not have noticed it until somebody pointed it out to us, *the relationships between the elements are exactly the same in both groups*. Remember, in the study of groups what we are really concerned with is the relationships between the objects, not the objects themselves. A close examination of the two groups in question here points that the elements of the two groups have been named differently (I, A, B. C, D, and E in one case, R_0, R_1, R_2, F_1, F_2 and F_3 in the other), but the relationships between the elements (as embodied in the two multiplication tables) are exactly the same. Since the relationships are more important than the elements names, a mathematician would consider these two groups *essentially the same*. He or she would say that these two groups are *isomorphic*.

Isomorphic groups are of interest because they enable mathematicians to make connections between groups which may not have been obvious on the surface. For example, suppose you know a lot of information about a certain group, but very little about a second group. If you can prove that the two groups are isomorphic, you suddenly know just as much about the second group as you did about the first! The relationships between the elements of the second group will be exactly the same as those in the first group, which we know more about. It is worth pointing out that this is a dominant theme in mathematics. When a mathematician studies any new structure, something he or she knows little about, it is unusual to start from scratch and develop lots of results about this structure. Often a much more fertile attack is to show that your system (the group, or whatever it is you are studying) is isomorphic to something that you are more familiar with. The relationships that you know about in the familiar system will then give you important insights into the unfamiliar one.

Exercises

1. Verify each of the entries in Table 7.12.

2. Verify that the group postulates hold for the system of symmetries of the equilateral triangle given in this section.

3. It was shown that the group of symmetries of the equilateral triangle is not Abelian because $R_1 \circ F_1 \neq F_1 \circ R_1$. Find all other pairs of elements in this group such that $X \circ Y \neq Y \circ X$.

4. If two finite groups are isomorphic do you think that it is necessary for them to have the same number of elements? Justify your answer.

7.6 Chapter Review

Important Terms to Know

Abelian Group	complex numbers	linear equation
addition modulo five	cubic equation	multiplication modulo five
associative law	degree	polynomial equation
axis of symmetry	Galois Theory	quadratic equation
biquadratic equation	group	quartic equation
clock arithmetic	group postulates	quintic equation
closure	identity	solution by radicals
commutative group	inverse	symmetry of the square
coefficient	isomorphic group	symmetry of an equilateral triangle
commutative law		

Important Names to Know

Abel, Neils Henrik	Cayley, Arthur	Jordan, Camile
Bell, Eric Temple	Ferrari, Ludovico	Tartaglia, Niccolo
Cardano, Gerolamo	Galois, Evariste	

Review Questions

1. Explain how the focus in group theory is different from the focus in many other topics of elementary mathematics.

2. Discuss how the contributions of Abel and Galois proved that there was a fundamental difference between polynomial equations of degree four and those of degree five or more.

3. Explain how you can find the identity for a finite group by inspecting the multiplication table for that group.

4. In your own words, explain why postulate **P2** (the associative law) is generally the most difficult one to verify.

5. Describe the difference between an Abelian and a non–Abelian group.

6. Explain what it means for two groups to be isomorphic.

Chapter Eight

The Computer Age

"The real danger is not that computers will begin to think like men, but that men will begin to think like computers."

Sydney J. Harris

Chapter Eight: **THE COMPUTER AGE**

Chapter Outline

8.0 Introduction

8.1 Historical Perspective
 Digital versus Analog Computers
 The Abacus
 The Slide Rule
 Early Mechanical Calculators
 Control of the Machine – Punched Cards and Data Storage
 Other Advances
 Modern Electronic Computers
 First Generation Machines
 Second Generation Machines
 Third Generation Machines
 Fourth Generation Machines

8.2 Computer Functions
 Input
 Storage
  Internal Storage
  External Storage
 Processing
 Output

8.3 The Role of the Computer
 Numerical Applications
 Clerical Applications and Data Processing
  The Airline Industry
  Other Examples of Data Processing
 Pattern Recognition
  The Turing Test
 Simulation

8.4 Modern Trends in Computing
 Home Computing
 Office Computing
 Scientific Computing
 Neural Networks, Expert Systems, and Artificial Intelligence
 The Arts

8.5 Chapter Review

8.0 Introduction

There is no modern invention that has changed the world more than the electronic computer. It has changed the way we learn, revolutionized the workplace, and transformed the way we entertain ourselves. Computers assist us in writing office memos, in designing the machines of the modern world, and in bringing us cable television services. A little thought will show how we take for granted many aspects of today's life which would be impossible without this invention.

There's no doubt that the computer has had a tremendous impact on the development of the modern world. With this has come an increased dependence on the computer, a dependence that many feel is highly undesirable. An understanding of the computer's influence on society and an unbiased appraisal of its positives and negatives will be essential to anyone hoping for success in the years to come. Recognizing the powers and limitations of the computer may be one of the most important skills in the years to come.

A better understanding of what a computer is and how it has become an essential part of man's lifestyle is the theme of this chapter. In attempting to achieve this understanding we will need to probe the relationship between man and machine, and even how computers have affected our relationship with other people. In addition, recent investigations in both the natural and social sciences have led to a new understanding of how the human brain works. In these investigations the computer has played a key role, not only in the processing of large amounts of information, but also as a model of how thought processes may be carried out. The computer provides a model which can be compared and contrasted with the way our own brains process information. Such comparisons have illuminated our understanding of how our own brains operate, and indicate how the computer's influence reaches far beyond the office, the classroom, and the home.

8.1 Historical Perspective

Broadly speaking, *a computer is any device which assists in calculations*. This means that the meaning of the word has evolved over the years as technology has improved our computing devices and made them more efficient. Using the word in the modern sense, "computer" implies reference to a powerful, generally electronic, digital machine. However, for the purposes of this section the word "computer" will be used to mean any device which receives input, stores and processes data, and supplies output. By using this definition we will not only be able to trace the history of computers far into the past, but we will also be able to investigate the interesting sequence of events and interrelationship of ideas that have led to the development of the modern invention.

Digital versus Analog Computers

Before proceeding, a distinction between *analog* and *digital* computing devices needs to be made. In the modern sense the word "computer" refers almost exclusively to digital machines, that is, machines that convert input into digital (numerical) form for later storage and processing. Since the 1960's most computing devices have been replaced by digital machines, which are *cheaper* and *more dependable* than the earlier analog devices.

Analog machines, which process information and make decisions without converting it into numerical form, were in common use before 1960. These devices sense a variable input, for example a voltage or a temperature, and based on the strength of this input decide what action is to be taken. A common example of such a machine would be a heating and air-conditioning system which, based on the temperature, turns on the heat or air-conditioning to keep a room at some desired constant temperature. The controlling mechanism, in this case a thermostat, senses the room's temperature and does *not* convert it into digital form. Instead, the temperature is converted into a reading on a gauge. This reading determines the action that the system is to take, that is, whether to turn on the heat or the air-conditioning.

Analog scales, not all of which are associated with computers, are familiar to most of us. These scales are continuous rather than discrete. The scales on mercury thermometers and old-fashioned wristwatches are analog scales. Mercury thermometers move from $97°$ to $98°$ by *continuously flowing* through all of the values in between, not by jumping through a small number of intermediate values (that is, *not* by jumping from $97°$ to $97.1°$ to $97.2°$ and so on without hitting the values in between). Similarly, an analog wristwatch does not jump from $11:31$ to $11:32$ without flowing through all of the times in between. The scale on a digital wristwatch does make the sudden change between these two times rather than a flowing change. The "jumps" made by the digital watch are the indication that you are dealing with a digital scale.

There are many places where the replacement of the older analog scales with the more modern digital device is apparent. There are now probably more digital watches and clocks around than the analog kind. Speedometers and odometers in late model cars and trucks are more likely to be digital than the analog style that used to be common. Digital thermometers are now taking over in hospitals, almost completely replacing the mercury thermometer there.

The Abacus

One of the earliest mechanical computing instruments was the *abacus*. The earliest forms of this tool were developed in the East more than 5000 years ago, but it was eventually introduced into Europe where it was still in common use until the seventeenth century. As Hindu-Arabic notation for numbers became popular in Europe, the use of the abacus declined. It is still used in the Middle East, China, and Japan.

The Abacus uses beads strung on wire to keep track of numbers. It can be used to perform the basic arithmetical operations quickly. Each wire represents a different place value, with the beads above the bar representing "five" and those below representing "one." In the diagram below the beads are set to represent the number 82,309.62. Note how a bead is counted only if it has been moved toward the center bar.

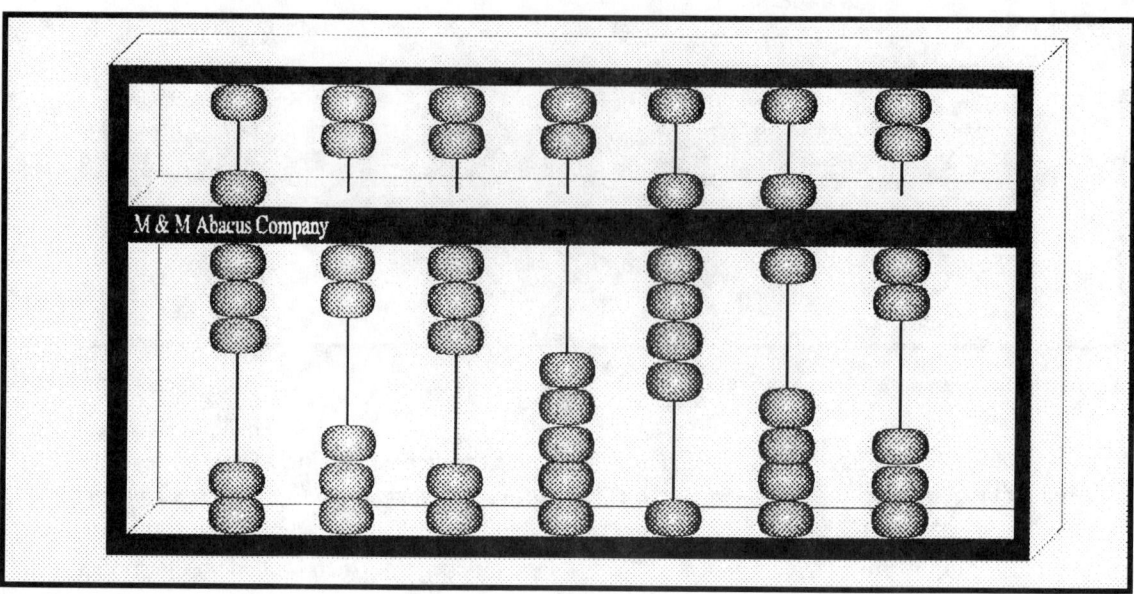

Figure 8.1 Representation of 82,309.62 on the Abacus.

The Slide Rule

In the late sixteenth and early seventeenth centuries a new mathematical invention, the *logarithm*, provided the foundation for a new mathematical calculator, *the slide rule*. The invention of logarithms is credited to a Scotsman, John Napier, who was looking for a way of simplifying the complicated computations that often come up in the study of astronomy. He is also credited with devising another instrument, called *Napier's Bones* or *Napier's Rods*, which could be used to multiply numbers mechanically.

To understand how logarithms could give rise to the slide rule, a very brief introduction to how logarithms work will be useful. Essentially, *a logarithm is an exponent*. If you recall the rules for exponents from elementary algebra you remember the following two rules:

1. $a^m \cdot a^n = a^{m+n}$
2. $\dfrac{a^m}{a^n} = a^{m-n}$

This is all you need to know to understand the connection between logarithms and the slide rule: Exponents (that is, logarithms) convert multiplication of two expressions with the same base into addition (the addition of the exponents). Similarly, they convert division into subtraction. This means that we can convert a *multiplication* problem into *addition of lengths*, lengths which represent the exponents of the factors to be multiplied. This addition of lengths can be achieved mechanically by moving sliding scales so that the lengths can be added visually. An illustration of how this process could be used to multiply 2 by 3 is shown in Figure 8.2.

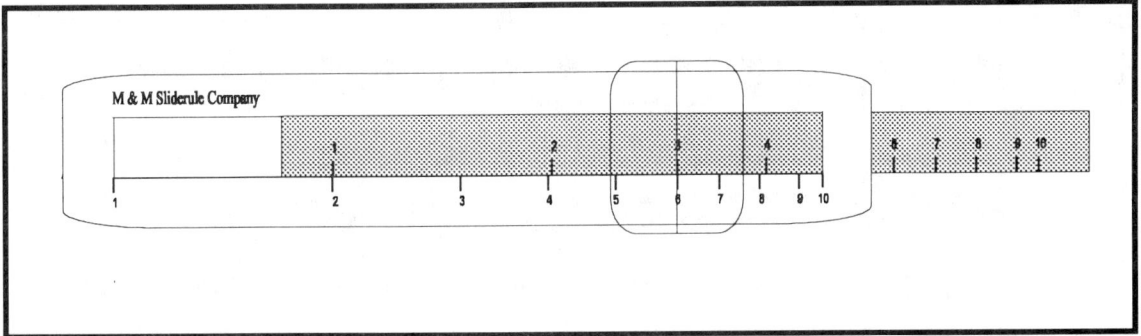

Figure 8.2 Two Times Three is Six!

Note that the inner sliding scale and the outer fixed scale are the same. These scales have been marked off "logarithmically" so that *adding their lengths is equivalent to adding the exponents of the expressions which they represent.* The "1" on the inner sliding scale is moved so that it is directly over the first factor of the product, 2. The second factor in the product, 3, is then located on the sliding scale using the cross–hair. The answer, 6, is found directly below it on the fixed scale. We have just multiplied 2 by 3 and gotten the answer, 6, by using the slide rule.

Slide rules could also be used to divide, raise to powers, extract roots, and perform many other arithmetical operations.

Robert Bissaker built the first slide rule in 1654. They were used extensively in the classroom and by engineers into the 1970's when they were replaced by pocket calculators. Despite the fact that slide rules are rarely used anymore, the mathematical invention that they were based upon, the logarithm, still plays an important role in mathematics and the sciences.

Early Mechanical Calculators

The next in the sequence of events which eventually led to the modern computer was the development of the first mechanical calculators. The first of these was completed by Blaise Pascal, a man who is noted for his achievements in mathematics, physics, theology, and philosophy. Although Pascal is now best known for establishing the basis for modern probability, for discovering Pascal's Principle in physics, and for his theological tracts *Les Provinciales* and *Penses,* during his lifetime his invention of the mechanical calculator was thought to be his greatest achievement.

Pascal's work on the calculator took place between 1642 and 1644 when he was between nineteen and twenty–one years old. He developed the device in order to assist his father, a mathematician who had been appointed the local administrator at Rouen. Pascal's desire was to develop a machine which would eliminate the drudgery of calculation, thus leaving him more time to devote to the more fulfilling aspects of mathematics and his other interests.

Pascal's machine, which was only capable of addition and subtraction, consisted of dials and cogs which could be set to enter numbers six digits or less. The dial was turned to change its value, and moving the dial beyond "9" to "0" would automatically increase the value of the dial in the next position in a manner similar to the way an analog odometer works in a car. Although the design of Pascal's machine was perfect, the technology of the times was not up to the task of building a reliable machine. Slipping gears made his machine undependable and inefficient.

Another brilliant thinker of the seventeenth century, Gottfried Wilhelm von Leibniz, also invented a mechanical calculator. Leibniz' fame, however, was also not due to his invention. He is more well known for his philosophical ideas, which have been further developed by many modern philosophers, and for his invention of calculus (independent of Isaac Newton) around 1675.

Leibniz introduced his calculator, *The Stepped Reckonner*, in 1673. Although it improved on Pascal's basic design, it too was inefficient and unreliable. In fact, it would be nearly two hundred years before reliable calculating machines would be commercially available.

Although Leibniz' machine was undoubtedly very important, another of his ideas had an even greater impact on modern computing. Leibniz seems to be one of the first, if not the first, European to propose the representation of numbers as powers of two. This gives rise to the binary number system, an alternative to the customary decimal system which we all learned in grade school. The binary number system is used almost exclusively in modern computer work.

This section on mechanical calculators would not be complete without mention of the English mathematician Charles Babbage. Babbage's first attempt to build a calculator occurred in 1812 when he designed his *Difference Engine*. He abandoned this attempt four years later when it became clear that the amount of time and money that would have to be spent to complete this project would be enormous. Undaunted, Babbage moved on to an even more ambitious project, the *Analytical Engine*. Both of Babbage's machines were critical successes but practical failures, designs which the technology of the time could not attain. Despite the fact that his machines were not built during his lifetime, Babbage is credited with the invention of this forerunner of the modern digital computer.

Although many of his contemporaries considered Babbage to be a crackpot, his machines foreshadowed modern machines in many ways. The analytical engine had a storage area, and was the first machine able to modify its program. Indeed, the Analytical Engine is considered to be the first "programmable" machine. Another modern feature of this machine's plan was the way data and instructions were to be input into the machine: through the use of punched cards.

One person who definitely would not have considered Babbage to be a crackpot was Lord Byron's daughter Ada, Countess of Lovelace. In addition to helping Babbage raise money for his projects, Ada Lovelace is attributed the honor of being considered the first computer programmer. If the Analytical Engine were ever built it would have been controlled by programs written by Ada, who now has a modern computer language named for her.

Control of the Machine – Punched Cards and Data Storage

Although the advances mentioned above were very important to the development of the modern electronic computer, other developments were necessary in order for the modern machine to evolve. For example, Babbage's idea of using punched cards to control his calculating machine was not a new one. In fact, it had been around in one form or another for nearly a hundred years.

Probably the earliest attempt at the control of machinery through the use of holes punched in paper occurred in the year 1725. It was then that a Frenchman, Basil Bouchon, added a mechanism called a "drawboy" to his loom in order to determine which cords should be drawn to create a specific pattern. The idea of the drawboy was not new with Bouchon; what was new was that the drawboy would be controlled by the holes which had previously been punched into the paper tape rather than a human assistant. The perforations in the paper would be used to select certain needles, which controlled the thread. This controlled selection would then lead to the desired pattern in the textile. Changing the roll of paper tape (and the pattern of the holes) would change the design produced by the loom. You may be more familiar with this idea in the "player piano" which is based on the same principle. The main difference between the two machines is that in the player piano the holes select different keys rather than needles, producing a musical design instead of a geometrical one. Paper tape similar to Bouchon's was still in use to control computing machinery well into the 1970's.

Another French inventor, Joseph–Marie Jacquard, made improvements on Bouchon's loom in 1801. The result was the *Jacquard Attachment*, which could be used to control a loom. The input for this attachment was in the form of punched cards which controlled the mechanism in a way similar to the way Bouchon's paper tape had been used. The similarity to the use of punched cards in the computing machines of the 1980's and earlier is striking. In the computer each punched card represented one instruction to the machine, while in Jacquard's loom each card represented one "throw of the shuttle."

Another of the reasons for using punched cards has been for *data storage*. Although Babbage's machines were designed to use punched cards to store data, the first person to really use this idea in a big way was Herman Hollerith, an American statistician. Hollerith worked for the United States government, compiling the censuses during the last decades of the nineteenth century. While working on the 1880 census, Hollerith and others realized that the practices which they were employing were quickly becoming outdated. A large number of immigrants had entered the country between 1880 and 1890. Unless some new techniques were applied the 1890 census would never be completed before it was time to start the next census ten years later.

Hollerith's response to this problem was to develop a new method for storing data, representing it by holes punched in cards. When processed, each card could be scanned electronically. The position of the holes on the card (now called Hollerith cards) would stand for various attributes of the person represented by that particular card (the person's gender, religion, ethnic background, age, etc.). An electronic counting machine could then easily compile and analyze all of the data needed for the census. The improved method which he developed enabled the Census Bureau to tabulate and check the figures for the 1890 census in a fraction of the time it would have otherwise taken. Hollerith later left the employ of the United States government and used his ideas to form a private company which later became known as International Business Machines (IBM).

Other Advances

Before the modern computer could become a reality a few more breakthroughs needed to fall into place. Two of these breakthroughs, uncovered by George Boole and Claude Shannon, supplied the answers to the last problems that needed to be solved.

George Boole, a nineteenth century British mathematician, was the first to apply algebraic principles to the study of logic. Boole's variables were binary, that is, could take on only two values (for example, a light can only be on or off; a sentence only true or false). Many of the results in the chapter on logic were due to George Boole. In fact, this field now goes by the name *Boolean Algebra*.

In 1938 Claude Shannon, an American, extended Boole's ideas to show that logical analysis and the analysis of electronic circuits are equivalent. This meant that electronic circuits could be used to simulate logic and arithmetic. This was the last piece needed to complete the solution of a very complex puzzle. What has been called The Computer Age could now begin. Things would now start to move very quickly.

Modern Electronic Computers

Because of Shannon's new insight, and spurred on by the need for high-speed computing equipment to support the war effort, the modern electronic computer would soon be a reality. The Mark I was developed by Howard Aiken in 1944. Although this machine was classified as *electromechanical* and therefore was not fully electronic, it was an impressive advance nonetheless. This machine was not really programmable, so it could be classified as nothing more than a giant calculator. Data was input using punched cards.

For many years Aiken's machine was considered the first of the modern computers, although such clear-cut distinctions are often over-simplifications. A mechanical machine invented in 1939 at Iowa State University by John Atansoff is now sometimes honored with this designation.

Since those early days computers have gone through a swift evolution into today's super machines. In order to follow this development, computer historians have classified machines by "generation," although advances are now moving so fast as to blur the distinction between generations. It is also important to keep in mind that sometimes there is no universal agreement among experts as to exactly where one generation ended and the next began.

First Generation Machines

In 1946 the first of the *fully electronic* computers, ENIAC, was completed. It was developed by J. Presper Eckert and John W. Mauchly of the University of Pennsylvania, and it replaced the electromechanical relays of the Mark I with *vacuum tubes*. This increased the speed of the computer, making it approximately 1000 times as fast as the electromechanical machine. Compared to today's machines the computer was still very large and suffered from problems with overheating.

It was during this period that an American mathematician, John von Neumann, working with others at the Institute for Advanced Study at Princeton, rediscovered Babbage's "stored–program computer" concept, allowing for the processing of program instructions in the same way as numerical data. This meant that programs no longer had to be "hardwired" into computers, but could be introduced as *software*. This was a major advance; for one thing, it allowed programs to be "self–modifying," reinventing the idea that Lovelace and Babbage had originally introduced. The concept of *artificial intelligence*, which depends on a machine being able to "learn" from its mistakes, owes its existence to this concept.

Other machines designed during this period were impressive, although many had a single objective. For example, machines were developed by the British for the express purpose of decoding secret messages.

The most famous computer of this era, UNIVAC, was probably the first of the widely used commercially available computers. UNIVAC's were used for many of the technical tasks of the 1950's, from the compilation of the census to the first computer–generated predictions of a Presidential election on national television in 1960. By this time the first generation of computers was already on its way out. Although UNIVACs would be used profitably for many more years, the second generation of computers would have many advantages over its ancestors.

Second Generation Machines

The second generation of computers began in 1958 with the introduction of the *transistor* into computer circuitry. The transistor had been developed more than ten years earlier by Robert Shockley, J. Bardeen, and H.W. Brittan at Bell Laboratories. The perfection of the transistor allowed for the replacement of vacuum tubes by the transistor, thus cutting down the size of the computer while increasing its dependability and speed. Almost all of the circuits in the computer were now controlled by transistors, and it could operate as much as twenty times as fast as a first generation machine. In addition to the increase in the raw speed of the computer, the replacement of vacuum tubes by the transistor also led to a marked decrease in the amount of heat generated by the computer. This meant that it could be operated for longer periods of time without having to worry about breakdowns.

Third Generation Machines

The third generation of computers lasted from the mid 1960's through the 1970's. It was characterized by more miniaturization. The *integrated circuit* was introduced, and the first personal computers, or desk–top machines, made their appearance. Integrated circuits, which could replace thousands of transistors and other electronic devices with a single device, revolutionized the computer industry once again. Large *main–frame* computers could now become incredibly powerful, while more modest machines would become smaller and smaller. The most important advance of this generation was Ted Hoff's invention of the *microprocessor*, which enabled the placement of a computer's entire processing unit onto a single chip.

Some consider the introduction of the *time sharing environment* to be the distinguishing characteristic of the third generation machine. This environment consists of operating systems which

allow more than one program to use the computer at the same time. Those who feel that this is the defining characteristic of the third generation would consider the Burroughs B5500 the first machine of this generation, since it introduced this capability.

Fourth Generation Machines

Many computer historians consider the computers of the 1980's to be fourth generation machines. The technology of this generation, sometimes called VLSI (for *Very Large–Scale Integration*), is characterized by improved silicon chips, both smaller and more efficient than the third generation. The fourth generation has also been called the *age of micro–miniaturization.*

Fourth generation computers process data more than 500 times as fast as second generation machines. Supercomputers process data that would have taken hundreds of years if done manually in mere minutes. Machines more powerful than UNIVAC are now the size of a notebook. In less than fifty years we have undergone a revolution whose effects are more wide ranging than the industrial revolution of the eighteenth and nineteenth centuries.

Whether the terminology of numbered generations will continue to be used is questionable. A fifth generation of future machines with the ability to "think" and to reason in human terms has been proposed, but is not yet here. These machines would have *Artificial Intelligence*, or A.I. The question of what Artificial Intelligence is, that is, what it means for a machine to think in human terms, is the object of a considerable amount of research by computer scientists, engineers, biologists, and psychologists.

Questions to Discuss

1. List and discuss some advantages and disadvantages that digital scales have over analog scales. Focusing on a specific example (for example, digital versus analog wristwatches) might help fix your ideas.

2. Explain why the analog machine called a thermostat satisfies the definition of "computer" given in the introduction. Explain why a mercury thermometer does not.

3. What is the reason that digital machines have largely replaced the earlier analog machines?

4. Explain how logarithms can be used to simplify the operations of multiplication and division.

5. What distinguished the Analytic Engine from earlier computing devices?

6. Characterize each of the different generations of electronic computers by giving the major advance that distinguishes it from the other generations.

8.2 Computer Functions

There are certain functions which all machines classified as digital computers are capable of performing. As mentioned in section 8.1, these operations are the ability to *accept input*, the ability to *store data*, the ability to *process data*, and the ability to *output results*. All of these have undergone considerable improvement in recent years.

The block diagram shown in Figure 8.3 is a simplified illustration of how these operations interact with each other.

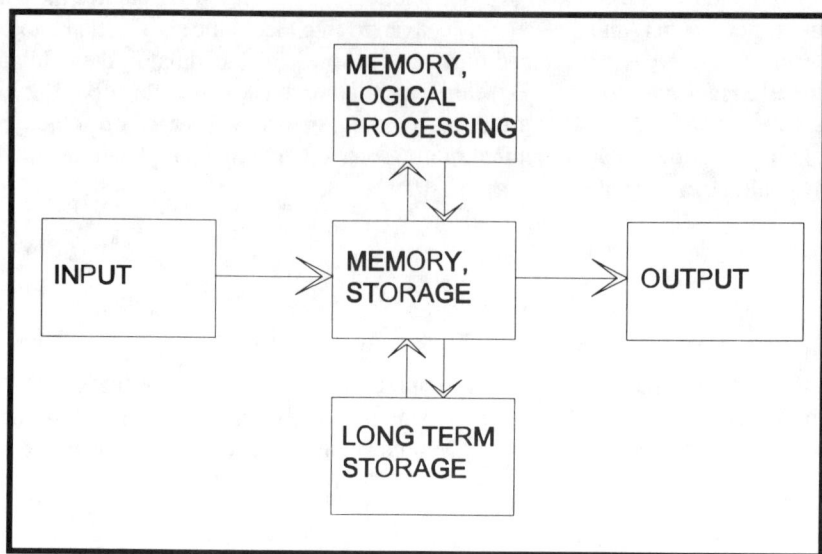

Figure 8.3 Relationship between the functions of a computer.

Information is input into the computer and stored. The stored data is processed and returned to storage. Finally, when the results are ready they may be stored in long–term storage (on disc or tape, for example), or output in some other form. Note that the information could move back and forth from processing to storage many times before it is finally output.

Input

Any information entered into a computer is called *input*. The computers you are probably most familiar with, the desktop computers (personal computers), have much of their information entered through a keyboard, but many other methods of entering information are common. Punched cards using holes to code information were first used in computers by Babbage, but were still commonly used until quite recently. Other ways of inputting information into computers include joysticks, mice, optical scanners, disc or tape drives, CD–ROM drives, and modems. Microphones may be used to input audio information directly. Some computers can even accept data that has been handwritten. The need for different input devices has developed from the different settings where computers are now used, the type of information that needs to be processed, and personal preference.

As an example, consider the problem of inputting the price of an item (data) at the check–out stand of a supermarket or a department store. In order to accomplish this quickly and accurately, scanning devices called *bar code readers* have been developed. The current technology allows a cashier to read the bar code on purchased items by passing a laser scanner over the bar code. The price of the item has now been input into the clerk's computer for later processing. In fact, in this case quite a bit more happens, since the swipe with the laser scanner also informs the store's computer that another particular item has been purchased. This information can be processed and eventually used to keep track of inventory, so restocking decisions can be made.

When you wish to transfer data over long distances a device known as a *modem* is often the choice. In this case the data to be introduced into your computer already needs to be in electronic form in another computer. The data to be transferred needs to be transformed into sound waves by using the modem. After traveling through telephone lines to its destination (your computer), it is then decoded

using another modem. This transforms it back into a form appropriate for input into your computer. The word "modem" comes from the way in which this device is utilized. It mo‌dulates the data, converting it into sound waves suitable for transmission over telephone lines. Then it de‌modulates the sound waves, again transforming them. This time the sound is converted into electronic signals that can be read by the computer. The word "modem" is a shortened form of the expression "modulator–demodulator."

Disc drives, tape drives, and CD ROM drives are other devices used for inputting information into computers. In these cases the information that you are inputting was stored on some type of medium (disc, tape, or CD ROM) either by your computer or by some other computer. The information that is input in this way could be either data or programs.

Storage

After information has been input into a computer it has to be stored, so that it will be ready for processing when the computer needs it. Storage may be internal, in the computer's main memory, or external, in disc, tapes, CD ROM's, etc. that can be removed from the computer and stored separately.

Internal Storage

Each computer has a limited amount of RAM, *random access memory*, where internal storage takes place. RAM is sometimes called *volatile memory* because data stored there is easily changed, and, in fact, will disappear completely when the machine is turned off. However, before a program can be run or data can be processed it must first be loaded into RAM. Increasing the amount of a computer's RAM will allow the computer to run larger programs and to process more data quickly.

External Storage

Since the programs and data stored in RAM are volatile, other external storage devices are needed in order for computers to be useful. For example, suppose you are playing a computer game and you now decide that you want to do some work using a Word Processing program. Loading the Word Processing program into RAM will "overwrite" the computer game so that the game will no longer be available to you. The Word Processor has now taken over the internal memory in the computer and is in command of the memory that the game had been using. Later on, when you shut the computer off, the Word Processor will also be expelled from memory.

If you want to play your computer game or operate your Word Processing program at some later date, you'll need to reload it into RAM. In order to accomplish this you'll need to have the program saved on some kind of external storage device. The most common of these storage media used in personal computers are hard discs, floppy discs, tapes, and CD ROM's. Most of these devices store data magnetically (CD ROM's and some other more modern devices are exceptions, since they store data optically). These devices have the advantage of being more permanent than RAM. Essentially they allow you to keep data and programs "out of the way" when they aren't being used. This frees up RAM, which is then available for more immediate tasks.

A complete understanding of how these external storage devices work is not necessary for this brief discussion. Suffice it to say that information is stored on the discs and tapes. This information is coded in much the same way that recorders can code audio or video information into magnetic signals so that it can later be decoded and played back by a tape player or VCR. The tape (or disc) contains many magnetic particles that can be oriented in one of two ways, either in the North–South orientation or in the

East–West orientation. These orientations are codes for either 0 or 1. In this way these magnetized particles can be used to represent messages in the binary number system which is used in all computers.

Processing

In order for computers to accomplish the many amazing achievements we ask of them, the data and programs which we have stored in RAM need to be processed. This is carried out in the CPU, the *Central Processing Unit*. In modern machines this unit is a single chip which keeps track of where the data and the instructions that are being worked on are stored. It performs a limited number if arithmetic and logical operations. The main power of the CPU is not in its versatility, but in its speed. Some Pentium® chips can perform 120 million or more operations per second, making them approximately 25,000 times as fast as Eckert and Mauchly's ENIAC. New chips promise even greater speeds – and lets not forget that we are talkiing about desktop machines here, not massive main–frames.

Output

Just as information can be input in many ways, there are also many methods for outputting data. The most common output devices are the computer monitor and the printer. Output can be sent to storage devices, such as discs, for later use in other programs or even other machines. In recent years human speech has been simulated, allowing computers to communicate in verbal form. Another output device is the plotter, which is used to produce graphs for mathematical and scientific work.

Small Group Exercise

Compare and contrast the ways computers and humans accomplish the following:

- Input
- Storage of data
- Processing of data
- Output

Also, discuss the relative efficiency of the two groups at each of the four tasks.

Questions to Discuss

1. What are the functions which are common to all electronic computers? Describe the devices which are used to carry out these functions.

2. Distinguish between a computer's internal and external storage. Give some advantages and disadvantages of each.

3. Describe the connection between the computer's storage of information in magnetic form and the binary number system.

8.3 The Role of the Computer

The number of tasks we ask the computer to do for us is increasing on a daily basis. From the beginning computers have been asked to assist us with high speed calculations which they can perform more quickly and accurately than humans. Later applications included more clerical chores such as word processing and filing. More recently computers have moved into the creative fields of the arts and humanities by assisting in the composition of art and music. We have now reached a point where almost no part of our lives is unaffected by the presence of computers, so much so that any attempt at listing the applications of computers will naturally be incomplete. Similarly, any attempt at classifying computer applications will meet with limited success, since many modern computer programs seem to cross the lines that were traditionally set up to classify software usage. Consider this section as an attempt at showing just how ubiquitous computers have become, how their importance has grown, and how dependent on them we have become.

For the purposes of this section we will consider the roles that the computer plays in *numerical applications*, *clerical applications*, *pattern recognition*, and *computer simulation*.

Numerical Applications

As you might guess, the earliest applications of computers were primarily numerical. Just the name of Eckert and Mauchly's machine, the Electronic and Numerical Integrator and Calculator, is enough to impress this upon us. In fact, the government was interested in the development of early computers principally in order to assist in the computation of the artillery tables needed for the war effort. Machines could produce these tables faster and more accurately than ever before. Other applications of computers, such as their use in coding and decoding secret messages, were also primarily numerical tasks.

Many years have past, but many of the applications that computers are asked to work on are still numerical. *Spreadsheets* have always been popular programs on the personal computer. These programs allow the user to manipulate numerical data in such a way as to predict the consequences of various courses of action, enabling him or her to decide which would be the best. They are used to plan major reorganizations by large corporations, or simply to keep track of the family budget. Statistical assistants, such as SPSS (*Statistical Package for the Social Sciences*) have been used for many years to analyze numerical data.

Clerical Applications and Data Processing

Another of the early applications for computers was in the classification and organization of data. This role, called *data processing*, is still a major reason why computers became a dominant factor in the 1950's, 1960's and 1970's. Whenever large amounts of data need to be prepared you'll find computers on the job helping to produce reports, to prepare payrolls, to keep track of and evaluate credit.

The first commercially produced computer, UNIVAC, was commissioned by the United States government in 1951 for just such data processing tasks. Originally designed by Eckert and Mauchly for use by the United States Bureau of the Census, UNIVACs took over many of the government's data processing jobs of the 1950s. In fact, the major appeal of this machine to the government was that it was capable of performing these data processing tasks as well as the numerical jobs handled by the earlier machines.

The Airline Industry

One of the first major applications of the computer outside of the federal sector was in the airlines industry. In 1939 commercial airlines carried less than two million passengers on approximately 340 airplanes. Ten years later in 1949 there were over a thousand commercial aircraft in use and nearly seventeen million passengers were flying annually. Unless they got help, it would be literally impossible to keep track of the industry in another ten years, with the passenger reservation system a particular problem. The airline industry was being seriously challenged by its own success.

A chance meeting between two executives from IBM and American Airlines during a cross-country flight in 1953 changed the way the airlines, and just about every other industry, would do business in the future. As the story goes, the two executives started a conversation when it was discovered that they both had the same name, Smith. Before the flight had landed the airline executive had described the nightmares that his industry was experiencing with its scheduling and reservations system, and the IBM executive realized that the computers that his company was manufacturing for the government would be just the tool needed to help solve some of these problems. It wasn't long before IBM had made a proposal to American Airlines to computerize its reservation system and American Airlines had accepted it. Work began on the system in 1956, it was delivered in 1962, and by the time all the bugs were worked out in 1964, a new, efficient reservation system, called *SABRE*, was in place.

SABRE revolutionized the airlines reservations system. It was now possible for airlines employees to keep track of the status of reservations right up to the time of departure. This was important, because last minute cancellations had been causing serious problems with the old reservations system. It had not been uncommon for seats that were in demand to go unsold because sales representatives were not aware of the cancellation making the seat available. In fact, before automating their system one airline estimated that its "sold-out" flights were running at less than 85% capacity because of last minute cancellations. After putting the computer on the job to control reservations, that figure jumped to well over 90%. Most airlines executives now agree that the reservations system designed by IBM for American Airlines was not just a matter of saving money by increasing efficiency, but a necessity if the industry was to survive in the form we know it.

By 1964 *SABRE*'s bugs were cleaned up and the system was working efficiently. For the first time a passenger could make plane reservations, rent a car, and make hotel reservations, all within a matter of seconds. Since they knew that passengers would soon be demanding this kind of convenience, the other airlines soon followed American Airlines' lead and either started their own computerized reservations system or bought into the system designed for American. All airlines now have similar systems, which are interconnected for added versatility.

Other Examples of Data Processing

Other examples of data processing can be found all around us.

- Telephone listings are compiled and updated via the computer.
- Company payrolls are processed.
- Monthly, quarterly, and annual reports for large corporations are assembled.
- Banks keep track of large numbers of deposits, withdrawals, and interest payments.
- Police gain access to large databases of information allowing them to identify and locate suspects.
- The military keeps track of where personnel with certain qualifications are located so that they can be moved to wherever they are needed.
- Placement tests are scored and their scores analyzed.
- Inventory is controlled by keeping track of the location of stock for later retrieval. In fact, the actual retrieval may be accomplished by using computer controlled robots.
- Data base programs keep track of records (for example, tax records) for easy access.

- Word Processing programs allow for the quick and efficient composition of memos, letters, and other business communications.

These and other applications are classified as data processing because they correspond to human tasks which are normally thought of as clerical in nature. Data is classified and organized, and although some numerical processing may be done, this is generally not the main purpose of the job.

Pattern Recognition

Pattern Recognition is a computer process which attempts to do more than simply classify data or compute arithmetical results. It deals with identifying connections that go beyond the clerical, and it attempts to imitate the type of processing that goes on when the human brain tackles a problem or develops a creation. Currently computers are not as good at this as they are at the simple clerical and numerical functions, but it is important to understand just how much more difficult this task is. We aren't asking the computer to simply remember where it filed something, or even to follow the small number of steps required in solving a linear equation. We're asking it to analyze patterns and maybe even draw conclusions. Some examples of pattern recognition that people participate in are the composition of music, poetry and art work; the understanding of the historical connections between events; and even the identification of a friend's voice when they call on the telephone.

As an example, some very talented people called composers know how to put together sounds in a way that many of us find pleasant. Is it possible to somehow get a computer to analyze these great works, identify the types of patterns which we would find pleasing, and write new, original music that's as good as (or even better than) the man made compositions? Right now, the answer is "no." Some computer music has been written, but critics probably would not classify it as very good. On the other hand, critics do definitely classify it as music.

A couple of points need to be emphasized here. First of all, the music we are talking about here is definitely written by the computer, not by the programmer. In some sense it would be more appropriate to say that the programmer "taught" the computer how to write the music rather than to give the programmer credit for writing the composition. The amount of participation by the computer, however, is up to the programmer/composer. It is also possible to consider situations where the composer simply uses the computer as a tool to assist him or her in the construction of the composition. See the end of this chapter for some examples of how the computer has been used as a composer's assistant in the arts.

The second point is that I've heard many people display a superior attitude, proclaiming how much better people are than machines because of the fact that composers are better than computers at things like writing music. Most of the people with this attitude have never composed any music, let alone good music. So although it may be accurate to say that mankind as a whole is more imaginative or more original than computers in producing music or art, on an individual basis it seems as though the machine outshines most of us.

The example of the composition of music shows the difference between the clerical and numerical uses of the computer and its use in pattern recognition. In pattern recognition the computer is used to try to imitate the creativity, the originality, some might say the spirit of man. Whether or not a computer could ever accomplish such a task is a difficult question. One problem that is almost immediately encountered is this: Who decides if the computer has accomplished this elusive task? If people can't agree among themselves what good music, or art, or literature is, how can we possibly judge whether a computer has equaled the masters in this? It's certainly not simply a matter of checking where a piece of music stands on some numerical scale to see if it qualifies as great.

This is one of the problems that confronts researchers in the relatively new field of *Artificial Intelligence*. The questions being asked in this field deal with the possibility of getting computers to approximate human thought and creativity. Recent research indicates that this may be more difficult to achieve than many once thought. The reason for this is that apparently decisions made by human beings are not totally logical but take many other factors into consideration as well. Some of these other factors

include experience, intuition, spirit, and emotion. Is it possible to get a machine which is primarily logical to "understand" what emotions and intuition are?

You can see that the questions which are considered in the field of Artificial Intelligence are difficult. Just because you give a computer an IQ Test and it scores at some reasonably high level is not enough evidence to convince most people that the computer is "intelligent" — nor should it be. Some other standard is needed, some other method of judging when a machine is "thinking." Some of the modern research is dealing with related questions, such as:

1. What are the major accomplishments of humankind? Is it possible to get computers to do similar things?
2. If we want computers to simulate the output of the human brain (for example, write a great piece of music), is it necessary to design a computer whose processor more closely mirrors that of the human brain? This is complicated by the fact that research indicates that the human brain contains about twelve billion neurons, the relays that the brain uses to transfer information. Even the largest computers contain only a small fraction of this storage and processing power, but transmit the information millions of times faster. Is it possible to use this speed to make up for the "design deficiencies" that need to be overcome?
3. How do we judge how well the computer or the computer program is doing?
4. Do we even want computers to emulate human thought? Maybe we would be better off heeding Mary Shelley's warnings in *Frankenstein*, where she warned us to be aware of the dangers inherent in run–away technology.

Even programs that don't employ full Artificial Intelligence techniques may be using them in some limited capacity. For example, in word processing the concept of a spelling checker is not particularly new. The spelling checkers used in most word processing programs would not be considered Artificial Intelligence, but are simply clerical in nature. Each word in your document is simply compared to a list of words in a file stored on a disc to see if it appears there. If it doesn't, the word is displayed as a possible spelling error for the user to either correct or accept. Grammar checkers are another question entirely. Here the computer attempts to analyze your sentences to see if it thinks they make sense. If the rules of grammar seem to have been broken, the grammar checker will notify the user of a possible error and even recommend possible changes. Computers may not be able to write good sentences yet, but at least they can recognize one when they see it.

Other places where pattern recognition is used are: the identification of sound patterns, which is needed if computers are going to be able to understand human speech; the identification of visual patterns, enabling computers to identify a particular person from a scanned photograph; and handwriting analysis. Notice that it is often the things that humans have very little trouble with, such as the identification of a person on sight or by the sound of their voice, that computers seem to have the most trouble with.

The Turing Test

Let's take a closer look at one of these questions, that of judging the accomplishment of the computer in human terms. Many benchmarks have been suggested. Some have recommended that computers could be considered to be "intelligent" when they can produce great art, great music, or write a good poem. Some would even be satisfied by a reasonable sentence! As mentioned above, such "standards" are really not effective, since there is no clear–cut distinction between good and bad art and literature.

It's also been recommended that the game of chess could be used as a gauge, since chess is difficult enough that playing a good game must require a significant amount of thought. It should be pointed out here that a chess playing computer does employ pattern recognition, since the game has so many possibilities. Simply listing all possible outcomes of a move to determine whether or not it is good would be impossible, even for a lightning fast computer. The computer needs to make a decision on

whether or not to make a move based on the analysis of the resulting pattern of the pieces. It was once suggested that if a computer could beat the world chess champion that machines would have reached some new threshold, that we would now be closer to a real thinking machine. In fact, in 1996 a machine beat the world chess champion in a game for the first time, although the human player won the match. Now that there are prospects of a machine actually winning the world chess championship in the near future, people no longer seem willing to accept this as a test of intelligence.

In any case, one of the human qualities mentioned above has been achieved in chess playing computers. Sophisticated programs can "learn" from their mistakes, thus gaining the "experience" that they need to improve. If a computer analyzes its play of a game and determines where it made its mistake you can be sure that, unlike a human, it won't be making that mistake again! Programs with this capability are called *learning programs*.

One of the more interesting tests for computer intelligence was proposed by Alan Turing in 1936, and now goes by the name *Turing Test*. It's interesting that Turing's thoughts on this subject preceded the world's entrance into what is now considered the computer age.

Turing was a brilliant British mathematician and logician whose theoretical contributions were essential to the early development of computers. His insights in the area of machine intelligence showed a level of understanding that has been matched by few people in history.

The Turing test is performed by placing a person alone in a room with two terminals connecting him or her to the outside. One of these terminals is connected to a computer, while the other is connected to a human. The person in the room does not know which terminal is which. The purpose of the exercise is for the person in the room to try to discover which terminal is connected to the computer and which is connected to the human by asking questions of them through the terminals. If the person in the room cannot make a determination as to which is which, or if he or she guesses incorrectly, that computer is judged to have passed the Turing Test. Turing's opinion was that such a machine was performing human–like thought processes.

Simulation

Computer simulation is another of the more recent uses for computers. In a computer simulation the idea is to build a "model" of a real life situation inside the computer. This is done in order to test the model to see how it reacts to certain stimuli, to train someone in the use of technical equipment, to test hypotheses, or simply for amusement.

As an example consider one of the more popular categories of computer software now, the flight simulator. This allows the user to experience some of the excitement of flying an airplane by simulating the conditions that a pilot faces in the cockpit. More advanced versions of flight simulators such as these are actually used to test and train pilots. The advantages of this are obvious: Pilots can be trained without expending valuable equipment or endangering lives. Some simulations such as these have gotten so good that they have been given the name *Virtual Reality*.

Other simulations are not nearly so realistic – nor do they attempt to be. These might be used to test ideas before putting them into action in a real–life situation. These simulations might be used to test military strategy before an attack, to test a company's economic strategy before a major change in their pricing policy, or to study the effects of a change in a nation's tariff policies before changing its laws. The advantages of such simulations are obvious. You can use them to test a course of action without the risks characteristic of a real–life test. If a computer simulation uncovers possible problems in your strategy which were unforeseen, it's possible that you might decide to reject that strategy, or to make changes in it before you put it into operation. More about this type of simulation is discussed in chapter 4.

Scientists have used computer simulations such as these extensively in recent years. One such simulation consisted of introducing different conditions into a simulation of the environment of the woolly mammoth to determine which of these conditions might have led to the extinction of these animals ten thousand years ago. By changing the conditions of the computer environment it was possible to determine

just what effect such factors as global warming, human predation, and changes in available plant life might have had on the mammoth populations. Although it isn't possible to prove conclusively just which of these factors may have played significant roles in the demise of the mammoth, possible scenarios can be tested to see how they could have impacted the population. After studying simulations such as these it is now believed that much of what has been learned about the effect of the environment on mammoth populations can be used in helping to stave off the possible extinction of the mammoth's living relatives, the African and Asian elephants. Other simulations have been used to test geologic theories concerning earthquakes, volcanoes, and plate tectonics.

Another kind of simulation is also employed in modern business. Prototypes of expensive equipment, such as airplanes, spaceships, or automobiles, are now "built" and tested on computer. This allows for the perfection of a design without actually going through the expense of building and testing of actual working models.

Questions to Discuss

1. List the four applications of computers discussed in the text. Give some original examples of each.

2. Outline how the introduction of the electronic computer revolutionized the airline industry's reservation system.

3. Compare and contrast the four applications of computers covered in the text. In particular, describe the distinguishing features of data processing (clerical applications) and pattern recognition.

4. Describe the purpose of the Turing test and how it attempts to carry out this purpose.

5. Identify some possible problems with the Turing Test. What modifications would you make on the Turing Test in order to try to eliminate these problems?

6. What possible reasons could you find for the fact that computers have trouble with those things that are easy for humans? Some examples are the identification of someone's voice or their face.

7. Discuss possible problems which could come up with simulations used to test economic or scientific hypotheses. Use a specific business situation or the woolly mammoth scenario described above to clarify your explanation.

8. Discuss possible problems which could come up in using computer simulations to test prototype designs for new airplanes or cars. Do you think it would be possible to design and test an airplane without building *any* working models?

8.4 Modern Trends in Computing

Fed by the computer, the world around us is changing at breakneck speed. Having given rise to this change in our world, the computer now needs to keep up with our growing appetite for faster and more powerful computing machines. Things are now changing so fast that some people refuse to buy computers simply because they think they will be out of date in a few months.

Home Computing

Home computing is said to have started in June 1977 with the introduction of the Apple II microcomputer. This is credited with being the first fully-assembled machine generally available to the public. Although some earlier machines had been marketed, they had been designed as kits for hobbyists to put together, and most were not general purpose machines. Some of these didn't even have keyboards and had no way to save programs. If you had a good idea, you would have to reenter your program from the beginning every time you wanted to run it! The Apple II, Commodore's PET, and the Radio Shack TRS-80 were all early machines that were popular in the home and the education market.

Modern personal computers have changed considerably from those early days. IBM, the computer giant which had concentrated on large business machines for many years, decided to enter the home computer market in the 1980's, introducing its IBM PC in 1981. With the power of IBM behind the personal computer, the idea of what a home computer was for would change drastically almost over night. In its first year the IBM PC sold over 800,000 units, and even more amazingly, *Time* magazine named the computer as its "Man of the Year." The power of the machines increased tremendously and their size decreased just as dramatically. Essentially, people were now able to work on their most important office machine at home. Since there was now very little difference between home and business machines, connecting them through modems made it possible for people to report for work without leaving the house. Many new in-home small businesses centered around the computer also emerged.

Although IBM has never been tops in home computer sales, almost all computers built since their move into the home computer market have adopted any hardware standards set by that company. With the notable exception of Apple's Macintosh, just about any home computer looking for general acceptance needs to "IBM compatible."

Because of the close similarity between home and office machines it has become very hard to differentiate between them. Many users employ Word Processing, Data Base Management, and Spreadsheet programs at home now, despite the fact that each of these programs were originally designed to satisfy office needs. The machine used in the home may need to be a bit more versatile in order to satisfy the family's entertainment and home research requirements, but as people get used to the power and speed that they have at their fingertips in the office they find it very difficult to settle for less at home.

In recent years the addition of CD-ROM drives to many home computers has greatly increased their capabilities. CD-ROMs allow computers to read large amounts of data stored on compact discs. This has made it possible to transfer the data necessary to display photographs and even movies on your computer monitor. Other compact discs contain entire reference books (such as encyclopedias, almanacs, and dictionaries), interactive games, or novels. CD-ROMs and other devices which allow for the storage of large amounts of data in a very compact form have given home computers an incredible amount of power. By the way, ROM stands for "Read Only Memory." You may use CD-ROM drives to read the information that has been stored on the discs, but you cannot alter that information.

Office Computing

The modern office is the place where computers of all different sizes meet. Large corporations have been comfortable working with large "main-frame" computers ever since American Airlines put the IBM 360 to work on its SABRE reservation system mentioned earlier in this chapter. Although main-frames are still used by large corporations, governments, and wherever high-powered computer muscle is needed, more and more they are being replaced by minicomputers, microcomputers (also called desktop computers and personal computers), laptop computers (including machines labeled as portable, notebook, and subnotebook computers), and even pocket organizers. The modern computerized office in most large companies, colleges, and governmental agencies may contain many desktop units which are connected to a large main-frame computer that coordinates their efforts. The main-frame could store many large and powerful programs for office use, thus relieving the desktop machines of this burden. In addition, the

output from these could be stored on the main-frame where it could be shared with other authorized users within the company. A setup such as this is called a *network*.

By far the most useful software in the business environment is the *word processor*. In fact, without the word processing capabilities of computers it's hard to see how computers would have ever achieved the popularity that they have today. Many companies produced machines for this one specific purpose, but now the desktop computer, both cheaper and more versatile, has replaced these machines in most office environments. In fact, it's almost impossible to find a typewriter in most offices anymore.

The power and speed of the modern computers make them more important than ever in today's fast-paced business world. Periodic reports requiring the analysis of extensive amounts of data can be prepared in a more timely manner than ever before. These reports are often accompanied by slick charts, graphs, and other graphics in order to make the report more easily understood. The desktop computer could play an important role at every level in the preparation of such a report.

In the business world size is fast becoming a more important attribute than either power or speed. When a business person leaves the office he or she can essentially take that office with him or her in the form of a laptop computer. These machines are battery operated, allowing them to be used just about anywhere. They have enough storage power to hold even large business programs on their hard drives, and their speed is very close to the desktop units. They also generally contain built-in modem and FAX capabilities allowing communication with the home office when that's necessary. Micro-miniaturization has had its most obvious impact here, in the business sector.

Scientific Computing

The electronic computer was developed primarily to assist scientists and engineers in attacking the more difficult problems in their disciplines. Now they are used for everything from word processing and data storage (the same capabilities used in the business world) to the complex simulations used to predict the course of hurricanes and even local thunderstorms. Now that the enormous power and speed of modern machines has become more and more accessible, scientists are finding more and more applications for them. To try to understand just how powerful the modern machines are, consider this: In 1986 machines that were able to process $50,000,000$ data transfers per second (called "fifty megahertz") would have been classified as *Supercomputers*. Such machines probably could not even be afforded by large universities, and access to them was restricted to a few lucky scientists. In 1996 machines operating at 120 megahertz and faster are available as desktop machines and are routinely sold through mail order for less than $\$3000$! These machines are within the reach of just about any scientist who needs one. In fact, nowadays to be considered a super computer the machine has to be operating at billions of Hertz (thousands of megahertz). The fact that this speed and power is so readily available is changing the way science is being done.

Networking has multiplied the power of desktop computers even more. Networks have been used in business and educational environments, but they have truly revolutionized scientific computing. A few years ago if more computer power was needed there would have been only one response to the problem: build a faster, more powerful machine. Now this is not considered the only answer. More power is often available by hooking together existing machines so that their combined strength can be applied to the problem. This is called *parallel processing*. In a classic example of how this can work, hundreds of machines connected informally through the Internet worked together to factor a large number. The factorization of very large numbers turns out to be a much more difficult task than most would think, and it had been estimated that factoring this number would take hundreds of years on existing machines. Through the cooperation of these machines the job was done in just a few months! Although this might not seem like an important accomplishment, it actually is quite significant. The factorization of large numbers allows us to crack certain types of secret codes which have been used in the corporate community. The ability to factor large numbers quickly may make these coding techniques obsolete, and require that more complicated techniques be employed in the future.

Neural Networks, Expert Systems, and Artificial Intelligence

Neural Networks are another modern development. This takes the network concept one step further by attempting to use computers in a way that is more like the human brain. The neural network idea grew from an understanding that the human brain does not process information in a linear way. In some sense, the brain accepts many different stimuli and processes them "in parallel." It is working on *many facets of the problem at once* rather than sequentially moving from one task to the next only after the previous job is completed. The old ideas of computer programming stuck to the more sequential, linear model, only moving on to the next task when the previous one had been completed. Neural networks allow for a number of computer processors to work on different aspects of a problem at the same time. The results of this work are eventually integrated to get to the final solution. Neural networks are a better model for the way we currently understand the way the human brain works than the old-fashioned linear computer processor.

Neural networks have proved to be a very powerful tool in the analysis of difficult problems. Some feel that the development of neural networks is a significant step in the evolution of artificial intelligence.

Another of the advances in the field of artificial intelligence has been the growth of *Expert Systems*. Expert systems are designed to store an enormous amount of information about a restricted topic. Problems can be solved by having the computer compare a real-life situation to known schemes in the data base. Doctors might use a set-up like this to help diagnose a patient's illness by comparing their symptoms with those in the expert system. When the expert system thinks it has a match between the symptoms and a possible illness, it can report the match to the doctor in order for him or her to verify the result. Similar systems are also in use by automobile mechanics and electronics repairmen.

It is absolutely impossible to guess where all of this might be leading. Researchers from only ten years ago would probably be amazed by what has been accomplished in such a short time. What is certain is that computers will increase in speed and power even more in the future, and the problems that engineers and scientists will be solving with them will be bigger and more difficult than ever.

The Arts

In the earlier section on pattern recognition we discussed attempts at using computers to emulate the creative powers of the human brain. Although the results of most of these investigations have been unsatisfactory in that the art and music which has been produced primarily through the computer has been very primitive, this does not mean that the computer has no role as a tool in these areas. In fact, the computer is now seen as a valuable assistant by many in the art world.

An example illustrating the use of the computer as a "composer's assistant" is Kenneth Lampl's *Statiphony for Wind Ensemble*. He has this to say about his composition:

> As the title suggests, it is a Symphony for Wind Orchestra constructed with the use of statistical procedures. My interest in this position stems from the notion of treating musical texture not in terms of a hierarchy of individual contrapuntal or homophonic parts, but in having each individual function as a single grain in a larger mass or cloud of sound. The most logical selection for defining the procedures for which these masses are to be subjected was statistical manipulation via the computer. The use of such computer regulated procedures allow us the flexibility and precision to define sonic entities not only in terms of their pitch, rhythm, and timbre, but also their density, rate of change and degree of order or chaos. This is the third of such statistical-based pieces and is focused on the idea of a perpetual transformation of its material by static and dynamic accumulation. These continuous processes are then interrupted by sometimes violent eruptions in the musical fabric. The eruption of chaos in a world moving toward order.

Other musicians, such as the accomplished cellist Yo-Yo Ma have been known to use the computer with stunning effect in their work.

Another, more recognizable use of the computer as an artistic assistant would be its use in the field of commercial art. One example here is the use of fractals in much of the animation that is currently employed in television commercials and even in motion pictures. Chapter 9 gives more information on this topic.

> ### *Small Group Exercise*
>
> Discuss Lampl's quote. Note in particular how he is willing to use the computer as a tool in the construction of his compositions, and even finds it "natural." Also, take note of the way the computer enables him to get at characteristics of the music which he would not find accessible without its help, and his reference to the modern scientific concept of chaos.
>
> Comment on the way that projects such as this close the perceived gap between science and technology and the arts and humanities. How does some knowledge of both worlds increase the ability of the artist to create and the ability of the observer to appreciate?

> ### *Questions to Discuss*
>
> 1. Explain how the office main–frame can be used to coordinate the efforts of many workers on personal computers.
>
> 2. Describe how new advances in computing have influenced the scientific community.
>
> 3. Explain why neural networks seem to be a better model for the human brain than earlier attempts at artificial intelligence.
>
> 4. Many works of science fiction have themes concerning themselves with the dangers of "thinking machines" taking over civilization. Is this something that we need to be concerned with, or at least aware of? Give some examples of specific science fiction movies or books where this theme is used, and comment on the believability of the plot in these cases.

8.5 Chapter Review

Important Terms to Know

abacus	ENIAC	numerical applications
analog computer	expert system	optical scanner
Analytical Engine	Hollerith card	output devices
Apple II	input devices	parallel processing
artificial intelligence	integrated circuit	pattern recognition
bar code reader	International Business Machines	personal computer
binary number system	Jacquard attachment	RAM
Boolean Algebra	joystick	SABRE
CD-ROM	keyboard	slide rule
clerical applications	learning program	software
computer chip	logarithm	spreadsheet
computer generation	main-frame	SPSS
computer simulation	Mark I	Stepped Reckonner
CPU	micro-miniaturization	storage devices
data base management	microcomputer	time sharing
data processing	microprocessor	transistor
data storage device	minicomputer	Turing test
desktop computer	modem	UNIVAC
disc drive	mouse	vacuum tube
Difference Engine	Napier's bones	virtual reality
digital computer	Napier's rods	VLSI
drawboy	network	volatile memory
electromechanical computer	neural network	word processing program
electronic computer		

Important Names to Know

Ada, Countess of Lovelace	Bouchon, Basil	Napier, John
Aiken, Howard	Eckert, J. Presper	von Neumann, John
Atansoff, John	Hoff, Ted	Pascal, Blaise
Babbage, Charles	Hollerith, Herman	Shannon, Claude
Bardeen, J.	Jacquard, Joseph-Marie	Shockley, Robert
Bissaker, Robert	Leibniz, Gottfried Wilhelm von	Turing, Alan
Boole, George	Mauchly, John W.	

Review Questions

1. What distinguishes an analog computer from a digital computer? Which of these types is the more common type of computer in operation today?

2. List the computer generations along with the advance or characteristic that made each of these generations possible.

3. Discuss the reasons why you think pattern recognition is more difficult to achieve than data processing.

4. Give some examples from your own experience where computers have been used to assist artists in the completion of their work.

5. Why do neural networks model the working of the human brain better than the earlier computer networks had?

Chapter Nine

Geometry

"... there is no branch of mathematics, however abstract, that may not someday be applied to phenomena of the real world."

Nikolai Ivanovich Lobachevsky

Chapter Nine: GEOMETRY

Chapter Outline

9.0 Introduction

9.1 Historical Perspective

9.2 The Geometry of Euclid
- *The Special Status of Geometry*
- *Definitions*
- *Postulates and Axioms*
- *Theorems*

9.3 Plane Analytical Geometry and Other Developments
- *The Coordinate System*
- *Locating Points*
- *The Utility of Analytical Geometry*
- *Projective Geometry*

9.4 Non–Euclidean Geometry
- *Girolamo Saccheri's Attempt; Reducio ad Absurdum*
- *The Birth of Non–Euclidean Geometry*
- *Riemannian Geometry*
- *A Model for Elliptic Geometry*
- *A Model for Hyperbolic Geometry*
- *Use of the Models*
- *Differences in Theorems*

9.5 Modern Geometry; Fractals
- *Symmetry*
- *Mandelbrot's Contribution*
- *The Nature of Self–Similarity*
- *The Self–Similarity of Nature*
- *Fractal Growth*
- *Fractal Models of Other Processes*

9.6 Chapter Review

9.0 Introduction

Geometry is one of the oldest branches of mathematics. The word, which comes from the Greek words ge (earth) and metria (measure), reflects the original practical goals of the subject. However, it wasn't long before the Greeks had transformed the subject into a totally new type of study, one in which the still young discipline of logic played a central role. This was *Plane Euclidean Geometry*, the subject still studied by high school students today, over two thousand years later.

Although we will take a brief look at Euclidean geometry, most of our efforts will be focused on more modern developments. The most important of these was the discovery of non–Euclidean geometry in the nineteenth century, although many more recent discoveries have had important consequences both within and outside mathematics.

9.1 Historical Perspective

The earliest recorded occurrence of anything resembling modern geometry goes back to ancient Egypt and Mesopotamia. Their geometry was practical; it was used to survey land in order to levy taxes. Although their geometry would have to be considered primitive by modern standards, the Egyptians did have surprising knowledge of some advanced results, including some idea of the Pythagorean Theorem.

Many areas of modern Western thought can trace their origins to the classical Greek era of the last thousand years before the birth of Christ. The Greeks made their mark in many fields, and their contributions in art, drama, science, philosophy, and mathematics are still studied and have a definite impact to this day. Their contributions to the field of geometry have to rank among their greatest accomplishments. The approach to the subject taken by Euclid in his *Elements* was used as a model for almost all elementary geometry texts for over two thousand years, and its axiomatic method has served as a guide for study in all of the sciences and philosophy.

While Euclidean geometry serves as model for the study of modern mathematics, generalizations of the subject have changed the subject over the years. The first of the major modifications of geometry came in the 17th century when two French mathematicians and philosophers, René Descartes and Pierre de Fermat, developed analytic geometry. This new subject connected algebra and geometry in a way that enabled each of these important mathematical disciplines to be used as an aid in solving difficult problems in the other field. Analytic geometry also turned out to be the foundation which was an essential ingredient in Isaac Newton and Gottfried Wilhelm Leibniz' formulation of calculus later in the 17th century. As we shall see, the other breakthrough of the 17th century, projective geometry, also had far-reaching consequences.

The big revolution in geometry came in the 19th century with the discovery of non–Euclidean geometries. These new geometries proved to have many applications, and have played a large part in the revolutions that have taken place in many areas in mathematics and science during the twentieth century. Two of these applications are the use of non–Euclidean geometries as an aid to navigation, and the primary role that they played in the development of the Theory of Relativity by Albert Einstein. As such they play an important role in man's understanding of the structure of the universe.

In the twentieth century geometry has moved in many new and unexpected directions. There is topology, sometimes called rubber sheet geometry. In this branch of geometry shape is no longer important, but other spatial properties of objects take on added significance. Network theory (or graph theory) is a branch of topology which could be used to answer questions concerning the best path for a coast–to–coast phone call or for the prioritization of tasks to complete a construction project. Finally, there is the latest craze in geometry, fractal geometry, which some think is the vanguard for a whole new understanding of the way our brains process information. Fractal geometry has already had commercial applications within the industrial world, where it has been used to generate much of the computer graphics seen in the movies and on television. Already fractal geometry has had a large impact within mathematics and in other subjects.

9.2 The Geometry of Euclid

The early development of geometry by the Greeks reflected their belief in the power of the intellect. Man *strives for perfection*, but generally the attainment of this ideal is not possible because of the inaccuracy of his senses. Certainly this was a problem with the natural sciences, since their study required experimentation and observation. If there were any subject where man could *achieve perfection* it would have to be a very special branch of knowledge, one that depended on the mind rather than the senses.

The Special Status of Geometry

Geometry was to be this special subject. The plan was to start with a limited number of *accepted truths*, which Euclid called *axioms* and *common notions*. (Euclid's axioms are now called *postulates*, while his "common notions" are what we now call *axioms*.) These "accepted truths" were supposed to be self–evident. That is, they should be so obvious that no one would even consider challenging them. After listing these the work of geometry could begin, with the proving of theorems. Theorems would be deduced from the axioms and postulates through logical demonstrations, those valid arguments which we studied earlier in the chapter on logic. This rigorous structure would allow no errors to occur in geometry, since valid arguments only admit true conclusions when the hypotheses are true. Since the hypotheses of the arguments could only be axioms or postulates (assumed true) or previously proved theorems (proved true), *the conclusion to any logical demonstration in geometry would have to be true.* In this way geometry would always achieve true conclusions, and perfection would be attained.

The Greeks realized that the special status of geometry would only come at a price. The "things" of geometry — points, lines, triangles, circles, and so on, are ideals which can exist only in our minds. Any actual construction made by man would only be a crude approximation of these ideal objects. Thus the theorems of geometry did not deal with concrete, everyday objects, but with imaginary concepts. Geometry would no longer be the practical science of the Egyptians, but the incredible triumph of the classical Greek mind. It would stand as a memorial to the great accomplishments of the classical Greeks.

Definitions

Actually carrying out this reasonable sounding program is more easily said than done. First there was the problem of defining the basic concepts of the subject. For example, Euclid defined a point as something which "has no part," a line (that is, a curve) as something which has "length but no breath," and a straight line as one which "lies evenly with its points." These definitions have been criticized for being vague, but Euclid was actually facing an impossible task. Definitions should describe things in terms of other, hopefully more familiar, concepts. As we trace these concepts further and further back we must eventually get to a starting point, some agreed upon beginning where the basic concepts in question have some accepted (possibly intuitive) meaning. In modern mathematics these basic building blocks are accepted as *undefined terms*, and their meanings may even be considered irrelevant. Thus the emphasis in modern geometry is not necessarily on the objects themselves, but rather in the relationships between them.

Postulates and Axioms

The other problem faced by the developers of Euclidean geometry was to construct the list of agreed upon truths, that foundation upon which the rest of geometry would be built. As mentioned earlier, these should be beyond dispute since they would be used to prove the other truths of geometry, the theorems. Presumably all truths about geometry would be in either Euclid's list of assumed truths or in his list of theorems. *The essential difference between a postulate and a theorem was that the postulate was accepted as true* (because it was obvious), *while a theorem needed to be proved true* (presumably because it was not obvious). It is not known which mathematicians made the decisions concerning which statements would be permitted as postulates (that is, which statements were "obvious enough") but it probably wasn't Euclid himself, since the subject was already well developed when Euclid wrote the *Elements*.

To give some idea of the flavor of what Euclid was doing we will take a quick look at the postulates and axioms of Euclidean geometry, followed by a couple of theorems. The fifth postulate, also called the parallel postulate, is replaced by a simplified version of the original parallel postulate. This version is given because it should be easier to visualize.

EUCLID'S POSTULATES
1. Given any two points there is a line segment connecting them. (Euclid assumed without actually stating it that there was only one line connecting the two points.)
2. A line segment may be extended indefinitely in both directions (forming a line).
3. A circle can be constructed if we are given its center and a point on it.
4. All right angles are equal.
5. (*The parallel postulate*) If we are given a line ℓ and a point P not on ℓ, then there is one and only one line that goes through P which is parallel to ℓ.

EUCLID'S AXIOMS
1. Things equal to the same thing are equal to each other.
2. If equals are added to equals the results are equal.
3. If equals are subtracted from equals the results are equal.
4. Things that coincide with one another are equal.
5. The whole is greater than any part.

The main distinction between an axiom and a postulate is that postulates deal with geometric concepts, while axioms are more general. For our purposes this distinction is not important enough to warrant further comment, and we will generally refer to all of the accepted truths as postulates.

A quick look at the list of postulates would seem to indicate that if the main purpose in constructing it was to come up with a list of indisputable truths, then the authors of the list did a pretty good job. In fact, with the exception of the parallel postulate no one even considered doubting any of the statements on the list for over 2000 years. Even when doubts were expressed concerning the parallel postulate they dealt not with its truth, but rather with the question of whether or not it was obvious enough to be considered a postulate.

The amazing thing is just how much can be proved from this short, innocent looking list of statements. The geometers of the day had some idea of what they wanted to prove, and this brief list of accepted truths, along with logic, was enough to prove just about any statement about geometry that they believed to be true.

Theorems

For example, by measuring the angles of many triangles the Greeks had reason to believe that the sum of the angles in any triangle was $180°$ (of course the Greeks didn't measure angles in terms of degrees). If geometry were really going to become the perfect science they had hoped it would be, then they ought to be able to prove this. With the help of the parallel postulate this is easily accomplished. Note that if they could not prove this, but were still absolutely sure that it was true, then Euclid could have agreed to add the statement "The sum of the angles in any triangle is 180°" to his list of postulates. This wouldn't be very attractive because *this statement*, although just as believable as the postulates, *is not nearly as obvious.*

It is interesting to note that if Euclid had decided to replace the parallel postulate with the statement "The sum of the angles of any triangle is $180°$," then the parallel postulate could have been proven as a theorem. What this means is that the parallel postulate could have been replaced by the statement "The sum of the angles of any triangle is $180°$" *without changing any of the provable truths* of the system. There are many other similar choices that could have been made, and the final decision on what should be a postulate and what should be a theorem is, from the modern mathematical point of view, quite arbitrary. From the Greek point of view, however, this choice would not be arbitrary. If a statement were not obvious the Greeks simply could not make it a postulate.

Two additional examples of theorems may give some idea of the types of things that can be proved in Euclidean geometry. The first of these is the famous Pythagorean Theorem.

Pythagorean Theorem: If the three sides of a triangle have lengths a, b, and c, and if the angle opposite side c is a right angle (that is, $90°$), then $a^2 + b^2 = c^2$. (It is also true that if $a^2 + b^2 = c^2$, then the angle opposite side c must be a right angle.)

Again, although this theorem is believable, it would be hard to make an argument for this being obvious. Thus this should be a theorem (which it is) rather than a postulate.

The last example of a theorem we'll give deals with congruence of triangles. You may have seen it written in shorthand notation as $SSS \cong SSS$.

Theorem: If the three sides of one triangle are equal in length to the corresponding sides of a second triangle, then the two triangles are congruent. (That is, the two triangles can be rotated and moved so that they exactly coincide.)

Euclidean geometry was the supreme example of a system devised by man, and went essentially unchanged and unchallenged for over 2000 years. Later we will see what happened when the challenge finally did come in the 19th century.

> *Questions to Discuss*
>
> 1. Outline the reasons why the Greeks believed geometry was the perfect discipline. What was the feature of geometry that allowed for this distinction from other fields of study, such as the physical and natural sciences?
>
> 2. Explain the necessity for undefined terms in the development of geometry.
>
> 3. Explain the need for postulates and axioms in the development of geometry. (Hint: If there were no statements which were accepted truths, what would you use for the hypotheses of your first theorem?)
>
> 4. Describe the similarities and differences between postulates and theorems.
>
> 5. Explain the role that logic played in the Greek development of geometry.

9.3 Plane Analytic Geometry and Other Developments

It would be many years before anybody approached geometry from any point of view which was significantly different from the Greeks. In the seventeenth century, when these new perspectives finally did come, they would be vital to the development of many other fields.

In 1673 the French mathematician and philosopher René Descartes and his contemporary countryman Pierre de Fermat introduced *analytic geometry*, an important new way of using geometry to solve problems. Their method now goes by the name *Cartesian coordinates* (or rectangular coordinates) and has become an important part of the elementary algebra curriculum in high schools and colleges.

What Descartes and Fermat had discovered was a simple but ingenious method for converting algebraic problems, which are often hard to visualize, into a geometric form, called a *graph*. This would enable people to spot relationships which may have been difficult or impossible to spot in a maze of algebraic symbols.

The Coordinate System

The key to Descartes system of geometry was a *coordinate system* which involved a method for identifying each point on a plane (that is, flat surface). Once this is done he showed how this coordinate system could be used to construct pictures, or graphs, of algebraic equations. In this way an algebraic relationship between two variables would be represented by a curve in the plane. By examining these curves (for example where they are rising or falling or where two such curves cross), important information about the algebraic relationship could be gathered. Since these algebraic relationships came up in many fields (such as physics, economics, biology, and so on), this procedure could be useful in analyzing many subjects. It should also be pointed out that in addition to giving a convenient way of visualizing algebraic problems, analytic geometry also gives us a way of translating geometric problems into algebraic form. This means that the solution of some geometric problems, which might have required some spatial or logical insight, could now be solved in an alternative way, through the manipulation of algebraic symbols.

Since it is assumed that most students are familiar with the fundamentals of graphing, only a brief review is given here. After that we will take a look at a few places where graphical analysis has proved to be beneficial.

284   Chapter Nine: **GEOMETRY**

Locating Points

Points are located by giving two numbers, called the x and y coordinates of the point. These numbers identify where the point is with relation to a fixed (but arbitrary) point called the *origin*. The x coordinate is listed first, and it indicates how many units to the right or left of the origin the point is located. (A positive x coordinate indicates a point to the right of the origin, while a negative x coordinate indicates a point that is to the left of the origin.) The second coordinate, or y coordinate, would indicate the number of units above (positive) or below (negative) the origin that your point lies. For example, referring to Figure 9.1, point A is two units to the right of the origin and four units above it, so it has the coordinates (2,4). Point B is 2.5 units to the left of the origin and 0 units above it, so it has coordinates (-2.5,0). Finally, the point C is 2 units to the left of the origin and 3.5 units below it, so it has coordinates (-2,-3.5).

Notice the bold horizontal and vertical lines given for reference in the picture. They are called the x–axis and the y–axis. Coordinates can be measured along these axes to determine the location of points. The units used to measure along these axes can be any convenient quantities, such as inches, millimeters, dollars, or seconds.

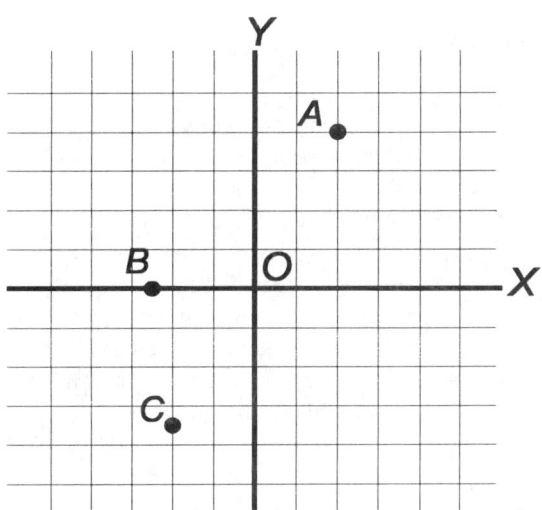

Figure 9.1 The Cartesian coordinate system.

The Utility of Analytic Geometry

The following examples are given in order to give some indication of the usefulness of analytic geometry.

Example #1: Analysis of Supply and Demand.

The graph (see Figure 9.2) shows two curves, called the *supply and demand curves*, for a specific product. To see how the analysis of this particular problem goes, we will consider two specific examples. Suppose that some external force (such as government regulation) sets the price of this particular item at $2. Locating the value of "2" on the "price axis" (the vertical axis), move horizontally across until you hit the supply curve. When you hit the curve, move vertically down to see where you intersect the "quantity axis." This will occur at approximately 9 (which represents a quantity of 900,000 units). *This means that a price of $2 will result in industry supplying 900,000 units* of this product. Similarly, we could use the graph to locate the demand that a $2 price would produce by moving horizontally across from "price = 2" to the demand curve, and we see that *a price of $2 would induce a demand of*

approximately 11 (which corresponds to a demand of eleven-hundred thousand units, or 1.1 million units). Thus, if the price is set at $2 about 200,000 consumers will be unhappy because they would be willing to purchase the product at this price, but not enough items would be produced for them to get one.

On the other hand, suppose that the price of the item were set at $4 instead of $2. Moving horizontally across from "price = 4," we intersect the demand curve at a quantity of about 7 and the supply curve at a quantity of approximately 14. (That is, moving horizontally along from "price = 4," we hit the demand curve vertically up from "quantity = 7" and we intersect the supply curve vertically up from "quantity = 14".) This means that at a price of $4 there will be a demand for only 600,000 units, while 1,400,000 units will be supplied. This time industry will be unhappy, because they have supplied 800,000 units that there is no market for. Note that as the price of the item goes up, the number of people willing to buy the item will go down, while the number of items supplied by business goes up.

The place where the supply and demand curves cross (at a production of about ten hundred-thousands, or one million units, and a price of about $2.25) is called the equilibrium point ($2.25 is called the equilibrium price). If there are no external forces setting prices in the marketplace, the market for this product will move towards the equilibrium point through competition, because this is the only place where supply and demand for the product are equal.

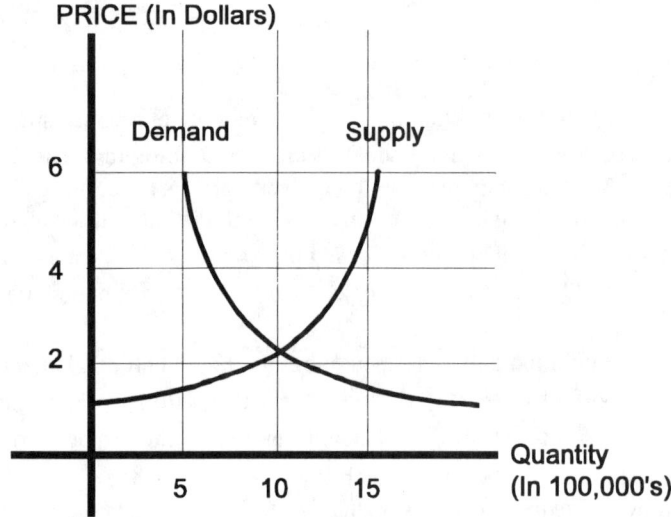

Figure 9.2 An analysis of supply and demand.

Although actually finding a point like this through the analysis of equations would be difficult, at least finding an approximation for this point could be simplified with the use of graphical techniques. Certainly a student's understanding of the concept of equilibrium point is enhanced by the use of the graphs. For this reason, graphs are studied extensively in elementary economics courses.

Example #2. The height of a thrown ball.

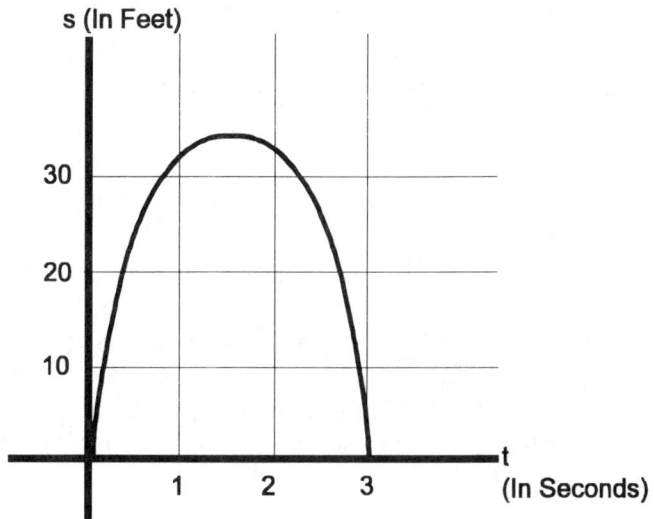

Figure 9.3 The height s of a thrown ball after t seconds.

This graph compares the height of a ball thrown into the air with the number of seconds since the ball was released. (Note that t and s are used instead of x and y, but this changes nothing in the analysis of the problem.) Just as in the last problem, we can compare values on the vertical axis to the corresponding values on the horizontal axis. For example, to determine how high the ball will be after one second, locate "time = 1" on the horizontal axis, move vertically up until you intersect the curve, then move horizontally across to the "height" axis. This shows that the object will be at a height of about 32 feet after 1 second has elapsed.

Note how easy it is to determine certain important facts about the flight of the ball by glancing at the graph. For example, the ball will be rising for the first 1.5 seconds of its flight, falling for the next 1.5 seconds, and will reach a maximum height of about 36 feet. This information could also be found through the application of calculus to the equation of this curve, which is $s = -16t^2 + 48t$, but the visual presentation is much easier to follow and requires much less study.

Example #3. Growth of a Bacterial Colony.

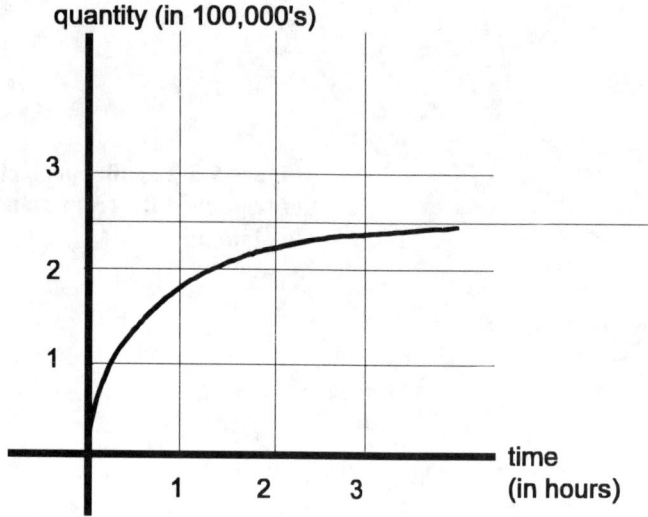

Figure 9.4 The growth of a bacterial colony.

The graph in this example shows how the number of bacteria that are present in a bacterial colony changes with the passage of time. Again, certain important features of the analysis are easy to identify from the graph. For example, the number of bacteria in the colony will approach 250,000 units (called the carrying capacity of the medium). If we let q represent the quantity of bacteria present, then the line $q = 250,000$ is called an asymptote of the curve (in this case it represents the number of bacteria that the colony will approach, but never attain).

Analyzing this problem algebraically would require the use of exponential functions, another concept best studied within the context of a calculus course.

These examples, and others which you could find daily by flipping through the newspaper, give some idea of just how useful Descartes' invention has become in the modern world.

Projective Geometry

Projective geometry is included here because of its importance outside mathematics and because it has at least a superficial relationship to analytic geometry. Although projective geometry didn't achieve maturity as a branch of mathematics until the 19th century, some important findings were made by the Frenchmen Girard Desargues and Blaise Pascal in 1639 and 1640, just a bit before analytic geometry was getting its start.

As a field, projective geometry is concerned with the projection of figures (especially points and lines) from one plane to another. This projection may be accomplished either through parallel lines (parallel projection) or through lines that meet at a point (central projection). Examples of these types of projections are shown in Figures 9.5 and 9.6.

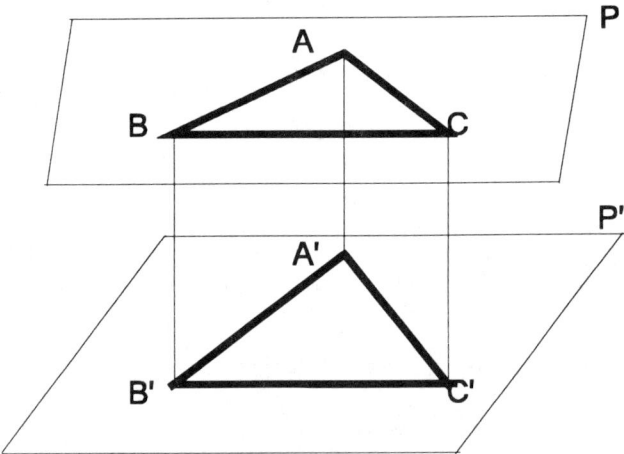

Figure 9.5 Parallel projection of triangle ABC from plane P to plane P'.

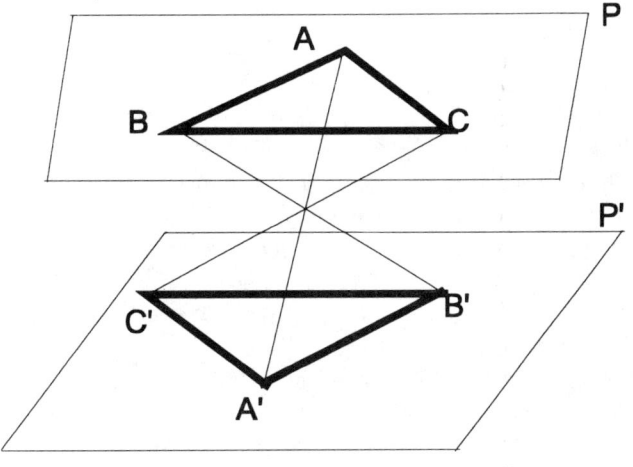

Figure 9.6 Central projection of triangle ABC from plane P to plane P'.

    The development of this subject has influenced and been influenced by the field of art. Early in the Renaissance period the Italian architect and engineer Filippo Brunelleschi rediscovered the concept of projection, which had been known to the classical Greeks and Romans but had apparently been forgotten. Although his procedure for projection was primitive and not mathematical, he did understand how this projection system worked, and as such was one of the first modern Western artists to manage to get perspective into his work. Although he probably was not an accomplished artist, he did teach his projective system to a number of artists of the period, and for the first time in the modern era accurate artwork began to appear. Artists such as Albrecht Dürer and Leonardo da Vinci and sculptors such as Donatello finally had the tool they needed to infuse realism into their paintings and reliefs. Some artists, such as Dürer, even wrote treatises on how geometry could be used to improve their work.

    Although projective geometry has come a long way over the years, remnants of Brunelleschi's system still persist today in a procedure that is taught in modern painting and drawing classes. This procedure involves *viewing the subject to be painted through a grid similar to the Cartesian coordinate system* (a sort of transparent graph paper), while *a second grid is drawn on the canvas*. The image within each small square is then "projected" by the artist from the field of vision to the canvas.

    We might point out that not only projective geometry, but other general mathematical strategies are employed when using this technique. For example, a typical mathematical tactic is to take a large, unmanageable problem and to break it up into a series of smaller, simpler problems. The problem of

perspective may be unmanageable when viewing an entire scene. However, when the scene is broken up into a number of smaller problems by the gridlines, the human mind is able to focus and solve the smaller scale problems.

Questions to Discuss

1. Compare and contrast the axiomatic method of Euclidean geometry with the methods of analytic geometry.

2. Give some examples of how you have seen graphs used as an aid in the transferring and analysis of information.

3. Carl Sagan has called analytic geometry "the corpus callosum of mathematics." (The corpus callosum connects the right hemisphere of the brain, which controls spatial reasoning, with the left hemisphere of the brain, which controls analytical reasoning.) Comment on this.

4. Discuss the interrelationship between projective geometry and the use of perspective in art.

5. Compare and contrast Descartes' system for identifying points in the plane with the method used for finding the position of a point on the Earth's surface by giving its latitude and longitude. (Hints: What corresponds to "positive" or "negative" when referring to longitude? latitude? What do the x and y axes become when referring to a map?)

9.4 Non–Euclidean Geometry

For the two thousand years following Euclid's documentation of the axiomatic system of geometry it seems that there was some dissatisfaction with the setup. Although the logical foundation of the system was certainly not challenged and most of the axioms and postulates were beyond suspicion, one postulate, the parallel postulate, was the subject of some controversy. It appears that the problem was that although people were willing to believe that the postulate was true, some were unwilling to believe that it was obvious enough to be a postulate. The result of this was a large number of attempts to prove the parallel postulate from the other, more acceptable, axioms and postulates of geometry. In other words, what people were unwilling to accept as a postulate would simply have to be proved as a theorem.

Before proceeding to the one attempt at proving the parallel postulate that is worthy of mention (both because it contained no logical flaws and because it can be understood fairly easily), it should be pointed out that many modern historians believe that Euclid himself was not happy with the parallel postulate. As evidence of this they point out that the first twenty–eight theorems of the *Elements* are proved without any reference to it. It appears that he wished to organize his work in such a way that even if this postulate were eliminated, a good portion of the book would still be usable for some new approach. That portion of geometry which can be proved without reference to the parallel postulate is now called *absolute geometry*, since theorems proved in this way are provable in both Euclidean geometry and the non–Euclidean geometries which were eventually developed in the nineteenth century.

Girolam Saccheri's Attempt; Reducio ad Absurdum

One attempt at proving that the parallel postulate was a consequence of the other axioms and postulates took a far different path than the other attempts. This was a proof which was masterminded by Girolamo Saccheri, a Jesuit logician who lived in the 17th and 18th centuries.

What made Saccheri's attempt different from the others was his use of a logical principle called *reducio ad absurdum*. This procedure would be used to prove that a statement was true by an indirect method rather than a direct one.

Suppose that S is a statement which you wish to prove is true. Instead, make the assumption that S is false. If through logic you could then show that this assumption leads to a contradiction, that contradiction would show that your assumption (that S is false) must have been faulty. The only alternative that is left is that S must be true (as we had originally hoped to prove). Essentially you are proving that something is true by showing that its falsity is untenable (because assuming that it is false leads to a contradiction).

To apply this strategy to the parallel postulate problem, Saccheri attempted to prove that the parallel postulate is true by showing that denying it must lead to a contradiction. This was carried out by listing all of the "theorems" which one could deduce if one denied the parallel postulate rather than accepting it as Euclid had. It was clear to Saccheri that once this were done, a careful examination of these "theorems" would lead him to the inevitable contradiction which he knew had to be there.

Unfortunately, the contradiction Saccheri labored so hard to find would not be so easy to uncover. In fact, little did he realize that there was no logical contradiction there at all! Saccheri, however, believing that Euclid's was the only true geometry, refused to consider that this could be possible. He found his "contradiction," but it was not the logical contradiction which he had expected to find. Instead, he found a series of statements which he believed to be *physically impossible*, and he used this to vindicate Euclid.

Although he did not realize it, *Saccheri had failed in his attempt* to show that the parallel postulate could be logically proved from the other postulates. The conclusions which he had deduced from the denial of the parallel postulate, those same statements which he had dismissed as physically impossible, were, in fact, theorems of a new type of geometry which is now called hyperbolic geometry. Saccheri's failure to see this was a product of the fact that these statements were so unlike the "truths" which he knew from Euclidean geometry. Thus, they seemed impossible to him. One could say that the statements which he found *were* impossible in the Euclidean world which Saccheri believed in and knew so well. But he was now in a new world, a strange world which he had no experience with. In this world these seemingly impossible statements actually were true! Saccheri's *failure to find a logical contradiction* really did mean that he had failed in his quest to prove that Euclidean geometry was the only true geometry. But what he had accomplished was even more astounding than what he had attempted and failed to carry out. He had proved a number of theorems in a new type of geometry. Unfortunately, he didn't realize that he had done this.

The Birth of Non-Euclidean Geometry

In the early 19th century the Hungarian János Bolyai was one of the first to realize that the parallel postulate could not be deduced from the other postulates. In fact, the parallel postulate is *independent* of the other postulates, which means that neither it nor its denial can be proved from the other axioms and postulates. This means that you could choose either the parallel postulate or its negation, and the resulting system would be logically viable in either case. Of course the system that resulted from choosing the parallel postulate would be different from the one that you would get if you chose its denial, but there would be no logical way of deciding which of these two systems is the "correct" one. Although Saccheri would not have liked Bolyai's new system, from a logical point of view it was just as good as Euclid's. (Bolyai himself could not prove this. It was later shown that although neither of the

two systems could be proved consistent, it could be proved that if Euclid's system was consistent, then so was Bolyai's. That is, if no contradiction could ever be proved in Euclid's system, then no contradiction could ever be proved in Bolyai's system either. Thus the decision on which geometry was the correct one was not a logical decision, but would have to based on some other criteria.)

To understand why this realization by Bolyai was such a monumental accomplishment, let's take another look at the fifth postulate (or at least the version of the fifth postulate that was given in section 9.2).

> **Postulate #5:** If we are given a line ℓ and a point P not on ℓ, then there is one and only one line that goes through P which is parallel to ℓ.

How would it be possible to deny this postulate? If there isn't to be one line through P that is parallel to ℓ, then that must be because there is either no parallel to ℓ through P, or because there is more than one parallel to ℓ through P. Both of these possibilities seemed so unreasonable to people that most people weren't even willing to consider them. In fact, Saccheri's analysis did eliminate the first alternative as impossible, since he showed that *the "no parallel" option was logically impossible* if all of the other postulates and axioms were adopted as Euclid had written them. But the second alternative, *the "more than one parallel" option*, as distasteful as it seemed, *could not be eliminated through logic alone*.

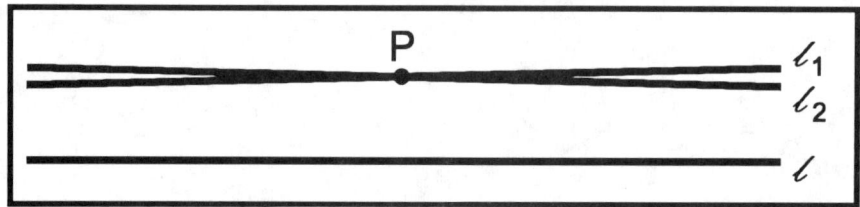

Figure 9.7 Lines ℓ_1 and ℓ_2 both go through P. Could both be parallel to ℓ?

Figure 9.7 gives an indication of the problem. Lines ℓ_1 and ℓ_2 both go through P. Is it possible to believe that if both are extended indefinitely that neither of the two would ever intersect with ℓ?

The surprising and (possibly) totally unexpected answer to this question is "yes"! It is *possible* to believe this. That is not to say that we must believe that straight lines work this way, but it is to say that we may. The question goes back to what we believe a line actually is. Recall that in the modern view the term *line* is undefined. Furthermore, *even our experience of how lines work* (or how we think they should work) *is local*. The whole idea of lines "extending forever" is something that we as humans couldn't actually carry out, even if it were possible to construct a perfect line segment (that is, portion of a line).

It is important to note a change in our attitude toward what geometry is here. In the above explanation we looked toward our *experience* to help us decide what properties we expect of lines. Should this be allowed? Remember, geometry was expected to be the perfect branch of knowledge primarily because it was *not* to depend on experience. Geometry was to be the perfect logical deductive system because it did not depend on the senses, but only on logic. It would not only be unfair to make a decision now which was based on our human, fallible senses, but it would destroy the perfection of the system and drop geometry down to the same level as any of the empirical sciences. There might be nothing wrong with this, as long as you understood that this was what you were doing, and accepted the fact that you were giving up on the Greek ideal of perfection. If, on the other hand, you reject the ability to rely on experience, then both of the systems must stand as equally acceptable geometries. Although one of the geometries might be more useful than the other, from the theoretical point of view both would stand on an equal footing.

One would expect that János Bolyai would have achieved considerable notoriety for his insight into a problem which had baffled mathematicians for 2000 years, but such was not the case. His father,

Farkas Bolyai, sent a copy of his son's publication to Karl Freidrich Gauss, one of the greatest mathematicians of all time, only to find that Gauss himself had already discovered non–Euclidean geometry even before János was born! Gauss, however, had not published his findings, probably because he expected these ideas to be criticized by the conservative mathematical community. In the meantime a Russian mathematician named Nikolai Ivanovich Lobachevski independently published a similar paper and is also credited with the co–discovery of the first of the non–Euclidean geometries.

Riemannian Geometry

During the second half of the 19th century another mathematician, a German named Bernhard Riemann, discovered another new geometry, one that revived the previous "no parallel" alternative (see above). Rather than use the denial of the parallel postulate that Bolyai and Lobachevski had used (that is, there is more than one parallel to ℓ through P), Riemann tried the other possible denial: There is no parallel to ℓ through P. In other words, Riemann's alternative could be thought of as saying that no lines are parallel — that is, that all lines must eventually cross. As previously mentioned, when combined with the other postulates of Euclidean geometry this would yield an inconsistent system, one in which a contradiction could be deduced. However, it turned out that this problem would be remedied by making a relatively minor change in one of the other postulates. The result was another geometry, now called *elliptic geometry*, which also could logically stand on an equal footing with the other two known geometries.

A Model for Elliptic Geometry

Even putting the logical justification of elliptic geometry aside, Riemann's geometry had an almost immediate practical value. If we consider the surface of the Earth to be a perfect sphere, then this two dimensional surface would not satisfy the principles of Euclidean geometry, since these rules were made to work on flat surfaces, or planes. With the proper interpretation of undefined terms such as *point* and *line*, this surface would be found to model the postulates of Riemannian geometry. Once this is accepted, the practicality of this geometry is evident, since it could be used to solve problems dealing with navigation on the surface of the Earth. This would give Riemannian geometry a practical as well as a theoretical justification.

The first question which comes up is this: What would the interpretation of the word *line* be if we restrict ourselves to moving on the surface of the Earth? To answer this question two properties of lines from Euclidean geometry were transferred to see what they should mean on the surface of a sphere. Lines should have the following properties:

1. Any two points should determine a unique line.
2. The shortest path between two points should be a line segment.

This second property gave the clue that was needed, since it was well known that the shortest path between two points on the Earth's surface was a *great circle* — a circular path that had the same center as the Earth. Although the first property could not quite be satisfied (two antipodal points, for example the north and south poles, have infinitely many great circles connecting them — in this case the great circles are called lines of longitude), a solution to this problem turned out to be reasonably simple. In any case, it is reasonable to believe that Riemannian geometry is satisfied on this surface because any two great circles must cross (Think of what happens if you slice an orange through its center twice. Not only will the two great circles have to cross, they'll have to cross twice, at two antipodal points.). In this way Riemann's elliptic geometry was given not only an abstract, theoretical meaning, but also a practical one.

A Model for Hyperbolic Geometry

Once the model for elliptic geometry is understood (and seen to be a simple sphere), it makes sense to try to construct a model for Bolyai's hyperbolic geometry. This time, however, some determination is needed before the appropriate model can be found. A clue here might come from comparing the two models we already know. The model for Euclidean geometry, the plane, is perfectly flat. This surface is said to have zero curvature. The model for elliptic geometry, the sphere, bulges out. This surface is said to have positive curvature. It seems reasonable that if we could find a model for hyperbolic geometry that it would bend in the opposite direction, that is, inward. Such a surface, called a *pseudosphere*, is pictured in figure 9.8.

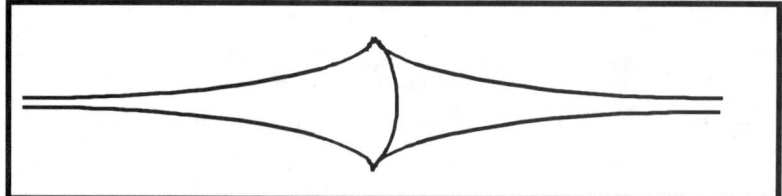

Figure 9.8 The pseudosphere.

If this is the best we could do to find applications for hyperbolic geometry I think that everyone would agree that it wouldn't be the most useful tool ever discovered by man. After all, how often does someone run into a pseudosphere? Still, Bolyai's discovery does have its uses. Early in the 20th century, when Albert Einstein was developing his *theory of relativity*, he needed some way of explaining why light rays followed the paths that he predicted they would. Although space is three dimensional rather than two dimensional, he thought of space as a geometric arena where the word *line* was interpreted to mean *ray of light*. His theory, which has revolutionized man's understanding of the universe, acknowledged that space might satisfy the postulates of non–Euclidean geometry, that is, that space might require that light rays travel along curves. Although it is not clear that space will have the same properties in all regions of the universe, experiments in this region of the universe seem to support the opinion that our area of space satisfies the laws of hyperbolic geometry.

Use of the Models

Thus we have not only a logical justification for all three types of geometry, but practical justifications as well.

If we were working on a flat surface, or something very nearly flat, then Euclid's geometry would be appropriate for solving problems. For example, if I wanted to take some measurements and plan a garden in my backyard, it's unlikely that I would want to take the curvature of the Earth into account in my calculations. I would assume that my backyard were flat (although I know that this is not exactly true), and use Euclidean geometry.

If I were a navigator on an aircraft who was planning a trip from New York to Paris, however, the curvature of the Earth would definitely have to be taken into account. Elliptic geometry would probably be much more useful to me in solving this problem. The most efficient path from New York to Paris would simply be the unique great circle joining these two points.

Finally, if instead of going to Paris we were going to Proxima Centauri (at least in our minds; other than the sun, Proxima Centauri is the closest star to our planet, but it is still 4.3 light years away), then we may well need to use hyperbolic geometry to plan our trip.

All three geometries turn out to be not only logically defensible, but useful as well.

Differences in Theorems

Although all three of the geometries discussed in this section are based on logic, the postulates, or basic assumptions of the three systems differ. Thus, the theorems which can be deduced in the three systems also differ. For example, it is well known that in Euclidean geometry the sum of the angles of any triangle must equal 180°. In elliptic and hyperbolic geometry this is not the case. For example, in elliptic geometry the sum of the angles in any triangle must be more than 180°. (See Figure 9.9.)

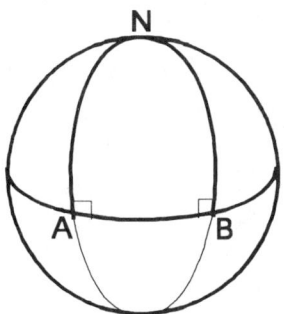

Figure 9.9 Each line of longitude crosses the equator at a **90°** angle forming a triangle whose angles total more than **180°**.

It can also be shown that the sum of the angles of any triangle in hyperbolic geometry must be less than 180°.

There are many other differences in the theorems which may be proved in the three geometries. For example, in elliptic geometry it can be proved that all lines are of finite length. With results which at first glance seem as strange as this, it is not surprising that Saccheri dismissed non–Euclidean geometries as describing impossible situations.

Questions to Discuss

1.
    (a) Explain how mathematicians can justify the study of three types of geometry (the geometry of Euclid, the geometry of Riemann, and the geometry of Bolyai) when each gives results which are not in agreement with others?

    (b) In light of your answer to part (a), why do you think the study of Euclidean geometry remains so prevalent in high schools today, even though we know that there are other geometries which are just as valid?

2.   Kahlil Gibran said: "Say not, 'I have found the truth.' but rather 'I have found a truth.'" Explain how what we have learned about non–Euclidean geometry can help us to better understand Gibran's words.

3.   A student once wrote: "non–Euclidean geometry is the invention of crazy mathematicians who needed something to teach their liberal arts students. Its main purpose is to give students a headache."

    Answer this student's criticism, giving reasons why the study of non–Euclidean geometry is meaningful for liberal arts majors.

> 4. In order to emphasize the abstract nature of geometry, the famous mathematician David Hilbert said "One must be able to say at all times — instead of points, lines, and planes — tables, chairs, and beer mugs." Explain what he meant, and in so doing, compare and contrast this more modern view with the classical Greek notion of geometry.
>
> 5. Compare and contrast Euclidean and non–Euclidean geometries. Consider their foundations, their use of logical principles, and the theorems that are proved in the different geometries.
>
> 6. Discuss the connection between non–Euclidean geometries and the theory of relativity.

9.5 Modern Geometry; Fractals

Just as the idea of self–reference has revolutionized logic and provided insights into our understanding of human thought, a similar idea, called "self–similarity," promises to open up new frontiers in geometry. A self–similar object, one of a class of objects known as *fractals*, is one which appears to be the same no matter what magnification is used to view it. Like self–referentiality, some mathematicians believe that the study of fractals may give some insight into human thought processes and enable us to better understand how the human mind works. However, fractals also have had an impact on more popular endeavors, such as animation for science fiction movies and television commercials. In fact, the use of fractals by graphics artists is now so commonplace that an important part of their training requires them to learn how to use the computer packages which are employed in the generation of fractal images. Other applications of fractals include the construction of models of the human circulatory system, the analysis of stock market trends, and population growth models. Finally, their study is intimately related to two new branches of applied mathematics, *chaos theory* and *catastrophe theory*.

Symmetry

Webster's Third New International Dictionary defines symmetry as "beauty of form or arrangement arising from balanced proportion" or as "Correspondence of size, shape, and relative position of parts that are on opposite sides of a dividing line or median plane or that are distributed about a center or axis."

In his book *Art and the Computer,* Melvin L. Prueitt suggests that perhaps people enjoy pictures that display symmetry because of the bilateral symmetry of our own bodies. Whether this is the case of not, there's no doubt that people have studied natural symmetry and employed it their art, architecture, poetry, and music for thousands of years. With the introduction of the computer, the artist has been given a new tool to help in his or her creation of symmetrical or near symmetrical graphic images.

Mandelbrot's Contribution

In 1982 Benoit Mandelbrot published *The Fractal Geometry of Nature*, in which he expressed his idea that another kind of symmetry was an important ingredient in the way people observe and perceive the world. This "super symmetry", called *self–similarity*, had been around in simple form for many years, but it was only with the development of the personal computer in the 1970's and 1980's that more complicated and useful fractal images could be produced efficiently.

In order to get some idea of what a *fractal* is, we will show how to construct one of the simplest of fractals, called the *von Koch snowflake*. The "actual" snowflake is constructed only after an "infinite number of steps," (meaning that it can never actually be constructed through the process described below) but we will have an approximation of what it looks like if we stop the process after a few steps.

The process starts with an equilateral triangle (that is, a triangle with all three sides equal; see Figure 9.10 below).

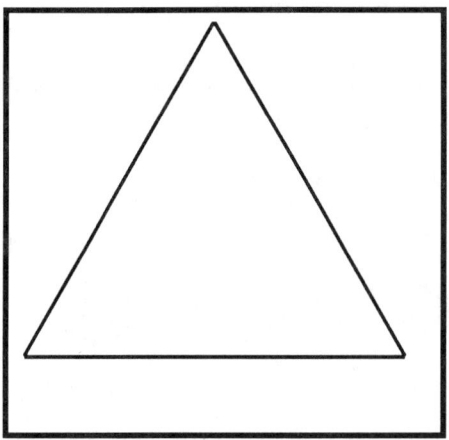

Figure 9.10 Start of the von Koch snowflake construction. Three sides of length one unit; perimeter is three units.

We will be modifying this triangle by constructing a new triangle over the middle third of each of its sides. After doing this we will then erase the base of each of the new triangles which coincides with a side of the original triangle. The result of this operation is shown in Figure 9.11 below. We will call this the first approximation of von Koch's snowflake.

Figure 9.11 First approximation to von Koch's snowflake. Twelve sides of length $\frac{1}{3}$ unit; perimeter is 4 units.

Before proceeding let's make a couple of observations. First of all, each side of the original triangle has been replaced by ─╱‾╲─ , which has a total of four edges. Thus the new figure has four times as many sides as the original figure, or twelve sides. Second, each side in the new figure is one–third as long as the sides of the original figure, so at the end of the process the perimeter has grown from 3 units to $12 \cdot \frac{1}{3} = 4$ units.

We now continue on to the next steps. Following the mathematician's conviction that "anything that has been done once can be repeated over and over again," each of the steps that follow will be carbon copies of the first step in the process, which we have just completed. Starting with the end product of the first step (again, see Figure 9.11), we again trisect each side of the figure and build a new equilateral triangle on the middle segment. That is, we again replace each edge of the figure with ⎯⎯⎯/\⎯⎯⎯ . The result is shown in Figure 9.12.

Figure 9.12 Second Approximation to von Koch's snowflake. Forty–eight sides of length $\frac{1}{9}$ unit.; perimeter is $5\frac{1}{3}$ units.

Again, note that each side in the previous figure has been replaced by four new edges, so the figure now has $12 \cdot 4 = 48$ sides; also, each side has length one–third of length of the side of that in the previous figure. Thus each side in this figure has length $\frac{1}{3} \cdot \frac{1}{3} = \frac{1}{9}$ unit. This gives a perimeter of $48 \cdot \frac{1}{9} = 5\frac{1}{3}$ units.

One more iteration is about as far as we can be expected to go. Again, we replace each edge from the last step in the process with ⎯⎯⎯/\⎯⎯⎯ . This yields Figure 9.13, below, with four times as many sides as the previous figure, each of which is one–third as long.

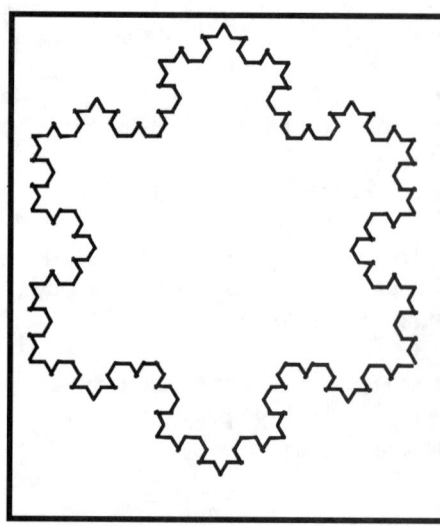

Figure 9.13 Third approximation to von Koch's snowflake. One hundred ninety–two sides of length $\frac{1}{27}$ unit. Perimeter is $7\frac{1}{9}$ units.

Although we won't go any further with this construction, it is clear that the steps which we have performed could be repeated any number of times. (Anyone trying to go any further should enlist the aid of some kind of computer drawing program. The detail required to construct even one more step by hand will try the patience of even the most determined.) However, even if we don't construct any further images, we can still make some interesting comments about the figures. At least the following two statements are evident:

1. At each step we get a figure with four times as many sides as the one in the previous step.
2. At each step we get a figure whose sides are one–third as long as they were in the previous step.

Thus, the next step would give a figure that has $192 \cdot 4 = 768$ sides, each of which has length $\frac{1}{3} \cdot \frac{1}{27} = \frac{1}{81}$ units (which is the reason that we didn't actually try to construct the next approximation). The perimeter of this figure would be $768 \cdot \frac{1}{81} = 9\frac{13}{27}$ units.

It would be interesting to know how big the perimeter of this snowflake gets after six, eight, or any number of steps, and there actually is an easy way of determining this.

To figure out the perimeter of the nth approximation to von Koch's snowflake (that is, the figure that you get after applying the above procedure n times), note the following:

1. The original figure's three sides would have been multiplied by four a total of n times. Thus, it would have $3 \cdot 4^n$ sides.
2. The length of each side would have been divided by three (that is, multiplied by one–third) a total of n times, which means that each side would have length $\frac{1}{3^n}$ units.

To figure out the perimeter of this nth approximation to von Koch's snowflake, simply multiply the number of sides by the length of each side. This gives a perimeter of $3 \cdot 4^n \cdot \frac{1}{3^n}$, or $3 \cdot \left(\frac{4}{3}\right)^n$ units.

One interesting thing about this is that as n gets larger and larger, this perimeter grows without bound (a mathematician would say that it approaches infinity). For example, after applying this procedure 10 times we would get a perimeter of $3 \cdot \left(\frac{4}{3}\right)^{10}$, or approximately 53 units. If we apply the procedure 100 times, we get a perimeter of $3 \cdot \left(\frac{4}{3}\right)^{100}$ units, which is more than nine trillion units!

(Nine trillion inches would be about 147 million miles, or more than 1.5 times the distance from the earth to the sun.)

Loosely speaking, the von Koch snowflake is the "limiting curve" which would be "constructed" by applying the procedure described above an unlimited number of times. The analysis given above shows that the perimeter of this figure is infinite, although it turns out that the area enclosed by the figure is finite!

Although this might seem shocking, mathematicians knew about curves that acted similarly before fractals were discovered. Fractals, however, have an even more remarkable property, which not only characterizes them, but also is the source of many useful applications.

The Nature of Self-Similarity

The other remarkable property shared by the von Koch snowflake and other fractals was hinted at earlier. If any portion of the snowflake is magnified, the magnified region will look exactly like a portion of the original object. That is, if you used a magnifying glass to view one section of the snowflake, you would see exactly the same pattern that you would see when looking at the unmagnified figure. The magnifying process could be repeated again and again, but the results would always be the same, no matter what level of magnification is used.

Although the simplicity of the von Koch snowflake makes its construction easy to understand, it might not be possible to fully appreciate the self–similarity concept by studying this example. Two other fractal curves, *Self–Squared Fractal Dragon* (Figure 9.14) and the spiral image in Figure 9.15, may make this concept clearer. Careful examination of the swirls that make up these figures shows that they are constructed from other swirls, while each of these swirls is composed of other, still smaller swirls. This process can be continued indefinitely, but the result will always be the same—swirls composed of other swirls. As we shall soon see, it is here where the connection with many naturally occurring structures can be made.

Figure 9.14 SELF-SQUARED FRACTAL DRAGON.
From FRACTAL MOUNTAINS THAT NEVER WERE: An imitation of nature created by Richard F. Voss. From *The Fractal Geometry of Nature* by Benoit B. Mandelbrot (Yale University) New York: W.H. Freeman 1982. Reprinted with permission.

Figure 9.15 A fractal spiral image.
From FRACTAL MOUNTAINS THAT NEVER WERE: An imitation of nature created by Richard F. Voss. From *The Fractal Geometry of Nature* by Benoit B. Mandelbrot (Yale University) New York: W.H. Freeman 1982. Reprinted with permission.

The Self-Similarity of Nature

There are two reasons why fractals have recently become a hot topic both inside and outside the mathematical community. The first reason has already been mentioned. Although fractals, at least in primitive form, have been around for quite a while, it was the personal computer which made them easy enough to generate in a routine way. In fact, Benoit Mandelbrot's method of producing fractal curves uses such simple equations that its almost impossible to believe that they could result in such beautiful and inspiring images.

The second reason why fractals may be important is Mandelbrot's belief that fractals give us a better understanding of our perception of the form of many natural structures. Images very closely related to the self–similar figures discussed above can be used to generate realistic looking counterfeit representations of clouds, shorelines, mountains, trees, and many other natural objects. Other examples, given by John Allen Paulos in *Beyond Numeracy*, include the surface of battery electrodes, the spongy interior of intestines and lung tissue, and the diffusion of liquid through semi–porous clay. In fact, such fractal images often look more realistic to us than the real thing. If Mandelbrot is right, it may be that the human brain expects to see more regularity in some objects (such as shorelines and clouds) than is actually there, and when the image gives us what we are looking for, we are fooled into thinking that the abstract image is more perfect than the real thing. The other possible theory, which is subscribed to by many, is that certain natural forces work in ways which form some objects (such as mountains, shorelines, and so on) in a way which causes them to exhibit this nearly self–similar feature.

It should be pointed out that the images that are used in modeling natural structures are not really self–similar in the sense described above. Instead, they are given some statistically imposed variation

which makes the charade even more believable. What this means is that if a small portion of the image is magnified, the result would not be *exactly* the same as another portion of the image. The magnified portion would, however, bear a striking resemblance to the rest of the figure, in much the same way that variations resemble each other in musical compositions. In fact, fractals have been used in the creation of computer music and art. There is no doubt about one thing: Fractal geometry does a much better job of modeling certain natural objects than Euclidean geometry does.

The fractal images shown in Figures 9.16 and 9.17 show just how powerful this method of generating graphics can be. After viewing just a few of these images it is easy to see how fractals have played a large part in science fiction movies such as *Star Trek II – The Wrath of Kahn*.

Figure 9.16 FRACTAL MOUNTAINS THAT NEVER WERE
From FRACTAL MOUNTAINS THAT NEVER WERE: An imitation of nature created by Richard F. Voss. From *The Fractal Geometry of Nature* by Benoit B. Mandelbrot (Yale University) New York: W.H. Freeman 1982. Reprinted with permission.

Figure 9.17 EARTH-LIKE PLANET VIEWED FROM A MOON.
From FRACTAL MOUNTAINS THAT NEVER WERE: An imitation of nature created by Richard F. Voss. From *The Fractal Geometry of Nature* by Benoit B. Mandelbrot (Yale University) New York: W.H. Freeman 1982. Reprinted with permission.

Fractal Growth

It is not really clear to scientists why fractals, the product of a purely mathematical operation with no apparent connection with the visible world, should be such good models of so many natural phenomena. One theory, presented by Leonard Sander in the January 1987 issue of *Scientific American*, is that so many natural objects grow in a way that causes them to take on a fractal or nearly fractal form.

Fractal growth would occur when large numbers of small particles, moving in a random way, come into contact with each other. Upon contact, these particles would adhere to each other forming clusters, and the object would grow as more and more of these particles come together. Some objects which may grow in this way are soot deposits and the damp spots which occur as water seeps through porous objects.

This process can be easily simulated by computer, and researchers hope that a study of fractals may lead to a better understanding of the physical properties of objects which grow in this way.

Fractal Models of Other Processes

In addition to the specific applications of fractals listed above, at least one mathematician, Rudy Rucker, has proposed the idea of using fractal structure as a metaphor for human consciousness. Just as tree branches (another naturally occurring fractal–like structure) reach out, forming a sprawling, hazy pattern, so to our thoughts and conversations branch out in ways that are vague and ill–defined. By focusing (that is, magnifying) on any portion of our consciousness we find a logical structure that is somewhat similar to what we would find in any other area. Again, magnifying, or getting deeper and

deeper into the thought processes doesn't seem to change things much. The same nebulous logical structure seems to be present no matter how deep you go. More about this topic can be found in John Allen Paulos' *Beyond Numeracy*.

Fractals have caused a controversy in the mathematical community in recent years. Some mathematicians feel that they are part of the next revolution in the sciences, one that will change our understanding of the structure of the universe. Others feel that fractals are mostly fluff with very little substance and that there is very little real mathematics going on here at all. It is not likely that this dispute will be settled soon, but that shouldn't keep us from admiring the beauty of these intricate, beautiful figures.

Small Group Exercise

Discuss the similarities and differences between self–reference and self–similarity. What is the significance of objects containing copies of themselves in all of this?
Hint: See the exercises at the end of section 1.8.

Questions to Discuss

1. Discuss the popularity of fractal geometry, taking both its mathematical and commercial applications into consideration in your explanation.

2. The argument given in this section shows that the perimeter of the van Koch snowflake is infinite. Explain why the area enclosed by this curve is finite.

9.6 Chapter Review

Important Terms to Know

absolute geometry	geometry	Pythagorean theorem
analytic geometry	graph	rectangular coordinates
axiom	graph theory	reducio ad absurdum
Cartesian coordinates	hyperbolic geometry	self-similarity
catastrophe theory	line	supply curve
chaos theory	network theory	symmetry
congruent	non-Euclidean geometry	theorem
coordinate system	origin	theory of relativity
demand curve	perspective	topology
Elements	postulate	undefined terms
Euclidean geometry	projective geometry	von Koch snowflake
fractal geometry	pseudosphere	

Chapter Nine: GEOMETRY

Important Names to Know

Bolyai, Janos
Brunelleschi, Filippo
da Vinci, Leonardo
Desargues, Girard
Descartes, Rene
Donatello
Durer, Albrecht

Einstein, Albert
Euclid
Fermat, Pierre de
Gauss, Karl Fredrich
Leibniz, Gottfried Wilhelm von
Lobachevski, Nicolai Ivanovich

Mandelbrot, Benoit
Newton, Isaac
Pascal, Blaise
Pythagoras
Riemann, Bernhard
Saccheri, Girolamo

Review Questions

1. Comment on the Greek belief in the special status of geometry. Why would the Greeks have believed geometry to have a higher status than one of the natural or physical sciences? How has modern thinking changed this opinion?

2. Make a time line that illustrates the growth of the various branches of geometry. Include all branches discussed in the chapter.

3. How did projective geometry influence advances in the art world?

4. Compare and contrast the Greek development of geometry with the earlier geometry of Egypt and Mesopotamia.

5. What other branch of mathematics, also developed by the Greeks, played a significant role in the development of geometry? Comment as to the importance of this discipline with regard to the Greek vision of geometry's importance.

6. Discuss how non–Euclidean geometry and fractals can help one describe the physical world around them in December (Christmas time). Use specific objects. Assume you live in the northern hemisphere.

Chapter Ten

Probability and Counting

"... the race is not to the swift, nor the battle to the strong ... but time and chance happeneth to them all."

Ecclesiastes 9:11

Chapter 10: PROBABILITY AND COUNTING

Chapter Outline

- **10.0 Introduction**
- **10.1 Historical Perspective**
- **10.2 The Fundamental Counting Principle**
- **10.3 Permutations**
- **10.4 Combinations**
  - *More Complex Combinations*
  - *Pascal's Triangle*
- **10.5 Counting Trees**
- **10.6 Counting Problems**
  - *Duplicate Items*
- **10.7 Types of Probabilities**
  - *Preliminaries*
  - *Basic Notation*
  - *Classical Probability*
  - *Relative Frequency Probability*
  - *Subjective Probability*
- **10.8 Probability Problems and Basic Facts**
  - *Facts about Probability*
  - *Complements*
  - *Probability Involving "or"*
  - *Probability of Independent Events*
- **10.9 Odds**
  - *Converting Odds to Probabilities*
  - *Converting Probabilities to Odds*
- **10.10 Chapter Review**

10.0 Introduction

We are all familiar with games of chance. How do people determine the odds for a horse race? What is the likelihood you will win at the blackjack table or slot machine at a casino? The weatherman reports that there is a 70% chance of rain today. What does that mean exactly and how did he arrive at that figure? These and other questions like these refer to the topic of probability.

Often, when we compute a probability, we need to have an exact count of how many possible ways there are to achieve something or how many combinations of things are possible. This is the area of counting or *combinatorics*. This is the area we will turn to first.

10.1 Historical Perspective

Probability has been studied for hundreds of years. One of the first systematic computations of probabilities was presented in the book *Liber de Ludo Aleae* by Girolamo Cardano in the sixteenth century.

The theory of probability has since been applied to many areas. In 1654 a friend asked Blaise Pascal, a French mathematician, a question dealing with rolling a die. Pascal worked on this problem and corresponded on this matter with Fermat, another French mathematician. Their correspondence became the beginnings of modern probability theory.

The mathematician known as the founder of probability theory lived during this time period as well. He is Jacques Bernoulli (1654–1705). In 1713 he wrote *Ars conjectandi*. This is the earliest substantial volume on probability theory. In this work he included a general theory of combinations and permutations and what is known as the Law of Large Numbers.

Abraham DeMoivre was a French Huguenot who taught mathematics privately in England. He was mainly interested in developing general procedures and notations for probability theory. In the eighteenth century DeMoivre discovered a very important and useful distribution, known as the normal distribution, while studying games of chance. Pierre Simon de Laplace also developed the normal distribution independently of DeMoivre. Laplace applied it to astronomical observations. Laplace gave much to the theory of probability, for he considered it from all aspects and at all levels.

In the nineteenth century a Belgian scientist by the name of Adolphe Quetelet introduced the use of probabilistic models into many sciences.

In 1929, a Russian mathematician named A. N. Kolmogorov published a set of axioms that could be used to develop probability theories.

The recent developments in probability theory have included Markov chain theory (involving computer simulations of real events) and Rasch procedures which are used to predict the odds of producing correct answers in psychological testing.

10.2 The Fundamental Counting Principle

Suppose you had three shirts, a red, a blue, and a yellow shirt and four pairs of jeans, indigo blue, white, black, and stone–washed. Further, suppose that each shirt coordinated with each pair of jeans. How many outfits could you create just using these shirts and jeans?

One way we could approach this problem is to make a listing of the different possible outfits. We have done this in Table 10.1 below.

SHIRT	JEANS
red	indigo blue
red	white
red	black
red	stone–washed
blue	indigo blue
blue	white
blue	black
blue	stone–washed
yellow	indigo blue
yellow	white
yellow	black
yellow	stone–washed

Table 10.1 All possible outfits

This list is complete and we found twelve distinct outfits. Notice that there were 3 shirts from which to choose and 4 jeans. The number of shirts times the number of jeans, or 3(4), is 12. This is the *Fundamental Counting Principle*.

Fact: If there are a possible ways to do the first thing and b possible ways to do the second thing and c possible ways to do the third thing, there are $(a)(b)(c)$ possible distinct groupings of the three items.

This above fact can be expanded to as many different items as we wish. Just keep multiplying by the number of that item.

We can take our above example and also select a pair of shoes to wear. Suppose we have sneakers or brown shoes from which to choose. Now how many distinct outfits are possible? (Some may look more appealing to the eye than others.) For each outfit listed above, we can choose sneakers or brown shoes. There were 12 before, so now there are 24. If we used the Fundamental Counting Principle we would have had:

(shirts) (jeans) (shoes)
(3) (4) (2) = 24.

This principle enables us to find the NUMBER of distinct groupings possible without listing all of the possible groupings. Would you want to list all of the possible groupings if you had 20 shirts and 8 jeans and 9 pairs of shoes?

There are times when you need to create listings. This is when you need to know more than just how many groupings there are. If a complete listing is needed, then this principle is not going to be

enough. We will return to this problem later, in section 10.5. Until then, use the Fundamental Counting Principle when you only need the number of groupings, and create a list as we did above when needed.

Example 1. A club contains 36 men and 32 women members. Of the male members, 25 have been in the club 7 or more years. Of the female members, 26 have been in the club at least 7 years.

(a) They need to elect a president and a vice–president. One person cannot hold both positions. In how many different ways can they elect a president and a vice–president?

(b) They need to elect a president and a vice–president. The president must be in the club at least 7 years. No one can hold both offices. In how many different ways can this be done?

Solution

(a) Since we only need to know the NUMBER of possible ways this can be done, we do not need to list all of the possibilities. We can apply the Fundamental Counting Principle. Anyone can be president, so there are 36+32 members who can be president, or 68. Everyone can be vice–president except the person who was elected president because no one can hold both positions. Thus, 68−1=67 people can be vice–president. Therefore, there are $(68)(67) = 4,556$ distinct possibilities.

(b) Again, we only need to find the NUMBER of possible ways and not the actual ways, thus we will apply the Fundamental Counting Principle once again. But now the president must be in the club a minimum of 7 years. There are only 25 men and 26 women who have been in the club that long. These are the only people eligible to run for president. Therefore, there are 25+26=51 people who can be president. Everyone except the person elected president can be vice–president. So, there are 68 members and of these, 68−1=67 are eligible to be vice–president. Thus, there are $(51)(67)=3,417$ distinct possibilities.

Exercises

1. Sally has five different gifts to give her five friends. In how many different ways can she give the gifts?

2. To use an automated teller machine you must generally enter a four digit code using the digits 0 through 9. How many different codes are there?

3. If a club consists of 53 members, 47 of which have been members at least two years, in how many different ways can a president, vice president, and secretary be chosen if

   (a) no one can hold more than one office?
   (b) no one can hold more than one office and the president must be a member at least two years?

4. A telephone number consists of seven digits. The first digit cannot be 0 or 1.

   (a) How many different telephone numbers are possible?
   (b) Suppose we now include an area code of three digits, the first of which cannot be 0 or 1. How many different telephone numbers are now possible?

5. A code for a home alarm consists of seven digits from 0 through 9.

(a) How many different codes are possible?
(b) How many different codes are possible if the first digit cannot be 0?
(c) How many different codes are possible if no digits may be repeated?

6. A college identification number consists of three letters followed by four digits. How many different college identification numbers are possible?

7. Sally takes an eight question multiple–choice test where each question has four choices. How many different ways can she mark her answer sheet if she answers every question?

8. A license plate consists of three letters followed by three digits.

(a) How many different license plates are possible?
(b) If none of the digits may be zeros, how many different license plates are possible?

9. Gloria and Jim are planning their wedding reception. The caterer offers them a choice of three soups and a choice of six entrees. How many different combinations of soup and entree are possible?

10. A professor is creating a test bank of questions. There are ten different types of questions. Of each type, there are four possible problems as choices. How many different tests are possible if each test consists of one problem of each type?

11. A driver's license number consists of one letter followed by fourteen digits. How many different driver's license numbers are possible?

12. A security code consists of three letters followed by five digits.

(a) How many different codes are there if no letters and no digits may be repeated?
(b) How many different codes are there if the letter "o" and the number "0" may not be used?
(c) How many different codes are there if the letter "o" and the number "0" may not be used and repetition of letters and digits is not allowed?

10.3 Permutations

Before we can explore *permutations*, we need to look at an operation known as *factorial*.

Definition: n *factorial*, denoted $n!$, is defined by

$$n! = n(n-1)(n-2)(n-3)\cdots(3)(2)(1).$$

Consider $6!$, read six factorial. This is equal to $6(5)(4)(3)(2)(1) = 720$.

Definition: $0! = 1$.

Recall the Basic Order of Operations,
Grouping Symbols
Exponents
Multiplication and Division from left to right

Addition and Subtraction from left to right

Factorials, just like exponents, must be calculated before multiplication and division and just after grouping symbols.

Example 2. Find each of the following:

(a) 5! (b) 8! (c) (10−3)!
(d) 6! − 4! (e) 6 − 4! (f) 7! − 0!

Solution:
(a) 5! = 5(4)(3)(2)(1) = 120
(b) 8! = 8(7)(6)(5)(4)(3)(2)(1) = 40,320
(c) (10 − 3)! = 7! = 7(6)(5)(4)(3)(2)(1) = 5,040 (We must perform the operation within the parenthesis first.)
(d) 6! − 4! = 6(5)(4)(3)(2)(1) − 4(3)(2)(1)
    = 720 − 24 = 696
(e) 6 − 4! = 6 − 4(3)(2)(1) (We find 4! before we subtract.)
    = 6 − 24 = −18
(f) 7! − 0! = 7(6)(5)(4)(3)(2)(1) − 1 (Recall that 0! = 1.)
    = 5,040 − 1 = 5,039

Sometimes the way we list items in a grouping makes a difference and other times it does not. When the order does change the meaning of the grouping, it is called a *permutation*. If the order does not change the meaning of the grouping, it is called a *combination*.

Consider a club consisting of five members, Jean, Jeff, George, Sally, and Mary. This club elects a president and a vice–president. If we were to list some of the possible outcomes of the election, two of them (with the president listed first) would be:

Jean, Mary
Mary, Jean

Clearly, these two listings would not mean the same thing. In the first listing Jean is the president and Mary is the vice–president, but in the second listing Mary is the president and Jean is the vice–president. Thus, the order in which one lists the names changes the meaning, so both listings are different and distinct. This, therefore, is a permutation.

Now consider the same club with the same members, only this time they will choose two members to represent their club on a committee. Again, consider the same two listings as before,

Jean, Mary
Mary, Jean

Are they now distinct? The first listing means that Jean and Mary are on the committee. The second listing also means that Mary and Jean are on the committee. They both represent the same selection, thus this is not a permutation. It is called a combination.

Suppose we need to know how many different permutations are possible. The number of permutations is denoted P. We have the following fact to help us with this computation.

Fact: The number of *permutations* of n things taken r at a time is denoted $_nP_r = \dfrac{n!}{(n-r)!}$.

312   Chapter 10: **PROBABILITY AND COUNTING**

With permutations, no repetition of items is permitted.

We will return to our club listed above. Recall that our club was very small; it consisted of the set of members:

{Jean, Jeff, George, Sally, Mary}.

Let's find all of the possible ways to elect a president and a vice–president. We have made this list in Table 10.2 below.

PRESIDENT	VICE–PRESIDENT
Jean	Jeff
Jean	George
Jean	Sally
Jean	Mary
Jeff	Jean
Jeff	George
Jeff	Sally
Jeff	Mary
George	Jean
George	Jeff
George	Sally
George	Mary
Sally	Jean
Sally	Jeff
Sally	George
Sally	Mary
Mary	Jean
Mary	Jeff
Mary	George
Mary	Sally

Table 10.2 All possible ways to elect a president and vice–president

This list does account for all the possible ways to choose the president and vice–president because it allows each person to be the president in four different ways. The four different ways correspond to the four possible vice–presidents that could be matched with the president.

As you can see, there are twenty different ways to do this. This listing was tedious. If we needed to know the actual ways, this listing would be necessary. Suppose instead, we only need to know how many ways this can be done. Then listing is not the best method. We will use the above fact. Here, $n = 5$ because there are 5 members in this club from which to choose, and $r = 2$ because we will choose 2 people from the club, one to be president and one to be vice–president. Therefore, we have:

$$_nP_r = \frac{n!}{(n-r)!}$$

$$_5P_2 = \frac{5!}{(5-2)!} = \frac{5 \cdot 4 \cdot 3 \cdot 2 \cdot 1}{3!} = \frac{120}{3 \cdot 2 \cdot 1} = \frac{120}{6} = 20.$$

This number is not surprising.

Example 3. The following example refers to the seven days of the week.
(a) Janet wants to go shopping one day, to the library another day, and to the movies a third day. She can only do one of these activities each day. How many different ways can she do all three activities in a week?
(b) Janet wants to go shopping three days of the week. In how many different ways can she do this?

Solution:
(a) If Janet goes shopping Monday, to the library Tuesday, and to the movies Wednesday, this would be listed: Monday, Tuesday, Wednesday.
On the other hand, the listing: Tuesday, Monday, Wednesday, represents the case where she goes shopping Tuesday, to the library Monday, and to the movies on Wednesday. Thus, if we rearrange the days listed, the meaning changes. This is a permutation problem. We only want to know how many ways she can do this, so we will not list all of the ways but use the above fact. There are seven days in a week, so $n = 7$. We need to choose three of those days, thus $r = 3$. Therefore,

$$_7P_3 = \frac{7!}{(7-3)!} = \frac{7!}{4!} = \frac{7 \cdot 6 \cdot 5 \cdot 4 \cdot 3 \cdot 2 \cdot 1}{4 \cdot 3 \cdot 2 \cdot 1} = \frac{5,040}{24} = 210.$$

This can be done in 210 different ways.

(b) Janet just wants to go shopping three of the days of the week. Thus, the listing Monday, Tuesday, Wednesday and the listing Tuesday, Wednesday, Monday represent the same thing. Listing both would be repetitive. This is called a combination problem. For now, the only method to find the number of distinct ways to do this would be to list all of the possible ways. Let S represent Sunday, M represent Monday, T represent Tuesday, W represent Wednesday, R represent Thursday, F represent Friday, and A represent Saturday. The possibilities are:

S,M,T	S,M,W	S,M,R	S,M,F	S,M,A	S,T,W
S,T,R	S,T,F	S,T,A	S,W,R	S,W,F	S,W,A
S,R,F	S,R,A	S,F,A	M,T,W	M,T,R	M,T,F
M,T,A	M,W,R	M,W,F	M,W,A	M,R,F	M,R,A
M,F,A	T,W,R	T,W,F	T,W,A	T,R,F	T,R,A
T,F,A	W,R,F	W,R,A	W,F,A	R,F,A	

Later, when we discuss counting trees, we will see that these are the only ways to list the days in a way that will satisfy this problem.
As we can see there are only 35 different ways to go shopping three days of the week.

Exercises

1.   Evaluate each of the following:

(a) $0!$
(b) $1!$
(c) $9!$
(d) $12 - 4!$
(e) $(12 - 4)!$
(f) $12! - 4!$
(g) $\dfrac{12!}{4!}$
(h) $\dfrac{10!}{9 - 3!}$
(i) $\dfrac{10!}{(9 - 3)!}$
(j) $\dfrac{12!}{5!}$
(k) $11 - 5!$
(l) $(11 - 5)!$

(m) $11! - 5!$ (n) $\dfrac{12!}{12-9!}$ (o) $\dfrac{12!}{(12-9)!}$

2. Evaluate each of the following:
   (a) $_7P_2$ (b) $_{10}P_5$ (c) $_8P_3$
   (d) $\dfrac{_9P_3}{_9P_5}$ (e) $\dfrac{_{10}P_4}{_{10}P_5}$

3. Sally has seven different gifts to give seven of her friends. In how many different ways can she give the gifts?

4. Suppose Sally has seven of the the same gift to give her friends. She has ten friends, but she can only give seven of them a gift. In how many different ways can she give the gifts to seven of her friends?

5. A club consists of 58 members. A president and a treasurer are to be chosen. No one can hold both offices. In how many distinct ways can this be done?

6. Can the permutation rule be applied to either part of exercise #3 from section 10.2? Explain.

7. Three prizes will be awarded to three different people. The first prize is for $1,000. The second prize is for $500 and the third prize is for $100. There are 13 people eligible for the prizes. In how many different ways can the prizes be awarded?

8. There are nine finalists in a dancing competition. One person will get first, one second, one third, and one fourth place. In how many different ways can this occur?

9. In how many ways can a contractor build different models on five available lots if there are seven models from which to choose?

10. How many different ways can six people be seated in a row?

11. There are seven children dancing in a performance. They must exit in a single line. In how many different ways can they line up to exit?

10.4 Combinations

The last example we looked at in the previous section dealt with Janet going shopping three days of the week. We decided that this was a *combination*. We had no formula to help us compute the number of different ways this could be done, so we listed all of the different combinations possible. We will return to this problem again. In that example, we found that there were 35 different ways Janet could go shopping on three days of the week. This number is much smaller than the number of ways to go shopping, to the library, and to the movies. We found that there were 210 ways to do that. Notice that 35 is much smaller than 210. That is because we do not count rearranging the three items in a different order. Remember, order doesn't matter in a combination. Therefore, in a permutation, for example,

S,M,T and S,T,M and M,S,T and M,T,S and T,S,M and T,M,S

are all distinct listings. But, in a combination these are all considered to be the same event. Therefore, in a combination there is only one such grouping and not 6. We can find the number of combinations by dividing the number of permutations by $r!$. The number of combinations is denoted by C. Thus,

$$_nC_r = \frac{_nP_r}{r!} = \frac{\frac{n!}{(n-r)!}}{r!} = \frac{n!}{(n-r)!} \cdot \frac{1}{r!} = \frac{n!}{(n-r)! \cdot r!}.$$

We have the following fact to help us with the computation of combinations.

Fact: The number of *combinations* of n things taken r at a time is denoted $_nC_r$, where

$$_nC_r = \frac{n!}{(n-r)! \cdot r!}.$$

Note that the value of $_nC_r$ is simply the value of $_nP_r$ divided by $r!$. This division cuts down the value to account for the fact that rearrangements are to be eliminated.

Now we will return to Janet. Recall that we found that Janet could go shopping three days of the week in 35 different combinations of days. This we decided was a combination, and we found this number by listing all of the possible combinations (tedious!). Let us now apply the above fact. There are seven days in the week from which to choose, so $n = 7$, and Janet chooses three days, so $r = 3$. Thus,

$$_nC_r = \frac{n!}{(n-r)! \cdot r!}$$

$$_7C_3 = \frac{7!}{(7-3)! \cdot 3!} = \frac{7!}{4! \cdot 3!} = \frac{7 \cdot 6 \cdot 5 \cdot 4 \cdot 3 \cdot 2 \cdot 1}{4 \cdot 3 \cdot 2 \cdot 1 \cdot 3 \cdot 2 \cdot 1} = \frac{5{,}040}{144} = 35.$$

Small Group Exercise

Recall that we said that $_nC_r = \frac{_nP_r}{r!}$. Show that this is true for Janet in the above example by computing the number of permutations first. Recall that Janet wishes to go shopping three days of the week.

Before we look at our next example, we will review the contents of a standard deck of 52 cards. Such a deck consists of cards in four suits: diamonds, hearts, clubs, and spades. For each suit, there is a 2, 3, 4, 5, 6, 7, 8, 9, 10, Jack, Queen, King, and Ace. Thus, there are 13 cards of each suit. Since there is a 3 of diamonds, 3 of hearts, 3 of clubs, and 3 of spades, there are four 3's in a deck.

Example 4. Consider a standard deck of 52 cards.

 (a) How many different 5 card hands are possible?
 (b) How many different 7 card hands are possible?

Solution:

(a) Since the listing

5 of hearts, 2 of diamonds, 3 of clubs, 10 of spades, and Jack of clubs

refers to the same hand as the listing

2 of diamonds, 5 of hearts, 3 of clubs, Jack of clubs, and 10 of spades

this is a combination problem. There are 52 cards in the deck from which to choose, so $n = 52$. We will choose 5 cards, so $r = 5$. Thus, the number of different 5 card hands is

$$_nC_r = \frac{n!}{(n-r)!\cdot r!}$$

$$_{52}C_5 = \frac{52!}{(52-5)!\cdot 5!} = \frac{52 \cdot 51 \cdot 50 \cdot 49 \cdot 48 \cdot 47!}{47!\cdot 5!} = \frac{52 \cdot 51 \cdot 50 \cdot 49 \cdot 48}{5 \cdot 4 \cdot 3 \cdot 2 \cdot 1}$$

$$= \frac{311,875,200}{120} = 2,598,960.$$

(Notice that 52! and 47! are too large for our calculator display. That is why we needed to do some reducing before we multiplied. This will come in handy often.)

There are 2,598,960 different 5 card hands.

(b) Again, this is a combination, only now $r = 7$ because we will choose 7 cards, not 5. We will need to reduce again before multiplying.

$$_nC_r = \frac{n!}{(n-r)!\cdot r!}$$

$$_{52}C_7 = \frac{52!}{(52-7)!\cdot 7!} = \frac{52 \cdot 51 \cdot 50 \cdot 49 \cdot 48 \cdot 47 \cdot 46 \cdot 45!}{45!\cdot 7!}$$

$$= \frac{52 \cdot 51 \cdot 50 \cdot 49 \cdot 48 \cdot 47 \cdot 46}{7 \cdot 6 \cdot 5 \cdot 4 \cdot 3 \cdot 2 \cdot 1}$$

We still have a problem. The number in the numerator is still too large. We need to reduce even further. Notice that $\frac{49}{7} = 7$, $\frac{48}{6 \cdot 4 \cdot 2} = 1$, $\frac{50}{5} = 10$, and $\frac{51}{3} = 17$. Removing these factors we have:

$$\frac{52 \cdot 17 \cdot 10 \cdot 7 \cdot 1 \cdot 47 \cdot 46}{1} = 133,784,560.$$

Question to Discuss

In the above example, part (b), we were able to divide every factor in the denominator into a factor in the numerator. Will this always be the case in a combination problem? In a permutation problem? Explain your reasoning clearly in complete sentences.

More Complex Combinations

Sometimes a counting problem involves separate pieces, where each piece is a combination. When this happens the total number of combinations is equal to the product of the combinations of the separate pieces.

Example 5. Suppose we are in a diner. There are specials tonight. There is a choice of 7 entrees. Each entree comes with a choice of soup or salad, coffee or tea, and a choice of dessert. There are 6 choices for dessert. How many different dinners are possible?

Solution:

This is a combination problem. Whether we choose soup and chicken or chicken and soup, we will be eating the same dinner. Thus, the order does not matter. There is no repetition, because no item can be ordered more than once (you can't order an entree more than once, and you can't order two cups of coffee). However, this is a more complex counting problem because it has separate pieces — 4 to be exact. What are the four separate parts? They are: soup or salad; entree; beverage; and dessert. We find each of these four separate combinations and then find their product.

SOUP OR SALAD: $n = 2, r = 1$

$$_nC_r = \frac{n!}{(n-r)! \cdot r!}$$

$$_2C_1 = \frac{2!}{(2-1)! \cdot 1!} = \frac{2!}{1! \cdot 1!} = \frac{2 \cdot 1}{1 \cdot 1} = 2.$$

ENTREE: $n = 7, r = 1$

$$_7C_1 = \frac{7!}{(7-1)! \cdot 1!} = \frac{7!}{6! \cdot 1!} = \frac{7 \cdot 6 \cdot 5 \cdot 4 \cdot 3 \cdot 2 \cdot 1}{6 \cdot 5 \cdot 4 \cdot 3 \cdot 2 \cdot 1 \cdot 1} = \frac{5,040}{720} = 7.$$

BEVERAGE: $n = 2, r = 1$

This is $_2C_1 = 2$, the same value that we computed under "soup or salad."

DESSERT: $n = 6, r = 1$.

$$_6C_1 = \frac{6!}{(6-1)! \cdot 1!} = \frac{6!}{5! \cdot 1!} = \frac{6 \cdot 5!}{5! \cdot 1!} = \frac{6}{1} = 6.$$

Now we find the product of these four combinations.

PRODUCT: $_2C_1 \cdot {_7C_1} \cdot {_2C_1} \cdot {_6C_1} = 2 \cdot 7 \cdot 2 \cdot 6 = 168.$

There are 168 different dinner combinations.

Chapter 10: PROBABILITY AND COUNTING

Pascal's Triangle

The following array of numbers is known as *Pascal's Triangle*:

```
                        1
                     1     1
                  1     2     1
               1     3     3     1
            1     4     6     4     1
         1     5     10    10    5     1
      1     6     15    20    15    6     1
                        ⋮
```

This triangle continues in this manner. Before we begin referring to Pascal's Triangle, keep in mind that in all references we will begin counting with the number zero. For example, the top row is referred to as "row zero" and the row below that is called "row one." The same holds true when referring to the entries in a row. The far left entry is referred to as "entry zero," while the next entry is called "entry one." The first two rows, referred to as row zero and row one respectively, consist of 1's. Every row begins and ends with 1. In row two, (the third row from the top), entry zero is 1, then entry one is 2 (the sum of the two numbers in the row above it), and entry two is 1. In row three, (the fourth row from the top), entry zero is 1, entry one is 3 (which is the sum of the 1 and 2 immediately to the left and right of this number in the row above it), entry two is 3 (which is the sum of the 2 and 1 immediately to the left and right of this number in the row above it), and entry three (or last entry on the right) is 1.

Also, notice the following:

$$_0C_0 = \frac{0!}{(0-0)! \cdot 0!} = \frac{0!}{0! \cdot 0!} = \frac{1}{1 \cdot 1} = 1.$$

$$_1C_0 = \frac{1!}{(1-0)! \cdot 0!} = \frac{1!}{1! \cdot 0!} = \frac{1}{1 \cdot 1} = 1.$$

$$_1C_1 = \frac{1!}{(1-1)! \cdot 1!} = \frac{1!}{0! \cdot 1!} = \frac{1}{1 \cdot 1} = 1.$$

$$_2C_0 = \frac{2!}{(2-0)! \cdot 0!} = \frac{2!}{2! \cdot 0!} = \frac{2}{2 \cdot 1} = 1.$$

$$_2C_1 = \frac{2!}{(2-1)! \cdot 1!} = \frac{2!}{1! \cdot 1!} = \frac{2}{1 \cdot 1} = 2.$$

$$_2C_2 = \frac{2!}{(2-2)! \cdot 2!} = \frac{2!}{0! \cdot 2!} = \frac{2}{1 \cdot 2} = 1.$$

$$_4C_2 = \frac{4!}{(4-2)! \cdot 2!} = \frac{4!}{2! \cdot 2!} = \frac{24}{2 \cdot 2} = \frac{24}{4} = 6.$$

$$_6C_3 = \frac{6!}{(6-3)! \cdot 3!} = \frac{6!}{3! \cdot 3!} = \frac{720}{6 \cdot 6} = \frac{720}{36} = 20.$$

Notice too, that

$_0C_0 = 1$ and the row zero, entry zero in the triangle is also 1.

$_1C_0 = 1$ and the row one, entry zero in the triangle is also 1.
$_1C_1 = 1$ and the row one, entry one in the triangle is also 1.
$_2C_0 = 1$ and the row two, entry zero in the triangle is also 1.
$_2C_1 = 2$ and the row two, entry one in the triangle is also 2.
$_4C_2 = 6$ and the row four, entry two in the triangle is also 6.
$_6C_3 = 20$ and the row six, entry three in the triangle is also 20.

Do you see the pattern yet? What is the value of $_5C_3$? It is the same as the row five, entry three in Pascal's Triangle, which is 10. This means that you can use Pascal's Triangle as a quick way of finding the value of $_nC_r$. It is the same as the row n, entry r in Pascal's Triangle.

Question to Discuss

Using Pascal's Triangle,

(a) extend the triangle to include row twelve.
(b) find each of the following using the triangle wherever possible:
$_{11}C_5$, $_{11}C_8$, $_{12}C_0$, $_{12}C_3$, $_{12}C_6$, $_{12}P_5$.
(c) for each row, find the sum of the entries of that row. Do you see a pattern? What is the pattern? What do you conjecture to be the sum of the entries of row thirteen? row fifteen? row twenty –five?
(d) expand $(a+b)^2$, $(a+b)^3$, and $(a+b)^4$. Now, compare the coefficients of each term with Pascal's Triangle. Do you see a pattern? What is the pattern, if any? (Remember, $(a+b)^2 \neq a^2 + b^2$. $(a+b)^2 = (a+b)(a+b)$.)

Exercises

1. Compute each of the following:

   (a) $_6C_5$
   (b) $_8C_2$
   (c) $_9C_3$
   (d) $_9P_3$
   (e) $\dfrac{_5C_2}{_5C_2}$
   (f) $\dfrac{_9C_5}{_9P_5}$
   (g) $\dfrac{_{10}C_6}{_{10}C_3}$

2. Six light bulbs from a shipment of twelve are to be tested for defects. In how many ways can this be done?

3. Six cards are drawn from a standard deck of 52 cards without replacement. In how many ways can four jacks and two eights be drawn?

4. Seven cards are drawn from a standard deck of 52 cards without replacement. In how many ways can three queens, two fours and two aces be drawn?

320   Chapter 10: **PROBABILITY AND COUNTING**

5.   A history test consists of two parts. In the first part you must answer five of the six essays. On the second part you must answer four of the seven questions. In how many different ways can this be done?

6.   How many different five–member committees can be formed from the 100 US senators?

7.   A box contains ten red, three blue, seven green, and four white bingo chips. Eight chips are selected at random. In how many ways can

   (a) this be done?
   (b) the selection include two of each color?
   (c) the selection consist of only red chips?
   (d) the selection consist of only white chips?
   (e) the selection consist of three blue, four green, and one red chip?

8.   A department of a large college consists of 21 full–time members and 16 part–time members. A book committee is to be formed consisting of six full–timers and two part–timers. How many different committees of this composition are possible?

9.   A bag of m & m's ® contains 28 red, 15 blue, 12 green, 34 brown, and 30 yellow m & m's. Twenty m & m's are to be selected at random.

   (a) In how many ways can this be done?
   (b) In how many ways can the selection include 10 red and 10 brown m & m's?

10.   Extend Pascal's Triangle to include row ten. Find $_{10}C_8$ using Pascal's Triangle. Now compute it using factorials.

11.   Using Pascal's Triangle, find $_9C_7$.

12. $_nC_r = \dfrac{_nP_r}{r!}$. Solve this for $_nP_r$. Now, use Pascal's Triangle to find $_8P_5$.

10.5 Counting Trees

Sometimes we not only need to know how many different groupings there are, but exactly what the make–up of each grouping is. This is especially true when dealing with probability problems. Any listing that is constructed methodically will do. We will examine the method of constructing *counting trees*. This method will ensure that no possible grouping is overlooked and no grouping is listed twice.

Let us consider a very small club of five members. Its set of members is

{Mary, George, Harry, Jim, Karen}.

This club needs to elect a president and a vice–president. We know by the counting principle that this can be done in $5(4) = 20$ ways. Let's find all 20 of the different permutations. This is what is called a two task problem. The first task is to elect a president and the second task is to elect a vice–president. Since

we have two tasks, we will need two columns, each column representing one of the tasks. If the problem had four tasks, we would need four columns.

We will begin by labeling each column. Then we will list all of the possibilities for our first task, electing a president. Do this in some methodical way, such as alphabetically, or in the order they appeared above. At this point we have:

PRESIDENT	VICE–PRESIDENT	RESULTING GROUP (president, vice–president)
Mary		
George		
Harry		
Jim		
Karen		

Now we will draw branches stemming from the person listed as president to each of the possible vice–presidents who could go with that president. For example, if Mary is president, then George, Harry, Jim, or Karen can be vice–president. We list their names opposite Mary under the column headed VICE–PRESIDENT. Then we draw lines from Mary to each of these four. Continue in the same manner for each of the other possible presidents. The result is shown in Figure 10.1.

322   Chapter 10: **PROBABILITY AND COUNTING**

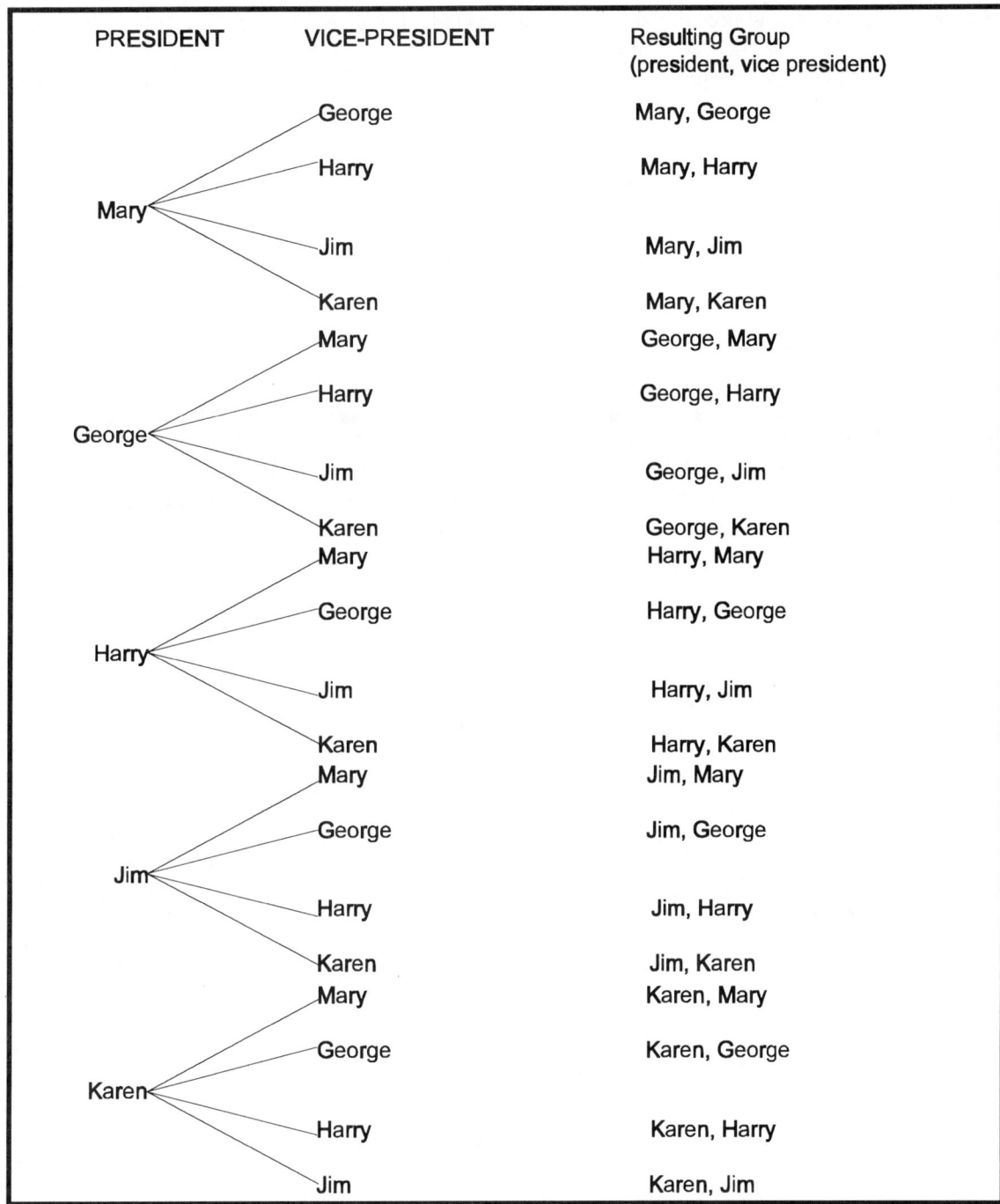

Figure 10.1 A tree of presidents and vice–presidents.

The twenty possible ways of electing a president and a vice-president have all been listed in the last column of this figure.

Example 6. Find all of the three digit odd numbers less than 400 that have a 2, 3, 4, or 5 in the tens place and have no duplicate digits.

Solution: We will construct a counting tree. This is a three task problem. First, we need to find the hundred's digit (we'll put this in the first column), then the ten's digit (the second column), and finally the one's digit (the third column). We begin by labeling the three columns. The first digit can be any

integer from 1 to 3 inclusive. (Why not 0? Why not 4 through 9?) The second digit can only be a 2, 3, 4, or 5 and cannot have the same digit as that in the first column. (For example, if the first digit is 2, the second digit must be either 3, 4, or 5. It cannot be a 2 because we already used 2 for the first digit). The third digit must by a 1, 3, 5, 7, or 9 because it must be an odd number, and this digit cannot be the same as the digits in the first or second column. (For example, if the first digit is 3 and the second digit is 5, then the third digit can either be a 1, 7, or 9. It cannot by a 3 or a 5 because then we would have duplicate digits.)   This tree is reproduced as Figure 10.2

324   Chapter 10: **PROBABILITY AND COUNTING**

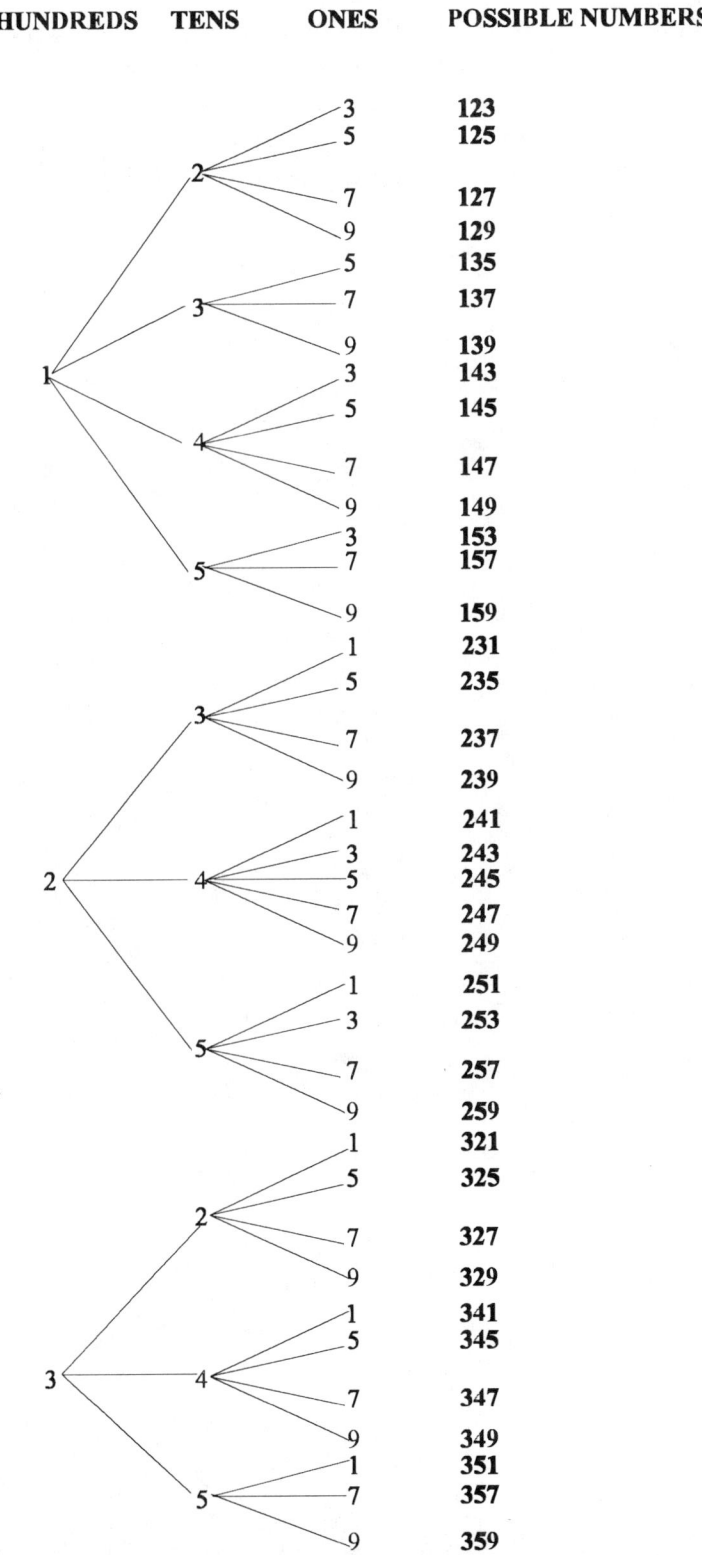

Figure 10.2 Three Digit Numbers.

Exercises

1.   Find all of the two digit even numbers less than fifty.

2.   Construct a counting tree to find all of the two digit even numbers less than fifty that have no repeating digits.

3.   A club consists of the members Jean, Jim, George, Peter, Katie, and Mary. Find all of the possible ways to elect a president, vice president, and treasurer if no one can hold more than one office and the president must be male.

4.   Three fair coins are tossed. Construct a counting tree to find all of the possible ways of getting each of the following.:

   (a) at least two tails
   (b) fewer than three heads
   (c) no more than one head

5.   Construct a counting tree to determine all the three digit even numbers that have no duplicate digits and have a 2, 4, or 7 in the hundred's place.

6.   Construct a counting tree to determine all of the four digit odd numbers less than 3,000 with no repeating digits and a 7 in the hundred's place.

10.6 Counting Problems

We have seen three methods, depending on the type of problem, that enable us to count the number of ways items can be arranged without listing them all. These three methods are the Fundamental Counting Principle, Permutations, and Combinations. How does one determine which method to use? The following summary may help.

FUNDAMENTAL COUNTING PRINCIPLE
- Repetition is allowed.

PERMUTATION
- Repetition is NOT allowed.
- Order matters, that is, abc and bac are considered to be distinct groupings.

COMBINATION
- Repetition is NOT allowed.
- Order does not matter, that is, abc and bac are NOT considered to be distinct groupings.

Example 7. The State needs to decide if it will have enough different license plate numbers for all of its motorists. It is considering three possible ways of assigning the numbers and wants to know which of these ways, if any, will enable it to assign a number to every car. There are 25 million registered vehicles in the State. The possibilities they are considering are:

   (a) three digits followed by three letters

(b) two digits followed by three letters followed by two digits. The digits cannot be zeros and there is no repetition of letters or digits.

(c) two digits followed by four letters. The digits cannot be zeros and there is no repetition of letters or digits.

Solution:

(a) There is no mention about repetition, so it cannot be assumed that repetition is not allowed. Thus, repetition is allowed. Therefore, we should use the Fundamental Counting Principle. This is the only rule that we have which allows repetition. Thus, we have

(digit) (digit) (digit) (letter) (letter) (letter)
(10) (10) (10) (26) (26) (26) = 17,576,000 possible license plates.

Note that $17,576,000 < 25,000,000$.

(b) There is no repetition and order does matter. If we use permutations this is a multi-step problem, where the first step considers the digits and the second step considers the letters (see below for this approach).

Instead we can use the Fundamental Counting Principle to reduce this to a one step problem. Zero is not to be used, so we only have the digits 1 through 9 to choose from for the first digit, or nine choices. For the second choice, we cannot use the digit that we just selected, so we have $9 - 1 = 8$ choices left. Next we get to select a letter. Since there are no restrictions on which letter we may choose, there are 26 possibilities for this selection. For the next letter we have only $26 - 1 = 25$ choices left, since we are not permitted to repeat the first letter chosen. Continuing in this way we find that there are

(digit) (digit) (letter) (letter) (letter) (digit) (digit) =
(9) (8) (26) (25) (24) (7) (6) = 47,174,400 possible license plates. Note that $47,174,400 > 25,000,000$.

This problem could be calculated using permutations. There is no repetition and the order does matter, that is, 98ABC75 is a different plate from the license plate 89ABC75. If we use permutations, we split the problem into the product of two permutations, one for the digits and one for the letters. (We do not need three permutations, because multiplication is commutative.)

The permutation for the digits is calculated with $n = 9$, (why not 10?), and $r = 4$ (we need to choose 4 digits all together). Thus, we have:

$$_nP_r = \frac{n!}{(n-r)!}$$

$$_9P_4 = \frac{9!}{(9-4)!} = \frac{9!}{5!} = \frac{362,880}{120} = 3,024.$$

The permutation for the letters is calculated with $n = 26$ and $r = 3$ (because we need to choose 3 letters). Thus, we have:

$$_{26}P_3 = \frac{26!}{(26-3)!} = \frac{26!}{23!} = \frac{26 \cdot 25 \cdot 24 \cdot 23!}{23!} = \frac{26 \cdot 25 \cdot 24}{1} = 15,600.$$

Their product is the number of possible license plates possible, or

(3,024) (15,600) = 47,174,400.

This is the same result as we found using the Fundamental Counting Principle.

(c) In this case, there are two digits followed by four letters, no repetition, and the digits cannot be zeros. Again, we have two choices. We can use the Fundamental Counting Principle or we can use a product of permutations, one for digits and one for letters. We will examine both methods.

Using the Fundamental Counting Principle, we have:

(digit) (digit) (letter) (letter) (letter) (letter)

(9) (8) (26) (25) (24) (23) = 25,833,600 different license plates. 25,833,600 > 25,000,000.

If we use permutations, we will first compute the permutation for the digits. In this case, there are nine digits from which to choose, so $n = 9$ and we need to choose two digits, thus $r = 2$. We have:

$$_nP_r = \frac{n!}{(n-r)!}$$

$$_9P_2 = \frac{9!}{(9-2)!} = \frac{9!}{7!} = \frac{362,880}{5,040} = 72.$$

The permutation for the letters has $n = 26$, because there are 26 letters from which to choose, and $r = 4$, because we need to choose four letters. We now have:

$$_{26}P_4 = \frac{26!!}{(26-4)!} = \frac{26!}{22!} = \frac{26 \cdot 25 \cdot 24 \cdot 23 \cdot 22!}{22!} = \frac{26 \cdot 25 \cdot 24 \cdot 23}{1}$$
$$= 358,800.$$

Therefore, there are (72) (358,800) = 25,833,600 different license plates.

We can finally answer the question. Recall that there are 25 million vehicles in the state which need license plates. The first option will only create 17,576,000 different license plates, which is too few. The second option will create 47,174,400 different license plates. This is many more than needed and would leave room for growth in the state. The third option will create 25,833,600 license plates. This is also more than 25 million. Thus, the only feasible options would be options (b) and (c). Option (b) may be better since it leaves room for many additional motorists in the years to come.

Example 8. Sally is in the Newest Wave CD Store. She has enough money to purchase 3 CD's.

(a) Sally really likes 9 CD's. She can purchase only 3. In how many different ways can this be done?

(b) Sally is shopping for presents for her friends. She sees 9 CD's they would like. She will buy one CD for Fred, a different CD for Linda, and a still different CD for Marisa. In how many different ways can this be done?

Solution:

(a) In this case Sally is going to purchase 3 CD's. If she purchases abc or bac, she has made the same purchase (each of a, b, and c stand for a particular CD). Thus, order doesn't matter and there is no repetition (she isn't going to purchase 2 of the same CD for herself). Thus, this is a combination problem. (Why?) In this case, $n = 9$ (she likes 9 CD's) and $r = 3$ (she will purchase 3 of them).

$$_nC_r = \frac{n!}{(n-r)! \cdot r!}$$

$$_9C_3 = \frac{9!}{(9-3)! \cdot 3!} = \frac{9!}{6! \cdot 3!} = \frac{362,880}{720 \cdot 6} = \frac{362,880}{4,320} = 84.$$

Sally can purchase 3 CD's out of 9 for herself in 84 different combinations.

(b) Sally is still purchasing 3 CD's out of 9, except this time it is for three of her friends. It states that she will be buying different CD's for each friend, so there is no repetition. The purchase of *abc* will mean that Fred receives CD *a*, Linda receives CD *b*, and Marisa receives CD *c*. If, however, she purchases *bac*, then Fred receives CD *b* (not *a*), Linda receives CD *a* (not *b*), and Marisa receives CD *c*. In this case it is clear that the order the CD's are listed does matter, since it changes the recipient of a particular CD. Thus, this is a permutation. As before, $n = 9$ and $r = 3$.

$$_nP_r = \frac{n!}{(n-r)!}$$

$$_9P_3 = \frac{9!}{(9-3)!} = \frac{9!}{6!} = \frac{362,880}{720} = 504.$$

Sally can purchase 3 different CD's for her friends in 504 different ways.

Question to Discuss

In each case below, design a complete story problem so that the answer is the value given.
(a) $_{11}C_7$
(b) $_8P_2$
(c) $(24)(23)(22)(9)(9)$
(d) $_{13}C_2 \cdot {_5C_3}$

Duplicate Items

Sometimes a problem involves duplicate items (2 or more of the same thing). To give you an example of what we mean by duplicate items, consider the following:

Example 9. Consider the word SEED. In how many different ways can the letters in the word "SEED" be arranged (not necessarily to form a new word).
Solution:
Since we have no technique yet, we will list all of the different arrangements of the letters.

SEED SEDE SDEE EESD EEDS ESED ESDE EDES EDSE DEES DESE DSEE

We have found 12 different arrangements of the letters in the word "SEED". The reader should convince himself or herself that these are the only arrangements possible for these letters, and that all of these are distinct.

It wasn't too difficult to find all of the arrangements for a short word like SEED where there is a duplicate "E." However, it would be a rather long and tedious task to list all possibilities for a word such as STATISTICS or SUPERFLUOUS. We have the following fact to help us.

Fact: Suppose you have n items. Item one appears k_1 times, item two appears k_2 times, item three appears k_3 times, and so on. The last item, item z, appears k_z times. Then, the number of different arrangements of these n items is equal to:

$$\frac{n!}{k_1! \cdot k_2! \cdot k_3! \cdots k_z!}$$

We will now use this fact to find the number of different arrangements of the letters in the word "SEED". This word consists of 4 letters. Thus, $n = 4$. The letter "S" appears once, so $k_1 = 1$. The letter "E" appears twice, so $k_2 = 2$. The letter "D" appears once, so $k_3 = 1$. Computing the value given in the above fact gives

$$\frac{4!}{1! \cdot 2! \cdot 1!} = \frac{24}{1 \cdot 2 \cdot 1} = \frac{24}{2} = 12.$$

Therefore, there are 12 different arrangements of the letters in the word "SEED," the same number of arrangements that we found when we listed them.

Example 10. How many different arrangements are there of the letters in the word "STATISTICS"?

Solution: The word "STATISTICS" consists of 10 letters, thus $n = 10$. The letter "S" appears three times, so $k_1 = 3$. The letter "T" appears three times, so $k_2 = 3$. The letter "A" appears once, so $k_3 = 1$. The letter "I" appears twice, so $k_4 = 2$. The letter "C" appears once, so $k_5 = 1$. The number of different arrangements of the letters is equal to:

$$\frac{10!}{3! \cdot 3! \cdot 1! \cdot 2! \cdot 1!} = \frac{3{,}628{,}800}{6 \cdot 6 \cdot 1 \cdot 2 \cdot 1} = \frac{3{,}628{,}800}{72} = 50{,}400.$$

Exercises

1. A college with 10,953 students needs to assign student identification numbers. Which of the following ways will meet their needs?

    (a) five digits with no repetition and the first digit cannot be zero.
    (b) four digits with no repetition.
    (c) four digits with no repetition and the first digit cannot be zero.
    (d) four digits and the first digit cannot be zero.

2. Carl must choose two of his twenty five students to represent the class on a panel. In how many different ways can this be done?

3. There are thirty girls competing in a gymnastics competition. Eight will be chosen as finalists. In how many different ways can this be done?

4. There are fifteen girls competing in a dancing competition. The judge will place one girl in first, one in second, and one in third. In how many different ways can this be done?

5. A bag contains seven apples and nine oranges. Four are randomly selected. In how many ways could you get

(a) four apples
(b) four oranges
(c) exactly three apples
(d) three oranges and one apple
(e) more apples than oranges

6. How many different "combinations" are possible on a combination lock having 35 numbers on the dial? (Note: Repetitions are allowed and a "combination" requires three numbers. Also, note that since the order that you enter the numbers into the lock is clearly important, we find that "combination locks" are misnamed. They should be called "permutation locks.")

7. Consider the set { $, ?, !, +, =, *}. How many subsets are there

(a) with three elements?
(b) with four elements, containing the element "?"?

8. How many different arrangements are there for the letters in each of the following words?

(a) mommy
(b) Canada
(c) superfluous
(d) excellent

9. A club consists of 50 members. Twenty-eight of these members are male. Fifteen of the male members and ten of the female members have been in the club at least five years. The club membership is to elect a president, treasurer, and secretary. In how many different ways can this be done if no one may hold more than one office and

(a) the president must be a member of the club for a minimum of five years?
(b) none of the men are willing to be secretary of the club?

10. Three students in a class of 42 are needed to represent the class in a debate. In how many different ways can the class be represented in the debate?

10.7 Types of Probabilities

Preliminaries

Before we can begin an examination of the types of probabilities, we need to understand several key terms from probability theory. The first such term is *experiment*.

Definition: An *experiment* is a controlled environment.

An example of an experiment would be tossing a coin fifty times and counting how many times heads occurred and how many times tails occurred. Another example of an experiment would be calling 100 people in Ohio and asking them who they favor in an upcoming gubernatorial election. In both of these cases, we are keeping tally of the results in a controlled environment.

When we toss a fair coin there are two possibilities, that is, either heads or tails can occur. We say that there are two possible *outcomes*. One outcome is heads and the other is tails.

When we roll a fair coin, there are six possibilities, that is, we can roll a 1, 2, 3, 4, 5, or 6. We say that there are six possible outcomes. Each of these numbers is an outcome.

Definition: An *outcome* is a result of an experiment. The set of all outcomes contains all of the possible results of an experiment.

We are calling for a poll for a gubernatorial election in Ohio. If there are two candidates for governor of Ohio in an upcoming election, then there are two outcomes (assuming everyone chooses one of the two candidates). Each of these candidates is an outcome of the experiment.

If we take a subset of the set of all outcomes, the result is an *event*. Consider rolling a fair die. We listed the set of all possible outcomes as

$$\{1, 2, 3, 4, 5, 6\}.$$

All of the following are subsets of this set and are, therefore, events:
  roll an even number
  roll a two
  roll a number less than 4
  roll a number between 2 and 5.

Definition: An *event* is a collection of outcomes.

Example 11. There are 8 red marbles, 6 blue marbles, 4 white marbles, and 2 black marbles in a jar. One marble is drawn from the jar.

   (a) List the set of all possible outcomes.
   (b) List all of the outcomes that would satisfy each of the following events:
       A draw a red marble
       B draw a red or a blue marble
       C draw a white and a black marble
       D draw a green marble
       E draw a red or blue or white or black marble

332   Chapter 10: **PROBABILITY AND COUNTING**

Solution:
  (a) The set of all possible outcomes is {red, blue, white, black}.
  (b) The only outcome that would satisfy event A is   red.
    Since the word "or" means one or the other or both conditions are satisfied, the outcomes that would satisfy event B are   red, blue.
    No outcome would satisfy event C because none of the marbles in the jar are both white and black at the same time. (Remember the word "and" means both conditions must be satisfied.)
    No outcomes would satisfy event D because there are no green marbles in the jar.
    All of the outcomes satisfy event E because every marble in the jar is either red, blue, white, or black.

Small Group Exercise

Consider a standard deck of 52 cards. One card is drawn.

(a) List all of the possible outcomes.
(b) Give an example of 5 different events.
(c) Give an example of an event that is also an outcome. If this is not possible, explain why.
(d) Give an example of an event that cannot also be an outcome. If this is not possible, explain why.
(e) Give an example of an outcome that cannot also be an event. If this is not possible, explain why.
(f) Can all outcomes also be events? Explain your reasoning.
(g) Can all events also be outcomes? Explain your reasoning.

Basic Notation

In order to refer to an event, we will name an event with a capital letter. For example, consider rolling a die. We can name some events as follow:

EVENTS: A consists of rolling an even number.
          B consists of rolling a number between 2 and 5.

Now when we refer to the event "rolling an even number" we do not have to rewrite that entire phrase. We can just write an "A".

There is standard notation that is used to represent a probability. P(event) stands for the probability of an event and has a numerical value.

Using the above events for rolling a die, "$P(A)$" represents the probability that event A occurs. $P(A)$ is a number.

WORD OF CAUTION: $P(C) = \dfrac{4}{5}$ means the "probability of event C occurring is $\dfrac{4}{5}$."

$P(C) \neq P\left(\dfrac{4}{5}\right)$. $P(C) = P\left(\dfrac{4}{5}\right)$ is **_MEANINGLESS_**! This would read "the probability of event C is equal to the probability of event $\dfrac{4}{5}$." There is no such thing as "event $\dfrac{4}{5}$"!

There are three different types of probabilities. For some circumstances, only one or two of the types may be reasonable. At times, one type is best. The three types of probabilities are:

Classical Probability
Relative Frequency Probability
Subjective Probability

Classical Probability

Classical probability requires that all of the outcomes have an equal chance of occurrence. This means that one outcome does not have a greater chance of occurring that any other outcome.

For example, if you throw a fair coin then both heads and tails have an equal chance of occurring. If, on the other hand, you throw a two–headed coin, then heads and tails do not have an equal chance of occurring. It is much more likely it will land heads than tails (actually, heads is on both sides of the coin, so it is impossible for the coin to land tails up).

Consider rolling a die. If it is a fair die, a 1 has just as much chance of occurring as a 2, or a 3, or a 4, or a 5, or a 6. Each outcome is equally likely to occur. If the die is weighted, then one side is more likely to land face up and thus one outcome is more likely to occur than the others.

Classical probability is very accurate in discussing games of chance and other situations, however the outcomes must be equally likely to occur. Thus, you cannot use this type of probability if one outcome is more likely to occur than some other outcome.

Fact: The *classical probability* that event A occurs is defined as:

$$P(A) = \frac{\text{number of outcomes that satisfy event } A}{\text{number of all possible outcomes}}$$

given that all of the outcomes are equally likely to occur.

Example 12. Billy tosses a coin. Find the probability that the coin lands

(a) heads up
(b) tails up.

Solution: There are two possible outcomes for this problem: heads or tails. Thus, the number of all possible outcomes is 2. This will be the denominator in each of the calculations.

(a) The number of outcomes that satisfy the event that the coin lands heads up is one, heads. Therefore
$$P(\text{heads up}) = \frac{1}{2}.$$

(b) The number of outcomes that satisfy the event that the coin lands tails up is one, tails. Therefore
$$P(\text{tails up}) = \frac{1}{2}.$$

Example 13. Megan rolls a die. Find the probability of each of the following events.
EVENTS: A roll an even number
          B roll a two

334   Chapter 10: **PROBABILITY AND COUNTING**

C roll a number between 3 and 5
D roll a number greater than 6
E roll a number less than 3
F roll an odd number or an even number
G roll an odd number and an even number

Solution: Since the problem makes no mention of a weighted die, we will assume the die is an ordinary die, and therefore, all outcomes are equally likely. The set of all possible outcomes is

$$\{1, 2, 3, 4, 5, 6\}.$$

The number of possible outcomes is 6. Therefore, the denominator for the calculation of each probability is 6.

The outcomes satisfying event A, roll an even number, are 2, 4, and 6. There are 3 such outcomes. Thus, we have:

$$P(A) = \frac{3}{6} = \frac{1}{2} = 0.5.$$

The outcome satisfying event B, roll a two, is 2. There is only one such outcome, so we have:

$$P(B) = \frac{1}{6} = 0.1\overline{6}.$$

(You should not write 0.16 because $\frac{1}{6} \neq 0.16$)

The outcome satisfying event C, roll a number between 3 and 5, is 4. We cannot include the outcome 3 because 3 is not between 3 and 5, nor is 5. Thus

$$P(C) = \frac{1}{6} = 0.1\overline{6}.$$

There are no outcomes that satisfy event D, roll a number greater than 6. None of the numbers on a die are greater than 6. Therefore, the number of outcomes satisfying event D is 0. We have:

$$P(D) = \frac{0}{6} = 0.$$

Notice that event D cannot possibly occur, and therefore its probability is zero.

The outcomes satisfying event E, roll a number less than 3, are 1 and 2. We have:

$$P(E) = \frac{2}{6} = \frac{1}{3} = 0.\overline{3}.$$

The outcomes satisfying event F, roll an odd number or an even number, are 1, 2, 3, 4, 5, and 6. Remember the word "or" means that only one of the conditions needs to be met to include that outcome. Thus we have:

$$P(F) = \frac{6}{6} = 1.$$

Notice that event F is certain to happen. Thus its probability is one.

There are no outcomes satisfying event G, roll an odd number and an even number. The word "and" means that both conditions must be met to be included. There are no numbers that are both even and odd. Therefore

$$P(G) = \frac{0}{6} = 0.$$

Small Group Exercise

Two dice are rolled.

(a) List the set of all possible outcomes.
(b) Find the probability of each of the following events:
    A the sum of the faces up is 3
    B the sum of the faces up is an even number
    C the sum of the faces up is less than 12
    D the sum of the faces up is between 5 and 11

Relative Frequency Probability

The second type of probability is *relative frequency probability*. This is sometimes referred to as *empirical probability*. This type of probability is determined by the actual observations of an experiment. An experiment is conducted and the number of times each outcome occurs is recorded.

Fact: The *relative frequency probability* that event A occurs is defined as:

$$P(A) = \frac{\text{number of times event } A \text{ has occurred}}{\text{total number of times the experiment was conducted}}$$

Example 14. A die was rolled 75 times. The number of times each outcome occurred is given in Table 10.3

Outcome	Occurred
1	13
2	11
3	11
4	12
5	14
6	14

Table 10.3 The results of rolling a die 75 times

Chapter 10: PROBABILITY AND COUNTING

Find the relative frequency probability of each of the following events:

events A roll a 4
               B roll an even number
               C roll a number less than 5

Solution: The experiment was conducted 75 times, thus the denominator of each probability will be 75. A four was rolled 12 times, therefore we have

$$P(A) = \frac{12}{75} = \frac{4}{25} = 0.16.$$

If you rolled a 2, 4, or a 6, you rolled an even number. We know from Table 10.3 that a 2 was rolled eleven times, a 4 was rolled twelve times, and a 6 was rolled fourteen times. Thus, we have

$$P(B) = \frac{11 + 12 + 14}{75} = \frac{37}{75} = 0.49\bar{3}$$

If you rolled a number less than 5, you rolled either a 1, 2, 3, or a 4. From Table 10.3 we know that a 1 was rolled thirteen times, a 2 was rolled eleven times, a 3 was rolled eleven times, and a 4 was rolled twelve times. Thus

$$P(C) = \frac{13 + 11 + 11 + 12}{75} = \frac{47}{75} = 0.62\bar{6}$$

We found in a previous example the classical probability of rolling an even number to be 0.5. Just now, we found the relative frequency probability to be $0.49\bar{3}$. These values, though not equal, are very close. This is because we rolled the die a large number of times so the fraction representing the relative frequency probability of rolling an even number is stabilizing around 0.5. This is an instance of an important principle known as the *Law of Large Numbers*. This principle does not state that if you roll a die ten times, you should roll an even number five of those times. It applies to an experiment being conducted a large number of times. It predicts the relative frequency probability over the long run, not for a few trials.

Small Group Exercise:

Toss a coin 25 times and record the number of times the coin lands heads up and the number of times the coin lands tails up. Find the classical and relative frequency probabilities for the event heads and for the event tails. Discuss why they are different. Which is more accurate? Why? Relate this to the Law of Large Numbers. Now redo this, tossing the coin 50 times. 100 times.

Subjective Probability

The third type of probability, *subjective probability*, refers to one's educated belief as to the likelihood an event will occur. It is an educated hypothesis based upon past experience and knowledge. It may be different from someone else's subjective probability. Also, this type of probability cannot be checked. It is used for "one–shot" situations. For example, the director of a summer camp may estimate the probability a new food program will have a positive effect upon the number of applicants for camp next year. No one can check his estimate. He is basing it upon the many past experiences he has had.

Exercises

1. Roll a die. Find the probability of each of the following events:

    A   roll an odd number
    B   roll a number between 2 and 6
    C   roll a number less than 1
    D   roll a number less than 3 or greater than 4
    E   roll an even number less than 5
    F   roll a number less than 4 and greater than 3

2. Draw a card from a standard deck of 52. Find the probability of each of the following events:

    A   draw a red card
    B   draw a jack
    C   draw a black queen
    D   draw a green card

3. Which type of probability is each of the following?

    (a) The weatherman predicts the probability it will rain tomorrow is 0.3.
    (b) A jar is filled with Ping–Pong balls numbered from 1 through 65. The probability an even numbered ball is drawn is found.
    (c) 600 residents are phoned and asked if they prefer Foodshop, Shop Well, or Pathmade. The probability Foodshop is chosen is determined.
    (d) Based upon past years' calls for faulty furnaces, the area gas company predicts that the probability a furnace will not light is 0.34.
    (e) The probability of an individual winning the state lottery is determined.

4. A telephone company surveys 1,000 calls and returns how many times the phone rings before a phone is answered either by a person or an answering machine. After 8 rings the caller hangs up and the phone is considered not answered. The results are given in the following table:

NUMBER OF RINGS	NUMBER OF CALLS
1	25
2	200
3	175
4	325
5	125
6	70
7	30
8	25
not at all	25

Find the probability of each of the following events:

- *A*   no one answers
- *B*   it is answered in fewer than four rings
- *C*   it is answered in four rings
- *D*   it is answered in more than two rings
- *E*   it is answered in more than four rings

5. Based upon your experiences in previous mathematics courses, what is the probability you will earn an A in this course? What type of probability did you use?

6. Estimate each of the following probabilities:

(a) The probability you will get a flat tire the next time you drive a car.
(b) The probability the price of a postage stamp will increase within the next 12 months.
(c) The probability it will rain tomorrow.
(d) The probability you will buy a new coat.

7. When tossing a coin, the probability it will land heads up is 0.5. Does this mean that if a coin is tossed twice, one head will appear? If not, what does it mean?

8. Explain in your own words the Law of Large Numbers.

9. A community's birth record shows $2,000$ births last year, of which, $1,236$ were females.

(a) What is the probability the next child born in the community will be a girl?
(b) What type of probability is this?
(c) What is the probability the next child born in the community will be a boy?

10. In a survey, a sample of $1,200$ students were asked to rate the cafeteria's food service as good, fair, or poor. The results were as follows.

Number of Students	Rating
221	good
481	fair
293	poor
205	no opinion

Find the probability the next person will rate it as

(a) good.
(b) poor.
(c) have no opinion.

10.8 Probability Problems and Basic Facts

Facts About Probability

Regardless of which type of probability you use, there are some basic facts that apply in all situations.

Fact 1: The probability of an event is always a real number between 0 and 1 inclusive.

The probability of an event cannot be negative and cannot be greater than one.

Fact 2: The probability of an event that cannot happen is zero.

If it is impossible for the event to occur, then the probability that the event occurs is equal to 0.

Fact 3: The probability of an event that is certain to happen is one.

If the event is definitely going to happen, then the probability the event occurs is equal to 1. For example, if we toss a two–headed coin (heads on both sides), then $P(\text{tails}) = 0$ and $P(\text{heads}) = 1$.

Fact 4: The sum of the probabilities of all possible outcomes is equal to 1.

For example, if we are rolling a die, then
$P(\text{rolling a 1}) + P(\text{rolling a 2}) + P(\text{rolling a 3}) + P(\text{rolling a 4}) + P(\text{rolling a 5}) + P(\text{rolling a 6}) = 1.$

Example: Given below in Table 10.4 are ten of the many endangered mammals and their range.

MAMMAL	RANGE
Asian wild ass	Asia
Bobcat	central Mexico
Ozark big–eared bat	U.S.
Brown or grizzly bear	U.S.
Chinese river dolphin	China
Gorilla	Africa
Leopard	Africa and Asia
Ocelot	U.S.
Utah prairie dog	U.S.
Tiger	Asia

Table 10.4 Endangered mammals and their range

Find the probability of each of the following events:

event: A a mammal named on the list lives in Asia
          B a mammal named on the list lives in England
          C an animal named on the list is a mammal

Solution: We will use classical probability theory. There are ten mammals listed, so the denominator in each of our probabilities is 10. Since the Asian wild ass, the leopard, and the tiger all live in Asia, the numerator for the probability of event A is 3. Therefore $$P(A) = \frac{3}{10} = 0.3$$
None of the mammals listed lives in England, thus event B is impossible. Therefore, $P(B) = 0$.
All of the animals listed are mammals, thus event C is certain to occur. Therefore, $P(C) = 1$.

What does it mean to say that the probability of one event is greater than the probability of another event? Suppose $P(A) = 0.4$ and $P(B) = 0.8$. We know that $0.8 > 0.4$, and thus $P(B) > P(A)$. This means that event B is more likely to occur than event A.

Complements

The *complement* of an event is a bit like the opposite.

> **Definition**: The *complement* of an event A is the event that A does not occur; it is denoted by $\overline{A}$.

For example, suppose we toss a coin and event A is that we toss heads. Then the complement of A is that we toss tails. If we do not toss heads, then we must toss tails. Suppose instead we roll a die and event A is that we roll a number less than 5, i.e. 1, 2, 3, or 4. Then the complement of A is that we do not roll a number less than 5 or, stated another way, that we roll a number greater than or equal to 5, that is, 5 or 6. Notice, if we put A together with the complement of A we have every possible outcome. Also notice that A and the complement of A never share any outcomes. Therefore, we have the following fact:

> **Fact:** $P(A) + P(\overline{A}) = 1$ or $P(\overline{A}) = 1 - P(A)$ or $P(A) = 1 - P(\overline{A})$.

Sometimes it is easier to find the probability of the complement of A than it is to find the probability of event A. That is when these facts come in handy.

Example: Roll a standard die. Find the probability of each of the following events:

event A roll a number that is not a 4
        B do not roll an even number

Solution: Rolling a number that is a 4 is the complement of rolling a number that is not a four. Thus,

$$P(A) = 1 - P(\overline{A}) = P(\text{rolling a four}) = 1 - \frac{1}{6} = \frac{5}{6}.$$

If you do not roll an even number, then you must roll an odd number. The possible odd numbers you can roll are 1, 3, and 5. Thus, $P(B) = \frac{3}{6} = \frac{1}{2}$.

Example: It is known that $\frac{1}{3}$ of all incoming freshman at a certain school will never graduate. What is the probability that an incoming freshman in this school will graduate?

Solution: Graduating and not graduating are complements. Thus, $P(\text{graduate}) = 1 - P(\text{not graduate})$. Thus, $P(\text{graduate}) = 1 - \frac{1}{3} = \frac{2}{3}$.

Probability Involving "or"

Suppose someone asks us to pick a number between 1 and 20 inclusive. What is the probability the number picked is even or is less than 7? This is a *compound probability* problem.

Definition: A *compound probability* involves the words "or" or "and".

We will begin by dealing with those problems that involve the word "or". We have the following fact:

Fact: $P(A \text{ or } B) = P(A) + P(B) - P(A \text{ and } B)$.

Let's reconsider the situation just stated. Someone asks us to pick a number between 1 and 20 inclusive. What is the probability the number picked is even or is less than 7? We can think of event A as picking an even number and event B as picking a number less than 7. We find the probability of event A and the probability of event B and add those two probabilities together. Then we subtract the probability that the number is both even and less than 7. We do this because we counted those possibilities twice and we should have only considered them once. In this example, the $P(A) = P(\text{even number}) = \frac{10}{20} = \frac{1}{2}$. The $P(B) = P(\text{number less than } 7) = \frac{6}{20} = \frac{3}{10}$. Now we need to find the numbers that are even and less than 7. They are 2, 4, and 6. There are three of them. Thus, $P(\text{even and less than } 7) = \frac{3}{20}$. Finally, we have:

$$P(\text{even}) + P(\text{less than } 7) - P(\text{even and less than } 7) = \frac{10}{20} + \frac{6}{20} - \frac{3}{20} = \frac{13}{20}.$$

Note that this agrees with a "direct" attack on the problem. If we count up the number of outcomes that satisfy the event "even or less than 7" we see that it is satisfied by the outcomes in the following list:

1, 2, 3, 4, 5, 6, 8, 10, 12, 14, 16, 18, 20.

Thus

$$P(\text{even or less than seven}) = \frac{\text{the number of outcomes that satisfy even or less than seven}}{\text{number of possible outcomes}} = \frac{13}{20}$$

Example: A card is drawn from a standard deck of 52 cards. Find the probability that the card is red or is a queen.
Solution: This is a compound probability involving the word "or". The first event is that the card is red. The second event is that the card is a queen. Half of the 52 cards in the deck are red, so there are 26 red cards in the deck. There are four queens in the deck. Two queens are also red, that is the queen of hearts and the queen of diamonds. Thus, $P(\text{red and queen}) = \frac{2}{52}$. Therefore, we have:

$$P(\text{red or queen}) = P(\text{red}) + P(\text{queen}) - P(\text{red and queen}) = \frac{26}{52} + \frac{4}{52} - \frac{2}{52} = \frac{28}{52} = \frac{7}{13}.$$

Sometimes, the probability of A and B is equal to zero. Then, the two events do not share any outcomes. When this occurs, the events are said to be *mutually exclusive*.

Definition: Two events are *mutually exclusive* if it is impossible for the two events to occur at the same time.

When two events are mutually exclusive, then $P(A \text{ and } B) = 0$. Thus, for two mutually exclusive events A and B: $P(A \text{ or } B) = P(A) + P(B)$. This is only true if the events are mutually exclusive!

Example: A card is drawn from a standard deck of 52 cards. Find the probability that the card is red or black.
Solution: The card cannot be red and black at the same time, thus these two events are mutually exclusive. Thus, we have

$$P(\text{red or black}) = P(\text{red}) + P(\text{black}) = \frac{26}{52} + \frac{26}{52} = \frac{52}{52} = 1.$$

Since this probability is equal to 1, this is certain to happen. All cards are either red or black, so one is certain to choose a card that is red or black.

Probability of Independent Events

If two events are *independent*, then we do not need to know what happened on the first event in order to find the probability that the second event occurs.

Definition: Two events are *independent* if the occurrence of either event does not in any way affect the probability of the occurrence of the other event.

For example, suppose we draw two cards from a standard deck of 52 cards with replacement. This means we draw one card, look at it, and put it back in the deck before we draw the second card. In this case the drawing of the two cards are independent events. It does not matter which first card was drawn. Every card has an equal chance of being drawn the second time. Note that if we did not replace the first card before drawing the second card then the events would not be independent.

Suppose I was interested in the probability of drawing two aces. I draw one card and the probability that it is an ace is $\frac{4}{52}$. I do not put that card back in the deck. If the first card I drew was an ace then the probability I draw an ace the second time is $\frac{3}{51}$. But, if the first card was not an ace, then the probability the second card is an ace is $\frac{4}{51}$. These two probabilities are not the same. These events are *not* independent. I need to know what happened with the first event before I can calculate the probability of the second event. In what follows we will only concern ourselves with independent events. "And" probability problems for dependent events are much more complicated and are dealt with in a course on probability and statistics.

Fact: If events A and B are independent, then $P(A \text{ and } B) = P(A) \cdot P(B)$.

This is known as the *multiplication rule*.

Example: Two cards are drawn from a standard deck of 52 cards with replacement. What is the probability that two spades are drawn

Solution: Since the cards are drawn with replacement, the two events are independent. The probability of drawing a spade from a deck of 52 cards is $\frac{13}{52} = \frac{1}{4}$. Thus, we have:

$$P(\text{spade and spade}) = P(\text{spade}) \cdot P(\text{spade}) = \frac{1}{4} \cdot \frac{1}{4} = \frac{1}{16}.$$

Example: A spinner has equal sized slices for each of the letters a, b, c, d, e, f, g, o. The spinner is spun three times. Find the probability the spinner lands on a c the first spin, e the second spin, and g the third spin.

Solution: Since the spinner has equal sized slices for each of the letters, we can use classical probability. (Why is this?) These events are independent, because the sector where the spinner lands the first time does not affect the probability of where it will land the next time. So, we can use the multiplication rule above.

$$P(c \text{ and } e \text{ and } g) = P(c) \cdot P(e) \cdot P(g) = \frac{1}{8} \cdot \frac{1}{8} \cdot \frac{1}{8} = \frac{1}{512}.$$

Exercises

1. The probability of an individual being chosen for a local cheering squad is 0.687. What is the probability that an individual is not chosen?

2. The name of a past Secretary of Defense for the United States is selected from the following list (Table 10.5).

SECRETARY OF DEFENSE	HOME STATE
James V. Forrestal	New York
Louis A. Johnson	West Virginia
George C. Marshall	Pennsylvania
Robert A. Lovett	New York
Charles E. Wilson	Michigan
Neil H. McElroy	Ohio
Thomas S. Gates Jr.	Pennsylvania
Robert S. McNamara	Michigan
Clark M. Clifford	Maryland
Melvin R. Laird	Wisconsin
Elliot L. Richardson	Massachusetts
James R. Schlesinger	Virginia
Donald H. Rumsfeld	Illinois
Harold Brown	California
Caspar W. Weinberger	California
Frank C. Carlucci	Pennsylvania
Richard B. Cheney	Wyoming
Les Aspin	Wisconsin

Table 10.5 Past Secretaries of Defense and their home states

Find the probability of each of the following:

(a) A Secretary of Defense was from New York.
(b) A Secretary of Defense was from the United States.
(c) A Secretary of Defense was not from New York.
(d) A Secretary of Defense was from Pennsylvania or Wisconsin.
(e) A Secretary of Defense was from Florida.
(f) The last name of a Secretary of Defense begins with the letter "R".

3. A card is drawn from a standard deck of 52 cards. Find the probability of choosing:

(a) a black card or a jack
(b) a jack or a ten
(c) a green card
(d) a black face card (A face card is an ace, jack, queen, or king.)

4. Which, if any, of the four parts of problem 3 above are mutually exclusive? Explain.

5. A die is rolled twice. What is the probability of

(a) rolling two even numbers?
(b) rolling an even number the first time and a number less than 3 the second time?
(c) rolling a number less than 7 both times?

6. Which of the following situations are independent? Explain.

(a) Draw two marbles from a box that contains 6 white marbles, 4 green marbles, and 5 red marbles.
(b) Select a number between 1 and 10 inclusive. Then, choose a number between 1 and 10 inclusive again.

(c) Select two different numbers between 1 and 20.

7. A bag contains 8 red marbles, 6 blue marbles, 7 green marbles, and 5 white marbles. Find the probability of each of the following:

(a) drawing a yellow marble?
(b) drawing a red or blue marble?
(c) Two marbles are drawn with replacement. What is the probability the first marble is green and the second marble is white?

8. Table 10.6 gives the probability that the speed of a car will be in the given range at a particular point on a highway.

Speed	Probability
under 45 mph	0.01
45 – 54 mph	0.09
55 – 64 mph	0.48
65 – 74 mph	0.27
75 mph or over	0.15

Table 10.6 The probability the speed of a car will be in a given range

Find the probability that the speed of a car will be:

(a) under 55 mph
(b) between 55 mph and 74 mph inclusive
(c) under 75 mph
(d) over 54 mph
(e) over 64 mph

9. In a certain office there are 60 secretaries. Of these, 35 can type, 18 can take shorthand, and 8 can do both.

(a) What is the probability a secretary in the office cannot type?
(b) What is the probability a secretary in the office cannot take shorthand?
(c) What is the probability a secretary in the office can type or take shorthand?

10. 50% of coffee drinkers use sugar, 60% use cream, and 40% use both.

(a) What is the probability a person uses sugar or cream?
(b) What is the probability a person does not use sugar?
(c) What is the probability a person uses neither?

10.9 Odds

Closely related to the idea of probability is that of *odds*. We read about them often in newspapers and magazines. You may have heard something like: the odds of winning the pick four lottery are 1 in 12,959,999. Although odds are quoted in our newspapers and TV media nearly daily, there is a great misunderstanding among many people about just what odds are. They are not probabilities.

The probability that an event occurs is equal to the ratio of the number of outcomes favoring an event to the total number of outcomes. The odds in favor of an event occurring is also a ratio. However, it is the ratio of the number of outcomes favoring an event to the number of outcomes against an event. The ratios are not the same. Their values are not equal.

Fact: The *odds in favor* of an event are given by:

$$\frac{\text{number of outcomes favorable to the event}}{\text{number of outcomes unfavorable to the event}}.$$

The *odds against* an event are given by:

$$\frac{\text{number of outcomes unfavorable to the event}}{\text{number of outcomes favorable to the event}}.$$

As with classical probability, all outcomes are assumed to be equally likely. Since the odds of an event is a ratio, the ratio is often expressed in the form $a{:}b$ or a to b.

Example: It is known that 4 out of every 7 people with a certain condition benefit from a new medication. What are the odds a person with this condition will benefit from this new medication?

Solution: Since we are finding the odds someone will benefit we are looking for the odds in favor of the event. The number of outcomes favorable is the number who benefit, which is 4. The number of outcomes unfavorable is the number who do not benefit, $7 - 4 = 3$. Thus, the odds of benefiting from this new medication are $4{:}3$ or 4 to 3.

Note that $\frac{4}{3} > 1$. Odds do not have to be a number between 0 and 1 inclusive.

Note that odds are expressed in the form $a{:}b$, or a to b, or $\frac{a}{b}$ where $a \geq 0$ and $b \geq 0$. In this case it is possible that $\frac{a}{b}$ could be greater than 1.

Example: A shirt is randomly selected from a closet containing 4 blue shirts, 3 red shirts, and 5 white shirts. What are the odds against choosing a blue shirt?
Solution: The number of outcomes that are unfavorable to choosing a blue shirt are 8 (3 red and 5 white). The number of outcomes that are favorable to choosing a blue shirt are 4. The odds against choosing a blue shirt are therefore $8{:}4$ or $2{:}1$.

WORD OF CAUTION: Odds are expressed as a numerical ratio. Therefore, $2{:}1$ remains as $2{:}1$. The number 2 is not a ratio. Also, the ratio $7{:}3$ remains $7{:}3$ and does not become $2\frac{1}{3}$.

Converting Odds to Probabilities

Sometimes we are given the odds and we need to know the probability. Odds can be converted to probabilities fairly easily.

> **Fact**: Let the number of favorable outcomes be a and number of unfavorable outcomes be b. Then the total number of outcomes is equals to $a + b$. If the odds in favor of an event occurring are $\frac{a}{b}$, then the probability of success is $P(\text{success}) = \frac{a}{a+b}$.

The reason for this is simple. While odds compare the number of favorable outcomes to the number of unfavorable outcomes, probability compares the number of favorable outcomes to the total number of possible outcomes (both favorable and unfavorable).

Example: The odds of winning a certain drawing are 3 to 28. Find the

(a) probability of winning the drawing.
(b) probability of losing the drawing.

Solution: Since the odds in favor of winning the drawing are 3 to 28, then $a = 3$ = the number of favorable outcomes and $b = 28$ = the number of unfavorable outcomes.

(a) The probability of winning is
$$\frac{\text{number of favorable outcomes}}{\text{total number of outcomes}} = \frac{a}{a+b} = \frac{3}{3+28} = \frac{3}{31}.$$

(b) The probability of losing is
$$\frac{\text{number of unfavorable outcomes}}{\text{total number of outcomes}} = \frac{b}{a+b} = \frac{28}{3+28} = \frac{28}{31}.$$

Example: The odds that someone will be born gifted (with an IQ over 130) are 1:49. Find the probability that someone will be born gifted.
Solution: Since the odds in favor are 1:49, the number of favorable outcomes, or a, is 1 and the number of unfavorable outcomes, or b, is 49. Thus, the probability of being gifted is

$$\frac{\text{number of favorable outcomes}}{\text{total number of outcomes}} = \frac{1}{1+49} = \frac{1}{50}.$$

Converting Probabilities to Odds

Sometimes we are given the information in terms of probabilities and we need to find the odds. We have the following fact to help.

348   Chapter 10: **PROBABILITY AND COUNTING**

Fact: If $P(\text{success}) = \dfrac{a}{c}$, then the number of favorable outcomes is a and the total number of outcomes is c. Therefore, the number of unfavorable outcomes is $c - a$. Thus, $b = c - a$. Therefore, we have

odds in favor of this event are

$$\frac{a}{c-a} = \frac{a}{b}$$

and

odds against this event are

$$\frac{c-a}{a} = \frac{b}{a}.$$

Example: The probability someone will earn an A in a certain English course is 0.35. Find the odds of earning an A in the course and the odds of not earning an A in the course.

Solution: Since the probability of earning an A is $0.35 = \dfrac{35}{100}$, the number of favorable outcomes, or a, is 35 and the total number of outcomes, or c, is 100. Thus, $b = c - a = 100 - 35 = 65$. Therefore, we have the following:

odds of earning an A are $\dfrac{a}{b} = \dfrac{35}{65} = \dfrac{7}{13}$ or 7 to 13.

odds of not earning an A are $\dfrac{b}{a} = \dfrac{65}{35} = \dfrac{13}{7}$ or 13 to 7.

Exercises

1. A die is rolled. What are the odds of:

    (a) rolling a 4?
    (b) not rolling a number less than 3?
    (c) rolling an even number?
    (d) rolling an odd number less than 5?

2. If the odds of winning a raffle are 2 to 159, find the probability of

    (a) winning the raffle.
    (b) losing the raffle.

3. If the probability of placing in a contest is 0.18, find the odds of placing.

4. If the probability it will rain today is 0.26, what are the odds it will not rain today?

5. The odds a team will win are 8 to 3. What is the probability the team will lose?

6. A police department estimates that the probability a thief is armed with a gun is 0.15. What are the odds a thief is armed with a gun?

7. If $P(A) = \dfrac{1}{3}$,

(a) what are the odds in favor of A?
(b) what are the odds against A?
(c) what is $P(\overline{A})$?

8. If the odds in favor of A are 5 to 8, what is $P(A)$?

9. Explain in your own words using complete sentences what we mean when we say

(a) "The probability we will win is $\dfrac{3}{8}$."
(b) "The odds we will win are 3 to 8."

10.10 Chapter Review

Important Terms to Know

classical probability	event	odds
combination	experiment	outcome
combinatorics	factorial	Pascal's Triangle
complement	Fundamental Counting Principle	permutation
compound probability	independent	probability
counting trees	Law of Large Numbers	relative frequency
duplicate item	multiplication rule	subjective probability
empirical probability	mutually exclusive	

Important Names to Know

Bernoulli, Jacques	Fermat, Pierre de	Pascal, Blaise
Cardano, Girolamo	Kolmogorov, A. N.	Quetelet, Adolphe
De Moivre, Abraham	Laplace, Pierre Simon de	

Review Questions

1. Summarize when a counting problem is a permutation and when it is a combination.

2. When is it best to use each of the following:

   The Fundamental Counting Principle

   $${}_nP_r = \frac{n!}{(n-r)!}$$

   $${}_nC_r = \frac{n!}{(n-r)!\cdot r!}?$$

3. What are the three types of probabilities? Define each type and give an example of when each type may be used.

4. Consider a twelve sided block. Each side is a different color. The colors of the sides are yellow, pink, red, blue, green, brown, black, purple, orange, white, tan, and teal. Such a block is known as a dodecahedron, and when tossed, each side coming up is equally likely.

   (a) State an event that has probability

       (1)   0.

       (2) $\frac{1}{12}$.

       (3)   1.

   (b) State two events A and B that are mutually exclusive. Find the $P(A)$, $P(B)$, and $P(A$ or $B)$.

   (c) State two events C and D that are not mutually exclusive. Find $P(C)$, $P(D)$, and $P(C$ or $D)$.

   (d) State two events E and F that are independent. Find $P(E)$, $P(F)$, and $P(E$ and $F)$.

5. Explain the difference between probabilities and odds. If the probability an event will occur is 0.4, what are the odds it will occur?

Small Group Exercise

Consider the game of Monopoly. First recall how it is played. Players take turns rolling a pair of dice. The number of dots showing on the dice determines the number of squares around the board the player will move. All players start from the square labeled "Go." The first twelve squares are labeled Mediterranean Avenue, Community Chest, Baltic Avenue, Income Tax, Reading Railroad, Oriental Avenue, Chance, Vermont Avenue, Connecticut Avenue, Just Visiting Jail, St. Charles Place, and Electric Company.

(a) Why is the first player most likely to land on the square labeled Chance?
(b) If the player doesn't land on Chance first, where is the player most likely to land?
(c) You have landed on Oriental Avenue. It is now your turn to roll again. What are the odds you will land on Connecticut Avenue?
(d) What is the probability a player will land on Mediterranean Avenue on the first roll?

Chapter Eleven

Statistics

"Statistics are like a bikini. What they reveal is suggestive, but what they conceal is vital."

Aaron Levenstein

Chapter Outline

11.0 Introduction
11.1 Historical Perspective
11.2 Some Basic Terminology
11.3 Sampling
Quota Samples
Random Samples
Systematic Samples
Stratified Samples
Unrepresentative Samples
11.4 Graphs
Pie Charts
Bar Charts
Histograms
Frequency Polygons
Scatter Plots
11.5 Measures of Central Tendency
The Mean
The Median
The Mode
11.6 Measures of Dispersion
The Range
The Standard Deviation
11.7 The Truthfulness of Statistics and Graphs
11.8 Modern Methods
11.9 Chapter Review

11.0 Introduction

Statistics is the science of gathering, analyzing, and interpreting data. Statistics helps us to graphically understand data and to clarify the numerical implications of data that have been obtained in an experiment. How do we interpret the graphs we see in the paper? What do the findings in a study really mean? We have tested a possible new medication on a number of patients — are the findings significant? The ad reads "Four out of five doctors recommend it." Should I also use it? Statistics is the science that enables us to answer these questions.

11.1 Historical Perspective

Statistics comes from the Latin word statisticus, meaning "of the state." Originally statistics was associated with numbers that were gathered for the governments to use. For thousands of years, governments have been taking censuses. A census is a gathering of statistical data. There was a census even in the time of Mary and Joseph. That is why they traveled to Bethlehem.

The first census taken in the United States was in 1790. We now have a census taken every ten years in the U.S. It is used for many purposes today. For example, the number of seats for each state in the House of Representatives is determined from information gathered in the census.

Today statistics are used to regulate the economy, for public opinion polls, and for the theory of tests and measurements in the field of education. The statistical theory of tests and measurements enables educators to compare the achievements of individuals from different backgrounds.

Originally, everyone concerned was polled when gathering data. Today there are methods that enable us to obtain these statistics using relatively small samples. While William S. Gossett was a student, he produced some of the first results concerning small samples. He published his work under the name "Student." His work, known as the Student's t-test, is a very useful statistical tool.

John Gaunt was a London merchant. He was the first person to make statistical predictions from a set of data. He noted in 1662 that more male babies were born than female babies. He also noted, however, that eventually the number of both sexes comes to be about the same.

Insurance companies make use of such mortality statistics. Life insurance companies rely upon the accuracy of mortality tables in determining their premium rates.

Carl Friedrich Gauss (1777–1855) developed the statistical method of Least Squares. This method is widely used today in such fields as astronomy, biology, physics, and the social sciences. Gauss is sometimes said to be the last person to have mastered mathematics. Since then the field of mathematics has grown too large for any one person to master.

One field of inferential statistics, known as regression analysis, enables one to compare quantities or variables to discover relationships that may exist between them. Francis Galton, who lived from 1822 to 1911, developed early notions of regression and correlation. He discovered a very useful statistic known as the correlation coefficient and he posed the problem of multiple regression.

Every day we can find statistics which are quoted in newspapers and magazine articles. They are used by many professionals in numerous fields, including researchers, scientists, political pollsters, advertisers, and educators to name just a few.

11.2 Some Basic Terminology

Data refers to the information that we are collecting. For example, if we phone 500 people and ask them what their age is, their replies would be our data. This is *raw data*.

For example. If we have a list of 500 ages and nothing has been done with these figures yet, that would be called "raw data.". We use the science of statistics to then generate graphs, calculate and analyze some meaningful figures, and draw conclusions.

Definition: *Statistics* is the branch of mathematics that deals with collecting, organizing, analyzing and interpreting numerical data.

We use *statistics* to basically make sense of the raw data. We seldom see the raw data in any materials we read. The raw data was organized into the graphs we see printed in the paper, and used to calculate the statistics we see quoted, such as "25% of the community is in support of this issue."

We usually begin by trying to determine something about a group. For example, we want to predict the election results for an upcoming gubernatorial election in the state of Missouri. The *population* is the collection of all people, animals, or things with which we are dealing. In this example, the population would be all registered voters in the state of Missouri. They are the people who will determine the next governor of that state. As another example, suppose we wanted to determine the average midterm exam grade for a statistics class. The population would consist of the midterm exam grades of all students in that statistics class. Suppose, as a final example, we want to determine what the best selling car was in America this past year. Our population would consist of every car sold in America in the past year.

Definition: The *population*, or *sample space*, is the collection of all people, animals, or things in which we are interested.

Sometimes, the population is extremely large or widespread. It can be either very difficult or impossible to select each item in the population. In these instances, we select a representative *sample* with which to work. It would be very expensive and time consuming, if not impossible, to reach every registered voter in Missouri to question their voting intentions. Therefore, we would only speak with some of the registered voters in Missouri. These that we select would make up the sample.

Definition: A *sample* is a subset of the population.

We do not always need to select a sample. If our population is the midterm exam grades of all students in a particular class, we would not draw a sample. We would use all of the class' exam grades in our calculations. When we calculate using the population, we have determined a *parameter*.

> **Definition**: A *parameter* is a calculation based on the population.

If, however, we use sample data for our calculations, the result of our calculation is referred to as a *statistic*.

> **Definition:** A *statistic* is a calculation based on the sample.

The terminology, parameter and statistic, enables us to know whether the entire population or just a sample was used in the calculation.

If our sample is representative of our population, then our statistic can be used to predict or describe the population. If our sample is not representative, then there is no relationship between the behavior of the sample and that of the population. We will consider sampling in our next section.

Exercises

1. Answer "true" or "false."

    (a) A parameter describes a sample space.
    (b) Raw data is organized into graphs.
    (c) If we want to determine the average life expectancy of poodles, the population would consist of all dogs in the world.
    (d) A sample is always representative of the population.

2. What is the difference between a parameter and a statistic?

3. When should one use a sample instead of the population?

4. What is the difference between data and raw data?

11.3 Sampling

When choosing a sample, it is essential that the sample be representative of the population. You can think of the sample as being a mini population. Then, and only then, are the calculated statistics valuable and meaningful. The sample cannot be *biased*.

There are various ways in which to choose a sample. We will consider four of those ways here.

Quota Samples

Quota samples have been generated since 1935, when George Gallup used them to help predict the next president. When choosing a sample using this technique, one makes sure the proportion of the sample that has a specific characteristic is the same as the proportion of the population with that characteristic. For example, if 53% of the population were female, then 53% of the sample would also be female. Characteristics such as race, sex, and political party affiliation were considered by George

Gallup in 1935. This type of sampling seems like a very good idea. It did in 1935, also. However, there can be problems with this type of sampling.

This type of sampling was used in the Gallup polls to predict the next president in the 1948 election between Thomas Dewey and Harry Truman. The poll predicted that Dewey would win the election. The Chicago Tribune even went to press before all of the counts were in with a head line reading "Dewey Defeats Truman." But, after the votes were all counted, it was found that Truman had actually won the election. The sample did not make the right prediction.

What went wrong? If you look back in history, you will find that the predicted percentages of votes for each candidate were close in margin. Also, consider how a quota sampling is generated. You select various characteristics. What characteristics do you choose? How many characteristics do you choose? Do you consider each characteristic separately, such as race and then religion, or in a combination, such as all Asian Muslims? Do you see the possible problems with such a sampling?

There are other types of sampling techniques. We will take a look at one technique which is very useful.

Random Samples

Suppose we just throw everyone's name in a hat and draw five hundred names. Seems rather simple, doesn't it. That is basically what *random sampling* is. The people or items in the sample are chosen at random. In this way, every item or person in the population has an equal chance of being chosen. The key here is to draw a large enough sample to keep it from being biased or unrepresentative of the population.

Usually we do not throw everyone's name in a hat. For example, you can assign each person or item a number and then choose a specific number of numbers. This was often accomplished using a Random Number Table. However, in the age of computers, computer programs now often choose the random numbers. Many modern calculators even have this capability.

The next type of sampling we will consider is systematic sampling.

Systematic Samples

With *systematic sampling*, every nth item is chosen. The first item chosen to sample is random. So, for example, if we were going to sample a box of screws to approximate how many defective screws there were in the box, we could test the fifth screw and every eleventh screw after that. This works well if we choose the items from the entire population and every nth item is constructed by the same person or machine. If every nth item was constructed by the same machine, then the sample would be biased to that machine and not representative of the entire population. If, for example. a given machine selected every eleventh item, then we would not want to choose every eleventh item, but possibly every ninth item.

The last type of sampling we will consider here is stratified sampling.

Stratified Samples

When using *stratified sampling*, one breaks the population into categories, or *strata*, and then chooses a random sample from each strata. One common strata is "geographical region." In polling for an upcoming presidential election, one strata might be "the state." This strata may be broken down into two cities, two suburbs, and a rural town. Then a random sample of people would be phoned in those five

particular areas in each state. Not every city in the state would be sampled, only some (in this example two).

This type of sampling works well, is representative, and cost effective. Thus, it is widely used today.

Unrepresentative Samples

For a statistic to be meaningful and representative of a population, it cannot be biased. It also must be large enough. If a sample is too small, then the statistics may very well not be even close to the actual parameters they are trying to represent. For example, if the population consists of $1,000,000$ people, then a sample of size 5 would not be representative. There are procedures that are used to determine the minimum sample size needed to be representative. We will not investigate those procedures here. However, they are essential. If the sample is not representative, then you do not know anything more about the population than you did before you began.

Exercises

For exercises # 1 through 5, state what type of sampling each is.

1. A new form of a nonaspirin children's medication is to be tested against a well-known product. Every fourth child in the sample will receive the new test product. All others will receive the well-known product. The children and parents will not know which they are using for control purposes.

2. A sample of raccoons from our national parks is to be studied for health purposes. The percentage of raccoons in the sample from a given park will match the percentage of national raccoons in that given park.

3. A well known magazine wants to sample some of its readers in the northeast. All subscribers in that area are assigned a number and a computer generated list of $1,000$ numbers is used to select those to be sampled.

4. A sample is to be drawn in New Jersey to see if department store preference is related to level of education. Level of education is broken into high school, some college, college degree, masters degree, and Ph.D. A set number of people from each grouping are chosen to be in the sample.

5. A college alumni office wants to sample graduates from the last twenty years. Each graduate is assigned a number. The computer generates a list of $5,000$ numbers. These graduates are sampled.

6. What are some of the problems with quota sampling?

7. What must one be careful of when using a systematic sample?

8. What does it mean for a sample to be unrepresentative? biased?

9. Give an example of a biased stratified sample.

10. Explain in your own words why the quota sample in the 1948 presidential election did not accurately predict the election results.

358 Chapter 11: **STATISTICS**

11.4 Graphs

There are two main types of statistics: *descriptive statistics* and *inferential statistics*. Inferential statistics deal with the analyzing of data and information. We will not deal with this type of statistics here. These are very widely used and meaningful and are dealt with in full semester and full year courses on statistics after the ground work is laid.

We will spend the remainder of the chapter considering descriptive statistics. Descriptive statistics are used to describe data. Various graphs, measures of central tendency, and measures of dispersion are all descriptive statistics. In this section, we will consider various graphs that you will see in reading a newspaper or article.

Pie Charts

The first type of graph is called the *pie chart* because it is shaped like a pie, that is, round. You have probably seen pie charts numerous times in your readings. A pie chart is used to demonstrate graphically how a number of items are proportioned into categories. The key here is that the data is in percentage form before the graph is constructed. Figure 11.1 is a pie chart for the household budget given in Table 11.1.

ITEM	MONTHLY PAYMENT
Mortgage	$1,400
Car Payment	$ 350
Car Insurance	$ 180
Gasoline	$ 150
Utilities	$ 110
Food	$ 250
Entertainment	$ 75
Miscellaneous	$ 100

Table 11.1 Household Budget

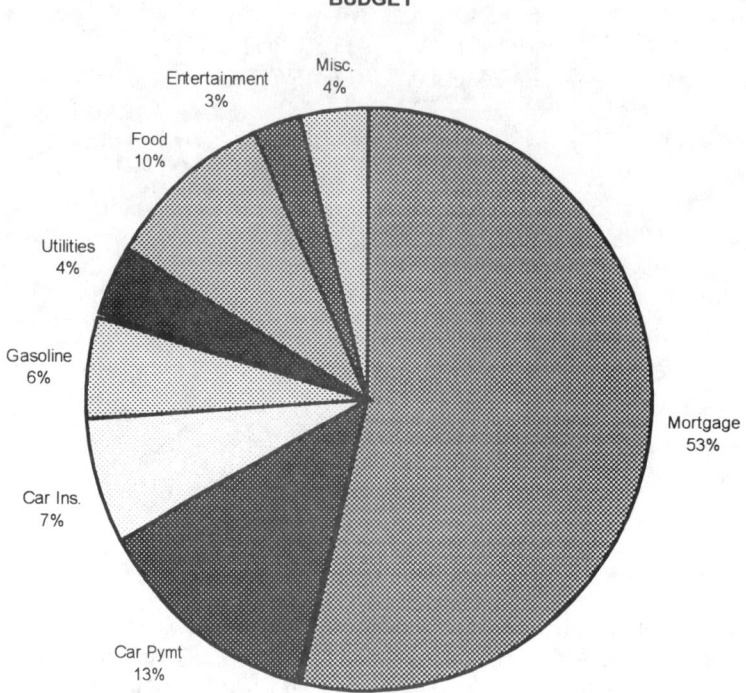

Figure 11.1 Pie chart for the Household Budget

Notice that the pie is divided into eight pieces, the same as the number of categories. Further, notice that each piece is labeled with the category name and percentage, that is the percentage of the monthly income spent on that item. Suppose we wanted to take the raw data and construct a pie chart. We would begin by converting the data into percentages. We will total the monthly payment column to find our total monthly earnings, divide each monthly payment by that total amount, and then multiply the result by 100 to find its corresponding percentage. We find the following:

	HOUSEHOLD BUDGET		
ITEM	MONTHLY PAYMENT	PERCENTAGE OF INCOME	
Mortgage	$1,400	53.5%	$\left(\dfrac{1400}{2615}\right) \approx 0.535$
Car Payment	$350	13.4%	$\left(\dfrac{350}{2615}\right) \approx 0.134$
Car Insurance	$180	6.9%	
Gasoline	$150	5.7%	
Utilities	$110	4.2%	
Food	$250	9.6%	
Entertainment	$75	2.9%	
Miscellaneous	$100	3.8%	
Total:	$2,615	100%	

Next, we partition the pie into eight categories, where the size of each piece of pie is the same percentage of the entire circle as that category is of the total income. Mark the center of the circle first and cut slices from there, just as with a pizza. Sometimes it is easier to slice the largest piece first and work in descending order. For example, if we begin with the largest percentage, mortgage, we would cut this piece a little bit more than half the size of the pie since 53.5% is a little more than half.

A pie chart is a useful graph that gives a good visual picture of how something is divided (or where all the money is going in this case). However, the number of categories should be kept small, between 5 and 10 categories inclusive.

Bar Charts

This second type of graph, the *bar chart*, is also a common graph that appears often in newspapers and magazines. Recall our monthly budget from earlier, Table 11.1. The bar chart for this information looks like Figure 11.2 below.

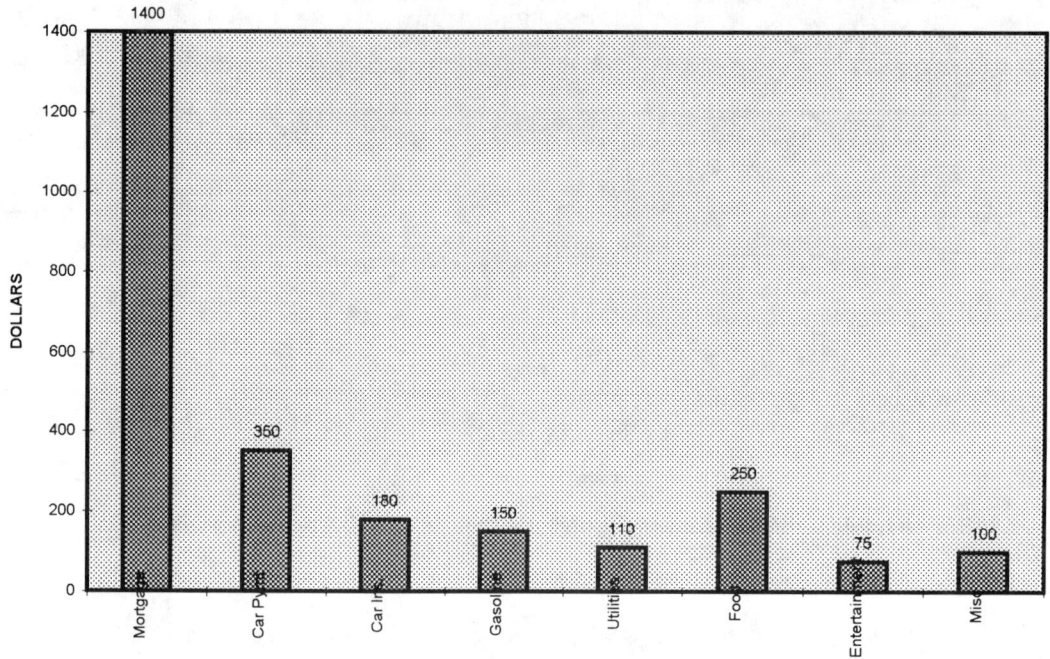

Figure 11.2 Bar chart for the Household Budget.

Notice, there is a vertical axis and a horizontal axis making this looks like the first quadrant in the xy–plane. We begin by making a small marking on the horizontal axis for each category and labeling each with the title of the category. These markings should be an equal distance apart. Then, we mark the vertical axis in equal increments. Letting each marking denote one unit would be monstrous for this problem, so we pick a more useful increment, every $200, and we label this axis "dollars". It is important that the vertical axis be divided in equal increments. If this is not done, the graph will not give an acurate visual picture of where the money is being spent!

Next, a rectangle is drawn over each category, with the marking on the horizontal axis as the center of the base of the rectangle. The height of the rectangle is the amount of money spent on the category. Since the exact amount will not be clear from the height (only an approximate amount will be), sometimes the exact amount is written at the top of each rectangle. This is not necessary. Each rectangle should have the same width and there should be a space between each rectangle. These spaces should also be of equal width.

Notice that in a bar chart one of the axes must be numerical but the other does not have to be.

Sometimes a bar chart is constructed sideways. This is especially true when there are numerous categories as in Figure 11.3.

362   Chapter 11: **STATISTICS**

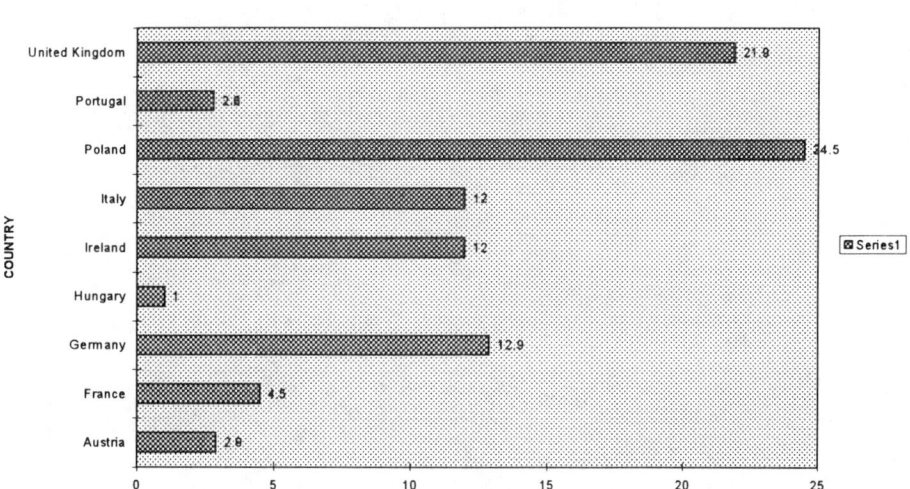

Figure 11.3 Bar chart depicting European immigration to the United States for 1992

Histograms

In our next type of graph, we again draw a vertical axis and a horizontal axis, but this time, each axis is labeled numerically. The horizontal axis indicates the observed values and the vertical axis indicates the *frequency*. The frequency is the number of times a value is observed.

Suppose forty households are sampled and asked how many cars they have in their household. Table 11.2 gives how many households reported having no cars, 1 car, 2 cars, and so forth.

NUMBER OF CARS	NUMBER OF HOUSEHOLDS
0	4
1	5
2	12
3	10
4	6
5	3
total number of households sampled	40

Table 11.2 Number of cars per household.

Figure 11.4 is a *histogram* depicting this information.

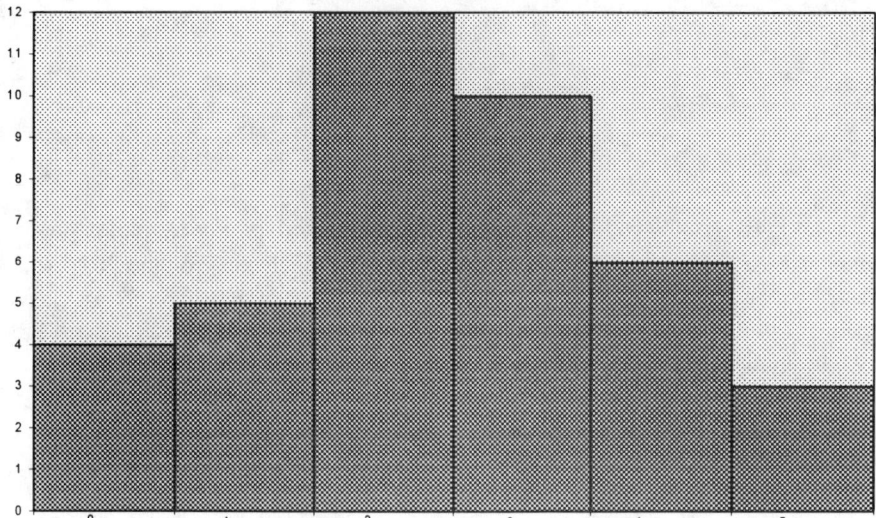

Figure 11.4 Histogram depicting the number of cars per household.

Notice the horizontal axis is marked for each of the possible number of cars (0 is the origin) and that these markings are spaced evenly. The horizontal axis is labeled "number of cars." The vertical axis is marked in increments of one unit. This is different from the bar chart. When reading a histogram, one can read the frequency from the height of the rectangle because the vertical axis is divided in increments of one unit. The vertical axis is labeled "number of households". Again, a rectangle is drawn over each marking on the horizontal axis so that the marking is in the center of the base and all rectangles are of the same width. The height of each rectangle is the frequency. However, there is usually no space between the rectangles with a histogram. If there is a frequency of zero, the top of the rectangle is the horizontal axis. If one were to draw a rectangle, no matter how low, it would give it a height and thus the frequency would have to be greater than or equal to one.

Suppose we look at a second example. This time we will consider sampling 20 patients and asking them how long they had to wait in a doctor's office before being seen. Further suppose they gave the following times (in minutes):

15	22	55	28	10	8	15	35	32	15
51	5	20	38	40	30	39	22	37	18

Notice that there are many different values, with very few repeating. Thus, a histogram like the one above would not be very helpful. Therefore, we begin by constructing a chart known as a *frequency distribution*. This chart will eventually enable us to construct a histogram. To begin, we break the raw data into *classes* or *intervals*. These intervals should be of equal width. It is best to have between 6 and 15 intervals inclusive whenever possible. The more data, the more intervals usually used. Each piece of data should fit into exactly one interval and only one interval.

If we consider the data above, the smallest is 5 and the largest is 55 and there are 20 pieces of data. That isn't very many. Thus, we should have a small number of classes, say 6. Since 5 is so small, we will begin the first interval at 1 and let each interval have a width of 10 (contain 10 integers). Thus, we have the following classes:

CLASSES
1 – 10
11 – 20
21 – 30
31 – 40
41 – 50
51 – 60

Notice that each class has the same width and that no two classes overlap. For example, the second interval could not be 10 – 20 because then you would not know in which class to place a 10 (the first class or the second). Also, the first class should contain the smallest piece of data and the last class should contain the largest piece of data. Now, we *tally* the data. That is, we place a "|" in a class for each piece of data. Then we count the tally marks for each class and record that number in the frequency column. For example, since 15 is between 11 and 20 inclusive, we place a tally mark, "|", in class two. Then we consider the next piece of data, 22. This is between 21 and 30 inclusive, so we place a tally mark in class three. We continue in this fashion and we have the following Frequency Distribution given in Figure 11.5.

CLASSES	TALLY	FREQUENCY
1-10	|||	3
11-20	⊬|	5
21-30	||||	4
31-40	⊬||	6
41-50		0
51-60	||	2

Figure 11.5 Frequency distribution for waiting times

Notice that if we total the frequency column we have 20, the exact number of pieces in our sample. We need one more piece of information before we can construct our histogram. We need to find the *midpoint* of each class. To find the midpoint, we find the sum of the *lower class boundary* and the *upper class boundary*. Then we divide that sum by 2. For example, the midpoint of the first class, 1 – 10, is $\frac{1+10}{2} = \frac{11}{2} = 5.5$

Thus, we have the midpoints for each interval given in Figure 11.6.

CLASS	MIDPOINT
1 – 10	5.5
11 – 20	15.5
21 – 30	25.5
31 – 40	35.5
41 – 50	45.5
51 – 60	55.5

Figure 11.6 Midpoints for each class of Figure 11.5

Now we are ready to construct the histogram. We draw our two axes. On the horizontal axis we make a marking for each class midpoint, making sure the markings are equally spaced apart, and label each marking with the value of the midpoint for that class. We label this axis "Waiting Times." Next, we mark the vertical axis from 1 to 6 in increments of one, and label these markings. (We use 6 because that is the largest frequency of all classes.) We label the vertical axis "Frequency". We draw rectangles of

equal width with no spaces between them. Each rectangle has the marking on the horizontal axis as the center of the base and a height equal to the frequency for that class. All rectangles should have the same width. We have now constructed this histogram in Figure 11.7 below.

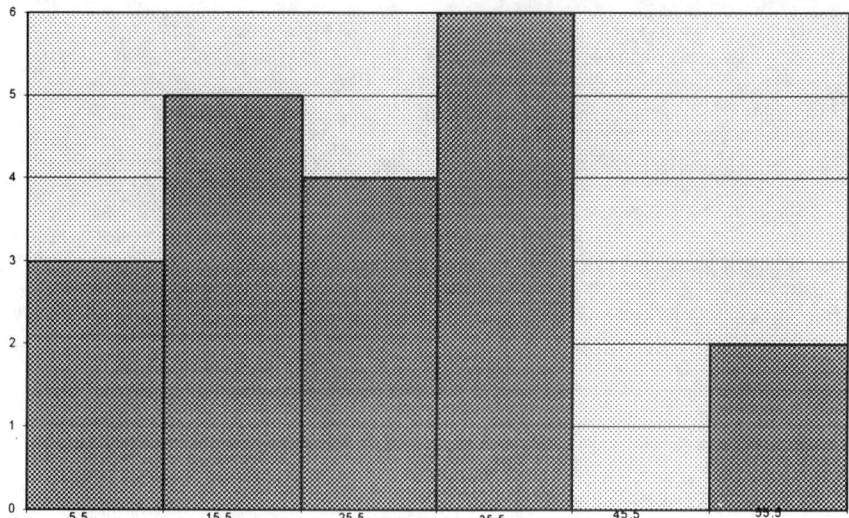

Figure 11.7 **Histogram depicting waiting times.**

The next type of graph we will consider is related to the histogram and is known as a *frequency polygon*.

Frequency Polygons

The frequency polygon is constructed in a similar manner to the histogram. Let's reconsider our example of number of cars per household. The information was given in Table 11.2. To begin constructing a frequency polygon for this sample data, we label our axes in the same manner as we did for the histogram in Figure 11.4. "Number of cars" will be plotted on the horizontal axis and "number of households" will be plotted on the vertical axis. However, we will not draw rectangles. Instead, we place a dot over each marking on the horizontal axis, the height of the dot being equal to the number of households that were found to have that many cars. For example, since four households were found to have no cars, we place a dot over the marking labeled "0" at a height of 4. Then, we connect these dots. To finish the polygon, we draw a straight line from the origin to the first dot plotted and then a line from the last dot plotted to the horizontal axis. That finishes the frequency polygon. The frequency polygon for the data above is now given in figure 11.8.

366   Chapter 11: **STATISTICS**

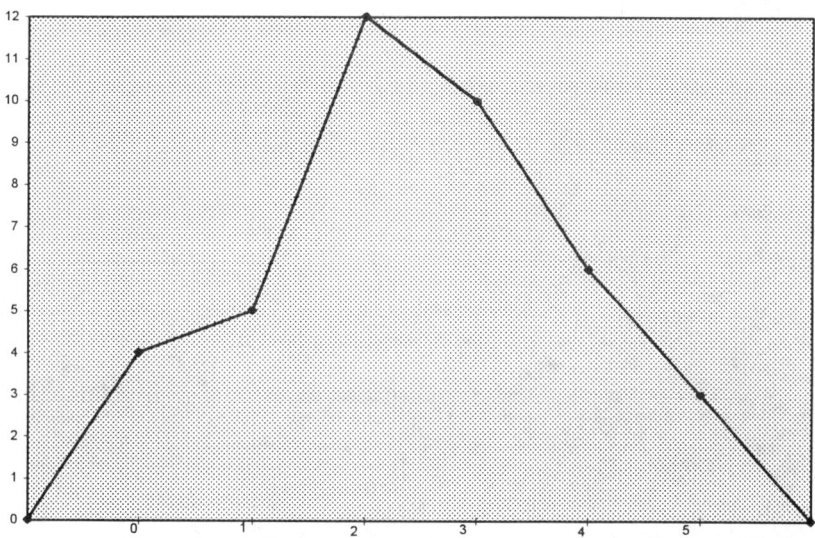

Figure 11.8 Frequency polygon representing the number of cars per household.

We will create one more frequency polygon, this time for grouped data. Recall our waiting times sample data that we constructed into a frequency distribution. Recall, we developed the frequency distribution with midpoints given in Table 11.3.

CLASSES	TALLY	FREQUENCY	MIDPOINT
1 – 10	|||	3	5.5
11 – 20	⊬⊤⊓	5	15.5
21 – 30	||||	4	25.5
31 – 40	⊬⊤⊓ |	6	35.5
41 – 50		0	45.5
51 – 60	||	2	55.5

Table 11.3 Frequency distribution of waiting times

We follow the same procedure as we did in constructing the previous frequency polygon in Figure 11.8, except we label the horizontal axis with the values of the midpoints of each class. Figure 11.9 is the frequency polygon for Table 11.3.

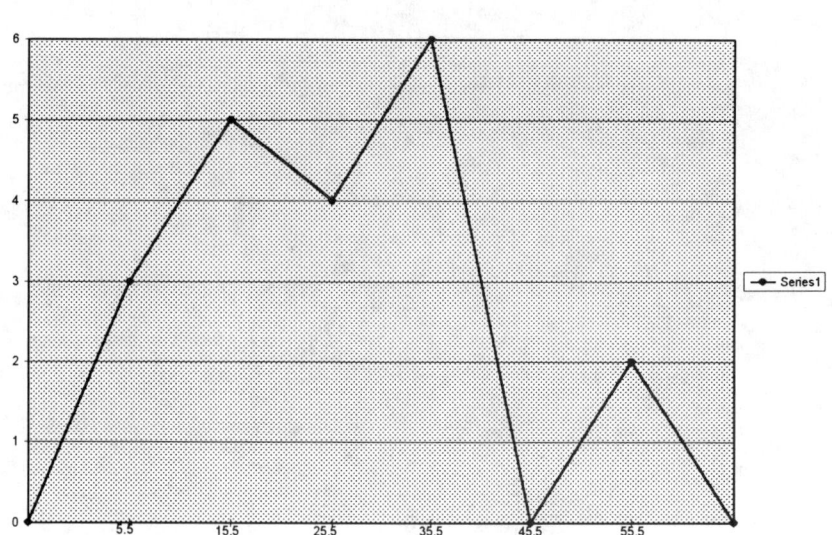

Figure 11.9 Frequency Polygon representing waiting times

The last type of graph we will consider here is known as the *scatter plot*.

Scatter Plots

Before we can construct a scatter plot, we need to define two additional terms — the *independent variable* and the *dependent variable*. The independent variable is the variable whose value is set; it is not dependent upon the value of the other variable. For example, suppose we consider the number of hours a student studies and the test score the student earns. The number of hours the student studies is the independent variable. That does not depend upon what score the student earns the next day. He or she studied just so many hours, and that's that. However, the test score the student earns depends upon the number of hours the student studied, and is thus the dependent variable.

Consider the sample data given in Table 11.4 below.

NUMBER OF HOURS OF STUDYING	STUDENT'S TEST SCORE
4	75
8	100
6	90
7	91
2	68
0.5	35
6	86
5	82
4	78
9	98

Table 11.4 Study hours and test scores.

We plot the points (independent variable, dependent variable) in the first quadrant of the xy-plane. Thus, we will plot the following points:

(4, 75) (8, 100) (6, 90) (7, 91) (2, 68) (0.5, 35) (6, 86) (5, 82) (4, 78) (9, 98)

That gives us the scatter plot in Figure 11.10.

368   Chapter 11: **STATISTICS**

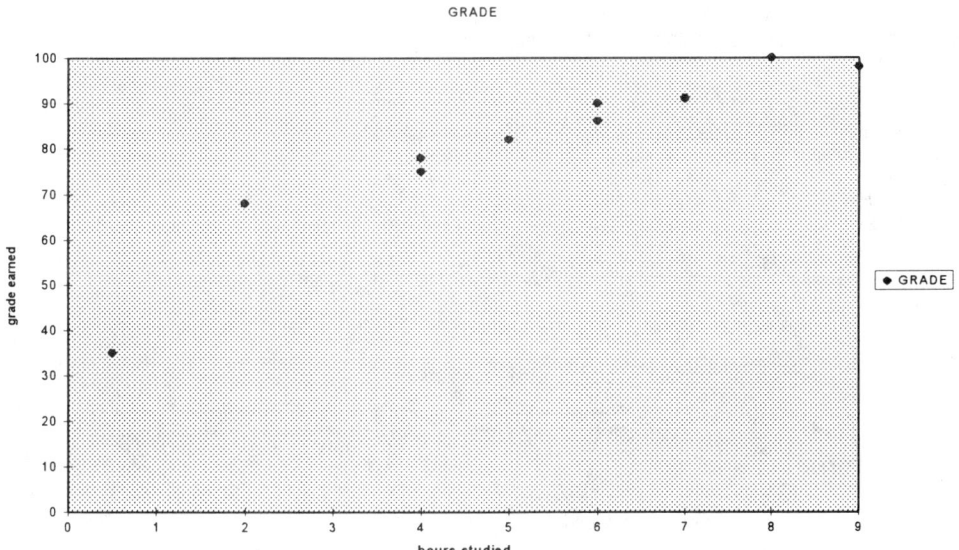

Figure 11.10 Scatter plot of number of hours of studying and grade

If we look closely, we can envision drawing a straight rising line near these data points. It would look something like Figure 11.11.

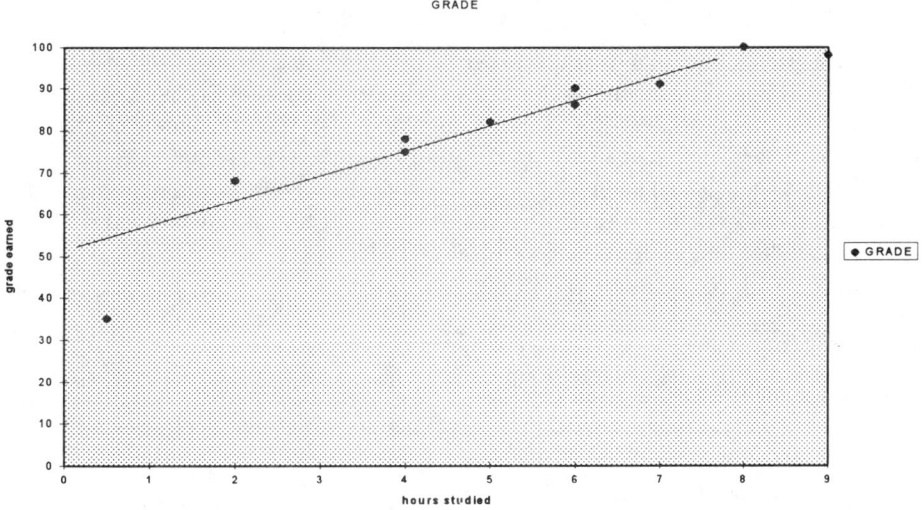

Figure 11.11 Possible regression line drawn on scatter plot

We are able to sketch a straight line passing through or near the data points. Therefore, we say there is a *linear relationship* between the number of hours spent studying and the grade earned. This is true whether it be a rising line, like the one above, or a falling line.

Sometimes, the data doesn't seem to hover around a straight line. At other times, though, a curve seems to fit the data well, as in the Figure 11.12 below.

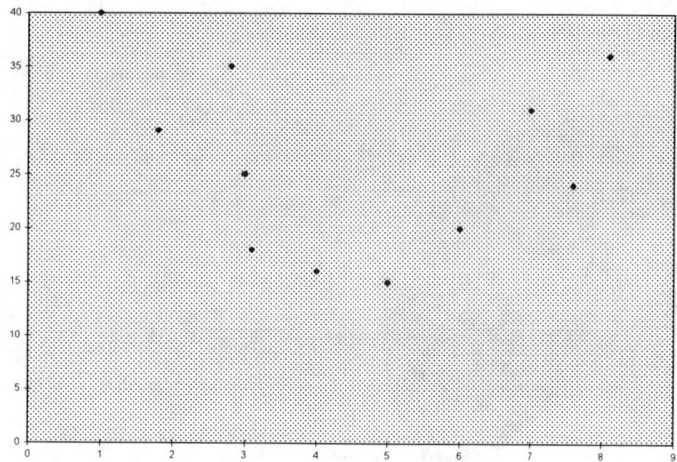

Figure 11.12 Curvilinear relationship

In cases such as this we say there is a *curvilinear relationship*.

At other times, there doesn't seem to be any type of relationship in the data, as in Figure 11.13.

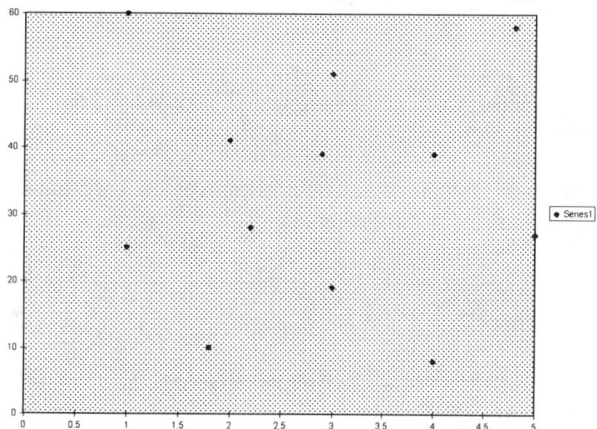

Figure 11.13 No relationship between the data

There are other types of statistical graphs that we have not covered here. These graphs described here are the types you will probably encounter the most often.

Exercises

1. The pie chart in Figure 11.14 illustrates the percentage of students at a local community college receiving degrees in various majors in the last five years.

370   Chapter 11: **STATISTICS**

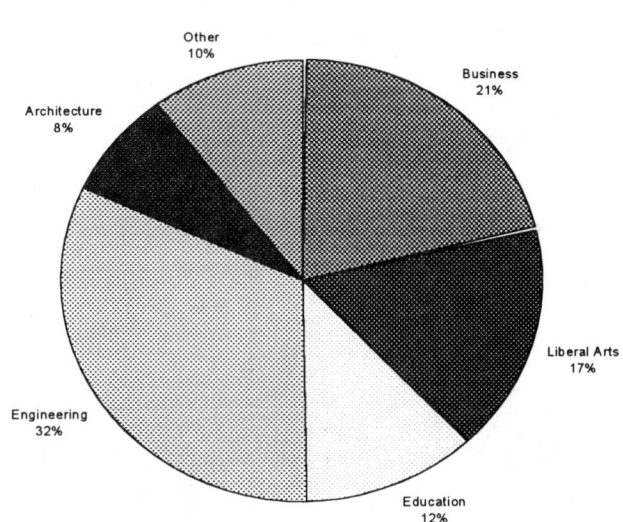

Figure 11.14 Percentage of students receiving degrees in various majors

(a) In which major were the most degrees awarded in the last five years?
(b) If 4,762 students have received degrees in the last five years, determine approximately the number of degrees awarded for each major listed.

2.   There are six candidates on a town ballot for town councilman. Table 11.5 gives the percentage of votes each received in the election. Construct a pie chart for this information.

NAME	% OF VOTES
Darcy	8%
Docherty	11%
Lane	46%
Markwith	5%
Pallitto	30%

Table 11.5 Town council election results

3.   At a large college 634 students were enrolled in a given history class and received a passing grade in the course for a given semester. The number of students receiving each passing grade is given below in Table 11.6.

GRADE	NUMBER OF STUDENTS
A	28
B+	67
B	98
C+	136
C	152
D+	86
D	67

Table 11.6 Grade distribution of a History class

Draw each of the following for this data set:
(a) pie chart
(b) bar chart

4. Using the bar chart in Figure 11.15, answer the following questions.

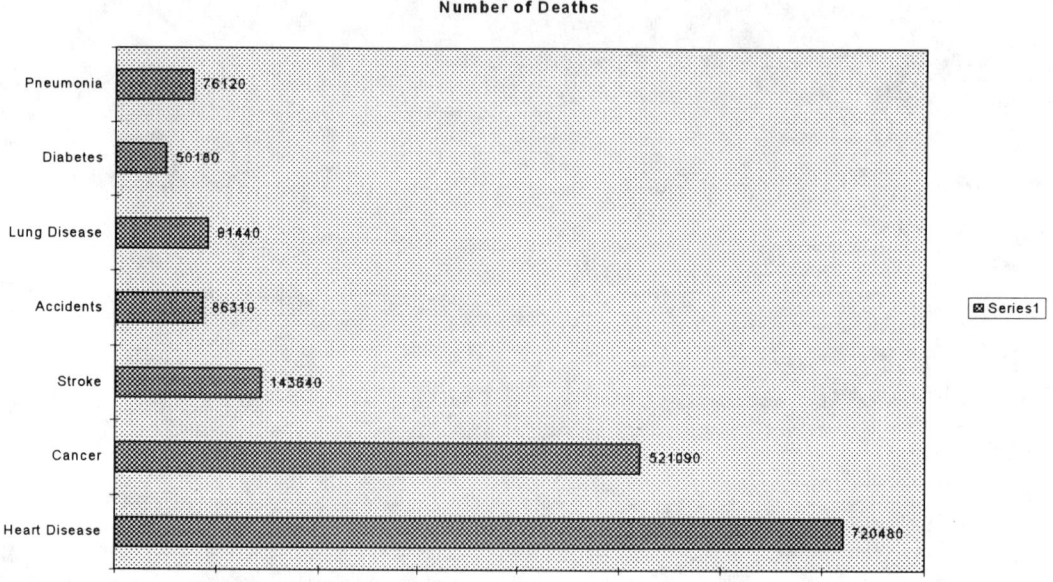

Figure 11.15 **Leading causes of death**

(a) What was the leading cause of death?
(b) How many people died of one of the causes listed?
(c) How many more people died from heart disease than from cancer?

5. Find examples of four different types of graphs from a recent magazine or newspaper and label each as a pie chart, bar chart, histogram, frequency polygon, or scatter plot.

6. Discuss the similarities and differences between a bar chart and a histogram.

7. Twenty five people were surveyed in a philosophy class in a community college and asked their age. Their responses are given below.

21	28	31	63	21	27	19	18	26	32
49	33	21	32	20	38	25	39	24	48
18	41	26	28	42					

(a) Create a frequency distribution for this data with the first class of 18 – 24.
(b) Construct a histogram for this data.
(c) Construct a frequency polygon for this data.

8. For each scatter plot given in Figure 11.16, state whether there appears to be a linear relationship, a curvilinear relationship, or no relationship. If there is a linear relationship, sketch a possible line through the data. If there is a curvilinear relationship, sketch a possible curve through the data.

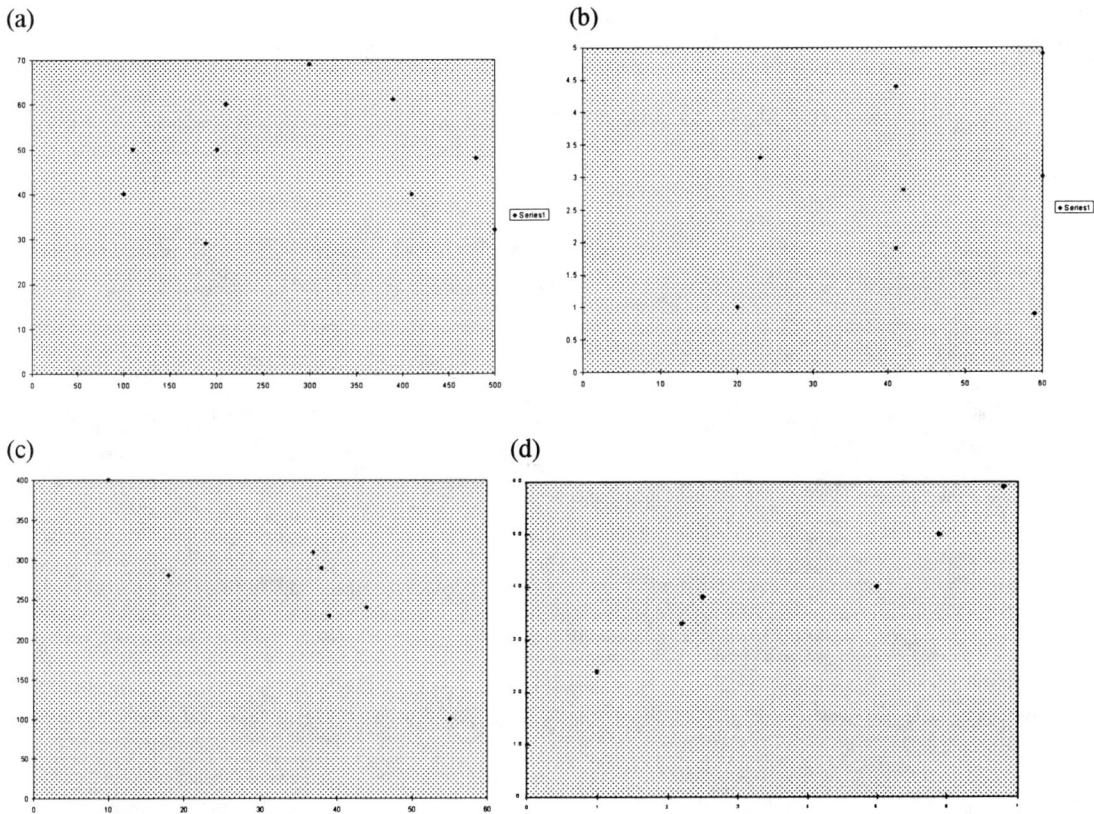

Figure 11.16 Scatter plots for exercise 8.

9. For the data given in Table 11.7,

WEIGHT	AGE
31	4
31	3
37	5
36	4
45	5
45	6
50	7
32	4
47	6
59	8

Table 11.7 Weight and age distribution for exercise 9.

    (a) What is the independent variable?
    (b) What is the dependent variable?
    (c) Sketch a scatter plot for this data.
    (d) What type of relationship if any does there appear to be?

10. Thirty people were surveyed and asked their weight. Their responses are given below.

128	128	186	212	109	141	185	175	124	191
138	138	176	265	121	138	196	135	107	280
161	155	150	191	132	155	203	125	188	201

(a) Create a frequency distribution for this data with the first class of 105 – 125.
(b) Construct a histogram for this data.
(c) Construct a frequency polygon for this data
(d) In constructing a scatter plot, what should the independent variable be: weight or age?
(d) Construct a scatter plot for this data.
(e) Does there appear to be a linear relationship between age and weight? Explain.
(f) Does there appear to be a curvilinear relationship between age and weight? Explain.

11.5 Measures of Central Tendency

Graphs are very useful, however they are not always the preferred means of conveying information. Suppose a student approaches a professor and asks how the exam scores were. The professor is not going to grab paper and pencil and draw a graph. But he or she might mention an average or other statistical measures. There are times when numerical values are very useful in describing data.

There are two types of numerical values we can calculate — those that tell us something about where the values fall and those that tell us how the values are spread out. The first type are known as *measures of central tendency* and we will investigate a few of these in this section. The second type are known as *measures of dispersion* and we will investigate some of those in section 11.6.

The measures of central tendency we will discuss here are the *mean*, the *median*, and the *mode*. These are easy to compute and also very useful in helping to describe the center of a distribution.

The Mean

This is sometimes referred to as the *average*. This is found by summing all of the data values and dividing the sum by the number of pieces of data.

We will assume we are working with sample data. We let n stand for the number of pieces of data in our sample, or the *sample size*. The other symbol we will see sometimes is $\sum_{i=1}^{n}$. This stands for "the sum of."

For example, suppose we have a class of fifteen students with the following midterm exam grades:

86, 75, 81, 99, 93, 70, 61, 42, 58, 69, 73, 77, 82, 94, 93.

Then, $n = 15$ because there are 15 grades in our sample. We let x_i represent the ith exam grade on our list. For example, $x_1 = 86$, $x_2 = 75$, $x_3 = 81$.

374   Chapter 11: **STATISTICS**

> **Fact**: $\sum_{i=1}^{n} x_i = x_1 + x_2 + x_3 + \ldots + x_n$.

Example. Using this fact and the grades listed above, find each of the following

(a) $\sum_{i=1}^{15} x_i$,   (b) $\sum_{i=1}^{5} 2x_i$.

Solution:

(a) $\sum_{i=1}^{15} x_i = x_1 + x_2 + x_3 + \ldots + x_{15} =$
$86 + 75 + 81 + 99 + 93 + 70 + 61 + 42 + 58 + 69 + 73 + 77 + 82 + 94 + 93 = 1{,}153.$

(b) $\sum_{i=1}^{5} 2x_i = 2x_1 + 2x_2 + 2x_3 + 2x_4 + 2x_5 = 2(86) + 2(75) + 2(81) + 2(99) + 2(93) = 868.$

Now, we are ready to compute the mean. The formula for the mean of a sample is given now.

> **Definition**: The *mean* of a sample is denoted $\bar{x}$, where $\bar{x} = \dfrac{\sum_{i=1}^{n} x_i}{n}$. n is the sample size.

We will now find the mean of the fifteen exam scores given previously. Recall that we already found that $\sum_{i=1}^{15} x_i = 1{,}153$. Therefore, the sample mean is

$$\bar{x} = \frac{\sum_{i=1}^{15} x_i}{15} = \frac{1{,}153}{15} \approx 76.867.$$

Example. The ages of the students in a psychology class are given below. Find the mean age of the students.

18, 21, 33, 28, 41, 27, 24, 26, 20, 24, 49, 31, 36, 25.

Solution: There are 14 ages given, therefore $n = 14$. We now find the sample mean as follows.

$$\bar{x} = \frac{\sum_{i=1}^{14} x_i}{14} = \frac{18 + 21 + 33 + 28 + 41 + 27 + 24 + 26 + 20 + 24 + 49 + 31 + 36 + 25}{14}$$
$$= \frac{403}{14} \approx 28.786.$$

Sometimes the mean is not the most representative measure of central tendency. Consider the following example.

Example: The following exam grades were recorded for a statistics course.

82, 85, 91, 86, 97, 92, 76, 78, 22.

Calculate the mean and discuss why this is not representative of how the class performed.
Solution: There are 9 grades, thus $n = 9$. The mean is found as follows:

$$\bar{x} = \frac{82+85+91+86+97+92+76+78+22}{9} = \frac{709}{9} \approx 78.778.$$

This is not representative of the class. Notice that only two people scored below 78.778 and seven scored above it. A matter of fact, there were scores of 91, 92, and 97. Why, then, is our mean so low? The grade of 22 caused it. No other student scored any where near as poorly. The score of 22 is adversely affecting the mean. This is known as an *extreme value*. An extreme value is a data value that is either much smaller or much larger than the other data values. When there is an extreme value, the mean is not a good choice for measuring the central value. This brings us to our next measure of central tendency, the *median*.

The Median

When there is an extreme value, the median is often a useful and more representative value for describing the center of sample data. The *median* is the middle value. To calculate the median, we begin be rearranging the data in numerical order from smallest to largest. We will do that now as our last example. Recall that our exam scores were:

82, 85, 91, 86, 97, 92, 76, 78, 22.

We will now rearrange these grades so that they are listed in numerical order from smallest to largest.

22, 76, 78, 82, 85, 86, 91, 92, 97.

The median is the middle value in this list. Since there are nine grades in our data and since nine is an odd number, the median is simply the middle value on our newly arranged list, or 85. That definitely seems much more representative!

What if there is an even number of data values? We begin the same way — rearranging the values in ascending order. Then we find the mean of the middle two values. Let's consider an example now.

Example: Find the median for the following ages of people in a room.

9, 8, 21, 11, 7, 5, 10, 6.

Solution: Do you see why we do not want to find the mean? There is an extreme value of 21 which is much larger than any other value in our data set. We will now find the mean. First, rearrange the data in ascending order.

5, 6, 7, 8, 9, 10, 11, 21.

The sample size is 8, an even number, therefore we find the mean of the middle two values. The middle two values are 8 and 9. We find the mean of these two values (find their sum and divide the sum by 2).

$$\frac{8+9}{2} = \frac{17}{2} = 8.5.$$

The median is 8.5.

Sometimes a score or scores are repeated numerous times. Then, we may want to compute the mode, the last measure of central tendency we will consider here.

The Mode

The *mode* is the value or values that appears the most often in the data set. If no values are repeated, there is no mode.

Example: Find the mode of each data set.

(a) 86, 58, 91, 86, 69, 92, 91, 86, 82, 78
(b) 10, 12, 9, 7, 22, 31, 18
(c) 66, 54, 43, 66, 54, 76, 68, 66, 79, 54, 43
(d) 118, 121, 132, 143, 118, 112, 125, 161, 157, 121, 118, 132, 121, 132, 160
(e) 2, 3, 4, 3, 2, 4, 2, 4, 3

Solution:
(a) The data value 86 appears three times and 91 appears twice. All other data values appear only once. Since 86 appears more often than any other value, 86 is the mode. (Note: 91 is not the mode because it does not appear as often as 86.)
(b) Every data value appears only once. There is NO mode.
(c) The data values 66 and 54 appear three times and 43 appears twice. All other data values appear only once. Since 66 and 54 appear the same number of times and more often than all other data values, the mode is 66 and 54. This is known as a *bimodal distribution* because it has two modes.
(d) The data values 118, 121, and 132 all appear three times each, which is more often than any other value in the data set. Therefore, the mode is 118, 121, and 132. There are three modes, thus this is known as a *trimodal distribution*.
(e) Every data value appears exactly three times. Therefore, no value appears more often than any other values. Thus, there is NO mode.

NOTE: A data set may have no mode, one mode, two modes, three modes, or more than three modes.

> **Small Group Exercise**
>
> Consider the following problem: Mary comes to her professor complaining about her grade in a course. Mary received a C+ and she believes she should have received a B. Her average test grade was a 79. She argues to the professor: "I only missed a B by one point. Why didn't you give me a B?" Mary's test grades were 82, 72, 81, 83, and 77. What is the problem with Mary's argument?

The mean, the median, and the mode are measures of central tendency. They help us to describe the center of a data set or distribution and only the center. Sometimes we also need to describe the spread of values in a distribution. Measures of dispersion enable us to describe the spread and we will turn our attention to them in section 11.6.

Exercises

1. Answer "True" or "False"

   (a) A distribution may have more than one mean.
   (b) A data set must have a median.
   (c) The median is always one of the pieces of data.
   (d) Some data sets have a mode.
   (e) The mode is always an actual piece of data.

2. Compute the mean, median, and mode for each data set below. Explain which measure of central tendency is the most representative for each set of data.

   (a) 83, 98, 92, 85, 92, 81, 88
   (b) 121, 132, 145, 112, 118, 138
   (c) 11, 10, 7, 9, 7, 12, 15, 7, 3, 6
   (d) 165, 163, 172, 181, 176, 165, 168
   (e) 77, 87, 92, 81, 38, 75, 91, 77, 98
   (f) 50, 48, 43, 62, 57, 42, 53, 50, 62, 41
   (g) 28, 18, 18, 21, 26, 31, 33, 38, 41, 35, 27, 25

3. Listed below are the Smith's monthly telephone charges for a six month period. Find the mean and the median telephone charge. Which is more representative and why?

$28.37	$33.45	$59.95
$42.31	$35.78	$30.29

4. Frank has taken six quizzes in his philosophy course. His quiz average is 82. Find the sum of his six quiz grades.

5. Construct a data set consisting of five pieces of data with a mean of 35 such that no two pieces of data are the same.

6. Construct a data set consisting of six pieces of data with a mean, median and mode of 81.

7. Consider the data set: 5, 5, 5, 6, 6, 6, 7, 7, 7. If one 6 is changed to a 5, which of the following will change: mean, median, mode?

8. Consider the data set: 1, 2, 3, 6, 6, 8, 10, 11.

   (a) Find the mean, median, and the mode.
   (b) Change the 10 to a 5. Find the mean, median, and the mode.
   (c) Which of the three measures of central tendency were affected by the change made in part (b)?
   (d) Using the original data set for this problem, change the 11 to 7. Which of the following would change as a result: the mean, the median, the mode?

9. Carl is taking a psychology course. He will take five exams in the course. A mean average of 60 on the five exams is needed to pass the course. He has taken the first four exams and has earned the following grades: 76, 43, 62, 51.

   (a) What is the lowest grade he can earn on the fifth exam and still pass the course?
   (b) Can he earn a C in this course? (He needs a mean average of 70 to earn a C.) If so, what is the lowest grade he can earn on the fifth exam and still earn a C in this course?
   (c) If the lowest of the first four exam grades is dropped, can he earn a C in this course? If so, what is the lowest grade he can earn on the fifth exam and still earn a C in this course?
   (d) If the lowest of the first four exam grades is dropped, what is the highest mean average he can have in this course?

10. Bill has taken five exams so far in his history class. He scored 85, 91, 96, 84, and 88. What is the lowest grade Bill can earn on the sixth (and last exam) so he will have an A average in the course? (An A requires a 90 or better average.)

11. Sally has taken five exams so far in her biology class. She scored 85, 91, 96, 84, and 83. She would like to earn an A in the course. There is only one exam left to take. Her grade will be the average of the six exam grades. (An A requires a 90 or better average.) Can Sally earn an A in the course? If so, what is the lowest grade she can earn on the sixth exam? If not, explain.

11.6 Measures of Dispersion

The measures of central tendency we studied in the previous section help us to describe the center of a distribution or data set. Sometimes we also need to describe the way the values are spread. *Measures of dispersion* enable us to do this. The measures of dispersion we will discuss here are the *range* and the *standard deviation*.

To see why the spread might be important, consider the following two data sets:

DATA SET A: 79, 80, 84, 76, 85, 91, 65
DATA SET B: 51, 100, 91, 48, 95, 83, 92.

Both of these distributions have the same sample mean, 80. Yet, if you look closely, they do not look very similar. The smallest score in data set A is 65, yet the smallest for data set B is much smaller, 51. Data set A has most of the scores near each other. In data set B the scores are widely spread. Although their means are the same, these two distributions are quite different.

The Range

The range is the easiest measure of dispersion to compute. To compute the range one simply finds the difference of the largest and smallest values of the distribution.

> **Fact:** The *range* is computed as follows:
>
> RANGE = largest value – smallest value.

Example: Compute the range for the two data sets given above. Recall that the two distributions were:

DATA SET A: 79, 80, 84, 76, 85, 91, 65
DATA SET B: 51, 100, 91, 48, 95, 83, 92.

Solution:

DATA SET A: The largest data is 91 and the smallest is 65. Thus, the range is computed as follows:

RANGE = 91 – 65 = 26.

DATA SET B: The largest data is 100 and the smallest is 51. Thus, the range is computed as follows:

RANGE = 100 – 51 = 49.

The ranges of these two data sets are not at all similar. Twenty six is a much smaller number than forty nine, especially when you consider that the largest score is only one hundred.

Although the range gives us an idea of how far apart the scores are spread, that is all it tells us. It only gives us information about the spread between the largest and smallest scores and tells us nothing about the scores in between them. Consider for example the following two distributions:

DATA SET C: 40, 50, 48, 100, 91, 95, 90, 88, 60
DATA SET D: 95, 88, 76, 72, 83, 58, 35, 38, 75

The range for both of these sets is 60, (For data set C the range was computed as 100 – 40. For data set D the range was computed as 95 – 35.) Although the ranges are the same, the distributions are quite different. In the first distribution all of the data is either between 40 and 60 inclusive or between 88 and 100 inclusive. There are no scores between 60 and 88. However, in the second distribution, the scores are all spread out and not just on either extreme.

Although the range is easy to compute, it tells us the least of all the measures of dispersion. This is because it only uses two of the distribution's values in its computation, that is the largest and the smallest pieces of data. The other data have no part in the calculation of the range. The next measure of dispersion uses all of the data in its calculation.

The Standard Deviation

The standard deviation is the most commonly used measure of dispersion. It will be computed by applying a series of steps. First, we will give the actual definition.

Definition: The *standard deviation of a sample*, denoted by *s*, is the square root of the *variance*, or squared deviations from the mean. The formula is:

$$s = \sqrt{\frac{\sum_{i=1}^{n}(x_i - \bar{x})^2}{n-1}}.$$

Recall that n is the sample size and that $\bar{x}$ is the sample mean. It is important to note here that this is the standard deviation of the sample. If we are finding the standard deviation of the population the formula changes slightly. The standard deviation would then be denoted by the Greek lowercase letter σ and the denominator of the fraction would be N, the size of the population, and not $n - 1$. Here are the steps to follow in the calculation of the standard deviation of a sample.

STEPS TO COMPUTE THE STANDARD DEVIATION OF A SAMPLE:
1. Compute the mean of the distribution.
2. Make a chart with three columns. In the first column, labeled x, write each of the sample values.
3. In the second column, labeled $x - \bar{x}$, write the difference of each data value and the mean.
4. In the third column, labeled $(x - \bar{x})^2$, record the square of each value in the second column.
5. Find the sum of the third column.
6. Take the sum just found in step 5 and divide it by $n - 1$, (one less than the sample size). This is the value of the variance.
7. Take the square root of the quantity found in step 6.

Example: Find the standard deviation of each samples:

DATA SET A: 79, 80, 84, 76, 85, 91, 65
DATA SET B: 51, 100, 91, 48, 95, 83, 92

Solution:
DATA SET A: We begin by finding the mean of sample A.

$$\bar{x} = \frac{79 + 80 + 84 + 76 + 85 + 91 + 65}{7} = \frac{560}{7} = 80.$$

Now, form Table 11.8.

x	$(x - \bar{x})$	$(x - \bar{x})^2$
79	$79 - 80 = -1$	$(-1)^2 = 1$
80	$80 - 80 = 0$	$(0)^2 = 0$
84	4	16
76	−4	16
85	5	25
91	11	121
65	−15	225
	sum:	404

Table 11.8 Table for the calculation of the standard deviation of Data Set A.

Next, we take the sum we found in column three, 404, and divide it by one less than the sample size. Since this is a sample of size 7, we divide by 7 − 1 or 6. Thus, we see that

$$\text{variance} = \frac{404}{6} = 67.\overline{3}$$

The only thing left to do is to take the square root of the variance and we will have found the standard deviation. Thus,

$$s = \sqrt{67.\overline{3}} \approx 8.2057$$

DATA SET B: We will now find the standard deviation for sample distribution B. Recall, we begin by finding the mean of the sample.

$$\bar{x} = \frac{51 + 100 + 91 + 48 + 95 + 83 + 92}{7} = \frac{560}{7} = 80.$$

Now, we form Table 11.9.

x	$(x - \bar{x})$	$(x - \bar{x})^2$
51	$51 - 80 = -29$	$(-29)^2 = 841$
100	$100 - 80 = 20$	$(20)^2 = 400$
91	11	121
48	−32	1024
95	15	225
83	3	9
92	12	144
	sum:	2764

Table 11.9 Table for the calculation of the standard deviation of Data Set B

Next, divide this sum, 2,764, by one less than the sample size, $n - 1 = 7 - 1 = 6$, and we have the variance.

$$\text{variance} = \frac{2764}{6} = 460.\overline{6}$$

Finally, we take the square root of the variance and we will have found the standard deviation.

$$s = \sqrt{460.\overline{6}} \approx 21.4631$$

Recall that we began this section by considering two data sets that have the same mean yet have a much different spread in their respective data. We just calculated the standard deviation of these two data sets in the previous example. We found the standard deviation of data set A to be approximately 8.2057 and that of data set B to be approximately 21.4631. Notice that the standard deviation we found for data set A is much smaller than what we calculated for data set B. This is because the standard deviation measures how much the data differs from the mean. The larger the difference, the larger the standard deviation. Thus, the results of our calculation of the standard deviations agree with our observation at the beginning of the section. Then we had observed that data set A had most of the scores near each other, unlike data set B. Now we have found that data set A has a much smaller standard deviation than that of B. The data in A do not differ from the mean as much as the data in B.

Exercises

1. Compute the range, variance, and standard deviation of each data set below.
   (a) 121, 132, 145, 112, 118, 138
   (b) 28, 18, 18, 21, 26, 31, 33, 38, 41, 35, 27, 25
   (c) 50, 48, 43, 62, 57, 42, 53, 50, 62, 41
   (d) 11, 10, 7, 9, 7, 12, 15, 7, 3, 6
   (e) 83, 98, 92, 85, 92, 81, 88, 52
   (f) 9, 8, 6, 2, 9, 6, 5, 6, 7
   (g) 1.03, 1.1, 1.2, 1.7, 1.82, 1.41

2. Answer "True" or "False".
   (a) The range is the easiest measure of dispersion to compute.
   (b) The standard deviation is a measure of central tendency.
   (c) One computes the standard deviation of a sample the same way one computes the standard deviation of a population.
   (d) The variance is a measure of dispersion.
   (e) Every piece of data is used in the computation of the range.

3. Compare the ages of the following two classes.

   class A: 33, 38, 28, 24, 18, 29, 30, 42, 49, 29
   class B: 36, 30, 24, 21, 29, 38, 32, 46

4. Compare the test scores of two sections of a philosophy course.

   section 001: 82, 88, 98, 76, 53, 61, 59, 48, 32, 18, 83, 78, 77, 71
   section 002: 81, 92, 76, 71, 69, 85, 84, 48, 53, 68, 66, 65, 58, 12, 62

5. Construct a distribution with seven pieces of data and a range of eighteen.

6. If a data set has a standard deviation of $s = 9.87$, find its variance.

11.7 The Truthfulness of Statistics and Graphs

Statistics are very useful. They can also be just as damaging. They can be misleading. In large part this depends upon the way the statistics are presented. Sometimes statistics that are quoted in advertisements are misleading. The markings on an axis of a graph may be altered to lead the reader to a certain conclusion. Statistics may be quoted without all of the supporting information. That is what we want to examine here. Reader beware!

For example, consider an advertisement for a brand of gum that states "... four out of five dentists recommend" it. How large was the sample? Did they question five dentists and four of them recommended this gum or did they sample 1,000 dentists and find that 800 recommended it? The statistics from a sample size five are not very convincing. I'm sure we could find four dentists to recommend almost any particular item. Finding 800 out of 1,000 is much different, especially if the sample is representative of all dentists. Information has been omitted. Thus, this advertisement is considered statistically misleading. It misleads one to conclude that chewing this brand of gum is highly recommended by dentists.

Besides omitting some information, advertisements may also contain ambiguous words such as "many" or "largest" or "average". We already know that there are several different averages. They are computed differently and result in different values very often. When the word "average" is used, the reader does not know which calculation was used. It may not be the mean with which we are most familiar. For example, an employer may say that the average salary raise was $2,000 while the workers' union may say the average raise was $1,200. They may both be telling the truth. They each calculated a different average. They each used the average that best made their point. Most readers assume the average was calculated as the "mean" because that is the most familiar one.

Suppose a company advertises that they are the largest such company. What exactly do they mean? Do they have the most stores, the largest acreage, the largest number of employees, or the largest profit? The reader doesn't know. However, the reader reads the word largest and associates it with what the reader thinks the company means and may think "larger is better." Just what the advertiser was counting on the reader doing.

Graphs may also be misleading. Consider the two graphs given in Figure 11.17.

384   Chapter 11: **STATISTICS**

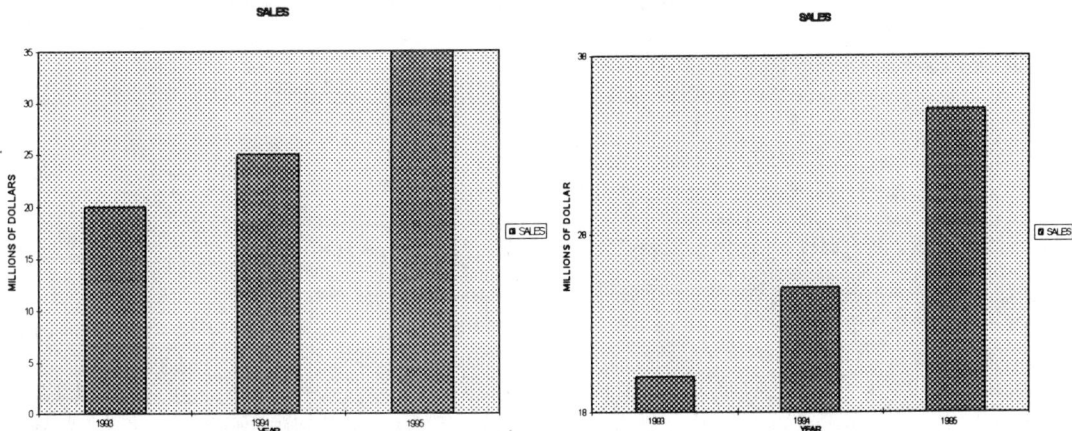

Figure 11.17 Two bar charts depicting the same information

In the first graph of Figure 11.17, there appears to be a modest raise in sales for each year. In the second graph there appears to have been a huge jump in sales from 1993 to 1995. Yet, look at these two graphs more closely. The vertical axes are marked differently. That is why it looks like the company did so much better in the second graph than in the first. In fact in 1993 sales were 20,000,000 and in 1995 sales were 35,000,000 for both graphs. If the company really wants to impress you they may use the second graph. They are not lying with the second graph. They figure that most readers will not read the markings on the vertical axis to notice that it starts at 18,000,000 and not 0.

Let's consider one more pair of graphs. Consider the two graphs given in Figure 11.18.

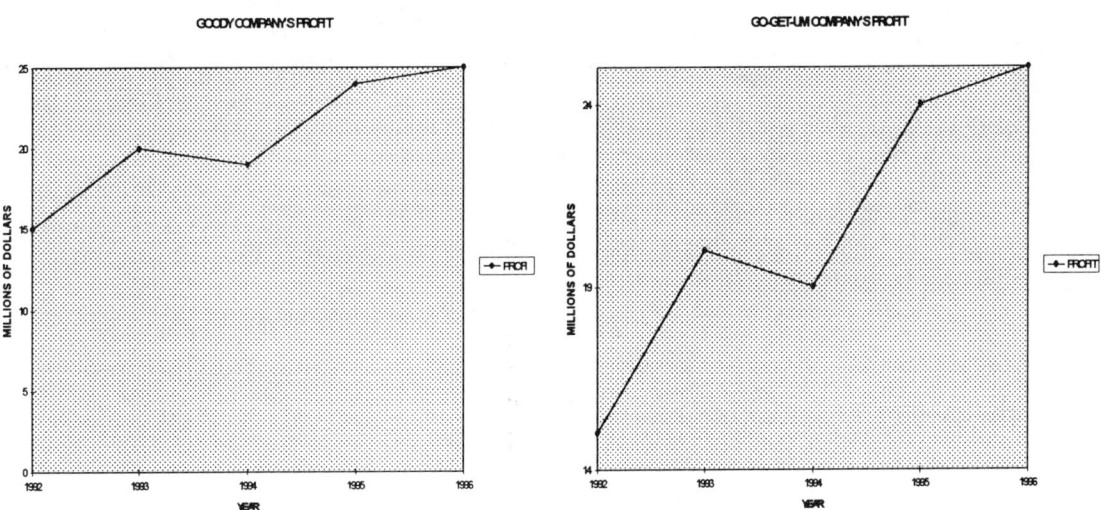

Figure 11.18 Two line graphs depicting the same information

Which company had a greater increase in profits from 1992 to 1996, the first company, Goody Company, or the second company, Go–Get–Um Company? From the two graphs in Figure 11.18, it appears that Goody Company had a modest increase and that Go–Get–Um Company had a really large jump in profits. Actually, they had the same profits for each of the years plotted. In 1992 they both had $15,000,000 in profit and in 1996 they both had $25,000,000. Look closely at the vertical axis's scale. In the first graph it is marked from 0 to 25. But, in the second graph it begins with 14 and not 0.

Again, if a company wants to make its jump in profit look more impressive than another, it could mark the vertical axis as we did in the second graph. It is misleading.

Not all advertisements are misleading, but many are. Some advertisements are misleading but not *statistically misleading*. Do you understand the difference? Reader beware!!!

Exercises

1. Explain what it means for something to be statistically misleading?

2. Find three recent advertisements in the local paper or a magazine that are statistically misleading. Explain in one to three paragraphs just why each advertisement is statistically misleading.

3. Find two graphs from a current local paper or magazine that are statistically misleading. Explain in one to three paragraphs why each is statistically misleading.

4. How can an advertisement be misleading but not statistically misleading? Find an example of such an advertisement.

11.8 Modern Methods

Computer software packages have eased the computation, analysis, and presentation of statistics. What was once done with paper and pencil is now done with the aid of computers. There are numerous software packages on the market just for statistics, such as Minitab, SPSSx, and SAS to name just a few. If you take a statistics course after this you may be introduced to a package such as Minitab. It is relatively easy to use and yet quite powerful.

The graphs created in this chapter were constructed using a computer software package. With the aid of computers, three dimensional graphs can be constructed quite easily. Consider the graphs in Figures 11.19 and 11.20 below.

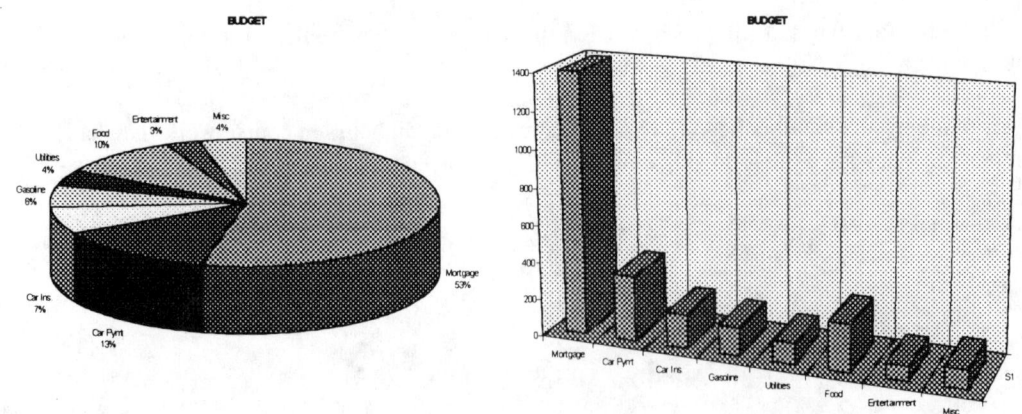

Figure 11.19 A pie chart.   **Figure 11.20 A bar chart.**

Figures 11.19 and 11.20 above where both created using a computer software package. Figure 11.19 is a three–dimensional pie chart and Figure 11.20 is a three–dimensional bar chart. The computer has changed statistical analysis and presentation dramatically.

11.9 Chapter Review

Important Terms to Know

average	intervals	sample
bar chart	linear relationship	sample size
biased	lower class boundary	sample space
bimodal distribution	mean	scatter plot
classes	measures of central tendency	standard deviation
curvilinear relationship	measures of dispersion	statistic
data	median	statistics
dependent variable	midpoint	statistically misleading
descriptive statistics	mode	strata
extreme value	parameter	stratified sample
frequency	pie chart	systematic sample
frequency distribution	population	tally
frequency polygon	quota sample	trimodal distribution
histogram	random sample	upper class boundary
independent variable	range	variance
inferential statistics	raw data	

Important Names to Know

Francis Galton   Carl Friedrich Gauss   William S. Gossett
John Gaunt

Review Questions

1. Describe the four types of samples studied in this chapter. What are the advantages and disadvantages of each?

2. Forty students at a small college were asked how many credit hours in course work they had already completed. They gave the following counts.

```
38   15   63   15   26   42   36   10
32   12   48   12   36   22   41    6
12   36   45   18   32   12   20    9
 8   52   41   27   48   28   18   21
 0   58   36   28   46   33   15   18
```

(a) Create a frequency distribution for this data with the first class interval of $0 - 8$.
(b) Construct a histogram for this data.
(c) Construct a frequency polygon for this data.
(d) In what interval(s) did the most student responses fall?
(e) What is the mode of this distribution?

(f) What is the mean of this distribution?
(g) What is the median of this distribution?
(h) Which measure of central tendency is the most representative of this distribution and why?
(i) What is the range of this distribution?

3.   Construct two sets of data such that all of the following hold:

- both have a mean of 40,
- the range of one set of data is 60 and the range of the other set of data is 35,
- each set of data contain ten pieces of data,
- the median of each set of data is 36.

4.   Explain in words what we mean by the standard deviation of a sample. Give an example to support your explanation. (Do not describe the procedure for finding the standard deviation.)

Solutions, Answers, and Hints to Selected Exercises

CHAPTER 1

Section 1.3 (page 14)

1. (For Table 1.4): The entries in columns 1 and 2 are the same for every truth table containing the two variables p and q. The entries in column 3 are obtained by applying the "working rule for conjunction" to the entries in columns 1 and 2. The entries in column 4 are obtained by applying the "working rule for negation" to the entries in column 3 (that is, by switching them from T to F or from F to T).

Section 1.4 (page 16)

1. To get column 3, negate (that is, reverse the truth values) in column 1. To get column 4, apply the working rule for disjunction to columns 2 and 3.

Section 1.8 (page 24)

1. Construct the truth table shown:

p	q	$p \Rightarrow q$
T	T	T
T	F	F
F	T	T
F	F	T

Remove the shaded rows. Row 2 is removed because a hypothesis (in fact either of them) is false in this row. Row 4 is removed since a hypothesis is false in this row (q is false in this row).
    In the resulting table (consisting of the unshaded rows) we find that the conclusion of this argument may be false. Therefore the argument is invalid.

3. Valid.

CHAPTER 2

Section 2.2 (page 39)

1. (a) This is not a set since it is not well–defined.
    (c) This is a set.
    (e) This is not a set.
2. (a) A has cardinality zero — $n(A) = 0$ — since it has no elements.
    (c) $n(C) = 0$.
    (e) $n(E) = 2$. (E has two members.)
4. (a) $\{a,e,i,o,u,y\}$
    (c) $\{5,-5\}$
5. (a) $\{x|x \text{ is a positive even integer}\}$
    (c) $\{x|x \text{ is the square a n non–zero integer}\}$

Section 2.4 (page 44)

1. (a) $A \cup B = \{1,2,3,5,7,9,11,111113,15,17,19\}$. This is the set of all elements which are in either A or in B or in both.
   (c) $B - A = \{1,9,15\}$. This is the set of all elements which are in B but not in A.
3. (a) A' is the set of books which have less than 500 pages.
   (c) $A \cap B$ is the set of hard–cover books that have 500 pages or more.
   (e) $A \cap B'$ is the set of all soft–cover books with at least 500 pages.
   (g) $(A \cap B)'$ is the complement of the set of hard–cover with 500 pages or more. To be in this set a book needs to be a soft–cover book or have less than 500 pages (or both).

Section 2.5.1 (page 50)

1. (a) These people must be in the "classical music lovers" region but not in the "rock lovers" region. This means that they must be in region II.
   (c) Regions II and III.
   (e) Region IV.
   (g) Regions II, III, and IV.
2. (a) These people are members of C, so they enjoy classical music; they are members of R, so they like rock music; and they are members of W, so they also like rap music. Therefore this region represents the set of all people who like classical, rock, and rap music.
   (c) This is the set of all people who like classical music but not rock music nor rap.
   (e) This is the set of all people who like classical music and rap.
   (g) This is the set of all people rock music, and in addition, they like either classical music or rap, but not both.
   (i) This is the set of all people who like any two of the three types of music listed, but they do not like all three.
   (k) This is the set of all people who like no more than one of the three types of music listed. (They like one type, or none.)
3. (d) (A comment on the last part of the problem.) Since you aren't told whether or not the 45–year old housewife is a college freshman, you don't have enough information to accurately place her "x." You might want to place in on the boundary of two regions to show that she might be a member of either one.

Section 2.5.2 (page 59)

1.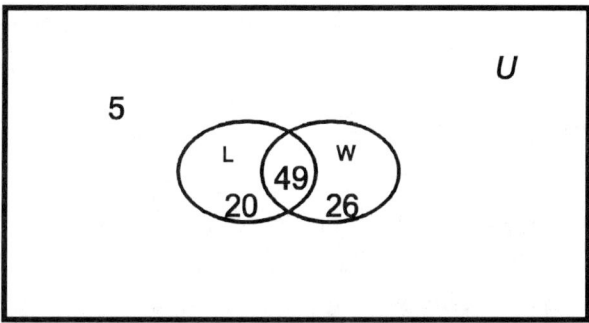

   In the diagram, $L = \{x | x \text{ likes logic puzzles}\}$ and $W = \{x | x \text{ likes word puzzles}\}$.
   (a) 5
   (c) 26
   (e) 95

3. Hint: Make a survey diagram and in each region enter the *percentage* of people polled who fit into that class.

4.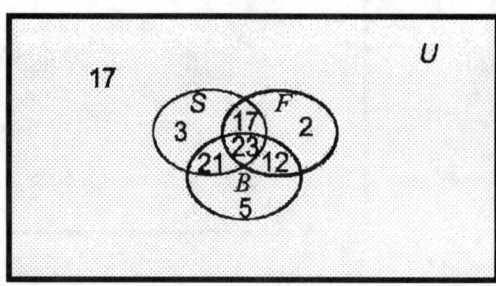

In the diagram, $S = \{x \mid x \text{ would participate in swimming}\}$, $F = \{x \mid x \text{ would participate in finger painting}\}$, $B = \{x \mid x \text{ would participate in basketball}\}$.

(a) 17 (c) 78 (e) 80
(g) 81 (i) 20 (k) 3
(m) 5   (o) 73

Section 2.5.3 (page 66)

1. (a)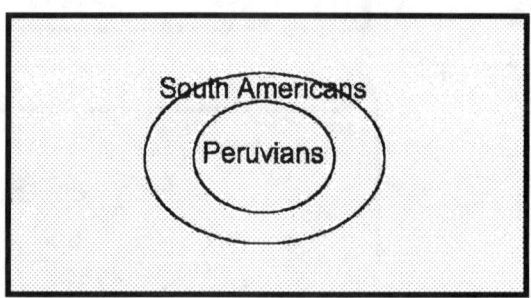

   (c)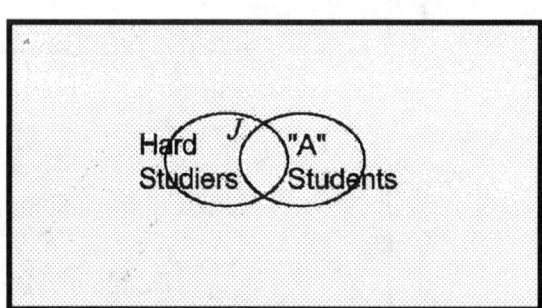

   J represents Jean.

   (e)

(g)

(i)

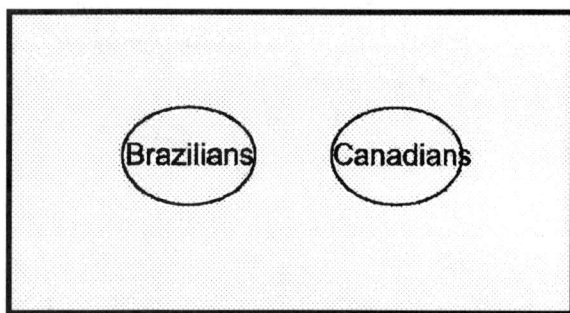

(Other diagrams are possible.)

2. (a)

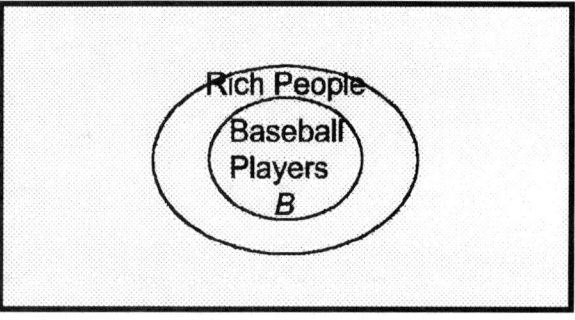

This argument is valid (B for Babe must be in the "rich" circle).

(c)

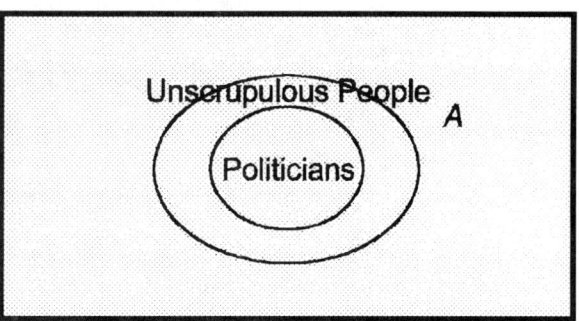

This argument is valid.
    (e) Not valid
    (g) Not valid
    (i) Valid
    (k) Valid.

CHAPTER 3

Section 3.2 (page 79)

1. (a) conditional, $x = -\dfrac{7}{2}$
   (c) conditional, $x = -9$
   (d) contradiction, no solution
   (f) identity, all real numbers
   (g) conditional, $x = -3$
   (j) conditional, $x = 3$
   (l) conditional, $x = 1$
2. (a) 98
   (b) no
   (c) 48
5. (a) yes
   (b) no
7. b,c,d,e

Section 3.3 (page 83)

1. (a) $x < 5$
   (b) $x \leq -\dfrac{31}{6}$
   (d) all real numbers
   (e) $-7 < x \leq -7$
2. Dinner must cost less than $20.67.

Section 3.4 (page 91)

1. $x = 2, y = -3$
3. no solution
5. $x = -37, y = 13$
7. $x = -1, y = 3$
9. all points on the line $10x - 4y = 8$
10. (a) $3,000 in sales; salary of $420.

Section 3.5 (page 93)

1. (a) A; 3, 4, $\dfrac{1}{3}$
   (b) A is 3×3, B is 2×3, C is 3×1, D is 3×4
   (c) no
   (d) yes; C is a column vector
   (e) -3
3. (a) True
   (b) True
   (c) False

Section 3.6 (page 103)

1. A, G, J

4. $\begin{bmatrix} 5 & -1 & -1 \\ 11 & 11 & -4 \\ -13 & 14 & -4 \end{bmatrix}$

6. $\begin{bmatrix} 8 & -3 & -2 \\ 11 & 13 & 0 \\ -19 & 22 & -13 \end{bmatrix}$

8. $\begin{bmatrix} 2 & 2 & 12 \\ -4 & -4 & 2 \\ 6 & -2 & 0 \\ 8 & 0 & 4 \end{bmatrix}$

9. $\begin{bmatrix} \frac{3}{2} & 1 \\ -1 & \frac{1}{2} \\ -\frac{1}{2} & -\frac{3}{2} \end{bmatrix}$

11. $\begin{bmatrix} 0 & -3 & -1 \\ -11 & -8 & 12 \\ 1 & 2 & -15 \end{bmatrix}$

12. $\begin{bmatrix} 14 & 7 \\ -8 & -10 \\ -25 & 23 \end{bmatrix}$

15. $\begin{bmatrix} -33 & 48 & -51 \\ -12 & 8 & -15 \\ 9 & -8 & -7 \\ 0 & 8 & -22 \end{bmatrix}$

17. $\begin{bmatrix} 7 \\ -7 \end{bmatrix}$

21. $\begin{bmatrix} 2 & 4 \\ -1 & 3 \\ 5 & -8 \end{bmatrix}$

23. $\frac{1}{3} \cdot \begin{bmatrix} 1 & 3 \\ -6 & 2 \end{bmatrix}$

Section 3.7 (page 112)

1. $x = 3, y = -4$
3. no solution
5. all points on the line $6x - 24y = 48$
7. $x = -2, y = 5$
9. $x = \dfrac{1}{3}, y = -\dfrac{2}{3}$
11. $x = 13, y = -2$
14. $x = 1, y = 2, z = 4$
16. $x = -1, y = -1, z = 3$

Section 3.8 (page 116)

5. $x = -4, y = -2$
7. $x = \dfrac{1}{2}, y = 8$
9. $-22, -39, -54, 0, -10, -17, -42, -77, -104$
11. Math is fun!

CHAPTER 5

Section 5.2 (page 156)

1. (a) Natural number, whole number, integer, real number, rational number
   (b) Integer, real number, rational number
   (c) Whole number, integer, real number, rational number
   (d) Real number, rational number
   (e) Real number, rational number
   (f) Natural number, whole number, integer, real number, rational number
   (g) Real number, irrational number
   (h) Real number, rational number
   (i) Real number, irrational number
2. (a) True
   (b) True
   (c) False
   (d) False
   (e) True
   (f) True
   (g) True
   (h) True
   (i) False
   (j) False
   (k) False
   (l) False
   (m) True
   (n) True
   (o) True
   (p) True
   (q) False

396 SELECTED ANSWERS

    (r) False
    (s) False
    (t) False

Section 5.3 (page 162)

1. (a) False
   (b) True
   (c) False
   (d) False
   (e) False
   (f) True
   (g) True
   (h) True
   (i) True
   (j) False
3. $\{1, 2, 3, 4, 6, 8, 12, 24\}$
6. 11 and 13, 17 and 19
9. 3, 7, 15, 31, 127
10. (a) $12 = 5 + 7$
    (b) $22 = 11 + 11$
    (d) $13 = 2 + 11$
    (e) $21 = 2 + 19$
11. No

Section 5.4 (page 169)

3. (a) True
   (b) True
   (c) False
4. (a) Divisible by: 2, 3, 4, 6, 8, 9, 12
   (c) Divisible by: 2, 4, 5, 7, 8, 10
   (e) Divisible by: 2, 3, 5, 6, 7, 9, 10
5. (a) $2^2 \cdot 3^2 \cdot 5$
   (c) $2^4 \cdot 3^2 \cdot 7$
   (e) $2 \cdot 3^2 \cdot 5^3$
6. (a) 5,040
   (c) 7,560
   (e) 840
7. (a) 36
   (c) 36
   (e) 28

Section 5.5 (page 173)

1. (a) Set of divisors is $\{1, 2, 3, 6, 9, 18\}$; set of proper divisors is $\{1, 2, 3, 6, 9\}$
   (c) Set of divisors is $\{1, 2, 11, 22\}$; set of proper divisors is $\{1, 2, 11\}$
   (e) Set of divisors is $\{1, 2, 3, 5, 6, 10, 15, 30\}$; set of proper divisors is $\{1, 2, 3, 5, 6, 10, 15\}$

(g) Set of divisors is {1, 2, 4, 8, 16, 32}; set of proper divisors is {1, 2, 4, 8, 16}
3. The set of proper divisors of 16 is {1, 2, 4, 8} and the sum of the proper divisors is $1 + 2 + 4 + 8 = 15 \neq 16$.
5. (a) abundant
   (c) deficient
   (e) abundant
   (g) deficient
6. (a) The sum of the proper divisors of 21, $1 + 3 + 7 = 11$, is not equal to 18.

Section 5.6 (page 176)

1. (a) Add 5 to any term to get the next term.
   (b) Multiply a term by -3 to get the next term.
   (c) Multiply a term by $\dfrac{1}{2}$ to get the next term.
   (f) Compute the terms two at a time by first adding 4 and then adding 1.
2. $-98,415$
3. (a) $a_2 = 8$; $a_5 = 26$
   (b) $a_2 = 6$; $a_5 = -6$
5. (a) 4, 5, 6, 7, 8
   (b) $\dfrac{1}{3}, \dfrac{2}{3}, 1, \dfrac{4}{3}, \dfrac{5}{3}$
   (e) 3, -6, -9, -12, -15

Section 5.7 (page 188)

1. (a) geometric, $r = 4$
   (c) arithmetic, $d = \dfrac{1}{2}$
   (e) geometric, $r = -\dfrac{1}{2}$
   (g) geometric, $r = -3$
   (i) arithmetic, $d = -3$
   (k) arithmetic, $d = -4$
2. (a) 786,432
   (c) $\dfrac{21}{2}$
   (e) $\dfrac{3}{32}$
   (g) $-78,732$
   (i) -33
   (k) -13
3. (a) $-1,048,575$
   (c) $\dfrac{165}{2}$
   (e) $-32,736$

SELECTED ANSWERS

    (g) −59,048

    (i) −195

    (k) 50

5. (a) arithmetic

   (b) Hint: Use the formula from the section for S_n, the sum of the first n terms of an arithmetic sequence.

7. $23,800; $206,500

9. $800; $75,600

Section 5.8 (page 193)

1. (a) 21

   (c) 144

   (e) 377

2.   143

3. (a) 196,418

   (b) 46,368

7. $\dfrac{5}{3} \approx 1.67$

9. (a) yes; 27, 44, 71, 115

   (c) no

Section 5.9 (page 202)

1.   30, 42, 56

2. $1 + 2 + 3 + 4 + 5 = \dfrac{5 \cdot 6}{2}$

6.

15	16	11
10	14	18
17	12	13

9.   See next page.

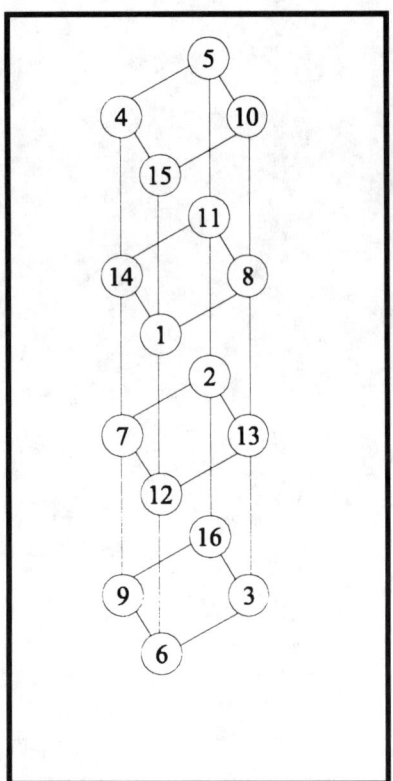

CHAPTER 6

Section 6.3 (page 214)

1. Repetitive system; no base; no placeholder.
2. (a) 3,020
   (c) 200,030
3. (a) ∩∩∩ ||||||||
   (c) 999999 ||

Section 6.4 (page 217)

1. (a) CMLIV
   (c) MMXCVIII
   (e) $\overline{\overline{IX}}$
2. (a) 1,002
   (c) 97
   (e) 344
3. Repetitive system; no base; no placeholder.

Section 6.5 (page 221)

1. (a) 1,201

(c) 381
2. (a) ▽▽▽   <<▽▽▽
    (c) ▽   ▽▽▽   ▽▽

Section 6.6 (page 224)

1. (a) 3,721
   (b) 381

2. (a) $\dfrac{\bullet\bullet}{\bullet\bullet}$

   $\dfrac{\bullet\bullet\bullet}{\bullet\bullet}$

   (c) $\dfrac{\bullet}{\overline{\overline{}}}$

   $\bullet\bullet\bullet$

3. Positional system; basic base of twenty with an auxiliary base of five; yes.

CHAPTER 7

Section 7.3 (page 237)

1. $A^{-1} = B;\ B^{-1} = A$

3. Since $I \times I = I, C \times C = I, D \times D = I$, and $E \times E = I$, the elements $I, C, D,$ and E are all their own inverse.

5. The only such element is 0.

Section 7.4 (page 239)

1. Use row–1 and column–1 (that is, the row and column headed by 1.)

3.
element	inverse
1	1
2	3
3	2
4	1

5. This is an Abelian group. The identity is E, and both O and E are their own inverse.

7. Since the sum of two even numbers is even, **P1** is satisfied. 0 is an even integer, and acts as the identity, so **P3** is satisfied. **P4** is satisfied, the inverse of any element of the set being its opposite. Can you explain why **P2** must be satisfied and why the group must be Abelian?

Section 7.5 (page 247)

2. Hint: Verify the group postulates by using Table 7.12.

3. Hint: Again, use Table 7.12.

CHAPTER 10

Section 10.2 (page 309)

1.   120
3. (a) 140,556
   (b) 124,644
5. (a) 10,000,000
   (b) 544,320
   (c) 604,800
7.   65,536
9.   18
12. (a) 471,744,000
    (c) 208,656,000

Section 10.3 (page 317)

1. (a) 1
   (b) 1
   (c) 362,880
   (d) −12
   (e) 40,320
   (g) 19,958,400
   (i) 5,040
2. (a) 42
   (b) 30,240
   (d) $\dfrac{1}{30}$
3.   5,040
5.   3,306
8.   3,024
11.   5,040

Section 10.4 (page 319)

1. (a) 6
   (b) 28
   (d) 504
   (e) 1
   (g) $\dfrac{7}{4}$
3.   288
5.   210

402 SELECTED ANSWERS

8. 6,511,680
11. 36

Section 10.5 (page 325)

2. 10, 12, 14, 16, 18, 20, 24, 26, 28, 30, 32, 34, 36, 38, 40, 42, 46, 48
4. (a) T,T,H; T,H,T; H,T,T; T,T,T
   (b) T,T,T; H,T,T; T,H,T; T,T,H; H,H,T; H,T,H; T,H,H
   (c) T,T,T; H,T,T; T,H,T; T,T,H

Section 10.6 (page 329)

1. only part a
4. 2,730
5. (a) 840
   (b) 3,024
6. 42,875
7. (a) 20
   (b) 10
8. (a) 20
   (b) 120
   (d) 30,240
9. (a) 58,800
   (b) 51,744

Section 10.7 (page 337)

1. $P(A) = \frac{1}{2}$, $P(B) = \frac{1}{2}$, $P(C) = 0$, $P(D) = \frac{2}{3}$, $P(E) = \frac{1}{3}$, $P(F) = 0$
3. (a) subjective
   (b) classical
   (c) relative frequency
4. $P(A) = \frac{1}{40}$, $P(B) = \frac{2}{5}$, $P(C) = \frac{13}{40}$, $P(D) = \frac{3}{4}$, $P(E) = \frac{1}{4}$
9. (a) $\frac{309}{500}$
   (b) relative frequency
   (c) $\frac{191}{500}$
10. (a) $\frac{221}{1200}$
    (b) $\frac{293}{1200}$
    (c) $\frac{41}{240}$

Section 10.8 (page 343)

1. 0.313
2. (a) $\frac{1}{9}$
   (b) 1
   (c) $\frac{8}{9}$
   (d) $\frac{5}{18}$
   (e) 0
   (f) $\frac{1}{9}$
4. only part b
5. (a) $\frac{1}{4}$
   (b) $\frac{1}{6}$
   (c) 1
6. only part b
8. (a) 0.1
   (b) 0.75
   (c) 0.85
   (d) 0.9
   (e) 0.42
9. (a) $\frac{5}{12}$
   (b) $\frac{7}{10}$
   (c) $\frac{3}{4}$

Section 10.9 (page 348)

1. (a) 1 : 5
   (b) 2 : 1
   (c) 1 : 1
   (d) 1 : 2
3. 9 : 41
5. $\frac{3}{11}$
7. (a) 1 : 2
   (b) 2 : 1

404 SELECTED ANSWERS

(c) $\dfrac{2}{3}$

8. $\dfrac{5}{13}$

CHAPTER 11

Section 11.2 (page 355)

1. (a) False
   (b) True
   (c) False
   (d) False

Section 11.3 (page 357)

1. systematic sampling
3. random sampling
5. random sampling
7. You do not want every nth item chosen to have been constructed from the same group.

Section 11.4 (page 369)

1. (a) Engineering
   (b) 1,000 in Business, 810 in Liberal Arts, 571 in Education, 1,524 in Engineering, 381 in Architecture, 476 in other degrees
3. (a)

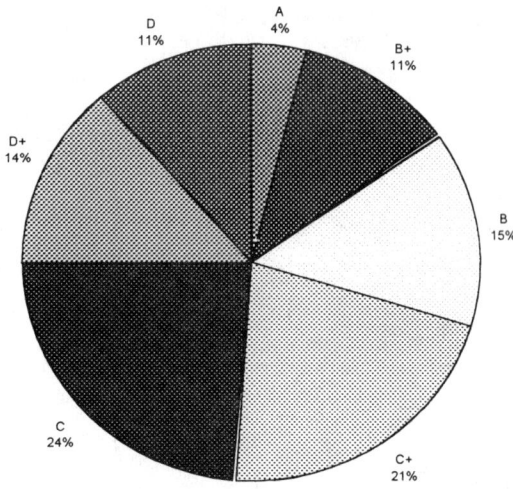

History Class Grade Distribution

(b)

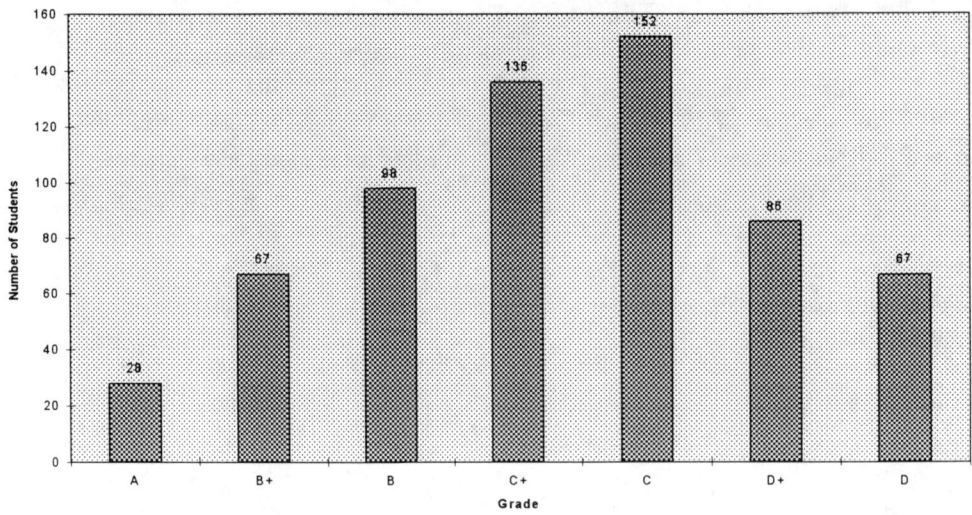

4. (a) heart disease
   (b) 1,679,260
   (c) 199,390
8. (a) curvilinear
   (b) no relationship
   (c) linear
   (d) linear
9. (a) age
   (b) weight
   (c)

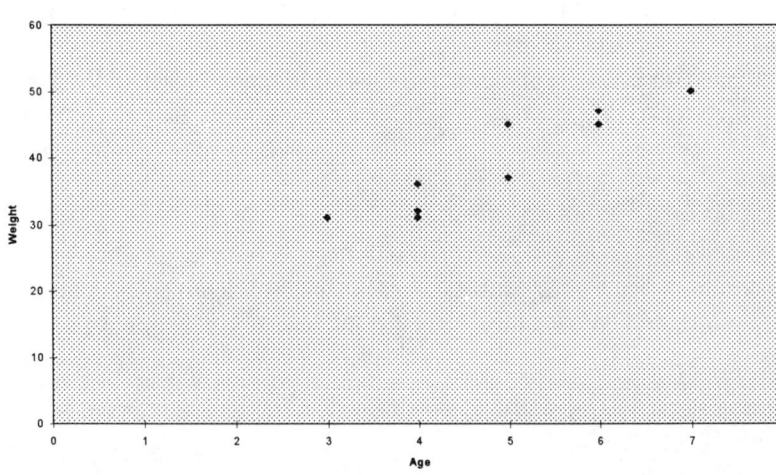

   (d) linear relationship

Section 11.5 (page 377)

1. (a) False
   (b) True

406 SELECTED ANSWERS

      (c) False
      (d) True
      (e) True

2. (a) mean ≈ 88.43; median $= 88$; mode $= 92$. The mean and the median are the most representative.
      (c) mean $= 8.7$; median $= 8$; mode $= 7$. The mean is the most representative.
      (e) mean ≈ 79.6; median $= 81$; mode $= 77$. The median is the most representative.
      (g) mean ≈ 28.4; median $= 27.5$; mode $= 18$. The median is the most representative.

4.   492

7.   mean and mode

8. (a) mean $= 5.875$; median $= 6$; mode $= 6$.
      (b) mean $= 5.25$; median $= 5.5$; mode $= 6$.
      (c) mean and median
      (d) mean

10.   96

Section 11.6 (page 382)

1. (a) range $= 33$; variance $= 150$; standard deviation ≈ 12.25
      (c) range $= 21$; variance ≈ 46.2; standard deviation ≈ 6.8
      (e) range $= 45$; variance ≈ 187.4; standard deviation ≈ 13.7
      (g) range $= 0.81$; variance $= 0.10964$; standard deviation ≈ 0.33

2. (a) True
      (b) False
      (c) False
      (d) True
      (e) False

3.   The mean age of both classes is the same, 32. However, the median age of each class is different. The median age of Class A is 29.5 but the median age of Class B is 31. Class B has no modal age, but the modal age of Class A is 29. The youngest and oldest person are both in Class A. The range of ages of Class A is 31, whereas the range of ages of Class B is only 25. Thus, the ages in Class A have a larger spread than those of Class B. The standard deviation of the ages in Class A is approximately 8.97 and the standard deviation of the ages in Class B is approximately 7.98.

6.   97.4169

Section 11.7 (page 385)

1. Something is statistically misleading when it cites statistics in a deliberately deceptive way either by omitting information, using vague words, or modifying the axes of a graph in a way that might be misunderstood by the reader.

Index

addition method, 86, 87, 89
abacus, 244, 245
Abel, Neils Henrik, 233, 237
Abelian Group, 237–239, 241, 232, 247, 248, 250
absolute geometry, 289
abundant, 172
Ada, Countess of Lovelace, 257
addition modulo five, 238, 240
additive system of numeration, 211, 215
Ahmes Papyrus, 215
Aiken, Howard, 258
aleph–null, 38, 68
amicable, 172, 173
analog computer, 254, 256, 260, 274
analytic geometry, 279, 283, 284, 287, 289
Analytical Engine, 257
Anderson, Goran, 147
antecedent, 14
Apple II, 270
Aristotle, 3, 4, 30
arithmetic sequence, 177–183
artificial intelligence, 259, 260, 266, 267, 272
associative law, 235, 237, 239, 240, 250
Atansoff, John, 258
average, 354, 355, 373, 377, 383
avoidance game, 144, 146
axiom, 280, 281, 283, 289–291
axis of symmetry, 244, 245

Babbage, Charles, 257–259, 261
bar chart, 360, 361, 384, 385
bar code reader, 261
Bardeen, J., 259
base, 210–212, 216, 219, 222, 223, 226

Bell, Eric Temple, 231
Bernoulli, Jacques, 307
biased, 355, 356, 357
bimodal distribution, 376
binary number system, 257, 248, 263
biquadratic equation, 232
Bissaker, Robert, 256
Blackett, P.M.S., 123
Bolyai, Janos, 277, 290–294
Boole, George, 4, 256
Boolean Algebra, 258
Borel, Emile, 125
Bouchon, Basil, 257
break–even point, 91
Brunelleschi, Filippo, 288

Cantor, Georg, 35, 36, 38, 67, 68
Cardano, Girolamo, 232, 307
cardinality, 38
Carroll diagram, 45
Carroll, Lewis, 45
Cartesian coordinates, 283, 284, 288
catastrophe theory, 295
Cayley, Arthur, 74, 92, 234
CD–ROM, 261, 262, 270
chaos theory, 295
Chu Shih–chieh, 196
ciphered system, 212
classes, 363, 364
classical probability, 333–336, 340, 343, 346
clerical applications, 264, 266, 267, 269
clock arithmetic, 241
closure, 235, 238
coefficient, 232

Cole, Frank, 161
column vector, 93, 98, 99, 102, 113, 115, 116
combination, 307, 310, 311, 313–317, 325, 327, 330, 349
combinatorics, 307
common difference, 177, 178
common ratio, 182, 183, 186
commutative group see Abelian group
commutative law, 234, 237
commutative, 95, 98
complement, 34, 43, 340
complex numbers, 232
composite, 155, 158, 165
compound inequality, 82
compound probability, 341, 342
computer chip, 259, 260, 263
computer generation, 258–260, 275
computer simulation, 126, 140, 142, 264, 268, 269, 271
conclusion, 3, 4, 14, 17, 20
conditional equation, 14, 77, 79
conflicting interests, 141, 143
congruent, 282
conjecture, 161
conjunction, 5–8
consequent, 14
consistent system, 84, 87
constraint, 128–134, 137–139
contradiction, 16, 77, 79, 83
contrapositive, 17, 18
converse, 17, 18
coordinate system, 283, 284, 288
corner point rule, 134, 135, 150
counting trees, 313, 320
CPU, 263
crazy loop, 26
Cretan Paradox, 5
cryptography, 114–117
cubic equation, 232, 233
curvilinear relationship, 369

da Vinci, Leonardo, 288
Dantzig, George, 124, 138
data base management, 265, 270, 272
data processing, 264–266, 269, 275
data storage device, 257, 258, 271
data, 353–359, 363–369, 375, 376, 378–382
De Moivre, Abraham, 307
De Morgan, Augustus, 4
deficient, 172
degree, 232, 233, 237, 250

demand curve, 284, 285
dependent system, 89, 110
dependent variable, 367
Desargues, Girard, 287
Descartes, Rene, 74, 279, 283, 287, 289
descriptive statistics, 358
desktop computer, 261, 263, 270, 271
Difference Engine, 257
digit, 163, 164
digital computer, 253, 254, 257, 260, 274
dimension, 93–98
Diophantus, 73, 74
direct reasoning, 22, 23
disc drive, 261–263, 267
disjoint sets, 42, 45, 46
disjunction, 9, 25
divisible, 157, 163, 164
divisor, 157, 162, 170, 171, 172
Dodgson, Charles – see Carroll, Lewis
Domineering, 147, 148
Donatello, 288
double inequality, 82
drawboy, 257
duplicate item, 322, 328
Durer, Albrecht, 288

Eckert, J. Presper, 259, 263, 264
Einstein, Albert, 280, 293
electromechanical computer, 258, 259
electronic computer, 253, 257, 258, 260, 263, 269, 271
element, 36–43, 46, 47, 52–54, 68, 92, 94, 96
Elements, 279, 281, 289
empirical probability, 335
empty set, 37, 42, 46, 47, 63, 64
ENIAC, 259, 263
Epimenides' Paradox, 5
equal sets, 40, 41
equation, 73–119
Eratosthenes, 159
Euclid, 155, 156, 158, 168, 279–282, 289–291, 293, 294
Euclidean geometry, 279–282, 290, 292–295, 301
Euler circle, 45, 62, 63, 64, 66
Euler, Leonhard, 45, 62–66, 69, 155, 171
even, 155, 157, 158, 161, 164, 171
event, 315, 331–336, 339–343, 345–347, 350
experiment, 331, 335, 336
expert system, 272
extreme value, 375

factor, 157, 158, 165–168, 170
factorial, 310, 311, 320
fallacy, 3, 4, 30
feasible region, 134, 135, 137–139
Fermat, Pierre de, 156, 161, 279, 283
Ferrari, Ludovico, 232
Fibbonacci – see Leonardo of Pisa
Fibonacci number, 191–195, 205
Fibonacci sequence, 155, 175, 189, 191, 192, 194, 195
finite set, 55, 58, 68, 69
forecasting, 123, 124, 140
fractal geometry, 280, 295, 296, 299–303
frequency distribution, 363–366
frequency polygon, 365–367
frequency, 362–364
friendly, 172, 173
Frogs and Toads, 149, 150
Fundamental Counting Principle, 308, 309, 325, 326, 350

Galileo, 67
Galileo's paradox, 67, 68
Galois Theory, 233
Galois, Evariste, 233, 250
Galton, Francis, 354
game theory, 123–126, 141–150
Gardner, Martin, 145, 147
Gaunt, John, 353
Gauss, Carl Freidrich, 155, 189, 292, 353
geometric sequence, 177, 182, 184, 186
geometry, 277–304
Gödel, Kurt, 25, 26
Goldbach, Christian, 161, 204
golden number, 193
Gossett, William, 353
graph theory, 280
graph, 283
greatest common factor, 168
group postulates, 235, 247, 249
group, 231–256
grouping system, 211, 215

hieratic, 215
histogram, 362–365
Hoff, Ted, 259
Hofstadter, Douglas, 26, 28, 29
Hofstadter's Law, 30
Hollerith card, 258
Hollerith, Herman, 258
hyperbolic geometry, 290, 293, 294

hypothesis, 14, 17

identity matrix, 92–94, 103, 113
identity, 77, 83, 90, 235–241, 250
incomplete information, 141–143
Incompleteness Theorem, 24, 25
inconsistent system, 88, 111
independent variable, 367
independent, 342, 343
indirect reasoning, 24
inequality, 80–83, 118
inferential statistics, 354, 358
infinite set, 35, 38, 67–69
input devices, 258, 261, 262
integers, 155
integrated circuit, 259
International Business Machines, 258
interplay of logic and chance, 141, 143
intersection, 41, 42, 49, 50
intervals, 363, 364
inverse, 17, 18, 112–117, 235, 236, 238–241, 247
invertible, 113, 115
irrational numbers, 156
isomorphic group, 247, 249, 250

Jacquard attachment, 257
Jacquard, Joseph–Marie, 257
Jordan, Camile, 233
joystick, 261

keyboard, 261, 270
Kolmogorov, A. N., 307

Laplace, Pierre Simon de, 307
Law of Large Numbers, 307, 336, 338
learning program, 268
least common multiple, 167
Leibniz, Gottfried Wilhelm von, 4, 256, 257, 279
Leonardo of Pisa, 189
Liar Paradox, 5, 25–28
line, 281, 287, 291–293
linear equation, 73–119, 232
linear programming, 123, 124, 126–139, 150
linear relationship, 368
Lobachevski, Nicolai Ivanovich, 292
logarithm, 255, 256, 260
logical connective, 5, 6, 8, 9
logical equivalence, 12
lower class boundary, 364

magic number, 196–198, 200

magic square, 194, 196–200
magic, 173
main–frame, 259, 263, 270, 271, 273
main diagonal, 92–94
Mandelbrot, Benoit, 295, 300–302
Mark I, 258, 259
material implication, 9, 14, 15, 17, 30
mathematical logic, 3
matrices, 92–119
matrix, 92–119
Mauchly, John W., 259, 263, 264
mean, 373–378, 380–383
measures of central tendency, 358, 373–378
measures of dispersion, 358, 373,377–383
median, 373, 375–378
membership, 39, 40
Mersenne prime, 161, 171
Mersenne, Father Marin, 161
micro–miniaturization, 260, 271
microcomputer, 270
microprocessor, 259
midpoint, 364, 366
minicomputer, 270
mode, 373, 376–378
model, 125–128, 141, 142, 151
modem, 261, 262, 270
modified positonal system, 217
Mohammed ibn–Musa al–Khwarizmi, 73
Morgenstern, Oskar, 125, 141–143, 150
mouse, 261
multiple, 157, 159, 160, 167, 200
multiplication modulo five, 240, 241
multiplication rule, 343
multiplicative system, 211, 213
multiplier, 211
mutually exclusive, 342

Napier, John, 255
Napier's bones, 255
Napier's rods, 255
natural numbers, 155, 156, 158
negation, 9, 10, 29
network theory, 280
network, 271, 272, 275
neural network, 272
Newton, Isaac, 279
Nicomachus of Gerasa, 194
non–Euclidean geometry, 279, 280, 289–291, 293–295
nonrepeating, 156
nonsingular, 113
nonterminating, 156

null set, 37
number theory, 153–204
number, 209–227
numeral, 209–227
numeration system, 209
numerical applications, 264, 266

objective function, 128, 129, 134, 137
odd number, 157, 161
odds, 307, 308, 345, 346, 347, 350
one–to–one correspondence, 68
operations research, 123–141, 150
optical scanner, 261
optimization problem, 124
order, 93
origin, 284
outcome, 331–335, 339–342, 345–347
output devices, 263

palindromic number, 197, 198
paradox, 5, 25–30
parallel processing, 271
parameter, 354, 355, 357
Pascal, Blaise, 155, 195, 196, 256, 257, 287
Pascal's triangle, 155, 195, 198, 318–320
pattern recognition, 264, 266–269, 272, 275
perfect number, 170, 171, 172
permutation, 307, 310–316, 321, 325–327, 328, 330
personal computer, 259, 261, 262, 264, 270, 274
perspective, 288, 289
pie chart, 358–360, 385
placeholder, 213, 216, 219, 222–226
Plato, 155
polynomial equation, 231–233, 250
population, 354–357
positional system, 212, 213, 223, 227
postulate, 280–283, 289–293
premise, 4
prime factorization, 165, 167
prime number, 157–161, 165, 166, 171, 204
probability, 307–350
product mix, 138
projective geometry, 279, 287–289, 304
proper divisor, 170–172
proposition, 5
pseudosphere, 293
Pythagoras, 279
Pythagorean theorem, 279, 282

quadratic equation, 232

quartic equation, 232
Quetelet, Adolphe, 307
queuing theory, 123, 124, 139–141
quintic equation, 233
quota sample, 355, 356

RAM, 262, 263
random sample, 356
range, 378, 379
rational numbers, 156
raw data, 354, 355, 359, 363
real numbers, 156
rectangular coordinates, 283
reducio ad absurdum, 290
relative frequency, 333, 335, 336
relative positional system, 219, 222
repetitive system, 211, 215
reverse tic–tac–toe, 143, 144, 146
Rhind Papyrus, 215
Riemann, Bernhard, 292–294
Rosetta Stone, 214
roster method, 37, 41, 42, 43
row vector, 93, 98
Russell, Bertrand, 25

SABRE, 265, 270
Saccheri, Girolamo, 290, 291, 294
sample size, 357, 373, 376, 380, 381
sample space, 354
sample, 354–357, 364–367, 373–375, 380, 383
scalar, 95
scatter plot, 367, 369
scheduling problem, 124, 138
search patterns, 123, 124
self–reference, 25–27
self–similarity, 295, 296, 299, 301, 303
sequence, 155, 173–195, 204
set, 35–69
set–builder notation, 37–39
set difference, 43
Shannon, Claude, 268
Shockley, Robert, 269
sieve of Eratosthenes, 159, 160
Sim, 145–149
Simmons, Gustavus J., 145, 146
simplex method, 124, 138
singular, 113
sinking funds, 123, 140, 141
slide rule, 265, 266
software, 269, 268, 271
solution by radicals, 232

solution, 73, 74
spreadsheet, 264, 270
SPSS, 264
square matrix, 92, 113
standard deviation, 378, 380
statement, 5–12, 17–26
statistic, 355, 357
statistically misleading, 383, 385
statistics, 353–387
Stepped Reckonner, 257
storage devices, 257–263, 270, 271
strata, 356
strategy, 125, 141–145, 150
stratified sample, 356, 357
subjective probability, 333, 337
subset, 39, 40, 45, 62–64, 67, 68
substitution method, 84, 85
subtraction principle, 217
supply curve, 284, 285
survey diagram, 52, 53, 56, 69
syllogism, 4, 20
symmetry of an equilateral triangle, 248, 249
symmetry of the square, 243–245
symmetry, 295, 296
systematic sample, 356

tally, 364, 366
tangled hierarchy, 26
Tartaglia, Niccolo, 232
tautology, 16
term, 174–195
theorem, 161, 279–283, 289, 290, 294, 295
theory of relativity, 280, 293, 295
time sharing, 259
topology, 280
transistor, 259
transportation problem, 124, 138
trimodal distribution, 376
truth table, 4, 7, 8, 10–24, 30
Turing test, 267–269
Turing, Alan, 268
twin primes, 160

undefined terms, 281, 283, 291, 292
union, 41–43, 50
UNIVAC, 259, 260, 264
universal sets, 38, 43, 44, 48, 51
upper class boundary, 364

vacuum tube, 259
valid argument, 3, 4, 20–25, 30

variance, 380–382
vector, 93, 98, 113, 115
Venn diagram, 35, 45–49, 50, 62, 69
Venn, John, 45, 69
virtual reality, 268
VLSI, 260
volatile memory, 262
von Koch snowflake, 296, 299
von Neumann, John, 125, 141–143, 150, 259

well–defined, 36
Whitehead, Alfred North, 25
whole numbers, 155–157
Wiles, Andrew, 161
Wittgenstein, Ludwig, 3, 25, 36
word processing program, 262, 264, 266, 267, 270, 271

Preface

Every book has its pre-history and so has this one. The work on my doctoral dissertation *Solomonic State Officials* (Lund, 1971) led me to see that the problems connected with the legal position of the king and with the royal jurisdiction in ancient Israel deserve to be investigated. Having devoted some time to a projected monograph on this subject (cf. ZAW 84/1972, 292) I found it necessary to go into the question of the civil and sacral legitimation of the king during the period of the early monarchy. I originally planned a brief chapter on this question, mainly in the form of a discussion of the pertinent research. I soon found, however, that the problem would have to be made the subject of an investigation on its own merits. The present volume constitutes the result of this undertaking. I pray that the truth may be served and not hindered by this work, devoted as it is to a theme that is one of the most central in the Old Testament.

The work on this book was begun in the spring semester of 1973 and was completed in the spring semester of 1976. Ch. 1–3 have been revised to profit by the most recent literature (notably the works by Görg and Veijola from 1975). The remaining chapters have only been updated by means of additional references in the notes.

The work has been carried out during my term of appointment as a docent at the University of Lund. The Old Testament Research Seminar at Lund under the chairmanship of Professor *Gillis Gerleman* and, during his sabbatical leave in the autumn of 1975, of Dr *Bo Johnson* has proved a stimulating milieu for research work. The original and challenging research of my colleagues has been an incentive to my own efforts. I extend my sincere thanks to all of them for criticism and inspiration. Professor Gerleman has kindly allowed me to use two of his forthcoming papers. I thank Dr *Sam. Nyström* for private discussions.

My thanks are also due to a number of other scholars and friends. I have had the benefit of the experienced instruction and advice of Professor *Jørgen Læssøe* (Copenhagen) in matters of Assyriology. He has read the section of my work devoted to a discussion of Akkadian texts on anointing (ch. 10.3.1). Other parts of my work were read and criticized by Professor *Aelred Cody* (O.S.B., Rome), Dr *Jakob Grønbæk* (Copenhagen) and Dr *Bernard Jackson* (Edinburgh). I also wish to thank Professor *Helmer Ringgren* (Upsala) for his kindness in sending me the proofs of his forthcoming TWAT article on *ḥayā* and Professor *Gösta Vitestam* (Lund) for a discussion in his Semitic Research Seminar of my treatment of 2 S 23,1–7.

I am greatly indebted to Miss *Eva Strömberg*, research assistant for Old Testament studies at Lund. She took on the laborious task of checking all the references in the manuscript except for some minor sections that I had already personally checked. She also prepared the bibliography for publication. I am also indebted to Mr *Bertil Evertsson*, Mrs *Margaret Greenwood Petersson*, Mrs *Britta Hyllstam* and Mr *Sixten Hyllstam* who have read the proofs.

It was necessary, of course, to consult native Englishmen to correct my English. Thus Mrs *Barbara Lindberg* looked at ch. 6-8 and 11-12 and Mr *Kevin Benn* at ch. 10. Most of the work, however, has been looked through by Mrs *Margaret Greenwood Petersson* who also subjected the whole of my manuscript to a final inspection. I am greatly indebted to her for the most unselfish way in which she has spent time and skill in making my English style clearer.

I also wish to thank the staff of Messrs. *Wallin & Dalholm* and of *Lunds Fotosätteri* for their co-operation and skill and for having mastered the considerable typographical problems involved with such success. The passages in Greek and Hebrew script were typed for the offset printing by Mrs *Birgit Ödvall*. The publication of my work was made possible by a substantial grant from *Statens Humanistiska Forskningsråd*.

Finally I must put on record the constant, patient encouragement of my wife, *Solvi*. She means more to my research work than I am able to express. To her this book is dedicated.

Lund, June 1976
Tryggve N.D. Mettinger

Contents

(N.B. A summary appears at the end of each chapter.)

Preface	7
Introduction	13

PART ONE
The Sources

Introduction: The Deuteronomistic Historical Work	19
Literature and Political Propaganda	22
Ch. 1. The Succession Narrative	27-32
Ch. 2. The History of David's Rise to Power	33-47

1. The Opening of the HDR 33
2. Abigail's Speech 35
3. *Tendenz*, Purpose and Date 38
4. The Conclusion of the HDR 41
   1. 2 S 5,17-25 and 6,1-23 42
   2. The Redactional Position of the Prophecy of Nathan 42
      1. The Language of the Prophecy of Nathan 43
      2. The Contents and the HDR 43
      3. Previous Allusions to David's Future Kingship 44

Ch. 3. The Prophecy of Nathan (2 S 7,1-29)	48-63

1. Survey of Research 48
2. The Deuteronomistic Layer 51
3. The Solomonic Document and Its Dynastic Redaction 52
4. Characteristic Features. Purpose and Date 56
   1. Verse 13 and the Reference to the Temple 56
   2. Verse 16: A "House" for David or for Solomon? 57
   3. Questions of Date 60
   4. Royal Ideology: Son of God and *nagîd* 61

Ch. 4. Saul's Anointing as Nagid (1 S 9,1 – 10,16)	64-79

1. Tensions and Patterning (*Berufungsschema*) 64
2. Saul and the Spirit 68
3. The Promise of Kingship 70
4. The Contents of the Two Layers 72
5. *Sitz im Leben* and Date 74

Ch. 5. The Traditions Concerning Saul's Kingship (1 S ch. 8–12)   80-98

1. The Deuteronomistic Framework   80
2. The Tradition in 1 S 11,1-15   83
    1. Editorial Links   83
    2. Historical *Quaestiones Facti*   85
3. The Tradition in 1 S 10,17-27   87
    1. Samuel as the Last Saviour   88
    2. Samuel as a Representative of Genuine Yahwism   92

Ch. 6. The Royal Psalms   99-105

1. The Royal Psalms. A Delimitation   99
2. The Question of Court Style   102

PART TWO
The Civil Legitimation of the King

Introduction   107

Ch. 7. The Participation of the Elders and the Assembly at the Royal Investitures   111-130

1. The Popular Assembly in Northern Israel   111
    1. Passages Concerning Saul   111
    2. David and "the Elders of Israel"   114
    3. The Assembly at Shechem. The Investitures of Omri and Jehu   115
2. The Popular Assembly in Judah   118
    1. From David to Solomon   118
        1. David   118
        2. Adonijah and Solomon   119
    2. The "Divided Monarchy". The Judaean ʽăm haʼaræṣ   124

Ch. 8. Acclamation and the Royal Covenant   131-150

1. The Acclamation: An Elliptic Oath   131
2. The Royal Covenant   137
    1. The Davidic Kings and the Northern Tribes   138
    2. The Question of a Royal Covenant in Judah   141
        1. The Investiture of Joash   142
        2. Leadership and Covenant in the Period before David   145

PART THREE
The Sacral Legitimation of the King

Ch. 9. The Divine Designation and the Problem of Nagid — 151-184

1. Designation as *nagîd*. The Biblical Material. Survey of Research. 152
2. A Secular Use of the Term *nagîd* 158
3. The Theologization. Its Background and Purpose 162
   1. The Date of the Theologization 162
   2. The Place and Purpose of the Theologization 167
4. Further Semantic Aspects: Syntagmatic and Paradigmatic Relations 171
5. The Problem of Earlier Conceptions of Divine Designation 174
6. Saul's Designation in 1 S 10,17-27 179

Ch. 10. The Anointing of the King — 185-232

1. *Status Quaestionis*. Survey of the Evidence 185
2. The Historical Development 194
   1. Saul and the Northern Kingdom 194
   2. David and Solomon. The Term *mašîᵃḥ* 198
   3. The "Divine" Anointings 203
3. The Efficacity of the Rite 208
   1. Oil and Contractual Relations in the Ancient Near East 212
      1. Oil as a Diplomatic Symbol 212
      2. Anointing in Business Contracts 216
      3. Anointing as a Nuptial Rite 217
      4. The "Anointing of Liberation" 221
   2. Oil and Contractual Relations in Ancient Israel 224

Ch. 11. The Royal Charisma — 233-253

1. The Martial Charisma of Saul 234
2. The "Hearing Heart" of Solomon 238
3. David and the Spirit in 1 S 16,13 246
4. The Royal Charisma in Other Texts 248

Ch. 12. Divine Sonship and the Davidic Covenant — 254-293

1. The Lyrical Echoes of the Prophecy of Nathan 254
   (Ps 89; Ps 132; 2 S 23,1-7; Ps 2 and 110)
2. The Divine Sonship of the King 259
   1. Divine Sonship and Divine Kingship 259
      (2 S ch. 7; Ps 2; Ps 89; Ps 110)
   2. The *Interpretatio Israelitica* 265
      1. Adoption and Performatives 265
      2. Democratization and *nagîd* 267
      3. King, *Urmensch* and Image of God 268

3. The Davidic Covenant 275
   1. The Conditioning of the Promise in the Dtr Redaction 276
      1. The Conditional Series (DtrN and Ps 132) 276
      2. The Unconditional Series (Ps 89; 2 S 23,5; Jer 33,20-21) 278
      3. The Use of the Word *b^{e}rît* 282
   2. The Davidic Covenant in the Pre-Exilic Period 283
      1. The Royal Anointing 283
      2. The Prophecy of Nathan 284
      3. The Terms *ḥoq* and *ʿedût* (Ps 2,7; 2 R 11,12) 286
      4. The King and the Law 289

Concluding Remarks — 294-297

Excurses: — 298-308
1. The Dualism of Israel 298
2. Covenant, Contract and *b^{e}rît* 301
3. The Problem of a Cultic Renewal of Kingship 304

Survey: The Development of the Prose Traditions — 309

Abbreviations. Technical Remarks — 310

Bibliography — 312-332

Indexes — 333 ff.
1. Biblical and Jewish Sources 333
2. Ancient Near Eastern Sources 337
3. Oriental Words 338
4. General Index 340

Introduction

Theories are nets: only he who casts will catch.

(Hypothesen sind Netze, nur der wird fangen, der auswirft.)

Novalis

(1) *The Task and its Limits.* – There is no danger that the informed reader will underestimate the importance of the subject matter of this volume. Israelite kingship has a bearing on the entire political, religious and cultural development of ancient Israel. As is well known the problems raised by this institution have given rise to an extensive literature which cannot be surveyed here.[1] Suffice to say that there is a dichotomy between those scholars who base their views primarily on the Psalms and the Prophets and who emphasize the sacral character of Israelite kingship,[2] and those who lay more stress on the prose material of the historical books and stress the secular aspects of the institution.[3]

This previous research provides the background, the landscape against which any attempt to design a new understanding of Israelite kingship must be silhouetted. However, the scientific atmosphere of the seventies is, I am sure, somewhat different from that of some decades ago when Israelite kingship was most intensely debated. It is sufficient to only hint at the new interest taken in the idea of the covenant ever since the fifties and at the growing awareness of the importance of the Deuteronomistic problem. It will be my task to formulate the new problems that the new *Forschungslage* has raised and also to envisage the old problems in the new forms which they assume when refracted into new shapes through the new scientific atmosphere.

The various questions of detail will be formulated in due course at their appropriate place in my discussion. Here I shall only draw attention to two different sets of problems which have been of particular moment in the general organization of my work.

(a) One concerns the interdependence of the civil and sacral aspects of the legitimacy of the king.[4] Is it, for instance, possible to find cases when

---

[1] For surveys of research see *C.M.Edsmann* (in: La regalità sacra, Leiden 1959: 3 ff.) and *H.-J.Kraus* (Geschichte der historisch-kritischen Erforschung des Alten Testaments, Neukirchen 1969: 460 ff.). A bibliography is found in *K.-H.Bernhardt* (1961: 307 ff.).

[2] References in *Ringgren* (²1969: 220 note 2).

[3] References in *Ringgren* (op. cit. 220 note 1).

[4] I am well aware that ancient Israel had a high degree of cultural integration. Nevertheless, I find it necessary and even possible to make such distinctions as that between sacral (civil) and secular. On such problems in the study of religions see *Å.Hultkrantz* (1973: 9-15).

the lack of civil legitimacy (dynastic rights, recognition by the popular assembly, etc.) has been compensated by an added emphasis on the sacral legitimacy (e.g. by reference to divine election)? Do we find cases when one particular notion or rite displays connections with both the civil and the sacral side of kingship?

In this connection, I wish to emphasize the point that I make a distinction between "divine kingship" and "sacral kingship". The term "divine kingship" should be used in a narrow sense and only when the idea of an identity between king and God is found so that the king holds the position of *deus incarnatus* on earth. The king can then be seen as having divine descent, and he can be made the object of a cult. When this requisite is not at hand, the king can nevertheless be regarded as chosen by God in some way or other. This may be termed "sacral kingship". Here it should also be noted that I do not reserve the term "Messiah" for the eschatological figure but agree with other scholars who have adopted the Old Testament use of "Messiah" as a royal title for the historical king.[5]

(b) The other set of problems concerns the historical development of the conceptions involved. Only an awareness of the possibility that we have to do with a dynamic historical development can save us from the danger of Procrustean generalizations, so often paid tribute to in studies of Israelite kingship. Any reconstruction that is not based on a source-critical evaluation of the material will almost of necessity give an anachronistic picture of the whole, combining features that are relevant to widely different periods. Thus what I set out to undertake is a historical investigation, in which the procedure of historical reconstruction is carried out on the basis of a source critically ascertained foundation. An important question will here be this: is the "*Hochmessianismus*" (by which I refer to the royal ideology of texts such as 2 S ch. 7) a reality existing from the beginning of the monarchy or is it a later development, perhaps not to be found until at the time around the exile? Is this form of royal ideology the result of Deuteronomistic "*Gemeindetheologie*"?

This definition of the task determines the material to be used. Even if one does not subscribe to the dictum of a well-known historian *quod non est in actis non est in mundo*, it is important to use as wide a selection of evidence as possible. I shall therefore try to pay due attention both to the material in the Psalms and to that in the historical books. The material contained in the prophetic books will, however, be used with some reserve. The reason for this is mainly that my prime interest concerns the first centuries of the monarchy, while the prophetic material is relevant only for the later centuries. It is to be hoped that the source-critical assessment of

---

[5] Cf. *Engnell* (1943: 43 note 3) and *Ringgren* ([2]1969: 222 note 8). Contrast *Mowinckel* (1956: 3 ff., 451 f.).

the material in Samuel and Kings, carried out with the tools of redaction criticism etc., will provide new criteria for the handling of the evidence in the Psalms, which is from the historian's point of view more elusive material. I shall thus pay heed to the relation between the various redactional stages in Samuel and Kings and the material in the Psalms.

This investigation has its limits. First, my study is an examination of the civil and sacral aspects of the royal *investitures*. One could well make a general study of the status of the king, his judicial position, and so forth. However, since I plan to write a monograph on the king as judge (see preface), I feel justified in restricting myself here to the royal investitures, which indeed provide the essential material for a study of the legitimation of royal power in ancient Israel.

Secondly, it is not my task to study the question of the origin of Israelite kingship as an institution. I am not here concerned with the genetic problem. I do not intend to interpret the royal ideology of Israel by working inwards from the wide periphery of the *Umwelt* of ancient Israel. Instead, I shall try to understand Israel from within, through a historical analysis of the biblical material itself.

Thirdly, my task is not that of the comparatist. Just as the genetic problem is a legitimate one, so should Israel be studied as part of its ancient Near Eastern *milieu*. But such a study cannot be carried out until the kingship of each particular culture has been studied on its own. It is this more restricted task that I have taken on for ancient Israel.

(2) Methodological Considerations. Arrangement of Presentation. – The above definition of the nature of the undertaking determines the method to be used. A historical investigation must use historical method. I wish to make two points here:

(a) There is in present-day Old Testament scholarship an increasing interest in methodological questions. The latest decade and a half brought about what I should like to term a "linguistic revival" of Old Testament research. Also questions of other methodological steps and procedures have been discussed. Scientific "cross-fertilization" has alway been an important incentive to the progress of research. For my own part I think that much can be learnt from our colleagues within the field of history. Indeed, the current discussion within the discipline of history of the methodological and historico-philosophical aspects of the work of the historian has much to give to the student of ancient Israel. And much that has long been commonplace to the historians certainly deserves a more alert interest on the part of the exegetes.[6]

---

[6] A select bibliography of literature on historical method is to be found in *H.P.Clausen* et al. ("Et udvalg af historiemetodisk litteratur" in: Historie. Jyske samlinger N.S. 7/1966-67,

I shall here only indicate some pertinent points of my methodological approach. It is a truism to say that it is important to make a distinction between the picture that the historical sources purport to suggest and the actual historical reality behind these sources. It is often believed that historical reconstruction on the basis of historical evidence consists in illuminating the reality from the sources, a reality the main features of which are more or less taken for granted. In actual fact, however, the proper procedure is this: to attempt to reconstruct a reality that can explain the historical evidence.[7] We have no other access to the historical past than the historical evidence that is part of it.

There are two different ways of *using* historical evidence:[8] All historical evidence can be used as *Überreste*, as relics of the historical past. When we are concerned with source material that is the result of human activity this way of using it means to understand it as (the result of) an action or as the expression of an attitude of the originator. Some types of historical evidence can also be used as *Tradition* of the historical past. When historical evidence is used in this way, the interest of the scholar is concentrated on the subject matter. If we take for instance a Deuteronomistic text dealing with the kingship of Saul (e.g. 1 S ch. 8), to use this passage as *Tradition* would imply to draw conclusions on the subject matter of this passage, on what Samuel said on a certain occasion. On the other hand, to use it as *Überrest* means to regard it as the expression of a certain attitude of its originator, whether this belonged to the Deuteronomistic movement or not.

That historiography may serve the purposes of political propaganda was pointed out several decades ago by G.Monod.[9] And the method of using a narrative source as *Überrest* and to see in it an expression of the ideology of the period to which it belongs, was used with considerable success by E.Bernheim.[10] We must thus be aware of the possibility that evidence can sometimes be seen as an expression of the intentions and the political will of its originators or as an expression of the current ideology of the period to which it belongs. These are possibilities that I shall test on the evidence to be discussed.

77-91). Here the reader will find references to the classic works by *E.Bernheim, J.G.Droysen* and *Langlois–Seignobos*. Scandinavian readers will find valuable information in *P.Renvall* (Den moderna historieforskningens principer, Stockholm 1965), *O.Dahl* (Grunntrekk i historieforskningens metodelære, Oslo 1967), *S.Langholm* (Historisk rekonstruksjon og begrunnelse, Oslo ²1970) and *R.Torstendahl* (Historia som vetenskap, Stockholm ²1971). Note also the series of studies Studier i historisk metode, started in 1966. General historico-philosophical problems are dealt with by *K.-G.Faber* (Theorie der Geschichtswissenschaft, München ²1972).

[7] See *Langholm* (op. cit. p. 17).
[8] For the following see for instance *Langholm* (op. cit. p. 21 ff.).
[9] See *G.Monod* (Études critiques sur les sources de l'histoire carolingienne, Paris 1898).
[10] See *E.Bernheim* (Mittelalterliche Zeitanschauungen in ihrem Einfluss auf Politik und Geschichtsschreibung, Tübingen 1918).

This approach to the historical evidence raises a difficult historico-philosophical problem, viz. that of *homo historicus*. In economics *homo oeconomicus* governed by the desire for profit is a prominent concept used in economic theory. There are important differences between this *homo oeconomicus* and what could be called *homo historicus*, governed by the desire for power and acting with cold rationality.[11] It is obvious that man does not always act in a rational way. But as far as I can see the historian must assume that man generally does this. The empirical exceptions to the rule must make the historian less confident of his own results, but there is no methodological procedure that can eliminate this source of error except for making allowance for this when discussing obviously pathological personalities.

(b) The other point I wish to make is this: Scholars of various disciplines display a growing awareness of the necessity of pursuing their studies within a structuralistic-functionalistic perspective. This trend can be found in linguistics, in sociology, in history and in comparative religion, to mention but a few examples.[12] The present study can be seen as part of this more comprehensive picture. I shall try to see the problems in a holistic perspective. To be sure, this is nothing new within biblical scholarship.[13] What is new is only that I shall try to lay greater stress on this aspect than is generally done. I shall thus be concerned not with the genetic question of the ultimate origin of Israelite kingship and its most characteristic expressions at the level of ideology, but with the historical development of the ideas connected with Israelite kingship seen as parts of a configurational whole.[14] It is this holistic approach that has led me to try to find the interdependence of the civil and sacral side of kingship (see for instance the chapters on the anointing and on *nagîd*) and to study the ideas of divine sonship and the Davidic covenant as mutually related parts of a configuration of beliefs. This holistic approach can also be seen in my treatment of linguistic problems (for instance in the discussion of the semantic relations of the word *nagîd*).

In a well-known work Thomas S. Kuhn stressed the role of anomaly in scientific discovery. The paradigm theory or the disciplinary matrix for the scholarly opinion on a complex of problems has the character of a whole, into which the different data must fit. Discrepancies or anomalies are symptoms of the need for revision or even a sign that the paradigm needs to be replaced by a new one.[15] Inspired by Kuhn I have tried to locate the ano-

---

[11] See for instance the remarks made by S. Björklund ("Dikt och vetande i historieskrivningen", Scandia 31/1965, 189-226, esp. p. 207 f.).
[12] For this trend in the study of comparative religion see Å.*Hultkrantz* (1973: ch. 3).
[13] Cf. for instance *Mowinckel* (in: La regalità sacra, 1959: 286 ff.), *Bernhardt* (1961: 66) and *Soisalon-Soininen* (SEÅ 33/1968, 55 ff.).
[14] For this terminology see Å.*Hultkrantz* (1973: 101 ff., esp. p. 113 and 116).
[15] T.S.*Kuhn* (The Structure of Scientific Revolutions, Chicago ²1970, reprint 1975). I wish to thank Mrs Heike Friis, Copenhagen, who called my attention to this work.

malies and to handle them in a constructive manner. This requires an adjustment of the theory so that the anomalous becomes the expected. This, too, is part of my general holistic approach.

Finally a few words on the general disposition of this work. The historical evidence consists of texts which will be subjected to a source-critical analysis in Part One. For practical reasons, however, I shall discuss some particular questions of this nature in a later part of my work (see ch. 9.5). Part Two will deal with the civil legitimation of the king. I shall here discuss the role of the popular assembly at the royal investitures, and the nature of the royal acclamation and of the royal covenant with the people. In Part Three the sacral aspects of Israelite kingship will be dealt with. It is to be noted that the rite of anointing makes a point of intersection between the sacral and civil sides of kingship. I have decided to discuss the anointing in Part Three and also to deal here with its secular aspects. The chapter on the anointing is preceded by a chapter on divine designation and followed by discussions on the royal charisma and the conceptions of divine sonship and Davidic covenant.

PART ONE

The Sources

Introduction

Historical conclusions must be based on historical evidence. The first part of this investigation will be devoted to a source-critical sifting of the evidence to determine the date, purpose and nature of the extant material. This will be done in a series of chapters, each devoted to a separate segment of the material. Before entering on a detailed discussion of these questions, some introductory comments on the Deuteronomistic Historical Work and on the phenomenon of historical literature as a vehicle of political propaganda are in place.

The Deuteronomistic Historical Work. – Our prose material is found in what M.Noth calls the Deuteronomistic Historical Work.[1] Later research has tended to see subsequent redactional activity in this work in addition to a main composition. In a work on the sources of the Books of Kings that was written independent of Noth, Jepsen had already queried the fact of a single redactional stage.[2] During the last decade and a half further indications of redactional complexity have been found. Beyerlin adduced facts appertaining to the frame sections in the Book of Judges[3] and Helga Weippert studied the framework of the Books of Kings,[4] both arguing that the theory of redactional unity in the sense of Noth could no longer be upheld. In a study of some sections of Jos–Jud, R.Smend argued for the existence of a "nomistic" redactor (DtrN).[5] In a major contribution, W.Dietrich (1972) disclosed a number of passages, particularly in Kings, where the activity of a "prophetic" redactor (DtrP) is to be seen. As regards texts of special interest to our inquiry here, Dietrich finds the activity of

---

[1] *Noth* (ÜSt 1943). The theory of such a work has been criticized from time to time, cf. *Eissfeldt* (Introduction p. 241 ff.) and the literature mentioned by *W.Dietrich* (1972: 145 note 144). In my opinion, the critics have not been able to disprove the basic soundness of Noth's views.
[2] *Jepsen* (1953). The publication of this work was delayed by the war.
[3] *Beyerlin* (FsWeiser 1963: 1-29). Cf. *W. Richter* (1964).
[4] *H.Weippert* (Bibl 53/1972, 301-339).
[5] *R.Smend* (Fs vonRad 1971: 494-509). Smend finds this DtrN in Jos 1,7-9; 13,1b-6; Jos ch. 23; Jud 2,17.20–21.23; Jud 1,1–2,9. See further *Dietrich* (1972; cf. RB 81/1974, 604) and *Veijola* (1975: 127 note 1).

this redactor in 2S 12,1-14; 1R 11,29ff. and 1R 14,7-11.[6] According to Dietrich, whose general view I accept as basically correct, we have to reckon with a Deuteronomistic Historical Work which has subsequently been subjected to two redactions, DtrP and DtrN. However, I am less confident than Dietrich that both the bulk of the work and the two redactions are exilic,[6a] but this particular problem is of little importance here. In my own discussions, I shall use the following sigla:

HDR   the History of David's Rise to Power (David's *Aufstieg*).
SN   the Succession Narrative (*Thronfolgegeschichte*).
Dt   the Deuteronomic Law with its old paraenetic framework in Dt ch. 5–28.
Dtr   as an adjective: Deuteronomistic;
      as a noun: the authors or redactors of sections or layers in the spirit of Dt, for instance in Dt ch. 1–4, Jos ch. 23 or 2R 17,7ff. The following suggested specifications are to be noted:
      DtrH the Deuteronomistic Historical Work.
      DtrP the prophetic redactor/redaction.
      DtrN the nomistic redactor/redaction.

The use of the adjectives "Deuteronomic" and "Deuteronomistic" should be kept apart, the first word being used for Dt, the other for DtrH, DtrP or DtrN.

The fact that King David appears in the Dtr material of the Books of Kings[7] makes it natural to raise the question of the possibility of Dtr contributions to the texts about David in the Books of Samuel too. In general Noth and later scholars have been very reluctant to assume the presence of Dtr material in 1–2 S.[8] The first step in another direction was taken by A.Carlson (1964). This scholar does not recognize the existence of, for instance, a pre-Deuteronomistic Succession Narrative (p. 131 ff.). On the whole Carlson's attitude to the possibility of disclosing pre-Dtr stages of the material in 2S is extremely pessimistic (p. 43). In 2S, he sees a methodical composition of a "D-group" (a group of Deuteronomists). The image of David to be seen in this material is mainly a fruit of the Messianic ideas of this "D-group" (p. 263ff.). For instance the prophecy of Nathan is

---

[6] See *Dietrich* (1972, for 2S ch. 12 p. 127 ff., for 1R ch. 11 p. 15 ff., 54 f. and for 1R ch. 14 p. 10 f., 51 ff).

[6a] Cf. the literature cited by Dietrich (p. 145 note 143) and see also *Cross* (1973:274 ff.).

[7] See e.g. 1R 11,13.32.36; 15,4 and cf. *vonRad's* study from 1947 (now in GesStud ²1961: 189 ff. esp. p. 198 f.). See also *Cross* (1973:278 ff.) and *Veijola* (1975:5).

[8] See *Noth* (ÜSt p. 61 ff.), *Nübel* (1959:123), *Grønbæk* (1971:271). For *Mildenberger* see the survey in *Veijola* (1975:8 note 25). For a brief survey of research on the Books of Samuel, see *Veijola* (1975:5 ff.).

assessed as a Dtr piece of literature through and through (p. 97 ff.). Carlson makes a number of observations that have proved useful to subsequent research. However, a major objection to his approach is that while writing redaction history he attempts to do this without the necessary literary critical work.[9] Dispensing with this essential process he plunges straight into compositional analysis and tradition history, stages that should follow a literary critical analysis of the redactional layers.

In this respect Veijola has made a very original contribution with his monograph *Die Ewige Dynastie* (1975).[9a] Veijola writes redaction history using the tools of literary criticism. Starting from 1 R ch. 1–2, he elaborates a Dtr strand (mainly belonging to DtrH) in the texts about David in 1–2 S. He assumes (p. 127 ff.) that it was the Deuteronomists that first used the titles '*æbæd* and *nagîd* of David. In the latter case they applied to David the title used for Saul in the old pre-Dtr tradition in 1 S 9,1–10,16 (p. 129). The Dtr depict David as a righteous and innocent king (1 S 25,26.31.33; 2 S 3,28-29.38-39; p. 130 ff.). In particular, the idea of an eternal dynasty is assumed to be of Dtr origin (2 S 7,11 ff.; 1 R 2,31-33.44-45; see p. 134 ff. and esp. p. 72 ff.). Thus the most important characteristics of David as a sacral king are to be ascribed to Dtr elaboration. Veijola's work can be seen in a more comprehensive setting. In Old Testament research one can now discern a pan-Deuteronomistic trend. To mention but one example only, Kutsch and Perlitt[10] hold the Dtr responsible for the theological use of $b^e r\hat{\imath}t$. Veijola attempts a similar explanation of the most characteristic features of the Davidic ideology.

We shall return to a more detailed discussion of an alleged Dtr revision of texts in the HDR and the SN relevant to this study. Some general reflexions are, however, in place here.

(1) Literary critical analysis does not dispense with the need of taking into account the character of the material that existed prior to a Dtr revision. It must be remembered that at least three different entities are involved: (a) the oldest source material of the authors of the HDR and the SN, (b) the contributions made by the authors of these two works and (c) the Dtr material. It seems to me that Carlson and Veijola have not always paid due attention to the characteristic features of the HDR and the SN but tend to all too hastily ascribe to the Deuteronomists material that has a bias that would well suit the purposes of the authors of the earlier literary works.

(2) It is necessary to distinguish between redaction criticism and *Tradi-*

---

[9] See *Veijola* (1975: 13).
[9a] Cf. my review (SvenskTKv 52/1976, 42-44).
[10] The papers by Kutsch have now been collected in *Kutsch* (1973). For the latter scholar see *Perlitt* (1969).

tions- or *Überlieferungsgeschichte*.[11] Thus if it can be proved with a high degree of probability that a particular passage is redactional, this by no means settles the question of the origin of the material. A section placed in its final context by the Dtr may well contain considerably older material.[12]

(3) Peculiarities of language and style are important indications of Dtr affiliations. Here two points should be kept in mind. (a) Our knowledge of the Hebrew of ancient Israel is sadly lacking. The Old Testament is only a fragment of a reality to which we have no other access (except for some epigraphic material). As for quantity, we must remember that there is more material preserved from the period around the time of the exile (Dt, Jer, Ez, Is ch. 40–66, the Priestly Code, etc.) than from earlier periods. Consequently there may be an intrinsic tendency for a study of the distribution of linguistic phenomena to show that a given item was used in the "late" period.[13] (b) Statistic probability must also be considered. Can we say anything at all on the basis of four or five occurrences of a given word?[14] If a lexical item appears four times in Dtr texts is this sufficient grounds for assessing a fifth occurrence of the same item? This of course does not mean that linguistic observations are irrelevant. On the contrary, they can be of great value.[15] They must, however, be interpreted with caution.

(4) To demonstrate from compositional analysis that a given text has a major role in the DtrH, as has apparently the prophecy of Nathan, does not necessarily mean that the text is itself of Dtr origin. By means of literary devices, such as prefiguration, etc. the Deuteronomists may have placed an old item of tradition so as to make it stand out in relief.

Literature and Political Propaganda. – Before entering on an assessment of the SN and the HDR, a few comments are necessary concerning some particular purposes that the literature of the Solomonic and early post-Solomonic periods may have been designed to fill. On two different points there must have been a strong need for legitimation.

---

[11] My distinction between *Traditionsgeschichte* and *Überlieferungsgeschichte* is made in agreement with *Barth–Steck* (1971: 37 ff., 70 ff.). I use the first term for the history of traditional contents or whole complexes of ideas. *Traditionsgeschichte* could also be called "Vorstellungsgeschichte" (op. cit. p. 71). With *Überlieferungsgeschichte* I refer to the history of an oral unit of tradition, whether a very small piece or a whole complex of tradition. I use the English term "traditio-historical" for either of these two aspects.

[12] Thus *Smend* (Fs vonRad 1971: 508) points out that Jud 1,1–2,5 although placed here by DtrN probably contains pre-Dtr tradition.

[13] I cannot free myself from the suspicion of having paid too little attention to this aspect in my paper on the nominal pattern $q^e tull\bar{a}$ (JSS 16/1971, 2-14).

[14] On the statistical study of literary vocabulary, see esp. *Yule* (1944).

[15] I think, for instance, that the chapter on *Sprachgebrauch* in *Dietrich* (1972: 64 ff.) is a most valuable contribution to the subject of Dtr language and style.

(1) The nature of Solomon's accession to the throne was such that it required justification. The remarkable fact that it was Solomon and not one of his elder brothers that succeeded to the throne clearly called for an explanation.[1] In the SN the final part describes events in connection with Solomon's investiture (1 R ch. 1–2 ptm). Here, Solomon's claim to the throne is derived from (a) an oath that David is said to have sworn to Bathsheba to the effect that her son Solomon should succeed him (1 R 1,13.17.28-30) and (b) David's confirmation of this oath through his designation of Solomon as *nagîd* (1,35).

It is difficult to assess the historicity of these items of information. It is possible that David's weakness for Bathsheba had led him to make certain concessions concerning the future of their son Solomon. On the other hand, it would appear that Bathsheba does not remember that David had sworn a formal oath but had to be "reminded" of this by Nathan. There is no other information to be found in the SN that David had formally designated his son heir apparent. If this had taken place before the crisis related in 1 R ch. 1, the SN would probably have recorded something that was such an important occasion in the history of the young monarchy. It is therefore probable that what the SN says concerning Solomon's designation as *nagîd* ($w^{e^\jmath}otô$ $ṣiwwîtî$ $lihyôt$ $nagîd$ ..., 1 R 1,35), is a performative utterance and is to be understood as meaning "and I hereby appoint him *nagîd* ..." (see ch. 9.2 at the end). This interpretation is also in agreement with what we are told of David's attitude towards Adonijah. This prince took deliberate steps to seize power after David. Although it seems that this had been known for some time, David showed no reaction (1 R 1,5ff.), which would have been strange if he had previously designated Solomon as *nagîd* or privately sworn an oath to Bathsheba.

But even a formal designation of Solomon by the aged David (1 R 1,35) is difficult to establish as a historical fact. The witnesses present on the solemn occasion were all supporters of Solomon's: Zadok, Nathan, and Benaiah (1 R 1,32). Thus it cannot be precluded that the designation of Solomon as *nagîd* by David was a fabrication to suit the purposes of the Solomon party to justify Solomon's claims to the throne against those of Adonijah. In any case this designation as *nagîd* is the only verification of Solomon's claims, and it is therefore probable that the Solomon party argued from this position from the outset. Thus, whether historical or not, the statement on Solomon as *nagîd* can be traced back to the days of the

---

[1] For the following, cf. *Mildenberger* (1962: 75ff.). Mildenberger holds that (a) Solomon was never designated by David and (b) David was already dead, when Solomon took the throne. On this last point I don't agree. As for his first point, I am highly sceptic about some of Mildenberger's arguments but have myself found additional evidence for a similar conclusion.

accessional crisis. It is certainly not a fabrication of the author of the SN, which will suffice for the purposes of this present study. It is also of some importance in understanding the title *nagîd* to which a special chapter will be devoted. It can also be noted that later Rehoboam and Jehoshaphat are said to have designated their successors (2 Ch 11,18-23; 21,2-4). But these later cases of designation cannot be adduced as proof that David had done the same.

An analysis of the very act of investiture (1 R 1,32-40) reveals some remarkable features: Solomon came to the throne without the normal acclamation of the assembly and without a royal *b^erît* (below 7.2.1.2 and 8.2.1). From this point of view his legitimacy was clearly deeply controversial.[1a]

It is also worth considering Adonijah and his party in this context. Even if the statement on David's designation of Solomon were historically reliable, something which can be called in question, some sort of a justification *post festum* for such a remarkable arrangement would certainly be highly desirable from Solomon's point of view because of Adonijah's exceptionally strong position from the outset.

There are indications that the normal order of succession would conform to the principle of primogeniture. Jonathan, Ishbosheth, Amnon and Absalom illustrate this. Therefore, the fact that Adonijah ranked above Solomon with respect to age must not be overlooked (1 R 1,6; 2,15.22). Another important factor is that the Adonijah party (Adonijah, Joab and Abiathar) had particularly strong ties with the nation's past.[2] Joab was commander of the national militia whereas Benaiah was commander of the Cherethites and the Pelethites. In this connection a most important circumstance is that Abiathar represented a link with pre-Jerusalemite cultic institutions. He was probably the son of Saul's oracle priest (1 S 14,3; 22,20 accepting the current identification of Ahijah with Ahimelech) and it was he who brought the ephod to David (1 S 23,6).[2a] Adonijah himself was one of the sons born to David at Hebron (2 S 3,2-5) whereas Solomon was born in the new capital, Jerusalem (2 S 5,14).

All this must be kept in mind when we utilize the Succession Narrative as a historical source, since this literary work dates from the days of Solomon.

(2) The other matter of importance to be considered is the permanent state of tension existing between the two halves of the Davidic kingdom, which was constitutionally a personal union. The evidence for this structural dualism is examined separately in excursus no 1. This tension resulted in a need to justify the Jerusalemite claim to sovereignty over the whole nation,

---

[1a] As was stressed by *Fohrer* (ZAW 71/1959, 6 f.).
[2] See e.g. *Ahlström* (VT 11/1961, 120 ff.). On the possible antecedentia of one of Solomon's main adherents, the priest Zadok, see *Cody* (1969: 88 ff.).
[2a] Contrast *Veijola* (1975: 39 ff.).

i.e. over the northern as well as the southern tribes. To refer to this claim is to refer at the same time to the claims of the Davidic lineage as opposed to rival forces. Reasons for the motivation and support of these claims were of course particularly strong after the dissolution of the personal union,[2b] but it is to be noted that the dualism did not originate in developments after Solomon's death but was a structural peculiarity of an earlier date.[3] These aspects are important to remember when discussing the History of David's Rise.

It goes without saying that we must reckon with the possibility that the historical literature from this period can contain features shaped to suit the needs of political propaganda, motivated by historical circumstances such as those mentioned above. There would be nothing new or surprising in this. Well-known precedents are found, for example, in Egypt. Two literary works from the beginning of dyn. XII (beginning of the second millennium B.C.) provide particularly eloquent examples, viz. the Prophecy of Neferti and the Instruction of Amen-em-het.[4] The *Prophecy of Neferti*[5] purports to relate how King Snefru of dyn. IV sought entertainment and how a lector-priest, Neferti, foretold the downfall of the Old Kingdom and the re-establishment of law and order by a new king, Ameni. This Ameni is clearly none other than Amen-em-het I, the founder of dyn. XII. The literary work which contains the prophecy of his coming is obviously a piece of propaganda commissioned by his government to provide numinous legitimacy[6] to a man whose claims to the throne could not be based on royal descent. The *Instruction of Amen-em-het*[7] applies to a similar dynastic crisis, arising after the murder of Amen-em-het in a palace conspiracy. His son, Sen-Usert I, managed to seize power in spite of this. Taken at face value, the Instruction of Amen-em-het contains the political testament of the old king and his advice to his son. It also confirms Sen-Usert's claims to the throne. That historically this was a justification *post festum* is obvious from the fact that the instruction refers to the conspiracy which led to the death of Amen-em-het.

There is almost certainly no historical connection between these two Egyptian literary works and the historical writings from the Solomonic era

---

[2b] See *Mettinger* (1971:39), *Mauchline* (VT 20/1970, 287 ff.), and *Grønbæk* (1971:20,23, 273 ff.).

[3] That this dualism was felt also during Solomon's reign can be seen in the list of Solomon's districts, see *Mettinger* (1971:111 ff.).

[4] On the political literature of the twelfth Egyptian dynasty see esp. *Posener* (1956) and *R.J.Williams* (FsMeek 1964: 14-30). Among Old Testament scholars who have drawn attention to comparative material such as this can be mentioned *Lipiński* (1967: 83 ff.) and *Whybray* (1968: 105 ff.).

[5] Translation: *ANET*³ (p. 444 ff.). Comments: *Posener* (1956: 21-60).

[6] I follow here the classification in civil and numinous legitimacy. See *Sternberger* (1968).

[7] *ANET*³ (p. 418 f.), *Posener* (1956: 61-86).

in Israel, but they are most instructive in showing the mechanisms at work in a situation where a monarch feels the need for legitimation.

We shall now go on to consider the nature and relative age of the Old Testament texts which comprise the material of the historical part of this investigation.

Note the survey on p. 309.

CHAPTER I

The Succession Narrative

Of the two great historical works, the History of David's Rise and the Succession Narrative the latter is the older. During the last decade in particular Rost's conclusions (1926) concerning the purpose and character of this work have been called in question.[1] To come to grips with these problems it is necessary to raise anew the question of the compass of the work. In this connection the two key passages are 1 R ch. 1–2 and 2 S ch. 12. Must we assume extensive Dtr elaborations in these chapters?[2] And is it necessary to speak of an anti-Solomonic and anti-Davidic bias in the parts that belong to the SN in these chapters?[3]

There is almost general agreement that the conclusion of the SN is to be looked for somewhere in 1 R ch. 1–2.[3a] Rost considered that the SN concluded with these two chapters almost entirely in their present form.[4] M.Noth, on the other hand, saw in ch. 2 a series of "Nachträge". First, the kernel of the testament of David (2,5-9) was added, then the two comprehensive sections 2,13-35 and 2,36-46 and, finally, he also found traces of Dtr revision.[5] Veijola takes a third path and assumes that an anti-Solomonic narrative in ch. 1–2 was revised by the Dtr. Thus the whole of the testament of David in 2,1-9 as well as 31b-33.44-45 are judged to be of Dtr origin, to mention only the most important points in Veijola's analysis.[6]

None of these suggestions are quite convincing. Rost gives us a conclusion of the SN with some remarkable inner discrepancies (below). Noth makes the work end with a section (1.49-53) that really calls out for a conti-

---

[1] For the theory that there was actually such a unified literary work (*Thronnachfolge Davids*), see esp. *Rost* (1926=1965: 119-253), *vonRad* (GesStud ²1961: 159 ff.), *Whybray* (1968), and *Thornton* (ChQR 169/1968, 159-166). Recent critics such as *Carlson* (1964: 131ff.), cf. *Blenkinsopp* (VTSuppl 15/1965, 44ff.) *Flanagan* (JBL 91/1972, 172ff.) and *Schulte* (1972: 138ff.) have not been able to produce convincing arguments against it. Recently *Delekat* (ZAWBeih 105/1967, 26ff.) has tried to demonstrate that the work has an anti-Solomonic bias (cf. *Noth*, Könige p. 39f.). The same line of thought is now also taken up by *Würthwein* (1974). For reasons to which I shall return below I do not find these studies convincing.
[2] On 1 R ch. 1–2 see *Veijola* (1975: 16 ff.), on 2 S ch. 12 *Dietrich* (1972: 127 ff.).
[3] So *Würthwein* (1974).
[3a] *Mowinckel's* contention (ASTI 2/1963, 11ff.) that 1 R ch. 1–2 belong to what follows was rightly criticized by *Schulte* (1972: 169).
[4] *Rost* (1926: 86ff.). As later additions he counted 1 R 2,1-4(2-4). 27b. (p. 91).
[5] *Noth* (Könige p. 8-11).
[6] *Veijola* (1975: 16ff. esp. 19ff.).

nuation. And Veijola assumes that 1 R ch. 1–2 crudely and without any extenuating circumstances relate a series of political murders committed by Solomon, which would indeed be a strange conclusion to a work that Rost assumed to have a pro-Solomonic *Tendenz*.[7]

A solution to the problem must explain the following circumstances. (1) The passage on Adonijah (1,41-53) must belong to its continuation in 2,13 ff. (2) There is a certain incongruity between David's testament (2,1-9) and the sections that relate the execution of David's injunctions. The testament mentions the sons of Barzillai (v. 7) who do not, however, appear again in 2,13 ff. The testament does not mention Adonijah and Abiathar who on the other hand appear in 2,13 ff. The testament does not denote Amasa as "commander of the army of Judah" as in 2,32. Thus there is a certain lack of agreement between the testament and 2,13-46. (3) A certain discrepancy between 1,41-53; 2,13-46 on the one hand and 1,1 ff. on the other should be noted. From 1,4 it seems that Abishag was not taken into the royal harem. From 2,22 f. it appears that she was. Since Bathsheba had already been introduced as "the mother of Solomon" in 1,11 the repetition in 2,13 seems somewhat superfluous. (4) The concluding formula is repeated three times in ch. 2, viz. in v. 12.35(LXX).46.

To account for these observations it is necessary to advance a new theory concerning the conclusion of the SN: the final section of this work comprised (a) Solomon's designation and anointing (1,1-40), (b) David's testament except for Dtr accretions (2,5-9), the beginning of it now being lost and (c) the concluding formula in 2,12. The work did not, however, contain the sections on the political murders. Thus 1,41-53 and 2,13-46 are secondary, and here 2,31b-33.44-45 are still later Dtr additions. This hypothesis accounts for the internal discrepancies in ch. 1–2. The SN appears as a beautifully rounded off work, a complete whole. It contained nothing about the incriminating circumstances in connection with the executions of Solomon's enemies. Instead, the testament of David provides the work with a very good justification of the most problematic of these murders, that of Joab and that of Shimei.

I thus disagree with Veijola's suggestion that the whole of the testament of David is Deuteronomistic.[8] On the other hand Veijola is right in his conclusion that 2,31b-33.44-45 and 2,24 did not originally belong to the SN. Thus the conclusion of the SN did not contain any allusions to the prophecy of Nathan except perhaps in the concluding formula in 2,12 (cf. 2 S 7,12b). The Dtr elaborations in 2,31b-33.44-45 should be seen in connection with

---

[7] *Rost* (1926: 128).
[8] I cannot find that *Veijola's* arguments on p. 28 prove anything as regards the corpus of the testament of David (1 R 2,5-9). That there are Dtr traces in the first verses of the chapter is, however, clear.

2 S 3,28-29.38-39. We are here faced with sections inserted by the Dtr in order to connect the SN and the HDR, sections in which the Dtr tendency to stress the innocence of David appears.[9] As for 1 R ch. 1, it must be concluded that v. 46-48 did not belong to the SN. These verses are possibly an addition to what is already a secondary passage, v. 41-53. On the other hand I cannot subscribe to the view that 1,35-37 are secondary. There is indeed no reason for taking Solomon's designation as *nagîd* as a Dtr addition to the SN.[10]

In spite of statements to the contrary[11] there is no reason for seeing an anti-Solomonic bias in the final section of the SN. The passages on the political murders (2,13-46) do not belong to this work. What Fohrer termed Solomon's "Staatsstreich von oben"[12] has been disguised in a way that makes the reader assume that Solomon was acclaimed king in the normal manner by a popular assembly (1,39). Nor can I see why it should be difficult to consider the details of David's oath to Bathsheba (1,13.17.28-30) as part of a work with a pro-Solomonic bias. The point in v. 11-40 is that, according to the narrator, David's word supports Solomon's claim to the throne. It matters little here how this formal designation (v. 29-30.35) was obtained. What matters is that David's oath is irrevocable. A comparison could be drawn with Isaac's blessing of Jacob (Gn ch. 27).

A section that is probably of Dtr origin is 2 S 17,5-14. It is not necessary to go into detail here. The secondary character of this passage has been demonstrated by Würthwein,[12a] and for the formulation *habî' ra'ā 'ăl X* as an indication of Dtr authorship, W.Dietrich is referred to.[12b]

Let us now turn to 2 S ch. 12. Of the modern scholars Carlson and Dietrich have argued that the passage v. 1-14 was placed here by the Dtr.[13] It is true that there is a perfect connection between 11,27b and 12,15b. But there are no literary tensions that force us to take 12,1-14 to be secondary in its entirety. It is quite sufficient to regard v. 7b-10a (or 7b-12) as secondary.[14] David's behaviour in 12,15b-22 would be difficult to understand if not seen

---

[9] See *Veijola* (1975: 30ff.). – On the other hand, I regard it as unnecessary to assume a Dtr hand in 2 S 16,11-12 and 19,22-23 as Veijola does (p. 33ff.).
[10] *Veijola* (p. 16f.) overlooks the fact that the title *nagîd* is here used in a secular sense that is otherwise not attested in Dtr sections. He also overlooks that the dualism of Israel–Judah is attested also in v. 34 (LXX) and not only in v. 35. Note also that v. 35 (*nagîd*) is closely linked with v. 20 (*lᵉhăggîd*), which verse Veijola does not take to be secondary.
[11] See *Delekat* (ZAWBeih 105/1967, 26ff.), *Würthwein* (1974: 11ff.), and *Veijola* (1975: 26).
[12] *Fohrer* (ZAW 71/1959, 6f.).
[12a] *Würthwein* (1974: 40ff.).
[12b] *Dietrich* (1972: 72f.).
[13] *Carlson* (1964: 140ff. esp. 160), *Dietrich* (1972: 127ff.). Cf. *Würthwein* (1974: 24f.).
[14] For details see *Rost* (1926: 92ff.) and *Dietrich* (loc. cit.). Cf. *Thornton* (ChQR 169/1968, 162f.).

against the background of v. 1-14 (apart from the secondary section).[15] And it is not entirely correct to say that 11,27b is a literary link that reveals a Dtr hand.[16] The phrase *wăyyeră' hăddabar be'ênê X* is well known from contexts that can hardly be said to be of Dtr origin.[17] Dietrich's contention that 12,1-14 was placed here by DtrP meets with a difficulty in the fact that there are no *Erfüllungsvermerke* for the woe oracles in v. 10.11.14, although such formulations concerning the fulfilment of an oracle are characteristic of DtrP.[18] Impossible to substantiate is also the suggestion that v. 24b-25 is the result of Dtr elaboration.[19]

In 2 S ch. 12, I take only v. 7b-10a (7b-12?) to be of Dtr origin. Thus the reference to David's anointing (probably by Samuel) that is found in v. 7b was not in the SN. The corpus of ch. 12, however, has a very important function in the SN. David's adultery and his meeting with Nathan was not included by the narrator to inform us of David's moral weakness. Instead the details of the chapter are strictly subordinated to the general pro-Solomonic *Tendenz* of the SN. The death of the child is mentioned in connection with the statement that *YHWH hæ'ᵃebîr* David's sin (v. 13-14). Gerleman has argued that this does not mean simply that God "took away" the sin but more specifically that he "made the punishment pass over" to the child.[20] The death of the child implies that the Davidic dynasty does not bear the blame in the matter of Bathsheba. The author of the SN is also anxious to make it clear that Solomon is not to be mistaken for the illegitimate child. That this child died is probably a historically dependable fact in particular if Gerleman is correct in his argument that the birthname of the second child, *šelomō*, means "sein Ersatz" and denotes Solomon as a compensation for the child that died.[21]

Thus the birth and death of the illegitimate child are immediately followed by Solomon's triumphal entry on the scene. Together with Solomon his good genius Nathan appears and receives an oracle to the effect that the auspicious name Jedidiah should be added to the birthname that David gave his son (2 S 12,24-25). This name Jedidiah purports to present Solomon as one chosen by God from the beginning.

---

[15] Cf. *Seebass* (ZAW 86/1974, 210 note 18).
[16] As does *Dietrich* (1972: 132) and *Würthwein* (p. 24).
[17] See Gn 21,11; 38,10; 1 S 8,6; 18,8.
[18] See *Dietrich* (p. 22 ff.).
[19] This was held by *Carlson* (1964: 161). Cf. *Würthwein* (1974: 29).
[20] See *Gerleman* in a study to be published in the forthcoming Festschrift for W. Zimmerli.
[21] See *Gerleman* (ZAW 85/1973, 13). Gerleman argues from his understanding of the root *š-l-m* as basically connected with retribution (in positive and negative sense). If Gerleman is right, it becomes impossible to follow *Honeyman* (JBL 67/1948, 22 f.), who assumed that Jedidiah was the private name and Solomon the throne name. The information in the text that David himself gave the child the name Solomon is reliable.

As for the beginning of the SN, we cannot be as certain. Possibly 2 S ch. 9 was preceded by the passage 2 S 21,1-14.[22] An interesting but very difficult question is whether the prophecy of Nathan in some form was part of the work. Rost argued in favour of such a conclusion on the basis of 1 R 2,24.[23] As we have seen, however, this verse does not belong to the SN. On the other hand the conclusion of the SN in 1 R 2,12 could contain an allusion to 2 S 7,12b. From the point of view of composition an opening with the prophecy of Nathan in some form would fit in very well with 2 S ch. 12 (Solomon as Jedidiah) and also with the conclusion of the work with Solomon's accession to the throne. It can be noted here that there is a pro-Solomonic *skopos* in 2 S 7,12-13. On the whole, however, there is too little evidence to allow for certain conclusions on this point.

That I agree with Rost on the basically pro-Solomonic character of the SN appears from what has been said. The work was written *in majorem gloriam Salomonis*.[24] The aim is to justify and uphold the claims of Solomon himself, not primarily the Davidic dynasty.[25] The *leit-motif* of the work is expressed in the words "who shall sit on the throne?" (1 R 1,20.27). The purpose of the narrator is to relate how it came to pass that David was succeeded by Solomon[26] and to defend Solomon with regard to the most incriminating of the political executions during his first years.

The date of the work must be placed during the reign of Solomon. The dissolution of the personal union after Solomon's death is nowhere hinted at. We must probably assign a date to the SN during the early part of Solomon's reign[27] when Solomon was in particular need of support. However, since the testament of David refers to the execution of Shimei (1 R 2,8 f.), the elapse of the first three years of Solomon's reign is presupposed if we can trust the information given in 1 R 2,39. Besides, if the prophecy of Nathan in its original form actually made up the opening of the work, this could be another indication of the *post quem*, namely if this original form of the prophecy contained the allusion to the building of the temple which is now found in 2 S 7,13. The building of the temple was begun in the fourth year of Solomon's reign (1 R 6,1).

---

[22] See for instance *Carlson* (1964: 198 ff.).
[23] *Rost* (1926: 105 f.).
[24] *Rost* (1926: 128).
[25] On this point I disagree with *Whybray* (1968: 53).
[26] See esp. *Rost* (1926: 86 f.), *Whybray* (1968: 50 ff.), and *Thornton* (ChQR 169/1968, 159 ff.).
[27] I here agree with *Rost* (1926: 127) and *Whybray* (1968: 53 f.) among others.

Summary

(1) The compass of this historical work has been discussed. I suggested the theory that it ended with 1 R 1,1-40 (Solomon's designation by David and his anointing), 2,5-9 (the kernel of David's testament), and 2,12 (concluding remark). The sections on Solomon's political murders (1,41-53; 2,13-46) display a number of tensions and were therefore considered to be secondary. As for the beginning of the SN, I called attention to the possibility that an original, pro-Solomonic kernel of the prophecy of Nathan made up its opening (cf. below ch. 3).

(2) I did not agree with those scholars who suggested that the whole of 2 S 12,1-14 has been inserted by DtrP. Instead, I argued that here only v. 7b-10a (7b-12?) are secondary. The reference to David's anointing is found in this secondary section (v. 7).

(3) The intention of the work is to legitimate and defend Solomon. The concluding part of it exonerates Solomon from the political murders in connection with the accessional crisis. 2 S ch. 12 relates how David's punishment for committing adultery with Bathsheba was transferred to the child so that the Davidic dynasty was innocent. It is also an important point in this narrative that Solomon cannot be identified with the child borne in adultery. This child died, and Solomon was named by David as its substitute ($š^e lomō$).

(4) The SN was probably composed during the early part of Solomon's reign, although we must allow for the elapse of at least a few years after his accession to the throne.

CHAPTER II

The History of David's Rise to Power

Research into the History of David's Rise (HDR) has made important progress thanks to Weiser and Grønbæk.[1] The work of these two scholars prove that an attempt to distinguish between two major strands in these traditions[2] is problematic. Texts that may or may not belong to this work contain highly important information concerning the nature of kingship (designation as *nagîd*, divine anointing, the *b*^{e}*rît* to the popular assembly). It is therefore necessary to devote some space to a discussion of the compass, purpose and date of this work. As for the compass it is in particular necessary to take a stand to Veijola's theory that a Dtr redaction is responsible for much of what is said about the king in these texts.

1. The Opening of the HDR

For a discussion of the royal anointing, it is particularly important to make sure whether the passage on Samuel's anointing of David (1 S 16,1-13) belongs to the HDR or is a later addition. This makes it necessary to discuss the opening of the work. The old established idea is that the HDR begins with the passage telling how the Spirit of the Lord departed from Saul (1 S 16,14 ff.). Since, however, this passage refers back to 16,13 and since it would be a torso without the passage relating how the Spirit came over David through Samuel's anointing, Weiser holds that 16,1-13 also made up part of the work.[3] Grønbæk agrees on this point but holds that the rejection of Saul should also be included, and so he counts 15,1–16,13 as the great opening section of the HDR.[4] Veijola returns to the former theory that the work begins with 16,14 and asks if ch. 15 and 16,1-13 are not traditions of prophetic origin, first inserted into the Deuteronomistic Historical Work by DtrP, ch. 15 perhaps being provided with some additions by this redactor

---

[1] The major work on this is now *Grønbæk* (1971). Also of importance is *Weiser's* study (VT 16/1966, 325-354). One can also mention *Nübel* (1959), *Mildenberger* (1962, with many valuable observations but with general conclusions which are less convincing), *Ward* (1967, summarized in Diss. Abstr. 27/1966-67, 4336 A), *L.Schmidt* (1970: 120 ff.), *Rendtorff* (Fs vonRad 1971: 428 ff.) and *Conrad* (ThLZ 97/1972, 321 ff.). For a discussion of David's career on the basis of Grønbæk's work, see *Lemche* (DanskTT 38/1975, 241 ff.).
[2] This attempt was made by *Nübel* (1959) and *Mildenberger* (1962).
[3] See *Weiser* (1966: 149 f. and VT 16/1966, 325 f.).
[4] *Grønbæk* (1971: 25 ff., 37 ff.). This scholar sees Dtr traces in 1 S 15,2.6 (p. 271).

himself.⁵ Since, as we have just seen, the mention of Samuel's anointing of David in 2 S 12,7 does not belong to the SN, there would then be no early reference to it.

The present position of 14,52 is strange. It fits badly into the Dtr passage 14,47-51. On the other hand it seems to point forward to 16,14 ff. which describes how David came to Saul's court. Thus 15,1 – 16,13 seems to have been inserted into this material. Are we entitled to think that the HDR opened with 14,52; 16,14 ff. and that the long section in between was inserted by a late redactor (DtrP)? Or is it preferable to conclude that it was the author of the HDR who was responsible for the inclusion of the material describing Saul's rejection and David's anointing?

An indication in favour of the latter alternative is found in the fact that there are various connections between this material and what can be safely judged as belonging to the HDR. David's Amalekite campaign in ch. 30 should thus be seen against the background of the similar campaign fought by Saul (15,1-9).⁶ The symbolism of the robe in 18,4 (Jonathan handing over his "royal" $m^{e'}îl$ to David) seems to form another point of connection, especially if the tearing of the robe in 15,27 refers to Saul's robe⁷ whether it was Saul himself or (more probably) Samuel who tore it. The rending of (15,27) and handing over of (18,4) a piece of the royal apparel would symbolize the transference of kingship from Saul and his son to someone else, to David.⁸ The departing of the Spirit from Saul (16,14 cf. 18,10.12) connects in a natural way with the information given in 16,13 that the Spirit of the Lord came upon David from the day of his anointing. Above all, it is worthwhile noting that the HDR speaks repeatedly of Saul as the $maši^aḥ$.⁹ In a work of clearly pro-Davidic and anti-Saul bias this way of referring to Saul would be remarkable, if the reader were not to assume that David could lay claim to the status of "anointed" *a fortiori*. This presupposition of the whole work is voiced in 16,1-13. By including this tradition the author makes David appear from the outset as "the secret Messiah".

The conclusion that 16,1-13 made up part of the work finds support in the observation that the hand of DtrP is only to be found in one particular section of ch. 15. Opinion is divided on whether or not this chapter is a

---

⁵ *Veijola* (1975: 102 note 156).
⁶ See *Grønbæk* (1971: 51, 202).
⁷ So *Hylander* (1932: 200). Especially Samuel's interpretation of this as a sign ("the Lord has torn the kingdom of Israel from you this day", v. 28) suggests an analogy between the kingdom and the robe which implies that the latter also belonged to Saul.
⁸ An inner connection also seems possible if *Grønbæk* (1971: 40 ff.) is right in his assumption that it was Samuel who tore his own robe. However, Grønbæk argues mainly from the idea of the inviolability of the king, which does not seem to provide a conclusive argument.
⁹ 1 S 24,7.11; 26,9.11.16.23; 2 S 1,14.16.

literary unity.[10] On two points in particular there are discrepancies within the chapter. (a) There are two different ideas of God's repenting. In v. 11 (cf. 35b) it is said that God regrets that he has made Saul king. In v. 29 comes the solemn assurance that God "will not lie or repent". (b) In v. 24-26 Saul confesses his sin and asks Samuel to return with him, which Samuel refuses to do. Compared with this, v. 30-31 are a strange repetition, but also an inconsistency since here Samuel grants Saul his wish. It therefore seems that v. 10-26.35b were not originally in the chapter. In addition, it is this particular section that shows the mark of DtrP. The formula in 15,10 $wăyhî\ d^eb\check{a}r\ YHWH\ 'æl\ X\ (Wortereignisformel)$ is typical of DtrP.[11] The prophetic argument in v. 22-23 fits in well with such an origin of the section. I therefore conclude that the section under discussion is secondary and was inserted in its present position by DtrP. The following section v. 27-35a probably had a beginning that DtrP left out in favour of his own insertion, v. 10-26.35b. This redactor used a similar technique in 1 R ch. 11.[12] On the other hand there is no indication that DtrP placed the whole of 15,1–16,13 in its present position.

As we shall see in another section of this study (ch. 9.5) there is reason to believe that 16,1-13 was not composed by the author of the HDR but originally made up an independent tradition. Indeed its only connection with ch. 15 is the link in 15,35a+16,1a.

As regards the beginning of the HDR it can thus be concluded that the work contained 15,1–16,13 except for the passage that was later inserted by DtrP (15,10-26.35b).

2. Abigail's Speech

The next section deserving of special attention is the meeting of Abigail and David, and here the passage 1 S 25,28-31 is of especial interest to us, since it contains the promise of a dynasty to David (v. 28), mention of David as *nagîd* (v. 30) and, in addition, a vivid metaphor for the divine protection of the king ("the bundle of the living", v. 29). Grønbæk assumes that this passage can be ascribed to the author of the HDR,[13] while Veijola holds

---

[10] *Weiser* (ZAW 54/1936, 4) holds that only v. 25-30a are an intrusion. *Stoebe* (1973: 282) regards the chapter as "im wesentlichen einheitlich". *Seebass* (ZAW 78/1966, 149ff.), on the other hand, assumes a far-reaching literary disunity. On this chapter see also F. *Stolz* (1972: 136ff.).

[11] See *Dietrich* (1972: 71f.). The use of this formula in 2 S 24,11 may be due to DtrP, see *Veijola* (1975: 112, 115), and the same perhaps holds for 2 S 7,4. Note that in these instances of the formula as also in 1 S 15,10.16, there is a revelation by night.

[12] 1 R 11,29-39 was inserted into an old narrative, elements of which are still found in v. 26-28.40, but with the kernel left out, see *Dietrich* (1972: 54f.).

[13] *Grønbæk* (1971: 174).

that these verses make up part of a Dtr strand to which he attributes v. 21-22.23b.24b-26.28-34.39a.[14]

Be as it may it seems clear that the oldest, pre-redactional material was a narrative of David's meeting with Abigail, the purpose of which was to make known the extraordinary merits of the future wife of David.[15] This thread appears in v. 1-24a.27.28a: Abigail comes to David, throws herself down at his feet; sharing the guilt of her husband Nabal she offers a present to David and his men to make good her husband's lack of generosity. This thread, however, is not taken up again until v. 35 where David receives her gift. The section v. 28b-34, consisting of Abigail's speech (v. 28b-31) and David's praise (v. 32-34), breaks the connection between Abigail's offering the gift and David's acceptance of it. There is in Abigail's speech in v. 28-31 a new *skopos* as compared with the older strand of tradition: David's future kingship and the innocence of David. Thus, v. 28b-34 seem to be of a secondary nature in relation to the old narrative. The same may also be true of v. 24b-26, but this question is of minor interest to us.

Within the secondary section, v. 32-34 (and v. 39a) are of Dtr origin.[16] But what of v. 28b-31? There are only two alternatives to be taken into serious consideration: either that this passage is Deuteronomistic or that it derives from the author of the HDR. The arguments that Veijola[17] adduced in favour of the first alternative are not conclusive. The formulation *băyit næ'ᵃᵉman* (v. 28) can though need not be an indication of Dtr authorship. It is apparently a fixed formulation and is also found in 1 S 2,35 and 1 R 11,38, that are probably Deuteronomistic.[18] The formulation in 1 S 25,28 depends on the prophecy of Nathan (2 S 7,16: *wᵉnæ'măn bêtka*).[19] If, as Veijola holds, this verse in the prophecy of Nathan can be ascribed to the Dtr[20] the same would seem to hold for the formulation in 1 S 25,28. If not, 1 S 25,28 may well contain an old formulation that was later used by the Dtr (1 S 2,35; 1 R 11,38). Thus, this point cannot be cleared up until we have studied the prophecy of Nathan. The same holds for the words *'æt hăṭṭôbā* in 1 S 25,30 which are dependent on 2 S 7,28.[21] If this verse in the

---

[14] *Veijola* (1975: 47 ff.).
[15] Cf. *Grønbæk* (1971: 174).
[16] If David's praise in v. 32a (cf. v. 39) is Dtr (see *Veijola* p. 52 f.), it seems reasonable to assume that the expression *măštîn bᵉqîr* (v. 34) is an indication of the same provenance of the section, since this is otherwise used in Dtr contexts in 1 R 14,10; 16,11; 21,21; 2 R 9,8 (see *Veijola* p. 51). Thus, the whole of 1 S 25,32-34 is probably due to the Dtr. The section is not indispensable in its context. However, in 1 S 25,22 the words *măštîn bᵉqîr* may be a gloss, as appears from a comparison with Num 9,12, and need not imply that v. 22 as a whole is Deuteronomistic.
[17] *Veijola* (1975: 52 f.).
[18] On 1 S 2,27-36 see *Veijola* (1975: 35 ff.). On 1 R 11,29-39 see *Dietrich* (1972: 15 ff., 54 f.).
[19] Cf. *L.Schmidt* (1970: 122).
[20] *Veijola* (1975: 73).
[21] See *L.Schmidt* (1970: 122). Veijola does not mention this point.

prophecy of Nathan is Dtr,[22] the reference in 1 S 25,30 is probably from the same hand, in which case it is important to note that its syntactic position in this verse could be taken to indicate that it is a gloss.[23] If 2 S 7,28 were shown to belong to the HDR, the occurrence in Abigail's speech would derive from the same author.

In my opinion these are the most interesting indications of a Dtr hand in v. 28-31. Veijola's other arguments do not carry as much weight.[24] If Dtr authorship of v. 28-31 cannot be regarded as proved, we must count with the possibility that the author of the HDR was responsible for the insertion of v. 28-31 into the old narrative. In this way this author too can be regarded as having reworked the material relating to Abigail and David. In Veijola's analysis, he disappears from the picture in ch. 25. The development of 1 S ch. 25 may have been as follows: (1) An old narrative about David and Abigail is preserved in v. 1-24a.27.28a.35-38.39b-44. (2) The author of the HDR added v. 28b-31 (and perhaps even v. 24b-26 if these are not Dtr) in order to subordinate his source material to his special *skopos*: David's future kingship and his freedom from blood-guilt. (3) A Dtr redactor added David's praise in v. 32-34.39a. He perhaps also inserted into v. 30 a reference to the *ṭôbā* in 2 S 7,28 thus placing the promise in v. 28-31 in relief. However, this is so far only provisional. It is also necessary to study the prophecy of Nathan to assess correctly 1 S ch. 25 (see ch. 2.4.2).

Just as in 1 S ch. 25 there is also a hint at the dynasty in 20,12-17.42b, one of the texts referring to a covenant between Jonathan and David. Veijola also ascribes this text to the Dtr, as also the similar material in 23,16-18 and 24,18-23a. He holds that these sections were inserted by the Dtr to link the HDR and the SN.[25] These passages are indeed of secondary character in relation to the oldest material. Now, whether or not 23,16-18 and 24,18-23a are Dtr, the same does not necessarily hold for the passage 20,12-17.42b. That this section, where David promises Jonathan to show mercy to his descendants, is somehow related to the tradition contained in the SN concerning David's pardon of Meribbaal (2 S ch. 9; cf. 2 S 21,7),

---

[22] See for instance *Cross* (1973: 254 note 154) and *Veijola* (1975: 74).
[23] See *Stoebe* (1973: 450). In 1 S 24,19 a similar construction is found in a passage that Veijola (p. 90 ff.) takes to be of Dtr origin.
[24] To make a distinction between the reality of the YHWH-war in 1 S 18,17 and its "theoretische Repristinierung" in 25,28 (*Veijola* 1975: 52) seems a little far-fetched. As for the formulation "take vengeance with one's own hand" (v. 31 LXX), there is only one occurrence of this outside 1 S ch. 25, namely in Jud 7,2. Even if Dtr, this single occurence does not prove anything. As for the title *nagîd*, I find it impossible to share Veijola's conviction that not only 1 S 13,14 but also 2 S 5,2; 6,21; 7,8 are due to Dtr elaboration. For my reasons see below on the conclusion of the HDR and my chapter on the title *nagîd*. As for David's innocence (*Veijola* p. 53 f.), this feature clearly plays a part in other places of the HDR (see 1 S 24,1-16; ch. 26; 2 S 1,1-16; 3,22-39; 4,1-12) and therefore need not be of Dtr origin.
[25] *Veijola* (1975: 81 ff.).

goes without saying. But this connection need not be of a literary nature as Veijola holds. Even if 2 S 21,7 (which links with 1 S 20,42b) is of Dtr origin[26] this does not automatically imply that 1 S 20,42b (and 20,12-17) is of the same provenance. Moreover the linguistic indications, which would seem to point to a Dtr origin for 1 S 20,12-17.42b do not seem to be conclusive.[27] Thus, it remains an interesting but so far unproved hypothesis that this passage is the result of Dtr elaboration. The bias of the passage would quite as well suit the purposes of the author of the HDR.

3. Tendenz, Purpose and Date

To allow a discussion of the conclusion of the HDR, it is necessary at this point to treat the purpose and date of the work. In doing this, I shall provisionally argue from the old established idea that the conclusion of the work is found in 2 S 5,10. Later on, we shall see that there are reasons to also include some further sections.

In an attempt to understand the HDR from internal evidence, Grønbæk has demonstrated that the intention of the work is to describe David as the man elected by God to succeed Saul to the throne. Saul stands out as rejected by the Lord. His office was to be taken over by one who was his superior, i.e. by David (1 S 15,27 f.; 16,14 ff.; 18,10-12).[28] The divine election of David is emphasized by the recurrent phrase $YHWH$ $‘immô$, indicating that the Lord was with David. This *Beistandsformel* plays an important role in the HDR.[29] It represents the Lord as standing behind the course of events that led up to David's seizure of power.

[26] See *Veijola* (1975: 108).
[27] To *Veijola's* arguments (p. 84) the following can be said. (a) The designation of God as $YHWH$ $’a^{e}lohê$ $yiśra’el$ (20,12) also appears in pre-Dtr contexts (e.g. Jud 5,3.5; 1 S 14,41; 23,10-11). (b) The special type of oath in which the speaker refers to himself by name is so sparsely attested that it does not prove anything. Of the four occurrences I hold 2 S 3,9 and 1 R 1,30 to be pre-Dtr. (c) The *Beistandsformel* with a phrase of comparison is also too sparsely attested to say anything. Besides, it occurs in 1 R 1,37, which I cannot take to be Dtr. (d) While $‘ad$ $‘ôlam$ is used by the Dtr it also occurs in other layers of the Old Testament, as appears from a glance at the concordance.
[28] See *Grønbæk* (passim, esp. p. 271-277). *Mildenberger* speaks of two different tendencies in the material: (a) an interest to legitimate Davidic claims to sovereignty over Northern Israel as well (1962: 170, 177), and (b) the representation of Saul as a man rejected by God and replaced by David (e.g. p. 12). The first tendency was ascribed by Mildenberger to an early narrative about Saul and David, and the second to a nebiistic revision from the days of Isaiah. It is the great merit of *Grønbæk* to have demonstrated that these two tendencies are but aspects of one and the same basic interest: to justify David as the lawful successor to Saul and thereby as king over all Israel.
[29] The assertive use of this phrase is found in 1 S 16,18; 18,12.14.28; 2 S 5,10 (cf. 2 S 7,3.9). The promissory use of it is found in 1 S 17,37; 20,13. On this subject see *Preuss* (ZAW 80/1968, 139 ff., esp. 148 ff.) and *Grønbæk* (1971: 79 f.). Note also *D. Vetter* (1971). *Nielsen* (VTSuppl 7/1960, 71 f.) suggests that the phrase was an echo of a coronation ritual, practised at the royal sanctuary of Jerusalem.

Various other features are stressed, that contribute to this impression of David as the legitimate successor to Saul. The circumstances that led to his taking over of Saul's oracle priest, Abiathar, are dealt with at length (1 S ch. 21–22).[30] His frequent consultation of the oracle shows that the various steps taken by him are in accord with the purposes of the Lord. Saul's royal *nezær*, his diadem, is brought to David after the battle on Mount Gilboa (2 S ch. 1). David is said not only to have married Saul's second daughter but also to have received Saul's promise to marry Merab, the eldest one (1 S 18,17 ff.).[31]

There is thus an unmistakable tendency to suggest a continuity between Saul and David. Here the actual historical situation presented a problem to the writer. As Buccellati has demonstrated, even Saul's kingship was in principle dynastic.[32] That is to say that the natural successor to Saul was his eldest son, Jonathan, and not David. The way in which this dilemma is solved by the author reveals much of the intention of the work.

In 1 S 18,3-4 we read that Jonathan and David made a $b^e r\hat{\imath}t$ and that Jonathan "stripped himself of the robe [$h\breve{a}mm^{e'}\hat{\imath}l$] that was upon him, and gave it to David, and even his sword and his bow and his girdle". The deep and beautiful symbolism of this seems to have been overlooked so far.[33] It seems to me that the motif here has royal overtones. The rending of a robe, probably that of Saul, in 1 S 15,27f. signified the rejection of Saul and the transition of his kingdom to David. Seen in the light of the fact that the word $m^{e'}\hat{\imath}l$ can denote a royal robe,[34] Jonathan's robe is part of his princely apparel. When he hands it over to David he at the same time gives up and transfers his particular position as heir apparent. There is thus a legal symbolism in the act.[35] The author of the HDR solves his problem by representing David as the man to whom Jonathan, of his own free will, transferred his position as heir apparent.

In all his dealings with the house of Saul, David is depicted as guiltless. This feature is stressed to show that he was no usurper of the throne. Through his compositional arrangement, the writer stresses the historical connection between the death of a Saulide and David's seizure of power over Judah and the northern tribes respectively. Thus, his anointing as king

---

[30] On this, see the valuable analysis by Grønbæk (1971: 127 ff.).
[31] See Grønbæk (p. 107 f.). Note also *Morgenstern's* interesting hypothesis (JBL 78/1959, 322-325) that the strange lack of continuity in the Edomite king list (Gn 36,31-39) may be explained on the assumption that each successive king was the son-in-law of his predecessor.
[32] *Buccellati* (1967: 195 ff.).
[33] Even *Grønbæk* seems to have overlooked it although it provides evidence in support of his theory.
[34] See 1 S 24,5.12; Ez 26,16. Cf. also 2 S 13,18 (the king's daughters).
[35] A similar thought is expressed in 1 S 23,17. According to *Veijola* (1975: 88 ff.) this belongs to a Dtr section.

over Judah (2 S 2,1-4) is preceded by the battle on Mount Gilboa, David's execution of the Amalekite, who claimed to have killed Saul, and his lamentation over Saul and Jonathan. He was not anointed king over the northern tribes (2 S 5,1-3) until after the death of Ishbaal.

In the two scenes in which we meet David in a situation where it would have been possible for him to have killed Saul, the same loyalty is stressed by the contrast to others who did not respect the inviolability of Saul as the anointed of the Lord (1 S 24,5; 26,8-9). In this connection one can also mention the death of Abner. This is described in some detail to show that David was free from involvement and thus bore no blame (2 S 3,22 ff.).[36]

The author of the HDR is thus anxious to show that David's seizure of power was unimpeachable. It took place by the will of God. The work also reveals a particular interest in the relations of the northern tribes to Saul and David respectively. There was early an attachment between David and both the northern and the southern tribes (1 S 18,6.16). As God's own elect David became king over a pan-Israelite kingdom. He was anointed over both Judah and Israel. Now, it can be inferred that Saul was never king of Judah in the full sense of the word; the author of the HDR, however, purports to convey the impression that he was (see excursus no 1 on the dualism between Judah and Israel). It seems probable to me that Saul's royal title was actually *mælæk yiśra'el* (1 S 24,15; 26,20; 29,3), and that "Israel" was used here in its narrow sense as a designation of the kernel of the northern tribes. There are indications that the use of "Israel" in the pan-Israelite sense is later than the days of Saul.[37] In its narrow sense, however, the word also occurs in connection with Solomon's designation as *nagîd* (1 R 1,35).

Historically, Saul was king of the northern tribes, but the author of the HDR tries to impress on his readers the idea that Saul's kingdom comprised Judah as well as Israel. We are entitled to say that the make-up of David's actual kingdom has been reflected backwards to the days of Saul. Some very particular reason must lie behind this, an interest to demonstrate that the Davidic supremacy over a kingdom of pan-Israelite dimensions was not a novelty but a heritage from the days of Saul, a heritage that became David's through divine intervention.

The background and nature of this interest must of course be understood from the period of composition. Both Ward and Grønbæk have argued that

---

[36] I agree with *Veijola* (1975: 30 ff.) that 2 S 3,28-29.38-39 are of Dtr origin, but the tendency to stress David's guiltlessness is already present in the pre-Dtr material as Veijola is also well aware of.

[37] See *S. Herrmann* (1973: 189 f. with literature). However, I do not agree with this scholar that this usage is as late as the period after the fall of the Northern Kingdom. It is found several times in the HDR which is to be dated considerably earlier.

the work was composed in the first decades after Solomon's death.[38] This suggestion accounts for precisely this feature in the work. It is hard to assume a date during the reign of Solomon for a work that depicts the ideal king as not guilty of bloodshed (contrast Solomon's executions of his enemies). On the other hand, the assumption of a late date during the days of Jehu[39] cannot account for the characteristic features of the work. These features make sense in the period immediately following Solomon's death. The reflecting backwards of the extent of David's kingdom to the days of Saul is one of two important elements in a literary attempt to legitimate the Davidic, Jerusalemite claims to total supremacy over "all Israel" after the dissolution of the personal union.[40] The other important element in this is the remarkable stress on a continuity between Saul and David. This particular accent can be seen as an expression of the idea that Saul's kingship could not be taken up by a northern usurper (Jeroboam); God himself had transferred it to David. It should be noted that this dating of the HDR ties in with and receives further support from the results of my examination of the title *nagîd*.

4. The Conclusion of the HDR

We are now in a position to take up the question of the conclusion of the HDR. The classical opinion is that this is to be found in 2 S ch. 5 (5,10 to be more exact).[41] But a few scholars have held that 2 S ch. 7 also made up part of the work.[42] That the material in ch. 8 was put in its present position by the Dtr is easily seen from 8,1a.14b-15.[43] The passage on David's wars in this chapter probably serves to demonstrate the Deuteronomistic theory that David was not permitted to build the temple because of his wars (1 R 5,17). It was therefore inserted after the prophecy of Nathan in which the building of the temple has a certain role. However, the contention that all the material in 1 S 5,17–8,18 was inserted here by the Dtr[44] must be seriously questioned. Of course, this would give the HDR a very anaemic ending, hardly equal to the one of the SN as disclosed above. But there are more specific reasons.

---

[38] *Ward* (1967) and *Grønbæk* (1971: esp. p. 20-23, 273-277).
[39] So *Conrad* (ThLZ 97/1972, 321 ff.).
[40] This was hinted at by *Mildenberger* (1962: 170, 177) and was developed by *Grønbæk* (1971: esp. p. 20-23, 273-277).
[41] Most recently this opinion has been held by *Grønbæk* (1971: 256 ff.) and by *Veijola* (1975: 98 f.).
[42] See *Mildenberger* (1962: 119–121, 151), *Weiser* (VT 16/1966, 342 ff.) and *Rendtorff* (Fs vonRad 1971: 435 f. note 24).
[43] See *Veijola* (1975: 95 f.)
[44] As *Veijola* (p. 94-105) holds.

1. 2 S 5,17-25 and 6,1-23

That 2 S 5,17-25 and 6,1-23 were transmitted together appears from a number of *verba associandi*.[45] And with the word *'ôd*, "again", 6,1 links with 5,17 ff.[46] Within this section 5,17–6,23 there are some features deserving attention.

(a) The designation of the ark is not *'arôn berît YHWH* as we would expect in a passage handled by the Dtr (cf. for instance 1 S 4,3-5). It is simply *'arôn ha' aelohîm* (6,2.4.6.7) or *'arôn YHWH* (6,10.15.17).

(b) The statement in 5,21 that David and his men took with them the idols of the Philistines seems strange in a passage inserted by the Dtr. One would rather have expected them to burn them (as in the Chronicler's version 1 Ch 14,12) or bury them and not simply carry them away as spoil.

(c) The passage on David's victories over the Philistines in 5,17-25 appears as the fulfilment of the divine promise mentioned in 2 S 3,18 that David would save Israel from the hand of the Philistines (Abner to the elders of Israel). If this promise belongs to the HDR,[47] as I shall later argue it does, its fulfilment in 5,17 ff. is reasonably part of the same work.

(d) The motif of the consultation of the oracle, which is the common mark of the two originally independent traditions in 5,17-25, is a further indication that the section under discussion belongs to the HDR where its role is of importance. It is worthwhile noticing that Grønbæk felt that 5,17-25 must belong to the HDR, but since he assumed that this work ended in 5,10 he was forced to resort to the theory that 5,17-25 had been transposed from its original position after 5,3 to its present place by a redactor.[48] If one assumes that the HDR did not conclude with 5,10 this theory is superfluous.

2. *The Redactional Position of the Prophecy of Nathan*

The material itself supports the conclusion that 5,17–6,23 was not placed here by a Dtr redactor but was part of the original HDR. What is then to be said of the prophecy of Nathan? The question of the literary integrity of this text and of possible Dtr accretions will be taken up below. What I am concerned with here is only who is responsible for placing the prophecy of Nathan in its present context. That a pre-Deuteronomistic strand is to be found in this text, is generally admitted.[48a] The question now is this: are

---

[45] Note e.g. *parăṣ* (5,20; 6,8) and see further *Carlson* (1964: 58 ff.).
[46] See *Veijola* (p. 101).
[47] *Veijola* (p. 60 ff.) argues that 2 S 3,17-19 is a Dtr passage. On this I do not agree (see below), but I appreciate his insight (p. 103) that there is a connection between 3,18 and 5,17 ff.
[48] *Grønbæk* (1971: 250-254). For a reaction, see *Veijola* (p. 98).
[48a] *Carlson* (1964: 97 ff.) seems to hold that the text as a whole is Dtr. Otherwise, scholars who stress the Dtr elements of the chapter admit that there were earlier stages, see *Cross* (1973: 254 ff.) and *Veijola* (1975: 77 f.).

we entitled to think that some form of the prophecy of Nathan was included in the SN (as the opening of this work) or in the HDR (as its conclusion).[48b]

(1) The *language* of the prophecy of Nathan makes it very hard to assume that more than possibly a kernel made up the opening of the SN. The *Beistandsformel* (*YHWH 'im*) is found in 2 S 7,3.9 in its assertive use. This use is known from the HDR but not from the SN.[49] A pregnant and rare term that occurs in 2 S 7,8 (cf. 6,21) is *nagîd*. The use of this term to denote divine designation is in agreement with its use in the HDR (2 S 5,2; 6,21; cf. 1 S 25,30). On the other hand the SN has a different use of it since there it is David who designates Solomon *nagîd* (1 R 1,35). Similarly, the divine name *YHWH* (*'ᵃᵉlohê*) *ṣᵉba'ôt* (2 S 7,8.26.27; cf. 6,2.18) does not occur even once in the SN but is found three times in the HDR (1 S 15,2; 17,45; 2 S 5,10). The phrase *galā 'ozæn*, found in 2 S 7,27 (=1 Ch 17,25), is found 13 times in the Old Testament: In addition to the two texts already mentioned we find it once in Ruth (4,4) and in 1 S 9,15 (pre-Dtr Saul tradition), three times in Job (33,16; 36,10.15) and four times in texts clearly belonging to the HDR (1 S 20,2; 22,8 *bis*; 22,17) to which we may also add the two cases in 1 S 20,12.13 if the passage 20,12-17 is part of the HDR. By contrast the phrase does not occur at all in the SN.

(2) The *contents* of the prophecy of Nathan give positive indications of a connection with the HDR. The situation in 2 S ch. 7 (the king sitting in his palace, planning to build a house for the ark of God) presupposes the facts found in the preceding chapters: the conquest of Jerusalem, the building of the palace (5,6-9.11), and the bringing of the ark to the new capital (ch. 6). The stress on the election of David and the rejection of Saul (7,8-9.15) points back to 6,16.20-23 where Michal's barrenness stands out clearly as a very marked expression of the rejection of Saul: not even through his daughter Michal would Saul be given a descendant to the throne. Here, in 2 S 6,20-23 and 7,9ff. we have only the final *fermat* of the brilliant tune played throughout the HDR. One also notes that the royal title used by Michal of David, "the king of Israel" (6,20), is Saul's title in the HDR (1 S 24,15; 26,20; 29,3) used here in Michal's utterance to express the continuity between Saul and David, a theme of infinite importance to the author of the HDR. In the same way, the stress on the legitimacy of the Davidic dynasty in the prophecy of Nathan would seem to form a natural part of the argument of the author of the HDR. If we recall that this work was probably written during the decades immediately after Solomon's death, that is, shortly after the dissolution of the political ties that existed

---

[48b] Both alternatives are rejected by *Veijola* (1975: 100f.).

[49] Cf. above, note 29. The assertive use is not found in the SN. The promissory use is attested twice (2 S 14,17; 1 R 1,37).

between the northern and the southern tribes, it is not difficult to find reasons for a dynastic accent in the conclusion of the work. What could be more natural in a situation where the northern half of the Davidic kingdom seceded and chose a new king, than to stress the point of divine election not only of David personally but also of the dynasty? As we have already seen the author of the HDR wanted to ascribe to David the divine right to a pan-Israelite kingdom. The stress on the dynasty makes perfect sense as a prerequisite of the argument that the situation under David was to be normative for the period where the author himself lived – that the divine right of the kings of David's lineage related to a pan-Israelite kingdom.

(3) Finally, the various *allusions to David's future kingship* and his status as *nagîd* must be examined. As L.Schmidt pointed out, all but one (2 S 3,18) point forward to and presuppose the prophecy of Nathan.[50]

2 S 3,9-10 contains Abner's words to Ishbaal concerning a divine promise to David of a kingdom comprising all Israel, from Dan to Beer-sheba. What we have here is not a Dtr formulation but a very clear expression of the tendency of the HDR: David as elected by God to be king over all Israel.[51] The next promise, found in 2 S 3,18, contains a text-critical problem. This can be solved if we suppose that the original formulation did not contain $b^e y\check{a}d$.[52] The verse speaks of David as the saviour of Israel and purports to depict him in unbroken continuity with Saul who was also given the task of saving Israel from the Philistines (1 S 9,16). Thus, we can also here discern the hand of the author of the HDR. The secondary formulation with $b^e y\check{a}d$ and with the verb in the first person ('*ôšîª*', see app.) is due to Dtr elaboration and expresses a Dtr spiritualization of human achievements.[53] Apart from $b^e y\check{a}d$, the formulation of the MT is pre-Deuteronomistic. It belongs to the HDR and forms a promise that points forward to its fulfilment in 2 S 5,17ff., which is also part of the same work. One should note the title "servant", used of David in 2 S 3,18. Although it could be from the same Dtr hand as was responsible for the insertion of $b^e y\check{a}d$ nothing precludes the assumption that it was actually found in the original formulation in the HDR.[54]

2 S 5,1-2 speaks of "all the tribes of Israel" coming to David at Hebron. There is no reason to take this to be of Dtr origin. On the contrary, the for-

---

[50] See *L.Schmidt* (1970: 120ff.). On these promises see also *Grønbæk* (passim). *Veijola* (1975: 59ff.) takes all of them to be due to the Dtr.

[51] I am not convinced by the arguments adduced by *Veijola* (1975: 59f.) for a Dtr authorship. Abner's words that he will personally transfer the kingship to David are hardly in agreement with the Dtr tendency to spiritualize human achievements found in 2 S 3,18.

[52] See most recently *L.Schmidt* (1970: 136).

[53] I thus do not agree with *Veijola* (p. 60ff.) that the verse as a whole is due to the Dtr. For the Dtr spiritualization of human deeds, see 2 S 23,10.12 and cf. *Veijola* (p. 123).

[54] Cf. 1 S 23,10-11 and contrast *Veijola* (p. 127f.) who contends that the Dtr were responsible for the use of this title for David.

mulation "we are your flesh and blood" expresses the idea of the attachment of all the northern tribes to David which the author of the HDR is so anxious to stress. The divine utterance, quoted in v. 2, "you shall be shepherd of my people Israel, and you shall be *nagîd* over Israel", points back to 1 S 16,1-13 where the young shepherd David is taken from the sheep, but also foreshadows the prophecy of Nathan where we find both the rare use of *ra'â* for a leader (v. 7 for the judge) and the word *nagîd* (v. 8 for David). The formulation in 5,2 is clearly dependent on 7,7-8.[55] Thus if the words in 5,2 are pre-Deuteronomistic (and make up part of the HDR) the same early date holds *a fortiori* for the formulations in 2 S 7,7-8.

Finally, David's self-legitimation in 2 S 6,21 is a further expression of the intentions of the author of the HDR and must originate from that work. The rejection of Saul's family and the divine election of David as *nagîd* belong with the above-mentioned formulations by the author of the HDR as do pearls on a necklace.[56]

Thus a series of allusions to the divine election of David goes through the HDR like the thread of Ariadne. The implications of the anointing by Samuel (1 S 16,1-13) stand out as a secret yet generally recognized piece of knowledge.[57] The different formulations just studied make part of a very delicate structure. The work opened with a section that contained David's anointing by Samuel, continued with a series of highlights pointing forward to the prophecy of Nathan and concluded with some form of this prophecy of Nathan (to be more nearly determined below). Thus, it opened with David's election and ended with the transference of this preferential status to the Davidic dynasty.

If this conception of the HDR, its compass and purpose, is in the main correct then nothing stands in the way of the words of Abigail in 1 S 25,28-31 forming another highlight, formulated by the author of the HDR. Indeed, Abigail's words fit into the series of allusions to David's divine election and foreshadow the triumphant finale of the work with its stress on the Davidic dynasty.

The passages in the prophecy of Nathan (2 S ch. 7) that are presupposed in or else carry the marks of belonging to the HDR are the following: v. 7 (*ra'â*, cf. 2 S 5,2), v. 8 (*nagîd*), v. 9 (*Beistandsformel*), v. 11b.16 (the sure house, cf. 1 S 25,28) and v. 28 (*tôbā*, cf. 1 S 25,30). The implications of these observations will be kept in mind in the investigation of the prophecy of Nathan, to which I shall now turn.

---

[55] See *L.Schmidt* (1970: 124 f.).
[56] *Veijola's* arguments for a Dtr authorship (p. 68) do not convince. The title *nagîd* is pre-Dtr in 1 S 9,16; 10,1; 1 R 1,35; 2 S 5,2. The verb *bahăr* is used in pre-Dtr formulations about the king in 1 S 10,24; 2 S 16,18. And "das Nebeneinander von Sauls Verwerfung und Davids Sonderstellung" certainly creates no problem for including the verse in the HDR.
[57] Cf. *Hertzberg* (I & II Samuel p. 258).

Summary

The HDR was discussed with particular attention to the recent contributions by Grønbæk and Veijola.

(1) It was concluded that the HDR comprised 1 S ch. 15–2 S ch. 7. I agreed with Grønbæk that the rejection of Saul and the anointing of David by Samuel (1 S 15,1–16,13) were part of the work but suggested that within this section 15,10-26.35b have been inserted by DtrP. As for the conclusion of the work, I disagreed with the general opinion, defended most recently by both Grønbæk and Veijola, that the work ended in 2 S ch. 5 with David's conquest of Jerusalem. Also 5,17-25; 6,1-23 and, in particular, a pre-Dtr form of the prophecy of Nathan made up the conclusion of the work.

(2) As for the purpose and date of the work, I agreed with Grønbæk. David is described as the one chosen by the Lord to be king over Israel. He is depicted as Saul's legitimate successor. His loyalty and innocence in his dealings with Saul and his family are stressed. The work was composed during the decades immediately after Solomon's death and the dissolution of the personal union between Judah and Israel. One of the major concerns of the author was to justify the claims of the Davidic kings in Jerusalem to supremacy not only over Judah but also over Israel. The author achieves this in the following way:

a. The actual extent of the David's dominion (Judah and Israel) is reflected backwards to the days of Saul. Historically Saul was king over Northern Israel only but is depicted in the HDR as king over Judah as well.

b. An unbroken continuity between Saul and David is suggested. As Saul's successor David inherited sovereignty over all Israel.

c. The emphasis on the concept of the Davidic dynasty (1 S 25,28; 2 S 7,11b. 16) serves to establish every new Davidic king as the divinely commissioned heir of the pan-Israelite kingdom of David.

(3) For the purposes of this study, the following points are of particular importance:

a. The anointing of David by Samuel in 1 S 16,1-13 was included in the HDR and within this work had the essential function of depicting David as being the secret Messiah from the outset.

b. A pre-Dtr form of the prophecy of Nathan formed the conclusion of the HDR. The implications of this will be pursued in detail in the next chapter.

c. There are a number of highlights in the work that allude to David's position as the chosen one of the Lord designated to become king (1 S 25,28-31; 2 S 3,9-10; 5,1-2; 6,21). The term *nagîd* plays an important part in these (exception: 2 S 3,9-10). These sections cannot be regarded as Dtr insertions but already existed in the HDR and have a function in the

literary structure of this work. The bias of the work is clearly expressed in these passages. I am therefore inclined to draw the conclusion that they were the work of the author of the HDR. I shall revert to this problem in my treatment of the term *nagîd* (see ch. 9.3).

CHAPTER III

The Prophecy of Nathan (2 S 7,1-29)

1. Survey of Research

The vast literature on the prophecy of Nathan[1] shows that the amount of research that has gone into understanding this text is in proportion to its exceptional importance. Any new attempt at interpretation must be made against the background of earlier research, which I shall first outline to give a general idea of the lie of the land.[2] In the following survey, the references are to the literature mentioned in note 1.

Rost's contribution (1926: 47-74) determined the course of much of the subsequent research. He takes as his point of departure David's prayer (v. 18-29) and assumes that it contains an early tradition, possibly from the days of David, that was later enriched by the Dtr passage v. 22-24. The kernel is found in v. 27 which contains an oracle to David not mediated through Nathan (p. 63 f.). In the central part of the text, v. 8-17, Rost maintains that v. 11b and v. 16 contain the oldest version of the prophecy of Nathan. For lack of any indication to the contrary he dates this kernel to the days of David (p. 63). The major part of this section (v. 8-11a.12.14.15. 17) forms a later strand dating from the days of Isaiah (p. 64 f.). The promise of the temple in v. 13a is a late insertion of Dtr origin (p. 65, 67).

In addition to other difficulties in Rost's analysis, his view that v. 11b.16 are an original kernel and that v. 8-11a.12.14.15.17 are a later strand must be considered. Is it feasible that an oracle that originally promised an "eternal" dynasty to David (v. 11b.16) would later have been reduced to an oracle applying to David's immediate successor?[3]

Rost's influence can still be seen in the contributions of Kutsch and Poulssen while at the same time important modifications are to be noted. According to Kutsch there is (a) an old kernel to be found in v. 11b, whereas (b) the rest of the chapter is a unity, although (c) v. 13a is a Dtr insertion. Poulssen in his turn

---

[1] Except for the commentaries see *Rost* (1926: 47-74), *Mowinckel* (SEÅ 12/1947, 220-229, pagination as in the Lindblom Festschrift), *v.d.Bussche* (ETL 24/1948, 354-394), *Simon* (RHPhR 32/1952, 41-58), *S.Herrmann* (WZLeipzGes.spr. Reihe 3/1953-54, 51-62 esp. 57 ff.), *Noth* (GesStud I, ²1960: 334-345), *Fohrer* (ZAW 71/1959, 9f.), *Kutsch* (ZThK 58/1961, 137-153), *Ahlström* (VT 11/1961, 113-127, esp. 126f.), *Tsevat* (HUCA 34/1963, 71-82), *Schreiner* (1963: 75-101), *Caquot* (VTSuppl 9/1963, 213-224), *Gese* (ZThK 61/1964, 10-26. esp. 21 ff.), *Carlson* (1964: 97-128), *Weiser* (ZAW 77/1965, 153-168), *McCarthy* (JBL 84/1965, 131-138), *Tsevat* (Bibl 46/1965, 353-356), *Clements* (1965 A: 55-61; 1965 B: 56-66), *Calderone* (1966), *Poulssen* (1967: 43-55), *Weinfeld* (JAOS 90/1970, 184-203; 92/1972, 468 f.), *L.Schmidt* (1970: 146-159), *Seybold* (1972: 26-45), *F.M.Cross* (1973: 241-265), *Veijola* (1975: 68-79) and *Görg* (1975: 178-271).

[2] For other notes on previous research see *Cross* (1973: 241 ff.), *Veijola* (1975: 68 ff.) and *Görg* (1975: 178 ff.).

[3] For this and other objections see *Veijola* (1975: 69 f.).

assumes two different complexes, viz. v. 5-11a and v. 11b-16. Like Rost, he identifies the old kernel in v. 11b.16. These two complexes were brought together when v. 13 was added, viz. during the reign of Solomon. Thus v. 13 is not a late Dtr accretion but is considerably older and serves to legitimate the temple (p. 48 ff.).

Ever since the forties there has been a growing tendency to see more of literary homogeneity in the chapter. Thus Mowinckel took the text as a whole, including v. 13a, as a theological *aition* from the days of Solomon composed to explain why David did not build a temple (p. 224). S.Herrmann's theory from the fifties that the genre of the text is that of the royal novel (p. 57 ff.) became an important argument in the hands of those who uphold the literary unity of the text. Noth (p. 342 ff.) accepted it, and Weiser in particular (p. 154 ff.) argued for a Solomonic date of the text as a whole on the basis of Herrmann's definition of the genre.

Herrmann's theory was later criticized.[4] There are two difficulties in particular connected with it. First, contrary to what we should expect from the alleged Egyptian model, the divine message comes to David through a third party, the prophet Nathan. In spite of statements to the contrary (Rost above, Görg below) it seems difficult to dissociate Nathan from the oracle in its original form, as will appear from my analysis below. Secondly, it is an essential element of the royal novel that the king's plans are carried through. In the Israelite text, however, David is prevented from carrying out his intentions. In recent years alternative suggestions have been advanced by Calderone (1966) and Seybold (p. 35 ff.), both arguing in favour of a covenantal structure, whereas Weinfeld (p. 184 ff., esp. 190 ff.), proceeding along similar lines, draws attention to the promissory, unconditional type of covenant known from the royal grants recorded on the *kudurru* stones.

However, the line from Herrmann was continued by M.Görg (178 ff.). This scholar founds his comparison with Egyptian material on a literary critical analysis of the prophecy of Nathan. According to Görg the text began with v. 1-7 in a form in which the prophet Nathan was not mentioned, a form that contained a direct revelation to David.[5] This *Grundbestand* continues in 8b.9.11b*.12-16.18-22a.25-29, while v. 8a.10.11aβ.11b.17.22b-24 constitute a later strand (p. 205). Thus Görg assumes the existence of an original version containing both the divine promise of a dynasty and the king's response. This original form also comprised the promise of the building of the temple in v. 13a (p. 197 ff., 222), that has often been taken as Deuteronomistic. As for genre, Görg compares the earliest version with emancipated Egyptian literature containing individual elements of the structure of the royal novel, such as "The Decree or Blessing of Ptah upon Ramesses II and III" and "The Prophecy of Neferti" (p. 234 ff.).

Another line of research has stressed the Dtr elements of the prophecy of Nathan. This is in line with a general interest in recent years in Dt and the Dtr literature. A.Carlson, whose attitude is very pessimistic concerning the possibility of reconstructing a pre-Dtr cycle of traditions of David in the Books of Samuel, takes the same position as regards the prophecy of Nathan (p. 97 ff.). McCarthy puts aside the question of possible literary sources in an attempt to demonstrate that the pericope belongs to the series of major Dtr speeches and similar passages, which determined the structure of the entire DtrH.

F.M.Cross (1973: 241 ff., esp. 249 ff.) also stresses the function of the text in the overall structure of the DtrH and points to the Dtr idiom in it. But Cross is also aware of the necessity of posing the question for pre-Dtr strands in the text. Accord-

---

[4] See *Kutsch* (ZThK 58/1961, 151 ff.), *Cross* (1973: 247 f.) and *Veijola* (1975: 71 f.).
[5] *Görg* (p. 187). Cf. *Rost* (1926: 68 ff., cf. p. 63).

ing to him the text contains two pre-Dtr oracles: (a) the "old oracle" of Nathan in v. 1-7 and (b) the "eternal decree" in v. 11b-16. Both are old, although the first displays some Dtr features (p. 254 ff.). A third section, v. 8-11a, reflecting some older material, is not an integral part of either oracle but forms a Dtr link connecting v. 1-7 with v. 11b-16 (p. 254). The prayer of David in v. 18-29 is Dtr throughout (p. 247).

T.Veijola, although mainly interested in the Dtr redactions of the Books of Samuel, is also alive to the possibility of the presence of old material in the prophecy of Nathan. His point of departure is an alleged literary discrepancy between v. 12b (wăhªkînotî 'æt mămlăktô) and v. 13b (wᵉkonăntî 'æt kissê' mămlăktô 'ăd 'ôlam). The latter is secondary, and extends the horizon of the text beyond the limits of the original oracle which was only concerned with David's immediate successor (p. 72 f.). V. 13a with the promise of a house for the name of the Lord is also taken to be secondary and belonging to the same strand as v. 13b (p. 72). To this secondary stratum belong also v. 11b.16, which display the same extended horizon.

Proceeding along these lines Veijola reaches the following conclusion. The old material used by the Deuteronomists contained two oracles. (a) One of these was a prophetic veto on the plans to build a temple (v. 1a.2-5.7), which the Deuteronomists modified by making the prohibition appear only provisional saying that the temple was built for the name of the Lord and not as his dwelling place (p. 78). (b) The other oracle consisted of v. 8a.9.10.12.14.15.17 and was concerned with David and his immediate successor although the latter was not mentioned by name. By the insertion of v. 13, the Dtr redactor identified this as the builder of the temple, Solomon. By the insertion of v. 11b.16, this redactor also extended the horizon of the promise to refer to an eternal Davidic dynasty (p. 78). This material reflects two Dtr redactions. The text owes v. 11b.13.16.18-21.25-29 to DtrH and v. 1b.6.11a.22-24 to DtrN (p. 74 ff.).

These efforts to come to grips with the Dtr material in the pericope are deserving of attention. Veijola's attempt to distinguish between two different horizons is certainly noteworthy. But the discrepancy between v. 12 and v. 13 is only apparent. Furthermore, it is strange that an oracle applying to David's immediate successor should not have referred to Solomon until in a late, Dtr redaction. Veijola's conclusion that there are traces of DtrN in the pericope is also problematic. According to Veijola (p. 142) this redactor made the promise conditional (1 S 13,13-14; 1 R 2,3-4; 8,25; 9,4-5). It is difficult to believe that this alleged redaction of 2 S ch. 7 would have left the unconditional promise (v. 14b-15) untouched. One particular problem is also the relation between v. 1-7 and v. 11b-16. Both Cross and Veijola assume two different, and as it seems originally independent, oracles. Were they first brought together in the DtrH? An indication to the contrary seems to be the observation that there are certain connections between 8-11b.16.28 in particular and the History of David's Rise. In my own analysis I shall try to do justice to the conclusion reached above that the prophecy of Nathan in some form or other constitutes the concluding part of this work of history (see above ch. 2.4.2).

The fact that the prophecy of Nathan forms a pivotal passage in the general structure of the DtrH and fits into the series of major Dtr speeches and similar passages, does not preclude the possibility that there is older material preserved in 2 S ch. 7. I shall now first try to isolate what can with some certainty be determined as a Dtr strand in this text. After this I shall

investigate the literary integrity of the older material and then, finally, study the purpose and background of this pre-Dtr material.

2. The Deuteronomistic Layer

The part of the pericope in which scholars have seen most Dtr redaction is David's prayer in v. 18-29. Carlson, Cross and Veijola consider this to be Dtr throughout.[6] It is true, indeed, that there is Dtr material in v. 18-29. It is important to note, however, that this is concentrated to a passage beginning in v. 22. Rost, and later Noth, recognized the Dtr character of v. 22-24.[7] This passage is marked by its Dtr phrases[8] and this phraseology is also found in v. 25 (*heqîm dabar*[9]). The passage also stands out by reason of its Dtr ideology. While the remainder of David's prayer and the preceding oracle revolve around David and the Davidic dynasty, the whole concern of v. 22b ff. is "the great and terrible things" of God on behalf of Israel in the past, at the time of the Exodus.[10] The confession in v. 22-24 can be compared with the Dtr confessions in Jos 2,9-11; 9,9-10.[11] The praise of the uniqueness of the Lord (22b) and of His deliverance of the people from Egypt (v. 23) are also well-known Dtr motifs. Thus, v. 22b-25 have the Dtr marks of language and content.

In addition other observations make it probable that v. 22b-26 are an insertion. V. 22b opens abruptly in "we-style", which is not found in the rest of the chapter. It refers to Israel while the rest deals with David and his dynasty. And v. 25 containing the prayer asking God to establish His word (with the Dtr phrase *heqîm dabar*) is a remarkable repetition of the prayer asking for fulfilment of the divine promise in v. 28-29. If v. 22b is the beginning of the insertion then where is the end? – It is to be found in v. 26, since v. 27 forms the continuation of v. 22a. Moreover v. 27 opens in the same way as v. 22b with a *kî*.

My conclusion is thus that v. 18-22a.27-29 belong to a pre-Dtr stratum of the prophecy of Nathan, and that only v. 22b-26 are a Dtr interpolation.[11a] In its pre-Dtr form David's prayer forms a literary unity. No inner discrepancies are to be noted in it. The conclusion that the section in

---

[6] See *Carlson* (1964: 128) and *Cross* (1973: 247). *Veijola* (1975: 74 ff.) takes v. 22-24 to be due to DtrN and the rest of the verses 18-29 to be due to DtrH.

[7] See *Rost* (1926: 49) and *Noth* (ÜSt p. 64).

[8] Note the use of *padā*, see *Stamm* (1940: 21), the complete "Bundesformel" in v. 24, see *Smend* (1963 B: 5) and "the great and terrible things" in v. 23 (cf. Dt 10,21).

[9] See Dt 9,5; 1 S 3,12; 1 R 2,4; 6,12; 8,20 etc. and cf. *Veijola* (1975: 75).

[10] As was pointed out by *Weinfeld* (1972: 38 the note). Cf. Dt 10,21.

[11] On these confessions in Jos, see *Bächli* (1970, 21-26).

[11a] It is also possible that the vocalization of the noun *hgdwlh* as a $q^etullā$ form (cf. *Mettinger*, JSS 16/1971, 2ff.) in v. 21 (cf. v. 23) was imposed by the Dtr redactor on an original *hăgg^edolā*.

David's prayer that referred to Israel is an insertion has a bearing on the assessment of v. 1-17: it is reasonable to conclude that v. 10-11a are also an insertion made by the same hand.[12] Here we see the same interest in the people of Israel. What is said of the enemies is also a strange repetition of v. 9a where these have already been accounted for. And the rest-motif in v. 11a strikes a well-known Dtr chord.[13] It occurs again in v. 1b ($w^e YHWH\ henî^aḥ\ lô\ missabîb\ mikkāl\ 'oybâw$), which should therefore also be taken to be Dtr.

Thus of v. 1-17 I take v. 1b.10-11a to be Deuteronomistic. It is, of course, tempting to assume the same origin for the *Wortereignisformel* ($wăyhî\ d^ebăr\ YHWH\ 'æl\ X$) in v. 4, but this is perhaps to go too far.[14] The same holds for the Exodus formula in v. 6.[15] In any case, it is of no importance to this study whether there are Dtr traces in these two verses or not. Important, however, is the problem of whether the significant verses 11b and 16, containing the promise of a Davidic dynasty, are due to Dtr redaction as Veijola holds. This question will be answered in the following discussion of the pre-Dtr material.

3. The Solomonic Document and Its Dynastic Redaction

When we now turn to the older material of v. 1-17, the first question concerns its literary integrity. A preliminary observation of great importance is that there are actually two different *skopoi* in this old material. (a) One is found in v. 8-11.16 where David and the election of the Davidic dynasty is the theme and the central term *băyit* denotes the dynasty (11b.16). (b) The other is found in v. 12-15, where the interest is focussed on Solomon and the building of the temple. These verses refer quite distinctly to an individual. And the Chronicler stresses this by defining *zæră'* as *'ašær yihyæ̂ mibbanêka* ("who is among your sons", 1 Ch 17,11). In v. 12-15 the word *băyit* refers to the temple (v. 13) and not to the dynasty.

Both these *skopoi* are held together by the ambiguous use of *băyit*. In this word, the two *skopoi* overlap. If the argument of v. 8-11.16 runs that David is not to build a house for the Lord, but that the Lord will build one for David, then the logic behind v. 12-15 is that David is not going to build a house for the Lord, but that Solomon is to do this. This implies that both *skopoi* are somehow related to what is said in v. 1-7. Though it is not

---

[12] I here agree with *Görg* (1975: 191 ff.).
[13] See Dt 12,10; 25,19; Jos 21,44; 23,1; 1 R 5,18 and cf. *vonRad* (GesStud ²1961: 101 ff.).
[14] See *Veijola* (1975: 112 note 39). In general, however, the occurrences of this formula are late, see *Dietrich* (1972: 71 f.).
[15] See *W.Gross* (ZAW 86/1974, 440f.) who takes 2S 7,6 to be pre-Dtr. Contrast *Veijola* (1975: 77) who takes the whole v. 6 to be a Dtr interpolation.

difficult to see which of these two *skopoi* that v. 1-7 originally served to express. This passage, where God prohibits David to build a temple, finds its proper continuation in v. 12-15. There is a line of thought running through v. 1-7.12-15: David was not to build the temple, but one of his offspring was to do so. Moreover, this line of thought is stressed by the remarkably close correspondence between God's question to David in v. 5 and the promise of the temple in v. 13:[16]

v. 5:   האתה תבנה לי בית לשבתי
v. 13:   הוא יבנה [לי] בית לשמי

The parallelism is perfect once we read *lî* in v. 13 on the basis of the LXX and the Chronicler (1 Ch 17,12). At some stage in the development of the text, reading both *lî* and *lišmî* was felt to be tautological, and so *lî* fell out from Samuel in the MT and *lišmî* from the Chronicles in the MT.[17] The LXX of 2 S 7,13 has preserved both of them correctly.

Some other features of v. 1-17 may also be relevant to the question of its literary integrity. The word *zæră'* in v. 12 is strangely ambiguous. Taken in connection with v. 11b (the dynasty of David), this word takes on the character of a collective and must denote the whole Davidic line of kings (cf. Ps 89,30-33; 132,12). But since v. 12-15 are held together by one particular *skopos*, which is not the one found in v. 11b, it becomes more natural to read v. 12 and *zæră'* in conjunction with v. 13 which speaks of the man who was to build the temple. Then *zæră'* appears to denote an individual. It is true that Budde took the allegedly collective sense in it to indicate that v. 13 must be an insertion.[18] However, it is to be remembered, that *zæră'* is also found in a singular sense referring to an individual in Gn 4,25; 1 S 1,11, a use that was also known to St Paul.[19] That the word *zæră'* in v. 12 is to be understood primarily in its individual sense is in agreement with the use of the expression *'ªšær yeṣe' mimme'êka* (v.12), which refers to an individual in the two other occurrences (Gn 15,4; 2 S 16,11). If this is correct there is indeed a certain discrepancy between v. 11b (the dynasty) and v. 12-13 (Solomon) which becomes acute in the word *zæră'* in v. 12.

It may also be observed that v. 16, which expresses the dynastic *skopos* of the text, stands in a slight tension to v. 12-15 insofar as the second person

---

[16] This correspondence between v. 5 and v. 13 was noted by *Caspari* (1926: 482), *Carlson* (1964: 109) and *Görg* (1975: 221). *Noth's* objection (GesStud I, ²1960: 335 f.) is not valid, as appears from my conclusion below that the distinction *lᵉšibtî* – *lišmî* was imposed on v. 1-7 (cf. v. 13) in order to make an originally definite prohibition against a temple appear only provisional.

[17] I owe this explanation to Dr *Bo Johnson*, Lund.

[18] *Budde* (Samuel p. 232).

[19] See Gal 3,16.

in the singular ("your house" etc.) appears a little suddenly after the "seed" has been mentioned in the third person in v. 12-15. Moreover, while v. 11b.16 speak of an everlasting dynasty, there is no mention of this in v. 12-15. On the contrary the "seed" is a single king, Solomon according to v. 13.

It is remarkable that there is no reference to v. 13 and the building of the temple in the whole section comprising David's prayer. If, as Veijola holds, both v. 13 and v. 18-29 were the work of the Deuteronomists, this fact is very strange. We must look for an explanation of the absence of the temple from David's prayer.

Finally, it is important to note that the actual opening of Nathan's prophetic oracle to David is in v. 4-5. Thus there is a strange repetition in v. 8 which contains a new opening, although nothing indicates that Nathan has been interrupted or that he has otherwise finished the speech begun in v. 5.

The question of the literary integrity of the pre-Dtr material must be answered on the basis of these observations. And there is only one answer that accounts for all of them: there are two different layers in the pre-Dtr material. (a) One consisted of v. 1-7.12-15 (to suggest a preliminary compass[20]) and could be termed the Solomonic layer since it centres on Solomon and the temple. (b) The other consisted of v. 8.9.11b.16 (as will be remembered, we found that v. 10-11a were Dtr). This could conveniently be termed the Davidic-dynastic layer.

Our next question will naturally be concerned with the relative age of these two layers. Has one of them the character of a commentary on the other? Evidence favours the conclusion that the Solomonic layer is the older. The fact that there is a continuous line of thought in v. 1-7.12-15 is important to note. There is also a close formal connection between v. 5 and v. 13. This connection was made considerably less obvious by the insertion of v. 8.9.11b. V. 11b in particular contains the new motif of the dynasty which dissolves the original connection between v. 5 and v. 13. It is the dynastic motif of v. 11b that makes *zæră'* in v. 12 ambiguous. In the Solomonic layer the "seed" is an individual. V. 11b creates the present tension between the individual and the collective sense of the word *zæră'*. We can therefore conclude that the Solomonic oracle was later submitted to a redaction that imposed a new Davidic-dynastic *skopos* on the old kernel of the text. A promise that primarily concerned Solomon as an individual, was extended so as to be valid for the whole Davidic dynasty by means of v. 11b.16. The traces of this development that remain seem to me to imply that we are here concerned with a literary process and that the Solomonic layer was already in existence as a written document.

---

[20] V. 14b-15 probably belong to the Davidic redaction, see below.

A glimpse at David's prayer in v. 18-22a.27-29 is sufficient to show which of the two layers of v. 1-17 this belongs to. Everything in David's prayer revolves around the promise of a Davidic dynasty; there is no mention of Solomon or the temple in it and David's prayer is thus part of the dynastic redaction of the older Solomonic promise. That there is no reference to v. 13 is not because v. 13a is a Dtr insertion as has often been held.[21] On the contrary, the temple was actually mentioned in the Solomonic promise, its absence in David's prayer being due to a redaction that imposed a new *skopos* on the text.

If the relative age of the two layers can thus be determined as (1) the Solomonic document and (2) its Davidic-dynastic redaction, we can now go a step further by making use of the conclusion reached above in the discussion on the HDR that this great work of history had the prophecy of Nathan (in some form or other) as its concluding block. Some sections of the prophecy of Nathan were presupposed by other passages in the HDR, viz. v. 7-9.11b.16.28. Since these verses (except for v. 7) are all due to the dynastic redaction it follows that the HDR presupposed and contained the prophecy of Nathan in its dynastic redaction. That is to say the major part of the chapter (except for v. 1b.10-11a.22b-26 which are Dtr) constituted the triumphant finale of the HDR. Indeed, I would like to venture to suggest that the dynastic redaction of the prophecy of Nathan is the work of the author of the HDR. Even so, the dynastic redaction of this text was carried out prior to the composition of the HDR, since it is presupposed in various passages (see ch. 2.4.2.3).

This conclusion regarding the relation of the dynastic redaction to the HDR is interesting from two different points of view. (a) It follows that there is no reason to assume traces of a Dtr redaction in Abigail's speech in 1 S 25,28-31. This speech refers to the prophecy of Nathan as a *tôbā* (v. 30) and thereby presupposes 2 S 7,28 which is not Dtr but the outcome of the dynastic redaction. The same speech (in v. 28) also refers to the "sure house" of 2 S 7,16, the linking of which with David is due to the same dynastic redaction (see below ch. 3.4.2).

(b) If the Davidic-dynastic redaction of the Solomonic prophecy of Nathan is presupposed in the HDR and now forms part of this work, there follows a most interesting conclusion for the old Solomonic document: it must be still older than the HDR which is taken to have been composed in the decades immediately after Solomon's death.

---

[21] Cf. *Rost* (1926: 56) to mention a representative example.

4. Characteristic Features. Purpose and Date

So far we have distinguished the two layers of the pre-Dtr prophecy of Nathan and have found that what we have here is a Davidic-dynastic redaction of an old Solomonic prophecy of Nathan. The conclusion that the prophecy of Nathan originally applied to Solomon fits in perfectly with what is said regarding Nathan in connection with Solomon's birth (2 S 12,25: Jedidiah) and the accessional crisis (1 R ch. 1). Some additional observations pertaining to the Solomonic document can now be made.

1. Verse 13 and the Reference to the Temple

The usual excision of v. 13a, *hû' yibnæ* [*lî*] *băyit lišmî*, as a Dtr insertion is unwarranted as appears from its interrelation with v. 5b. The possibility always remains that *lišmî* in v. 13a (and then of course also the corresponding element in v. 5b, *lᵉšibtî*) can be put down to Dtr redaction,[22] a point of no great importance to the present study. However, it may well be that the contrast between the temple as the abode of the Lord (v. 5) and the temple as a place for the more spiritual presence of His name (v. 13) was part of an early defence from the days of Solomon, of the theological acceptability of the temple.[23] Actually, a theological criticism of the temple is taken up in v. 6-7 which refer to the old nomadic conception of YHWH as a god who had never taken his abode in a house (*yašăb*) but always in a tent, as S.Nyström has pointed out.[24] Although the temple was built as a *Wohntempel* (cf. 1 R 8,12 f.: *makôn lᵉšibtᵉka*), it is possible that, quite early, recourse was taken to the theological distinction between God's personal presence and that of His name in defence of the Solomonic temple. And the theology of the divine *šem*, that is of considerable importance in Dt and Dtr writing, may well have more ancient roots than is generally supposed.[25]

---

[22] See 1 Ch 17,12 and cf. *Gese* (ZThK 61/1964, 22 f.) who does not, however, see the implications for v. 5. – As I pointed out above, there are no text-critical difficulties in assuming that v. 13a originally had both *lî* and *lišmî*.

[23] On the prohibition against David's plan to build a temple, see esp. *Schreiner* (p. 80 ff., esp. 89 ff.) and *Weiser* (ZAW 77/1965, 158), who both distinguish between *Wohntempel* and *Erscheinungstempel*. Note also *Clements* (1965 A: 55-61) and *Ahlström* (VT 11/1961, 113 ff.).

[24] *S.Nyström* (1946: 125).

[25] Note the following indications: (a) The use of Akkadian *šakānu šumšu*, "to place one's name", as an expression for taking possession of something, in the Amarna letters EA 287, 60-63 and 288,5-7 which are both letters from Jerusalem. (b) The early use of *hizkîr šem* for similar purposes in Ex 20,24 (see *Mettinger* 1971: 54). (c) The fact that there is a clear connection between the ark and the name of the Lord since the name YHWH was regarded as having been called out (*qara'* Niph), over the ark (2 S 6,2). – On this subject, see *Schreiner* (1963: 158-164) who nevertheless takes v. 13a to be Dtr (p. 76), *Weiser* (ZAW 77/1965, 163 note 28), *Görg* (1967: 117 ff.), *W.Richter* (1970: 117 note 55) and *Görg* (1975: 222).

Whatever the case may be it is an inescapable fact that the Solomonic document contained a reference to the temple, as is borne out by the correspondence between v. 5 and v. 13. The main point in this Solomonic document is not, however, a legitimation of the temple. The reference to the temple in v. 13a serves above all to identify Solomon as the particular son of David whose kingdom God was to establish (v. 12b), as the one referred to in the promise of divine sonship (v. 14). The main purpose of the Solomonic document is not so much to demonstrate the theological acceptability of the temple (even if this motif is probably present) as to legitimate Solomon through the divine proclamation $'^a n\hat{\imath}\ 'æhy\bar{æ}\ l\hat{o}\ l^e 'ab\ w^e h\hat{u}\ yihy\bar{æ}\ l\hat{\imath}\ l^e ben$ (v. 14).

2. Verse 16: A "House" for David or for Solomon?

A close reading of v. 16 provides us with still another expression of the same intention. We concluded above that this verse is the result of the Davidic redaction. David is the one spoken to ("*your* house" etc.), and the utterance takes up the thread from v. 11b. In this "Davidic" form, occurring in the MT, v. 16 must be part of the dynastic redaction. In actual fact, however, the LXX has a different reading, a point that is generally overlooked in the scholarly literature.[26] The LXX reads the third person ("*his* house" etc.), the "house", "kingdom" and "throne" thus being denoted as *Solomon's*. The textual evidence can be tabulated thus:

2 S 7,16		1 Ch 17,14	
MT	LXX (B)	MT	LXX (B)
ונאמן	καὶ πιστωθήσεται	והעמדתיהו	καὶ πιστώσω αὐτὸν
ביתך	ὁ οἶκος αὐτοῦ	בביתי	ἐν οἴκῳ μου
וממלכתך	καὶ ἡ βασιλεία αὐτοῦ	ובמלכותי	καὶ ἐν βασιλείᾳ αὐτοῦ
עד עולם	ἕως αἰῶνος	עד העולם	ἕως αἰῶνος,
לפניך	ἐνώπιον ἐμοῦ,		

---

[26] *H.v.d.Bussche* (ETL 24/1948, 391) noted it and even preferred to think that v. 16 originally referred to Solomon, although he did not connect this insight with the question of real redaction of the text.

כסאך	καὶ ὁ θρόνος αὐτοῦ	וכסאו	καὶ θρόνος αὐτοῦ
יהיה	ἔσται	יהיה	ἔσται
נכון	ἀνωρθωμένος	נכון	ἀνωρθωμένος
עד עולם	εἰς τὸν αἰῶνα.	עד עולם	ἕως αἰῶνος.

That the *lᵉpanêka* of the MT is to be corrected into *lᵉpanay* is easy to see (*kaph* through dittography of the first letter of the following word). As for the suffixes of the three nouns "house", "kingdom" and "throne", there is a very firm textual tradition which attests to the third singular. Except for Aquila, Theodotion and Symmachus, who probably represent a correction based on the same textual tradition as that found in the MT, the whole LXX tradition for 2 S 7,16 attests to the third singular. The reading of the Chronicler ("and I will appoint him over my house and over my kingdom for ever and his throne shall be established for ever"[27]) is due to a theocratic re-interpretation of the prophecy of Nathan.[28] Even so the version of the Chronicler (in the MT as well as in the LXX) agrees with the LXX of 2 S 7,16 in relating the utterance to Solomon and not to David.

How can this textual variation in v. 16 between the MT ("your house", i.e. David's) and the LXX ("his house", i.e. Solomon's) be explained? The reading of the LXX could of course be secondary and have arisen from the strange oscillation between Solomon and the Davidic dynasty. On the other hand the possiblity must be faced that we have here one of the probably very rare occasions when a textual variation reflects the redaction history of a given passage. In this case the LXX reading has preserved a tradition that goes back to the original Solomonic document of Solomon's legitimation: "And his house and his kingdom shall be made sure for ever before me; his throne shall be established for ever." The MT on the other hand is the result of the dynastic redaction.

It is then also interesting to note that the "Solomonic" version of v. 16 is presupposed in Solomon's words in 1 R 2,24, where Solomon thanks God – "who has established me and placed me on the throne of David my father, and who has made me (*lî*) a house, as he promised". The suggestion (BHK³ app.) to emend to *lô* to introduce a reference to David is unwarranted since the verse seems to record the original form of 2 S 7,16.

The concept of the Davidic dynasty is prominent in the dynastic redaction. The original promise of a "house" for Solomon, the promise that the

---

[27] My own translation.
[28] Cf. 1Ch 28,5; 29,23; 2 Ch 9,8; 13,8 and see *Poulssen* (1967: 172). – On the Septuagint of Chronicles, see *Gerleman* (1946) and *Allen* (1974).

royal line would continue through him (v. 16 in its Solomonic form), is like a tune that has been transposed into a different key by altering the signature. The function of the "signature" is fulfilled by v. 11b, which was added by the dynastic redaction. This formulation, "and hereby the Lord declares to you that he will make you a house",[29] has been put before the original promise to Solomon in v. 12-16. It fulfils the task of transposing this original promise into a promise of a dynasty to David. Consequently, the short melody of the Solomonic tune must end on this new note, and so we find the suffixes in v. 16 changed to the second person singular. This transfers the reference from Solomon to David. It is this use of v. 11b as what could perhaps be called a pre-positive element to introduce v. 12-16 *and* the alteration of the suffixes in v. 16 that explain the strange oscillation between individual and collective in *zæră'*.

Within the Solomonic section v. 12-16 the reference to the misbehaviour of the king and his chastisement (v. 14b-15) probably belongs to the dynastic redaction, since it seems improbable that the Solomonic document should have contained this feature. Moreover the rejection of Saul mentioned in v. 15 is a motif well known from the HDR. This motif is used here to provide a contrast to the Davidic king who was never to be rejected by God but only punished.

The result of this analysis can then be summarized in the following survey:

---

[29] My own translation. I take *wᵉhiggîd* to be a *perfectum declarativum*. I am not convinced by the suggestions made by various scholars (see most recently *Cross* 1973: 256 and *Görg* 1975: 195f.) to depart from the MT of 2 S 7,11b, except that an original *wᵉhayā* at the beginning of v. 12 was mistaken for *yhwh* (and taken to belong to the end of v. 11b) or that this *wᵉhayā* in v. 12a fell out after an original *yhwh* in v. 11b (cf. 2 S 7,12 LXX and 1 Ch 17,11 MT and LXX which attest to this *wᵉhayā*). – To read the first person instead of the third (*wᵉhiggîd*) leads to the suggestion of either *wa'āggîd* as in 1 Ch 17,10 (the MT) or *w'gdlk* (to be vocalized as a piel or a hiphil) on the basis of καὶ αὐξήσω σε (1 Ch 17,10 LXX). In both cases we are left with an imperfect. In my opinion a *perfectum declarativum* is more fitting for the solemn proclamation, and this we have in the MT of 2 S 7,11b.

The Solomonic promise	The dynastic redaction
v. 1a.2-7: David's plan to build a house for YHWH. Revelation to Nathan: David is not to do this. References to theological objections to the temple (*y-š-b*).	*v. 3: Beistandsformel.*
	v.8-9.11b: Historical retrospect. David is elected *nagîd*. YHWH promises to build David a "house" (a dynasty).
v. 12-14a: Solomon is David's "seed". Identified through the commission to build the temple, Solomon is the one who is alluded to in the promise of divine sonship (v. 13-14).	*v. 14b-15:* Disobedience results in punishment but not in rejection as in the case of Saul.
v.16*: A house for Solomon, suffixes in the third singular (cf. LXX).	*v. 16*:* The verse is brought into line with the Davidic-dynastic redaction through a change of the suffixes into the second singular: a house for David as in the MT.
v.17: Conclusion	
	18-22a.27-29: David's prayer, revolving around the promise of a dynasty to David.

3. Questions of Date

The relative age of the two layers has already been commented on, but some further remarks can be appended here. The Solomonic document is from the time prior to the composition of the HDR (the decades immediately after the death of Solomon). On the other hand the reference to the temple points to a date when this building existed. Thus, we have reason to believe that the Solomonic prophecy of Nathan is from the days of Solomon's reign, a date that fits in excellently with its obvious purpose of legitimating Solomon. Whether this Solomonic oracle formed the actual opening of the SN is impossible to say, although this would provide the SN with a proper beginning, something that scholars have so far looked in vain for. In this case it would be natural to see a connection between 2 S 12,25 (Nathan calls Solomon Jedidiah) and the promise of divine sonship in the original prophecy of Nathan (v. 14).

Another observation pertaining to the age of the material is that originally v. 1-7 probably comprised an independent oracle, perhaps from the reign of David, that was incorporated into the Solomonic document. This oracle probably implied a definite rejection of David's plans to build a temple (see v. 6-7). It was given a new accent when the Solomonic promise imposed upon it the distinction between a *Wohntempel* ($l^e\check{s}ibt\hat{\imath}$, v. 5) and an *Erscheinungstempel* ($li\check{s}m\hat{\imath}$, v. 13), an observation that incidentally makes it even less probable that $li\check{s}m\hat{\imath}$ is a Dtr accretion.

The dynastic redaction, comprising the dynastic promise in v. 11b.16, cannot possibly date from David's own reign. It belongs to the period of the composition of the HDR, shortly after the death of Solomon. To find a very marked dynastic accent in a piece of literature from this period is quite natural since the Davidic supremacy had then been challenged by the line of Northern Israelite kings. It is also interesting to note that the dynastic version of the text displays no particular interest in denoting David himself as "son" of God. It is important, however, that every new Davidic king on the throne of Jerusalem stands out as holding this privilege of divine sonship.

4. Royal Ideology: Son of God and nagîd

Our new interpretation of the process of growth behind the present form of 2 S ch. 7 is of course highly important to the study of the sacral legitimacy of the king. In the old Solomonic document of legitimation the relation between king and God is seen in the categories of divine sonship. We shall return to this subject in due course and only point out here that the formulation with the preposition l^e ($l^e\:ab - l^eben$) seems to indicate that this is to be understood in a metaphorical sense. In addition to the divine sonship the Solomonic document also mentions the divine support of the king (v. 12b. 13b.16).

In its dynastic redaction the prophecy of Nathan speaks of divine sonship for every new king of David's lineage. But now a new key word has been introduced in addition to *ben*. God took David "from the pasture, from following the sheep"[30] so that he would be *nagîd* over Israel (v. 8). A highly significant result of this investigation is that the formulation about David as *nagîd* (v. 8) is later than the formulation found in the Solomonic oracle about Solomon as "son" of God (v. 14). The implications of this will be followed up in the chapter devoted to the important title *nagîd*.

---

[30] I find it quite impossible to accept *Gottlieb's* suggestion (VT 17/1967, 197) that 2 S 7,8 should refer to a cultic humiliation of the king: "Ich entferne dich hiermit aus deiner Stellung als Hirte", the term "Hirte" then being used of the position as king. Whether it is possible or not to find allusions in the OT to a cultic suffering of the king it is out of question to take 2 S 7,8 to be one of them.

Summary

The previous attempts to come to grips with the problems of the prophecy of Nathan have been found to be unsatisfactory. It has therefore been necessary to work out an entirely new interpretation of this crucial text.

(1) I used the same procedure as that adopted in an excavation: to define first the most recent stratum and then proceed to the earlier levels. The most recent stratum represents a Dtr redaction of a pre-Dtr text and is found in v. 22b-26 and also in v. 1b.10-11a.

(2) The pre-Dtr material contains two different layers. The original prophecy of Nathan was a document from the reign of Solomon concerned with the legitimacy of this king. This document contained the material now found in v. 1a.2-7.12-14a.16*.17. The point in this document is that one particular son of David is to enjoy the privilege of divine sonship (v. 14a). That this son is none other than Solomon appears from the reference to the building of the temple (v. 13). There is here a close connection between v. 5 and v. 13 with a marked correspondence between these at the levels of both form and content. The "house" in v. 16 was here connected with Solomon (suffix in the third singular as in the LXX) and not with David. I drew attention to the interesting possibility that this pro-Solomonic prophecy of Nathan formed the opening of the SN, a work that was found to have a pro-Solomonic purpose. I also mentioned the possibility that v. 1-7 contain an originally independent oracle from the days of David aiming at a definite rejection of David's plans to build a temple. This feature was then modified in the Solomonic document through the contrast between a house $l^e\check{s}ibt\hat{i}$ (v. 5) and a house $li\check{s}m\hat{i}$ (v. 13).

(3) The Solomonic prophecy of Nathan was later, probably in the decades immediately after Solomon's death, subjected to a dynastic redaction, the traces of which are now found in v. 8-9.11b.14b-15.16*.18-22a.27-29. Here it is no longer Solomon that comes to the fore but the divine election of David (v. 8-9) and his dynasty (v. 11b.16.18-22a.27-29). The original link between v. 5 and v. 13 has here been broken through v. 11b with the emphasis now on $b\breve{a}yit$ as "dynasty". This new feature caused the ambiguity now found in $z\ae r\breve{a}^\epsilon$ in v. 12, which, while originally referring to Solomon, has here been extended to comprise the whole Davidic dynasty.

(4) In this dynastic form the prophecy of Nathan was utilized as the final building stone by the author of the HDR. We have earlier found that the allusions to David's divine election and his future kingship in the HDR presuppose the prophecy of Nathan (ch. 2.4.2.3). It is then important to note that these passages rely on the prophecy of Nathan in its new, dynastic form. Since this dynastic redaction is clearly later than the original Solomonic document, there is slight probability that these passages in the HDR record promises that were actually made to David. The conclusion reached

in the previous chapter that these passages were probably formulated by the author of the HDR is thus substantiated by the above analysis of the prophecy of Nathan. Indeed, I even suggested the possibility of the same author being responsible for the dynastic redaction of this text.

(5) There is in the Solomonic document and in its later dynastic redaction a slightly different type of royal ideology. In the former the emphasis was on the promise of divine sonship to Solomon (v. 14a). This feature is also contained in the dynastic redaction, but here the new term *nagîd* (v. 8) has been introduced to denote the king as the chosen one of the Lord. This agrees with the use of the same term in the HDR in 1 S 25,30; 2 S 5,2; 6,21, an observation that I shall return to in a later discussion of this term.

CHAPTER IV

Saul's Anointing as Nagid (1 S 9,1 – 10,16)

The correct interpretation of 1 S 9,1 – 10,16[1], which relates Saul's anointing as *nagîd*, is of great significance for the study of the sacral status of the king. In the traditions of King Saul, this text holds place of precedence similar to that of the prophecy of Nathan and of the dream at Gibeon in the traditions of David and Solomon. The text in 1 S 9,1 – 10,16 contains a sacral legitimation of King Saul. In the subsequent discussion of the antecedent designation as *nagîd*, of the anointing of the king and of Saul's royal charisma conclusions will have to be based on this text. It is thus essential to discuss in some detail the problems connected with its use as historical evidence.

Some of the verses in this text can be regarded as redactional links. Thus 10,8 where Samuel tells Saul to go to Gilgal and wait for him there for seven days, appears to point forward to 13,7b ff. The role of 9,13b seems to be similar.

1. Tensions and Patterning (Berufungsschema)

The corpus of the text contains some tensions, the explanation of which is highly important to the general apprehension of it. The most important are the following ones:

1. The *skopos* of the narrative is obviously the anointing of Saul. But there is also in it another peak, namely the recovery of the lost asses.[1a]
2. The seer, whom Saul and his servant consulted about the lost asses of Kish, appears first as an anonymous "man of God" (9,6-8). It would seem that this local seer is from the town (v. 6). Later on in the text, however, this seer is recognized as being Samuel (9,14 ff.; 10,14-16). Further, it becomes clear that Samuel has only come to the town for a short visit in connection with a sacrificial feast (9,12).
3. There are tensions within the formulations about the signs. Samuel predicts three signs (10,2-6), but the fulfilment of one only is mentioned (10,9a. 10 ff.).

---

[1] For a survey of the research on this text, see *L.Schmidt* (1970: 58 ff.). On the general problem of the various traditions concerning the establishment of the institution of kingship in Israel see for a survey of research *Langlamet* (RB 77/1970, 161-200).

[1a] See now especially *W.Richter* (1970: 43-45).

4. As regards this fulfilment of the third sign, there is a discrepancy between 10,5 and 10,9. According to 10,5 this was to take place when Saul had left Samuel and arrived at Gibeah. According to v. 9, it took place immediately, while Saul was still with Samuel.
5. There is also a difference between the MT and the LXX. While both the MT and the LXX speak explicitly of "signs" in the plural (10,7.9) the LXX contains in 10,1b an additional passage that speaks of one single sign. This passage is not found in the MT but should nevertheless be considered original (see below).
6. It seems that 10,9b forms the conclusion of the narrative, but in spite of this 10,10 ff. comes as a continuation.
7. This continuation of the narrative (10,10-13a) has a more negative view of Saul's relations with the ecstatic prophets than that expressed in 10,5 ff.

Of these observations nos 6 and 7 suggest that the etiology of the *mašal* in 10,10-13a is a later insertion. But what can be said of the other tensions in the text?

Hertzberg assumes that the narrative had two primary forms, native to different places. One told how Saul when searching for the asses was promised the crown by an unknown seer. The other described a visit by Saul to Samuel and dealt particularly with the anointing.[2] A new important trend in the study of this text was initiated by Stoebe who assumes a kernel dealing with the recovery of the asses. In one sense, this kernel points to Saul's future kingship. Because of the loss of the asses the future leadership of Saul's house was at stake since asses were the riding animal *par préférance* of the nobility of Israel. In the process of oral transmission this kernel was given a new *skopos*: the secret anointing was introduced into the narrative at a time when the anointing was a *sine qua non* for the legitimacy of the king.[3] A similar approach has also later been taken by other scholars.[4] There is now an emerging consensus according to which the secret anointing of Saul belongs to a later strand in the text. This strand has features in common with the type of call narratives known for instance in

---

[2] *Hertzberg* (1964: 78 f.). Cf. *Seebass* (ZAW 79/1967, 157 f.). However, the unity of 1 S 9,1–10,16 had been questioned decades ago by e.g. *H.Tiktin* (1922: 13) and *I.Hylander* (1932: 133 ff.). – *Weiser* (1962: 48 ff.) regards the narrative as essentially a unity, though 10,2-13 is said to be secondary (57 ff.).
[3] *Stoebe* (VT 7/1957, 362-370, esp. 364 ff.; 1973: 65, 200 f.).
[4] *Schunk* (1963: 85 ff.), *Macholz* (1966, unpublished dissertation, for which see *Boecker* 1969: 14 f.), *W.Richter* (1970: 13-56, esp. 43-45), *L.Schmidt* (1970: 58-102), *B.C.Birch* (JBL 90/1971, 55-68) and *J.M.Miller* (CBQ 36/1974, 157 ff.). – *Wildberger* (ThZ 13/1957, 451-455) suggested to take the passage about the anointing as *nagîd* (9,22–10,1.3.4) as being the kernel of the narrative and the rest of it as being unhistorical embroidery. This is to turn things upside down.

connection with Moses (Ex ch. 3) and Gideon (Jud 6,11-24). These features together constitute the *Berufungsschema*.[5]

The main elements of this *Berufungsschema* of the call narratives can be defined as follows:

1. Reference to the affliction of the people: (a) "... for I have seen [the affliction of] my people" (9,16, according to LXX), cf. Ex 3,7 and compare Jud 6,13. (b) "... because their cry has come to me" (9,16b), cf. Ex 3,(7.)9.
2. Commission (*Retterformel*): καὶ σὺ ἄρξεις ἐν λαῷ Κυρίου, καὶ σὺ σώσεις αὐτὸν ἐκ χειρὸς ἐχθρῶν αὐτοῦ κυκλόθεν (10,1 LXX). This commission is also referred to in 9,16a: "He shall save my people from the hand of the Philistines", cf. Jud 6,14 (Ex 3,10).
3. Objection: "Am I not a Benjaminite, from the least of the tribes of Israel?" (9,21), cf. Ex 3,11 and Jud 6,15.
4. Reassurance of divine assistance (*Beistandsformel*): "... for God is with you", (10,7b), cf. Ex 3,12 and Jud 6,(12.)16.
5. Sign: καὶ τοῦτό σοι τὸ σημεῖον (10,1 LXX).

Here we must consider the variant readings in 10,1. In this verse the LXX offers a text that is considerably longer than that of the MT (in the following, the parts of the Greek that correspond to the MT have been underlined):

<u>Οὐχὶ κέχρικέν σε Κύριος εἰς</u>   הלוא
ἄρχοντα ἐπὶ τὸν λαὸν αὐτοῦ, ἐπὶ
Ἰσραήλ; καὶ σὺ ἄρξεις ἐν λαῷ
Κυρίου, καὶ σὺ σώσεις αὐτὸν ἐκ
χειρὸς ἐχθρῶν αὐτοῦ κυκλόθεν.
καὶ τοῦτό σοι τὸ σημεῖον
<u>ὅτι ἔχρισέν σε Κύριος</u>   כי משחך יהוה
<u>ἐπὶ κληρονομίαν αὐτοῦ</u>   על נחלתו
<u>εἰς</u> ἄρχοντα·   לנגיד

The Peshitta attests to the short text of the MT, while the Vulgate has placed part of the LXX plus after a rendering of the first verse which agrees with the MT.

As is well known the reading of the LXX is often preferred to the MT in

---

[5] See *Zimmerli* (1969: 17; this fascicle was published as early as 1955, see the preface), *Kutsch* (ThLZ 81/1956, 75-83, esp. 79f.), *W.Richter* (1970: esp. 136ff.), *L.Schmidt* (1970: 88ff.) and *Birch* (JBL 90/1971, 61ff.). The critical remarks by *Seebass* (ZAW 79/1967, 163 note 36) against the assumption of the pattern in 1S 9,1ff. fail to convince. Richter's study of the elements of the pattern is particularly valuable.

10,1.[6] So far this opinion has been based more on scholarly intuition than on conclusive argument. The above observations (nos 2 and 5) that certain formulations of the *Berufungsschema* are lacking in the MT but have been preserved in the LXX present conclusive evidence in favour of the reading of the LXX. This aspect has hitherto been overlooked in the discussions of the textual problem. There are three points to be noted here:

(a) In 9,16 the LXX reading τὴν ταπείνωσιν τοῦ λαοῦ μου favours the restoration *'æt* [*'ᵃnî*] *'ammî*, which in turn corresponds exactly to the reference to the affliction in Ex 3,7.

(b) In 10,1 the LXX has a reference to the commission in its proper place, addressed directly to Saul, while this element is absent from the MT in 10,1. It is also to be noted that the divine commission mediated by a prophet at the anointing is paralleled at the anointing of Jehu (2 R 9,3.6-10).

(c) In the LXX (10,1) the phrase καὶ τοῦτό σοι τὸ σημεῖον corresponds exactly to the reference to the sign in Ex 3,12 (*wᵉzæ lᵉka ha'ôt*, cf. also 1 S 14,10). Here the reference to the sign is in the singular, whereas the reference in 10,7.9 (both MT and LXX) is in the plural. The LXX has here preserved a *lectio difficilior*. The tension between the singular and plural in the reference to the sign must be accounted for in the following investigation.

We can therefore conclude that 10,1 should be read according to the LXX. The shorter text of the MT can be readily explained by the assumption that a scribe's eye passed from the first *mᵉšaḥᵃka YHWH* to the second.

The parts of the text, expressing the new *skopos* of the anointing of Saul as *nagîd*, have been defined in somewhat different ways:

W.Richter: 9,14aβb.15-17.20-21; 10,1-7 (1970: 52).
L.Schmidt: 9,13aγ.14b-17.20-21.22b-24a; 10,1.13b-16 (1970: 101).
B.Birch: 9,15-17.20-21.(25-26).27 – 10,1 (LXX).5-8.16b (p. 68).

I agree on the essential correctness of the general approach. The presence of the twofold *skopos* and of other tensions in the present text thus finds a natural explanation. This means that the anointing of Saul as *nagîd* belongs to a more recent stratum of the text and not to the old kernel. For the purposes of this investigation it is of particular importance to decide where Saul's charismatic endowment (10,5-9) and the probable allusion to Saul's future kingship (9,20b) belong. It must be stated here that I find it somewhat difficult to accept the recent tendency to explain these two features as be-

---

[6] To mention only a representative sample the LXX is preferred by *Wellhausen* (1871: 72 f.), *S.R.Driver* (1890: 59), *Budde* (1902: 66), *P.Dhorme* (1910: 82), *A.Schulz* (1919: 144) and *Hertzberg* (1964: 77). The MT is preferred by *Ehrlich* (III: 201) *Weiser* (1962: 57 note 22) and *Stoebe* (1973: 197, 205).

longing to the *nagîd* stratum of the text. These points must therefore be discussed at some length.

It is clear that God's command to Samuel to anoint Saul (9,15-17) and its execution (9,27–10,1, with the text corrected according to the LXX) owe their place in the text to the new *skopos*. The same seems to be true of Saul's objection (9,21) and the reassurance of help (10,7b) which both belong to the *Berufungsschema*.

2. Saul and the Spirit

Of the more problematic passages we shall first consider 10,2-9, where the coming of the Spirit over Saul is of particular interest. The two encounters predicted for Saul in 10,2-4 must be attributed to the original tradition. In the kernel of the text (a) the search for the asses and in connection with this the concern of Kish for his son (9,5) and (b) the lack of bread (9,7) play a prominent part.[6a] These two features recur in 10,2-4. Thus these verses belong to the kernel of the tradition.

V. 8 has already been explained as a redactional link but the rest of v. 5-9 remains a problem, the solution of which has been looked for in different directions. Richter and Birch both ascribe v. 5-7 to the *nagîd* layer.[7] L.Schmidt on the other hand explains v. 5-6 as due to the redactor, who included the etiology of the *mašal* (10,10-13a) in its present place in the text, while he considers v. 7 and 9 to be original.[8] Neither of these two explanations carry conviction.

As we have already seen the sign of the *Berufungsschema* is found in the LXX in 10,1 and is in the singular. The plurality of signs in 10,7.9 is due to the fact that the original narrative mentioned several signs (10,2 ff.). The *Berufungsschema* with one single sign was applied to a narrative in which there were several.

The gift of the Spirit is not elsewhere an element of the *Berufungsschema*. It does not appear at all in connection with the call of Moses, and in the case of Gideon, endowment with the Spirit (Jud 6,34) does not seem to stand in any relation to the preceding call, which is depicted by means of the pattern. There is also a difference in terminology between Gideon's endowment with the Spirit and Saul's: *labăš* in Jud 6,34 as compared with *ṣalăḥ 'ăl* in 1 S 10,6. This being so it is reasonable to argue that the Spirit in 1 S 10,6 is not due to the pattern but is an element of the original tradition. At this point of the argument we can therefore ascribe to the original narrative v. 2-4, v. 9b and the essential elements of v. 6.

[6a] On this *L.Schmidt* (1970: 66) and *Birch* (p. 59) agree.
[7] *Richter* (1970: 52), *Birch* (p. 65).
[8] *L.Schmidt* (1970: 66, 112f., 117).

As for v. 7 we have already noted that the reassurance of divine assistance, "for God is with you", is probably due to the *Berufungsschema*. This, however, does not necessarily imply that the whole of the verse belongs to the *nagîd* layer. The following observations prove this unwarranted.

The verb *ṣalăḥ* is used in a number of places to describe the coming of the Spirit over a human being. Formulations saying that the Spirit *ṣalăḥ* *'ăl PN* occur in the following instances: Jud 14,6.19; 15,14 (of Samson); 1 S 10,6.10; 11,6; 18,10 (of Saul); 1 S 16,13 (of David). In the three cases where the expression is used of Samson the Spirit came upon him as the *immediate* prelude to a deed of valour. Now, it can be shown as probable that in 1 S 10,7 the command to "do whatever your hand finds to do" expresses an exhortation to Saul to act according to his strength and perform a deed of valour.[9] This means that in the present text there is also a direct link between the coming of the Spirit (expressed by *ṣalăḥ* v. 6) and a feat of bravery (v. 7). This implicit connection is destroyed if, like Schmidt, we try to ascribe the whole of v. 6 to the redactor who introduced the etiology in v. 10-13a into the text. The only part of v. 7 that can belong to the *nagîd* layer is the reassurance of divine assistance at the end of it ("for God is with you"). The rest must belong to the old narrative.

The original tradition, we can conclude, contained three different signs, and the last of these (v. 6-7) placed Saul with Samson. Here the original narrative agrees with 1 S ch. 11, which contains an obviously very old tradition of a mighty deed of Saul's as a manifestation of the Spirit. And also there we find the characteristic terminology *wăttiṣlăḥ rûᵃḥ* ... *'ăl* ... (11,6).

It still remains to discuss v. 5 and 9. It immediately strikes the reader that the two verses differ in the point of time for the fulfilment of the third sign. According to v. 5 f. this was not to occur until Saul had left Samuel and arrived at Gibeah. According to v. 9, the "turning" of the heart, which must be regarded as worked by the Spirit (cf. v. 6b), was immediate, i.e. before Saul left Samuel. The probable explanation of this is that the formulation "when he turned his back to leave Samuel, God gave him another heart" (v. 9a) is due to the revision of the original narrative. It seems that v. 9a expresses the idea of a very close connection between the anointing and the Spirit. Since the signs spoken of in the original narrative were retained the reference to the Spirit could not be placed immediately after the anointing in 10,1. The statement in 10,9a that Saul was still with Samuel when God turned his heart is made "by way of compensation" to underline the proximity in time between the anointing and the coming of the Spirit. (See also ch. 9.5.)

---

[9] Cf. Jud 9,33 and see *L.Schmidt* (1970: 74 ff.). According to Schmidt (p. 79), this is the *Ziel* of the original tale.

As mentioned above L.Schmidt took v. 5-6 to belong with the etiology of the *mašal* in v. 10-13a.[9a] This conclusion does not carry conviction. In the first place the immediate and original connection between the Spirit (v. 6) and the deed of valour (v. 7) must not be broken. This has been demonstrated above. Secondly, the attempt to disentangle v. 5 from the two preceding signs destroys the epic structure of the narrative. Each sign is marshalled by an encounter with a different number of persons, first two men (v. 2), then three (v. 3) and finally a whole band of prophets (v. 5). Thus v. 5 is the necessary climax of a series of three encounters.

Accordingly, the analysis of the passage under discussion (10,2-9) shows that the major part of it belongs to the original tradition (v. 2-7.9b). Only the reassurance of divine assistance (v. 7b) and the statement that Saul's heart was turned while he was still with Samuel (v. 9a) are due to the revision. And v. 8 is a still later redactional gloss.

3. The Promise of Kingship

Let us now consider the passage on Saul's encounter with Samuel and the sacrificial meal (9,18-24). Allowing for the difficulties connected with the analysis of this passage the following can be stated.

In the passage v. 18-21 the first two verses clearly belong to the original narrative. That Saul's objection (v. 21) belongs to the *Berufungsschema* and is therefore to be linked with the *nagîd* stratum can also be easily seen. The difficulty lies with v. 20. There is a unity of motif in the two halves of this verse, since the motif of the property of the house of Saul in v. 20a is developed in v. 20b. The first half of the verse speaks of the asses, and in the second half Saul and his *bêt 'ab* are promised *kål ḥæmdăt yiśra'el*. This formulation contains a beautiful ambiguity. The word *ḥæmdā* can mean *both* the desirable object, a sense that gave the primary impetus to its use after v. 20a speaking of the asses, *and* the desire itself. Taken in the latter sense the promise says that Israel's whole desire is concentrated on Saul and his ancestral house.

Recent treatments agree that v. 20 belongs to the *nagîd* layer.[10] The arguments for this attribution, however, seem to be inconclusive. The presence of the objection in v. 21 does not prove that its logical corollary, the promise in v. 20b, is late. Saul's objection can well have been appended to a promise found in the original narrative.[11]

[9a] L.Schmidt (1970: 112f.).
[10] See W.Richter (1970: 28, 52), L.Schmidt (1970: 67f.) and Birch (p. 62f., 68).
[11] Contra Birch (p. 62f.).

As for v. 20a, it has been said that the Hebrew perfect conveys a preterite sense so that the asses are said to *have* been found. This in turn would imply a conflict between v. 20a on the one hand and v. 19b and 10,2 on the other. We would thus have a conflict between 20a and verses belonging to the kernel of tradition so that 20a must belong to the revision.[12] Such a view, however, is simply due to a misapprehension of the functions of the Hebrew conjugations, which express aspect rather than tense.[13] Another argument has been that the three-day period in 20a is in conflict with the description of the long journey in 9,4f.[14] This argument does presuppose that the number three is to be taken in its literal sense. Now, this may not be the case, since the number three plays a conspicuous role in the original narrative. There are three signs in 10,2-9, one of which consists of three men carrying three kids, three loaves of bread and a skin of wine respectively (10,3). The "three days" in 9,20 fit well into this pattern. It seems that the actual number is imposed by the style and is not meant to be taken literally. The alleged "tension" is then more apparent than real and v. 20a may thus well belong to the old narrative.

The implicit promise "And for whom is *kål hæmdăt yiśra'el*? Is it not for you and for all your father's house?" (v. 20b) must reasonably be an allusion to Saul's future kingship. No doubt, the *nagîd* layer of the text is directly concerned with Saul's royal status. But this does not mean that all hints to Saul's kingship must belong to that layer of tradition. It should be kept in mind that the original narrative, however old it may be, played its role and had its main function after Saul had already become king. Then his youth became an interesting topic for tradition. This means that the basic tradition may well have contained the promise to Saul of "future" kingship.

Another question in this connection is the import of *bêt 'ab* (v. 20b). In all probability this expression contains a dynastic hint. This feature can have had a polemic function at the time when kingship had gone over to David. But there is nothing to prevent us from assuming that this element in the text is older than the *nagîd* stratum. Since Saul's kingship was historically intended to be dynastic, there is no difficulty in assuming a date as early as Saul's own reign for this reference to his "house".

The observations concerning the important v. 20 can then be summed up as follows: The arguments adduced in support of the opinion that v. 20 belongs to the *nagîd* layer have been found to be insufficient. On the contrary, there is no difficulty in assuming that v. 20a-b belongs to the strand of tradition that existed before the incorporation of Saul's anointing as *nagîd*.

Moreover, a positive indication in favour of this attribution is found in the three signs (10,2-9), all belonging to the original narrative. The first two of these (v. 2-4) refer to the affair of the asses. It is then to be expected that the third sign, the coming of the Spirit (v. 5ff.), has a corollary in the first part of the narrative. If so the only point that offers itself is the promise in v. 20b. And then this promise must belong to the original strand of tradition.

The sacrificial meal in 9,22ff. (cf. v. 12-13), at which Saul is offered a seat

---

[12] So *L.Schmidt* (1970: 67f.).
[13] For recent research on this problem see the survey by *Mettinger* (ASTI 9/1973, 73 ff.).
[14] *W.Richter* (1970: 17, 28).

of honour and is given the most valuable pieces of meat, appears as an anticipation of a coronation banquet.[15] It falls in line with the custom at royal investitures (1 S 11,15; 16,1-13; 2 S 15,7-12; 1 R 1,9). The same can be said of the thirty especially invited guests who perform the function of obligatory representatives of the people (see below ch. 7). The reference to Saul's kingship in 9,22 ff. is then more direct than the vague allusion in 9,20b. One could therefore feel tempted to ascribe the sacrificial meal to the *nagîd* layer which is concerned with Saul's legitimation for kingship.[16] The fact that the sacrificial meal is a feature adduced to explain why Samuel came to the town that particular day,[17] seems to support this conclusion, since the seer of the original narrative appeared to live in the town (9,6). On the other hand one cannot exclude the possibility that a meal played some part in the original narrative. In its present elaboration, however, the sacrificial meal probably belongs with the anointing.

4. The Contents of the Two Layers

We are now in a position to summarize the contents of the narrative at the two discernible stages of tradition: in its old form and after the inclusion of Saul's anointing as *nagîd*. The *original narrative* told how young Saul consulted a local seer about the lost asses belonging to his father Kish. This local seer promised that he would find the asses and also intimated Saul's future rank. This intimation took the form of a vague allusion (9,20b) and was not vested in a prophetic oracle in contradistinction to the anointing oracle of the *nagîd* layer (9,27 f.). Whether or not a meal played a part in the basic tradition cannot be determined with certainty.

Saul was granted three signs. Two of these (10,2-4) are related to the affair of the asses. The third, the gift of the Spirit, is meant to substantiate the seer's promise to Saul of future elevation. The gift of the Spirit can be seen as an allusion to a royal charisma. In this connection two points are most important to note:

(a) This royal charisma is directly linked with a military deed. It is thus conceived of in the categories of a more martial ideal of kingship than we find later in the Solomonic period, when the royal charisma was understood essentially as royal wisdom, particularly judicial wisdom, as is evidenced by 1 R ch. 3.[18]

---

[15] As was properly observed by *L.Schmidt* (1970: 84 f.).
[16] As does *L.Schmidt* (p. 84 f.).
[17] 9,12. Actually, Samuel is not mentioned until v. 14, but the coming of the man was found above to be linked with Samuel and not with the kernel of tradition.
[18] Note also the fact that 2 S ch. 14 (the woman from Teqoa) is part of the Succession Narrative, which dates from Solomon's reign.

(b) The connection between the anointing and the gift of the Spirit, so familiar from other texts (1 S 16,1-13; Jes 61,1-3), is not at hand in the original tradition. This mentioned the Spirit but not the anointing. The connection between the two emerged as the result of the process of tradition.

The *narrative in its developed form* with Saul's anointing as *nagîd*, formulated in the characteristic phrases of the *Berufungsschema*, points to Saul's future kingship in much more explicit terms than in the original. A feature already present in the basic tradition has thus been accentuated. The seer now takes the shape of the well-known Samuel. In a revelation, this man of God had received express instructions to anoint Saul *nagîd* over Israel. Before this commission was carried out Saul was invited to a meal that is depicted as a coronation banquet with representatives of the people expressly listed as present. The rite of anointing took place on the following morning, and this was accompanied by a solemn prophetic oracle (9,27–10,7), immediately after which God turned Saul's heart (10,9) implying the fulfilment of the promise of the Spirit.

The original tradition offered itself to the imposition of the *Berufungsschema*. The three signs granted by the local seer in the original tradition (10,2-9) could conveniently be subsumed under the single sign of this pattern (10,1 LXX). The formal elements of Saul's objection and of the reassurance of divine assistance have been appended to details of the original tradition that can be regarded as natural items for such elaboration. The objection (9,21) was thus added to the seer's allusion to Saul's future elevation, and the promise of divine help (10,7b) to the seer's exhortation to Saul to perform a deed of valour.

We must then pose the question as to whether the contents of the *nagîd* layer derive from preceding tradition or have been formulated *ad hoc* as an interpretation of the basic narrative.

Two observations are relevant here. First, one can note the technique displayed by the *nagîd* layer. The *Berufungsschema* stands out as a naked skeleton. As we have just observed, its elements have been appended to details of the original tradition, apparently as a commentary of sorts. This seems to indicate that much in the *nagîd* layer is due to literary fiction.

Secondly, even if the anointing seems to be epic in itself, we shall not overlook one essential circumstance: the place where this important act is said to have been performed is not named which indicates that the story of the anointing cannot derive from local tradition.

Therefore, it would be a highly precarious undertaking to use the statements about the anointing of Saul as historical evidence for the actual course of events. The elements of the *nagîd* layer cannot be explained as derived from tradition.

5. Sitz im Leben and Date

After looking at the contents we can proceed to the **question** of the setting in life of the tradition in its elaborate form. In this form the story has several features that point to a *Sitz im Leben* in prophetic circles.

In the original tradition the seer's utterance concerning Saul's future kingship (9,20b) is worded as a vague and ambiguous allusion. In the *nagîd* stratum, this is not so. Here Samuel says expressly to Saul that he is going to let him hear the word of God (*wᵉ'ăšmî'ᵃka 'æt dᵉbăr 'ᵃᵉlohîm*).[19] Then follows in 10,1-7 what must be denoted as a prophetic oracle, or more exactly an oracle of anointing:

> Has not the Lord anointed you to be *nagîd* over his people, over Israel? And you shall reign over the people of the Lord and you will save them from the hand of their enemies round about. And this shall be the sign to you that the Lord has anointed you to be *nagîd* over his heritage ... (10,1 LXX).

There are also some other features that may equally well belong to this prophetic web. Thus, Samuel had received a revelation in advance to the effect that Saul was to appear in the town and that he was to anoint this young man as *nagîd 'ăl 'ămmî yiśra'el* (9,15-16). The revelation by night is described by the phrase *galā 'ozæn* (9,15). This is not a typically prophetic expression but one notes that prophetic revelations could be described as an opening of the ear (Jes 50,4-5).

If 9,9 is not a later gloss[20] but an explanation by the narrator[21] it must belong to the *nagîd* layer. What is here most interesting to us is not first and foremost the equation *ro'æ – nabî'*[21a] but the expression *darăš 'ᵃᵉlohîm*. As Westermann has demonstrated this terminology is connected with an institution, viz. the consultation of God through a prophet. This prophetic institution took the place of the old consultation of the Urim and Thummim which was referred to by the term *ša'ăl bᵉYHWH*.[22]

In the *nagîd* layer Samuel thus appears as a prophet. He is depicted in the same categories in 1 S ch. 1–3 (esp. 3,1.7.20f.) and ch. 15 (v. 10.16. 22).[23] Samuel's anointing of Saul is remarkably similar to the anointing of Jehu by a disciple of Elisha. Both acts are carried out by a prophet. The term *păk hăššæmæn*, "vial of oil", is the same. It occurs indeed only here in these two contexts (1 S 10,1; 2 R 9,1.3). Otherwise we find the

---

[19] Note Jer 18,18, which links the "word" with the prophet. See further the evidence advanced by *v.Rad* (ThAT II, ³1962: 93ff. esp. 100) and *Lindblom* (1962: 108ff.).
[20] As is held by *W.Richter* (1970: 18f. with note 20, p. 23).
[21] So *Jepsen* (1934: 100).
[21a] The seer is also called *'îš (ha)'ᵃᵉlohîm* (v. 6 etc.). The equation of this designation with *nabî'* is clear from 1 R 13,11.18.
[22] *Westermann* (KuD 6/1960, 2-30).
[23] On Samuel as a prophet see e.g. *Jepsen* (1934: 99-114) and *R.Press* (ZAW 56/1938, 177-225).

qæræn hăššæmæn (1 S 16,1.13; 1 R 1,39). And in both cases we hear of a prophetic oracle over the new king, directly stating what his commission involves (1 S 10,1 LXX; 2 R 9,3.6-10).

Samuel's designation of Saul is a *prophetic designation of the future king*. It can therefore be compared with Ahijah's designation of Jeroboam I.[24] In that case as well a prophet appears as the agent of YHWH. We are faced with a designation in advance. And this designation is linked with the title *nagîd* (1 R 14,7), precisely as is Samuel's designation of Saul.

We can thus discern a line of prophetic designations of kings:

Saul, designated by	Samuel	1 S 9,1 ff. *nagîd*
David, "	"	1 S 16,1 ff.
Jeroboam I, "	Ahijah	1 R 11,29 ff. *nagîd* (14,7)
Baasha, "	Jehu	1 R 16,2 *nagîd*
Jehu "	unknown prophet	2 R 9,1 ff.

It would be tempting to include among these cases the prophecy of Nathan in its original pro-Solomonic form. But this text is of a different kind and does not contain a designation proper.

To this can be added that the *Berufungsschema* has further prophetic affiliations which need not be adduced here, since this particular question has been studied in detail by W.Richter.[25]

There is then ample evidence which leads to the conclusion that the elaborated version of 1 S 9,1–10,16 with the designation in advance of Saul had its setting in life in prophetic circles: the horizon[25a] is a prophetic one; the conceptions derive from prophetic circles. There is also reason to believe that these circles are to be looked for among the northern tribes. The call of Gideon (Jud 6) is a northern tradition as is also Saul's consultation about the lost asses.[26]

The question of the date of the tradition in the original and in the elaborated forms is of great interest to our study but is admittedly a very difficult one. As for the basic tradition, nothing is to prevent us from assuming that it was already in existence at a very early date, as early as Saul's own reign. When Saul had proved to be a good warrior and had established his reputation as a hero of Israel his youth became an interesting topic for tradition. Whether Saul's encounter with the unknown seer is historical or not[27]

---

[24] 1 R 11,29-39; 14,2.7. On the question of the original compass of the Ahijah complex see *Noth* (ÜSt p. 79, 81), who counts roughly the following to this narrative: 1 R 11,29-31.36-37; 12,1-31; 14,1-18, and *W.Dietrich* (1972: 15 ff. and 54 f.) who takes the whole of 11,29 ff. to be Deuteronomistic. See also *Seybold* (1972: 58 ff.).

[25] *W.Richter* (1970: 173 ff., 176 ff.).

[25a] For the term "horizon", see *W.Richter* (1971: 117 f.).

[26] See *W.Richter* (1970: 165, 176-181).

[27] The alternative is preferred by *L.Schmidt* (1970: 79 f.), who even says: "Die Sage stellt somit eine Ätiologie der Erfolge Sauls dar" (p. 79).

there is a clear topical connection between Saul's well-known success as a warrior and the exhortation of the seer to perform a deed of valour (10,7).

As for the date of the tradition in its elaborated form[28] it seems possible to work out certain limits within which we must keep.

(1) An *ante quem* is found in the fact that the HDR contains certain features which more or less clearly presuppose acquaintance with 1 S 9,1–10,16 in its elaborate form. This gives a lower limit for the date somewhere in the first decades after Solomon's death. The following points deserve attention here:

(a) *Saul as the Anointed One in the HDR*. – We find in the HDR various allusions to an anointing of Saul. As I have already argued that 1 S ch. 15 (except for v. 10-26.35 b) is part of the HDR[29] the reference to Saul's anointing by Samuel in 15,1 is interesting in this connection (in v. 17 the anointing belongs to the section that was inserted by DtrP). Besides, the HDR contains several references to Saul as the *mašiᵃḥ*.[30] This use of the term for Saul is not found prior to the HDR. The question now is: where did the author of the HDR obtain his information that Saul had been anointed? The reading of the LXX in 1 S 11,15, according to which Samuel anointed Saul at Gilgal, does not come into question as original. This reading is due to a deliberate alteration of the MT. Precisely as in 2 R 11,12, the translator did not like the idea that it was the people that proclaimed someone king, and therefore he introduced a singular subject.[31] We are therefore left with the statements about Samuel's anointing of Saul in the *nagîd* layer of the text under discussion as the only probable source for the references in the HDR. And in this connection an observation of importance to my later discussion of the royal anointing is that the references to Saul's anointing in the HDR are based on the anointing in 1 S 10,1 and thus cannot be ascribed a source value of their own.

(b) *1 S 19,18–20,1a*. – In 9,1 ff. the etiology of the *mašal* (*Saul inter prophetas*, v. 10-13a) is later than both the original tradition and the *nagîd* layer.[32] The passage 19,18 ff. is somewhat of a parallel to 10,10-13a.

---

[28] For this *W.Richter* (1970: 52, 176) suggests a date at the beginning of Saul's public career. *L.Schmidt* (1970: 95-97) argues for a date after Solomon's death and the dissolution of the personal union. – It should be stressed here that my own conclusion, although similar to that of *L.Schmidt*, is based on wholly different and, it is to be hoped, more convincing arguments.

[29] See above ch. 2.1.

[30] 1 S 24,7.11; 26,9.11.16.23; 2 S 1,14.16.

[31] As was observed by *Kutsch* (1963: 54). On the LXX in 1 S 11,1-15 se also below ch. 5.2.1.

[32] This is evident from the obvious conclusion contained in 10,9 and from the fact that v. 10-13a take a critical view of the prophetic ecstasy as distinguished from v. 5 which is in a context that is clearly favourable to it. For treatments of the *mašal* and the etiology see *Eppstein* (ZAW 81/1969, 287 ff.), *Sturdy* (VT 20/1970, 206 ff.), *Lindblom* (ASTI 9/1973, 30 ff.), *L.Schmidt* (1970: 103 ff.) and *Grønbæk* (1971: 114 ff.).

Moreover, it is a reversal of what 10,1-9 says of Saul's endowment with the Spirit. In both cases the Spirit is a divine manifestation. In 10,1-9 it gives Saul strength to carry out his feat of bravery. In 19,18 ff. it works in the reverse: it makes Saul helpless and drives him to strip off his clothes. These clothes are the clothes of a king, who now lies naked, incapable of anything at all.[33] Instead, the Spirit is on the side of David who is now the true anointed one of YHWH.

(c) *2 S 3,18.* – As L. Schmidt has pointed out the formulation here that David "shall save my people Israel from the hand of the Philistines"[33a] purports to present David as the counterpart of Saul. Only in 1 S 9,16 and 2 S 3,18 does the saviour formula occur with "my people" as the object.[34]

(2) The indications of a *post quem* are less certain.

(a) *The anointing.* – As we have seen, there are strong indications that Saul's anointing by Samuel was not derived from tradition but is literary fiction. The texts offer no other independent piece of evidence that Saul was anointed. Now, because there was every reason to tell of Saul's anointing in traditions positive to him, we are here entitled to argue *e silentio* and assume that since none of the old traditions of Saul refer to his anointing this was not a historical fact. The reworking which brought the feature of Saul's anointing into the text, can then be assumed to be from the time when the rite of anointing was a *sine qua non* for the legitimacy of the king. Since David, Absalom (2 S 19,11) and Solomon had been anointed it can be inferred that anointing had been a prerequisite of the royal status at least from the days of Solomon and was conceivably already so at the end of David's reign.[35]

(b) *The title nagîd.* – Anticipating the results of my study of the title *nagîd* (below ch. 9.1-4), it can be said here that this title apparently did not exist as early as is often taken for granted. The oldest occurrence is probably that in 1 R 1,35 in the Succession Narrative (of Solomon). The spiritualization of the term came later. The theological use of it in connec-

---

[33] *Stoebe* (1973: 368 f.) has rightly interpreted 1 S 19,18 ff.
[33a] On the textual problem see above ch. 2.4.2.3.
[34] *L. Schmidt* (1970: 136 ff.). Note also *Schmidt's* wellfounded deletion of $b^ey\check{a}d$ in 2 S 3,18 (loc. cit.). On the relation between the two passages see also *Grønbæk* (1971: 239). – A further observation to be made here is that the formulations with *nagîd* in 2 S 7,8 and 1 S 10,1 (LXX) display an interesting similarity insofar as the preposition after *nagîd* is repeated:
2 S 7,8: *nagîd 'ăl 'ammî 'ăl yiśra'el.*
1 S 10,1: εἰς ἄρχοντα ἐπὶ τὸν λαὸν αὐτοῦ ἐπὶ Ἰσραήλ. Cf. also 2 S 6,21. That ἄρχων stands for *nagîd* here where no Hebrew *Vorlage* is preserved is proved by the use of this Greek word to render a Hebrew *nagîd* in 1 S 9,16 and 10,1b.
[35] The Jotham fable which refers to anointing in Jud 9,8.15 would seem to favour a different conclusion, but see below ch. 10.2.1. at the end.

tion with David as appointed by God to be *nagîd* belongs to the HDR. Admittedly, 1 S 13,14 stands outside this context, but it seems difficult to assume that this reference should be of considerably earlier date.[35a] The references to Saul as *nagîd* (1 S 9,16; 10,1 including the ἄρχων of the LXX in 10,1) seem to lie somewhere in between the Succession Narrative and the HDR. We then have a *post quem* in the first half of Solomon's reign.

(c) *The pan-Israelite colouring.* – An indication which would seem to motivate an adjustment of this lower limit to a still later date is to be found in the fact that there is a marked pan-Israelite colouring in the reference to Saul's dominion. YHWH orders Samuel to anoint Saul *l^enagîd 'al 'ămmî yiśra'el* (1 S 9,16; cf. 10,1 MT and LXX). This phrase expresses a theological concept and not the actual, constitutional situation as is the case with other formulations, which tell that David was anointed king over Judah and Israel separately (2 S 2,4; 5,3) or that Solomon was appointed heir designate of Israel and Judah (1 R 1,35). My discussion of the literary expressions, particularly in the HDR, of the tensions between the North and the South after Solomon's death, and of the claims to pan-Israelite dominion, makes it tempting to take the pan-Israelite formulations as an indication of a date from this period.

The evidence for the date of the interpretative strand then remains inconclusive. This strand must be earlier than the HDR, which is from the last decades of the tenth century. It is probably later than the SN from the middle of the same century. The pan-Israelite formulations favour a still later date, when the tensions between the North and the South gave a particular impetus to formulate claims to total supremacy.

Summary

(1) The observation of a number of tensions in the text led to the conclusion that an old tale about Saul's search for his father's lost asses had been reworked to comprise also an anointing by Samuel. Still later than this reworking is the inclusion of the etiology of the *mašal* in 10,10-13a. The elaborate version that tells of Saul's anointing as *nagîd* has a number of conventional features in common with the call narratives. These features are part of the *Berufungsschema*. This technique of patterning a narrative composition can be readily associated with oral tradition, although we cannot exclude the possibility that such patterning may occur in the process of written transmission.[36] From the presence of this pattern

---

[35a] See *Veijola* (1975: 55 ff.).
[36] On the general question of narrative patterns see *D.M.Gunn* (VT 24/1974, 286 ff.), who does not however discuss the *Berufungsschema*.

in the text I argued that the longer text of the LXX in 1 S 10,1 is to be preferred to the MT.

(2) Of the text in its present form the following parts belong to the layer containing Saul's anointing as *nagîd*: 1 S 9,14b-17.21; 9,27−10,1; 10,7bβ.9a. This layer identifies the unknown seer as Samuel. It tells of the divine commission to anoint Saul as *nagîd*, Saul's protest, the carrying out of the anointing, the promise of divine help, and it also tells that Saul is immediately filled with the Spirit of God. On two essential points I disagreed with the opinion of other scholars on this layer in the text:

a. The promise to Saul of future elevation (9,20b) did not belong to it but was part of the original tradition.

b. The three signs in 10,2-7 and in particular that of the Spirit also belong to the original tradition.

(3) As for the type of royal ideology found in each of the two layers of tradition I conclude that even the original tale testifies to the conception that Saul had been chosen in advance by God for his royal office (see 9,20b). The gift of the Spirit in the same basic tradition is closely connected with the exhortation to perform a deed of valour (10,7). This means that the royal charisma was conceived in the categories of a more martial ideal of kingship than is found in the Solomonic period.

(4) The interpretative strand with Saul's anointing as *nagîd* adds emphasis to the idea of Saul's divine election. We find here a formal, divine designation in advance, vested in a prophetic oracle (9,27 f.). The reference to Saul's kingship, already present in the original tale, is underlined through the anointing by Samuel. It is important to note that here, just as in the prophecy of Nathan, the title *nagîd* is used in a more recent layer of tradition with a more elaborate royal ideology than that found in the original layer.

(5) The original tale probably dates from the reign of Saul. The indications for the date of the interpretative strand of tradition are inconclusive but point to a date near Solomon's death. From the beginning the tradition is a northern one. Particular marks of the elaborate version reveal that prophetic circles stand behind the idea of Saul's anointing as *nagîd*. This anointing as *nagîd* is not due to an old tradition but is probably fictitious.

CHAPTER V

The Traditions Concerning Saul's Kingship (1 S ch. 8–12)

The cycle of texts dealing with the rise of the monarchy in Israel (1 S ch. 8–12) raises a number of difficult problems.[1] Sometimes an attitude of despair is taken as regards the possibility of unravelling the actual course of events from these chapters.[1a] The hypothetical nature of the following attempt to interpret these chapters must be emphasized. It will be possible, however, to utilize the findings on 1 S 9,1–10,16 (above ch. 4) and on the relation between the tradition of the lot-casting at Mizpah in 10,17-27 and the traditions of the two anointings carried out by Samuel in 9,1–10,16 and 16,1-13 respectively (below ch. 9.5). This will, it is hoped, give us a better idea of the material in 1 S ch. 8–12.

1. The Deuteronomistic Framework

That much in these chapters is due to the redactional and compositional work of the Deuteronomists is clear.[2] The central part of the cycle in its final Deuteronomistic form is the lot-casting and acclamation at Mizpah (10,17 ff.). This ancient pre-Dtr tradition was provided with a brief introduction by the Deuteronomists (v. 18-19a).

The framework consisting of 7,2–8,22 and ch. 12 holds an important place in the Dtr composition. This framework serves to express the negative, Dtr attitude to the events at Mizpah when Saul became king (10,17 ff.). In ch. 7, the passage on Samuel's victory over the Philistines at Mizpah is of interest to us. It is true that this tradition has a function in the Dtr overall perspective: this divine act of salvation functioned to demonstrate that the installation of a king at Mizpah was uncalled for.[3] But it would be wrong to take 7,7-14 to be a Dtr accretion. And it would be equally wrong to read it as a report of actual historical events in the days of Samuel. A victory of such proportions (7,13-14) would have been inconceivable in the days of Samuel. And *if* Samuel had really won such a victory, the

---

[1] For a survey of the extensive literature on the traditiohistorical, literary and historical problems see *F.Langlamet* (RB 77/1970, 161 ff.). Not included in this survey is *Boecker* (1969).
[1a] See for instance *A.Alt* (KS II, 13 ff. esp. 15).
[2] This aspect was stressed particularly by *M.Noth* (ÜSt 54 ff.) and by *Boecker* (1969). A criticism of Noth was attempted by *A.Weiser* (1962).
[3] So *Stoebe* (1973: 173).

messengers from Jabesh (ch. 11) would have gone to him with their request for help. As is well known the reign of Saul was a period of recurrent hostilities between Israel and the Philistines, the final subjection of whom, referred to in 7,13, was actually effected by David. The tradition in 7,7-14 presupposes the military success of this king. As Weiser has pointed out this tradition aims at minimizing the importance of David's military achievements by representing Samuel as the real deliverer.[4] Thus, David's subjection of the Philistines gives the *a quo* for the date of this tradition. As for the terminus *ad quem*, it should be noted that Weiser's observation makes it difficult to attribute this tradition to the Deuteronomists, since the Dtr attitude to David is a positive one.[4a] The fact that during the days of the personal union there was already a northern opposition to David and his dynasty (2 S 20,1; 1 R 12,16) means that there is every reason to presume a date during the reigns of David or Solomon for this tradition.

In ch. 8, the *mišpāṭ hămmælæk* (8,9.11 ff.) cannot be used as historical evidence for the history of the early monarchy on the arguments presented by Mendelsohn, who contends on the basis of Ugaritic material that 1 S 8,11 ff. afford an authentic picture of Canaanite feudal kingship.[5] This passage could be authentic in the mouth of Samuel only if he were the representative of an anti-monarchic movement which does not seem to have been the case.[6] It may well be, however, that 1 S 8,11 ff. reflect actual, historical experiences of the northern tribes during the reign of Solomon, as has been pointed out.[7] One indication is the northern opposition to Solomon's policy that found expression at the assembly at Shechem (1 R ch. 12). In its present form the passage 1 S 8,11 ff. is probably Dtr. A comparison with the law of the kingdom in Dt 17,14-20 shows that 1 S 8,11 ff. are designed to express a Dtr criticism of certain aspects of the monarchy,[7a] a criticism that also has the function of denigrating Saul and his kingship[7b] although, from the historical point of view, a criticism such as this would have been much more appropriate in connection with Solomon's aggrandisement. The statement of the people in 8,20 that the king should "go out" before them and fight their battles should probably be connected with the statement in Jos 23,3.10 that YHWH had fought for Israel. Jos ch. 23 rounds off and ends an epoch in the Deuteronomistic History. 1 S ch. 8 has a similar central function within this work. After the interlude of the judges a new epoch commences. Therefore there is a correspondence between the two

---

[4] So *Weiser* (1962: 22f.). – *Blenkinsopp* (1972: 79) thinks that we are instead concerned with a polemic reediting of an account of a victory won by Saul. The consequences of the victory (1 S 7,14), however, apply rather to David's final subjection of the Philistines. See also *W.Richter* (1964: 124 note 46), whose criticism of Weiser does not convince me.

[4a] See for instance the positive mention of David in the Deuteronomistic passages 1R 11,4.12.13; 14.8; 15.3-5; 2 R 18,3; 22,2 and cf. *vonRad* (GesStud 189 ff.), *Clements* (VT 24/1974, 406 ff.) and *Veijola* (1975: 5).

[5] *I.Mendelsohn* (BASOR 143/1956, 17ff.).

[6] As was pointed out by *H.Wildberger* (ThZ 13/1957, 458).

[7] See for instance *Ed.Nielsen* (1965: 104) and *Clements* (VT 24/1974, 403-405). I cannot see that *Weiser* (1962: 37 ff.) has managed to rule out this possibility.

[7a] See *Boecker* (1969: 26 ff.). It seems to me that two different lines converge in the Deuteronomistic criticism of kingship: (a) the old sheikh ideal, see *Nyström* (1946: 78-82, 163-167) and *Bernhardt* (1961: 114 ff., 154 ff.) and (b) the conception, connected with the idea of the YHWH-war, of YHWH as the saviour of His people, see *Boecker* (1969: 32 ff.) and *W.H.Schmidt* (Fs vonRad, 1971: 440 ff.). According to this theory, which is certainly later than a., the king usurps the position of YHWH as the saviour of the people.

[7b] See *Clements* (VT 24/1974, 398-410, esp. 406 ff.).

statements about God and the king respectively fighting for Israel and this points to a Dtr hand.[8]

That 1 S ch. 12 holds an important place in the Deuteronomistic History has been demonstrated by Noth.[9] In the first part of the chapter, where it is said that Samuel has not "taken" certain things from the people, the verb *laqăḥ* (v. 3-5) effects a hook-word connection with 8,11 ff. This connection is probably to be regarded as an intentional device of the Deuteronomists.[10] In v. 7 ff. we are faced with a legal case, the point of which is quite in the spirit of the Deuteronomists. As Boecker has pointed out, the intention is here to demonstrate that it was not because YHWH had forsaken his people that they took recourse to the new institution of the monarchy.[11] This chapter then expresses a Dtr attitude to the monarchy.

Nevertheless, even this part of the Dtr framework contains potentially old material of interest to the present investigation. There are particularly two points that we should pay attention to. First, there is the singular enumeration of men in v. 11 comprising: Jerubbaal, Bedan, Jephthah and Samuel.[11a] That this list purports to enumerate a number of saviours appears from the mention of Jerubbaal and Jephthah. That it is not of Dtr origin can also be seen. In a list with that provenance one would not expect to find Samuel, who does not figure at all in the Book of Judges in its Dtr redaction. And the same holds for Bedan (who is not to be emended into Barak). Evidently this series of saviours is different from the one known from the book of Judges of later days. An illuminating suggestion has been made by Fohrer who assumes that there was an original form of a pre-Dtr book of saviours ("Retterbuch"), that contained stories about the men mentioned in 1 S 12,11. This book was then revised before being subjected to Dtr elaboration.[12] Thus we can assume that v. 11 contains very old material.

The same seems to be at least possible for v. 12. Here the people's request for a king is linked with the Ammonite threat:

---

[8] See *Boecker* (1969: 32 ff.).
[9] *Noth* (ÜSt 5, 59 f.). See also *Boecker* (1969: 61 ff.). It is quite possible that in ch. 12 more is old than these two scholars are willing to admit. There is no point in discussing the whole problem here. I shall limit myself to v. 11-12, which are of a certain interest to us.
[10] See *Boecker* (1969: 70).
[11] *Boecker* (1969: 72 ff.). As for the well-known problem of the grammatical structure of 1 S 12,14 Boecker (p. 78-80) has made the interesting suggestion that v. 14 and v. 15 have a parallel structure so that just as v. 15 has an *apodosis* (starting with $w^e hay^e t\bar{a}$), so has v. 14 (starting with *wihyitæm*). There is, however, still another overlooked possibility, viz. to understand v. 14 as lacking an *apodosis*, if namely *'im* is here taken to be used in the same way as Akkadian *šumma* for instance in the Vassal Treaties of Esarhaddon (ed. *Wiseman* p. 33 lines 62, 73 and passim through the bulk of the text). Here *šumma* alone is used to express positive statements in a treaty text (note the treaty features in 1 S ch. 12) and can be rendered "you swear that...". Contrast the normal use of *šumma lā* for positive statements, see *vonSoden* GAG (§ 185 g).
[11a] The reading of "Samson" instead of "Samuel" (LXX bc; Peshitta) seems to depend on the contention that Samuel could not have talked of himself. But this point of view is of course relevant only if 1 S ch. 12 is authentic in the mouth of the historical Samuel, which is not the case. Besides, "Samuel" is indisputably the *lectio difficilior*, since Samuel is not known from the saviours in the Book of Judges. I therefore consider "Samuel" to be the original reading. On the problem of Bedan, cf. *Zakovitch* (VT 22/1972, 123-125), who suggests that Jephthah also had the name Bedan.
[12] *G.Fohrer* (Einl. 1969: 230). Note also what *Weiser* (Einl. 1966: 139) has to say about two parallel traditions in the narratives about Gideon and Jephthah.

And when you saw that Nahash the king of the Ammonites came against you, you said to me [i.e. Samuel], 'No, but a king shall reign over us,' when the Lord your God was your king.

This does not fit in with ch. 8, where the people's request is motivated by the poor state of domestic affairs. Thus, it is hardly a Dtr elaboration[13] but rather an old tradition.[14] On the other hand there is a slight difference from ch. 11,1 ff., insofar as nothing is said there of the people's request in connection with Saul's Ammonite campaign. But 11,1 ff. and 12,11-12 agree on one essential point: both traditions connect Saul's monarchy with the period of the saviours.[15]

2. The Tradition in 1 S 11,1-15

We can now turn to the pre-Dtr traditions. As I have already dealt with 9,1–10,16, I shall now first discuss 11,1-15 and then the *skopos* of 10,17-27. A discussion of the connections between the tradition in 10,17-27 and the traditions of Samuel's anointing of Saul and David will be found in the chapter on divine designation (see ch. 9.5-6). My conclusion on this question is that of these three traditions the oldest is that of the lot-casting at Mizpah (10,17-27). The tradition of Samuel's anointing of David (16,1-13) is somewhat later. The most recent of these is the elaborate tradition of Saul's anointing as *nagîd* in 9,1–10,16.

1. Editorial links

There has long been almost general agreement that 1 S 11,1 ff. (Saul's rescue of Jabesh) contain the oldest and most reliable tradition dealing with the course of events that immediately preceded his "coronation".[16] Immediately before this comes the passage on the lot-casting at Mizpah (10,17 ff.). Nevertheless, the events mentioned in this text are not presupposed in 11,1 ff. In spite of the obvious fact that 10,17 ff. purport to tell that the whole assembly had acclaimed Saul king after the lot-casting at Mizpah, nothing in 11,1 ff. so much as hints at the proceedings at Mizpah. The messengers from Jabesh do not reveal any knowledge of the fact that Saul had

---

[13] Contra *Noth* (ÜSt 60) and *Boecker* (1969: 75 f.). On the other hand it is of course clear that 1 S 12,11-12 has a function within the Deuteronomistic argument of the chapter: in a situation in which the people earlier used to cry to YHWH for help, they ask for a king. This was rightly seen by *Boecker* (1969: 76). But this observation does not necessitate the conclusion that v. 12 is Deuteronomistic.

[14] So *Weiser* (1962: 75 f., 86) and *Stoebe* (1973: 237 f).

[15] In 1 S 12,11-12 the Ammonite threat and the request of the people are represented against the background of the series of saviours. In 11,1 ff. Saul's rescue of Jabesh takes on the character of a deed of a saviour, and the root y-$š$-$'$ is used (v. 3.9.13, cf. 10,27). On 11,1 ff. from this aspect, see *Alt* (KS II, 22).

[16] See for instance *Soggin* (1967: 41 ff.) and *Langlamet* (RB 77/1970, 167 with note 26, and p. 197). The affection that the inhabitants of Jabesh showed to Saul and his family (1 S 31, 11 ff.; 2 S 2,4 ff.; 21,11 ff.) speaks strongly for the historicity of 1 S 11,1 ff.

already been made king over Israel. The LXX has tried to lessen the tension by having the messengers go "to Gibeah, to Saul", whereas the undoubtedly original reading preserved in the MT is "to Gibeah of Saul" (v. 4). Nor do the people seem to know anything about what is said to have happened at Mizpah; not even Saul himself does. This means that we must understand 11,1 ff. as an independent tradition that originally had no connection with the Mizpah tradition.

In 11,15 it is the people that act at the coronation of Saul. Samuel is not mentioned at all at the decisive moment. If Samuel was present, as is implied by v. 12-14, it is remarkable that he has no role at the sanctuary of Gilgal (v. 15).[17] It is interesting to see how the LXX in v. 15 lets Samuel and not the people make Saul king. This reading has probably arisen from the need to make v. 12-14 and v. 15 more consistent as regards Samuel's role, although there may be other reasons as well.[18] It then seems that v. 12-14 were not originally at home in the tradition that relates Saul's rescue of Jabesh. The purpose of this addition is revealed by v. 14 which tells of the renewal of the kingship. This is obviously a secondary harmonization of the two traditions concerning the lot-casting at Mizpah and Saul's rescue of Jabesh, two traditions that are at variance on the question of when Saul was made king. By making the latter occurrence appear as a renewal of the former the redactor tried to get out of the dilemma. On this view, one must also conclude that Samuel slipped into the text in 11,12-14 as part of the Mizpah tradition in which he is a prominent figure. I then conclude that the passage 11,12-14 is the result of editorial activity its purpose being to harmonize ch. 11 with the Mizpah tradition.[19]

The objection could be made that Samuel is already present in 11,7. This observation, however, is not sufficient to overthrow the preceding conclusions. The continuation of the narrative shows that Samuel is not taken into account at all except in the editorial passage v. 12-14. It is Saul who musters the people at Bezek (v. 8), and in 9a it is Saul who speaks to the messengers from Jabesh.[20] Thus, the evidence indicates that $w^{e'}\check{a}\underbar{h}\check{a}r\ \check{s}^{e}m\hat{u}'el$ (v. 7) is an intruder in the text, occasioned by the mention of Samuel in 10,17 ff. and 11,12-14.[21]

Also the passage about the lot-casting contains some sentences that seem to be redactional. The proceedings at Mizpah come to a natural end, when Samuel sends the people home (10,25). The question in 10,27 "how can this man save ($h\hat{o}\check{s}\hat{\imath}^{a'}$) us?" points forward to 11,12-13 where the people want to have the recalcitrant scoundrels put to death, but where Saul motivates his clemency by a reference to the act of salvation ($t^{e}\check{s}\hat{u}^{'}\bar{a}$) that YHWH had wrought. Thus, 10,27 anticipates

---

[17] This was seen by *Wildberger* (ThZ 13/1957, 449).
[18] It is possible that the Septuagint translators preferred the idea of a single sacral person making someone king (1 S 11,15; 2 R 11,12) to the idea of the people acting at this procedure (so the MT ibid.), see *Kutsch* (1963: 54).
[19] In this conclusion I agree with, for instance, *Wellhausen* (1871: 77), *Budde* (1902: 73) and others. It is inconceivable to me how *Bernhardt* can take the Mizpah and Jabesh traditions as a single unit (1961: 142 with note 1).
[20] The singular *wăyyomær* should be read with the LXX in v. 9a. This reading is generally preferred.
[21] Even *Weiser*, who argues for the role of Samuel in connection with the investiture at Gilgal, considers Samuel is a gloss in 1 S 11,7 (1962: 71).

the editorial link at the end of ch. 11. Since further 10,26-27 belong together, it is natural to take both verses as a redactional link of the same origin as 11,12-14.[22]

Three things can be said of the editorial connection of 10,17 ff. and 11,1-11.15, which is brought about by the two editorial pieces 10,26-27 and 11,12-14. (a) It makes the conclusion of the Jabesh episode (11,15) appear as only a renewal of the kingship that Saul is said to already have received at Mizpah. (b) It motivated this renewal of the kingship by referring to opposition to Saul. By taking up the *môšîaʿ* motif from the Jabesh tradition (11,3 cf. v. 9) it presented the triumph at Jabesh as a victory, the possibility of which had earlier been questioned (10,27). As we have already noted this tendency towards a harmonization was carried still further by the LXX in 11,4.15. (c) Because of its very positive attitude towards Saul's kingship this editorial link can hardly have been created by the Dtr. This in turn indicates that 10,17 ff. and 11,1 ff. were already connected with each other before the Dtr redaction. What existed before this redaction was not only isolated traditions about Saul.

2. *Historical Quaestiones Facti*

The above considerations show that in treatments of historical questions 11,1-11.15 must be dealt with independent of the editorial material in v. 12-14.[23]

Some scholars have argued that Saul did not become king in connection with his Ammonite campaign,[24] a conclusion that I am not prepared to accept. Although the passage 11,1-11 appears to be beautifully rounded off and does not require the continuation in v. 15, this verse which deals with the king-making does not in any way contradict the report on the campaign (v. 1-11). It is important to note that this verse is a stumbling block to accepting the Mizpah tradition (10,17 ff.) which also concludes with the installation of Saul as king. It can be suspected that the pre-Dtr redactor (above) would readily have omitted the sentence about the king-making at Gilgal (v. 15). The elimination of this sentence would have made the editorial

---

[22] Cf. *Weiser* (1962: 73 f.) who connects 10,27 with 11,12 f. *Boecker's* objection (1969: 56-58) that 10,27 belongs with v. 26 does not disprove this, since both v. 26 and v. 27 together should be taken as being editorial. – *Buber's* observation (Werke II: 788) of a possible connection between 1 S 14,45 (the people motivating clemency towards Jonathan with a reference to the *yᵉšûʿā* wrought by him) and 1 S 11,13 (similar motivation for clemency) does not make it impossible to take 11,12-14 as being editorial as Buber thinks it does. It is probable that 11,13, formulated at a later time, refers back to 1 S 14,45 and not vice versa as Buber holds.
[23] *Wildberger* (ThZ 13/1957, 448 ff.), *Weiser* (1962: 70) and *Beyerlin* (ZAW 73/1961, 188 f.) have felt that 1 S 11,1-11 is rounded off in itself, but the conclusions they infer from this seem open to doubt.
[24] See *Wildberger* (op. cit. 467), *Beyerlin* (op. cit. 189), and *Langlamet* (RB 77/1970, 197).

connection of the Mizpah and Jabesh traditions much easier. That the redactor did not do so, but instead brought about a harmonization by making 11,15 a repetition of the king-making at Mizpah, shows that 11,15 maintained its place with a stubbornness that calls for the respect of the historian. Besides, the tradition in 12,12 also connects Saul's kingship with the Ammonite threat. But it may be that 12,12 is somehow dependent on ch. 11.[25]

Since there is no obvious advantage in dissolving 11,15 from its connection with the Ammonite campaign, it seems wise to trust the tradition that Saul's kingship dates from the days of this military expedition. That after a magnificent victory such as that at Jabesh the participating tribes should go to a sanctuary to offer sacrifices does not fall out of the frame of what we otherwise know; and that the inspired leader of this military undertaking received an acclamation from his men and was raised to the position of permanent leader should not surprise us.

It seems to me that we should not read too much into the words wăyyămlikû šam 'æt ša'ûl (11,15). At this early date the verb himlîk probably did not have the sense of a concentrated expression for the carrying out of the rites in a royal ritual (such as anointing, the handing over of insignia and so forth) as is probable in later texts. The royal ritual was certainly something that was developed gradually, something that did not originally present itself as a fixed set of rites. Although final proof cannot be adduced it seems better to take himlîk in 11,15 to be a delocutive,[26] "to call someone king", than to be an expression for the carrying out of certain well-defined ceremonies in a royal ritual, that is hard to think of as existing right from the first moment of the monarchy. The word seems to refer to an acclamation whether this was phrased as $y^e\d{h}î$ hămmælæk (cf. 1 S 10,24) or as malăk ša'ûl (cf. 2 R 9,13).

If it is correct to assume that Saul actually became king after rescuing Jabesh, one should not overlook the implications of this tradition for the relation between divine election and human acclamation of the king. What goes before the acclamation is not a formal divine designation by lot-casting (as in the later Mizpah tradition 10,17 ff.) or a divine oracle mediated by a prophet (as in 9,1–10,16), but rather a course of events that in itself demonstrates that Saul was approved of by YHWH, that he had a charisma.

---

[25] As for 1 S 9,1–10,16 we have seen that 10,7 anticipates a heroic deed carried out by Saul. But this deed is not the victory over the Ammonites at Jabesh but that over the Philistine $n^e\d{s}îb$ at Geba-Gibeah in 1 S 13,4 (see also 10,5). This was pointed out by *J.M.Miller* (CBQ 36/1974, 159).

[26] With delocutive verbs I understand verbs that are related to a locution in discourse (cf. Engl. "to hail", "to welcome", "to sweetheart"). Such verbs are found in Hebrew in piel and hiphil, see *D.R.Hillers* (JBL 86/1967, 320ff.). For instance hi$\d{s}$dîq and hirši^a' are better described as delocutive verbs than as declarative ones.

There is here a difference that should not be overlooked. As the man who had led the successful campaign against the Ammonites, Saul appears as one who *could* be made king. Raised to the status of *nagîd* (9,1 ff.) Saul is denoted as the one who in fact *must* be made king, since this title implies divine designation in advance for the office of king. Thus in 11,1-11.15 we meet the conception of the divine election of the king in a very ancient form. This text takes us back to a point in time prior to the concept of the king's divine designation as *nagîd* and even designation by lot-casting.

3. The Tradition in 1 S 10,17-27

Even if we disregard the end of the pericope on the lot-casting at Mizpah which appears as an editorial link (10,26-27), it is impossible to treat this tradition as a source of information on the actual circumstances connected with Saul's kingship. The tensions between 10,17 ff. and 11,1 ff. are too strong to allow this. The tradition of Samuel's designation of Saul at Mizpah is designed for very particular purposes. It was shaped, not by the actual historical circumstances in connection with the beginning of Saul's kingship but by the needs of a later time characterized by a tension between different ideals of kingship. This certainly does not mean that 10,17 ff. is of no interest to us. On the contrary it may have important things to say about the conception of kingship among the northern tribes during the reigns of David or Solomon.

There is no real agreement on the age of the elements in this tradition. That some verses at the opening of the pericope (10,18-19a) are Dtr seems to be clear. Apart from this Boecker also claims most of the remainder of 10,17-27 for the Deuteronomists. Thus the lot-casting is taken to be a Dtr interpretation of the consultation of the Urim oracle, and the *mišpăṭ hămmᵉlukā* is also considered to be Dtr history writing.[27] On neither of these two points am I prepared to follow Boecker.

As for the lot-casting the analysis carried out below (ch. 9.6) will show that there is no need to distinguish between two different traditions in 1 S 10,19b-24 as has so often been done. And since there are indications that this one tradition is older than the tradition of Samuel's anointing of David (1 S 16,1-13) there can be no question of a Dtr tradition in the former, since the latter is already part of the HDR (see ch. 2.1 and ch. 9.5).

As for the second point, viz. the question of whether not only the *mišpăṭ hămmælæk* in 8,9.11 ff. but also the *mišpăṭ hămmᵉlukā* in 10,25 is Dtr, one should not overlook the difference between these two entities. First, there is a difference in the actual Hebrew terminology. Secondly, there is also a difference in contextual function. While the *mišpăṭ hămmælæk*

---

[27] Boecker (1969: 44 ff.; 50 ff.).

(8,9.11 ff.) is a sort of prophecy[28] that aims at showing how the monarchy was to degenerate and serves the purpose of being a warning to the people, there is nothing of all this in the *mišpăṭ hămmᵉlukă* (10,25). The latter constitutes the concluding part of the proceedings at Mizpah and is apparently seen as something positive. It seems probable that the term *mišpaṭ* has a different nuance in the two contexts. In 8,9.11 the *mišpăṭ hămmælæk* is best understood as "legal claims of the king" (cf. the *mišpăṭ hăkkóhᵃnîm* in 1 S 2,13; Dt 18,3), while the *mišpăṭ hămmᵉlukā* in 10,25 is to be understood as something like "Grundordnung des Königtums"[29]. Because of the differences it is reasonable to conclude that 10,25 is an earlier tradition taken over by the Deuteronomists.[30] Out of the *mišpăṭ hămmᵉlukā* in 10,25 the Deuteronomists created a premonitory prophecy (8,9.11 ff.).

It should be pointed out that not even the writing-down of the *mišpăṭ hămmᵉlukā* in 10,25 is necessarily a Dtr accretion. The *sepær* placed before God must not necessarily be understood as a book. It is more illuminating to take it to be an inscribed stele.[31] Since the idea of the erection of a stele before YHWH is known particularly in connection with the making of a covenant,[32] and since the word *mišpaṭ* would also be conceivable in a covenant context, it is most tempting to see in the *mišpăṭ hammᵉlukā* (10,25) a reference to a royal contract, an institution that is known from other texts (see ch. 8). Or at least it purports to tell that Saul's government was a legally regulated regime.

1. Samuel as the Last Saviour

Samuel has a most conspicuous role in the tradition of the lot-casting at Mizpah. As the preceding analysis of ch. 11 has shown Samuel was not mentioned at all in the original tradition of the Ammonite campaign and the "coronation" at Gilgal, and it must be concluded that historically Samuel had nothing to do with Saul's investiture at Gilgal (11,15). It is

---

[28] *Nielsen* (1965: 104).
[29] See *Boecker* (1969: 56) and esp. *G.Liedke* (1971: 93 note 5). For further examples of *mišpaṭ* as "Rechtsanspruch" and as "Ordnung" see Liedke (p. 92 ff. and 81 ff.).
[30] See *Noth* (ÜSt p. 58). Cf. *Ed.Nielsen* (1955: 122), who is very open to the possibility of pre-Deuteronomistic tradition.
[31] *Soggin* (Bibbia e Oriente 7/1965, 279 f.) has drawn attention to the fact that *spr* often means "inscription" in other West Semitic texts (cf. DISO p. 197). *Soggin* (Joshua, 1972: 225 f., 241) points out that the *sepær* in Jos 24,26 may well be an inscription on stone that was later understood as a book and that *tôrăt ᵃᵉlohîm* may be understood as a gloss that expresses this later understanding. In Ex 24,4 and Gn 31,45 such a stone, erected in connection with a covenant, is called a *măṣṣebā*. If the prohibiting of *măṣṣebôt* in Dt 16,22 is also valid for such stones as these, one is not inclined to take what is probably a stele in 1 S 10,25 to be a Deuteronomistic accretion.
[32] See the biblical references in the foregoing note.

important to note that this conclusion is also supported by the observation that neither does Samuel appear in the basic tradition of Saul and the unknown seer (9,1–10,16); it is only at a later stage of the development of this tradition that the seer is identified as Samuel (the *nagîd* layer), as was demonstrated above.

If the conclusion reached below is correct, viz. that the tradition of the lot-casting is older than the *nagîd* version of the tradition of Saul and the seer (ch. 9.5), we can conclude that 1 S 10,17 ff. contains the oldest extant tradition that connects Saul's kingship with Samuel.[33]

If Samuel's designation of Saul in 10,17 ff. is not a historical fact, one must ask why this tradition was created, what its purpose is. To answer this question it is necessary to ask in which capacity Samuel is thought to act in 10,17 ff. Later, when Samuel appears in the tradition of Saul's anointing as *nagîd*, he has prophetic features as is also the case in 1 S ch. 15 in the HDR. But it is hardly in this prophetic capacity that he acts in 10,17 ff.

A consideration of the various possibilities leaves as the most probable answer that in 10,17 ff. Samuel is to be understood primarily as *môšîaʿ*.

Here a word should be said about the distinction traditionally made between the "great judges", *môšîʿîm* (the charismatic saviour-heroes), and the "minor judges", *šopᵉṭîm* (the men enumerated in the list in Jud 10,1-5; 12,7-15 who are generally thought to have had judicial functions).[34] Latterly this distinction has become more difficult to uphold.[35] First, it seems increasingly probable that the verb *šapaṭ* has a much wider semantic range than was earlier assumed.[36] It could probably be used fairly early to denote an activity of the sort carried out by the charismatic heroes.[37] Secondly, there were men who seem to have combined the

[33] In this negative conclusion about Samuel's role in the establishment of Saul's kingship I am in disagreement with above all Wildberger and Weiser. *Wildberger* (ThZ 13/1957, 442-469 esp. 459 ff.) builds too much on 1 S 9,1–10,16 where, as I have pointed out, Samuel is not mentioned in the oldest strand of tradition. *Weiser* (1962: 25 ff. 37 ff. 69 ff.) also founds his historical conclusions on an analysis of the sources that I cannot agree with.

[34] This distinction is made by *Noth* (ÜSt 47-50; GesStud II: 71 ff.). In recent years it has been defended by *R.Smend Jr* (1963: 54), *W.Beyerlin* (FsWeiser p. 7). Cf. also *W.Richter* (1964: 116-131, esp. 130).

[35] See *T.Ishida* (RB 80/1973, 514-22) for a survey of research with numerous references to recent works. See also *Lemche* (1972: 78), *Hauser* (JBL 94/1975, 190 ff.) and *deGeus* (ZAW 84/1972, 383 f.). I must confess, however, that I do not consider the West Semitic use of *š-p-ṭ* in the sense of "to rule", "to govern" to be such a decisive argument against Noth's theory as does *Ishida* (p. 517).

[36] For a survey of research on this issue see *Liedke* (1971: 62 ff.).

[37] See *Seeligman* (VTSuppl 16/1967, 274 ff.) who finds indications for this in Ob v. 21; Jes 19,20; Hos 13,10. Seeligman suggests we understand 1 S 8,20 as "unser König möge uns helfen" (p. 276). On a pre-Deuteronomistic date for the sections belonging to the literary frame in Judges 3,7–11,33, see *Beyerlin* (FsWeiser 1963: 1-29); cf. also *Weiser* (Einl. 1966: 138). *Grether* (ZAW 57/1939, 119) denoted 2 S 7,11a as the first occurrence of *šopet* for the deliverer. However, v. 10-11a probably belong to the Dtr layer in 2 S ch. 7 (see above ch. 3.2). On the text-critical problem in v. 7 cf. *Ph. deRobert* (VT 21/1971, 116 ff.), who prefers the Mt.

functions of both a military and forensic nature. Jephthah is a notable example. He saved Israel from the Ammonite threat (Jud ch. 11) and is also included in the list of the so-called "minor judges" (Jud 12,7).[38] Joshua should also be remembered in this connection. It seems that his authority as a military leader (Jos 10,1 ff.) led to his acceptance as arbitrator in cases of a legal nature (Jos 17,14 ff.; cf. Jos 24).[39]

The passage on Samuel's lot-casting at Mizpah should be connected with the pre-Dtr elements in ch. 7 and ch. 12, where Samuel is also a prominent figure. Mizpah is the place for the lot-casting (10,17 ff.), it is the place of Samuel's victory over the Philistines (7,7-14), and although the place is not mentioned in ch. 12 it is better to also connect this chapter with the two other Mizpah traditions than with 11,1 ff.[40] One can in fact be justified in speaking of a series of pre-Dtr Mizpah traditions.

What is of particular interest to the present investigation is that in these traditions Samuel is depicted as the last great leader of pre-monarchic times. He combines the features of both the "great" and the "minor" judges, and since this distinction can no longer be upheld as being as clear-cut as before, there is no difficulty in finding features of these two kinds in one series of traditions. Judicial functions are thus found in 7,15-17 (cf. 8,1-3).[41] But it is above all as a military saviour that Samuel appears in the Mizpah traditions. Here belongs his victory over the Philistines (7,7-14). And 12,11 has a most remarkable enumeration of saviours: Jerubbaal, Bedan, Jephthah and Samuel. Here we are faced with Samuel as the last of the pre-monarchic saviours.[42]

Having advanced this far the connections are easier to discern. The historical kernel of tradition in 1 S 11,1-11.15 describes how a $môšî^a{}^c$ (cf. v. 3.9) was made king. There is already here an implicit affiliation between Saul and the earlier $môšî^cîm$. It is my conclusion that the creation of the tradition of Samuel's designation of Saul (10,17 ff.) aims at making this link still closer. Samuel, presented as the last of the pre-monarchic $môšî^cîm$ (12,11; 7,7 ff.), designates through lot-casting the first saviour-king. The great saviour deed of Samuel (7,7-14) forms a bridge between earlier saviour deeds and Saul's deed at Jabesh. Samuel is thus presented as a link between the pre-monarchic leaders and the monarchy of Saul. The

---

[38] On Jephthah see also below ch. 8.2.2.2.
[39] See esp. *Alt* (KS I, 187 ff.). Alt regards the mention of Joshua as original in Jos 10,1 – 11,15. Here Noth is somewhat reluctant, see *Noth* (Josua ²1953: 61, 67).
[40] As is traditionally done and most recently by *Stoebe* (1973: 235).
[41] *Wildberger* (ThZ 13/1957, 463 f.) stressed this feature and understood Samuel as "minor judge".
[42] I must here dissociate myself from *W.Richter* (1964: 123-25), who thinks that Samuel is depicted only as $šopet$ and not as $môšî^a{}^c$. The fact that this understanding of the material forces Richter to assume that "Samuel" in the enumeration of deliverers in 1 S 12,11 is due to corruption (p. 131 note 71), shows its weakness.

presentation of Samuel as having personally arranged the lot-casting at Mizpah serves to create something of an "apostolic succession": Saul is brought into line with the great pre-monarchic leaders.[43] This can be represented in the following manner:

SAVIOURS		SAUL
Jerubbaal		
Bedan		
Jephthah		
Samuel		
(1 S 12,11)		
Samuel's saviour deed at Mizpah (1 S 7,7-14)	→ Samuel arranges the lot-casting at Mizpah (1 S 10,17-27)	→ Saul's saviour deed at Jabesh (1 S 11,1-15)

It could be noted here, that the Deuteronomists altered the original tradition in 10,17.19b-25 by adding an introduction (v. 18-19a) using *môšîaʿ* of God Himself rather than of a man chosen by Him to act in this capacity, as the original tradition depicted Saul.[44] In fact, another peculiarity of the sources may also be due to this "anti-synergistic" tendency in the Dtr literature. The very passive role of Samuel in 1 S 7,7-14 and the linking of the verb *yašăʿ* with "our God" and not with Samuel in 7,8 may be the result of Dtr revision of a tradition that originally depicted Samuel as somewhat more militant.

What the texts in 1 S ch. 8–12 have to say about Samuel and Saul can be summarized in a few points.

(a) The oldest traditions originally contained nothing about Samuel in connection with the investiture of Saul (11.1-11.15; 9,1–10,16 before the *nagîd* reworking).

(b) 1 S 10,17 ff. contains the first tradition introducing the conception of Saul as leader designated by Samuel. The purpose of this tradition was to stress the continuity between Saul and the earlier saviours. When 10,17 ff. and 11,1 ff. were joined together Samuel was also inserted into ch. 11 (v. 7.12-14).

(c) Still later is the identification of Samuel with the seer who promised future kingship to Saul when he was only a youth (9,1–10,16 in the *nagîd* version).

---

[43] Thus, I do not agree with *W.Richter* (1964: 130 note 63), who speaks of the line *šopeṭ* – king as represented by 1 S 7; 8; 10,17 ff. and the line *môšîaʿ* – king as handed over in 1 S 9,1–10,16. I hold that the first series of texts lays stress on the continuity between the saviours and Saul. I also think that there was less difference between *šopeṭ* and *môšîaʿ* than Richter believes.

[44] Cf. *Richter* (1964: 108).

(d) So firmly rooted was Samuel in the pre-Dtr traditions about Saul that the Dtr could not leave him out. His designation of Saul, however, is excused as due to the people's request for a king (8,4 ff.).

2. Samuel as a Representative of Genuine Yahwism

We have then an idea of the import of the role of Samuel in the tradition of the lot-casting at Mizpah. I shall now take the liberty of advancing some further reflections of a more inferential nature. The dating of the tradition in 10,17 ff. is a difficult problem. On the above understanding, 1 S 7,7-14 presupposes David's subjection of the Philistines. This gives an *a quo*, since it is most natural to assume that the tradition of Samuel's lot-casting at Mizpah is not earlier than the tradition of his saviour deed. Also the general observation that what is said in 10,17 ff. considerably diverges from the actual, historical course of events (cf. 11,1 ff.) suggests that this tradition can hardly be from a time when there were still people alive who could tell from their own experience that this was not a tradition that represented history "wie es eigentlich gewesen". This observation would seem to suggest the reign of Solomon as the earliest date. We also have an indication of the *ad quem* since the tradition in 10,17 ff. is older than that in 16,1-13, which was incorporated into the HDR, composed in the last decades of the tenth century B.C. (for this see ch. 9.5). Although admittedly inconclusive, these indications suggest the reign of Solomon as the date for this tradition.

As we have seen, the Mizpah tradition stresses the continuity between the deliverers and Saul. At the same time Samuel also represents a link between the old Shiloh traditions[45] and Saul's kingship. Samuel's allegiance to Shiloh needs no comment. His birth meant the fulfilment of a divine promise that his mother received at a visit to Shiloh (1 S ch. 1). He was brought up in the sanctuary of Shiloh and received divine revelations there (1 S ch. 2–3). That is to say that the tradition in 1 S 10,17 ff., which creates a connection between Saul's kingship and Samuel, thereby also implies an association with the traditions of the sanctuary at Shiloh, which held an important place in the religious life of pre-monarchic times. The ark was kept there for a considerable time. And in this connection it matters little whether historically the religious practices of Shiloh had a syncretistic element or not.[45a] David and Solomon gave a new course to the develop-

---

[45] On Shiloh see esp. *S.Holm-Nielsen* (Shiloh 1969: 56-59) and *Eissfeldt* (VTSuppl 4/1957, 138 ff.).

[45a] There is no agreement on whether the god of Shiloh was a local counterpart of Jerusalemite 'el 'ᵃᵉlyôn. The presence of the divine name 'al in the Song of Hannah (1 S 2,10) has been seen as an indication of this by *H.S.Nyberg* (ARW 35/1938, 368-70 and on 'al p. 329-45) and by *Ed.Nielsen* (1955: 316 and VTSuppl 7/1960, 63-65), while this conclusion has been questioned by *deVaux* (Bible et Orient 1967: 259 note 1) and by *S.Holm-Nielsen* (Shiloh 1969: 57 note 289). Whether the ark was of nomadic or Canaanite origin has been debated, see the literature quoted by *Lemche* (1972: 62).

ment of the Israelite religion through the innovations in the new capital, which also became the religious centre. As a man so closely linked with Shiloh Samuel certainly appeared as a true representative of the genuine Yahwistic tradition of the "good old days". Behind the image of Samuel in 1 S 10,17 ff. we can see the sanctuary of Shiloh materialize as an implicit challenge to the novel and therefore suspect institutions of Jerusalem.

It is true that David's monarchy could boast two features that could serve to connect it with the sacral institutions of the pre-monarchic period. (a) David took over Abiathar after Saul's massacre of the priests of Nob (1 S 22,20). This Abiathar was the son of Ahimelech who is generally taken to be identical with Saul's oracle priest Ahijah, who is said to be an Elide (1 S 14,3).[46] (b) David moved the ark to Jerusalem, a step of the utmost importance to the status of this town in the cultic life of the nation.[46a] Although David showed a certain deference to the past, his reign also saw the introduction of a radically new situation (transition from national state to territorial state, Jerusalem as capital, etc.), and during the reign of Solomon the change became still more apparent (note the temple).[46b]

The fact that the residence was moved from Hebron to Jerusalem was a step of great importance to the religious development of the kingdom. As can be inferred from Ps 110 and Gn ch. 14 the court of Jerusalem saw a line of continuity between the Davidic kings and the old, pre-Israelite traditions of Jerusalem.[47] In this connection Zadok is important. Zadok ranked among the foremost of David's men. He shared the position of priest with Abiathar (2 S 20,25 and cf. below note 48). He was the one who carried out the anointing of Solomon (1 R 1,39). Since Abiathar had supported the wrong candidate in the struggle for the throne and was banished to his native village (1 R 1,7; 2,26 f.), Zadok's position became still stronger under Solomon than under David. The fact that there is no acceptable genealogy for Zadok has led modern scholars to take him to be of non-Israelite descent. The theory that he was the last priest of pre-Davidic Jerusalem is well known. Of the various suggestions for Zadok's origin, this is indeed the

---

[46] See for instance *Grønbæk* (1971: 132f.).
[46a] See *Noth* (GesStud I: 172 ff.) and *Gunneweg* (VT 10/1960, 335-341, esp. 340).
[46b] See *Ahlström* (1963: 43ff.) and *Soggin* (1967: 84f.).
[47] I do not feel obliged to submit even a representative selection of the vast bibliography on these two texts. I shall only point out that *Schreiner's* remarks (1963: 117f.) have convinced me that Ps 110,4 cannot aim at legitimating Zadok's priesthood as a continuation of that of Melchizedek, as was held by *Rowley* (FsBertholet 1950: 461 ff.). I must also point out that I am not convinced by *Bernhardt's* arguments (1961: 91-102) against the assumption that there was a sacral kingship in pre-Davidic Jerusalem. What he says on the Amarna letters (p. 101) completely fails to pay attention to the very subservient tone which marks not least the letters from Jerusalem. Concerning the existence of a pre-Israelite temple in Jerusalem Bernhardt (p. 96f.) has not properly seen the possible significance of Araunah's *goræn* (2 S 24,18) or of the *bêt YHWH* which David enters in 2 S 12,20, on which items see *Ahlström* (VT 11/1961, 115f., 126).

one that solves most problems, even if it cannot be actually proved.[48] The name *ṣadôq* probably refers to a divine name connected with pre-Israelite Jerusalem.[49]

In 1 S 10,17-27 there are several features that assume interest if we pay attention to the circumstances in connection with Solomon's installation as king.

(1) The lot-casting implies a stress on Saul's divine designation in advance. In a most unambiguous way YHWH announces whom he has chosen for king. Solomon had no such divine designation. His right to the throne was motivated by referring to the decidedly human act of David when he made known that Solomon was to succeed him (1 R 1,35). What Solomon received at Gibeon (1 R ch. 3) was divine legitimation *a posteriori*.

(2) The Mizpah tradition is to demonstrate that Saul was acclaimed king by a great popular assembly, representing *kål šibṭê yiśra'el* (1 S 10,20). Solomon became king without the consent of such an assembly. The *'ăm* mentioned in connection with his investiture (1 R 1,39 f.) consisted of court functionaries and royal mercenaries and cannot be interpreted as representing the people (see ch. 7.2.1.2).

(3) As I have pointed out there is a certain possibility that the *mišpăṭ hămmᵉlukā* of the Mizpah tradition (1 S 10,25) refers to a contract between the king and the people or at least purports to tell that the government of Saul was a legally regulated regime. To Solomon, this was a very sensitive point. He became king without a contract with the people. His regime displayed absolutistic features. There must have been opposition to this among the northern tribes, an opposition that was finally voiced by the assembly at Shechem (1 R ch. 12), an assembly which was quite unwilling

---

[48] The identification of Zadok as a "Jebusite" was argued by *Bentzen* (1931: 8 ff.). There is now an extensive literature on this issue. For the pros and cons, see *Gunneweg* (1965: 98 ff.) and *Cody* (1969: 88 ff.), who are both basically in agreement with Bentzen.
— Evidently 2 S 8,17 cannot be used as genealogical information on Zadok. The probable reading here is not "and Zadok the son of Ahitub and Ahimelech the son of Abiathar" (so MT) but instead "and Zadok and Abiathar, the son of Ahimelech, the son of Ahitub"; see *Wellhausen* (1871: 176 f.) and *Gunneweg* (1965: 99, 104 ff.). The reason for assuming a corruption is that it was Abiathar and not Ahimelech who was the priest of David (2 S 20,25; 1 R 2,26) and this Abiathar was the son of Ahimelech (1 S 22,20; 23,6; 30,7). And besides, according to 1 S 22,20 only one Elide seems to have escaped Saul's massacre of the priests of Nob, namely Abiathar. The reading in 2 S 8,17 seems to display a wish to provide Zadok with an Elide genealogy, see *Gunneweg* (1965: 104 f.).
— Zadok is often taken to have been the last priest-king of pre-Israelite Jerusalem. This is not probable since it is hard to believe that David would have allowed the defeated king to occupy the position of priest in his own capital. Besides, there is also a possibility that Araunah was the last pre-Israelite king of the town, as *Ahlström* (VT 11/1961, 117 f.) argues, taking *'ᵃrăwnā hămmælæk* in 2 S 24,23 as a personal name + apposition. Note, however, the objections of Cross (1973: 210 note 58) to Ahlström's theory. On Araunah see also S.Yeivin (VT 3/1953, 149 with note 1).
[49] On this issue see *Ringgren* (1947: 85 f.).

to make Solomon's son Rehoboam king unless he first accepted certain conditions (see ch. 7.1.3 and 8.2.1).

(4) The proceedings at Mizpah were organized by Samuel, the last saviour and the leading representative of the old Shilonite traditions. Solomon was installed as king by Zadok, a feature that in northern eyes associated Solomon's kingship with the traditions of pre-Israelite Jerusalem. Samuel on the other hand represents an umbilical cord connecting Saul with Israel's past, with Shiloh[50] and with the saviours. Since Solomon's reign was particularly open to the influence of foreign culture,[51] Solomon was certainly vulnerable to the association of Saul to the genuinely Israelite tradition through Samuel.

The mention of Judah as fighting at Jabesh (1 S 11,8) should be considered here. The tribes that actually participated in Saul's Ammonite campaign certainly did not form a pan-Israelite amphictyony.[52] Personally I am inclined to suppose that only Benjamin, Ephraim-Manasseh (note the muster at Bezek between Shechem and Beth-shan v. 8) and Reuben and Gad (since the fight took place in Gilead) were involved. The insertion of Judah means an extension of this tradition to give it pan-Israelite dimensions. And this is conceivable at the stage when 11,1 ff. were connected with the Mizpah tradition, which ascribes pan-Israelite dimensions to the kingdom of Saul (1 S 10,20).

We saw that Samuel represented a connection between Saul and Shiloh. There is also an association of northern Israelite kingship with Shiloh in the case of Jeroboam I who was designated by the prophet Ahijah from Shiloh (1 R 11,29). This brings us to the oracle of Judah in Gn 49,10. It is not easy to say anything definite about this crucial text which has been the subject of endless speculation. However, I would like to draw attention to the possibility that this promise could date from the time shortly after Solomon's death. The promise that "the sceptre shall not depart from Judah" is dynastic in its nature. The mention of Shiloh implies that the northern tribes were not yet or no longer under the control of the Davidic kings. As will be remembered the period after Solomon's death was marked by (a) emphasis on the legitimacy of the Davidic dynasty, as is evidenced by the prophecy of Nathan in its elaborate dynastic form (above ch. 3) and by (b) Davidic claims to sovereignty over both Judah and Israel, as is seen from the HDR. It is possible that the oracle of Judah in Gn 49,10 can be explained from this situation of ideological wrestling between Judah and Israel.

Another prophecy that can perhaps be understood from the same ideological situation is the promise of "a sure house" made to the Zadokite priesthood (1 S 2,35). This promise, which is appended to the curse on the Elides, is probably to be assigned a somewhat earlier date than the oracle of Judah, perhaps shortly after Solomon's banishment of the Elide priest Abiathar (1 R 2,26 f.). We are here concerned with the idea that Shiloh and the Elides have been superseded by Jerusalem and the Zadokides.[53]

[50] Cf. in this connection *Eissfeldt* on "Siloh und Jerusalem" (VTSuppl 4/1957, 138 ff.). Eissfeldt does not, however, contrast the investitures of Saul and Solomon.
[51] This was most probably a period with a particularly strong Egyptian influence on Israel in the fields of royal administration and literature (wisdom, royal novel, etc.). See *Mettinger* (1971), where further references are given.
[52] See *Möhlenbrink* (ZAW 58/1940-41, 60-62) and *Wallis* (1968: 55 f.).
[53] Cf. the end of Ps 78 with the contrast Joseph – Shiloh (v. 60.67) over against Judah – Zion –

Summary

(1) The oldest and historically most reliable tradition dealing with the beginning of Saul's kingship is that in 1 S 11,1-11.15 according to which Saul became king after rescuing Jabesh. Already here Saul is seen as a man of the same type as the earlier saviours.

(2) This feature was stressed by the more recent tradition in 10,17.19b-25 of Samuel's lot-casting at Mizpah. Historically Samuel had nothing to do with Saul's investiture. The *skopos* of this tradition is to create a direct "apostolic succession" between Saul and Samuel, who is depicted in the Mizpah traditions as the last saviour (1 S 7,7-14; 12,11). It is very difficult to date this tradition more than approximately. The indications point to the reign of Solomon. My demonstration that the tradition in 10,17-27 is presupposed by the tradition of David's anointing by Samuel (16,1-13), which is now part of the HDR, shows that the former tradition cannot be later than the date of this literary work. The features of the tradition in 10,17 ff. make sense as directed against Solomon. Behind the figure of Samuel, we can see two genuinely Israelite institutions: (a) the line of divinely commissioned saviours and (b) the cult at Shiloh. The lack of continuity with traditional Israelite institutions such as these was characteristic in Solomon's days, and in these respects 1 S 10,17-27 touched upon a very vulnerable point. The *mišpāṭ hămmᵉlukā* is probably directed against Solomonic absolutism. The tradition of the assembly at Mizpah is connected with the earlier Jabesh tradition in 11,1-11.15 by means of two redactional links (10,26-27; 11,12-14) which attempt to harmonize the two traditions by making Saul's investiture at Gilgal (11,15) appear as a renewal of the kingship received at Mizpah (10,17 ff.).

(3) Still later is the tradition in 1 S 9,1–10,16 in its elaborate form with Saul as *nagîd*. Here, too, Samuel has the role of mediator of the divine designation, but here he appears as a prophet. Through this "prophetic" Samuel Saul receives a prophetic designation as *nagîd* (9,16.27 ff.).

(4) Finally, the above-mentioned material was incorporated into the Deuteronomistic history. Traces of this process are discernible above all in ch. 8 and 12. In the tradition in 10,17 ff. only a few introductory words (v. 18-19a) are Dtr. In spite of statements to the contrary the bulk of this tradition is not of Dtr origin.

(5) There has been a certain tendency in recent research to regard each of the main traditions of Saul's kingship as reflecting a particular historical

---

David (v. 68 ff.). The suggestions for the date of this psalm are at great variance. See recently *R.P.Carroll* (VT 21/1971, 133-150 esp. 144 ff.). With regard to what I have said above, it is interesting to note that *Eissfeldt* (1958: 26-43) argues for a date in the tenth century. However, as *S.Norin* points out in his forthcoming dissertation (Er spaltete das Meer, Lund 1976), there are also strong reasons for a dating in the Josianic period.

event on Saul's way to kingship over the northern tribes. Thus Wallis propounds the attractive suggestion that Saul's dominion was gradually extended and that the different investitures described in the texts refer to decisive acts in this historical development.[54] My analysis has shown that this theory, however attractive it may seem at first sight, cannot be upheld. First, it would be strange that Benjamin would then be concerned twice, since the traditions in 1 S 10,17-27 and 11,1-15 overlap as regards Benjamin. Secondly, as we have seen, the Mizpah tradition in 10,17-27 cannot be considered to be a record of actual historical events in connection with Saul's kingship. Thirdly, the anointing of Saul as *nagîd* (9,16; 10,1) is only found in a more recent layer of 9,1–10,16 and was not contained in the old folk tale about the lost asses.

(6) A reconstruction of the most probable course of events would be as follows:

1. Saul defeated the Philistine $n^e \c{s}îb$ at Geba-Gibeah in 1 S 13,4 (on the place name, see below ch. 11.2 at the end). The old folk tale about Saul's search for the lost asses and the three signs mentioned by the seer foreshadows this victory by mentioning the Philistine $n^e \c{s}îb$ (read the singular) in 10,5.[55] For obvious reasons, we must leave the question of the historicity of this old folk tale open. Saul's victory in 13,4 was later ascribed to Jonathan (13,3).
2. The rescue of Jabesh in ch. 11 took place after the event in 13,4 and perhaps also after the other events mentioned in ch. 13–14. The threat when Saul summoned the people to arms to Jabesh (the cutting of the oxen in 11,6-7) was thus backed up by the authority that Saul had gained through his earlier victory.[56]
3. Saul was made king only once, and this took place after his relief of Jabesh (11,15).

(7) The traditions of Saul's kingship testify to a development of the concept of the divine election of the king.

1. In 11,1-11.15 Saul appears as the man who was seized by the Spirit and who was thereby enabled to perform a deed of salvation. This showed the people that he was *approved of by YHWH*.
2. The tradition of the lot-casting at Mizpah shows the transition from the

---

[54] *Wallis* (1968: 45-66). Cf. also *Hauer* (JBL 86/1967, 306 ff.) and *Stoebe* (1973: 178).
[55] This point was made by *J.M.Miller* (CBQ 36/1974, 159).
[56] As was pointed out by *Miller* (p. 167f.). – I thus agree with Miller on two essential points, but I disagree with him concerning 10,8, which I take to be a late gloss, anticipating the Dtr section 13,7b-15a (contrast Miller p. 160f.), and concerning 10,26b-27 and 11,12-13, which Miller refuses to treat as a secondary framework (Miller p. 165 ff.), verses which I prefer to regard as redactional (see above ch. 5.2.1).

general idea of a divine election of the king to the concept of *the divine designation in advance*.

3. In its elaborate form with the anointing of Saul as *nagîd*, 9,1 – 10,16 is still later. Here a *prophetic oracle of designation* has taken the place of the lot-casting (9,27 ff.).

It is difficult to decide where Saul's meeting with the seer in the old folk tale belongs. This folk tale contains a hint of Saul's future kingship (9,10b) and a reference to the sign of the Spirit (10,5 ff.). It should be noted, however, that there is here no formal designation and no prophetic element.

CHAPTER VI

The Royal Psalms

1. The Royal Psalms. A Delimitation

The royal psalms in the Psalter are of obvious importance in the study of the sacral status of the king. The prophetic books in turn also contain material that is possible to draw on concerning problems under discussion.[1] It is essentially the same royal ideal which forms the basis for both the psalmists' way of depicting the reigning king and the prophets' way of painting the picture of the future Saviour. Nevertheless, when we feel that here the psalms have a major claim to our interest, this is for two reasons. First, it is from the methodological point of view a less risky undertaking to base conclusions concerning the reigning king on the royal psalms, where the future is of subordinate importance. Secondly, the prophetic texts in question are mainly from the last centuries of the monarchy of Judah. The interests of the present investigation are concentrated on the period before the classical prophets, and for this there is better chance of finding relevant material in the royal psalms, even if some of these may of course be late.

The questions of *Gattung* and *Sitz im Leben* in connection with the royal psalms are not easily answered. They cannot properly be said to form a *Gattung* of their own on the usual criteria for what constitutes a *Gattung*.[2] Actually, various *Gattungen* are represented among them, and different situations may be assumed to be their *Sitz im Leben*. The group is held together more by a common motif[3], which I should like to define in quite general terms as "the king and his God", than by a set of formal characteristics.[4]

---

[1] On the texts in the prophetic books, see the recent monographs by *Rehm* (1968) and *Seybold* (1972).

[2] I here refer to Gunkel's three criteria: texts belonging to the same *Gattung* should have the same *Sitz im Leben*, they should have a collection of ideas and moods in common and have a *Formensprache* in common, see *Gunkel–Begrich* (Einl. Ps. 1933: 22 f.).

[3] I here distinguish between theme (Germ. "Stoff") and motif (Germ. "Motiv"). I define theme with *E.Frenzel* (1966: 24): "Ein grösseres, aus einem oder mehreren Motivkomplexen erwachsenes stoffliches Gefüge mit festem Handlungsablauf, wie es die pragmatischen Dichtungsgattungen benötigen, wird als 'Stoff' im engeren Sinne bezeichnet." Cf. *W.Kayser* (^{14}1969: 56), who says: "Der Stoff ist immer an bestimmte Figuren gebunden, ist vorgangsmässig und zeitlich und räumlich mehr oder weniger fixiert." *Motif* is something different. Cf. *E.Frenzel* (1966: 12): "Das Motiv stellt ein stoffliches, situationsmässiges Element dar, dessen Inhalt knapp und allgemein formuliert werden kann, z.B. als der Mann zwischen zwei Frauen. ... Sie kann als Oberbegriff über ganze, festgefügte Stoffe, etwa den Graf-von-Gleichen-Stoff, den Medea-Stoff und den Ariadne-Stoff, gesetzt werden, und das Motiv erscheint dann in jedem einzelnen dieser Stoffe abgewandelt." Cf. *Kayser* (op. cit. p. 59 ff.).

[4] So *Mowinckel* (1951: 57), *vonRad* (ThAT ^{4}I: 331 note 1). Cf. what *E.Frenzel* says of the "artenprägende Kraft von Motiven" as a general phenomenon in literature (Frenzel 1966: 114 ff.).

Being aware of the effects of the "democratization" of isolated royal expressions makes it impossible to delimit the relevant material in the all-inclusive manner of certain Scandinavian scholars some decades ago.[5] If such psalms are set aside, where an intercession for the king only forms a subordinate element in a text that cannot in its entirety be described as a royal psalm,[6] we then feel justified in defining the group of royal psalms proper as being comprised of the following texts: Ps 2; 18; 20; 21; 45; 72; 89; 101; 110; 118 (?); 132; 144. Here I should also like to mention Jes 38,9-20 (Hezekiah). Besides, a text such as 2 S 23,1-7 ("the last words of David") is also of interest, even if it cannot properly be denoted as a royal psalm. This fairly narrow definition of the material of primary importance in the investigation does not imply that one can simply neglect other material. "Democratized" features should also be paid attention to, but here we are on more uncertain ground than when we deal with the royal psalms proper.

A survey of the various types of material in the royal psalms is illuminating. Three of these pieces are intercessions for the king (Ps 20; 72; 132[7]), and besides there are similar intercessions in texts that fall outside the group of royal psalms (Ps 61,7-8; 63,12; 84,10). Four of the royal psalms contain prayers voiced by the king himself (Ps 18; 144; 89; Jes 38). In Ps 101 we are faced with another piece recited by the king, but this time one that comes close to a negative confession of sin.[8]

The observation may seem to be too trivial to be put on record but should nevertheless be emphasized: this material clearly depicts the king as a man in submission to and dependent on the God of Israel.[9]

From Israel's neighbours we know of hymns addressed to the king. Thus the model letter in Pap. Anastasi II 5,6 ff. and IV 5,6 ff. and the morning hymn to Pharaoh provide unequivocal examples of hymns to the Egyptian sovereign.[10] There is nothing in the Old Testament that can suitably be compared with this.[11]

---

[5] For a survey of the psalms that these scholars subjected to a royal-ideological interpretation see *Bernhardt* (1961: 191 ff.).

[6] See Ps 61,7-8; 63,12; 84,10 (cf. Ps 28,8).

[7] That Ps 132 is an intercession for the king is all too often overlooked but appears from v. 1 and v. 10. Note that *hešîb panîm* (v. 10) is a phrase for "einen Bittenden abweisen", see 1 R 2,16.17.20 and cf. *GBL* (811 b sub 5). The reference to the two divine oracles in Ps 132 is made as part of the argument of the intercessor.

[8] See *Kaiser* (ZAW 74/1962, 195 ff.) for a valuable analysis in which he develops points made by *A.R.Johnson* in the first edition of his Sacral Kingship (1955: 104 ff. then most recently ²1967: 113 ff.). Note also the earlier hints by *Mowinckel* (PsSt II: 328 f. and 1951: 67, 77, 333 ff.), who, in contrast to Johnson and Kaiser, refrained from speaking of royal suffering in the cult (p. 570 ff.).

[9] Cf. *Posener's* stress on the same aspect of Egyptian kingship (1960: 23 ff.).

[10] On the model letter see below note 19. For the morning hymn to Pharaoh see *Erman* (1911: 15 ff. esp. 18) and cf. the expressions in the morning ceremonial in Pharaoh's field camp, see *Alt* (WO 1/1947, 2-4). Cf. also *Grapow* (²1960: 46 ff. and 50 ff.).

[11] Not even Ps 45.

A few psalms still remain to be mentioned, namely Ps 2; 21; 110. The last-mentioned consists of two oracles to the king.[12] Ps 2 is a proclamation made by the king, in which he refers to a divine oracle previously delivered to him. Ps 21 is of a very composite structure. It opens with a thanksgiving (v. 2-8), continues with an oracle to the king (v. 9-13),[13] and ends in a lament (v. 14).

Needless to say, I consider it difficult to agree wholeheartedly with the interpretation of the Psalms propounded by the English myth-and-ritual school and by Scandinavian scholars affiliated to the Upsala-circle[14]. But this does not mean that I find every criticism justified. Notably K.-H. Bernhardt (1961), who makes a number of valuable points, perpetrates several exaggerations in his attempt to issue a death-certificate for the study of the royal ideology in the Psalms. Bernhardt's refusal to admit that we do know the major elements of the coronation ritual (p. 259) is difficult to understand. What the Old Testament has got to say about various coronations cannot fairly be dismissed as "durchweg Sonderfälle von sehr unterschiedlichem Aufbau" (p. 259). Although these cases are surely remarkable from various points of view, we can easily discern certain basic elements, such as anointing and acclamation, although we do not know, of course, the whole outline of "die Normalzeremonie der Krönung".

Particularly weak are Bernhardt's arguments against the assumption of a ritual *Sitz im Leben* for the royal psalms (p. 291 ff.). That we do not have a complete synopsis of the number, outline and contents of the rites of the royal ritual, and the fact that we do not find any *Regieanmerkungen* in the texts, do not prove anything in this connection. The material has been sifted through the hands of the traditionists of the priestly theocracy of post-exilic times, and the fact that the monarchy was then long ago at an end, must have had its effects in this connection. The fact that the scholars criticized by Bernhardt often put forward mutually incompatible suggestions does not in itself falsify all their results, as Bernhardt sometimes seems to think. Of two contradictory proposals, only one needs to be false. And the fact that the outcome of the research criticized is a "Vielzahl paralleler 'Ritualteile'" is not *a priori* in conflict with the contention that "das offizielle Jerusalemer Originalritual kann nur eine Fassung gehabt haben" (p. 297). Bern-

---

[12] I do not agree with *Kraus* (Psalmen p. 754), who contends that Ps 110 contains three oracles. In my opinion there are only two. Instead of introducing a new oracle, v. 3 only continues the oracle begun in v. 1. The opening of the other oracle is found in v. 4. Thus each oracle is opened by an introductory formula, namely n^{e}°um YHWH and nišbā‛ YHWH. That v. 2 and 5 speak of YHWH in the third person and not in the first, does not invalidate this interpretation, cf. *Stamm* (FsGuggisberg 1973: 250), who adduces a number of examples of such a transition, e.g. Hos 1,7; Jes 8,5.7; 8.11.13; 11,9b; Jer 3,11-13. – In my statement above that the two oracles in Ps 110 are directed to the king I disagree with *Rowley* (Fs Bertholet 1950: 469f.), who argues that v. 4 contains a promise to Zadok. For a criticism of this theory see *Schreiner* (1963: 117f.) and cf. *Coppens* (1959: 344). The person adressed in Ps 110 is throughout the king.

[13] Some scholars prefer to see Ps 21,9-13 as directed to YHWH, so *D. Michel* (1960: 223) and *Fensham* (ZAW 77/1965, 198). For my own part I agree with *Tournay* (RB 66/1959, 177f.) and *Ridderbos* (1972: 182), who see in this part of the psalm an address to the king.

[14] With *D.A. Knight* (1973: 293 f.) I prefer to speak of an Upsala "circle" instead of an Upsala "school".

hardt's last-mentioned assertion may be true from the synchronic point of view, but diachronically we have to reckon with a development during a time spanning several centuries. It is symptomatic that Bernhardt is not able to put forward a real alternative to the ritual interpretation of the royal psalms. Indeed one fears that this would mean reverting to the interpretation of the Psalms adhered to in the period before Mowinckel.

I must therefore emphatically dissociate myself from Bernhardt's abortive attempt to create a gap between the royal ideology, as it was expressed in the actual royal ritual, on the one hand, and the picture of the king in the royal psalms on the other.[15] To reduce the contents of the royal psalms to "Motive ... , Bilder dichterischer Sprache, bestenfalls Anspielungen des Sängers auf Festerlebnisse und ähnliches" (p. 298 f.) is not a convincing way of accounting for the characteristics of this group of texts. The intrinsic conservatism in cult and ritual makes it much more natural to think that actual survivals of the royal rites of the first temple have come down to us in the royal psalms. And if most of these texts thus had their *Sitz im Leben* in the royal temple of the kings of Judah, they must be considered to form a material of first rate interest in the inquiry into the sacral position of the king.

2. The Question of Court Style

A special problem to be dealt with in connection with the royal psalms is that of *Hofstil*[16] or court style. Gressmann used the term in a very comprehensive way:

> Der Ausdruck Hofstil ist geeignet, alle Anschauungen, Redewendungen und Sitten zusammenzufassen, die am königlichen Hofe üblich sind, die nur in seiner Atmosphäre gedeihen und die daher ebenso notwendig zu ihm gehören wie Paläste, Frauenhaus, Prunkwagen, Leibwache und Steuern.[17]

Apparently, the Yahwistic faith was not apt to supply the young court first in Hebron and later in Jerusalem with all the necessary means to express the sacral legitimation of the monarch. This gap was filled by the conventions created at other courts in the ancient Near East.[18] During the early period it was probably mainly Egypt and its former vassal states on

---

[15] Bernhardt writes (1961: 298): "Die alttestamentlichen 'Königspsalmen' enthalten also nicht die 'ursprüngliche' Ideologie des Königsrituals und tragen ebensowenig die 'ursprüngliche' Ritualform der Königsideologie."

[16] This term seems to have been used for the first time in Old Testament scholarship by R.Kittel (ZAW 18/1898, 160). It plays a considerable part in the work by *Gressmann* (1929: 1-64). See also *Grzegorzewski* (1937). On the neo-Assyrian court style in Ps 45, see J.Mulder (1972: 95 ff., 148 ff.). For some notes on court style in Mari, see J.G.Heintz (Semitica 22/1972, 6-12).

[17] *Gressmann* (1929: 7).

[18] That ancient Near Eastern court style was taken up by Israel is now commonplace knowledge. An exception is R.E.Murphy (1948: 45-78), who tries to invalidate the arguments. The intention to uphold a traditional messianic interpretation of Ps 72 explains but does not add conviction to this position.

Canaanite soil that provided the models. Later on Assyria and Babylonia also appear in the picture.

As is shown by an Egyptian model letter (dyn. 19) and by "hymnic" portions in the Amarna letters from Abimilki of Tyre (EA 147,5-15.41-56), devotional formulae of hymnic character could have a place in Egyptian epistolary style.[19] As Albright has shown, the Egyptianisms in the Abimilki-letters suggest that these were written by an Egyptian scribe.[19a] The implications of this seem to be that diplomatic correspondence may have played a certain part in the diffusion of court style in the ancient Near East. It would lead too far, however, to enter into a discussion of this particular problem here.

Needless to say, regarding court style we are concerned with conventions fostered at the court. G.Posener, in his study *De la divinité du Pharaon* (1960) has rightly warned against the tendency of some scholars to take the court phraseology *ad litteram* (p. 6-12). One must always be aware of the possibility of an inflation of the values of this phraseology. Protocollary formulas are sometimes void of content; "le témoignage de piéte finit par devenir essentiellement un terme de politesse" (p. 6), a development that can be aptly illustrated by modern forms of address such as "Sa Sainteté", "Saint Père", etc. These observations are as valid for Israel as they are for Egypt.

Besides, there is also another fact that must not be ignored, viz. that in cases of borrowing there is always the possibility that formulae and expressions, the original significance of which had fallen into oblivion, were used in a new setting and were filled with a new content that was considered to be compatible with the Yahwistic faith.

Nevertheless, to dismiss the royal psalms as "mere" court style would be a somewhat cavalier way of handling the evidence.[20] It is interesting to note that Posener in his above-mentioned treatment of the Egyptian material expressly points out this danger.[20a] In this connection it seems wise to

---

[19] For the model letter see Pap. Anastasi II 5,6 ff. =IV 5,6 ff., text in *A.Gardiner* (Late Egyptian Miscellanies 1937: 15 and 40), translation in *R.A.Caminos* (Late Egyptian Miscellanies 1954: 48 f., 153). Note *A.Barucq* (1962: 247), who points out that "Le début du texte est plutôt un début de lettre. Le texte lui-même est nettement hymnique." – On the "hymnic" portions in EA 147, see *Albright* (JEA 23/1937, 197 ff.). This letter is dealt with in a forthcoming paper by *Cecilia Grave*, to whom I am indebted for having drawn my attention to the above-mentioned model letter.

[19a] See *Albright* (JEA 23/1937, 190-203, esp. 196 ff.).

[20] See the warnings voiced by *Engnell* (1943: 43 note 3) and *Mowinckel* (1951: 70). *Gressmann* was also aware of this danger, when he said that the word *Hofstil* should be taken to refer not only to subjective expressions of devotion or enthusiasm but also to "objektive, genau geregelte, feste Verpflichtungen, deren Zwang sich niemand ungestraft entziehen kann" (1929: 7).

[20a] "Si le scepticisme est permis en présence de certains excès de langage ou effets de rhétorique, il n'est pas de mise par exemple devant les scènes et les textes religieux des temples" (*Posener* 1960: 101).

dissociate oneself from Gressmann in his all too inclusive definition of Hofstil as comprising not only "Redewendungen und Sitten" but also "Anschauungen" fostered at the court (above). Thus, it seems commendable to distinguish here between style and contents and denote the former as court style and the latter as royal ideology. Now, it is of course in the abstract, possible that certain expressions of court style should be taken as mere conventions, not related to underlying ideas belonging to the royal ideology. That one should not, however, without further ado explain away the royal psalms as "mere" court style can be seen particularly clearly at two points.

(1) As has often been observed, the statements about the world-wide dominion of the Davidic king (Ps 2; 72) could perhaps be explained as being due to influence from the ancient Near Eastern court style. The actual extension of the Davidic empire, however, makes a factual point of departure for such expressions in the royal psalms.[21] Besides, statements of this kind should be seen in relation to the conception of the king as the vicegerent of YHWH. To God belong the peoples and the ends of the earth; he can delegate his power to whom he wants to.[22]

(2) Expressions referring to the inviolability of the king (e.g. in Ps 2 and 89) are certainly not to be interpreted as mere stylistic conventions. Information about legal cases, dealing with *crimina laesæ maiestatis* (2 S 1,1-16; 16,5-13 with 19,16-24) and other instances (such as 1 S ch. 24 and 26) should make us most cautious on this point.[23]

Summary

(1) The all-inclusive definition of the group of royal psalms propounded in some Scandinavian writing on the subject was rejected. A large proportion of the material consists of intercessions for the king and prayers voiced by him. Although some of the most sublime expressions of the king's sacral status are found in the royal psalms, we must thus conclude that the king even here is depicted as a man dependent on his God. By way of contrast, I drew attention to the Egyptian hymns addressed to the monarch. As for the *Sitz im Leben* of the royal psalms, I preferred to connect them with the royal ritual of the Israelite monarchy. In particular, I doubt the validity of Bernhardt's attempt to create a gap between the royal psalms on the one hand and the royal ritual and the royal ideology on the other.

---

[21] See *Kraus* (Psalmen p. 15 f.).
[22] Cf. *Mowinckel* (1951: 66). *Kraus* (Psalmen p. 15), and *vonRad* (ThAT ⁴I: 333).
[23] Against the background of such observations one feels tempted to denote much in the court style as being "verbal realities", using an expression that *F.Daumas*, in his review of Posener's above-mentioned work (RHR 160/1961, 139) applied to the Egyptian court style.

(2) It is necessary to distinguish between *Hofstil* and royal ideology. It is true that the whole phraseology of the royal psalms cannot be taken *ad litteram*. We always have to consider the possibility of an inflation of the values of a phraseology of this kind. Nevertheless, there are reasons not to dismiss the royal psalms as "mere" court style.

PART TWO

The Civil Legitimation of the King

Introduction

No one who studies the Israelite kingship can fail to notice what I should like to call a remarkable "synergism": according to the extant texts, both God and the people appear as involved and active parties in the making of a king. Thus the verb *himlîk*, "to make someone king" is used with both God and human beings as the grammatical subject.[1] That this "synergism" is not due to the ideas of later times but was already found in the early period of the monarchy, seems to appear from 2 S 16,18, where Hushai refers to Absalom as the man "whom the Lord and this people and all the men of Israel have chosen". The fact that the author of the Succession Narrative does not regard Absalom as the one chosen by the Lord but as a revolutionary, makes this utterance important, since it is then meaningful only as an expression of current contemporary beliefs connected with the appointment of a king.[2] The same combined activity of God and the people can be inferred from Hos 8,4, although the formulation is in the negative:

הם המליכו ולא ממני השירו ולא ידעתי

> They made kings, but not through me. They set up princes, but without my knowledge.

This is a criticism, not of kingship in general, but of such kingmaking that is not sanctioned by YHWH.[3]

The words in Dt 33,5 certainly refer to YHWH as king,[4] but even so they contain an interesting reflex of the role of the popular assembly in the making of a human king:

ויהי בישרון מלך
בהתאסף ראשי עם יחד שבטי ישראל

---

[1] The verb occurs with God as subject in 1 S 15,11.35; 1 R 3,7; 1 Ch 28,4; 2 Ch 1,8.9.11 and with a human as subject in the plural (cases referring to foreign kings not included): Jud 9,6.16.18; 1 S 11,15; 1 R 12,1 (=2 Ch 10,1); 12,20; 16,16.21; 2 R 10,5; 11,12 (=2 Ch 23,11); 2 R 14,21 (=2 Ch 26,1); 17,21; 21,24 (=2 Ch 33,25); 23,30 (=2 Ch 36,1); 1 Ch 11,10; 12,32.39; 29,22; 2 Ch 22,1.
[2] See *L.Schmidt* (1970: 181).
[3] See *H.W.Wolff* (Hosea ²1965: 178) and cf. *Gelston* (OTS 19/1974, 71 ff.).
[4] So recently *Seeligman* (VT 14/1964, 82 f.).

Then a king arose in Jeshurun,
when the chiefs of the people were assembled,
the congregation of the tribes of Israel.[5]

In this part of my investigation I shall study the role of the people in the making of a king. I shall then devote the next major section to the sacral legitimation of the king. I have found this to be a convenient way of organizing my work, although the existence of a development in certain conceptions could motivate a slightly different disposition from the one actually followed here.

"People" and *"elders"*. – The enthronement formula *himlîk 'æt* ... (*'ăl* ...), frequently occurring in the annal excerpts in the Books of Kings, normally appears with the subject in the plural.[6] In some cases the subject is specified, and we then find that a body denoted as *'ăm* has an important role as the subject of the verb *himlîk*: *kål ha'am* (1 S 11,15; cf. 10,23-25), *kål 'ăm yᵉhûdā* (2 R 14,21), and *'ăm ha'aræṣ* (2 R 21,24; 23,30).[7] All these expressions refer to the people or its representatives as an active party at the royal investitures. This tempts one to speak of a quasi-democratic feature of Israelite kingship.[8]

It should be noted that this acting party is never called *gôy*. The semantic difference between *'ăm* and *gôy* have already been studied by others[9] and there is no reason to undertake a new investigation here. Among the notable differences is that *gôy* often appears as a parallel to *mămlakā*.[10] A *gôy* can be made (*'aśā*), established (*natăn*), founded (*śîm*), or the like; while an *'ăm* just is as a physical fact.[11] In contrast to *gôy*, *'ăm* was originally a kinship term; and its original meaning seems to have been "uncle" (cf. Lev 21,1 ff.). This kinship connotation is preserved in expressions like *wăyye'asæp 'æl 'ămmâw*, "he was gathered to his kindred" (Gn 25,17 etc.) and *nikrăt me'ămmâw* (Ex 30,33.38). To quote Speiser *'ăm* was "essentially a term denoting close family connections, and hence secondarily the extended family, that is, people in the sense of a larger, but fundamentally consanguineous, body".[12]

A very interesting observation was made by L.Rost, who pointed out that *'ăm* denotes "die Mannschaft eines Volkes als Zusammenfassung

---

[5] My own translation. I take *yăḥăd* as a noun, cf. *HAL* (p. 387b).

[6] See above, note 1.

[7] Cf. also *ha'edā* in 1 R 12,20 (for other expressions for the assembly see v. 1.3.5.15).

[8] On quasi-democratic features in the Hebrew monarchies, see *E.Day* (AJSL 40/1923-24, 98-110), *Nyström* (1946: 79-82), *C.U.Wolf* (JNES 6/1947, 98-108), *Gordis* (A. Marx Jub. Vol. 1/1950, 369-88), *Malamat* (BA 28/1965, 34 ff.), *Soggin* (1967 passim) and *Tadmor* (1968: 46 ff.).

[9] See particularly *L.Rost* (FsProcksch 1934: 137 ff.) and *Speiser* (JBL 79/1960, 157 ff.). For further literature on *'ăm* see *Lohfink* (Fs vonRad 1971: 277 note 13).

[10] See e.g. 1 R 18,10; Jer 18,7.9; 2 Ch 32,15; and cf. Ex 19,6.

[11] See *Speiser* (p. 160).

[12] *Speiser* (p. 159).

der Verheirateten, auf eigener Scholle sitzenden Vollbürger mit dem Recht zur Dienstleistung im *Heerbann*, zur Teilnahme an der *Rechtssprechung* und zur Ausübung des *Kultes*".[13] Thus we meet the ʿăm both as the militia summoned to arms, and as the legal and cultic assembly.

Indeed, some of the royal investitures take place in a military setting. When considering such occasions, it must be kept in mind that Israel and Judah had a militia, a citizen army based on "general conscription".[14] The army was in principle the ʿăm. It is from this point of view that we must look at the investitures of Saul and Omri. After the battle at Jabesh the militia, denoted as *kål haʿam*, followed Saul to Gilgal and made Saul king. The fact that the people offered sacrifices only shows that the ʿăm, who shortly before had operated as the militia in the battle at Jabesh, could also act as cultic assembly. On a later occasion we are told that "all Israel made Omri, the commander of the army, king over Israel that day in the camp" (1 R 16,16).[15]

A term to be mentioned in connection with ʿăm is $z^eqenîm$, "elders".[16] In some of the passages which will now be studied, there is a strange oscillation between "the elders" and "the people".[17] This is partly due to the fact that the elders represent and embody the people in a way that is in line with the conception of "corporate personality". However, it would be wrong, at least for the period of the monarchy, to postulate an outright identification of the elders with the entire adult male population.[18]

In the study of the role of the people at the royal investitures, I shall proceed in the following order. First, I shall study a number of investitures and point out what is said in the texts about the participation of the popular assembly (ch. 7). Because of the structural dualism between Judah

---

[13] *Rost* (p. 147), my italics. See also *L.Köhler* (1931: 147).

[14] One cannot take it for granted that the militia lost its importance because of the use of professional soldiers. See *Knierim* (ZAW 73/1961, 167 ff.) and cf. *M.Weippert's* comment (ZAW 84/1972, 491 f.).

[15] For Solomon see below.

[16] On the elders in general see *J.L.McKenzie* (Bibl 40/1959, 522-540), *H.Berg* (unpubl. diss. 1959, mainly on "the elders of Israel"), *J.Dus* (Communio Viatorum 3/1960, 232-242 with some debatable conclusions), *v.d.Ploeg* (Fs H.Junker 1961: 175-191), and *J.M.Salmon* (unpublished diss. 1968: 395-417). On the elders in Mesopotamia, see *A.Walther* (1917: 52 ff.) and *H.Klengel* (Or 29/1960, 357-375). On the elders in Hatti, see *H.Klengel* (ZA 23/1965, 223-236).

[17] This is a feature found in a number of texts. See *v.d.Ploeg* (p. 185). In addition to his examples, one could also mention for instance 1 S 8,10.19.22. See also *C.U.Wolf* (JNES 6/1947, 98 ff.).

[18] Here I agree with *J.L.McKenzie* (Bibl 40/1959, 523 f., 535). In addition to the arguments advanced by this scholar, one should also note that the expression "elders of the people" (Ex 19,7; Nu 11,16.24; 1 S 15,30; Jes 3,14; Jer 19,1) is a difficulty to an outright identification of the elders with the adult male population. See also *v.d.Ploeg* (p. 185) and cf. *Salmon* (1968: 402 f.).

and Israel from early times I shall keep the investitures in the North (part 1) apart from those in the South (part 2). In connection with the investitures in Judah I shall also have to enter into a discussion of the well-known problem of the '*ăm ha'aræṣ*. After this I shall devote ch. 8 to a discussion of constitutional problems such as the character of the royal *bᵉrît* and the popular acclamation.

CHAPTER VII

The Participation of the Elders and the Assembly at the Royal Investitures

1. The Popular Assembly in Northern Israel

Already for the pre-monarchic period, there are points in the passages on Gideon, Abimelech and Jephthah that are of interest in the present investigation.[1] The first was offered sovereignty by "the men of Israel" but rejected the offer (Jud 8,22 f.).[2] Abimelech's kingship cannot be regarded as genuinely Israelite.[3] But it should be noted that he was invested with his power by an assembly of kål bă'ălê šekæm (Jud 9,6). This is sometimes regarded as a feudal assembly of honoratiores.[4] One could ask, however, if this assembly of landowners[5] does not come fairly close to the popular assemblies of later times in Israel and Judah. Finally, in the case of Jephthah it was the elders who went to offer him sovereignty and to bring him back from the land of Tob (Jud 11,4-11). They even made some sort of a contractual agreement with him and then brought him to Mizpah, where the 'ăm installed him l^ero'š ûl^eqaṣîn (11,9-11).[6]

1. Passages Concerning Saul

A general source-critical examination of the texts concerning Saul's kingship was submitted above in chapters 4 and 5, and for details I refer to the results achieved there. The passage that comes closest to depicting the actual participation of the assembly in Saul's investiture is 1 S 11,1-11.15. After the victory at Jabesh, all the people (kål ha'am, cf. also kål 'ănšê yiśra'el) went to Gilgal and made Saul king there (v. 15). Nothing is expressly said about an anointing of Saul or about the popular acclamation. These acts may be implied in the verb himlîk, but as for the anointing we shall later see that Saul was probably never anointed (see ch. 10.2.1). On the other hand, the text expressly mentions that the people offered z^ebaḥîm š^elamîm[7] before the Lord.

---

[1] On these see *Soggin* (1967: 11-25) with references to further literature.
[2] In spite of this there are royal features in Gideon. See *Wallis* (1968: 51).
[3] See *Alt* (KS II, 6) and *Soggin* (1967: 21 note 17). On Abimelech see also *H.Schmid* (Jud 26/1970, 1-11).
[4] For instance by *Soggin* (1967: 23 and 122).
[5] For this sense in bă'ăl, see *HAL* (137 a sub no 2).
[6] On ro'š as a title, see *Bartlett* (VT 19/1969, 1-10).
[7] On this type of sacrifice see most recently *Gerleman* (ZAW 85/1973, 11 ff.).

As we saw in our discussion of the source material, 10,17-27 is a passage that is unusually difficult to assess. I put forward the theory that the tradition found here serves the purpose of voicing a northern criticism of Solomonic absolutism. If this is correct the passage in question cannot be used as historical evidence for the constitutional role of the people at Saul's actual investiture. But even so it testifies to the constitutional ideal adhered to by the northern tribes during the Solomonic era.

According to this tradition Samuel summoned the people (*'ăm*) to Mizpah (v. 17). Then the text goes on to describe a procedure of lot-casting (v. 19b-22), that will be discussed in detail in the chapter on the divine designation of the king. The outcome of this sacral procedure is that Saul stands out as the one designated by God.

When Saul had been brought back from his hiding place, Samuel asked the people: *hărr^e'îtæm 'ašær bahăr bô YHWH kî 'ên kamohû b^{e}kål ha'am* (v. 24). The crucial point here is the semantic content of the verb *ra'ā*.[8] It has been suggested that Samuel's question refers to Saul's unusual height as a sign of his divine election.[9] The translation would then be something like: "Do you (now) see him whom the Lord has chosen?" However, there are strong reasons for giving a different interpretation. In a number of cases the verb *ra'ā* is used in a developed sense: "see" > "choose", "appoint" (cf. Ger. "aussehen", "ersehen").[10] The following occurrences of this verb can be cited as examples of this use:

Gn 7,1   *kî 'otka ra'îtî ṣaddîq l^{e}panăy* (God to Noah: "For you I have chosen to be righteous before me.").[11]

Gn 22,8 *'^{a}elohîm yir'æ̆ lô hăśśæ̆* (Abraham to Isaac).

Gn 41,33 *w^e'ăttā yeræ' păr'ō 'îš nabôn w^{e}hakam* (Joseph to Pharaoh).

1 S 16,1 *kî ra'îtî b^{e}banâw lî mælæk* (God to Samuel about the sons of Jesse). Cf. 1 S 16,17-18.

2 R 8,13 *hir'ănî YHWH 'otka mælæk 'ăl '^{a}ram* (Elisha to Hazael. Translate: "The Lord caused me to appoint you king over Aram.").[12]

2 R 10,3 *ûr^e'îtæm hăṭṭôb w^{e}hăyyašar mibb^{e}nê '^{a}donêkæm w^{e}śămtæm 'ăl kisse' 'abîw* (Jehu to the elders of Samaria).

It is well worth noticing that in the last three examples, the verb is used with reference to the appointment of kings. The same semantic develop-

---

[8] On the form in 1 S 10,24 see *Ges-K* (^{27}1902 § 22 s and 100 l).
[9] So *Budde* (1902: 72).
[10] Most of the following examples of *ra'ā* used in this sense were noted by *W.M.Clark* (VT 21/1971, 267f., 275f.).
[11] For a penetrating analysis of this verse see *Clark* (p. 261-280).
[12] This occurrence is discussed in detail by *Clark* (p. 275f.).

ment ("see" > "choose", "appoint") is attested for other verbs as well. Thus *ḥazā* is used in this way in Ex 18,21 (cf. v. 25), and the *hapax legomenon barā* II (1 S 17,8) provides another case.[13]

The possibility of interpreting the words in 1 S 10,24 to mean "do you *appoint* the one whom the Lord has chosen?" must thus be taken into account. What makes this interpretation not only possible but even probable is the context. Samuel's question is followed by the people's acclamation of Saul as king: *yᵉḥî hămmælæk* (v. 24). The interpretation of the question as "do you (now) appoint?" reveals the inner coherency of the course of events. When the divine designation of one single man had been established by means of the sacral lot, Samuel put a solemn and formal question to the people. This solemn question was not merely rhetorical that is whether the people were able to see (discern) whom the Lord had chosen. What Samuel's question implied was, whether or not the people were prepared to recognize the divine designation of Saul and appoint him king. The formal consent of the people was expressed by means of the acclamation.

Understood in this way, 1 S 10,24 displays the balance between the divine designation and the popular acclamation. The people play quite an active part in the proceedings. The acclamation is here not merely an act of salutation. It is a manifestation of the *vox populi*, a legal act through which one designated by God became *mælæk*.[14]

We can now turn to the third tradition of Saul, viz. that in 1 S 9,1–10,16. In its original form this tradition contained a narrative about Saul's consulting a seer about his father's asses. In a more recent form, probably from the decades immediately after Solomon's death, this tradition was expanded to also contain Saul's anointing as *nagîd*. The sacrificial meal in 9,22 ff. perhaps already had a role in the original narrative, but in its present form, depicted as something like a royal banquet, it is to be linked with the more recent stratum.

What is said about the people in other traditions has its corollary in what is said here about the participants at the sacrificial meal. There were about thirty men specially invited, *qᵉrû'îm* (v. 13.22). These are also denoted as *'ām* (v. 12.13.24). It is possible that in the tradition in its expanded form *qᵉrû'îm* alluded to "the elders of Israel".[15]

---

[13] On *barā* II see *Kutsch* (1973: 32f.). It is possible that *baḥār* displays the same semantic development. The senses "prüfen", "erwählen" are derived from a supposed original sense "genau ansehen" in *HAL* (p. 115a). Cf. also *Wildberger* (THAT 1/1971, 279 sub 2a). The same development is perhaps also present in Akkadian *(w)atû*, see *CAD* (vol. A:2 p. 518ff.).

[14] I thus disagree with *Weiser* (1962: 66 note 42), who thinks that the people is here depicted in a very passive role. For a clear distinction between designation by God and acclamation by the people see *Alt* (KS II, 23), who did not, however, notice the sense "appoint" in *ra'ā*.

[15] Cf. *Buber* (Werke II, 761 f.).

In this connection attention must be drawn to the word *môʿed* in 9,24. The common interpretation is that this means here "at the appointed time". I prefer to connect it with the term *qᵉrûʾîm* and to interpret it from the expressions *qaraʾ môʿed*, "to summon an assembly" (cf. Thr 1,15) and *qᵉriʾê môʿed*, "conveners of assembly" (Nu 16,2). As a matter of fact, Samuel speaks of the summoning of the people (*haʿam qaraʾtî*) in the same breath as he utters the word *lămmôʿed* (v. 24). At this assembly Saul was allowed to take the seat of honour *bᵉroʾš hăqqᵉrûʾîm* (v. 22).[16]

The assumption that what is said about the presence of the representatives of the people at the sacrifice in this case stands in direct relation to the investiture (although this takes place on the following day) – this assumption is corroborated by other texts which display the same collocation of people, sacrifice and investiture. In Absalom's case (2 S 15,7-12) there were two hundred men specially invited (again *qᵉruʾîm* v. 11), who certainly participated in the sacrifice (v. 12). A similar "coronation" sacrifice is mentioned for Adonijah (1 R 1,9), and here we also meet the *qᵉruʾîm* (1 R 1,41.49), but in this case the word does not refer to a popular assembly as we shall soon see.

2. David and "the Elders of Israel"

The investiture of Ish-baal may be passed over here, since we do not know whether it took place with the consent of the people or not (2 S 2,8-10). Instead, we can turn to David's investiture over the northern tribes. When David had already become king of Judah we are told in 2 S 3,17-21 that Abner negotiated with (a) *ziqnê yiśraʾel* (v. 17 f.) and (b) Benjamin (v. 19) in order to prepare the way for David's installation as king of Northern Israel as well. Abner then reveals to David his plans to have David invested with power by an assembly representing *kål yiśraʾel* (v. 21).

After the death of Ish-baal (2 S 4,1-12) this plan was carried out, although Abner had then been murdered by Joab. David's investiture over the tribes of Northern Israel is described in 2 S 5,1-3. The short passage contains some inner tensions. First, v. 3a is a repetition of v. 1a. Secondly, there is a slight shift in terminology from v. 1 with "all the tribes of Israel" to v. 3 with "all the elders of Israel".

Hertzberg takes the shift in terminology to indicate two different acts, the one in v. 1-2 having "more the nature of a preliminary action" undertaken by "the active and responsible men of the tribes", the second

---

[16] The idea that this was imagined as a secret assembly (*Buber*, Werke II, 761 ff. and *Wildberger*, ThZ 13/1957, 454) is connected with an interpretation of this tradition as commemorating an actual event in the life of Saul. As was seen above, I do not think that this can be said of the features contained in the *nagîd* layer of 1 S 9,1–10,16.

and decisive step being the one mentioned in v. 3, which was taken by the elders as an official body.[17] Others have solved the problem by the assumption of traces of redaction in the brief section.[18] Here, the observation that v. 2 alludes to the divine election of David in a way that is typical of the History of David's Rise is particularly helpful. The first two verses of the short section may therefore be attributed to the author of this historical work, while the original tradition of David's investiture over Israel is found only in v. 3.[19]

Our conclusions concerning David's actual investiture over the northern tribes must be based on this interpretation of the evidence. It was the elders of these tribes[20] who acted as the official representatives of the ʿăm. The course of events described in v. 3, falls into two separate actions, both of which are of pre-eminent constitutional significance. First David granted the elders a $b^e r \hat{\imath} t$ ($w \check{a} y y i k r o t \; l a h \hat{\ae} m \; h \check{a} m m \hat{\ae} l \ae k \; d a w i d \; b^e r \hat{\imath} t \; b^e h \hat{\ae} b r \hat{o} n \; l i p n \hat{e} \; Y H W H$). This refers to what I shall call the royal covenant, to which I shall devote a special investigation in the following chapter. Then the people "anointed David king over Israel".

Two preliminary observations about the royal anointing should be made here and these will be further pursued in the chapter on this royal rite. (a) The verb $ma\check{s}ăḥ$ appears in the plural, and the acting subject that carries out the rite is clearly "the elders of Israel" mentioned in the same verse. This is reminiscent of David's anointing over Judah, where the $'ăn\check{s}ê \; yehûdā$ appear as the acting subject behind the rite (2 S 2,4). (b) Since there are only two acts mentioned, one with the king as the subject, namely the granting of a $b^e r \hat{\imath} t$ to the elders, and the other with these elders as the subject, namely the anointing, we must ask whether there is an inner connection between these two constitutional acts, so that they mutually correspond.

3. The Assembly at Shechem. The Investitures of Omri and Jehu

The next occasion on which we hear of the representatives of the northern tribes taking part in acts related to the transference of royal power, is in connection with the assembly at Shechem after the death of Solomon (1 R ch. 12). The textual witnesses are at variance, and there are generally

---

[17] *Hertzberg* (Samuel p. 266f.).
[18] *Budde* (1902: 2!8) took the reference to the elders in v. 3a to be due to later redaction. *A.Schulz* (Samuel II, 54) took v. 1-2 to be "eine spätere Ausführung".
[19] See *Grønbæk* (1971: 248-250) and cf. above ch. 2.4.2.3.
[20] That "Israel" in v. 3 (cf. v. 1) historically refers to the northern tribes is evident from 2 S 2,1-4 and 3,17-21. Whether the author of the History of David's Rise used it in a pan-Israelite sense (so *Grønbæk* 1971: 246 ff. and cf. *Danell* 1946: 79 f.) is a different matter. – The Chronicler wholly suppressed David's investiture over Judah in 2 S 2,1-4 and presented the investiture over Israel in 2 S 5,1-3 as the sole narrative of David's investiture (1 Ch 11,1-3).

speaking three different versions of these events, namely the one found in the MT, the one found in the LXX in 11,43–12,24, and that of the LXX in 12,24a-z. Of these the MT is to be preferred.[21] Another problem is that of the tension between 12,2-3a.12 and the statement in v. 20. However, this problem is mainly relevant to a discussion of the historical sequence of events and has less bearing on an investigation of the constitutional position of the assembly versus royal power. I shall therefore not enter into a discussion of this problem here.[22]

The first point of interest to us is the negotiations between the king over Judah and the representatives of the northern tribes. It seems that after Solomon's death, Rehoboam became more or less automatically king of Judah (1 R 11,43). His sovereignty over the northern tribes was a different matter and required a separate investiture. The conditions were the same under David, who became king first of Judah and then of Northern Israel. Just as "the elders of Israel" had gone to Hebron to anoint David, so Rehoboam went to Shechem to receive the acclamation of the same tribes. And these tribes are said to have come to Shechem "to make him king" (12,1). As we shall see in a subsequent discussion of the royal covenant, the negotiations at Shechem are to be understood as dealing with the conditions which Rehoboam had to accept in order to receive the acclamation. The people (or elders), here denoted as *kål yiśra'el* (v. 1), *ha'am* (v. 5.12.15) and *ha'edā* (v. 20), are in opposition to the heir apparent as the other party in these negotiations. It stands to reason that the people had an extremely important role in the legal transference of royal power. They could even submit certain conditions, which the claimant to the throne had to accept.[23]

---

[21] For a survey of the research see *Debus* (1967: 68-80). On the LXX in 11,43–12,24 see esp. *Gooding* (VT 17/1967, 173 ff. and JBL 91/1972, 529 ff.), who stressed the superiority of the MT. As for the LXX in 12,24a-z, *Seebass* (VT 17/1967, 325 ff.) tried to use it for the purpose of historical reconstruction. However, *Debus* concludes from his detailed study (1967: 55-92) "dass die griechische Version nicht als über MT hinausführende historische Quelle gelten kann" (p. 90).

[22] Different solutions have been attempted. *Nielsen* (1955: 171 ff.) assumes two originally Shechemite traditions. One of them was concerned with the negotiations between Rehoboam and the elders of Israel (11,43; 12,1.3b-15.18-19). The other centred on Jeroboam's election (12,2-3a.20.25 ff.). *Debus* (1967: 19 ff., esp. 27) also assumes two different traditions: (a) 12,2-3a.20 give reliable information on Jeroboam's return and election, (b) 12,3b-16.18-19 form a popular narrative that is considerably less reliable. *Noth* (Könige p. 265 ff.) thinks of one single Jerusalemite tradition (p. 271), with v. 2-3a forming an addition (p. 273) as also does the mention of Jeroboam in v. 12 (p. 276). Cf. the LXX. *Gooding* (VT 17/1967, 180 f.) tries to explain the text as one consistent tradition without additions, by means of the hypothesis that there were actually two assemblies at Shechem shortly after each other. Jeroboam is supposed to have been called to the first one by his supporters in the tribe of Ephraim (cf. v. 2-3a), while he was officially summoned to the second assembly (cf. v. 20).

[23] A special problem is connected with the identity of the *z^eqenîm* and the *y^eladîm* whom Rehoboam took counsel with (v. 6.8). This problem has been discussed by *Malamat* (BA

The second point of interest to us has to do with Jeroboam. Quite apart from the problem of how to relate the statements in v. 2-3a.12 to the statement in v. 20, one thing is sufficiently clear, namely that Jeroboam was made king by an assembly:

> And when all Israel heard that Jeroboam had returned, they sent and called him to the assembly [ha'edā] and made him king over all Israel. (1 R 12,20)

The details handed down to us concerning the investiture of Omri are somewhat difficult to assess properly, but may nevertheless be relevant here. Zimri, who was commander of half the chariotry, slew King Elah in Tirzah, the capital (1 R 16,8 ff.). This is denoted as "conspiracy" (v. 9.20). The army, busy with the siege of Gibbethon, did not accept Zimri as king (v. 15 ff.) but instead made Omri king. This constitutional act was thus carried out by the army and took place in the military camp (v. 16). It seems to me that Zimri, who had a high position in the chariotry, relied on the professional troops, while Omri received the support of the non-professional militia, that acted as representing "all Israel" (v. 16-17) and that was also logically denoted as 'ăm (v. 15-16).[24] Since, as we have seen, the 'ăm could act both as militia and as a cultic and legal assembly, the events in connection with the investiture of Omri cannot be seen as the outcome of a clash between the army and the people. The investiture of Omri falls in line with the other ones where the people are reported to have played a significant role. The later conflict between Omri and Tibni (v. 21-22) need not present a difficulty for such an interpretation.

The last potential reference to the assembly of the Northern Kingdom occurs in connection with Jehu (2 R 9,1–10,31). Immediately on his anointing by a member of the prophetic guild of Elisha, Jehu was acclaimed king (wăyyitqe'û băššôpar wăyyo'merû mălăk yehû', 9,13). The problem is, however, that it is difficult to decide whether the army here consisted of the professional soldiers or of the militia. In the latter case, the officers (v. 5.11) could be men who held the position of elders in peace.

The role of an assembly is also presupposed in Jehu's ironical[25] letter to the elders and other prominent persons in Samaria, in which he summons them to take the fittest of the royal sons and set him on his father's throne (10,3; cf. v. 5).

During the period from Jehu to the fall of Samaria, we do not get any

---

28/1965, 34 ff., esp. p. 41 ff.), G.Evans (JNES 25/1966, 273 ff.), Debus (1967: 30 ff.), Noth (Könige p. 274 f.) and Lipinski (VT 24/1974, 430 ff.). My own position, which approaches that of Evans, is that the $z^eqenîm$ were princes of Solomon's generation and that the $y^eladîm$ were princes of Rehoboam's generation.

[24] Soggin (1967: 99) has misinterpreted this.
[25] So Galling (1929: 19).

details which could reveal anything concerning the extent to which the people still played an active role in the investitures. The general development of affairs, however, allows us to assume a growing tension between autocratic tendencies, represented by strong men supported by professional troops, and on the other hand the old quasi-democratic ideals.[26]

2. The Popular Assembly in Judah

1. From David to Solomon

In the North, ratification by the people was a *sine qua non* for the legitimate transference of royal power to a new man. Also in Judah, the people had a very strong position, but to judge from the evidence the investitures of Adonijah and Solomon took place without the convocation of a formal assembly. It seems, however, that these two cases only formed a constitutional interlude, since there is evidence to make it probable that the kings before and after Solomon were put on the throne by the people.

(1) *David*. – The texts mention three different investitures of David. First there is his secret investiture through his anointing by Samuel at Bethlehem (1 S 16,1-13). For certain reasons the discussion of this text will be postponed. Then there are his two official investitures at Hebron over Israel (2 S 5,1-3) and over Judah (2,1-4a). Here it is said that "the men of Judah came, and there they anointed David king over the house of Judah" (2,4a). This is strikingly similar to David's investiture over the tribes of Northern Israel by means of the anointing by the elders of these tribes in 5,3. Probably "the men of Judah" are to be identified as the elders of the *bêt yᵉhûdā* (cf. 2 S 19,12.15). We may guess that David's earlier distribution of spoils between "the elders of Judah" (1 S 30,26-31) was made with the conscious aim to prepare the way for his recognition by these.

There is also another text from which something of David's relations to the assembly of Judah can be inferred. It is the passage describing the events after Absalom's revolt and death, when David returned home (2 S 19,10-44). David had beaten Absalom with the help of his professional mercenaries.[1] The way back to Jerusalem lay open to him. But instead of returning by his own strength, relied on his professional soldiery, a possibility which David must have taken into account, he was anxious

---

[26] Cf. *Soggin* (1967: 102 f.).

[1] I agree with *Noth* (History ²1960: 201) and *Soggin* (1967: 75) that Absalom had the support of the militia, whereas David relied on the professional soldiers. Note 2 S 15,18 and cf. 8,18 and 20,23.

for an official manifestation of the loyalty of his people. This took place at the return over the Jordan in the form of an act that I would like to describe as a second "coronation". In spite of the fact that we do not hear of anointing and acclamation, there are other indications:

1. Absalom's revolt and investiture (2 S 15,7 ff.) meant the deposition of David. This is true (15,19) in spite of the fact that David is denoted as king in 19,10 ff.
2. David had fled the land (19,10) and was now about to return to it.
3. The role played by Gilgal in these events (19,16.41) is to be understood as being due to a conscious association with Saul's investiture at this place.[2]
4. As at investitures proper, the people here acted through their elders, "the elders of Judah" (19,12; cf. v. 15.17), who summoned David back to the throne.
5. On the very day of his return, David judged two legal cases (Shimei and Meribbaal). Especially in the first of these two cases (19,17-24), David's verdict of acquittal (*lo' tamût*, v. 24) bears the marks of a royal amnesty at the coronation.[3] It can be compared with the amnesty in 1 S 11,12-14[3a] and with that connected with the installation of a new high priest.[4] It is because of the special character of the day as a second "coronation" that David motivates his pardon of Shimei with the words "I am this day king over Israel" (19,23).

I conclude from these observations that David's negotiations with the elders of Judah in connection with his return after Absalom's revolt testify to the importance ascribed by David to the recognition and ratification by the popular assembly.

(2) Adonijah and Solomon. – David's eagerness to gain the acknowledgement of the people strongly contrasts with what we know about the investitures of Adonijah and Solomon. In the first case (1 R 1,5-31) we are told that Adonijah had the support of Joab, who was the commander of the militia. Since the militia was in principle the *'ăm*, it could be tempting to see the representatives of the people in the *śarê hăṣṣaba'*, found in the MT of v. 25. But in the first place, even if the plural of the

---

[2] This was stressed by K.*Galling* (ZDPV 66/1943, 147 f.).
[3] Cf. A.*Schulz* (Samuel II, 234) *Hertzberg* (Samuel 1964: 366) and *Macholz* (ZAW 84/1972, 170).
[3a] These verses belong to the redactional material connecting 11,1-11.15 with 10,17 ff. and it is thus impossible to use them as evidence for an actual amnesty proclaimed by Saul. But even so the verses in question presuppose the possibility of such an amnesty.
[4] See Nu 35,25.28; Jos 20,6.

MT should represent the better text, these men must reasonably belong to the "royal servants" in v. 9b, where it is said that of all the men of Judah, Adonijah invited only the royal servants to his sacrifice.[5] In the second place, the reading of the singular, *śăr hăṣṣaba'* (=Joab), is attested in the Lucianic text and fits better the order of enumeration in this verse. Therefore, we should probably read the singular.[5a] This means that at Adonijah's investiture there were a number of people present belonging to the royal court and to the royal officials but that as far as we can see there were no representatives of the people.

As for Solomon's investiture, it has already been pointed out that Solomon did not have the right of seniority, since Adonijah was older (1 R 1,6; 2,15.22), and we have also discussed the statement about a formal designation of Solomon as *nagîd* by David (see Part One the introduction). The question of the participation of the people in his investiture will be taken up here.

As regards 1 R 1,32-40 at first glance we get the impression that the people were duly represented at the investiture:

> Then they blew the trumpet; and all the people (*kål ha'am*) said, "Long live King Solomon!" (1 R 1,39; cf. v. 40)

But taken as a whole, the passage rather favours the assumption that Solomon's investiture took place as a private affair of the court.[6] Various observations make it difficult to see in the *'ăm* in v. 39-40 a formal assembly carrying out a constitutional act in the traditional sense of the participation of the people at the royal investitures.

(a) Those present on the occasion are specified as being Zadok, Nathan, Benaiah, the royal entourage (v. 32-33) and the Cherethites and the Pelethites (the mercenary troops, v. 38). It is this group that David orders to acclaim the new king (v. 34). This should be compared with David's return after Absalom's revolt, when David deliberately abstained from depending upon the support of the mercenaries. In strong contrast to this, the Cherethites and the Pelethites play a predominant part in Solomon's investiture. It is indeed an important factor that the militia could not be relied upon, since its commander, Joab, gave his support to Adonijah.

(b) It is also most important to note who carries out the rite of anointing. David was anointed by the representatives of the people, both at his investiture over Judah and at that over Israel (2 S 2,4; 5,3). In contrast to this, the anointing of Solomon is said to be carried out by Zadok and Nathan (v. 34) or by Zadok alone (v. 39). At Solomon's investiture the

---

[5] I here agree with *Montgomery–Gehman* (Kings p. 73), *Noth* (Könige p. 6, 19) and others.
[5a] As do *Burney* (Kings, repr. 1970: 7) and *Gray* (Kings 1964: 84).
[6] Cf. *Alt* (KS II, 61 f.), *Würthwein* (1936: 20 f.), *Fohrer* (ZAW 71/1959, 6 ff.), *D.G.Evans* (JNES 25/1966, 274 f.) and *Soggin* (1967: 76 f.).

anointing is thus carried out by one or two members of the court, by royal officials. The people have nothing to do with it.

(c) The statement about David's designation of Solomon as *nagîd* (1 R 1,35) also deserves attention here. If this information is historically reliable, the participation of the people would in any case have been reduced to the recognition of what was in fact a *fait accompli*. It is also expressly said that David "made Solomon king" (v. 43). This is a most remarkable use of *himlîk*, since this Hiphil regularly appears with the subject in the plural referring to the assembly.[7]

On the basis of these observations it must be concluded that the people were not formally represented at Solomon's investiture. It may be that the narrator, who seems to be concerned about Solomon's legitimacy, chose the word *'ăm* because of its established use in denoting the formal assembly acting at the transference of royal power. But nothing can hide the embarrassing fact that there is no referential truth behind the word. Either Solomon was made king through an autocratic act of the aged King David, by the mere *fiat* of the moribund king, *or* what is said about David's designation of Solomon as *nagîd* is only a fabrication to camouflage a *coup d'état* organized by Solomon and his supporters at court. In neither case was his investiture a constitutional act carried out by the people.

It is necessary here not only to establish facts but also to ask for explanations. How shall we account for the absence of the people in the cases of Adonijah and Solomon? In the latter case one could of course think of the fact that Joab, who was the commander of the militia, supported Adonijah. It also seems that for Solomon the matter was urgent, leaving no time for the convocation of an assembly. In the case of Adonijah things are different. This claimant to the throne had the right to succeed David to the throne, since normally the succession followed the principle of primogeniture. Adonijah had the initiative and would certainly have had the time to call together an assembly. And we should remember that he enjoyed the support of the commander of the militia. We must therefore look for other reasons for the absence of the assembly in this case.

It seems that the true explanation is that the assembly of Judah had lost something of its importance during the latter half of David's reign.[8] The evidence in support of this is to be found in the events connected with Absalom's rebellion (2 S 15,1–19,44). In spite of Albrecht Alt's state-

---

[7] For references see above. With the exceptions of 1 Ch 23,1 and 2 Ch 11,22 the kings of Israel and Judah do not appear as the subject of this Hiphil.
[8] As was pointed out by *D.G.Evans* (JNES 25/1966, 274).

ment to the contrary[9] it must be concluded that Absalom gained the support of both the northern and the southern tribes.[10] Alt's contention that Judah remained neutral cannot provide a convincing explanation of the relevant data:

1. Absalom chose Hebron for the place of his investiture (15,7 ff.). Besides 200 men from Jerusalem (denoted as $q^eru'îm$, 15,11) followed him. Even if these were innocent, the measures taken by Absalom seem to indicate that he seriously reckoned with the possibility of gaining support from Judah.
2. The decisive events took place in the Forest of Ephraim (18,6). This means that David had fled from Judahite territory, something that he would hardly have done if he had enjoyed the support of a considerable part of the population of Judah.
3. There was a Judahite element among Absalom's leading men: Ahithophel (see 2 S 15,12; Jos 15,51) and Amasa (see 2 S 17,25; 1 Ch 2,15-17).
4. The tribal militia appears to have taken sides with Absalom. David won his victory by means of his own mercenaries (15,18).[11] Here one can contrast it with the rebellion of Sheba. In that case the sources contain explicit information that the men of Judah remained loyal to David (2 S 20,2) and that he summoned them in order to pursue the rebel (20,4 ff.).
5. It could be that Ahithophel's advice to Absalom to choose "twelve thousand men" to pursue David (17,1) was meant to give a pan-Israelite expression to the opposition to David.

It appears from these observations that Absalom enjoyed broad popular support from both the North and the South. His rebellion was not an affair organized by a handful of the king's men. It was a revolution in the sense that it was a manifestation of a great number of the governed people against the governing authority, and this revolution was not limited to the one of the two parts of the kingdom.

More specifically, the text also informs us that the *elders* of both Judah and Israel must have been under grave suspicion for treason. First, "the elders of Israel" appear as a group at Absalom's side, listening to and choosing between the advice given by Ahithophel and Hushai. The advice of Ahithophel "pleased Absalom and all the elders of Israel" (17,4; cf. v. 15). It seems probable that this group of elders were those of the northern tribes, since "the elders of Judah" are explicitly referred to as such a little later (19,12). David was thus betrayed by precisely the same official body from the northern tribes that had earlier entered into a contractual agreement with him at his investiture over these tribes. This body of men was also then referred to as "the elders of Israel" (2 S 5,3).[12] The elders of Israel were then seriously involved on Absalom's side in the conflict, thereby committing what David must have regarded as treason.

---

[9] *Alt* (KS II, 56f.). Cf. also *Soggin* (1967: 75).
[10] So *Danell* (1946: 81f.), *Noth* (History ²1960: 201), *Evans* (JNES 25/1966, 274), *Bright* (History ²1972: 204f.), *Tadmor* (1968: 51) and *Bardtke* (FsElliger 1973: 1-8).
[11] See above, note 1. – These remain the main contours, even if 2 S 18,1 ff. would allow for at least some loyal members of the tribal militia to be included among the men at David's disposal. *Tadmor* (1968: 50) thinks that David here organized an entirely new army.
[12] For further references to "the elders of Israel" see *J.L.McKenzie* (Bibl 40/1959, 522 ff.).

Secondly, the elders of Judah also appear to be under serious suspicion for disloyal conduct. In a passage that deals with the events immediately before David's return (2 S 19,12-15) there are some interesting indications of this. David's message to "the elders of Judah" through Zadok and Abiathar has an unmistakable tone of reproach: "Why should you be the last to bring the king back to his house ... ?" (v. 12) This question is not introduced by *măddûaʿ*, which has a cognitive value and is used in real questions, but by *lammā*, which has emotional connotations and conveys a note of a reprimand.[13] The delay finds its most natural explanation in the assumption of an awareness among the elders of Judah that their behaviour had compromised them in the eyes of David. In a similar way, the statement that David "swayed [*naṭā* Hiph.] the heart of all the men of Judah" so that they summoned him to return (v. 15) provides a further indication that not even the elders of Judah remained loyal to David.

Although David's return after the victory over Absalom took the form of a second "coronation" with the participation of the elders, the conduct of the people and their elders in connection with the revolution of Absalom must have seriously undermined the position of the assembly during the latter half of David's reign. I believe that it is against this background that the absence of the assembly at Adonijah's investiture is to be seen.

A feed-back mechanism must be imagined here. The disloyalty of the people was probably instigated by certain absolutist features in David's government (interpreting "absolutism" as the rule of a government that is not effectively checked by non-governmental forces[14]). Quite generally, the period of the early monarchy certainly witnessed a contest between royal centralized institutions and older gerontocratic ones. It is sufficient to remind the reader here of what the new institution of the monarchy meant to the people in the form of public services and taxes, and of the implications of the Solomonic district system which I have discussed in a previous work.[15] At the same time, however, the disloyalty of the people contributed to the reinforcement of the absolutist tendencies, which came to a peak during the reign of Solomon.

Ratification by the people meant the civil legitimation of the king. Since the representatives of the people did not take part in Solomon's investiture, this was a departure from normal procedure. From this point of view the secondary tradition of David's anointing not by an assembly but by Samuel (1 S 16,1-13) can claim our interest. I shall not anticipate here my detailed discussion of this tradition (see ch. 9.5 and 10.2.3) but only mention that my investigation has led me to venture the hypothesis that

---

[13] On these two words see *Jepsen* (ZAWBeih 105/1967, 106-113) and for further remarks *Boecker* (Redeformen ²1970: 177 f.).

[14] For this definition see *Wittfogel* (1957: 106).

[15] See *Mettinger* (1971: 128 ff. and 111 ff. and note what is said on p. 118 ff. about the treatment of "the House of Joseph" in Solomon's district system).

this tradition was created as a justification of the remarkable mode of procedure at Solomon's investiture.

2. The "Divided Monarchy". The Judaean ʿăm haʾaræṣ

At the investitures of some Judaean kings "the people of the land", the *ʿăm haʾaræṣ* (in the following abbreviated as *a.h.*), are said to have had a role which lends itself to comparison with that of the people and elders in the previous period. Since scholarly opinion is divided as to the identification of this group or class of people[16] it will be necessary to discuss this much debated problem afresh. In the extant texts the *a.h.* appear three times at investitures.

(a) In 2 R ch. 11 the *a.h.* are mentioned repeatedly in connection with the coronation of Joash (v. 14.18.19.20).[17] In the text there is nothing explicitly said about the function of the *a.h.*, except that they blew the trumpets and took part in a solemn procession, bringing the king from the precincts of the temple to the palace (v. 19). There is no difficulty in understanding the role of the *a.h.* here as being fully in line with the presence of the representatives of the people at earlier coronations. One should note the possibility that the *coup d'état* of Jehoiada took place at a new year feast connected with the commencement of a new seven-year period (cf. v. 4).[17a] If this were so, then people from the whole country would naturally have been present in Jerusalem.

---

[16] *Würthwein* (1936), who offers the most comprehensive discussion on the subject so far, understands the term as referring to "die Gesamtheit der judäischen Vollbürger" (p. 16). A similar solution was hinted at by *Gillischewski* some years earlier (ZAW 40/1922, 137-142). *J.L.McKenzie* (1959 B) preferred to take the *a.h.* as "the totality within which all social classes outside the royal court are found" and "not as a particular social class" (p 208). *deVaux* (RA 58/1964, 167-172 and ²1965: 70-72) joined company with Würtwein, as also did *Soggin* (1967: 106-111; cf. VT 13/1963, 187-195). – More or less divergent views are held by other scholars. *Gordis* (JQR 25/1934-35, 237-259, esp. 243 f.) took the expression to denote "the rural inhabitants" as opposed to the urban population of Jerusalem. Cf. also *Ihromi* (VT 24/1974, 421-429, esp. 425 ff.). *Talmon* (1967) took the term very narrowly to refer to "a body of Judaeans in Jerusalem that rose to some power and importance which was ultimately derived from their loyalty to the Davidic dynasty" (p. 76). Talmon refused to regard the *a.h.* as "a democratic or otherwise constitutionally circumscribed institution" (loc. cit.). Rather it was "a fairly loosely constituted power group within the kingdom of Judah" (p. 75). *Nicholson* (JSS 10/1965, 59-66) could not offer more than a counsel of despair, when he concluded that "the term has no fixed and rigid meaning but is used rather in a purely general and fluid manner and varies in meaning from context to context" (p. 66). – As will be seen, the present writer is definitely more sympathetic to the approach of Würthwein than to that of Gordis, Talmon or Nicholson.

[17] For a discussion of the literary integrity of this chapter, see ch. 8.2.2.1. I am of the opinion that *a.h.* is original in v. 19 and 20 and that the people of Judah was involved in the *coup d'état* that was organized by the priest.

[17a] This possibility was stressed particularly by *Widengren* (JSS 2/1957, 7 and 12), who also referred to Dt 31,9 ff.

(b) On a later occasion the *a.h.* executed the royal officials who had conspired against King Amon and killed him. Upon that "the people of the land made Josiah his son king in his stead" (2 R 21,23-24). Here the *a.h.* are clearly linked with the acts circumscribed by the verb *himlîk*, "to make someone king". It should also be noted that the *a.h.* here acted in opposition to the court establishment in Jerusalem and that they were even able to execute high royal officials proved guilty of *lèse-majesté*.

(c) On the death of Josiah, the *a.h.* are once more seen in action in a similar context. The royal officials brought the dead king from Megiddo to Jerusalem and buried him there. But it was the *a.h.* who installed the new king:

> And the people of the land took Jehoahaz the son of Josiah, and anointed him, and made him king in his father's stead. (2 R 23,30)

Here the *a.h.* appear as the subject of both "anointing" and "king-making".

This context also yields information that may be of importance in the proper evaluation of the constitutional power of the *a.h.* To judge from the evidence, both Jehoiakim and Zedekiah, who became kings later on, were older than Jehoahaz.[18] The *a.h.* thus by-passed the elder brothers of Jehoahaz. We have no explicit information on the reasons for this.[18a] At first sight one could presume that Josiah had adopted an old right of the paterfamilias to disregard the law of primogeniture and establish a younger son in the position of first-born. This custom is known from Nuzi, Ugarit and Alalakh[19] and was probably also practised in Israel.[20] However, on further consideration this seems an improbable explanation. Evidently the basic principle in the succession to the throne was that of primogeniture.[21] And above all, it is difficult to imagine that the king behind the Josianic reform would himself have done something that was clearly prohibited by

---

[18] Quite apart from the question of whether Josiah had four sons (1 Ch 3,15) or – if the first-born did not die young – three (2 R 23,31-36; 24,17-18), it is sufficiently clear that Jehoahaz (=Shallum) was not the eldest son. Cf. 2 R 23,31.36 and note that in 1 Ch 3,15 which starts with the first-born, Shallum is mentioned last.

[18a] *Ihromi* (VT 24/1974, 421-429, esp. 425 ff.) holds that the *a.h.* supported princes whose mothers did not come from Jerusalem but from the country-side.

[19] See *Mendelsohn* (BASOR 156/1959, 38-40) and *Weinfeld* (JAOS 90/1970, 193 f.).

[20] See *Mendelsohn* (op. cit.), who refers to Gn 48,13-20 (Ephraim) and to Gn 49,3-4; 48,22; 1 Ch 5,1-2 (Joseph). If our sources of information are historically reliable this right was probably exploited by David when he appointed Solomon *nagîd* (1 R 1,35) and by Rehoboam when he chose Abijah for the same position (2 Ch 11,22), although he was not the eldest son (2 Ch 11,18-20). However, the possibility that 1 R 1,35 is a fabrication of Solomonic propaganda cannot be precluded.

[21] Adonijah's claims to the throne were motivated by his status as eldest living son (1 R 1,6; 2,15.22). The principle of primogeniture is clearly expressed in 2 Ch 21,3 and esp. 22,1. The same principle was in force in Edom (2 R 3,27). It seems difficult to agree with *de Vaux* (²1965: 101), who thinks that the king had more or less free choice between his sons if the first-born had died.

the Deuteronomic law (Dt 21,15-17). It seems therefore that the *a.h.* actually displayed a (constitutional?) power to by-pass the elder sons of the deceased king and to choose a younger one, and to do this in spite of the firmly established principle of primogeniture in the succession to the throne.

These three cases and the circumstances accompanying them make it important to provide an answer to the question of the identity of the *a.h.* during the period of the monarchy. And it is particularly important to evaluate the accuracy of Talmon's recent definition of the *a.h.* as a loosely organized pressure group consisting of a comparatively small number of individuals ("not more than a few hundreds"), a group that is "not to be viewed as a democratic or otherwise constitutionally circumscribed institution".[22]

(1) In order to form an opinion all the available evidence for the *a.h.* must be gone through. The term is attested 51 times in the MT.[23] Three of these cases must be eliminated for reasons of textual criticism,[24] and so 48 cases remain. The supposition that the *a.h.* consisted of a very small number of individuals is patently wrong. This group is numerous enough to need a recruiting officer of its own for the purpose of military conscription (Jer 52,25; 2 R 25,19).[25] Moreover, we also learn that the Egyptian tribute of 100 talents of silver and one talent of gold was raised with the help of a tax levied on the *a.h.* (2 R 23,31-35). Here the very size of the sum presupposes that the *a.h.* comprised the majority of the population of Judah. The term also appears in some enumerations where it seems to refer to the mass of the population apart from the civil and cultic officials.[26] One of these instances is Jer 34,19 which tells of the participation of the *a.h.* in the covenant ritual of walking between the halves of the calf. The *a.h.* are here identified as "all the people in Jerusalem" (v. 8), but this narrow definition can obviously be ascribed to the extraordinary fact that the city was under siege.[27]

The fact that the *a.h.* must have comprised the majority of the population is in agreement with what we know about the ʿăm in the period before Solomon's

---

[22] *Talmon* (1967, quotation from p. 76).

[23] The plural of the expression is not included in the following list:

2 R 11,14=2 Ch 23,13	2 x	Ez 7,27; 12,19; 22,29; 33,2;	
2 R 11,18 (cf. 2 Ch 23,17)	1 x	39,13; 45,22; 46,3.9	8 x
2 R 11,19=2 Ch 23,20	2 x	Jes 24,4	1 x
2 R 11,20=2 Ch 23,21	2 x	Zach 7,5	1 x
2 R 15,5=2 Ch 26,21	2 x	Hagg 2,4	1 x
2 R 16,15	1 x	Dan 9,6	1 x
2 R 21,24=2 Ch 33,25	4 x	Esr 4,4	1 x
2 R 23,30=2 Ch 36,1	2 x	Job 12,24	1 x
2 R 23,35	1 x	Gn 23,7.12.13; 42,6	4 x
2 R 24,14	1 x	Ex 5,5 (read with Sam.)	1 x
2 R 25,3=Jer 52,6	2 x	Lev 4,27; 20,2.4	3 x
2 R 25,19=Jer 52,25	4 x	Nu 14,9	1 x
Jer 1,18; 34,19; 37,2; 44,21	4 x		

[24] 2 R 24,14; Jes 24,4; Job 12,24.

[25] Here I prefer the reading in Jer 52,25, see *Mettinger* (1971: 20).

[26] Jer 1,18; 37,2; 44,21; Ez 22,26-29. I do not think, however, that one is justified in concluding from such instances that the *a.h.* also comprised persons not enjoying legal status (women, slaves, etc.).

[27] I find it appropriate to say here that I do not find *Gordis's* interpretation (above, note 16) compatible with the evidence.

death. The same holds for the fact that the *a.h.* can act as cultic and legal assembly and as tribal militia.

(a) In some contexts the *a.h.* can be understood as forming the cultic assembly.[28]

(b) The *a.h.* appear as the tribal militia in Jer 52,25 (=2 R 25,19), which reports that the Babylonians carried away and executed sixty men of the *a.h.* and did the same to "the secretary of the commander of the army who mustered the people of the land" (*soper šǎr hǎṣṣaba' hǎmmǎṣbi' 'æt 'ǎm ha'aræṣ*). This designation refers to a military scribe serving directly under the commander of the army, a scribe who was in charge of military conscription.[29] Here our term *a.h.* corresponds reasonably well to *'ǎm* used about the militia in other contexts.[30] The sixty men who were executed were probably heads of important families, who held leading positions in the tribally organized militia. In the same way, the *a.h.* are referred to as the militia burying fallen enemies in Ez 39,13. The same interpretation commends itself in Ez 7,27 and 33,2.

(c) We also find the *a.h.* as the legal assembly. A clear case of this is found in Lev 20,2-5. This passage deals with the procedure against those involved in child sacrifice, "playing the harlot after Molech" (v. 5). Anyone guilty of this was to be executed: "the people of the land shall stone him with stones (*yirg^{e}muhû ba'abæn*)". I should like to draw attention to the fact that this should be compared with two passages in Ezekiel dealing with a similar case, viz. Ez 16,35-43 and 23,36-49. Here we are also confronted with child sacrifice (16,36; 23,37.39), and throughout the two texts the sin is described in terms of whoredom and adultery. The punishment is also that of stoning, and it is described by the same locution as found in Leviticus: *ragǎm ba'æbæn* (Ez 16,40; 23,47). There can be no doubt that the crime, the law applied and the method of execution are identical in Leviticus and Ezekiel.[31] One must then also assume that the group carrying out the execution is one and the same. Then the variation in terminology between Leviticus and Ezekiel provides very valuable information, since what is denoted as the *'ǎm ha'aræṣ* in Leviticus is clearly referred to as a *qahal* in Ezekiel (16,40; 23,47). That is, the *a.h.* act as legal assembly.

It is probably in their capacity of legal assembly that the *a.h.* are accused of oppression of the poor, the needy and the sojourner *b^{e}lo' mišpaṭ* (Ez 22,29).

In Jer ch. 34,[32] the *a.h.* also appear in their capacity of legal assembly. This passage also offers an interesting glimpse of the constitutional position of the *a.h.* versus the king. The latter intended to proclaim *d^{e}rôr*, which involved the manumission of Hebrew debt slaves. The act in question affected the economic rights of the people. It is important to note that the king did not proceed by issuing an outright decree but made the people accept a solemn agreement to release their debt slaves (v. 8 ff.; v. 15). In this context the people appear under the designation *a.h.* (v. 19). As legal assembly, the *a.h.* are involved here in a solemn legal act under divine sanction.

It also seems to me that the capacity of the *a.h.* to act as legal assembly explains some of the steps taken in connection with the royal investitures. At the

---

[28] Zach 7,5; Jer 44,21; Ez 46,3.9; 45,22; 2 R 16,15; Lev 4,27.
[29] See *Mettinger* (1971: 20f.).
[30] For references see *Rost* (FsProcksch 1934: 145 note 3).
[31] On the points of similarity between Ezekiel and the Holiness Code in general see *Zimmerli* (Ezechiel I, 1969: 70*-79*).
[32] On this text see esp. *M.David* (OTS 5/1948, 63-79), *M.Kessler* (BZ 15/1971, 105-108) and *Kutsch* (1973: 8-9). On *andurāru* and *d^{e}rôr* see below (ch. 11.4 at note 78).

investiture of Joash the *a.h.* killed Mattan, the priest of Baal (2 R 11,18).[33] Further in their execution of the royal servants who had conspired against King Amon (2 R 21,24), the *a.h.* also seem to have acted as legal assembly.

(2) The cumulative weight of these observations makes it probable that in connection with the royal investitures in Judah, the *a.h.* represented the *vox populi* in the same way that the people did who took part in the royal investitures in the period before the death of Solomon. The question is then whether or not this conclusion is compatible with the data available for other coronations in Judah during the period of the "divided monarchy", cases where the *a.h.* are not mentioned.

At first glance the statement in 2 Ch 22,1 that Ahaziah was made king by "the inhabitants of Jerusalem"[34] would seem to complicate the general conclusion and favour a narrow definition of the *a.h.* Nevertheless, this would be a premature conclusion. The evidence studied so far makes it indeed necessary to adopt a broad definition of the *a.h.* as implying the majority of the people apart from the court and the priesthood. But within this whole a fraction can also be said to represent the whole and act in their name, as we saw in Jer ch. 34, where the term refers primarily to the inhabitants of Jerusalem (Jer 34,8.19).[35] My conclusion is therefore that in the case of Ahaziah the inhabitants of the capital acted on behalf of the *a.h.* as a whole.

Here we must also draw attention to the investiture of Uzziah. We are told that the father of this king, Amaziah, was murdered in a (court?) plot in Jerusalem (2 R 14,19). In this situation "all the people of Judah" immediately intervened and made Uzziah king in the place of his father (v. 21). This must be compared with two other situations, when the Davidic dynasty was threatened. In 2 R ch. 11 the *a.h.* appear in connection with the coronation of Joash. In 2 R 21,24 the *a.h.* put Josiah on the throne when king Amon had been murdered. There was apparently a special allegiance between the *a.h.* and the house of David (something that we must keep in mind when we discuss the royal covenant in Judah). It is then natural to infer that the *a.h.* are those referred to as "all the people of Judah" in connection with the coronation of Uzziah.

My *conclusions* concerning the *a.h.* may thus be summarized as follows: It is difficult to speak of classes in ancient Israel in the modern sense of groups conscious of their particular interests and being opposed to one another. One cannot say that the *a.h.* represented a particular class within the society of Judah. Nevertheless, the *a.h.* is a phenomenon that has to do with the horizontal stratification of this society. The *a.h.* are clearly distinguished from the royal court and from the priesthood. On the other hand the "lower" limit of the *a.h.* is not so clearly defined. We are probably not mistaken if we assume that the term denotes only those members

---

[33] That the verb *harăg*, which is the one used here, can denote judicial execution is clear from Ex 32,27; Lev 20,15-16; Nu 25,5; Dt 13,10.

[34] One cannot accept *Galling's* view (Chronik 1954: 132) that the expression *a.h.* was "verdächtig". The expression is actually used in other places in the Chronicles, see above, note 23.

[35] I do not think that the capital remained settled by "Jebusites" and court people only (so *Würthwein* 1936: 16 and *Alt*, KS II, 47 and III, 333f.). An interesting indication of the contrary circumstance is found in 1 Ch 9,1-34. Besides, there is the possibility that Jerusalem is not to be identified with ancient Jebus, see *J.M.Miller* (ZDPV 90/1974, 115-127).

of society who enjoyed legal status. Outside this group we find women, children, slaves and sojourners. Borrowing the terminology used by Gilissen[36] we may express this in the following way:

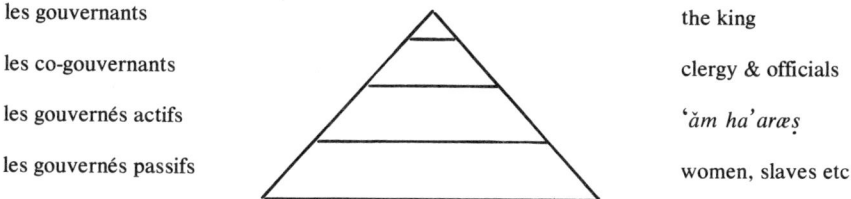

les gouvernants — the king
les co-gouvernants — clergy & officials
les gouvernés actifs — 'ăm ha'arœṣ
les gouvernés passifs — women, slaves etc.

The fact that the *a.h.* enjoyed a certain economic status fits into this picture. They were laid under tribute (2 R 23,35), and owned debt-slaves (Jer 34,19 and the context). They were accused of oppressing the poor (Ez 22,29). As attested by 2 R 23,30 and Jer ch. 34 the power of the *a.h.* was a "constitutional" check on governmental authority in Judah.[37] The participation of the *a.h.* in the royal investitures agrees with what we know of the investitures of Saul and David, and so there is a remarkable continuity in this respect. It could be observed, of course, that the expression *a.h.* does not appear in connection with the Northern Kingdom. But the phenomenon itself naturally existed there too. The term was presumably *gibbôrê hăḥăyil*, which is the expression used about those laid under tribute by Menahem (2 R 15,20).[38]

Summary

The participation of the people or its representatives (elders) at the royal investitures was a more or less constitutionally fixed feature of life in Israel and Judah.

(1) As for Northern Israel the three traditions of the investiture of Saul all stress the participation of the people. It was "the elders of Israel" who anointed David king over these tribes (2 S 5,3). After Solomon's death Rehoboam went to Shechem to be appointed king by these same tribes.

(2) In Judah, too, the assembly had a definite role in connection with royal investitures. Thus David was anointed king over "the house of Judah" by "the men of Judah" (2 S 2,4), a group that can probably be identified as "the elders of Judah" mentioned in 1 S 30,26-31. It seems

---

[36] *Gilissen* (1969: 68).
[37] Note also that even Abraham is said to bow down before the *a.h.* (Gen 23,7.12).
[38] *Würthwein* (1936: 15) paid due attention to this. On this term see esp. *v.d.Ploeg* (Vivre et penser 1/1941, 120-125), and *McKane* (1959). In 2 R 15,20 the sense is probably "landowner" as also in 1 S 9,1; 1 R 11,28; Ruth 2,1 (cf. 3,11).

that the position of the assembly of Judah was weakened during the reign of David, and this was probably because of the participation of the people of Judah in the rebellion of Absalom. The assembly was not present at the investitures of Adonijah and Solomon.

(3) However, the assembly of Judah regained its strong position during the period after Solomon's death. This can be seen from the participation of the 'ăm ha'aræṣ at the royal investitures (2 R ch. 11; 21,23-24; 23,30). It appears from these cases that there were strong ties between the people of Judah and the Davidic dynasty, so that the people took action in the case of plots against the king. The 'ăm ha'aræṣ cannot be regarded as a small pressure group. It has been found that the 'ăm ha'aræṣ could be summoned to arms and that they could act as both cultic and legal assembly. In these respects "the people of the land" corresponds to 'ăm in the previous period, and their participation in the royal investiture can be regarded as that of the popular assembly.

CHAPTER VIII

Acclamation and the Royal Covenant

It has been seen that the participation of the popular assembly was a normal feature of the royal investitures in ancient Israel. I shall now, in this final chapter on the civil legitimation of the king, study the constitutional significance of the participation of the assembly at the investitures. I shall first study how the *consensus populi* was expressed and then turn to the important and very intriguing problem as to whether there existed a covenant between the king and the people.

In dealing with the expressions of the concurrence of the people, we are actually concerned with two different rites, viz. the anointing of the king by the representatives of the people and the acclamation by the popular assembly. My study of the anointing of the king has led me to conclude that this was originally a secular (in the sense that it was not manifestly sacral) rite, that brought the king in relation to the people (2 S 2,4; 5,3). Only at a second stage of development was this rite regarded as the expression *par excellence* of the sacral legitimation of the king. For practical reasons I have chosen to treat all the evidence which has to do with the anointing of the king in one separate chapter, and this can be found below in Part Three of this study.

1. The Acclamation: An Elliptic Oath

According to Th. Klauser, the term "acclamation" can be defined as

> die oft rhythmisch formulierten u. sprechchorartig vorgetragenen Zurufe, mit denen eine Volksmenge Beifall, Lob u. Glückwunsch, oder Tadel, Verwünschung u. Forderung zum Ausdruck bringt.[1]

My task will be a limited one concerning only the acclamation of the king as an act immediately connected with the royal investiture.[2] The exclamation that occurs on such occasions cannot be regarded as a spontaneous

---

[1] *Th.Klauser* (RAC 1/1950, 216).
[2] For comments on the general phenomenon of acclamation of the leader by the subjects see *M.Weber* (GdS III: 2 ³1947: 763 ff.) and *J.Gilissen* (Rec. de la Soc. Jean Bodin 20/1970, 73 ff. and 22/1969, 83 ff.). See also the comprehensive article by *Th.Klauser* (RAC 1/1950, 216-233). For remarks pertinent to the royal acclamation in ancient Israel see *A.Alt* (KS II, 23), *deBoer* (VT 5/1955, 225-231), *D.Michel* (VT 6/1956, 40 ff., esp. 43-48), *Beyerlin* (ZAW 73/1961, 194 f.), *Lipiński* (1965: 348-361), *Gerleman* (THAT 1/1971, 551 f.) and *Ringgren's* forthcoming article on ḥayā (to appear in TWAT).

expression of joy but is part of the ceremony. This can be seen from the fact that David is said to have ordered an acclamation of Solomon (1 R 1,34.39).

The formula *malăk PN* has sometimes been taken to express a royal acclamation. It occurs in 2 S 15,10 (Absalom) and 2 R 9,13 (Jehu). Both cases deal with a usurper. In the case of Absalom, the exclamation in question is not part of the investiture but seems to be a summons to arms to his followers brought to them by messengers from Hebron. It is therefore questionable whether or not *malăk PN* can be regarded as a form of acclamation by the people.[3]

The acclamation proper, which was probably denoted by the term *t^{e}rû'ā*,[4] is quoted in the text as *y^{e}ḥî hammœlæk*. The phrase in question occurs eight times in all, two of these occurrences not being immediately connected with an investiture.

a) 1 S 10,24. When Saul had been designated by lot Samuel asked the people: "*hărr^e'îtæm* him whom the Lord has chosen?" I have argued above that the crucial verb does not mean "do you see?" but "do you (now) appoint?" The response of the people to this question is expressed in the words:

ויךעו כל העם ויאמרו יחי המלך

And all the people shouted, "Long live the king!"

b) 2 S 16,16. According to this verse David's "friend" Hushai greeted Absalom with the words *y^{e}ḥî hammœlæk*. This is one of the two cases where the formula is used outside a royal investiture (for the other see below *sub* d). But even here the words express some kind of recognition, since Absalom immediately answers: "Is this your loyalty (*hæsæd*) to your friend?" (v. 17).

c) 1 R 1,25. Nathan tells David of Adonijah's sacrifice:

> For he has gone down this day, and has sacrificed oxen, fatlings, and sheep in abundance, and has invited all the king's sons, Joab the commander of the army, and Abiathar the priest; and behold, they are eating and drinking before him, and saying, "Long live King Adonijah!"[5]

d) 1 R 1,31. The expression is used here as a polite phrase by Bathsheba to David: "May my lord King David live for ever!"

e) 1 R 1,34.39. David instructs Zadok, Nathan, and Benaiah to take the servants of the king, probably the members of the court and the royal

---

[3] On this point I agree with *Schreiner* (1963: 193 ff.) and *Lipinski* (1965: 372 ff.).
[4] Cf. 1 S 10,24 (*wăyyari'û kål ha'am*) and compare Nu 23,21 (*t^{e}rû'ăt mælæk*). See *P.Humbert* (1946: 20, 30-35) and cf. *Lipinski* (1965: 352 ff.).
[5] I quote RSV, which follows LXX *L* (see app.).

guard, and anoint Solomon king: "Then blow the trumpet, and say, 'Long live king Solomon!' " When this instruction has been carried out, this is described in the words:

Then they blew the trumpet; and all the people said, "Long live King Solomon!"

f) 2 R 11,12 (=2 Ch 23,11). Here the acclamation occurs in connection with the investiture of Joash:

Then he [the priest] brought out the king's son, and put the crown upon him, and gave him the testimony; and they proclaimed him king, and anointed him; and they clapped their hands, and said, "Long live the king!"

In order to understand the meaning of the acclamation of the people, we must have recourse to circumstantial evidence. A fact that should not be disregarded is that the same elements which are found in the acclamation are also found in an oath, viz. in the swearing by the life of the king.[6] One can mention for instance 2 S 14,19 which can be rendered: "By your own life, my lord the king... ($h\hat{e}$ $n\check{a}p\check{s}^e ka$ $^a don\hat{\imath}$ $h\check{a}mm\ae l\ae k$ $\,'im$ ...)."[6a] This oath comes close to swearing by the life of God. Moreover, there are cases when the life of God and the life of the king are juxtaposed in an oath as in 2 S 15,21: $h\check{a}y$ $YHWH$ $w^e h\hat{e}$ $^a don\hat{\imath}$ $h\check{a}mm\ae l\ae k$ $k\hat{\imath}$ ...[7] It is only persons of exceptional importance who are alluded to in oaths of this kind. In addition to the king we hear of priests,[8] prophets[9] and of Pharaoh[10]. This seems to indicate that the king has "life" in a particular sense of the word that distinguishes him from his subjects. Both oath and acclamation

---

[6] This was pointed out by *deBoer* (VT 5/1955, 228f.). As examples of this oath by the life of the king can be mentioned 1 S 17,55; 2 S 11,11; 14,19.

[6a] For understanding the element $h\check{a}y/h\hat{e}$ as a noun, "life", see *Greenberg* (JBL 76/1957, 34-39).

[7] Oath by the life of God e.g.: 1 S 14,39.45; 19,6; 25,34; 26,10.16. Oath by the life of God and king e.g.: 1 S 25,26; 2 S 15,21 (cf. 1 S 20,3). The thought pattern behind such oaths is discussed by *M.R.Lehmann* ZAW 81/1969, 83-86. Lehmann assumes behind this a basic blessing pattern "May I live forever/as long as God or King X, if I speak the truth." He finds this basic pattern in Dt 32,40f. I cannot agree on this point. In my opinion the point in this type of oath is that the life of God/the king is at stake in the case of perjury. The grammatical construction is $h\check{a}y$ $YHWH$ $\,'im$ ... for negative statements (1 S 14,45; 19,6 by the life of God; cf. 1 S 17,55; 2 S 11,11; 14,19 by the life of the king) and $h\check{a}y$ $YHWH$ $k\hat{\imath}$ ... for positive statements (1 S 14,39; 26,10; 26,16; by the life of God; 1 S 20,3; 2 S 15,21 by the life of both God and the king). The first-mentioned type is comparable to Akk. *liblut šarru šumma* ... , "may the king live if ... ", which is used for negative statements as appears from the context (EA 256,10-13). This suggests that the grammatical constructions mentioned above are by no means due to a "grammatical development based on analogy" as Lehmann is forced to think (p. 84) when he starts from Dt 32,40. The development was rather contrary to what Lehmann believes. – To swear by the life of God/the king is a well-known phenomenon in the ancient Near East.

[8] 1 S 1,26.

[9] 2 R 2,2.4.6; 4,30.

[10] Gn 42,15.

refer to the "life" of the king, which is "life" in the highest potency of the word.

This leads us to the question: is the acclamation more intimately linked with the oath than is generally believed? In his study of the acclamation, deBoer drew attention to the above-mentioned similarity and concluded that the acclamation implies something more than a mere wish for the welfare of the king. He who utters the oath places himself under the jurisdiction of the one to whom he refers in his oath. In a similar way, says deBoer, the acclamation is a formula by which it is recognized that the king has power over life and death; those who utter the acclamation thereby accept the king's exercise of this authority.[11]

Lipinski also ascribes great importance to the similarity between acclamation and oaths. He takes this similarity to imply that the acclamation is "de même ordre que les formules de serment". But he assumes a somewhat different nuance from deBoer. Those who utter the acclamation are thereby obliged on oath to respect the covenant between the king and the people.[12]

These interpretations must be seriously considered, but they suffer from lack of proof, insofar as neither deBoer nor Lipinski is able to point out more than a general similarity between acclamation and an oath, a similarity that does not amount to actual analogy.

However, their argument can be supported by an observation that has so far been overlooked in discussions on the subject. We know from the Amarna letters some instances where the Akkadian formula *libluṭ šarru*, "may the king live" (*balāṭu*, "to live" in the precative), is indisputably used as an oath.[13] In EA 256,10-13 it is even repeated to give added emphasis to the statement: *li-ib-lu-uṭ šarru^{ru} bēli-ia li-ib-lu-uṭ šarru^{ru} bēli-ia šum-ma* ... , "may the king my lord live, may the king my lord live, if [A is in the town B]." The formulation with *šumma* is clear enough. The context shows that the statement is a negative one: the speaker denies that A is in the town B; he has fled (line 6). There are also cases of the same oath formula with assertive particles: *libluṭ šarru^{ru} adi* ... (EA 85,39-40.86) and *libluṭ šarri^{ri} lū* ... (EA 289,37-38). Incidentally, the last-mentioned letter is one of those from ʿAbdu-Heba of Jerusalem. And EA no 256 is a letter from the middle Jordan valley.[13a]

Thus the Akkadian counterpart of *y^{e}ḥî hămmælæk* was used as an oath by scribes in Canaan during the Late Bronze Age, and even by the scribe who was attached to the court at Jerusalem. Now, since ellipsis in oaths

---

[11] See *deBoer* (VT 5/1955, 228-231, esp. 230 top and 231 bottom).
[12] See *Lipinski* (1965: 352).
[13] *CAD* (2/B p. 57 col. b) correctly describes it as an oath formula.
[13a] On EA no 256 see *Albright* (BASOR 89/1943, 7 ff.).

is a well-known phenomenon we can ask whether an interpretation of *yᵉḥî hǎmmǽlæk* as an abbreviated oath would agree with the evidence.

Let us first consider Bathsheba's words in 1 R 1,31. When David had renewed an earlier oath to make Solomon king, Bathsheba bowed with her face to the ground and made obeisance to the king and said: "May my lord King David live for ever!" Of course, these words could imply a polite phrase and express the thought that Bathsheba was not in a hurry to see her son as David's successor. On the other hand the words could well be interpreted as an oath, as an endorsement of David's oath "by the life of God", with the added reference to the life of David himself.

I should like to point out here the use of oaths in contractual settings; a covenant may be ratified by means of an oath.[14] Now, there are some indications that would seem to suggest that acclamation is concerned with a contractual relationship between the king and the people, that it expresses the people's obligation to the king.

In 2 R 11,12 the acclamation forms part of the investiture of Joash. Then follows a section that deals with the death of Athaliah (v. 13-15). After this passage we find v. 17 which mentions two different covenants, one of which is a covenant between the Lord and the king and the people, the other a covenant between the king and the people. As we shall see below there is reason to believe that the passage concerning the death of Athaliah and what is said in v. 17a concerning a covenant with the Lord forms a Dtr expansion of the original text. If this is correct then the reference to the acclamation in v. 12 was originally followed by the reference to the royal covenant which is now found in v. 17.

1 S 10,24 deals with the acclamation of Saul. When Saul had been designated by lot Samuel asked the people if they were prepared to appoint him king (see above ch. 7.1.1). The acclamation comes as the answer to this question. This shows that the acclamation had the character of a performative utterance. It was through the acclamation that Saul was here made king by the people. Although this text cannot be used as a source for conclusions concerning Saul's investiture, it nevertheless testifies to an ideal of kingship among the northern tribes according to which the acclamation was of central importance. The continuation of the text is also very illuminating:

> Then Samuel told the people the rights and duties of the kingship [*mišpǎṭ hǎmmᵉlukā*]; and he wrote them in a book and laid it up before the Lord.
> (1 S 10,25)

---

[14] See e.g. Gn 21,31-32 (cf. v. 22-24); 26,28.31; Jos 9,15 (cf. v. 16-20); 2 R 11,4; Ez 17,13.16.18-19. Compare also Gn 14,13 (*bǎ'ᵃlê bᵉrît*) with Neh 6,18 (*bǎ'ᵃlê šᵉbû'ā*). For discussion, see *Pedersen* (1914: 21-51, esp. 31 ff.), *Horst* (Gottes Recht, 1961: 293 f.), *G.M.Tucker* (VT 15/1965, 487 ff.) and *M.R.Lehmann* (ZAW 81/1969, 74 ff.).

This remark, which I take to be of pre-Dtr origin, hints at a contractually regulated relationship between the king and the people. The acclamation of the people forms a declaration, a solemn oath, that the people are willing to enter into this relationship.

Similarly, in 1 R 1,25 (Adonijah) the acclamation is mentioned together with what looks very much like a covenant meal.[15] Finally, 2 S 16,16-17 should not pass without notice. Here Hushai's words to Absalom are understood by this to be an expression of loyalty ($ḥæsæd$). The one who utters the acclamation thereby accepts a relationship of loyalty to the king.

This is all that is to be found in the scanty material that attests to the acclamation of the king. However, if we can find further evidence of the fact that the relationship between king and people was conceived in contractual categories, this would add to the probability of the suggested interpretation of the acclamation as forming an elliptic oath. As we shall soon see, this is actually the case: there is evidence of a royal covenant. At the same time our findings concerning the acclamation can serve as a preliminary step in the investigation of this matter.

This interpretation of the acclamation as an elliptic oath enables us to take a stand regarding the suggestion that the jussive in $y^eḥî\ hămmælæk$ is to be understood as having the force of an indicative, so that the expression would mean something like "the king is full of life or vital power".[16] To be sure, there are several examples of this use of a jussive form of other verbs where the jussive has the same meaning as an indicative.[17] However, in the Akkadian examples from the Amarna letters quoted above the oath in question clearly preserves the formal character of a wish: "may the king live, if [this is not so and so]". If the Hebrew formula is to be understood as corresponding to this the jussive then has the same force as the precative of the Akkadian formula.

The participation of the people at royal investitures and the popular acclamation of the king does not prove that we are dealing with an elective monarchy. The procedure does not form an election in the modern sense of the term. Nevertheless, the acclamation serves the purpose of expressing the *consensus populi*. Of course, the acclamation of the subjects may under certain conditions develop into a regular election, but it is a far cry to this as Max Weber points out.[18]

---

[15] Cf. Gn 26,30; 31,54. See also *W.T.McCree* (JBL 45/1926, 120ff.).

[16] This was suggested by *deBoer* (VT 5/1955, 230f.). The theory was accepted by *D.Michel* (VT 6/1956, 46 note 1) and *Beyerlin* (ZAW 73/1961, 194f.). *Gerleman* (THAT 1/1971, 552) also finds this theory probable but notes that a difficulty may be found in the imperatives in Dan 2,4; 3,9; 5,10; 6,7.22.

[17] See *Ges-K* (^{27}1902 § 109k) for examples.

[18] *MaxWeber* (GdS III: 2 ^{3}1947: 766).

Even if Israel and Judah were not elective monarchies the acclamation of the subjects is an act of some constitutional importance. Its true character may be better understood through a comparison with what has been termed *dinggenossenschaftliche Rechtsfindung*, that is, law-finding by the popular assembly or, if I may suggest a convenient English term: sodalic law-finding. This is known from various cultures and takes the form of an active participation of the *Umstand*. Max Weber describes this type of law-finding as

> die Teilnahme der nicht zu den Rechtshonoratioren gehörigen Rechtsgenossen an der Rechtsfindung in der Form, dass die Ratifikation des von den Urteilern gefundenen Rechtsspruchs durch ihre Akklamation als unentbehrlich galt und dass prinzipiell das Recht zur Urteilsschelte einem jeden Rechtsgenossen zustand.[19]

This sodalic type of law-finding is known from the earliest period of the Israelite monarchy (1 S 14,45; cf. also Jer ch. 26). Acclamation in connection with royal investiture as the constitutional ratification of the new king is only what one would expect in a society whose legal life is characterized by sodalic law-finding.

2. The Royal Covenant

In his essay on the various types of monocratic government in history, J.Gilissen attempted to use as one basis of subdivision the different types of foundations of the monocratic government. He distinguished between a military basis of power, and a religious, economic and contractual basis.[1] In the last case, there is some sort of a contractual relationship between the governing authority and those governed. The contract can be formal or informal. It can consist of mutual oaths or promises, the ruler's formal concession of certain rights to the people, or of a proper constitution. Gilissen also points out that the development of a feudal contract (the basis of a feudal monocracy) into a royal contract is known.[2]

I shall now discuss the question of a royal covenant in Israel and Judah, an undertaking that is facilitated by an important study by Fohrer.[3] The material consists primarily of 2 S 5,3 (David and the elders of Northern Israel) and 2 R 11,17 (Joash and the people of Judah). We shall, however, require additional evidence. In the following pages I shall organize the material separately for Israel and Judah, but when studying each separate piece of evidence I shall consider the following questions:

---

[19] See *MaxWeber* (Rechtssoziologie ²1967: 231-235, quotation from p. 231). See also the English translation of this work (Max Weber on Law in Economy and Society, 1954: 90ff.).

[1] See *J.Gilissen* (Rec. de la société Jean Bodin 20/1970, 5-135, esp. 93 ff.).

[2] *Gilissen* (op. cit. p. 112-116).

[3] See *Fohrer* (ZAW 71/1959, 1-22). See also *A.Alt* (KS II, 23, 41, 45, 58), *Noth* (GesStud I, ²1960: 26f., 151f.) and *Malamat* (BA 28/1965, 34ff.).

1. Was the $b^e rît$ in 2 S 5,3 mainly a means of establishing the personal union between Judah and Israel under David? That is, has this $b^e rît$ more to do with the relations between two groups of tribes – one represented by David, the other by its elders – than with the relations between the king and his subjects? Or shall we regard this $b^e rît$ as a case of what was more or less an institutional part of the royal investiture? This question is related to the next one.
2. Was there a royal covenant in Judah or not? It should be noted that while 2 S 5,3 mentions a $b^e rît$ granted by David to the elders of Israel nothing similar is said in connection with his investiture over Judah (2 S 2,4). To this can be added the fact that 2 R 11,17b, which is the only definite reference to a royal covenant in Judah, is not contained in some of the textual witnesses.
3. If there was a royal covenant was it normally renewed at each subsequent coronation or only in situations of dynastic crisis or change?
4. We must then also ask: what type of obligation are we dealing with – mutual or unilateral?

1. The Davidic Kings and the Northern Tribes

When David had been made king of Judah, Abner entered into negotiations with "the elders of Israel" and then separately with Benjamin aiming at persuading them to accept David as their king (2 S 3,17-19). Abner then went to David and said that he would gather all Israel to David "that they make a covenant with you" ($w^e yikr^e tû$ '$itt^e ka$ $b^e rît$, v. 21). It seems that Abner brought David some information about conditions which these tribes set forth as a proviso for accepting David as king (cf. $kål$ '$^a šær$ $tôb$ $b^{e\prime}ênê$ $yiśra'el$, v. 19b). In any case, when the elders of Israel later came to David at Hebron and these plans materialized, David made them a solemn promise:

> So all the elders of Israel came to the king at Hebron; $wăyyikrot$ $lahæm$ $hămmælæk$ $dawid$ $b^e rît$ at Hebron before the Lord, and they anointed David king over Israel. (2 S 5,3)

It is very important to note that "the elders of Israel" here denotes the elders of the northern tribes; David had already been made king of Judah. This important fact was overlooked by M. Noth, when he said:

> Das Königtum im Staate Juda ruhte rechtlich bis zu dessen Ende im Jahre 587 v. Chr. auf dem 2. Sam. 5,3 erwähnten Vertag mit David; ... .[4]

Another point to be noted is the expression used here: $kărăt$ $b^e rît$ l^e. This

---

[4] *Noth* (GesStud I, ²1960: 26 f.).

construction is attested extensively and normally expresses the obligation of the one who grants the $b^e r\hat{\imath}t$. There are only two exceptions to this (Jos 24,25; 2 R 11,4). If one does not want to count 2 S 5,3 among the rare exceptions, one must understand $b^e r\hat{\imath}t$ as denoting David's obligation to the elders of Israel.[5]

If one regards David's $b^e r\hat{\imath}t$ as a royal promise, it is natural to see a reciprocal relation between this royal vow and the anointing that is then carried out by the elders. The order of these two acts should not be overlooked. The king first grants the elders his $b^e r\hat{\imath}t$, and then they anoint him. A.Jepsen correctly saw this reciprocity between the $b^e r\hat{\imath}t$ and the anointing:

> Was David beschwört, ist also eine Art Wahlkapitulation, auf Grund deren er dann zum König gesalbt wird. Mir scheint, dass das Schema von Über- und Unterordnung hier überhaupt nicht recht passt; die Salbung geht von den Ältesten Israels aus und sie erfolgt erst, nachdem David seine Zusage in aller Form "vor Jahwe" beschworen hat.[6]

The above-mentioned passages make it clear that there was a covenant between David and the northern tribes. This covenant formed the basis of the personal union between Judah and Israel under David.[7] We have already seen that the investitures of Adonijah and Solomon took place without a proper representation of the people at the solemn act. We also found that Solomon was anointed by one or two royal officials and not by the people. We may therefore conclude that there was no covenant between Solomon and his people, and thus not with the northern tribes. Fohrer is justified when he speaks of Solomon's road to the throne as a "Staatsstreich ohne Wahl und Vertrag".[8]

Already appointed king of Judah (1 R 11,43), Rehoboam went to Shechem. Here the assembly of the northern tribes had gathered to make him king ($l^e h\breve{a}ml\hat{\imath}k\ '\hat{o}t\hat{o}$, 1 R 12,1). The text does not in plain words refer to a royal covenant, but there are several indications that the negotiations between Rehoboam and the assembly of Northern Israel dealt with the question of a covenant between the king and these tribes.[9] The following points should be paid attention to:

First, the assembly at Shechem put forward certain conditions which Rehoboam had to accept before being made king of Northern Israel:

> Your father made our yoke heavy. Now therefore lighten the hard service of your father and his heavy yoke upon us, and we will serve you. (1 R 12,4)

The last word is $w^e n\breve{a}\,'\breve{a}bd\varpi kka$, "and we will serve you". The formulation

---

[5] See *Kutsch* (1973: 22 f., cf. p. 56).
[6] *A.Jepsen* (in Verbannung und Heimkehr=FsW.Rudolph, 1961: 164).
[7] Cf. *Alt* (KS II, 43 ff., esp. 45).
[8] *Fohrer* (ZAW 71/1959, 7). *Noth* (Könige 1968: 40) disagrees, but hardly on good grounds.
[9] Cf. *Fohrer* (ZAW 71/1959, 8) and *Malamat* (BA 28/1965, 34 ff.).

can be compared with that in 1 S 11,1 about the negotiations between the Ammonite king and the citizens of Jabesh, where the latter say: "Make a treaty (*bᵉrît*) with us, and we will serve you (*wᵉnă'ăbdækka*)." And there are other contexts as well where the verb *'abăd* occurs in a covenantal setting.[10]

Secondly, it seems probable that the leadership of Gideon and Jephthah in the pre-monarchic period had a contractual basis (see below). The covenant between David and the elders of Israel in 2 S 5,3 falls into line with such cases. The historical value of the information in 2 S 5,3 is then very difficult to contest.[10a] On the contrary, 2 S 5,3 forms the background against which the proceedings at Shechem are to be interpreted. David had made a promise to the northern tribes. No similar agreement, however, was conceded by Solomon when he became king. At Shechem these northern tribes react against "the hard service" imposed upon them by Solomon, the nature of which has been discussed in an other work.[11]

Thirdly, Rehoboam's refusal to make formal concessions to the northern tribes, to make a formal royal promise, was met with the repudiation of the Davidic dynasty on the part of the assembly. This was expressed in the exclamation:

> What portion (*helæq*) have we in David?
> We have no inheritance (*năhᵃlā*) in the son of Jesse.
> To your tents, O Israel! (1 R 12,16)

This sounds like a reverberation of the words used by Sheba at his rebellion (2 S 20,1), words aimed at the nullification of the personal union between Northern Israel and Judah.[12] Here at Shechem the personal union between these groups of tribes, which had once been created by the covenant between David and the elders of Israel, was once and for all dissolved.[13] The fact that Rehoboam did not agree on the conditions of such a covenant as set forth by the assembly at Shechem, provides an explanation of the

---

[10] *Nielsen* (1955: 187 f.) called attention to the use of *'abăd* in two covenant contexts, namely Jos 24,15 and Jud 9,28.

[10a] The mention of a *bᵉrît* in 2 S 5,3 is not an invention by the author of the History of David's Rise. (a) There is no particular stress on any obligation of the northern tribes towards David. The stress is on David's promise to these tribes. (b) The negotiations at Shechem in 1 R ch. 12 make sense on the assumption that there was really a contract between David and the elders of Israel. (c) The *bᵉrît* in 2 S 5,3 does not stand out as an innovation, but falls into line with what can be inferred for the pre-monarchic and early monarchic period, see below on Jephthah and Saul.

[11] See *Mettinger* (1971: 128-139 and 118-120).

[12] See *Hertzberg* (Samuel 1964: 371), *Fohrer* (ZAW 71/1959, 5 f.) and *Malamat* (BA 28/1965, 39 ff.).

[13] It can be appropriate to quote *Fohrer's* words: "Wie das davidische Reich mit Hilfe des Königsvertrages zustande gekommen war, so zerbrach es an dessen Nichterneuerung" (p. 8).

fact that the procedure was interrupted and did not close with the acclamation of Rehoboam as king of Israel.

In connection with this discussion of the covenant between David and the northern tribes and the fact that it was not renewed by Solomon and Rehoboam a further point can be made, viz. that we may possibly find in the extant sources Northern Israelite opposition to this non-renewal of the covenant. As I have already pointed out it may well be that what is said in 1 S 10,25 about Samuel's reading of the *mišpāṭ hămmᵉlukā*, "the rights and duties of the kingship", in its very picture of legally regulated relations between Saul and his subjects intends to express Northern Israelite criticism of the hard conditions of Solomon's government.[14]

2. The Question of a Royal Covenant in Judah

We have seen that David sealed a covenant with the northern tribes when he became king of Northern Israel (2 S 5,3). We shall now turn to the problem of whether there was also a contractual basis for the kingship of the Davidides over Judah. The account of David's investiture over Judah is contained in 2 S 2,1-4. We are told that David and his men established a new political centre at Hebron. The investiture itself is described only in the following words:

> And the men of Judah came, and there they anointed David king over the house of Judah. (2 S 2,4)

Nothing is said about a royal covenant between the king and the Judaean tribes. Nevertheless, a number of circumstances should be contemplated.

The account is found in the History of David's Rise. At the time of the composition of this historical work after the death of Solomon, it was the claim of the Davidic kings to superiority over the northern tribes as well that was the problem. For a Davidic king to be the ruler of Judah was a natural circumstance. If a royal covenant existed between David and the people of Judah the silence of the sources could be explained from this.

But is it probable that there was such a royal covenant? – Let us consider the situation. In a recent study, Zobel has made it probable that there was already in the pre-monarchic period a territorial confederation of towns that formed a political unity, a *Gross-Juda*, with a gerontocratic constitution.[14a] The formation of this confederation can be inferred from the list of towns to which David sent shares of his spoils (1 S 30,26-31). It was the

---

[14] Cf. also Jud 9,15: "If *bæ'ᵃᵉmæt* you are anointing me king over you, then come and take refuge in my shade....." Here *'ᵃᵉmæt* could well be a covenant term in the same way as in Ps 132,11 where *HAL* (p. 67a) suggests "Treuschwur" as the translation. See also J.Maier (Kairos 11/1969, 32 f.).

[14a] See *Zobel* (VTSuppl 28/1975, 253-277).

elders of these towns (v. 26) who came to David and anointed him king at Hebron. They are then denoted as "the men of Judah" (2 S 2,4). These "men of Judah" appear at David's investiture as an already existing political body, capable of negotiations with their future leader. David did not impose his authority on a number of disparate tribal units. On the contrary, he was accepted as a leader by an already existing political confederation of towns in Judah. Under these circumstances it is natural to infer that the investiture was an act involving mutual obligations and concessions, briefly: an act of contractual significance.[14b]

We must then reckon with the probability that there was a contractual basis for the kingship of Judah. This general impression will now be tested. I shall first investigate the evidence from the later history of Judah and discuss the investiture of Joash in some detail. I shall then go back to the period before the monarchy and study the evidence for a contractual basis of political leadership during these days.

(1) The Investiture of Joash (2 R 11,4-20; cf. 2 Ch 23,1-21). – In the account of the investiture of Joash, there is a reference to a royal covenant between the king and the people:

> And Jehoiada made a covenant between the Lord and the king and the people, that they should be the Lord's people; and also between the king and the people. (2 R 11,17)

There are two different problems involved in the assessment of this verse. First, in the latter part of the verse the mention of the covenant between the king and the people is not found in the Lucianic text, and in the Syrohexaplaric text it is asterisked. Nor is it to be found in the corresponding place in the account of the Chronicler. However, we find in 2 Ch 23,3 a reference to the same covenant as that in 2 R 11,17b.

Secondly, there is reason to believe that there are two different strands in 2 R 11,4-20.[15] It is hard to believe that the destruction of the house of Baal was allowed to interrupt the natural sequence of the anointing of Joash (v. 12) and his enthronement in the palace (v. 20).[16] And the death of

---

[14b] Cf. *Alt* (KS II, 41) who says that the word "Bund" would have been appropriate and points out that David's going to Hebron and the coming there of the men of Judah belong together: "Der Initiative des einen entspricht die Initiative der anderen, und beide zusammen ergeben die gegenseitige Bindung, auf der das Staatswesen beruht."

[15] The integrity of the text has been questioned by among others *B.Stade* (ZAW 5/1885, 280-288), *Burney* (1903: 308), *Šanda* (Könige II, 1912: 134 ff.), *J.Gray* (1964: 511 ff.; ²1970: 566 ff.). For a different opinion see *W.Rudolph* (FsBertholet, 1950: 473-478), who regards only the mention of ʿam haʾareṣ in v. 14.18.19 as secondary (esp. p. 477), but even so Rudolph is forced to make certain *Umstellungen* in the text (p. 477 point 3).

[16] 2 R 11,19 has the verb *yašăb* in the qal while 2 Ch 23,20 has it in the hiphil: "And they set the king upon the royal throne."

Athaliah is related twice (v. 16 and v. 20). It is also possible to find in v. 13-18 an interest in the temple and in the exclusive attachment of the people to the Lord typical of Dtr writing.

For my own part I hold that broadly speaking v. 13-18 are due to later redaction,[17] and that this is connected with the composition of the Deuteronomistic Historical Work. Indications of this are to be found in the covenant between God and people[18] and the reference to the people as the people of the Lord,[19] both in v. 17a, and in the hatred of foreign cults expressed in v. 18. Also the stress on the fact that Athaliah was taken out of the temple and killed outside it (v. 15-16) points in the same direction. Certain features that may well contain reliable historical information have been elaborated by the redactor to enhance the impression that the investiture of Joash meant not only a constitutional reformation, but also a religious one similar to that of Josiah (see especially 2 R 23,1-3).[20]

This means that the reference to the covenant between the king and the people in v. 17b is now found in a secondary section. One is therefore tempted to disregard v. 17b as historical evidence for the actual investiture of Joash.[21] Three circumstances must, however, be taken into account here.

(1) The Chronicler contains a reference to a royal $b^e r\hat{\imath}t$ in the case of Joash, although this is found at the beginning of the Chronicler's account (2 Ch 23,3) and not in the same place as in Kings.

(2) The relation between v. 17a and 17b in Kings is somewhat strained, since as it now stands v. 17b is an obvious repetition. It should be noted that there is no reason for taking v. 17b to be of Dtr origin. If one assumes that v. 17b belonged to the original account, then the fact that it seems to be a repetition can be due to the revision that inserted the covenant with the Lord and the covenantal formula about Israel as the people of the Lord into v. 17a. The translator of the LXX had access to the elaborate formulation of v. 17 and then, quite naturally, found v. 17b to be a repetition and therefore omitted it. This is the view of M. Noth.[22]

(3) That some sort of an agreement between the people and the new king was entered into is probable when the nature of the situation is taken into account. In effect, the enthronement of Joash meant a renewal of the old ties between the people and the Davidic dynasty, ties that are also found in 2 R 14,17-21 and 21,23-24, where the people intervene in plots against the king.

---

[17] Probably v. 18b is also to be ascribed to the later expansion. The guards at the temple of the Lord make sense as a measure of precaution after the destruction of the house of Baal in v. 18a.
[18] What we have here is an expression of the Deuteronomistic covenant theology, on which see *Perlitt* (1969: 7-53).
[19] Cf. Dt 4,20; 7,6; 14,2; 27,9; 1 S 12,22.
[20] Cf. *J. Gray* (1964: 513; ²1970: 568).
[21] Cf. *B. Stade* (ZAW 5/1885, 283) and *S. Herrmann* (1973: 280).
[22] So *M. Noth* (GesStud I, ²1960: 151 with note 23). Cf. also *Montgomery–Gehman* (Kings 1951: 426).

I therefore maintain that the reference to a royal covenant in 2 R 11,17 and 2 Ch 23,3[23] has its most natural explanation in the assumption that this reference preserves historically reliable information. As part of the original account, v. 17 probably read

ויכרת יהוידע את הברית ⟨...⟩
בין המלך ובין העם

And Jehoiada closed the covenant between the king and the people.

I thus find it probable that the reference to a royal covenant in v. 17 was part of the original account. Its place was immediately after the sacral part of the investiture in v. 12 but before the enthronement in the palace, described in v. 19-20 (cf. above note 16).

It must be frankly admitted that the general understanding of the character of the investiture of Joash depends to a great extent on where the reference to the royal covenant in v. 17 belongs. Stade assumed that it belonged to the secondary section. According to him, the original account (which he defined as consisting of. v. 1-12.18b-20) told of a *coup d'état* which the priest carried out with the help of only the royal guard. The people of Judah are not supposed to have been involved in this. The investiture of Joash would then be of the same type as that of Solomon with anointing and acclamation by court officials and the royal guard.[24]

Apart from what I have said about v. 17, I believe that if the historical situation is considered this is somewhat difficult to accept. After a reign such as that of Athaliah's, the priest Jehoiada probably chose an opportunity for his action that gave the new king as strong a constitutional position as possible, that is, an occasion when the representatives of the people were present to participate in the investiture. When the prince had been hidden for six years, Jehoiada took action in the seventh (v. 3-4). If we assume that the occasion chosen was that of a feast of boots after a seven-year-period (cf. Dt 31,9-13), this would explain why precisely the seventh year was chosen.

Let us now turn to the obligation: is it mutual or unilateral? If we compare 2 R 11,17 with 2 S 5,3 two points stand out. (a) The royal contract is not mentioned in immediate connection with the anointing, as a prerequisite of this. On the other hand we find in 2 R ch. 11 a closely connected sequence of anointing, acclamation (v. 12), royal covenant (v. 17) and enthronement (v. 19). Both acclamation and enthronement are acts carried out by the people. (b) The formulation in 2 R 11,17 speaks of a covenant *bên*

---

[23] Note that this word *bᵉrît* in 2 Ch 23,3 does not form the Chronicler's counterpart of the covenant in 2 R 11,4, which is found in the Chronicler in 2 Ch 23,1.
[24] *Stade* (ZAW 5/1885, 280-288; esp. 283 and 287). Contrast *Gray* (²1970: 566).

hămmælæk ûbên ha'am, while 2 S 5,3 has the expression *karăt bᵉrît lᵉ*. The type of formulation found in 2 R 11,17 can be used of various types of obligations.[25]

The royal covenant in 2 S 5,3 probably implied mutual obligation, the king's promise being expressed by the term *bᵉrît* and the obligation of the people being symbolically expressed by the rite of anointing. I shall argue in my study of the royal anointing that this rite was originally carried out by the elders and that it expressed the obligation of the people. Later it was performed by the priest and was then conceived of as a sacral rite expressing the relationship between king and God. This change in the rite may explain the order in the case of Joash, where the anointing is separated from the royal covenant. Here, the royal covenant is the prerequisite not of the anointing (which was, in spite of the formulation, probably carried out by a priest), but of the enthronement carried out by the people. It seems probable that the obligation was mutual, and that the agreement of the people was expressed by means of the acclamation and enthronement. The formulation *karăt bᵉrît bên ... ûbên ...* is thus used in the same way as in 1 R 15,19a (cf. 2 S 21,7).

(2) Leadership and Covenant in the Period before David. – It has been found that there was probably a royal covenant between Joash and the people of Judah. I shall now turn to the period before David. Here there is unduly neglected evidence of a contractual basis of leadership in the North.

The most indisputable case is Jephthah. The account of his road to power is found in Jud 11,4-11.[26] (a) The negotiations between the elders and Jephthah in the land of Tob and (b) the solemn act at the sanctuary of Mizpah, in which the whole *'ăm* was involved, should be kept separate.

In the case of the Ammonite threat, the elders of Gilead went to Jephthah in the land of Tob to bring him back as leader in the war against the Ammonites. Their plan was to make Jephthah *qaṣîn* (v. 6). Jephthah apparently did not consider that a temporary leadership in times of war was sufficient to re-establish him as a worthy member of clan and tribe. He also wanted to become leader in times of peace (*ro'š*).[26a] He was willing to accept the task of military leader on this condition:

> If you bring me home again to fight with the Ammonites, and the Lord gives them over to me, I will be your head. (Jud 11,9)

---

[25] See *Kutsch* (1973: 25).
[26] For the following see *E. Täubler* (1958: 285-287).
[26a] For a general survey of the use of *ro'š* as a title in the OT, see *Bartlett* (VT 19/1969, 1-10). Contrary to Bartlett (p. 1-2) I prefer to count the cases in connection with Jephthah to the occurrences where this title is used for civil leadership.

The elders were willing to accept this. So much seems clear, whether we opt for one or the other of the two possible interpretations of their answer in v. 10b:

יהוה יהיה שמע בינותינו
אם לא כדברך כן נעשה

The first part of this utterance is generally assumed to refer to the calling on the Lord as witness and the second to contain an oath: "The Lord will be witness between us; we will surely do as you say." I should, however, like to draw attention to the possibility that the Lord is here invoked as judge. Such a legal use of the verb *šamă'* is found in Dt 1,16-17 (cf. 1 R 3,9.11; 2 S 14,17[27]), and the construction *šamă' bên* ... has a close semantic parallel in *šapăṭ bên*..., "to judge", "to arbitrate".[28] The words of the elders to Jephthah would then mean: "The Lord will judge between us if we do not act according to your word."

Then Jephthah and the elders went to the sanctuary of Mizpah. There the promise of the elders was solemnly ratified by the entire people:

> So Jephthah went with the elders of Gilead, and the people made him head and leader [*ro'š* and *qaṣîn*] over them; and Jephthah spoke all his words before the Lord at Mizpah. (Jud 11,11)

The compact was thus sealed at the local sanctuary of Mizpah, "before the Lord". The text does not give any details, but I agree with Täubler who assumes that the ratification by the people was expressed in the form of an acclamation and that Jephthah now repeated his earlier promise to the elders in response to this acclamation.[29] If this is correct we have here the same order between acclamation and "royal" covenant as is found in 2 R 11,12.17.

To summarize, we have in the case of Jephthah the mutual obligation of the leader and the people. Here, the leader puts his military talent at the disposal of the people; the people in turn promise to obey him as leader even in times of peace. The fact that this contractual agreement seems to have been sealed by acclamation is in agreement with the conclusions in the previous analysis of the acclamation.

The case of Saul is very similar to that of Jephthah. Saul is also the successful leader in battle who is being invested with permanent leadership. The people do not acclaim him king on the battlefield at Jabesh but go to the sanctuary of Gilgal, and "there they made Saul king before the Lord" (1 S 11,15). The solemn act of making Saul king implied obligations that needed the safeguard of divine supervision. That the term *bᵉrît* is not used

---

[27] See my discussion in the chapter on the royal charisma at note 42.
[28] For references, see the chapter on the royal charisma, note 42.
[29] *Täubler* (1958: 287).

in the brief account can, as A.Alt expressed it, "schwerlich mehr als ein Zufall sein".[30]

Thus, in the cases of Jephthah and Saul, we come in contact with contractual relations between the leader and the people, and at least in the former case the covenant was explicit with the formal ratification by the people and the express promise of Jephthah.

There are even some other probable cases in the pre-monarchic and early monarchic period. In 2 S 2,4b-7 it is related that David sent messengers to "the men of Jabesh" to express his deep satisfaction with their burying of Saul. David's message continues:

וגם אנכי אעשה אתכם הטובה הזאת

And also I will make with you this ṭôbā. (2 S 2,6)[31]

The expression ʿaśā ṭobā is the exact Hebrew counterpart of Akkadian ṭābūta epēšu itti..., "to make friendship by treaty with...".[32] Here ṭābūtu is a treaty term, and the same terminology appears in the phrase ṭūbtu u sulummû, "friendship by peace effected by treaty", with the term sulummû formed according to the nominal pattern purussû which is often used for legal terms.[33]

I assume that Hebrew ṭôbā has the same meaning of "treaty" as its Akkadian congruent[34] in the following cases:

2 S 2,6 with the construction ʿaśā ṭôbā ʾæt....

Dt 23,7 with the parallelism šalôm // ṭôbā, cf. Akkadian ṭūbtu u sulummû.[35]

Jer 33,9 with the construction ʿaśā ṭôbā ʾæt... and the parallelism ṭôbā // šalôm.[36]

2 S 7,28 where the term ṭôbā seems to be used as a covenant term to denote the dynastic promise.[37]

---

[30] *Alt* (KS II, 23).
[31] My own translation.
[32] See *Buccellati* (Bi e Or 4/1962, 233; not seen, known to me from Soggin 1967: 65 note 12). This interpretation is accepted by *HAL* (p. 356b).
[33] On this treaty terminology found in Akkadian, Aramaic and Hebrew, see *Buccellati* (above, note 32), *Moran* (JNES 22/1963, 173-176), *Hillers* (BASOR 176/1964, 46-47), *Fitzmyer* (Bibl 46/1965, 52-54), *Malamat* (BA 28/1965, 63f.) and *M.Fox* (BASOR 209/1973, 41-42). Textual references: for Akkadian ṭūbtu see *Moran* op. cit., for Aramaic ṭbtʾ see Sefire I C 4-5; I C 19-20; II B 2 and KAI 266,8=Adon (discussed by *Moran* and *Fitzmyer*, op. cit.). For Hebrew ṭôbā see below. – For the Akkadian nominal pattern purussû referred to above see *vonSoden* (FsKoschaker 1939: 199-207), and for its Hebrew counterpart, qᵉtullā, see *Mettinger* (JSS 16/1971, 2-14).
[34] For this terminology see *Mettinger* (1971: 2).
[35] Adduced by *Hillers* (op. cit.).
[36] Adduced by *Fox* (op. cit.).
[37] Adduced by *Malamat* (BA 28/1965, 64).

Jud 9,16 is also a probable case, see below.

There are then reasons for considering that the formulation in 2 S 2,6 refers to David's offer of a royal covenant to the citizens of Jabesh. The offer is motivated by the statement "for Saul your lord is dead, and the house of Judah has anointed me king over them" (v. 7). Thus David seems willing to accept the same obligation to protect Jabesh as Saul had assumed during his lifetime.[38]

Here one could perhaps also mention the case of Jerubbaal (Gideon).[39] Jotham concludes his famous fable with the words:

> Now therefore, if you acted in good faith and honour [$bæ'^{ae}mæt\ ûb^etamîm$] when you made Abimelech king, and if you have made a $tôbā$ with Jerubbaal and his house, and have done to him as his deeds deserved .... (Jud 9,16)[40]

It is tempting to bring forward this case in connection with the above-mentioned use of $tôbā$ as "treaty".[41] If this is correct, the leadership of Jerubbaal also had according to this text a contractual basis, but admittedly this remains in the wide realm of possibilities.

Let us now return to the question of a royal covenant in Judah. Although the term $b^erît$ did not occur in 2 S 2,4, reasons have been found for presuming that David's investiture over "the house of Judah", which was already an existing political confederation, was an affair of contractual significance. It has been discovered that there are cases of a contractual basis of leadership among the affiliated tribes of Northern Israel in the period prior to David. This means that David's covenant with the elders of Israel mentioned in 2 S 5,3 is not an innovation, which would have made the assumption of a similar covenant with Judah in 2 S 2,4 difficult to accept. We have also seen that the reference to a royal covenant closed between Joash and the people of Judah probably contains historically reliable information. Therefore, when all is said and done, I find the most probable conclusion to be that the Davidic kingship over Judah had from the beginning a contractual basis.

---

[38] It may be that before Saul's action the men of Jabesh tried to get a royal promise from Nahash the Ammonite, see 1 S 11,1b.

[39] According to *Haag* (ZAW 79/1967, 305-314) the identification of Jerubbaal with Gideon is secondary. The fact that Gideon rejected the offer of kingship (Jud 8,22) would then be irrelevant to the present discussion.

[40] My own translation. Note the parallel structure of v. 15 and v. 16-19.

[41] This sense was assumed in Jud 9,16 by *J. Maier* (Kairos 11/1969, 32 f.).

Summary

The constitutional significance of the participation of the people at the royal investitures has been studied. The lines converge to indicate that the relationship between the ruler and the people was conceived in contractual categories.

(1) While the king had to make certain concessions to the people, as can be seen from the promise (*b^erît*) that David made to the elders of Israel (2 S 5,3), the people expressed their ratification of the new king by means of acclamation and, in the case of David, anointing. This anointing, carried out by the people, will be discussed in the chapter on this royal rite. The acclamation took the form of the exclamation *y^eḥî hămmælæk*. The same elements occur in the oath sworn "by the life of the king". Starting from the observation that Akkadian *libluṭ šarru*, "may the king live", is used as an oath in the Amarna letters, and even in one from Jerusalem, I argued that the Hebrew royal acclamation was originally an elliptic oath. The jussive form *y^eḥî* does not have the sense of an indicative, as has been argued by some scholars; it retains the sense of a wish, precisely as the corresponding precative in the Akkadian formula. The royal acclamation, which had the character of an oath, meant the agreement on the part of the people to the contractual relationship with the king. In the acclamation we are not concerned with an election in the modern sense of the word, but none the less with a constitutionally significant expression of the *consensus populi*.

(2) The observations on the royal covenant agree with what was worked out for the acclamation. In a number of cases we have found evidence for a contractual basis of the authority of the ruler. The leader and the people accepted mutual obligations. In this respect, the covenant between David and the elders of Northern Israel (2 S 5,3) is no innovation. Nor was it primarily an affair between two tribal groups, even if the practical effect of this contractual agreement was that Judah and Israel became linked in a personal union under David. Just as in the other cases, both earlier and later, it was a covenant between the ruler and the people.

(3) In spite of little direct evidence I have found reasons for concluding that royal power also had a contractual basis in Judah. When David became king over "the house of Judah" and was anointed by "the men of Judah" (2 S 2,4), he was accepted as the leader of an already existing political confederation of towns, the representatives of which were strong enough to enter into negotiations with their future leader. A contractual agreement between David and the elders of Judah fits in perfectly with what was found for Jephthah and Saul. In this connection I discussed the use of *ṭobā* as a contractual term. I found that this term refers to a royal covenant in 2 S 2,6.

(4) It seems probable to me that the royal covenant was normally renewed at every new investiture. The various contractual features of the investiture (acclamation, anointing) are an indication of this. The obligations were probably mutual, the king granting the people his royal promise (cf. $b^e r\hat{\imath} t$ in 2 S 5,3)[42] and the people accepting the obligation to obey the king. The obligation of the people was expressed not only by means of the acclamation but also by means of the anointing, as long as this was carried out by the elders as in the case of David (2 S 2,4; 5,3).[43] This is an extremely important observation, the implications of which I shall have to return to in the study of the royal anointing.

(5) In two important cases a royal covenant was not closed. Solomon became king without making a royal covenant with the people and without ratification by the elders. After Solomon's death, his son Rehoboam was not willing to renew the royal covenant that David had closed with the elders of Northern Israel. His refusal to do this meant the end of the personal union established by David.

---

[42] For a general consideration of the possibility of the ruler binding himself see *Th.Geiger* (1947:305-311).

[43] Compare the reluctant hint by *Pedersen* (1914:62f.).

PART THREE

The Sacral Legitimation of the King

CHAPTER IX

The Divine Designation and the Problem of Nagid

Let us now turn to the sacral legitimation of the king and first discuss the question of the divine designation of the king. We shall then discuss the rite of anointing and the question of the royal charisma and finally the divine sonship of the king and the formulations referring to the Davidic covenant.

Divine designation in advance is mentioned for a number of kings of Israel and Judah:

Saul	1 S 9,1–10,16	Saul's anointing as *nagîd*.
	1 S 10,17-27	The lot-casting at Mizpah.
David	1 S 16,1-13	Samuel's anointing of David.
	2 S 7,8	Nathan's oracle concerning David: David chosen by God to be *nagîd* (cf. 1 S 25,30; 2 S 5,2; 6,21).
Jeroboam	1 R 11,29-39	Ahijah's oracle concerning Jeroboam (cf. 14,7 *nagîd*).
Baasha	1 R 16,2	Prophetic oracle concerning Baasha and his designation as *nagîd*.
Jehu	2 R 9,1-13	Jehu anointed king by one of the members of the prophetic guild of Elisha.

The picture one gets from a first survey of the extant sources is one of bewildering complexity. There are, for instance, two wholly different and unrelated accounts of a divine designation of Saul. The one tells of a prophetic designation as *nagîd* and the other of a lot-casting. Whereas in the HDR, David's designation is repeatedly referred to by the term *nagîd*, this title does not occur in connection with his anointing by Samuel. On the other hand it is the key term in the passage on Saul's anointing by the same man of God. The picture of Samuel is also a different one. In connection with the anointing of Saul he takes on prophetic stature, while this is

hardly the case in the passage dealing with the anointing of David. Such are the intricacies, to mention but a few, that we find in the material. One of our main concerns in the following investigation will be to answer the questions when, where and why was the conception of a divine designation of the king developed? In particular, were such conceptions known during the reigns of Saul, David and Solomon?

The analysis of the material will be carried out in two main steps. First, I shall discuss the material for the designation as *nagîd*. As can already be seen from the brief survey above, the role of this term in the sources is considerable. A more accurate definition of this term would imply an important step forward in the understanding of the sacral position of the king. The problems connected with the title *nagîd* will therefore be subjected to a detailed analysis. One of the main results of this part of the study is that the conception of the divine designation as *nagîd* derives from the period after Solomon's death. This leads us to the second part of the investigation in which I shall pose the question for earlier ideas of the divine designation of the king.

1. Designation as Nagid. The Biblical Material, Survey of Research

There are in the MT 44 instances of the word *nagîd*. Of these, one is suspect on text-critical grounds, viz. 1 Ch 27,4 where the text of the LXX, which omits the word, seems to offer a better reading than the MT. Apart from the cases found in the MT the longer text of the LXX in 1 S 10,1 should be included, since the LXX is here to be preferred to the MT (above, ch. 4.1). On the other hand, there is no temptation to emend the MT and read *nagîd* in 2 Ch 6,6 or 1 S 16,6 (cf. BHK³ app.). There are thus 44 occurences in all to be studied. Of these the references to royal designations in Samuel and Kings are of immediate concern to us, but so that my conclusions will be founded on as broad a basis as possible I shall study the whole of the material and utilize my observations for the interpretation of the import of the term in passages dealing with the kings of the early monarchy. The distribution of the term is as follows:

The Saul Cycle, the HDR and the SN

1 S 9,16; 10,1 (in 10,1 I follow the longer text of the LXX): By divine commission Samuel anoints Saul *nagîd*.

1 S 13,14: Samuel rejects Saul and says that YHWH sought out a man after His own heart and appointed him to be *nagîd* over His people.

1 S 25,30: Abigail refers to David's status as *nagîd*.

2 S 5,2 (=1 Ch 11,2): "All the tribes of Israel" come to David at Hebron

to make him king over Israel. The word *nagîd* is embedded in a divine oracle.

2 S 6,21: David says to Michal that YHWH chose him above Saul and his house and appointed him *nagîd*.

2 S 7,8 (=1 Ch 17,7): Nathan conveys a divine oracle to David: "Thus says the Lord of hosts, I took you ... that you should be *nagîd* over my people, over Israel; ...."

1 R 1,35: David says to Zadok, Nathan, and Benaiah: "I hereby appoint him [i.e. Solomon] to be *nagîd* over Israel and Judah."[1]

Miscellaneous Texts apart from Chronicles

1 R 14,7: The prophet Ahijah instructs the wife of Jeroboam I to tell her husband: "Thus says the Lord, the God of Israel: 'Because I exalted you from among the people, and made you *nagîd* over my people Israel, ...'"

1 R 16,2: The prophet Jehu receives a divine revelation of doom on the house of Baasha: "Since I exalted you out of the dust and made you *nagîd* over my people Israel, ..."

2 R 20,5: YHWH instructs Isaiah: "Turn back, and say to Hezekiah the *nagîd* of my people, Thus says the Lord, the God of David your father...."

Jes 55,4: David as *nagîd*.

Jer 20,1: Pashhur, the priest, as *paqîd nagîd* in the house of YHWH.

Ez 28,2: The prophet is ordered to convey an oracle to the *nagîd* of Tyre.

Ps 76,13: $n^e gîdîm//m^e lakîm$.

Job 29,10: $n^e gîdîm//śarîm$, v. 9.

Job 31,37: "... like a *nagîd* I would approach him [i.e. God]."

Prv 8,6: $n^e gîdîm$ '$^a dăbber$, which Gemser takes to mean "Edles rede ich."[1a]

Prv 28,16: If one accepts the emendation of $w^e răb$ to read $yareb$[2] (Hiph. of *rabăb*), there is no reason to delete *nagîd*[3]. The rendering should be: "A *nagîd* who lacks understanding increases oppression...."

Dan 9,25: "the coming of an anointed one, a *nagîd*".

Dan 9,26: "the people of the *nagîd* who is to come".

Dan 11,22: "the *nagîd* of the covenant".

---

[1] For a motivation of this translation see below under 2.

[1a] *Gemser* (1963: 44). *Ringgren* (1962: 37) also adheres to the same interpretation. For a slightly different opinion see *Grollenberg* (RB 59/1952, 40-42), followed by *McKane* (1970: 345).

[2] *Ringgren* (1962: 109).

[3] As does *Gemser* (1963: 99).

Chronicles and Neh.

a) *nagîd* in connection with royal status:

1 Ch 5,2: "... though Judah became strong among his brothers, and a *nagîd* was from him, yet the birthright belonged to Joseph."[4]

1 Ch 11,2=2 S 5,2 (above).

1 Ch 17,7=2 S 7,8 (above).

1 Ch 28,4: David says: "... for he chose Judah as *nagîd*, and in the house of Judah my father's house, and among my father's sons he took pleasure in me to make me king over all Israel."

1 Ch 29,22: "And they made Solomon the son of David king the second time, and they anointed him as *nagîd* for the Lord, and Zadok as priest."

2 Ch 6,5: "... and I chose no man as *nagîd* over my people Israel;"

2 Ch 11,22: "... and Rehoboam appointed Abijah the son of Maacah to be *ro'š*, to be *nagîd* among his brothers, for he intended to make him king."[4a]

b) *nagîd* used of tribal leader or military chief:

1 Ch 12,28: "Jehoiada, the *nagîd* of Aaron" included in a list of "the divisions of armed troops who came to David in Hebron" (v. 24).

1 Ch 27,16: "for the Reubenites Eliezer the son of Zichri was *nagîd*".

2 Ch 19,11: The supreme court in Jerusalem, instituted by Jehoshaphat, had two presidents. One of these was Zebadiah, the *nagîd* of the house of Judah, who had competence for "the king's matters".

1 Ch 13,1: *kål nagîd* used as inclusive term for various sorts of military *śarîm*.

2 Ch 11,11: Rehoboam puts *n^{e}gîdîm* in his fortresses.

2 Ch 32,21: "*kål gibbôr ḥåyil w^{e}nagîd w^{e}śar* in the camp of the king of Assyria".

c) *nagîd* in connection with tasks at the sanctuary:
Neh 11,11; 1 Ch 9,11.20; 26,24; 2 Ch 28,7; 31,12.13; 35,8.

This general survey in itself leads to some observations. In 1 S–2 R the title is used only of persons who were already or who later became kings. Nevertheless the word does not seem to be just a synonym of *mælæk*. There is in 1 S 9,16; 10,1 and in 1 R 1,35 a distinction between *nagîd* and *mælæk*. It is generally God who appoints a *nagîd*. In two cases, however, a king appoints a son of his to be *nagîd*. Thus David appointed Solomon *nagîd* (1 R 1,35) as did Rehoboam with Abijah (2 Ch 11,22).

---

[4] I do not find it necessary to deviate from the MT as does *Rudolph* (1955:42f.) who emends the end of the verse to read *w^{e}håbb^{e}korā lô lo' l^{e}yôsep*, "and the birthright belonged to him, not to Joseph".

[4a] My own translation.

Although the figure (44 X) is too low to allow for reliable conclusions *e silentio* it is important to note certain gaps in the distribution.

(a) The title is never used of a leader of pre-monarchic times. The first person to be thus denoted is Saul (1 S 9,16; 10,1).

(b) It is strange that the title, which has a prominent role in the earliest historical writings, does not appear at all in the royal psalms. It is found only once in the whole of the Psalter and then not for the king of Jerusalem but in the plural, for foreign sovereigns (76,13). As the title is the key word for the divine election of David in the prophecy of Nathan (2 S 7,8) it is most remarkable that not even Ps 89, that clearly echoes Nathan's oracle, contains an occurrence of the word *nagîd*. These circumstances would be difficult to explain if the word had had a role in the royal ritual of the coronation. On the other hand one must ask whether some other term in Ps 89 conveys a sense similar to that of *nagîd* in the prophecy of Nathan. A perusal of the psalm gives two possible alternatives at this point: *baḥîr* (v. 4) and *bᵉkôr* (v. 28). Which of these it is that stands in semantic relation to *nagîd* will be discussed later.

(c) In 1 S 9,1–10,16 the anointing of Saul as *nagîd* is the very *skopos* of the text. In a second text (1 S 16,1-13), Samuel also anoints David. But here nothing is said of David as *nagîd*.

(d) The word occurs in connection with David's investiture as ruler over Northern Israel (2 S 5,2) but not in connection with his anointing as ruler over Judah (2 S 2,1-4).

(e) The prophet Ahijah speaks of Jeroboam's elevation as a *nagîd* designation (1 R 14,7), but the term does not occur in the passage which claims to report what happened at this designation (1 R 11,29-39).

(f) The term does not occur in the passage on the prophetic anointing of Jehu (2 R 9,1-13).

The most important scholarly opinions on the subject are as follows:[5]

In his famous study of the "Staatenbildung" (1930) Albrecht Alt[6] based his interpretation of the title on the traditions of Saul, in which he found a clear distinction between the divine designation through which Saul became *nagîd* (1 S 9,16; 10,1) and the acclamation of the people, through which Saul became *mælæk*.[7] Alt took the term to mean "Kundgegebener" (a passive participle) and to denote the charismatic leader as the one designated by YHWH. Solomon's designation by David in

---

[5] For contributions on the philological problem, see below section 2. The following brief survey only includes contributions that (a) are particularly thoroughly argued and/or (b) have played a considerable part in the scholarly debate, as is the case with Alt's brief remarks (below). For full references to the literature see *W.Richter* (BZ 9/1965, 71 f. the notes) and *Langlamet* (RB 77/1970, 188 note 154).

[6] *Alt* (KS II, 23 with note 2).

[7] For this *Alt* refers to 1 S 11,15 but see preferably 1 S 10,24.

1 R 1,35 was interpreted as a transgression so that David here infringed upon the divine prerogative to designate the king.[8] For more than three decades Alt's interpretation served as the central point in a scholarly consensus.[9]

Wolfgang Richter's study in 1965[10] marshalled in a new epoch in the discussion. Richter here drew attention to the fact that the title is often embedded in a formula. 1 S 13,14, to quote but one example, has the typical wording: *wăyṣăwwehû YHWH l^{e}nagîd 'ăl 'ămmô*. The constituent elements of this formula are: a verb (normally with God as the subject) + *(l^e)nagîd* + the preposition *'ăl* + the sphere of dominion denoted as God's *'ăm* (or in one case *năḥ^{a}lā*, 1 S 10,1).[11] According to Richter, *nagîd* and *mælæk* denoted two originally different positions of rank. The use of *năḥ^{a}lā* and *'ăm* in the formula led Richter to the conclusion that the word was originally a tribal title.[12] It gradually underwent semantic expansion to denote the leader of the whole of Northern Israel. The connection between *nagîd* and the saviour formula (*Retterformel*)[13], attested in 1 S 9,16 and 10,1 (for the latter see LXX), indicates a link between *nagîd* and the YHWH war (p. 78 ff.). And so *nagîd* can be defined as a successor of the "saviour" of pre-monarchic Israel (p. 81 f.). Richter finds the oldest occurrences of the title in 1 S 9,16; 10,1, where an original pre-monarchic connection between anointing and *nagîd* is still preserved (p. 76). He expressly dissociates himself from Alt's suggestion to understand *nagîd* as the person designed to be king (p. 82 note 41).

In a new perusal of the material, Ludwig Schmidt (1970: 141-171) went a step further than Richter and tried to substantiate the hypothesis that *nagîd* originally

---

[8] *Alt* (KS II, 62 note 1).

[9] See *W.Richter* (BZ 9/1965, 71 f. note 5) for references. – A brief criticism of Alt's interpretation of *nagîd* was offered by *Thornton* (JThSt 14/1963, 8), whose paper is only concerned with the alleged evidence for charismatic kingship during the period of the divided monarchy (p. 2 note 1). Thornton writes: "There is no necessary reason to suppose that this word [i.e. *nagîd*] as used in the book of Kings has any particular connotation of some special divine designation or endowment with some God-given 'charisma'" (p. 8). And he goes on to say that if the title ever had a particular technical meaning when applied to kingship its meaning was probably "heir-apparent to the throne". – On the first point Thornton is, in my opinion, mistaken. On the second he has hit on an essential truth but, regrettably, does not draw the consequences of his insight.

[10] *W.Richter* (BZ 9/1965, 71-84). *Vorarbeiten* to that study were published in *Richter* (1963: 286-93). – I find no reason to discuss here the theory of *A.Carlson* (1964: 52-55) that *nagîd* is a "Deuteronomic alternative to *mælæk*", on which see Richter's refutation (BZ 19/1965, 74 note 9). Nor shall I devote space to *Glück's* unhappy combination of *nagîd* and *noqed* (VT 13/1963, 144-50), already criticized by *Gese* (ZThK 61/1964, 13 note 7) and by *Richter* (p. 72 f. note 7).

[11] In this connection I want to draw attention to *Richter's* general methodological discussion of "geprägte Elemente" (1971: 99 ff.), which he defines as "formal gleichgebaute Wortverbindungen oder Wortgruppen" which occur repeatedly (p. 99). Within this entity Richter differentiates: "Eine geprägte Wendung liegt vor, wenn sich die festgeprägte Wortverbindung auf ein literarisches Werk beschränkt; sie ist hier Ausdruck der Ansicht eines Autors. Eine Formel liegt vor, wenn sich die festgeprägte Wortverbindung in mehr als einem literarischen Werk findet..." (p. 101). Note also what Richter says on the importance of this distinction for conclusions concerning "Sitz in der Literatur" and "Sitz im Leben" (p. 117 f.).

[12] *Richter* (BZ 9/1965, 77) defines *năḥ^{a}lā* as "das einem Stamm vom Amphiktyonieverband zugebilligte Erbland" and *'ăm* as "die dazugehörigen freien, waffenfähigen, besitzenden Männer".

[13] For a definition and description see *Richter* (1963: 149 ff., 215).

denoted the chief of the tribal militia (*Heerbannführer*) of pre-monarchic times. Historically, Saul, David and Solomon bore the title in their capacity of chief of the militia. The title, according to Schmidt, forms a connection between the early monarchy and the institutions of the tribal period. Later on the military connotations of the title were lost, and it was used chiefly to describe the king's position as subordinate to YHWH. On two points Schmidt agrees with Richter: that the title derives from the tribal period and that it denoted a military function.

One must here make some critical reflections. First, both Richter and Schmidt are committed to the theory that the title is pre-monarchic and is a heritage from the tribal period. That the title should owe its existence to the institution of the monarchy is regarded by Schmidt as "von vorneherein unwahrscheinlich" (p. 142). However, this cannot be taken as a matter of course. The neglected fact that the title is not attested for a single person during the period of the judges[13a] commends caution here. If Richter and Schmidt were right one would expect to find not only *šôpeṭ* and *qaṣîn* but also *nagîd*.

Secondly, these scholars seem to base their conclusions on tacit assumptions regarding the relative chronology of the occurrences. Thus Alt takes as his point of departure Saul's anointing as *nagîd*. David's designation of Solomon (1 R 1,35) is evaluated as a deviation from established custom. And Richter clearly holds the Saul passage to be the earliest of the extant sources.[14] Schmidt is more cautious here, but is not concerned with which is the oldest text that contains an occurrence of *nagîd*. One must be fair here and admit that it is not to be expected that these scholars should found their conclusions on the basis of a full-length discussion of the isagogic problems in the Books of Samuel. Our understanding of these, however, has been deepened by recent research.

Thirdly, the contention that the military connotations of the title provide an indication of its origin could be called in question. The evidence adduced to support this theory can be summarized in two points: (a) 1 S 9,16 and the LXX in 10,1 contain the saviour formula. Further, 2 S 7,8 appears in a context which contains a reference to the defeat of the enemy (v. 9 ff.). Since the connection between *nagîd* and the YHWH war are not found in passages that are considered to be dependent on these two, this connection is presumed to be original.[15] (b) The word *'ām*, which is an integral part of the *nagîd* formula, is taken to mean "Heerbann".[16]

[13a] Attention was drawn to this circumstance by *S.Herrmann* (1973: 178); cf. *Langlamet* (RB 77/1970, 191).

[14] *Richter* (BZ 9/1965, 76 and cf. 1970: 176).

[15] *L.Schmidt* (1970: 152).

[16] *W.Richter* (BZ 9/1965, 77) and *L.Schmidt* (1970: 154). Cf. *Smend* (Theologische Studien 68/1963, 19).

As for the first of these two points the saviour formula proves nothing. And the tacit assumptions concerning the relative chronology of the occurrences must be questioned. As will be seen the oldest occurrence is probably that in 1 R 1,35.[17]

As regards the second argument, I shall here only point out that the suggestion "Heerbann" is not altogether well founded for the sense of ʿăm in the formula nagîd ʿăl ʿăm YHWH. As we shall see it is much more probable that this word denotes Israel not as the "army" of but as the "family" of YHWH.

Postscript. – After I had completed this chapter in September 1974,[17a] Lipinski published a brief but important "short note" on *nagîd* (VT 24/1974, 497-499). This scholar argues that 1 R 1,35 is the oldest occurrence, that Solomon was the first historical *nagîd* and that the title denotes the Crown prince. It is of worth that we have independently arrived at the same basic interpretation of the development of the title. The priority is Lipinski's, but unlike him I have dealt with the question of the date, place and purpose of the theologization of the term and have also studied its semantic relations and its etymology. – A work which also appeared after the completion of this chapter is that by Veijola (1975), who takes most of the occurrences of the title in Samuel and Kings to be due to the work of the Dtr. I have added a note on this below in section 3.1.

2. A Secular Use of the Term Nagid

The problem of the meaning of the word *nagîd* is an intriguing one. The nominal pattern, which provides the morphological basis for the word, does not indicate whether we are concerned with an active or a passive formation, since the pattern *qatîl* contains both (a) the active participle *qatîl* and (b) the passive participle (**qătîl>*) *qatîl*.[18] The occurrences in the Phoenician Nora inscription[19] or the Aramaic treaties from Sefire (III,10)[20] do not contribute much to our understanding of the problem. Even the problem of which root is involved is so far not settled. In his study of 1930 Alt apparently interpreted the word *nagîd* as a derivative of the verb *higgîd* and took it to be a Qal passive participle: "Kundgegebener".[21] Joüon on

---

[17] The relative chronology of the sources in which the word *nagîd* occurs will be discussed in detail below *sub* 2 and 3.

[17a] It was discussed by the Old Testament seminar at Lund on the fourth of October 1974.

[18] See *Barth* (1894: 182-86). Barth himself lists *nagîd* under the active participle: "Sager" (p. 184 e). See further *Ges-K* (^{27}1902 § 84 al), *Bauer – Leander* (p. 470), and *Moscati et al.* (1964: 146).

[19] Published and commented upon by *B.Peckham* (Or 41/1972, 457-68). The word occurs in line 7 of the inscription (see p. 459).

[20] Text and translation most recently in *Fitzmyer* (1967: 98-99), commentary ibid. (p. 112). See also *DISO* (p. 174). Donner admits the possibility of reading *ngdy* but prefers to read *ngry*, cf. Akkadian *nāgiru* (KAI II, 268). On Akkadian *nāgiru* see *Mettinger* (1971: 57 f.).

[21] *Alt* (KS II, 23 with note 2).

the other hand suggested deriving the word from the preposition *nægæd* and to understand *nagîd* as "celui qui est devant les autres", "préposé".[22] Still another path was chosen by Glück who took *nagîd* to be a root variant of *nôqed* and argued that the word denotes the king as the shepherd of his people.[23] It is quite clear that so far no suggested solution of the linguistic problem has won universal approval. Is it possible to advance further observations that can settle the controversy?

In a number of cases the appointment as *nagîd* takes place by direct divine command although a prophet may act as mediator. We are here faced with a very distinctive use, and one that is of considerable importance in the sources. The majority of the occurrences in 1 S – 2 R belong here. In the following I shall refer to this as the theological use of the title.

Now, theological conceptions are often expressed in the secular terms of this-worldly matters. The "indirect", metaphorical or elevated senses of words used in theological contexts can often be regarded as derived from more "direct" and secular ones. Thus semantic treatments often give historical priority to secular senses although statistically they are sometimes sparsely attested. In treatments of the root *h-ṭ-'*, which has a central role in the semantic field "sin", priority is often given to the secular sense "miss (the mark)".[23a] Behind the use of *sᵉgullā* denoting Israel as the possession of YHWH lies the secular use of this word to denote the innermost sphere of the property of an earthly sovereign, his royal treasury.[24] In the same way, an earthly institution may provide the basis of a *theologoumenon* as is the case in the divine lawsuit (*rîb*).[24a] The examples could easily be multiplied. They suffice to show that it is not out of place to ask whether the description of the king as *nagîd* through divine appointment also has a secular basis.

From the purely statistical point of view, the "normal" procedure is no doubt that YHWH appoints somebody *nagîd*. An occurrence that does not conform to this is 1 R 1,35 where we are told of David's designation of Solomon as *nagîd*. Alt's conclusion that David here infringes upon divine prerogative has become widely accepted.[25] According to this opinion,

---

[22] *Joüon* (Bibl 17/1936, 229-33).
[23] *Glück* (VT 13/1963, 144-50). For criticism see above, the literature referred to in note 10 at the end.
[23a] See Jud 20, 16 and Prv 19,2.
[24] See 1 Ch 29,3 and Eccl 2,8.
[24a] There is perhaps a slight difference between this example and the preceding ones. If *Würthwein* (ZThK 49/1952, 1-16) is right, the divine lawsuit is patterned on a cultic institution. *Boecker* (1964: 71-94, esp. 91 ff.), connects it with the procedure of the city gate. In any case, the basis is provided by an earthly institution.
[25] *Alt* (KS II, 62 note 1). He was followed by among others *E.Rosenthal* (JJS 9/1958, 9), *W.Richter* (BZ 9/1965, 77) and *Noth* (1968: 25). – *Schmidt's* criticism (1970: 159ff.) does not remove the difficulties.

David's act represents an abuse, a deviation from an old established custom. However, this idea of a deliberate infringement on divine rights is in itself problematic. The fact that Solomon's appointment as *nagîd* is related in a literary work that is concerned with demonstrating the legitimacy of this king, viz. the Succession Narrative, is not favourable to such a supposition. On the other hand, if we reverse the problem, this passage no longer constitutes a difficulty: it can be regarded as a case of a secular use of *nagîd* that offered the basis for a subsequent theologization. The crucial words run:

ואתו צויתי להיות נגיד על ישראל ועל יהודה

The secular connotations of the title manifest themselves in two ways. (a) David, and not a prophet or YHWH Himself, is the one who pronounces the decisive word. (b) The area of competence of the *nagîd* is not described theologically as *'al 'am YHWH* but in a secular, constitutional terminology referring to the two entities united in the personal union through David: *'al yiśra'el we'al yehûdā*.[26] If one is looking for a secular use that could have offered the basis for the theological connotations of the title, 1 R 1,35 is indeed a most interesting indication.

In spite of statements to the contrary,[27] this is not an isolated occurrence. The same secular use of the title is also found in 2 Ch 11,22:

ויעמד לראש רחבעם את אביה בן מעכה לנגיד באחיו
כי להמליכו

And Rehoboam appointed Abijah the son of Maacah as chief prince among his brothers, for he intended to make him king.

It may well be that David and Rehoboam actually designated their successors and raised one of the princes to the status of *nagîd*.[28] 1 R 1,35 and 2 Ch 11,22 anyhow report a secular designation: it is the reigning king who is said to appoint one of his sons *nagîd*. The title in question denotes the heir-designate, the Crown prince. We see here the peculiar relation between *nagîd* and *mælæk*. There is a clear distinction: as *nagîd* Abijah is not yet *mælæk*. At the same time, the connection is evident: precisely in his capacity of *nagîd* Abijah is to become *mælæk*. The title may convey the

---

[26] The fact that the MT of the preceding verse (1 R 1,34) has only "Israel" should not make us suspicious of v. 35, since in v. 34 a "Judah" is most probably to be restored on the basis of the Lucianic text.

[27] Cf. *L.Schmidt* (1970: 159): "Nur hier setzt ein Mensch und nicht Jahwe zum nagid ein, ..."

[28] I here agree with *Rudolph* (1955: 232 f.; 265) in his opinions on 2 Ch 11,18-23 and 21,2-4. – *Noth* (ÜSt 143 note 1) regards both passages in Chronicles as additions and the contents as historically questionable. *Galling* (1954: 106; 130) connects the contents with the times of Josiah.

notion of a free choice on behalf of the reigning king. Solomon was clearly not the eldest living prince (1 R 1,6; 2,22).[29]

The texts then tell of two cases of a royal *Nachfolgerdesignation*, to use the terminology of Max Weber[30], and in both cases the term *nagîd* is used (1 R 1,35; 2 Ch 11,22). A third such designation is found in 2 Ch 21,1-3, where it is said that Jehoshaphat gave his sons various gifts together with fortified cities in Judah; "but he gave the kingdom to Jehoram because he was the first-born" (v. 3). Although the word *nagîd* is not used here, it is nevertheless a question of heir-designate. Note also that in this case the designation conformed to the principle of primogeniture.

This formal designation of the heir to the throne is paralleled by a corresponding institution in Assyria. Here the king designated one of his sons — not necessarily the eldest. The designation was confirmed by the priests and the militia, and the Crown prince took up his abode in a special house, the *bît redûti* ("Nachfolgehaus").[30a]

On the basis of these observations we are justified in concluding that David's designation of Solomon as *nagîd* is not a deviation from the pattern of an already established theological usage. On the contrary, this occurrence is to be regarded as a case of a secular use of *nagîd*. Moreover, scholars have so far also overlooked the fact that 1 R 1,35, seen in its context, may offer a clue to the linguistic analysis of the title. David's decisive words *we'otô ṣiwwîtî lihyôt nagîd 'al yiśra'el we'al yehûdā* convey his answer to the request of Bathsheba:

> And now, my lord the king, the eyes of all Israel are upon you, to tell (*lehǎggîd*) them who shall sit on the throne of my lord the king after him.
> (1 R 1,20)

There is here an unmistakable connection between the request that David should announce (*lehǎggîd*) whom he wished to see as his successor and his designation of Solomon as *nagîd* in v. 35. If 1 R 1,20.35 is not a secondary explanation of an already established title the original sense of which had fallen into oblivion (a possibility that can be ruled out, as we shall see) we may conclude that the title is a Qal passive participle of the same root as is found in the verb *higgîd*.

This observation concerning the connection between Bathsheba's request and David's formal announcement also prepares the way for a correct syntactic assessment of 1 R 1,35. This verse does not refer to an earlier designation, as is often thought. David's words instantly bring about the

---

[29] According to 2 Ch 11,20 Abijah was the son of Maacah whom Rehoboam married after Mahalath (v. 18). This could suggest that Abijah was not the eldest son of Rehoboam.
[30] M.Weber (GdS III: 1 p. 143; cf. III: 2 p. 763 ff.).
[30a] See *Cardascia* (1970: 353 f.) and *AHw* (p. 134a and 981b). Note the occurrences in the vassal treaties of Esarhaddon (ed. *Wiseman* p. 29-59 passim, comments ibid. p. 4, 7).

state of things that they speak of. They are to be understood as a performative utterance[31]. The perfect *ṣiwwîtî* can only be taken as a case of the so-called *perfectum declarativum* ("Perfekt der Koinzidenz"):[32] "... and I hereby appoint him to be *nagîd* over Israel and Judah".

3. The Theologization. Its Background and Purpose

1. The Date of the Theologization

Instead of comprising a problematic deviation from a theological pattern, 1 R 1,35 is a most valuable case of the secular use of *nagîd*. This leads us to the problem of the development of the term. Let us first consider the relative age of the two separate uses, the theological and the secular. The assumption that the theological use is the older one immediately touches upon a problem in 1 R 1,35. We would then probably have to infer that David had infringed upon a divine right. However, once we assume that the secular use is the older one, a supposition that has high prior probability, 1 R 1,35 is accounted for. We are, in that verse, not faced with an abuse but with a use that is "normal" in the sense that it is the original use of the term. Thus, the probable development was not from the theological use to the secular but instead from the secular use to the theological.

The question of the relative age of the occurrences in the extant sources is interrelated but not identical with the question of the age of the two usages. Solomon's designation as *nagîd* is contained in the SN, which was composed at the beginning of Solomon's reign. As we noted above, there are also reasons to suppose that the designation of Solomon as *nagîd* was not invented by the author of this work but can be traced back to the critical days at the end of David's life, whether David actually did designate Solomon or whether this was only a fabrication of the Solomon party in the interests of propaganda.

The theologization of the title is presupposed by the HDR.[32a] This work was composed in Jerusalem some time before the hostilities between the kingdoms of Judah and Israel came to an end during the reigns of Asa and Baasha. The theologization of the title must have taken place before this, which gives a lower limit for the date of this semantic process. But what of the upper limit? Are there any indications for the *a quo*?

It is often taken for granted that the occurrences of *nagîd* describing the divine election of Saul and David are older than the SN and that the

---

[31] On performative utterances see above all the study by *J.L.Austin* (Philosophical Papers, 1961: 220 ff.). See also *M.Furberg* (Locutionary and Illocutionary Acts. A Main Theme in J.L. Austin's Philosophy, 1963: 187 ff.).

[32] As did in fact Noth (1968: 25) although without reference to 1 R 1,20.

[32a] See the theological use of the title in 1 S 25,30; 2 S 5,2; 6,21; 7,8.

title was actually used during the reigns of these two kings. But is this really evident? – The dating of the HDR to the decades after Solomon's death means that a number of occurrences are found in a work that is later than the SN. 1 S 25,30; 2 S 5,2; 6,21 and 7,8 which denote David as *nagîd* all belong to the HDR. Besides, these occurrences are all found in contexts that betray the intention of the author.[33] One is therefore inclined to conclude that the use of *nagîd* is here due to the author of this work and not to preceding tradition.

The possible evidence for a theological use before the composition of the SN then shrinks considerably. We are left with two texts: 1 S 9,1–10,16 (with the title in 9,16 and 10,1) and 1 S 13,7b-15a (with the title in v. 14). It is impossible to avoid the question as to whether these two texts can carry the burden of proof of the opinion that *nagîd* was used before Solomon's days to denote the divine designation of the king. I am strongly inclined to answer this question in the negative.

In 1 S 13,7 ff. Samuel, in reproach to Saul for his cultic misconduct, announces the appointment of someone else as *nagîd* (v. 14). This passage must then reasonably presuppose Saul's appointment to this rank in 1 S 9,16; 10,1. The composition of 13,7 ff. even led to the inclusion of a secondary redactional link in the text dealing with Samuel's anointing of Saul (10,8). The question of the date of 13,7 ff. is thus directly linked with that of the date of the *nagîd* layer in 9,1–10,16. If a date after a certain point of time, for instance Solomon's designation as *nagîd*, appears to be probable for that layer, the same holds *a fortiori* for 13,7 ff.[33a]

I have already pointed to two notable features of the *nagîd* layer in 9,1 ff. (above ch. 4.5). Saul is furnished with a royal anointing, in spite of the fact that historically he was not anointed king. His dominion is depicted as being of pan-Israelite dimensions, in spite of the fact that he was only king in the full sense of that word over the northern tribes. This, of course, does not conclusively prove but can be taken to indicate a date when anointing was a *sine qua non* for the legitimacy of the king and one when the tensions between North and South made it natural to express claims to pan-Israelite sovereignty. I found a date during the reign of Solomon or during the decades after his death to be consonant with these requirements.

The validity of these considerations can now be tested from another angle. Let us return for a moment to the SN. This is a literary work of considerable length which aims to demonstrate the legitimacy of Solomon. In this work, the title *nagîd* is used once only, and then as a secular term for the one designated by the reigning king (1 R 1,35). There is not a single occurrence of the title as a theological term in this work of history. Only some decades later it plays a role as a key word for divine designation

---

[33] On 1 S 25,28-30 and 2 S 5,1-2 see *Grønbæk* (1971: 174, 248 f.). On 2 S 6,21 and 7,8 see above ch. 2.4.2.3 and ch. 3.
[33a] 1 S 13,13-14 is due to DtrN, see now *Veijola* (1975: 55 ff.).

in the HDR. Now, if one holds that *nagîd* was used as a theological term already before the SN, this literary work assumes the character of an unexplainable parenthesis. Why should the term not be used here? And why is it not used in the episode where Nathan hints at Solomon's position as the beloved one of YHWH, giving him the name Jedidiah (2 S 12,24-25), a passage that clearly points forward to Solomon's future kingship? The situation, depicted in that passage, could very well have been embroidered as the occasion for an outright divine designation as *nagîd*.

There are, theoretically, mainly two different ways of accounting for this. *Either* there must have been some particular reason for the author of the SN not to use *nagîd* in a theological sense that was already an established one, *or* one must conclude that the theological use is to be dated after the SN. Now, one cannot of course deny that our knowledge of the historical situation is highly incomplete. Some circumstance unknown to us may have lead the author to avoid the term. Nevertheless the second possibility deserves particular attention. Taken on its own, the argument from the silence of the SN does not weigh very heavily, but together with other indications that point in the same direction it assumes importance and can provide a stone in the foundation of a historical conclusion that can claim a reasonable degree of probability: that the theological use of *nagîd* is later than the composition of the SN. This conclusion also explains the fact that the term is not used in the "Solomonic" kernel of 2 S ch. 7 (v. 8 is due to the dynastic redaction).

Nathan's auspicious words over the child Solomon betray a theology of election that lends itself to comparison with that in the seer's words to Saul (1 S 9,20) in the original tale of Saul's search for the lost asses before the revision which brought the anointing as *nagîd* into the text. But they cannot be brought into line with the pregnant formulations concerning Saul as *nagîd* in 1 S 9,16; 10,1.

A third approach to the problem is to focus attention on the two occurrences of the secular use of the term. In 1 R 1,35 the word *nagîd* seems to be used for the first time as a title of the heir-designate. Bathsheba asks David *lᵉhăggîd* a successor to the throne. David answers by designating Solomon as *nagîd*. 2 Ch 11,22 gives us the last time that *nagîd* is attested as a term in connection with a king's designation of a son of his as heir-apparent to the throne. This occurrence refers to Rehoboam's designation of Abijah. Now, it seems that there was also later a formal designation of the crown prince (2 Ch 21,1-3). But there the term *nagîd* is not used. If the term in 2 Ch 11,22 has not been introduced by the writer but was in fact used at the act of designation referred to, this suggests that this secular use of *nagîd* became obsolete not long after the designation of Abijah. It is reasonable to connect this inferred disuse of *nagîd* as a term for secular

designation with its increasing use as a theological key word. To the same degree that the theological use with YHWH or his prophet as the acting subject established itself, the use of the term in connection with secular royal designation must have manifested itself as increasingly problematic.

This, of course, does not make it impossible to assume that the word can have been sporadically used as a theological term before Rehoboam's designation of Abijah, especially not in the North, but it makes it difficult to believe that the title had already found wide use in that sense.

There is indeed one northern context of interest here, a context where we would expect to find the title in its theological use but where we look in vain for it, viz. Jeroboam's designation by the prophet Ahijah (1 R 11,29-39). This prophetic designation of the future king is similar to Samuel's designation of Saul as *nagîd* (1 S 9,1–10,16), but the title *nagîd* is not mentioned. On the other hand the term is actually used of Jeroboam but later, in a context that reports his denunciation by the same prophet (1 R 14,7). It seems that the title was not used at the designation proper, but that this moment was later described and interpreted as a designation of Jeroboam as *nagîd*. May we assume that the title was not in use as a theological term at the very beginning of Jeroboam's reign but that the theologization emerged during that very period?

The HDR with its emphatic theological use of the term should be placed after Rehoboam's designation of Abijah. It would be very difficult to place that work of history, which is of Jerusalemite derivation[34], before this secular designation in the capital of Judah. This in turn is well in keeping with the conclusion that the HDR is to be dated to the last decades of the tenth century B.C. (above ch. 2.3).

Let us stop for a moment and draw the net together. From the methodological point of view, the task of the historian is not to illuminate with the help of the sources a historical past, the main features of which are already taken for granted, but rather the reverse: to reconstruct a past that explains as many features and peculiarities of the sources as possible. This is what I have tried to do here.

(1) We started from certain observations concerning an often misunderstood passage (1 R 1,35) and found that this occurrence of *nagîd* is best explained as a case of a secular use of the word in connection with the designation of the heir-apparent to the throne. The case of Abijah (2 Ch 11,22) required the same assumption. This secular use was judged to be the oldest one, providing the basis for a theologization of the term. So far our conclusions can claim a high degree of probability.

(2) Of a more inferential nature are our conclusions concerning the time when the word found use as a theological term. The circumstantial evi-

---

[34] On HDR and Jerusalem see *Grønbæk* (1971: 277 f.).

dence was found to be in favour of the conclusion that this was after the composition of the SN.

a. The word does not seem to have played any role in the "Solomonic" kernel of the prophecy of Nathan.
b. The word is not used as a theological term in the SN.
c. The reworking of the old folk tale in 1 S 9,1–10,16 to comprise Saul's anointing as *nagîd* can hardly be dated prior to the SN.
d. The HDR attests to the theological use of the term. This work is probably to be dated in the last decades of the tenth century.
e. The word seems to still have been used in its secular sense at a date during the reign of Rehoboam (2 Ch 11,22).
f. The term does not occur in the text that describes Ahijah's prophetic designation of Jeroboam (1 R 11,29-39), but it is used *post festum* to denote the sacral status of Jeroboam (1 R 14,7).

The date suggested for the theologization of the term must account for all these observations. There is only one solution that corresponds to this requirement: that it was during the last three or two decades of the tenth century, probably during the reign of Jeroboam I, that the title established itself as a theological term in connection with divine designation. It is to this period of time that our indications converge.

To which extent is the use of the title *nagîd* the result of Dtr elaboration of the sources?[35] – In my opinion the following occurrences are found in Dtr sections: 1 S 13,14;[35a] 1 R 14,7; 16,2;[36] 2 R 20,5. But the question of an underlying tradition is not thereby answered in the negative.

As appears above I hold that the title was actually used of Jeroboam I during his reign. No doubt the traditions of the prophet Ahijah have been handled and to a certain extent also shaped by Dtr circles. On the whole W.Dietrich has made a good case for the conclusion that Ahijah was not mentioned in DtrH and that the sections 1 R 11,29-39 and 14,1-18 were inserted into the Deuteronomistic Historical Work by the prophetic redactor (DtrP).[37] But even so this material probably has a pre-Dtr basis. The circumstance that Saul was given a fictitious prophetic designation as *nagîd* towards the end of the tenth century B.C. is understandable only if prophetic designation played a role within the royal ideology developed in the Northern Kingdom in this period. This suggests that Jeroboam was conceived of as having a prophetic designation. We therefore should not regard the tradition of his prophetic designation by Ahijah as entirely the result of Dtr fiction.[38]

---

[35] Cf. *A.Carlson* (1964: 52-55) who regards *nagîd* as a "Deuteronomic alternative to mælæk" but also assumes a tradition behind (54).
[35a] See *Veijola* (1975: 55 ff.).
[36] On 1 R 14,1-18 see *W.Dietrich* (1972: 10 f., 51 ff., 112 ff.). On 16,1-4 see most recently *Sebass* (VT 25/1975, 178 f.).
[37] Cf. note 36 and on 1 R 11,29-39 *Dietrich* (1972: 15 ff., 54 f.).
[38] I thus dissociate myself from *Noth* (1968: 245 f.). Cf. *Gray* (^{2}1970: 288), who assumes an old kernel in 1 R 11,29-32 and later expansion in v. 33-39.

Over against Veijola's recent attempt to define only the two occurrences of the title in connection with Saul in 1 S 9,16 and 10,1 as contained in old tradition and the rest of the occurrences in Samuel and Kings as Deuteronomistic,[38a] I have concluded that the occurences in 1 S 25,30; 2 S 5,2; 6,21; 7,8 belong to the HDR and are clearly pre-Dtr.[38b] Besides, if these occurrences were Dtr, we would expect to find a number of references to David as *nagîd* in the Dtr framework of the Books of Kings, and we would expect to find occurrences of *nagîd* in Ps 89 and 132 where a strong Dtr influence is to be seen (below ch. 12.1). But this is not the case.

The theological use of the title had its short *floruit* during the last decades of the tenth century B.C. It was then used for Saul (1 S 9,16; 10,1), for David (1 S 25,30; 2 S 5,2; 6,21; 7,8), for Jeroboam (1 R 14,7) and probably also for Baasha (1 R 16,2).

Our demonstration that the title was born out of the womb of the institution of the monarchy means that the idea, adhered to in recent literature on the subject, that the title has a pedigree from the pre-monarchic period must be given up. The title owes its existence to the institution of the monarchy. It was probably used for the first time about the heir-designate during the last days of David (1 R 1,35). It came into vogue as a theological term some decades later. This is why the term is not attested for the pre-monarchic period.

2. *The Place and Purpose of the Theologization*

I shall continue the investigation, keeping the theological use in the focus of attention. I have reached the conclusion that this title underwent a process of theologization some time during the last decades of the tenth century. But where did this happen, in which of the two kingdoms of Israel and Judah? And why did this happen? What was the term designed to express?

The probable answer to the first question is that this semantic process took place in the North. It is difficult to find any particular reason for Judah to subject the title to a theological interpretation; the secular use is also found down to the days of Rehoboam. On the other hand such an interest is easy to point out in the North as we shall soon see. Moreover, the earliest occurrences of the theological use derive from the North (1 S 9,16; 10,1), while the HDR is later than this.[39]

The material even indicates that it was among prophetic circles in the Northern Kingdom that this innovation was conceived of. The prophet

---

[38a] See *Veijola* (1975: 129, 139, 141 and the references in the index p. 163).
[38b] See above ch. 2.4.2.3 and ch. 3.2-3.
[39] The HDR presupposes 1 S 9,1–10,16 in its expanded form with the anointing as *nagîd*, see above ch. 4.5.

Ahijah, who designated Jeroboam, was a man of Northern extraction, to be more exact he was from Shiloh (1 R 11,29). The very sentence in which we find this designation described with the help of the word *nagîd* is formulated as a prophetic oracle: "Thus says the Lord, the God of Israel: 'Because I exalted you from among the people, and made you *nagîd 'ăl 'ămmî yiśra'el* ... " (1 R 14,7). On the prophetic affiliations and northern origin of the text that deals with Saul's designation as *nagîd* (1 S 9,1–10,16) enough has already been said earlier in this study. The whole text issues in a prophetic oracle, pronounced by Samuel to Saul (9,27–10,7). We may infer that the same prophetic circles in the North that fostered theological conceptions expressed by the key word *nagîd* were also responsible for working over the original folk tale in 1 S 9,1–10,16 to comprise Saul's formal call and elevation to the rank of *nagîd*.

The demise of the crown is always a delicate situation, in particular when a *homo novus* such as Jeroboam takes his seat on the throne. Jeroboam's claim to political legitimacy could not be based on heredity, as was the case with Solomon and Rehoboam. Instead, his claims were justified by reference to divine designation through the prophet Ahijah (1 R 11,29-39). If Solomon and Rehoboam could base their claims to the throne on dynastic rights, Jeroboam could base his claim on the divine word. We here see the dynastic and charismatic principles at work in Judah and Israel respectively. In both contexts we find the word *nagîd* used as a pregnant term for designation. In Judah, the king could elevate one of his sons to the status of heir-designate, *nagîd*. Prophetic circles in Northern Israel introduced the idea that YHWH, the Supreme King, could take one of His own people and designate him *nagîd*. It is tempting to see in the choice of this terminology for divine designation a tacit criticism of the secular institution of a human king designating his successor: God Himself and no one else was to decide who was to sit on the throne. The theological use of the term is thus a powerful expression of a theocratic ideal of kingship.[40]

The application of the title to Saul (1 S 9,16; 10,1) fits in with this political situation. This was probably a secondary development after the title had already been used for Jeroboam. To give Saul the same prophetic designation as *nagîd* created a theological continuity between two Northern kings who were not dynastically connected.

Above all, Jeroboam was thereby brought into line with the very first king of the tribes of Israel and Judah. Thus the reigns of David and Solomon constituted a parenthesis between two divine designations as *nagîd*, Saul's and Jeroboam's, so that the whole period between Saul and Jeroboam assumed the character of an ideological interlude. I therefore hold that the

---

[40] Cf. *E. Rosenthal* (JJS 9/1958, 8).

nagîd layer in 1 S 9,1–10,16 has grown out of the political situation that arose after Solomon's death and should be interpreted as an etiological justification of an actual historical use of the title *nagîd* for Jeroboam.

Each of the two different uses can then be linked with a particular *Sitz im Leben*. The secular use was fostered by court circles in Judah. Through the process of what I should like to call linguistic confiscation the term was then adopted by the northern tribes. It was there used in a new sense, as a theological key word for divine designation. This semantic process took place among prophetic circles. We are thus concerned with a piece of dynamic semantic history that has a continuation: the resumption of the use of the title by Judah. The claims expressed by the supporters of the new royal house in the North could not be left unchallenged.

This is indicated by the occurrences in the HDR, where the title has a very important role. Here the title is used in passages that in some way relate to David's future kingship:

1 S 25,30: Abigail uses the term in connection with David.
2 S 5,2: The tribes of Israel refer to a divine oracle that David was to become *nagîd*:
"And the Lord said to you, 'You shall be shepherd of my people Israel, and you shall be *nagîd* over Israel'."
2 S 6,21: David to Michal concerning his elevation as *nagîd*.
2 S 7,8: A divine oracle, pronounced by Nathan to David:
"Thus says the Lord of hosts, I took you from the pasture, from following the sheep, that you should be *nagîd* over my people, over Israel."

It is not difficult to see that here there is something that connects with the prophetic connotations of the title as used in the North. But at the same time one must conclude that Judah could not base its counterclaims on behalf of David (and his house) on the solid bedrock of an actual historical prophetic designation of David.

My preceding analysis of the prophecy of Nathan demonstrates that the divine oracle, pronounced by Nathan, that David should be *nagîd* (v. 8), belongs to the later interpretation of the original oracle. It is highly improbable that Nathan ever pronounced such an oracle to David about his status as *nagîd*. If this had been the case one would have to ask why this oracle had been appended secondarily to an oracle that originally referred to Solomon. It would no doubt have made an excellent topic for a literary representation of its own. And besides, why in that case did Nathan not pronounce a similar *nagîd* oracle to Solomon in 2 S 12,24-25, if he had done this in the case of David?

That the other occurrences of the term in the HDR are dependent on

the prophecy of Nathan has been demonstrated by L.Schmidt in a recent investigation.[41] It is thus impossible to find in this work of history mention of an actual historical occasion when David received prophetic designation as *nagîd*. One can hardly escape the conclusion that the use of *nagîd* is here due to a fiction that in turn is necessitated by the need to counterbalance the claims raised in the North.[42]

The term was excellently suitable for that purpose. Just as it had been used in the North to establish a continuity between two historically unconnected persons, viz. Jeroboam and Saul, so it was used in a similar way in Judah to establish a link between Saul and David.

There are two points to be made here. First, the continuity between Saul and Jeroboam, suggested by the use of the title in connection with them, was broken when the title was transferred from Saul to David. The application of the term to David was linked with the idea of the rejection of Saul and these two phenomena are mentioned together in two texts (2 S 6,21; 7,8.15).[43] At the date of the composition of the HDR (after Solomon's death), this implied that no king of Northern Israel could claim to have inherited the sceptre of Saul since Saul's sacral status had been transferred to David.[44] Secondly, when in this way the HDR made David the legitimate heir of Saul, David was depicted as "heir-apparent to the throne" of a kingdom comprising both Israel and Judah.[45] We here touch upon the *Tendenz* of the HDR to justify the claims of Jerusalem to sovereignty over the northern tribes as well.

---

[41] *L.Schmidt* (1970: 120 ff.). This is a most valuable part of Schmidt's study. *Grønbæk* concluded that 1 S 25,28-30 and 2 S 5,1-2 betray the intention of the author of the HDR (1971: 174, 249), but he did not discuss 2 S ch. 7 in this connection.

[42] That 1 S 13,14 does not offer a historical "point of Archimedes" so that one could find here an actual historical situation for a designation of David as *nagîd* is, I think, clear from the fact that the HDR nowhere refers to 1 S 13,7b-15a.

[43] In connection with this one should also note that the author of the HDR tried to stress that David did not usurp Jonathan's rights to the crown. Jonathan is said to have resigned from his status as heir apparent of his own free will. He transferred his position to David (1 S 18,3-4; 23,17; see above ch. 2.3). From what has already been said on the origin and development of the term *nagîd*, it is evident that this term could also be used to give further emphasis to this though: that David and no one else was heir-apparent to the throne of Saul, and this not by human will but by divine regulation.

[44] A problem connected with this is why the HDR does not stress the point that Benjamin joined Judah after Solomon's death, a fact that in itself could be adduced against the northern idea of a continuity between the Benjaminite Saul and the Ephraimite Jeroboam. – On Benjamin after Solomon's death, see *Schunck* (1963: 139-53). *Debus* (1967: 15-17) does not, I think, produce convincing evidence for the opinion that Benjamin was divided between Israel and Judah.

[45] That is, Saul's dominion did not historically include Judah. It was depicted in the HDR as doing so in order to motivate that David, as the successor of Saul, became king over "all Israel", so that thereby this and nothing less could be claimed for themselves by the Davidides after the dissolution of the personal union. See excursus no 1.

This explains one remarkable feature of the sources. While there is no mention of the term *nagîd* in connection with David's investiture as king over Judah (2 S 2,1-4), a divine oracle saying that David would be *nagîd* over Israel is quoted by "all the tribes of Israel" to motivate David's investiture over the northern tribes (2 S 5,1-3). This peculiar feature of the distribution of the word certainly arises from the fact that the term played its part in the war of propaganda between Judah and Israel after Solomon's death and was used in the HDR just to motivate the claims of Judah against those of the northern tribes.

4. Further Semantic Aspects: Syntagmatic and Paradigmatic Relations

My theory is that the word *nagîd* is a derivative of the root *n-g-d*, also found in *higgîd*, and is to be analysed as a Qal passive participle. I came to this conclusion after observing a previously overlooked connection between Bathsheba's request (1 R 1,20) and David's designation of Solomon (v. 35). The etymology[46] of the word is thereby clarified. A further investigation of the semantic relations of the word follows.

Modern linguistics tends to give priority to a relational definition of "meaning".[47] For our present purpose it is sufficient to point out that the meaning of any given word should be understood as "the meaning of the choice of that word in relation to other words in the same language at the same time".[48] A word has its place in *a system of relationships* which it contracts with other words in the vocabulary.

These relations are of two different kinds, syntagmatic and paradigmatic. The terminology can conveniently be defined as follows:

Syntagmatic relations are relations between a given word and other words which are used in contiguity with it, in for instance the same sentence.

Paradigmatic relations are relations of similarity or opposition with other words which might have been chosen in place of the word which *was* chosen.[49]

The following is a selective discussion insofar as I only intend to include some of the more outstanding semantic relationships. It should also be noted that this procedure will serve to test the validity of my general solu-

---

[46] On the term "etymology" and its varied use see *Barr* (OTS 19/1974, 1-28). I here use the term in the sense "historical tracing within an observable development" (see Barr p. 7 ff.) and not in the sense of "prehistoric reconstruction".

[47] See in particular *S.Ullmann* (1957: 65 ff.), *J.Lyons* (1971: 427 f. and passim) and *H.Geckeler* (1971: 41-83).

[48] I here quote *Barr* (1973: 122).

[49] On paradigmatic and syntagmatic relations see for instance *Lyons* (1971: 70-81; 428 f.). The formulations above are borrowed from *Barr* (1973: 122).

tion. The sign of a sound theory is that it solves more problems than it raises. If it can be shown that the theory I have advanced regarding the origin of *nagîd* solves problems connected with the syntagmatic and paradigmatic relations of the word this will further support the hypothesis.

A survey of the extant sources shows that the word *nagîd* appears in syntagmatic solidarity in particular with *ʿăm*. The construction *nagîd ʿăl ʿăm YHWH* is well known. If it could be demonstrated that the meaning of *ʿăm* in this formula is "tribal militia" ("Heerbann")[50] this would be a serious challenge to my hypothesis. However, this is not so. As N.Lohfink[51] has recently shown, it can be argued that *ʿăm* here means "relatives" and denotes Israel as the family of YHWH. This conclusion is based on the following observations. The word *ʿăm* originally meant "uncle" and then "the family connections of a man".[52] Now, we once find *nagîd* as *nagîd* over the *năḥᵃlā* of YHWH (1 S 10,1). In the same passage the more usual construction *nagîd ʿăl ʿăm (YHWH)* also occurs (9,16; 10,1 LXX). This indicates that *ʿăm* has here retained its original connotations of "family" since *năḥᵃlā* means "patrimony", "family inheritance in land"[53]. This interpretation of the formula also explains why later *ʿăm YHWH* often occurs together with a statement describing the relation between YHWH and Israel as that of father and son. This combination of motifs is an old one. It occurs in Nu 21,29 where the *ʿăm* of the god Chemosh is described as his sons and daughters.

These are the observations made by Lohfink. His analysis receives support from my own investigation which has made it probable that the title *nagîd* was originally used as a term for the heir-apparent designated by the reigning king. The basis of selection was here the *royal family* as it was one of the princes that was designated *nagîd*.[54] Similarly, when YHWH chose someone to be *nagîd* He took him from among the people, who were conceived of as being YHWH's royal family, elevating him above His other "sons".

That the author of the HDR lets "all the tribes of Israel" say to David that they are his "bone and flesh" and in the same breath speak of him as *nagîd* over Israel (2 S 5,1-2) agrees perfectly with this. As *nagîd* over

---

[50] So L.Schmidt (1970: 154). Similarly W.Richter (BZ 9/1965, 77). – It is true that *ʿăm* can have the sense "the militia of YHWH" (Jud 5,13 and possibly 2 S 1,12), but this sense soon became obsolete as was demonstrated by N.Lohfink (in Probleme Biblischer Theologie, 1971: 281 ff.; 294).

[51] See N.Lohfink (op. cit. 284 ff.).

[52] See GBL (p. 597) and especially Rost (1934: 142 f.) who argues on the basis of Lv 21,1 ff. See also Speiser (1967: 160 ff.).

[53] On this word see F.Horst (1961: 134-152). – Lohfink (op. cit. 283 f.) assumes that we are concerned with a split up phrase and that the formula was originally *nagîd ʿăl ʿăm YHWH wᵉʿăl năḥᵃlatô* (cf. 1 S 9,16; 10,1 according to the LXX).

[54] 1 R 1,35; 2 Ch 11,22. Note the formulation *nagîd bᵉʾæḥâw* in the latter text.

the people of YHWH David stands in a consanguineous, fraternal relation with the Northern Israelites. This also accounts for the syntagmatic relation between *nagîd*, *be'æḥâw* and *hăbbekorā* in 1 Ch 5,2.

We can thus discern three stages in the development of the *nagîd* formula. (a) The formulation in 1 R 1,35 is an example of the original secular use of the term, and as one might expect the title is here followed by a phrase reflecting the constitutional make-up of David's kingdom: Solomon is *nagîd* over Israel and Judah. (b) In connection with the theologization of the title it was placed in connection with *'ăm YHWH*, "the family of YHWH". This phrase was explained as "Israel" (1 S 9,16; 10,1 LXX; 2 S 6,21; 7,8).[55] (c) Later the element *'ăm* could be dropped so that only "Israel" remained (1 S 25,30; cf. 2 S 5,2).

We shall now turn to paradigmatic relations, that is, relations of similarity or opposition with other words which could have been chosen instead of the word that actually was chosen. I shall restrict myself to two points here. As was shown in a preceding chapter, it is necessary to assume two different stages in the development of the prophecy of Nathan (2 S ch. 7): an original kernel from the days of Solomon was made the subject of a later interpretation, which had the legitimation of the Davidic dynasty as its *skopos*. The mention of *nagîd* in v. 8 belongs to the interpretative layer. One can now ask whether the original kernel contained some basic term that could function as a natural point of departure for describing David as *nagîd*. The answer is simple. The term *nagîd* corresponds to the term *ben* in the kernel (v. 14). From what has been said this paradigmatic relation between *nagîd* and *ben* is natural in the sense that it can be understood as arising out of the original connotations of the title. He who became *nagîd* was of course one of the sons of the king. The word *nagîd* is a more precise specification of *ben*. David is not only the "son". He is more: the one chosen by God to inherit the throne of Saul. (See also ch. 12.2.2.2.)

The other point is that of Ps 89, a text that clearly echoes the prophecy of Nathan but where we must look in vain for the term *nagîd*. This surprising lacuna in the distribution of the word can now be accounted for. In Ps 89 the word *bekôr* (v. 28) has taken the place of *nagîd* in the prophecy of Nathan, the reason probably being that *nagîd* was beginning to lose its old connotation of "the one especially elected by God from all Israel, His royal family". This process can perhaps be seen in the fact that the formula *nagîd 'ăl 'ămmî ('ăl) yiśra'el*[56] could drop the element *'ăm*.[57]

It is probably this development that is responsible for the title not being used in connection with the prophetic designation of Jehu (2 R 9,1-13).

---

[55] It is possible that "Israel" is a later interpretative element, see W.Richter (BZ 9/1965, 77).
[56] Found in 1 S 9,16; 10,1 (LXX); 2 S 7,8; 1 R 14,7; 16,2; 1 Ch 11,2; 17,7.
[57] 1 S 25,30; 2 S 5,2

That this designation was of the same prophetic character as the designations of Jeroboam and Saul is seen in the fact that the representative of YHWH was a prophet. There is also a terminological peculiarity insofar as Jehu is made king over *'ăm YHWH* (v. 6). Thus a relic of the *nagîd* formula, developed in prophetic circles in Northern Israel, is also retained in this prophetic designation of a king. That the title itself does not occur here is probably the result of a semantic development that had led to a loss of its original connotations.

This new interpretation of the designation as *nagîd*, and of the linguistic problems raised by the title, has made it possible to find a satisfactory explanation for most of the peculiarities in the use of the title in the extant sources (the absence of the term in 1 S 16,1-13 will be discussed below). On the basis of an assessment of the date, nature and purpose of the sources I studied the use of the word *nagîd* during the early monarchy. The general reconstruction of the development of the title and its special function in political propaganda during the early monarchy is highly plausible. The fact that the theory accounts for the more important semantic relations of the word further supports the hypothesis.

5. The Problem of Earlier Conceptions of Divine Designation

That there was no divine designation as *nagîd* in the days of Saul, David or Solomon is, I believe, an inescapable conclusion from our investigation so far. Still less was there a divine designation as *nagîd* before the days of the monarchy, as has sometimes been suggested. The theologization of the title occurred in the North, in the days of Jeroboam I. This makes it imperative to try to go beyond this period and look for earlier conceptions of divine election of the king. Is it possible to find *traditions* that attest to the existence of such conceptions before the period when the idea of divine designation as *nagîd* came into vogue?

A case that immediately presents itself is 1 S 10,17-27, a passage which relates that Saul received his popular acclamation after his divine election had been established by lot. The question then is whether this tradition of divine election by lot is earlier or later than the concept of a divine designation as *nagîd*? Since Saul is also said to have a designation of the latter type (1 S 9,1–10,16) it is advisable to try to establish the date of the tradition found in 10,17-27 in relation to the tradition of Saul as *nagîd*.

If we simply place the two passages side by side the question of the relative ages of their respective traditions is impossible to answer. There is however one way out of this dilemma. When 1 S 16,1-13 (Samuel's anointing of David) is included the possibility of establishing a chronological sequence offers itself. In an unexpected manner this passage, in itself quite proble-

matic, provides the key to our problem at this point. The mutual relation of the two other traditions can be determined through an analysis of their relations to 16,1-13. We are thus faced with a case of traditio-historical trigonometry.

At first sight 1 S 16,1-13 seem to be later than and even dependent on 1 S 9,1-10,16.[57a] In support of this Grønbæk[58] adduced that (a) 1 S 16,1-13 are part of the HDR and seem to be from the hand of the author of this work; since the HDR as a whole is clearly later than 9,1-10,16 this would also hold for 16,1-13; (b) the passage under consideration seems to contain an unspoken criticism of the reference to Saul's imposing stature in 9,2 when God's rejection of Eliab is motivated by the divine recommendation to Samuel:

> Do not look on his appearance or on the height of his stature, because I have rejected him; for the Lord sees not as man sees; man looks on the outward appearance, but the Lord looks on the heart. (1 S 16,7)

Such a supposition is, however, open to objections. First, there are certain features found in 9,1 ff. that we should expect to recur in 16,1 ff. if Grønbæk's theory was correct. For instance, one would expect the emphasis in 16,1 ff. to be on the prophetic features of Samuel which is not the case. One would also expect to find the *Berufungsschema*, which has such an important role in 9,1 ff. Above all there is one circumstance that creates a serious problem, namely that Samuel does not anoint David *nagîd*, while Saul's anointing as *nagîd* is the very climax of 9,1 ff. This remarkable gap in the distribution of the term must be accounted for in some way or other. Grønbæk's theory does not solve this problem.

Secondly, if 16,1-13 had been influenced by 9,1-10,16 we should not expect to find a designation through a process of gradual elimination in this passage, but rather a direct divine announcement stating who was the elect one (cf. 9,15-16.27 ff.).

Thirdly, it is true that Eliab is something of a "new Saul", so that in his rejection Saul is denounced in effigy.[58a] It is, however, important to note that 16,7 need not necessarily contain a criticism of 9,2. It can just as well be directed against the tradition in 10,17-27 where Saul's stature is emphasized in v. 23.[59]

We must then ask: is any connection indicated between 10,17-27 and 16,1-13, and if so where does it lie? It is true that Samuel is depicted as the

---

[57a] In the following I speak of 1 S 9,1-10,16 as it stands out *after* the new *skopos* of Saul's anointing as *nagîd* had put its stamp on the narrative but before the etiology of the *mašal* (10,10-13) had been added.
[58] *Grønbæk* (1971: 68-76, esp. p. 72-74).
[58a] See below, note 64.
[59] It is possible that 9,2 is due to 10,23b. See *W.Richter* (1970: 25 with note 48).

last saviour in 10,17 ff. (above ch. 5.3.1), which is not the case in 16, 1 ff. Nevertheless, there are a number of similarities between these two traditions. In 16,1 ff. Samuel arranges a sacrifice and thereby takes on a priestly character reminiscent of 10,17 ff., where he apparently arranges not only the casting of lots conforming to the alternative lay procedure but even a priestly *ša'ăl*-consultation.[60] Still more specific is the circumstance that 16,1 ff. also mention a procedure that is very *similar* to that in 10,17 ff. though *differing* markedly from the designation through a performative prophetic oracle and simultaneous anointing in 9,1 ff. (see 9,27–10,7). In the tradition of David's election we are faced with something that comes close to casting lots to decide between simple alternatives ("yes" or "no"). Through a process of elimination David is finally revealed as the chosen one of God. The words about God's "finding" of David in Ps 89,21 probably refer to this procedure in 1 S 16,1-13. Note also that 10,17-27 have the established terminology for this procedure (*q-r-b* and *l-k-d*),[61] whereas this is not so in 16,1 ff.

A striking similarity is also that both Saul and David are absent at a certain point in the narrative and have to be brought to the scene of action. Saul had hidden himself among the baggage, while David was keeping the sheep. The motif of the humility of the elected one of YHWH thus manifests itself in a similar manner in both traditions.

Here we can compare 16,11 (*hᵃtămmû hănnᵉ'arîm*, "Is this the full number of the young men?"[62]) with 10,22 (*hᵃba' 'ôd hᵃlom 'îš*, "Is there yet a man to come hither?"[62a]). Both sentences comprise a question: can the procedure be closed or is there still someone missing?

Another similarity between the two traditions is that both use the term *mælæk* (10,24b; 16,1b) but not *nagîd* as do 9,16 and 10,1. Also, the word *baḥăr* has a central position in both cases denoting God's election of the king (10,24; 16,8 ff.) whereas this verb does not occur in 9,1 ff.

If we add to this the above observation that 16,7 ("do not look on his appearance") provides yet another point of contact, although one of opposites (cf. 10,23), the conclusion that these two traditions contain similarities that are more than casual is inevitable. Since it is impossible to find

---

[60] See below, note 61. Note also that the LXX in 1 S 10,22 expressly states that Samuel carried out this consultation. – It is true that there are priestly features in the figure of Samuel in 1 S 9,1–10,16 (the sacrificial meal), but these features are there subordinate to the prophetic ones.

[61] See Jos 7,14-18 and 1 S 14,40-42. The terminology for the two types of lot casting, the alternative lay-type and the priestly Urim consultation, has been studied by *Lindblom* (VT 12/1962, 164-78).

[62] My own translation.

[62a] Translation after RSV the note.

a common denominator for the two traditions[63] we must infer that these similarities are due to the influence of one tradition on the other. The direction of this influence is clear from the fact that the tradition concerning David is in opposition to 10,17-27. The motivation in 16,7 for the "rejection"[64] of Eliab is directed against the mention of Saul's *eloquentia corporis* in the tradition of his divine election:

> Then they ran and fetched him from there [i.e. the baggage]; and when he stood among the people, he was taller than any of the people from his shoulders upwards. (1 S 10,23)

Just as the "anti-thesis" presupposes the "thesis" so 16,7 presupposes 10,23. That is, the tradition in 16,1-13 is later than that in 10,17-27. One could perhaps add here that the emphasis in 16,1 ff. on the initiative of YHWH could contain an unspoken criticism of the more "synergistic" procedure in 10,17 ff. of the popular acclamation of king.[65]

We can therefore conclude that the tradition in 10,17-27 is older than that in 16,1-13 and has helped to shape it. Judaean tradition in 16,1 ff. has adopted ideas from northern tradition in 10,17 ff.

Having arrived at this point in the analysis it is natural to ask for the relation between the traditions in 16,1-13 and 9,1–10,16. The importance of this is due to the fact that if 16,1 ff. should prove to be older than 9,1 ff. this would *a fortiori* also hold good for 10,17-27, which are older than 16,1 ff. That is to say 10,17 ff. would contain conceptions of the divine election of the king that would without doubt precede the concept of a divine designation as *nagîd*.

That the traditions of the anointing of Saul and David by Samuel are connected has long been admitted. So far, however, research has not been able to give a convincing answer to the question of a possible dependency. The hypothesis that 16,1 ff. is dependent on 9,1 ff. raises difficulties.[66] On the other hand the hitherto overlooked possibility that the tradition of the anointing of David should actually have influenced the tradition of the anointing of Saul in 9,1 ff. provides us with a theory that explains a number of remarkable features in the sources.

---

[63] The possibility that both texts are due to actual history (that Samuel really designated both Saul and David) can be ruled out. On 1 S 10,17-27 see above ch. 5.3 and on 16,1-13 see below ch. 10.3.

[64] Note the use of *ma'ăs* in 16,7. God's treatment of Eliab is more than "non-election". It amounts to rejection. Note that Eliab here appears in the role of a new Saul.

[65] This all the more if I am right in my conclusion (ch. 7.1.1) that the verb *ra'ā* in both 16,1 and 10,24 is to be taken in the sense of Germ. "aussehen" ("choose"). If so, there is a stress in 16,1 on God as the subject of this verb compared with the people as the subject in 10,24.

[66] This solution, recently suggested by *Grønbæk* (1971: 68-76), was criticized above.

Both traditions are about an anointing by Samuel. In 16,13 this anointing is directly linked with the coming of the Spirit over David. It is clear from 10,1-9 that the hand that formed the tradition of the anointing of Saul was at pains to establish the same connection in this case. The three signs of the original tale made this difficult: according to 10,5 f. Saul would receive the Spirit later, when he had returned to Gibeah. The desired contiguity of anointing and Spirit was supplied by 10,9a, though at the cost of being contradictory to the original account found in 10,5 f. According to 10,9a Saul's heart was "turned" while he was still with Samuel. The fact that this feature was introduced though admitting of a contradiction indicates that the contiguity of anointing and Spirit from 16,13 was present in the mind that shaped the formulations about Saul.

The motifs of the beauty and humility of the elect one, known from 10,17 ff. and 16,1 ff., are also found in 9,1 ff. (see 9,2 and 9,21). The sacrificial feast in 9,1 ff. has taken on more spectacular proportions than in 16,1 ff. and appears as something in the style of a royal banquet.

One prominent feature of the two earlier traditions has been dropped, viz. the procedure of elimination through lot-casting. In 1 S 9,1 ff. something new has come instead. Here Samuel's role is that of the prophet, and the fact that Saul is the chosen one is made known to him in a revelation before Saul comes to the town (9,15 f.) and is disclosed to Saul in a direct prophetic oracle (9,27 – 10,7). The *Berufungsschema* is imposed on the old narrative of Saul's search for the asses. And most important, Saul is designated *nagîd* over the people of God.

Here we have the explanation of the remarkable fact that 16,1-13 form a lacuna in the distribution of the word *nagîd* in the extant sources. This passage was not composed by the author of the HDR. The tradition of Samuel's anointing of David had an independent existence before it was included in this work.[67] It is even older than the *nagîd* layer in 9,1 – 10,16. It was formed before the theologization of the term *nagîd* had taken place. The implications of this for the understanding of 16,1-13 will be pursued in the chapter on the royal anointing.

We are now in a position to answer the question of whether the tradition of Saul's divine election through lot-casting is older or later than the tradition of his anointing as *nagîd*. The relative chronology of the traditions contained in the three passages involved in this discussion has been established simply through the application of a classic logical principle. What has so far been said can be summarized in two propositions and a conclusion:

---

[67] Contra *Grønbæk* (1971: 74). – *Stoebe* (VT 7/1957, 365) rightly saw that the two texts 1 S 9,1 – 10,16 and 16,1-13 have something in common, but he did not pursue the question and mistook the difference in terminology (*nagîd – mælæk*) to mean that there was no direct connection between them.

(a) The tradition in 10,17-27 is older than that in 16,1-13.
(b) The tradition in 16,1-13 is older than that in 9,1 – 10,16.
(c) Thus the tradition in 10,17-27 is older than that in 9,1 – 10,16.

For the convenience of the reader, the points of similarity and difference between the three passages that have been discussed are summarized here:

1 S 10,17-27	*1 S 16,1-13*	*1 S 9,1 – 10,16*
Samuel and a priestly Urim consultation	Samuel as priest	Samuel as priest and prophet
Lot-casting v. 19b-21 Urim consultation v. 22	Lot-casting	
"Is there yet a man to come hither?" v. 22	"Is this the full number of the young men?" v. 11	
Saul's stature v. 23	David's beauty v. 12 Polemics against Saul's beauty v. 7	Saul's stature 9,2
Humbleness: Saul hides himself among the baggage v. 22	Humbleness: David is keeping the sheep v. 11	Humbleness: Saul's protest 9,21
The verb *baḥăr* v. 24 The noun *mælæk* v. 24	The verb *baḥăr* v. 8 ff. The noun *mælæk* v. 1	
	Samuel anoints David v. 13	Samuel anoints Saul 10,1
	Immediate endowment with the Spirit v. 13	Immediate "turn" of Saul's heart 10,9
	Sacrificial meal v. 2 ff.	Sacrificial meal depicted as a royal banquet 9,12-13.22 ff.
		Berufungsschema and *nagîd*

6. Saul's Designation in 1 S 10,17-27

The preceding analysis has led to the conclusion that 1 S 10,17-27 contain the oldest tradition of a royal designation in ancient Israel. Traces of a Dtr hand are found in v. 18-19a.[68] Likewise, v. 26-27 are also redactional although of an earlier, pre-Dtr date.[69]

The ancient kernel relates two different procedures.[70] First we hear

---

[68] Cf. *Noth* (ÜSt p. 57 f.) and *Boecker* (1969: 35-44).
[69] See above ch. 2.1 and 2.3.
[70] These two procedures can be distinguished on the basis of the terminology. The lay procedure uses the terms *qarăb* and *lakăd*, while a key term in connection with the priestly Urim oracle is *ša'al b^{e}YHWH*. On these two types see especially *Lindblom* (VT 12/1962, 164-178). On the *ša'ăl*-consultation see also *Westermann* (KuD 6/1960, 10 ff.). As for 1 S 10,22 I find it hard to agree with *Lindblom* (p. 165 note 1) who assumes that here a seer or cult prophet is speaking on behalf of YHWH. It is much more natural to take the divine answer to be mediated by the Urim oracle, so most recently *B.Johnson* (ASTI 9/1973, 25).

(19b-21) that Samuel arranged for lot-casting according to the alternative lay procedure, and that Saul was taken by lot. Then a priestly Urim consultation gave the answer that Saul was to be found among the baggage (v. 22). When he was brought before Samuel it is said that he stood out from the rest of the people by reason of his exceptional height (v. 23).

Two things are remarkable in the passage as it now stands. First, in v. 21b the chosen man is nowhere to be found. This does not seem to harmonize with what was said earlier, since we must assume that the men of the family of the Matrites were "brought near" *in figura*.[71] Secondly, v. 22 ("Is there yet a man to come hither?") is strangely unrelated to the context.

A well-known attempt to solve these problems is that made by Eissfeldt who assumes that two different traditions of Saul's divine designation have been intertwined. Unlike the designation through the alternative lot procedure in 19b-21, a reminiscence of an account in which the divine oracle pointed out as the future king the man who stood head and shoulders above the rest of the people is to be assumed in v. 22 f. When no one appeared to fulfil this requirement the people asked the question in v. 22: "Is there yet a man to come hither?" Then would come the reference to the baggage, which enabled the people to find Saul.[72] This ingenious hypothesis has been accepted by a number of scholars and was further developed by Boecker who assumes that the passage about the lot procedure (19b-21) is a Deuteronomistic interpretation of the consultation of the Urim oracle in v. 22.[73]

Nevertheless, I hold that the possibility and probability of a wholly different understanding of the crucial v. 22 can be demonstrated. Although textual emendation runs the risk of developing into a science where the consonants count for little and the vowels for nothing, I think that a good case can be made for the following restoration:

MT:	הֲבָא עוֹד הֲלֹם אִישׁ
LXX (B)	Εἰ ἔρχεται ὁ ἀνὴρ ἐνταῦθα
reconstruction:	הָבָה עוֹד הֲלֹם הָאִישׁ

The MT is generally taken to mean: "Is there yet a man to come hither?" In spite of two minor variations the LXX attests to the same general comprehension of the meaning of the utterance. The text as it is reconstructed above should be rendered: "Oh, bring the man here again!"

---

[71] So *Hertzberg* (1964: 88).

[72] *Eissfeldt* (1931: 7).

[73] *Boecker* (1969: 44-48), cf. already *Noth* (ÜSt p. 58). Eissfeldt's analysis was also accepted in its main outlines by among others *Hylander* (1932: 126 f.). *Hertzberg* (1964: 88) and *Seebass* (ZAW 77/1965, 288 note 9). – For critical remarks on Eissfeldt's theory see *Budde* OLZ 34/1931, 1059 f.) and *Stoebe* (1973: 217 f.).

(a) An original *habā* (*hbh*) was mistaken for *hᵃba'* (*hb'*). We are probably concerned here with an early *Hörfehler* during the oral stage of transmission.[74] If, as I hold, the tradition of Saul's divine election by lot contributed to form the tradition contained in 1 S 16,1-13, it could well be that the latter tradition presupposes the former in its slightly distorted form represented by the MT. An indication of this is perhaps to be found in 16,11 (see above). The use of this verb as found in the present verse is not an isolated case. In one other passage the word is also construed with *hᵃlom* (Jud 20,7). And on one other occasion we find the word used in connection with an oracular consultation, viz. in 1 S 14,41: *habā tamîm*, "give a true decision"[74a].

(b) The word *'ôd* need not necessarily mean "besides", "yet". It can also be translated as "again".[75]

(c) The reading *ha'îš* (instead of *'îš*, MT) is attested in the LXX, the Targum and the Peshitta.

Thus the crucial words of v. 22 appear as an integral part of the context. The tradition relates the following course of events: (1) Samuel arranged for lot-casting. (2) When Saul, who was present *in figura* at this procedure, was taken by lot he immediately disappeared and hid himself among the baggage. (3) The problem of where he had hidden himself could not be solved by means of the alternative lot-casting procedure. Instead, a consultation of the divine Urim oracle was arranged, which probably answered by means of some alphabetic device which had to be interpreted by a priest.[76] The crucial part of v. 22 contains the prayer to God to reveal Saul's hiding place: "Oh, bring the man here again!" This connects with the preceding part of the text. It is a natural request under the circumstances. It also connects with what follows: "Behold, he has hidden himself among the baggage" (v. 23). This interpretation helps us see the original unity of the text: the question and the answer were congruent. It is thus wholly unnecessary to assume that two different accounts of Saul's divine designation have been secondarily intertwined.

Finally some words about the use of *bahār* to denote divine designation. Saul is described in 1 S 10,24 as *'ᵃšær bahăr bô YHWH*. It is reasonable

---

[74] Our case has probably nothing to do with the use of *aleph* as *mater lectionis* for *ā*. On this use of *aleph* see *Cross–Freedman* (1952: 69, 33 f., 59).

[74a] *Lindblom's* translation (VT 12/1962, 173). It is the merit of Lindblom to have made probable (a) that the short text of the MT is to be preferred to that of the LXX in 1 S 14,41 and (b) that the lot-casting in 14,38-42 is of the civil type performed by the laity, while that in v. 36f. is of the priestly type (p. 172-177). One can thus note that the oracular consultations in 1 S 10,22 and 14,41 are of different types, but this does not seem to affect the interpretation of 1 S 10,22 given above.

[75] Gn 18,29; 2 S 12,23; Jer 3,1; Job 14,7.

[76] On this see *E.Robertson* (VT 14/1964, 67-74) and *B.Johnson* (ASTI 9/1973, 23-29).

to suppose that from the very beginning of the monarchy the king was in some way or other regarded as one chosen by God, even if this is not stated explicitly in one of the oldest traditions (1 S 11,1 ff.). Even in the texts from the tenth century B.C. we meet the verb *baḥăr* used in this sense. The author of the HDR speaks of David as chosen by God (2 S 6,21). Still earlier is an occurrence in the SN (2 S 16,18)[77]. The tradition of Samuel's anointing of David states emphatically that God has chosen the king (1 S 16,8-10). This tradition is to be dated still earlier than the composition of the HDR as we have just seen. In my opinion it may well be from the days of Solomon. Earlier again is the statement about Saul's divine election in 1 S 10,24.[78] Thus, 1 S 10,24; 2 S 16,18 and 1 S 16,8-10 seem to be the earliest occurrences in the extant sources of *baḥăr* for the divine election of the king.[79]

Conclusion. – Apart from some Dtr accretions 1 S 10,17-27 contain a single tradition of Saul's divine designation. There is no reason to assume an echo of a tradition of a divine oracle referring to the height of the chosen one. A new suggestion for the reading of v. 22 makes it probable that the lot-casting according to the civil lay procedure and the Urim consultation are two subsequent steps in a continuous series of proceedings.

Summary

One of the conclusions reached in ch. 5 was that the conception of the divine election of the king had undergone a development. In this chapter we have discussed the most distinctive form of this idea, i.e. the conception of a formal divine designation in advance and the use of the title *nagîd* to denote the king as set apart by God for this office.

(1) There is no scholarly agreement of opinion on the linguistic interpretation of the title *nagîd*. The observation of a connection between 1 R 1,20, where David is asked to proclaim (*leḥăggîd*) a successor, and 1 R 1,35 where Solomon is proclaimed *nagîd*, makes it probable that the word is to be understood as a Qal passive participle of the common root *n-g-d*. The sense of the term is then "the one proclaimed", "the one designated".

---

[77] On 2 S 16,18 see the important remarks by *L.Schmidt* (1970: 180f.), who concludes that the statement is not due to the author of the Succession Narrative but to preceding tradition.

[78] This conclusion is based on the above analysis of the relative chronology of the traditions in 1 S 10,17-27; 16,1-13 and 9,1–10,16.

[79] The use of *baḥăr* for divine election of the king is discussed by *Wildberger* (THAT I, 280-83) and *Seebass* (TWAT I, 595-98). According to *Seebass* (col. 597) the word *baḥăr* disappears from the language of kingship from the time of David. This is patently wrong, as is demonstrated by the occurrence in 2 S 6,21 in the Aufstieg.

(2) Contrary to what is often held the term was probably not used in the pre-monarchic period as a title denoting the leader of the people. The oldest occurrence in the extant sources is that in 1 R 1,35. Here the word is used as a secular term for the crown prince as designated by the reigning king (cf. 2 Ch 11,22). That David in this way infringed upon a divine prerogative cannot be upheld.

(3) The theological use of the term to express divine designation came later. This theological use had its short floruit towards the end of the tenth century B.C. By means of "linguistic confiscation" the originally secular title was borrowed from the Jerusalemite court by prophetic circles of the northern tribes. Here belong the references to Saul (1 S 9,1; 10,16). However, as the result of "semantic re-capturing", the word was also used as a theological term in Judah. This chapter in its semantic history can be studied in the occurrences in the HDR where it refers to David (1 S 25,30; 2 S 5,2; 6,21; 7,8). If this dating of the theological use of the term is correct, Grønbæk's dating of the HDR to the decades after Solomon's death is confirmed. It is also immediately probable that the references to Jeroboam and Baasha as *nagîd* (1 R 14,7; 16,2 both in Dtr sections) are connected with a tradition and that these kings were actually claimed by their supporters to have been designated by God. It is then probable that the term served to create an ideological continuity between Saul and Jeroboam, who of course were not connected dynastically.

(4) An analysis of the semantic relations of the word at the syntagmatic and paradigmatic levels lends further support to my new interpretation. There is an intrinsic connection between the secular use of the word to denote designation within the royal family and the theological use of it in the formula *nagîd 'ăl 'ăm YHWH*, where *'ăm* denotes Israel as the (royal) family of the Lord. This formula is relevant to the discussion of the kingship of the Lord in the Old Testament. When the word *'ăm* lost its familial connotations *nagîd* apparently ceased to be used as a theological term. Other words such as $b^e k\hat{o}r$, "first-born", were then better fitted to express these ideas (cf. Ps 89,27-28).

(5) Earlier conceptions of divine designation prior to the use of the word *nagîd* as a theological term were investigated. The conclusion was that the three important traditions of a divine designation found in the material on Saul and David arose in the following order: (a) the lot-casting at Mizpah, 1 S 10,17-27, (b) Samuel's anointing of David, 1 S 16,1-13, (c) Samuel's anointing of Saul as *nagîd*, 1 S 9,1–10,16.

(6) The tradition of the lot-casting at Mizpah thus precedes the concept of divine designation as *nagîd*. A new solution of the textual crux in 1 S 10,22 resulted in an understanding of v. 19b-24 as depicting a single course of events. There is no need to presume that this passage was derived

from two different traditions. In 1 S 10,17-27 lot-casting has the same significance as later the prophetic word has in revealing the will of God in connection with designation as *nagîd*.

On *nagîd* and the king as the "son" of God see below, ch. 12.2.2.2.

CHAPTER X
The Anointing of the King

The anointing of the king was the essential element of the royal ritual. The king is "the Lord's anointed", $m^e\check{s}\hat{i}^ah$ *YHWH*. An investigation of the history and contents of this royal rite is therefore an undertaking, the complexities and ramifications of which must not hold us back from an attempt to come to grips with the historical evidence. The present study of the matter will be organized in the following manner: Since there are already numerous studies of the royal anointing, I shall begin with a brief survey of previous research. After this I shall enter on my own discussion, which I shall open with a preliminary sorting of the basic concordance material in order to get a firm hold of the evidence, its general nature, its distribution and the character of the problems involved. After this a new reconstruction of the historical development and a fresh assessment of the import of the rite of anointing will be attempted. Comparative material will be consulted in due time to throw light on particular aspects of the Israelite evidence.

1. Status Quaestionis. Survey of the Evidence

In the following brief survey of research on anointing, I shall concentrate on different opinions held on the biblical material.[1] Although the opinions propounded vary widely, one can nervertheless discern certain general characteristics.

In his study of 1898, Weinel argues that all kings of Judah and Israel were anointed and that the rite was carried out by a priest (p. 20-27). The custom is held to have been taken over from the Canaanites (p. 52f.). The act of anointing is interpreted as conferring holiness on the king and making him partake in the life of YHWH (p. 54). This sacral interpretation of the anointing was later upheld by C.R.North and M.Noth. – Cothenet's lengthy article is remarkable for bringing together a mass of extra-biblical evidence. Cothenet observes among other things

---

[1] The most important discussions of the subject are found in the following works: *H.Weinel* (ZAW 18/1898, 1-82), *C.R.North* (ZAW 50/1932, 13-17), *D.Lys* (Études théologiques et religieuses 29/1954 no 3 p. 1-54), *M.Noth* (GesStud ²1960: 319-322), *E.Cothenet* (DBSuppl 6/1960, 701-732), *E.Kutsch* (1963), *R.deVaux* (Mél. E. Tisserant I, 1964: 119-133, esp. p. 129ff.). *K.R.Veenhof* (BiOr 23/1966, 308-313), *J.A.Emerton* (JSS 12/1967, 122-128), *E.Lipinski* (1967: 45-52), *L.Schmidt* (1970: 172-188) and *F.Hesse* (ThW vol. 9, fascicles 8/9 1972 p. 485-500). – The ancient Near Eastern material is discussed particularly by Cothenet, Kutsch and Veenhof in the above-mentioned contributions.

that an anointing is attested for Pharaoh's officials in Egypt and for Egyptian vassals in Syria, but he fails to develop the realization that there is probably an inner connection between these two types of anointing (cols. 709; 714). More recently, both Kutsch and deVaux have used this to illuminate the biblical evidence. As for the meaning of anointing as an Israelite royal rite, Cothenet stresses the connection between the anointing and the charisma of the Spirit in the cases of Saul's and David's anointings by Samuel (col. 719f.).

The most comprehensive study so far of anointing in Israel and its neighbours is found in the monograph by E. Kutsch, *Salbung als Rechtsakt* (1963). This work contains an extensive survey of ancient Near Eastern material that was later supplemented by Veenhof in his review. In an introductory chapter, Kutsch discusses the meaning of anointing in general every-day life. Here he tries to elaborate a distinction between the strengthening and the purifying effect of oil. He then applies this basic distinction to the material for his main topic, namely "Salbung als Rechtsakt". In its aspect of "purification" anointing denotes "liberation" (p. 16-33). Here Kutsch lists the anointing of a female slave at Ugarit in connection with her manumission, the anointing of buyer and seller in connection with a transaction, the anointing of the participants in a covenant meal at Mari and the anointing of a girl when she is given in marriage in the Amarna letters and the Middle Assyrian Laws. According to Kutsch, the anointing of the High Priest in post-exilic Judaism belongs to this type of anointing as "purification" = "liberation". The anointing liberates and separates the priest from the people for the service of the Lord (p. 22ff.). The anointing of the High Priest is not to be explained as due to a transference of the royal anointing to the head of state of post-exilic times (p. 25).

The other major group of cases contains instances of anointing as a "strengthening", as conferring power, authority and glory (p. 37-70). Here belongs the anointing of officials in Egypt and of Egyptian vassals in Syria (p. 34 ff.). While there was no anointing of kings in Mesopotamia or Egypt (p. 40ff.) there is clear evidence for it in Hatti (p. 36ff.) and Israel (p. 52ff.) And this use of anointing at the installation of the king is to be seen as a case of anointing denoting authorization. In the Israelite material Kutsch makes further refinements. He thus distinguishes between two different kinds of royal anointing. (a) There is an anointing carried out by the people. Here the anointing creates a relation between the people and the king. It conveys an authorization of the king by the people. As an integral element of the coronation ritual of Judah, the rite of anointing was consistently of this "plural" type with the people as the acting subject. This type of anointing represents the Hittite practice and is due originally to Hittite influence. (b) The cases where YHWH or a prophet appear as the subject that carries out the act correspond to the Egyptian anointing of officials and vassals. The knowledge of this Egyptian custom has probably reached Israel through Canaanite mediation. In the Israelite rite YHWH has taken the place of Pharaoh as sovereign (p. 56f.). The cases of this second type of anointing are not to be understood as recording actual historical instances. Instead, we are here faced with a secondary *theologoumenon* (p. 57 f.). – In the interpretation of the expression $m^e\check{s}i^ah$ *YHWH*, Kutsch argues (p. 60ff.) on the basis of Jes 45,1 that this expression does not (not even during the period of the monarchy) presuppose the rite of anointing, but is only meant to express a particular relation between the king and YHWH. – Very similar opinions on the subject as a whole are held by F. Hesse in his contribution to Kittel's *Wörterbuch*.

Independent of Kutsch, deVaux, too, elaborated an analogy between the anointing of officials and vassals of Pharaoh and the anointing of the Israelite king. In contrast

to Kutsch, however, he laid emphasis on the anointing as a rite to express vassalage. To deVaux, the anointing is the sacrament which makes the king the vassal of YHWH (p. 119; 129 ff.). According to this scholar, the conceptual frame of the divine vassalage of the Israelite king also embraces the Davidic $b^e r\hat{\imath}t$, understood in analogy with the political treaties (p. 124 ff.), and the use of the terms *nagîd* and *'æbæd* denoting the king (p. 120 ff.). This study by deVaux is clearly a fruit of the interest taken by Old Testament scholars during the fifties and early sixties in the whole complex of treaty and covenant.

In a postscript (p. 133 note 68), deVaux takes exception to the monograph by Kutsch. His disagreement is emphatic. The Israelite kings are called "the Lord's anointed" in texts that are certainly old, and this because they were actually anointed by a representative of God. Texts of this nature should be given priority over texts that seem to indicate that the anointing was carried out by a collective (the elders, etc.). The rite must have been carried out by a single agent, and it is the passages that seem to convey a different impression which create a problem and which should be explained. (On deVaux, cf. below note 57.)

In his chapter on anointing, Ludwig Schmidt (1970: 172-188) tries to bridge the gap between a sacral interpretation of the anointing (Weinel, Noth and others) and a more "secular" understanding of it as an act through which the people confer authority on the king (Kutsch). A study of the passage on Solomon's anointing (1 R ch. 1) leads Schmidt to the conclusion that the agent who carries out the rite is normally a priest (p. 176 f.). In cases where a collective appears as the subject performing the anointing the usage is imprecise. In spite of this, in Israel the act was not primarily understood as a sanctification or a consecration of the king. David's twofold anointing, over Judah and over Israel, shows that the effect of the rite was less to confer a new quality on the king than to invest him with a new office. If the anointing had meant basically a consecration, bringing about a particular relation to God, then the second anointing could not have conveyed anything new and would thus have been meaningless (p. 179 f.).

According to Schmidt there is a very specific relation between the acting of God and the acting of the people in the anointing. 2 S 19,11 seen in conjunction with 2 S 16,18 is held to show "dass zumindest zu Beginn des israelitischen Königtums die Initiative und Zustimmung des Volkes mit der Wahl Jahwes gleichgesetzt wurden" (p. 182). A second stage in the development is shown by 1 S 16,1-13 (Samuel anoints David). Here, the divine and human activity, which were originally identified, have been separated (p. 183 f.) and the anointing has taken on a new sense as a consecration of the king for the service of the Lord. The anointing of the post-exilic priests has developed from this new understanding of the royal anointing, represented by the tradition of Samuel's anointing of David (p. 186). As for the origin of the rite, Schmidt thinks that it was taken over from the Canaanites (p. 179; 193; 197). The suggestions advanced by deVaux are not commented on, since Schmidt has overlooked this contribution.

This survey of the research devoted to the subject shows one thing: there is no consensus. Kutsch's monograph remains important but appears as a highly controversial contribution to the discussion (cf. the reviews by Veenhof and Emerton and the criticism by deVaux). As for the main problem of how to understand the actual import of the rite, we can broadly speak of three different opinions:

1. The "sacral" interpretation. The anointing brings about a particular relation between God and the king (Weinel and others). According to deVaux, the anointing creates a relationship of vassalage.
2. The "secular" interpretation. The anointing means the authorization of the king by the people (Kutsch).
3. The mediating position. L.Schmidt tries to come beyond this alternative by suggesting that both aspects (God and people as acting) coexist from the beginning and become separate only at a later stage.

As is well known, there are quite a few words connected with the semantic fields of "to anoint" and "fatness – oil". One could mention for instance *sûk*, *mišḥā*, *šæmæn*, *mišman*, *dæšæn* and *yiṣhar*. It has been necessary to pay attention to the whole of this material,[1a] but I shall not burden the presentation with a survey of the occurrences of each of these words. Observations connected with these lexical items will be utilized in their proper place. What I shall do here is to survey the material for the two terms that are most intimately connected with the royal anointing, viz. the verb *mašăḥ* and the noun *mašîᵃḥ*.

The noun *mašîᵃḥ* has the following distribution in the Old Testament.

The Saul cycle

1 S 12,3.5.

The History of David's Rise

1 S 16,6: Samuel's anointing of David.
1 S 24,7 (*bis*): 24,11: David uses the word of Saul in the cave.
1 S 26,9.11.16.23: David of Saul, when he spares his life again.
2 S 1,14.16: David of Saul to the Amalekite *ger*.
2 S 1,21: David's *qînā* over Saul: *magen ša'ûl bᵉlî mašîᵃḥ băššamæn*, probably meaning that Saul's shield was "not anointed with oil", cf. Jes 21,5. The form is possibly due to a misrepresentation of an original *mašûᵃḥ*.[2]

The Succession Narrative

2 S 19,22: Shimei has "cursed the Lord's anointed".[2a]

Psalms

Ps 2,2; 18,51 (=2 S 22,51); 20,7; 28,8; 84,10; 89,39.52; 105,15 (=1 Ch 16,22); 132,10 (=2 Ch 6,42); 132,17.

[1a] See *Kutsch* (1963: 6–15).
[2] As is read by 21 MSS. Note that yodh and waw were easily confused in certain periods. – The verse belongs to the "song of the bow". It is possible that v. 17-27 were inserted by the Dtr, see *Carlson* (1964: 47 ff.) and *Grønbæk* (1971: 221 f.). But even so this dirge may be an authentic element in the pre-Dtr material.
[2a] Cf. ch. 1 note 9.

1 S 2,10: The Song of Hannah.
Hab 3,13: The Prayer of Habakuk.
Thr 4,20: *rûᵃḥ 'appênû mᵉšîᵃḥ YHWH*.

Miscellaneous texts

1 S 2,35: The oracle concerning the house of Eli.
2 S 23,1: The Last Words of David.
Jes 45,1: "Thus says the Lord to his anointed, to Cyrus...."
Dan 9,25.26
Lev 4,3.5.16; 6,15: of the High Priest.

The verb *mašăḥ* is used with various objects, animate and inanimate. For our purposes we are interested in the anointing of kings which I shall therefore survey.

The Saul cycle

1 S 9,16; 10,1 (three times, since I take the longer text of the LXX to be correct in 10,1). All three instances belong to the *nagîd* layer and deal with Samuel's anointing of Saul as *nagîd*. The Spirit comes over Saul (10,9).
1 S 11,15: The LXX has the reading καὶ ἔχρισεν Σαμουὴλ ἐκεῖ τὸν Σαοὺλ εἰς βασιλέα where the MT has *wăyyămlikû šam 'æt ša'ûl*.

The History of David's Rise

1 S 15,1.17: Samuel speaks to Saul about his anointing.[2b]
1 S 16,3.12.13 God to Samuel: "And you shall anoint for me [*lî*] him whom I name to you." Samuel anoints David. The Spirit comes over David. The anointing is the consummation of divine election. The verb *mašăḥ* stands in opposition to *ma'ăs* (v. 7) and *lo' baḥăr* (v. 8 ff.).
2 S 2,4: "And the men of Judah came, and there [i.e. at Hebron] they anointed David king over the house of Judah."
2 S 2,7: In David's message to Jabesh.
2 S 3,39: The words *wᵉ'anokî hăyyôm răk ûmašûᵃḥ mælæk* are problematic. Various possibilities have been suggested, the most attractive being "and I am this day weak though anointed king". Probably Deuteronomistic.[3]
2 S 5,3: The elders of Israel come to David at Hebron, *wăyyikrot lahæm hămmælæk dawid bᵉrît ... wăyyimšᵉḥû 'æt dawid lᵉmælæk 'ăl yiśra'el*.
2 S 5,17: The Philistines learn of this anointing.

[2b] Note that v. 17 belongs to a Dtr section, see above ch. 2.1.
[3] See ch. 2 note 36.

The Succession Narrative

2 S 12,7: Nathan to David: "Thus says the Lord, the God of Israel, 'I anointed you king over Israel, and I delivered you out of the hand of Saul....' " Probably Deuteronomistic.[4]

2 S 19,11: "But Absalom, whom we anointed over us, is dead in battle."

1 R 1,34.39.45: Solomon's anointing, carried out by Zadok (and Nathan?) with oil from the tent.

Other instances in the Books of Kings

1 R 5,15: Hiram's first embassy to Solomon. According to the LXX, Hiram, King of Tyre, sent his servants to anoint Solomon.

1 R 19,15.16: Elijah receives the divine commission to anoint Hazael, Jehu and Elisha.

2 R 9,3.6.12: The anointing of Jehu by one of the sons of the prophets that belonged to the guild of Elisha.

2 R 11,12: The anointing of Jehoash. The MT has the verb *mašăḥ* in the plural, while the LXX presents the priest as the agent who carried out the anointing.

2 R 23,30: The anointing of Jehoahaz by "the people of the land".

Miscellaneous texts

Jud 9,8.15: The trees anoint a king over themselves in the Jotham fable.

Jes 61,1: "The Spirit of the Lord God is upon me, because the Lord has anointed me to bring good tidings to the afflicted."[4a]

Ps 45,8: "Therefore God, your God, has anointed you with the oil of gladness above your fellows." The expression is perhaps purely metaphorical.

Ps 89,21: "I have found David, my servant; with my holy oil I have anointed him."

1 Ch 11,3 (=2 S 5,3).

1 Ch 14,8 (=2 S 5,17).

1 Ch 29,22: "And they made Solomon ... king the second time, and they anointed him $l^eYHWH\ l^enagîd$, and Zadok as priest."

2 Ch 22,7: Jehu "whom the Lord has anointed to destroy the house of Ahab".

2 Ch 23,11: In contradistinction to the parallel in 2 R 11,12 the Chronicler lets Jehoiada and his sons carry out the anointing of Jehoash.

In addition to these instances of the anointing of kings, a number of occurrences in the Pentateuch refer to the anointing of the High Priest: Ex 28,41; 29,7; 30,30; 40,13.15; Lev 7,36; 8,12; 16,32; Nu 3,3; 35,25. The anointing of

---

[4] See ch. 1 after note 19.

[4a] Whether this text refers to a royal or prophetic person, its linking of the anointing and the Spirit should be noted. On this text see particularly *Zimmerli* (FsGalling 1970: 321 ff.).

weapons in the YHWH-war seems to be presupposed in Jes 21,5 (cf. 2 S 1,21). Jacob anointed the *maṣṣēbā* that he erected at Bethel (Gn 31,13; cf. 28,18; 35,14). A number of instances in Ex–Nu, easily found in Lisowsky, deal with the anointing of other cultic objects.

Important observations of typical features on the one hand and irregularities on the other may already be made after this preliminary sorting out of the material.

The noun māšîªḥ. – There is only one instance where this word is not used as a title, viz. 2 S 1,21 (of Saul's shield), where it may be a textual corruption. When it appears as a title, the grammatical construction is very striking. Only in two very late occurrences do we find the word used in the absolute state (Dan 9,25⁵.26). In all the other instances the word appears in syntagmatic solidarity[5a] with *YHWH*, either expressed by a suffix referring to *YHWH*[6] or by a construct relation which likewise brings the anointed one in relation to the God of Israel: *mᵉšîªḥ YHWH*[7] or, once, *mᵉšîªḥ ᵃᵉlōhê yaʿᵃqōb*[8]. This means that the word is a very specific term to denote the relation between king and God. There is no evidence for syntagmatic solidarity between this term and a designation of the land or the people, a point where the title *mælæk* displays a marked contrast.

The distribution of the noun *māšîªḥ* in the extant sources also reveals some interesting features. The word seems to have been in use throughout the period of the "divided" monarchy down to the exile.[9] A cumulation of occurrences is found in (a) the HDR and (b) the Psalms. This last observation points to a marked difference from *nāgîd* which occurs only once in a psalm, and then in the plural. In the HDR the word *māšîªḥ* is used not only of David but also of Saul. Remarkably few occurrences are found in the SN (only 2 S 19,22) and in the prophetic literature (only Hab 3,13 – actually in a psalm – and Jes 45,1). With regard to the distribution, one must ask when the word came into use as a title used of the king. One should also ask whether or not the title was used in Northern Israel, since no northern king except Saul is denoted as *māšîªḥ*.

The verb māšaḥ. – As for syntagmatic solidarities, one notes that the verb very often occurs with the preposition *lᵉ* + a title. The act of anointing thus brings about a change of status. The expression *māšaḥ lᵉmælæk* is the

---

[5] In Dan 9,25 the word *nāgîd* is probably an apposition of *māšîªḥ*, see F.Hesse (TWNT 9: 491 with note 52).
[5a] For the definition, see ch. 9.4.
[6] 1 S 2,10.35; 12,3.5; 16,6; Ps 2,2; 18,51 (=2 S 22,51); Ps 20,7; 28,8; 84,10; 89,39.52; 105,15 (=1 Ch 16,22); Ps 132,10 (=2 Ch 6,42); Ps 132,17; Hab 3,13; Jes 45,1.
[7] 1 S 24,7.11; 26,9.11.16.23; 2 S 1,14.16; 19,22; Thr 4,20.
[8] 2 S 23,1.
[9] Note the occurrences in the royal psalms, in Hab 3,13 and in Thr 4,20.

most common of these constructions,[10] but we also find *mašaḥ lenagîd*,[11] *lekohen*,[12] and *lenabî*'[13]. The royal anointing is also referred to by the elliptic expression in 2 S 19,11 when the people speak of Absalom as the one *'ašær mašaḥnû 'alênu*.

There is a rich variety of subjects of the verb:

God anoints:
  Saul: 1 S 10,1; 15,17.
  David: 2 S 12,7; Ps 89,21 Probably the anointing by Samuel in 1 S 16,1-13.
  Jehu: 2 R 9,3.6.12; 2 Ch 22,7 The act was carried out by a prophet.
  Note also: Ps 45,8; Jes 61,1.

Samuel anoints:
  Saul: 1 S 9,16; 10,1 (cf. 11,15 LXX).
  David: 1 S 16,3.12.13.

A prophet anoints:
  1 R 19,15.16; cf. 2 R 9,3.12.13 (Jehu); 1 R 1,34.45 (Solomon).

A priest anoints:
  Solomon: 1 R 1,34.39.45 Note Nathan's prophetic cooperation.
  Jehoash: 2 Ch 23,11 Cf. 2 R 11,12 with the assembly as the active subject.

The people or their representatives anoint:
  David: 2 S 2,4 (*'ănšê yehûdā*); 2 S 2,7; 5,3 = 1 Ch 11,3 (*ziqnê yiśra'el*); 2 S 5,17.
  Absalom: 2 S 19,11.
  Solomon: 1 R 5,15 (but note the LXX); 1 Ch 29,22.
  Jehoash: 2 R 11,12 Cf. 2 Ch 23,11 with the priest as the subject.
  Jehoahaz: 2 R 23,30 The *'ăm ha'aræṣ* as the subject.
  Note also: Jud 9,8.15 The trees in the Jotham fable.

It is easy to discern two major groups in this material:
1. Cases where the people or its representatives appear as the performer of the rite.
2. Cases where God is said to have acted through a human intermediary (Saul's and David's anointings by Samuel; Jehu's anointing by one of the prophets).

The two groups overlap only in one single person: David, who is described as having been anointed by Samuel (1 S 16,1-13) and by the representatives of Judah and Israel (2 S 2,4; 5,3). How is one to account for these different anointings of David?

In the cases of what I shall call the "divine" anointings of Saul, David

---

[10] Jud 9,15; 1 S 15,1.17; 2 S 2,4.7; 12,7; 1 R 1,34.45; 5,15; 19,15.16; 2 R 9,3.6.12; 1 Ch 11,3; 14,8.
[11] 1 S 9,16; 10,1; 1 Ch 29,22.
[12] 1 Ch 29,22.
[13] 1 R 19,16.

and Jehu, one can with some justification speak of acts carried out without the presence of the popular assembly. These "divine" anointings create a problem. Do they represent actual historical cases of designation in advance (deVaux), or are they expressions of a certain attitude to kingship among particular circles in ancient Israel (Kutsch)? And what is the relation between these three cases and Solomon's anointing, where we also look in vain for the participation of the popular assembly?

To this must be added a further observation: There is a surprising contrast between the verb and the noun. As we saw in the survey of the grammatical subjects, the verb connects the anointing both with the popular assembly and with God. The noun $maši^ah$, on the other hand, links the king exclusively with God. Any comprehensive interpretation of royal anointing must account for this discrepancy.

The above survey of grammatical subjects also points to another problem. An institutionalized rite such as anointing must have acquired a certain degree of stability with regard to the persons involved. Therefore, the very manifoldness of the subjects that occur together with the verb creates a problem. Are we to think that the oil was normally poured on the head of the king by a priest, a prophet or the leading elders of the people?

It is also worthwhile surveying the kings that appear as the object of the verb:

Saul: 1 S 9,16; 10,1; 15,1.17 (11,15 LXX).
David: 1 S 16,13; 2 S 2,4.7; 3,39; 5,3.17; 12,7; Ps 89,21; 1 Ch 11,3; 14,8.
Absalom: 2 S 19,11.
Solomon: 1 R 1,34.39.45; 5,15; 1 Ch 29,22.
Jehu: 1 R 19,16; 2 R 9,3.6.12; 2 Ch 22,7.
Jehoash: 2 R 11,12; 2 Ch 23,11.
Jehoahaz: 2 R 23,30.

The anointing of Jehoahaz (2 R 23,30) and the occurrence of the noun $maši^ah$ in Thr 4,20 seem to indicate that the rite of anointing was practised in Judah down to the exile. Only two of the kings above belong to the North, viz. Saul and Jehu, and in both cases we are concerned with "divine" anointing without the participation of the assembly. Nothing at all is said about the anointing of Jeroboam I, neither by God in connection with Ahijah's prophetic designation of the future king (1 R ch. 11), nor by the assembly at Shechem (1 R ch. 12). Is this lacuna to be explained on the theory that the mention of an actual anointing has been found uninteresting or embarrassing so that it has been left out by the Dtr, *or* are we justified in taking it that this king was never anointed? This raises the problem of the royal anointing in the North: was it practised or not, and if

so, was it practised from Saul right down to the last king over the northern tribes?

Irregularities in the distribution of a word are always important. Therefore, we should also take note of the prophecy of Nathan. This passage contains a retrospect of God's gracious dealings with David (2 S 7,8 ff.). The anointing of David by Samuel (1 S 16,1-13) would certainly have made a very natural point of reference here. But there seems to be no allusion to it in the words of Nathan in 2 S ch. 7.

The most important task of all is of course to arrive at an understanding of the actual meaning of the rite of anointing. Is there any connection between the anointing of kings and the anointing of priests and sacred objects? What does the use of oil actually imply?

2. The Historical Development

1. Saul and the Northern Kingdom

The analysis begun in the above survey of the distribution of the material will now be deepened. Let us first study the historical development of the rite within Israel, as far as it can be traced, and then pursue the problem of its import against the background of the historical development. In my opinion some premature conclusions are due to the fact that sufficient attention has not been paid to the possibility that an actual development can be inferred from the material.

It is sometimes asserted that all kings of Israel and Judah were anointed right from the beginning.[14] In our survey of the material, however, we found reason to ask whether the royal anointing was firmly established as a custom in the North.[15] The problem of the age of this royal rite in ancient Israel is of course of no small interest in a study such as this, and this problem is linked up with the question of whether Saul was anointed or not.

Whether historical or not, the report of the anointing of Jehu by one of the prophets (2 R 9,1 ff.) would be meaningless to the citizens of Northern Israel if anointing was not normally practised there. Otherwise it would be incomprehensible that just the rite of anointing would be said to make Jehu king.[16] But this does not imply that all anointings were carried out by a

---

[14] See for instance *Weinel* (ZAW 18/1898, 21 ff.) and *deVaux* (Mél. Tisserant 1/1964, 129).

[15] *Kutsch* (1963: 60) holds that anointing was not or only rarely practised in the north, since anointing was to him normally an act carried out by the people. According to him, the people can hardly have anointed the king in the case of a usurpation, which so often occurred in the north.

[16] See *L.Schmidt* (1970: 184f.) as opposed to *Kutsch* (1963: 59), who thinks of a singular prophetic act which does not permit any conclusions concerning the institution. On the text about Jehu's anointing see also *H.Chr.Schmitt* (1972: 139-152).

prophet. It is only a general indication that anointing was the essential ✓ royal rite in the Northern Kingdom in the ninth century B.C. For the period prior to this there is the strange silence in 1 R ch. 11–12 concerning a possible anointing of Jeroboam I. On the other hand, we are told that "the elders of Israel" anointed David at Hebron (2 S 5,3). This statement is found in the HDR which was composed, to be sure, in the period after Solomon's death. Nevertheless, it seems difficult to explain David's anointing as king over the northern tribes as a fabrication of the author of this work of history.[17] But can this instance be taken to testify to a northern practice of anointing? It rather seems that the anointing is here carried out in deliberate conformity to the Judaean anointing of David (2 S 2,4). David's two anointings are a "symmetric" expression of David's installation over a dual monarchy comprising Judah and Israel in a personal union.

So far there is nothing to prevent us from inferring that anointing was not practised in the North until after Jeroboam I. We must ask: is this really in keeping with the numerous passages that seem to hint at an anointing of Saul? Let us first look at the instances in the Saul cycle in 1 S ch. 8–12. Here, Saul is twice called $mašîah$ in 1 S 12,3.5. However, this is in the Dtr framework of this cycle of texts, and besides, there is in these particular two verses a hook-word connection ($laqăh$) with the Dtr section in 1 S 8,11 ff. This connection is probably to be regarded as a deliberate device of the Deuteronomists.[18] Therefore, these two verses are of little importance as evidence for a possible anointing of Saul.

Neither can the text concerning Saul's anointing as $nagîd$ by Samuel (1 S 9,1–10,16) be adduced as proof that Saul was actually anointed. My previous investigations make it unnecessary to go into details here. It is sufficient to refresh our memory on the following points: (a) The study of the tradition of this anointing (above ch. 4) shows that anointing as $nagîd$ belongs to a later remoulding of the original tradition concerning Saul and the unknown seer. (b) We also saw (ch. 9.5) that the tradition in its final form with anointing as $nagîd$ is dependent on the tradition of Samuel's anointing of David (1 S 16,1-13). The anointing of Saul probably duplicates the anointing in the older tradition of David. (c) The analysis of the title $nagîd$ (ch. 9) points in the same direction. This title came into use in connection with David's designation of Solomon. It was not used in connection with the king before this. Its use in 1 S 9,16 and 10,1 even represents a secondary spiritualization of the term as an expression denoting divine designation, and this process cannot possibly be thought to have taken place as early as the days of Saul. All this together indicates that the tradi-

---

[17] See *Grønbæk* (1971: 250) for indications that there is "eine konkrete Überlieferungsgrundlage" behind 2 S 5,3.
[18] See *Boecker* (1969: 68-70).

tion of Saul's anointing as *nagîd* must not be used as independent historical evidence that Saul was actually anointed.

In the MT of the Saul cycle, there is thus nothing that can provide a basis for the conclusion that Saul was anointed. In the LXX there is a reading in 1 S 11,15 according to which Samuel anointed Saul at Gilgal. But the LXX is alone in this and hardly preserves the original reading.[19] On the contrary, the LXX reading is here the result of the tendency, already found in the Hebrew tradition, to harmonize the tradition in 1 S 11,1 ff. with that in 1 S 10,17 ff.[20] The LXX merely goes a step further by introducing Samuel in 11,15 as well.

After this examination of the text of the Saul cycle, we turn to the HDR. In 1 S 15,1 Samuel says: "The Lord sent me to anoint you *l^emælæk* '*ăl 'ămmô 'ăl yiśra'el*". This refers to an anointing of Saul by Samuel, and the phrase '*ăl 'ămmô*, which echoes the typical formula *nagîd 'ăl 'ăm YHWH* (see above ch. 9.4), is but another indication that it is Saul's anointing as *nagîd* that is here referred to. What then remains to be discussed is the references in the HDR where Saul is referred to as *mašîªḥ*. We are here concerned with three different contexts:

(a) 1 S 24,7.11 where David uses the word denoting Saul when he spares his life in the cave at En Gedi.
(b) 1 S 26,9.11.16.23, when David spares Saul's life a second time.
(c) 2 S 1,14.16 where David uses the title for Saul when he accuses the Amalekite *ger* of *lèse-majesté*.

The fact that the title is here used to express the certainly very old idea that the king is inviolable[21] should not mislead us to argue that we are here faced with instances of *mašîªḥ* that are as old as this idea in Israel. It is true that the inviolability of the king is very often implicit in this title, but the idea in question is not exclusively linked with the title. It goes without saying, of course, that the sovereign was inviolable, whether anointed or not. There is every reason to believe that the great leaders of pre-monarchic times enjoyed the same legal status although they were not anointed.[22] In the final analysis, the instances of *mašîªḥ* referring to Saul in the HDR cannot be taken as independent evidence that Saul was anointed (see also below on the date of the term *mašîªḥ*). If there is an

---

[19] See for instance *Wellhausen* (1871: 77), *Budde* (1902: 76), *A.Schulz* (1919: 164) and *Stoebe* (1973: 223).
[20] Samuel is introduced in the redactional link 1 S 11,12-14 and then also in the gloss in 11,7. See above ch. 5.2.1.
[21] I hope to be able to return to the subject of the inviolability of the king in a projected monograph "Messiah and *mišpaṭ*".
[22] Cf. Ex 22,27: "You shall not revile God, nor curse a ruler (*naśî'*) of your people" (*RSV*). For a very special interpretation of this verse see *Brichto* (1963: 150-158) who compares it with the expression "to eat the *asakku* (of a king or a god)", attested in the Mari letters.

allusion in 1 S 15,1 to Saul's anointing as *nagîd* by Samuel, then the occurrences of *mašîªḥ* referring to him should almost certainly be taken to have the scene in 1 S 10,1 as their corollary. Moreover, these formulations about Saul probably derive from the author of the HDR.

There is only one possible conclusion: there is no tradition from the days of Saul that this king was ever anointed. Indeed the later indications all seem to be bound up with the tradition of Saul's anointing as *nagîd*. And this tradition in turn cannot be taken as evidence supporting conclusions concerning the actual historical circumstances in the case of Saul (cf. ch. 4.5). Our conclusion as to the state of affairs in the extant sources is thus a negative one.

We have now reached a point where we have to look for the historical reality: is it possible to argue from this silence in our sources that Saul was not anointed? Here we must be less positive. Historical conclusions *e silentio* can never claim definite certainty, since our actual knowledge of the period under discussion is of course extremely fragmentary after three thousand years. We can never control all the factors involved. But if we argue on the basis of the extant sources, and this is the only thing we can do, then we may note two circumstances. On the one hand, as is shown by the HDR, at the time of the composition of this work (the decades after Solomon) there was no interest in Judah in suppressing any mention of an anointing of Saul. On the other hand, northern traditionists must have had fairly strong reasons for preserving the memory of the actual anointing of Saul, if any such had occurred. It is thus difficult to see why an anointing of Saul should have passed unmentioned. Therefore we can feel entitled to infer that Saul was never anointed. This is the most probable conclusion from the evidence. This gap was later filled in by the tradition of his anointing as *nagîd* by Samuel.

We are now in a position to summarize our conclusions concerning the practice of anointing among the northern tribes.

(1) It can be demonstrated with a high degree of certainty that the extant sources do not contain any independent tradition concerning an actual anointing of Saul.

(2) Although, owing to the nature of the matter, it is not possible to adduce final proof, it seems highly probable that Saul was never anointed.

(3) Royal anointing came into practice later among the northern tribes, probably during the period between Jeroboam I (who is not said to have been anointed) and Jehu.

The theory of an anointing as *nagîd* practised in the pre-monarchic period[23] can therefore be ruled out as untenable. A different question is how to evaluate the Jotham fable, where the role of anointing is considerable

---

[23] This theory was propounded by *W.Richter* (1963: 289 ff. and BZ 9/1965, 76 and 83).

(Jud 9,8.9.15). This tradition, probably handed down among the northern tribes, should, however, not be exploited as proof that anointing was practised among the northern tribes right from the beginning. The Jotham fable is either a reflexion of conditions in the Canaanite city states (although this seems less probable since the evidence for royal anointing among the Canaanites is so scant, EA no 51) *or* it is to be disentangled from its present context[24] and evaluated as an expression of opposition to the harsh rule of one of the first kings in the North after Solomon.[24a]

2. David and Solomon. The Term *mašîaḥ*

Against the background of the above conclusions concerning Saul, there are strong reasons for believing that the first royal anointing among the Israelites was that of David. It is therefore of particular interest to try to get as clear a picture as possible of the circumstances in the case of David. As a matter of fact, the two reports about David's anointing by "the men of Judah" (2 S 2,4) and by "the elders of Israel" (2 S 5,3) are found in the HDR, a source that is more recent than the SN, which tells of Solomon's anointing (1 R ch. 1). Nevertheless, there is no reason to doubt what is said in the HDR about these two investitures of David. These two anointings were carried out at an old sanctuary, Hebron. But the texts say nothing about the participation of a priest. On the contrary, the very expressions point to a democratic initiative and to the role of the people in connection with the rite. In 2 S 5,3 we hear of the *ziqnê yiśra'el*, and one can suspect that the *'ănšê yᵉhûdā* in 2 S 2,4 are more or less the same men as the *ziqnê yᵉhûdā*, to whom David had earlier sent shares of the spoil (1 S 30,26). Now, we know that the HDR lays considerable stress on the divine legitimation of David. It is enough to recall Samuel's anointing of David and the divine promises, pronounced by various persons. Seen against this background, the formulations referring to an anointing by the people take on interest. It is difficult to explain these as the outcome of the general tendency of that work of history. On the contrary, they should be trusted as being historically reliable.[25] Moreover, as we shall see these formulations about David as anointed by the people should probably be taken at their face value.[26]

---

[24] So particularly *W.Richter* (1963: 248 ff., cf. 282 ff.) and *B.Lindars* (JThS 24/1973, 355 ff). For further notes on the Jotham fable see *E.Nielsen* (1955: 145 ff.), *E.H.Maly* (CBQ 22/1960, 299 ff.), *K.-H.Bernhardt* (1961: 145 f.), *Boecker* (1969: 27 f.) and *Zenger* (1971: 97 ff.).

[24a] This alternative is preferred by *Zenger* (1971: 131).

[25] I thus disagree with *Grønbæk* (1971: 223) when he takes 2 S 2,1-4a to be "vom Verfasser konstruiert".

[26] Opinions are divided on this point. *Kutsch* (1963: 53 ff.) stressed the role of the people so as to take the plural expressions *ad litteram*. On the other hand *L.Schmidt* (1970: 176; 180) took the plural expressions to be "eine ungenaue Ausdrucksweise" throughout. See below ch. 10.2.3 at the end.

If David's actual anointings over Judah and Israel are said by the traditions to have been carried out by the leading representatives of the people, it is strange to see that the HDR through the very structure of its general composition tends to minimize the importance of these two acts. By incorporating the tradition of David's anointing by Samuel (1 S 16,1-13), the author suggests an internal relation between a preceding designation of the future king by God and David's subsequent anointings over Judah and Israel. After the divine act carried out by Samuel, the anointings at Hebron by the people appear as mere confirmations of what had already been decreed by YHWH. And one need merely cast a glance at the three passages involved (1 S 16,1-13; 2 S 2,1-4; 5,1-3) to see what is really important to the author of the HDR. The anointing by Samuel is represented in detail, while considerably less space is devoted to the anointings carried out by the people.

In the introductory discussion of the material, we saw that there are other instances of a collective appearing as the active subject of the verb *mašăḥ*. As a matter of fact, these do not exclusively refer to David, but later kings such as Jehoash (2 R 11,12) and Jehoahaz (2 R 23,30) also appear to be anointed by a similar collective. It seems that we are here concerned with a linguistic usage that became established in the days of David. The extent to which we are entitled to conclude that the kings were always anointed by the people (as Kutsch holds for sure) is a different problem to which we shall revert in a while.

With this in mind the word *mašîᵃḥ*, to which I shall now turn, is very remarkable. There is nothing in the use of it that implies a relation between the king and the people. It would even be correct to say that this term denotes the king as very definitely set apart from the rest of the people, since it signifies his status as linked with God and thus inviolable. In two different contexts we meet the expression *šalăḥ yăd bimšîᵃḥ YHWH*[27] referring to something that David refused to do against Saul. Such a crime would bring *ḥalîlă*, an expression that Gerleman translates as "Zerfliessung" ("mouldering"), i.e. death,[28] over the sinner. In Ps 105,15 *mašîᵃḥ* is used in the plural to denote the patriarchs as inviolable: *'ăl tiggeᶜû bimšîḥay*, "touch not my anointed ones". It should be remembered that the verb *nagăᶜ* often has a legal overtone of "interfering with the legal rights of a person".[29] The one who "puts forth his hand against the Lord's anointed"

---

[27] 1 S 24,7.11; 26,9.11.23.
[28] *Gerleman* pers. comm. The subject will be treated by him in a forthcoming study. For the formula *ḥalîlă lî min* + *inf.* he suggests the translation "mouldering will be my share from doing so and so".
[29] See Gn 26,11.29; Jos 9,19; 2 S 14,10; Jer 12,14; Zach 2,12; Job 1,11; Prv 6,29; Ruth 2,9. See also *H.Schulz* (1969: 103 f.), who says: "nagăᶜ im rechtlichen Sinne ist also ein Antasten der Rechtssphäre des Betroffenen" (p. 104).

will not be "guiltless" (*mî šalăḥ yadô bimšîªḥ YHWH wᵉniqqā*, 1 S 26,9). There are also here unmistakable legal connotations (note *naqā*[30]). Therefore, the mention of a crime committed against the king as directed against the Lord's anointed immediately strikes a note of strong indignation.[31] The relation between God and the king is one of particular intimacy. God grants the anointed one the hearing of his prayers[32] and "salvation" (the root *y-š-ʿ*)[33]. As we have already noted, the title *mašîªḥ*, with but two late exceptions, appears throughout in syntagmatic relations with *YHWH* (construct relations or suffix). The anointed one is the Lord's anointed. The corollary is that the Lord is denoted as the king's God.[34]

The distribution of the title *mašîªḥ*[35] is worthy of particular attention. It occurs 10 times in the HDR. In addition there are 16 occurrences in texts that can be denoted as psalms. Only 8 occurrences fall outside these two groups.[36]

From this it can be concluded that the use of the term became firmly established at the latest during the decades after Solomon's death when the HDR was composed. The indications for a *post quem* are more difficult to pin-point. Since in all probability Saul was never anointed, it seems rather difficult to assume that the title came into use during his reign already. This conclusion may receive further support from a remarkable case of *mašîªḥ* in David's *qînā* over Saul. Here the word is used not as a title but as a pure verbal noun about Saul's shield as not being anointed with oil, *bᵉlî mašîªḥ băššamæn* (2 S 1,21). It is very interesting to note that *mašîªḥ* and not *mašûªḥ* – as we would expect[37] and as 21 MSS have it – is used in this way. The possibility cannot be ruled out that we have in the MT a textual corruption (above, note 2). However, if *mašîªḥ* is original, then 2 S 1,21 is most easily understood as belonging to a period prior to the semantic separation of *mašîªḥ* and *mašûªḥ*, which resulted in the former being used exclusively as a title. If we can assume that David's *qînā* is authentic, there is reason to believe that *mašîªḥ* had not yet firmly established itself as a title at the beginning of David's reign. On the top of this there is the remarkable fact that the title appears only once in the

---

[30] In its legal sense Hebrew *naqā* (*naqî*) almost perfectly corresponds to Akk. *zakû* (*zakûtu*). Cf. *CAD* (21/Z p. 23 ff.). For a special study of MB *zakûtu* see F.R.Kraus (FsM.David 2/1968, 9ff.).

[31] 2 S 1,14.16 (the Amalekite *ger* who killed Saul); 2 S 19,22 (Shimei); Ps 89,52.

[32] Ps 20,7 (cf. Ps 84,10; 132,10).

[33] Ps 20,7; 28,8; Hab 3,13 (cf. Ps 132,17 and 1 S 2,10).

[34] "My God": 2 S 24,24; Ps 89,27 (David); 1 R 5,18f.; 8,28 (Solomon). "Your God": 1 S 13,13; 25,29; 2 S 14,11; Jes 7,11; Ps 45,8. On this see C.R.North (ZAW 50/1932, 22) and especially H. Vorländer (1975: 231 ff.).

[35] I here disregard 2 S 1,21 (of Saul's shield) and the instances about the High Priest in Lev.

[36] 1 S 2,35; 12,3.5; 2 S 19,22; 23,1; Jes 45,1; Dan 9,25.26.

[37] Cf. Ex 29,2; Lev 2,4; 7,12; Nu 3,3; 6,15 (cf. Jer 22,14).

SN (2 S 19,22), which in my opinion was composed in the first half of Solomon's reign. With all due caution we can then formulate our conclusion in the following way: The title came into use at the earliest during David's reign. Its sparse occurrence in the SN and the cumulation of occurrences in the HDR favour the conclusion that the title did not come into vogue until the early days of Solomon.

Let us now revert to the anointings of David. It should be noted that David was anointed twice, first over Judah and then over Israel. If the rite basically accomplished a new relation between God and the king, then the repetition would become problematic. The second anointing could then add nothing new to the first one.[38] It is therefore better to assume that the rite somehow effects the relation between the people and the king. Indeed, the expressions that depict the representatives of the people as the subject who carries out the rite are in good agreement with this. In the term *mašîᵃḥ*, on the other hand, the anointed one is somehow linked with God. Thus, we are here concerned with *two different conceptions of the rite*. The first, attested in connection with David's two anointings, may be termed *"secular"*. The second, attested by the use of *mašîᵃḥ* in the HDR, may be termed *"sacral"*. The fact that they can be separated from the point of view of chronology indicates that we should resolve the tension as being due to a *development* of the ideas connected with the rite. This process can aptly be described as *sacralization*. In passing, one may ask whether this is not an analogy of the semantic development of the title *nagîd*. We have already discussed the reasons for and the effects of that process. Is it possible to infer anything about the historical circumstances that caused or favoured the sacralization of the rite of anointing?

With this particular question in mind we shall now proceed to the anointing of Solomon. This is referred to in 1 R ch. 1, first in David's instruction to Zadok, Nathan and Benaiah (v. 32-37), then in the passage that describes the execution of David's order (v. 38-40), and finally it is hinted at by a member of the Adonijah party (v. 45). In comparison with the anointings of David, that of Solomon is remarkable from one particular point of view: the popular assembly is not present at the act. To be sure, the text speaks of "all the people" as the body that acclaimed Solomon king: *wǎyyo'mᵉrû kǎl ha'am yᵉḥî hǎmmælæk* (v. 39). But for once language cannot conceal facts. The context makes it clear that "all the people" comprised only Zadok, Nathan, Benaiah and the royal mercenaries or the Cherethites and the Pelethites (v. 38.44). It is quite in agreement with this when the priest Zadok, and not the elders of the people, is said to perform the rite of anointing. Indeed, the investiture of Solomon denotes the point of intersection between old semi-democratic institutions

---

[38] This was pointed out by *L.Schmidt* (1970: 179f.).

and new ones in which cooptation, heredity and dynasty deprive the people of a good deal of their legal prerogatives in connection with the installation of the king.

The development of the rite, mentioned above, can be described thus: the place originally held by the people has been taken over by God. In this process the anointing of Solomon has an important place. Here, the role of the people is drastically reduced. I shall not go so far as to suggest that the anointing of Solomon was basically a sacred act. A critically ascertained minimum position may be to hold that there are features of this anointing which make a subsequent sacralization quite understandable. Solomon's anointing has a potential sacrality.

First, the rite is now expressly said to have been performed by a priest, by Zadok. Since mediatorship between God and man is essential to Israelite priesthood, it is easy to imagine that such an anointing can at least later be interpreted as having been performed on behalf of God.

Secondly, the oil used for the purpose is said to have been fetched "from the tent" (v. 39). Now, we do not really know what is meant by this "tent". Various interpretations are possible[39] but at all events the "tent" seems to be some kind of sanctuary. In agreement with this Ps 89,21 speaks of God's "holy oil", used for the anointing of the king. In a sense this brings the royal anointings in line with the anointing of cultic objects and persons. Compared with David's two anointings this means something new, since David can hardly be supposed to have been anointed with such sacred oil "from the tent".

Thirdly, the appearance of a prophet, Nathan, is a further element that falls into line with the two above-mentioned observations. Although Zadok is the one who handles the horn of oil (v. 39) there is no reason to delete Nathan in David's order "and let Zadok the priest and Nathan the prophet there anoint him" (v. 34).[40] How are we then to imagine the role of Nathan? – An attractive suggestion is that he pronounced an oracle concerning Solomon at the moment of his anointing.[41] Rites always have two sides, viz. what the Greeks called τὰ δρώμενα, "what is being done", and

---

[39] *M.Görg* (1967:124-137, esp. 128 ff.) thinks that this "tent" is not identical with the Davidic "tent", where the ark was placed, and holds that *giḥôn* is to be emended to *gibʿôn*. This is, however, a suggestion that meets with various difficulties, see *Blenkinsopp* (1972:95). A possibility to be considered would be to connect the "tent" with a surmised YHWH sanctuary from the days of David. Cf. 2 S 12,20 and note that *ʾohæl* can be used of a temple (for instance Ps 15,1; 27,5; 61,5; Jes 33,20). For the possibility of a Davidic sanctuary see *Ahlström* (VT 11/1961, 126 f.).

[40] Note the unanimous textual attestation of reading "Nathan", and note that a verb in the singular (like *ûmašăḥ*) can be used in the first position about a subject in the plural, see *BrSynt* (§ 50a). I therefore agree with *Šanda* (1911:20). *Montgomery – Gehman* (1951:77) and *Noth* (1968:24), who retain Nathan in 1 R 1,34. Others take Nathan to be an addition so *Weinel* (ZAW 18/1898, 23 f.), *Benzinger* (1899:7) and *L.Schmidt* (1970:176 f.).

[41] See *Noth* (1968:24).

τὰ λεγόμενα, "what is being said". The presence of the prophet Nathan calls attention to the nature of the words accompanying the rite, although they have not been handed down here. It is also a well-known fact that oracles of anointing are found in other texts: 1 S 9,27–10,7 (Saul); 2 R 9,3 (Jehu); Ps 2,7-9; 110,1-3. If Nathan pronounced such an oracle this would explain why he is mentioned in direct connection with the anointing in 1 R 1,34 although it is quite clear from v. 39 that Zadok is the one who is responsible for "what is being done".

In its expanded form, the end of the SN (above ch. 1) testifies to the convention of speaking of the anointing as having been carried out by a whole body of persons, and this in 1 R 1,45. While Nathan is to be retained in v. 34, the same does not hold for v. 45. Here ṣadôq hăkkohen wᵉnatan hănnabî' is probably a gloss, although generally attested in the manuscripts. The group of persons present at the anointing is mentioned in v. 44: Zadok, Nathan, Benaiah and the Cherethites and the Pelethites. After the anointing the same group of persons went up (wăyyă'ᵃlû) from Gihon to the city. The verb 'ala in v. 45 must refer to the same persons as those mentioned in v. 44. But the gloss in v. 45 cuts this connection and makes only Zadok, Nathan and Benaiah leave the scene at the conclusion of the act. My conclusion is therefore that the original reading was: wăyyimšᵉḥû 'otô lᵉmœlæk bᵉgihôn wăyyă'ᵃlû miššam ... .[42] If this is correct, then we have here a case when an anointing carried out by a priest is referred to by a formulation in the plural. Quite clearly, the plural here is not to be taken *ad litteram*. But we are not thereby entitled to think that this holds for all cases where the verb "anoint" appears with a plural subject.[43] On the contrary the use of the plural is to be seen as resulting from a stubborn convention (cf. 2 R 11,12; 2 R 23,30) that must have had some basis in reality.

In conclusion, then, Solomon's anointing holds a very important place in the material. It is of a different character from that of David's since there is no assembly of elders present. At one point the difference is quite tangible: the anointing of David created a particular relation between David and the people and was carried out for Judah and Israel separately. The personal union between Judah and Israel continued to exist during the reign of Solomon, but Solomon was nevertheless anointed only once.

3. The "Divine" Anointings

Three kings are expressly said to have been anointed by God, viz. Saul, David and Jehu. I shall call these cases "divine" anointings. The cases of Saul and Jehu provide the clue to the statements about David's divine anointing. Both Saul and Jehu are anointed by human intermediaries, but these anointings are also described as enacted by God himself (1 S 10,1; 2 R 9.3.6.12). Then it is probable that the formulations about a divine

---

[42] Cf. *Weinel* (ZAW 18/1898, 24) and *L.Schmidt* (1970: 176).
[43] Contra *L.Schmidt* (1970: 176, 180).

anointing of David in Ps 89,21 and 2 S 12,7 refer to an anointing carried out by a human intermediary. Through its very wording, 2 S 12,7 points to an anointing that precedes David's adventures with Saul: "I anointed you king over Israel, and I delivered you out of the hand of Saul; . . . ."[44] There is here a tacit reference to the inviolability of the anointed one as the explanation of the fact that David was able to outlive Saul. Therefore, this anointing of David must be the one mentioned in 1 S 16,1-13. There are then three anointings that are described as having been carried out by God:

Saul's anointing by Samuel (1 S 10,1).
David's anointing by Samuel (1 S 16,13; cf. Ps 89,21; 2 S 12,7).
Jehu's anointing by a prophet (2 R 9,6).

Since the term $maši^ah$ links the king exclusively with God, it is natural to infer that it has something to do with this conception of the divine anointing of the king. We have already estimated the probabilities for the chronological assessment of the terminology $m^eši^ah\ YHWH$. We found that this terminology was probably developed during the reign of Solomon. Let us now attempt to come to grips with the date and background of the conception of the divine anointing of the king.

From our previous investigations[44a] it appears that the passage concerning David (1 S 16,1-13) is the one of these three cases that must be judged to contain the oldest tradition of such a divine anointing. We found that the tradition of David's anointing by Samuel preceded that of Saul's, and we were able to work out the following chronological sequence:

1. 1 S 10,17-27   Saul's election and acclamation
2. 1 S 16,1-13   David's divine anointing
3. 1 S 9,1 – 10,16 Saul's divine anointing as *nagîd*
4. the HDR   (the author of which used 1 S 16,1-13)

The absolute age of the tradition in 1 S 16,1-13 is of course impossible to determine. Nevertheless, the above-mentioned chronological sequence provides an *ante quem*. The tradition in question is older than both the HDR and the tradition of Saul's anointing as *nagîd*. This takes us back as far as the end of Solomon's reign. To find a *post quem* is more difficult. The only thing that can be said is that the tradition in 1 S 16,1-13 must be later than that in 1 S 10,17-27, something that does not, however, offer a definite point of time. In my discussion of the source material I pointed out that 1 S 10,17-27 cannot be read as a report of actual events, and suggested

---

[44] I here agree with *A.Schulz* (1920: 129) and *Hertzberg* (1964: 313). *Budde* (1902: 255) is of a different opinion: the anointing in 2 S 12,7 need not refer to 1 S 16,13.
[44a] See ch. 9.5.

that this tradition should be seen against the background of Solomon's investiture, as a plea for the rights of the people in relation to royal power.

Now, it is widely recognized that the passage concerning David's anointing by Samuel (1 S 16,1-13) is also difficult to exploit as a source of information about actual events in the life of David.[45] But as to the reason for the existence of this tradition, the commentators are at a loss to explain it. Since there are indications of a date as early as Solomon's reign I should like to submit the following hypothesis: the tradition of David's anointing by Samuel was created to meet the need for a historical precedent for Solomon's investiture. Solomon was anointed without the participation of the popular assembly, and he became king in spite of the disturbing fact that he lacked the right of primogeniture. As his senior Adonijah was the more probable candidate. A number of features in 1 S 16,1-13 support this theory.

First, the figure of Samuel deserves attention. From other traditions we know him as a judge and as a seer/prophet, but here one is inclined to see him more as a priest (the sacrifice), although he cannot historically have been a priest in any genuine sense.[46] If our tradition had anything to do with Solomon's investiture, then it is easy to see that a priestly Samuel, without his qualities of judge and prophet, is an apt counterpart of the priest who performed Solomon's anointing.

Secondly, there is no trace here of a "synergism" between God and the people. We are not faced with the combination of divine election and popular acclamation found in the tradition of Saul in 1 S 10,17-27. Even this feature makes the tradition of David fit into the picture as a historical precedent for the procedure at Solomon's anointing. The anointing of David in 1 S 16,1-13 is not carried out by a popular assembly. We are not concerned with a public act. David is anointed in privacy. The whole story is theocentric. The initiative is God's, and Samuel only acts as God's representative when he carries out His order.

Thirdly, it is clear that in the tradition concerning David there is a certain stress on the circumstance that the human principle of primogeniture is superseded by divine election. Eliab, the first-born (1 S 17,13), would normally have been the one to be chosen. But here God prefers the very youngest of the sons of Jesse. The older sons are eliminated one by one until we come to David whose election is so improbable that he is not even present. There is here a striking similarity with the case of Solomon. Three

---

[45] See for instance *Budde* (1902:114), *Caspari* (1926:188 top), and *Stoebe* (1973:303). The latter says that we have here "weniger alte Überlieferung als theologische Absicht".
[46] See *Cody* (1969:72-80, esp. 78f.). The "seer" in the LXX of 1 S 16,4 is probably a harmonization with 1 S 9,1-10,16 where there are both priestly and (still more) prophetic features in Samuel.

of his brethren, older than himself, Amnon Absalom and Adonijah, were one by one eliminated through the course of events. Perhaps it is not by chance that the same number are mentioned by name in the tradition concerning David, viz. Eliab, Abinadab and Shamma (v. 6-9). Solomon and David are thus presented as having the disadvantage of not being able to base their claim to the throne on the principle of primogeniture. But God is not bound by such human principles. He acts freely in His election. The tradition of David's anointing by Samuel is nothing less than a condensed parallel of the events of the drama of the Davidic Succession which led up to the investiture of Solomon.

Fourthly, we can add that there is even a case of almost verbal similarity between the divine anointing of David and the investiture of Solomon:

1 R 1,39: ויקח צדוק הכהן את קרן השמן
מן האהל ויםשח את שלמה

1 S 16,13: ויקח שמואל את קרן השמן
ויםשח אתו ...

This should not be mistaken for definite proof of connection, the missing link in the chain of arguments. But although it does not elevate my theory to the rank of established fact it does, in fact, point in the same direction. It should be noted that the expression *qæræn hăššæmæn* is only found in these two passages, while we find *păk hăššæmæn*, "flask of oil", in 1 S 10,1 and 2 R 9,1.3.

The cumulative weight of these different indications should not be disregarded by the scholar who seeks an explanation of the tradition contained in 1 S 16,1-13. If the main lines of my argument are correct then this tradition should be considered in conjunction with what we know of Solomon's investiture and with the tradition of Saul in 1 S 10,17-27. The last-mentioned tradition speaks of Saul, designated by God and acclaimed king by the assembly, as the antithesis of Solomon. The tradition of David's anointing by Samuel provides a precedent for the procedure at Solomon's investiture and resolves the "Solomonic dilemma" by implying (a) that the absence of the assembly does not detract from the fact of divine election and (b) that the rite of anointing is in itself the sign of election. If, as I have suggested, the tradition in 1 S 10,17-27 is directed against Solomon, it is also understandable why 1 S 16,1-13 not only offers a precedent for anointing without the participation of the popular assembly, but also – in Eliab's rejection in v. 7 – is a direct criticism of the tradition of Saul in 1 S 10,17-27.

What we hear about the anointing in 1 S 16,1-13 can be summarized in the following points:

1. The connection between the popular assembly and the rite of anointing

has been dissolved. Instead, the anointing is said to have been performed by a man who is manifestly a man of God with a special divine commission. It is in no way public[47] and is not accompanied by popular acclamation.
2. The anointing does not bring about a relation between the king and the people. Instead, it has the character of a consecration for YHWH: "... and you shall anoint for me [*lî*] him whom I name to you" (v. 3). *The rite has become sacralized.*
3. The anointing amounts to a visible sign of the divine *election* of the king. Election terminology is of considerable importance in the passage (*ma'ăs – bāḥăr* in v. 7-10). The anointing seals the divine election of David.
4. There is an immediate connection between the anointing and the bestowal of the *charisma* of the Spirit. (v. 13). The charisma is closely related to the rite itself. There are no immediate spectacular manifestations of it. From the point of view of this tradition the question of how one could know that David had the Spirit could only be answered: because he was anointed. That the royal charisma of the Spirit did not have an intrinsic and original connection with the rite of anointing is shown by 1 S 11,1-11 and by the tradition of Saul and the unknown seer in its ancient form before the incorporation of Saul's anointing as *nagîd* (1 S 10,2 ff.). In the tradition of David's anointing by Samuel (1 S 16,1-13), *the charisma has become ritualized* and, I should like to add, it has also become routinized,[47a] stripped of its earlier dramatic manifestations.

Up to the time when the conception of Saul's anointing as *nagîd* emerged, the story of David's anointing by Samuel appeared as a narrative relating the "first" royal anointing among the Hebrew tribes. This tradition is to be classified as a *cultic legend*, a *hieros logos* for the custom of anointing the king. This custom was originally of a secular character but is here derived from a divine injunction and is interpreted as a profoundly sacral rite. The etiological element should not be overlooked. This cultic legend provides "historical" justification for a development of the rite that was initiated by the anointing of Solomon.

Before we turn to the problem of what the anointing was held to bring about, the efficacy of the rite, some concluding reflections on the subject performing the rite can be appended:

---

[47] Note also the possibility that *bᵉqæræb 'æḥâw* in 1 S 16,13 means "from the midst of his brothers", see *A.Schulz* (1919: 248) and *Hertzberg* (1964: 139).
[47a] Cf. *MaxWeber* on "die Veralltäglichung des Charisma" (GdS III:1, ³1947: 142 ff. Note especially what he says on "Amtscharisma" and the transference of this through a hierourgical act). See also below ch. 11.

(1) One could of course be tempted to think that David had been anointed by his priest, Abiathar, and that mention of the participation of this man had been suppressed by the author of the HDR since at the time of the composition of this work the Zadokides ruled the cultic community.[48] Nevertheless, it seems that there was very little of sacral character in David's anointings over Judah and Israel (2 S 2,4; 5,3). As has earlier been pointed out[49] the very fact that David was anointed twice complicates a sacral interpretation. The most attractive alternative is that David's anointings create a new relation of obligation between him and the people. Therefore, *if* the rite was performed by the priest, this individual certainly acted in the name of the people and only after the people had somehow expressed its recognition of the candidate for the throne. But if we also consider the fact that the fairly persistent convention of using the verb *mašăḥ* in the plural must have had a quite specific background in historical reality, then the balance of probabilities must be said to be in favour of the conclusion that the people, acting through their leading elders, actually performed the rite in the case of David.

(2) In the case of Solomon it is clearly an individual, a priest, that performs the decisive act. The same is true of the divine anointings of Saul, David and Jehu, albeit the agent has the character of a prophet in the cases of Saul and Jehu. The anointing is now held to bring about a relation between God and the king. It is not difficult to see that this new interpretation of the rite had a very great impact on the language. The noun *mašîaḥ* is thus never associated with the land or the people, but only with God. This being so, I consider it probable that from Solomon onwards the rite was performed by a priest. The plural formulation in 2 R 11,12 (MT) cannot nullify this conclusion. To be sure, one must agree with Kutsch that this verse in the MT is to be preferred to that of the LXX and to the parallel in 2 Ch 23,11 (anointing by a priest).[50] But against the background of what has been said above, it is most difficult to agree with this scholar that this instance makes it impossible to hold that the kings of Judah were normally anointed by the High Priest.[51] In particular, it should be noted that Solomon's anointing, so obviously carried out by an individual, is also referred to as performed by a collective (1 R 1,45 text. emend.).

3. The Efficacy of the Rite

I have repeatedly denoted the royal anointing as a rite. In doing so I understand "rite" as "die sozial stereotypisierte, zur Regelform gewordene Ablaufsganzheit eines als korrekt geltenden Verhaltens"[52]. It is to be noted that a rite can be profane as well as sacred.[52a] I shall now turn to the problem of the efficacy of the rite of royal anointing in ancient Israel, that is, I shall ask what the rite was held to bring about. We cannot of course here feel

---

[48] Cf. what *Grønbæk* (1971: 127-143) says of 1 S ch. 21–22.

[49] *L.Schmidt* (1970: 179f.). Nevertheless, the same scholar unduly generalizes from the anointing of Solomon: "1 Kön 1 belegt auch, dass Stellen, an denen eine Mehrzahl als Subjekt der Salbung auftritt, auf eine ungenaue Ausdrucksweise zurückgehen" (p. 176).

[50] See *Kutsch* (1963: 54) for details. Note that the Chronicler has so to speak "moved the atnach".

[51] *Kutsch* (1963: 54f.).

[52] So *W.E.Mühlmann* (RGG³ 5/1961, 1 127).

[52a] See *Å.Hultkrantz* (1973: 21ff.).

satisfied with a broad and non-specific definition of this rite as a *rite de passage*, a ritualized change of status. While this definition is correct, it is necessary to carry the analysis still further and ask if there were other uses of oil in the ancient Near East that can have provided a frame of reference, uses whose significance may be illuminating in the present case. We must here be aware of the fact that the interpretation of a rite always involves very subtle problems. Scholars of comparative religion often point out that it is virtually impossible to arrive at a definite understanding of certain ancient rites.

The problems of (a) the origin and (b) the nature of the rite as practised *in situ* in Israel must be kept strictly apart as two different questions. Thus, even if the rite was adopted under foreign influence, it may well be that it assumed a profoundly new significance in Israel. We must reckon with the possibility of what A.L.Kroeber has termed *stimulus diffusion*.[52b]

The anointing of kings was not practised in Egypt or Mesopotamia. However, it is attested for Hatti. Kutsch suggested that the Israelite anointing by the people goes back to Hittite influence.[53] This seems feasible enough, but as soon as we realize that this influence must have been mediated by the Canaanites, as Kutsch believes, certain problems emerge. To be sure, the Jotham fable with its plural formulations could be taken to attest to a Canaanite custom with the people anointing the king, but the uncertainty as regards the date and origin of this fable makes such an interpretation far from conclusive. The only unequivocal testimony to a royal anointing among the Canaanites is found in EA 51,4-9, where it is said that Thutmose III made Taku king of *Nuḫašše* and anointed his head with oil. Now, this anointing corresponds to the Egyptian practice of anointing officials at their installation.[54] The anointing of Taku is thus to be seen as a rite of vassalage. This is an isolated example, and we do not know if other Canaanite royal anointings were of the same nature, but if such was the case, two points must be made:

(a) The royal anointing of the Hittites hardly had this character of rite of vassalage.[55] Besides, as H.M.Kümmel has pointed out, one text that seems to speak of the reigning king as designating his successor by anointing him, makes Kutsch's interpretation problematic when he takes the Hittite anointing to express the authorization of the king by the nobles.[56] Thus it seems difficult to establish a

---

[52b] See *A.L.Kroeber* (1952: 344 ff.), and cf. *Å.Hultkrantz* (1973: 180).
[53] *Kutsch* (1963: 56).
[54] See *Cothenet* (DBS 6: 714), *Kutsch* (1963: 34 f.), and *deVaux* (Mél. Tisserant 1/1964, 131 f.). Further references for such anointing of Egyptian officials are found in *W.Helck* (Lexikon der Ägyptologie 1,2/1973, 228), and several cases are adduced by Redford in his survey of Egyptian scenes of investiture (1970: 209 ff.).
[55] See *Kutsch* (1963: 36 ff.) and *H.M.Kümmel* (1967: 43 ff.).
[56] See *H.M.Kümmel* (1967: 44 f.) criticizing *Kutsch* (1963: 38 f.). The above-mentioned text is

connection between the Hittite anointing and the rite known from Canaan. It also seems that the similarities between the Hittite rite and the Israelite may be more superficial than one has been inclined to think.

(b) An interpretation of the origin and import of royal anointing in Israel must account for David's anointing, as this is to be understood according to the historical analysis above as a rite carried out "in the name of the people". Whether deVaux's interpretation of the anointing as a rite that made the king the vassal of YHWH is suitable or not for the later idea of anointing, deVaux actually made the mistake of overlooking this development in the rite.[57] The Egyptian anointing of officials and vassals, which this scholar drew attention to, gives no immediate clue to the understanding of the Israelite rite.

It is quite possible that the practice of royal anointing among the Canaanites was of importance as a general *impetus* when the rite was taken up in Israel. But for reasons stated above, this influence is then restricted to the formal level as a case of *stimulus diffusion*. It seems difficult in this way to shed light on the principles underlying the rite.

The biblical texts speak of different performers of the rite. On the one hand we find the people and on the other the priest, who is subsequently considered as acting in the name of God. This means that we find the people and God as the "ultimate" performers of the rite. It is then a remarkable circumstance that the king was conceived of as standing in contractual relation to both the people and YHWH. We have already discussed the covenant between king and people, and the "Davidic covenant" will be discussed in an ensuing chapter. It may be sufficient to say here that there are traces of this conception of a contractual relation between the king and YHWH in certain formulations in the prophecy of Nathan (in its dynastic redaction) and in the choice of the terms *ḥoq* and *'edût* (Ps 2,7; 2 R 11,12), and that this conception found its crowning expression in the use of the term *bᵉrît* to denote the divine promise to David.[58]

We can then speak of a remarkable co-variation of the conceptions of who was the ultimate performer of the rite of anointing *and* the conceptions of the king's contractual relations, a circumstance that has so far escaped notice. Our observations can be summarized thus:

KBo XVI 25 recto 51ff., now reproduced in *Kümmel* (p. 44). The other important text on Hittite anointing is the ritual for the substitute king, KUB XXIV 5+IX, 13 recto 19f., now found in *Kümmel* (p. 10), cf. *ANET*³ (p. 355 col. b).

[57] See *deVaux* (Mél. Tisserant I, 1964: 129-133). – The difference between the solution suggested by deVaux and the one set forth in the present study should not be overlooked. I am critical of deVaux particularly on the following points: (a) He overlooked the development in the rite and based his conclusions on an unhistorical understanding of the Biblical evidence. (b) His frame of reference was all too narrowly restricted to relations of vassalhood. (c) He built his conclusions almost exclusively on EA no 51 and supposed an Egyptian influence behind the Israelite rite.

[58] See ch. 8 and ch. 12.3. For my general "covenant terminology", see excursus no 2.

anointing: ultimate performer	*covenant: parties involved*
the people	– the people
God	– God

I have tried to demonstrate that the rite of anointing underwent a process of development. In the early monarchy, the king was anointed in the name of the people. Even at this early stage we find the conception of a royal covenant between king and people. But there are no traces in the earliest traditions of a contractual relation between the king and God. Later God was envisaged as the ultimate performer of the rite, and then we also find traces of the conception of a contractual relation between the king and God. It seems then that the ideas related to anointing and covenant form what students of comparative religion would call a *configuration of beliefs*.[59]

It is obvious that this type of formal similarity between two sets of ideas does not necessarily presuppose an original, organic connection between the two. However, the observation is striking enough to rouse our suspicions and make us formulate the question: was the efficacy of the rite of anointing to establish a community – whether on the level of an exchange relation or on the more qualified level of a contractual relation – between the performer and the recipient in the rite?[59a]

Although unduly neglected, there is in the ancient Semitic material a use of unction that is linked with the establishment of an exchange relation and even of a contractual relation. This use of unction is attested for cases both of parity and of vassalage. That is to say, it may well account for both David's anointing by the people and for the subsequent theological reflection on the anointing as carried out by God. It occurs in very different settings, at the conclusion of a purchase of land, at the contraction of a marriage, as a manifestation of friendly international relations or human submission under a god. Some of these cases, the anointing of buyer and seller at a business transaction and the anointing of the bride, are understood by Kutsch as cases of anointing as "Reinigung – Freimachung", analogous to the case in the Akkadian text from Ugarit RS 8.208, where a female slave is anointed by her master as a token of her liberation.[60] As we shall see, this interpretation is hardly convincing. Instead, a contractual interpretation of such instances should be seriously considered.

---

[59] See the chapter "Funktionalism och konfigurationell forskning" in Å.*Hultkrantz* (1973: 101-118, esp. 111 ff. and 116 f.).
[59a] On exchange relations and contractual relations, see excursus no 2.
[60] This case is treated by *Kutsch* (1963: 16 ff.). For further evidence see *Veenhof* (BiOr 23/1966, 310).

1. Oil and Contractual Relations in the Ancient Near East

That anointing, just as eating and drinking created a general sense of fellowship is evidenced by some lines in the series *Utukkū lemnūti* Tabl. IV col. V 34 f. (CT XVI 11):

> Whether [you are a demon saying]: "I want to eat with him today [Sum.: daily]", or: "I want to drink with him today", or: "I want to anoint myself with him today", or: "I want to cloth myself with him today...".[61]

Similarly, as a token of hospitality, bread, water, a garment and oil are offered to Adapa in Anu's heaven.[62] In both cases, however, the persons anoint themselves. For obvious reasons we are more interested in the present study in cases where the rite has a reciprocity or transitivity.

(1) Oil as a Diplomatic Symbol. – Of great interest to us is the use of oil in international relations, not as merchandise or as tribute but as a diplomatic symbol. The text KBo I 14 – probably a letter from Hattusilis III to the Assyrian king Shalmaneser I[63] – states that it was customary for kings to send oil when a new king assumed kingship in a neighbouring country:

> Did not [my father] send the proper presents [*šul-ma-na-ti*] to you? [But] when I assumed kingship, you did not send[63a] me an ambassador. Still, it is customary [*pár-ṣú*] that – kings assume [king]ship, and the kings, his peers [*mi-iḫ-ru-šú*], send him the proper [pres]ents [on that occasion], a royal gown [*lu-bu-ul-ta ša šarru-ut-ti*], fine [oil] for anointing [*ša na-ap-šu-ši*]. But you did not do such a thing today. (KBo I 14 verso 4-10[64])

Here, the sending of oil and a royal gown[64a] is an act of diplomatic courtesy. The oil signifies peace, friendship and fellowship between the two countries. Whether a sort of contractual relation is also involved we do not know.

This, however, seems to be the case in one of the Amarna letters from Alashiya, which I here quote together with Knudtzons translation:

> (42) *ù lu-[ú en-ni]-pu-uš ki-it-tu*
> *i-na bi-[ri-]ku-ni ù*
> $^{am\bar{e}lu}$ *mār ši-ip-(!)ia a-na maḫ-ri-qa*
> (45) *ji-li-ku ù* $^{am\bar{e}lu}$ *mār ši-ip-ri-ka*
> *a-na maḫ-ri-ia ji-li-ku ša-ni-tú*
> *šamnē ù kitê a-na mi-nim la-a*

---

[61] The translation quoted is that by *Veenhof* (BiOr 23/1966, 310 col. a).

[62] See the Adapa myth, lines 29 ff. and 60 ff., text in *Knudtzon* (EA no 356), translation in *ANET*³ (p. 102). For this understanding of the anointing in the Adapa myth, see *Th.Jacobsen* (AJSL 46/1930, 201-203).

[63] See *Goetze* (1940: 31 f.).

[63a] I have here corrected the misprint "sent" in Goetze's translation.

[64] The translation is that by *Goetze*, who also presents the text (Kizzuwatna 1940: 28 f.).

[64a] It is possible that the royal garment represents the person of the sender, cf. *J.M.Munn-Rankin* (Iraq 18/1956, 92) and *Petschow* (RLA III/1957-1971, 319 col. b).

tu-wa-ši-ru-ni a-na ku[-t]ú⁶⁴ᵇ ù ša
te-ri-šu at-ta ù a-[na-k]u id-di-nu
(50) ù al-lu-ú ḫa-ba-na-at[ša]šamna ṭāba
ma-la-at a-na ta-pa-ki a-na [qa-qa]-di-ka
uš-ši-ir-ti i-nu-ma tu-ša-ab a-na ⁱˢᵘkussî
šarruʳᵘ -[t]a-ka

(42) Und es mög[e gesc]hehen, was recht ist, (43) zwisc[h]en uns, und (44) mein Bot[e] möge vor dich (45) kommen, und dein Bote (46) möge vor mich kommen! Ferner: (47) warum hast du mir nicht Öl und kitû (48) gesandt zu . . . . . ? Das, worum (49) du gebeten hast, habe doch i[ch] gegeben, (50) und ich habe sogar eine . . . . . , [die] von gutem Öl (51) voll ist, gesandt zum Ausgiessen auf deinen (52) [Kop]f, jetzt da du sitzest auf dem Throne (53) deines Königtums.

(EA 34,42-53⁶⁵)

A number of points are still obscure, but the situation seems to be as follows: The king of Alashiya (prob.=Cyprus⁶⁶) has heard that a new Pharaoh, probably Amenophis IV,⁶⁷ has assumed kingship and therefore expresses his intention to send a rich gift (EA 33,9 ff.). EA 34 presupposes a complaint from Pharaoh that the messenger with the promised gift has not yet arrived (EA 34,9-10). The king of Alashiya excuses himself that he did not know of Pharaoh's (coronation-?) feast (34,11-12). He renews his promise to send a gift, now reduced to 100 talents of copper (cf. EA 35,12 ff.). In a following list, he enumerates what he wants from Egypt, among other things he mentions (line 24 f.) 17 jars (ḫabannatu=Egypt. hbn.t⁶⁷ᵃ) of fine oil and 4 kitê šarri, that is, four pieces of royal linen=Egyptian šs nsw.⁶⁸ The end of the passage quoted above (line 46 ff.) is not altogether lucid. Either the king of Alashiya reproaches his addressee for not sending "oil and linen", or, he quotes a second complaint from his addressee (cf. line 8-9) that the king of Alashiya has not sent the things mentioned.⁶⁹ Since "oil and linen" occur in line 24 f., I think that the first alternative is the more probable one. The oil, sent from the king of Alashiya (line 50 ff.), should not be regarded as merchandise. The "one jar full of perfumed oil, to pour on your head, now when you are sitting on the throne of your kingdom" has the same sense of a symbolic gift as in the letter KBo I 14, quoted above.

A study of the context reveals that this symbolic delivery of oil should be regarded as a token of friendship and fraternity. Kutsch's interpretation

---

⁶⁴ᵇ *Ebeling* (Glossar, EA vol. II p. 1443) reads *ana ku-tam*: "Bedeutung unbekannt".
⁶⁵ Text and translation from *Knudtzon* (EA). The item is discussed by *Kutsch* (1963: 67).
⁶⁶ See *O.Weber* (EA vol. II p. 1076 f.).
⁶⁷ See *Weber* (EA vol. II p. 1078).
⁶⁷ᵃ See *vonSoden* (AHw p. 302b), *CAD* (6/Ḥ p. 7) and for Egyptian *hbn.t* Erman–Grapow (II: 487).
⁶⁸ See *CAD* (8/K p. 474 col. a sub 3').
⁶⁹ The text is understood in the former way by *Knudtzon* (see the translation quoted above) and by *deVaux* (Mél. Tisserant 1/1964, 130) and in the latter way by *Kutsch* (1963: 67).

of it as an act of diplomatic courtesy[69a] is not wrong but can be qualified in a particular sense. The international relations between Egypt and Alashiya have been discussed by Y.L.Holmes, who points out that there was a position of equality between the two countries.[70] The king of Alashiya speaks to Pharaoh as his "brother".[71] This takes on significance when compared with the other cases in the Amarna letters when the king of Egypt is called "brother" by a foreign ruler.[72] The vassal does not use this word about his Egyptian overlord. However, Holmes overlooked that there is an indication that the king of Alashiya suggested the conclusion of a formal treaty. This is found in EA 34,42-46, where the meaning can be more exactly defined than appears from Knudtzon's translation (above): *ù l[ú en-ni]-pu-uš kittu ina bi[rī]kuni*, "and a treaty should be made between us (?) (and my messenger should go to you and your messenger should come to me)"[73]. The phrase *kitta epēšu*, occurs in three other cases in the Amarna letters with the sense "to make a treaty".[74] And *kīma ki-ti* in EA 105,21 means "according to the agreement/treaty". It even seems that the treaty suggested came into existence between Egypt and Alashiya, since the king of the latter country takes the liberty of expressing a concern that Egypt might not engage in relations with Shanhar or the king of Hatti: *it-ti-šu-nu la ta-ša-ki-in* (EA 35,49-50). The kind of ellipsis here can be inferred from the formulation *ù inanna iš-ku-nu ki-it-ta ina berīšunu*, "and now they have made a treaty with each other" (RS 17.123, 5-6).[75] Thus we may conclude that EA 35,49-50 contains a formal request from the king of Alashiya to the Egyptian king not to make an alliance with certain other states: "do not make a treaty with them".

The relation between the symbolic gift of oil and the contraction of an international treaty in EA 34[76] should not be seen as meaning that the gift of oil implies ratification of the treaty. Oil is not here what in German would be called a *Perfektionszeichen*. From the text it seems that the king of Alashiya has already sent the oil and now as a second step suggests a

---

[69a] *Kutsch* discusses this and other cases under the heading "Überreichung von Salböl als Akt der Huldigung" (1963: 66 ff.). From the context it appears that he uses "Huldigung" in the non-technical sense of "Zuwendung von 'Ehre'" (p. 68) and not in the sense of a vassal's recognition of his lord.

[70] Y.L.*Holmes* (AOAT 22/1973, 91 ff., esp. 96). Holmes does not discuss the question of oil or the possibility of an actual treaty (see below).

[71] Note the introductory addresses in EA nos 33–35 and 37–39.

[72] See *Holmes* (op. cit. p. 97 for references). For the same usage in other texts, see *J.M.Munn-Rankin* (Iraq 18/1956, 76 ff.).

[73] This is the translation of *CAD* (4/E p. 211 sub *epēšu* with *kittu*). *Holmes* (op. cit.) overlooked this possibility of an outright treaty.

[74] See EA 83,24 f.; 125,39 f.; 138,53 (cf. 132,33). See also *CAD* (4/E p. 211 and 8/K p. 471 f. sub litt. e).

[75] This text is found in *PRU IV* (p. 230 f.).

[76] This interesting connection has been overlooked in previous discussions of the text.

treaty. The oil is a token of peace and goodwill that can be developed into a formal contract.

Let us leave EA 34 for the inscription on the statue of Idrimi, king of Alalakh.[77] Due to the poor state of preservation, a probable case in this text has to remain hypothetic. Here, too, the context deals with international relations. Idrimi says in line 42 ff. that he has sent a messenger to the Hurrian king Barattarna in order to accept renewed vassalage under him.[78] The Hurrian king listens to a description of the former services (*mānaḫtu* from *anāḫu* I "to toil", "to become tired"[79]) and of the former oath (*māmītu*) between the two countries. Then follows an interesting but textually not altogether certain statement, which S.Smith in his official publication of the text read LÚ *šu-ul-mi-ia im-da-ḫar*[79a] (line 54-55), which means "he received (accepted) the man of my peace". Smith frankly admitted by means of an asterisk in his edition that LÚ was an uncertain reading. Goetze, in his review of Smith's edition, suggested the alternative reading NI which is the Sumerogram for *šamnu*, "oil".[80] The resulting translation would then be "he received (accepted) the oil of my peace". A new inspection of the original is necessary to settle the point, if it is possible to settle at all. But some points can be made: (a) It is not clear why Barattarna's receiving of the messenger should be mentioned here at the end of the passage. The acceptance of "oil of peace" would certainly make sense just here. The offering and acceptance of oil would then signify the assumption of friendly and peaceful relations between the two countries. (b) The phrase *šaman šulmija* would have a parallel in a new Ugaritic text in which *šmn šlm* occurs (UT 603 verso 4[81]). These observations do not prove but certainly support reading *šaman šulmija* in Idrimi line 54 f. If this is correct, we have here a case where the acceptance of "oil of peace" is the symbol of a resumed treaty relation between the two countries. The oil is not here sent on the occasion of a coronation, but as a token of

---

[77] For the text see *S.Smith* (The Statue of Idrimi 1949: 16). Discussions of this most difficult text are found in *Albright* (BASOR 118/1950, 14 ff.) and *A.Goetze* (JCS 4/1950, 226 ff.). In all essentials I agree with *A.L.Oppenheim* in his translation of the passage under discussion (ANET³ p. 557), which is to be preferred to the translation submitted by S.Smith.

[78] I cannot agree with *Goetze* (op. cit. p. 228 note 20) who speaks of "the equality of the two parties". The whole context and particularly the "service" points to a vassal treaty.

[79] See *vonSoden* (AHw p. 601). *Albright* (op. cit. p. 18) translated the word "the conditions of peace", apparently deriving it from *nâḫu*.

[79a] I have corrected the obvious printing error *im-da-har*.

[80] *Goetze* (JCS 4/1950, 228 col. b).

[81] This text (=RS 24.245) was published as text no 3 by *Virolleaud* in Ugaritica V (p. 556-559). *Gordon* refers to it under the UT number UT 603. For the bibliography of the text se *Rainey* (JAOS 94/1974, 193) and for Rainey's own views ibid. (p. 188 f.). On the basis of UT 603, the same reading *šmn šlm* can now be restored in ʿ*nt* II 31 f. – As for *šulmu/šlm*, note that words for grace and friendship are important in the ancient Near Eastern covenant terminology, cf. *Weinfeld* (JAOS 93/1973, 191 ff.).

submission and readiness to accept the obligations of a treaty, in this case a vassal treaty.

The same could be said of some lines in the Assyrian ritual col. I.[82] There is no explicit contractual relation here, but the underlying conception seems to be contractual. Before the coronation of the Assyrian king, there goes the proclamation "Ashur is king!" (line 29). The prince goes to the temple and prostrates himself before the god while a robe and a bowl of oil are placed before the feet of the image (lines 30-37). He accepts the status of vassal of the god.

Let us now leave the international sphere for cases of unction in connection with contractual relations of two specific types, viz. business and marriage.

(2) Anointing in Business Contracts. – The Mari text ARM VIII 13[83] is a business contract and records a purchase of land. The seller "bestows" (*in-ḫi-il* from *naḫālu*, corresponding to Hebr. *naḥăl*) the field on the buyer. Likewise the buyer "bestows" a certain amount of money on the seller. The terminology makes it probable that the text deals with a piece of land that was in principle inalienable and that the transaction is of the type that G.Boyer termed "vente déguisée" so that the case is comparable to the sales adoptions at Nuzi.[84] The end of the text reads:

ka-ra-am i-ku-lu	They have eaten from the [same] platter,
ka-sa-am iš-tu-ú	drunk from the [same] goblet,
ù ša-am-na-am	and anointed each other
ip-ta-šu	with oil.
	(ARM VIII 13 verso 10 ff.[85])

Kutsch singles out the first two actions, the eating and the drinking, as forming a "Bundesmahl" but prefers to see the anointing as an additional legal rite with a different sense, as a case in point of anointing as "Reinigung – Freimachung", a declaration that the contracting parties are "clean" from claims in connection with the transaction concerned.[86] Veenhof on the other hand holds that the anointment of both parties, just as the common meal, established a community between them and "created a sphere in which the sale could take place".[87] I agree on the general correctness of Veenhof's interpretation, but I am sceptical of the way in which he interprets the act of anointing as a *preparation* for the transaction. The order

---

[82] For text and translation see *K.Fr.Müller* (Das assyrische Ritual 1937: 8f.).
[83] ARM VIII 13 is discussed by *G.Boyer* (in ARM vol. VIII p. 194ff.), *Kutsch* (1963: 19f.) and *Veenhof* (BiOr 23/1966, 309f.).
[84] *G.Boyer* (op. cit. p. 194), cf. *F.Horst* (FsW.Rudolph 1961: 151f.).
[85] For a translation, cf. *CAD* (8/K p. 239 col. b) and *Veenhof* (BiOr 23/1966, 309 col. b).
[86] *Kutsch* (1963: 19f.).
[87] *Veenhof* (op. cit. p. 309 col. b).

seems to be a different one. The next item to be discussed is helpful on this point.

This is a text from about 1800 B.C. from the archives of the Sin temple at Khafajah, ancient Tutub, in the Diyāla region east of the Tigris.[88] The text in question is a business contract concerning a field. Here, the *bukānu* formula (*bukānam šūtuq*)[88a] is immediately followed by the mention of the anointing. This was a mutual anointment. As Kutsch has argued against R.Harris, the reading of the original is correct: *ša-am-na qá-qá-sú-nu pa-ši-iš*. Thus, "their heads", the head of both seller and buyer, were anointed with oil.[89]

As for the meaning of the rite in this text, Kutsch understands it in the same way as he takes ARM VIII 13: anointing as liberation (from claims). Veenhof relies on the same interpretation as he suggested for the Mari text. However, to say that the anointing in the text from Khafajah creates a sphere in which the sale could take place seems a little awkward. The *bukānu* rite signifies the ratification of the contract. If the anointing were preparatory to the transaction it would hardly have been mentioned after the *bukānu* formula. It should be noticed that the anointing perfects the agenda in the two contracts. And at this place one expects a rite of ratification rather than preparation for the sale. I would therefore say that in both contracts the anointing has the contractual character of a rite of ratification, of a *Vertragsperfektion*, to use a convenient German term.

(3) Anointing as a Nuptial Rite. – While anointing may already have occurred as a nuptial rite among the Sumerians,[90] the indisputable evidence[91] is found in the marriage correspondence of the Amarna Pharaohs and of Ramses II, and besides in the Middle Assyrian Laws (=MAL) from roughly the same period[92].

a) MAL § 42-43: The father of the bridegroom anoints the bride. A detailed discussion is given below.

b) EA 11,16-18:[93] The two representatives of the Egyptian king anoint the

---

[88] Published by *R.Harris* (JCS 9/1955, 92 text no 59).

[88a] On the *bukānu* formula, see *Edzard* (ZA 60/1970, 8 ff.). The form *šūtuq* is an Š stative of *etēqu*.

[89] *Kutsch* (1963: 19). *R.Harris* suggested the reading *qá-qá-sú*, deleting *-nu* (loc. cit.).

[90] For the possible reference see *Diakonoff* (RA 52/1958, 9) and cf. *Greengus* (JCS 20/1966, 71 note 105).

[91] The list of occurrences submitted by *Kutsch* (1963: 28 f.) is now to be supplemented by that of *Landsberger* (FsM.David 2/1968, 80 the note), who does not, however, discuss the matter. – The reason why I leave out EA 1,98 is that in this text the father of the bride is responsible for the oil used for the girl, so that we may here have a case of the cosmetic non-ritual use of unction as was suggested by *O. Weber* (EA vol. II p. 1018).

[92] The tablets of the laws are from the reign of Tiglath-Pileser I in the 12th century B.C., but the laws themselves may go back to the 15th century, cf. *T.J.Meek* (ANET³ p. 180).

[93] For restoration and translation see *Landsberger* (loc. cit.).

daughter of Barnuburiash, king of Karduniash. There is no mention of a *tirḫātu*.

c) EA 29,22-23: The messenger of Pharaoh brings oil for the head of the bride, the daughter of Tusratta of Mitanni. Anointing and the handing over of the bridal money *uno acto*.

d) EA 31,11-16[94]: The messenger of Pharaoh anoints the daughter of the king of Arzawa. Mention of a *zuḫalalija* of gold.

e) KUB III 63,15 f.: Ramses II quoting a letter to himself from Hattusilis III:

> Lasse Leute kommen um [gutes Feinöl aufs Haupt mei]ner [Tochter] zu giess[en] und möge [man s]ie ins Haus des Grosskönigs, des Königs von Ägypten, [bringen!][95]

f) KUB III 24+59, 5-7: From the same correspondence of Ramses II:

> Als man gutes Feinöl auf das Haupt der Tochter g[oss,] da hat man [den(?)] Unterweltsgöttern [. . . . .] weggenommen; an jenem Tage wurden die zwei grossen Länder zu einem Lande und ihr, die beiden Grosskönige, wurdet zu einer Brüderschaft.[96]

g) KUB XXVI 53,4[97]

Various interpretations have been suggested for this nuptial rite. Kutsch is of the opinion that it should be compared with the anointing of a female slave at her manumission[98] and holds that the anointing of the bride is to be understood as her " 'Reinigung', 'Freimachung' aus der Muntgewalt ihres Vaters"[99]. There is, however, one serious drawback connected with this interpretation: the case of the female slave would make us expect the former master of the bride, her father, to perform the rite. This is not the case. Instead it is the representatives of the bridegroom (in MAL his father) who carry out the anointing.[100] Veenhof, on the other hand, suggests interpreting the rite as a demonstration by the future husband of his love and care and a promise to account for her livelihood.[101] This does not seem quite impossible, especially since we know that "food, oil, and clothing" were the standard commodities required for the support of a wife in the ancient Near East.[102] But there is no direct evidence for such a significance in the texts where anointing occurs as a nuptial rite.

---

[94] See now the new publication and discussion by *LianeRost* (MIO 4/1956, 334 ff.).
[95] Transliteration and translation in *Edel* (JKIF 2/1952-53, 264 ff.).
[96] Transliteration and translation in *Edel* (op. cit. p. 269).
[97] See *Landsberger* (FsM.David 2/1968, 80 f. end of note 4).
[98] This case, known from Ugarit (RS 8.208), is discussed by *Kutsch* (1963: 16 ff.). Further evidence for this "anointing of liberation" is advanced by *Veenhof* (BiOr 23/1966, 310 col. b).
[99] *Kutsch* (1963: 27 ff., esp. p. 31).
[100] The attempt made by *Kutsch* (1963: 32 f.) to account for this alarming circumstance is hardly convincing.
[101] *Veenhof* (BiOr 23/1966, 310 col. b).
[102] See the texts quoted by *S.Paul* (1970: 56 ff.).

Now, if we study it carefully, one of these texts, the Middle Assyrian Laws, seems to offer a possible understanding of the rite that has so far been overlooked. The text is here given together with the translation by Th.J.Meek in ANET³ (p. 183 f.):

§ 42 (Col. VI 14 ff.)
(14) šum-ma awīlu i-na ūmi ᵐⁱ ra-a-ki
(15) šamna a-na qaqqad mārat awīli it-bu-uk
lu-ú i-na ša-ku-ul-te
ḫu-ru-up-pa-a-te ú-bi-il
tu-ur-ta la-a ú-ta-ar-ru

§ 43 (Col. VI 19 ff.)
(19) šum-ma awīlu lu-ú šamna a-na qaqqadi it-bu-uk
(20) lu-ú ḫu-ru-up-pa-a-te ú-bíl
māru ša aššata ᵗᵃ ú-di-ú-ni-šu-ni
lu-ú me-e-it lu-ú in-na-bi-it
i-na mārê ᵐᵉš -šu ri-ḫa-a-te
iš-tu eli māri rabê ê a-di eli māri
(25) ṣi-iḫ-ri ša-a 10 šanāte ᵐᵉš -šu-ni
a-na ša ḫa-di-ú-ni i-id-dan

§ 42 If a seignior poured oil on the head of a [nother] seignior's daughter on a holiday[103] or brought betrothal-presents on a festival, they shall not make any return [of the gifts].

§ 43 If the seignior either poured oil on [her] head or brought betrothal-presents [and] the son to whom he assigned the wife either died or fled, he may give [her] to whichever he wishes of his remaining sons from the oldest son to the youngest son who is at least ten years old.[104]

These two paragraphs deal with the contraction of an "inchoate marriage"[105]. The fact that the anointing of the bride and the offering of the *ḫuruppu*-gifts are described disjunctively (note *lū*, "or", in line 16 and 20) is of particular interest to us. This can be understood in two different ways. Either, we are faced with two alternative modes of contracting the marriage. Or, we can assume with Driver and Miles that both the anointing of the bride and the offering of the gifts were part of one and the same ceremony, but that the contract was regarded as binding if performance of either of these acts could be proved.[106] Also in the last case, which seems the more probable, it seems that the significance of the anointing can be illuminated by a correct understanding of the nature of the *ḫuruppu*-gifts, since both items have the same legal effect.

[103] The difficult *rāki* in *ina ūmi rāki* is to be understood as the adj. *rāqu*, "empty" (=Bab. *rēqu*), see most recently *Landsberger* (Fs M.David 2/1968, 79f. note 4) contrary to *Driver – Miles* (1935: 482) and *Greengus* (JCS 20/1966, 61 note 34).
[104] For the Assyrian text, see *Driver – Miles* (1935: 410). For legal comments see *Driver – Miles* (1935: 180 ff.) and cf. *Cardascia* (1969: 209 ff.).
[105] Cf. *Driver – Miles* (1935: 173-186).
[106] *Driver – Miles* (1935: 180 f.).

The decisive lines run *lū ina šākulte ḫuruppāte ubil* (lines 16-17). The etymology of *ḫuruppu* may still be open to some doubts, but on the basis of the occurrences so far known there can be little doubt that the word denotes a sort of plate or dish. Thus von Soden: "eine Metallschüssel" (AHw p. 360). Whether the root is the same as that found in *hᵃrûpâ*, attested in post-biblical Hebrew with the sense "designated", "betrothed",[106a] remains to be seen, but it is an interesting possibility. That the word *šākultu* is a derivative of *akālu*, "to eat", goes without saying. It can be rendered "feeding", "banquet".[107] Cardascia thus translates the two lines as a statement concerning the case that the father of the bridegroom "a apporté des plats [nuptiaux] pour la fête".[108] I therefore agree with Landsberger, when he circumscribes the contents of lines 16-17 as "eine von der Seite des Bräutigams in das Haus der Braut gebrachte Mahlzeit".[109]

We then find that MAL § 42-43 refer to what the ethnologists would call a mutual ingestion. Something similar is also known from the Laws of Eshnunna, where § 27 (cf. § 26) stipulates that the bridegroom has to arrange *kir-ra-am ù ri-ik-[sa-]tim a-na a-bi-ša ù um-mi-ša*, "contract and a *kirru* for her father and/or her mother".[110] The word *kirru* has attracted considerable attention in recent years and can now be understood as meaning "drinking party".[111] In addition to these paragraphs in the MAL and the Laws of Eshnunna, there are further cases known of what has been called "ein Hochzeitsmahl mit rechtsverbindlicher Wirkung".[112]

I thus agree with Landsberger that the *šākultu* of the MAL and the *kirru* of the Laws of Eshnunna contribute "zum Sinnbild der Verschwägerung".[113] Since the meal in question, as a gift on the part of the bridegroom comes close to the usual *tirḫātu*, "bridal-money", it should perhaps be remembered that the Sumerian synonym of *tirḫātu* is NÍG.MUNUS.SÁ, which can be literally rendered "Verschwägerung", since MUNUS.SÁ is the bridegroom or the brother-in-law.[114] Indeed, Hebrew *hᵃtunnā* offers a close semantic parallel. This lexical item means "marriage", "wedding", and is a denominative from *ḥatan*, "daughter's husband", "son-in-law".

It is here, in the contractual context of such nuptial rites, that the anointing of the bride belongs. Against the background of the contractual character of the marriage expressed in these rites, and against the background of the use of unction in other contractual settings in the ancient Near Eastern material, it is natural to understand the anointing of the bride, not as a "purification", a symbolic liberation of the bride from the

---

[106a] *Jastrow* (Dictionary p. 500).
[107] See *Landsberger* (Fs M.David 2/1968, 82: "Speisung") and *Cardascia* (1969: 209 note c: "banquet").
[108] *Cardascia* (1969: 209).
[109] *Landsberger* (op. cit. p. 82).
[110] Text in *R.Yaron* (The Laws of Eshnunna 1969: 32) and in *A.Goetze* (The Laws of Eshnunna, 1956: 76).
[111] See *Landsberger* (op. cit. p. 75 ff.). Earlier discussions are found in *F.R.Kraus* (JEOL 16/1959-62, 24 f.: "Einstand") and *Greengus* (JCS 20/1966, 62-66: "libation").
[112] *Landsberger* (op. cit. p. 84).
[113] *Landsberger* (op. cit. p. 82).
[114] See *Landsberger* (op. cit. p. 95).

authority of her father (so Kutsch) but as a contractual rite. Besides, one should note that the anointing signifies an obligation of the party responsible for the rite. The case that the side of the bride fails to fulfil the contract is regulated in MAL § 31, while § 42-43 deal with the case that the side of the bridegroom fails, for instance through the death of the bridegroom, in which case the bridal gifts of precious stones and other non-consumptabilia shall normally not be restored, if there are other male relatives (brothers or sons) of the deceased bridegroom, who can assume the obligations. Thus, the unction (and the meal) signify the obligation of the subject performing the rite. Unction and meal perform the ratification of the contract and have the character of a *Vertragsperfektion* just as in the business contracts already discussed.

The correctness of this contractual interpretation is also borne out by KUB III 24+59,5 ff. (above *sub* f). This text describes the day of anointing the bride as a day when two countries "became one country" and two kings "became one brotherhood". Such formulations in the texts themselves stand out as a proper exegesis of the actual meaning of the rite.

(4) The "Anointing of Liberation". – The cases studied do not make up an exhaustive inventory of the whole ancient Near Eastern material for ritual anointing. There is for instance also the very important use of unction as a legal symbol in connection with the manumission of slaves.[115] I would like here to call attention to the possibility that his "anointing of liberation" and the contractual type studied above stand in a complementary relation to each other. The occurrence of *acta contraria* is well known in the fields of law and magic. Thus, to mention some examples from the former field, "to seize the hem of the garment of PN" (*qaran ṣubāt PN ṣabātum*) is a menial gesture performed at the ratification of a treaty of vassalage. Its opposite "to let go of the hem of the garment of PN" (*qaran ṣubāt PN wuššurum*) denotes infidelity and breach of a treaty.[116] Likewise, while on the one hand contract tablets are sometimes – OB, MB (Kassite), and Nuzi – sealed with the *sissiktu* (the hem of a garment), on the other hand, it occurs in divorce proceedings that the husband cuts the *sissiktu* of his wife as a gesture of repudiation.[117] One could also ask if there was not a positive counterpart of the expression "to push away the hand" (*qātam napāṣum*) which refers to the rejecting of a hand previously clasped in friendship and is an expression of the breaking off of relations.[118]

---

[115] On this use see *Kutsch* (1963: 16-17). As appears from my own contribution I disagree on most of the cases discussed by Kutsch in the rest of his chapter. Kutsch's interpretation of the anointing of the Israelite High Priest in Lev 7,36 as a case of purification-liberation (on the assumption that the syntactical construction is *mašaḥ min...*) collapses on a comparison with Lev 7,34f. and Ex 29,28.

[116] See *J.M.Munn-Rankin* (Iraq 18/1956, 91 f.).

[117] See *Munn-Rankin* (op. cit. p. 92) and *Petschow* (RLA III/1957-71, 321).

[118] See *Munn-Rankin* (op. cit. p. 86). Cf. Ez 17,18; 2 Ch 30,8; 2 R 10,15.

I am inclined to think that the seemingly very disparate types of "anointing of liberation" and the gift of oil as a vassal rite (above *sub* 1) form another pair of such *acta contraria*. In the vassal rite it is the inferior party who offers the unction, as in Idrimi and the Assyrian Ritual (EA 51 where Pharaoh anoints a vassal king represents the Egyptian practice of anointing officials). The anointing of liberation, performed by the owner of the slave, could then be seen as a reversal of the rite of vassalage. The oil is being "returned".

We have studied the contractual use of oil in the ancient Near East. In contractual relations the obligation has an important place, as I have pointed out in my excursus on these relations. Before leaving the extra-biblical material, I shall therefore say some concluding words precisely on the connection between oil and obligation. The following cases can be discerned.

(1) The performer of the rite normally assumes obligation. He pledges himself to the other party involved. There are three subdivisions here:

a. In *parity* relations, such as the business contracts, both parties accept an obligation and consequently anoint each other.
b. When the stronger party anoints the weaker, we are faced with a *promissory* type of contractual relation. Thus in the nuptial anointing, where the party responsible for the anointing thereby assumes obligation. The stronger party does not thereby make himself a vassal of the weaker but assumes obligation towards the bride.
c. When the weaker party is responsible for the unction we can speak of an *obligatory* type of contractual relations in which the vassal has to oblige himself. Thus in Idrimi and in the Assyrian Ritual the weaker party offers unction as a token of submission.

(2) There is also a wholly different type of anointing not contained in the material treated above, and this is the case when the recipient of the rite is thereby placed under obligation. This type should be seen against the background of the occurrence of an acted-out conditional curse in connection with a covenant. This latter feature is aptly illustrated by the following examples:

a. The mutilation of a spring lamb in the treaty between the Assyrian king Ashur-nirari VI and Mati'ilu of Arpad col. I 10 ff.: "This head is not the head of a lamb, it is the head of Mati'ilu, ... This shoulder is not the shoulder of a spring lamb, it is the shoulder of Mati'ilu."[119]

[119] The text is found in *Weidner* (AfO 8/1932-33, 18 f.). For a translation see *ANET³* (p. 532 f.). For comments see *D.J.McCarthy* (1963: 70 ff.). Cf. also *Polzin* (HThR 62/1969, 227 ff.) on Hebrew *hôqă'* as denoting the punishment for the violation of a covenant.

b. The killing of an ass in Mari (*ana ḫa-a-ri-im qa-ta-li-im*, ARM II 37,6).[120]
c. A whole series of magical rites in Sefire I recto 35-42 from which the following can be quoted: "Just as this wax is burned by fire, so may Matî['el be burned by fi]re! ... And just as a man of wax is blinded, so may Matî['el] be blinded! [Just as] this calf is cut in two, so may Matî'el be cut in two...."[121]
d. To "touch the throat" [*napištam lapātum*] is attested several times in Mari.[122] There can be no doubt that this, too, was a gesture symbolic of the fate of the treaty-breaker.[123]

Further examples could easily be adduced, also from the covenant rites of the Old Testament.[124]

It is against this background that we should see the use of oil in connection with an oath.[125] In the Vassal Treaties of Esarhaddon (lines 622-625) we find the characteristic formulation:

> Just as [this] oil enters your flesh, so may they [scil. the gods] make this oath enter your flesh, the flesh of your brothers, your sons and daughters.[126]

This text should be compared with what is said in an Old Testament text of the wicked man:

> He clothed himself with cursing as his coat,
> may it soak into his body like water [*wăttabo' kămmăyim b^eqirbô*],
> like oil into his bones [*w^ekăššæmæn b^e'aṣmôtâw*]! (Ps 109, 18)

In both texts, the penetration of oil into the body is symbolic of the curse. But the Old Testament text has a further element: water (cf. Nu 5,16 ff.). This association of water and oil in connection with a curse sheds light on the custom of swearing "by water and oil", known for instance from Neo-Assyrian risk-clauses[127] and from the Vassal Treaties of Esarhaddon (line 155).

This use of oil as what I would like to call "oil of curse" is not to be confused with the type discussed above. The oil of curse brings an obliga-

---

[120] For comments see *McCarthy* (op. cit. p. 53ff.).
[121] For text and translation see *J.A.Fitzmyer* (The Aramaic Inscriptions of Sefire 1967: 14 ff.). See also *ANET³* (660 col. a).
[122] See *CAD* (9/L p. 84f.).
[123] See the comments of *Munn-Rankin* (Iraq 18/1956, 89f.).
[124] See *Kutsch* (1973: 44ff.).
[125] *Veenhof* (BiOr 23/1966, 312f.) has the merit of having collected the following material and demonstrated the function of oil as a ritual, conditional curse.
[126] For the text see *Wiseman* (The Vassal-Treaties of Esarhaddon, 1958: 77). The translation above is that by *E.Reiner* (ANET³ p. 540).
[127] For these see *K.Deller* (Bibl 46/1965, 349ff.). Deller suggests the translation: "If the pledge dies [or] flees – by water [and] oil, by snake [and] scorpion – [this risk] rests upon his/her owner/father" (p. 350 note 1). However, the true character of this as a promissory oath was first seen by *Veenhof* (BiOr 23/1966, 312). For further occurrences of oath "by water and oil", see *vonSoden* (AHw p. 1157 sub *šamnu* 1 litt. f.).

tion over the recipient of the rite. It is to be noted that this type is also attested as a vassal rite. In the Vassal Treaties of Esarhaddon, lines 622 ff. quoted above, the vassals who had to swear the oath were smeared with oil, which penetrated into their flesh, just as the conditional curse would do in case of transgression of the stipulations of the treaty.

Pharaoh's anointing of Taku of *Nuḫašše* (EA no 51) is problematic. This anointing of an Egyptian vassal in Syria corresponds to the anointing of Pharaoh's officials in Egypt. The Egyptian material for the interpretation of this is extremely scanty and permits no safe conclusions. H. Bonnet, however, thinks that the anointing in such cases was a symbol of authority, of the delegation of royal powers.[127a] As far as I am aware, there is no reason to argue for a contractual interpretation of the anointing of Egyptian officials and vassals, and to the best of my knowledge, formal treaties between Pharaoh and his vassal kings are also unknown. Because of the configuration in the Old Testament material of the royal anointing and the king's covenants with the people and with God, it is the contractual use of oil that is important to us. Thus EA no 51 can hardly shed light on our problems.

2. *Oil and Contractual Relations in Ancient Israel*

Our next task is to investigate the evidence for the contractual use of oil in the Old Testament. As a matter of fact there are some relevant passages, although most of these have been overlooked in earlier treatments of the symbolic import of unction.

There are three references to Jacob's anointing of the stone at Bethel (Gn 28,18; 31,13; 35,14). One of these instances contains an interesting indication of a connection between Jacob's anointing of the stone and the making of a vow. God says to Jacob:

> I am the God of Bethel, where you anointed a pillar [*'ašær mašăḥta šam mașșebā*] and made a vow to me [*'ašær nadărta lî šam nædær*]. (Gn 31,13)

The two elements of ointment and promise also occur in Gn 28,18.20-22. On my definition of a contractual relation as existing when one, or both, parties assume obligation (see excursus no 2), we are justified in saying that the events at Bethel provide a contractual setting for Jacob's anointing of the stone. It must also be remembered that in some contexts the words *nædær*, "promise", and *bᵉrît*, "obligation", are commutable. Thus, the well-known expressions *heqîm bᵉrît* and *heper bᵉrît*[128] are matched by *heqîm nædær* (Nu 30,14 f., cf. 30,8.10.12) and *heper nædær* (Nu 30,9.13 f.). And

---

[127a] See *RÄRG* (p. 648 f.).
[128] On *heper bᵉrît*, see W. Thiel (VT 20/1970, 214 ff.).

that a *măṣṣebā* can have a function in a contractual setting appears from Gn 31,45.[129] There is thus reason to conclude that the efficacity of the anointing performed by Jacob was not primarily a sanctification or a consecration of the stone, but was to establish a contractual relation between Jacob and God. This passage is quite in line with extra-biblical material discussed above.

Two texts in the Old Testament attest to the symbolical delivery of unction as a diplomatic gesture of friendship and preparedness to enter into more established diplomatic relations. In Hos 12,2[130] the making of a *bᵉrît* and the sending of oil appear in parallelism. I translate the verse as follows:

> Ephraim assumes relations with the wind [*roʿæ*[131] *rûᵃḥ*]
> and pursues the east wind all day long,
> heaping up treachery and havoc;
> they make a treaty [*bᵉrît*] with Assyria,
> and at the same time,[132] oil is brought to Egypt [*wᵉšæmæn lᵉmiṣrăyim yûbal*[133]].

The context describes Ephraim's treachery against God (v. 1). The present verse deals with a double-dealing in human matters of foreign affairs. While having a formal treaty with Assyria, Ephraim brings oil to Egypt. The parallelism with *kărăt bᵉrît* makes it clear that this delivery of oil is to be seen as a diplomatic gesture and not as a commercial affair or as a tribute. Either it is meant as a first step on the way to a formal treaty, or it should be understood as the ratification of such a treaty. The latter is regarded as impossible by W.Rudolph, who argues that Ephraim cannot have a treaty with both Assyria and Egypt.[134] This, however, is to overlook the very point of the context, which expatiates on Ephraim's perfidy against God and men.

The other passage has hitherto been wholly overlooked, viz. the reading of the LXX in 1 R 5,15 which has never, as far as I am aware, been taken

---

[129] Within Gn 31,43-54 *Kutsch*, partially following Gunkel, has elaborated a "Steinhaufen-Rezension" and a "Masseben-Rezension" (1973: 61 ff.). Gn 31,45 belongs with the latter strand in the text. Here also belong Jacob's promise of loyalty to Laban's daughters (v. 50), his sacrifice and his covenant meal (v. 54). Thus, even if the *măṣṣebā* in v. 45 should not primarily be connected with v. 44 with the *bᵉrît* and the *ʿed* (which means "pact", cf. Akk. *adê* and Aramaic *ʿdy*, and not "witness", see *Volkwein* BZ 13/1969, 36) the context is clearly covenantal.

[130] D.J.McCarthy (VT 14/1964, 215 ff.) called attention to the contractual meaning of the oil in this text.

[131] From *raʿā* II, "Verkehr m. jem. pflegen" (*GBL* p. 766 col. b), "associate with" (*BDB* p. 945 col. b). As occurrences of this verb I list: Prv 13,20; 28,7; 29,3; Hos 9,2; 12.2.

[132] The simultaneity is expressed by *wᵉ* ... *wᵉ* in v. 2b.

[133] The verb *yûbal* is to be analysed as *yabăl* in the Hoph. imperf. *K.Deller's* suggestion (Bibl 46/1965, 349 ff.) to take it as *balăl*, "mix", in the qal passive seems very improbable to me. Against this suggestion see also *Veenhof* (BiOr 23/1966, 312).

[134] W.Rudolph (1966: 226 with note 11).

seriously. The LXX (B and the Lucianic group boc2e2) contains the remarkable statement that Hiram of Tyre sent messengers to anoint Solomon. The MT, which is universally preferred as the best reading, says instead that when Solomon had been anointed King Hiram sent messengers to him.

MT	LXX B (L)
וישלח חירם	Καὶ ἀπέστειλεν Χειρὰμ
מלך צור	βασιλεὺς Τύρου
את עבדיו	τοὺς παῖδας αὐτοῦ
אל שלמה	(L:τοῦ) χρίσαι τὸν Σαλωμὼν
כי שמע כי אתו משחו	ἀντὶ Δαυεὶδ
למלך תחת אביהו	τοῦ πατρὸς αὐτοῦ,
כי אהב היה חירם	ὅτι ἀγαπῶν ἦν Χειρὰμ
לדוד	τὸν Δαυεὶδ
כל הימים	πάσας τὰς ἡμέρας.

It is not difficult to see that here it is the LXX that claims the status of *lectio difficilior*. Nevertheless, the material presented above surprisingly makes this reading appear as a most possible one. And this possibility once granted, the MT stands out as the smoothened text, purged from the difficulty of a Tyrian anointing of Solomon.

Indeed, we do not need to rely only on the comparative material. The context itself shows that the setting of this diplomatic anointing is indisputably contractual.[135] It seems that there were already close diplomatic ties between David and Hiram. This is probable from 2 S 5,11 and from the statement in 1 R 5,15 that "Hiram always loved David" (*'oheb hayā ḥiram leḍawid*). From both biblical and comparative material it appears that "love" is a contractual term.[136] What Hiram tried to achieve through his embassy to Solomon was probably the renewal of an already existing treaty. In any case the outcome was a treaty between Hiram and Solomon. This can be concluded from 1 R 5,26: *wayhî šalom bên ḥiram ûben šelomō wayyikretû berît šenêhæm*. Here, *berît* is a contractual term. And *šalôm* also has this sense. This use of *šalôm* has parallels in the Akkadian

---

[135] The various indications of a formal treaty between the Israelites and the Tyrians are competently dealt with by *Fensham* (VTSuppl 17/1969, 71 ff.). This scholar, however, fails to appreciate the diplomatic implications of the ointment and expressly states that he prefers the MT in 1 R 5,15.

[136] See 1 S 18,1-4; 20,16-17; 2 Ch 19,2. For comments with particular attention to the comparative material see *Moran* (CBQ 25/1963, 77-87). See also on Hebrew *'ahăb* J.A.Thompson (VT 24/1974, 334 ff.) and *Ackroyd* (VT 25/1975, 213 f.).

treaty terminology (*sulummû* and *salīmu*[137]) and is attested in other Old Testament texts as well.[138] The mutual services rendered by the contracting parties show that we are concerned with a parity treaty. Hiram sends building material for Solomon's temple. Solomon delivers wheat and oil (1 R 5,25) and also cedes a number of towns to Hiram (1 R 9,10-14). The position of equality between the two can also be seen from the fact that Hiram calls Solomon "my brother" (1 R 9,13).[139] Indeed, it still shines through in the *b^{e}rît 'aḥîm* in Am 1,9.[140]

If we combine these clear indications of a diplomatic, contractual setting of the anointing mentioned in the LXX of 1 R 5,15 with the evidence found in extra-biblical texts such as KBo I 14 and EA no 34, then the conclusion seems hard to escape that the LXX has here preserved the original reading. The reason for the development of the reading contained in the MT and other versions is probably that the diplomatic anointing was mistaken for the investitorial act in connection with Solomon's "coronation". Since the circumstances in connection with this were known (1 R 1,32-40) and since nothing indicated Tyrian participation, the statement about the anointing in 1 R 5,15 took the character of an erratic block to be removed. Nevertheless, the LXX (BL) preserved this original reading, thus attesting to a contractual use of oil in the days of Solomon.

We can now assess our positions and draw a conclusion. Our observations concerning the efficacy of the rite can be summarized in the following points:
1. We found that various difficulties are connected with the attempts made to explain the Israelite royal anointing as due to an originally Hittite (Kutsch) or Egyptian influence (deVaux). If the rite was taken up under foreign influence, we are faced with a case of stimulus diffusion, so that the definition of a certain culture as the origin has little to contribute to the understanding of the efficacy of the rite as practised in Israel.
2. Instead, we have called attention to a new aspect: the surprising configuration of the conceptions related to the royal anointing (by the people and by God) and the king's covenants (with the people and with God).

---

[137] See *J.M.Munn-Rankin* (Iraq 18/1956, 85f.) and *Fensham* (op. cit. p. 77). Cf. further on *sulummû* vonSoden (AHw p. 1057 col. a and Studia et Documenta 2/1939, 205: the formal entry into a state of friendship through the act of a contractual agreement). Note that the nominal pattern of this word is *purussû*, frequently occurring in legal terms. On *salīmu* see vonSoden (AHw p. 1015f.). Note *salīmam šakānum*, "to establish friendship", and *salīmam epēšum*, "to make friendship", used in the sense "to conclude a treaty".
[138] See Dt 23,7; Jos 9,15; Jud 4,17; 1 S 7,14; Jes 27,5; Jer 33,9; Ob v. 7.
[139] On the diplomatic use of "my brother" see *Munn-Rankin* (Iraq 18/1956, 76ff.) and *Holmes* (AOAT 22/1973, 97).
[140] See *J.Priest* (JBL 84/1965, 400ff.).

This observation inspired us to investigate the ancient Near Eastern material from a new angle.
3. In this extra-biblical material we found that anointing can have a contractual meaning. In certain cases, the unction even has the symbolic import of a *Vertragsperfektion*.
4. The Old Testament passages just discussed show that the same meaning is also attested for unction in Israel.
5. Our conclusion concerning the efficacy of the rite must be based on these observations. Since there is a contractual meaning in anointing both in the ancient Near East and in Israel itself, it is highly probable that the configuration of royal anointing and the king's covenants is not due to mere chance, that the royal anointing of ancient Israel was a contractual rite.

We can now, finally, revert to the anointing of Israelite kings and look for traces of this contractual significance of the rite when applied to kings. The earliest cases of royal anointing among the Israelites are found in connection with David's investitures over Judah (2 S 2,1-4) and over Israel (2 S 5,1-3). The latter passage indeed gives a glimpse of the connection between unction and agreement:

> So all the elders of Israel came to the king at Hebron; *wăyyikrot lahæm hămmælæk dawid b^{e}rît* at Hebron before the Lord, and they anointed [*wăyyimš^{e}ḥû*] David king over Israel. (2 S 5,3)

As was already pointed out in the discussion of the royal covenant with the people (above ch. 8). David here grants the people a promise. It has been said that the context is not susceptible to the interpretation as dealing with mutual obligations of both the king and the people.[141] Such a statement overlooks precisely the contractual implications of the anointing carried out by the representatives of the people. There is here a marked reciprocity: David grants the people his royal promise. In immediate conjunction with this the elders perform the anointing. By performing the rite the elders thereby accept an obligation towards David, precisely as we have seen that anointing works as a legal rite in other connections. David's *b^{e}rît* to the elders and their anointing of him belong together and establish a reciprocal contractual relation between the king and his people. One could thus say that the anointing represents the people's homage to the king, the term "homage" being understood in its technical sense of "formal public acknowledgement of allegiance".[142] Consequently, the information that David was anointed king over Israel adds further support to my main theory.

[141] See *Kutsch* (1973: 55 ff.).
[142] So *The Concise Oxford Dictionary* (Oxford ^{5}1964: 581).

In 2 S 2,1-4 (David's investiture over Judah) nothing is said about a $b^e rît$ by David to his people. But as I have already pointed out (ch. 8.2.2), the situation is best understood as that of the closing of a royal covenant. It therefore seems natural to take the anointing to have the same significance as in 2 S 5,3.

Also after the rite has taken on its new meaning as ultimately carried out by God himself, there are some interesting traces of its contractual sense. Thus Ps 89,39-40 says:

> But now thou hast cast off and rejected,
> thou art full of wrath against thy anointed.
> Thou hast renounced the covenant with thy servant
>   [$ne'\check{a}rtā\ b^e rît\ {}^c\check{a}bd\ae ka$];
> thou hast defiled his crown [$nizrô$] in the dust.

On the background of our previous observations, one is inclined to presume that the association of wrath against the $maš\hat{\imath}^a\d{h}$ and renouncement of his covenant is not purely casual.[143]

In this connection Ps 105,15 also deserves attention. Here, the patriarchs are called "my anointed ones" and the reference to the anointing is made to authenticate a claim to inviolability. If we remember that this statement occurs in a covenantal context (v. 7-15), then the explanation may be that God's covenants with Abraham and with David have been telescoped so that the covenant with the fathers has been depicted as a covenant established through God's anointing of these.

The tradition of David's anointing by Samuel (1 S 16,1-13) is a very early exponent of the rite as a sacred act. Here one looks in vain for explicit covenant terminology. But once one remembers the established connection between election and covenant, the election terminology of this passage deserves attention as an indication of the covenantal character of the anointing. The verb $ra'\bar{a}$ has such a sense in v. 1 and possibly also in v. 7 ("see" > "choose", "appoint", above ch. 7.1.1). And the pair $ba\d{h}\check{a}r - ma'\check{a}s$ is used to denote the election and its opposite (see v. 1.7-10).

The change in the rite and its "ideology", from the profane anointing carried out by the people to the sacred rite performed in the name of God, can be judged to be due to the fact that a new subject carried out the rite from Solomon onwards: the High Priest. The covenant takes on a new dimension: the king becomes the vassal of YHWH through the anointing. We are now faced with the Davidic covenant between God and king, which must be distinguished from the royal covenant between king and people. It seems to me that we should not here look primarily for a model in the vassal rites, known from extra-biblical material. It is not necessary to assume the

---

[143] One may also ask whether $\d{h}\ae s\ae d$ in Ps 18,51 (=2 S 22,51) is not to be taken as a similar indication when it is said that God makes $\d{h}\ae s\ae d$ to his anointed.

existence of such a model. Instead the idea of a covenant between God and king, of the king as the vassal of YHWH, can be explained as due to an autochtonous development. The present investigation has led to three conclusions:

1. The anointing has a contractual efficacity.
2. The performer of the rite pledges himself to the recipient.
3. There was a change in the subject (performer) of the rite from the elders to the priest, who was subsequently considered to act in the name of God.

We have here all the ingredients necessary for the development of the conception of a contractual relation between God and king. It seems reasonable to assume that when the rite had reached the point of development when it was imagined to be ultimately performed by God, then the idea of a divine covenant presented itself. In such a covenant between God and king the latter necessarily takes the position of vassal. Furthermore, if the *leitmotiv* of the rite was the contractual obligation of the performer towards the recipient we should also expect that in its oldest form the Davidic covenant with God is of the promissory type: God, who is the subject behind the rite, pledges himself to the king. My observations at this point also seem to provide a new criterion for dating the idea of the Davidic covenant: *if* there is a genetic connection between the rite of anointing and the dogma of this covenant, then the latter cannot be prior to that stage in the development of the rite when God was conceived of as the active subject, that is, not before Solomon.

Summary

(1) In the introductory survey of previous research we found that three different interpretations of the royal anointing prevail among modern scholars: the "sacral" interpretation, the "secular" interpretation and the mediating position or the attempt to combine sacral and secular aspects as coexistent from the beginning. The investigation makes it very difficult to agree entirely with any one of these interpretations. Instead, I have found reason to argue that there was a *development* in the rite which has been overlooked in previous research. The development of the rite is to be described in the following manner:

a. The anointings of David over Judah and over Israel were performed by the leading elders of the people. The plural formulations in connection with later investitures are a survival on the level of language of this early form of the rite.
b. The investiture of Solomon is a pivotal point in the development. To be sure, Solomon's investiture was an extraordinary case. For certain reasons the popular assembly was never convoked. Instead, Solomon

was anointed by the priest Zadok. However, the role of the priest became an institutional feature in the rite.

c. Soon enough, the priest was conceived of as acting in the name of God. YHWH was referred to as the ultimate subject performing the rite. The idea of a "divine anointing" was developed, first for David (1 S 16,1-13) and then for Saul (1 S 9,1-10,16; the *nagîd* layer). In this connection, 1 S 16,1-13 is of particular interest. I suggested that this tradition was an etiology for the procedure at Solomon's investiture, supplying a defence of the election of one who did not have the right of seniority and explaining why the convocation of the popular assembly was not a prerequisite. As a result of the conception of the divine anointing of the king the term *mašîaḥ* became a key term to denote the king in his relation to God.

(2) In the discussion of the *efficacy* of the rite, a functionalistic, holistic approach enabled me to see a *configuration* of the royal *anointing* (performed first by the people and then by God) and the two basic *covenant* relations of the king (with the people and with God). This observation led to the question of a possible interaction between these two entities. I was able to demonstrate that ritual anointing had a contractual significance in the ancient Near East and in Israel itself. Proof of this was found in a number of documents and deeds in the extant cuneiform material, such as business and marriage contracts and texts dealing with international affairs. Some neglected Old Testament passages were also found to require the same contractual interpretation of the symbolic significance of oil. The anointing carried out in connection with the manumission of slaves also seems understandable within this contractual frame of reference, if we assume that this "anointing of liberation" and the vassal rite of offering oil to the overlord are to be interpreted as *acta contraria*. The contractual interpretation of the symbolic significance of oil is a key to the understanding of the development of the "ideology" unfolded in connection with the rite. The *leitmotiv* of the royal anointing was the obligation of the performer towards the recipient of the rite. Thus, in the anointings of David over Judah and over Israel, the people pledged themselves to the king. Later, when God was conceived of as the ultimate subject performing the rite, the contractual significance must presumably have implied a covenant between God and king, the Davidic promissory covenant. *If* the rite was the starting point for the development of the conception of the Davidic covenant, then we have here a most interesting case of a rite preceding a related dogma.

(3) The genetic question of the historical origin of the Israelite royal anointing is a separate problem.

a. The suggestion that it derived from a pre-monarchic anointing as *nagîd* (W. Richter) must be ruled out.

b. That the rite is due to influence from the Egyptian custom of anointing officials and vassals (deVaux) is incompatible with the original form of the rite in Israel. David's anointing in no way made him a vassal of his people. Besides, there is no need to see the later idea of the king as the vassal of YHWH as the result of foreign influence. This conception was probably due to an autochtonous development in Israel.
c. Kutsch suggested deriving the anointing by the people from ultimately Hittite influence. This suggestion has the advantage of not being entirely impossible. A difficulty to be remembered, however, is that in that case Canaan must have been a mediating link. But the only evidence for the anointing of a Canaanite king is found in EA no 51, which seems, however, to be a case of the Egyptian anointing of officials and vassals.

CHAPTER XI
The Royal Charisma

The present chapter will be devoted to a discussion of the royal charisma. Here I shall deal with the conception of the king's endowment with the Spirit of God and with the idea of his divine wisdom. I shall not, however, discuss the post-exilic roots of New Testament Wisdom christology. The outline of this chapter is as follows: after some introductory remarks on the definition of "charisma", I shall first discuss the passages concerning Saul and the Spirit of God (1 S 10,5 ff.; 11,6 ff.), then the passages about Solomon's dream at Gibeon (1 R 3,4-15) and David's anointing by Samuel (1 S 16,1-13), and finally append a few remarks on some other relevant passages. There is a vast literature dealing with, on the one hand the Spirit of God and on the other wisdom in the Old Testament. It is not my task to enter into a broad investigation of these general problems.[1] The present undertaking must be confined to what is relevant to the understanding of Israelite kingship.

It is well known that Max Weber has given us the conceptual tools for an investigation of this kind.[2] Leaning on Weber, we can define charismata as specific gifts of body and spirit which are conceived of as supernatural in the sense that they are not accessible to everyone.[3] Where charismatic leadership is at hand, we find "die ausseralltägliche Hingabe an die Heiligkeit oder die Heldenkraft oder die Vorbildlichkeit einer Person und der durch sie offenbarten oder geschaffenen Ordnungen".[4] For apparent

---

[1] On the Spirit see *Volz* (1910), *Hehn* (ZAW 43/1925, 210 ff.), *Linder* (1926), *Jepsen* (1934: 12 ff.), *R.Koch* (1950), *Gerleman* (RGG³ 2/1958, 1270f.), *Lys* (1962) and the articles in the Biblical dictionaries. As for wisdom in general, it is not possible to list here even the most representative works. On royal wisdom there are however some studies to be mentioned, namely those by *Noth, Porteous* and *Scott* in the Rowley *Festschrift* (VTSuppl 3/1955). Cf. also *Goodenough* (JBL 48/1929, 169 ff.).
[2] See *Weber's* discussion of "charisma" (GdS III,1 ³1947: 124, 140-148 and III,2 ³1947: 753-778). An English translation of a number of Weber's texts on charisma is now found in *S.N.Eisenstadt* (ed.), Max Weber on Charisma and Institution Building (1968).
[3] *Weber* (GdS III,2: 753). A somewhat wider definition of "charisma" was suggested by *E.Shils*: "the quality which is imputed to persons, actions, roles, institutions, symbols, and material objects because of their presumed connection with 'ultimate,' 'fundamental,' 'vital,' order determining powers" (Intern. Enc. of the Soc. Sciences 2/1968, 386). Cf. also the discussion by *Shils* (The American Sociological Review 30/1965, 199-213). Shils has, in the above definition, rightly seen the connection between charisma and mana, but for my purposes his definition is too wide.
[4] *Weber* (GdS III,1: 124).

reasons, charismatic leadership is an unstable type of authority. The leader has to provide perpetual authentication of his charisma by means of, for instance, miracles or heroic deeds. According to Weber, the charisma is a typical "Anfangserscheinung". When royal authority begins to assume institutional firmness, this is accompanied by the process of a routinization of the charisma (*Veralltäglichung des Charisma*).[5] An epiphenomenon of this is the reification (*Versachlichung*) of the charisma. This involves a dissociation of charisma from a particular individual, making it an objective, transferable entity. Out of a strictly personal gift develops a quality that may be transferred or acquired. Thus the charisma can be thought of as being linked with a particular dynasty and transferred by the blood (*Erbcharisma*), or it can be thought of as being linked with a particular office and transferable by means of a hierourgical act, for instance the rite of anointing (*Amtscharisma*). I wish to stress that in the following I do not reserve the term "charisma" for ecstatic phenomena. The charisma may well manifest itself in the undramatic gift of the God-inspired wisdom of the judge.

1. The Martial Charisma of Saul

Writing in the vein of Max Weber, Albrecht Alt emphasized the importance of charismatic leadership in ancient Israel and particularly the charismatic character of Saul's kingship as a continuation of the leadership of the charismatic heroes known from the Book of Judges. Other scholars have expressed a similar opinion, while still others have assumed a more cautious attitude.[6] Strong criticism was launched by Beyerlin against Alt. This scholar does not refuse to speak of a royal charisma in the case of Saul, but he contends that it cannot be brought into line with that of the heroes of the previous period. Saul's endowment with the Spirit in 1 S 10,2-16 has nothing to do with divine equipment for a heroic achievement and is thus of a different kind from that of the preceding heroes. It would seem easier to establish a connection on the basis of 1 S 11,6 ff., but here Saul's endowment with the Spirit has nothing to do with his kingship mentioned in v. 15, says Beyerlin.[7] While Saul does not have the charisma of the great judges

---

[5] *Weber* (Gds III,1: 143,147; III,2: 771 ff.). As *T.Parsons* pointed out (apud Eisenstadt 1968: 51 note 6), Weber used *Charisma* and *Alltag* in two senses. On the one hand, of the extraordinary and temporary as opposed to the every-day and routine; on the other hand, the sacred as opposed to the profane.

[6] See *Alt* (KS II: 1-65, esp. p. 17, 22 ff. and 116-134). Among his followers one could mention *Soggin* (ThZ 15/1959, 410 ff.; ZAW 75/1963, 54 ff.; and his monograph 1967: 44 ff. and passim) and *Stoebe* (1973: 533 ff.; cf. 180 and 208). The more reluctant position was taken by *Wildberger* (ThZ 13/1957, 468 note 60), *Beyerlin* (ZAW 73/1961, 186-201), *F.Stolz* (1972: 131 with note 11) and *J.M.Miller* CBQ 36/1974, 172 f.).

[7] *Beyerlin* (ZAW 73/1961, 186 ff., esp. 188 f.).

he has a charisma by virtue of his anointing (10,1-16). The most important expression of this charisma is his inviolability (1 S ch. 24 and 26), all according to Beyerlin.[8]

It appears from the preceding analysis of the source material on Saul that there are indeed two different traditions. In 1 S 10,5 ff. the coming of the Spirit is one of the signs mentioned by the seer, and the setting is a "nebiistic" one: when Saul meets a band of prophets the Spirit is to come over him. In 11,6 ff. there is a very vivid description of Saul's fury, kindled by the Spirit, but nothing is said about prophets. It is indeed tempting to follow Beyerlin and to see here two profoundly different conceptions of the Spirit. Moreover, Beyerlin is not alone in this interpretation of the material. Thus Linder saw in 11,6 ff. a "shophetic" conception of the Spirit, similar to that described in the Book of Judges,[9] according to which the Spirit means a divine endowment with heroic strength and qualities of leadership. In 10,5 ff. Linder found a different, "nebiistic" conception. Here we are not concerned with divine endowment for a particular task but with an exercise of piety.[10]

It is against this background that the following questions must be seen:
(a) Do the texts really represent two different conceptions of the Spirit?
(b) What is the connection between the Spirit and Saul's kingship?

1 S 10,2-16. – When discussing Saul my preceding analysis of 1 S 9,1– 10,16 can be profited from. According to this the section 10,10-13a can be disregarded as being a late insertion in the text. In its most original form the tradition contained a narrative describing Saul's visit to an unknown seer. This old narrative contained among other things the seer's allusion to Saul's future kingship (9,20b) and the three signs (10,2-7), one of which was the Spirit of God. This narrative was later expanded to also contain Saul's anointing as *nagîd* (10,1). The statement about the immediate fulfilment of the sign of the Spirit in 10,9 is contained only in this expanded form of the tradition.[11]

Let us now bring these results to bear upon the problem of the charisma. In the first place: was there originally a connection between the charisma

---

[8] *Beyerlin* (p. 190 ff.). – For a criticism of Alt, see also *Thornton* (JThSt 14/1963, 1 ff.) and *Buccellati* (1967: 195 ff.), who criticize in particular Alt's theory of a structural difference between the monarchies of Israel and Judah. Buccellati dissolves the traditional tension between charisma and dynasty by speaking of Saul's charisma as dynastic (p. 199) and David's dynasty as charismatic (p. 211 f.). I agree with Buccellati that Saul's kingship was already dynastic in principle (cf. also his study in Bi e Or 1/1959, 99-128). On these questions see also *L.Schmidt* (1970: 200 ff.).
[9] Jud 3,10; 6,34; 11,29; 13,25; 14,6.19; 15,14.
[10] *Linder* (1926: 1 ff., esp. 9 f.).
[11] See above ch. 9.5 after note 66. Note that also 10,8 is an addition to the text (cf. 13,7b-15a).

and the *anointing*, as Beyerlin contends? – The answer must be no. Since the anointing is due to a later expansion of the tradition, there is no original link between the Spirit and the anointing. I can also refer to the conclusion reached in the chapter on the royal anointing, viz. that Saul was never anointed. This negative conclusion that the coming of the Spirit in 10,5 ff. was not originally related to the anointing in 10,1 does not, however, preclude the existence of a link between endowment with the Spirit and Saul's *kingship*. Such a connection is made probable by the observation that both the seer's promise of future kingship (9,20b) and the signs (10,2-7) belong to the original narrative. Moreover the signs, and particularly the sign of the Spirit, confirm the seer's words. But this is something different from a connection between the charisma and the rite of anointing, which is only brought about by the expansion of the tradition to contain the formulations about the anointing and the immediate fulfilment of the promise of the Spirit (10,1.9).

Secondly, we must ask whether the charisma in 10,5 ff. is really profoundly different from that in 11,6 ff. The character of the charisma in 10,5 ff. can be defined from various observations. One indication is found in the use of the word *hitnăbbe'* in 10,5.6. A comparison with instances such as 1 S 18,10 f. (Saul "prophesies" and tries to kill David), Jer 29,26 (the "prophet" as $m^e\check{s}ugga'$,[12] cf. 2 R 9,11; Hos 9,7) and 1 R 18,29 (the raving of the "prophets" of Baal) makes it probable that *hitnăbbe'* in this context means "to be filled with prophetic rapture".[13] If thus 10,5 ff. refer to prophetic rapture (and not to prophetic mediation of a divine message) as the essence of the experience of the Spirit, its exact character must be defined from the context itself.

Two details deserve attention here. First the strange exhortation in v. 7 to "do whatever your hand finds to do" should be understood as a summons to perform a heroic deed, as I have already pointed out. Secondly, v. 5 speaks of the Philistine $n^e\d{s}\hat{\imath}b$[14] ("governor" or "garrison"). This anticipates 13,4 where it is said that Saul defeated the $n^e\d{s}\hat{\imath}b$ of the Philistines.[15] It must be concluded from these observations that the prophetic rapture in 10,5-7 is clearly related to a definite task, viz. to perform a heroic deed. Consequently, even if there are differences between 10,5 ff. and 11,6 ff., the case is certainly overstated if one assumes that there are two different conceptions of the Spirit. The prophetic rapture in 10,5 ff. was no lethargic ecstasy.

---

[12] For the sense "be mad" in this word, see 1 S 21,15f.
[13] Cf. *Jepsen* (1934: 5ff.).
[14] Read the singular, see the app. and cf. 13,3-4.
[15] This point was stressed by *J.M.Miller* (CBQ 36/1974, 159). *Stoebe* (1973: 207), too, saw that 10,5-7 points forward to a heroic deed.

1 S ch. 11. – Does perhaps also 1 S 11,6 ff. contain features which make the contrast to 10,5 ff. appear more superficial than is generally believed? According to 11,6 ff., the Spirit[16] came over Saul, "and his anger was greatly kindled" (cf. Jud 14,19).[16a] The text then goes on to tell how Saul cut the oxen into pieces and summoned the people. A *păḥăd YHWH* fell upon the people so that they came out as one man. This is something quite different from the sacral panic which otherwise strikes the enemies with confusion.[16b] The *păḥăd* that came over the Israelites in 1 S 11,7 is evaluated as a positive phenomenon comparable to the prophetic rapture in 10,5 ff. The prophetic rapture was there a contagious ecstasy. Even others who were not members of the band of prophets were effected (cf. 1 S 19,20 ff.). In the same way, after Saul had been filled with the Spirit in 11,6, the entire people were taken over by the *păḥăd YHWH* and went out to conquer the Ammonites.[17] Thus, from the point of view of 11,6 ff. as well, the theory of a profound difference between 10,5 ff. and 11,6 ff. must be questioned. Moreover, just as the Spirit in 10,5 ff. was related to Saul's kingship, so is the situation similar in 11,6 ff. It has been found earlier that 11,15, which describes how Saul was made king at Gilgal, cannot be disentangled from v. 1-11.[18]

Both problems that I set out to solve have now found an answer. (a) The two traditions of Saul and the Spirit both contain something that can perhaps best be described as a charismatic fury which made Saul capable of performing a heroic act.[19] (b) In both cases the charisma is somehow related to Saul's kingship. In neither of them, however, is it brought into connection with the rite of anointing until at a later stage of the development of the tradition (10,1.9). A further observation can be made. It is possible that the two traditions of Saul refer to two subsequent events and thus to two different charismatic experiences, one of which enabled Saul to conquer the Philistine *neṣîb* and the other to conquer the Ammonites. If this is so, one cannot fail to notice the limited effect of the charisma. We are clearly dealing with charismatic endowment for one limited task. But at the same time, this pouring of the Spirit over Saul proves that he is the chosen one of God and provides a charismatic legitimation of his authority.

---

[16] The MT has *rûaḥ 'aelohîm* but note that the LXX, the Targum and the Vulgate favour the reading *rûaḥ YHWH* found in two manuscripts.

[16a] On *ḥara 'ăp* see *Mettinger* (ASTI 9/1973, 65 f.). I now find that my conclusions are supported by the semantic development in the word *rûaḥ*, which means both "Schnauben" (Job 4,9) and "Zorn" (Jud 8,3; Prv 16,32; 29,11 etc.) See *GBL* (p. 748 col. b sub 1b).

[16b] On this see *J. Becker* (1965: 66 ff.).

[17] This point concerning the *păḥăd* was seen by *F. Stolz* (1972: 131 with note 12).

[18] See ch. 5.2.2.

[19] Cf. the heroic ecstasy of the berserker.

The question of continuity between Saul and the charismatic heroes of the Book of Judges (cf. Jud 3,10; 6,34; 11,29; 13,25; 14,6.19; 15,14) is a complicated one. It is not possible here to undertake the examination of the literary and traditio-historical questions raised by the material in Judges, which would be necessary in order to enable us to deal more confidently with the problem concerned. It is true that Jud 3,10 belongs to the Dtr framework. And 6,34 and 11,29 (about Gideon and Jephthah) can be ascribed to the redactor of a pre-Dtr 'Retterbuch' and is not found in the most original material.[20] But it can by no means be taken for granted that such a 'Retterbuch' is as late as suggested by Richter who dates it efter Jehu.[21] Thus much has to be left open here. That a connection between Saul and these charismatic heroes was imagined as being at hand seems to be a probable conclusion.[22] We do not know, however, whether this idea of a continuity was found right from the beginning of Saul's activity, or whether Saul's experiences of the Spirit were only later reflected backwards into the days of the earlier heroes so that these were only later attributed endowment with the Spirit. It would seem wise, however, not to dismiss the first alternative too hastily.

2. The "Hearing Heart" of Solomon

Saul received the Spirit of God before he became king. In contrast to this nothing is said about Solomon's endowment with divine gifts until after he had been installed in his office. The passage in question is 1 R 3,4-15 describing the inaugural revelation of Solomon's reign: his dream at Gibeon.[23] Here the following problems will claim my attention: (a) What is the nature of Solomon's charisma, particularly as compared with that of Saul? (b) The event takes place at the great *bamā* of Gibeon (v. 4). This already shows that the passage is not merely a fabrication of the Deuteronomists. At the same time we must ask why Gibeon of all places is just where Solomon receives his charisma. From the point of view of the modern historian, this question must be reduced from one with metaphysical implications to the more modest formulation as to whether Gibeon had already certain connections with Israelite kingship. (c) Finally, we must ask whether the passage shows

---

[20] So *F.Stolz* (1972: 127).
[21] *W.Richter* (1963: 340). This dating is based mainly on the number seventy in Jud 9,5 and 2 R 10,6. A point on which I am also inclined to disagree is Richter's contention that the endowment with the Spirit is a fixed part of a traditional literary *Schema* for the description of the Holy War (1963: 175 ff., esp. 179 f.). For critical remarks on this point see *F.Stolz* (1972: 129 note 3).
[22] Cf. how Saul stands out as a *môšîaʿ* in 1 S 11,3. Note that this connection is not made in the original narrative about Saul and the seer. There it is only found in the revision (1 S 9,16; 10,1 LXX). Note also the occurrence of the word *ṣalāḥ* about the Spirit, which almost seems like a catchword that connects the traditions about Saul (cf. 1 S 10,6; 11,6) with those about Samson (Jud 14,6.19; 15,14). On the sense in *ṣalāḥ* see *J.Blau* (VT 7/1957, 100 f.): "spalten, überschreiten, über jemanden kommen, gelingen". For a different opinion on the sense see *Joüon* (MuB 1925: 39 f.).
[23] For the literature on 1 R 3,4-15 see *Noth* (1968: 42). See now also *Fensham* (1967: 67-70), *Zalevsky* (Tarbiz 42/1973, 215-258) and especially *Görg* (1975: 16-115).

any interrelations with the dynastic oracle contained in the prophecy of Nathan. In particular: what are we to understand from the formulation in 1 R 3,6b about Solomon as the son of David on the throne of Jerusalem?

Let us first study the integrity of the text by literary critical methods[24] and let us concentrate upon the points of special interest to the present investigation. It is well known that the Chronicler contains a parallel version (2 Ch 1,3-13)[25] which differs remarkably from that found in Kings. For instance, the version of the Chronicler does not contain the apparently Dtr elaborations found in Kings.[26] This does not mean, however, that the Chronicler offers the narrative in its original pre-Dtr form. That this is not the case is made clear above all by the fact that the beautiful structure of the corpus of the text, which Görg recently drew attention to,[27] is no longer contained in the Chronicler. On one particular point, however, the Chronistic version will be useful to us, as we shall presently see.

That the version contained in 1 R 3,4-15 shows traces of Dtr redaction is immediately seen from v. 14a, which has a conditional formulation of the divine promise that in a natural way falls in line with the similar formulations of the dynastic promise studied below in ch. 12.3.1. I therefore consider v. 14a to be of Dtr origin. The same conclusion can be applied to the latter half of v. 6. The intermediate part of this verse (that is, the whole section comprising $k\check{a}$'$^a\check{s}ær$ $hal\check{a}k$... $h\check{a}ggad\hat{o}l$ $h\check{a}zz\bar{æ}$) displays Dtr phraseology.[28] And it is not found in the Chronicler. Also, the very last part of v. 6 about the son of David on the throne is missing in the Chronicler's version. From the point of view of content it can be profitably compared with the Dtr references to the dynastic promise studied in ch. 12.3.1. It is therefore natural to conclude that this final part of v. 6 can also be ascribed to Dtr redaction.[29] As for some other details in the text, I admit that the words ‘$\check{a}mm^eka$ '$^a\check{s}ær$ $bah\check{a}rta$ in v. 8 may well be of the same origin.[30] On the other hand, I find it difficult to agree with those who contend that v. 10 is an insertion,[31] or that the words leb $hakam$ $w^enab\hat{o}n$ in v. 12 are of Dtr origin[32].

One of my above questions immediately receives its answer from this analysis, viz. that concerning a possible connection with the prophecy of Nathan. If it is correct that the final part of v. 6 can be ascribed to Dtr redaction, there is nothing in the text that contains a reference to the dynastic promise, and it may be inferred that the tradition of Solomon's

---

[24] Cf. particularly *Burney* (Kings, repr. 1970: 27 ff.), *Noth* (1968: 44 ff.) and *Görg* (1975: 16 ff., 25 ff., 32 ff.).
[25] For convenient comparison of the text of Kings and Chronicles (MT and LXX) see *Vannutelli* (1931: 194 ff.). *Burney*, too, gives the parallel Hebrew texts (p. 29 f.).
[26] Notably 1 R 3,6 (from: "because he walked before thee..."), 3,8 (the expression "thy people whom thou hast chosen") and 3,14 (the entire verse).
[27] *Görg* (1975: 37 ff., esp. 45). Note the role of the verb $\check{s}a$'$\check{a}l$ in structuring the composition. On the king's prerogative to ask something from God cf. Ps 2,8; 20,6; 21,5. Note the contrast between Ps 21,5 and 1 R 3,11.
[28] For references see ch. 12.3.1 note 8.
[29] This is not the general opinion, but see *Burney* (p. 30).
[30] See *Noth* (1968: 45).
[31] So *Noth* (p. 44) and *Görg* (1975: 29).
[32] So *Burney* (p. 31).

dream at Gibeon came into being before the dynastic revision of the prophecy of Nathan in the early post-Solomonic period. Now, it may be that the expression *nă'ăr qaṭon* (v. 7) is an allusion to the divine sonship of the king. In that case there could be a connection with the original oracle of Nathan, but this is a problem that cannot be settled on the basis of our present state of knowledge. The important and obvious observation is that the tradition of the dream at Gibeon precedes the legitimation of the whole dynasty in the oracle of Nathan in its secondary, dynastic form.

I thus regard a Solomonic date as probable. It is then interesting to note that the passage displays well-known affinities to Egyptian literature. The genre is that of the Egyptian royal novel, with similarities particularly with the Egyptian "Sphinx Stela".[33] And an expression such as *leb šome^a'* has Egyptian parentage.[34]

My main concern is of course to define the nature of Solomon's charisma. According to two different traditions Saul's charisma made him a successful warrior. His charisma was a martial one. Solomon's divine gift is of a different nature. What he asked from God was a "hearing heart" (*leb šome^a'*, v. 9). It is worth noticing that the Egyptian counterpart of this expression is found in a wisdom text.[35] God's performative utterance in v. 12 in answer to Solomon's request also defines such a heart as "wise": "Behold, I hereby give you a wise and discerning heart (*leb ḥakam w^{e}nabôn*)".[36] However, if we are thus concerned with some kind of wisdom, there are still different possibilities open. Is Solomon's "hearing heart" a charisma that is oriented in the direction of nature wisdom, judicial wisdom, practical wisdom ("Erfahrungsweisheit"), or theological wisdom (theodicy etc.)? An answer to this question is to be found in the context.

When God refers to Solomon's request he says that Solomon asked for *habîn lišmo^a' mišpaṭ* (v. 11). This points to a judicial charisma, an impression that is strengthened by the definition of the "hearing heart" as *leb šome^a' lišpoṭ 'æt 'ămm^{e}ka l^{e}habîn bên ṭôb l^{e}ra'* (v. 9). It is true that *ṭôb – ra'* is sometimes used as a merismus to express totality. If this were the sense here Solomon would ask for omniscience. This interpretation is not suitable here. Since there are indications of a legal interpretation of Solomon's charisma, it must be pointed out that there are other

---

[33] For the text see *W.Helck* (Urkunden der 18. Dynastie, Heft 19, 1957, 1539a–1544). Translation in *ANET*³ (p. 449). On the genre in question see *S.Herrmann* (WZLeipz 3/1953-54, 51 ff.) and *Görg* (1975: 51-65). I am not convinced by *Fensham's* objections (1967: 67 ff.) since they are based on the Dtr sections of the text.

[34] See *H.Brunner* (ThLZ 79/1954, 697 ff.) and *Görg* (1975: 82 ff.). Görg also finds other Egyptian affinities in the text (see particularly p. 100 ff., 105 ff.).

[35] The Instruction of the Vizier Ptah-hotep, lines 545-554. For a translation see *ANET*³ (p. 414 col. a). Cf. *Görg* (p. 82 ff.).

[36] My own translation. The perfect *natătti* is evidently a performative.

instances of *ṭôb–raʿ* that suggest a legal nuance in this expression.[37] In Gn 31,24.29 God tells Laban that he must not "speak with Jacob from good unto evil".[38] The following brusque exchange of words suggests that Laban did not understand this to mean that he was to say "nothing", as would have been the case if the formulation expressed totality. The point is rather that Laban may have a legitimate claim, but he is not allowed to pursue it. In the same way 2 S 13,22, where Absalom did not speak with Amnon "from evil unto good", refers to Absalom's failure to take legal action.[39] Likewise, Dt 1,39 speaks of "children, who this day have no knowledge of good or evil", which we are to understand as referring to minors who have not reached the age of legal "responsibility".[40] I would like to suggest that the same interpretation should be considered for Jes 7,16.

The conclusion from these observations must be that Solomon asked for judicial wisdom, for the faculty to discern between good and evil. In order to specify this charisma still more we shall now have to ask in which direction Solomon's "hearing" in v. 9.11 goes. Is the "hearing heart" directed towards God or towards the litigant parties in a lawsuit? In the first case the king receives renewed instruction from God for every new legal case he has to judge. In the second, the charisma is even greater and allows the king to take a more "independent" position; the charisma is then a permanent endowment that enables him to discern between "good and evil" as each case arises.

The problem is not easy to solve, but a glance at the use of the verb *šămăʿ* seems to indicate which alternative is favoured. Of the cases where this verb is used with legal connotations[41] two are particularly relevant here. In Dt 1,16 and Jud 11,10 we find the construction *šămăʿ bên*..., which in both cases refers to arbitration between litigating parties, cf. the close semantic parallel *šăpăṭ bên*..., "to arbitrate".[42] This throws light on our text and on 2 S 14,17. Compare the following formulations:

1 R 3,9	לב שמע לשפט את עמך להבין בין טוב לרע
3,11	ושאלת לך הבין לשמע משפט
2 S 14,17	כמלאך האלהים כן אדני המלך לשמע הטוב והרע
14,20	כחכמת מלאך האלהים לדעת את כל אשר בארץ

---

[37] For the following see the penetrating study by *W.M.Clark* (JBL 88/1969, 266-278, note the observations on phraseology on p. 267 note 6).
[38] *Clark* (p. 269).
[39] *Clark* (loc. cit.).
[40] *Clark* (p. 274).
[41] See Dt 1,16.17; Jud 11,10; 2 S 14,16(?).17; 15,3; 1 R 3,9.11; Prv 21,28; 25,10(?); Job 31,35.
[42] For *šăpăṭ bên* ... see e.g. Gn 16,5; 31,53; Ex 18,16; 1 S 24,13.16 and see the discussion in *Liedke* (1971: 63 ff.).

Of these formulations that in 2 S 14,17 should be our starting point. The context is well known: the legal case brought before David by the woman from Tekoa. The woman asks for "the word of my lord the king" (v. 17a), for a legal decision to be made by the king to settle the dispute. In doing this she relies on the king's supernatural gift (cf. the comparison $k^e m \check{a} l' \check{a} k\ ha' {}^{ae} l \bar{o} h \hat{\imath} m$) to judge lawsuits. This divine faculty of the king is described in striking agreement with the text in 1 R ch. 3 as "hearing" (v. 17) and as "wisdom" (v. 20). And just as in the case of Solomon, David's ability to "hear good and evil" and his "wisdom" are expressions of one and the same charisma, even if the scope in v. 20 probably extends beyond legal matters. Now, in v. 20, David's wisdom is directed "downwards" and enables the king "to know all things that are on earth". Then, David's hearing has presumably the same "downward" direction towards matters on earth. It follows that David's ability "to hear what is good and what is evil"[43] should be taken in the sense of a supernatural sensitiveness to his subjects, which enables him to discern which of the two parties in a lawsuit is in the right and which is not.[44]

It should be remembered that the Succession Narrative, where 2 S ch. 14 belongs, is a work from Solomon's reign. This makes it probable that the allusions to David's judicial wisdom in the passage concerning the woman from Tekoa show influence from the language that was used about Solomon's charisma. In any case, the similarities between 1 R 3,4-15 and this passage grant that the interpretation of David's "hearing" in the latter is a valuable help in the interpretation of Solomon's "hearing heart". Just as David's ability to "hear" in 2 S 14,17, so Solomon's "hearing heart" is directed "downwards". It is the faculty to discern between "good and evil" ($l^e h a b \hat{\imath} n\ b \hat{e} n\ t \hat{o} b\ l^e r a'$, 1 R 3,9; cf. v. 11). Solomon has this gift as a permanent possession. Something of God's own wisdom has been delegated to him (cf. 1 R 3,28).

Incidentally, this conclusion has a bearing upon the translation of the text. The "hearing heart" does not stand for an attitude of pious subordination and obedience to God (cf. Germ. "Hörigkeit") but for a charismatic sensitivity (cf. Germ. "Hellhörigkeit"), given once and for all, and which enables Solomon to settle justly every legal case that comes before him.[45]

---

[43] As is seen from this translation I contemplate the possibility that the article serves the purpose of introducing a relative clause, a function that the article can have when it is appended to a participle or an adjective (cf. *HAL* 226 col. a sub 3 and *Ges-K* [27]1902: § 126 k).

[44] I thus disagree with *Hoftijzer* (VT 22/1972, 441) who takes the expression as indicating totality.

[45] The Swedish translation of 1917 is mistaken when it translates the "hearing heart" as "ett hörsamt hjärta". The correct translation is "ett lyhört hjärta".

My conclusions lead me to question Noth's interpretation of 1 R ch. 3. According to this scholar there is something of secularized Enlightenment over the whole thing. His main argument is that the legal decision of the king (cf. 1 R 3,16-28) now takes the place of the old sacral procedure of lot-casting. According to Noth, there is a profound difference between lot-casting as a sacral means of settling a difficult case and the reliance on a human judge who finds his way by virtue of his "wisdom".[46]

The following comments can be made. There were in ancient Israel two different types of lot-casting, a lay procedure, and a priestly procedure by consulting the Urim-Thummim oracle.[47] Both were apparently regarded as a sacral means of settling disputes. The lay procedure may have survived Solomon, but it is correct that the priestly Urim-Thummim consultation *ša'al b^{e}YHWH/be'lohîm*) seems to have ended with David.[48] However, this does not justify the conclusion that reliance on the king's judicial wisdom means a secularization of the legal life. For some unknown reason[49] the Urim-Thummim consultation came to an end. When Solomon takes over cases that were formerly settled in this way he does this not as a usurper of divine prerogatives but according to 1 R 3,4-15 as a person with a specific charisma endowed for this purpose.

Noth tries to substantiate his case by pointing out that it is mostly late texts that bring wisdom into relation with God,[50] but has to admit that we find in the traditions of Solomon "schon verhältnismässig früh die Bezeichnung der Weisheit Salomos als einer Gabe Gottes".[51] Solomon's dream at Gibeon speaks in clear language here. The king's equipment for his task as supreme judge is manifestly a charisma. This feature is also found in other texts. In Prv 16,10 we find the remarkable saying:

קסם על שפתי מלך במשפט לא ימעל פיו

Oracle is on the lips of the king;
his mouth does not fail in judgement.[52]

---

[46] *Noth* (VTSuppl 3/1955, 230-237=GesStud II, 1969: 104 ff.). Cf. *Porteous* (VTSuppl 3/1955, 247-261) who is more aware of the divine character of Solomon's wisdom.
[47] See especially *Lindblom* (VT 12/1962, 164 ff.) on the terminology connected with these two procedures.
[48] Note the remarkable silence concerning Urim consultations from Solomon onwards. See *Westermann* (KuD 6/1960, 10 ff., 27 ff.) and cf. Mishnah, Sotah 9,12.
[49] One should consider the possibility that this has something to do with the replacement of Abiathar with Zadok, since the Elides seem to have close links with the oracle. Note that no Urim consultation is reported for David until after Saul's massacre of the priests of Nob, when Abiathar went over to David bringing the ephod (1 S 22,20; 23,2.6). Cf. *B.Johnson* (ASTI 9/1973, 28).
[50] *Noth* (VTSuppl 3/1955, 232 ff.).
[51] *Noth* (p. 235). – Except for 1 R 3,4-15, one should consider 3,28; 5,9; 10,24.
[52] My own translation.

We do not know the date of this saying but it probably dates from the time of the monarchy, presumably prior to the Dtr period.[53] What is meant by *qæsæm* is made particularly clear by two facts: (a) The root is used in connection with oracular consultation by means of the *t^erapîm* (Zach 10,2; 1 S 15,23; cf. Ez 21,26). (b) It is also used in connection with prophecy (Mi 3,6-7.11; cf. Jes 3,2; Jer 14,14). – The king's legal decision has the same quality of inerrancy as is attached to oracular consultations and prophetic utterances.[54] In the same way the king's word is an inspired word. It is an expression of a charisma.

The saying just cited may well be compared with a statement found in "The Last Words of David", which although found in a late text expresses a traditional view:

> The Spirit of the Lord speaks by me,
> his word is upon my tongue (2 S 23,2).[55]

It is said in Dt 1,17 that "the judgment is God's" (*hămmišpaṭ le'lohîm hû'*).[56] The administration of justice belongs ultimately to God. But on earth, the king has the role of mediator. In his judicial task the king is the vicegerent of God, and so the psalmist says of him in immediate connection with his "sceptre of righteousness": "Your throne is God's for ever and ever."[57] It is against this background that the psalmist prays for the new king in Ps 72:

> O God, endow the king with *mišpaṭæ̀ka*,
>   and give thy righteousness to a king's son,
> that he may judge [*yadîn*] thy people rightly
>   and deal out justice to the poor and suffering. (Ps 72,1-2)[57a]

The conclusion I have drawn from these considerations is that whatever can be said concerning a "Solomonic Enlightenment" (vonRad) the king's judicial wisdom is decidedly of a charismatic nature. Noth's contraposition of the old priestly Urim-Thummim consultation and the new reliance on the king's judicial wisdom disregards the essential point of the matter: the judicial wisdom of the king is a charismatic gift.[58] Indeed, this faculty to discern "between good and evil" grants the king a quality of incomparableness on earth (1 R 3,12), it renders him to some extent "like God" (cf. 2 S 14,17.20; Gn 3,5.22; cf. 1 R 3,28).

---

[53] Cf. Dt 18,10; Jer 14,14 where the root *q-s-m* occurs in very negative contexts.
[54] On *ma'ăl*, "act unfaithfully", see *Knierim* (THAT 1/1971, 920 ff.).
[55] For a discussion of *dibber b^e*, see *S.R.Driver* (1890: 274 f.).
[56] On Dt 1,17 see *Cazelles* (VTSuppl 15/1966, 110 ff.).
[57] For this interpretation of Ps 45,7 see *Mulder* (1972: 33 ff.).
[57a] Translation according to *NEB*.
[58] Cf. *Goodenough's* view (JBL 48/1929, 169-205, esp. 194 ff.) that the Israelite king was regarded as the nomos empsychos.

Of the questions connected with Solomon's charisma one has still to be answered, viz. that concerning the role of Gibeon. Is it possible that Gibeon had certain ties with Israelite kingship even before Solomon's days?

A scrutiny of 1 S 10,5 shows that this possibility must be considered. According to this verse Saul was to receive the Spirit of God at *gib'ăt ha'ᵃelohîm*. We are also informed that there was a *bamā* at this place and a band of prophets who had perhaps more established links with this sanctuary. Finally, there was also a Philistine *nᵉṣîb* here. Whether the word means "governor" or "garrison" it certainly indicates some sort of Philistine "military presence".

According to general opinion the place in question is none other than Gibeah of Saul and is to be identified with *tell el-fūl*.[59] In recent writing there is, however, a growing dissatisfaction with this solution.[60] I consider the following facts deserving of particular attention:

1. It can by no means be taken for granted that *tell el-fūl* was Saul's native village. According to 2 S 21,14 the family tomb was located at *ṣela'*, which is probably to be identified with *ḥirbet ṣelāḥ*, between Jerusalem and *el-ǧîb*.[61]
2. The genealogy of the family of Saul is found within that of the Gibeonites in 1 Ch 8,29-40; 9,35-44.[62] This seems to reflect a Benjaminite settlement of Gibeon, in which the family of Saul was also involved. It is difficult, however, to decide whether this settlement took place in the pre-monarchic period[63] or is to be connected with Saul's action against the Gibeonites mentioned in 2 S 21,1 ff. (cf. 2 S 4,3 about Beeroth, which was also a Gibeonite town, Jos 9,17).
3. It is natural to expect from the context in 2 S ch. 21 that the sons of Saul were executed at Gibeon. According to the MT of v. 6 they were hung up *bᵉgib'ăt ša'ûl bᵉḥîr YHWH*. Instead of "at Gibeah" the LXX has here "at Gibeon". According to the LXX the execution was then carried out "at Gibeon of Saul, the chosen one of the Lord".[64] Thus, according to a pre-Massoretic textual tradition, Gibeon is linked with Saul.

---

[59] So most recently *Stoebe* (1973: 198).
[60] Two different points are to be kept apart here. (a) As regards Gibeath-haelohim in 1 S 10,5 some scholars have identified it with Gibeon see *Bruno* (1923: 53 ff.), *v.d.Born* (OTS 10/1954, 201 ff.), *Blenkinsopp* (1972: 59; VT 24/1974, 5; as a possibility) and *Demsky* (BASOR 212/1973, 26 ff.). *J.Simons* (1959: 311 f.) distinguished Gibeath-haelohim from Gibeah of Saul. (b) The identification of Saul's home village, Gibeah of Saul, with *tell el-fūl* has been severely criticized by *J.M.Miller* (VT 25/1975, 145 ff.) who prefers modern *ǧeba'*, while *Demsky* (esp. p. 31) still opts for *tell el-fūl*.
[61] Cf. *Simons* (1959: 177 and map no 1). The place is also mentioned in Jos 18,28 and probably also hides behind the name in 1 S 10,2.
[62] For a discussion of this point see *Demsky* (BASOR 202/1971, 16 ff.; cf. ibid. 212/1973, 26 ff.). Cf. also *Blenkinsopp* (1972: 58 f.).
[63] So *Demsky* (BASOR 202/1971, 18 note 10; ibid. 212/1973, 27) who identifies Gibeon *and* Gibeah with *el-ǧîb* and connects the Israelite settlement of Gibeon with Jud ch. 19 and 21,23.
[64] Thus there is no reason to emend the Hebrew text to read *bᵉgib'ôn bᵉhar YHWH* (so BHK³ app.), an emendation that is due to the supposed difficulties in linking Saul with Gibeon!

4. That there was a *bamā* at Gibeon is well known (*hăbbamā hăggᵉdôlā*, 1 R 3,4; cf. 2 S 21,9). This *bamā* is probably to be identified with modern *nebi ṣamwīl*, only two kilometres south of *el-ǧīb*.⁶⁵ This land mark is one of the most impressive geographical formations in the whole area.
5. From the point of view of Philistine strategy *el-ǧīb* would be a more natural choice for a *nᵉṣîb* than *tell el-fūl*.⁶⁶ Gibeon was the administrative centre of the Benjaminite territory west of the watershed. It had good supply lines connecting it with the coast, whereas *tell el-fūl* could easily be cut off from the coastal plain.
6. It should be remembered that geographical names have often developed from appellatives. Originally, *gibʻā, gibʻôn* and *gæbaʻ* are appellatives from the same root. In 1 S 10,10 *hăggibʻā* is the same hill as referred to in 10,5 as *gibʻăt haʾᵃᵉlohîm*, a fact that indicates that this place name retains some of its appellative force: the Hill of God. As for *gibʻôn*, I should like to draw attention to the possibility that the word formation is to be compared with the Akkadian use of the ending *-ān(um)*, which is used "zur Hervorhebung bestimmter, oft individueller Vertreter der durch das Grundwort bezeichneten Art oder Gattung" (cf. *šarrāqānum*, "Dieb im bestimmten fall")⁶⁷. In this case *gibʻôn* would come close to *hăggibʻā*.

This state of affairs does not permit me to speak of more than probabilities. The hypothesis advanced by some scholars that Saul tried to make Gibeon the capital of the young monarchy⁶⁸ deserves close attention. Whether it proves correct or not I am inclined to think that the place where Saul received his charisma, the Hill of God, was no other place than the high place of Gibeon. If this is so then we find a geographical link between the traditions on the charisma of Saul and Solomon. Although Saul's charisma was martial and Solomon's consisted of judicial wisdom, the choice of Gibeon for Solomon's inaugural revelation may have served its purpose in the respect that it suggests an ideological continuity.

3. David and the Spirit in 1 S 16,13

As Weber pointed out the charisma is a typical "Anfangserscheinung", subjected to gradual "Veralltäglichung" or routinization. The text describing David's anointing by Samuel is a good illustration of this. Here David receives the Spirit in immediate association with the anointing:

> Then Samuel took the horn of oil, and anointed him in the midst of his brothers; and the Spirit of the Lord came mightily (*wăttiṣlăḥ*) upon David from that day forward. (1 S 16,13)

⁶⁵ See e.g. *Blenkinsopp* (1972: 81 ff., 98 ff.).
⁶⁶ For details see *Demsky* (BASOR 212/1973, 27 f.).
⁶⁷ Quotation from *vonSoden* (GAG page 70). – I have not been able to consult the recent (unpublished) dissertation by *B.Gross* on noun formations with the afformatives *-an, -ôn* in Biblical Hebrew, see Elenchus (55/1974, 432).
⁶⁸ See *Hylander* (1932: 262), *Schunck* (1963: 131 ff.) and *Blenkinsopp* (VT 24/1974, 1 ff.). Cf. *Nielsen* (1955: 302 note 1). – However, *Demsky* still identifies Saul's capital as *tell el-fūl* (BASOR 212/1973, 31) and *Miller* as modern *ǧebaʻ* (VT 25/1975, 165).

My conclusion concerning the date of this tradition agrees with the view that it represents a more recent conception of the charisma than the passages on Saul in 1 S 10,5 ff. and 11,6 ff. I argued that it probably dates from the reign of Solomon and suggested that it represents an etiology for the procedure at the anointing of this king (ch. 9.5 and 10.2.3). This tradition probably does not commemorate an actual event in David's life, in which case there is no tradition from the early monarchy concerning David and the Spirit of God. What is said in 2 S 14,17.20 regarding David's supernatural wisdom is probably due to a "Solomonic" colouring of David, as we found above. It may be added that the idea of a divine anointing of the king did not emerge until after the reign of David. David himself was anointed by the people (2 S 2,4; 5,3). David was probably by virtue of his actual extraordinary talents already regarded as a charismatic in his lifetime (cf. the *Beistandsformel* above ch. 2 note 29). But there was probably no tradition concerning a particular event marking his endowment with the Spirit (contrast Saul and Solomon!).

Three points are to be noted concerning David and the Spirit in 1 S 16,13. First, there are no direct or spectacular manifestations of the charisma. There is not the same stress on the immediate authentication of the charisma as in the traditions concerning Saul. The charisma in 1 S 16,13 is not divine equipment for one limited action but is a perpetual attribute of the king (cf. Solomon).

Secondly, the charisma is here transferred by means of a hierourgical act, the rite of anointing. We find that reification (*Versachlichung*) of the charisma that Weber described as an epiphenomenon of its routinization. Note that this aspect of the charisma as being linked with a specific rite is not found in Solomon's dream at Gibeon, nor in the Saul cycle until at a later stage in the development of the tradition. In its developed form the tradition of Saul and the seer contains a reference to an anointing of Saul. And now a rather forced connection between the rite and the charisma is attempted (1 S 10,1.9; cf. ch. 9.5). As we noted, this later attempt to connect Saul's charisma with the rite was influenced by the tradition of David's anointing where this connection is original.

Thirdly, the tradition of David's anointing by Samuel was later taken up by the author of the History of David's Rise and incorporated into this work, which was probably composed during the decades immediately after Solomon's death. We now find the idea that the Spirit of the Lord departed from Saul. Indeed, by means of the compositional arrangement, the author brings this into immediate association with Samuel's anointing of David in 16,13:

> Now the Spirit of the Lord departed from Saul, and an evil spirit from the Lord tormented him. (1 S 16,14)

We can compare this with 19,23 f. where Saul, overcome by the Spirit, strips off his robe. The contrast between this and the traditions in 10,5 ff. and 11,6 ff. is most striking. There Saul was enabled by the Spirit to perform a heroic deed. In 19,23 f. the very opposite happens: Saul is incapacitated and is forced to lie naked "all that day and all that night".[69]

At this stage of development, there is a direct association between charisma and succession. In the History of David's Rise, it is the charisma of Saul that has been transferred to David (1 S 16,13-14). This aspect was not found in the tradition of David's anointing by Samuel read as an isolated unit. The connection between charisma and succession can also be seen in some other persons who are described as charismatics. Thus, given the opportunity to ask something of Elijah, Elisha says: "I pray you, let me inherit a double share of your spirit" (2 R 2,9).[70] The relation between Moses and Joshua is expressed in similar terms:

> And Joshua the son of Nun was full of the spirit of wisdom, for Moses had laid his hands upon him. (Dt 34,9)[71]

4. The Royal Charisma in Other Texts

Finally, I shall draw attention to some further instances mostly in the wisdom literature and in the prophets, which speak of royal wisdom or of the king as being endowed with the Spirit of God. In some of these cases a connection with the king's judicial task is to be found. In Prv ch. 8 Wisdom says:

> I have counsel and sound wisdom, I have insight, I have strength.
> By me kings reign, and rulers decree [$y^e\hat{h}\hat{o}q^e\hat{q}\hat{u}$] what is just;
> by me princes rule, and nobles govern the earth. (Prv 8,14-16)

It is the same Wisdom that says in v. 22 that the Lord "begat"[72] her. Jer 23,5 on the righteous Branch from David's line deserves to be mentioned here:

> ... and he shall reign as king and deal wisely [$w^e hi\acute{s}k\hat{i}l$],
> and shall execute justice and righteousness in the land.

The judicial function of the wise king is also reflected in Prv 20,26 (cf. 20,8 and Jer 15,7). Most interesting in this connection is, of course, Jes ch. 11 which deals with the future Davidic ruler:

---

[69] This contrast was observed by *Stoebe* (1973: 368 f.).
[70] Cf. Dt 21,17.
[71] Cf. Nu 27,18 and Nu 11,17.25.
[72] For the sense "beget" in *qanā* in Prv 8,22 cf. Gn 4,1 and cf. *ḥîl* (polal) in Prv 8,24 f. See also *Ringgren* (1947: 99 ff.).

> And the Spirit of the Lord shall rest upon him,
>> the spirit of wisdom and understanding [ḥåkmā ûbînā],
>> the spirit of counsel and might [ʿeṣā ûgᵉbûrā],
>> the spirit of knowledge and the fear of the Lord. (Jes 11,2)

The words in the third stichos echo the name of the future ruler in Jes 9,5: *pælæʾ yôʿeṣ ʾel gibbôr ʾᵃbî ʿăd śăr šalôm*. The question now is whether "the spirit of counsel and wisdom" is to be understood in a martial sense or not. Wildberger opts for the alternative suggestion on the grounds that the ruler referred to in 9,5 is "Prince of Peace".[73]

Two facts must, however, be taken into account here. First, the phrase "counsel and wisdom" in itself strongly speaks in favour of a martial interpretation (cf. *ʿeṣā ûgᵉbûrā lămmilḥamā* in 2 R 18,20) and the word *gᵉbûrā* is used several times referring to a king's military ability (1 R 15,23; 16,5.27 etc.). Secondly, the expression *śăr šalôm* is indeed open to a martial interpretation too: "Prince of Revenge" or "Prince of Tribute."[74] The most natural interpretation of the discussed phrase in Jes 11,2 is therefore that it refers to the charisma of a hero.

But there is also another aspect of the charisma of the future ruler of Jes ch. 11. His judicial activity is clearly expressed in the continuation of the passage (v. 3-4). It is then natural to connect the *rûᵃḥ ḥåkmā ûbînā* with this aspect of his tasks, as the charisma of the future ruler in his capacity of supreme judge (cf. *leb ḥakam wᵉnabôn* in 1 R 3,12). It is not difficult to see what this means: the two lines from the martial charisma of Saul and the judicial one of Solomon have merged in the image of the ruler in Jes ch. 11.

I shall now turn to the Servant Songs. When dealing with other important characteristics of this enigmatic figure it must not be forgotten that the Servant of the Lord displays royal features. These royal affinities are to be seen particularly in the first Servant Song. I suggest translating Jes 42,1 as follows:

> Behold my servant, whom I hold,
>> my chosen in whom my soul delights;
> I hereby give[75] my Spirit upon him,
>> he will bring forth justice [*mišpaṭ*] to the nations.

The scene probably depicts the presentation of the Servant before the heavenly council and his installation in his office. In connection with his installation, the Servant receives the charisma of the Spirit. From our point of view it is particularly interesting to find that *mišpaṭ* is a key term in the text. I shall not enter here upon a discussion of the vexed

---

[73] *Wildberger* (1972: 449).
[74] See *Gerleman* (ZAW 85/1973, 10).
[75] I take the perfect *natăttî* to be a performative.

problem of the exact sense of this word in each of the three verses where it occurs in the first Servant Song (v. 1.3.4).[76] Suffice it to say that there is a natural connection between the charisma of the Spirit and the mission of the Servant to administrate *mišpaṭ*. Just as the Servant has a royal charisma, so can his mission be described in royal terminology.

For reasons which I shall not discuss here I am inclined to believe that 42,5-9 are also closely connected with the first Servant Song. If this is correct the possibility that the task mentioned in v. 7 to free prisoners is also connected with the charisma in v. 1, should be considered. A connection between this charisma and a task of that nature can clearly be seen in Jes ch. 61:

> The Spirit of the Lord is upon me
>   because the Lord has anointed me;
> he has sent me to bring good news to the humble,
>   to bind up the broken-hearted,
> to proclaim liberty [d^eror] to captives
>   and release to those in prison. (Jes 61,1)[77]

As in Jes ch. 42 one should not overlook the royal categories used about the figure described in ch. 61. Here belong not only the anointing but also the proclamation of d^eror. The royal proclamation of d^eror is known from Jer 34,8.15.17. The Israelite institution is evidently an offshoot of a much older one in Mesopotamia known from cuneiform sources that speak of $(an)durāru$, which denotes a "Zustand der Lastenbefreiung, Freistellung von Abgaben."[78] Since an- is a formative we have in $(an)durāru$ the etymon of the Hebrew term d^eror.

That the Spirit of God was the endowment *par préférence* of the political leader can also be seen in the case of Joseph:

> Now therefore let Pharaoh select a man discreet and wise, and set him over the land of Egypt. (Gn 41,33)

> And Pharaoh said to his servants, "Can we find such a man as this, in whom is the Spirit of God?" So Pharaoh said to Joseph, "Since God has shown [$hôdî^a$] you all this, there is none so discreet and wise as you are." (Gn 41,38-39)

The wisdom of Joseph, which makes him suitable for his task as a statesman, is a divine gift of the Spirit, a charisma. In this case the charisma is not restricted to the judicial sphere but extends to administration in general.

---

[76] See *Elliger* (Jesaja II, Lief. 3/1971, 205 ff.), *Beuken* (VT 22/1972, 1 ff.) and *JörgJeremias* (VT 22/1972, 31 ff.).
[77] Translation according to *NEB*.
[78] *vonSoden* (AHw p. 50). On the Mesopotamian institution see *J.Lewy* (EI 5/1958, *21 ff.). On Jes 61,1 see *Zimmerli* (FsGalling, 1970: 321 ff.). Cf. also *Lemche* (VT 26/1976, 38 ff. esp. p. 56). Note that Lemche mentions a forthcoming paper on the subject of d^eror (p. 41 note 11).

The connection between Spirit/wisdom and the office of judge is attested by the tradition in the Pentateuch dealing with the judicial reform of Moses. This is found in three different versions (Ex 18,13-27; Nu 11,10-30; Dt 1,9-18).[79] A traditio-historical connection between these three texts can be seen for instance in the use of the root *n-ś-'* to denote that Moses carried the people (Ex 18,22; Nu 11,11.13.14; Dt 1,9). This burden became too great for Moses, and a decentralization of the office of judge was therefore to take place. What is of interest to us is that according to Dt 1,13.15 these new judges were to have wisdom, although nothing is said there about this wisdom as a charismatic endowment. It is striking that the version in Numbers does not mention wisdom. There is, however, in Numbers a strong emphasis on the charisma of these new judges:

> Then the Lord came down in the cloud and spoke to him, and took some of the spirit that was upon him and put it on the seventy elders; and when the spirit rested upon them, they prophesied. (Nu 11,25)

According to the Pentateuch the great leaders (Joseph, Moses and Joshua) and the Mosaic judges had a charisma for their task. It must, however, be left to future research to study the question of whether the Solomonic conception of the royal charisma has not left an imprint on the expressions used by the Pentateuchal traditions at this point.

Another question raised by the material studied in this chapter also deserves the attention of future research. As we shall see (ch. 12.2.3), there is probably a link between the royal ideology and the conceptions connected with primaeval man and the angelic beings. From our present point of view it is thus a remarkable fact that primaeval man has wisdom (Job 15,7-8) and that this wisdom may at times be described as the ability to recognize "good and evil" (Gn 3,5.22). In both Job and Gn this is a type of wisdom that properly belongs to the heavenly beings (cf. Prv 30,3 and 2 S 14,17.20). The possibility of an inner connection between the conception of the charismatic wisdom of the king and the conception of the wisdom of the heavenly beings and of primaeval man cannot be dismissed and certainly deserves to be investigated in detail.

Summary

We studied the passages that deal with the divine endowment of Saul, David and Solomon. The conceptual tools for this investigation were borrowed from Max Weber who provided the definition of the notion of

---

[79] I know of no comprehensive study of this tradition in its various forms. However, on Ex 18,13 ff. see *Knierim* (ZAW 73/1961, 146 ff.) and on Dt 1,9-18 cf. *Cazelles* (VTSuppl 15/1966, 97 ff.). The questions involved certainly deserve further study.

charisma and the theory of the *Veralltäglichung* and *Versachlichung* of the charismatic gift.

(1) Saul's endowment with the Spirit of the Lord is mentioned in two mutually independent traditions (1 S 10,5 ff.; 11,6 ff.). I have reason to disagree with those scholars who see two different conceptions of the Spirit in these traditions. The effects of endowment of the Spirit are the same: a charismatic fury (compare the heroic ecstasy of the berserker) that enabled Saul to achieve heroic feats, in the first case the defeat of the Philistine $n^e\d{s}ib$ (probably at Gibeon=*el-ǧīb*; cf. 1 S 10,5; 13,4) and in the second the defeat of the Ammonites at Jabesh. In both instances the Spirit is somehow related to Saul's (future) kingship, but in neither case was there originally a link between the charisma and the rite of anointing. Such a connection was brought about only at a later stage of the development of the tradition of Saul and the seer through the inclusion of 10,1.9. As far as historicity is concerned I assume that these two traditions of Saul and the Spirit have a basis in actual events in Saul's life.

(2) The tradition of Solomon's dream at Gibeon (1 R 3,4-15) already existed before the dynastic redaction of the prophecy of Nathan. Since 1 R 3,6b is probably due to a Dtr redaction of Solomon's dream, there is no allusion in the original text to the dynastic promise in 2 S 7,11.16. Solomon's dream is obviously concerned with his legitimation as an individual. His charisma is described as a "hearing heart" and consists of judicial wisdom (not omniscience). In this "hearing heart" I saw primarily not an expression of obedience to divine instructions for each new legal case but the charismatic sensitivity of Solomon, directed "downwards" to his subjects, a charisma given in permanent possession. This interpretation was made probable by a study of David's judicial wisdom in the passage concerning David and the woman from Tekoa (2 S ch. 14). Unlike Noth I emphasized the manifestly charismatic nature of Solomon's judicial wisdom. Finally, I drew attention to the possibility of a geographical link between the tradition of Solomon's charisma and that of Saul's in 1 S 10,5 ff., since the Hill of God and Gibeon (*el-ǧīb*) are probably the same place.

(3) A surprising result of the investigation is that there is no tradition concerning a charismatic endowment of David that can be used as evidence of a historical event in the life of this king. 2 S 23,1-7 (where the Spirit is referred to in v. 2) is probably a late composition from the exilic period (see below ch. 12.1). David's wisdom in 2 S ch. 14 is probably painted in the colours of the Solomonic era. And the tradition of David's anointing by Samuel (1 S 16,1-13) was presumably created for purposes other than the commemoration of a historical event. This tradition provides a very good example of what Max Weber called the *Versachlichung* of the charisma, since here the charisma is linked with a hierourgical act, the rite of anointing.

(4) Of other passages where a reference to the divine endowment of the king is found, Jes 11,1-9 deserves attention. Here the future Davidic ruler possesses both the martial charisma of Saul and the judicial wisdom of Solomon. I also observed a connection between the Spirit of God and the mission associated with *mišpaṭ* in the case of the Servant of the Lord. Finally I drew attention to a possible connection between the conception of the wisdom of the king and that of primaeval man and the heavenly beings.

CHAPTER XII

Divine Sonship and the Davidic Covenant

It is my aim in the following chapter to analyse the implications of divine sonship and of the Davidic covenant for the sacral status of the king. I shall study these ideas not in isolation but as interrelated parts of a *configuration* of beliefs. My approach will thus be a *holistic* one.[1] The natural point of departure for this undertaking is the prophecy of Nathan. In the above analysis of this text I reached the conclusion that (a) an old document with Solomon's personal legitimation as its *skopos* (2 S 7,1a.2-7. 12-14a.16*.17) has been subjected to (b) a dynastic redaction which introduced a new angle: emphasis on David and the Davidic dynasty (v. 8-9. 11b.14b-15.16*. 18-22a.27-29). At the second stage of its development this text contains both the conception of the divine sonship (found in v. 14 already in the original Solomonic document) and the embryo of the conception of the divine covenant with David (the dynastic promise in v. 11b.16). A similar "symbiosis" of the two ideas can be found in Ps 89 which has the sonship in v. 27 f. and the covenant in v. 29-38. There can be no doubt that the prophecy of Nathan is a point of intersection. Its relations to Ps 89 must be studied. Likewise, we shall have to investigate the connection between this text and Ps 132 and 2 S 23,1-7. In the present chapter I shall first discuss the relationship between the prophecy of Nathan and these three texts (are they earlier or later than the two pre-Dtr forms of 2 S ch. 7?) and then proceed to the question concerning the meaning of the ideas of divine sonship and the Davidic covenant. (For a discussion of terminological questions in connection with the Davidic covenant, see excursus no 2.)

1. The Lyrical Echoes of the Prophecy of Nathan

Psalm 89. – The first problem concerns the age of the relevant lyrical passages in relation to the prophecy of Nathan.[1a] Especially Psalm 89 has

---

[1] On configurational research within the field of comparative religion see Å.*Hultkrantz* (1973: 101 ff.).
[1a] *vonRad* (ZAW 58/1940-41, 217 f.) took all the royal psalms to be later than the prophecy of Nathan. Cf. *Schreiner* (1963: 102). As we shall see, this opinion is probably in need of certain revision. On 2 S ch. 7 and Ps 89, 132 and 2 S 23,1-7 see especially *Caquot* (VTSuppl 9/1963, 213 ff.) and *W.H.Schmidt* (Fs vonRad 1971: 444 ff.).

been discussed in this connection, and opinion is divided on the question as to whether this psalm is older or later than the prophecy of Nathan.[2] The evidence is decidedly in favour of the conclusion that the psalm is the more recent text.

(a) While according to my definition of "contractual relation" (excursus no 2) it would seem justified to say that 2 S ch. 7 is in itself implicitly contractual (and covenantal),[3] this feature of the promise has been made more explicit by means of outspoken covenantal terminology in Ps 89. The term $b^e rît$ is used repeatedly in the psalm (v. 4.29.35) to denote the promise of the prophecy of Nathan. This explicitly covenantal character is also borne out by the reference to God's oath in the psalm (v. 4.36.50) and to the "witness" to this oath (v. 38). The use of $hæsæd$ is also revealing in this connection:

2 S 7,15   וחסדי לא יסור ממנו
Ps 89,34   וחסדי לא אפיר מעמו

Here, in a line that is a close parallel to a formulation in the prophecy of Nathan, Ps 89 has a wording that recalls the technical expression *heper $b^e rît$*, which occurs particularly in Dtr and related texts.[4]

(b) In the original Solomonic prophecy of Nathan David's "seed" (2 S 7,12) is an individual, Solomon. In the dynastic redaction the "seed" is David's dynasty. Similarly, in Ps 89,30 f. the "seed" is defined as David's sons, that is, his dynasty.

(c) In the dynastic redaction of the prophecy of Nathan, there is a formulation (2 S 7,14b-15) stating that if the king commits iniquity God will chasten him but will not withdraw his $hæsæd$ (see above). Ps 89,31-34 are formulated in a way that makes one suspect a direct dependency on 2 S ch. 7, and so far a dependency on the dynastic redaction of this text is indicated.

(d) We can, however, go a step further and add to this that the psalm has developed the formulation concerning the king's iniquity (*'ašær $b^e hă'aw\eth ô$*, 2 S 7,14b) in a very specific manner: Ps 89,31 f. use the Dtr terminology expressing violation of the Mosaic Law. One must then ask: are there perhaps any traces in the psalm of the final, Dtr redaction of the prophecy of Nathan? This question should be answered in the af-

---

[2] For the opinion that Ps 89 precedes the prophecy of Nathan see *Ahlström* (1959: 182 ff.) and *Lipinski* (1967: 70, 77 and passim). On the other hand many scholars consider Ps 89 to be later, see *J.Coppens* (1968: 47 ff.), *N.M.Sarna* (Studies and Texts 1/1963, 29 ff.), *Perlitt* (1969: 51) and *W.H.Schmidt* (Fs vonRad 1971: 446).
[3] Note also that *ṭôbā* in 2 S 7,28 may be a covenant term, see *A.Malamat* (The Biblical Archaeologist Reader 3/1970, 195 ff. esp. p. 197).
[4] On this expression see *W.Thiel* (VT 20/1970, 214 ff.).

firmative: it is difficult to avoid the conclusion that Ps 89,23 (*ûbæn 'ăwlā lo' y^e'ănnænnû*) is dependent on 2 S 7,10 (*w^elo' yosîpû b^enê 'ăwlā l^e'ănnôtô*), which has been found to belong to the Dtr layer of the text.

This comparison of the psalm and 2 S ch. 7, made on the basis of my analysis of the latter (above ch. 3), is thus very illuminating. The inescapable conclusion is that the psalm cannot be dated to before the late preexilic period. It represents a re-working of the prophecy of Nathan in the spirit of the Dtr movement. However, it would not be wise to argue from the lament in v. 39 ff. that the psalm as a whole presupposes the experiences of the exile. While the hymn (v. 6-19) and the dynastic oracle (v. 20-38) are neatly integrated and form a unity, as has been demonstrated by J.-B.Dumortier,[5] one looks in vain for such elaborate connections between the lament and the body of the psalm. Thus, the lament could well be secondary in relation to the corpus of the psalm.[6]

Ps 132. – This psalm has also been dated to quite different periods,[7] but must reasonably be of a fairly late date. This is indicated above all by Dtr affinities. Here belong *bă'^{a}bûr dawid 'ăbdæka* (v. 10),[8] *p^erî bæṭæn* (v. 11),[9] the use of *baḥăr* referring to Zion (v. 13)[10] and finally David's lamp, his *ner* (v. 17)[11]. The Dtr formulation in v. 12 makes the keeping of the Mosaic Law[12] the stipulation for the dynastic promise of v. 11.

[5] *Dumortier* (VT 22/1972, 176 ff.). Dumortier offers a convincing criticism of *Lipinski* (1967) who argued that not only the lament (v. 39 ff.) but also the cosmic hymn (v. 6-19) is later than the royal oracle (v. 1-5.20-38). Lipinki's point of departure is the fragment 4 Q Ps 89, published by *J.T.Milik* (RB 73/1966, 94 ff.). As opposed to Lipinski, Dumortier demonstrates (a) that the cosmic hymn and the royal oracle are neatly integrated (esp. p. 186 ff.) and (b) that the section v. 29-38 is structured through the device of inclusion in a way that makes the sequence of the verses in the MT the only possible one (p. 189 ff.).

[6] This position is taken by e.g. *Dumortier* (VT 22/1972, 176 note 4). A handful of scholars hold the whole psalm to be a literary unity, so *Mowinckel* (PsStud III, 36), *A.R.Johnson* (²1967: 106 ff.), *Ahlström* (1959: 139 ff., 153), *J.M.Ward* (VT 11/1961, 323 ff., 339) and *Sarna* (Studies and Texts 1/1963, 33).

[7] Notably *H.Gese* (ZThK 61/1964, 16 f. and Fs vonRad 1971: 78 f.) and *F.M.Cross* (1973: 232 ff.) take Ps 132 to be from the early monarchical period. Gese regards the psalm as pre-Dtr dating from the early pre-exilic period, and holds 2 S ch. 7 to be "eine spätere Uminterpretation im deuteronomischem Geiste" (loc. cit. 1971). On the other hand, the Dtr features of Ps 132 were stressed by *Caquot* (VTSuppl 9/1963, 221 ff.), *Coppens* (1968: 52), *W.H.Schmidt* (Fs vonRad 1971: 446 f. note 17) and *Veijola* (1975: 134). For a form-critical study of this psalm see *Fretheim* (JBL 86/1967, 289 ff.).

[8] Cf. 1R 11,12.13.32.34; 15,4; 2R 8,19; 19,34; 20,6 (all these with l^e*mă'ăn*) and see vonRad (GesStud I, ²1961: 198 ff.).

[9] See *Caquot* (VTSuppl 9/1963, 222) who pointed out that six occurrences of nine are found in Dt (Dt 7,13; 28,4.11.18.53; 30,9).

[10] Cf. the expression "the place which the Lord your God will choose" (Dt 12,5.11 etc.) and see *W.H.Schmidt* (Fs vonRad 1971: 446 f. note 17).

[11] See 1R 11,36; 15,4; 2R 8,19 and cf. *Veijola* (1975: 118 f.).

[12] As *Perlitt* (1969: 52 with note 1) points out, it is impossible to agree with *Kraus* (Psalmen II, ²1961: 886), who has the Davidic covenant in mind. On the contrary, Ps 132,12 could be compared with Dt 17,18-19.

This psalm presupposes the existence of the prophecy of Nathan. The mention of David's dynasty, his "sons", in v. 11-12 reflects the dynastic revision of the earlier text. A possible echo of the Dtr verse 2 S 7,10 may, however, be found in v. 1b of the psalm ($z^ek\hat{o}r$ YHWH l^edawid 'et kål 'unnôtô), but this is uncertain.

A similarity to Ps 89 is found in the oath in v. 11. But there are two other features in Ps 132 that distinguish it from 2 S ch. 7 and Ps 89. (a) There is no mention of the divine sonship of the king. (b) The keeping of the Law is made the stipulation for the Davidic promise ('im $yišm^er\hat{u}$ banêka $b^er\hat{i}t\hat{i}$ ..., v. 12). There is some tension between this formulation and the unconditional promise in v. 11 ($nišbă$' YHWH l^edawid '$^{ae}mæt$ lo' yašûb $mimmænnā$). The apparent explanation is that we have in v. 11 one of the foundation stones taken over and used by the psalmist. The condition in v. 12 represents a development that is later than the explicitly unconditional formulation, found in 2 S 7,14b-15.

2 S 23,1-7 – "The Last Words of David" is also a text the date of which is a matter for dispute.[13] I find it difficult to believe that this passage should be older than the prophecy of Nathan in its dynastic redaction,[14] since this is probably alluded to in v. 5. And this dynastic promise is interpreted here by means of the covenant term par excellence, $b^er\hat{i}t$ (v. 5), just as in Ps 89. The expression $b^er\hat{i}t$ 'ôlam (v. 5) could of course be compared with the formulations in ancient Near Eastern material concerning the eternal validity of gifts and grants.[15] But the closest parallel in the epigraphic material is found in the Phoenician incantation from Arslan Tash from the 7th century B.C. ('lt 'lm, "eternal oath")[16], and the other occurrences in the Old Testament of $b^er\hat{i}t$ 'ôlam all date from the end of the 7th century or later.[17] One can also mention the use of $ṣamăh$ concerning the prosperity of the dynasty (v. 5) which is reminiscent of Jer 23,5; 33,15; Zach 3,8. However, there are no Dtr features in 2 S 23,1-7, a fact that distinguishes it from Ps 89 and 132. Nor is there mention of the divine sonship, in contrast with 2 S ch. 7 and Ps 89. The distribution of the expression $b^er\hat{i}t$ 'ôlam suggests a date roughly contemporary with the P-

---

[13] *Procksch* (BWAT 13/1913, 112-125) dates it to the time of David, *Cross* (1973: 234 ff., cf. 237 note 81) to the tenth century, *Caquot* (VTSuppl 9/1963, 218) to the Solomonic era, H.S.*Nyberg* (ARW 35/1938, 384 ff.) to the reign of Ahaz, *Mowinckel* (ZAW 45/1927, 58) to the days of Hezekiah or Josiah, and *Perlitt* (1969: 50 f.) seems to presume a still later date.
[14] Against *vonRad* (ThAT I, ⁴1962: 323).
[15] For references see *Weinfeld* (JAOS 90/1970, 199).
[16] KAI 27,9-10. *Weinfeld* (Bibl 56/1975, 127) drew attention to this.
[17] In addition to 2 S 23,5, $b^er\hat{i}t$ 'ôlam occurs in Gn 9,16; 17,7.13.19; Ex 31,16; Lv 24,8; Nu 18,19; 25,13 (all in P), and in Jes 24,5; 55,3; 61,8; Jr 32,40; 50,5; Ez 16,60; 37,26; 1 Ch 16,17; and Ps 105,10. Cf. *Perlitt* (1969: 50 with note 6). For the exilic date of Ps 105 see S.*Norin* (in *Er spaltete das Meer*, forthcoming doctoral dissertation, Lund).

writings. This in turn links up with the fact that no condition is appended to the promise in v. 5.[18]

Ps 2 and 110. – So much for the most evident lyrical echoes of the prophecy of Nathan. On one most characteristic point there is, however, a similarity between this text and two psalms that have not been mentioned so far, viz. Ps 2 and 110. These psalms both allude to the status of the king as "son" of God, as does also 2 S 7,14 from the first "Solomonic" form of the prophecy of Nathan down through the two main redactions. It is, however, quite impossible to demonstrate any form of interrelationship between the Solomonic prophecy of Nathan and these two psalms. However, one point deserves attention: the conception of the Davidic dynasty is not found in these two psalms, nor in the oldest Solomonic prophecy of Nathan. This is an important fact that links up with certain other observations:

a. In the prophecy of Nathan the divine sonship of the king (v. 14) is the very *skopos* of the original Solomonic promise. In the dynastic redaction the emphasis has been transposed from this to the new element of the Davidic dynasty (v. 11b.16*). This can be seen particularly clearly in David's prayer (v. 18-22a.27-29), which is the result of the dynastic redaction. Although this redaction has retained the mention of the divine sonship in v. 14, everything in David's prayer revolves around the dynastic promise.
b. The Dtr framework of the Books of Kings contains a number of references to the dynastic promise, but the divine sonship is not mentioned here (see 1 R 2,3-4; 3,6; 9,4-5; 11,38).
c. Both sonship and dynasty play a part in Ps 89. But the sonship is expressed here by means of the special term $b^e k\hat{o}r$ (v. 28), and there can be no doubt that the climax of the psalm is reached in the passage dealing with the unconditional covenant (v. 29-38).
d. Ps 132 lays great stress on the dynastic promise but does not mention the divine sonship of the king.
e. Even if Kutsch and Perlitt probably overstate their case when they try to show that the theological use of $b^e r\hat{\imath}t$ is a Dtr innovation, the evidence clearly indicates that the conception of the Mosaic covenant came to the fore during the Dtr period (see excursus no 2). The elaboration of the dynastic promise as a $b^e r\hat{\imath}t$ in Ps 89 and 2 S 23,1-7 (cf. the oath in Ps 132) is clearly in line with the added emphasis on $b^e r\hat{\imath}t$.
f. In addition to this comes the fact that the conception of the people as the son(s) of God often appears in the prophetic writings from the middle

---

[18] On the unconditional character of the covenants in P, see *Zimmerli* (Gottes Offenbarung, ²1969: 205-216) and cf. also *Kutsch* (1973: 102-115).

of the eighth century B.C. down to the Babylonian exile. This makes one doubt that the conception of the king as the son of God was productive during the same period.[19]

Together with the above-mentioned observation about Ps 2 and 110, these observations may be explained on the hypothesis that the place held by the conception of the divine sonship of the king was gradually taken over by the conception of the dynastic promise as a covenant made by God with David. The historical course of development described the line *from* divine sonship *to* Davidic covenant. It was probably during the Solomonic era that the conception of the divine sonship of the king found its first formulations in Israelite literature (Ps 2 and 110 and the Solomonic version of the prophecy of Nathan).

My conclusions from the discussion of the lyrical echoes of the prophecy of Nathan can be summarized in the following points:

1. It is possible that Ps 2 and 110 are older than the dynastic redaction of the prophecy of Nathan.
2. It is highly probable that the other texts which have been discussed here, viz. Ps 89; 132; and 2 S 23,1-7, are from a later period than the dynastic redaction of the prophecy of Nathan. A date during the late pre-exilic and exilic periods is indicated.
3. It is probable that the conception of the divine sonship of the king was of significance during the Solomonic era. It seems however that the Davidic covenant was an increasingly important element of royal ideology during the late pre-exilic and exilic periods.[19a]

2. The Divine Sonship of the King

1. Divine Sonship and Divine Kingship

The question of divine kingship in Israel and the ancient Near East is one that has attracted considerable attention in the literature. Various definitions of "divine kingship" are possible. I should like to suggest that the term be used in a narrow sense and only when there is a sense of identity between the king and the god so that the king holds the position of *deus incarnatus* on earth. The king can then be thought of as being of divine descent (cf. *hieros gamos*). He may also be the object of a cult.[19b] The Israelite conception of the divine sonship of the king is such that it suggests

---

[19] This was pointed out by *deBoer* (OTS 18/1973, 204). For references and discussion of Israel as the "son(s)" of God, see *deBoer* (ibid. p. 195 ff.) and *Schlisske* (1973: 116 ff.).
[19a] Cf. the hints in *vonRad* (GesStud ²1961: 211) and *S.Herrmann* (1965: 101).
[19b] Cf. *Bernhardt* (1961: 73-78 with the notes).

that the conception of divine kingship was also found in ancient Israel. It is therefore important to decide in which sense the divine sonship of the king is to be interpreted: was divine sonship conceived in mythological categories, or was it understood in legal, adoptianic terms. This is the problem to which I now turn, and I shall try to answer it on the basis of a perusal of the primary evidence, i.e. 2 S ch. 7, Ps 2, Ps 89 and Ps 110.[20]

(1) *2 S ch. 7.* – Of the two pre-Dtr forms of the prophecy of Nathan the Solomonic version comprised v. 1a.2-7.12-14a.16*.17. The divine sonship motif is found in v. 14a: *'ᵃnî 'æhyæ̃ lô lᵉ'ab wᵉhû' yihyæ̃ lî lᵉben*. Apart from strict identity, such phrases with *hayā lᵉ... lᵉ...* can also denote metaphorical relations (e.g. Ex 4,16: Moses is to be "as God" to Aaron; cf. Ex 13,9 and Jer 31,9). Thus, G.Cooke translates 2 S 7,14a: "I shall be *to* him *for* a father, and he shall be *to* me *for* [as] a son."[21] The statement in v. 12, also belonging to the kernel of the text, that Solomon goes forth from the body of David (*'ᵃšær yeṣe' mimme'ǣka*) supports such a metaphorical interpretation of the divine sonship. One should also note that the verb used is not *yalăd* but the more neutral *hayā*.

In its dynastic redaction, the prophecy of Nathan also comprised v. 8.9.11b.14b-15.16*.18-22a.27-29. While in the Solomonic version, the promise of divine sonship is expounded in v. 16* as implying divine protection (*wᵉnæ'măn bêtô...*), the dynastic redaction adds a formulation concerning filial obedience to God (v. 14b). However, the demand for obedience is not made a *sine qua non* for the promise of a dynasty. In v. 14b-15, the dynastic redaction contains an explicit formulation on the unconditional character of the divine promise in the prophecy of Nathan. Even if the king is disobedient he will remain the "son" of God in contrast to the *bᵉnê 'adam*, who execute punishment (v. 14).

While in the Solomonic version it is only Solomon who is depicted as "son" (cf. 1 Ch 22,8-10; 28,6), the dynastic revision (esp. v. 11b.16) makes every new Davidic king appear as "son". Although David himself is not denoted "son", it would certainly be wrong to infer that David was imagined by the redactor to enjoy a lesser degree of sacral status than his descendants. Thus in Ps 89,27 f. David is denoted as the first-born.

---

[20] Quite a lot has been written on the divine sonship of the king. See *Noth* (GesStud I, ²1960: 222 ff.), *G.Cooke* (ZAW 73/1961, 202 ff.), *G.Fohrer* (ThW 8/1967, 340-354), *Donner* (OrAnt 8/1969, 113 f.), *M.Görg* (Theologie und Glaube 60/1970, 413 ff.), *Weinfeld* (JAOS 90/1970, 189 ff.), *Schlisske* (1973: 78 ff.), *deBoer* (OTS 18/1973, 188 ff.) and *Görg* (1975: 258 ff.). Note also the articles on *ben* and *'ab* in the theological dictionaries. References to earlier works are found in *deFraine* (1954: 271 ff.).

[21] *G.Cooke* (ZAW 73/1961, 207). – This metaphorical feature is thus found already in the Hebrew OT. Contrast *deBoer* (OTS 18/1973, 192 f.), who suggests that is was introduced by the Targum.

What holds for the latter kings *a fortiori* also holds for David in 2 S ch. 7. Because of this it is important to note that David's human attributes are emphasized. His divine election occurred at a definite point in time: God "took" him from the sheep (v. 8). In this connection the term *nagîd* (v. 8) is also of interest. It is a specification of the "son" in v. 14 as the "firstborn", the one who is to inherit the crown after Saul. Since *nagîd* denotes a status, reached through divine designation, through a divine act of election, this word also hints at the human attributes of the king.

(2) Ps 2. – The psalms can be treated according to the order in which they appear in the canon, and we thus start with Ps 2.[22] In this psalm, the statement about the divine sonship is its very core. It is the contents of the *ḥoq*[23]. The phrase *bᵉnî 'ăttā 'ᵃnî hăyyôm yᵉlidtîka* is a solemn, performative utterance,[24] and the perfect *yᵉlidtîka* can be said to be a case of what I prefer to call *perfectum performativum*.[25] In this case the performative utterance initiates the king's status as son of God at the same moment that it is pronounced. The word order puts the emphasis on God as the speaking subject: *'ᵃnî hăyyôm yᵉlidtîka* (cf. the stressed *bᵉnî*). The same word order is also found in v. 6: *wă'ᵃnî nasăktî*[26] *mălkî* ... .

Two observations show that the king's status as "son" is initiated at a definite point in time. (a) V. 7b is formulated as a performative utterance. (b) The use of the word *hăyyôm*, "this day", is to be compared here with that in other instances to indicate the formal initiation of a legal contract (Ruth 4,9-10; Gn 25,31.33).[27] We can see here that the utterance points

---

[22] In addition to the literature mentioned in *Kraus* (Psalmen I, ²1961: 11), the following contributions can be mentioned: *Engnell* (Fs Johs.Pedersen 1953: 85 ff.), *G.H.Jones* (VT 15/1965, 336 ff.), *N.Poulssen* (1967: 55 ff.), *Soggin* (FsEichrodt 1970: 191 ff.), *M.Görg* (Theologie und Glaube 60/1970, 413 ff.), *Brownlee* (Bibl 52/1971, 321 ff.) and *Schlisske* (1973: 88 ff.).

[23] According to *vonRad* (GesStud I, ²1961: 205 ff.) the *ḥoq* in Ps 2,7 and the *ʿedût* in 2 R 11,12 correspond to the Egyptian *nḫb.t*. For a discussion of these questions, see below ch. 12.3.2.3.

[24] A performative utterance performs the legal act which it is the purpose of the instrument to perform. Such an utterance is therefore "operative" in a specific manner. On performative utterances see esp. *J.L.Austin* (Philosophical Papers 1961: 220 ff.).

[25] This use of the Hebrew perfect is found e.g. in *natăttî*, "I hereby give you..." (Gn 1,29; 1 R 3,12). It can be regarded as a subdivision of the so-called coincidence case (cf. *BrSynt* § 41 d and *H.S.Nyberg*, Hebreisk Grammatik, 1952, § 86 j). Cf. also *Gardiner* (Egyptian Grammar, ³1973, § 414: 5).

[26] The verb *nasăktî* is generally taken to be a form of *Gesenius' nasăk* I, "ausgiessen" (p. 507 b), which is used of libations, and is assumed to refer to the installation of the king through a libation (cf. *KBL* p. 620 a). Probably starting from this basic understanding of the word *Cazelles* (SEÅ 39/1974, 48 f.) speaks of a baptism of the king. *H.Gese* (Fs vonRad 1971: 81 f.) on the other hand changes the vocalization into *nᵉsăkkotî*, a form of *sakăk*, "weave together", "form".

[27] Cf. *G.M.Tucker* (CBQ 28/1966, 42-45) and *Weinfeld* (JAOS 90/1970, 190 note 55). Note the formula *ištu ūmi annî* ("from today") in the Akkadian documents from Alalakh and Ugarit.

forward: not with regard to his descent but with regard to his future task, the king is proclaimed "son" of God.[28]

The passing of kingship made the insurgency of the vassals possible (v. 1-3). There is in Ps 2 an intentional contrast between the rebellion of the "kings of the earth" (v. 2) and the divine sonship of the Israelite king. As son, the king is also heir and inherits the "nations" and the "ends of the earth" (v. 8). Thus, the king enjoys world-wide dominion, as "he who sits in heaven" (v. 4) has delegated his power to him. In contrast to the "kings of the earth", the "son" enjoys fatherly protection from God himself. The suffixes in Ps 2 serve to express the close relationship between the king and his God. Thus "YHWH and his anointed" are treated as a unity in v. 2; and v. 3 speaks of "their bonds" and "their cords". When God speaks of the king he refers to him as "my king" (v. 6) and "my son" (v. 7). And God refers to the king's capital, Zion, as "my holy hill" (v. 6).

(3) *Ps 89.* – In Ps 89,27-28, the king is described as $b^ek\hat{o}r$. The delicate literary structure of this psalm makes it imperative to study this utterance in its proper context. Apart from the concluding lament the psalm consists of an introduction (v. 1-5), a cosmic hymn (v. 6-19) and a royal oracle (v. 20-38). This royal oracle in turn falls into two parts, v. 20-28 and v. 29-38. The latter part contains the covenantal dynastic promise and I shall return to this later in connection with the Davidic covenant. My immediate interest will be focussed on v. 20-28, a section that ends with the following lines (v. 27-28):

הוא יקראני אבי אתה אלי וצור ישועתי
אף אני בכור אתנהו עליון למלכי ארץ

The context makes it clear that here it is David himself who is spoken of as $b^ek\hat{o}r$ (contrast 2 S ch. 7 where Solomon is the "son").

Let us first refer the statement concerning the sonship to the immediate context (v. 20-28) and then to the preceding part of the psalm, the cosmic hymn (v. 6-19). Although it has so far passed unnoticed it seems that the passage v. 20-28 consists of a series of inclusions with v. 24 as the central utterance: "I will crush his foes before him and strike down those who hate him."

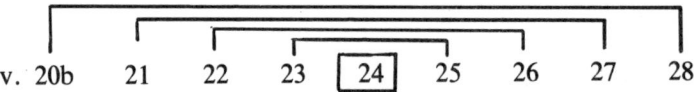

Thus, v. 22 (God's hand with the king) and v. 26 (the king's hand on the sea) correspond to each other. So do v. 21 (*maṣa'tî dawid 'ăbdî*...) and v. 27 (*hû' yiqra'enî 'abî 'attā*). The filial relationship in v. 27 f. means that

---

[28] So *Schlisske* (1973: 91).

David's status as God's "servant" in v. 21 is raised. For the sake of consequence v. 28 must correspond to v. 20b. This observation lends support to the recent suggestion that the word ʿezær in v. 20b should be congruent to the Ugaritic ǵzr, "boy", "warrior", and the words šiwwîtî ʿezær ʿăl gibbôr hᵃrîmôtî baḥûr meʿam translated "I exalted a stripling over the man of war, I raised up a young man from the people".[29] There is also here in v. 20 and 28 an intensification: the young and inexperienced stripling is not only placed above the warriors (v. 20) but is even installed as $b^e k\hat{o}r$, as ʿælyôn lᵉmălkê ʾaræṣ (v. 28). From this study of v. 20-28 it then appears that (a) the formulation referring to the king as $b^e k\hat{o}r$ is a supreme expression of his divine election and (b) this implies God's paternal protection of the king against his enemies.

What is said of the king's status in v. 20-28 must also be considered in connection with the cosmic hymn to YHWH in v. 6-19. It is due to J.-B. Dumortier that attention has been drawn to the close connection between these two sections of the psalm.[30] These links make the king's dominion on earth appear as the reflexion of God's cosmic supremacy. The first part of the cosmic hymn (v. 6-9) describes God as the head of the heavenly assembly, denoted as qᵉhăl qᵉdošîm, bᵉnê ʾelîm, and sôd qᵉdošîm. The Lord is not denoted ʿælyôn in Ps 89, but elsewhere this name describes Him as the head of the divine council (cf. Ps 82,6). Thus, when the divine sonship of the king is expounded as implying that he is ʿælyôn over the kings of the earth (v. 27 f.), the connection is unmistakable: the king does on earth what God does in heaven. One is almost tempted to speak of the king as "the image and likeness of God" on earth. The cosmic hymn also speaks of God as ruling over the sea and of his victory over răḥăb (v. 10-11).[30a] This power he delegates to the king: wᵉšămtî băyyam yadô ûbănnᵉharôt yᵉmînô (v. 26). And God's mighty arm that scatters the enemies in the hymn (v. 11b) strengthens the king in the royal oracle (v. 22).

Ps 89 thus contains extremely strong expressions describing the sacral position of the king. Nevertheless even here the king remains manifestly a human being. He is raised from the people (v. 20b). He calls the Lord his God and his rock of salvation (v. 27). It is possible that the word $b^e k\hat{o}r$ was chosen to retain this human side of the king. Because of its well-known associations this term was very apt in denoting the king as a

---

[29] See *P.D.Miller* (UF 2/1970, 159 ff., esp. 165), *Rainey* (Orient and Occident, 1973: 139 ff., esp. 141) and *F.M.Cross* (1973: 258 note 173). For Ugaritic ǵzr see *UT* (Glossary no 1956) and *Aistleitner* (WB no 2138). On the term "congruent", see *Mettinger* (1971: 2).

[30] See *Dumortier* (VT 22/1972, 186 ff.). *Ahlström* (1959: 108) made the observation on a connection between v. 10 and v. 26 but did not develop this insight.

[30a] Ps 89,10-11 possibly allude to the exodus and not to the creation, see *S.Norin* (*Er spaltete das Meer*, forthcoming doctoral diss., Lund).

manifestly human being who belongs to the Lord.³¹ If this is correct, then it should be noted that there is a possible correspondence between the last verse in the passage concerning the king's election (v. 28) and the last verse of the cosmic hymn, which contains a parallel statement: "For our shield belongs to the Lord, our king to the Holy One of Israel" (v. 19; cf. Ps 84,10).

*(4) Ps 110.*³² – The textual crux in Ps 110,3 is generally assumed to hide a formulation referring to the king as the son of God.³³ Least alteration is needed, if v. 3b is read in the following manner:

בהדרי קדש מרחם משחר לְךָ טל יְלִדְתִּיךָ

In holy array from the womb of the dawn³⁴ go forth;
  as the dew I have begotten you.³⁵

It should be seriously doubted that this reflects the idea of a *hieros gamos*. On the contrary, *mišḥar* and *šăḥăr* (the latter in Jes 14,12: *bæn šăḥăr*) could hardly be taken to denote a goddess.³⁵ᵃ The Ugaritic *šḥr* is a male god. And *bæn šăḥăr* in Jes 14,12 does not perhaps mean more than "matutinal", which would have a parallel in Job 38,7: *kôkᵉbê boqær* // *bᵉnê ʾᵃᵉlohîm*. I therefore regard a figural interpretation of Ps 110,3 as the most probable. This interpretation is also supported by Job 38,28 f. (cf. 38,8), where God's production of natural phenomena is described in the figure of paternity: "Has the rain a father, or who has begotten the drops of dew? From whose womb did the ice come forth, and who has given birth to the hoarfrost of heaven?"³⁶

The closeness between God and king is also stressed in Ps 110. Both are denoted as *ʾadôn* (v. 1.5). The king is summoned to sit at the right hand of the Lord (v. 1), something that is reminiscent of representations in Egyptian art depicting the king and a god sitting on the same throne.³⁷ Ps 110,1 should be compared with Ps 45,7 (*kisʾᵃka ʾᵃᵉlohîm ʿôlam waʿæd*). As far as I can

---

³¹ I find *Ahlström's* remarks on *bᵉkôr* (1959: 111 ff.) very valuable, although this scholar seems to overestimate the sacral implications.
³² In addition to the commentaries and the literature mentioned in *Kraus* (Psalmen II, ²1961: 752) note *Caquot* (Semitica 6/1956, 33 ff.), *Bernhardt* (1961: 232 ff.), *G.Cooke* (ZAW 73/1961, 218 ff.), *Schreiner* (1963: 112 ff.), *Poulssen* (1967: 55 ff.), *K.Homburg* (ZAW 84/1972, 243 ff.) and *Schlisske* (1973: 94 ff.).
³³ For a textual criticism of v. 3 see conveniently *Kraus* (Psalmen II, ²1961: 753) and *G.Cooke* (ZAW 73/1961, 218 ff.).
³⁴ In retaining the word *mišḥar* I follow *HAL* (p. 609a) and take this word to be a ma-nomen.
³⁵ This agrees with *Cooke* (p. 221 f.) except that I retain *mišḥar*.
³⁵ᵃ *McKay* (VT 20/1970, 456 ff.) tries to demonstrate that Ps 110,3 reflects an ancient belief in a personalized feminine Dawn. But this is very doubtful and cf. besides *P.C.Craigie* (ZAW 85/1973, 223-225, esp. p. 224).
³⁶ Cf. *Cooke* (p. 224).
³⁷ See *O.Keel* (Bildsymbolik, 1972 p. 233, 240, 246 f.).

see J.Mulder has put a very good case for the interpretation of this as an ellipsis the equivalent of which would be *kis'ᵃka kissê 'ᵃᵉlohîm 'ôlam wa'æd*, "your throne is Elohim's throne for ever and ever".[38] Thus, the king sits on the throne of God, invited to share His power. The king is God's co-regent, exercising delegated divine power. Just as in Ps 2 and Ps 89 there is also in Ps 110 a contrast between the threat of the enemies and the divine sonship because of which the king enjoys divine protection (v. 1b.2b.5.6).

This perusal of the texts justifies the conclusion that the divine sonship of the Israelite king was not conceived in mythological categories. The king was not considered to be of divine descent. His divine sonship commenced at a definite point in time and was brought about by a performative utterance of God. In the next section I shall discuss the question of whether the divine sonship was understood in adoptianic categories.

2. The Interpretatio Israelitica

(1) Adoption and Performatives. – I am inclined to agree with those scholars who maintain that the Israelite conception of the divine sonship of the king is due to Egyptian influence.[1] The filial relationship between the Egyptian king and the god was conceived in mythological categories with the emphasis on the physical descent of the king from the god who begat him.[1a] It is important to note that it is not in this mythological form that we find the conception of divine sonship in the Israelite texts. Divine sonship has been subjected to an *interpretatio israelitica*. Indeed, it does not seem to be out of place to interpret this process as a case of de-mythologization.

In general the scholars have interpreted the divine sonship of the Israelite king in an adoptianic sense.[2] This interpretation has been challenged. Thus H.Donner has drawn attention to the fact that the legal material preserved in the Old Testament does not deal with the practice of adoption. It is true that some narratives have often been taken as supporting the theory that adoption was known in Israel, but Donner prefers to interpret these cases as legitimation within Family Law. According to Donner the divine

---

[38] See *J.Mulder* (1972: 33-80). In addition to the references cited there, I would also refer to Ps 92,11.

[1] See ch. 12.2.3 note 28.

[1a] For the myth see esp. *H.Brunner* (Die Geburt des Gottkönigs, 1964).

[2] Most recently, this view has been defended by *G.Cooke* (ZAW 73/1961, 202 ff.), *Weinfeld* (JAOS 90/1970, 189 ff.) and *Boecker* (ZAW 86/1974, 86 ff.). On adoption as a legal custom in the *Keilschriftrecht* see above all *M.David* (1927) and *H.Donner* (OrAnt 8/1969, 87 ff.). Donner underlines the necessity to distinguish between *adoptio*, "'Annahme an Kindesstatt' gewaltunterworfener Personen" and *arrogatio*, "'Annahme an Kindesstatt' gewaltfreier Personen" (p. 88).

sonship of the Israelite king should not be interpreted in the legal sense of an *adoptio filii loco*. It is "ein auf die Ebene der Metapher transponiertes mythisches Element", which Israel had taken over from Egypt.[3] G.W.Ahlström and M.Görg also object to the adoptianic interpretation but they prefer to speak of "Neugeburt" or "Wiedergeburt".[4]

Although there is a genetic connection with the mythological sonship of the Egyptian king, there is nevertheless in the Israelite material an emphasis on the proclamation of the sonship not as an epiphany of the king but as a first recognition, as a kind of adoption on the part of God. It is very tempting to see this as a deliberate adaptation and re-interpretation of the Egyptian mythological conception. The emphasis on the human nature of the king in 2 S 7,12 and Ps 89 deserves attention. Moreover, Ps 2,7 makes it clear that the status of the king as "son" begins at a definite point in time (note *hăyyôm* and the sonship as resulting from a performative utterance). Similarly, Ps 89 contains the formulation "I will make him the first-born" (*b^{e}kôr 'ætt^{e}nehû*, v. 28), which speaks of a status bestowed upon the king through a divine act of will, and not of a right held by descent. It is also an important factor that the Akkadian diplomatic vocabulary is rooted in the familial sphere. Thus, relations between states can be defined as *abbūtu* ("fathership"=suzerainty), *mārūtu* ("sonship"=vassalage) or *aḫḫūtu* ("brotherhood"=parity relation).[5] The use of familial metaphors was thus well known in the royal-national sphere, and it is certainly not a prerequisite for the use of such a terminology that the legal practice of the country in question should include the custom of adoption. In any case, king Ahaz can say to Tiglath-pileser that he is his "servant" and "son" (2 R 16,7). Although *adoptio filii loco* was probably not practised by the Israelites, the divine sonship of the king can be interpreted in adoptianic terms, insofar as it denotes a filial relationship between the king and his God that must not be interpreted in mythological terms, but that comes into being at a definite point in time, through a divine act of will.

Does Ps 2,7 contain an adoption formula? – As we have seen, the phrase *b^{e}nî 'āttā 'ănî hăyyôm y^{e}lidtîka* (Ps 2,7) is a performative utterance. From the moment these words were pronounced (by a priest or a cultic prophet) the king is the "son" of God. This is illuminated by the similar use of performative utterances within *Keilschriftrecht*. Thus, in the Middle Assyrian Laws, a man who wants to marry

[3] *Donner* (op. cit. esp. p. 104-114, quotation from p. 114). Donner admits (p. 114) that in Israel this cannot have been understood in the sense of a physical begetting.
[4] *Ahlström* (1959: 112) and *M.Görg* (Theologie und Glaube 60/1970, 413 ff.). In his review of Ahlström Å.*Sjöberg* (SEÅ 25/1960, 102) points out that the conceptions of both "Neugeburt" and adoption may well be present side by side in Ps 2,7. – *deBoer* (OTS 18/1973, 204), too, is sceptical of the adoptianic interpretation.
[5] See esp. *J.M.Munn-Rankin* (Iraq 18/1956, 68 ff.). Cf. also *Lipinski* (1967: 58 ff.), *Weinfeld* (JAOS 90/1970, 194), *Fensham* (FsAlbright 1971: 121 ff.), and *Y.Holmes* (AOAT 22/1973, 97).

his concubine shall veil her in the presence of witnesses and say "she is my wife" (MAL § 41).[6] Similarly, a marriage could be dissolved through the utterance of the formula "you are not my wife".[7] As far as adoption is concerned the situation seems to be comparable. An adoption could be dissolved if the adoptive parents said "you are not our son" (VAT 926,24-25).[8] M.David assumes that there was a corresponding formula when formally entering into an adoptive relationship and refers to CH § 170-171.[9] Here a man legitimates the children that his female slave has borne to him, and this he does by saying "you are my sons".[10] In spite of the sparse attestation, it seems that performative utterances occurred both at the establishment and at the dissolution of adoption contracts.[11] Thus, even if we cannot go so far as to call the phrase in Ps 2,7 an adoption formula since we cannot speak of a formula on the basis of a single occurrence, it nevertheless appears that the function of the phrase as a performative utterance in establishing a legal relationship corresponds with what we can conclude about the legal customs within cuneiform law.

(2) Democratization and nagîd. – Some of our findings concerning the title *nagîd* (see especially ch. 9.4) are also relevant here. We have found that in the prophecy of Nathan the old Solomonic kernel contained the saying about the king as "son" of God (2 S 7,14), while the dynastic redaction introduced the term *nagîd* (v. 8). According to my interpretation, this term first denoted the royal son who was appointed Crown prince, and then the one whom God designated. There are thus familial connotations in the word. This semantic aspect becomes manifest in the formula *nagîd ʿăl ʿăm YHWH* where, as we have seen, the word *ʿăm* denotes Israel as the "family" of the Lord. In this connection, one should also note 1 S 10,1 where Samuel anoints Saul as *nagîd* over God's *năḥªlā*.

It is therefore natural to regard the symbiosis of the two terms *ben* and *nagîd* in the prophecy of Nathan as being due to a semantic relationship between these words. Both denote the king's relation to God as filial. But there is one important difference. The use of the word *ben* does not in itself presuppose the existence of other "sons". This is, however, the case with *nagîd*. The expression *nagîd ʿăl ʿăm YHWH* hints at a filial relation to God not only for the king but also for his people, since *ʿăm* denotes Israel as the "family" of the Lord. The word *nagîd* thus conveys more "democratic" connotations than the word *ben*. The king is *primus inter pares*.

---

[6] Text in *R.Borger* (Babylonisch-assyrische Lesestücke, II, 1963: 53) translation e.g. in *ANET*³ (p. 183, *T.J.Meek*).
[7] See *C.Kuhl* (ZAW 52/1934, 102 ff.) and *Driver–Miles* (The Babylonian Laws I p. 402 f.).
[8] Text in *M.David* (1927: 43). For the case that the adoptive son says "you are not my father" see the same text, lines 17 ff., and CH § 192.
[9] *M.David* (1927: 78-81).
[10] Text in *Borger* (op. cit. p. 30 f.), translation e.g. in *ANET*³ (p. 173, *T.J.Meek*).
[11] See also *Boecker* (ZAW 86/1974, 88 f.).

The tendency represented by the choice of the term *nagîd* was expressed in new ways during the subsequent centuries of the "divided monarchy". It seems that during this period, we are witness to a "democratization" of some of the conceptions of the royal ideology. If the Israelite king was denoted as the image of God in certain court circles for a short period during the Solomonic era (below), then the conception of *imago Dei* is an example of such a democratization. In a similar way, the use of the word *ben* to denote the king was later extended to include the whole people as "son(s)" of God. The oldest occurrences are probably those in Hosea (2,1; 11,1). In Ex 4,22-23 the same use is found in an addition to a J-E section.[12] There are a number of other occurrences,[13] but there is nothing to indicate that this use of "son(s)" for Israel should be earlier than the eighth century B.C. The semantic development of *baḥăr* describes a similar course. Its earliest use referring to divine election concerns the king.[14] The corresponding use concerning the divine election of the people is not attested until in Dt and Dtr writings.[15] And although *baḥăr* is used here in a casual and unstressed way that makes one suspect that this use of the word concerning the people is somewhat older, it probably represents an extension, a "democratization" of the earlier "royal" use.[16] Thus, the "democratization" of the divine sonship of the Israelite king is probably due to a general tendency in the theological development during the last pre-exilic centuries, but even so, the "democratization" of the sonship can be seen as the ultimate *interpretatio israelitica* of an originally mythological conception.

3. King, Urmensch and Image of God

In spite of the fact that the expression *ben 'el* or *ben (ha)'ᵃᵉlohîm* is not used for the king, the Old Testament speaks in various ways about the divine sonship of the king, as we have seen. We have here reached a point where it becomes natural to look for the relationship between the king and "the sons of God", the heavenly beings, an inquiry that will lead us to the *Urmensch*. One can note, for instance, that the power that God bestows upon both the "Son" and the "sons" is described as an inheritance. The

---

[12] See *Schlisske* (1973: 161). Note, however, that Schlisske also says: "Der Titel wird so selbstverständlich verwendet, dass er als längst bekannt gelten muss" (p. 161).
[13] For a discussion see *Schlisske* (p. 116 ff.) and *deBoer* (OTS 18/1973, 195 ff.). I am not inclined to think that the cases in Dt 32,5.19 are earlier than those in Hosea. For a balanced discussion of the date of Dt 32, see *G.E.Wright* (FsMuilenburg 1962: 26 ff.).
[14] 2 S 16,18 (the SN), 2 S 6,21 (the HDR) and 1 S 10,24.
[15] See *Seebass* (TWAT 1/1973, 603 cf. 606) and *Wildberger* (THAT 1/1971, 284 f.).
[16] Cf. *Wildberger* (op. cit. col. 285).

Son receives the nations as his heritage (Ps 2,8). Similarly, *'ælyôn* distributes the peoples between the "sons of God" (Dt 32,8-9[1]) as an inheritance. In the main stream of Old Testament tradition, the king has apparently been regarded at the most as comparable with a heavenly being. There is no identification. Thus, in the Succession Narrative, David is compared with a *mǎl'ak*. Mephiboshet says to David: *wǎ'donî hǎmmælæk k^{e}mǎl'ǎk ha'^{ae}lohîm* (2 S 19,28). Two utterances, made by the woman from Tekoa, reveal that this comparison above all refers to the wisdom of the king. In 2 S 14,17 she says: *kî k^{e}mǎl'ǎk ha'^{ae}lohîm ken '^{a}donî hǎmmælæk lišmo$^{a\text{'}}$ hǎṭṭôb w^{e}hara'*.[2] And in 14,20 the wording goes: *wǎ'donî ḥakam k^{e}ḥåkmǎt mǎl'ǎk ha'^{ae}lohîm lǎdǎ'ǎt 'æt kål '^{a}šær ba'aræṣ*. The difference in formulation is significant. The first of the woman's statements refers to the judicial wisdom of the king. The second extends the knowledge of the king from the judicial sphere to royal knowledge of human affairs in general,[3] perhaps even to a sort of omniscience. At bottom, the first utterance (14,17) is a condensed repetition of 1 R 3,9: *w^{e}nåtǎtta l$^{e\text{'}}$åbd^{e}ka leb šome$^{a\text{'}}$ lišpoṭ 'æt 'åmm^{e}ka l^{e}habîn bên ṭôb l^{e}ra'*.[4] Similar comparisons with an angelic being are found later in the History of David's Rise (1 S 29,9; cf. v. 4) and in Zach 12,8.

The two verses quoted above from 2 S ch. 14 remind us of the knowledge of the elohim-beings in Gn ch. 3: *k$^{e\text{'}}$åḥåd mimmænnû lǎdǎ'ǎt ṭôb wara'* (v. 22; cf. v. 5). In this connection Job 15,7-8[5] is also relevant. According to Job the *Urmensch* (*ri'šôn 'adam*) had access to the divine council (*sôd '^{ae}lô^{a}h*)[6] and so acquired the divine wisdom of the elohim-beings (cf. Prv 30,3).

That royal categories are used in the description of the First Man can easily be seen from Gn 1,26-28[7] and from Ps 8,6 ff.[8] And Ps 8 also says that man was made only a little less than the elohim-beings.[9] In fact, the affinity

---

[1] I follow the LXX reading in v. 8, now supported by the well-known fragment from Qumran. See *Skehan* (BASOR 136/1954, 12 ff.) and most recently *Schlisske* (1973: 58 ff.).
[2] For a bibliography on the "knowledge of good and bad" see *Westermann* (Genesis, Lief. 5/1972, 328, discussion p. 328 ff.).
[3] See *W.M.Clark* (JBL 88/1969, 266 ff. esp. 268 f.).
[4] *Clark* (p. 269). Cf. 1 R 3,28.
[5] On this text see *Ringgren* (1947: 89 ff.).
[6] For *sôd* as a designation of the divine council see also Ps 89,8 and Jer 23,18.22. For literature on *sôd* see *G.Cooke* (ZAW 76/1964, 39 note 74).
[7] See e.g. my remarks in ZAW 86/1974, 412 ff. (with literature).
[8] The following recent studies on Ps 8 may be noted: *W.H.Schmidt* (ThZ 25/1969, 1 ff.), *Soggin* (ASTI 8/1970-71, 106 ff.), *Tournay* (RB 78/1971, 18 ff.), *Loretz* (UF 3/1971, 104 ff.), *Ringgren* (SEÅ 37-38/1972-1973, 16 ff.) and *J.J.Stamm* (FsGuggisberg 1973: 247 ff.).
[9] *J.J.Stamm* (op. cit.) points out that the translation "wenig geringer als Gott" is quite possible for Ps 8,6 (cf. *Schmidt*, op. cit. p. 11). But even if this is so I regard the "angelic" translation as much more probable.

between king, the First Man and angelic beings[10] can also be substantiated by the study of two other texts, Ez ch. 28 and Jes ch. 14. It should be kept in mind, however, that these two texts deal with foreign kings, not Israelite kings.

In Ez ch. 28, it is particularly the *qînā* for the king of Tyre (v. 11-19) that is of interest to us.[11] It would be outside the scope of this work to discuss this passage in detail. It is really "a Pandora's box of problems" (H.G.May). To a certain extent every interpretation of this text must remain hypothetical.

In v. 14 and 16, there is a notable difference between the MT and the LXX, and the latter is generally preferred.[11a] According to the LXX there are two different beings in the garden of God, (a) the First Man and (b) the cherub. There are, however, certain indications that the LXX here offers a rather free interpretation.[12] It is practical to start with v. 16. The crucial word here is *wa'ăbbædka*. This is often emended to the third person and the cherub taken as its subject. However, this form of *'abăd* makes sense as a Piel perfect in the first person singular,[13] and then the suffix must refer to the cherub so that this is the object: "and I banished you, you overshadowing cherub, from the midst of the stones of fire."[13a] Thus, the MT here identifies the cherub with the being that was expelled. From this we can proceed to v. 14. Here it should first be noted that it is not necessary to follow the LXX and revocalize the first word, *'ăt*, into *'ét*, "with". At least eight cases of *'ăt* for the personal pronoun in the second masculine are known (among others Nu 11,15; Dt 5,27[13b]). But how are we then to interpret the syntactic structure of v. 14? If we allow for just one improvement of the MT, altering the vocalization of *bᵉhăr* into *bahar* (with the article), then the structure can be interpreted in the following manner:

את כרוב ממשח הסוכך ונתתיך בָהָר
קדש אלהים היית בתוך אבני אש התהלכת

[10] On the subject cf. Bentzen (1948), Engnell (SEÅ 22-23/1957-1958, 265 ff.), H.G.May (FsMuilenburg 1962: 166 ff.). These scholars, however, all neglect the "angelic" implications. One who does pay attention to the king's affinity to the elohim beings is *Mowinckel* (1956: 76 ff.), but he does not here discuss the connection with the *Urmensch*.

[11] For literature on Ez ch. 28 see *Zimmerli* (Ezechiel vol. 2/1969 p. 661 f., 671) and note further *K.Yaron* (ASTI 3/1964, 28 ff.), *H.G.May* (op. cit.) *N.C.Habel* (Concordia Theol. Monthly 38/1967, 516 ff.) and *H.J.vanDijk* (1968).

[11a] However, *Widengren* in a number of works (references in ZAW 86/1974, 423 note 58) has opted for the MT. So also does *H.J.vanDijk* (1968: 119, 121).

[12] In the LXX, v. 13b and 14a are taken together so that Man is created together with the cherub. This is difficult because of v. 15. In particular, the LXX seems to have left out certain difficult words that have been preserved in the MT, viz. *mimšăḥ hăssôkek* and *hithăllakta* in v. 14 and *hăssôkek* in v. 16.

[13] So Bauer-Leander (370 m).

[13a] My own translation.

[13b] See Bauer-Leander (248 e) for further references.

If we should attempt a translation it would be something like this:

You were the anointed[14] cherub, shadowing widely,[15]
and I placed you on the mountain.
You were the holy property[16] of God;
you walked among the stones of fire.

A difficulty can be seen in the fact that v. 13a (cf. 16b) seems to favour the segmentation $b^eh\check{a}r$ $qod\mathit{æ}š$ $'^{ae}loh\hat{\imath}m$ $hay\hat{\imath}ta$, "you were on the holy mountain of God", in v. 14. But there is nothing to say that this interpretation is absolutely necessary, and moreover it creates a difficulty as regards $\hat{u}n^et\check{a}tt\hat{\imath}ka$, which finds a natural function on the above interpretation. The interpretation suggested above has some clear advantages over the LXX interpretation. (a) It explains v. 14 and v. 16 without altering more than the vocalization of one single word. This does not apply to the LXX (cf. note 12). (b) It gives a $q\hat{\imath}n\bar{a}$-metre, which suits v. 12, according to which we are here concerned with a dirge for the king of Tyre. (c) Structurally there is an interesting correspondence between the lines $'\check{a}tt\bar{a}$ $\d{h}\hat{o}tem$ $t\mathring{a}kn\hat{\imath}t\ldots$ (v. 12) and $'\check{a}t$ $k^er\hat{u}b$ $mimš\check{a}\d{h}$ $\d{h}\check{a}ss\hat{o}kek\ldots$ (v. 14), both of which open with a pronoun in the emphatic position and both containing a predicative expression about the being walking in the garden of God.

Thus the MT of Ez 28,11-19 speaks of a being depicted as both king, First Man and cherub. To identify this being as a cherub is in line with the above-mentioned comparisons between the king and a $m\check{a}l'\check{a}k$ $ha'^{ae}loh\hat{\imath}m$. Despite not infrequent statements to the contrary, this identification of the being in the garden of God with a cherub is not a difficult one. The preceding section, which also deals with the king of Tyre, says that he denoted himself $'el$ (v. 1) and $'^{ae}loh\hat{\imath}m$ (v. 14). To describe this royal being as a cherub in v. 14 is only a different way of ranking him with the heavenly beings. Such a use of $k^er\hat{u}b$ can be compared with the use of the word $s^erap\hat{\imath}m$ in Jes ch. 6 to refer to the heavenly court of YHWH. The situation in Jes ch. 6 is, of course, to be seen against the background of such scenes as that in 1 R 22,19 ff. The description of a royal figure as a cherub has a parallel in Jes 14,12-15, where $h\hat{e}lel$ $b\mathit{æ}n$ $š\check{a}\d{h}\check{a}r$ (v. 12) also appears as an elohim-being, his designation being analogous to that of the

---

[14] I would like to suggest taking $mimš\check{a}\d{h}$ to be an otherwise not found noun derived from $maš\check{a}\d{h}$, "to anoint". For a different suggestion see *vanDijk* (1968: 119).

[15] Cf. 1 R 8,7 and 1 Ch 28,18.

[16] It is true that a revocalization of $qod\mathit{æ}š$ to $q^edoš$, "a Holy One", would be conceivable. The MT, however, makes sense and seems to give a parallel of v. 12b., where $\d{h}\hat{o}tem$ is probably to be taken to be an active participle, "sealer", referrring to the figure in the garden of Eden as the signet and thus a particularly precious possession of God. I thus don't agree with *vanDijk* (1968: 113 ff.) who takes $\d{h}wtm$ to contain an enclitic *mem* and to be cognate with Aramaic $\d{h}wh$, "serpent".

sons of God as the "morning stars" (*kôkᵉbê boqær*) in Job 38,7. The identification of the being in Ez ch. 28 with the cherub also agrees with the reference to the place where he dwells as "the mountain (of God")" in v. 14 and 16. This is no doubt the *hăr môʿed*, the place of the divine council of Jes 14,13 (cf. Job 15,7-8). Note also the *'ăbnê 'eš* (see note 17).

The royal characteristics of the being in Ez ch. 28 are unmistakable. He is described as "the king of Tyre" (v. 12). He wears a royal pectoral (v. 13).[17] He is a *kᵉrûb mimšăḥ*, which possibly means "an anointed cherub".[18] Just as the Israelite king is described as belonging to God in a specific way (Ps 89,19.28; see above), so is this being denoted as "the holy property [*qodæš*] of God" in v. 14 and as a signet in v. 12 (cf. Jer 22,24; Hag 2,23).

The being in Ez ch. 28 is also described as the *Urmensch*. He has a number of features in common with Adam in Gn ch. 2-3.[19] The text mentions his creation (v. 13.15), that he dwelt in the garden of Eden (v. 13), his blamelessness from the day of his creation until the day when iniquity was found in him (v. 15), his expulsion from the garden of God (v. 16), and that he became ashes (v. 18). Just as the First Man in Job 15,7-8 acquires divine knowledge, the royal figure in Ez ch. 28 is in the same way distinguished by his wisdom (v. 12b.17).

The locality mentioned in Ez ch. 28 deserves attention. It is a double exposure showing both the garden of the First Man (v. 13) and the mountain of God where the elohim-beings dwell (v. 14.16; cf. Jes 14,13).

The following table shows the features that are of interest to us:

	Gn ch. 2-3	Ez 28,11-19	Jes 14,9-15
the First Man	+	+	
king	(+)[20]	+	+
elohim-being		+	+
garden of Eden	+	+	
mountain of God		+	+[21]
fall/expulsion	+	+	+

[17] See *Widengren* (esp. 1955: 26-27). Similarly, *Zimmerli* (p. 683 f.; cf. 673 ff.) refers to a "Prachtgewand". *H.J.vanDijk* (1968: 116 ff.), however, does not refer to a garb but to a wall with precious stones that surrounds the garden of Eden. This scholar thus equates the stones in v. 13 with the *'ăbnê 'eš* in v. 14.16. It is then difficult to account for the similarity between the enumeration in v. 13 and Ex 28,17-20. Besides, as *Zimmerli* points out (p. 685 f.) it is more natural to take the "stones of fire" to denote "Lichtwesen", angelic beings among whom First Man had his dwelling on the mountain of God (cf. Job 15,7-8). Perhaps the seraphim of Jes ch. 6 were glowing beings of light.

[18] See above note 14.

[19] See esp. *N.C.Habel* (Concordia Theol. Monthly 38/1967, 522 ff.) for a comparison with Gn ch. 2-3. Unlike Habel (p. 519) I regard the royal features in First Man in Ez 28 as belonging to the tradition that lies behind this passage and not to the application of this tradition to the king of Tyre.

[20] The royal features are less prominent in Gn 2,4b-3,24 than in 1,26 ff. But just as in 1,26 ff. Adam has dominion over the animals in 2,19 f. (note he gives them names). Note also that the name of one of the streams is Gihon (v. 13) and cf. 1 R 1,33 ff.

[21] Here the mountain is the place *hêlel* strives to get to (Jes 14,13).

The same affinity between the king and the First Man also seems to be evident in Mi 5,1, where the future ruler is depicted as a new David "whose origin is from of old, from ancient days" (*ûmôṣa'otâw miqqædæm mîmê 'ôlam*). And the affinity between the king and the divine beings seems to recur in Jes 9,5 in the name *'el gibbôr*. As it appears from Dt 10,17 and Jer 32,18 a divine epithet has been applied here to the king.[22] However, Ps 45,7 does not belong here, since this verse means that the throne of the king is God's throne forever, as J.Mulder has made probable.[22a]

The divine sonship of the king is known from Mesopotamia.[22b] However, the fact that the idea is found in the Canaanite epic of Keret is perhaps still more interesting. Here we are particularly concerned with UT no 125[23], which has been understood to contain a *qînā* for king Keret.[24] Although El is called "father of mankind" (*ab adm*, Keret lines 37 and 151), the divine sonship of Keret is of a more specific kind. Men usually die, but this was not expected of Keret:

Wilt thou die then, father, like the mortals, ...
How can it be said, "A son of El is Keret,
An offspring of the Kindly One, and a holy being"?
Shall, then, a god die.
An offspring of the Kindly One not live? (UT no 125,17-23)[25]

Keret is son of El (*bn il*, line 20) and a holy being (*qdš*, line 22). It is interesting to note that according to another text Keret has failed to judge the cause of the widow and to provide for and protect other *personæ miserabiles*.[26] This is reminiscent of the misconduct of the sons of God in Ps 82, but we do not know whether there is an inner connection between this "sin" of Keret and the imposition of mortality.

The question of sacral kingship in Ugarit[27] certainly deserves further study. In the present state of our knowledge it is, however, impossible to say more than that the epic of Keret describes the heroic past of Ugarit, and that nothing of the divine sonship of the king is known from the texts relevant to the study of the Late Bronze Age Ugarit.

The opinion that the conception of the divine sonship of the Israelite king was formulated primarily under Egyptian influence is maintained by several

---

[22] I am not convinced by *M.Rehm's* attempt (1968: 149 ff. esp. 155 f.) to argue for a mitigatory rendering of this name.
[22a] See *J.Mulder* (1972: 33 ff.).
[22b] See *R.Labat* (1939: 53 ff.).
[23] This text is also found in *Herdner* (Corpus no 16; p. 71 ff.), *J.Gray* (The Krt Text 1955: 18 ff.) and *G.R.Driver* (Canaanite Myths and Legends, 1956: 40 ff.). For a study of the compositional structure of the epic of Keret as a whole see *H.Sauren–G.Kestemont* (UF 3/1971, 180 ff.).
[24] *H.Gottlieb* (DanskTT 32/1969, 88 ff.).
[25] I follow *Ginsberg's* translation (ANET³ p. 147).
[26] UT no 127,45 ff., translated in *ANET³* (p. 149).
[27] The only studies known to me are those by *J.Gray* (Ugaritica 6/1969, 289-302), and *J.Coppens* (FsBöhl 1973: 81-89). Cf. also the remarks made by *M.Liverani* (Le Palais et la Royauté, 1974: 338-341).

scholars.[28] In this connection there are certain indications that deserve very close attention.

1. We know of a number of things borrowed from Egypt[29] in the field of government offices,[30] coronation ritual[31] and court literature[32]. The borrowing of the conception of the divine sonship of the king has here a natural frame.
2. In Egypt, the king is at one and the same time the son of and the image of Amon-Re.[33] To be the image of Amon-Re was a royal prerogative.
3. It seems highly probable that the Israelite conception of *imago Dei* has its roots in the Egyptian conception of the divine sonship of the king.[34] The democratization of this conception took place on Israelite soil.[35]
4. As we have seen, in some late Old Testament texts there is an interesting affinity between king and First Man.

These observations make it probable that (a) the related Egyptian conception of the divine sonship of the king and that of *imago Dei* were taken over by Israel as a conceptual unit and that (b) the Israelite king was originally denoted not only "son" but also the "image" of God. It is natural to interpolate this intermediary stage between the Egyptian conception of the king as the image of Amon-Re and the democratization of this in the late P-writings in Israel.[36] It is true that H.S.Nyberg tried to find an allusion to the king as the image of God in 2 S 23,3b,[37] but this interpretation rests on an unnecessary emendation and, moreover, it does not fit into the context. Admittedly there are no texts to attest to the king as being *imago Dei*. My conclusion rests solely on the above deducible argument. What we find in the texts is at the most some polemical hints, as in Jes 14,14 where *hêlel* tries to make himself like the Most High (*'æddămmæ*

---

[28] Cf. *vonRad* (GesStud I, ²1961: 209 ff.), *Wildberger* (ThZ 16/1960, 314 ff.), *G.Cooke* (ZAW 73/1961, 213 f.), *M.Görg* (Theologie und Glaube 60/1970, 413 ff.) and *H.Donner* (OrAnt 8/1969, 113).

[29] For a survey of the Egyptian influence on Israel, see *R.J.Williams* (VTSuppl 28/1975, 231 ff.).

[30] On the government officials see *Mettinger* (1971), where I demonstrate that the Egyptian model of the office of the Israelite "house-minister" is *mr pr wr*, "High Steward", and not the Egyptian vizier as has previously been held, and that the Israelite "friend of the king" holds an office corresponding to that of the Egyptian *rḫ nśw.t* and not to that of the Egyptian *śmr* (p. 70-110 and 63-69). These new equations have now been accepted by the Egyptologist *R.J.Williams* (VTSuppl 28/1975, 236-237).

[31] See most recently *Williams* (p. 234 f. with literature).

[32] See *Mettinger* (1971: 140 ff.) and *Williams* (p. 238 ff.) with the literature mentioned there.

[33] See *Mettinger* (ZAW 86/1974, 403-424, p. 412 f. with literature).

[34] *Mettinger* (ZAW 86/1974, 413 ff. with references to earlier literature).

[35] *Mettinger* (op. cit. p. 415 f.; cf. p. 412 note 21).

[36] On the influence of the tabernacle theology in this connection see *Mettinger* (op. cit p. 403 ff.).

[37] *H.S.Nyberg* (ARW 35/1938, 379 f.).

l^e '*ælyôn*), an endeavour that fails completely, as seen when the shades in Sheol say to him: "You have become like us!" (v. 10). Similarly, there is perhaps also a polemical hint against the conception of the king as *imago Dei* in Ps 89,7 (note that Ps 89 is a royal poem).

3. The Davidic covenant

The expression "Davidic covenant" is a stock phrase in scholarly discussions of the royal ideology.[1] In a number of instances the dynastic promise to David in the prophecy of Nathan is in fact alluded to as a $b^e rît$: 2 S 23,5; Jer 33,21; 2 Ch 13,5; 21,7; Ps 89,4.29.35.40. The only possible instance in the Dtr Historical Work would be 1 R 8,23 but it is better to connect this case of $b^e rît$ with the Mosaic covenant (cf. v. 21) or with the patriarchal covenant and the gift of the land (cf. Dt 7,12). If $b^e rît$ had here denoted the Davidic promise, one would expect to find the same term in the other references in the DtrH to the promise to David (see below), but this is not the case. The conclusion that the DtrH does not refer to the Davidic promise as a $b^e rît$ seems justifiable.[2] In line with the use of $b^e rît$ referring to this promise is the description of the same promise[3] as an oath: Ps 89,4.36 (cf. v. 38); Ps 132,11.[4]

The justification of rendering $b^e rît$ with "Bund" or "covenant" has been questioned by Jepsen and Kutsch.[5] These scholars have seen something very essential, when they stress the connotations of "Zusage" or "Verpflichtung" in $b^e rît$. However, as I pointed out in excursus no 2, the absolute distinction made by Kutsch between "Bund", "Abkommen" on the one hand and "Verpflichtung" on the other seems questionable. Thus I shall continue here to translate $b^e rît$ in a number of texts with "covenant".[6] In my opinion, the expression "Davidic covenant" is not made obsolete as a term used in scholarly discussions by the recent contributions to the interpretation of $b^e rît$. It should be noted that in the present study the term "Davidic covenant" is used for the promise of God to David, and the term "royal covenant" for the promise of the king to the people (e.g. 2 S 5,3).

During the last few decades the Davidic covenant has been the subject of a number of studies,[7] but there is a depressing lack of consensus. A num-

---

[1] See *vonRad* (GesStud I, ²1961: 202, originally published in 1947) and the studies by Rost, Gunneweg and others mentioned below in note 7.
[2] I here agree with *Perlitt* (1969: 48, 50).
[3] In Ps 110,4 the oath refers to the priestly status and not to the dynastic promise.
[4] On the conceptual closeness between $b^e rît$ and oath see *Pedersen* (1914: 21-51) and *G.M.Tucker* (VT 15/1965, 488 ff.).
[5] See *A.Jepsen* (in: Fs W.Rudolph 1961: 161 ff.) and *E.Kutsch* (1973: 1 ff.).
[6] Cf. *M.Weinfeld* (Bibl 56/1975, 120 ff., esp. p. 124 f.).
[7] See *Rost* (ThLZ 72/1947, 129 ff.), *Sekine* (VT 9/1959, 47 ff.), *Gunneweg* (VT 10/1960,

ber of problems remain to be settled. We shall have to wrestle with above all the following ones: How is the strange absence of the term $b^e rît$ in the prophecy of Nathan itself to be explained? Is it due to mere chance, or is the use of $b^e rît$ to denote this promise a later terminological innovation? And how can the strange fact be explained that the prophecy of Nathan contains an expressly unconditional formulation of the promise (2 S 7,14-15), while other passages such as Ps 132,12 are expressly conditional?

1. The Conditioning of the Promise in the Dtr Redaction

In the first part of the present chapter I have already attempted to relate a number of texts to the prophecy of Nathan. It was found that those poetic texts that contain allusions to the dynastic promise were all later than the dynastic redaction of 2 S ch. 7 (Ps 89; Ps 132; 2 S 23,1-7). I shall now try to reach more precise conclusions, and in order to do this I shall also include the remaining prose material found in the Dtr Historical Work in the discussion. A first glance at the passages that allude to the dynastic promise reveals that a distinction can be made between those in which the promise is linked to a condition and those where this is not the case.

(1) The Conditional Series. – The original promise, found in the layer of the dynastic redaction of 2 S ch. 7, is expressly unconditional:

> When he commits iniquity, I will chasten him with the rod of men, with the stripes of the sons of men; but I will not take my steadfast love [$ḥæsæd$] from him ... . (2 S 7,14-15)

In contrast to this the passages mentioning a condition are all of a later date and represent a secondary development. As a matter of fact all these instances except one are found in redactional material which can be attributed to the Deuteronomists. The exception is Ps 132, but even this shows Dtr influence (ch. 12.1). We thus have here material that can be easily delimited and that can, within a margin of mere decades, be dated to about 600 B.C. It is therefore logical to start with this material and then, at the next stage of the investigation, bring the unconditional texts into relation with this.

Within the conditional series, one can distinguish between formulations where keeping the Law is the condition and those of another type such as in 1 R 8,24-26 where the condition reads:

> There shall never fail you a man before me to sit upon the throne of Israel, if only [$răq$ 'im] your sons take heed to their way, to walk before me as you have walked before me. (1 R 8,25)

335 ff.), *deVaux* (Mél. Tisserant 1, 1964: 119 ff.), *Gese* (ZThK 61/1964, 10 ff.), *S.Herrmann* (1965: 92 ff.), *Perlitt* (1969: 47 ff.), *W.H.Schmidt* (in: Fs vonRad 1971: 444 ff.), *Seybold* (1972), *Kutsch* (1973: 115 ff.), *F.M.Cross* (1973: 219-273) and *Veijola* (1975: 134 ff.).

This conditional formulation of the promise is found in a Dtr section and is probably of Dtr origin.[7a] The same can be said of 1 R 3,6, where we find Dtr formulations.[8] Here too the formulation is implicitly conditional[9] although its scope is restricted to the generation after David.

With the exception of Ps 132, the references to the keeping of the Law as the condition, and to which I now turn, are probably all due to the work of the nomistic redactor, DtrN.[10] Here belong 1 S 13,13-14; 1 R 2,3-4; 6,11-13; 9,4; 11,38.[11] It is strange to find that one psalm, Ps 89,31 ff., has this nomistic language (*tôrā, mišpaṭîm, ḥuqqôt, miṣwôt*), although the promise is expressly unconditional. This creates a problem which I shall try to account for presently. On the other hand Ps 132 does contain a nomistic formulation of the conditional promise:

> If your sons keep my covenant and my testimonies which I shall teach them, their sons also for ever shall sit upon your throne. (Ps 132,12)

This nomistic formulation of the dynastic promise must be correlated with the series of references in DtrN. In this connection further observations can be made. First, Ps 132 contains the formulation "for thy servant David's sake" (*bă'ăbûr dawid 'ăbdæka*, v. 10). This phrase sounds like a reverberation of the well-known *lᵉmă'ăn dawid ('ăbdî)* which occurs in just these sections from DtrN in the Dtr Work of History.[12] Secondly, the psalm also mentions "the lamp" of David (*'arăktî ner limšîḥî*, v. 17). It is true that this "lamp" also occurs in the pre-Dtr 2 S 21,17,[13] but the fact that it also occurs in three of the passages inserted by DtrN containing the expression *lᵉmă'ăn dawid*[14] should not be overlooked. Thus, Ps 132 has in common with the nomistic redaction of the Dtr Historical Work not only the nomistic conditioning of the promise but also certain formulations about David. From this it can be inferred that Ps 132 is dependent on DtrN and is of a later date than the redaction of the Dtr Historical Work. If Dietrich is correct in his dating of DtrN to shortly after the pardon of Jehoiachin[15]

[7a] For a survey of opinions on 1 R 8,14-53 see *M.Görg* (1975: 131 f. note 74).

[8] For *halăk lᵉpanêka* cf. 1 R 2,4, for *ûbiṣdaqā ûbᵉyišrăt lebab* cf. Dt 9,5 and for *wăttišmăr lô 'æt hăhæsæd* cf. Dt 7,9.12 and 1 R 8,23. See *Burney* (1970: 30), *Noth* (Könige 1968: 50 f.) and *Görg* (1975: 34).

[9] Note *kă'ăšær halăk ...lᵉpanêka*.

[10] On this nomistic redactor, DtrN, and what derives from him see above part one: introduction note 5.

[11] On 1 S 13,13-14 see *Veijola* (1975: 55 ff.), on 1 R 2,3-4 see *Veijola* (p. 25), on 1 R 6,11-13 see *W.Dietrich* (1972: 71 note 23), on 1 R 9,4-5 *Dietrich* (p. 72 note 35) and *Görg* (1975: 129 f.) and on 1 R 11,38 *Dietrich* (p. 19 f., 28 f.).

[12] See 1 R 11,12.13.32.34; 15,4; 2 R 8,19; 19,34; 20,6. Cf. *Dietrich* (1972: 19 f., 28 f.) and *Veijola* (1975: 141 note 99).

[13] For the pre-Dtr date of this, see *Veijola* (1975: 118 f.).

[14] See 1 R 11,36; 15,4; 2 R 8,19 and cf. *Veijola* (1975: 142) and *Dietrich* (1972: 19, 28 f.).

[15] See *Dietrich* (1972: 142 f.).

this would give a *post quem* for Ps 132 in the exilic period. But the arguments for this dating are weak. Dietrich bases his conclusion on 2 R 25,27-30 which he assumes to have been written by DtrN. Therefore, I shall refrain from expressing an opinion on the question of the date and make only the general observation that whether pre-exilic or not DtrN is late and Ps 132 still later.

It appears from what has been said that all formulations with a conditional form of the dynastic promise are in some way connected with Dtr redactional work. We can thus trace a development of the dynastic promise where we find at the one extreme the specifically unconditional wording of 2 S 7,14-15 and at the other the nomistic conditioning of the promise in DtrN and in Ps 132. The attempt to reconstruct a totally different development (from an originally conditional covenantal royal ideology with Ps 132 at the beginning of the time scale) is thus definitely unwarranted.[16]

(2) The Unconditional Series. – As we have already seen, the formulation in the prophecy of Nathan is expressly unconditional (2 S 7,14-15). Similarly, there is a very strong emphasis on the unconditional nature of the promise in Ps 89,29-38. As has been pointed out by Dumortier,[17] this passage is marked by a series of inclusions around the central formulation in v. 33-34 which is a reverberation of 2 S 7,14-15:

```
        ┌──────┬──────┬──────┬──────┐
 v. 29-30   31-32  │33-34│  35-36   37-38
```

There is thus a direct correlation between v. 30 ("I will establish his line for ever") and v. 37 ("his line shall endure for ever"). And v. 32 with the formulation "if they [scil. his children] violate my statutes" is taken up in v. 35 with the words "I will not violate my covenant". The whole arrangement serves the purpose of putting the central utterance in v. 34 in high relief:

(29) My steadfast love I will keep for him for ever,
    and my covenant will stand firm for him.
(30) I will establish his line for ever
    and his throne as the days of the heavens.
(31)   If his children forsake my law
    and do not walk according to my ordinances,
(32)   if they violate my statutes
    and do not keep my commandments,
(33)   then I will punish their transgression with the rod
    and their iniquity with scourges;

---

[16] I thus dissociate myself from *Cross* (1973: 232-237, 264 f.).
[17] See *J.-B.Dumortier* (VT 22/1972, 189 ff.).

(34) but I will not remove from him my steadfast love,
or be false to my faithfulness.
(35) I will not violate my covenant,
or alter the word that went forth from my lips.
(36) Once for all I have sworn by my holiness;
I will not lie to David.
(37) His line shall endure for ever,
his throne as long as the sun before me.
(38) Like the moon it shall be established for ever;
it shall stand firm while the skies endure.

I have already pointed out the strange fact that this passage (see v. 31-32) contains the nomistic language known from DtrN. However, in contrast to the conditional formulation of the promise in DtrN Ps 89 has the promise in an emphatically unconditional form. Thus, while Ps 89 seems to presuppose the formulations found in DtrN, it takes a profoundly different view regarding the validity of the promise. One can hardly escape the conclusion that Ps 89 offers a deliberate alternative to the conditional formulations known from DtrH and DtrN, and thus it becomes natural to date Ps 89 still later than DtrN and to assume a date in the exilic period. On the assumption of such a date for Ps 89, the concluding lament (v. 39-53) has a natural function and appears as an integral part of the whole.

The passage containing "The Last Words of David" (2 S 23,1-7)[18] presents a problem in this connection. Here v. 5 speaks of a $b^e rît$ $^c ôlām$, but the question is whether this is implicitly linked to a condition. The crucial utterance is found in v. 5 which reads as follows:

כי לא כן ביתי עם אל
כי ברית עולם שם לי
ערוכה בכל ושמרה
כי כל ישעי וכל חפץ
כי לא יצמיח

The main problem here is connected with the import of the first words $kî$ lo' $kēn$ $bêtî$ $^c im$ $^,ēl$. Various interpretations have been suggested. Thus, some scholars find a sense of "firmness" in $kēn$.[19] On the other hand, Nyberg and deBoer interpreted lo' $kēn$ in the sense of "nicht recht",

---

[18] On 2 S 23,1-7 see *Procksch* (BWAT 13/1913, 112ff.), *Mowinckel* (ZAW 45/1927, 30ff.), *Nyberg* (ARW 35/1938, 377ff.), *Cazelles* (Mél. A.Robert 1956: 131ff.), *deBoer* (VTS 4/1957, 47ff.), *Caquot* (VTS 9/1963, 217ff.), *A.Carlson* (1964: 254ff.), *H.N.Richardson* (JBL 90/1971, 257ff.), *D.N.Freedman* (ibid. 329f.) and *Cross* (1973:234ff.). – On the date of this text see above ch. 12.1.

[19] *A.Carlson* (1964: 256) translates: "Yes, firm indeed is my house with God, ..." Cf. *H.N.Richardson* (JBL 90/1971, 259): "Truly, my house is established by God, ..." The exact linguistic derivation of $kēn$ is not stated by these scholars.

"Unrecht" (cf. for instance Jer 23,10; Prv 15,7).[20] The latter translates: "Supposé que ma maison ne soit pas juste envers Dieu, aurait-il fait avec moi une alliance durable, ... ?" If we interpret it in this way the formulation concerning the $b^e rît \, ‘ôlam$ is implicitly conditional.

I hope to present my own interpretation of the whole passage in greater detail elsewhere.[21] Here it can suffice to say that a most important clue to understanding it has so far been overlooked: the trivial fact that the word *ken* in v. 5 is part of a structural grid system of semantic relations. On the one hand it points back to the comparative particle k^e in the first word of v. 4: $ûk^{e’}ôr$. This verse contains a positive simile that illustrates what the author wants to say about the prosperity of the royal house. On the other hand, it also points forward to $k^e qôṣ$ in v. 6, which offers a contrast consisting of a simile introduced by an adversative *waw*: $ûb^e liyyă\,‘ăl\,k^e qôṣ$. Thus, v. 5 must be understood as being part of the overall structure of the poem. My observations concerning this structure would seem to justify the following interpretation of v. 4-7:

(4) And as the sun shines forth at daybreak [$ûk^{e’}ôr\,boqær$],
 [as] a morning without clouds after dawn,
 [as] after rain grass [comes] from the earth –
(5) Is it that my house is not so with God,
 when He has granted me an everlasting covenant,
 set forth in order, in all, and secured?
 Is it that all my happiness and all [my] desire –
 is it that He will not cause it to prosper?
(6) But godless men – like thorns [$k^e qôṣ$] thrust away are they all,
 for not by hand do you take [them].
(7) But the man who touches them
 arms himself with iron and the shaft of a spear.
 And they are utterly consumed by fire < ... >

I therefore find it unnecessary to assume that the two last cola of v. 4 are "corrupt, perhaps hopelessly corrupt"[22]. On the contrary, they are quite comprehensible. The two cola form a beautiful chiasmus, and the preposition *min* in both *minnogăh* and *mimmaṭar* has a temporal sense: "after". It follows that v. 4 functions as a positive illustration of v. 5. It speaks of the intrinsic and indisputable connection between dawn and brilliant sunshine, between rain and grass. And similarly, v. 5 speaks of the connection between $b^e rît\,‘ôlam$ and the prosperity of the house of David. That *yiš‘î* and *ḥepæṣ* refer to the "house", the dynasty, mentioned at the be-

---

[20] H.S.Nyberg (ARW 35/1938, 381 f.) translates: "Fürwahr, verkehrt verhält sich mein Haus zu ’El." Cf. deBoer (VTSuppl 4/1957, 54). A.Caquot (VTSuppl 9/1963, 217) is critical but does not motivate his position.
[21] See the forthcoming Festschrift for H.Ringgren (SEÅ 41-42/1976-77).
[22] So *Cross* (1973: 235 note 73).

ginning of v. 5 is suggested by the use of *ṣamāḥ* which has close parallels in Jer 23,5; 33,15; Zach 3,8. Needless to say, the word *ken* in the phrase *kî lo' ken bêtî 'im 'el* simply means "so". It is thus impossible to find an allusion to the moral quality of the ruler as a condition for the *b^{e}rît 'ôlam* in v. 5. The formulation contains no explicit or implicit condition to the dynastic promise.

The Davidic dynasty enjoys divine protection. This aspect acquires a very pregnant expression in v. 1 of this passage, where David is denoted *m^{e}šî^{a}ḥ 'ᵃelohê yă'ᵃqob ûn^e'îm z^{e}mirôt yiśra'el*. The parallel shows that *z^{e}mirôt yiśra'el* is a designation for God. The word *z^{e}mirôt* is probably cognate with the Ugaritic *ḏmr*, which denotes a class of troops, and the Amorite *zmr* found in Amorite names with the sense "to protect".[23] The plural should be understood as a so-called intensive plural. One could compare it with, for instance, the name of the beast in Job 40,15, *b^{e}hemôt*, which has been explained as such a plural with the sense "the Beast, par excellence".[24]

The suggestion has been made that the redactor DtrN inserted 2 S 22,1-51 *and* 23,1-7 in their present place.[25] It is true that the psalm in ch. 22 shows traces of having been handled in the spirit of DtrN.[26] If, on the other hand, we look at 23,1-7 we cannot fail to notice the central importance of the term *b^{e}rît* (v. 5), a term that the nomistic redactor does not otherwise use for the Davidic promise. If he had read 23,1-7 he would probably have taken up this terminology. Moreover, if 23,1-7 had been handled by the nomistic redactor, he would probably have appended a condition to the promise, as he has done elsewhere (see above). This makes it less probable that DtrN was responsible for the *compositional arrangement* comprising 2 S 22,1–23,7. However, *the psalm* in ch. 22 shows traces of this redactor. Since the two passages 22,1-51 and 23,1-7 must reasonably have been included at the same time (note the inclusion structure of 2 S ch. 21–24 and note the associative link between *ḥæsæd.... 'ăd 'ôlam* in 22,51 and *b^{e}rît 'ôlam* in 23,5), it can be inferred that "The Last Words of David" gained its present place some time *after* DtrN, probably in the exilic period.

Ps 89 speaks of the Davidic covenant as made *sola gratia*. And my analysis of 2 S 23,5 has shown that there is no condition for the covenant in this verse. The passage Jer 33,14-26, which is probably post-exilic,[27] continues in the same tradition. One should here pay attention to the ingenious formulation of v. 20-21:

---

[23] See *UT* Glossary (no 727) and *Huffmon* (1965: 187 f.) and cf. *Cazelles* (Mél. A.Robert 1956: 131 ff. esp. 134 ff.) and *H.N.Richardson* (JBL 90/1971, 261 ff.).
[24] See *M.Pope* (Job 1965: 268).
[25] See *Veijola* (1975: 120-124).
[26] Note *Veijola's* observations (loc. cit.) on v. 1.21-25.51. Veijola's explanation that v. 21-25 derives from a Dtr hand seems convincing.
[27] See e.g. *W.Rudolph* (Jeremia ³1968: 217 ff. esp. 219).

> If you break [*'im taperû*] my covenant with the day and my covenant with the night, ... , then also [*găm*] my covenant with David my servant may be broken [*tupăr*] ... .[27a] (Jer 33,20-21)

The formulation seems to presuppose the conditional promise of the Dtr writings and at the same time it makes a deliberate re-interpretation of this. The Dtr structure of the utterance with a conditional clause has been preserved, but the contents have been re-modelled in a deep and purposeful manner. What seems at first sight to be a divine threat is in the final analysis an unconditional promise.

These observations concerning the reformulations of the dynastic promise are significant and help us to see the dynamic development of the Davidic ideology. The original formulation was specifically unconditional (2 S 7,14-15). At the second stage of development the Deuteronomists appended a condition to the promise. Admittedly, we cannot find a *post quem* for the composition of "The Last Words of David" (2 S 23,1-7), but the observations made seem to favour the conclusion that this text was formulated during the exilic period. This means that from the exilic period onwards the original unconditional formulation of the promise was reverted to as the normative form (Ps 89; 2 S 23; Jer 33).

(3) The Use of the Word b^{e}rît. – The Davidic promise has a definite role in the Dtr literature of late pre-exilic and exilic times. Although in this literature the word *b^{e}rît* is a key term in connection with the Mosaic Law it is not used here for the Davidic covenant. The use of this word for the Davidic covenant seems to be post-Dtr. It occurs in five passages. Of these, 2 Ch 13,5; 21,7 and Jer 33,21 belong to the post-exilic period. Ps 89 (v. 4.29.35.40) belongs to the exilic period. The one remaining case is 2 S 23,5 (*b^{e}rît 'ôlam*, cf. Jes 55,3). This passage cannot bear the burden of being proof of the conviction that the Davidic promise was termed *b^{e}rît* prior to the exile. It is worth noting that Isaiah does not use the word *b^{e}rît* for the Davidic promise. Nor does the Dtr Historical Work. I must conclude that the word *b^{e}rît* is not attested as a term for the Davidic covenant until the exilic period, nor was it in all probability used in this way before that period.[28]

It should be noted that *b^{e}rît* is only used, when the promise is unconditional. It is a term that stresses the validity of the promise as a legally safeguarded commitment. As for the *b^{e}rît 'ôlam* in 2 S 23,5 it should be

---

[27a] *RSV* translates "if you can break". Against the background of the other texts I find it better to see this verse as a promise disguised as a threat and then the translation offered above commends itself.

[28] On this point I agree with *Noth* (GesStud I, ²1960: 122), *S.Herrmann* (1965: 100f.), *Perlitt* (1969: 47-53) and *Kutsch* (1973: 115ff., esp. 118).

compared with the covenants with Noah and with Abraham, both of which are described in the Priestly Code as an "eternal covenant" (Gn 9,16; 17,7.19). If, as Kapelrud maintains, the similarities between P and Deutero-Isaiah should be taken to suggest an exilic date for the Priestly Code,[29] then passages from broadly the same period speak of a $b^e rît$ '$ôlam$ for Noah, Abraham and David. Here Jes 55,3 should also be noted. In this passage the people are granted an eternal covenant which is a renewal of the Davidic covenant.[29a] This stress on the eternal validity of the covenant found in different exilic texts is probably to be understood from the exilic situation.

2. The Davidic Covenant in the Pre-Exilic Period

I found that as far as terminology is concerned the exilic period was a formative era for the Davidic promise. Not until then was the promise denoted by the legal term $b^e rît$. We must then ask: what was the situation in the pre-exilic period? A contractual relationship between God and the king is expressed in the dynastic promise in the prophecy of Nathan. But is it possible to find further traces of the contractual and covenantal character of the relationship between God and king in the pre-exilic period, although the term $b^e rît$ was not used until later? Was the use of $b^e rît$ due to a reconceptualization, or was similar legal terminology already in use during the period of the monarchy?

(1) The Royal Anointing. – In my study of the royal anointing I found indications that made me infer that this rite had a contractual efficacy. Royal anointing in Israel can be interpreted against the background of the ancient Near Eastern use of oil for the ratification of contracts. At his investiture over the northern tribes David granted the people a promise ($b^e rît$), and then the people, probably acting through their elders, anointed him king over Israel (2 S 5,3). The king's promise and the anointing carried out by the people correspond as reciprocal acts of contractual import. I have tried to make it feasible that there was later a transformation in the conception of the rite so that YHWH was regarded as the one who performed it, acting through a priest. Even if we do not find a promise made to God by the king here, it is probable that the rite had the same basically covenantal meaning and that it implied that God pledged himself to the king. Thus after this transformation of the rite the royal anointing presented a characteristic expression of a contractual relation between king and God.

---

[29] See *Kapelrud* (ASTI 3/1964, 58 ff.). For the same dating of P see also *Eitz* (diss. 1969, summarized in ZAW 82/1970, 482) and *Cross* (1973: 323 f.). *A.Hurvitz* recently suggested, on the basis of the language, a still earlier, pre-exilic date for P (RB 81/1974, 24-56). The post-exilic dating is still defended by *J.G.Vink* (OTS 15/1969, 1-144).

[29a] On Jes 55,3-5 see *Eissfeldt* (FsMuilenburg 1962: 196 ff.).

(2) The Prophecy of Nathan. – The prophecy of Nathan has been understood as being a covenantal text. K.Seybold suggests that the structure of the prophecy of Nathan corresponds to the treaty formulary with a "historical prologue" (v. 8 ff.) and a stipulation in the case of violation of the covenant (v. 14b). He also maintains that the terms '*ăbdî* (v. 5.8), *ben* (v. 14) and *ḥæsæd* (v. 15) are used here against a covenantal background. And he concludes that in this light, the Davidic covenant appears to be stamped by the Sinaitic covenant.[30]

However, 2 S 7,14-15 say that even if the king errs his position will be assured. This is obviously contrary to what we know from the formal treaties.[31] Besides, the stress in 2 S ch. 7 is on the promise of God and not on the obligation of the king as would be expected if the structure were actually that of the vassal treaties. One could therefore ask with Weinfeld whether the Davidic promise is not closely associated with another type of contractual text, viz. the royal land grant, the classical form of which is found in the texts on the *kudurru* stones.[32] However, while there are similarities in formulation between the neo-Assyrian grants and the late Dtr references to the Davidic promise,[33] it is more debatable whether such similarities exist between the prophecy of Nathan itself and the land grants.[33a] Even if the royal grants provide interesting comparative material, one should probably not conclude that they provided the model for the Davidic promise in 2 S ch. 7.

Thus caution is necessary regarding the question of whether the literary form of 2 S ch. 7 is influenced by the vassal treaty or the royal grant. Nevertheless, certain terms in 2 S ch. 7 can be of interest.

One of these terms is *ḥæsæd* in v. 15. The allusion to this verse in Ps 89,34 represents an explicitly contractual interpretation of *ḥæsæd* (*wᵉḥăsdî loʾ ʾapîr meʾimmô*). The same contractual implication in *ḥæsæd* is found in other texts as well.[33b] We must therefore keep an open mind as to the possibility that *ḥæsæd* has a contractual meaning even in 2 S 7,15.

A fact that supports this interpretation of *ḥæsæd* is that the text contains other potentially contractual features. Thus, the occurrence of the word *ṭôbā* in v. 28

---

[30] See *Seybold* (1972: 35-44, 163 ff.). Cf. *Calderone* (1966).
[31] As was pointed out by *D.McCarthy* (1972: 51).
[32] See *Weinfeld* (JAOS 90/1970; 184 ff. and ibid. 92/1972, 468 f. and his article in TWAT 1/1973, esp. col. 799). It is hard to say whether Weinfeld holds that the prophecy of Nathan in itself betrays influence of the grant type of texts or whether only the later Dtr formulations of the promise do this.
[33] This was pointed out by *Weinfeld* (JAOS 90/1970, 185-189).
[33a] Another problem may be that the curses, which are a salient feature of the *kudurru* texts, are not found in 2 S ch. 7. But admittedly there are *kudurru* texts without curses, see *Steinmetzer* (1922: 254 ff., esp. 257).
[33b] See 1 S 20,8; 1 R 3,6; 8,23; Jes 55,3; Mi 7,20; Dt 7,9.12. On *ḥæsæd* in general see *Stoebe* (THAT 1/1971, 600 ff.).

should probably be compared with the use of *ṭôbā* as a contractual term, which I have already discussed in my chapter on the royal covenant with the people.[34]

The word *ṭôbā* is found in David's prayer, a section which can be attributed to the dynastic redaction of the prophecy of Nathan. Even *ḥæsæd* occurs in a passage due to the work of the same redactor (v. 15). This could be taken to suggest that the dynastic redaction emphasized the contractual aspects of the original Solomonic promise. This impression is strengthened by an observation concerning the use of *'æbæd* referring to David as the "servant" of God in this text. This term occurs a number of times in David's prayer in the form "your servant". It occurs twice in the form "my servant" in v. 5.8. While v. 8 belongs to the dynastic revision, v. 5 is part of the original Solomonic document. However, it is then interesting to note that the pleonastic formulation in v. 5 (*'æl 'ăbdî 'æl dawid*) makes one suspect that *'æl 'ăbdî* was perhaps added by the redactor.[35] In that case, God's designation of David as "my servant" would correspond to David's designation of himself as "your servant" both belonging to the dynastic redaction of the text.[36]

This is of interest since we know that in the ancient Near East various words for "servant", "slave" were used to denote the vassal in a treaty between two states.[37] The Hebrew word *'æbæd* is given the same meaning. Thus, 2 S 10,19 speaks of "all kings who were servants of Hadadezer", and in 2 R 16,7 Ahaz sends messengers to Tiglath-pileser saying "I am your servant and your son". Therefore, perhaps Ps 89,4 does not contain a semantic innovation when it states: "I have made a *covenant* with my chosen one, I have *sworn* to David my *servant*." On the contrary, I am inclined to think that in the dynastic redaction of 2 S ch. 7, the word *'æbæd* is already used to express the covenantal subordination of the king to the Lord.

The prophecy of Nathan in its pre-redactional form had its *skopos* in the utterance about the king as "son" of God (v. 14). Our observations so far make us ask: could the word *ben* also be interpreted in a similar way? As I have already pointed out, the use of "son" referring to the king was probably borrowed from Egypt where it has a role in the royal ideology. Nevertheless, from Semitic texts we are familiar with the use of "son" to denote the vassal in a political relationship. Thus, in the Amarna letters, the vassal sometimes speaks of his overlord as his "father" and of himself as the "son" of the great king.[38] It may therefore be of some interest that two of the psalms where the divine sonship of the Israelite king is alluded to contain implicit references to the kingship of the Lord (Ps 2,4; Ps 110,1). And in Ps 89, the designation of the Lord as "father" (v. 27) relates back to the designation of David as "servant" (v. 21), since these two verses correspond in the inclusional structure of the passage v. 20b-28. Besides, as we have seen, the term "servant" has covenantal connotations in v. 4. One should also note that the passage that

---

[34] Cf. also *Malamat* (The Biblical Archaeologist Reader 3/1970, 197).

[35] In which case the pleonastic formulation in v. 5 influenced the formulation of v. 8.

[36] *Veijola* (1975: 127 ff.) holds that the use of *'æbæd* as a title of honour (unlike *'ăbdᵉka* of humility) is due to a Dtr redactor. It is correct that "servant" is a favourite term for Moses, Joshua and David in the Dtr literature, but I do not dare to go as far as assuming that all the occurrences in connection with David are late. In my opinion 2 S 3,18 and the prophecy of Nathan testify to the pre-Dtr use. On 2 S 3,18 see my remarks in the chapter about the HDR (ch. 2.4.2.3).

[37] See *deVaux* (Mél. Tisserant I, 1964: 123 f.).

[38] See EA 73,1-3.35-38 (cf. line 42); 82,1-4 (cf. also 44,1-5; 96,1-4; 158,1-2.11-16.34) and see *Fensham* (FsAlbright 1971: 121 ff.).

mentions the father – son relationship is immediately followed by the central covenantal passage v. 29-38. It is therefore not an impossibility that although originally borrowed from Egypt, the designation of the king as "son" of God soon became associated with the diplomatic use of "son" to denote the legal status of a vassal under a great king.

As far as the prophecy of Nathan is concerned, my conclusion is that although the compositional structure of the text should not be deduced from the pattern of the political treaty or the royal grant, certain terms seem to stress the legal nature of the relationship between God and the king, and this feature of the text is mainly due to the dynastic redaction.

(3) The Terms ḥoq and ʿedût (Ps 2,7 and 2 R 11,12). – According to vonRad, these two terms denote the Israelite counterpart of the Egyptian royal protocol, the five-fold titulary (*nḫb.t*).[38a] K.Kitchen disagrees saying that this is only a titulary, consisting of five great names (*rn wr*), and that the Israelite *ḥoq/ʿedût* is hardly comparable to this, since the Israelite *ʿedût* seems to contain a proclamation of the divine sonship of the king.[39] A fact which has been overlooked in this connection and which makes me agree with vonRad is that the fifth part of the Egyptian titulary is generally introduced by the epithet "son of [the sun-god] Re", a name that was borne by the king even before his accession, and which denoted him as the son of the god.[40] This fits in well with Ps 2,7 where the *ḥoq* apparently contains a declaration of the divine sonship of the king. One should also note that the Egyptian fivefold name seems to lie behind Jes 9,5-6.[41]

vonRad's solution is the most attractive one for Ps 2,7. The word *ḥoq* thus probably refers to the royal "protocol", the legal effect of which is the king's adoption as "son" of God. It is important to note that it is the word *ḥoq* that was chosen for this purpose. Even if it does not express a mutual agreement or a divine demand upon the king,[42] it seems to me that the word has here a sense of divine "Ordnung", which comes close to the sense of *bᵉrît* as "legally safeguarded promise".[43] One can compare this with Ps 105,10 where *ḥoq* and *bᵉrît* appear in parallel. Thus, even if we are not concerned with the dynastic promise in Ps 2,7 but with the divine sonship of

---

[38a] See *vonRad* (GesStud ²1961: 205 ff.).
[39] See *K.Kitchen* (1966: 106 ff.).
[40] See *A.Gardiner* (Grammar ³1973: 71 ff., esp. 74).
[41] See *vonRad* (GesStud ²1961: 211 f.), *Alt* (KS II, 219), *Wildberger* (ThZ 16/1960, 314 ff.) and *R.J.Williams* (VTSuppl 28/1975, 234 f.). I am inclined to disagree with *Zimmerli* (VT 22/1972, 249 ff.), who thinks that there were originally only four names in Jes ch. 9. – It is also possible that a "great name" was known in Ugarit, see UT 1007.
[42] *G.H.Jones* (VT 15/1965, 336 ff.) is a little too eager to find an aspect of divine demand on the king in Ps 2.
[43] For a full discussion of the root *ḥ-q-q* see *Liedke* (1971: 154-186, on Ps 2,7 see p. 172 f.).

the king, we also find here contractual overtones in the expression used to express the relationship between king and God.

The *'edût*[44] at the coronation of Joash offers almost insurmountable problems to the scholar. Whereas formerly an emendation of *h'dwt* to *hṣ'dwt* (*hăṣṣe'adôt*, "armlets") was not seldom made,[45] vonRad suggests that a designation of the royal protocol of Ps 2,7 can also be seen here.[46] Other scholars such as A.R.Johnson and deVaux have suggested that *'edût* is a document embodying the basic terms of the Davidic covenant.[47] The formulation *wăyyitten 'alâw 'æt hănnezær we'æt ha'edût* must guide our interpretation of *'edût*. We are apparently concerned with something that is put on the king. This problematic item is mentioned together with the *nezær* and is called *'edût*.

While fully aware of the wide margin of uncertainty, I should nevertheless like to suggest a new hypothesis. It is a well-known fact that there is a certain connection between the royal and the priestly apparel.[48] It is therefore interesting to note that on his turban the priest had a *nezær* (Ex 29,6; 39,30; Lev 8,9). The texts also mention a golden "flower", *ṣîṣ*, with the legend *qodæš l^eYHWH* (Ex 28,36; 39,30). It should be remembered that the word *nezær*, which is usually translated "crown", "diadem", actually has the sense of "consecration". An identification of the *nezær* and the *ṣîṣ* seems to be at hand in Ps 132,18 (*we'alâw yaṣîṣ nizrô*), and a comparison of Ex 28,36 with 29,6; 39,30 and Lev 8,9 points in the same direction suggesting that *nezær* and *ṣîṣ* refer to one and the same thing, the golden plate on the forehead of the priest with the inscription *qodæš l^eYHWH*.[49] Now, there are indications that some items of the priestly dress ultimately derive

---

[44] On *'edût* in general in the Old Testament see *Mowinckel* (NTT 61/1960, 118-126) and *Volkwein* (BZ 13/1969, 18-40, on 2R 11,12 p. 27-30).

[45] Cf. 2 S 1,10 and see *Wellhausen* (Composition ³1899: 292f. note 2). For further references see *A.R.Johnson* (²1967: 23 note 4).

[46] *vonRad* (GesStud ²1961: 205 ff.). – I should also like to mention the following interpretations. *Ed.Nielsen* (1965: 31, cf. VTSuppl 7/1960, 73) took *'edût* to have originally been a decadic coronation oracle (comparable to the *ḥoq* in Ps 2,7) that was later interpreted by the Dtr as the decalogue. *Widengren* (JSS 2/1957, 6) understood it to be the tablets of law from the beginning and thus tried to substantiate his interpretation of the king as mediator of the law. For a criticism of Widengren see *Bernhardt* (1961: 250-252 with the notes). *Z.W.Falk* (VT 11/1961, 88ff.) saw it as a piece of jewellery, perhaps an amulet (cf. the Babylonian Talmud Sanh. 22a) that symbolized the covenant. *J.Maier* took it to denote the Urim and the Tummim (Kairos 11/1969, 37). *S.Yeivin* (IEJ 24/1974, 17-20) read *wh'dt ḥrs* in Jehawmelek (=KAI no 10) line 5. He derived this word and Hebrew *'edût* from the root *'-d-y* (cf. *ᵃdî*, "ornaments") and assumed that the *'edût* was a head cover, fashioned in the shape of a winged and tailed sun disc. – Those who interpret *'edût* as a document could perhaps have referred to Job 31,35-36 where a *sepær* is worn like a crown on the head.

[47] See *A.R.Johnson* (²1967: 23ff.) and *deVaux* (Mél. Tisserant I, 1964: 127f.). This is the interpretation that *Volkwein* (BZ 13/1969, 31) holds to be the most probable one.

[48] See *Widengren* (1955: 24ff.) and *Noth* (GesStud ²1960: 317f.).

[49] As was pointed out by *Noth* (Exodus 1962: 225f. and GesStud ²1960: 317 note 18).

from the royal apparel. This seems to be the case with the pectoral of the priest. Such royal pectorals are known from pre-Israelite Syro-Palestine and were probably also worn by the Israelite kings.[50] The turban, *miṣnæpæt*, is found as part of the royal dress in Ez 21,31. And the *nezær* is also well known as part of the royal insignia (2 S 1,10; 2 R 11,12; Ps 89,40; 132,18).

If my argument is correct the king, like the priest, had on his forehead a golden plate with an inscription on it, indicating his close relation to the God of Israel. This conclusion is made particularly probable by the observation that the golden "flower" of the priest ultimately corresponds to the uraeus serpent on the crowns of the Egyptian kings.[51] Thus the word *nezær* in 2 R 11,12 refers to this golden "flower". But what about the word *'edût*? There seem to be two possibilities. Either it refers to the golden plate and indicates some special aspect of it, or else it refers to the inscription. The difference is minimal.

But the question of the sense of the word *'edût* is not thereby settled, since sense and reference should be kept apart. The occurrences in the P-writings, where the word is a term for the two tablets of the ark, and the occurrences in Dt and Dtr writings, where it is one of the terms for the Law, do not seem to offer much help. In the main, there seem to be two possible senses in 2 R 11,12. The word is either used here in the sense of "testimony", "confirmation", attested in Sir 31,23; 36,20 (Strack's numbering),[51a] or else the Hebrew word should be compared with the Akkadian *adû*, generally found in the plural, *adê*, which means "oath"[52] and which is a terminus technicus for treaty and treaty stipulations.[53] To assume a connection between the Akkadian *adê* and the Hebrew *'edût* seems to be a satisfactory explanation of the use in Dt and Dtr of *'edût* referring to the Law. This observation makes the second alternative the more attractive possibility. We can therefore assume that *'edût* in 2 R 11,12 denotes that the golden "flower", or the inscription on it, was a symbol of a covenantal relationship between king and God. My analysis also explains Ps 89,40:

Thou hast renounced the *bᵉrît* with thy servant;
thou hast defiled his *nezær* in the dust.

---

[50] See *Widengren* (1955: 26 ff. with the references in note 57).
[51] See *Noth* (Exodus 1962: 226). On the Egyptian crowns see *Abubakr* (1937), on the uraeus see *RÄRG* (844 ff.). On the flower on the forehead of the Israelite priests see also *A.deBuck* (OTS 9/1951, 18 ff.).
[51a] So does *Mowinckel* (NTT 61/1960, 119 f.).
[52] See *AHw* (p. 14).
[53] For this comparison *adê*/*'edût*, see *GBL* (p. 565 col. b), *Widengren* (1955: 94 note 69) and *Wiseman* in his edition of the Vassal-Treaties of Esarhaddon (1958: 81). This was taken up by *deVaux* (Mél. Tisserant I, 1964: 127 f.) and by *Volkwein* (BZ 13/1969, 31 ff.). Cf. also Aramaic *'dy'*, attested in the Sefire texts, see *Fitzmyer* (1967: 188 references, 23 discussion).

Here, the *nezær* is the symbol of the Davidic covenant. In 2 R 11,12 the same aspect is expressed by calling the same *nezær* '*edût*.

(4) The King and the Law. – It is necessary to add to this discussion of Ps 2,7 and 2 R 11,12 some remarks on the king and the Mosaic Law. Jewish mediaeval exegesis connected 2 R 11,12 with the injunction in Dt 17,18-19 that the king should have a copy of the Law. Both Rashi and R.Levi ben Gershon understood '*edût* in 2 R 11,12 to refer to a copy of the Law and quote Dt 17,19 in support of this.[54] As appears from what I have said above, I do not think that the pre-Dtr formulation in 2 R 11,12 should be interpreted in this way, and there is no evidence that it was interpreted in this way even by the Dtr redactors.

On the other hand there is some evidence of an attempt, made in the spirit of the Dtr movement, to juxtapose the king and the Law. The injunction that the king should have a copy of the Law and "read in it all the days of his life" (Dt 17,18 f.) is never alluded to in the old pre-Dtr source material. However, there are traces of it in certain redactional insertions and arrangements. The most obvious instance is found in 1 R 2,3 where David commands Solomon to follow the Mosaic Law. On good grounds, this verse may be taken to be due to the work of the nomistic redactor DtrN, which fits in with the fact that Jos 1,7-9 (with similar formulations about Joshua and the Mosaic Law) have been ascribed to the same redactor.[54a] Further evidence is found in the traces of a redactional connection between Ps 1 and Ps 2.[55]

It is a well-known fact that there is an old tradition, attested by the Western text in Acta 13,33, by the Babylonian Talmud Berakoth 9b and by other witnesses as well, that Ps 1 and Ps 2 together constitute "the first Psalm".[56] There are, in fact, links between Ps 1 and Ps 2. Thus, the word '*ăšrê* opens Ps 1 and recurs in the last line of Ps 2, forming a kind of inclusion. The verb *hagā* forms another verbal link (1,2; 2,1). The juxtaposi-

---

[54] See *Miqra'ôt gᵉdôlôt* vol. Z on 2R 11,12. Cf. the Babylonian Talmud Sanh. 22a according to which the king fulfils Dt 17,18-19 by wearing an amulet on his arm. Cf. the rendering of the Targum of 2S 1,10: *ṭôṭepta'*. I wish to thank Dr T.Kronholm, Uppsala, for a valuable discussion on this post-Biblical material.

[54a] See *Veijola* (1975: 25) and *Smend* (Fs vonRad 1971: 494 ff.).

[55] For modern discussions on the relations between Ps 1 and Ps 2 see *Lund* (AJSL 49/1932-33, 293 ff.) who assumed an original unity, *Brownlee* (Bibl 52/1971, 321 ff.) who assumes that we are concerned with two originally independent psalms that were united at the time of the exile (p. 332 ff.) and *Bardtke* (FsBöhl 1973: 1 ff.) who assumes that the final form of Ps 1 and 2 is the result of editorial activity about 200 B.C. (p. 17). In this connection it may be noted that *Engnell* (FsPedersen 1953: 85-96, esp. 91 ff.) argues that Ps 1 is a *Fürstenspiegel*. But Engnell arrives at this result on the basis of an alleged tree-of-life motif in Ps 1. He does not comment on the old tradition of a connection between Ps 1 and 2. He is expressly critical of Lund's suggestion of a connection (Engnell p. 90 note 17).

[56] For further details see *Brownlee* (Bibl 52/1971, 321 note 2) and *Bardtke* (FsBöhl 1973: 1 ff.).

tion of *dæræk* and *'abăd* is a further example (1,6; 2,12). Brownlee is therefore probably right when he questions the view that Ps 1 was prefixed as an introduction to the entire Psalter.[57] Instead, he suggests that "Ps 1, though originally only didactic, was aptly joined to and knitted together with Ps 2 for the coronation of one of the last kings of Judah, who thereby pledged himself to fulfil the Deuteronomic law".[58]

Although the contention that this arrangement was made for liturgical purposes in connection with a particular coronation remains unproved, the observation that the redactional arrangement reflects the Dtr outlook is most helpful (cf. Dt 17,18-19; Jos 1,7-9). For my own part, I should like to put forward the suggestion that the *hoq* in Ps 2,7 (*'ªsapp^erā 'æl hoq YHWH*), which originally denoted the royal protocol (see above), has been subjected to a Dtr interpretation by means of the redactional arrangement that combined Ps 1 and Ps 2. The king's proclamation of the *hoq* (2,7) is interpreted in Ps 1,2 as meditating (*hagā*) on the Law day and night. It seems that in this way the original connection in Ps 2,7 between the *hoq* and the divine sonship has been loosened up so as to make the sonship appear more as a motivation for the king's commitment to the Law than as the consequence of the proclamation of the royal protocol.[59]

An aspect which is interesting in this connection is that there are apparent links between Ps 1,2-3 and Jos 1,8. Now, Jos 1,7-9 have been ascribed to the nomistic redaction of the Dtr Historical Work.[60] It is the same redaction that we found to have influenced Ps 132 with its nomistic formulation of the condition attached to the promise. As for the relation between Ps 1 and Jos 1,8, a simple comparison does not reveal which influenced the other. But the most probable assumption is that the injunction of Dt 17,18-19 forms the background of the formulations of the nomistic redaction of the Dtr Historical Work to which Jos 1,7-9 belong, and that both Ps 1 and Ps 132 in turn show influence from this nomistic redaction.

---

[57] *Brownlee* (p. 325).
[58] *Brownlee* (p. 332). – *Bardtke*, who suggested a date around 200 B.C. for the union of the two units, overlooked the relevance of Dt 17,18-19 and Jos 1,7-9 for the problem.
[59] Cf. Dt 14,1 where divine sonship motivates obedience and cf. the use of *huqqîm* in for instance Dt 4,40; 26,17; 27,10. On this word see further *Braulik* (Bibl 51/1970, 51ff.).
[60] See *Smend* (Fs vonRad 1971: 494ff.).

Summary

Because of the apparent links between the divine sonship and the Davidic covenant I found it appropriate to study these two conceptions together.

(1) This attempt to study these two conceptions in the context of their interplay and not in isolation led to the conclusion that there was a development in the royal ideology *from* an early interest in divine sonship (Ps 2 and 110; the Solomonic kernel in 2 S ch. 7) *to* an emphasis on the Davidic dynastic promise (references below under point 6). I was able to decide with a high degree of probability that in Ps 89 and 132 and in 2 S 23,1-7 we are concerned with lyrical echoes of the prophecy of Nathan in its dynastic version. These texts are thus all later than the first redaction of 2 S ch. 7.

(2) The Israelite conception of the divine sonship of the king was probably formulated primarily under the influence of Egyptian mythological conceptions. Nevertheless we must conclude that in Israel we are not concerned with divine kingship. On point after point we have noted how the formulations tend to stress the fact that the divine sonship of the king has a definite moment as its starting-point and that in his capacity of "son", too, the king remains a human being. We noted for instance the metaphorical formulation in 2 S 7,14 and the expression $b^ek\hat{o}r\ 'ætt^eneh\hat{u}$ in Ps 89,28 where both the noun and the verb are revealing. The verb shows that we are concerned with a status attained through a divine act of will, and the noun that the king is of this-worldly origin although as "son" he is elected and consecrated. It was also found that similar aspects were stressed through the performative utterance in Ps 2,7 ($'^an\hat{i}\ h\breve{a}yy\hat{o}m\ y^elidt\hat{i}ka$). It was also found probable that the term *nagîd* expressed an *interpretatio israelitica* of the Egyptian conception of the divine sonship of the king. We are actually concerned with a process of de-mythologization of the originally mythological conception. Finally, the conception of the divine sonship of the king was democratized to comprise the whole people.

(3) I examined the affinities between king and *Urmensch* and drew attention to the possibility that, for a short period at least the Israelite king was regarded as the image of God. As for the problematic passage Ez 28,11-19 the identification of the king in the garden of God with the cherub, as found in the Massoretic text, was preferred to the distinction found in the LXX.

(4) As "son" of God, the king belongs to the sphere in which God in a specific manner manifests his fatherly concern and exercises fatherly authority.[61] Both a privilege and an obligation are thus involved. As "son", the king enjoys divine protection and help. This feature is found in all the most important texts. As "son", the king also participates in the power of

---

[61] For a similar formulation see *deBoer* (OTS 18/1973, 205).

God and exercises delegated divine power. His sovereignty on earth is a replica of that of God in heaven (Ps 89 and 110). But divine sonship also implies filial obedience, although this obedience is not a *sine qua non* for the legitimacy of the king (2 S 7,14-15). Just as the political vassal is the "son" of the suzerain (2 R 16,7), so is the king in a position of dependency on and subordination to his heavenly Overlord.

(5) The Davidic promise was not denoted by the term $b^e r\hat{\imath} t$ until the exilic period. This raised the question of whether the contractual relationship between king and God was formulated by means of legal terminology even in the pre-exilic period. This question was answered in the affirmative, although the fact that the material is far from abundant commends caution and does not permit us to speak of more than a certain degree of probability for this conclusion. The structure of the prophecy of Nathan cannot be said to repeat that of the vassal treaties or of the royal grants known from the extra-biblical material. Nevertheless, the occurrence of certain terms such as $\underline{t}\hat{o}b\bar{a}$, $\d{h}\ae s\ae d$ and $\ `\ae b\ae d$ made me inclined to believe that the dynastic redaction stressed the covenantal aspects of the oracle of Nathan. In this connection attention was also drawn to the divine anointing of the king, to the $\d{h}oq$ in Ps 2,7 and to the $\ `ed\hat{u}t$ in 2 R 11,12. I suggested that $\ `ed\hat{u}t$ refers to the golden "flower" on the head of the Israelite king or to the inscription on this golden plate. This conclusion was reached on the basis of circumstantial evidence concerning the apparel of the High Priest. In spite of certain rabbinic interpretations to this effect, the $\ `ed\hat{u}t$ in 2 R 11,12 has nothing to do with the Mosaic Law. However, attempts in the Dtr spirit to juxtapose the king and the Law were found in 1 R 2,3-4 and in the combination of Ps 1 and 2.

(6) The period around the exile meant two new things for the development of the Davidic covenant. (a) An attempt was made to append a condition to the promise that was originally unconditional (2 S 7,14-15). That this attempt was made is borne out by a number of references in the nomistic redaction of the Dtr Historical Work (1 S 13,13-14; 1 R 2,3-4; 6,11-13; 9,4; 11,38) and by Ps 132,12 which is still later (cf. 1 R 3,6; 8,25). But probably under the influence of the national catastrophe of the exile, the original unconditional formulation and the principle of *sola gratia* were soon reverted to: Ps 89,29-38; Jer 33,20-21. Here also belongs 2 S 23,5 as my analysis of this verse showed. (b) Probably in connection with this return to the unconditional formulation of the promise the latter was denoted as $b^e r\hat{\imath} t$, a term that only occurs in connection with unconditional formulations of the Davidic promise (2 S 23,5; Ps 89,4.29.35.40; Jer 33,21; 2 Ch 13,5; 21,7). This was only a terminological innovation and does not seem to have implied any profound reconceptualization of it.

This is the yield of the present chapter. The questions involved, however,

certainly deserve to be further studied. To mention only one problem that I have not found possible to discuss here but which merits attention in future: how are we to assess the relation between the Davidic covenant and the Mosaic and patriarchal covenants? Are there points of contact and can we presume influence and interplay?[62]

---

[62] For comments on the relation with the Sinaitic covenant see the survey in *Seybold* (1972: 11 ff.) and Seybolds's own discussion. Seybold himself concludes that the importance of the Davidic covenant was "das Königtum in die Ordnung des Sinaibundes einzubeziehen" (p. 165). I am not quite convinced by this. The whole question should be taken up anew with due attention to the theories of *Perlitt* (1969) and *Kutsch* (1973). – The question of the relation with the patriarchal covenant seems also to be unsettled. See most recently *R.Clements* (1967: esp. 47 ff.) and *N.E.Wagner* (FsWinnett 1972: 117 ff. esp. 131 ff.).

Concluding Remarks

In the introduction to this work I pointed out two sets of problems that demanded special attention, viz. (1) that of the historical development of the conceptions and rites involved and (2) that of the interdependence of the civil and sacral aspects of kingship. Some general considerations follow.

(1) In the interest of historical differentiation I subjected the two historical works dealing with the early monarchy, viz. the History of David's Rise to Power and the Succession Narrative, to source-critical scrutiny with particular attention to purpose, *Tendenz* and date. The History of David's Rise, which contains important formulations referring to the king as *mašîᵃḥ* and as *nagîd*, was found to be a work from the decades after Solomon's death. The examination of the prophecy of Nathan, a passage of crucial importance, yielded some noteworthy results. We found an original document from Solomon's reign that depicted Solomon as the "son" of God. A later dynastic redaction added emphasis on the Davidic dynasty and described David as *nagîd*. The results of the study of 1 S 9,1–10,16 linked up with this. Here an original folk tale related how Saul consulted an unknown seer who promised him kingship and gave three signs as the confirmation of this promise. Saul's anointing as *nagîd*, however, is the result of later elaboration. The more studied form of the tradition of Saul and the seer dates from the period around Solomon's death.

I then studied separately the various procedures, rites and conceptions related to the civil and sacral legitimation of the king. I concluded that the popular assembly was of less importance during the second half of David's reign and during Solomon's. Thus Solomon became king without the participation of the representatives of the people.

Although owing to the nature of the evidence a number of questions cannot be answered, I am inclined to believe that the royal ideology developed along the following lines. – *Saul* was an outstanding warrior, and two old traditions (1 S 10,5 ff. and 11,1-11.15) ascribe his feats of arms to a charismatic gift. The traditions of a divine designation of Saul (*nagîd*; the lot-casting), however, are both later. Nevertheless Saul's success as a warrior was proof that Saul was approved of by the Lord. – The sources give a fairly clear picture as regards *Solomon*. The tradition of Solomon's dream at Gibeon in 1 R ch. 3 ascribes charismatic wisdom to this king. Of somewhat later date is the affirmation of Solomon's divine sonship in the old, Solomonic kernel of the prophecy of Nathan. It also seems probable that for a short period at least Solomon was described as the image of God.

– In *the post-Solomonic era* the conception of the divine sonship of the king became less important. We found reason to speak of a demythologization of this conception. The king was now described as designated *nagîd* by God. The conception of the Davidic covenant between God and the king became increasingly important and received its most characteristic formulation (as a *b*ᵉ*rît*) during the Deuteronomistic era.

The reign of *David* is a blank. The situation as regards the historical evidence for the state of affairs during this period demands close attention. The main sources are the History of David's Rise to Power and the Succession Narrative, both being historical works of a later date and designed for quite specific purposes. I maintain that the passages expressing a Davidic *Hochmessianismus* (such as 1 S 25,28-31; 2 S 5,1-2; 6,21; and the dynastic version of 2 S ch. 7) are redactional and hardly derive from genuinely Davidic tradition. The formative role of the author of the HDR is important in these passages. The royal psalms that are affiliated with the prophecy of Nathan (Ps 89; 132) are dependent on the dynastic redaction of 2 S ch. 7 and cannot be used as historical evidence for the royal ideology during the reign of David.

The conception of divine designation was first applied to Saul and Jeroboam in connection with the tensions between the North and the South that led to the dissolution of the personal union. Not until later was this conception of divine designation as *nagîd* applied to David by the author of the HDR. It is also important to note that David's anointings as king over Judah and over Israel (2 S 2,1-4; 5,3) expressed civil recognition by the people and not a sacral legitimation of David for his office. The tradition of David's anointing by Samuel (1 S 16,1-13) can be interpreted as an etiology for Solomon's investiture without the participation of the popular assembly.

It would be wrong, however, to conclude that the *Hochmessianismus* connected with David's name is the result of Deuteronomistic *"Gemeindetheologie"*. It was formulated during the Solomonic and early post-Solomonic periods. As for the actual situation during the life of David, we must confess to be at a loss. So much can be said, David's military success assured him of a position as a charismatically gifted warrior in the eyes of his people, as a man approved of by the Lord as the *Beistandsformel* (*YHWH ʿimmô*) says.

(2) A main result of this investigation is that the civil legitimation of the king was of greater significance in the cases of Saul and David than is generally recognized. Contractual categories are essential as expressions of the relation between king and people. The king's promise to the people, his *b*ᵉ*rît*, had a corollary in the acclamation by the people which was an elliptic oath, and in the anointing by the people which also implied the

people's obligation towards the king. Thus the conception of the royal covenant, the covenant between the king and the people, was of significance during the early monarchy.

Solomon became king without the recognition of the representatives of the people. It is therefore interesting to note that Solomon's reign and the early post-Solomonic era constituted a period when certain important expressions of the sacral legitimacy of the king were developed. One can here mention the conception of the divine sonship of the king, found in the Solomonic kernel of the prophecy of Nathan. We also found that certain civil categories were subjected to a process of "theologization". Thus the term *nagîd*, which originally denoted the heir designated by the reigning monarch (1 R 1,35), was allowed to function as a term for divine designation as in the well-known cases referring to Saul and David. The rite of anointing underwent a similar process. Originally the royal anointing expressed the civil legitimation of the king, as in the case of David's anointings over Judah and Israel. From Solomon onwards the rite was carried out by the priest who was subsequently considered as acting in the name of God. The anointing then expressed the sacral legitimation of the king, and the word *mašîaḥ* came into use as a term for the king in his particular relation to God. As I have pointed out there may be a genetic relation between this new conception of the rite of anointing and the Davidic covenant, since both in Israel and in the ancient Near East oil has a symbolical function as expressing a contractual relation.

Finally, some suggestions for further research should be made. The question of the origin of Israelite kingship and of its terminology should be raised anew. Here the term *mælæk* deserves particular attention. (One should also investigate the strange fact that Hebrew has *mælæk*, "king", and *śăr*, "official", while Akkadian has *šarru*, "king", and *māliku*, "counsellor".) The question of the king's position in the legal life of ancient Israel also deserves detailed investigation (cf. above, the preface). Here one should contrast Saul as *primus inter pares* in the case of Jonathan (1 S ch. 14), and Solomon and David in whom divine wisdom is internalized. In this connection I should also like to suggest that the problems related to royal wisdom should be considered anew with particular regard to the conceptions of royal wisdom found among the surrounding peoples. A thorough discussion of the Old Testament passages expressing a critical attitude to kingship is needed (cf. F.Crüsemann in ZAW 85/1973, 280). A number of studies have already been devoted to the different covenants known from the Old Testament. A study of these covenants, especially the Davidic, Patriarchal and Mosaic covenants, not as isolated units but as potentially interrelated parts of a configurational whole is still a *desiderat-*

um. Such a study, of course, must not overlook making the necessary diachronic refinements. Disintegrated or democratized royal features (cf. above, ch. 12.2.2) deserve further investigation. In this connection attention should be paid to the royal features of the Servant of the Lord and the post-exilic High Priest. An unduly neglected problem is that of Dtr material in the Psalms (cf. above, ch. 12). It seems probable that fresh points could be gained from an investigation that relates such Dtr material in the Psalms to the different Dtr redactions of the DtrH. Some most interesting results of the present investigation are connected with the symbolical meaning of oil in the ancient Near East and in Israel. Unction can serve as a legal symbol. We here touch upon a whole set of problems that can probably still yield a number of interesting results: legal symbols and symbolical procedures of legal import in the biblical world. I have repeatedly drawn attention to the role of performative utterances (note the use of the perfect in this connection and cf. General Index *sub* Performative utterances). The linguistic, legal and philosophical aspects of such utterances deserve a thorough treatment. Thus the present investigation has raised a number of new problems. It is my hope that future research will try to come to grips with these.

Excursus no 1. The Dualism of Israel

When studying the constitutional peculiarities of ancient Israel, due attention must be paid to the deep dualism between the North and the South. Alt in particular stressed this dualism during the monarchy of David and Solomon and maintained that during the reigns of these two kings North and South were united in a personal union.[1] The events at Shechem after the death of Solomon (1 R ch. 12) cannot, according to Alt, be described as a schism within the kingdom but has to be understood as the dissolution of this personal union.[2]

This dualism is clearly attested in the texts. David first became king over Judah (2 S 2,1-4a) and then over Israel (5,1-3). The "men of Israel" and the "men of Judah" are mentioned as two distinct entities in connection with David's return after the rebellion of Absalom (2 S 19,41-44) and in connection with the Davidic census (2 S 24,1.9). The rebellion of Sheba clearly stands out as an abortive attempt to dissolve the ties between North and South (2 S 20,1-2; cf. 1 R 12,16). A hint of the dualism is also preserved in the designation of Solomon as $nagîd$ $‘al$ $yiśra’el$ $w^e‘al$ $y^ehûdā$ (1 R 1,35), which may well be a reflection of an official titulary which has not come down to us due to the chances of preservation.[3] As I have tried to show elsewhere, the common assertion that Judah was not included in the Solomonic system of districts is almost certainly wrong. This means that the absence of Judah in the list of districts (1 R 4,7-19) cannot be taken as a testimony to the dualism. Nevertheless, the way in which the tribes in the Ephraimite hill country were dealt with in this district system offers evidence to the need to keep a check to the dualistic tendencies.[4] The fact that after Solomon's death his son Rehoboam had to go to Shechem to receive the acclamation of the Northern tribes (1 R ch. 12), shows that in spite of Solomon's administrative measures these tribes had managed to preserve a considerable degree of independence and national feeling.

Buccellati has tried to show that this dualism was not original but was a gradual development towards the end of David's reign,[5] a conclusion that is closely linked with his opinion that Israel, that is the Northern and the Southern tribes together, was a political unity even in the pre-monarchic period, although he admits there were two major groups of tribes, a northern and a southern one.[6] Allegiance to YHWH was certainly a feature that linked

---

[1] *Alt* (KS II, 33-65 and 116-134). Cf. the objections of *Buccellati* (1967: 146-160).
[2] *Alt* (KS II, 65).
[3] On this and other points in connection with the royal titulary as reflecting the dualism cf. *Buccellati* (1967: 156 f.).
[4] *Mettinger* (1971: 111-127).
[5] *Buccellati* (1967: 146-155, esp. 153 f.).
[6] *Buccellati* (1967: 111-125). This scholar avoids the term amphictyony (p. 114).

Judah with the other tribes at a very early date,[7] but recent discussion *pro et contra* Noth's theory of an amphictyony makes a political unity increasingly problematic.[8] There is no reason for us to enter on the general aspects of the amphictyony discussion; it is sufficient here to concentrate on Judah.

That Judah is included within the system of tribal borders set down in Jos ch. 13-19[9] does not prove that it belonged to the pre-monarchic Israel.[10] The possibility remains that the "minor" judge Ibzan (Jud 12,8-10) came from Bethlehem of Judah,[11] but the Bethlehem of Ibzan may equally well be that in Zebulun (Jos 19,15). Apart from this the theory that the office of the "minor" judges was a central office is open to doubt.[12] The notice that Samuel installed his sons in Beer-sheba (1 S 8,1-3) should warn us from seeing Judah as wholly isolated from the rest of the tribes, but at the same time it is probably because of particular links between this place and the North[13] rather than ties between Judah as a whole and these tribes.[14]

The status of Judah during the reign of Saul presents an intriguing problem. A factor that complicates the assessment of the evidence is the traditio-historical evaluation of the material, which consists mainly of the History of David's Rise to Power (above ch. 2). Grønbæk has dated this literary work to the decades after Solomon's death.[15] The main purpose of the writer was to justify the claims of the Davidic kings of Judah to supremacy over the northern tribes after the dissolution of the personal union.[16] According to Grønbæk one must therefore count with the possibility that features in this work that seem to convey the impression that Saul was king over Judah as well, are due to a projection of the picture of David's kingdom back to the days of Saul. The intention is to depict David as (a) the legitimate heir to Saul's throne and consequently (b) sovereign over

---

[7] *R.Smend* (1967: 59).
[8] The main proponents of the amphictyony theory revived by *Noth* (1930) are: *vonRad* (1951), *R.Smend* (1967 and EvTh 31/1971, 623-30), and *Buccellati* (above note 6). The most important criticism was launched by: *Eissfeldt* (KS II, 64-80; KS III, 159-67, esp. 163 ff.; and CAH, new edition fasc. 32/1965, 12-17), *Mowinckel* (ZAWBeih 77/1958, 129-50), *Orlinsky* (OrAnt 1/1962, 11-20), *S.Herrmann* (ThLZ 87/1962, 561-74; VTSuppl 17/1969, 139-158), *Fohrer* (ZAWBeih 115/1969, 84-119), *deVaux* (HThR 64/1971, 415-36), *Mayes* (VT 23/1973, 151-70) and *deGeus* (ZAW 84/1972, 383 f.). A survey of the discussion is found in *Lemche* (1972) who sides with the critics.
[9] On this see esp. *Alt* (KS I, 193-202).
[10] The argument was advanced by *R.Smend* (1967: 61), but see the criticism by *deVaux* (1971: 509).
[11] As suggested by *R.Smend* (1967: 61).
[12] See *W.Richter* (ZAW 77/1965, 40-72) and *Mayes* (VT 23/1973, 162-164).
[13] See Am 5,5; 8,14 and see *Zimmerli* (1932: 25 ff.).
[14] Actually Beer-sheba was situated within the territory of Simeon (Jos 19,2). On the evidence for a historical connection between Simeon and the north see *E.Nielsen* (1955: 259 ff.).
[15] *Grønbæk* (1971: esp. 277).
[16] *Grønbæk* (1971: 19 ff., 260 f., 274, and passim). On this *Conrad* (op. cit.) also agrees.

both North and South.[17] Another factor which Wallis has drawn attention to in this context is that a secondary (not historical) extension of the kingdom of Saul to assume pan-Israelite dimensions could be the result of (a) interpreting the "great" judges, the "saviours", as pan-Israelite leaders and (b) conceiving Saul's kingdom as a link between the "great" judges and the kingdom of David.[17a] Unfortunately, scholars who have argued in favour of Judah's belonging to the kingdom of Saul[18] have not paid due attention to such source critical questions. The indications that at first sight would seem to support the contention that Saul reigned over Judah as well are mainly the following:[19]

1. 1 S 11,8 stating that Judah sent troups to the help of Jabesh.
2. 1 S 15,1-9.12: Saul's raid on the Amalekites to the south of Judah. Judah sent troups (v. 4). The notice about Saul's *măṣṣebā* at Carmel (v. 12).
3. 1 S 17,1.52: Saul's wars against the Philistines to the west of Judah.
4. 2 S 21,2: The notice that Saul's action against the Gibeonites was dictated by his zeal "for the people of Israel and Judah".
5. 1 S 17,12 ff., stating that Isai of Judah sent sons to the war.
6. 1 S 18,16 saying that both Israel and Judah loved David.
7. 1 S chapters 23 ff., telling of David's flight from Judah to escape Saul and of Saul's freedom to move all over Judah.
8. The impression, conveyed by the material as a whole, that Saul regarded David as a rival to the throne.
9. Gibeah as the capital since it was close to the boundary between the northern and southern tribes.

Of these points I think that no 9 is dubious. That Saul made Gibeah his capital was probably owing to the fact that he owned land here (1 S 11,4 ff.). On the other hand, even if one doubts the historicity of the statements in 1 S 11,8 and 15,4 (points 1 and 2 above),[20] the historicity of all the other above-mentioned particulars cannot reasonably be questioned. It is not possible to explain all of them as the outcome of *Tendenz* on the part of the author of the History of David's Rise. Nor would it be possible to argue that the belt of unconquered territories between Judah and the Rachel tribes (Jud 1,21.29.35) wholly separated Judah from the northern tribes. These

---

[17] *Grønbæk* (1971 esp. 274).
[17a] *Wallis* (1968: 64 f.).
[18] *Danell* (1946: 74 f.), *Schunck* (1963: 124-129), *Aharoni* (1967: 254-58).
[19] A number of points are enumerated by *Schunck* (1963: 124-29).
[20] The mention of Judah in 1 S 11,8 seems to be an example of "die Ausweitung eines begrenzten Ereignisses auf gesamtisraelitische Verhältnisse" says *Stoebe* and points to the very high number (*šᵉlošim ʾælæp*) as a way of underlining pan-Israelite participation in the fight (Stoebe 1973: 227 f.; cf. p. 222). *Hauer* (JBL 86/1967, 307 note 11) judges the number as surprisingly low, since Judah accounts for only 10% of Saul's muster, and says that this testifies to "the tenuous ties between 'Israel' and 'Judah' ".

territories were gradually assimilated, a process in which the battle of Michmash may have been a decisive point.[21] The question then becomes whether any of the above-mentioned points *requires* Saul's *full* kingship over Judah for its explanation. In my opinion the answer is no. My conclusion is that there were ties of loyalty between Saul and Judah and which gradually became stronger, but that Saul was not king over Judah in the same full sense of the word as he was over Benjamin and Ephraim.[22] What we hear of Judah and Israel as two distinct political entities (although united in a personal union) during the reigns of David and Solomon were only expressions of a structural dualism that existed prior to these kings and that later manifested itself in the dissolution of the personal union after Solomon's death.

Excursus no 2. Covenant, Contract and Berit

In biblical studies, the terms "covenant" and "contract" are used almost *promiscue*.[1] In English and American jurisprudence, however, the terms are distinct. According to *Black's Law Dictionary*, the term "covenant" denotes:

> An agreement, convention, or promise of two or more parties, *by deed* in writing, signed, sealed, and delivered, by which either of the parties pledges himself to the other that something is either done or shall be done, or stipulates for the truth of certain facts.[2]

The same authority defines "contract" as:

> A promissory agreement between two or more persons that creates, modifies, or destroys a legal relation.[3]

In both cases we are concerned with agreements, but in the case of a covenant the agreement is "by deed in writing". For various reasons a distinction of this type is less fruitful in studies of ancient Israel. In a study of Old Testament material G.M.Tucker suggests using "contract" of "private legal and economic agreements, such as conveyances, deeds, or work contracts".[4] According to him contracts belong to the sphere of activity which in modern times is considered as civil law in contrast, for instance, to trea-

---

[21] See *Mayes* (VT 23/1973, 170).
[22] Cf. *Alt* (KS II, 19 f. note 3) and *Smend* (1967: 58 col. a). Whether 2 S 2,9 is only valid for the days of Ish-baal or reflects the actual extension of Saul's kingdom (so *Grønbæk* 1971: 226 ff.) is difficult to judge. I have found it wise not to build much on this verse, on which see also *Wallis* (1968: 63 f.).
[1] *G.M.Tucker* (VT 15/1965, 487) called attention to this.
[2] *H.C.Black*, (Black's Law Dictionary [4]1968: 436).
[3] Op. cit. (p. 394).
[4] *G.M.Tucker* (VT 15/1965, 487-503, quotation from p. 487).

ties that are political agreements. He then works out a difference in structure between what he calls "covenant" and "contract". The covenant is based on the oath-pattern and is often solemnized by a conditional self imprecation. It did not require the presence of witnesses or the participation of the court. With contracts, attestation, almost invariably by several witnesses, holds a central place.[5]

The differences are not always absolutely clear-cut. Thus the international treaties may be said to form a category of their own in which the oath is essential, but where we also find witnesses. But even so the above distinction is based on fundamental characteristics in the material itself. I therefore prefer this terminology to other possible alternatives. I thus speak of a covenant between God and Israel, between God and David, between David and Jonathan and between the king and the people, to mention some characteristic examples. In doing this I disregard the question of whether we are here concerned with agreements "by deed in writing" or not.

While making this distinction between covenant and contract I use the term "contractual" in the very broad sense of promissory agreements between parties. On my understanding a *contractual relation* is at hand, where one or both parties take on an obligation.[6] I hold what modern sociologists call *exchange relations* distinct from this. These are informal relations implying a certain degree of commitment and loyalty but lacking an enforceable obligation.[7] Our terminology can then be summarized as follows:

exchange relations	*contractual relations*
	a. covenant (oath)
	b. contract (witnesses)

The distinction between covenant and contract thus reflects two different types of attestation. But there is also a difference in enforcement. The oath of a covenant implies that the covenant is to be enforced by the divine court, while a contract attested by witnesses is to be enforced by the human court.[7a] If we disregard this distinction between covenant and contract and instead focus our attention on the type of relation, the following distinctions can be made:

1. *parity* relations, when the parties enjoy equal status and both accept an obligation.

---

[5] On the covenant form p. 488 ff. and on the contract form p. 497 ff.
[6] Cf. *Pedersen's* definition of $b^e rît$ (1914: 33 f.), in which he lays particular emphasis on the "Gegenseitigkeit und Verpflichtung" (p. 34). For a survey of the various interpretations of $b^e rît$, see *Kutsch* (1973: 1 ff.).
[7] On exchange relations see the work by *P.M.Blau* (1964).
[7a] This essential distinction between the two types of enforcement was pointed out to me by *Bernard S.Jackson* (in a letter of 1976-04-11, quoted by permission).

2. *vassalage*, when one of the parties is superior to the other. Within this type we can further distinguish between
   (a) the *obligatory* type, when the stronger party imposes an obligation on the other party involved.
   (b) the *promissory* type, when the superior party himself takes on an obligation.[8]

The ancient Near Eastern material,[9] so often cited for comparison in biblical studies, consists of parity treaties, vassal treaties and (land) grants. The land-grant type has found its classical expression in the inscriptions on the *kudurru* stones (boundary stones).[10] The following picture emerges:

Type of relation	*Type of text*
1. parity	parity treaty
2. vassalage	
(a) obligatory type	vassal treaty
(b) promissory type	(land) grant

The form of the Mosaic covenant, particularly the form it takes in the literary structure of the Book of Deuteronomy, has often been compared with the treaty form found in ancient Near Eastern diplomacy. Weinfeld has argued for a structural analogy between God's covenants with Abraham and with David on the one hand and on the other hand the ancient Near Eastern land grants in which the suzerain himself takes on the obligation and where the curses are directed not against the vassal but against any third party violating the rights of the vassal.[11] The structural similarity is interesting, but the question of whether this similarity is the result of influence from the land-grant type on the Israelite form cannot yet be regarded as settled. For my own part I prefer to take up an attitude of caution on this point.

Some remarks on the terminology of the sources are appropriate here.[12] In recent years Jepsen and Kutsch have propounded a new theory regarding the term $b^e r\hat{i}t$. Jepsen points out that when this word is used in connection with relations between men (or groups of men) it denotes "eine feierliche, vor Jahwe übernommene Selbstverpflichtung, eine Zusage, ein Versprechen an einen anderen". When used for relations between God and man

---

[8] This distinction between the obligatory and the promissory type is found *in nuce* in *Clements* (1967: 53 f.), although this scholar uses the term "law covenant" for the obligatory type. The observation was fully developed by *Weinfeld* (JAOS 90/1970, 184 ff.; 92/1972, 468 f.). Note also the other contributions by *Weinfeld*, his monograph (1972: 59 ff.) and his article on $b^e r\hat{i}t$ in TWAT (1/1970-73, 781 ff.).

[9] An important work on ancient Near Eastern diplomacy is the monograph by *Kestemont* (1974), which came to my notice too late to be utilized in the present investigation.

[10] See now *Weinfeld* (JAOS 90/1970, 184 ff. with literature) and cf. *Mettinger* (1971:101 ff.).

[11] See *Weinfeld* (JAOS 90/1970, 184 ff.; 92/1972, 468 f.).

[12] For a survey of the "covenant terminology" in the ancient Near East see *Weinfeld* (JAOS 93/1973, 190 ff.).

it can also denote "eine feierliche Zusage Gottes".[13] Kutsch proceeds from this point and submits a fresh investigation of all the Old Testament material. This leads him to suggest "Verpflichtung" as the basic sense of the term $b^e rît$. Important to Kutsch is that the word should not be translated as "Bund" ("covenant"). It denotes not the relation between two parties but the obligation.[14]

The observations of Jepsen and Kutsch on the basic sense of the word $b^e rît$ are convincing. The difference between the unspecified promise and the $b^e rît$ is that the latter is a solemn vow, a legally safeguarded promise; $b^e rît$ is a legal category. However, Kutsch's attempt to do away with translations such as "Bund" or "covenant" is less convincing. If $b^e rît$ does not denote the relation itself it certainly denotes the most important element in a contractual relation, viz. the obligation. The formal promise called $b^e rît$ creates a legal, contractual relation. Thus $b^e rît$ is implicitly a relational term, a circumstance that commends caution as regards the premature elimination of the traditional renderings of $b^e rît$.[15]

I thus basically agree with Jepsen and Kutsch on the semantic content of the term $b^e rît$. A related question which has also been discussed in recent literature is that of the theological use of this term to denote the relation between God and Israel. Perlitt and Kutsch argue with great emphasis that the events at Sinai were not termed "covenant" in the pre-monarchic period and that $b^e rît$ was used as a theological category mainly in the Deuteronomistic era.[16] This problem is not important to the present investigation. My personal reaction, however, is that these scholars have perhaps gone a step too far when they try to eliminate cases such as Hos 6,7 and 8,1. But no one can now question the fundamental observation that $b^e rît$ had its floruit as a theological term in the seventh and sixth centuries B.C.

Excursus no 3. The Problem of a Cultic Renewal of Kingship

Some kind of a cultic renewal of kingship has often been imagined to exist in ancient Israel. If such a renewal of kingship at one of the annual festivals could be made probable, and if the main motifs of this festival could be defined, this would probably further our understanding of the sacral aspect of Israelite kingship. Kingship has a considerable role in the cultic life of several peoples of the ancient Near East. In Egypt, the coronation was first

---

[13] *A.Jepsen* (Fs W.Rudolph 1961: 161-179, quotations from p. 178).
[14] See the essays collected in *Kutsch* (1973, esp. p. 1 ff.).
[15] Cf. *Weinfeld* (Bibl 56/1975, 120-128, esp. p. 123-125).
[16] See *Perlitt* (1969) and *Kutsch* (1973: 51-92). Cf. also *L.Wächter* (ThLZ 99/1974, 801-816). For critical remarks see *D.McCarthy* (Bibl 53/1972, 110-121) and *Weinfeld* (Bibl 56/1975, 125 ff.).

commemorated annually. Later this yearly celebration was replaced by the ḥb-śd festival.¹ Whether Canaan knew of such a renewal of kingship is, for lack of conclusive evidence, a very intriguing question, but there are some indications that so was the case.² Also in Hatti, kingship and cult are closely linked together.³ From Mesopotamia we know of the Babylonian *akītu* festival, the rites of the fifth day of which comprised a cultic humiliation of the king that meant an annual submission to and re-election by the god.⁴

In Israel as well there was apparently a close connection between kingship and cult. That the royal psalms are found in the Psalter at all would seem to suggest that these texts were used not only on the rare occasions when a new king was placed on the throne but had a more central place in the cultic life of the nation. The impact of the royal traditions on the prophetic hope of a future Saviour also indicates that these traditions were firmly embedded in the cultic life of Judah and thus points to the same thing.

(a) There is ample evidence of the close ties between the kings and the temple of Jerusalem.⁵ The king holds the ultimate responsibility for this institution.⁵ᵃ The temple can be defined as a royal national sanctuary. It was built and maintained by the kings. It was built on ground that David had acquired for that specific purpose. The very architecture is revealing. Not only was there a striking proximity of temple and palace but they were even enclosed by the same wall (1 R 7,12).⁶ The leading priests appear in the lists of royal officials in the Books of Samuel and Kings,⁷ which means

---

¹ See *H.Bonnet* (RÄRG p. 400). For details on this festival see *Bonnet* (ibid. p. 158 ff.), *Frankfort* (1948: 79 ff.) and *Fairman* (Myth, Ritual and Kingship, 1958, p. 81 ff.).

² See *J.Gray* (Ugaritica 6/1969, 300) who suggests that names such as Ethbaal and Jezebel can connect with instances in the Ugaritic texts that can be interpreted as speaking of a renewal of the power of Baal, namely UT 49 III, 20-21 (=Herdner Corpus no 6) and UT 49 IV, 39-40 (=Herdner Corpus no 6). See also *J.Coppens* (FsBöhl 1973: 87) and especially *J.C.deMoor* (1972). Note also *Kapelrud's* study published as early as 1940 (NTT 41/1940, 38 ff.).

³ See *Gurney* (Myth, Ritual, and Kingship, 1958, p. 109) on the "regular festivals" of the goddess Arinna, who "directs kingship and queenship". Note also the *nuntariyašḫaš*, a royal progress passing from town to town, when the king returned from a campaign. According to *Furlani* (RLA III, 44) there was also a feast celebrated on the completion of a six-year period of government.

⁴ For the textual evidence, see *Thureau-Dangin* (Rituels Accadiens 1921: 127-154); *ANET*³ p. 331 ff. For discussions see *S.A.Pallis* (1926), *R.Labat* (1939: 161 ff.), *Frankfort* (1948: 318 ff.) and *S.Smith* (Myth, Ritual, and Kingship, p. 22-73). Smith's attempt (p. 55) to reconstruct a series of 30-year intervals in the Assyrian eponym lists, similar to the intervals between the Egyptian sed festivals, seems questionable.

⁵ The question of king and cult is dealt with by among others *Mowinckel* (PsStud II, 111 ff., 114, 298 ff. and 1956: 80 ff.), *Widengren* (1955: ch. 1-3, to mention but one of his contributions), *Grønbæk* (DanskTT 20/1957, 1 ff.), *A.R.Johnson* (²1967: 102 ff.), *Ahlström* (1959 passim) and *Cody* (1969: 87-107).

⁵ᵃ See particularly *N.Poulssen* (1967: 11 ff.) who also gives further biblical references for what follows. Note also *H. Vorländer* (1975: 240 ff.).

⁶ On this wall see also *Mettinger* (1971: 34 note 56).

⁷ See 2 S 8,17-18; 20,25-26; 1 R 4,2. On these lists of officials see *Mettinger* (1971).

that the priests were on the royal pay roll. The king had the right to appoint and dismiss priests (1 R 2,26-27.35). In the early monarchy the priests were strongly pro-monarchic and pro-Davidic (Ebiathar[8]; Zadok[9]). That the king also had the treasury of the temple[10] at his disposal only adds to the same picture. The relations between the temple and the palace being of this nature it would certainly not be astonishing if the cultic procedures at the royal, national sanctuary took on forms that also served to propagate the interests of the Davidic dynasty.

(b) Although the king is never denoted *kohen*, he sometimes takes on cultic duties.[11] He can carry out a sacrifice[12] and pronounce the blessing.[13] If the king thus appears in the cult and plays a part in it, one must ask to what extent he represents God or the people. Some scholars cling to the idea that the king enacted the role of YHWH.[14] But a more attractive assumption is the one propounded by Mowinckel, viz. that the king had the role of David, while YHWH was represented by the ark, his words being spoken by a cultic prophet.[15] If this is correct it becomes impossible to speak of a cultic identification of the king with God.

What can be inferred from the evidence cited so far is that the links between kingship and the cultic establishment were such that an annual festival in which kingship and dynasty were celebrated appears as a natural, integral part of the picture. But is there more conclusive evidence?

(c) A number of scholars have tried to substantiate the theory of a yearly, cultic humiliation of the king similar to the rite on the fifth day of the Babylonian *akītu* festival.[16] The suffering of the Servant in Deutero-Isaiah could perhaps be interpreted as being connected with the royal aspect of this complex and enigmatic figure, but it does not necessarily imply an Israelite cultic reality.[17] Ps 89 and 18 have been cited as evidence that royal suffer-

[8] Ebiathar had strong personal ties with David after the massacre at Nob (1 S 22,20).
[9] Zadok belonged to the Solomon party in 1 R ch. 1.
[10] See 1 R 15,18; 2 R 12,19; 16,8; 18,15.
[11] On the priestly functions of the king see especially *Cody* (1969: 98-107) and *deVaux* (Ancient Israel p. 113 f.). Note also *Widengren* (1955: ch. 1-3).
[12] See 2 S 6,13.17; 23,16; 24,22-25; 1 R 3,4.15; 8,5.62 ff.; 9,25; 10,5; 2 R 16,12 ff. Traces of this are still found in Ezekiel (44,3; 45,16-17.22 ff.; 46,2 ff.; cf. Jer 30,21). It is true that some of these instances are capable of the interpretation as indirect action, i.e. a sacrifice ordered by the king but not carried out by him personally. But all of these cases should probably not be understood in this way. *Widengren* (1955: 34 ff.) has drawn attention to a passage in the Samaritan liturgy, where the king has an interesting role (The Samaritan Liturgy ed. *Cowley* vol. 2 p. 782 ff.). On this see also *Mowinckel* (1956: 72 note 2).
[13] See 2 S 6,18; 1 R 8,14.55 f.
[14] So for instance *Engnell* (1943: 174 ff.) and *Widengren* (1955: 75 f.).
[15] *Mowinckel* (1956: 82-84 and cf. 1959: 291).
[16] See *A.R.Johnson* (1935: 98 ff., and ²1967: 106 ff.), *Engnell* (1943: 176), *J.Grønbæk* (DanskTT 20/1957, 5 ff.), *Ahlström* (1959: 139-153, esp. 141 f.) and *Kaiser* (ZAW 74/1962, 195-202). *Ringgren* (1966: 235 ff.) is inclined to think along these lines. Critical is *Mowinckel* (1951: 570 ff.).
[17] See *Engnell* (SEÅ 10/1945, 31 ff.).

ing was known during the period of the monarchy.[18] This remains an interesting possibility but one cannot escape the impression that these two psalms can also, and perhaps more naturally, be connected with the occasions of a successful campaign (see Ps 18,38 ff.) or a lost battle (see Ps 89,43-45). Moreover it can be argued that Ps 89 contains Dtr features and is of exilic date (see ch. 12.1 and ch. 12.3.1.2). There are also difficulties in interpreting a group of psalms containing the motif "Through Death to Life" such as Ps 22; 69 and others, as supporting the theory of a ritual humiliation of the king,[19] since most of these psalms can hardly be regarded as royal texts. The most remarkable piece of evidence is found in Ps 101, in which the king describes his righteous ways.[20] The *qînā* metre of this psalm should not be overlooked. In *matăy* (v. 2), the psalm contains an element which indicates the *Gattung* of the psalms of lament. Both elements would fit into the context of a negative confession similar to the confession of the king in the *akītu* festival. The only difficulty with this interpretation is the observation that the *tôrā* liturgies (Ps 15; 24,3 ff.) seem to lead us to expect in such a confession the use of the perfect for an accidental relation between the grammatical subject and the action, whereas Ps 101 actually uses the imperfect.[21] It may be that in this psalm, the imperfect is used specifically to express a substantial relationship between the king and his righteousness. This being so it is extremely difficult to judge whether Ps 101 is an affirmation of the rule which the king is wont to exercise (expressed in the context of an annual renewal of kingship) *or* a vow indicating the type of rule the king proposes to exercise. The fact that the mood in promises is either the imperfect (cf. Ps 101) or cohortative[22] favours the latter alternative.

The evidence thus remains inconclusive.[23] A cultic suffering on the part of the king in a yearly renewal of kingship would perhaps not constitute a wholly inconceivable element in Israelite kingship. However, as far as I can see, we must admit that there is a lack of positive evidence for such a practice in ancient Israel.

---

[18] For instance by *Johnson* in his works cited in note 16.
[19] For such an interpretation of these psalms see *Ringgren* 1956: 54 ff. and 1966: 235 f. Ringgren expresses himself with caution well aware of the hypothetical character of the argument.
[20] For a valuable analysis of Ps 101 see *Kaiser* (ZAW 74/1962, 195 ff.) who develops points made by *A.R.Johnson* in the first edition of his Sacral Kingship (1955: 104 ff.). Note also the earlier hints by *Mowinckel* (PsSt II, 328 f. and 1951: 67, 77, 333 ff.), who nevertheless refrains from speaking of a cultic humiliation of the king (1951: 570 ff.).
[21] See *D.Michel* (1960: 236 and 118 ff.).
[22] See *Gunkel–Begrich* (Einl. Ps. 1933: 248) for occurrences.
[23] *Otzen* (1964: 193 f.) suggested the possibility that Zach 13,7 could be seen in the light of a cultic suffering of the king but wisely admits the hypothetical character of this suggestion. *Gottlieb* (VT 17/1967, 190-200) argued that 2 S 7,8 can be explained in the same way. I find Gottlieb's theory impossible (cf. above, ch. 3 with note 30).

(d) In my opinion Kraus's theory of an annual festival on Mount Zion to celebrate the royal dynasty[24] also remains within the realm of the hypothetical. On the basis of my results two points can be made here. First, as regards 2 S ch. 6–7 these two passages are linked in the HDR and form the concluding block of this historical work (above, ch. 2.4 and ch. 3). But this unity is secondary and is not found until the early post-Solomonic period, when the HDR was composed. In its original Solomonic, form the prophecy of Nathan had no links with the tradition contained in 2 S ch. 6 and laid no particular emphasis on the Davidic dynasty, a feature that is due to the dynastic redaction. Thus, the combination of 2 S ch. 6 and ch. 7 cannot be cited as evidence of a royal festival on Mount Zion during the reigns of David or Solomon. Secondly, Ps 132 is important to Kraus's argument. However, as I pointed out above (ch. 12.3.1.1) this psalm displays Dtr influence and is of late origin (even if some material in it may be older). In conclusion: whether or not there was a royal festival of Zion during the period of the "divided monarchy", the evidence cannot sustain the theory that such a festival was celebrated during the early monarchy.

In conclusion: it may well be that there was an annual festival in which kingship and dynasty were celebrated. It must be frankly admitted, however, that there is no conclusive evidence to prove this theory. Thus, in the final analysis the question must be left open.

---

[24] See *Kraus* (1951). For a criticism of Kraus see *N.Poulssen* (1967:64 ff.).
Postscript: For a somewhat different opinion on the questions discussed in this excursus see now *J.J.Eaton*, Kingship and the Psalms (1976).

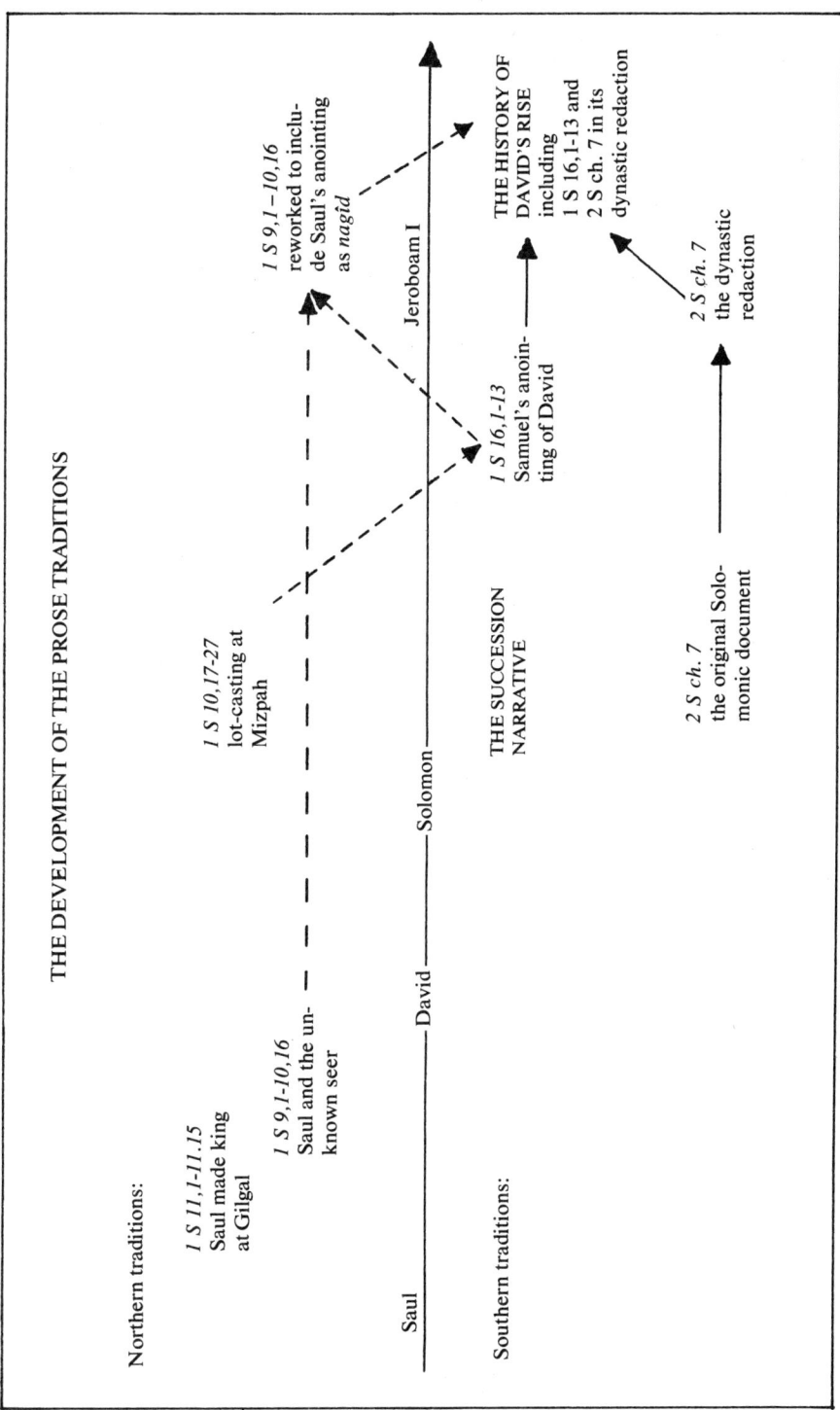

Abbreviations. Technical Remarks

I have used the abbreviations listed in the *Abkürzungsverzeichnis* of the Biblischer Kommentar Altes Testament, Neukirchen (1968). These abbreviations are essentially the same as those found in RGG³, in the Elenchus Bibliographicus Biblicus and in Eissfeldt's Introduction. In addition to these abbreviations I have also used the following:

AOAT	Alter Orient und Altes Testament
BDB	Fr.Brown – S.R.Driver – Ch.A.Briggs, A Hebrew and English lexicon of the Old Testament... based on the lexicon of W.Gesenius. (1907) corrected impr. London 1957
CT	Cuneiform Texts from the Babylonian tablets ... in the British Museum
DISO	Ch.-F.Jean – J.Hoftijzer, Dictionnaire des inscriptions sémitiques de l'ouest. Leiden 1965
Dt, Dtr	See above Part One: the introduction
EA	J.A.Knudtzon, Die El-Amarna-Tafeln (VAB 2:1-2), Leipzig 1907-1915
Fs	Festschrift
GBL	W.Gesenius – F.Buhl, Hebräisches und aramäisches Handwörterbuch über das Alte Testament. 17 Aufl. Leipzig 1921
HAL	Hebräisches und aramäisches Lexikon zum Alten Testament von L.Koehler und W.Baumgartner. 3 Aufl. neu bearbeitet von W.Baumgartner..., Leiden 1967 –
HDR	The History of David's Rise to Power (see ch. 2)
KBo	Keilschrifttexte aus Boghazköi
KUB	Keilschrifturkunden aus Boghazköi
MAL	The Middle Assyrian Laws
NEB	The New English Bible
RSV	The Revised Standard Version
vonSoden GAG	W. vonSoden, Grundriss der akkadischen Grammatik... samt Ergänzungsheft (AnOr 33+47), Roma 1969
SN	The Succession Narrative (see ch. 1)
THAT	E.Jenni (ed.), Theologisches Handwörterbuch zum Alten Testament, vol. 1, München ... 1971
TWAT	G.J.Botterweck – H.Ringgren (ed.), Theologisches Wörterbuch zum Alten Testament, vol. 1, Stuttgart 1973
UF	Ugarit Forschungen
UT	C.H.Gordon, Ugaritic Textbook (AnOr 38), Roma 1965
VAT	Museum signature Berlin: Vorderasiatische Abteilung Thontafeln Berlin

The Latin abbreviations of the names of the books of the Bible have been used. References to passages (even to LXX) follow the numbering of the Hebrew text. I have in general rendered the biblical passages according to the Revised Standard Version; deviations from this principle have been indicated in the notes.

Transliteration (and transcription): Biblical Hebrew according to the system

adopted by ZAW (with the exception that *yodh* is rendered by *y*), Ugaritic according to C.H.Gordon, Ugaritic textbook (1965) and Akkadian according to the CAD system. For technical reasons it has been necessary to use the signs ă (instead of ă̄) and ā, ū, etc. (instead of ā̄, ū̄, etc.), and ᵃᵉ for *ḥatep sᵉgôl*.

Names: Biblical names of persons and places according to the RSV, other ancient Near Eastern names generally according to ANET and Arabic place names according to J.Simons, The geographical and topographical texts of the Old Testament (1959).

Brackets have been used in the following manner:
[ ] restorations of the text or explanatory addition.
[...] damaged or unintelligible passage.
< > later glosses, etc., to be deleted from the text.
... (without brackets) to indicate that part of the quotation has been left out.

Bibliography

N.B. Standard works like lexica and grammars which are listed in the *Abkürzungsverzeichnis* of Biblischer Kommentar Altes Testament have not been included in the bibliography. Entries marked with an asterisk came to my notice after the completion of my manuscript.

A. Sources

Biblia Hebraica..., ed. R.Kittel. Textum Masoreticum curavit P.Kahle. Editionem tertiam denuo elaboratam ad finem perduxerunt A.Alt et O.Eissfeldt. Stuttgartiae 1937.
Biblia Hebraica Stuttgartensia... editio funditus renovata... ediderunt K.Elliger et W.Rudolph. Textum Masoreticum curavit H.P.Rüger. Masoram elaboravit G.E.Weil.
  Liber Genesis, praeparavit O.Eissfeldt. Stuttgart 1969.
  Exodus et Leviticus, praeparavit G.Quell. Stuttgart 1973.
  Liber Jesaiae, praeparavit D.Winton Thomas. Stuttgart 1968.
  Liber Jeremiae, praeparavit W.Rudolph, Stuttgart 1970.
  Liber XII Prophetarum praeparavit K.Elliger. Stuttgart 1970.
  Liber Psalmorum, praeparavit H.Bardtke. Stuttgart 1969.
The Samaritan Liturgy vol. 1-2. Ed. by A.E.Cowley. Oxford 1909.
Die Sprüche Jesus', des Sohnes Sirachs. Der jüngst gefundene hebräische Text mit Anmerkungen und Wörterbuch (Schriften des Institutum Judaicum in Berlin vol. 31). Ed. by H.L.Strack. Leipzig 1903.
Libri Synoptici Veteris Testamenti seu Librorum Regum et Chronicorum Loci Paralleli. Ed. P.Vannutelli. Romae 1931.
The Old Testament in Greek..., ed. by A.E.Brooke, N.McLean and H.St.J.Thackeray, vol. 1-9. Cambridge 1906-1940.
Septuaginta..., ed. A.Rahlfs, vol. 1-2. Stuttgart 1935.
Vetus Testamentum Syriace... ed. S.Lee. Londini 1823.
Translatio syra Pescitto Veteris Testamenti ex Codice Ambrosiano... ed. A.M.Ceriani. Mediolani 1876-1883.
The Bible in Aramaic... ed. by A.Sperber, vol. 2: The Former Prophets according to Targum Jonathan. Leiden 1959.
Milik, J.T., Fragment d'une source du Psautier (4 Q Ps 89). RB 73/1966, 94-106.
[The Mishnah:] *šiššā sidrê mišnā*, ed. Ch. Albeck. Jerusalem 1958-1959.
The Mishnah. Translated... by H.Danby. Oxford (1933) repr. 1958.
Monumenta Hebraica. Monumenta Talmudica... ed. K.Albrecht, S.Funk, N.Schlögl. Zweiter Band: Recht. Bearbeitet von Salomon Gandz. Wien... 1913.
Der babylonische Talmud... ed. L.Goldschmidt. Berlin 1897-1935.
The Babylonian Talmud... transl. into English... under the editorship of I.Epstein. London 1935-1952 (repr. 1961).
Miqra'ôt gᵉdôlôt 'im šᵉlošîm ûšᵉnayim pêrûšîm, vol. 1-10. New York repr. 1951.

Borger, R., Babylonisch-assyrische Lesestücke (vol. 1-3). Roma 1963.
Boyer, G., Textes juridiques (ARM vol. 8). Paris 1958.

Brunner, H., Die Geburt des Gottkönigs. Studien zur Überlieferung eines altägyptischen Mythos (Äg Abh vol. 10). Wiesbaden 1964.
Caminos, R.A., Late-Egyptian miscellanies (Brown Egyptological Studies vol. 1). London 1954.
Cardascia, G., Les lois assyriennes (Littératures anciennes du Proche-Orient). Paris 1969.
Donner, H. – W.Röllig, Kanaanäische und aramäische Inschriften, vol. 1-3. Wiesbaden 1962-1964.
Driver, G.R., Canaanite myths and legends. Edinburgh 1956.
Driver, G.R. –J.C.Miles, The Assyrian laws. Edited with translation and commentary. Oxford 1935.
– The Babylonian laws. Edited with translation and commentary. Vol. 1 2nd ed., Oxford 1956, vol. 2, Oxford 1955.
Edel, E., KUB III 63, ein Brief aus dem Heiratskorrespondenz Ramses' II. JKlF 2/1952-1953, 262-273.
Erman, A., Hymnen an das Diadem der Pharaonen (Aus den Abhandl. d. königl. preuss. Akad. d. Wiss.). Berlin 1911.
Fitzmyer, J.A., The Aramaic letter of king Adon to the Egyptian Pharaoh. Bibl 46/1965, 41-55.
– The Aramaic inscriptions of Sefire (Biblica et Orientalia vol. 19.). Rome 1967.
Gardiner, A., Late-Egyptian miscellanies (Bibl. Aegyptiaca vol. 7). Bruxelles 1937.
Goetze, A., The laws of Eshnunna. AASOR 31/1951-1952. Published New Haven 1956.
Gordon, C.H., Ugaritic Textbook (AnOr vol. 38). Roma 1965.
Gray, J., The krt text in the literature of Ras Shamra (Documenta et Monumenta, OrAnt vol. 5). Leiden 1955.
Harris, R., The archive of the Sin temple in Khafajah (Tutub). JCS 9/1955, 31-88; 91-120.
Helck, W., Urkunden der 18. Dynastie. Heft 19. Historische Inschriften Thutmosis' IV. und biographische Inschriften seiner Zeitgenossen. Berlin 1957.
Herdner, A., Corpus des tablettes en cunéiformes alphabétiques découvertes à Ras Shamra-Ugarit de 1929 à 1939 (Mission de Ras Shamra vol. 10.). Paris 1963.
Jean, Ch.-F., Lettres diverses (ARM vol. 2). Paris 1950.
Keel, O., Die Welt der altorientalischen Bildsymbolik und das Alte Testament. Zürich... 1972.
Knudtzon, J.A., Die El-Amarna-Tafeln. Anmerkungen und Register bearbeitet von O.Weber und E.Ebeling (VAB vol. 2: 1-2). Leipzig 1907-1915.
Kümmel, H.M., Ersatzrituale für den hethitischen König (Studien zu den Boğazköy-Texten vol. 3). Wiesbaden 1967.
Müller, K.Fr., Das assyrische Ritual (MVG vol. 41: 3). Leipzig 1937.
Peckham, B., The Nora inscription. Or 41/1972, 457-468.
Pritchard, J.B., Ancient Near Eastern texts relating to the Old Testament. 3rd ed. with supplement. Princeton 1969.
Rost, Liane, Die ausserhalb von Boğazköy gefundenen hethitischen Briefe. MIO 4/1956, 328-350.
Schaeffer, C.F.-A., Le palais royal d'Ugarit, vol. 4. Paris 1956.
Smith, S., The statue of Idri-mi (Occasional Publications of the British School of Archaeology in Ankara). London 1949.
Thureau-Dangin, F., Rituels accadiens. Paris 1921.
Virolleaud, Ch., Les nouveaux textes mythologiques et liturgiques de Ras Shamra

(XXIVᵉ Campagne, 1961). In: Ugaritica vol. 5 (=Mission de Ras Shamra vol. 16). Paris 1968, p. 545-606.
Weidner, E.F., Der Staatsvertrag Aššurniraris VI. von Assyrien mit Mati'ilu von Bît-Agusi. AfO 8/1932-1933, 17-34.
Wiseman, D.J., The Vassal-Treaties of Esarhaddon (Iraq 20/1958, part 1). London 1958.
Yaron, R., The laws of Eshnunna. Jerusalem 1969.

B. Literature

Abubakr, Abd el Monem Joussef, Untersuchungen über die ägyptischen Kronen. Diss. Berlin 1937. Glückstadt... 1937.
Ackroyd, P.R., The verb love-'āhēb in the David-Jonathan narratives – a footnote. VT 25/1975, 213-214.
Aharoni, Y., The land of the Bible. A Historical geography. London 1967.
Ahlström, G.W., Psalm 89. Eine Liturgie aus dem Ritual des leidenden Königs. Lund 1959.
– Der Prophet Nathan und der Tempelbau. VT 11/1961, 113-127.
– Aspects of syncretism in Israelite Religion (Horae Soederblomianae vol. 5). Lund 1963.
Albrektson, B., History and the gods. Lund 1967.
– Prophecy and politics in the Old Testament. In: H.Biezais (ed.), The myth of the state (Scripta Instituti Donneriani Aboensis vol. 6). Stockholm 1972, p. 45-56.
Albright, W.F., The Egyptian correspondence of Abimilki, prince of Tyre. JEA 23/1937, 190-203.
– Two little understood Amarna letters from the middle Jordan valley. BASOR 89/1943, 7-17.
– Some important recent discoveries: alphabetic origins and the Idrimi statue. BASOR 118/1950, 11-20.
Allen, L.C., The Greek Chronicles, vol. 1-2 (VTSuppl 25 and 27). Leiden 1974.
Alt, A., Höfisches Zeremoniell im Feldlager der Pharaonen. WO 1/1947, 2-4.
– Kleine Schriften, I-III. München 1953-1959.
Amsler, S., David, roi et messie (Cahiers théologiques, vol. 49). Neuchatel 1963.
Artzi, P., "Vox populi" in the El-Amarna tablets. RA 58/1964, 159-166.
Austin, J.L., Philosophical Papers. Oxford 1961.
Bächli, O., Zur Aufnahme von Fremden in die altisraelitische Kultgemeinde. In: H.J.Stoebe (ed.), Wort-Gebot-Glaube (Fs W.Eichrodt). Zürich 1970, p. 21-26.
Bardtke, H., Samuel und Saul. Gedanken zur Entstehung des Königtums in Israel. BiOr 25/1968, 289-302.
– Erwägungen zu Psalm 1 und Psalm 2. In: M.A.Beek et al. (ed.), Symbolae Biblicae et Mesopotamicae (Fs F.M.Th.Böhl). Leiden 1973, p. 1-18.
– Erwägungen zur Rolle Judas im Aufstand des Absalom. In: Gese H.–H.P.Rüger (ed.), Wort und Geschichte (AOAT vol. 18=Fs K.Elliger). Kevelaer... 1973, p. 1-8.
Barr, J., Hebrew lexicography. In: Studies on Semitic lexicography (=Quaderni di Semitistica 2/1973), p. 103-126.
– Etymology and the Old Testament. OTS 19/1974, 1-28.
Barth, H.–O.H.Steck, Exegese des Alten Testaments. Leitfaden der Methodik. Neukirchen... 1971.

Barth, J., Die Nominalbildung in den semitischen Sprachen. 2nd ed. Leipzig 1894.
Bartlett, J.R., The use of the word ro'š as a title in the Old Testament. VT 19/1969, 1-10.
Barucq, A., L'expression de la louange divine et de la prière dans la Bible et en Egypte (Institut Français d'archéologie orientale, Bibliothèque d'étude vol. 33). Le Caire 1962.
Becker, J., Gottesfurcht im Alten Testament (AnBibl vol. 25). Romae 1965.
Begrich, J., vide Gunkel.
– Gesammelte Studien zum Alten Testament. Herausgegeben von Walter Zimmerli (ThB vol. 21). München 1964.
Bentzen, Aa., Studier over det zadokidiske præsteskæbs historie (Festskrift udgivet af Københavns Universitet). København 1931.
– Messias. Moses redivivus. Menschensohn (AThANT vol. 17). Zürich 1948.
Berg, H., Die "Ältesten Israels" im Alten Testament. Diss. Ev. Theol. Fak. Univ. Hamburg 1959. Unpublished.
Bergman, J., Zum "Mythus vom Staat" im alten Ägypten. In: H.Biezais (ed.), The myth of the state (Scripta Instituti Donneriani Aboensis vol. 6). Stockholm 1972, p. 80-102.
Bernhardt, K.-H., Das Problem der altorientalischen Königsideologie im Alten Testament (VTSuppl 8). Leiden 1961.
Beuken, W.A.M., Mišpāṭ. The first servant song and its context. VT 22/1972, 1-30.
Beyerlin, W., Das Königscharisma bei Saul. ZAW 73/1961, 186-201.
– Gattung und Herkunft des Rahmens im Richterbuch. In: Tradition und Situation (Fs A.Weiser). Göttingen 1963, p. 1-29.
Birch, B.C., The development of the tradition on the anointing of Saul in I Sam 9: 1 – 10: 16. JBL 90/1971, 55-68.
*– The choosing of Saul at Mizpah. CBQ 37/1975, 447-457.
Black, H.C., Black's Law Dictionary. Definitions of terms and phrases of American and English jurisprudence, ancient and modern. 4th ed. St. Paul, Minnesota 1968.
Blau, J., Homonyme und angeblich homonyme Wurzeln II. VT 7/1957, 98-102.
Blau, P.M., Exchange and power in social life. New York... 1964.
Blenkinsopp, J., Theme and motif in the Succession History (2 Sam. XI 2 ff) and the Yahwist corpus. VTSuppl 15/1965, 44-57.
– Gibeon and Israel. The role of Gibeon and the Gibeonites in the political and religious history of early Israel (SOTS Monograph Series vol. 2). Cambridge 1972.
– Did Saul make Gibeon his capital? VT 24/1974, 1-7.
Boecker, H.J., Redeformen des Rechtslebens im Alten Testament (WMANT vol. 14). Neukirchen... 1964 (2nd ed. 1970).
– Die Beurteilung der Anfänge des Königtums in den deuteronomistischen Abschnitten des 1. Samuelbuches (WMANT vol. 31). Neukirchen 1969.
– Anmerkungen zur Adoption im Alten Testament. ZAW 86/1974, 86-89.
Boer, P.A.H. de, "Vive le roi!" VT 5/1955, 225-231.
– Texte et traduction des paroles attribuées à David en 2 Samuel xxiii 1-7. VTSuppl 4/1957, 47-56.
– The son of God in the Old Testament. OTS 18/1973, 188-207.
Born, A. van den, Etude sur quelques toponymes bibliques. OTS 10/1954, 197-214.
Braulik, G., Die Ausdrücke für "Gesetz" im Buch Deuteronomium Bibl 51/1970, 39-66.
Brichto, H.Ch., The problem of "curse" in the Hebrew Bible (JBL Monograph Series vol. 13). Philadelphia 1963.

Bright, J., A history of Israel. 2nd ed. London 1972.
Brownlee, W.H., Psalms 1-2 as a coronation liturgy. Bibl 52/1971, 321-336.
Brunius, T., "Wie es eigentlich gewesen". Leopold von Ranke och hans slagord. Scandia 29/1963, 392-401.
Brunner, H., Das hörende Herz. ThLZ 79/1954, 697-700.
Bruno, A., Gibeon. Leipzig... 1923.
Buber, M., Werke. Zweiter Band. Schriften zur Bibel. München... 1964.
Buccellati, G., Da Saul a David. Bibbia e Oriente 1/1959, 99-128. (Not seen. Known from Beyerlin, ZAW 73/1961, 196 f.)
– II Sam 2,5-7. Bibbia e Oriente 4/1962, 233. (Not seen. Known from Soggin, Königtum (1967), p. 65, note 12.)
– Cities and nations of ancient Syria. An essay on political institutions with special reference to the Israelite kingdoms (Studi Semitici vol. 26). Roma 1967.
Buck, A., de, La fleur au front du grand-prêtre. OTS 9/1951, 18-29.
Budde, K., Die Bücher Samuel (KHC vol. 8). Tübingen... 1902.
– Review of O.Eissfeldt, Die Komposition der Samuelisbücher (Leipzig 1931). OLZ 34/1931, 1056-1062.
Buhl, M.-L.–S.Holm-Nielsen, Shiloh. The Danish excavations at Tall Sailūn, Palestine, in 1926, 1929, 1932 and 1963 (Publications of the National Museum, Arch-Hist.Ser. I, vol. 12). Copenhagen 1969.
Burney, C.F., Notes on the Hebrew text of the Books of Kings. (1903) repr. New York 1970.
Bussche, H. van den, La texte de la prophétie de Natan sur la dynastie davidique. ETL 24/1948, 354-394.
Calderone, P.J., Dynastic oracle and suzerainty treaty (Logos vol. 1). Manila 1966.
Caquot, A., Remarques sur le psaume CX. Semitica 6/1956, 33-52.
– La prophétie de Nathan et ses échos lyriques. VTSuppl 9/1963, 213-224.
Cardascia, G., La royauté en Mésopotamie. Rec. Soc. Bodin 20/1970, 335-356.
Carlson, R.A., David, the chosen king. Stockholm 1964.
Carroll, R.P., Psalm LXXVIII: Vestiges of a tribal polemic. VT 21/1971, 133-150.
Caspari, D.W., Die Samuelbücher (KAT vol. 7). Leipzig 1926.
Cazelles, H., David's monarchy and the Gibeonite claim (II Sam XXI, 1-14). PEQ 87/1955, 165-175.
– La titulature du roi David. In: Mélanges Bibliques A. Robert. Paris 1956, p. 131-136.
– Institutions et terminologie en Deut. I 6-17. VTSuppl 15/1966 (Congress Geneva 1965), 97-112.
– De l'idéologie royale. The Journal of ancient Near Eastern society of Columbia University 5/1973 (=The Gaster Festschrift), 59-73.
– Jesajas kallelse och kungaritualet. SEÅ 39/1974, 38-58.
Clark, W.M., A legal background to the Yahwist's use of "good and evil" in Genesis 2–3. JBL 88/1969, 266-278.
– The righteousness of Noah. VT 21/1971, 261-280.
Clements, R.E., God and temple. Oxford 1965. (=1965A).
– Prophecy and covenant (Stud. in Bibl. Theol. vol. 43). London 1965. (=1965 B).
– Abraham and David. Genesis XV and its meaning for Israelite tradition (SBT second series vol. 5). London 1967.
– The deuteronomistic interpretation of the founding of the monarchy in I Sam. VIII. VT 24/1974, 398-410.
Cody, A., A history of Old Testament priesthood (AnBibl vol. 35). Rome 1969.

Conrad, J., Zum geschichtlichen Hintergrund der Darstellung von Davids Aufstieg. ThLZ 97/1972, 321-332.
Cooke, G., The Israelite king as son of God. ZAW 73/1961, 202-225.
– The sons of (the) god(s). ZAW 76/1964, 22-47.
Coppens, J., Les apports du psaume CX (Vulg. CIX) à l'idéologie royale Israélite. In: La regalità sacra. Leiden 1959, p. 333-348.
– Le messianisme royal (Lectio divina vol. 54). Paris 1968.
– L'idéologie royale ougaritique. In: M.A.Beek et al. (ed.), Symbolae Biblicae et Mesopotamicae (Fs F.M.Th.Böhl). Leiden 1973, p. 81-89.
Cothenet, E., Onction. DBSuppl 6/1960, 701-732.
Couroyer, B., Dieu ou roi? Le vocatif dans le psaume XLV (vv. 1-9). RB 78/1971, 233-241.
Craigie, P.C., Helel, Athtar and Phaethon (Jes 14 12-15). ZAW 85/1973, 223-225.
Cross, F.M., Jr., Canaanite myth and Hebrew epic. Essays in the history of the religion of Israel. Cambridge Mass. 1973.
Cross, F.M. Jr.–D.N.Freedman, Early Hebrew orthography. A study of the epigraphic evidence (American Oriental Series vol. 36). New Haven 1952.
Danell, G.A., Studies in the name Israel in the Old Testament. Uppsala 1946.
Daumas, F., Le sens de la royauté égyptienne. A propos d'un livre récent (Review article on G.Posener, De la divinité du Pharaon, 1961). RHR 160/1961, 129-148.
David, M., Die Adoption im altbabylonischen Recht (LRSt vol. 23). Leipzig 1927.
– The manumission of slaves under Zedekiah. OTS 5/1948, 63-79.
Day, E., Was the Hebrew monarchy limited? AJSL 40/1923-1924, 98-110.
Debus, J., Die Sünde Jerobeams. Studien zur Darstellung Jerobeams und der Geschichte des Nordreichs in der deuteronomistischen Geschichtsschreibung (FRLANT vol. 93). Göttingen 1967.
Delekat, L., Tendenz und Theologie der David-Salomo-Erzählung. In: F.Maass (ed.), Das Ferne und nahe Wort (ZAWBeih 105=Fs L.Rost). Berlin 1967, p. 26-36.
Deller, K., šmn bll (Hosea 12,2). Additional evidence. Bibl 46/1965, 349-352.
Demsky, A., The genealogy of Gibeon (I Chronicles 9:35-44). BASOR 202/1971, 16-23.
– Geba, Gibeah, and Gibeon – an historico-geographic riddle. BASOR 212/1973, 26-31.
Dhorme, P., Les livres de Samuel (Études bibliques). Paris 1910.
Diakonoff, I.M., Some remarks on the "reforms" of Urukagina. RA 52/1958, 1-15.
Dietrich, W., Prophetie und Geschichte. Eine redaktionsgeschichtliche Untersuchung zum deuteronomistischen Geschichtswerk (FRLANT vol. 108). Göttingen 1972.
Dijk, H.J. van, Ezekiel's prophecy on Tyre (Biblica et Orientalia vol. 20). Rome 1968.
Donner, H., Adoption oder Legitimation? Erwägungen zur Adoption im Alten Testament auf dem Hintergrund der altorientalischen Rechte. OrAnt 8/1969, 87-119.
Driver, S.R., Notes on the Hebrew text of the Books of Samuel. Oxford 1890.
Dumortier, J.-B., Un rituel d'intronisation: Le Ps. LXXXIX 2-38. VT 22/1972, 176-196.
Dus, J., Die "Ältesten" Israels. Communio Viatorum 3/1960, 232-242.
Edzard, D.O., Die bukānum-Formel der altbabylonischen Kaufverträge und ihre sumerische Entsprechung. ZA 60/1970, 8-53.
Ehrlich, A.B., Randglossen zur hebräischen Bibel. 7 vols. Leipzig 1908-1914.

Eissfeldt, O., Siloh und Jerusalem. VTSuppl 4/1957, 138-147.
- Das Lied Moses Deuteronomium 32 *1-43* und das Lehrgedicht Asaphs Psalm 78 samt einer Analyse der Umgebung des Mose-Liedes (BAL Phil.-hist. Klasse vol. 104: 5). Berlin 1958.
- Der Beutel der Lebendigen. Alttestamentliche Erzählungs- und Dichtungsmotive im Lichte neuer Nuzi-Texte (BAL Phil.-hist. Klasse vol. 105: 6). Berlin 1960.
- The promises of grace to David in Isaiah 55: 1-5. In: Anderson, B.W.–W.Harrelson (ed.), Israel's prophetic heritage (Fs J.Muilenburg). New York 1962, p. 196-207.
- Kleine Schriften. Ed. by Sellheim, R.–F.Maass, vol. 1 and 2. Tübingen 1963 and 1966.
- The Old Testament. An introduction. Transl. by P.R.Ackroyd. Oxford 1965.
Eitz, A., Studien zum Verhältnis von Priesterschrift und Deuterojesaja. Diss. Heidelberg 1969, publ. 1970. (Not seen. Known from the summary in ZAW 82/1970, 482.)
Elliger, K., Jesaja II (BKAT vol. 11). Neukirchen... 1970-.
Emerton, J.A., Review of E.Kutsch, Salbung als Rechtsakt (1963). JSS 12/1967, 122-128.
Engnell, I., Studies in divine kingship in the ancient Near East. Uppsala 1943.
- Till frågan om Ebed Jahve-sångerna och den lidande Messias hos "Deuterojesaja". SEÅ 10/1945, 31-65.
- "Planted by the streams of water." Some remarks on the problem of the interpretation of the psalms as illustrated by a detail in Ps. I. In: Studia orientalia Ioanni Pedersen. Hauniae 1953, p. 85-96.
- Die Urmenschvorstellung und das Alte Testament. SEÅ 22-23/1957-1958, 265-289.
Eppstein, V., Was Saul also among the prophets? ZAW 81/1969, 287-304.
Evans, G., Rehoboam's advisers at Shechem, and political institutions in Israel and Sumer. JNES 25/1966, 273-279.
Fairman, H.W., The kingship rituals of Egypt. In: S.H.Hooke (ed.), Myth, ritual and kingship. Oxford 1958, p. 74-104.
Falk, Z.W., Forms of testimony. VT 11/1961, 88-91.
Fensham, F.C., Ps 21 – A covenant song? ZAW 77/1965, 193-202.
- Legal aspects of the dream of Solomon. In: Fourth World Congress of Jewish Studies. Papers vol. 1. Jerusalem 1967, p. 67-70.
- The treaty between the Israelites and Tyrians. VTSuppl 17/1969, 71-87.
- Father and son as terminology for treaty and covenant. In: H.Goedicke (ed.), Near Eastern Studies in honor of W.F.Albright. Baltimore... 1971, p. 121-135.
Finet, A., Le pouvoir et les dieux en Mésopotamie. In: Le Pouvoir et le Sacré (=Ann. du Centre d'Étude des Religions vol. 1). Bruxelles 1962, p. 75-82.
Fisher, L.R.–F.B.Knutson, An enthronement ritual at Ugarit. JNES 28/1969, 157-167.
Flanagan, J.W., Court history or succession document? A study of 2 Samuel 9–20 and 1 Kings 1–2. JBL 91/1972, 172-181.
Fohrer, G., Der Vertrag zwischen König und Volk in Israel. ZAW 71/1959, 1-22.
- Altes Testament – "Amphiktyonie" und "Bund"? ThLZ 91/1966, 801-816; 893-904. Repr. in id., Studien zur alttestamentlichen Theologie und Geschichte 1949-1966 (=ZAWBeih 115). Berlin 1969, p. 84-119.
- Geschichte der israelitischen Religion. Berlin 1969.
- Einleitung in das Alte Testament. 11th ed. Heidelberg 1969.

- διός B. Altes Testament. TWNT 8/1969, 340-354.
Fox, M., ṭôb as covenant terminology. BASOR 209/1973, 41-42.
Fraine, J. de, L'aspect religieux de la royauté israélite (AnBibl vol. 3). Roma 1954.
Frankfort, H., Kingship and the gods. Chicago 1948, 4th impr. 1962.
Freedman, D.N., vide Cross Jr.
- II Samuel 23: 4. JBL 90/1971, 329-330.
Frenzel, E., Stoff- und Motivgeschichte (Grundlagen der Germanistik vol. 3). Berlin 1966.
Fretheim, T.E., Psalm 132: A form-critical study. JBL 86/1967, 289-300.
Furberg, M., Locutionary and illocutionary acts. A main theme in J.L.Austin's philosophy (Gothenburg Studies in Philosophy vol. 1). Göteborg 1963.
Furlani, G., "Fest bei den Hettitern." RLA 3/1957-1971, 43-47.
Galling, K., Die israelitische Staatsverfassung in ihrer vorderorientalischen Umwelt (AO vol. 28: 3-4). Leipzig 1929.
- Bethel und Gilgal. ZDPV 66/1943, 140-155.
- Die Bücher der Chronik, Esra, Nehemia (ATD vol. 12). Göttingen 1954.
Geckeler, H., Strukturelle Semantik und Wortfeldtheorie. München 1971.
Gehman, H.S., vide Montgomery.
Geiger, Th., Vorstudien zu einer Soziologie des Rechts (Acta Jutlandica. Aarsskrift for Aarhus universitet vol. 19: 2). Aarhus 1947.
Gelston, A., Kingship in the Book of Hosea. OTS 19/1974, 71-85.
Gemser, B., Sprüche Salomos (HAT vol. 16). 2nd ed. Tübingen 1963.
Gerleman, G., Studies in the Septuagint II. Chronicles (LUÅ N.F. Avd. 1 Band 43 nr 3). Lund 1946.
- Geist II. Geist und Geistesgaben im AT. RGG vol. 2, 3rd ed. Tübingen 1958, col. 1270-1271.
- ḥjh leben. THAT 1/1971, 549-557.
- Die Wurzel šlm. ZAW 85/1973, 1-14.
- Schuld und Sühne. Erwägungen zu 2. Sam. 12. (To be published in the forthcoming Festschrift for W.Zimmerli.)
- Der Sinnbereich "fest-los(e)" im Hebräischen. (Forthcoming in ZAW.)
Gese, H., Der Davidsbund und die Zionserwählung. ZThK 61/1964, 10-26.
- Natus ex virgine. In: H.W.Wolff (ed.), Probleme biblischer Theologie (Fs G.von Rad). München 1971, p. 73-89.
Geus, C.H.J. de, De richteren van Israel. Theol Tijdschrift 20/1965, 81-100.
Gilissen, J., Les rapports entre gouvernés et gouvernants, vus à la lumière de l'histoire comparative des institutions. Rec. Soc. Bodin 22/1969, 5-140.
- Essai d'étude comparative de la monocratie dans le passé. Rec. Soc. Bodin 20/1970, 5-135.
Gillischewski, E., Der Ausdruck ʿăm haʾaræṣ im AT. ZAW 40/1922, 137-142.
Glück, J.J., Nagid-shepherd. VT 13/1963, 144-150.
Goedicke, H., Die Stellung des Königs im Alten Reich (ÄgAbh vol. 2). Wiesbaden 1960.
Goetze, A., Kizzuwatna and the problem of Hittite geography (Yale Oriental Series vol. 22). New Haven 1940.
- Review of S.Smith, The statue of Idri-mi (London 1949). JCS 4/1950, 226-231.
Goodenough, E.R., Kingship in early Israel. JBL 48/1929, 169-205.
Gooding, D.W., The Septuagint's rival versions of Jeroboam's rise to power. VT 17/1967, 173-189.
- Jeroboam's rise to power: a rejoinder. JBL 91/1972, 529-533.

Gordis, R., Sectional rivalry in the kingdom of Judah. JQR N.S. 25/1934-1935, 237-259.
- Democratic origins in ancient Israel - the biblical ʿēdāh. In: A.Marx Jubilee Volume vol. 1. New York 1950, p. 369-388.
Görg, M., Das Zelt der Begegnung. Untersuchung zur Gestalt der sakralen Zelttraditionen Altisraels (BBB vol. 27). Bonn 1967.
- Die "Wiedergeburt" des Königs (Ps 2,7 b). Theologie und Glaube 60/1970, 413-426.
- Gott-König-Reden in Israel und Ägypten (BWANT vol. 105). Stuttgart... 1975.
Gottlieb, H., Die Tradition von David als Hirten. VT 17/1967, 190-200.
- Likklagen over Krt, II K I-II. Dansk TT 32/1969, 88-105.
Grapow, H., Wie die alten Ägypter sich anredeten, wie sie sich grüssten und wie sie miteinander sprachen (Deutsche Akad. d. Wiss. zu Berlin, Schriften der Sektion für Altertumswiss. vol. 26). 2nd ed. Berlin 1960.
Gray, J., Canaanite kingship in theory and practice. VT 2/1952, 193-220.
- I & II Kings. A commentary (OTL). London 1964 (2nd ed. 1970).
- The legacy of Canaan (VTSuppl 5). 2nd ed. Leiden 1965.
- Sacral kingship in Ugarit. In: Mission de Ras Shamra tome XVII=Ugaritica VI. Paris 1969, p. 289-302.
Greenberg, M., The Hebrew oath particle ḥay/ḥē. JBL 76/1957, 34-39.
Greengus, S., Old Babylonian marriage ceremonies and rites. JCS 20/1966, 55-72.
Gressmann, H., Der Messias (FRLANT vol. 43). Göttingen 1929.
Grether, O., Die Bezeichnung "Richter" für die charismatischen Helden der vorstaatlichen Zeit. ZAW 57/1939, 110-121.
Grollenberg, L., A propos de Prov., VIII, 6 et XVII,27. RB 59/1952, 40-43.
Grønbæk, J.H., Kongens kultiske funktion i det forexilske Israel. Dansk TT 20/1957, 1-16.
- Die Geschichte vom Aufstieg Davids (1. Sam. 15 - 2. Sam. 5). Tradition und Komposition (Acta Theologica Danica vol. 10). Copenhagen 1971.
Gross, W., Die Herausführungsformel - Zum Verhältnis von Formel und Syntax. ZAW 86/1974, 425-453.
Grzegorzewski, K., Elemente vorderorientalischen Hofstils auf kanaanäischem Boden. Diss. Köningsberg 1937.
Gunkel, H.-J.Begrich, Einleitung in die Psalmen (Göttinger Handkommentar zum Alten Testament. Erg.band zur II. Abteilung). Göttingen 1933.
Gunn, D.M., Narrative patterns and oral tradition in Judges and Samuel. VT 24/1974, 286-317.
Gunneweg, A.H.J., Sinaibund und Davidsbund. VT 10/1960, 335-341.
- Leviten und Priester (FRLANT vol. 89). Göttingen 1965.
Gurney, O.R., Hittite kingship. In: S.H.Hooke (ed.), Myth, ritual and kingship. Oxford 1958, p. 105-121.
Haag, H., Gideon-Jerubbaal-Abimelek. ZAW 79/1967, 305-314.
Habel, N.C., Ezekiel 28 and the fall of the first man. Concordia Theological Monthly 38/1967, 516-524.
Hauer, C.E.Jr., Does I Samuel 9,1-11,15 reflect the extension of Saul's dominions? JBL 86/1967, 306-310.
Hauser, A.J., The "minor judges" - a re-evaluation. JBL 94/1975, 190-200.
Hehn, J., Zum Problem des Geistes im alten Orient und im Alten Testament. ZAW 43/1925, 210-225.
Heintz, J.G., Langage prophétique et "style de cour" selon *Archives Royales de Mari X* et l'Ancien Testament. Semitica 22/1972, 6-12.

Helck, W., "Amtseinsetzung." In: Lexikon der Ägyptologie. Band I, Lief. 2., col. 227-228. Wiesbaden 1973.
Herrmann, S., Die Königsnovelle in Ägypten und Israel. Ein Beitrag zur Gattungsgeschichte in den Geschichtsbüchern des Alten Testaments. WZ Leipzig 3/1953-1954, ges.-sprachwiss. Reihe, Heft 1, p. 51-62.
- Das Werden Israels. ThLZ 87/1962, 561-574.
- Die prophetischen Heilserwartungen im Alten Testament. Ursprung und Gestaltwandel (BWANT vol. 5: 5). Stuttgart 1965.
- Autonome Entwicklungen in den Königreichen Israel und Juda. VTSuppl 17/1969, 139-158.
- Geschichte Israels in alttestamentlicher Zeit. München 1973.
Hertzberg, H.W., I & II Samuel. A. commentary (OTL). Transl. by J.S.Bowden. London 1964.
Hesse, F., $m\check{s}\d{h}$ und $ma\check{s}\hat{i}^a\d{h}$ im Alten Testament. ThW vol. 9, Lief. 8/9 1972, p. 485-550.
Hillers, D.R., A note on some treaty terminology in the Old Testament. BASOR 176/1964, 46-47.
- Delocutive verbs in biblical Hebrew. JBL 86/1967, 320-324.
Hoftijzer, J., David and the Teqoite woman. VT 20/1970, 419-444.
Holmes, Y.L., Egypt and Cyprus: Late Bronze Age trade and diplomacy. In: H.A.Hoffner Jr. (ed.), AOAT vol. 22 (=Fs C.H.Gordon). Neukirchen... 1973, p. 91-98.
Holm-Nielsen, S., vide Buhl.
Homburg, K., Ps 110 1 im Rahmen des judäischen Krönungszeremoniells. ZAW 84/1972, 243-246.
Honeyman, A.M., The evidence for regnal names among the Hebrews. JBL 67/1948, 13-25.
Horst, F., Gottes Recht. Gesammelte Studien zum Recht im Alten Testament. Ed. by H.W.Wolff (ThB vol. 12). München 1961.
- Zwei Begriffe für Eigentum (Besitz): $n\ddot{a}\d{h}^a l\ddot{a}$ und $^a\d{h}uzz\bar{a}$. In: A.Kuschke (ed.), Verbannung und Heimkehr (Fs W.Rudolph). Tübingen 1961, p. 135-156.
Huffmon, H.B., Amorite personal names in the Mari texts: a structural and lexical study. Baltimore 1965.
Hultkrantz, Å., Metodvägar inom den jämförande religionsforskningen. Stockholm 1973.
Humbert, P., La "terou'a". Analyse d'un rite biblique (Université de Neuchatel. Recueil de travaux publié par la faculté des lettres vol. 23). Neuchatel 1946.
Hurwitz, A., The evidence of language in dating the Priestly Code. RB 81/1974, 24-56.
Hylander, I., Der literarische Samuel-Saul-Komplex (1 Sam 1–15) traditionsgeschichtlich untersucht. Uppsala... 1932.
Ihromi, Die Königinmutter und der 'amm ha'arez im Reich Juda. VT 24/1974, 421-429.
Ishida, T., The leaders of the tribal leagues "Israel" in the premonarchic period. RB 80/1973, 514-530.
Jacobsen, Th., The investiture and anointing of Adapa in heaven. AJSL 46/1930, 201-203.
Jacobsohn, H., Die dogmatische Stellung des Königs in der Theologie der alten Ägypter (ÄF vol. 7). Glückstadt... 1939.
Jastrow, M., A Dictionary of the Targumim, the Talmud Babli and Yerushalmi, and the Midrashic Literature, 1-2. New York... 1926.

Jepsen, A., Nabi. Soziologische Studien zur alttestamentlichen Literatur und Religionsgeschichte. München 1934.
- Die Quellen des Königsbuches. Halle (Saale) 1953.
- Berith. Ein Beitrag zur Theologie der Exilszeit. In: A.Kuschke (ed.), Verbannung und Heimkehr (Fs W.Rudolph). Tübingen 1961, p. 161-179.
- Warum? Eine lexikalische und theologische Studie. In: F.Maass (ed.), Das ferne und nahe Wort (ZAWBeih 105=Fs L.Rost). Berlin 1967, p. 106-113.
Jeremias, J., mišpaṭ im ersten Gottesknechtslied (Jes XLII 1-4). VT 22/1972, 31-42.
Johnson, A.R., The role of the king in the Jerusalem cultus. In: S.H.Hooke (ed.), The labyrinth. London 1935, p. 73-111.
- Sacral kingship in ancient Israel. Cardiff 1955 (2nd ed. 1967).
Johnson, B., Urim und Tummim als Alphabet. ASTI 9/1973 (publ. 1974), 23-29.
Jones, G.H., "The decree of Yahweh (Ps. II 7)." VT 15/1965, 336-344.
Joüon, P., Notes lexicographiques hébraïques. MUB vol. 10:1. Beyrouth 1925, p. 39f.
- Notes de lexicographie hébraïque. Bibl 17/1936, 229-233.
Kaiser, O., Erwägungen zu Psalm 101. ZAW 74/1962, 195-205.
Kapelrud, A.S., Jahves tronstigningsfest og funnene i Ras Sjamra. NTT 41/1940, 38-58.
- King David and the sons of Saul. In: La regalità sacra. Leiden 1959, p. 294-301.
- The date of the Priestly Code (P). ASTI 3/1964, 58-64.
Kayser, W., Das sprachliche Kunstwerk. 14th ed. Bern 1969.
Kessler, M., The law of manumission in Jer 34. BZ 15/1971, 105-108.
Kestemont, G., vide Sauren.
- Diplomatique et droit international en Asie occidentale (1600-1200 av. J.C.) (Publication de l'Institut Orientaliste de Louvain vol. 9). Louvain... 1974.
Kitchen, K., Ancient Orient and Old Testament. London 1966.
Kittel, R., Cyrus und Deuterojesaja. ZAW 18/1898, 149-162.
Klauser, Th., Akklamation. RAC 1/1950, 216-233.
Klengel, H., Zu den šībūtum in altbabylonischer Zeit. Or 29/1960, 357-375.
- Die Rolle der "Ältesten" (LU^{meš} ŠU. GI) in Kleinasien der Hethiterzeit. ZA 23/1965, 223-236.
Knierim, R., Exodus 18 und die Neuordnung der mosaischen Gerichtsbarkeit. ZAW 73/1961, 146-171.
- Die Messianologie des ersten Buches Samuel. EvTh 30/1970, 113-133.
- m'l treulos sein. THAT 1/1971, 920-922.
Knight, D.A., Rediscovering the traditions of Israel. The development of the traditio-historical research of the Old Testament, with special consideration of Scandinavian contributions (Society of Biblical Literature, Diss. Series vol. 9). Missoula 1973.
Knutson, F.B., vide Fisher.
Koch, R., Geist und Messias. Wien 1950.
Köhler, L., Die hebräische Rechtsgemeinde (Festrede des Rektorats... Zürich 1931). In: Der hebräische Mensch. Tübingen 1953, p. 143-171.
Kraus, F.R., Briefschreibübungen im altbabylonischen Schulunterricht. JEOL VI: 16/1959-1962. Leiden 1964, p. 16-39.
- Ein mittelbabylonischer Rechtsterminus. In: J.A.Ankum et al. (ed.), Symbolae ivridicae et historicae (Fs M.David) vol. 2. Leiden 1968, p. 9-40.
Kraus, H.-J., Die Königsherrschaft Gottes im Alten Testament (BHTh vol. 13). Tübingen 1951.
- Psalmen (BKAT vol. 15: 1-2). 2nd ed. Neukirchen... 1961.

Kroeber, A.L., The nature of culture. Chicago 1952.
Kuhl, C., Neue Dokumente zum Verständnis von Hosea 2,4-15. ZAW 52/1934, 102-109.
Kutsch, E., Gideons Berufung und Altarbau Jdc 6,11-24. ThLZ 81/1956, 75-83.
– Die Dynastie von Gottes Gnaden. Probleme der Nathanweissagung in 2. Sam 7. ZThK 58/1961, 137-153.
– Salbung als Rechtsakt im Alten Testament und im alten Orient (ZAWBeih 87). Berlin 1963.
– Verheissung und Gesetz. Untersuchungen zum sogenannten "Bund" im Alten Testament (ZAWBeih 131). Berlin... 1973.
Labat, R., Le caractère religieux de la royauté assyro-babylonienne (Études d'Assyriologie vol. 2). Paris 1939.
Landsberger, B., Jungfräulichkeit: ein Beitrag zum Thema "Beilager und Eheschliessung" (mit einem Anhang: Neue Lesungen und Deutungen im Gesetzbuch von Ešnunna). In: J.A.Ankum et al. (ed.), Symbolae ivridicae et historicae (Fs M.David) vol. 2. Leiden 1968, p. 41-105.
Langlamet, F., Les récits de l'institution de la royauté (I Sam., VII–XII). RB 77/1970, 161-200.
– Review of W.Dietrich, Prophetie und Geschichte (1972). RB 81/1974, 601-606.
Lehmann, M.R., Biblical oaths. ZAW 81/1969, 74-92.
Lemche, N.P., Israel i dommertiden. En oversigt over diskussionen om Martin Noths "Das System der zwölf Stämme Israels" (Text og tolkning vol. 4). København 1972.
– Davids vej til tronen. DanskTT 38/1975, 241-263.
– The manumission of slaves – the fallow year – the sabbatical year – the jobel year. VT 26/1976, 38-59.
Lewy, J., The biblical institution of $d^e rôr$ in the light of Akkadian documents. EI 5/1958, 21*-31*.
Liedke, G., Gestalt und Bezeichnung alttestamentlicher Rechtssätze. Eine formgeschichtlich-terminologische Studie (WMANT vol. 39). Neukirchen... 1971.
Lindars, B., Jotham's fable – a new form-critical analysis. JThS 24/1973, 355-366.
Lindblom, J., Lot-casting in the Old Testament. VT 12/1962, 164-178.
– Prophecy in ancient Israel. Oxford (1962) repr. 1967.
– Saul inter prophetas. ASTI 9/1973 (publ. 1974), 30-41.
Linder, S., Studier till Gamla Testamentets föreställningar om anden (Arbeten utgivna med stöd av Vilhelm Ekmans universitetsfond vol. 32). Uppsala... 1926.
Lindhagen, C., The servant motif in the Old Testament. Uppsala 1950.
Lipinski, E., La royauté de Yahwé dans la poésie et le culte de l'ancien Israël (Verhandelingen v. d. koninklijke Vlaamse acad. voor Wetenschappen... van België. Klasse der Letteren Jaarg. 27: 55). Brussel 1965.
– Le poème royal du Psaume LXXXIX 1-5.20-38 (Cahiers de la Revue Biblique vol. 6). Paris 1967.
– Le récit de 1 Rois XII 1-19 à la lumière de l'ancien usage de l'hébreu et de nouveaux textes de Mari. VT 24/1974, 430-437.
Liverani, M., La royauté syrienne de l'âge du bronze récent. In: P.Garelli (ed.), Le palais et la royauté (XIXe Rencontre Assyriologique Internationale 1971). Paris 1974, p. 329-356.
Lohfink, N., Beobachtungen zur Geschichte des Ausdrucks ʿam $YHWH$. In: H.W.Wolff (ed.), Probleme biblischer Theologie (Fs G.vonRad). München 1971, p. 275-305.
Loretz, O., Psalmenstudien. UF 3/1971, 101-115.

Lund, N.W., Chiasmus in the Psalms. AJSL 49/1932-1933, 281-312.
Lyons, J., Introduction to theoretical linguistics. Cambridge (1968) repr. 1971.
Lys, D., De l'onction à l'intronisation royale. Études théologiques et réligieuses 29/1954 no 3,1-54.
- Rûach. Le souffle dans l'Ancien Testament (Études d'histoire et de philosophie religieuses vol. 56). Paris 1962.
McCarthy, D.J., Treaty and covenant. A study in form in the ancient oriental documents and in the Old Testament (AnBibl vol. 21). Rome 1963.
- Hosea XII 2: Covenant by oil. VT 14/1964, 215-221.
- II Samuel 7 and the structure of the Deuteronomic History. JBL 84/1965, 131-138.
- Old Testament covenant. A survey of current opinions. London 1972.
- Review of L.Perlitt, Bundestheologie im Alten Testament (1969). Bibl 53/1972, 110-121.
McCree, W.T., The covenant meal in the Old Testament. JBL 45/1926, 120-128.
Macholz, G.Ch., Die Stellung des Königs in der israelitischen Gerichtsverfassung. ZAW 84/1972, 157-182.
- Zur Geschichte der Justizorganisation in Juda. ZAW 84/1972, 314-340.
*- Nagid - der Statthalter, "praefectus". In: K.Rupprecht (ed.), Sefer Rendtorff (Fs R.Rendtorff), Dielheimer Blätter zum Alten Testament, Beih 1. Dielheim 1975, p. 59-72.
McKane, W., The gibbôr ḥayil in the Israelite community. Glasgow university oriental soc. Transactions 17/1959, 28-37.
- Proverbs. A new approach. Philadelphia 1970.
McKay, J.W., Helel and the Dawn-goddess. VT 20/1970, 451-464.
McKenzie, J.L., The elders in the Old Testament. Bibl 40/1959, 522-540.
- The "people of the land" in the Old Testament. In: Akten des 24. Internationalen Orientalisten-Kongresses München 1957. Wiesbaden 1959, p. 206-208.
Maier, J., Urim und Tummim. Recht und Bund in der Spannung zwischen Königtum und Priestertum im alten Israel. Kairos 11/1969, 22-38.
Malamat, A., Organs of statecraft in the Israelite monarchy. BA 28/1965, 34-65. Repr. in: Campbell, E.F.Jr.-D.N.Freedman (ed.), The Biblical Archaeologist Reader, vol. 3. New York 1970, p. 163-198.
Maly, E.H., The Jotham fable - anti-monarchial? CBQ 22/1960, 299-305.
Mauchline, J., Implicit signs of a persistent belief in the Davidic Empire. VT 20/1970, 287-303.
May, H.G., The king in the garden of Eden. A study of Ezekiel 28: 12-19. In: Anderson, B.W.-W.Harrelson (ed.), Israel's prophetic heritage (Fs J.Muilenburg). New York 1962, p. 166-176.
Mayes, A.D.H., Israel in the pre-monarchy period. VT 23/1973, 151-170.
Mendelsohn, I., Samuel's denunciation of kingship in the light of the Akkadian documents from Ugarit. BASOR 143/1956, 17-22.
- On the preferential status of the eldest son. BASOR 156/1959, 38-40.
Mettinger, T., Solomonic state officials (Coniectanea Biblica OT Series vol. 5). Lund 1971.
- The nominal pattern "q^{e}tullā" in biblical Hebrew. JSS 16/1971, 2-14.
- The Hebrew verb system. A survey of recent research. ASTI 9/1973 (publ. 1974), 64-84.
- Abbild oder Urbild? "Imago Dei" in traditionsgeschichtlicher Sicht. ZAW 86/1974, 403-424.
- Review of T.Veijola, Die ewige Dynastie (Helsinki 1975). SvenskTKv 52/1976, 42-44.

Michel, D., Studien zu den sogenannten Thronbesteigungspsalmen. VT 6/1956, 40-68.
- Tempora und Satzstellung in den Psalmen (Abhandlungen zur evangelischen Theologie vol. 1). Bonn 1960.
Mildenberger, F., Die vordeuteronomistische Saul-Davidüberlieferung. Diss. Tübingen 1962. Unpublished.
Miller, J.M., Jebus and Jerusalem: A case of mistaken identity. ZDPV 90/1974, 115-127.
- Saul's rise to power: some observations concerning 1 Sam 9: 1-10: 16; 10: 26- 11: 15 and 13: 2 - 14: 46. CBQ 36/1974, 157-174.
- Geba/Gibeah of Benjamin. VT 25/1975, 145-166.
Miller, P.D.Jr., Ugaritic ġzr and Hebrew ʿzr II. UF 2/1970, 159-175.
Möhlenbrink, K., Sauls Ammoniterfeldzug und Samuels Beitrag zum Königtum des Saul. ZAW 58/1940-1941, 57-70.
Montgomery, J.A.-H.S.Gehman, A critical and exegetical commentary on the Books of Kings (ICC). Edinburgh 1951.
Moor, J.C.de, New Year with Canaanites and Israelites (Kamper Cahiers vol. 21: 1-2). Kampen 1972.
Moran, W.L., The ancient Near Eastern background of the love of God in Deuteronomy. CBQ 25/1963, 77-87.
- A note on the treaty terminology of the Sefire stelas. JNES 22/1963, 173-176.
Morenz, S., Ägyptische und davididische Königstitulatur. ZÄS 79/1954, 73-74.
Morgenstern, J., David and Jonathan. JBL 78/1959, 322-325.
Moscati, S. (ed.), An introduction to the comparative grammar of the Semitic languages. Phonology and morphology (Porta Linguarum vol. 6). Wiesbaden 1964.
Mowinckel, S., Psalmenstudien II. Das Thronbesteigungsfest Jahwäs und die Ursprung der Eschatologie. Kristiania 1922.
- Psalmenstudien III. Kultprophetie und prophetische Psalmen. Kristiania 1923.
- "Die letzten Worte Davids" II Sam 23 1-7. ZAW 45/1927, 30-58.
- Natanforjettelsen i 2 Sam. kap. 7. SEÅ 12/1947, 220-229.
- Offersang og sangoffer. Oslo 1951.
- He that cometh. Transl. by G.W.Anderson. Oxford 1956.
- "Rahelstämme" und "Leastämme"? ZAWBeih 77/1958, 129-150.
- General oriental and specific Israelite elements in the Israelite conception of the sacral kingdom. In: La regalità sacra. Leiden 1959, p. 283-293.
- Loven og de 8 termini i Sl 119. NTT 61/1960, 95-127; 129-159.
- Israelite historiography. ASTI 2/1963, 4-26.
Mulder, J.S.M., Studies on Psalm 45. Oss 1972.
Munn-Rankin, J.M., Diplomacy in Western Asia in the early second millennium B.C. Iraq 18/1956, 68-110.
Murphy, R.E., A study of Psalm 72 (71) (The Catholic University of America Studies in Sacred Theology, Second Series vol. 12). Washington 1948.
Nicholson, E.W., The meaning of the expression ʿäm haʾaræs in the Old Testament. JSS 10/1965, 59-66.
Nielsen, E., Shechem. A traditio-historical investigation. Copenhagen 1955.
- Some reflections on the history of the ark. VTSuppl 7/1960, 61-74.
- Die zehn Gebote. Eine traditionsgeschichtliche Skizze (Acta Theol. Danica vol. 8). Kopenhagen 1965.
Norin, S., Er spaltete das Meer. (Diss. Lund. Forthcoming in Coniectanea Biblica).
North, C.R., The religious aspects of Hebrew kingship. ZAW 50/1932, 8-38.

Noth, M., Überlieferungsgeschichtliche Studien. Die sammelnden und bearbeitenden Geschichtswerke im Alten Testament. Halle (Saale) 1943, 3rd ed. Darmstadt 1967.
- Gott, König, Volk im Alten Testament. ZThK 47/1950, 157-191. Repr. in id., Ges Stud I (ThB vol. 6). 2nd ed. München 1960, p. 188-229.
- Das Buch Josua (HAT vol. 7). 2nd ed. Tübingen 1953.
- Die Bewährung von Salomos "göttlicher Weisheit". VTSuppl 3/1955 (=Fs H.H.Rowley), 225-237. Repr. in id., Ges Stud II (ThB vol. 39). München 1969, p. 99-112.
- Gesammelte Studien zum Alten Testament (ThB vol. 6). 2nd ed. München 1960. (=Ges Stud I)
- The history of Israel. London (1958) 2nd ed. 1960.
- Exodus. A commentary (OTL). Transl. by J.S.Bowden. London 1962.
- Könige (BKAT vol. 9: 1). Neukirchen... 1968.
- Gesammelte Studien zum Alten Testament II. Ed. by H.W.Wolff (ThB vol. 39). München 1969. (=Ges Stud II)
Nübel, H.-U., Davids Aufstieg in der Frühe israelitischer Geschichtsschreibung. Bonn 1959.
Nyberg, H.S., Studien zum Religionskampf im Alten Testament. ARW 35/1938, 329-387.
- Hebreisk Grammatik. Uppsala 1952.
Nyström, S., Beduinentum und Jahwismus. Eine soziologisch-religionsgeschichtliche Untersuchung zum Alten Testament. Lund 1946.
Orlinsky, H.M., The tribal system of Israel and related groups in the period of the judges. OrAnt 1/1962, 11-20.
Otzen, B., Studien über Deuterosacharja (Acta Theol. Danica vol. 6). Copenhagen 1964.
- b^{e}liyyă'äl. TWAT 1/1973, 654-658.
Pallis, S.Aa., The Babylonian Akîtu festival (Det Kgl. Danske Videnskabernes Selskab. Hist.-fil. meddelelser vol. 12: 1). København 1926.
Paul, S.M., Studies in the Book of the Covenant in the light of cuneiform and biblical law (VTSuppl 18). Leiden 1970.
Pedersen, J., Der Eid bei den Semiten (Studien zur Gesch. u. Kultur des islamischen Orients Heft 3), Strassburg 1914.
Perlitt, L., Bundestheologie im Alten Testament (WMANT vol. 36). Neukirchen ... 1969.
Petschow, H., Gewand(saum) im Recht. RLA III/1957-1971, 318-322.
Plein, I., Erwägungen zur Überlieferung von 1 Reg 1126-1420. ZAW 78/1966, 8-24.
Ploeg, J.van der, Le sens de gibbôr hail. Vivre et penser 1/1941, 120-125.
- Les šot^{e}rim d'Israël. OTS 10/1954, 185-196.
- Les anciens dans l'Ancien Testament. In: Lex tua veritas (Fs H.Junker). Trier 1961, p. 175-191.
Pope, M.H., Job (The Anchor Bible vol. 15). New York 1965.
Porteous, N.W., Royal Wisdom. VTSuppl 3/1955 (=Fs H.H.Rowley), 247-261. Repr. in id., Living the mystery. Collected Essays. Oxford 1967, p. 77-91.
Posener, G., Littérature et politique dans l'Égypte de la XIIe dynastie (Bibliothèque de l'École des hautes Etudes vol. 307). Paris 1956.
- De la divinité du Pharaon (Cahiers de la société asiatique vol. 15). Paris 1960.
Poulssen, N., König und Tempel im Glaubenszeugnis des Alten Testaments (Stuttgarter Biblische Monographien vol. 3). Stuttgart 1967.

Press, R., Der Prophet Samuel. ZAW 56/1938, 177-225.
Preuss, H.D., "... ich will mit dir sein!" ZAW 80/1968, 139-173.
Priest, J., The covenant of brothers. JBL 84/1965, 400-406.
Procksch, O., Die letzten Worte Davids. In: Fs R.Kittel (BWAT vol. 13). Leipzig 1913, p. 112-125.
Rad, G.von, Erwägungen zu den Königspsalmen. ZAW 58/1940-1941, 216-222.
– Der heilige Krieg im alten Israel (AThANT vol. 20). Zürich 1951.
– Gesammelte Studien zum Alten Testament (ThB vol. 8.) München 1961.
– Theologie des Alten Testaments. Vol. 1 4th ed., vol. 2 3rd ed. München 1962.
Rainey, A.F., ilānu rēṣūtni lillikū! In: H.A.Hoffner Jr. (ed.), AOAT vol. 22 (=Fs C.H.Gordon). Neukirchen 1973, p. 139-142.
– The Ugaritic texts in Ugaritica V. JAOS 94/1974, 184-194.
Redford, D.B., A study of the biblical story of Joseph (VTSuppl 20). Leiden 1970.
Rehm, M., Der königliche Messias im Licht der Immanuel-Weissagungen des Buches Jesaja (Eichstätter Studien N.F. I). Kevelaer 1968.
Rendtorff, R., Beobachtungen zur altisraelitischen Geschichtsschreibung anhand der Geschichte vom Aufstieg Davids. In: H.W.Wolff (ed.), Probleme biblischer Theologie (Fs G.vonRad). München 1971, p. 428-439.
Richardson, H.N., The last words of David: Some notes on II Samuel 23:1-7. JBL 90/1971, 257-266.
Richter, W., Traditionsgeschichtliche Untersuchungen zum Richterbuch (BBB vol. 18). Bonn 1963.
– Die Bearbeitungen des "Retterbuches" in der deuteronomischen Epoche (BBB vol. 21). Bonn 1964.
– Die nāgîd-Formel. BZ 9/1965, 71-84.
– Zu den "Richtern Israels". ZAW 77/1965, 40-72.
– Die sogenannten vorprophetischen Berufungsberichte (FRLANT vol. 101). Göttingen 1970.
– Exegese als Literaturwissenschaft. Göttingen 1971.
Ridderbos, N.H., Die Psalmen. Stilistische Verfahren und Aufbau. Mit besonderer Berücksichtigung von Ps 1–41 (ZAWBeih 117). Berlin 1972.
Ringgren, H., Word and Wisdom. Studies in the hypostatization of divine qualities and functions in the ancient Near East. Lund 1947.
– The Messiah in the Old Testament (SBT vol. 18). London 1956.
– Sprüche (ATD vol. 16:1). Göttingen 1962.
– Israelite religion. Transl. by D.Green. London 1966. 2nd impr. 1969.
– Psalm 8 och kristologien. SEÅ 37-38/1972-1973, 16-20.
– ḥayā (To appear in TWAT.)
Robert, Ph.de, Juges ou tribus en 2 Samuel VII 7? VT 21/1971, 116-118.
Robertson, E., The 'ūrīm and tummîm; what were they? VT 14/1964, 67-74.
Rosenthal, E.I.J., Some aspects of the Hebrew monarchy. JJS 9/1958, 1-18.
Rost, L., Die Überlieferung von der Thronnachfolge Davids (BWANT vol. 42). Stuttgart 1926.
– Die Bezeichnungen für Land und Volk im Alten Testament. In: Festschrift Otto Procksch. Leipzig 1934, p. 125-148.
– Sinaibund und Davidsbund. ThLZ 72/1947, 129-134.
– Das kleine Credo und andere Studien zum Alten Testament. Heidelberg 1965.
Rowley, H.H., Melchizedek and Zadok (Gen 14 and Ps 110). In: W.Baumgartner et al. (ed.), Festschrift Alfred Bertholet. Tübingen 1950, p. 461-472.
Rudolph, W., Die Einheitlichkeit der Erzählung vom Sturz der Atalja (2 Kön 11).

In: W.Baumgartner et al. (ed.), Festschrift Alfred Bertholet. Tübingen 1950, p. 473-478.
- Chronikbücher (HAT vol. 21). Tübingen 1955.
- Hosea (KAT vol. 13:1). Gütersloh 1966.
- Jeremia (HAT vol. 12). 3rd ed. Tübingen 1968.

Salmon, J.M., Judicial authority in early Israel: An historical investigation of Old Testament institutions. Diss. Princeton Theol. Sem. 1968. University Microfilms, Ann Arbor 1969.

Šanda, A., Die Bücher der Könige (Exegetisches Handbuch z. Alten Testament vol. 9: 1-2). Münster 1911-1912.

Sarna, N., Psalm 89: A study in innerbiblical exegesis. Studies and Texts, Brandeis Univ. (P.W. Lown Inst.) 1/1963, 29-46.

Sauren, H. –G.Kestemont, Keret, roi de Ḫubur. UF 3/1971, 180-221.

Schlisske, W., Gottessöhne und Gottessohn im Alten Testament. Phasen der Entmythisierung im Alten Testament (BWANT vol. 97). Stuttgart... 1973.

Schmid, H., Die Herrschaft Abimelechs (Jdc 9). Judaica 26/1970, 1-11.

Schmidt, L., Menschlicher Erfolg und Jahwes Initiative. Studien zu Tradition, Interpretation und Historie in Überlieferungen von Gideon, Saul und David (WMANT vol. 38). Neukirchen 1970.

Schmidt, W.H., Gott und Mensch in Ps. 8. ThZ 25/1969, 1-15.
- Kritik am Königtum. In: H.W.Wolff (ed.), Probleme biblischer Theologie (Fs G.von Rad). München 1971, p. 440-461.

Schmitt, H.Ch., Elisa. Traditionsgeschichtliche Untersuchungen zur vorklassischen nordisraelitischen Prophetie. Gütersloh 1972.

Schreiner, J., Sion-Jerusalem. Jahwes Königssitz (StANT vol. 7). München 1963.

Schulte, H., Die Entstehung der Geschichtsschreibung im Alten Testament (ZAWBeih 128). Berlin 1972.

Schulz, A., Die Bücher Samuel, I-II (EH vol. 8). Münster 1919-1920.

Schulz, H., Das Todesrecht im Alten Testament. Studien zur Rechtsform der Mot-Jumat-Sätze (ZAWBeih 114). Berlin 1969.

Schunck, K.-D., Benjamin. Untersuchungen zur Entstehung und Geschichte eines israelitischen Stammes (ZAWBeih 86). Berlin 1963.

Scott, R.B.Y., Solomon and the beginnings of Wisdom in Israel. VTSuppl 3/1955 (=Fs H.H.Rowley), 262-279.

Seebass, H., Traditionsgeschichte von I Sam 8, 10 17 ff. und 12. ZAW 77/1965, 286-296.
- I Sam 15 als Schlüssel für das Verständnis der sogenannten königsfreundlichen Reihe I Sam 9 1 – 10 16 11 1-15 und 13 2 – 14 52. ZAW 78/1966, 148-179.
- Die Vorgeschichte der Königserhebung Sauls. ZAW 79/1967, 155-171.
- Zur Königserhebung Jerobeams I. VT 17/1967, 325-333.
- Die Verwerfung Jerobeams I. und Salomos durch die Prophetie des Ahia von Silo. WO 4/1968, 163-182.
- bāḥar. TWAT 1/1973, 592-608.
- Nathan und David in II Sam 12. ZAW 86/1974, 203-211.

Seeligman, I.L., A psalm from pre-regal times. VT 14/1964, 75-92.
- Zur Terminologie für das Gerichtsverfahren im Wortschatz des biblischen Hebräisch. VTSuppl 16/1967 (=Fs W.Baumgartner), 251-278.

Sekine, M., Davidsbund und Sinaibund bei Jeremia. VT 9/1959, 47-57.

Seybold, K., Das davidische Königtum im Zeugnis der Propheten (FRLANT vol. 107). Göttingen 1972.

Shils, E., Charisma, order, and status. American Sociological Review 30/1965, 199-213.
- Charisma. Intern. Encycl. of the social sciences 2/1968, 386-390.
Simon, M., La prophétie de Nathan et le temple. RHPhR 32/1952, 41-58.
Simons, J., The geographical and topographical texts of the Old Testament. Leiden 1959.
Sjöberg, Å., Review of G.W.Ahlström, Psalm 89 (Lund 1959). SEÅ 25/1960, 97-108.
Skehan, P.W., A fragment of the "Song of Moses" (Deut. 32) from Qumran. BASOR 136/1954, 12-15.
Smend, R., Jahwekrieg und Stämmebund. Erwägungen zur ältesten Geschichte Israels (FRLANT vol. 84). Göttingen 1963. (=1963 A)
- Die Bundesformel (Theologische Studien Heft 68). Zürich 1963. (=1963 B)
- Gehörte Juda zum vorstaatlichen Israel? In: Fourth World Congress of Jewish Studies. Papers vol. 1. Jerusalem 1967, p. 57-62.
- Zur Frage der altisraelitischen Amphiktyonie. EvTh 31/1971, 623-630.
- Das Gesetz und die Völker. Ein Beitrag zur deuteronomistischen Redaktionsgeschichte. In: H.W.Wolff (ed.), Probleme biblischer Theologie (Fs G.vonRad). München 1971, p. 494-509.
Smith, S., The practice of kingship in early Semitic kingdoms. In: S.H.Hooke (ed.), Myth, ritual and kingship. Oxford 1958, p. 22-73.
Soden, W.von, Nominalformen und juristische Begriffsbildung im Akkadischen: Die Nominalform 'qutullā'. In: Studia et documenta ad iura Orientis Antiqui vol. 2 (Fs P.Koschaker). Leipzig 1939, p. 199-207.
Soggin, J.A., Zur Entwicklung des alttestamentlichen Königtums. ThZ 15/1959, 401-418.
- Charisma und Institution im Königtum Sauls. ZAW 75/1963, 54-65.
- Der judäische 'am-ha'areṣ und das Königtum in Juda. Ein Beitrag zum Studium der deuteronomistischen Geschichtsschreibung. VT 13/1963, 187-195.
- Osservazioni a due derivati della radice *spr* in ebraico. Bibbia e Oriente 7/1965, 279-283.
- Das Königtum in Israel. Ursprünge, Spannungen, Entwicklung (ZAWBeih 104).
- Berlin 1967.
- Zum zweiten Psalm. In: H.J.Stoebe (ed.), Wort-Gebot-Glaube (Fs W.Eichrodt). Zürich 1970, p. 191-207.
- Zum achten Psalm. ASTI 8/1970-1971, 106-122.
- Joshua. A commentary (OTL). Transl. by R.A.Wilson. London 1972.
Soisalon-Soininen, I., Begreppet funktion i gammaltestamentlig traditionsforskning. SEÅ 33/1968, 55-67.
Speiser, E.A., "People" and "nation" of Israel. JBL 79/1960, 157-163.
- Oriental and biblical studies. Ed. by J.J.Finkelstein. Philadelphia 1967.
Stade, B., Miscellen. 10. Anmerkungen zu 2 Kö. 10-14. ZAW 5/1885, 275-297.
Stamm, J.J., Erlösen und Vergeben im Alten Testament. Eine Begriffsgeschichtliche Untersuchung. Bern 1940.
- Zur Frage der Imago Dei im Alten Testament. In: Neuenschwander, U.–R.Dellsperger (ed.), Humanität und Glaube (Gedenkschrift K.Guggisberg). Bern 1973, p. 243-253.
Steck, O.H., vide Barth.
Steinmetzer, F., Die babylonischen Kudurru (Grenzsteine) als Urkundenform (Studien z. Gesch. u. Kultur des Altertums vol. 11: 4-5). Paderborn 1922.
Sternberger, D., Legitimacy. Intern. Encycl. of the social sciences 2/1968, 244-248.

Stoebe, H.J., Noch einmal die Eselinnen des *ķîš* (1 Sam IX). VT 7/1957, 362-370.
- *ḥæsæd* Güte. THAT 1/1971, 600-621.
- Das erste Buch Samuelis (KAT vol. 8: 1). Gütersloh 1973.
Stolz, F., Jahwes und Israels Kriege. Kriegstheorien und Kriegserfahrungen im Glauben des alten Israels (AThANT vol. 60). Zürich 1972.
Sturdy, J., The original meaning of "Is Saul also among the prophets?" (1 Samuel X 11,12; XIX 24). VT 20/1970, 206-213.
Tadmor, H., "The people" and the kingship in ancient Israel: the role of political institutions in the biblical period. Cahiers d'histoire mondiale 11/1968, 46-68.
Talmon, S., The Judaean ʿam haʾareṣ in historical perspective. In: Fourth World Congress of Jewish Studies. Papers vol. 1. Jerusalem 1967, p. 71-76.
Täubler, E., Biblische Studien. Die Epoche der Richter. Ed. by H.-J.Zobel. Tübingen 1958.
Thiel, W., *Hēfēr bᵉrît*. Zum Bundbrechen im Alten Testament. VT 20/1970, 214-229.
Thompson, J.A., The significance of the verb *love* in the David-Jonathan narratives in 1 Samuel. VT 24/1974, 334-338.
Thornton, T.C.G., Charismatic kingship in Israel and Judah. JThS 14/1963, 1-11.
- Solomonic apologetic in Samuel and Kings. The Church Quarterly Review 169/1968, 159-166.
Tiktin, H., Kritische Untersuchungen zu den Büchern Samuelis (FRLANT N.F. vol. 16). Göttingen 1922.
Tournay, R., Recherches sur la chronologie des psaumes. 3. Une liturgie d'intronisation (Psaumes XX et XXI). RB 66/1959, 161-190.
- Le psaume VIII et la doctrine biblique du nom. RB 78/1971, 18-30.
Tsevat, M., Studies in the Book of Samuel. III. The steadfast house: What was David promised in II Sam. 7: 11b-16? HUCA 34/1963, 71-82.
- The house of David in Nathan's prophecy. Bibl 46/1965, 353-356.
Tucker, G.M., Covenant forms and contract forms. VT 15/1965, 487-503.
- Witnesses and "dates" in Israelite contracts. CBQ 28/1966, 42-45.
Ullmann, S., The principles of semantics. Oxford... 2nd ed. 1957, repr. 1967.
Vaux, R.de, Le roi d'Israël, vassal de Yahvé. In: Mel. E.Tisserant vol. 1 (=Studia e Testi vol. 231). Città del Vaticano 1964, p. 119-133.
- Le sens de l'expression "peuple du pays" dans l'Ancien Testament et le role politique du peuple en Israël. RA 58/1964, 167-172.
- Ancient Israel. Its life and institutions. Transl. by J.McHugh. 2nd ed. London 1965.
- "Le lieu que Yahvé a choisi pour y établir son nom." ZAWBeih 105/1967, 219-228.
- Bible et Orient. Paris 1967.
- Histoire ancienne d'Israël. Paris 1971.
- La thèse de l'"amphictyonie israélite". HThR 64/1971, 415-436.
Veenhof, K.R., Review of E.Kutsch, Salbung als Rechtsakt (1963). BiOr 23/1966, 308-313.
Veijola, T., Die ewige Dynastie. David und die Entstehung seiner Dynastie nach der deuteronomistischen Darstellung (Ann. acad. scient. fennicae ser. B vol. 193). Helsinki 1975.
Vetter, D., Jahwes Mit-Sein ein Ausdruck des Segens (Arbeiten zur Theologie I: 45). (Not seen. Known from Saebø, ThLZ 98/1973, 26-27.)
Vink, J.G., The date and origin of the Priestly Code in the Old Testament. OTS 15/1969, 1-144.

Volkwein, B., Masoretisches ʿēdūt, ʿēdwōt, ʿēdōt – "Zeugnis" oder "Bundesbestimmungen"? BZ 13/1969, 18-40.
Volz, P., Der Geist Gottes und die verwandten Erscheinungen im Alten Testament und im anschliessenden Judentum. Tübingen 1910.
Vorländer, H., Mein Gott. Die Vorstellungen vom persönlichen Gott im alten Orient und im Alten Testament (ATAO vol. 23). Kevelaer... 1975.
Wächter, L., Die Übertragung der Berîtvorstellung auf Jahwe. ThLZ 99/1974, 801-816.
Wagner, N.E., Abraham and David? In: Wevers, J.W. –D.B.Redford (ed.), Studies on the ancient Palestinian world (Fs F.V.Winnett). Toronto 1972, p. 117-140.
Wallis, G., Geschichte und Überlieferung. Gedanken über alttestamentliche Darstellungen der Frühgeschichte Israels und der Anfänge seines Königtums. Berlin 1968.
Walther, A., Das altbabylonische Gerichtswesen (LSS vol. 6: 4-6). Leipzig 1917.
Ward, A.R.L., The story of David's rise: A traditio-historical study of I Samuel XVI 14–II Samuel V. Diss. Vanderbilt 1967. Summarized in: Diss. Abstr. 27/1966-1967 no 4336. A.
Ward, J.M., The literary form and liturgical background of Psalm LXXXIX. VT 11/1961, 321-339.
Weber, M., Grundriss der Sozialökonomik. III. Wirtschaft und Gesellschaft vol. 1-2. 3rd ed. Tübingen 1947.
– Max Weber on Law in economy and society. Ed. by M.Rheinstein. Transl. from M.Weber, Wirtschaft und Gesellschaft 2nd ed. 1925 by E.Shils and M.Rheinstein (20th century legal philosophy series vol. 4). Cambridge Mass. 1954.
– Rechtssoziologie. Ed. by J.Winkelmann. 2nd ed. Neuwied... 1967.
– Max Weber on charisma and institution building. Selected papers. Ed. and with an introduction by S.N.Eisenstadt. Chicago... 1968.
Weinel, H., mšḥ und seine Derivate. ZAW 18/1898, 1-82.
Weinfeld, M., The covenant of grant in the Old Testament and in the ancient Near East. JAOS 90/1970, 184-203. (add. ibid. 92/1972, 468-469.)
– Deuteronomy and the deuteronomic school. Oxford 1972.
– bᵉrît. TWAT 1/1973, 781-808.
– Covenant terminology in the ancient Near East and its influence on the West. JAOS 93/1973, 190-199.
– Bᵉrît – Covenant vs. obligation. Review article on E.Kutsch (1973). Bibl 56/1975, 120-128.
Weippert, M., "Heiliger Krieg" in Assyrien und Israel. ZAW 84/1972, 460-493.
Weippert, H., Die "deuteronomistischen" Beurteilungen der Könige von Israel und Juda und das Problem der Redaktion der Königsbücher. Bibl 53/1972, 301-339.
Weiser, A., Samuel. Seine geschichtliche Aufgabe und religiöse Bedeutung. Traditionsgeschichtliche Untersuchungen zu 1. Samuel 7–12 (FRLANT vol. 81). Göttingen 1962.
– Die Tempelbaukrise unter David. ZAW 77/1965, 153-168.
– Einleitung in das Alte Testament. 6th ed. Göttingen 1966.
– Die Legitimation des Königs David. Zur Eigenart und Entstehung der sogen. Geschichte von Davids Aufstieg. VT 16/1966, 325-354.
Wellhausen, J., Der Text der Bücher Samuelis. Göttingen 1871.
– Die Composition des Hexateuchs und der historischen Bücher des Alten Testaments. 3rd ed. Berlin 1899.
Westermann, C., Die Begriffe für Fragen und Suchen im Alten Testament. KuD 6/1960, 2-30.

- Genesis (BKAT vol. 1:1). Neukirchen... 1974.
Whybray, R.N., The Succession Narrative (SBT second series vol. 9). London 1968.
Widengren, G., Sakrales Königtum im Alten Testament und im Judentum (Franz Delitzsch-Vorlesungen 1952). Stuttgart 1955.
- King and covenant. JSS 2/1957, 1-32.
Wildberger, H., Samuel und die Entstehung des israelitischen Königtums. ThZ 13/1957, 442-469.
- Die Thronnamen des Messias, Jes. 9,5 b. ThZ 16/1960, 314-332.
- $b\d{h}r$ erwählen. THAT 1/1971, 275-300.
- Jesaja (BKAT vol. 10:1). Neukirchen... 1972.
Williams, R.J., Literature as a medium of political propaganda in ancient Egypt. In: The seed of wisdom (Fs T.J.Meek). Toronto 1964, p. 14-30.
- "A people come out of Egypt." An egyptologist looks at the Old Testament. VTSuppl 28/1975, 231-252.
Wittfogel, K.A., Oriental despotism. A comparative study of total power. New Haven 1957.
Wolf, C.U., Traces of primitive democracy in ancient Israel. JNES 6/1947, 98-108.
Wolff, H.W., Dodekapropheton 1 Hosea (BKAT vol. 14:1). 2nd ed. Neukirchen ... 1965.
Wright, G.E., The lawsuit of God: A formcritical study of Deuteronomy 32. In: Anderson, B.W.–W.Harrelson (ed.), Israel's prophetic heritage (Fs J.Muilenburg). New York 1962, p. 26-67.
Würthwein, E., Der ʿamm haʾarez (BWANT vol. 4:17). Stuttgart 1936.
- Der Ursprung der prophetischen Gerichtsrede. ZThK 49/1952, 1-16.
- Die Erzählung von der Thronfolge Davids – theologische oder politische Geschichtsschreibung? (Theologische Studien vol. 115). Zürich 1974.
Yaron, K., The dirge over the king of Tyre. ASTI 3/1964, 28-57.
Yeivin, S., Social, religious and cultural trends in Jerusalem under the Davidic dynasty. VT 3/1953, 149-166.
- Ēdūth. IEJ 24/1974, 17-20.
Yule, G.U., The statistical study of literary vocabulary. Cambridge 1944.
Zalevsky, Z., The revelation of God to Solomon in Gibeon. Tarbiz 42/1973, 215-258. (Hebrew, English summary, p. I.)
Zenger, E., Ein Beispiel exegetischer Methoden aus dem Alten Testament. In: J.Schreiner (ed.), Einführung in die Methoden der biblischen Exegese. Würzburg 1971, p. 97-148.
Zimmerli, W., Geschichte und Tradition von Beerseba im Alten Testament. Diss. Göttingen. Göttingen 1932.
- Gottes Offenbarung (ThB vol. 19). 2nd ed. München 1969.
- Ezechiel (BKAT vol. 13:1-2). Neukirchen... 1969.
- Das "Gnadenjahr des Herrn". In: Kuschke, A.–E.Kutsch (ed.), Archäologie und Altes Testament (Fs K.Galling). Tübingen 1970, p. 321-332.
- Vier oder fünf Thronnamen des messianischen Herrschers von Jes. IX 5b.6. VT 22/1972, 249-252.
Zobel, H.-J., Beiträge zur Geschichte Gross-Judas in früh- und vordavidischer Zeit. VTSuppl 28/1975, 253-277.

Indexes

1. Biblical and Jewish Sources

(N.B. The biblical index is selective.)

Genesis
1,26-28	269
ch. 2-3	272
3,5.22	244, 251
28,18-22	224
31,13	224
41,33	250
41,38-39	250
49,10	95

Exodus
ch. 3	66 f.
4,22-23	268
18,13-27	251
18,21	113

Leviticus
7,36	221 n.
20,2-5	**127**

Numbers
11,10-30	251
21,29	172

Deuteronomy
1,9-18	251
1,16-17	146
1,17	244
17,18-19	**289**
21,15-17	126
23,7	147
31,9-13	144
32,8-9	269
33,5	107
34,9	248

Joshua
1,7-9	19 n., 289 f.
2,9-11	51
9,9-10	51

Judges
6,11-24	66 f.
9,6	111
9,8.9	198
9,15	141 n., 198
9,16	148
10,1-5	89
11,4-11	**145 f.**
12,7-15	89

I Samuel
2,35	95
7,7-14	80 f., 90 f., 92
ch. 8–12	**80 ff.**
ch. 8	81
9,1–10,16	64 ff., 113 f., **151 ff.**, **174 ff.**, 195
9,18-24	**70 ff.**
9,24	114
9,27–10,7	203
10,1	66 f., 67, 167 ff., 172, 203 ff., 247, 267
10,2-16	**234 ff.**
10,2-9	**68 ff.**
10,5	236, **245 f.**
10,7	236
10,8	64
10,9	235, 247
10,17-27	83 ff., 87 ff., **112 f.**, **174 ff.**, **179 ff.**
10,24	112 f., **132 ff.**, 182
10,25	**87 f.**, 135, 141
10,26-27	**84 f.**, 97 n.
11,1-15	**83 ff.**
11,1	140
11,6	**234 ff., 237 f.**
11,7	84
11,12-13	97 f.
11,12-14	**84**, 119
11,15	86, 146 f., 196
12,11	**82**

12,12	86	5,10	38
12,14-15	**82 n.**	5,17-25	**42**
12,24-25	164	ch. 6–7	308
13,4	97, 236	ch. 6	42 ff.
13,7-14	64, 163, 152 ff.	6,21	**45**, 153 ff., 169, 170, 182
13,13-14	277, **152 ff.**	ch. 7	14, **41 ff.**, **48 ff.**, **173**, 239, 254 ff., 260 f., 266 f., 284 f.
14,41	181	7,1	52
14,45	85 n., 137	7,4	35 n.
14,52	34	7,5	**56 f.**
15,1–16,13	**33 ff.**	7,7	45
15,1	196	7,8	45, 61, 61 n., **151 ff.**, 169, **267**
15,27	34	7,9	45
16,1-13	**33 ff.**, 45, 123 f., **174 ff.**, 199, **204 ff.**, 229, **246 ff.**	7,10-11	52
16,14	**247 f.**	7,11	45, 59, 59 n.
16,14 ff.	34	7,12-15	**52 ff.**
18,3-4	**39**	7,12-13	31
18,4	34	7,12	266
19,18–20,1	76 f.	7,13	**52 ff., 56 f.**
19,23 f.	248	7,14-15	276, 170
20,12-17	37 f.	7,16	36, 45, **52 ff., 57 ff.**
23,16-18	37	7,18-29	51 f.
24,7	196, 199	7,28	36 f., 45, 147
24,11	35 n., 196, 199	8,17	94 n.
24,15	40	ch. 9	37
24,18-23	37	ch. 12	**29 f.**
ch. 25	**35 ff.**	12,1-14	20
25,28-31	**35 ff.**	12,7	204
25,30	152 ff., 169	12,20	202 n.
26,9	201	12,24-25	169
26,9.11.16.23	196, 199	12,25	56, 60
26,20	40	14,17	146, **241 f.**, 251, 269
30,26-31	118, 141 f.	14,19	133
		14,20	**241 f.**, 251, 269
II Samuel		15,1–19,44	**121 ff.**
		15,7-12	114
1,14.16	196	15,10	132
1,21	200	15,21	133
2,1-4	40, **118, 141 f.**, 298	16,16	**132 ff.**
2,4	138, **198 ff.**, 228 f.	16,18	182
2,6	**147**	17,5-14	29
3,9-10	44	19,10-44	**118 ff.**
3,17-21	114, 138	19,16	119
3,18	**42, 44**, 77	19,17-24	119
3,28-29	40 n.	19,23	119
3,38-39	40 n.	19,28	269
ch. 5	**41 ff.**	19,41	119
5,1-3	40, **114 f.**, 298	20,1	140
5,1-2	**44 f.**, 172 f.	21,6	245
5,2	153 ff., 169	21,7	37 f.
5,3	**137 ff., 198 ff., 228 f.**	22,1-51	281

23,1-7	**257 f., 279 ff.**
23,2	244
23,3	274

I Kings

ch. 1–2	**23 f., 27 ff.**
1,5-31	**119 f.**
1,9	114
1,20	161
1,25	**132 ff.**
1,31	**132 ff.**
1,32 ff.	**94 ff., 120 ff., 201 ff.**
1,34	**132 ff.**
1,35	**23,** 121, 153 ff., **159 ff.,** 164, 173, 298
1,39	132 ff., 206
1,45	**203**
2,3-4	277
2,3	289
2,24	28, 58
3,4-15	**238 ff.**
3,6	277
3,9	146, 269
3,11	146
3,16-28	343
3,28	244
5,15-26	**225 ff.**
6,11-13	277
8,24-26	276
9,4	277
11,29 ff.	20, 35 n., 75, **151 ff.,** 165, 277
11,38	
ch. 12	**115 ff., 139 f.,** 298
14,7-11	21
14,7	165, 168
16,2	**151 ff.**
16,8 ff.	**117**
16,16	109

II Kings

2,9	248
9,1–10,13	117
9,1-13	**151 ff.,** 173, 194
9,3.6.12	203 ff.
9,13	132
10,15	221 n.
ch. 11	**124**
11,4-20	**142 ff.**
11,12	**133 ff.,** 208, 286 ff.
11,17	**137 ff.**
11,18	128
14,17-21	143
14,19	128
15,20	129
16,7	266, 285
21,23-24	**125,** 143, 148
21,31-35	126
23,1-3	143
23,30	129, 135
23,35	129
25,19	**126 f.**

Isaiah

7,16	241
9,5-6	273, 286
11,2	**248 f.**
14,9-15	264, **271 f.** 274
42,1	249
55,3	257, 282
61,1	250

Jeremiah

23,5	248
ch. 26	137
33,9	147
33,14-26	281 f.
ch. 34	**127**
34,19	126, 129
52,25	**126 f.**

Ezekiel

16,35-43	127
17,18	221 n.
21,13	288
22,29	127, 129
23,36-49	127
ch. 28	**270 ff.**

Hoseah

2,1	268
8,4	107
11,1	268
12,2	**225**

Micah

5,1	273

Psalms

1+2	**289 f.**
2	101, **258 f.**, **261 f.**
2,4	285
2,7	266, **286**, **290**
2,7-9	203
2,8	269
8,6 ff.	269
18	100, 306 f.
20	100, 101
21	101
45,7	100, 264, 273
61,7-8	100
63,12	100
72	100, 104
72,1-2	244
82	273
84,10	100
89	155, 167, **173**, **254 ff.**, **262 ff.** 266, 306 f.
89,4	285
89,7	275
89, 21	202, 204
89,27-28	260, **262 ff.**, 272, 285
89,29-38	**278 f.**, 284
89, 34	284
89, 39-40	229
101	307
105,15	199, 229
109,18	223
110	93 n, 101 n. **258 f. 264 f.**,
110,1-3	203
132	100, 100 n., 167, **256 f.**, 290, 308
132, 12	**277 f.**
132,18	187

Proverbs

8,14-16	248
16,10	**243 f.**
20,26	248
30,3	251, 269

Job

15,7-8	251, 269, 272
31,35-36	287 n.
38,7	264, 272
38,28-29	264

I Chronicles

5,2	273
17,10	59 n.
17,14	**57 f.**
22,8-10	260
28,6	260

II Chronicles

3,1-13	239
11,22	154 ff., **160 f.**, **164 f.**
21,1-3	161
22,1	128
23,1-21	142 ff.
23,11	133 ff., 208
30,8	221 n.

Acts

13,33	289

Ecclesiasticus (Sir.)

31,23	288
36,20	288

Qumran

4 Q Ps 89	256 n.

Mishnah

Sotah 9,12	243 n.

Babylonian Talmud

Berakoth 9b	289
Sanhedrin 22a	287 n, 289 n.

Miqra'ôt gᵉdôlôt

on 2 R 11,12	289 n.

The Samaritan Liturgy, p. 306 n.

2. Ancient Near Eastern Sources

EGYPT

Decree or Blessing of Ptah	49
Instruction of Amen-em-het	25
Instruction of Ptah-hotep	240 n.
Pap. Anasti II 5,6 ff.	100, 103 n.
IV 5,6 ff.	100, 103 n.
Prophecy of Neferti	25
Sphinx Stela	240

SYRO-PALESTINE

Canaanaic and Aramaic Inscriptions

KAI 10,5	287 n.
27,9-10	257
266,8	247 n.
Nora inscription	158
Sefire I A 35-42	223
I C 4-5	147 n.
19-20	147 n.
II B 2	147 n.
III 10	158

Amarna letters

11,6-18	217
29,22-23	218
31,11-16	218
34	227
34,42-53	**212 f.**
35,49-50	214
51	198, 209, 224
73,1-3	285 n.
73,35-38	285 n.
82,1-4	285 n.
85,39-40	**134**
105,21	214
147,5-15.41-56	103
256,10-13	**134**
287, 60-63	56 n.
288,5-7	56 n.
289,37-38	**134**

Ugarit

Gordon, Ugaritic Textbook

49 III, 20-21.39-40	305 n.
125,17-23	**273**
127,45 ff.	273 n.
603 v. 4	**215**
1007	286 n.
'nt II,31 f.	215 n.
RS 8.208	211, **221**
17.123,5-6	214
24.245	215 n.

HATTI

KBo I 14	**212**, 227
KUB III 24+59,5-7	218, 221
III 63,15 f.	218
XXVI 53,4	218

MESOPOTAMIA

Ashur-nirari VI, treaty I 10 ff.	222
Assyrian Laws (MAL)	
§ 41	267
§ 42-43	217, **219 ff.**
Assyrian Ritual I 30-37	**216**
Esarhaddon, Vassal treaties	161 n.
155	**223**
622-625	**223**
Eshnunna, Laws of § 27	220
Hammurabi, Code of § 170-171	267
Idrimi, Statue of 42 ff., 54-55	**215**
Khafajah (Tutub) R.Harris no 59	**217**
Kudurru stones	284, 303
Mari, ARM	
II 37,6	223
VIII 13 v. 10 ff.	**216**
Utukkū lemnūti	212
VAT 926,24-25	267

3. Oriental Words

HEBREW

baḥăr	**182, 268**
bᵉkôr	**173, 262 ff.**
bᵉrît	115, **137 ff.**, 224, **228 f.**, 258, 275 ff., 282 f., 301 ff.
bᵉrît 'ôlam	**257,** 257 n.
gibbôrê hăḥăyil	129
gib'ôn	246
dᵉrôr	127, 250
heqîm dabar	51
zᵉmirôt yiśra'el	281
zæră'	**52 ff.**
hayā: yᵉḥî	**131 ff.**
ḥăy	133
ḥê	133
halîlā lî	199
ḥoq	286, 290
ḥarā 'ăp	237 n.
ḥæsæd	255, 284
ṭôb–ra'	240 f.
ṭôbā	36 f., **147 f., 284 f.**
yăḥad	107 f.
yᵉladîm	116 n.
leb šomeă'	**240 ff.**
lammā	123
mašiᵃḥ	76, **191, 196 f., 199 ff., 204,** 208
mišpăṭ hămmælæk	81
hămmᵉlukā	87 f.
mô'ed	114
mᵉ'îl	39
naba' Hitp.	236
nagîd	21, 23 f., 29, 37 n., 43, 61, **67 ff., 72 ff.,** 77, **151 ff.,** 261, 267 f.
năgă'	199
nezær	**287 ff.**
nôqed	159
'abăd	139 f.
'æbæd	285
'ed	225 n.
'edût	**286 ff.**
'ezær	263
'ăm	108 ff., 158, 172 f.
'ăm ha'aræṣ	**124 ff.**
păḥăd	237
ṣîṣ	**287 ff.**
qæsæm	244
ra'ā	**112 f.**
śăr šalôm	249
šalôm	226 f., 227 n., 249
šᵉlômō	30
šamă'	**146**
šamă' bên...	**146, 241**
šapăṭ bên...	241
tᵉrû'ā	132

AKKADIAN

abbūtu	266
adê	225 n., 288
aḫḫūtu	266
andurāru	250
-ānum (ending)	246
balāṭu	133 n., 134
bīt redûti	161
bukānu	217
ḫuruppu	219 f.
kittu	214
mānaḫtu	215
napištam lapātum	223
qaran ṣubāt PN ṣabātum/wuššrurum	221
qātam napāṣum	221
salīmu	227
sissiktu	221
sulummû	147, 227
šumma	82 n.
tirḫātu	220
tabūtu	147
tūbṭu	147
ūmu: ištu ūmi annî	261 n.
watû	113 n.
zakû/zakûtu	220 n.

ARAMAIC

tbṭ'	147 n.
'dy'	225 n., 288 n.

UGARITIC

ab adm	273
ḏmr	281
ġzr	263 n.

SUMERIAN

NÍG.MUNUS.SÁ	220

EGYPTIAN

mr pr wr	274 n.
rḫ nśw.t	274 n.
hbn.t	213
śmr	274 n.
šs nsw	213

4. General Index

(D indicates that a definition is given)

Abigail   35 ff.
Abijah   164
Absalom   122 f.
Absolutism   123 (D)
Acclamation   131 (D), 113, 131 ff., 146
Acta contraria   221 f.
Adonijah   119 ff.
Adoption   265 n. (D), 260 ff., 265 ff.
Adoption formula   266 f.
Ahaziah   128
Amphictyony   299, 299 n.
Amtscharisma   234
Angels   See:
   Elohim-beings and Heavenly council
Anointing   76, 115, 145, 185 ff., 235 f., 272, 283
Anomaly and scientific discovery   17
Araunah   94 n.
Army   109, 117, 120
Baptism of the king   261 n.
Beistandsformel   See: Formulae
Berufungsschema   64 ff., 73
Book of Judges   238
Call pattern   See: Berufungsschema
Canaan   209, 273, 305
Charisma   233 (D), 207, 233 ff., 246 ff., 248
Cherub   271
Conditional promise   276 ff.
Configuration of beliefs   17, 211, 254
Contractual relation   301 ff. (D), 210 ff., 222
Coronation   274, 286 ff.
Court style   102 ff.
Covenant   301 ff. (D), 125 f., 131 ff., 137 ff., 210 ff.
   Davidic c.: 230 ff., 254 ff., 275 ff.
   Mosaic c.: 258, 284, 293 n.
   Patriarchal c.: 229, 293 n.
   Royal c.: 131 ff., 137 ff.
   See also: $b^e r\hat{\imath} t$.
Covenant meal   136
Crown   287, 288, 288 n.
Crown prince   160 f.
David   33 ff., 114 ff., 118 f., 138 f., 141 f., 175 ff., 198 ff., 228 f., 230, 242, 246 f., 247 ff.

Davidic dynasty   See: Dynasty
Delocutive verbs   86 n. (D), 86
Democratization of royal categories   267 f.
Demythologization   265
Deuteronomistic literature   14, 16, 19 ff., 27 ff., 34 ff., 48 ff., 80 ff., 87 f., 135, 143, 166 f., 239, 276 ff., 254 ff., 289 f., 304.
   DtrN: 19 f., 178 f., 281.
   DtrP: 19 f., 30, 35.
Diplomatic correspondence 103, 212 ff., 266
Divine designation   97 f., 113, 151 ff.
Divine election   97, 151 ff., 254 ff., 266, 268. See also: *baḥăr*.
Divine kingship   14 (D), 259 ff.
Divine sonship   61, 240, 254 ff., 285
Dualism Israel – Judah   298 ff.
Dynasty   21, 36, 37, 39, 43 f., 52 ff., 57 ff., 71, 275 ff.
Egypt   185 ff., 209 n., 232, 264, 273 f., 286, 288, 304
Elides   243 n.
Elohim-beings   251, 269 ff.
Erbcharisma   234
Etymology   171 n. (D)
Elders   108 ff., 109 n., 114 ff., 116 n., 121 ff.
Exchange relation   302 (D)
Festival of Zion   308
First Man   See: Urmensch
Formulae   156 n. (D)
   Adoption formula   266 f.
   Beistandsformel: 38, 38 n., 43, 45, 66.
   Wortereignisformel: 35, 52
Gibeah   245 f.
Gibeon   238 ff., 245 f.
Heavenly council   263, 269, 269 n.
Hieros gamos   264
Hieros logos   207
High Priest   202, 208, 221 n., 229, 231, 287 ff.
Hiram of Tyre   225 ff.
Historical method   15 ff.

History of David's Rise 33 ff. and passim
Hittites 209 f., 212, 232, 305
Hofstil 102 ff.
Holistic approach 17 f.
Homage 228
Homo historicus 17
Horizon, as literary term 75
Image of God 263, 268 ff.
Imperfect 307
Inclusion 262, 278 f.
Insignia See: Royal i.
Jedidiah 30
Jehu 117, 173 f., 194 f.
Jephthah 145 f.
Jeroboam 165, 168 f.
Jerusalem 93
Joash 142 ff.
Joseph 250
Josiah 125 n.
Judah 118 ff., 141 ff., 298 ff.
Judicial wisdom 241 ff.
Judges 85, 88 ff., 238
Jurisdiction 127 f., 137, 240 ff., 148 ff.
Keilschriftrecht 265 n., 266
King
  Identity with God? 306 f.
  as "first-born". See: $b^ek\hat{o}r$.
  as "heir": 262, 268 f.
  as judge: 240 ff., 248 ff.
  as "servant" of the Lord: 285
  as "son" of God. See: Divine sonship.
  and cult: 304 ff., 305 n.
  and the Law: 289 f.
  and the temple: 305 ff.
  See also: Royal...
Kingship of God 168, 172 ff., 244, 263
Legal assembly 127 f., 137
Legal symbolism 39
Legal symbols 185 ff. See also: Insignia.
Lot casting 176 ff., 179 ff., 243 f.
Marriage rites 217 ff.
Messiah, Messianic. Use of the terms: 14. See also $maši^ah$.
Mesopotamia 186, 212, 216 ff., 273, 305
Mosaic Law 276 ff.
Moses 251
Motif vs. theme 99 n. (D)

Mythological conceptions 266
Nachfolgerdesignation 161
Name theology 56, 61
New Year festival 304 ff.
Nominal patterns
  purussû 147
  qatîl 158
Northern Israel 111 ff., 138 ff., 167 ff., 298 ff.
Oath 131 ff.
Omri 117
Pan-Israelite claims 24 f. 38 n., 40 f., 78
Paradigm 17
Paradigmatic relations 171 ff.
Paradise See: Urmensch
Perfect 161, 240 n., 249 n., 307
Perfectum performativum 261, 261 n.
Performative utterances 261 n. (D), 23, 59, 59 n., 135, 162, 176 f., 240, 240 n., 249 n., 261, 261 n., 265 ff.
Personal union 138, 298
Political propaganda, 16, 22 ff., 25
Popular assembly 107 ff., 111 ff., 131 ff.
Priestly Code 283
Primaeval Man 251, 268 ff.
Primogeniture 24, 120, 125
Prophecy, Prophetic circles 74 ff., 167 ff., 236
Ritualization of charisma 207
Ratification of contracts 214 ff.
Redaction criticism 21 f.
Rehoboam 139 f.
Retterbuch 238
Revolution 122 (D)
Rite 208 (D)
Rite de passage 209
Routinization of charisma 207, 234, 246 ff.
Royal
  apparel: 287 f.
  banquet: 114
  covenant, see: Covenant
  insignia: 286 ff.
  novel: 49, 240
  pectoral: 288
  suffering: 306 ff.
  wisdom: 240 ff., 269 ff.
Sacral kingship 14 (D)
Sacralization 158 ff., 201

Samuel 64 ff., 88 ff., 92 ff., 174 ff., 205
Saul 64 ff., 80 ff., 111 ff., 146 f., 168 ff., 177, 194 ff., 234 ff., 299 f.
Saviours 85, 88 ff.
Semantic relations 171 ff.
Servant of the Lord 249 f., 306
Shiloh 92 ff.
Sodalic lawfinding 137 (D)
Solomon 23 f., 27 ff., 30, 52 ff., 93 f., 119 ff., 159 ff., 201 ff., 226 f., 238 ff., 258 f.
Son of God See: Divine sonship
Spirit 68 ff., 233 ff., 246 ff.
Stimulus diffusion 209 f.
Structuralistic approach 17
Succession Narrative 27 ff. and passim
Suffering See: Royal s.
Synergism 107, 177

Syntagmatic relation 171 ff.
tell el-fūl 245 f.
"Tenses" See: Imperfect and Perfect
Theme vs. motif 99 n. (D)
Theocratic ideal 168
Traditionsgeschichte 22 n. (D), 21 f.
Treaty 302
Treaty terms 147 f.
Überlieferungsgeschichte 22 n. (D), 21 f.
Upsala circle 101 f.
Uraeus 288
Urim See: Lot-casting
Urmensch 251, 268 ff.
Uzziah 128
Wisdom 240 ff., 269 ff.
Zadok 93 f.
Zion 308